W9-CDG-543

Thru the Bible with J. Vernon McGee

By J. Vernon McGee

Compiled from previous publications by J. Vernon McGee.

Published in Nashville, Tennessee, by Thomas Nelson, Inc., Publishers and distributed in Canada by Lawson Falle, Ltd., Cambridge, Ontario.

Library of Congress Cataloging in Publication Data

McGee, J. Vernon (John Vernon), 1904–1988
Thru the Bible with J. Vernon McGee.

Based on the Thru the Bible radio program.
Includes bibliographies.
Contents: v. 2. Joshua—Psalms.
1. Bible—Commentaries. I. Thru the Bible (Radio program) II. Title.
BS491.2.M37 1982 220.7 81-3930
ISBN 0-8407-4979-1 Royal AACR2
ISBN 0-8407-4974-0 Nelson

Printed in the United States of America

25 - 03

Thru the Bible with J. Vernon McGee

By J. Vernon McGee

VOLUME II
Joshua—Psalms

Thomas Nelson Publishers
Nashville

TABLE OF CONTENTS

PREFACE

The radio broadcasts of the Thru the Bible Radio five-year program were transcribed, edited, and published first in single-volume paperbacks to accommodate the radio audience. From the beginning there was a demand that they be published in a more permanent form and in fewer volumes. This new hardback edition is an attempt to meet that need.

There has been a minimal amount of further editing for this publication. Therefore, these messages are not the word-for-word recording of the taped messages which went out over the air. The changes were necessary to accommodate a reading audience rather than a listening audience.

These are popular messages, prepared originally for a radio audience. They should not be considered a commentary on the entire Bible in any sense of that term. These messages are devoid of any attempt to present a theological or technical commentary on the Bible. Behind these messages is a great deal of research and study in order to interpret the Bible from a popular rather than from a scholarly (and too-often boring) viewpoint.

We have definitely and deliberately attempted "to put the cookies on the bottom shelf so that the kiddies could get them."

The fact that these messages have been translated into many languages for radio broadcasting and have been received with enthusiasm reveals the need for a simple teaching of the whole Bible for the masses of the world.

I am indebted to many people and to many sources for bringing this volume into existence. I should express my especial thanks to my secretary, Gertrude Cutler, who supervised the editorial work; to Dr. Elliott R. Cole, my associate, who handled all the detailed work with the publishers; and finally, to my wife Ruth for tenaciously encouraging me from the beginning to put my notes and messages into printed form.

Solomon wrote, ". . . of making many books there is no end; and much study is a weariness of the flesh" (Eccl. 12:12). On a sea of books that flood the marketplace, we launch this series of THRU THE BIBLE with the hope that it might draw many to the one Book, *The Bible*.

J. VERNON MCGEE

The Book of

JOSHUA

INTRODUCTION

In the Book of Genesis Israel was born. In the Book of Exodus Israel was chosen. In the Book of Numbers the nation was proven. In the Book of Leviticus it was brought nigh by the blood. In Deuteronomy it was instructed. Now in the Book of Joshua it faces conflict and conquest.

The Book of Joshua completes the redemption of Israel that was begun in Exodus. Exodus is the book of redemption *out* of Egypt; Joshua is the book of redemption *into* the Promised Land.

The key word in the Book of Joshua is *possession*. God had given the children of Israel their land in an unconditional covenant. To Abraham He had said, "And I will give unto thee, and to thy seed after thee, the land wherein thou art a stranger, all the land of Canaan, for an everlasting possession; and I will be their God" (Gen. 17:8). However, Israel's possession of the land was conditional. There was conflict and there was conquest. They had to fight battles and lay hold of their possessions. And, as Joshua reminded them in his final message before his death, their obedience to the Word of God would determine their continued possession of the land.

The Talmud says that Joshua wrote all but the concluding five verses, which were written by Phinehas. Joshua was the successor to Moses. He was a great general. Born a slave in Egypt, he was forty years old at the time of the Exodus out of Egypt. He was eighty years old when he received his commission as Moses' successor and one hundred ten years old at his death. Joshua had already gained prominence during the wilderness wanderings. When they were attacked by the army of Amalek, it was Joshua who organized the men into an army that fought off Amalek. Joshua served as a minister or servant to Moses. References to him in that connection reveal his loyalty to Moses and his devotion to God. At Kadesh-Barnea he was one of the twelve men who went to spy out the land of Canaan. He is one of the two spies that returned with a favorable report in full confidence that God would give them the land.

Joshua's name means "Jehovah saves." The same word in the New Testament is *Jesus*. Joshua was a man of courage, dependence upon God, faith, leadership, enthusiasm, and fidelity. He is a type of Christ in his name and in his work. As another has said, "Joshua shows that a man of average ability may become a leader in the church. Joshua received his call not in flaming letters written across the sky, but from an older man who knew God and knew Joshua, and saw that he was fitted by God to be a leader."

The Book of Joshua has a very practical application to the believer today. The Promised Land cannot be a type of heaven since heaven is not a place of conflict and conquest. Heaven is received as a gift of the grace of God. Rather, the Promised Land represents the place to which believers are brought right here in this world today. The Book of Joshua corresponds to the Epistle to the Ephesians in the New Testament where we see that the believer is blessed with all spiritual blessings. The practical possession and experience of them depends upon conflict and conquest. These are never attained through the energy of the flesh, but through the power of the Holy Spirit in the yielded life of the believer. The Book of Joshua is the pattern, and it illustrates the method by which the believer can possess what God has given to him.

OUTLINE

I. Land Entered, Chapters 1–12
- A. Commission and Command of Joshua, Chapter 1
- B. Contact of Spies with Rahab, Chapter 2
- C. Crossing the Jordan River, Chapter 3
- D. Construction of Two Memorials, Chapter 4
- E. Conditioned for Conquest, Chapter 5
- F. Center of Land Attacked, Chapters 6–8
  1. Conquest of Jericho, Chapter 6
  2. Conquest of Ai, Chapters 7–8
- G. Campaign in the South, Chapters 9–10
  1. Compact with the Gibeonites, Chapter 9
  2. Conquest of Five Kings of Amorites, Chapter 10 (*Miracle of sun*)
- H. Campaign in the North, Chapter 11 (*Conclusion of Joshua's leadership in war*)
- I. Conquered Kings Listed, Chapter 12

II. Land Divided, Chapters 13–22
- A. Command of Joshua Is Terminated; Confirmation of Land to the Two and One-half Tribes, Chapter 13
- B. Caleb Given Hebron, Chapter 14
- C. Consignment of Land to the Tribes of Israel, Chapters 15–19
- D. Cities of Refuge, Chapter 20
- E. Cities for Levites, Chapter 21
- F. Command to the Two and One-half Tribes to Return Home; Construction of Altar to "See To," Chapter 22

III. Last Message of Joshua, Chapters 23–24
- A. Call to Leaders of Israel for Courage and Certainty, Chapter 23
- B. Call to All Tribes of Israel for Consecration and Consideration of Covenant with God; Death of Joshua, Chapter 24

CHAPTER 1

***THEME:** Commission and command of Joshua*

In the first twelve chapters of Joshua the Promised Land is entered. Then in chapters 13–21 we see the land divided. The book concludes with the final message of Joshua to his people.

The great theme of Joshua is *possession*. In this first chapter we will see what is meant by that.

The chapter opens with the Lord personally giving Joshua his commission and his command.

Now after the death of Moses the servant of the LORD it came to pass, that the LORD spake unto Joshua the son of Nun, Moses' minister, saying [Josh. 1:1].

The first word of this verse, *Now*, should be translated "And," which connects it with the final chapter of Deuteronomy. *And* is a connective. The minute a speaker says *and*, he has to keep talking because *and* connects something that has gone before with something that is coming. This supports the theory that Deuteronomy 34 was written by Joshua.

Moses my servant is dead; now therefore arise, go over this Jordan, thou, and all this people, unto the land which I do give to them, even to the children of Israel [Josh. 1:2].

"Moses my servant is dead." As we have seen, Moses was not essential to lead the children of Israel into the land. In fact, he could not bring them into the Land of Promise. Moses represented the Law and the Law cannot save us. The Law is a revealer and not a redeemer. It shows us that we are sinners. The Law was never a savior. Moses could not lead Israel into the land because of his failure. The problem was not with the Law but with Moses just as the problem is with us. The Law reveals that we have fallen short of the glory of God. "Moses my servant is dead." Only Jesus our Savior, our Joshua, can lead us into the place of blessing He has for us.

This verse tells us that the land was given to Israel. Israel's ownership was unconditional. God promised it to Abraham and his offspring. God reaffirmed His promise again and again in the Book of Genesis. In the Book of Deuteronomy God made the Palestinian covenant with Israel which gave them the land as an everlasting possession.

Every place that the sole of your foot shall tread upon, that have I given unto you, as I said unto Moses [Josh. 1:3].

God has given them the land. The land is theirs, but their enjoyment of it depends upon their taking possession of it. That part of the land upon which they walked would belong to them. Comparatively speaking, we have been told in Ephesians 1:3 that we are blessed with all spiritual blessings in the heavenlies. Unfortunately, very few Christians lay hold of the spiritual blessings that belong to them.

Years ago a certain Englishman moved to the United States. Soon after he arrived he dropped out of sight. One day his uncle in England died and left him about a five-million dollar estate. Scotland Yard went about trying to locate the man whose last address had been in Chicago. They searched for him but never found him. Later I heard that he was found one morning frozen to death in an entryway of a cheap hotel. He could not afford twenty-five cents for a room although he was heir to five million dollars! He did not claim what was his. He did not lay hold of what belonged to him.

Although God gave Israel the Promised Land, they never possessed all of it. As a matter of fact, Israel got very little of the land. Many Christians today are like Israel in that they are blessed with all spiritual blessings and yet they die like bums in a doorway without claiming those blessings as their own. What a tragedy that is. The Book of Joshua is going to tell us how to lay hold of our possessions. Because there will be conflict, we are told in Ephesians 6 to put on the whole armor of God. We have a spiritual enemy fighting against us. "For we wrestle not against flesh and blood, but against principalities, against powers, against the rulers of the darkness of this world, against spiritual wickedness in high places" (Eph. 6:12). Ours is a spiritual enemy.

We will have to wear the whole armor of God. The victory has to be won. However, you and I don't get the victory; the Lord Jesus Christ gets the victory. We will get what Israel got—deliverance and possessions. Every victory Israel gained was given by God. If you and I ever win a victory, He will win it for us. We will, by faith, enter into these wonderful possessions.

From the wilderness and this Lebanon even unto the great river, the river Euphrates, all the land of the Hittites, and unto the great sea toward the going down of the sun, shall be your coast [Josh. 1:4].

God gave Israel 300,000 square miles of land and the most they ever claimed was 30,000 square miles. They did not do very well, did they? They took possession of about one-tenth of what God had given them. That is about the same amount of spiritual possessions claimed by believers today.

There shall not any man be able to stand before thee all the days of thy life: as I was with Moses, so I will be with thee: I will not fail thee, nor forsake thee [Josh. 1:5].

Joshua, average man that he was, needed to be encouraged. God encouraged him here in a most wonderful way. God says, "I won't desert you. Just as I was with Moses, I'll be with you."

Be strong and of a good courage: for unto this people shalt thou divide for an inheritance the land, which I sware unto their fathers to give them.

Only be thou strong and very courageous, that thou mayest observe to do according to all the law, which Moses my servant commanded thee: turn not from it to the right hand or to the left, that thou mayest prosper whithersoever thou goest [Josh. 1:6–7].

Twice God says to him, "Be strong and of a good courage." He is encouraging him.

Now notice something that is all important:

This book of the law shall not depart out of thy mouth; but thou shalt meditate therein day and night, that thou mayest observe to do according to all that is written therein: for then thou shalt make thy way prosperous, and then thou shalt have good success [Josh. 1:8].

There were no written Scriptures before Moses, and God communicated to Moses by speaking with him face to face. But Moses had faithfully recorded all that God had given to him so that the first five books of the Bible were available to Joshua and the people of Israel. In it God had given them all they needed to know to enter the land. They were not to depart from it. They were to meditate on it and observe to do it.

Have not I commanded thee? Be strong and of a good courage; be not afraid, neither be thou dismayed: for the LORD thy God is with thee whithersoever thou goest [Josh. 1:9].

Joshua is to take the Word of God in one hand and a sword in the other. He is to move out by faith. God encourages him again to be strong and courageous.

Friends, like Joshua, we as believers need to be strong and courageous. We need to possess our spiritual possessions by faith. Remember we are in enemy territory.

Then Joshua commanded the officers of the people, saying [Josh. 1:10].

Joshua took charge, and he didn't do it by presumption but in confidence. He did it because God told him to do it.

God had told Moses He would be with him. When Moses returned to Egypt, after spending years in Midian, he was fearful, but God said, "Now therefore go, and I will be with thy mouth, and teach thee what thou shalt say" (Exod. 4:12). This is God's method. When God called Jeremiah in a dark and difficult day, He said, "And they shall fight against thee; but they shall not prevail against thee; for I am with thee, saith the LORD, to deliver thee" (Jer. 1:19). We need the kind of conviction and courage spoken about in Hebrews 13:6, "So that we may boldly say, The Lord is my helper, and I will not fear what man shall do unto me." When David first said these words, which were quoted in Hebrews from Psalm 118:6, he turned his mind and heart away from that which was seen to that which was unseen. It means that he became occupied with the living and true God. He recognized the spiritual bond that was between him and the Lord. His soul was "bound up in a bundle of life with God." He could say, "The Lord is my helper." David knew that the Lord could deliver him.

Joshua believed God. God had encouraged him and told him to step out. The Word of God was to be his authority. It was not to depart out of his mouth. He was to meditate on it. He was to do what was written in the Word. That is the formula of faith.

Pass through the host, and command the people, saying, Prepare you victuals; for within three days ye shall pass over this Jordan, to go in to possess the land, which the LORD your God giveth you to possess it [Josh. 1:11].

Israel's ownership of the land is unconditional, but Israel's possession of it is conditional. Israel had to take the land. The key word of the Book of Joshua is not *victory*—it is God who gets the victory. The key word is *possession*. Israel was to possess the land.

A little later on, when Israel got into the land, the manna ceased and they ate the old corn of the land. That would be corn they captured from the enemy, old corn, because they hadn't had a chance to grow it. As you recall, they had to gather manna every day. Manna would not keep. If it was kept for more than one day, it became unfit to eat. The children of Israel had to gather manna every morning. That is why we are told in Ephesians 5:18 to be filled with the Spirit. Being filled with the Spirit is not a one-time job. You do not go to the gas station once and tell the attendant to fill up your tank and then seal the tank because you will never need more gas. That would be presumption. In fact, it would be foolish and stupid. There are many Christians, however, who think that they can have one experience and that is it. My friend, if you are going to walk with Him and live for Him, you will need a *daily* filling of the Holy Spirit of God. In fact, since you fill up the physical man three times a day, it would not be a bad idea to fill up the spiritual man three times a day. We all need a constant filling of the Holy Spirit, a looking to Him, and a resting upon Him.

And to the Reubenites, and to the Gadites, and to half the tribe of Manasseh, spake Joshua, saying [Josh. 1:12].

These two and one-half tribes did not cross over the river to settle there, and we find their defection very early. Moses was still alive when they came to the east bank of the Jordan, and you will find that they made a request recorded in Numbers 32:1–5: "Now the children of Reuben and the children of Gad had a very great multitude of cattle: and when they saw the land of Jazer, and the land of Gilead, that, behold, the place was a place for cattle; the children of Gad and the children of Reuben came and spake unto Moses, and to Eleazar the priest . . . saying . . . Wherefore, . . . if we have found grace in thy sight, let this land be given unto thy servants for a possession, and bring us not over Jordan." This was the specific request of two and one-half tribes. They were asking for land on the wrong side of the Jordan River.

Remember the word which Moses the servant of the LORD commanded you, saying, The LORD your God hath given you rest, and hath given you this land.

Your wives, your little ones, and your cattle, shall remain in the land which Moses gave you on this side Jordan; but ye shall pass before your brethren armed, all the mighty men of valour, and help them;

Until the LORD have given your brethren rest, as he hath given you, and they also have possessed the land which the LORD your God giveth them: then ye shall return unto the land of your possession, and enjoy it, which Moses the LORD'S servant gave you on this side Jordan toward the sunrising [Josh. 1:13–15].

Joshua is reminding them that Moses had given them permission to live on the east side of Jordan on the condition that their army would help the other tribes possess their land on the west of the river. This they agree to do.

And they answered Joshua, saying, All that thou commandest us we will do, and whithersoever thou sendest us, we will go.

According as we hearkened unto Moses in all things, so will we hearken unto thee: only the LORD thy God be with thee, as he was with Moses.

Whosoever he be that doth rebel against thy commandment, and will not hearken unto thy words in all that thou commandest him, he shall be put to death: only be strong and of a good courage [Josh. 1:16–18].

Perhaps you are asking the question, Well, what is wrong with dwelling on the east side of the River Jordan? Is it so essential to cross over the river? Is not the east bank of the Jordan River part of the Promised Land? Such questions are pertinent and require that we look at the passage of Scripture in which lies the account of the crossing of the Jordan River, which we will do shortly.

Crossing the Jordan River was symbolic of the death and resurrection of Jesus Christ. Under no condition, however, does it set forth *our* physical death. We often sing the old song, "On Jordan's Stormy Banks I Stand." To begin with, that is not a stormy stream; neither do you and I stand on the stormy banks. Christ alone was nailed to that cross and, hanging there, bore all the storms of the judgment of sin. When the storms of judgment fell on Him, they fell on us. The River Jordan speaks of *sanctification*, and the death of Christ was for our sanctification.

In the Book of Judges we find out that the two and one-half tribes made a big mistake staying on the wrong side of Jordan. Also, when Christ crossed the Sea of Galilee and came to the country of the Gadarenes, He found the Jews in the pig business. They started off wrong on the wrong side of the Jordan River.

Many Christians are in the pig business today and are frustrated. They ought to enter into the rest He has provided in His death and resurrection.

CHAPTER 2

***THEME:** Contact of spies with Rahab*

Here we are introduced to a woman, a very shady character. She was a prostitute, and her name is Rahab. The remarkable fact is that in the New Testament she is listed with those who are commonly called the heroes of faith. "By faith the harlot Rahab perished not with them that believed not, when she had received the spies with peace" (Heb. 11:31). I do not like to think of Hebrews 11 as a record of *heroes* of faith because that puts the emphasis on humanity. I like to put the emphasis upon faith. The men and women recorded there illustrate what faith did in all ages under all circumstances in their lives. For us it means that faith can do the same thing for us, seeing "we also are compassed about with so great a cloud of witnesses" (Heb. 12:1).

Another startling fact is that Rahab is in the genealogy of Christ! The New Testament opens with that genealogy, and you don't read five verses of the New Testament until you come to this woman's name. How did she get into the genealogy of Christ? She got there by faith.

As you can see, the chapter before us introduces a remarkable woman.

And Joshua the son of Nun sent out of Shittim two men to spy secretly, saying, Go view the land, even Jericho. And they went, and came into an harlot's house, named Rahab, and lodged there [Josh. 2:1].

Notice that two spies are sent in. You may be thinking that this is another mistake. Earlier they had sent the spies to see if they could take the land. Now they are being sent, not to see if they can take the land, but to find the best way to enter the land. The purpose is entirely different, you see.

Rahab, a citizen of Jericho, opens her home to the spies.

And it was told the king of Jericho, saying, Behold, there came men in hither to-night of the children of Israel to search out the country.

And the king of Jericho sent unto Rahab, saying, Bring forth the men that are come to thee, which are entered into thine house: for they be come to search out all the country.

And the woman took the two men, and hid them, and said thus, There came men unto me, but I wist not whence they were:

And it came to pass about the time of shutting of the gate, when it was dark, that the men went out: whither the men went I wot not: pursue after them quickly; for ye shall overtake them.

But she had brought them up to the roof of the house, and hid them with the stalks of flax, which she had laid in order upon the roof.

And the men pursued after them the way to Jordan unto the fords: and as soon as they which pursued after them were gone out, they shut the gate [Josh. 2:2–7].

She told her king an outright lie to protect these men. And in doing so, she actually jeopardized her own life. Now why would she put her life on the line like this? She didn't have to. She is in a business, by the way, where anything goes. Why did she lie to her own people and protect the enemy?

Before we see the answer to that question, let me raise another question. Is it possible to condone Rahab's action? Scripture is very clear on the fact that we, as children of God, are to obey authority and those that have the rule over us. Rahab certainly did not do that. I do not think we could call her a child of God until sometime after this experience. That would be one explanation. However, there is another explanation that I consider meaningful to us today.

A believer should certainly obey the authorities and those who have rule over us. A Christian should be the most law-abiding citizen in the land. But when the laws of a state conflict with God's revealed will, then the Christian has no choice but to obey the command of God. This was the experience of Peter and John when the authorities attempted to silence them in their witness for Christ, ". . . Whether it be right in the sight of God to hearken unto you more than unto God, judge ye. For we cannot but speak the things which we have seen and heard" (Acts 4:19–20). The believer is to obey the Word of God today rather than the word of man. That should be our attitude as children of God.

Now we will let Rahab answer our first question: why did she lie to protect the enemy?

And before they were laid down, she came up unto them upon the roof;

And she said unto the men, I know that the LORD hath given you the land, and that your terror is fallen upon us, and that all the inhabitants of the land faint because of you [Josh. 2:8–9].

She gives an insight into the thinking of the Canaanites at that time. The word is out that a great company of people is coming into that land. They believe they are going to take the land. The population is stirred up, and they are afraid. This is the report that Rahab gives the spies. I guess she was in a position to get all the gossip, and she could see that all of her people were terrified because of Israel's advance.

For we have heard how the LORD dried up the water of the Red sea for you, when ye came out of Egypt; and what ye did unto the two kings of the Amorites, that were on the other side Jordan, Sihon and Og, whom ye utterly destroyed [Josh. 2:10].

Notice: "We have heard how the LORD dried up the water of the Red sea for you." How long ago was this? That happened forty years before they arrived at the Jordan River! During those forty years God had been giving the people of Canaan an opportunity to turn to Him. How do we know that? Because God had said to Abraham that his seed would be strangers in a foreign land for four hundred years; then in the fourth generation they would come again because ". . . the iniquity of the Amorites is not yet full" (Gen. 15:16). That was 420 years before this. In other words, God was going to give the people of Canaan 420 years to decide whether or not they would turn to Him.

The critic declares that the God of the Old Testament was a great big bully, that He was cruel and barbaric. When God gave the people of Canaan 420 years to repent, in my opinion, that is long enough. But God extended the time by forty more years and saw to it that they heard how He had revealed Himself by delivering His people from Egypt. God did not destroy a people that had not heard about Him. He gave them ample opportunity to turn to Him. My question, Mr. Critic, is—how much longer do you think God should have given them?

In the New Testament God has not changed. He has made it very clear that those who reject Jesus Christ are going to hell. Does it shock you to hear that in this very "civilized" society that discounts the existence of hell? When God's judgment falls, I am sure there will be some soft-hearted and soft-headed folk on the sideline who will say, "He should have given them more time." More time? My friend, over 1900 years have gone by. God is patient; He is slow to anger; He is merciful. How much longer do you want Him to give us? He has been giving the world ample opportunity to turn to Christ.

The harlot said, "We have heard." And notice the reaction.

And as soon as we had heard these things, our hearts did melt, neither did there remain any more courage in any man, because of you: for the LORD your God, he is God in heaven above, and in earth beneath [Josh. 2:11].

Not only did they hear this, but they knew it was true. Even so, they did not turn to God.

There are a great many people today who know as a historical fact that Jesus Christ died, was buried, and rose again, but they are not saved. What saves you? It is trusting Him as your personal Savior. It is to have a personal relationship with Him.

Now that's not all Rahab said.

Now therefore, I pray you, swear unto me by the LORD, since I have shewed you kindness, that ye will also shew kindness unto my father's house, and give me a true token:

And that ye will save alive my father, and my mother, and my brethren, and my sisters, and all that they have, and deliver our lives from death.

And the men answered her, Our life for yours, if ye utter not this our business. And it shall be, when the LORD hath given us the land, that we will deal kindly and truly with thee [Josh. 2:12–14].

She not only believed, but she is acting on that belief. This is her reason for putting her life in jeopardy to protect enemy spies. She heard; she believed; then she acted upon her belief.

This is salvation, friend. When you hear the Gospel, the good news of what Christ has done for you, you must not only believe it as a historical fact, you must trust Christ yourself.

So this woman trusted the fact that God was going to give them that land. She turned to the living and true God. "By faith the harlot Rahab perished not with them that believed not, when she had received the spies with peace" (Heb. 11:31).

The spies promise to spare all of her family that is with her in the house when Jericho is attacked.

Behold, when we come into the land, thou shalt bind this line of scarlet thread in the window which thou didst let us down by: and thou shalt bring thy father, and thy mother, and thy brethren, and all thy father's household, home unto thee [Josh. 2:18].

And if the king of the city of Jericho had turned to God, he would have been saved. In fact, the whole city could have been spared if they had believed in God.

Now we will look at the final verses of this chapter, the report of the spies.

So the two men returned, and descended from the mountain, and passed over, and came to Joshua the son of Nun, and told him all things that befell them:

And they said unto Joshua, Truly the LORD hath delivered into our hands all the land; for even all the inhabitants of the country do faint because of us [Josh. 2:23–24].

You see, the spies' report is entirely different from the spies who went into the land forty years earlier. It is not a question now whether or not they will go into the land. They *are* going in. "All the inhabitants of the country do faint because of us" is the information they got from Rahab the harlot.

CHAPTER 3

***THEME:** Crossing the Jordan River*

Crossing the Jordan River into the land of Canaan was a major turning point as far as the faith of the Israelites was concerned. Almost forty years earlier the children of Israel had faced a similar crisis, but they had failed. To slip away into the wilderness of Sinai by crossing the Red Sea required some faith. However, to invade the land of Canaan by crossing the Jordan River took a great deal more faith because, having once crossed the river, there would be no possibility of escape. Once in the land, they would have to face the enemy with their armies, chariots, and walled cities. The entire nation took this step together in complete commitment to God.

And Joshua rose early in the morning; and they removed from Shittim, and came to Jordan, he and all the children of Israel, and lodged there before they passed over.

And it came to pass after three days, that the officers went through the host;

And they commanded the people, saying, When ye see the ark of the covenant of the LORD your God, and the priests the Levites bearing it, then ye shall remove from your place, and go after it.

Yet there shall be a space between you and it, about two thousand cubits by measure: come not near unto it, that ye may know the way by which ye must go: for ye have not passed this way heretofore [Josh. 3:1–4].

God commanded Joshua and the children of Israel to cross over the Jordan River. When they went over the Jordan River, it was quite different from their crossing the Red Sea. When they crossed the Red Sea, Moses went down to the water and smote it with his rod. All that night the waters rolled back. But when they crossed the Jordan River, it was actually a greater miracle, for it was at flood stage and their crossing caused a holding back of the waters that were rushing to the Dead Sea.

Also something new has been added. The ark is to go down far ahead of the people, three thousand feet, which is almost a mile; and it is to be carried by priests who are to come to the edge of the Jordan River and stand there.

And as they that bare the ark were come unto Jordan, and the feet of the priests that bare the ark were dipped in the brim of the water, (for Jordan overfloweth all his banks all the time of harvest,) [Josh. 3:15].

When the priests came to the edge of the Jordan River, the flow of water was restrained as if a dam had been put over it. The waters that were this side of it passed on down, and before long there was a dry passage. This is one of the greatest miracles recorded in Scripture.

This was the spring of the year. That land had two rainy seasons: in the fall and in the spring. The spring rains were most abundant. The Jordan was at flood stage. It is entirely possible that the people on the west side of Jordan felt that they had several days, or maybe several weeks, before the Israelites could get across the river. They probably felt that there was no immediate danger. Some of them, however, may have had a lurking fear, knowing that forty years earlier these people had crossed the Red Sea.

That the waters which came down from above stood and rose up upon an heap very far from the city Adam, that is beside Zaretan: and those that came down toward the sea of the plain, even the salt sea, failed, and were cut off: and the people passed over right against Jericho.

And the priests that bare the ark of the covenant of the LORD stood firm on dry ground in the midst of Jordan, and all the Israelites passed over on dry ground, until all the people were passed clean over Jordan [Josh. 3:16–17].

Note that the priests moved to the center of the Jordan River and stood there holding the ark until all of the children of Israel had passed over. The Israelites crossed the river at Jericho, but the waters were dammed up way back to the city of Adam. Now I have never been able to locate the city of Adam. What is the meaning of this city? Well, friend, it is the city we all came from in the sense that Adam is the father of the human family and by Adam came death. What was taking place at the Jordan River represented the death and resurrection of Christ and His work on the cross. It not only reached forward over 1,900 years to where you and I are, but it also reached back to Adam and the beginning of the human family. That is the picture we have here.

Now the ark is one of the finest types of the Lord Jesus Christ given in the Old Testament, although there are several that are conspicuous and outstanding. The ark had been in the very heart of Israel's camp for forty years during the wilderness march. Every night when they came into camp, the entire twelve tribes of Israel camped about the ark. It was the very center. But now, for the first time, that which speaks of Christ goes ahead to the Jordan River and enters it first.

As has already been stated, Christ goes before us in death. Of course He goes with us in life—as we pass through this world, He is with us. But He went before us in death; and when our Lord entered death, He entered it for you and for me.

CHAPTER 4

THEME: *Construction of two memorials*

Twelve men are appointed to take twelve stones out of the Jordan River, and twelve other stones are set up in the midst of the Jordan River as a memorial. The priests carrying the ark pass over the river, and the water of the river returns to its normal flow. God magnifies Joshua.

And it came to pass, when all the people were clean passed over Jordan, that the LORD spake unto Joshua, saying,

Take you twelve men out of the people, out of every tribe a man,

And command ye them, saying, Take you hence out of the midst of Jordan, out of the place where the priests' feet stood firm, twelve stones, and ye shall carry them over with you, and leave them in the lodging place, where ye shall lodge this night [Josh. 4:1–3].

This is something that they did. And here is what happened.

And the children of Israel did so as Joshua commanded, and took up twelve stones out of the midst of Jordan, as the LORD spake unto Joshua, according to the number of the tribes of the children of Israel, and carried them over with them unto the place where they lodged, and laid them down there [Josh. 4:8].

The twelve stones taken out of Jordan and put on the west bank of the river were a reminder of God's tremendous power on Israel's behalf.

And Joshua set up twelve stones in the midst of Jordan, in the place where the feet of the priests which bare the ark of the covenant stood: and they are there unto this day [Josh. 4:9].

That is, the stones were there when Joshua wrote this record.

Now this section has great spiritual significance for us today. In an attempt to get the full significance of this, I am quoting from Phillips' book (which is not a translation, but is an interpretation), Romans 6:1–4: "Now what is our response to be? Shall we sin to our heart's content and see how far we can exploit the grace of God? What a ghastly thought! We, who have died to sin—how could we live in sin a moment longer?" Now when did we die to sin? "Have you forgotten that all of us who were baptized into Jesus Christ were, by that very action, sharing in his death? We were dead and buried with him in baptism, so that just as he was raised from the dead by the splendid revelation of the Father's power so we too might rise to life on a new plane altogether." My friend, may I say to you that Christ went into death for you and me, and that is set before us here in the Book of Joshua. Twelve stones were put into the water of death. Those twelve stones were placed in Jordan to speak of the death of Christ. And the twelve stones taken out of Jordan and put on the west bank of the river represent the resurrection of Christ.

The Lord Jesus Christ died over 1,900 years ago, and Paul makes it clear in the sixth chapter of Romans that we are *identified* with Him in His death. It is too bad that the word *baptize* was transliterated and not translated. It is a Greek word *baptizo*, and its primary meaning here has no connection with water. It speaks of identification. We are identified with Christ in His death; and when He died, my friend, He died for us. His death was our death. When He arose from the dead, then we arose from the dead. And we are joined today to a living Christ. It is only in the measure that we are joined to Him that you and I can enjoy all spiritual blessings. I trust that you realize that. We have become identified with Him!

Now, when the children of Israel crossed over the river, they became citizens of Palestine. They became forever identified with that land—so much so, that today, even at this hour, they speak of the Jew in Palestine. And when he is out of that land, he is spoken of as the "wandering Jew." Let us tie this fact up with another great fact: When you, my friend, came to Christ and accepted Him as your Savior, His death became your death and His resurrection your resurrection. When you "wander" from this identity, even briefly, think of the tragic meaning.

Paul wrote a blessed truth to the Ephesians: "But God, who is rich in mercy, for his great love wherewith he loved us, Even when we were dead in sins, hath quickened us together with Christ, (by grace are ye saved;) And hath raised us up together, and made us sit together in the heavenly places in Christ Jesus: That in the ages to come he might shew the exceeding riches of his grace in his kindness toward us through Christ Jesus" (Eph. 2:4–7). When He died, He died for your sin that you might have life; and when He came back from the dead, His life was then your life. Now you are joined to the living God. My friend, that is one of the great truths of the Word of God.

And the people came up out of Jordan on the tenth day of the first month, and encamped in Gilgal, in the east border of Jericho.

And those twelve stones, which they took out of Jordan, did Joshua pitch in Gilgal.

And he spake unto the children of Israel, saying, When your children shall ask their fathers in time to come, saying, What mean these stones?

Then ye shall let your children know, saying, Israel came over this Jordan on dry land [Josh. 4:19–22].

If we carry the spiritual lesson out in this passage, our conclusion can only be that we are to teach our children the Gospel. The business of parents is to give their children the Gospel. There is no privilege like that of a parent leading his child to a saving knowledge of Christ. My wife had the privilege of leading our daughter to the Lord. This is the responsibility of parents.

For the LORD your God dried up the waters of Jordan from before you, until ye were passed over, as the LORD your God did to the Red sea, which he dried up from before us, until we were gone over:

That all the people of the earth might know the hand of the LORD, that it is mighty: that ye might fear the LORD your God for ever [Josh. 4:23–24].

What God did for the children of Israel He did for their benefit, your benefit, and mine. He did it that all the people of the earth might know that the hand of the Lord is indeed mighty. This purpose was graphically fulfilled as soon as the Canaanites heard the news that the children of Israel had crossed over Jordan.

Some of the important things to remember in this chapter are that the ark goes before and divides the Jordan River—not the rod of Moses. The ark goes before, carried by priests. Christ goes before us through death but also goes with us through this life. Jordan is typical of Christ's death, not ours.

CHAPTER 5

***THEME:** Fear falls upon the Amorites; a new generation is circumcised; the divine visitor—captain of the host*

In this chapter we learn that the rite of circumcision was performed; the manna ceased and they began to eat the old corn of the land; finally, Joshua was confronted by the unseen Captain of the "host of the LORD"—Joshua needed this vision at this time. These three things are important to see.

FEAR FALLS UPON THE AMORITES

And it came to pass, when all the kings of the Amorites, which were on the side of Jordan westward, and all the kings of the Canaanites, which were by the sea, heard that the LORD had dried up the waters of Jordan from before the children of Israel, until we were passed over, that their heart melted, neither was there spirit in them any more, because of the children of Israel [Josh. 5:1].

Because the Jordan River was at flood stage, the Amorites and Canaanites did not expect the Israelites to cross over. They expected them to cross over after the flood season was over. They probably thought they had quite a bit more time to prepare for battle, and it was a shock for them to discover that God had enabled Israel to cross Jordan.

A NEW GENERATION IS CIRCUMCISED

At that time the LORD said unto Joshua, Make thee sharp knives, and circumcise again the children of Israel the second time.

And Joshua made him sharp knives, and circumcised the children of Israel at the hill of the foreskins.

And this is the cause why Joshua did circumcise: All the people that came out of Egypt, that were males, even all the men of war, died in the wilderness by the way, after they came out of Egypt.

Now all the people that came out were circumcised: but all the people that were born in the wilderness by the way as they came forth out of Egypt, them they had not circumcised [Josh. 5:2–5].

The new generation had neglected the rite of circumcision, which was the badge of the Abrahamic covenant. The Abrahamic covenant, you remember, gave Israel the land of Canaan. They had neglected to observe this rite during those years of wandering through the wilderness.

For the children of Israel walked forty years in the wilderness, till all the people that were men of war, which came out of Egypt, were consumed, because they obeyed not the voice of the LORD: unto whom the LORD sware that he would not shew them the land, which the LORD sware unto their fathers that he would give us, a land that floweth with milk and honey.

And their children, whom he raised up in their stead, them Joshua circumcised: for they were uncircumcised, because they had not circumcised them by the way.

And it came to pass, when they had done circumcising all the people, that they abode in their places in the camp, till they were whole.

And the LORD said unto Joshua, This day have I rolled away the reproach of Egypt from off you. Wherefore the name of the place is called Gilgal unto this day [Josh. 5:6–9].

Both in spirit and in reality the children of Israel had not kept the rite of circumcision, which was the sign of the Abrahamic covenant. The children of Israel had walked forty years in the wilderness until all of the men that had come out of Egypt, who were men of war, had died. The Lord had given them children, and they are the ones whom Joshua circumcised. At this time, God rolled away the reproach of Egypt. The "reproach of Egypt" means that during the latter years of the Egyptian bondage this rite had been neglected, and the neglect had continued during the wilderness wanderings. Therefore, the place where Joshua circumcised the children of Israel was called *Gilgal*, which means "a rolling."

And the children of Israel encamped in Gilgal, and kept the passover on the fourteenth day of the month at even in the plains of Jericho [Josh. 5:10].

It was in the spring of the year, at the time of the latter rains, that Israel performed the rite of circumcision and then celebrated the Passover. The reproach of Egypt was rolled away from Israel. God had promised to give the descendants of Abraham the land, and the promise was about to become a reality.

All of this has a spiritual message for us today. The old nature is no good. The old nature cannot inherit spiritual blessing. The old nature cannot even enjoy spiritual blessing. The old nature will not like Canaan, nor anything in the heavenlies. In Galatians 5:17 Paul says, "For the flesh lusteth [which is literally *wars*] against the Spirit, and the Spirit against the flesh: and these are contrary the one to the other: so that ye cannot do the things that ye would." Paul found that there was no good in the old nature. He also discovered that there was no power in the new nature (see Rom. 7). The circumcision of the children of Israel recognized these facts.

And they did eat the old corn of the land on the morrow after the passover, unleavened cakes, and parched corn in the selfsame day.

And the manna ceased on the morrow after they had eaten of the old corn of the land; neither had the children of Israel manna any more; but they did eat of the fruit of the land of Canaan that year [Josh. 5:11–12].

Manna was a picture of Christ we are told in the New Testament. Jesus said, "Your fathers did eat manna in the wilderness, and are dead. This is the bread which cometh down from heaven, that a man may eat thereof, and not die. I am the living bread which came down from heaven: if any man eat of this bread, he shall live for ever: and the bread that I will give is my flesh, which I will give for the life of the world" (John 6:49–51). Manna represents Christ in His death. He is the One who came down to this earth "to give his life a ransom for many."

When Israel arrived in Canaan, the manna ceased, and they began to eat the old corn of the land.

THE DIVINE VISITOR—CAPTAIN OF THE HOST

And it came to pass, when Joshua was by Jericho, that he lifted up his eyes and looked, and, behold, there stood a man over against him with his sword drawn in his hand: and Joshua went unto him, and said unto him, Art thou for us, or for our adversaries?

And he said, Nay; but as captain of the host of the LORD am I now come. And Joshua fell on his face to the earth, and did worship, and said unto him, What saith my lord unto his servant?

And the captain of the LORD's host said unto Joshua, Loose thy shoe from off thy foot; for the place whereon thou standest is holy. And Joshua did so [Josh. 5:13–15].

This is the call and commission of Joshua. It is the same as Moses' call on the plain of Midian at the burning bush. Moses was told to remove his shoes, for the ground upon which he stood was holy (Exod. 3:5). The children of Israel had crossed the Jordan River and were camped on the other side. One morning Joshua probably got up and looked over the scene. It was an impressive sight. There were the camps of all twelve tribes of Israel around him. As he looked at it, I think he swelled with a little pride. He was the one in charge, and GHQ was in his tent now. Then he happened to look down at the edge of the camp, and he saw someone with a drawn sword. Joshua may have thought, *There is someone down there who doesn't seem to know that I am the general here. I'd better go down there and put that fellow in his place!* So he walked down there and, according to our translation, said, "Art thou for us, or for our adversaries?" Now in good old Americana he said, "What's the big idea? Who gave you an order to draw a sword?" Then that One, whom I believe was the pre-incarnate Christ, turned to him, and when He turned, He said, "Nay; but as captain of the host of the LORD am I now come!" Notice the reaction of Joshua. He fell on his face before Him.

You see, Joshua learned that GHQ was not in his tent after all. It was at the throne of God. *God* was leading them. Actually, he was not captain of the hosts of the Lord; he was under Someone else. And he would be taking orders from Him. We shall be seeing this in the next chapter as he marches the army around the city of Jericho for seven straight days. If you had stopped Joshua on the sixth day and said, "Look, General Joshua, this is a silly thing to be doing," he probably would have said, "That's exactly what I think." "Then why are you doing it? You are in command here." Joshua would say, "You are wrong. I take my orders from Someone above me. I am only a buck private in the rear ranks. I am doing this because I have been commanded to do it."

CHAPTER 6

***THEME:** Conquest of Jericho*

Now that we have come to the actual conquest of the Promised Land, let's look again at the events that led up to it.

The children of Israel have now crossed the Jordan River in a most remarkable manner, and they have entered the land. The Jordan is a quiet little stream in the summertime, but it is a rushing torrent during the rainy seasons. As you recall, the ark of the Lord, carried by the priests, went before them. The ark, of course, represents the presence of Christ. When the feet of the priests reached the Jordan, the waters rolled back; then they stood in the midst of the river, with the ark on their shoulders, while all the people passed over Jordan and the memorial stones were set up.

Now the people of Israel are camped on the west side of the bank of the Jordan River. What a glorious, wonderful anticipation awaits them! This is the land God had promised to give them, a land of milk and honey. It is the land they have been told to possess.

Obviously, their hearts are thrilled with it. Surges of anticipation and joy go through them.

They have been conditioned for conquest by circumcision, which was the token of the covenant God made with Abraham. Part of that covenant was that they were to have that land. You recall that Joshua made sharp knives for the circumcision.

What application does this have to your life and mine? To me the sharp knives speak of the Word of God, which ". is quick, and powerful, and sharper than any two-edged sword . . ." (Heb. 4:12). It is able to divide. In our country today all the morality lines are rubbed out, but there is still black and white in the Word of God. We need to get back to Bible morality, because there is no blessing to this nation or any people until they come back to the Word of God.

Another conditioning for conquest had been the vision of the Captain of the hosts of the Lord. General Joshua is going to take orders from above.

Now the first step of conquest is Jericho, and we see that the tactic is to divide the land. By taking the cities of Jericho and Ai, the center of the land will be theirs; then they will move into the south. This method of dividing the land is a method that was followed, it seems, by great generals from that day to this. They divide the enemy, then take them piecemeal. It was used in the Civil War, in World War I, and in World War II. However, the *method* for taking Jericho would not be used again. Let's look at it.

Now Jericho was straitly shut up because of the children of Israel: none went out, and none came in [Josh. 6:1].

Jericho was prepared for the attack of the Israelites. They did not think the Israelites would arrive as quickly as they did, but they shut up the city and prepared for attack.

And the LORD said unto Joshua, See, I have given into thine hand Jericho, and the king thereof, and the mighty men of valour.

And ye shall compass the city, all ye men of war, and go round about the city once. Thus shalt thou do six days.

And seven priests shall bear before the ark seven trumpets of rams' horns: and the seventh day ye shall compass the city seven times, and the priests shall blow with the trumpets.

And it shall come to pass, that when they make a long blast with the ram's horn, and when ye hear the sound of the trumpet, all the people shall shout with a great shout; and the wall of the city shall fall down flat, and the people shall ascend up every man straight before him [Josh. 6:2–5].

The day comes for the beginning of the campaign. Joshua follows the Lord's instructions exactly.

And it came to pass, when Joshua had spoken unto the people, that the seven priests bearing the seven trumpets of rams' horns passed on before the LORD, and blew with the trumpets: and the ark of the covenant of the LORD followed them.

And the armed men went before the priests that blew with the trumpets, and the rereward came after the ark, the priests going on, and blowing with the trumpets.

And Joshua had commanded the people, saying, Ye shall not shout, nor make any noise with your voice, neither shall any word proceed out of your mouth, until the day I bid you shout; then shall ye shout.

So the ark of the LORD compassed the city, going about it once: and they came into the camp, and lodged in the camp [Josh. 6:8–11].

The city of Jericho is prepared. Undoubtedly there are soldiers on the wall and watchmen at the gate. The military brass and its staff are in the city getting reports from the wall. Finally the word comes, "Here comes the enemy." Joshua and the army of Israel are marching toward the city. In front of the procession is the ark carried by the priests, and the priests carry horns. A watchman on the wall cries, "Here they come. Let's get ready. They apparently are going to attack at the gate!" So the forces of Jericho gather at the gate. They are ready for battle if the gate is broken down.

Then a strange thing happens. The watchman calls down, "They're not going to attack here. They made a turn and they are going to attack at another place!" So the army on the inside shifts, and I think they march around on the inside. They are informed by those on the wall, "They are here . . . they are here . . . they are here." The Israelites go all the way around, and instead of attacking, they go back into camp! You can be sure of one thing: there is a huddle that night of the king and the military brass.

And Joshua rose early in the morning, and the priests took up the ark of the LORD.

And seven priests bearing seven trumpets of rams' horns before the ark of the LORD went on continually, and blew with the trumpets: and the armed men went before them; but the rereward came after the ark of the LORD, the priests going on, and blowing with the trumpets.

And the second day they compassed the city once, and returned into the camp: so they did six days [Josh. 6:12–14].

The next day the Israelites give a repeat performance. The watchman on the wall cries out, "Here they come again." Then the Israelites march around the wall and go back to camp. Each day for six days they do the same thing. By the sixth day, the midnight oil had burned long and late in the Pentagon inside Jericho. The army on the outside was tired of marching around the wall. Maybe some of the children of Israel were saying, "What we are doing looks foolish!" If you had asked Joshua why he was doing this, he probably would have replied, "I take my orders from the Captain of the hosts of the Lord. This is what He has told me to do and I am doing it."

And it came to pass on the seventh day, that they rose early about the dawning of the day, and compassed the city after the same manner seven times: only on that day they compassed the city seven times [Josh. 6:15].

So on the seventh day the Israelites march around the wall again. The people of Jericho heave a sigh of relief when they get clear around. The army inside the wall has made its circuit, too, and is relieved that it is over for the day. Everyone sits down to rest—when all of a sudden the watchman says, "Wait a minute, they are going to march around again." So the Israelites make the circuit again. They do it a third and a fourth time. . . .

And it came to pass at the seventh time, when the priests blew with the trumpets, Joshua said unto the people, Shout; for the LORD hath given you the city.

So the people shouted when the priests blew with the trumpets: and it came to pass, when the people heard the sound of the trumpet, and the people shouted with a great shout, that the wall fell down flat, so that the people went up into the city, every man straight before him, and they took the city [Josh. 6: 16, 20].

The walls of Jericho fell down flat. I had the privilege of going to Jericho with a very special Arab guide who had worked with both John Garstang and Kathleen Kenyon; they had led archaeological expeditions in unearthing the ancient city of Jericho. Garstang and Kenyon disagreed as to the dates of the wall. But it had fallen down and was flat—that was obvious. Since this Arab guide had worked with both expeditions, I asked him what he thought as to the date of ancient Jericho. He went along with Garstang, and his reasoning was that when Garstang got there, he was probably not as scientific and didn't do quite the job that Kenyon did. Because he disturbed everything, it would be impossible for anyone coming later to arrive at an accurate estimation. Well, I'll let them argue that. All I'm interested in is that the Word of God says the walls fell down flat—and the evidence is there today. The faith of the believer does not rest upon the shovel of the archaeologist. "By faith the walls of Jericho fell down, after they were compassed about seven days" (Heb. 11:30).

Jericho represents the *world* to the believer. It is strong and formidable and foreboding—the conquest depends upon faith: "For whatsoever is born of God overcometh the world: and this is the victory that overcometh the world, even our faith" (1 John 5:4). Hebrews 11 reveals how faith worked in all ages in the lives of God's choicest servants as they met the world head-on and overcame by faith.

We hear the song, "Joshua Fit the Battle of Jericho." The question is—did he? No, he did not. He didn't fight at all. He just marched around the city. Who did the fighting? God did that, friend, and I think any other explanation is ridiculous. Some say that an earthquake took place at that psychological moment when the priests blew the trumpets and all the people shouted, and the shock toppled the walls. Others say that the constant marching of the children of Israel around the wall loosened the wall and it fell down. Well, you can believe that if you want to. I like it the way it is told in the Word of God. God got the victory; Israel got the possession.

A great problem that many believers have today is that they are trying to "fit the battle of Jericho" and overcome the world. But you and I need to start taking orders from the Captain up yonder, the Captain of our salvation.

Now notice two more things briefly. The first is that Rahab was spared.

But Joshua had said unto the two men that had spied out the country, Go into the harlot's house, and bring out thence the woman, and all that she hath, as ye sware unto her.

And the young men that were spies went in, and brought out Rahab, and her father, and her mother, and her brethren, and all that she had; and they brought out all her kindred, and left them without the camp of Israel.

And Joshua saved Rahab the harlot alive, and her father's household, and all that she had; and she dwelleth in Israel even unto this day; because she hid the messengers, which Joshua sent to spy out Jericho [Josh. 6:22–23, 25].

True to their promise, they saved Rahab and all her family that was with her in the house.

Note also that Joshua pronounced a curse on anyone who would rebuild that city.

And Joshua adjured them at that time, saying, Cursed be the man before the LORD, that riseth up and buildeth this city Jericho: he shall lay the foundation thereof in his firstborn, and in his youngest son shall he set up the gates of it [Josh. 6:26].

We will see when we study 1 Kings 16 that Jericho was rebuilt. And the curse came upon the man who rebuilt it and upon his son.

Before we leave this chapter, notice the explicit command of God, as relayed by Joshua, was that nothing was to be salvaged in the city but the silver, gold, vessels of bronze and iron, which were to be placed in the treasury of the Lord. No soldier was to take anything for himself.

And ye, in any wise keep yourselves from the accursed thing, lest ye make yourselves accursed, when ye take of the accursed thing, and make the camp of Israel a curse, and trouble it [Josh. 6:18].

We will see in the next chapter that somebody snitched at the battle of Jericho.

CHAPTER 7

***THEME:** Defeat at Ai*

The worst enemy that you have is yourself. He occupies the same skin that you occupy. He uses the same brain that you use in thinking his destructive thoughts. He uses the same hands that you use to perform his own deeds. This enemy can do you more harm than anyone else. He is the greatest handicap that you have in your daily Christian life.

There are two factors that make dealing with this enemy doubly difficult. In the first place, we are reluctant to recognize and identify him. We are loath to label him as an enemy. The fact of the matter is most of us rather like him. The second problem is that he is on the inside of us. If he would only come out and fight like a man, it would be different, but he will not. It is not because he is a coward, but because he can fight better from his position within.

Nations, cities, churches, and individuals have been destroyed by the enemy within. Russia fell to the Communists, not because of the German pressure on the outside, but because of this doctrine fomenting on the inside.

There comes out of ancient history an authentic narrative, long held in the category of mythology, that the city of Troy held off the Greeks for ten long, weary years. Finally the Greeks sailed away leaving a wooden horse. The Trojans took that wooden horse within their gates, and that was the undoing and destruction of Troy.

In a similar way churches are wrecked from within, not from forces without. The Lord

Jesus Christ, in letters to the seven churches in Asia Minor, gave them certain warnings; yet not one of these churches received warning as to the enemy on the outside. He said: ". . . Thou hast there some that hold the teaching of Balaam. . . . So hast thou also some that hold the teaching of the Nicolaitans in like manner" (Rev. 2:14–15 ASV). Also He warned: "But I have this against thee, that thou sufferest the woman Jezebel, who calleth herself a prophetess; and she teacheth and seduceth my servants to commit fornication, and to eat things sacrificed to idols" (Rev. 2:20 ASV). Christ said to these churches (in effect), "You have something within that is bringing about your own destruction." Disloyalty and unfaithfulness in the church today is hurting God's cause more than any enemy that is on the outside. The devil can only hurt our churches from the inside, not from the outside.

Also, my friend, an individual can be destroyed from the inside. Alexander the Great was probably the greatest military genius who has moved armies across the pages of history. There has been no one like him. Before the age of thirty-five he had conquered the world, but he died a drunkard. He had conquered the world, but he could not conquer Alexander the Great. There was an enemy within that destroyed him.

The only battle that the children of Israel lost in taking the Promised Land was a battle in which the defeat came, not from without, but from within. When the children of Israel entered the Promised Land, not many enemies, but three conspicuous and outstanding ones stood in their way. They were Jericho, Ai, and the Gibeonites. These three enemies of Israel prevented Israel's enjoyment and possession of the Promised Land. The land was there. God had told them that it was theirs. God had given them the title deed in His promise to Abraham. To Joshua He had said, "Every place that the sole of your foot shall tread upon, to you have I given it, as I spake unto Moses" (Josh. 1:3 ASV). God was saying to them, "It is yours, go in, possess, and enjoy that which you take."

What a lesson that is for us today. These people were given a land that was made up of three hundred thousand square miles, and even in their best days they only occupied thirty thousand square miles. Christians have been given all spiritual blessings. But how many of them, Christian, are you enjoying today? How many of them are really yours? You have the title to them, but have you claimed them and are you enjoying them as He intended? Think of the many Christians who are blessed with all spiritual blessings and yet are living as if they are spiritual paupers. God has made them available to us but, if we are to get them, there are battles to be fought and victories to be won. In fact, the Epistle to the Ephesians closes with the clanking of armor and the sound of battle, with the call to put on the whole armor of God.

In Joshua 7 and 8, defeat and victory at Ai represent the flesh in the believer. The sin of Achan was sin in the camp. Steps in sins of flesh are: I saw—physical; I coveted—mental; I took—volitional. There will be no deliverance until sin is dealt with in the life of a believer.

Now let us look at the text.

But the children of Israel committed a trespass in the accursed thing: for Achan, the son of Carmi, the son of Zabdi, the son of Zerah, of the tribe of Judah, took of the accursed thing: and the anger of the LORD was kindled against the children of Israel [Josh. 7:1].

This verse tells us that the children of Israel committed a trespass but it was one man, Achan, who committed the sin. The whole nation had to suffer because of what Achan did. This is interesting because many people stand on the outside and criticize the church. They talk about the failure of the church and its apostasy. I do some of this myself. But, my friend, talking about the church as a member is one thing, and standing on the outside doing nothing is quite another. If the church is failing and is in a state of apostasy (and it is), then you and I are implicated in it as members of the church. If one member suffers, then all members suffer. "And whether one member suffer, all the members suffer with it; or one member be honoured, all the members rejoice with it" (1 Cor. 12:26).

And Joshua sent men from Jericho to Ai, which is beside Beth-aven, on the east side of Beth-el, and spake unto them, saying, Go up and view the country. And the men went up and viewed Ai.

And they returned to Joshua, and said unto him, Let not all the people go up; but let about two or three thousand men go up and smite Ai; and make not all the people to labour thither; for they are but few [Josh. 7:2–3].

Jericho represents the world; Ai represents the flesh. Some saints are marching around Jericho, blowing trumpets as they talk about being separated Christians. But they are as negative as anyone could be as they declare, "We don't do this, and we don't do that." In fact, they do a spiritual strip-tease—they put off everything that seems to them to be worldly. They have overcome the world. But what about the flesh, friends? Some of the most dangerous people in the church are the super-duper saints who talk about having overcome the world, but they are defeated at Ai. Some of them have the meanest tongues imaginable. I was a pastor for forty years, and I could tell you story after story about the antics of the super-duper saints. The flesh has many people in tow. They think they are living the Christian life. In fact, they talk about living the victorious life, yet they do not even know what it is. The victorious life is *His* life. He is the One who gets the victory and not us.

The children of Israel were in the flush of victory. They had overcome Jericho. Although it was God's victory, in a short time Israel thought of it as their victory. Joshua sent some of his men to look at Ai. After looking the city over carefully, they said, "Ai is nothing compared to Jericho." When I was in that land, I looked at it through binoculars—we didn't even go up to it. It is a little old place and doesn't amount to much.

So there went up thither of the people about three thousand men: and they fled before the men of Ai.

And the men of Ai smote of them about thirty and six men: for they chased them from before the gate even unto Shebarim, and smote them in the going down: wherefore the hearts of the people melted, and became as water [Josh. 7:4–5].

Israel was defeated by the men of Ai. You and I are defeated by the flesh. We cannot use the same tactics to overcome the flesh as we use to overcome the world. The Israelites did not recognize their weakness. The apostle Paul recognized his weakness when he said, "For I know that in me (that is, in my flesh,) dwelleth no good thing: for to will is present with me; but how to perform that which is good I find not" (Rom. 7:18). Have you found out, my Christian friend, that you have no strength or power within yourself? You cannot live the Christian life, and God never asks you to. God wants to live the Christian life through you. In Romans 7 Paul discovered that there was no good thing in his old nature. He also found out that there was no power in his new nature. The new nature wants to live for God but does not have the power to do it. In Romans 8 we are introduced to the Holy Spirit of God. It is only when we are filled with the Holy Spirit of God that we can live the Christian life.

And Joshua rent his clothes, and fell to the earth upon his face before the ark of the Lord until the eventide, he and the elders of Israel, and put dust upon their heads.

And Joshua said, Alas, O Lord God, wherefore hast thou at all brought this people over Jordan, to deliver us into the hand of the Amorites, to destroy us? would to God we had been content, and dwelt on the other side Jordan! [Josh. 7:6–7].

We have heard this song before. Joshua is singing the blues. He learned the lyrics in the wilderness with the children of Israel. Joshua did not sing this song in the wilderness, but he is singing now. He cannot understand why he lost the battle. So he tears his clothes and cries out:

O Lord, what shall I say, when Israel turneth their backs before their enemies!

For the Canaanites and all the inhabitants of the land shall hear of it, and shall environ us round, and cut off our name from the earth: and what wilt thou do unto thy great name? [Josh. 7:8–9].

Listen to what the Lord said. It is getting right down to the nitty-gritty.

And the Lord said unto Joshua, Get thee up; wherefore liest thou thus upon thy face? [Josh. 7:10].

He says to Joshua, "Get up off your face, and cut out all this whining in sackcloth and ashes." There are Christians who spend their prayer time whining before the Lord. It won't do any good, friend. We need to get at the root of the problem.

Israel hath sinned, and they have also transgressed my covenant which I commanded them: for they have even taken of the accursed thing, and have also

stolen, and dissembled also, and they have put it even among their own stuff [Josh. 7:11].

Joshua did not know that Israel had sinned. He did not have the spiritual discernment that was in the early church. When Ananias and Sapphira lied about their property in Acts 5, the Holy Spirit brought it out immediately. The early church was sensitive to sin.

God told Joshua that sin was in the camp and he would have to deal with it.

In the morning therefore ye shall be brought according to your tribes: and it shall be, that the tribe which the LORD taketh shall come according to the families thereof; and the family which the LORD shall take shall come by households; and the household which the LORD shall take shall come man by man [Josh. 7:14].

The tribe of Judah and the family of the Zarhites were found to be guilty.

And he brought his household man by man; and Achan, the son of Carmi, the son of Zabdi, the son of Zerah, of the tribe of Judah, was taken [Josh. 7:18].

Israel had to go through this long procedure in order to find the guilty party. It was difficult for them to distinguish evil in the camp. For us, also, it seems to be difficult to distinguish evil in the church. Church members seem to be the most blind to evil in their own communities. They can see evil in a night club downtown or in a liquor store or in some politician, but they cannot see sin in their family or church. How tragic that is.

And Joshua said unto Achan, My son, give, I pray thee, glory to the LORD God of Israel, and make confession unto him; and tell me now what thou hast done; hide it not from me.

And Achan answered Joshua, and said, Indeed I have sinned against the LORD God of Israel, and thus and thus have I done:

When I saw among the spoils a goodly Babylonish garment, and two hundred shekels of silver, and a wedge of gold of fifty shekels weight, then I coveted them, and took them; and, behold, they are hid in the earth in the midst of my tent, and the silver under it [Josh. 7:19–21].

Notice the steps of Achan's sin. He saw, he coveted, he took. These are the steps of the sin of the flesh. Gossip, criticism, envy, and jealousy are all sins of the flesh. They cause strife and trouble. For instance, criticism builds up your ego. It calls attention to yourself. It makes you look better than the person you are criticizing. The old sin of the flesh sees, covets, and then takes.

Now what does Achan do when he is confronted? He confesses. He lays it right out. For believers today, how are we going to overcome the flesh? We have to deal with sin in our lives.

You remember that the way we overcome the world is by faith. But that isn't the way we overcome the flesh. We want to have fellowship with God; we want to be filled by the Holy Spirit that we might serve Him. Now how are we going to have fellowship with Him? How are we going to have power in our lives? John's first epistle makes it clear the way we *can't* do it: ". . . God is light, and in him is no darkness at all. If we say that we have fellowship with him, and walk in darkness, we lie, and do not the truth" (1 John 1:5–6). If you say you are having fellowship with Him and are living in sin, you are not kidding anybody. You certainly are not having fellowship with Him, and you know it. Now suppose we say we have no sin. "If we say that we have no sin, we deceive ourselves, and the truth is not in us" (1 John 1:8). But what are we to do? "If we confess our sins, he is faithful and just to forgive us our sins, and to cleanse us from all unrighteousness" (1 John 1:9). You see, you cannot bring God down to your level. And friend, you cannot bring yourself up to God's level. The thing to do is to keep the communication open between you and God. And the only way you can do it is by confessing your sin. John adds, "If we say that we have not sinned, we make him a liar, and his word is not in us" (1 John 1:10). That is strong language, friend. God says if we say we have no sin we are lying. And I believe He is accurate. But what do we do about it? We are to confess our sins.

How are we to do that? True confession does not deal in generalities. Spell it out as Achan did: "I saw them; I coveted them; I took them." Tell God everything that is in your heart—just open it up to Him. You might as well tell Him because He already knows all about it.

Mel Trotter told about a man on the board of his Pacific Garden Mission, a doctor, who, when he prayed would say, "Lord, if I have sinned, forgive my sins." Mel Trotter got tired of listening to that. Finally he went to the doctor and said to him, "Listen, Doc, you say, 'If I have sinned.' Don't you know whether or not you have sinned?" The doctor said, "Well, I guess I do." "Don't you know what your sin is?" "No," the doctor said, "I don't know what it is." Mel Trotter said, "If you don't know, then *guess* at it!" The next time the doctor prayed, Mel said, he guessed it the first time! It is amazing, friends, the way we beat around the bush even in our praying. Just go to God and tell Him exactly what your sin is. That is confession. There can be no joy in your life; there can be no power in your life; there can be no victory in your life until there is confession of sin.

And Joshua said, Why hast thou troubled us? the LORD shall trouble thee this day. And all Israel stoned him with stones, and burned them with fire, after they had stoned them with stones.

And they raised over him a great heap of stones unto this day. So the LORD turned from the fierceness of his anger. Wherefore the name of that place was called, The valley of Achor, unto this day [Josh. 7:25–26].

This is a serious situation, and it is emphasized for believers in the New Testament. "For if ye live after the flesh, ye shall die: but if ye through the Spirit do mortify the deeds of the body, ye shall live" (Rom. 8:13). There are many Christians who are not living. Dwight L. Moody put it in this quaint way, "People have just enough religion to make them miserable." There are miserable saints because they do not deal with the sin in their lives. The apostle Paul said, "For if we would judge ourselves, we should not be judged. But when we are judged, we are chastened of the Lord, that we should not be condemned with the world" (1 Cor. 11:31–32). If we don't judge ourselves, God has to step in and judge us, and His judgment is sometimes pretty serious. I can tell you from experience what the judgment of God is in my own life. And it will do no good to complain and whine like Joshua did. The thing to do is to go to God and get the miserable thing straightened out. When we confess our sin to Him and turn from it, then we experience the joy of the Lord.

CHAPTER 8

THEME: *Victory at Ai; Joshua reads the blessings and cursings*

As we have seen in chapter 7, Israel suffered an ignoble defeat at the little city of Ai, and the reason for the defeat was sin in the camp. Now the sin has been dealt with, and God is prepared to give Israel the victory.

VICTORY AT AI

And the LORD said unto Joshua, Fear not, neither be thou dismayed: take all the people of war with thee, and arise, go up to Ai: see, I have given into thy hand the king of Ai, and his people, and his city, and his land [Josh. 8:1].

Notice that God says to take *all* the men of war when they go against Ai. As we have said, Ai represents the flesh. The flesh is the greatest enemy you have, and you need all the resources you have to get the victory.

And thou shalt do to Ai and her king as thou didst unto Jericho and her king: only the spoil thereof, and the cattle thereof, shall ye take for a prey unto yourselves: lay thee an ambush for the city behind it [Josh. 8:2].

You will recall that at the battle of Jericho they were not to take any of the prey or the spoil for themselves. But here God tells them to take what they want. Why the difference? Well, we now know that in Jericho social diseases were running rampant. Joshua didn't know about disease germs, but God did.

Note that God tells Joshua to take Ai by ambush.

So Joshua arose, and all the people of war, to go up against Ai: and Joshua chose out thirty thousand mighty men of valour, and sent them away by night.

And he commanded them, saying, Behold, ye shall lie in wait against the

city, even behind the city: go not very far from the city, but be ye all ready:

And I, and all the people that are with me, will approach unto the city: and it shall come to pass, when they come out against us, as at the first, that we will flee before them,

(For they will come out after us) till we have drawn them from the city; for they will say, They flee before us, as at the first: therefore we will flee before them.

Then ye shall rise up from the ambush, and seize upon the city: for the LORD your God will deliver it into your hand [Josh. 8:3–7].

As we read on, we see that the strategy worked just as Joshua planned, and the city of Ai fell easily into the hands of Israel.

Because Ai represents the flesh, we learn from this episode great spiritual lessons. First of all there must be a recognition of the enemy and his potential. We must realize that the greatest enemy you and I have is *ourselves*. I hear folk saying, "The devil made me do it." Well, he didn't. It is that flesh of yours which is responsible.

Second, we must examine very carefully the reasons for our defeats. Primarily the reason for defeat is our dependence upon our own ability. You remember that the spies said to Joshua, "You will need only about two or three thousand men to overcome little Ai." And we think the flesh will be easy to overcome. We depend on ourselves to do it. We will have to come to the same place to which Paul came when he cried, "O wretched man that I am! who shall deliver me from the body of this death?" (Rom. 7:24).

My friend, you and I cannot control the flesh. Only the Spirit of God can do that. The tragedy is that thousands are trying to control and eradicate it in their own strength. You might as well take a gallon of French perfume out to the barnyard, pour it on a pile of manure, and expect to make it into a sand pile in which your children might play. You cannot improve and control this thing we know as the flesh or the sin nature. God says you cannot. Only the Holy Spirit can control it.

Christ died not only that you might have salvation, but He died that this sin nature might be dealt with. ". . . God sending his own Son in the likeness of sinful flesh, and for sin, condemned sin in the flesh" (Rom. 8:3). This simply means that when Christ came to this earth, He not only died for your sins that you might have salvation, but He died to bring into judgment this old sin nature. Otherwise God could not touch us with a forty-foot pole, because we are evil. Christ died because I have a sin nature and you have a sin nature. The Holy Spirit could not touch us until Christ had paid that penalty. When the penalty was paid, and our sin nature was condemned, then the Holy Spirit could and did come into our lives and bring victory out of defeat. As Paul expressed it, "I am crucified with Christ: nevertheless I live; yet not I, but Christ liveth in me: and the life which I now live in the flesh I live by the faith of the Son of God, who loved me, and gave himself for me" (Gal. 2:20). The flesh, like Ai, will defeat us unless we are depending upon the power of the Holy Spirit to win the victory.

JOSHUA READS THE BLESSINGS AND CURSINGS

Then Joshua built an altar unto the LORD God of Israel in mount Ebal,

As Moses the servant of the LORD commanded the children of Israel, as it is written in the book of the law of Moses, an altar of whole stones, over which no man hath lift up any iron: and they offered thereon burnt offerings unto the LORD, and sacrificed peace offerings.

And he wrote there upon the stones a copy of the law of Moses, which he wrote in the presence of the children of Israel [Josh. 8:30–32].

We find that after the victory at Ai, Joshua built an altar unto the Lord God of Israel in Mount Ebal. Then the Israelites did what Moses had commanded, and Joshua read the blessings and cursings (see Deut. 11:26–32).

And afterward he read all the words of the law, the blessings and cursings, according to all that is written in the book of the law.

There was not a word of all that Moses commanded, which Joshua read not before all the congregation of Israel, with the women, and the little ones, and the strangers that were conversant among them [Josh. 8:34–35].

Note that the entire Law of Moses was read.

They did not read just a part of it; they read all of it. This was to be the law of the land, and it was time for Israel to be reminded of the conditions of God's covenant with her.

CHAPTER 9

***THEME:** Compact with the Gibeonites*

As Joshua began the conquest of the Promised Land, he faced three formidable enemies: Jericho, Ai, and the Gibeonites. These three enemies of Joshua represent the enemies of the Christian today. Jericho represents the *world*; Ai represents the *flesh*; and the Gibeonites represent the *devil*.

You will recall that Joshua's strategy was to first take Jericho, located right in the center of the land, then to take Ai which stood northeast of Jericho. To the south was an alliance of Gibeonites. Apparently they were next in the line of conquest. But the Gibeonites were clever, as we shall see.

And it came to pass, when all the kings which were on this side Jordan, in the hills, and in the valleys, and in all the coasts of the great sea over against Lebanon, the Hittite, and the Amorite, the Canaanite, the Perizzite, the Hivite, and the Jebusite, heard thereof;

That they gathered themselves together, to fight with Joshua and with Israel, with one accord [Josh. 9:1–2].

Undoubtedly these kings had planned to unite against the Israelites, but it seems that for some reason they failed to come together, and they did not succeed in stopping the invading army of Israel. This may explain the defection of the Gibeonites. Their thought was not to fight but to make a compact.

And when the inhabitants of Gibeon heard what Joshua had done unto Jericho and to Ai,

They did work wilily, and went and made as if they had been ambassadors, and took old sacks upon their asses, and wine bottles, old, and rent, and bound up;

And old shoes and clouted upon their feet, and old garments upon them; and all the bread of their provision was dry and mouldy.

And they went to Joshua unto the camp at Gilgal, and said unto him, and to the men of Israel, We be come from a far country: now therefore make ye a league with us.

And the men of Israel said unto the Hivites, Peradventure ye dwell among us; and how shall we make a league with you?

And they said unto Joshua, We are thy servants. And Joshua said unto them, Who are ye? and from whence come ye?

And they said unto him, From a very far country thy servants are come because of the name of the LORD thy God: for we have heard the fame of him, and all that he did in Egypt [Josh. 9:3–9].

The Gibeonites were very clever, and they were a bunch of liars. They pretended to be envoys from a far country when, in fact, they lived only a few miles from Jerusalem. They told Joshua that they really wanted to worship the living and true God. Then they called Joshua's attention—if it hadn't been noticed—to their old sacks and wineskins, their old shoes and threadbare clothing, and their moldy bread. It was all a hoax, but Joshua fell for it. God had ordered the Israelites to completely wipe out the people of the land and to make no treaties with them. Although it was Joshua's intent to obey God, he was deceived into making peace with the Gibeonites and actually making a league with them. Notice that neither Joshua nor the men of Israel asked the mind of God before entering into this alliance.

As you recall, Jericho represents the world. How do you overcome the world? By faith. Ai represents the flesh. How do you overcome the flesh? Not by fighting it, but by recognizing your weakness, confessing to God, and letting the Spirit of God get the victory. Remember that it was God who said, "I'm going to give you Ai."

Now we have the third enemy, the Gibeonites, who represent for us the devil. Since Ephesians in the New Testament corresponds to the Book of Joshua in the Old Testament, we find an important parallel here. "Put on the whole armour of God, that ye may be able to stand against the wiles of the devil" (Eph. 6:11). As the men of Israel should have been beware of the wiles of the Gibeonites, so the believer today should watch for the wiles of the devil. "For we wrestle not against flesh and blood, but against principalities, against powers, against the rulers of the darkness of this world, against spiritual wickedness in high places" (Eph. 6:12). Our real enemy today is not a flesh and blood enemy, but a spiritual enemy. He is Satan. Yet how many Christians even recognize him today? What does he do? He tries to trick you into following him. I am not sure that he is interested in making a drunkard or a drug addict out of you. I think he is ashamed of that crowd of his in the bars and in the sinful places of the world. He went to church last Sunday, and he will be there next Sunday. He wants to be religious, and he wants you to fall down and worship him. He is clever and many Christians are taken in by him. The devil can pull the wool over our eyes. In 2 Corinthians 2:11 Paul says, "Lest Satan should get an advantage of us: for we are not ignorant of his devices." Unfortunately, you and I are sometimes ignorant of his devices.

Now how do we overcome this enemy? James 4:7 says, "Submit yourselves therefore to God. Resist the devil, and he will flee from you." My friend, we need to submit ourselves to God—that's the first thing. Oh, how we need to stay close to Him in this day in which we live! Satan is out to deceive us as believers. He works wilily. Frankly, I am amazed at the stupidity of the saints today. They are taken in by every ruse imaginable. Do you know why religious rackets are flourishing? It is because Christians are supporting them without doing any investigation. We need to resist the devil. We are to have nothing to do with that about which we are not well informed. There is danger of being linked up with him today, just as the men of Israel in their naiveté became linked up with the Gibeonites.

When Israel discovered that the Gibeonites were neighbors, and had tricked them, they still honored the treaty they had made with them.

But all the princes said unto all the congregation, We have sworn unto them by the Lord God of Israel: now therefore we may not touch them.

This we will do to them; we will even let them live, lest wrath be upon us, because of the oath which we sware unto them [Josh. 9:19–20].

The treaty was honored in that day, although made under these circumstances. Now you may think these folk back here in the Old Testament were uncivilized, but notice that a man's word was very important. And that is the way God wants it today.

And the princes said unto them. Let them live; but let them be hewers of wood and drawers of water unto all the congregation; as the princes had promised them.

And Joshua made them that day hewers of wood and drawers of water for the congregation, and for the altar of the Lord, even unto this day, in the place which he should choose [Josh. 9:21, 27].

CHAPTER 10

***THEME:** Southern campaign: five kings conquered; the sun stood still*

In this chapter Joshua conquers five kings of the Amorites, as he continues the campaign in the south. He completes the campaign in the south by the destruction of Makkedah, Lachish, Libnah, Eglon, Hebron, and Debir.

This chapter contains the account of the long day of Joshua. "Did Joshua make the sun stand still?" is a question which is asked by skeptic and saint alike. Following are some explanations of the long day of Joshua which have been proposed:

1. It is the practice of some to avoid giving any interpretation. They ignore it entirely as if it were not worthy of comment.

2. Some treat the language as poetic (v. 12). This is to adopt a non-literal interpretation which dismisses the miraculous from the incident entirely. Those who hold to this view generally refer to Judges 5:20, ". . . the stars in their courses fought against Sisera." I refuse to dismiss this as poetic because we do not have enough information to state dogmatically that these are poetic statements and not matters of fact. It reminds us of the old bromide that poetic language is sometimes prosaic lying.

3. Some call this a miracle of refraction. The emphasis is placed on verse 13.

4. Some adopt the position that God stopped the entire solar system. They make Joshua's day 23 hours and 20 minutes. The other 40 minutes is found in 2 Kings 20:8–11, where the sun went ten degrees backward for a sign to Hezekiah that his life would be extended.

5. Some adopt the position that God blacked out the sun rather than continued its shining. The Berkeley Version translates it, "O Sun, wait in Gibeon." In the ASV the marginal reading is, "Sun, be silent." Maunder in the International Standard Bible Encyclopedia takes this position. Joshua had made a forced march all night (about forty miles), attacked the enemy from the rear—came suddenly upon them. It was July—about 105° or 120° in the shade, and there was no shade. Joshua did not want more sun—he wanted less sun.

6. The best explanation, it seems, is a combination of numbers 4 and 5. Joshua needed more light and less heat. God covered the sun with a storm of hailstones. God slowed down the earth (v. 12). "Upon Gibeon" indicates that the sun was directly over—bisecting Gibeon—and the moon was going down "in the valley of Ajalon." Gibeon is latitude 31 degrees, 51 minutes north.

This is a miracle.

THE MIRACULOUS DEFENSE OF GIBEON

The background for all the action in this chapter is the treaty Joshua made with the Gibeonites. Of course, he should not have made this treaty, but since he did, he felt bound to it.

> **Now it came to pass, when Adoni-zedec king of Jerusalem had heard how Joshua had taken Ai, and had utterly destroyed it; as he had done to Jericho and her king, so he had done to Ai and her king; and how the inhabitants of Gibeon had made peace with Israel, and were among them;**
>
> **That they feared greatly, because Gibeon was a great city, as one of the royal cities, and because it was greater than Ai, and all the men thereof were mighty.**
>
> **Wherefore Adoni-zedec king of Jerusalem sent unto Hoham king of Hebron, and unto Piram king of Jarmuth, and unto Japhia king of Lachish, and unto Debir king of Eglon, saying,**
>
> **Come up unto me, and help me, that we may smite Gibeon: for it hath made peace with Joshua and with the children of Israel [Josh. 10:1–4].**

These kings hear of the treaty Gibeon made with Israel, and they come against these Hivites—for that is what these Gibeonites were—to destroy them.

> **Therefore the five kings of the Amorites, the king of Jerusalem, the king of Hebron, the king of Jarmuth, the king of Lachish, the king of Eglon, gathered themselves together, and went up, they and all their hosts, and encamped before Gibeon, and made war against it [Josh. 10:5]**

So what do these Gibeonites do?

And the men of Gibeon sent unto Joshua to the camp to Gilgal, saying, Slack not thy hand from thy servants; come up to us quickly, and save us, and help us: for all the kings of the Amorites that dwell in the mountains are gathered together against us [Josh. 10:6].

They send an SOS to Joshua—come help us quickly!

So Joshua ascended from Gilgal, he, and all the people of war with him, and all the mighty men of valour.

And the LORD said unto Joshua, Fear them not: for I have delivered them into thine hand; there shall not a man of them stand before thee.

Joshua therefore came unto them suddenly, and went up from Gilgal all night [Josh. 10:7–9].

Joshua came to their rescue for, I think, two reasons. First, because of the treaty, he felt obligated. Second, after all he had been told to exterminate the enemy in that land. So his army took out after them. He used the tactic of surprise attack, and the Lord routed them before Israel.

Then spake Joshua to the LORD in the day when the LORD delivered up the Amorites before the children of Israel, and he said in the sight of Israel, Sun, stand thou still upon Gibeon; and thou, Moon, in the valley of Ajalon.

And the sun stood still, and the moon stayed, until the people had avenged themselves upon their enemies. Is not this written in the book of Jasher? So the sun stood still in the midst of heaven, and hasted not to go down about a whole day.

And there was no day like that before it or after it, that the LORD hearkened unto the voice of a man: for the LORD fought for Israel [Josh. 10:12–14].

We have already discussed the various interpretations of Joshua's long day in the opening remarks of this chapter. According to Joshua 10:12, I believe God stopped the entire solar system to accomplish this miracle. The sun became silent. Joshua wanted more daylight in which to fight; so God stopped the solar system and cut down the heat of the sun by a hailstorm.

God caused the sun to stand still so that Joshua might be victorious in battle. A certain professor once said, "It is ridiculous that God would stop the entire universe for one man." It may sound preposterous to some people, but God did it. He also sent His Son into the world to die for sinners, which was much more wonderful than stopping the sun. When God stopped the sun, He demonstrated His wisdom and power. When He sent His Son into the world to become a man and die on the cross, He displayed His love. If you were the only person that had ever been born, Christ would have died for you. The professor will say that is ridiculous also, and it is. But we have another word for it: grace. "For by grace are ye saved through faith; and that not of yourselves: it is the gift of God" (Eph. 2:8).

VICTORY AT MAKKEDAH

And Joshua returned, and all Israel with him, unto the camp to Gilgal.

But these five kings fled, and hid themselves in a cave at Makkedah.

And it was told Joshua, saying, The five kings are found hid in a cave at Makkedah.

And Joshua said, Roll great stones upon the mouth of the cave, and set men by it for to keep them:

And stay ye not, but pursue after your enemies, and smite the hindmost of them; suffer them not to enter into their cities: for the LORD your God hath delivered them into your hand [Josh. 10:15–19].

Remember that these kings and their people were given 420 years to make up their minds as to whether or not they would turn to God. Also God had made it known that He was giving the land to Israel and that He would save anyone who would turn to Him. Israel had to stay out of the land 420 years until the iniquity of the Amorites was full. That time had now come. God brought the children of Israel across the Red Sea not only for their sake, but also to demonstrate His redemption through power, as He had by blood that last night in Egypt when the angel of death passed over the homes on which the blood was on the doorposts. This was not only to convince the Egyptians that there was the living and true God amidst all the idols of

Egypt, but also to convince these people in the land. Remember that the harlot Rahab had said, "For we have heard how the LORD dried up the water of the Red Sea for you" (Josh. 2:10). She believed. Now if that woman believed, anybody could have believed God. However, these folk who are losing their lives did not believe. They had rejected God's mercy, and judgment is coming upon them. Friend, the message has never changed. God loves the world. God loves you and gave His Son. If you will believe on Him, you will not perish. Will you perish if you don't believe? Yes. That is what is happening to these folk. They just don't believe God. Now that may not sound nice to you, and you'd like to have it otherwise, but this is the way it is written in the Word of God.

And it came to pass, when they brought out those kings unto Joshua, that Joshua called for all the men of Israel, and said unto the captains of the men of war which went with him, Come near, put your feet upon the necks of these kings. And they came near, and put their feet upon the necks of them.

And Joshua said unto them, Fear not, nor be dismayed, be strong and of good courage: for thus shall the LORD do to all your enemies against whom ye fight [Josh. 10:24–25].

This is an impressive array of kings. Forty years prior to this time they caused Israelite spies to say, "We cannot enter the land. We will never be able to take it." Joshua had the captains of his army put their feet upon the necks of these kings to strengthen the heart of these people. They were frightened folk.

There was a whimsical story that came out of World War I when a certain hero, who had captured more German prisoners than any other, was being feted by some society folk in Nashville, Tennessee. One dear talkative dowager asked the hero, "How did you feel when you brought all of those soldiers in?" He replied, "I was scared to death!" This is how the Israelites felt. God wants to encourage them. Then Joshua slew the kings and hanged them on five trees.

And it came to pass at the time of the going down of the sun, that Joshua commanded, and they took them down off the trees, and cast them into the cave wherein they had been hid, and laid great stones in the cave's mouth, which remain until this very day [Josh. 10:27].

The Israelites could have left the kings in the cave and starved them to death. It was more humane to slay them, and they did. They could not turn them loose, and they had no prison in which to put them. Do you think we live in a more civilized day? What do you think about the lawlessness on every hand in our country? We are not in a position to criticize what the Israelites did. They did not have lawlessness, and they settled their problem in the only way they could with a sinful, wicked race. If these kings had been turned loose, they would have led a rebellion against Joshua that would have caused literally thousands of people to die.

After the kings were hanged, they were taken down from the trees. They were not left hanging overnight. Why? Because we are told, "His body shall not remain all night upon the tree, but thou shalt in any wise bury him that day; (for he that is hanged is accursed of God;) that thy land be not defiled, which the LORD thy God giveth thee for an inheritance" (Deut. 21:23). In the New Testament Galatians 3:13 says, "Christ hath redeemed us from the curse of the law, being made a curse for us: for it is written, Cursed is every one that hangeth on a tree." Christ was crucified, but they took Him down from the cross because it is written that cursed is everyone that hangs on a tree. He bore the curse of sin for you and me.

And Joshua smote them from Kadesh-barnea even unto Gaza, and all the country of Goshen, even unto Gibeon.

And all these kings and their land did Joshua take at one time, because the LORD God of Israel fought for Israel.

And Joshua returned, and all Israel with him, unto the camp to Gilgal [Josh. 10:41–43].

It is important to see that it is God who gave Israel victory and possession. Today our victory is in Christ. The victorious life is His life lived in us. Then we are blessed with all spiritual blessings, which are the possessions He has promised to us.

CHAPTERS 11–12

***THEME:** The northern campaign and the roster of conquered kings*

Chapter 11 contains the campaign in the north and the conclusion of Joshua's leadership in war.

And it came to pass, when Jabin king of Hazor had heard those things, that he sent to Jobab king of Madon, and to the king of Shimron, and to the king of Achshaph,

And to the kings that were on the north of the mountains, and of the plains south of Chinneroth, and in the valley, and in the borders of Dor on the west,

And to the Canaanite on the east and on the west, and to the Amorite, and the Hittite, and the Perizzite, and the Jebusite in the mountains, and to the Hivite under Hermon in the land of Mizpeh.

And they went out, they and all their hosts with them, much people, even as the sand that is upon the sea shore in multitude, with horses and chariots very many.

And when all these kings were met together, they came and pitched together at the waters of Merom, to fight against Israel.

And the LORD said unto Joshua, Be not afraid because of them: for to-morrow about this time will I deliver them up all slain before Israel: thou shalt hock their horses, and burn their chariots with fire [Josh. 11:1–6].

Jabin of Hazor in the north seems to have been the organizer. He sends out word to all the folk in that area to come against Joshua, because it is obvious now that he has overcome in the south and he is going to move to the north. And if he moves to the north, he will invade their land—which, of course, is exactly what he did.

As we have seen, Joshua's strategy was to split the land in two, then move into the south (which couldn't get help, you see, from the north). Now the northern kings come together.

So Joshua came, and all the people of war with him, against them by the waters of Merom suddenly; and they fell upon them [Josh. 11:7].

Joshua's strategy, after dividing the land in two, was to come upon the enemy suddenly. You will see that Alexander the Great and also Napoleon used these same tactics.

Joshua made war a long time with all those kings.

There was not a city that made peace with the children of Israel, save the Hivites the inhabitants of Gibeon: all other they took in battle [Josh. 11:18–19].

It was a long and bitter campaign.

Now in chapter 12 we are given the names of the kings which Israel conquered. Frankly, a chapter like this is not very exciting to me. But the thing that impresses me is the detail that the God of this universe has given in items like this. We would think that He would constantly be dealing with great issues in grandiose terms, but God gets right down to the nitty-gritty where you and I live.

There is a lesson for us here. You and I sometimes hesitate to take to God in prayer the little details of our lives. We think, *I ought not to talk to Him about things like that.* Well, friend, talk to Him about those things. He wants to hear them.

A professor who was very liberal in his theology, said to me one time, "You take the Bible literally." "Yes," I said. "You certainly don't believe that God has books up there that He is going to open and look at." I think I shocked him when I said, "I sure do." He keeps the record, friend. Here is a chapter about these kings. I know nothing about them, but God does. He has the record.

He has two books: the Book of Works and the Lamb's Book of Life. Your name is written in one of them, my friend. It is written in the Book of Life when you trust Jesus Christ as your Savior. Your name will never be written there by your own effort. If your name is in this book, you have eternal life in Christ.

There is also a Book of Works. It records the details of everything you have ever done. It is going to be embarrassing for many people when they discover that all they did was give a cup of cold water that cost them nothing.

Recently a dear brother, a retired preacher

with plenty of time on his hands, wrote me a twelve-page letter. I read it and much of the contents were meaningless to me. It mentioned places, people, and a church I knew nothing about. But God knows everything about that man and his life. He has it all written down. It is interesting to God. It adds real dimension to this life to realize that each little detail about His children is important to Him.

CHAPTER 13

THEME: *Confirmation of land to the two and one-half tribes*

Now Joshua was old and stricken in years; and the LORD said unto him, Thou art old and stricken in years, and there remaineth yet very much land to be possessed [Josh. 13:1].

We have passed only the halfway point in this book and we find that Joshua is already an old man and stricken in years. He is not going to be able to lead the children of Israel much longer. He is the leader God used to take the land, but the wars are over. He was about eighty years old when God called him, and now he is over one hundred years old. He had led Israel for many years. Time seems to have passed more quickly since Israel is in the land. The wilderness journey, by comparison, seemed long and drawn out. Now that Israel is in the land of milk and honey, they are laying hold of their possessions, and time passes quickly.

Friend, time would not pass so slowly for some people if they were living a life for God. My, how fast the time goes when you are serving Him! When I began my last pastorate, I was still a young man, and the twenty-one years just slipped by. Suddenly I discovered I was an old man and ready to retire. The most thrilling part of my ministry, however, has taken place since I retired. In my radio and conference ministry I have seen more results than at any time in my ministry. I have seen more of the hand of God, and I have been more conscious of His leading than at any time of my life. I think Joshua felt the same way.

From all outward appearances Israel seemed to be doing very well. They went into the land and drove a wedge right into the center of it. They conquered the south and went on to conquer the north, but the Lord reminded Joshua that there remained much land to be possessed. After doing a tremendous job, my friend, that will be true of you and me. It has been true of every servant of God; he will never accomplish all that he wished. In Philippians 3:12 Paul says, "Not as though I had already attained, either were already perfect: but I follow after, if that I may apprehend that for which also I am apprehended of Christ Jesus." God told Joshua that the land upon which the children of Israel walked would be theirs. They did not, however, walk on all of it. Neither will we ever be able to possess all of our spiritual possessions. I have met a few saints who think they have. They think there is nothing more for them to learn or do. They are satisfied with the life they are leading and have no desire to press on to ". . . the prize of the high calling of God in Christ Jesus" (Phil. 3:14).

The command of Joshua is terminated. He is no longer General Joshua. His next duty is to divide the land and especially to make sure that Moses' promises to the two and one-half tribes are confirmed.

Now therefore divide this land for an inheritance unto the nine tribes, and the half tribe of Manasseh,

With whom the Reubenites and the Gadites have received their inheritance, which Moses gave them, beyond Jordan eastward, even as Moses the servant of the LORD gave them [Josh. 13:7–8].

Joshua's commission (Josh. 1:6) not only included the subjugation of the land, but also the apportioning of it. He allocated not only those portions of Canaan that had already been conquered, but also those parts that were yet to be taken.

CHAPTER 14

THEME: *Caleb given Hebron*

The nine tribes and the half tribe are to have their inheritance by lot. Caleb, by privilege, obtains Hebron. Caleb, who was born a slave, was a spy with Joshua and brought back a favorable report the first time Israel came to Kadesh-Barnea. According to Joshua 14:11 Caleb had found the fountain of youth. He had: (1) Faith to forget the past; (2) Faith to face facts; and (3) Faith to face the future.

And these are the countries which the children of Israel inherited in the land of Canaan, which Eleazar the priest, and Joshua the son of Nun, and the heads of the fathers of the tribes of the children of Israel, distributed for inheritance to them.

By lot was their inheritance, as the LORD commanded by the hand of Moses, for the nine tribes, and for the half tribe [Josh. 14:1–2].

As you will see by the map, all the way from Dan to Beersheba the land is divided into tribes. Reuben, Gad, and the half tribe of Manasseh are on the east bank of the Jordan River. Then starting in the south and going north we have the tribes of Simeon, Judah, Benjamin, Dan, Ephraim, Manasseh, Issachar, Zebulun, Naphtali, Asher, and Dan.

As the LORD commanded Moses, so the children of Israel did, and they divided the land.

Then the children of Judah came unto Joshua in Gilgal: and Caleb the son of Jephunneh the Kenezite said unto him, Thou knowest the thing that the LORD said unto Moses the man of God concerning me and thee in Kadesh-barnea.

Forty years old was I when Moses the servant of the LORD sent me from Kadesh-barnea to espy out the land; and I brought him word again as it was in mine heart.

Nevertheless my brethren that went up with me made the heart of the people melt: but I wholly followed the LORD my God [Josh. 14:5–8].

Caleb was a man who "wholly followed the LORD." If you want a recipe for a long life and a good life, here it is.

And now, behold, the LORD hath kept me alive, as he said, these forty and five years, even since the LORD spake this word unto Moses, while the children of Israel wandered in the wilderness: and now, lo, I am this day fourscore and five years old.

As yet I am as strong this day as I was in the day that Moses sent me: as my strength was then, even so is my strength now, for war, both to go out, and to come in [Josh. 14:10–11].

Caleb is now eighty-five years old, and yet he can say that he is as strong as the day Moses sent him into Canaan as a spy! During the wilderness journey all of the first generation that came out of Egypt died except Caleb and Joshua. These men, along with ten other spies, brought back reports concerning the land of Canaan. The question was, "Could Israel conquer the land?" Joshua and Caleb were certain that with God's help Israel would be victorious in taking the land. The other ten spies saw giants in the land and wanted to return to Egypt. They wanted to go back to slavery, brickyards, the lash of the taskmasters, chains, shackles, and groaning under burdens. The Lord Jesus said, ". . . No man, having put his hand to the plough, and looking back, is fit for the kingdom of God" (Luke 9:62). God had called Israel to go into the land of Canaan, and Caleb believed it could be done.

During those forty years I suppose that often someone would say to Caleb, "Oh, brother Caleb, isn't it terrible out here in this wilderness! It is so hot—it's 118° today!" Caleb would say, "I really hadn't noticed. I guess it is pretty warm, but I was thinking about those grapes of Eschol that I saw. And I was thinking about the city of Hebron. Our father Abraham liked that place, and I like it. That's where I am going." Caleb, even in the wilderness, could think of the future. He had a great hope. It kept him young. Those forty years in the wilderness killed off the rest of the crowd, but they didn't do a thing to him but make him healthy. They grew old, and he grew young. The giants in the Promised Land made the others tremble—they thought of themselves as grasshoppers. But Caleb thought of God. There was freedom from fear in the heart of this man. As Martin Luther said, "One with

God is a majority." God was bigger than the giants.

Caleb reminds me of Adoniram Judson, the missionary who spent twelve years in Burma without a convert. The board that sent him out didn't sense the situation nor what a tremendous missionary they had in Judson; so they wrote him a very diplomatic letter, suggesting that he should come home. They asked him what the prospects in Burma were for the future. His reply was, "The future is as bright as the promises of God." His confidence in God was the reason he could stay in the wilderness of Burma all those years. Although he suffered a great deal and it took a long time for revival to break out, it finally did. His time was well spent.

Are you enjoying all the spiritual blessings that God has for you today? You say, "I have lots of trouble." I know that Christians have many troubles in the course of their lives. My heart goes out to them. But I always think of the testimony of a Negro man who said his favorite Bible verse was, "It came to pass." When puzzled people asked him what he meant by that, he replied, "When I get into trouble and problems pile up, I turn to my verse and know my troubles have not come to stay; they have come to pass." There are a lot of things you can complain about, friend, and I do my share also, but what about your hope? What about the future? Caleb for forty years in that wilderness was enjoying all the spiritual blessings that were his.

Because Caleb believed God and was a man of faith, he said:

Now therefore give me this mountain, whereof the LORD spake in that day; for thou heardest in that day how the Anakims were there, and that the cities were great and fenced: if so be the LORD will be with me, then I shall be able to drive them out, as the LORD said [Josh. 14:12].

You will recall in Genesis that Abraham went to Hebron which means "communion." It was a place of fellowship. Caleb had fellowship with God and now he wants to reside at Hebron.

And Joshua blessed him, and gave unto Caleb the son of Jephunneh Hebron for an inheritance.

Hebron therefore became the inheritance of Caleb the son of Jephunneh the Kenezite unto this day, because that he wholly followed the LORD God of Israel [Josh. 14:13–14].

Friend, someday we will be rewarded. We will not be rewarded according to the great amount of work done for God, nor according to our prominence and popularity. The important thing will be—did you wholly follow the Lord? Oh, that God's people would learn today that the most important thing in this life is to wholly follow the Lord! Caleb, man of God that he was, took Hebron. There were giants there, but he said, "That's the place I want. That's the very best spot!" Oh, that you and I might press toward the mark for the high calling of God in Christ Jesus.

CHAPTERS 15–19

***THEME:** Consignment of land to the tribes of Israel*

This section includes the apportionment of the Promised Land given to the tribes that settled on the west side of the Jordan River. Chapter 15 deals with Judah's portion; chapter 16 with Ephraim's portion; chapter 17 with Manasseh's portion; and chapters 18 and 19 with the portions of Simeon, Zebulun, Issachar, Asher, Naphtali, and Dan.

As important as this section was to the nation of Israel, it has no great significance to us. Therefore we shall lift out only the high points.

PORTION OF JUDAH

In chapter 14 we saw that Caleb was a member of the tribe of Judah and that God gave to him the city of Hebron. In chapter 15 we have more about this remarkable man. Also the boundaries of the entire tribe of Judah are given in this chapter.

And unto Caleb the son of Jephunneh he gave a part among the children of Judah, according to the commandment of the LORD to Joshua, even the city of

Arba the father of Anak, which city is Hebron.

And Caleb drove thence the three sons of Anak, Sheshai, and Ahiman, and Talmai, the children of Anak [Josh. 15:13–14].

You see, the land old Caleb wanted was in giant country, and he was as ready to take on the giants now as when he was a young man.

And he went up thence to the inhabitants of Debir: and the name of Debir before was Kirjath-sepher.

And Caleb said, he that smiteth Kirjath-sepher, and taketh it, to him will I give Achsah my daughter to wife.

And Othniel the son of Kenaz, the brother of Caleb, took it: and he gave him Achsah his daughter to wife.

And it came to pass, as she came unto him, that she moved him to ask of her father a field: and she lighted off her ass; and Caleb said unto her, What wouldest thou?

Who answered, Give me a blessing; for thou hast given me a south land; give me also springs of water. And he gave her the upper springs, and the nether springs [Josh. 15:15–19].

The total area of the tribe of Judah is marked out in the first of the chapter; then cities are mentioned. You'll have difficulty finding most of them on your map because they are way down in Negev.

PORTION OF EPHRAIM

Joseph was one of the twelve sons of Jacob, and his two sons, Ephraim and Manasseh, were each counted as a tribe. Because the tribe of Levi was the priestly tribe and was given no land, the total number of tribes inheriting the land was still only twelve tribes, rather than thirteen.

And the lot of the children of Joseph fell from Jordan by Jericho, unto the water of Jericho on the east, to the wilderness that goeth up from Jericho throughout mount Beth-el,

And goeth out from Beth-el to Luz, and passeth along unto the borders of Archi to Ataroth,

And goeth down westward to the coast of Japhleti, unto the coast of Beth-horon the nether, and to Gezer: and the goings out thereof are at the sea.

So the children of Joseph, Manasseh and Ephraim, took their inheritance [Josh. 16:1–4].

PORTION OF MANASSEH

As you may recall, the tribe of Manasseh was divided. Half of the tribe settled on the east bank of the Jordan, but the other half crossed over and are now given their portion.

There is a remarkable instance in this chapter concerning the children of Joseph, and Ephraim in particular.

And the children of Joseph spake unto Joshua, saying, Why hast thou given me but one lot and one portion to inherit, seeing I am a great people, forasmuch as the LORD hath blessed me hitherto? [Josh. 17:14].

Ephraim was complaining because they had not been given a very large portion of land. In fact, Ephraim was given only about half of what Manasseh received. There were many people in the tribe of Ephraim. Joshua belonged to this tribe, and the Ephraimites probably felt that he would do something to help. Joshua, however, did nothing. The land they inherited was mountainous. The country is as rugged as any through which I have traveled. They were not satisfied.

And Joshua answered them, If thou be a great people, then get thee up to the wood country, and cut down for thyself there in the land of the Perizzites and of the giants, if mount Ephraim be too narrow for thee [Josh. 17:15].

If you travel to this area today, you will find that the hills are as bare as they are in Southern California. What happened to all of the trees? The enemies that have come into this country down through the centuries have completely denuded the hills. There is a great campaign in Israel right now to plant trees in that region. When I visited there, I planted five trees; one for myself, one for my wife, one for my daughter, one for the church in which I served, and one for a Jewish friend. Trees will grow here because the land was once covered with them.

By the way, in Christ's day the Mount of Olives was also covered with trees. If there had been just a little clump of trees, as there is today, His enemies would not have had any

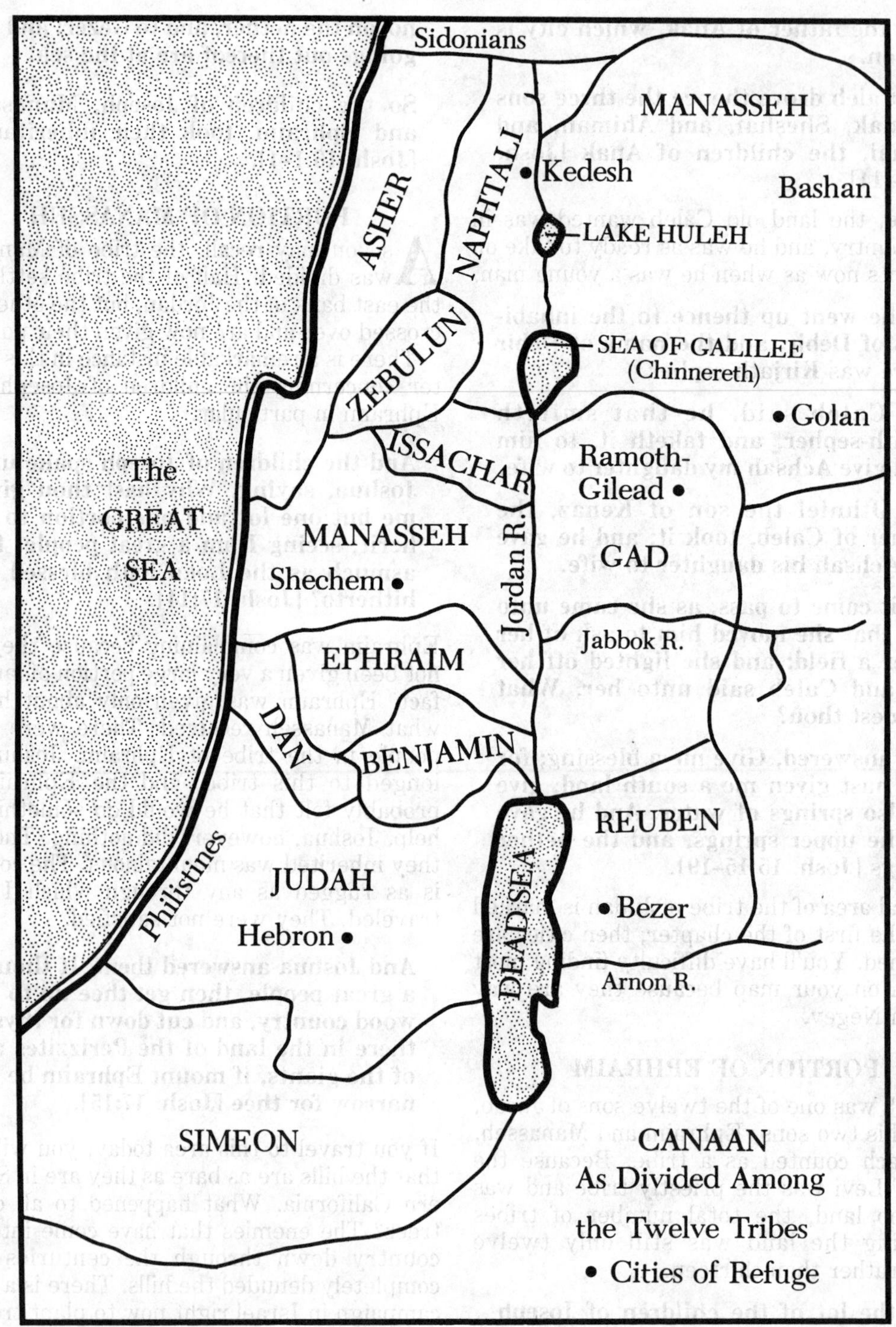

trouble finding Christ and His followers in the garden. Judas was needed to lead them through the jungle of trees and point out exactly where our Lord was.

Joshua's reply to his own tribe was noble.

And Joshua spake unto the house of Joseph, even to Ephraim and to Manasseh, saying, Thou art a great people, and hast great power: thou shalt not have one lot only:

But the mountain shall be thine; for it is a wood, and thou shalt cut it down: and the outgoings of it shall be thine: for thou shalt drive out the Canaanites, though they have iron chariots, and though they be strong [Josh. 17:17–18].

Joshua says, "If you don't like what you have, go up and possess the mountains. But remember there are giants in the land. You'll have to work; you'll have to fight. It's going to cost you something.

It is time we stopped complaining and possessed more land.

A great preacher from New York City once took a vacation in northern New York state. He went to church on Sunday in a small country town, and to his surprise the young pastor was preaching almost verbatim one of his published sermons. When the young man came out of the pulpit, and was greeting people at the door, the visiting pastor shook hands with him and asked, "Young man, I enjoyed your sermon this morning. How long did it take you to prepare it?" "Oh, it took me only about three hours," came his reply. "That is strange," said the famous preacher, "It took me about eight hours to prepare it."

It takes work to lay hold of spiritual possessions and blessings. Many years ago a student of mine entered the active ministry. He served in a church about three years and then came to see me. He was in distress because he said he was all preached out. I asked him how much time he spent studying and how long it took him to prepare a sermon. He told me that he did not spend much time studying and it took him about an hour to prepare a sermon. That was his problem. I spend anywhere from eight to twenty hours preparing a sermon. In order to lay hold of spiritual blessings, you are going to have to work hard. But remember that there is an enemy. There are giants in the land. Satan will trip you up if he can.

Another classmate of mine once complained to a professor about a book he was required to read. He claimed it was as dry as dust. "Well," said the professor, "why don't you dampen it with a little sweat from your brow?" This is a great argument for hard work. Joshua says to his tribe, "Don't come to me and complain. There is plenty of land for you. Go and get it."

THE TABERNACLE IS SET UP AT SHILOH

And the whole congregation of the children of Israel assembled together at Shiloh, and set up the tabernacle of the congregation there. And the land was subdued before them [Josh. 18:1].

The children of Israel pitched the tabernacle at Shiloh, a town in Ephraim. It was not, however to be the permanent place for the tabernacle because it was not the center of the land. God would choose a permanent site through David, which would one day be Jerusalem. But until the site changed, the children of Israel were to worship the Lord at Shiloh. The tabernacle remained in Shiloh during the whole period of the Judges.

DIVISION OF THE REMAINING LAND

Now Joshua gives a challenge.

And there remained among the children of Israel seven tribes, which had not yet received their inheritance.

And Joshua said unto the children of Israel, How long are ye slack to go to possess the land, which the LORD God of your fathers hath given you? [Josh. 18:2–3].

Seven of the tribes were standing around with their hands in their pockets. They said to Joshua, "What about this land? What are you going to give us?" Joshua told them, "You have been given a certain area. Go and possess your land. How long are you going to wait?"

This is also God's challenge to us. He has made available to us all spiritual blessings, but we are slack when it comes to claiming them. God has been so good to us. Oh, how we can thank Him for His grace, His love, His goodness, and His mercy. How wonderful He is! Why don't we move in and possess the land He has given to us?

After Joshua's challenge, the tribes began to move out and possess the land which had been allotted to them.

PORTION FOR BENJAMIN

The tribe of Benjamin received its inheritance between the land of Judah and the tribes of Ephraim and Dan.

PORTION FOR SIMEON

Out of the portion of the children of Judah was the inheritance of the children of Simeon: for the part of the children of Judah was too much for them: therefore the children of Simeon had their inheritance within the inheritance of them [Josh. 19:9].

As we saw in chapter 15, the tribe of Judah was given a special preference because it was the kingly tribe. It will be in that tribe that the capital of the nation, both religious and political, will be established. The capital city will become Jerusalem, and we will see that David is the one who made that choice.

Because the land allotted to Judah was more than it needed, the southern portion was given to Simeon.

PORTION FOR ZEBULUN, ISSACHAR, ASHER, NAPHTALI, DAN

The tribe of Zebulun received a portion of land that was landlocked in lower Galilee. The inheritance of Issachar went from Mount Tabor on the west to the southern part of the Sea of Galilee. It also included territory in the coastal region from north of Mount Carmel to the approximate area of Tyre and Sidon. The tribe of Naphtali settled in the area of eastern Upper and Lower Galilee. The territory of Dan was located between Benjamin and the Mediterranean Sea. Later some of the Danites migrated northward and settled near the northern part of Naphtali.

This section reveals how much detail God gave concerning Israel and the land. The land and the people go together. God not only gave them the land of Canaan, He also gave a particular area to a particular tribe. He gave each tribe a certain section of land. God was concerned about each individual and his possession.

In this God has a lesson for you and me today. It tells us that God is concerned about our personal lives. My friend, for Him your private life is not private—He knows you like a book. A rather godless neighbor said to me one day, "I want to go out into the desert where I can be by myself, and away from everybody." Well, that is a normal desire. We all need to get away from people once in awhile. But I reminded him—and I don't think he appreciated it—that he wouldn't get away from God. I said, "You can't run away from Him, brother. He will be right out there in the desert waiting for you." It is wonderful, friend, to get away from people like that, if we are getting away for fellowship with the Lord.

JOSHUA RECEIVES A SPECIAL PORTION

When they had made an end of dividing the land for inheritance by their coasts, the children of Israel gave an inheritance to Joshua the son of Nun among them:

According to the word of the LORD they gave him the city which he asked, even Timnath-serah in mount Ephraim: and he built the city, and dwelt therein.

These are the inheritances, which Eleazar the priest, and Joshua the son of Nun, and the heads of the fathers of the tribes of the children of Israel, divided for an inheritance by lot in Shiloh before the LORD, at the door of the tabernacle of the congregation. So they made an end of dividing the country [Josh. 19:49–51].

You would think that because Joshua was a man of God, had successfully led the children of Israel against the Canaanites, and had been victorious, that the Israelites would tell him that he could pick out any spot he wanted in which to settle. But that is not what happened. The Israelites did not offer him the choice spots in which to settle. Joshua made his own choice. It was a place called Timnath-serah. It was about eleven miles from Shiloh. It was a barren place, and one of the worst spots Joshua could have chosen. It reminds me of Abraham and Lot when they returned from the land of Egypt. Abraham said to Lot, "You pick any section you want and I will take what is left of this land." Lot took the very best and left Abraham holding the bag. This incident shows the character of these men. Joshua chose land that was similar to the backside of the desert. This is certainly a revelation of his character. It also reveals something about the Israelites. They were perfectly willing to let this man of God have a small, barren place as his portion.

In my opinion it is equally as shameful to see a church or Christian organization that has been served by a faithful worker, let that worker grow old and retire without making any arrangement for a pension for him. Cold-blooded business corporations take care of their employees when they retire, but God's people often fail to do this.

CHAPTER 20

***THEME:** Cities of refuge*

The cities of refuge set before us a vivid scene which has a remarkable lesson for us. God gave to the children of Israel commandment regarding setting aside certain cities for refuge. It is interesting that many tribes and many primitive people have had this same thing. Evidently this is something that was passed on to all mankind. The cities of refuge were for the protection of one who had killed another accidentally.

In the Hawaiian Islands, on the Kona coast of the Big Island, there is a place known as the City of Refuge. It was in use back in the days before Christianity came to the Islands, when the tribes were slaying each other and even offering human sacrifices. It is there as a tourist attraction today.

God's commandment for the establishment of cities of refuge was first given in Exodus 21:13: "And if a man lie not in wait, but God deliver him into his hand; then I will appoint thee a place whither he shall flee." Then explicit directions for the cities of refuge are given in Numbers 35—the entire chapter. "Then ye shall appoint you cities to be cities of refuge for you; that the slayer may flee thither, which killeth any person at unawares" (Num. 35:11).

Now that the children of Israel are in the Promised Land and each tribe has been allotted its portion of land, the Lord speaks to Joshua about assigning certain cities to be cities of refuge.

Speak to the children of Israel, saying, Appoint out for you cities of refuge, whereof I spake unto you by the hand of Moses:

That the slayer that killeth any person unawares and unwittingly may flee thither: and they shall be your refuge from the avenger of blood [Josh. 20:2–3].

If one man killed another, it would be one of two things. It would either be manslaughter —that is, the killing of another accidentally, or it would be premeditated murder. In Israel a murderer would be stoned to death. If in our society we had capital punishment for murder, with no "ifs" and "ands" about it, and the man who was guilty was executed quickly, it would save countless lives. We wouldn't be seeing our police officers shot down or storekeepers held up and murdered without mercy. My friend, God knows human nature. This was His law. However, if one killed another unintentionally, without premeditation, he is to be provided protection. There is an example given in Scripture of two men out in the woods, cutting down a tree. The axe head comes off the handle and strikes one of the men and kills him. Suppose the brother of the slain man says, "I know that man had it in for my brother. He did that purposely. I'm going to kill him!" That man wouldn't have a chance unless there was a place of refuge. So the man who had been responsible for the death would be given the opportunity of running to one of the cities of refuge.

And when he that doth flee unto one of those cities shall stand at the entering of the gate of the city, and shall declare his cause in the ears of the elders of that city, they shall take him into the city unto them, and give him a place, that he may dwell among them.

And if the avenger of blood pursue after him, then they shall not deliver the slayer up into his hand; because he smote his neighbour unwittingly, and hated him not beforetime.

And he shall dwell in that city, until he stand before the congregation for judgment, and until the death of the high priest that shall be in those days: then shall the slayer return, and come unto his own city, and unto his own house, unto the city from whence he fled [Josh. 20:4–6].

The city of refuge has a great spiritual lesson for you and me. The Lord Jesus Christ was slain. And the Scripture makes it clear that not only was the Lord Jesus Christ slain, but He is our city of refuge today. Speaking of Christ as our refuge, the writer of Hebrews says, "who have fled for refuge to lay hold upon the hope set before us." The reference, of course, is to those who, though conscious of their own sinfulness, have availed themselves of the salvation that was secured for them by our Lord upon the cross. All who find a refuge in Him are saved forever from the judgment of a holy God.

Now who is guilty of slaying Christ? The whole world is guilty. Both Jew and Gentile stand guilty before God as having participated in that which brought about the death of His Son. But Christ came to give Himself a ransom for all. And His sacrifice on the cross has opened up, as it were, a city of refuge for all who put their trust in Him.

It is absolutely wrong to try to blame the Jew for the crucifixion of Christ. He was not crucified on a Jewish cross; He was crucified on a Roman cross. But it is useless to pin the blame on any one people. One racial group is as guilty as another. We all are in the same position. We are all guilty.

Peter, in his second sermon to his Jewish brethren, said, "And now, brethren, I wot that through ignorance ye did it, as did also your rulers. But those things, which God before had shewed by the mouth of all his prophets, that Christ should suffer, he hath so fulfilled" (Acts 3:17–18). Therefore Peter could say to them, "Repent ye therefore, and be converted."

The apostle Paul makes it clear that the Gentiles are also guilty. "Howbeit we speak wisdom among them that are perfect: yet not the wisdom of this world, nor of the princes of this world, that come to nought. . . . Which none of the princes of this world knew: for had they known it, they would not have crucified the Lord of glory" (1 Cor. 2:6, 8).

According to these passages, God looks upon the whole world as guilty of the sin of manslaughter in connection with the death of Christ. To be specific, *you* are guilty. But you can point the finger right back at me and say, "*You* are guilty." But, thank God, His death made a city of refuge, a place for you and me to come.

As the song writer, George Keith, put it,

How firm a foundation, ye saints of the Lord
Is laid for your faith in His excellent Word!
What more can He say than to you He hath said,
To you who for refuge to Jesus have fled?

Have you fled to Jesus for refuge? There is protection there. What a wonderful chapter this is!

CHAPTER 21

THEME: *Cities for Levites*

The Levites were not given any land as were the other tribes. Instead they were given cities in the other tribes. They were scattered out so that they could minister to the people. Levi was the priestly tribe.

Then came near the heads of the fathers of the Levites unto Eleazar the priest, and unto Joshua the son of Nun, and unto the heads of the fathers of the tribes of the children of Israel;

And they spake unto them at Shiloh in the land of Canaan, saying, The LORD commanded by the hand of Moses to give us cities to dwell in, with the suburbs thereof for our cattle [Josh. 21:1–2].

Apparently they had a suburban problem in that day also. The Levites were to be given forty cities in which to dwell—all the way from Dan in the north to Beer-sheba in the south.

The division of the land is completed now.

And the LORD gave unto Israel all the land which he sware to give unto their fathers; and they possessed it, and dwelt therein.

And the LORD gave them rest round about, according to all that he sware unto their fathers: and there stood not a man of all their enemies before them; the LORD delivered all their enemies into their hand [Josh. 21:43–44].

The children of Israel now possessed the land of Canaan, but that was only a small segment of the land God had promised them. If they are to get any more land, they will have to go and possess it. The rule still stands that every place their feet stand upon will be theirs. That which the Israelites possess now, however, is free from the enemy and they can enter into rest.

The rest for us today is the rest of redemption. It is the rest that we desperately need. We live in an age of tension. There are many pressures, and if there is one thing that the average Christian needs, it is to enter into the rest God has provided.

As we shall see as we move into the Book of Judges, Israel failed to completely rid her possession of her enemies. Why? Because of her unbelief. Even Joshua could not give them the rest they needed since they failed to believe God and appropriate His power.

The writer to the Hebrews warns us about repeating Israel's failure: "There remaineth therefore a rest to the people of God. For he that is entered into his rest, he also hath ceased from his own works, as God did from his. Let us labour therefore to enter into that rest, lest any man fall after the same example of unbelief" (Heb. 4:9–11). How do you and I enter into that rest? By faith, that is the only way.

At the time of Christ, when Israel rejected Him as King and He rejected their cities, He gave a personal invitation which stands yet today, "Come unto me, all ye that labour and are heavy laden, and I will give you rest" (Matt. 11:28). That rest is the rest of redemption.

Now here in Joshua 21 the people have entered into the rest—at least temporarily—which God had provided for them. My, how wonderful it must have been after the long, weary journey through the wilderness and the warfare to take their possessions, to settle down on their own parcel of ground. What a thrill it must have been to cultivate it and eat the fruits of it.

CHAPTER 22

THEME: *The two and one-half tribes are sent home; they build the altar of witness*

As you will recall, the two and one-half tribes did not take their inheritance in the land with the other tribes. They remained on the east side of the Jordan River. They could have the inheritance they wanted only if they sent their armies into the land to help conquer it. This is what they did and, when the battle was won, they were free to return home.

> **Then Joshua called the Reubenites, and the Gadites, and the half tribe of Manasseh,**
>
> **And said unto them, Ye have kept all that Moses the servant of the LORD commanded you, and have obeyed my voice in all that I commanded you:**
>
> **Ye have not left your brethren these many days unto this day, but have kept the charge of the commandment of the LORD your God [Josh. 22:1–3].**

Just before the two and one-half tribes leave, Joshua calls them together and commends them for a job well done. He tells them that they have done a fine thing by helping their brethren. Then he gives them a warning.

> **But take diligent heed to do the commandment and the law, which Moses the servant of the LORD charged you, to love the LORD your God, and to walk in all his ways, and to keep his commandments, and to cleave unto him, and to serve him with all your heart and with all your soul [Josh. 22:5].**

These tribes are warned that even though they have chosen to dwell on the wrong side of the Jordan, they are still to follow the Mosaic system. After Joshua warns them about their duty, he dismisses them with a blessing.

> **So Joshua blessed them, and sent them away: and they went unto their tents [Josh. 22:6].**

The two and one-half tribes returned home.

> **And when they came unto the borders of Jordan, that are in the land of Canaan, the children of Reuben and the children of Gad and the half tribe of Manasseh built there an altar by Jordan, a great altar to see to [Josh. 22:10].**

They apparently built this altar on the west side of the Jordan River. It was an altar "to see to." That is a strange expression. Literally it means an altar "great to sight." This means that it could be seen from a great distance. It was an imposing structure. Bible scholars searched for the ruins of this altar on the east side of Jordan. But finally an archaeologist discovered the ruins on the west side of Jordan, and they are there today, located in a prominent place, a great altar in appearance. They built this monument to remind them of something. When the rest of the children of Israel heard what they had done, they became upset and gathered at Shiloh.

And when the children of Israel heard of it, the whole congregation of the children of Israel gathered themselves together at Shiloh, to go up to war against them [Josh. 22:12].

The children of Israel believed the two and one-half tribes were building an altar upon which to offer sacrifices. They thought it was an attempt to divide the nation.

Thus saith the whole congregation of the LORD, What trespass is this that ye have committed against the God of Israel, to turn away this day from following the LORD, in that ye have builded you an altar, that ye might rebel this day against the LORD?

Is the iniquity of Peor too little for us, from which we are not cleansed until this day, although there was a plague in the congregation of the LORD [Josh. 22:16–17].

The children of Israel accused the two and one-half tribes of building an altar to Baal. They remembered the time that Balaam had caused Israel to sin by seducing them to marry Moabite women and commit spiritual adultery. At that time God had judged them severely, and they were afraid it was going to happen again.

However, the two and one-half tribes give a good explanation for what they had done.

Then the children of Reuben and the children of Gad and the half tribe of Manasseh answered, and said unto the heads of the thousands of Israel,

The LORD God of gods, the LORD God of gods, he knoweth, and Israel he shall know; if it be in rebellion, or if in transgression against the LORD, (save us not this day,)

That we have built us an altar to turn from following the LORD, or if to offer thereon burnt offering or meat offering, or if to offer peace offerings thereon, let the LORD himself require it [Josh. 22:21–23].

They had not built an altar for the purpose of offering sacrifices. The altar was simply a reminder that they still belonged to the nation Israel. It may have been an enlarged model of the altar of burnt offering found in the tabernacle, but it was not intended for sacrifices.

And if we have not rather done it for fear of this thing, saying, In time to come your children might speak unto our children, saying, What have ye to do with the LORD God of Israel? [Josh. 22:24].

The two and one-half tribes were sincere in what they had done, and the nine and one-half tribes accepted their explanation.

And Phinehas the son of Eleazar the priest said unto the children of Reuben, and to the children of Gad, and to the children of Manasseh, This day we perceive that the LORD is among us, because ye have not committed this trespass against the LORD: now ye have delivered the children of Israel out of the hand of the LORD [Josh. 22:31].

The children of Israel realized that they had been hasty in accusing the two and one-half tribes. They remind me of some of us who are sometimes a little hasty. We say and do things we should not say and do, and we are sincere in thinking we are defending the Word of God when in reality we are not. The children of Israel made a mistake in coming against their brethren with thoughts of war.

And the children of Reuben and the children of Gad called the altar Ed: for it shall be a witness between us that the LORD is God [Josh. 22:34].

On the surface, the building of this altar sounds like a good idea, and many commentators have placed their seal of approval upon it. However, let's take more than a cursory look at this altar called "Ed." In the tabernacle was the brazen altar for sacrifices. There was to be no other. Deuteronomy 12:27 says, "And thou shalt offer thy burnt offerings, the flesh and the blood, upon the altar of the LORD thy God: and the blood of thy sacrifices shall be poured out upon the altar of the LORD thy God, and thou shalt eat the flesh." Israel was told to destroy all other altars. "But ye shall destroy their altars, break their images, and cut down their groves" (Exod. 34:13). There was to be but one exception, in Deuteronomy 27:4–8, where Israel is told to take twelve stones out of the Jordan River and put them up as a memorial. The two and one-half tribes never crossed over Jordan, and the river actually divided them from their brethren. This altar recognized that division. This altar was prima facie evidence that they were divided. It made way for the division later on. Right now Israel is divided east and west. It is nine and one-half tribes versus two and one-half tribes at this point, but later on it will be a north and south division with ten tribes in the north against two tribes in the south.

The brazen altar in the tabernacle, typifying the redemptive work of Christ, was a place of unity. And friend, I can meet with any man who will exalt Jesus Christ. In John 17:20–21 Jesus prayed, "Neither pray I for these alone, but for them also which shall believe on me through their word; That they all may be one; as thou, Father, art in me, and I in thee, that they also may be one in us: that the world may believe that thou hast sent me." There is an organic unity of those who are in Christ. The altar speaks of the death of Christ as a sacrifice.

As the two and one-half tribes built a bloodless altar which had divided Israel, today those who are liberal in their theology have divided the church. They have accused fundamentalists of being schismatic, but it is liberalism that has departed from the cross and the deity of Christ. They do not like an altar with blood. They have put up an "Ed," if you please. They worship at an altar where no sacrifice is to be offered. They have a "bloodless" Christ. Like the two and one-half tribes, their conduct reveals that they have departed from the truth. Our Lord said, "Ye shall know them by their fruits . . ." (Matt. 7:16). Several hundred years later the Lord Jesus crossed the Sea of Galilee and came to the country of the Gadarenes. The people living there were from the tribe of Gad, and they were still living on the wrong side of the Jordan River. Our Lord came upon a demon-possessed man dwelling in the tombs, and He cast the demons out of the man and gave them permission to enter a herd of pigs nearby. The Gadarenes were in the pig business! Can you imagine an Orthodox Jew in the pig business? They had failed to follow the commandments of God. They were on the wrong side of Jordan.

Liberalism has indeed divided the church. It has erected a beautiful altar, a "bloodless" Christ, one who never actually lived, one without deity, one without ability to save humanity.

My friend, have *you* crossed over Jordan? Have you entered into the rest of redemption which Christ offers?

CHAPTERS 23–24

THEME: *The last message of Joshua*

In chapter 23 Joshua calls the leaders of Israel to courage and certainty. Then in chapter 24 he calls to the tribes of Israel for consecration and consideration of the covenant of God. The chapter closes with the death of Joshua.

A deathbed message is becoming very familiar in the Word of God. You recall that Jacob called his twelve sons about him and gave prophecies concerning each of them. Then Moses called the twelve tribes—the sons are now tribes—to him and blessed them. Now Joshua, who has been their leader for forty years there in the Land of Promise, is giving them his final message before his death.

And it came to pass a long time after that the LORD had given rest unto Israel from all their enemies round about, that Joshua waxed old and stricken in age.

And Joshua called for all Israel, and for their elders, and for their heads, and for their judges, and for their officers, and said unto them, I am old and stricken in age:

And ye have seen all that the LORD your God hath done unto all these nations because of you; for the LORD your God is he that hath fought for you [Josh. 23:1–3].

You will notice that Joshua calls the people about him and says, "I am now ready to retire; I am a senior citizen, and I have some final words for you. You have seen what God has done for you."

Behold, I have divided unto you by lot these nations that remain, to be an inheritance for your tribes, from Jordan, with all the nations that I have cut off, even unto the great sea westward.

And the LORD your God, he shall expel them from before you, and drive them from out of your sight; and ye shall possess their land, as the LORD your God hath promised unto you.

Be ye therefore very courageous to keep and to do all that is written in the book of the law of Moses, that ye turn not aside therefrom to the right hand or to the left [Josh. 23:4–6].

Joshua is calling them to do what Moses had called them to do.

That ye come not among these nations, these that remain among you; neither make mention of the name of their gods, nor cause to swear by them, neither serve them, nor bow yourselves unto them:

But cleave unto the LORD your God, as ye have done unto this day [Josh. 23:7–8].

The grave danger of crossing the Jordan River, facing an enemy in a strange land, encountering the unknown on every hand, and meeting fear on every side, had kept Israel close to the Lord. Joshua recognized that now, since they had entered into rest and were enjoying prosperity and plenty, they would drift away from God. That is the story of human nature. It never changes.

At the time of this writing, I feel that the United States is facing a similar situation. After World War II, I was disturbed that God had judged Europe and even Russia and Korea. How these nations suffered, but we came through unscathed! While other nations went through a period of hardship, our nation entered an era of prosperity and affluence. I could not understand why God did not judge us. Then I realized that He was testing us with prosperity. The most dangerous period any people can go through is not the time of grave danger and suffering, but the time of peace and plenty.

This is the reason Joshua is giving Israel this charge. "God has done these wonderful things for you; now stay close to Him, and obey Him. If you do this, God will continue to bless you." Then he warns them what will happen if they turn from their God.

Take good heed therefore unto yourselves, that ye love the LORD your God.

Else if ye do any wise go back, and cleave unto the remnant of these nations, even these that remain among you, and shall make marriages with them, and go in unto them, and they to you:

Know for a certainty that the LORD your God will no more drive out any of these nations from before you; but they shall be snares and traps unto you, and scourges in your sides, and thorns in your eyes, until ye perish from off this good land which the LORD your God hath given you [Josh. 23:11–13].

He warns that God's judgment would be upon them.

Therefore it shall come to pass, that as all good things are come upon you, which the LORD your God promised you; so shall the LORD bring upon you all evil things, until he have destroyed you from off this good land which the LORD your God hath given you.

When ye have transgressed the covenant of the LORD your God, which he commanded you, and have gone and served other gods, and bowed yourselves to them; then shall the anger of the LORD be kindled against you, and ye shall perish quickly from off the good land which he hath given unto you [Josh. 23:15–16].

This is more of a prediction than a warning. As we well know, this prediction is now history.

In chapter 24 Joshua again gathers the people together, and they present themselves before the Lord. Joshua relays to them God's review of their history and His gracious dealings with them.

And Joshua said unto all the people, Thus saith the LORD God of Israel, Your fathers dwelt on the other side of the flood in old time, even Terah, the father of Abraham, and the father of

Nachor: and they served other gods [Josh. 24:2].

This reveals something that we didn't know before, although we suspected it. When God called Abraham from Ur of the Chaldees, He called him out of a home of idolatry. Terah, his father, we are told here, served other gods.

This raises the question: Why did God choose Abraham and make a nation from him? Let's consider the background. After the Tower of Babei, man totally departed from the Lord. No one served God—not even Terah the father of Abraham. When God confused the language, the people scattered in every direction, and they took with them a knowledge of the true and living God, which is the reason even pagan tribes today have a knowledge of the true God, although they do not worship Him. There was total apostasy after Babel.

Now what will God do that will be consistent with His person, His attributes, and His character? He could judge the human family and remove it from the earth. He could make the earth as bleak as the moon if He wanted to. But He didn't. He will recover mankind. He will begin with one man. That man was Abraham, who must have had a desire in his heart to know the living and true God. When God called him, He told him to leave Ur and all his family. Now we know why. Terah was an idolater. God called him away from all that in order to deal with him and make of him a nation through which the Messiah would come into the world.

Now God formed the nation in the brickyards of Egypt. (And, friends, if God is going to make anything of you and me, He will take us through the fire to do it. He won't use the molly-coddle of our contemporary churches, I can assure you!)

I sent Moses also and Aaron, and I plagued Egypt, according to that which I did among them: and afterward I brought you out.

And I brought your fathers out of Egypt: and ye came unto the sea; and the Egyptians pursued after your fathers with chariots and horsemen unto the Red sea.

And when they cried unto the LORD, he put darkness between you and the Egyptians, and brought the sea upon them, and covered them; and your eyes have seen what I have done in Egypt: and ye dwelt in the wilderness a long season [Josh. 24:5–7].

God continues to trace His care of them: delivering them from the Amorites who fought them and from Balaam who tried to curse them, bringing them across the Jordan and delivering them from the inhabitants of the land who fought against them.

And I have given you a land for which ye did not labour, and cities which ye built not, and ye dwell in them; of the vineyards and oliveyards which ye planted not do ye eat [Josh. 24:13].

Now the people of Israel are settled in the land. But, because they did not get rid of the civilization that was there, they are surrounded by idolatry. They are in real danger. Realizing this, Joshua calls them to a real dedication to God, a turning over of their lives completely to Him. Listen to him.

Now therefore fear the LORD, and serve him in sincerity and in truth: and put away the gods which your fathers served on the other side of the flood, and in Egypt; and serve ye the LORD.

And if it seem evil unto you to serve the LORD, choose you this day whom ye will serve; whether the gods which your fathers served that were on the other side of the flood, or the gods of the Amorites, in whose land ye dwell: but as for me and my house, we will serve the LORD [Josh. 24:14–15].

The more I know about Joshua, the better I like him. Through the years he has stood in the shadow of Moses so that we think he is a sort of miniature Moses. But Joshua is a man of great stature. God made no mistake in choosing this man. Although Joshua is an average man, this book reveals that an average man dedicated to God can be mightily used. He says to the nation, "Do you want to go back to the gods of your fathers, those pagan gods which they served? Or do you want to serve the gods of the Amorites? You can choose. But as for me and my house, we have made our choice; we are going to serve the Lord!" Friend, this was a tremendous challenge to all the tribes of Israel to consider their covenant with God.

Notice the response of the people.

And the people answered and said, God forbid that we should forsake the LORD, to serve other gods;

For the LORD our God, he it is that brought us up and our fathers out of the land of Egypt, from the house of bondage, and which did those great signs in our sight, and preserved us in all the way wherein we went, and among all the people through whom we passed [Josh. 24:16–17].

You would think that because of the fantastic way God worked with Israel they would stay close to Him and serve Him. It is easy to point a finger back about 3,580 years ago and say what a sorry lot Israel was. What terrible failures they were. What about us today? How close are we staying to the living God?

If ye forsake the LORD, and serve strange gods, then he will turn and do you hurt, and consume you, after that he hath done you good [Josh. 24:20].

God also has been so good to us that many people live in a lackadaisical manner without any regard as to the blessings He has showered upon them. Many people think they can do exactly as they please. It is true that He is a God of mercy, love, and comfort, but He is also a God of judgment.

And the people said unto Joshua, Nay; but we will serve the LORD [Josh. 24:21].

These sound like good intentions on the part of Israel, don't they?

So Joshua made a covenant with the people that day, and set them a statute and an ordinance in Shechem.

And Joshua wrote these words in the book of the law of God, and took a great stone, and set it up there under an oak, that was by the sanctuary of the LORD [Josh. 24:25–26].

In other words, what Joshua wrote was put on the same scroll that contained the five books of Moses.

This brings us to the death of Joshua.

And it came to pass after these things, that Joshua the son of Nun, the servant of the LORD, died, being an hundred and ten years old.

And they buried him in the border of his inheritance in Timnath-serah, which is in mount Ephraim, on the north side of the hill of Gaash [Josh. 24:29–30].

Joshua was buried in that barren place he had chosen for his inheritance.

And Israel served the LORD all the days of Joshua, and all the days of the elders that overlived Joshua, and which had known all the works of the LORD, that he had done for Israel.

And the bones of Joseph, which the children of Israel brought up out of Egypt, buried they in Shechem, in a parcel of ground which Jacob bought of the sons of Hamor the father of Shechem for an hundred pieces of silver: and it became the inheritance of the children of Joseph [Josh. 24:31–32].

At the time of Joshua's death he must have been held in high esteem because Israel served the Lord all the days of Joshua. This was the effect of his godly influence.

Joseph was the father of Ephraim and Manasseh. When these two sons left Egypt, they brought their father's bones with them and carried them for forty years in the wilderness. They had promised Joseph they would bury his bones in the Promised Land. Why? Because he was expecting to be raised from the dead in that land.

And Eleazar the son of Aaron died; and they buried him in a hill that pertained to Phinehas his son, which was given him in mount Ephraim [Josh. 24:33].

Aaron was the first priest to die; Eleazar was the second. The Book of Joshua is bound by death. It begins with the death of Moses and ends with the deaths of Joshua and Eleazar.

The thing that interests me in this verse, however, is the fact that they buried Eleazar in the hill that pertained to Phinehas, his son, which was given him in Mount Ephraim. The question is, "Where did Phinehas get this land?" The priests were given no land, and yet this man had acquired a nice little piece of real estate. Here is a beginning of departure from the living and true God, which will become obvious in the Book of Judges.

(For Bibliography to Joshua, see Bibliography at the end of Judges.)

The Book of

JUDGES

INTRODUCTION

The Book of Judges takes its title from the twelve men and one woman who served as judges during the period from Joshua's death to the time of Samuel.

This book was written later during the period of the monarchy, judging by the phrase which occurs four times, "In those days there was no king in Israel." It is possible that it was written by Samuel, but the actual writer is unknown.

All the judges were themselves limited in their capabilities. In fact, each one seemed to have some defect and handicap which was not a hindrance but became a positive asset under the sovereign direction of God. None of them were national leaders who appealed to the total nation as Moses and Joshua had done. The record is not continuous but rather a spotty account of a local judge in a limited section of the nation.

Backsliding and the amazing grace of God in recovering and restoring is the theme of Judges. *The New Scofield Reference Bible* gives the theme of the Book of Judges as "Defeat and Deliverance." This is unusually appropriate. There is, however, another aspect which this book emphasizes: disappointment.

The children of Israel entered the Land of Promise with high hopes and exuberant expectation. You would expect these people—who were delivered out of Egypt, led through the wilderness for forty years, and brought into the land with such demonstration of God's power and direction—to attain a high level of living and victory in the land, and in their lives. Such was not the case. They failed ignobly and suffered miserable defeat after defeat.

The Book of Judges is a philosophy of history. "Righteousness exalteth a nation: but sin is a reproach to any people" (Prov. 14:34).

1. Historically it records the history of the nation from the death of Joshua to Samuel, who was the last of the judges and the first of the prophets. It bridges the gap between Joshua and the rise of the monarchy. There was no leader to take Joshua's place in the way he had taken Moses' place. This was the trial period of the theocracy after they entered the land.

2. Morally it is the time of the deep declension of the people as they turned from God, the unseen Leader, and descended to the low level of "In those days there was no king in Israel: every man did that which was right in his own eyes" (compare Jud. 1:1 with 20:18). This should have been an era of glowing prog-

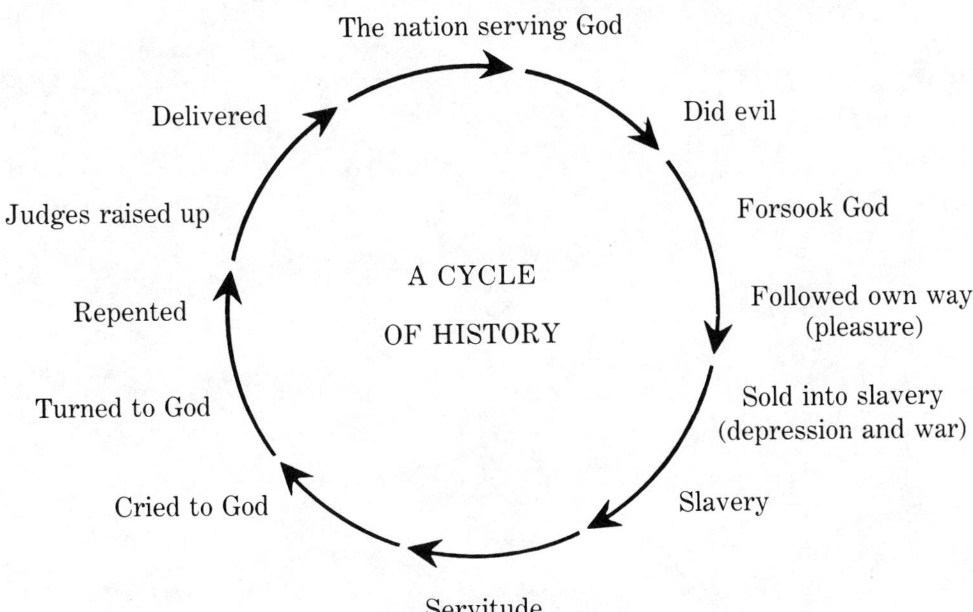

ress, but it was a dark day of repeated failure.

The "hoop" of Israel's history begins with the nation serving God. Then they take certain steps downward. They did evil in the sight of the Lord and served Baalim (see Jud. 2:11). They forsook the Lord, and they served Baal and Ashtaroth. The anger of the Lord was hot against Israel, and He delivered them into the hands of their enemies. Israel entered a time of servitude. Soon Israel cried out to God in their sad plight and distress. They turned to God and repented. God heard their prayers and raised up judges through whom they were delivered. Then again the nation served God.

Soon the same old story repeated itself. The children of Israel did evil, forsook God, followed their own pleasure, were sold into slavery, entered a period of servitude, cried out to God in their distress, turned to Him, judges were raised up, and Israel was delivered. The nation began serving God again, and they were once again at the top of the cycle. My friend, the hoop of history just turns over and over. You can follow that hoop right through the Bible, and it is still turning today. The old bromide "history repeats itself" is absolutely true.

The Book of Isaiah opens with God giving this philosophy of history. Isaiah outlines three steps that cause the downfall of nations: (1) spiritual apostasy; (2) moral awfulness; and (3) political anarchy, which is the final stage of any nation. These steps have destroyed nations down through history.

If you want to know just how up-to-date the Book of Judges is, listen to the words of the late General Douglas MacArthur: "In this day of gathering storms, as moral deterioration of political power spreads its growing infection, it is essential that every spiritual force be mobilized to defend and preserve the religious base upon which this nation is founded; for it has been that base which has been the motivating impulse to our moral and national growth. History fails to record a single precedent in which nations subject to moral decay have not passed into political and economic decline. There has been either a spiritual reawakening to overcome the moral lapse, or a progressive deterioration leading to ultimate national disaster."

OUTLINE

I. Introduction to Era of the Judges, Chapters 1–2

A. Condition of Nation after Death of Joshua (Revealed in Limited Victories of Tribes of Judah, Simeon, Benjamin, Manasseh, Ephraim, Zebulun, Asher, Naphtali, Dan), Chapter 1

B. God Feeds into Computer of History Israel's Cycle in Period of the Judges, Chapter 2

II. Era of Judges, Chapters 3–16

A. 1st Apostasy; Conquered by Mesopotamia; Delivered through Othniel, the Judge, 3:1–11

B. 2nd Apostasy; Conquered by Moabites and Philistines; Delivered through Ehud and Shamgar, the Judges, 3:12–31

C. 3rd Apostasy; Conquered by Jabin, King of Canaan, Delivered through Deborah and Barak, the Judges, 4:1–5:31

D. 4th Apostasy; Conquered by Midian; Delivered through Gideon, the Judge, 6:1–8:32

E. 5th Apostasy; Civil War; Delivered through Abimelech, Tola, Jair, the Judges, 8:33–10:5

F. 6th Apostasy; Conquered by Philistines and Ammonites; Delivered through Jephthah, Ibzan, Elon, Abdon, the Judges, 10:6–12:15

G. 7th Apostasy; Conquered by Philistines; Delivered Partially through Samson, the Judge, Chapters 13–16

III. Results of Era of Judges (Confusion), Chapters 17–21

A. Religous Apostasy (The Temple), Chapters 17–18

B. Moral Awfulness (The Home), Chapter 19

C. Political Anarchy (The State), Chapters 20–21

CHAPTERS 1–2

***THEME:** Introduction to the era of the judges*

Mentioned are nine of the twelve tribes, in chapter 1, in their failure to win a total victory in driving out the enemy. The three tribes not mentioned are Reuben, Issachar, and Gad. It must be assumed that they likewise failed. Each tribe faced a particular enemy. At no time was the entire nation engaged in a warfare against any particular enemy. The weakness of the tribes is first revealed in verse 3 where Judah called upon Simeon for help in his local situation.

THE CONDITION OF ISRAEL AFTER THE DEATH OF JOSHUA

Now after the death of Joshua it came to pass, that the children of Israel asked the LORD, saying, Who shall go up for us against the Canaanites first, to fight against them?[Jud. 1:1].

The weakness of the tribes is revealed from the word *go*. They asked the Lord what they should do and who would go for them against the Canaanites. The Canaanites were well entrenched in the land because the Israelites had failed to drive them out. They were a thorn in Israel's side during the reigns of Saul and David.

And the LORD said, Judah shall go up: behold, I have delivered the land into his hand [Jud. 1:2].

The Canaanites, apparently, were the principal enemy.

And Judah said unto Simeon his brother, Come up with me into my lot, that we may fight against the Canaanites; and I likewise will go with thee into thy lot. So Simeon went with him [Jud. 1:3].

At first this looks like a fine sign of cooperation between Judah and Simeon, and it was, but it was also a sign of weakness. The tribe of Judah had no business asking for help to drive the Canaanites out of their particular portion of land. With God's help they should have been able to do it. As a result, the Canaanites were never completely driven out of the land.

And Judah went up; and the LORD delivered the Canaanites and the Perizzites into their hand: and they slew of them in Bezek ten thousand men [Jud. 1:4].

You would think that after this first step of victory the people in Judah would be confident that God would deliver their inheritance into their hands.

And afterward the children of Judah went down to fight against the Canaanites, that dwelt in the mountain, and in the south, and in the valley.

And Judah went against the Canaanites that dwelt in Hebron: (now the name of Hebron before was Kirjath-arba:) and they slew Sheshai, and Ahiman, and Talmai.

And from thence he went against the inhabitants of Debir: and the name of Debir before was Kirjath-sepher [Jud. 1:9–11].

The town *Debir* was a center of culture for the Canaanite people. It is called the "town of books." I guess the library was there.

And Caleb said, He that smiteth Kirjath-sepher, and taketh it, to him will I give Achsah my daughter to wife.

And Othniel the son of Kenaz, Caleb's younger brother, took it: and he gave him Achsah his daughter to wife [Jud. 1:12–13].

Israel first took the hill country and held it the longest. The foothills, lying between the hill country and the coast, were the scene of constant fighting between Israel and the Canaanites. When the children of Israel settled in the Promised Land, they were subject to the influence and temptations of the Canaanite religion. It was a degrading religion, and they soon lapsed into idolatry and apostasy.

Whoever took this city was promised a reward, and in this case it was Caleb's daughter, Achsah. Grammatically, Othniel can be either Caleb's nephew or younger brother, but his marriage to Achsah would also classify him as a son-in-law. He undoubtedly was chosen as a judge because of his relationship to Caleb. Nepotism was prevalent even in that day. If he had been the son-in-law of Joe Doakes, he probably would never have become a judge. Many men today occupy positions of prominence, not because of their ability, but because of a certain relationship or circumstance. Napoleon called himself a man of destiny. He became prominent because of the times in which he was born. If he had lived in our generation, probably he would have been unknown. So it was with Othniel.

Nine of the twelve tribes mentioned in this chapter are mentioned in connection with failure. We have looked at the tribes of Judah and Simeon, and now Benjamin and Manasseh are the next to be considered. Failure is something that persisted in each one of the tribes.

And the children of Benjamin did not drive out the Jebusites that inhabited Jerusalem; but the Jebusites dwell with the children of Benjamin in Jerusalem unto this day [Jud. 1:21].

That is, at the time this record was written.

Neither did Manasseh drive out the inhabitants of Beth-shean and her towns, nor Taanach and her towns, nor the inhabitants of Dor and her towns, nor the inhabitants of Ibleam and her towns, nor the inhabitants of Megiddo and her towns: but the Canaanites would dwell in that land.

And it came to pass, when Israel was strong, that they put the Canaanites to tribute, and did not utterly drive them out.

Neither did Ephraim drive out the Canaanites that dwelt in Gezer; but the Canaanites dwelt in Gezer among them.

Neither did Zebulun drive out the inhabitants of Kitron, nor the inhabitants of Nahalol; but the Canaanites dwelt among them, and became tributaries [Jud. 1:27–30].

The report is failure for each of them.

Neither did Asher drive out the inhabitants of Accho, nor the inhabitants of Zidon, nor of Ahlab, nor of Achzib, nor of Helbah, nor of Aphik, nor of Rehob:

But the Asherites dwelt among the Canaanites, the inhabitants of the land: for they did not drive them out.

Neither did Naphtali drive out the inhabitants of Beth-shemesh, nor the inhabitants of Beth-anath; but he dwelt among the Canaanites, the inhabitants of the land: nevertheless the inhabitants of Beth-shemesh and of Beth-anath became tributaries unto them [Jud. 1:31–33].

And they chased Dan up into the hill country.

And the Amorites forced the children of Dan into the mountain: for they would not suffer them to come down to the valley [Jud. 1:34].

This is the Promised Land—God had given it to them! Yet not one tribe, apparently, was able to possess the land that God had given to it. How tragic!

THE CHILDREN OF ISRAEL ARE REBUKED FOR THEIR DISOBEDIENCE

And an angel of the Lord came up from Gilgal to Bochim, and said, I made you to go up out of Egypt, and have brought you unto the land which I sware unto your fathers; and I said, I will never break my covenant with you.

And ye shall make no league with the inhabitants of this land; ye shall throw down their altars: but ye have not obeyed my voice: why have ye done this?

Wherefore I also said, I will not drive them out from before you; but they shall be as thorns in your sides, and their gods shall be a snare unto you [Jud. 2:1–3].

I believe that the "angel of the Lord" is none other than the pre-incarnate Christ. God appeared in a form that could be perceived by the human senses. Although He had always met the need of His people, they had not obeyed His voice. This is the beginning of Israel's "hoop of history." They repeated the weary round of forsaking God, sinning, being reduced to servitude by the enemy, returning to God in repentance, being delivered by God-appointed judges, back to obedience to God.

GOD RAISES UP JUDGES

Nevertheless the Lord raised up judges, which delivered them out of the hand of those that spoiled them [Jud. 2:16].

Each time the nation hit bottom, God raised up a judge to deliver them.

CHAPTER 3

***THEME:** First and second apostasy; God delivers Israel from servitude through her judges: Othniel, Ehud, and Shamgar*

The children of Israel intermarried with the Canaanites, Hittites, Amorites, Perizzites, Hivites, and Jebusites among whom they lived. Israel did evil, forgot God, and served Baalim. God delivered them into slavery.

Othniel, the first judge, was raised up to deliver them. His only qualification seems to be that he was the nephew of Caleb and married his daughter.

Ehud, the second judge, was raised up to deliver Israel from the servitude of Eglon, king of Moab. His qualification was his being left-handed, which enabled him to gain the presence of the king without his concealed dagger being discovered.

Shamgar was the third judge, who was an expert with an ox goad. He used it as an instrument of war against the Philistines to deliver Israel.

All of the judges had some defect, some odd characteristic, or handicap which God used. The judges reveal that God can use any man who is willing to be used.

THE IDOLATRY OF ISRAEL BRINGS SERVITUDE

Now these are the nations which the LORD left, to prove Israel by them, even as many of Israel as had not known all the wars of Canaan;

Only that the generations of the children of Israel might know, to teach them war, at the least such as before knew nothing thereof;

Namely, five lords of the Philistines, and all the Canaanites, and the Sidonians, and the Hivites that dwelt in mount Lebanon, from mount Baal-hermon unto the entering in of Hamath [Jud. 3:1–3).

We find here that the Israelites had intermarried with the Canaanites, the Hittites, the Amorites, the Perizzites, the Hivites, and the Jebusites. They married into all the tribes, even though God had strictly forbidden it.

The five lords of the Philistines and the other tribes mentioned in this passage were enemies of the Israelites. As we proceed through the Old Testament, these enemies will appear time and time again. They were indeed a thorn in the flesh of the nation Israel.

And the children of Israel dwelt among the Canaanites, Hittites, and Amorites, and Perizzites, and Hivites, and Jebusites:

And they took their daughters to be their wives, and gave their daughters to their sons, and served their gods.

And the children of Israel did evil in the sight of the LORD, and forgat the LORD their God, and served Baalim and the groves [Jud. 3:5–7].

Instead of driving the Canaanites from the land, Israel shared it with them. Instead of maintaining their own beliefs and worship of God, they intermarried with the Canaanites and adopted their religious beliefs. The children of Israel lapsed into a period of apostasy.

Therefore the anger of the LORD was hot against Israel, and he sold them into the hand of Chushan-rishathaim king of Mesopotamia: and the children of Israel served Chushan-rishathaim eight years [Jud. 3:8].

Israel's idolatry resulted in chastisement. God sold them into slavery for eight years. They were oppressed to the point that they cried out to the Lord for help.

OTHNIEL, THE FIRST JUDGE

And when the children of Israel cried unto the LORD, the LORD raised up a deliverer to the children of Israel, who delivered them, even Othniel the son of Kenaz, Caleb's younger brother [Jud. 3:9].

How gracious and compassionate the Lord is! When the children of Israel cried unto Him for deliverance, He raised up Othniel to be the first judge.

And the spirit of the LORD came upon him, and he judged Israel, and went out to war: and the LORD delivered Chushan-rishathaim king of Mesopotamia into his hand; and his hand prevailed against Chushan-rishathaim.

And the land had rest forty years. And

Othniel the son of Kenaz died [Jud. 3:10–11].

Othniel was the first and one of the better judges. There is no great criticism leveled against him. He saved his people from the oppression of Chushan-rishathaim. The only thing is that he was not capable in himself. He did not become leader of Israel because of his outstanding ability but because he was Caleb's nephew and had married Caleb's daughter. And yet God used him. It is amazing what kind of men God will use. Maybe that is the reason He can use you and me. This book should certainly encourage us, friend.

All of the judges were "little men." There was not a big one in the lot. These men were used of God because they were—and I have to say it—odd characters. Their very oddness caused God to use them.

The biography of Othniel was that he was the son of Kenaz, who was Caleb's brother. The Spirit of God came upon him, and he delivered the children of Israel from oppression. He died. In a very few verses we have the life and death of this man. He had a lot going for him, but there was no glamour or anything spectacular connected with his life. Most biographies are much like this.

I met a man on the streets of Los Angeles, California, years ago who had written several fine biographies of Christian leaders of the past. He was working on a book about a present-day Christian leader, and I asked him how the work was coming along. He told me that he was having difficulty keeping the front page from rubbing against the back page. Apart from the birth and death of the man, there was little to say about him. Engraved on the tombstone of a dentist were the words: "Dr. John Smith filling his last cavity." That not only applies to dentists but to the rest of us as well.

Othniel was an ordinary man, but God came upon his simple life and made it something worthwhile. God can also touch our ordinary lives and make them worthwhile.

EHUD, THE SECOND JUDGE

And the children of Israel did evil again in the sight of the LORD: and the LORD strengthened Eglon the king of Moab against Israel, because they had done evil in the sight of the LORD [Jud 3:12].

Here goes the hoop rolling down through history again. The Israelites were serving God for awhile, then they turned their backs on Him and did evil in His sight.

Ehud was one of the judges God raised up to deliver Israel. He had very little ability. I cannot find that he did anything other than kill Eglon. He just happened to be left-handed, which gave him a marvelous opportunity to get rid of a man who was bringing all kinds of tragedy into the lives of the Israelites. Ehud was the instrument God used. His act of killing Eglon accomplished the purpose. God many times uses this method to cut out a cancer of sin in order to save the body of the people. Thousands of lives were saved because of what Ehud did.

Many people will say, "Well, our civilization would not permit something like this." No one can say this honestly, however, because we dropped an atomic bomb which killed men, women, and children. War is a terrible thing.

The remarkable fact is that the only advantage Ehud had was that he was left-handed. Friend, we don't have to have unusual ability to be used of God. Do you remember William Carey? He was a humble cobbler. Dwight L. Moody had little formal education. A friend gave me a cassette tape of Dwight L. Moody's voice, taken from a record. I had never realized what a wonderful voice he had—I would not have associated such a voice with the pictures I have seen of him. Although he did not have much of an education, he certainly sounded as though he did. Also I am reminded of G. Campbell Morgan. When he preached his first sermon in a particular church, he was turned down by the pulpit committee. They told him they did not think he could ever become a preacher. I certainly would have hated to have been responsible for that judgment because Dr. Morgan became one of the truly great Bible expositors of his time. All three of these men—Carey, Moody, Morgan—unpromising though they seemed, were mightily used by God.

Also there have been many men, humble men, who have been used by God in other capacities. J. C. Penney was the son of a preacher. When his father died, his mother was left without support because the church in that day did not provide a pension for a pastor's widow. He and his mother had to take in washing to exist. He resolved that some day he would make money to take care of his mother and also take care of poor preachers and their widows. Well, there is a place down in Florida named for Penney at which only retired preachers and their widows can live. God has used him in that way.

There is another man, a rancher, with

whom I used to hunt down on the Brazos River. He told me that as a young fellow he had staked a claim way out in west Texas on land that was so bad nobody wanted it. The weather was so rough he had to move his family into town, and he would sleep at night on his saddle blanket with a slicker over him and a trench around him to let the water drain off. He said, "People think I was lucky to hit oil on that land, but I prayed that if God would enable me to keep it and make money, I'd use it for Him." He did just that. He established a fund that has supported many a missionary in South America.

And he gathered unto him the children of Ammon and Amalek, and went and smote Israel, and possessed the city of palm trees [Jud. 3:13].

When the Israelites went against God's will, He delivered them into servitude. Then what happened?

So the children of Israel served Eglon the king of Moab eighteen years.

But when the children of Israel cried unto the LORD, the LORD raised them up a deliverer. Ehud the son of Gera, a Benjamite, a man lefthanded: and by him the children of Israel sent a present unto Eglon the king of Moab [Jud. 3:14–15].

Here we go again. The hoop is rolling. Israel cried unto the Lord and He raised up a deliverer. Who was he? He was Ehud, the son of Gera, a Benjamite, a left-handed man. This is a good one for you, friends. The only thing that this man had going for him was that he was left-handed, a southpaw!

But Ehud made him a dagger which had two edges, of a cubit length, and he did gird it under his raiment upon his right thigh.

And he brought the present unto Eglon king of Moab: and Eglon was a very fat man.

And when he had made an end to offer the present, he sent away the people that bare the present.

But he himself turned again from the quarries that were by Gilgal, and said, I have a secret errand unto thee, O king: who said, Keep silence. And all that stood by him went out from him.

And Ehud came unto him; and he was sitting in a summer parlour, which he had for himself alone. And Ehud said, I have a message from God unto thee. And he arose out of his seat.

And Ehud put forth his left hand, and took the dagger from his right thigh, and thrust it into his belly:

And the haft also went in after the blade; and the fat closed upon the blade, so that he could not draw the dagger out of his belly; and the dirt came out.

Then Ehud went forth through the porch, and shut the doors of the parlour upon him, and locked them [Jud. 3:16–23].

This is a brutal thing that took place. It certainly lacks the heroic or romantic. His name means "red hair" and he was left-handed. He made a dagger which had two edges and he hid it under his clothes on his right side. Now don't miss that. He was left-handed and would have to reach over on his right side to pull out the dagger. In that day almost everybody was right-handed, and they were searched on the left side to see if they carried a weapon. The king's Secret Service agents searched Ehud on the wrong side. He gained entrance by bringing a "present," which was probably the tribute. Eglon was a big fat king. After Ehud had given him the present, he pretended he had a secret to tell him. The king sent everyone else out of the room, thinking he was going to hear a very secret message. Instead, a bloody thing was about to happen. At a convenient moment, Ehud took out the dagger and plunged it into the king. He stuck him like you would a pig. The dagger was covered by the king's fat. Then Ehud locked the doors and left.

Ehud's act was not a cowardly one. It took courage to do what he did.

When he was gone out, his servants came; and when they saw that, behold, the doors of the parlour were locked, they said, Surely he covereth his feet in his summer chamber.

And they tarried till they were ashamed: and, behold, he opened not the doors of the parlour; therefore they took a key, and opened them: and, behold, their lord was fallen down dead on the earth [Jud. 3:24–25].

The servants of Eglon, king of Moab, waited around outside of the king's door. They saw that the parlor doors were locked and thought the king was asleep. They did not wish to disturb him. They kept thinking he would wake up. They waited so long they were very embarrassed. What happened? They finally opened the doors with a key and found Eglon dead.

And Ehud escaped while they tarried, and passed beyond the quarries, and escaped unto Seirath [Jud. 3:26].

All of the time the servants were waiting for their king to awaken, Ehud had an opportunity to escape. He left the land of Moab and went to another place, Seirath by name, where they could not find him.

And it came to pass, when he was come, that he blew a trumpet in the mountain of Ephraim, and the children of Israel went down with him from the mount, and he before them.

And he said unto them, Follow after me: for the LORD hath delivered your enemies the Moabites into your hand. And they went down after him, and took the fords of Jordan toward Moab, and suffered not a man to pass over.

And they slew of Moab at that time about ten thousand men, all lusty, and all men of valour; and there escaped not a man.

So Moab was subdued that day under the hand of Israel. And the land had rest fourscore years [Jud. 3:27–30].

SHAMGAR, THE THIRD JUDGE

As in the days of the judges, God still uses ordinary men who want to be used to accomplish His great purposes. God can use *you* if you want to be used, friends.

Now here is the third judge, Shamgar.

And after him was Shamgar the son of Anath, which slew of the Philistines six hundred men with an ox goad: and he also delivered Israel [Jud. 3:31].

In this case, it is not the man, it is the method that is remarkable. He used an ox goad, which is a very crude instrument. The Israelites just didn't have iron weapons; so he used that which he had.

I hear people say today, "Oh, we must have the best and the latest methods." It is fine to have good methods, but what about the message? It is wonderful to have airplanes that transport missionaries, but when the missionary gets to his field, is he giving out the Word of God? That's what I want to know. Television is great, but notice how it is prostituted today. The important thing is not the method, but the message.

An ox goad can be dedicated to God if it is in the right hands. Remember that God used the rod of Moses. He used a stone from the slingshot of David. And all Dorcas had was a needle and thread. Also there was a boy who had only five loaves and a few fishes. All of these things were given to God. Whatever you have, friend, if you will put it in His hand, He will use it. Think of these three judges who are mentioned in this chapter. They are three little men—plus God.

CHAPTER 4

THEME: *Third apostasy; God delivers Israel from oppression through Deborah and Barak*

DEBORAH AND BARAK

And the children of Israel again did evil in the sight of the LORD, when Ehud was dead.

And the LORD sold them into the hand of Jabin king of Canaan, that reigned in Hazor; the captain of whose host was Sisera, which dwelt in Harosheth of the Gentiles.

And the children of Israel cried unto the LORD: for he had nine hundred chariots of iron; and twenty years he mightily oppressed the children of Israel [Jud. 4:1–3].

After the death of Ehud, Israel again turned to idolatry, and a new period of oppression began. The Lord sold Israel into the hand of Jabin, king of Canaan. Sisera, captain of the host, had nine hundred chariots of iron. These chariots caused dread among the Israelites who had no such armaments. For twenty years Jabin oppressed Israel.

And Deborah, a prophetess, the wife of Lapidoth, she judged Israel at that time.

And she dwelt under the palm tree of Deborah between Ramah and Beth-el in mount Ephraim: and the children of Israel came up to her for judgment [Jud. 4:4–5].

Here we have a mother in Israel, Deborah, who is described as being both a prophetess and a judge. We are also told that she was the wife of Lapidoth, but I like to turn that around and say that Lapidoth was the husband of Deborah. She was quite a woman. She was raised up by God to judge Israel, and she called upon the general to get busy. He was not doing his job. He should go against the enemy that Israel might be delivered from slavery.

And she sent and called Barak the son of Abinoam out of Kedesh-naphtali, and said unto him, Hath not the LORD God of Israel commanded, saying, Go and draw toward mount Tabor, and take with thee ten thousand men of the children of Naphtali and of the children of Zebulun?

And I will draw unto thee to the river Kishon, Sisera, the captain of Jabin's army, with his chariots and his multitude; and I will deliver him into thine hand.

And Barak said unto her, If thou wilt go with me, then I will go: but if thou wilt not go with me, then I will not go [Jud. 4:6–8].

If there ever was a general who was a sissy, it was Barak. He should have been out in the thick of the battle, but here he is hiding behind a woman's skirt. Barak will not go into battle unless Deborah goes along. If this prophetess went with him, he felt he would be successful in battle. No wonder God had to use a woman in that day!

And she said, I will surely go with thee: notwithstanding the journey that thou takest shall not be for thine honour; for the LORD shall sell Sisera into the hand of a woman. And Deborah arose, and went with Barak to Kedesh [Jud. 4:9].

Deborah promised to go with Barak but told him that a woman would be the heroine of the battle.

THE DEATH AND DEFEAT OF SISERA

Deborah was a forthright woman who, as we shall see, wanted deliverance for her people. Barak called together his army, and they got ready to go against the enemy. God gave them the victory.

But Barak pursued after the chariots, and after the host, unto Harosheth of the Gentiles: and all the host of Sisera fell upon the edge of the sword; and there was not a man left [Jud. 4:16].

They exterminated the army.

Howbeit Sisera fled away on his feet to the tent of Jael the wife of Heber the Kenite: for there was peace between Jabin the king of Hazor and the house of Heber the Kenite [Jud. 4:17].

She was a Gentile.

And Jael went out to meet Sisera, and said unto him, Turn in, my lord, turn in to me; fear not. And when he had turned in unto her into the tent, she covered him with a mantle.

And he said unto her, Give me, I pray thee, a little water to drink; for I am thirsty. And she opened a bottle of milk, and gave him drink, and covered him.

Again he said unto her, Stand in the door of the tent, and it shall be, when any man doth come and inquire of thee, and say, Is there any man here? that thou shalt say, No.

Then Jael Heber's wife took a nail of the tent, and took an hammer in her hand, and went softly unto him, and smote the nail into his temples, and fastened it into the ground: for he was fast asleep and weary. So he died [Jud. 4:18–21].

Since the rest of his army was destroyed, Sisera's primary desire was to save his own life. Apparently the Canaanites had not bothered the Kenites, and Sisera believed he would be safe among these people. He went to the house of Heber, and his wife Jael offered the weary soldier hospitality. Her kindness led him to believe he could trust her. When he went to sleep, she took a tent pin and hammer and let him have it, friends. She got rid of him. This brought a great deliverance for Israel.

CHAPTER 5

***THEME:** The song of Deborah and Barak*

In the fourth chapter of Judges we saw the incident concerning Deborah. You will recall that they were dark days. In fact, it was dark all over the land. The incident concerning Deborah, Barak, and Jael took place in the northern part of Israel. God gave Israel a great deliverance. This song is one of praise to God and a rehearsal of the entire episode.

Then sang Deborah and Barak the son of Abinoam on that day, saying,

Praise ye the LORD for the avenging of Israel, when the people willingly offered themselves.

Hear, O ye kings; give ear, O ye princes; I, even I, will sing unto the LORD; I will sing praise to the LORD God of Israel.

LORD, when thou wentest out of Seir, when thou marchedst out of the field of Edom, the earth trembled, and the heavens dropped, the clouds also dropped water.

The mountains melted from before the LORD, even that Sinai from before the LORD God of Israel [Jud. 5:1–5].

Their song is very poetic, to be sure.

Deborah confesses that she is a mother in Israel and was not looking for a job at all. The fact that she took the lead is no reflection on her. She was God's choice. History affords many such examples. There was Molly Pitcher, the wife of a Revolutionary soldier, who, at the battle of Monmouth, manned the cannon at which her husband had just fallen. Other examples are Joan of Arc, the French heroine, and Zenobia, queen of Palmyra.

Deborah was one of the outstanding judges. She far exceeded Othniel in ability. It is an evidence of decline, however, when women come into the position of authority. It is a sign of weakness and of a flabby age. We have already seen that weak-kneed general, Barak. He was a sissy. He wanted to stay way back behind the fighting lines. In fact, he wanted to stay home and did not want to fight at all. Deborah had to agree to go with him before he was willing to go and battle the enemy.

Many years ago I heard Dr. Harry Ironside tell of a woman who was preaching in a park as he and one of his friends were walking by. His friend said, "It is a shame for a woman to get up and preach like that. I deplore it. She should not be doing that." Dr. Ironside replied, "I agree with you that it is a shame, not that a woman is preaching, but that there is not a man to take her place."

Regardless of what you might think (and I know I may sound very out of date, especially in this day of women's rights), America is paying an awful price for taking women into its defense system and into industry. I made this statement as far back as 1948, and I am no prophet, but I predicted a backwash of immorality if women left the home. Well, it certainly came to pass. First there was an epidemic of women shooting their husbands, deserting their children, becoming dope peddlers, and committing suicide. There are many things that are considered a menace in our country—inflation, crime, foreign aggression—but I feel that the greatest danger is that women are leaving their place in the home.

Deborah actually did not want to leave her home. However, Jabin was king of the Canaanites, and God had sold Israel into slavery to them. When the time of deliverance came, Barak, who commanded Israel's army, did not want to go into battle. God, however, promised victory. The victory was won, but it was an ignominious victory for Barak.

After the battle Deborah and Barak sang a song that was one of the first songs of the human race.

In the days of Shamgar the son of Anath, in the days of Jael, the highways were unoccupied, and the travellers walked through byways.

The inhabitants of the villages ceased,

they ceased in Israel, until that I Deborah arose, that I arose a mother in Israel [Jud. 5:6–7].

The song mentions Shamgar. He was the judge, you remember, that used an ox goad. He had judged during a time of lawlessness and grave immorality. It was not safe to walk the highways; the highways were unoccupied. Travelers walked through the byways because it was not safe to take the main route. It is becoming increasingly unsafe to travel today also. Women do not dare walk the streets at night alone. Deborah knew all about this kind of danger because lawlessness reigned in her day.

Then her song mentions the lack of leadership. Rulers had ceased to rule. There was no great man who could lead. Deborah was a mother. She had a mother's heart. Very candidly, she did not want to take the lead, but there was no man to assume the leadership. How tragic was this situation. She wanted something better for her children than what she saw about her. Because of her desire, she became a judge in Israel. She stepped out and took the lead in a day when her nation had denied God.

They chose new gods; then was war in the gates: was there a shield or spear seen among forty thousand in Israel? [Jud. 5:8].

Israel denied God—as men do today—only instead of becoming atheists, they became polytheists. They began to worship many gods. Think of the multitudes today that are living without God! Deborah did not want her children to grow up this way and that is why she stepped out as she did.

Do you remember the hopes that this country had after World War II? Everyone in the United States thought they were going to have peace at last. Many people thought they would live in peace and sin, and it would be nice. They forgot to read Psalm 85:10 which says, "Mercy and truth are met together; righteousness and peace have kissed each other." Friend, peace and righteousness do not even speak to each other today—I do not even think they know each other! It is interesting that God did not let us live comfortably in peace and sin. God did not let Israel live that way either. It is also interesting to note that Israel lacked a defense. They had nothing with which to meet the enemy. Deborah sang,". . . then was war in the gates: was there a shield or spear seen among forty thousand in Israel?" Israel had no help at all.

My heart is toward the governors of Israel, that offered themselves willingly among the people. Bless ye the LORD [Jud. 5:9].

The conditions were not all bad. There were some godly rulers. Deborah wanted them to know that she gave them her support. It was the godless crowd that she rejected.

Speak, ye that ride on white asses, ye that sit in judgment, and walk by the way.

They that are delivered from the noise of archers in the places of drawing water, there shall they rehearse the righteous acts of the LORD, even the righteous acts toward the inhabitants of his villages in Israel: then shall the people of the LORD go down to the gates [Jud. 5:10–11].

The gates were the place of assembly. Wherever people were going to meet, instead of talking about the common topics of the day, as they had in the past, they would talk about the righteous acts of God.

Awake, awake, Deborah: awake, awake, utter a song: arise, Barak, and lead thy captivity captive, thou son of Abinoam.

Then he made him that remaineth have dominion over the nobles among the people: the LORD made me have dominion over the mighty [Jud. 5:12–13].

After Israel's victory over the enemy, Deborah once again tells Barak to take command. But he does not take charge, and she has to continue as the leader. She found she had dominion over the mighty.

Out of Ephraim was there a root of them against Amalek; after thee, Benjamin, among thy people; out of Machir came down governors, and out of Zebulun they that handle the pen of the writer [Jud. 5:14].

The tribes now join in.

And the princes of Issachar were with Deborah; even Issachar, and also Barak: he was sent on foot into the valley. For the divisions of Reuben there were great thoughts of heart.

Why abodest thou among the sheepfolds, to hear the bleatings of the flocks? For the divisions of Reuben there were great searchings of heart [Jud. 5:15–16].

Some of the tribes didn't help. Reuben sent no reinforcements to the battle. They were not there to lend support when it was badly needed. They were neighbors and close by, but they did nothing. They felt like they should stay with their flocks and apparently did not trust someone else to watch their animals. They acted as if there was no war. They burned their draft cards and did not come. The tribe of Issachar, on the other hand, stood with Deborah and Barak.

Gilead abode beyond Jordan: and why did Dan remain in ships? Asher continued on the sea shore, and abode in his breaches [Jud. 5:17].

Dan was busy in commerce. The folk in that tribe did not want to come to the battle. Asher continued on the seashore. You know, human nature never changes. As in Deborah's day, many folk today have let their country down, and they should not have done that.

Zebulun and Naphtali were a people that jeoparded their lives unto the death in the high places of the field [Jud. 5:18].

These two tribes really fought.

The kings came and fought, then fought the kings of Canaan in Taanach by the waters of Megiddo; they took no gain of money [Jud. 5:19].

Israel had some allies that were formerly enemies. They helped at the waters of Megiddo which is near what will be Armageddon one day.

They fought from heaven; the stars in their courses fought against Sisera [Jud. 5:20].

I don't believe this is merely a poetic expression. My feeling is that it could truly be said that heaven, that God was against this enemy.

The river of Kishon swept them away, that ancient river, the river Kishon. O my soul, thou hast trodden down strength.

Then were the horsehoofs broken by the means of the prancings, the prancings of their mighty ones.

Curse ye Meroz, said the angel of the LORD, curse ye bitterly the inhabitants thereof; because they came not to the help of the LORD, to the help of the LORD against the mighty [Jud. 5:21–23].

Frankly, I cannot identify Meroz. However, one thing I know for sure and that is that I would not want to be an inhabitant of the city of Meroz. They did not come to help the work of the Lord and so they were cursed. Today, also, there are multitudes of folks who are not coming to help the work of the Lord.

Blessed above women shall Jael the wife of Heber the Kenite be, blessed shall she be above women in the tent [Jud. 5:24].

The heroine of the day was Jael, not Barak, in spite of her dastardly deed. But this was a time of war and the aftermath of war. All around was the holocaust of battle, broken bodies, and the fruit of war. Men's souls were blackened and scarred. The foliage of civilization was removed like thin veneer. Snarled and gnarled, the trunk of barbarianism was revealed. What Jael did was an awful thing. Woman has been created finer than man. There is something fine that has gone out of life today, and I think it centers in womanhood.

Now a mother's heart is revealed. Deborah remembers that Sisera, although he was the enemy, had a mother. And even though she extols Jael for what she did, she thinks of Sisera's mother.

The mother of Sisera looked out at a window, and cried through the lattice. Why is his chariot so long in coming? why tarry the wheels of his chariots?

Her wise ladies answered her, yea, she returned answer to herself,

Have they not sped? have they not divided the prey; to every man a damsel or two; to Sisera a prey of divers colours, a prey of divers colours of needlework, of divers colours of needlework on both sides, meet for the necks of them that take the spoil? [Jud. 5:28–30].

The mother of Sisera knew in her heart what had happened. She knew he had been slain. She had thought all of the time that he would be coming home, but he did not come. Even in this case, the heart of Deborah went out to this woman because she was a mother.

So let all thine enemies perish, O LORD: but let them that love him be as the sun when he goeth forth in his might. And the land had rest forty years [Jud. 5:31].

There have been mothers in the past who have overcome handicaps in evil days—evil days like those in which Deborah lived. Read the story of Augustine. He had a marvelous mother by the name of Monica, who prayed for him. He was a debauched college professor, and he finally came to the feet of Jesus Christ. There was also Susanna Wesley who prayed for her two sons, John and Charles Wesley. Now I am not talking about worshiping womanhood or motherhood, friend, but I do want to say that we are getting far away from God's conception of it. What a picture we have in Deborah and her song!

CHAPTERS 6–8

***THEME:** Fourth apostasy; God delivers Israel through Gideon*

Gideon is the next judge. He is called to his position in chapter 6. Chapter 7 tells how mightily God used him. He is one of the most interesting judges, although not the most outstanding. In reality none of the judges were great. They were little people, marked by mediocrity. Each one was insignificant, insufficient, and inadequate. Each one had some aberration in his life. Each one of them had a glaring fault, and sometimes that fault was the very reason God chose them and used them.

I would like to add some background to this incident with some very pertinent facts. The account of the judges was discounted by the critics for many years. They said because it was not in secular history, these events actually did not take place, and there was no situation in the past into which they could be fitted. But all of that has changed now because of the spade of the archaeologist and the scholarly work of men like Burney, Moulton, Breasted, and Garstang. These outstanding conservative scholars have given us the background for the Book of Judges.

Now we know that at this particular time in history Egypt was weak, very weak. It had been a world power, but it was weak because the pharaohs who were in office were weak men. Also there were internal problems and troubles. As a result, this nation was losing its grip upon its colonies. The nomadic tribes to the east of the Dead Sea and to the south of the Dead Sea began to push in. They pushed in because there was a drought in their land. They had experienced it there for several years. So these nomadic tribes of the desert began to encroach upon the territory of Israel. The Midianites and the Amalekites were among the Bedouins of the desert who came into the land. The story of Gideon opens with that.

ISRAEL SINS AND IS OPPRESSED BY MIDIAN

And the children of Israel did evil in the sight of the LORD: and the LORD delivered them into the hand of Midian seven years.

And the hand of Midian prevailed against Israel: and because of the Midianites the children of Israel made them the dens which are in the mountains, and caves, and strong holds [Jud. 6:1–2].

The Midianites and the Amalekites moved as a disorganized nomadic tribe. They were raiders. They would raid the crops and supplies of others. They generally took their families with them. In fact, they took all that they had with them. They would pitch their tents as they moved along. In this incident, we are not given numbers concerning them because no one in the world would have been able to number them—they were so disorganized. But by sheer numbers, and they were many, they overwhelmed the inhabitants of the land. The children of Israel fled from their homes and lived in caves and dens. There is abundant evidence in the land of Israel today that they lived in caves, especially during the period of the judges.

It is the same old story once again. Israel sinned and the hoop started moving. God had blessed the children of Israel under the administration of Deborah. When they sinned, God delivered them to Midian, and they cried out for deliverance.

For they came up with their cattle and their tents, and they came as grasshop-

pers for multitude; for both they and their camels were without number: and they entered into the land to destroy it [Jud. 6:5].

The Midianites came up against the children of Israel. They were like a plague of grasshoppers as they came into the land. They came "without number," which means that they had not been counted. They were such a large company that certainly the enemy could not count them. The Midianites saw that Israel had good crops, and they needed grain and foodstuff for themselves and for their animals.

The tribe of Manasseh, of which Gideon was a member, occupied the plain in which was located the Plain of Esdraelon (the place where Armageddon will be fought). Although they had occupied that territory, when these nomads came into that area, they took to the hills; they moved into the dens and into the caves up there. They had to. They saw their crops which they had left all taken by the enemy. This is the historical period into which the story of Gideon is cast.

And it came to pass, when the children of Israel cried unto the LORD because of the Midianites,

That the LORD sent a prophet unto the children of Israel, which said unto them, Thus saith the LORD God of Israel, I brought you up from Egypt, and brought you forth out of the house of bondage;

And I delivered you out of the hand of the Egyptians, and out of the hand of all that oppressed you, and drave them out from before you, and gave you their land;

And I said unto you, I am the LORD your God; fear not the gods of the Amorites, in whose land ye dwell: but ye have not obeyed my voice [Jud. 6:7–10].

Here goes Israel again, whining and complaining. But God is gracious and good. A prophet came and told them why they were in their present condition. They cried out to God, and God in mercy sent them another judge.

GIDEON, THE SIXTH JUDGE

Now at this juncture, God appeared to Gideon in a most embarrassing situation. We are told:

And there came an angel of the LORD, and sat under an oak which was in Ophrah, that pertained unto Joash the Abiezrite: and his son Gideon threshed wheat by the winepress, to hide it from the Midianites [Jud. 6:11].

Gideon is not introduced to us as a hero or an outstanding man. Do you know what he is doing? He is threshing wheat by the winepress. Now the winepress is the key to this entire situation. You see, in that day the winepress was always put at the foot of the hill because they brought the grapes down from the vineyard. Naturally, they would carry the heavy grapes downhill; they carried them to the lowest place. In contrast, the threshing floor was always put up on the top of the hill, the highest hill that was available, in order to catch the wind which would drive the chaff away. Here we find Gideon, down at the bottom of the hill, threshing. Now that would be the place to take the grapes, but that is no place to take your crop in order to do your threshing. Can you see the frustration of this man? Why doesn't he go to the hilltop? Well, he is afraid of the Midianites. He does not want them to see that he is threshing wheat. And you can imagine his frustration. There is no air getting to him down there, certainly no wind. So he pitches the grain up into the air. And what happens? Does the chaff blow away? No. It comes down around his neck and gets into his clothes making him very uncomfortable. There he is, trying his best to thresh in a place like that, and all the time rebuking himself for being a coward, afraid to go to the hilltop. I think he looked up there rather longingly and thought, "Do I dare go to the hilltop?" Gideon was having a very frustrating experience, but God was going to use this man. We will see why God used this kind of a man.

It was at that time that the angel of the Lord, which many of us believe was none other than the pre-incarnate Christ, appeared to him. We are told:

And the angel of the LORD appeared unto him, and said unto him, The LORD is with thee, thou mighty man of valour [Jud. 6:12].

Don't tell me, friend, that there is no humor in the Bible. Don't you think it sounds humorous to call Gideon a mighty man of valour? God has a wonderful sense of humor. The Bible is a serious book, of course. It deals with a race that is in sin, and it concerns God's salvation for that race. It reveals God as high and holy and lifted up. But God has a sense of humor and, if you miss that in the Bible, you will not find it nearly as interesting.

Jesus Christ has a great sense of humor. One day He said to the Pharisees, "Ye blind guides, which strain at a gnat, and swallow a camel" (Matt. 23:24). If you don't think that is funny, the next time you see a camel, look at it. A camel has more projections on it than some of our space vehicles. I rode a camel in Egypt and found out they even have horns. They also have the biggest Adam's apple in the world. They have pads on their knees, great big hoofs, and some have one hump, and some have two humps. Everywhere you look at them there is a projection. Can't you see these religious rulers trying to swallow camels? God indeed has a sense of humor.

One of the funniest things the Lord could have called Gideon was a mighty man of valour because he was actually a coward. I think that when Gideon looked up and saw Him and heard Him say, "Thou mighty man of valour," he looked behind him to see if there wasn't somebody else there, because that term did not apply to him. And then he turned to the angel and said, "Who? Me? Do you mean to call me a mighty man of valour when I am down here at the winepress pitching grain up into the air when I ought to be up yonder on top of the hill? If I were a mighty man of valour, that is where I would be, not down here. I am nothing in the world but a coward." The Lord does want to encourage him, of course, but the point is that it was a rather humorous title that the Lord gave to this man.

Well, God has called him now to this office to deliver his people, and He has called a most unusual man. This man is suffering from an inferiority complex.

> **And Gideon said unto him, Oh my Lord, if the LORD be with us, why then is all this befallen us? and where be all his miracles which our fathers told us of, saying, Did not the LORD bring us up from Egypt? but now the LORD hath forsaken us, and delivered us into the hands of the Midianites [Jud. 6:13].**

Now the angel of the Lord did not say that He was with *Israel* at this time; He was with Gideon. Frankly, He was not with Israel because of their sin. The angel said, "The Lord is with *thee*"—singular—with *you*, Gideon. But Gideon cannot believe that God would be with him. He wants to know where all those miracles are that their fathers had told them about. He believed that the Lord had forsaken Israel. He was as wrong as a man could be. The Lord had not really forsaken them; they had forsaken the Lord.

This man is in a bad state mentally and a bad state spiritually. Actually, he not only had an inferiority complex, he was skeptical, he was cynical, he was weak, and he was cowardly. That is this man Gideon. What a wrong impression is given of him today when he is described as a knight in shining armor, a Sir Lancelot, or a Sir Galahad. Why, he was nothing in the world but a Don Quixote charging a windmill, my beloved. He was the biggest coward that you have ever seen. But this was the man that God called.

> **And the LORD looked upon him, and said, Go in this thy might, and thou shalt save Israel from the hand of the Midianites: have not I sent thee? [Jud. 6:14].**

This is the call and commission of Gideon. It is a commission of courage. It is interesting to note, however, that even at this point Gideon did not believe God. Note what Gideon says:

> **And he said unto him, Oh my Lord, wherewith shall I save Israel? behold, my family is poor in Manasseh, and I am the least in my father's house [Jud. 6:15].**

Now consider for a moment the position Gideon occupies in his own thinking. He said in effect, "You certainly are not asking me to do this. To begin with, I belong to the nation Israel. We are now under the heel of the Midianites." It was bad enough to be under Egypt, but imagine being under these nomads of the desert, the Midianites! "We are in slavery. Here we are hiding, and here I am threshing at the foot of the hill. And you come and call *me?* Well, to begin with, the tribe of Manasseh (one of the sons of Joseph) is not noted for anything; we have had no conspicuous men. In the tribe of Manasseh, my family is not very well known. We are sort of ne'er-do-wells. We are not prominent folk. In my family I happen to be the very least one. You made a big mistake in calling me because you happen to have called the smallest pebble that is on the beach." Honestly, this man felt that he was the last man in Israel to be used of God. And do you know that he was right? He was the last man in Israel that God should have called.

Our problem today, friend, is that most of us are too strong for God to use. Most of us are too capable for God to use. You notice that

God uses only weak men, don't you? First Corinthians 1:26–27 tells us that this is so: "For ye see your calling, brethren, how that not many wise men after the flesh, not many mighty, not many noble, are called: But God hath chosen the foolish things of the world to confound the wise; and God hath chosen the weak things of the world to confound the things which are mighty." God used all of these judges but not because they were capable or outstanding. Does that encourage you, friend? Do you know why God does not use most of us? We are too strong. Most of us have too much talent for God to use us. Most of us today are doing our own will and going our own way. There are multitudes of people, talented people, people with ability, whom God is not using. Do you know why? They are too strong for God to use. Paul mentions this: "And base things of the world, and things which are despised, hath God chosen, yea, and things which are not, to bring to nought things that are: That no flesh should glory in his presence" (1 Cor. 1:28–29). There is something wrong with any Christian worker who is proud. God does not use the flesh. Anything that this poor preacher does in the weakness of the flesh and boasts about is despised by God. God hates it and cannot use it. God wants weak vessels, and that is the *only* kind He will use. God follows this policy so that no flesh will glory in His presence. When God gets ready to do anything, He chooses the weakest thing He can get in order to make it clear that He is doing it, not the weak arm of the flesh. That is God's method.

Remember Moses down in the bulrushes was only a little baby. Then look at Pharaoh Ramses II, the strongest of the pharaohs, who sat on the throne. He is the one who built the great cities of Egypt. Put the one down by the side of the other—the little weak, helpless baby and the powerful Pharaoh on the throne—and whom will you take? Of course you would take the Pharaoh because he is the strong one. But God took the little fellow in the bulrushes to demonstrate that He uses the weak things of the world to confound the wise.

Also God chose a man by the name of Elijah. Elijah was not a weak man, but he had to become weak. God had to put that man through a series of tests. He schooled him in the desert and finally forced him to listen to the still, small voice of God. And Elijah did not much care for still, small voices. This is the man who liked the three-ring circus, the fireworks, the noise and the fanfare, but God had to train him and let him know that He chooses the weak things of the world. After Elijah walked into the court of Ahab and Jezebel, he told them it would not rain for several years. Then God put him out by the brook Cherith. There as he saw the brook dry up, he found out that his life was no more than a dried-up brook. Later he looked down into an empty flour barrel, but he could sing the doxology. When he did, God fed him and the widow's family out of that empty flour barrel. Why? Because God chooses and uses weak things.

Then consider Simon Peter. Whoever would have chosen him? Why, everybody knew he was as weak as water, and our Lord said, "You are going to be a rock-man. I will make you as stable as a rock." I imagine everybody laughed when He said that. Even Simon Peter gave up on one occasion and said, "Depart from me, for I am a sinful man" (Luke 5:8). What he is really saying is this, "Why don't you give me up and go get somebody else? I am such a failure." But the Lord Jesus said, "Fear not; from henceforth thou shalt catch men" (Luke 5:10). In effect He said, "You are the very one I want. You are going to preach the first sermon on the day of Pentecost which will bring three thousand people to Me. I am going to demonstrate that I can use the weakest thing in the world." God always does that, my beloved. The interesting thing is, someone has said, that Nero was on the throne while Paul was being beheaded. At first glance, it looked like Paul had lost and Nero had won. But history had already handed down its decision. Men name their sons Paul and call their dogs Nero. This is quite interesting, is it not? God is choosing the weak things of this world.

Have you ever compared that little Baby in Bethlehem with Caesar Augustus who could sign a tax bill and the whole civilized world was taxed? Which would you pick? I would take the tax-gatherer every time because he seems to have a lot of power, but God took that little Baby in Bethlehem, for He was His Son. God always chooses that way.

Although Gideon was a very weak individual, God told him that he was the one who was going to deliver Israel. Yes, God is going to use Gideon, but first He must train him. Gideon had to overcome his fear and develop courage. He needed faith to help strengthen his feeble knees and make him patient. I want you to notice some of the training that he went through. He immediately, you see, was afraid; so God gave him his first lesson.

And the LORD said unto him, Peace be unto thee; fear not: thou shalt not die [Jud. 6:23].

He said, "Thou shalt not die," because Gideon feared that he would die after seeing God. And he told Gideon to go to his own hometown, to begin there by throwing over the altar of Baal, and burning the grove that was by it. All of this represented the worst sort of immorality.

GIDEON REPUDIATES BAAL: ISRAEL CALLED TO ARMS

Then Gideon built an altar there unto the LORD, and called it Jehovah-shalom: unto this day it is yet in Ophrah of the Abiezrites.

And it came to pass the same night, that the LORD said unto him, Take thy father's young bullock, even the second bullock of seven years old, and throw down the altar of Baal that thy father hath, and cut down the grove that is by it:

And build an altar unto the LORD thy God upon the top of this rock, in the ordered place, and take the second bullock, and offer a burnt sacrifice with the wood of the grove which thou shalt cut down.

Then Gideon took ten men of his servants, and did as the LORD had said unto him: and so it was, because he feared his father's household, and the men of the city, that he could not do it by day, that he did it by night [Jud. 6:24–27].

And so Gideon begins his adventure. Even with God's commission he is still afraid. Instead of obeying God in the bold daylight, he does it under the cover of darkness. But they find out who did it, and they are ready to execute Gideon. But God again delivers him.

Gideon is still hesitant. God has to overcome the fear. God has to develop courage and faith. God has to strengthen Gideon's feeble knees. It is a patient, long ordeal. The next step is to fill this man with His Spirit—God has always given a filling of the Spirit to the man that He uses.

But the spirit of the LORD came upon Gideon, and he blew a trumpet; and Abiezer was gathered after him [Jud. 6:34].

The blowing of the trumpet meant war. The minute he blew the trumpet, his people knew it meant war against the Amalekites, and they began to gather unto him.

Do you know what happened? Gideon got cold feet and went back to the Lord with a proposition.

And Gideon said unto God, If thou wilt save Israel by mine hand, as thou has said,

Behold, I will put a fleece of wool in the floor; and if the dew be on the fleece only, and it be dry upon all the earth beside, then shall I know that thou wilt save Israel by mine hand, as thou hast said.

And it was so: for he rose up early on the morrow, and thrust the fleece together, and wringed the dew out of the fleece, a bowl full of water [Jud. 6:36–38].

The next day Gideon went back (and I am of the opinion that he intended to do this all the time regardless of the outcome of the first test because if you put out a fleece here in California it would be damp, whereas the ground would be dry). He gave a two-way test that could not be gainsaid. He said, "Now, Lord, I will put out the fleece again. If You are really in this thing, put the dew around everywhere else and let the fleece remain dry." I am glad he did it that way because, frankly, I would be skeptical enough to believe it "just happened" the first time. Or let us say that it was natural for it to happen one way, but it was supernatural for it to happen the other way. This man asked God to put dew on the fleece and then for God not to put dew on the fleece. How gracious God was to Gideon. We will find that God will gradually school this man until He brings him to the place where Gideon can see that there is nothing in him. Then God will use him to win a mighty battle.

Now, looking back at verses 34 and 35, we see that men for his army had come to him from everywhere. When a trumpet is blown in Israel, it means war. And frankly, friend, he was the last man you would want to gather around. He certainly was not a man prepared to lead them into battle. So God begins to move in this man's life in a definite way, as we shall see in chapter 7.

THREE HUNDRED ALERT SOLDIERS ARE CHOSEN

Then Jerubbaal, who is Gideon, and all

the people that were with him, rose up early, and pitched beside the well of Harod: so that the host of the Midianites were on the north side of them, by the hill of Moreh, in the valley.

And the LORD said unto Gideon, The people that are with thee are too many for me to give the Midianites into their hands, lest Israel vaunt themselves against me, saying, Mine own hand hath saved me [Jud. 7:1–2].

Now Gideon goes out and looks at his army. He had thirty-two thousand men, and the thought in Gideon's mind is that this is not enough. The Midianites were like grasshoppers on the hills. They were disorganized, but by sheer numbers they would have overcome the Israelites. Therefore, his men were too few, and I think Gideon was ready to blow the trumpet again. But God said to Gideon, "You have too many men. I cannot give you the victory with thirty-two thousand men because you would boast and say that you did it in your own strength, power and might." No flesh is going to glory in God's presence. That is the reason God has to use weak instruments today. This is the method He continues to follow. He is going to cut down the number of the army.

Now therefore go to, proclaim in the ears of the people, saying, Whosoever is fearful and afraid, let him return and depart early from mount Gilead. And there returned of the people twenty and two thousand; and there remained ten thousand [Jud. 7:3].

Gideon had thirty-two thousand men and now he has lost twenty-two thousand of them! You may recall God's condition, as put down in the Mosaic system in the Book of Deuteronomy that if anyone was drafted into the army and was *afraid,* he could go home.

I have often wondered why Gideon did not go home. When he said, "All of you who are fearful and afraid," he could have said, "Follow me, because I am going home, I am more afraid than anyone here." He had to stay, however. God had commissioned him.

Now Gideon has only ten thousand men and that is enough to make anyone afraid. But God says, "Really, you still have too many men. You have to reduce this number. I cannot give you victory with this number of men in your army." So Gideon and his men went through another test.

So he brought down the people unto the water: and the LORD said unto Gideon, Every one that lappeth of the water with his tongue, as a dog lappeth, him shalt thou set by himself; likewise every one that boweth down upon his knees to drink.

And the number of them that lapped, putting their hand to their mouth, were three hundred men: but all the rest of the people bowed down upon their knees to drink water.

And the LORD said unto Gideon, By the three hundred men that lapped will I save you, and deliver the Midianites into thine hand: and let all the other people go every man unto his place [Jud. 7:5–7].

Do you know what we have here? It is one of the finest lessons concerning divine election and man's free will. This is the way they work together. God said to Gideon, "I am going to choose the men that I want to go with you, but the way I will do it is to let them make the choice. Bring them down to the water, and the ones who lap water like a dog, just going through and throwing it into their mouths, are the ones I have chosen. You can put aside those men who get down on all fours and take their time drinking. I don't want them."

Had we been there (ours is a great day for interviewing the man on the street), we could have had interviews with the men in Gideon's army. For example, let us take the man that is down on all fours. We would go up to him and say, "Brother, why did you get down on all fours?" "Well," he would reply, "I was just wondering why I didn't go home with the other crowd. I have been thinking this thing over and I have a wife and family, and I just do not think I ought to be here. I feel like I should have gone home. I have no heart for this." He made his choice, but God also made His choice. That is divine election and human free will. You see, God elects, but He lets *you* be the one to make the choice. Then we go to the man that lapped water like a dog, and went to the other side of the stream. "Why did you lap water like that?" we ask him. He says, "Where are the Midianites?" "Wait just a minute," we reply. "Why did you do that?" He replies, "Because I am with Gideon one hundred percent!" May I say to you that these three hundred men had a heart for battle. If you had said to any one of these three hundred men, "Say, did you know that God has elected you?" he would have replied, "I don't know what you are talking about. The thing is that I want to go after these Midianites!"

You can argue about divine election and free will all you want to, but it works. You cannot make it work out by arguing, but it sure works out in life, friend. Each one of the ten thousand men in Gideon's army exercised his free will. God did not interfere with one of them as far as their free wills were concerned. Today God, through His Son Jesus Christ, offers you the free gift of salvation. It is a legitimate offer. It is a sincere offer from God Himself. He says, "All that the Father giveth me shall come to me; and him that cometh to me I will in no wise cast out" (John 6:37). Now don't tell me that you can argue about election right now. You cannot. You can come to God if you want to come. If you don't come, I have news for you—you were not elected. If you do come, I have good news for you—you were elected. That is the way God moves.

Now these three hundred men often have been misunderstood. As a student, I went down to a little church in Georgia. When I got there, a dear little lady wearing a sunbonnet said to me, "Mr. McGee, we have here just a little Gideon's band." They didn't have a Gideon's band! They had the most discouraged, lazy folk I have ever seen in my life. That is not Gideon's band. Gideon's band was a group of dedicated men, willing to die to deliver Israel, men who had their hearts and souls in this matter. May I say to you that these men lapped up water like a dog because they were after the Midianites and not after water. They will drink after the battle is over.

I once watched a football game, and then I listened to the interview of the quarterback of the Arkansas team. Even after the game, he was so excited and so emotional that he took no credit for himself. He gave his team the credit for winning. He said, "We were determined to win." That is Gideon's band, friend, and that is the thing that is needed today in the church, if you please.

ISRAEL'S VICTORY OVER MIDIAN

But if thou fear to go down, go thou with Phurah thy servant down to the host:

And thou shalt hear what they say; and afterward shall thine hands be strengthened to go down unto the host. Then went he down with Phurah his servant unto the outside of the armed men that were in the host.

And the Midianites and the Amalekites and all the children of the east lay along in the valley like grasshoppers for multitude; and their camels were without number, as the sand by the sea side for multitude.

And when Gideon was come, behold, there was a man that told a dream unto his fellow, and said, Behold, I dreamed a dream, and, lo, a cake of barley bread tumbled into the host of Midian, and came unto a tent, and smote it that it fell, and overturned it, that the tent lay along.

And his fellow answered and said, This is nothing else save the sword of Gideon the son of Joash, a man of Israel: for into his hand hath God delivered Midian, and all the host [Jud. 7:10–14].

This is Gideon's final lesson before he goes into battle. He goes down to the edge of the camp and eavesdrops while two soldiers are talking. They frankly believe that God is going to deliver the Midianites into the hands of Gideon and his host. God permits Gideon to hear this conversation to encourage him just prior to the battle.

And he divided the three hundred men into three companies, and he put a trumpet in every man's hand, with empty pitchers, and lamps within the pitchers.

And he said unto them, Look on me, and do likewise: and, behold, when I come to the outside of the camp, it shall be that, as I do, so shall ye do. When I blow with a trumpet, I and all that are with me, then blow ye the trumpets also on every side of all the camp, and say, The sword of the LORD, and of Gideon.

So Gideon, and the hundred men that were with him, came unto the outside of the camp in the beginning of the middle watch; and they had but newly set the watch: and they blew the trumpets, and brake the pitchers that were in their hands.

And the three companies blew the trumpets, and brake the pitchers, and held the lamps in their left hands, and the trumpets in their right hands to blow withal: and they cried, The sword of the LORD, and of Gideon.

And they stood every man in his place

round about the camp: and all the host ran, and cried, and fled.

And the three hundred blew the trumpets, and the Lord set every man's sword against his fellow, even throughout all the host: and the host fled to Beth-shittah in Zererath, and to the border of Abel-meholah, unto Tabbath [Jud. 7:16–22].

This is the record given of Gideon's strategy. He divides his three hundred men into three groups. They are given three things: pitchers, lamps, and trumpets. The lamps were put inside the pitchers so that the light could not be seen, and they held them in one hand and their trumpets they held in the other hand. When they went into battle, their cry was to be, "The sword of the Lord and of Gideon." The interesting thing is that Gideon did not have a sword and neither did any of the three hundred men. You see they were under the rule of the Midianites, and the Midianites did not let them have an arsenal. They kept the weapons and the swords for themselves. So Gideon's strategy employed pitchers, lamps, and trumpets.

As we have said before, the Midianites and Amalekites were among the nomadic tribes of the desert. They had raided the land of Israel and seized their crops and supplies. They had a very loose organization. They moved as disorganized nomads through the desert and did not have an organized army. They had set a few guards about the camp but most of the people were asleep, here, there, and yonder. They did not expect to be attacked at night. To begin with, it is difficult to see at night. So Gideon posted his three hundred men in three groups around the camp. At a certain time they blew their trumpets and broke the pitchers so that the light shone out. Each trumpet represented the fact that there were probably several hundred of the enemy present. Imagine the Midianites waking out of a sound sleep. The first thing they did was start whacking with their swords in every direction. The Israelites did not have swords. All they did was hold the light so the Midianites could go after each other. It was a regular riot! The Midianites soon fled over the hills into the tall timber and out of that area. This gave Gideon and the Israelites a tremendous victory.

There are some wonderful spiritual lessons in this account. First of all, I would like to go back to this matter of the dew on the fleece. We need God today to do an interior decorating job on our lives. We need to ask Him for dew on our barren lives. In Hosea 14:5 God says, "I will be as the dew unto Israel: he shall grow as the lily, and cast forth his roots as Lebanon." God speaks about this subject several times. "And of Joseph he said, Blessed of the Lord be his land, for the precious things of heaven, for the dew, and for the deep that coucheth beneath" (Deut. 33:13). "The king's wrath is as the roaring of a lion; but his favour is as dew upon the grass" (Prov. 19:12). "By his knowledge the depths are broken up, and the clouds drop down the dew" (Prov. 3:20). Finally, in Psalm 133:1–3, God says, "Behold, how good and how pleasant it is for brethren to dwell together in unity! It is like the precious ointment upon the head, that ran down upon the beard, even Aaron's beard: that went down to the skirts of his garments; As the dew of Hermon, and as the dew that descended upon the mountains of Zion: for there the Lord commanded the blessing, even life for evermore." God has blessed in this way. We need that touch—that fresh touch. We need it like dew upon the rosebud and the grass in the morning. We need a tender touch.

Hosea 14:5 tells us that the lily is delicate. He, our Lord God, will come down upon us like rain upon the mown grass. Even when we are in trouble, and He has cut us down, He will come down upon us like rain. Our Lord could weep over Jerusalem, but do we weep today over sinners? The Publican could smite his breast and cry out about his sin, but what about us today? We need a touch from God that will make us strong and stable, grounded and settled. Oh that we could say with the psalmist, "My heart is fixed, O God, my heart is fixed: I will sing and give praise" (Ps. 57:7).

We need the dew of God upon our lives to bring purity into our lives. Peter tells us in 2 Peter 3:14, "Wherefore, beloved, seeing that ye look for such things, be diligent that ye may be found of him in peace, without spot, and blameless." This is what we need today. God only uses a clean cup. 1 Peter 1:16 says, "Because it is written, Be ye holy; for I am holy." God says this to us. "Having therefore these promises, dearly beloved, let us cleanse ourselves from all filthiness of the flesh and spirit, perfecting holiness in the fear of God" (2 Cor. 7:1). What a wonderful picture and lesson we have here.

Now let us look at another spiritual lesson concerning the pitchers. "But we have this treasure in earthen vessels . . ." (2 Cor. 4:7). Those pitchers represent the bodies of believers. That is what Paul means when he says, "I beseech you therefore, brethren, by the mercies of God, that ye present your bodies [your total personalities] a living sacrifice . . . unto God . . ." (Rom. 12:1). That is the reason we ought not to glory in any man. Paul says that. "Therefore let no man glory in men . . ." (1 Cor. 3:21). That is the earthen vessel. We have this treasure in earthen vessels—pitchers. Some of us are not broken and, as a result, the light does not shine through. It is not our light that we should shine, but the light of the Lord Jesus Christ. His light should shine through us. It can only shine in a broken life. We are to shine as lights in the world. Paul told the Philippians, "Do all things without murmurings and disputings: That ye may be blameless and harmless, the sons of God, without rebuke, in the midst of a crooked and perverse nation, among whom ye shine as lights in the world" (Phil. 2:14–15).

Let's look for a moment at the trumpets. First Corinthians 14:8 says, "For if the trumpet give an uncertain sound, who shall prepare himself to the battle?" This speaks of the testimony and witness of believers. The testimony and witness of believers must be certain and clear.

FORTY YEARS OF PEACE UNDER GIDEON

Chapter 8 is a continuance of the record of Gideon, the judge. Here you find events that came to pass after the remarkable deliverance that God gave Gideon over the Midianites. The children of Israel are free again and, as a result, they are prosperous. Zebah and Zalmunna, Midianite kings, have been pursued and slain. The Israelites are being blessed for the first time in a long time, and they are so grateful to Gideon for all that he has done that they want him to rule over them.

Then the men of Israel said unto Gideon, Rule thou over us, both thou, and thy son, and thy son's son also: for thou hast delivered us from the hand of Midian [Jud. 8:22].

This is the first indication given to us in Scripture that the children of Israel wanted a king to rule over them. God told them at the beginning that He did not want them to have a king like the nations round about them. But because Gideon had delivered them from bondage, they wanted him to accept the position of king. He apparently is the first one to have been offered this high position, and he turned it down. Later on we will discover that Israel asks for a king again. In fact, they insist upon having a king, and finally they demand one. Then God tells Samuel (who is the last of the judges and the first in the line of the prophets) that he is to anoint a king for them. Also God makes it clear that Israel is not rejecting Samuel, but is rejecting God. God wanted to rule over His people. The form of government for Israel was to be a theocracy. In this case, it was God who had used Gideon so remarkably, but it is Gideon who Israel wants to rule over them. They not only want Gideon to rule, but his son and his son's son also. This means that they want a king like the nations around them.

Notice the remarkable answer that Gideon gave the people.

And Gideon said unto them, I will not rule over you, neither shall my son rule over you: the LORD shall rule over you [Jud. 8:23].

Gideon certainly had learned a lesson; there is no question about it. This young man who threshed grain down by the winepress, recognized that he was a coward. He knew that it was God who had given him the victory. He knew he had no strength in himself to win the battle, but he realized God had raised him up for this purpose. Gideon was indeed a remarkable person. He is mentioned in Hebrews chapter 11 where the "Heroes of the Faith" are listed. In fact, he leads the list of judges. He is also ahead of David in the list. "And what shall I more say? for the time would fail me to tell of Gedeon, and of Barak, and of Samson, and of Jephthae; of David also, and Samuel, and of the prophets: Who through faith subdued kingdoms, wrought righteousness, obtained promises, stopped the mouths of lions, Quenched the violence of fire, escaped the edge of the sword, out of weakness were made strong, waxed valiant in fight, turned to flight the armies of the aliens" (Heb. 11:32–34). The writer of Hebrews says that time would fail to tell everything about these men, and he wanted to tell about Gideon. God raised up Gideon to perform an extraordinary task. It teaches us that any man or woman that God uses has to be used on God's terms. And He chooses the weak things of this world.

It seems as though each judge had some glaring weakness and in most cases God used it. Gideon's weakness was the fact that he was a coward. At times I have felt very close to this man in my ministry. When I became pastor of the great Church of the Open Door in Los Angeles, California, in 1949, I preached my first message on Gideon. I put myself in his class. I came to that congregation in weakness. The only reason I could see that God called me was because I was like Gideon—weak and cowardly. I have rejoiced in the fact that God did for me what He did for Gideon. God certainly was with me, and I have always been grateful to Him. I have discovered that when I get in the way (and I do sometimes), then I stumble and fall. But as long as I am willing to let God have His way, it is remarkable what He will do. I give God all of the glory for my radio ministry, friend. I never sought it. I did not start out after it. Like Topsy, it "just growed." God has blessed it, and I rejoice in it. He has been wonderful.

I wish we could end the story of Gideon here, but he had another weakness.

And Gideon had threescore and ten sons of his body begotten: for he had many wives.

And his concubine that was in Shechem, she also bare him a son, whose name he called Abimelech [Jud. 8:30–31].

Gideon had many wives and a concubine besides. He had a total of seventy-one sons. That is a real blot on this man's life. Now someone will say, as they did about Solomon, "*How* could God use a man like this and *why* did He use him?" Well, Gideon took these many wives and had all of these children after the battle. And the fact of the matter is that God used him in spite of this. God did not approve of what he did. The record makes it clear that his actions brought tragedy to the nation of Israel. The next chapter brings that out. God had forbidden intermarriage outside the nation. He had forbidden the Israelites to have more than one wife. God did not create several Eves for Adam. He created only one. God did not remove all of Adam's ribs. God took out only one rib.

Abraham, you remember, took a concubine, that little Egyptian maid named Hagar and, believe me, it caused trouble. God never sanctioned it. Through Abraham's son Isaac came the nation Israel. The Arabs are descendants of Ishmael, Abraham's son by Hagar. I talked to an Arab guide in Jericho who was very proud of the fact that he was a son of Abraham. He was also a Moslem. He said proudly, "I am a son of Abraham through Ishmael." That is true. That was the sin of Abraham, and God never blessed that, friend. God did not bless Solomon's actions in this connection, and He is not going to bless Gideon either. In fact, Gideon's actions split the kingdom and caused real tragedy. This is the blot in his life. God does not hide anything. God paints the picture of man as it is. Now if a friend of Gideon had been his biographer, he probably would have left this part of his life out of the story. God, however, did not. He paints mankind in all of his lurid, sinful color.

CONFUSION AFTER GIDEON'S DEATH

And it came to pass, as soon as Gideon was dead, that the children of Israel turned again, and went a-whoring after Baalim, and made Baal-berith their god.

And the children of Israel remembered not the LORD their God, who had delivered them out of the hands of all their enemies on every side:

Neither shewed they kindness to the house of Jerubbaal, namely, Gideon, according to all the goodness which he had shewed unto Israel [Jud. 8:33–35].

This is the same old story, is it not? The hoop of history continues to roll as it is rolling today. At first they were a nation who served God, then they did evil, forsook God, turned to Baal, and God sells them into slavery and servitude. Then they cry out to God. Then they repent, and God raises up a judge to deliver them. Here goes Israel again. As soon as Gideon was dead, the children of Israel, turned from God and went a-whoring after Baalim. That is the sad, sordid story of Israel, and also the story of His church today. This up and down business is the story of nations, churches, and individuals. Today many of us are just rolling a hoop through this world. One day we are up, and the next day we are down. God never intended our spiritual lives to be that way.

CHAPTERS 9–10

***THEME:** Fifth apostasy; Abimelech responsible for civil war*

THE CAREER OF ABIMELECH, GIDEON'S SON

This chapter records the story of Abimelech, the sinful and wicked son of Gideon and his concubine. You see, Gideon should not have had a concubine. It certainly caused trouble in the nation.

> **And Abimelech the son of Jerubbaal went to Shechem unto his mother's brethren, and communed with them, and with all the family of the house of his mother's father, saying,**
>
> **Speak, I pray you, in the ears of all the men of Shechem, Whether is better for you, either that all the sons of Jerubbaal, which are threescore and ten persons, reign over you, or that one reign over you? remember also that I am your bone and your flesh.**
>
> **And his mother's brethren spake of him in the ears of all the men of Shechem all these words: and their hearts inclined to follow Abimelech; for they said, He is our brother [Jud. 9:1–3.]**

This boy Abimelech is very ambitious. He had heard about the nation wanting Gideon to become ruler over them. Since he is a son of Gideon, he wants to become king. So he goes to his mother's people, who are in Shechem, and gets them to follow him.

> **And he went unto his father's house at Ophrah, and slew his brethren the sons of Jerubbaal, being three score and ten persons, upon one stone: notwithstanding yet Jotham the youngest son of Jerubbaal was left; for he hid himself [Jud. 9:5].**

Obviously, Abimelech is a wicked and brutal man. He does a horrible thing here.

Some Bible expositors rate Abimelech as a judge. He may have been a judge, at least it is said that he "reigned three years over Israel." Dr. James M. Gray wrote, "The usurped rule of Abimelech, the fratricide, is not usually counted [as a judge]." He brutally murdered the seventy sons of Gideon and set himself up as king. His abortive reign reveals, I feel, the truth of the statement in Daniel: ". . . the most High ruleth in the kingdom of men, and giveth it to whomsoever he will, and setteth up over it the basest of men" (Dan. 4:17). Even today when a good ruler comes into office, many folk say, "God raised him up." What about the wicked ruler? God permits him to come to the throne also. Do you know why? Because the principle is "like priest, like people." That is, people get the ruler they deserve. The people of Israel wanted this boy Abimelech to rule over them; and they got the calibre of man they deserved. Friend, when we look around our world today, we find this principle is still true.

Now we find that God judges Abimelech for the awful thing he did, and He also judges the men of Shechem for making him king and starting him out on such a course. Civil war ensued because there were many people who did not want Abimelech, of course.

> **And Abimelech came unto the tower, and fought against it, and went hard unto the door of the tower to burn it with fire.**
>
> **And a certain woman cast a piece of a millstone upon Abimelech's head, and all to brake his skull.**
>
> **Then he called hastily unto the young man his armour-bearer, and said unto him, Draw thy sword, and slay me, that men say not of me, A woman slew him. And his young man thrust him through, and he died.**
>
> **And when the men of Israel saw that Abimelech was dead, they departed every man unto his place.**
>
> **Thus God rendered the wickedness of Abimelech, which he did unto his father, in slaying his seventy brethren:**
>
> **And all the evil of the men of Shechem did God render upon their heads: and upon them came the curse of Jotham the son of Jerubbaal [Jud. 9:52–57].**

This is a sad ending for the life of Gideon who fathered this illegitimate son, Abimelech. God lifted Gideon from a very humble position to be the deliverer and judge of His people. How sad that a man who accomplished so much good should allow this in his life of which God did not approve and which resulted in civil war in Israel.

TOLA, THE SEVENTH JUDGE

Tola and Jair become the next judges. Maybe you have never heard of Tola. If you haven't, it is perfectly all right. He did nothing noteworthy.

And after Abimelech there arose to defend Israel Tola the son of Puah, the son of Dodo, a man of Issachar, and he dwelt in Shamir in mount Ephraim.

And he judged Israel twenty and three years, and died, and was buried in Shamir [Jud. 10:1–2].

What did Tola do? He died and was buried in Shamir. Not one thing is recorded about any achievements. Although he was a judge in Israel twenty-three years, there is not one thing that can be mentioned about the deeds of this man, from the day he was born to the day he died. All you have here is what is on his tombstone: "Born—died."

JAIR, THE EIGHTH JUDGE

And after him arose Jair, a Gileadite, and judged Israel twenty and two years.

And he had thirty sons that rode on thirty ass colts, and they had thirty cities, which are called Havoth-jair unto this day, which are in the land of Gilead.

And Jair died, and was buried in Camon [Jud. 10:3–5].

All that we are told about this man is that he had thirty sons and he bought each one of them a little donkey. He did not get them a Jaguar, Mustang, Pinto, or Cougar, he gave each boy a donkey. What a sight it must have been to see these thirty boys ride out of Gilead!

In Jair's story I can see three things: (1) prosperity without purpose; (2) affluence without influence; (3) prestige without power.

In that day a donkey was a mark of prosperity. That was the thing that denoted a man's wealth. For example, Judges 5:10 says, "Speak, ye that ride on white asses, ye that sit in judgment, and walk by the way." This verse speaks about the upper echelon, or the establishment. The donkey was a mark of wealth and was the animal that kings rode upon. There has always been a question about whether or not they had horses in that day. In Scripture the little donkey is the animal of peace and the horse is the animal of war (the horse was imported into that land). But the little donkey was actually the mark of prosperity and the mark of a king.

You remember that the Lord Jesus Christ rode into Jerusalem on a little donkey. We misinterpret Zechariah 9:9 which says, "Rejoice greatly, O daughter of Zion; shout, O daughter of Jerusalem: behold, thy King cometh unto thee: he is just, and having salvation; lowly, and riding upon an ass, and upon a colt the foal of an ass." Zechariah does not mean that the Lord Jesus is humble because He is riding on a little donkey. He is humble in spite of the fact that He is riding upon an animal which only kings ride. If He had not been King, it would really have been a presumption to ride into Jerusalem on that donkey as He did and receive all of the adulation and hosannas from the crowd that day.

Jair was obviously a man of wealth and prominence to be able to afford thirty donkeys. He gave each one of his sons a donkey, so he must have had a thirty-car garage! This was the mark of a benevolent father. He was generous, and I think he spoiled his sons. He got them what they wanted. They lived in the lap of luxury and with golden spoons in their mouths. Donkeys probably came in several models, and Jair bought each son the latest thing. But did these donkeys bring glory to God? Did they make Jair a better judge? Did they bring blessing to the people? Did any one of these boys go out as a missionary? No. They lived in Gilead.

It is true that there is nothing particularly wrong with donkeys. On the other hand, there is nothing particularly right with a man who is a judge and spends a whole lot of time with many boys and donkeys. This is important for us to see. Our Lord rode into Jerusalem on a little donkey to fulfill prophecy and to present Himself as King, and the hosannas were sung. Satan was angry and the religious rulers protested as Christ rode through the gate and into the city. But all of Jair's donkeys never lifted one hosanna. When these animals brayed, I think Satan smiled and the mob was entertained. Jair is a picture of prosperity without purpose, friend, and it is a dangerous thing. We see the same picture in the days of Noah when they were marrying and giving in marriage. This is also demonstrated in the account of Solomon sending out ships to bring back apes and peacocks—peacocks for beauty and apes for entertainment.

Years ago a high school class in the state of Washington came up with this motto for their graduating class: "Pep without purpose is piffle." Well, it is not much of a motto but it certainly expresses present-day conditions. We have prosperity but without purpose. May I ask you what the goal of your life is? Is it pointless? Is it aimless? Have you found life pretty boring? Shakespeare's Hamlet said,

"How stale, flat and unprofitable seem to me the uses of this world." What we need today is direction and dimension in our lives. We need a cause, and the cause of Jesus Christ is still the greatest challenge any man can have. Old Jair was some judge, wasn't he?

Jair's days were also marked by prestige without power. He was the outstanding man in the community. The traffic cops probably never gave any of his sons a ticket. But verse 5 does not speak of a monument for Jair. He was buried in an unknown spot. He never performed one conspicuous act. He never did a worthwhile deed. He never gained a victory. He may have had thirty donkeys, but he had no spiritual power. We are living in a day when the church has lost its power. What a picture we have in this man Jair.

Right before World War II, the city of Pasadena was having its annual Rose Parade. The float that was entered by the Standard Oil Company was covered with American Beauty roses. It was a sight to behold. The theme of the parade was, "Be prepared." Right in the middle of the parade the Standard Oil Company's float ran out of gas. It stopped right where I was viewing the parade. I couldn't help but laugh. If there was one float that should *not* have run out of gas, it was that one. Standard Oil Company should have had plenty of gas! As I looked at the float, I saw a picture of many Christians today. They are beautiful, but they have no power in their lives. They have beauty and prestige, but no power. That was judge Jair for you. He did nothing, died, and was buried.

EIGHTEEN YEARS OF SERVITUDE UNDER THE PHILISTINES AND AMMONITES

And the children of Israel did evil again in the sight of the LORD, and served Baalim, and Ashtaroth, and the gods of Syria, and the gods of Zidon, and the gods of Moab, and the gods of the children of Ammon, and the gods of the Philistines, and forsook the LORD, and served not him [Jud. 10:6].

You would think that after all their experiences, the Israelites would learn that when they turned to idolatry, trouble came upon them. Because of their idolatry, they went into slavery again—they served the Philistines and Ammonites for eighteen years. Human nature is fallen nature. Jeremiah has said, "The heart is deceitful above all things, and desperately wicked: who can know it?" (Jer. 17:9). You and I certainly do not know the heart. It is easier for us to point our finger back to these people who lived about one thousand years before Christ and say, "You did wrong," than it is for us to see what we are doing wrong.

How are we doing today, by the way? May I say that there is a frightful apostasy today in the church. Human nature is like that, and we are in a nation that is in trouble. We have tried every method, political scheme, and political party, and none of them has worked. What is wrong? We have gone to the wrong place for help. Only a turning to God will get us on the right path. I know that sounds square and out of date, but it sounded that way one thousand years before Christ also. The Israelites turned to other gods, refused to serve the living God, and look at what happened.

And the anger of the LORD was hot against Israel, and he sold them into the hands of the Philistines, and into the hands of the children of Ammon [Jud. 10:7].

God can afford to remove His instrument when that instrument fails Him. A great many people think that God has to have the church, even a particular church, and that God has to have America because it is sending out missionaries. May I say to you that God does not have to have any of us. He is not dependent upon us at all. We are, however, dependent upon Him.

Israel was probably at its lowest point at this time. Things were very bad for them.

And the children of Israel cried unto the LORD, saying, We have sinned against thee, both because we have forsaken our God, and also served Baalim [Jud. 10:10].

These people finally got so desperate that they turned to God. Here we see the same old story being acted out once again. It is the hoop of history that is rolling, and it is still rolling today. So then what happened?

And the LORD said unto the children of Israel, Did not I deliver you from the Egyptians, and from the Amorites, from the children of Ammon, and from the Philistines?

The Zidonians also, and the Amalekites, and the Maonites, did oppress you; and ye cried to me, and I delivered you out of their hand.

Yet ye have forsaken me, and served other gods: wherefore I will deliver you no more.

Go and cry unto the gods which ye have chosen; let them deliver you in the time of your tribulation.

And the children of Israel said unto the LORD, We have sinned: do thou unto us whatsoever seemeth good unto thee; deliver us only, we pray thee, this day.

And they put away the strange gods from among them, and served the LORD: and his soul was grieved for the misery of Israel [Jud. 10:11–16].

How merciful and gracious God is!

Then the children of Ammon were gathered together, and encamped in Gilead. And the children of Israel assembled themselves together, and encamped in Mizpeh.

And the people and princes of Gilead said one to another, What man is he that will begin to fight against the children of Ammon? he shall be head over all the inhabitants of Gilead [Jud. 10:17–18].

The Israelites lacked leadership. That is always characteristic of men, or of a generation, that has turned from God. Lack of leadership has definitely characterized our nation for the last twenty-five years. In fact, there has been a lack of leadership in the world for many years. We need vital leadership, but we cannot seem to find it. This was Israel's experience. Now they are going to turn to a most unusual man for guidance. Under normal circumstances they would not have turned to him at all.

CHAPTER 11

***THEME:** Jephthah, the ninth judge, and his rash vow*

Now Jephthah the Gileadite was a mighty man of valour and he was the son of an harlot: and Gilead begat Jephthah [Jud. 11:1].

The first thing that I would call to your attention is that he is an outstanding leader, but he has this black mark against him: he is illegitimate, the son of a harlot.

And Gilead's wife bare him sons; and his wife's sons grew up, and they thrust out Jephthah, and said unto him, Thou shalt not inherit in our father's house; for thou art the son of a strange woman [Jud. 11:2].

Proverbs 2:16 speaks of "the strange woman" whom the son should beware because harlots were strangers—that is, foreigners. Josephus tells us that Gilead's wife was a Gentile. Jewish writings have called her an Ishmaelite. So Jephthah was the son of a common heathen prostitute. Illegitimacy is a stigma that brands a person from birth, regardless of who he is. This man Jephthah was exiled. He was excommunicated and ostracized. According to Deuteronomy 23:2, the Law of Moses would also bar him from the congregation of the Lord.

Being an illegitimate child is a handicap, to be sure, but many men have overcome it. There are kings, emperors, generals, poets, and popes who have been illegitimate children. William the Conqueror, for example, signed his name "William the Bastard," for that is what he was. That is what Jephthah was also, and he overcame this handicap, as we shall see.

Then Jephthah fled from his brethren, and dwelt in the land of Tob: and there were gathered vain men to Jephthah, and went out with him [Jud. 11:3].

Jephthah had become a leader of a band of desperados. Here is this man with three hurdles to surmount before he can become a leader for his country: he is the son of a harlot; he has been exiled by his brethren; and he is the leader of a despised, rejected group. He is not a very likely man to be used; but, you see, God uses men like this. God moves in mysterious ways, and He chooses men that are despised in this world. God also humbles those whom He intends to use. He humbled Joseph, He humbled Moses, and He humbled David. Our Lord humbled Himself. He is "despised and rejected of men." He is the "Stone which the builders rejected," but which was made the head of the corner. His enemies said, "We will not have this Man reign over us." Yet God has highly exalted Him and given Him a name that is above every name.

There are those today, friend, who claim to be sons of God, but they are not. They are illegitimate in that they have not been born again. You can only become a legitimate son of God by trusting the Lord Jesus Christ.

Jephthah had been an exile, but now he is exalted.

And it came to pass in process of time, that the children of Ammon made war against Israel.

And it was so, that when the children of Ammon made war against Israel, the elders of Gilead went to fetch Jephthah out of the land of Tob:

And they said unto Jephthah, Come, and be our captain, that we may fight with the children of Ammon.

And Jephthah said unto the elders of Gilead, Did not ye hate me, and expel me out of my father's house? and why are ye come unto me now when ye are in distress?

And the elders of Gilead said unto Jephthah, Therefore we turn again to thee now, that thou mayest go with us, and fight against the children of Ammon, and be our head over all the inhabitants of Gilead [Jud. 11:4–8].

The elders of Gilead have made Jephthah a pretty good proposition.

And Jephthah said unto the elders of Gilead, If ye bring me home again to fight against the children of Ammon, and the LORD deliver them before me, shall I be your head?

And the elders of Gilead said unto Jephthah, The LORD be witness between us, if we do not so according to thy words [Jud. 11:9–10].

Jephthah makes things difficult for the elders of Gilead, but they have to swallow their pride and accept his terms. It was humiliating for the nation to appeal to this man whom they had exiled. And he makes it very clear that if he is going to be the judge and deliver them, then he is going to rule over them. Then he takes charge of things.

Then Jephthah went with the elders of Gilead, and the people made him head and captain over them: and Jephthah uttered all his words before the LORD in Mizpeh.

And Jephthah sent messengers unto the king of the children of Ammon, saying, What hast thou to do with me, that thou art come against me to fight in my land? [Jud. 11:11–12].

If you read the verses that follow this portion of Scripture, you will find an extended section where Jephthah outlines the way that the Ammonites came into the land. He makes it clear that the land really belonged to the Israelites who gained the land in a legitimate way. The Ammonites were, of course, attempting not only to drive the Israelites off the land, but were also trying to exterminate them. The same thing is happening in the land of Israel today. Especially since 1948 when Israel once again became a nation, the enemy has been trying to remove them from the land, exterminate them, actually drive them into the sea. I will not go over this section, but it will pay you to read it for the simple reason that Jephthah outlines a very sensible basis for Israel's occupation of the land. They had a legitimate claim to it.

Howbeit the king of the children of Ammon hearkened not unto the words of Jephthah which he sent him.

Then the spirit of the LORD came upon Jephthah, and he passed over Gilead, and Manasseh, and passed over Mizpeh of Gilead, and from Mizpeh of Gilead he passed over unto the children of Ammon [Jud. 11:28–29].

The king of Ammon totally rejects the paper that Jephthah apparently had sent to him. He said he would not accept what had been said. So Jephthah leads his army against the Ammonites. But when he passes through the land and gets a look at the enemy, he becomes a little fearful. Now he does something that under normal circumstances he probably would not have done. Remember that this man had spent years in exile and then suddenly he is exalted to the highest position in the land. He is made a judge. The natural reaction of a man who is suddenly elevated is excitement. In his excitement he makes a rash promise. Also remember that Jephthah did not have the light that we have today. He was one-half pagan with a heathen background. He did know God but not very well. God did not require him to make a vow.

And Jephthah vowed a vow unto the LORD, and said, If thou shalt without fail deliver the children of Ammon into mine hands,

Then it shall be, that whatsoever cometh forth of the doors of my house to meet me, when I return in peace from the children of Ammon, shall surely be the LORD'S, and I will offer it up for a burnt offering [Jud. 11:30–31].

His cause was just, and God had given Jephthah every assurance that he would be victorious. This man did not need to make a rash vow like this, because God had not put the victory on that basis. It was the hand of God that had elevated him to this high position. He should have recognized that, since God had brought him that far, He would see him through. In verse 29 of this chapter we were told that the Spirit of the Lord came upon him. He did not need to add anything to that. Can you imagine saying, "Whatever comes out to meet me I will deliver it to the Lord?" After all, suppose it had been a friend or a neighbor. He would have no right to dedicate or offer that individual to the Lord.

And Jephthah came to Mizpeh unto his house, and, behold, his daughter came out to meet him with timbrels and with dances: and she was his only child; beside her he had neither son nor daughter.

And it came to pass, when he saw her, that he rent his clothes, and said, Alas, my daughter! thou hast brought me very low, and thou art one of them that trouble me: for I have opened my mouth unto the LORD, and I cannot go back [Jud. 11:34–35].

Jephthah made a vow to God, and he feels that he cannot retract it.

The question is: did he offer his daughter in sacrifice? Let us look at this situation closely for a moment. The Scripture is silent concerning Jephthah's vow. It does not say whether he was right or wrong. Scripture never finds fault with him. In fact, Hebrews 11:32 says, "And what shall I more say? for the time would fail me to tell of Gedeon, and of Barak, and of Samson, and of Jephthae; of David also, and Samuel, and of the prophets." As you see, Jephthah is mentioned with a very fine group of men.

God's commandment is "Thou shalt not kill" (Exod. 20:13). God also gave rather specific instructions about offering children. We read in Deuteronomy 12:31: "Thou shalt not do so unto the LORD thy God: for every abomination to the LORD, which he hateth, have they done unto their gods; for even their sons and their daughters they have burnt in the fire to their gods." God says, "I won't ask you to do that, and you are *not* to do that, because it is pagan and heathen." God did not permit Abraham to offer Isaac. We need to recognize that fact. The whole point with Abraham and Isaac was how far Abraham was willing to go with God. As it turned out, he was willing to go all the way with God. Abraham lifted that knife and, as far as he was concerned, Isaac was a dead boy. But as far as God was concerned, He would not let Abraham kill his son.

The construction used in the language in verse 31 determines, I feel, the interpretation. Notice what Jephthah says, ". . . whatsoever cometh forth of the doors of my house to meet me, when I return in peace from the children of Ammon, shall surely be the LORD'S, and I will offer it up for a burnt offering." I am going to change the reading of the last phrase just a little. It can read, "or I will offer up a burnt offering." Now Jephthah said he would do one of two things: he would offer a burnt offering or he would offer a gift to the Lord.

Did he offer his daughter as a burnt offering? I do not think that he did. What is meant is that he set her apart to perpetual virginity. So here is Jephthah—he is illegitimate himself and he has only one daughter. He wants her to marry so he can have grandchildren. But his daughter is the one who comes forth through the doors to greet him, and he offers her up to the Lord. That means that she will never marry. You say to me, "Can you be sure of that?" Well, listen to what the girl says.

And she said unto him, My father, if thou hast opened thy mouth unto the LORD, do to me according to that which hath proceeded out of thy mouth; forasmuch as the LORD hath taken vengeance for thee of thine enemies, even of the children of Ammon [Jud. 11:36].

Notice that his daughter was obedient. She

said that she would do whatever he had promised the Lord.

And she said unto her father, Let this thing be done for me: let me alone two months, that I may go up and down upon the mountains, and bewail my virginity, I and my fellows [Jud. 11:37].

She did not understand his promise to be a burnt offering or sacrifice, but that she is not going to marry. Those are her intentions, and she is to bewail the fact of her virginity. She will not be presented as a bride to some man. Her life is to be dedicated to the Lord.

And he said, Go. And he sent her away for two months: and she went with her companions, and bewailed her virginity upon the mountains.

And it came to pass at the end of two months, that she returned unto her father, who did with her according to his vow which he had vowed: and she knew no man. And it was a custom in Israel.

That the daughters of Israel went yearly to lament the daughter of Jephthah the Gileadite four days in a year [Jud. 11:38–40].

This passage tells us that Jephthah's daughter did not get married. Instead she dedicated her life to the Lord. The word *lament* in verse 40 means "to celebrate." Every year for four days Jephthah's daughter was remembered in a special way. She was totally dedicated to the Lord and His service. There is no indication that she was made a human sacrifice. People have argued about this story for years. I am asked that question as much as any other question: "Did Jephthah offer up his daughter in sacrifice?" No, he did not, but that is not the point. God would not have permitted him to offer his daughter in a burnt sacrifice. The significant factor is that Jephthah kept his vow. His vow was something sacred. He did not trifle with it. It was a rash statement, to be sure, but it was not an idle boast. It was not a hollow promise. The Word of God has some severe and sharp things to say relative to making a vow. Notice what the Book of Ecclesiastes has to say about vows. "Be not rash with thy mouth, and let not thine heart be hasty to utter any thing before God: for God is in heaven, and thou upon earth: therefore let thy words be few. When thou vowest a vow unto God, defer not to pay it; for he hath no pleasure in fools: pay that which thou hast vowed. Better is it that thou shouldest not vow, than that thou shouldest vow and not pay" (Eccl. 5:2, 4–5). My friend, you will do well to promise God only what you think you can execute. I am afraid that there are many Christians who go through a little ceremony. Perhaps they go down to an altar after a service, and by lighting a candle they dedicate themselves to God. Some folk dedicate and dedicate themselves until it actually smells to high heaven! God says, "Don't be rash with your mouth." He says that you are a fool if you make a vow to Him carelessly. You might think that over, Christian friend, in the next dedication service you attend. Don't rush down to the altar and offer God everything if you don't mean what you are saying. Jephthah was an illegitimate child. His mother was a harlot. He had a sweet, lovely daughter and he wanted her to marry and have children. He unwittingly dedicated her to the Lord, but he kept his vow.

Christians today are notorious at making vows and breaking them. I noted this when I first began to move in Christian circles. As a young Christian, I went to a young people's conference and watched eighteen young people go forward and dedicate themselves to the Lord for full-time Christian service. I wouldn't go forward because I did not know whether I could make good my promise. May I say that out of all of those who dedicated themselves to the Lord's service that night, not one of them entered full-time service! Have you made a vow to God? If you have, He wants you to keep it. "It is a faithful saying: For if we be dead with him, we shall also live with him: If we suffer, we shall also reign with him: if we deny him, he also will deny us: If we believe not, yet he abideth faithful: he cannot deny himself" (2 Tim. 2:11–13). Oh, He keeps His Word. Let us keep our word. "But the Lord is faithful, who shall stablish you, and keep you from evil" (2 Thess. 3:3). My, how wonderful He is, and how foolish we are today! Jephthah should be a lesson to us today.

CHAPTER 12

***THEME:** Jealousy of Ephraim; Judges Ibzan, Elon, and Abdon*

EPHRAIM IS PUNISHED

And the men of Ephraim gathered themselves together, and went northward, and said unto Jephthah, Wherefore passedst thou over to fight against the children of Ammon, and didst not call us to go with thee? we will burn thine house upon thee with fire.

And Jephthah said unto them, I and my people were at great strife with the children of Ammon; and when I called you, ye delivered me not out of their hands.

And when I saw that ye delivered me not, I put my life in my hands, and passed over against the children of Ammon, and the Lord delivered them into my hand: wherefore then are ye come up unto me this day, to fight against me? [Jud. 12:1–3].

We have seen that the men of Ephraim also quarreled with Gideon (8:1) when he didn't summon them to help him rout the Midianites. Now in a hostile way, they demanded that Jephthah give them the reason why he did not ask for their help in the battle. The jealousy of Ephraim was a real infection that led to a defection. Later on, when the kingdom is divided into north and south, you will find out that Ephraim is the center of all of the rebellion. And it goes back to their jealousy.

There is jealousy in the church today. It is one of our greatest problems. Paul said, "Let nothing be done through strife or vainglory; but in lowliness of mind let each esteem other better than themselves" (Phil. 2:3). "Strife and vainglory" can be vanity and envy. These are two things that cause problems in churches today. When I hear some person in a church complain that it is not being run the way he thinks it should be, I wonder if he is jealous. When I find someone who is opposing the preacher all of the time, I suspect there is jealousy behind it.

Jealousy was the problem here. Jephthah had to protect himself. The men of Ephraim were going to burn his house down right over his head!

Then Jephthah gathered together all the men of Gilead, and fought with Ephraim: and the men of Gilead smote Ephraim, because they said, Ye Gileadites are fugitives of Ephraim among the Ephraimites, and among the Manassites.

And the Gileadites took the passages of Jordan before the Ephraimites: and it was so that when those Ephraimites which were escaped said, Let me go over; that the men of Gilead said unto him, Art thou an Ephraimite? If he said, Nay:

Then said they unto him, Say now Shibboleth: and he said Sibboleth: for he could not frame to pronounce it right. Then they took him, and slew him at the passages of Jordan: and there fell at that time of the Ephraimites forty and two thousand [Jud. 12:4–6].

The Gileadites were successful in defeating the Ephraimites, and they seized the Jordan fords so that the Ephraimites could not escape. Then they selected a password that would be difficult to pronounce because it contained a consonant which was not in the Ephraimite dialect. The word was *Shibboleth.* If a person's accent was not just right when he pronounced this word, he was in trouble. It is difficult for us to say certain words. *Shibboleth* was a word that was difficult for the Ephraimites to say because they could not put the "h" in it.

And Jephthah judged Israel six years. Then died Jephthah the Gileadite, and was buried in one of the cities of Gilead [Jud. 12:7].

Jephthah's death ended six eventful years.

IBZAN, THE TENTH JUDGE

The next three judges mentioned were practically zeros. They did nothing. Well, they did something, but they did not judge Israel as they should have done.

And after him Ibzan of Beth-lehem judged Israel.

And he had thirty sons, and thirty daughters, whom he sent abroad, and took in thirty daughters from abroad for his sons. And he judged Israel seven years.

Then died Ibzan, and was buried at Beth-lehem [Jud. 12:8–10].

This judge is from Bethlehem. Bethlehem was one of the cities of Judah in the south. Ibzan had thirty sons and thirty daughters. I would have thought that he would have worked at getting his daughters husbands instead of getting wives for his sons. I suppose that in the seven years that he was judge he did not have time to get his daughters husbands too. He did not have time to judge Israel either. In other words, Ibzan was a man who gave all of his time to his family. There is nothing wrong with that, but it was not what he was called to do.

There is a great deal of nonsense abroad today about the subject of responsibility. I once heard the story of a preacher who was on his way to a speaking engagement and his little son wanted to talk with him. He sat down and talked to his son and missed his speaking engagement. Many people applauded him for that. Well, my friend, that man was breaking an engagement and also he was spoiling a child. You can show love and interest in your children without breaking an engagement. There is a time when certain things have to be put first. I think he would have better served the boy if he had told him, "Your daddy has a speaking engagement and that is important. You would want your daddy to keep that appointment, wouldn't you?" I think the little fellow would have agreed. Then the father could have continued, "Now when I return, you and I will talk these things over, or tomorrow we can have a chat." That would have done more for the boy than what the father did. All he did was make a spoiled brat out of the youngster, as I see it. I know I sound like a square, but I do not approve of judge Ibzan's actions. He didn't do anything. He is a picture of mediocrity, to be sure.

ELON, THE ELEVENTH JUDGE

And after him Elon, a Zebulonite, judged Israel; and he judged Israel ten years.

And Elon the Zebulonite died, and was buried in Aijalon in the country of Zebulun [Jud. 12:11–12].

These two verses tell us all that we know about Elon. He did nothing—he didn't even have a large family. Apparently all that he did was twiddle his thumbs.

ABDON, THE TWELFTH JUDGE

And after him Abdon the son of Hillel, a Pirathonite, judged Israel.

And he had forty sons and thirty nephews, that rode on threescore and ten ass colts: and he judged Israel eight years.

And Abdon the son of Hillel the Pirathonite died, and was buried in Pirathon in the land of Ephraim, in the mount of the Amalekites [Jud. 12:13–15].

Abdon did nothing except "out-Jair" Jair. Talk about keeping up with the Jones family! As we have seen in chapter 10, Jair had thirty sons—but Abdon had forty sons and thirty nephews besides. It must have been quite a sight to see that man ride out of town with his sons and nephews. You would have seen a parade of Jaguars, Mustangs, Pintos, and Cougars like you had never seen before. They call the little donkey the "mocking bird" or "lark" of the desert because he can really bray. Just think of all of those braying donkeys! That is all Abdon contributed. That isn't much, friend.

We have quickly passed over the last three judges, Ibzan, Elon, and Abdon, because apparently they did nothing constructive as judges.

CHAPTERS 13–16

***THEME:** Seventh apostasy; Israel partially delivered through Samson*

FORTY YEARS OF SERVITUDE UNDER THE PHILISTINES

And the children of Israel did evil again in the sight of the LORD; and the LORD delivered them into the hand of the Philistines forty years [Jud. 13:1].

The repeated apostasy of Israel forms the setting for a time of oppression by the Philistines. The Philistines were probably the worst enemies that Israel had. This time their oppression lasted for forty years.

During this time we come to a judge that we cannot pass over. His name was Samson, and he was one of the most outstanding of the judges. He probably had more glorious opportunity than any man ever had. Everything was propitious for a career and a brilliant future, but he failed. That is the tragedy of this man's life. He came to judge during the seventh apostasy and is, in one sense, the last of the judges. Israel was conquered by the Philistines and was only partially delivered by Samson. The small civil war that began in Jephthah's day got bigger and bigger, and the Book of Judges ends in absolute confusion. During Samson's time of leadership we are given the secret of his success, the secret of his strength, and the secret of his failure. Again, let me repeat, never was a man born with a more glorious opportunity than this man.

BIRTH OF SAMSON, THE THIRTEENTH JUDGE

And there was a certain man of Zorah, of the family of the Danites, whose name was Manoah; and his wife was barren, and bare not [Jud. 13:2].

Zorah was a city between Dan and Judah, several miles west of Jerusalem. Manoah and his wife did not have any children because she was barren. So the birth of Samson was miraculous as was the birth of Isaac, or Joseph, or Benjamin.

And the angel of the LORD appeared unto the woman, and said unto her, Behold now, thou art barren, and bearest not: but thou shalt conceive, and bear a son.

Now therefore beware, I pray thee, and drink not wine nor strong drink, and eat not any unclean thing:

For, lo, thou shalt conceive, and bear a son; and no razor shall come on his head: for the child shall be a Nazarite unto God from the womb: and he shall begin to deliver Israel out of the hand of the Philistines [Jud. 13:3–5].

Before Samson was born, God marked him out. God raised him up to perform a gigantic task: he was to deliver Israel. The people of Israel were in a bad way because God had delivered them into the hands of the Philistines.

The angel of the Lord that appeared to the mother of Samson told her what her son was to be—a Nazarite. You will recall that back in the Book of Numbers we are told what constituted a Nazarite vow. It was threefold: (1) He was not to touch strong drink or use grapes in any form. Why? Because wine is a symbol in the Scriptures of earthly joy. It is to cheer the heart. The Nazarite was to find his joy in the Lord. Ephesians 5:18 says, "And be not drunk with wine, wherein is excess; but be filled with the Spirit." If we want to please Christ, we, too, are to find our joy in Him. In fact, joy is a fruit of the Holy Spirit—"But the fruit of the Spirit is love, joy, peace, longsuffering, gentleness, goodness, faith, Meekness, temperance: against such there is no law" (Gal. 5:22–23). Joy is one of the fruits the Holy Spirit wants to produce in your life and mine. (2) A Nazarite was not to cut his hair. Now what does that mean? In 1 Corinthians 11:14 Paul says, "Doth not even nature itself teach you, that, if a man have long hair, it is a shame unto him?" The Scripture says that long hair dishonors a man. A Nazarite, however, would be willing to bear the shame of long hair, and that is the reason a razor was not to touch his head. (3) He was not to go near a dead body. There were to be no natural claims upon him. He had to put God first, above his relatives and loved ones. The Lord Jesus said in Luke 14:26–27, "If any man come to me, and hate not his father, and mother, and wife, and children, and brethren, and sisters, yea, and his own life also, he cannot be my disciple. And whosoever doth not bear his cross, and come after me, cannot be my disciple." This simply means that we cannot put *anything* before Christ. This is something that we have lost sight of today.

Samson was a Nazarite. He was God's man, and that was the secret of the success he had. He was raised up for a great purpose, and his success was in God. Unfortunately he never succeeded in performing his God-appointed task. Did you notice what verse 5 said? Samson *began* to deliver Israel out of the hands of the Philistines. Success knocked at his door. He was a beginner, not a finisher. He began to deliver Israel, but he never finished the task.

There are many Christians like that. They make a great beginning, but they do not finish a task. Paul said to the Galatians, "Ye did run well; who did hinder you that ye should not obey the truth?" (Gal. 5:7). They started out with a bang and ended up with a fizzle. Many people *begin* to read the Bible, but many fall by the wayside. They just begin and don't go on with it. I have been a pastor for forty years, friend, and I have known lots of people who start something and never conclude it. They never finish what they are called to do.

And the woman bare a son, and called his name Samson: and the child grew, and the Lord blessed him.

And the spirit of the Lord began to move him at times in the camp of Dan between Zorah and Eshtaol [Jud. 13:24–25].

These verses tell us the secret of Samson's strength. Samson's strength was not in his arms, although he killed a thousand Philistines with those arms. His strength was not in his back, although he carried the gates of Gaza on his back, which was a remarkable undertaking. And Samson's strength was not in his hair, although he was weak when it was cut. Samson was strong only when the Spirit of God was moving him. Just cutting his hair off was not actually what weakened him. His hair was the badge of his Nazarite vow. The Spirit of God was not on him when his hair was cut. Why? Because he had failed in his vow. He had not made good.

We see advertisements of body builders which show the man before and after. The *before* picture always features a little dried up weasel. *After* he takes the tonic, we see a great big muscle-bound man. Even though many people have pictured Samson as a big bruiser, he was probably one of the worst sissies in or out of the Bible. I think he was a little, dried-up milquetoast type of man. His name means "little sun." He had long hair. He was a riddle maker. He played pranks like a schoolboy. He allowed women to make a fool of him. He was not a he-man. He was not the strongest man in the Bible. He was the weakest man. This fellow was tied to his mama's apron strings like a little sissy, and that is exactly what he was. Then when the Spirit of the Lord began to move him, he was strong. When the Spirit was not upon him, he was as weak as water.

The people in Samson's day wanted to know the source of his strength. They did not realize that God chooses the weak things of this world to accomplish His purposes. They marveled at Samson, "How can this little scrawny, milquetoast fellow, perform these feats of tremendous strength?" There was only one explanation—God did it.

SAMSON IS PROMISED A WIFE

It is amazing that the Spirit of God would come upon a man like this. But it is obvious that God moved through him. I feel that he was a sissy in every department of his life, and in chapter 14 we begin to see it.

And Samson went down to Timnath, and saw a woman in Timnath of the daughters of the Philistines.

And he came up, and told his father and his mother, and said, I have seen a woman in Timnath of the daughters of the Philistines: now therefore get her for me to wife [Jud. 14:1–2].

I submit to you that only a sissy would do a thing like that! Why didn't he go and talk to the woman and tell her that he loved her and wanted to marry her? Why didn't he go and talk to her father? In those days some sort of a business arrangement was always made when it came to marriage. Why didn't he take care of that himself? Well, he is a sissy, and mamma and papa had to arrange the marriage for him. This is Samson.

Then his father and his mother said unto him, Is there never a woman among the daughters of thy brethren, or among all my people, that thou goest to take a wife of the uncircumcised Philistines? And Samson said unto his father, Get her for me; for she pleaseth me well.

But his father and his mother knew not that it was of the Lord, that he sought an occasion against the Philistines: for

at that time the Philistines had dominion over Israel [Jud. 14:3–4].

Samson is going to use his marriage as a ruse in order that he might deliver Israel from the Philistines. He starts off well.

SAMSON SLAYS A LION AND GIVES A RIDDLE

Then went Samson down, and his father and his mother, to Timnath, and came to the vineyards of Timnath: and, behold, a young lion roared against him [Jud. 14:5].

We have been told that a Nazarite was to keep away from the grapes, but not Samson.

And the spirit of the LORD came mightily upon him, and he rent him as he would have rent a kid, and he had nothing in his hand: but he told not his father or his mother what he had done.

And he went down, and talked with the woman; and she pleased Samson well.

And after a time he returned to take her, and he turned aside to see the carcase of the lion: and, behold, there was a swarm of bees and honey in the carcase of the lion.

And he took thereof in his hands, and went on eating, and came to his father and mother, and he gave them, and they did eat: but he told not them that he had taken the honey out of the carcase of the lion [Jud. 14:6–9].

On his way to Timnath with his parents, Samson was attacked by a lion. The Spirit of the Lord came upon him during this time of emergency and he killed the lion with his bare hands. During another trip Samson went to look at the carcass of the lion and discovered a swarm of bees and honey in it. He scooped the honey out with his hands and ate it. He also gave some to his parents, but he did not tell them where he got it. Remember that having contact with a carcass was a violation of the Nazarite law.

So his father went down unto the woman: and Samson made there a feast; for so used the young men to do.

And it came to pass, when they saw him, that they brought thirty companions to be with him.

And Samson said unto them, I will now put forth a riddle unto you: if ye can certainly declare it me within the seven days of the feast, and find it out, then I will give you thirty sheets and thirty change of garments:

But if ye cannot declare it me, then shall ye give me thirty sheets and thirty change of garments. And they said unto him, Put forth thy riddle, that we may hear it.

And he said unto them, Out of the eater came forth meat, and out of the strong came forth sweetness. And they could not in three days expound the riddle [Jud. 14:10–14].

As was the custom, Samson put on a marriage feast. The feast was held at the bride's home. And all of the guests were Philistines. Riddles were a form of entertainment in those days, and Samson gave the guests a riddle. He gave them seven days in which to find the answer. If they guessed the riddle, then Samson would give them thirty linen garments and thirty cloaks. If they failed to guess the answer to his riddle, then they would have to give him thirty linen garments and thirty cloaks. Without knowing about the slain lion and the hive of bees in the carcass, there was no way the thirty guests could solve Samson's riddle.

SAMSON IS DECEIVED AND SLAYS THIRTY PHILISTINES

And it came to pass on the seventh day, that they said unto Samson's wife, Entice thy husband, that he may declare unto us the riddle, lest we burn thee and thy father's house with fire: have ye called us to take that we have? is it not so?

And Samson's wife wept before him, and said, Thou dost but hate me, and lovest me not: thou hast put forth a riddle unto the children of my people, and hast not told it me. And he said unto her, Behold, I have not told it my father nor my mother, and shall I tell it thee?

And she wept before him the seven days, while their feast lasted: and it came to pass on the seventh day, that he told her, because she lay sore upon him: and she told the riddle to the children of her people.

And the men of the city said unto him

on the seventh day before the sun went down. What is sweeter than honey? and what is stronger than a lion? And he said unto them, If ye had not plowed with my heifer, ye had not found out my riddle [Jud. 14:15–18].

The Philistines appealed to Samson's wife to help them find out the answer to the riddle. If she did not find out what his secret was, they threatened to burn down her father's house with her in it. Now the strongest weapon that a woman has is her tears, and Samson's wife turned hers on for seven days. I want to tell you that a woman who weeps for seven straight days, and at every meal, gets a little tiresome. Finally he had to give in and tell her the answer to the riddle. He was good at making wisecracks, too. He knew where these men got the answer to the riddle. Samson said, "If ye had not plowed with my heifer, ye had not found out my riddle." In other words, "You got the answer from my wife."

And the spirit of the LORD came upon him, and he went down to Ashkelon, and slew thirty men of them, and took their spoil, and gave change of garments unto them which expounded the riddle. And his anger was kindled, and he went up to his father's house [Jud. 14:19].

The Spirit of the Lord came upon Samson and he went down south to Ashkelon—Ashkelon is way down in the south. There he killed thirty men in order to get thirty changes of raiment that he needed to pay off his wager. Samson left in a pout. Notice that he doesn't take his wife with him. He is angry with her for giving away his riddle.

But Samson's wife was given to his companion, whom he had used as his friend [Jud. 14:20].

So the father of the girl gives her to the best man at the wedding!

SAMSON BURNS THE PHILISTINES CROPS

But it came to pass within a while after, in the time of wheat harvest, that Samson visited his wife with a kid; and he said, I will go in to my wife into the chamber. But her father would not suffer him to go in.

And her father said, I verily thought that thou hadst utterly hated her; therefore I gave her to thy companion: is not her younger sister fairer than she? take her, I pray thee, instead of her [Jud. 15:1–2].

After Samson's anger subsided, he went to visit his wife and brought a kid as a present. Her father informed Samson that he thought Samson no longer wanted her and so he had given her to his friend. Samson did not like this, of course.

And Samson said concerning them, Now shall I be more blameless than the Philistines, though I do them a displeasure.

And Samson went and caught three hundred foxes, and took firebrands, and turned tail to tail, and put a firebrand in the midst between two tails.

And when he had set the brands on fire, he let them go into the standing corn of the Philistines, and burnt up both the shocks, and also the standing corn, with the vineyards and olives [Jud. 15:3–5].

Samson apparently felt justified in vengeance on the Philistines. He caught three hundred foxes, tied their tails together and then tied a torch on the tails, set them on fire, and let the animals loose in the fields. Of course these foxes would really take out on a run, and they would scatter the firebrands everywhere. Actually, friend, this entire episode is like a prank a juvenile would play! Samson certainly doesn't look like God's man here!

Then the Philistines said, Who hath done this? And they answered, Samson, the son in law of the Timnite, because he had taken his wife, and given her to his companion. And the Philistines came up, and burnt her and her father with fire.

And Samson said unto them, Though ye have done this, yet will I be avenged of you, and after that I will cease.

And he smote them hip and thigh with a great slaughter: and he went down and dwelt in the top of the rock Etam [Jud. 15:6–8].

Notice that this is personal. This has nothing to do with his commission from God to deliver Israel from the Philistines. He is just avenging himself. His actions had nothing to do with delivering Israel. His revenge was personal.

SAMSON SLAYS ONE THOUSAND PHILISTINES

After smiting the Philistines with a great slaughter, Samson really had the enemy stirred up. They began looking for him, so he let his own people bind him with ropes in order to protect them from the Philistines.

And when he came unto Lehi, the Philistines shouted against him: and the spirit of the Lord came mightily upon him, and the cords that were upon his arms became as flax that was burnt with fire, and his bands loosed from off his hands [Jud. 15:14].

The men of Judah took Samson, their prisoner, to Lehi which was occupied by the Philistines. The enemy was overjoyed to see Samson being brought to them bound. Then he broke the bands as if they were nothing. Again we see the strength of this man—but not his own strength.

And he found a new jawbone of an ass, and put forth his hand, and took it, and slew a thousand men therewith [Jud. 15:15].

Samson grabbed the closest weapon, which was the jawbone of a donkey, and attacked the enemy. He killed one thousand of them. Notice the strength of this man. He could never have done such a thing in his own power of course; it was the Spirit of the Lord upon him that enabled him to do it. He is beginning to deliver Israel. If only he had kept that goal before him! But he did not, as we shall see in the next chapter.

SAMSON'S MORAL FRAILTY

Then went Samson to Gaza, and saw there an harlot, and went in unto her.

And it was told the Gazites, saying, Samson is come hither. And they compassed him in, and laid wait for him all night in the gate of the city, and were quiet all the night, saying, In the morning, when it is day, we shall kill him [Jud. 16:1–2].

What a playboy Samson was! The men of the city locked up the city and they said, "We'll get him in the morning."

And Samson lay till midnight, and arose at midnight, and took the doors of the gate of the city, and the two posts, and went away with them, bar and all, and put them upon his shoulders, and carried them up to the top of an hill that is before Hebron [Jud. 16:3].

Samson got up at midnight and found the gates of the city locked. So what did he do? He took the gate, posts, bar, and all, put them on his shoulders, and carried them away to the top of a hill that is before Hebron. That would have been about forty miles away. What he did sounds like the prank of a teenager or the trick of a college student. This boy Samson never did grow up. He has been called to deliver Israel with his mighty power, and all he does is use it for his personal advantage.

SAMSON AND DELILAH

And it came to pass afterward, that he loved a woman in the valley of Sorek, whose name was Delilah [Jud. 16:4].

That is the story of Samson. That is the downfall of Samson. That is the big failure in his life. That is the weak point in his life—"he loved a woman." No man falls suddenly into sin—he does it gradually.

There was a bank president in my congregation when I pastored a church in Texas. This man went with me to the local jail to hand out tracts and talk to the prisoners. Outwardly he was an outstanding man. One day he disappeared. He had gone on vacation. Suddenly the bank began to miss money. They could not believe that he had taken it. They tried to account for the loss in every other way, but they could not. They finally decided that he must be the one who took the money, and when he did not return from vacation, they began to search for him. After a complete investigation, they discovered that he had been taking money for years. No man falls suddenly into sin.

One of the greatest sins that destroys many a man today is this matter of illicit sex. That was Samson's sin—"he loved a woman whose name was Delilah." As far as we know, he made no attempt to marry her.

And the lords of the Philistines came up unto her, and said unto her, Entice him, and see wherein his great strength lieth, and by what means we may prevail against him, that we may bind him to afflict him: and we will give thee every one of us eleven hundred pieces of silver.

And Delilah said to Samson, Tell me, I pray thee, wherein thy great strength

lieth, and wherewith thou mightest be bound to afflict thee.

And Samson said unto her, If they bind me with seven green withs that were never dried, then shall I be weak, and be as another man [Jud. 16:5–7].

You may be sure that Delilah was more interested in the silver than she was in Samson. Once again the Philistine leaders had found a way to get to Samson.

Notice that he teases her at first. He begins to give her answers, but they are wrong answers. He broke the cords with no effort at all. Still his strength was not known.

And Delilah said unto Samson, Behold, thou hast mocked me, and told me lies; now tell me, I pray thee, wherewith thou mightest be bound.

And he said unto her, If they bind me fast with new ropes that never were occupied, then shall I be weak, and be as another man [Jud. 16:10–11].

Again he is playing with her; he is kidding her along. He allowed her to tie him up with ropes. Then when she cried, "The Philistines are upon thee, Samson," he broke the ropes like they were a thread. Now Delilah is really exasperated. She is frustrated with her boy friend.

And Delilah said unto Samson, Hitherto thou hast mocked me, and told me lies: tell me wherewith thou mightest be bound. And he said unto her, If thou weavest the seven locks of my head with the web.

And she fastened it with the pin, and said unto him, The Philistines be upon thee, Samson. And he awaked out of his sleep, and went away with the pin of the beam, and with the web [Jud. 16:13–14].

Now Samson is beginning to weaken. May I say to you, friend, this is the beginning of the end of this man. He is getting close to the truth now as he mentions his hair. But he is still teasing with her, and when she says, "The Philistines are upon thee, Samson," he picks the whole thing up and walks away with it.

And she said unto him, How canst thou say, I love thee, when thine heart is not with me? thou has mocked me these three times, and hast not told me wherein thy great strength lieth.

And it came to pass, when she pressed him daily with her words, and urged him, so that his soul was vexed unto death;

That he told her all his heart, and said unto her. There hath not come a razor upon mine head; for I have been a Nazarite unto God from my mother's womb: if I be shaven, then my strength will go from me, and I shall become weak, and be like any other man [Jud. 16:15–17].

This time Delilah tells Samson that if he *really* loved her he would tell her the secret of his strength. So Samson told her that he was a Nazarite. Long hair, as you remember, was a badge of this vow. His strength was not in his hair but in the Spirit of God who came upon him. Delilah sees what a fool he really is—and he is a fool.

And when Delilah saw that he had told her all his heart, she sent and called for the lords of the Philistines, saying, Come up this once, for he hath shewed me all his heart. Then the lords of the Philistines came up unto her, and brought money in their hand.

And she made him sleep upon her knees; and she called for a man, and she caused him to shave off the seven locks of his head; and she began to afflict him, and his strength went from him.

And she said, The Philistines be upon thee, Samson. And he awoke out of his sleep, and said, I will go out as at other times before, and shake myself. And he wist not that the LORD was departed from him [Jud. 16:18–20].

When Samson went to sleep, Delilah had one of the Philistines come in and shave off his hair. Then for the fourth time Delilah cried out, "The Philistines be upon thee, Samson!" This is the tragic time in the life of Samson. He awoke out of his sleep, thinking he would do as he had done before, but "he knew not that the Lord was departed from him." Friend, the strength was not in his hair; the strength was in the Spirit of the Lord who was upon him.

Friend, our spiritual strength today is not in ceremonies or in rituals. The strength of the believer is always in the Spirit of God —always.

Samson, called to be a judge for his people,

called to deliver his people from the oppression of the Philistines, is a carnal man. Now Ichabod (meaning "the glory is departed") is written over his life. He never raised an army. He never won a battle. He never rallied the men of Israel to him. Sex was the ruin of this man—this man who was chosen by God!

But the Philistines took him, and put out his eyes, and brought him down to Gaza, and bound him with fetters of brass; and he did grind in the prison house.

Howbeit the hair of his head began to grow again after he was shaven.

Then the lords of the Philistines gathered them together for to offer a great sacrifice unto Dagon their god, and to rejoice: for they said, Our god hath delivered Samson our enemy into our hand [Jud. 16:21–23].

Now we are coming to the tragic end of this man. After the Philistines captured Samson, they put out his eyes—blinded him—then forced him to do the work of a beast of burden in the prison. While he was in prison, his hair began to grow. He now has become a very repentant man.

The Philistines, of course, ascribe their victory over Samson to their god Dagon and hold a feast to celebrate.

SAMSON IS AVENGED IN HIS DEATH

And it came to pass, when their hearts were merry, that they said, Call for Samson, that he may make us sport. And they called for Samson out of the prison house; and he made them sport: and they set him between the pillars.

And Samson said unto the lad that held him by the hand, Suffer me that I may feel the pillars whereupon the house standeth, that I may lean upon them.

Now the house was full of men and women; and all the lords of the Philistines were there; and there were upon the roof about three thousand men and women, that beheld while Samson made sport [Jud. 16:25–27].

To make their victory celebration complete, the Philistines have Samson brought from the prison. Then they make a fool of him. About three thousand men and women watch Samson being tormented.

And Samson called unto the LORD, and said, O Lord GOD, remember me, I pray thee, and strengthen me, I pray thee, only this once, O God, that I may be at once avenged of the Philistines for my two eyes.

And Samson took hold of the two middle pillars upon which the house stood, and on which it was borne up, of the one with his right hand, and of the other with his left.

And Samson said, Let me die with the Philistines. And he bowed himself with all his might; and the house fell upon the lords, and upon all the people that were therein. So the dead which he slew at his death were more than they which he slew in his life.

Then his brethren and all the house of his father came down, and took him, and brought him up, and buried him between Zorah and Eshtaol in the buryingplace of Manoah his father. And he judged Israel twenty years [Jud. 16:28–31].

Samson was a failure. He *began* to deliver Israel—but he failed. He preferred to play with sin until the Spirit of God departed from him. Three significant verses tell his story:

1. Secret of Samson's *success*—
   For, lo, thou shalt conceive, and bear a son; and no razor shall come on his head; for the child shall be a Nazarite unto God from the womb: and he shall begin to deliver Israel out of the hand of the Philistines (Jud. 13:5).
2. Secret of Samson's *strength*—
   And the spirit of the LORD began to move him at times in the camp of Dan between Zorah and Eshtaol (Jud. 13:25).
3. Secret of Samson's *failure*—
   And she said, The Philistines be upon thee, Samson. And he awoke out of his sleep, and said, I will go out as at other times before, and shake myself. And he wist not that the LORD was departed from him (Jud. 16:20).

Note the parallel between the life of Samson and that of Jesus Christ:

Comparison:
1. Both births were foretold by an angel.
2. Both were separated to God from the womb.
3. Both were Nazarites.

4. Both moved in the power of the Holy Spirit.
5. Both were rejected by their people.
6. Both destroyed (or will destroy) their enemies.

Contrast:
1. Samson lived a life of sin; Jesus' life was sinless.
2. Samson at the time of death prayed, "O God, that I may be at once avenged of the Philistines for my two eyes." Jesus prayed, "Father, forgive them; for they know not what they do."
3. In death, Samson's arms were outstretched in wrath; In death, Jesus' arms were outstretched in love.
4. Samson died. Jesus Christ lives!

CHAPTERS 17–18

THEME: *Religious apostasy—the temple*

RELIGIOUS CONFUSION IN ISRAEL

In chapters 17–21 we have presented the philosophy of history that was mentioned at the beginning of this book. We have seen it illustrated in Judges as the hoop of history rolls over and over. It starts with Israel in the place of blessing. They are serving God. Then there is a departure from God and they do evil. They follow their own way. Then they are sold into slavery. In their slavery and servitude they cry out to God for deliverance. Then they turn to God and repent. Then God raises up judges to deliver them. Then Israel comes back to the place of blessing and becomes a nation that serves God. Just when everything is back in order, they lapse into sin and turn from God again. Altogether Israel went through seven apostasies. This gives us the philosophy of history. Every nation goes down in this order: (1) religious apostasy; (2) moral awfulness; (3) political anarchy. Deterioration begins in the temple, then to the home, and finally to the state. That is the way a nation falls.

This period of apostasy began in the tribe of Dan in their desire to enlarge their borders. It was another lapse into idolatry. It all can be traced to the home of Micah and his mother who spoiled him. The priest, hired by Micah to tend his idols, advised Dan to proceed with a selfish plan. This was the sweet talk of a hired preacher.

IDOLATRY IN EPHRAIM

And there was a man of mount Ephraim, whose name was Micah.

And he said unto his mother, The eleven hundred shekels of silver that were taken from thee, about which thou cursedst, and spakest of also in mine ears, behold, the silver is with me; I took it. And his mother said, Blessed be thou of the Lord, my son [Jud. 17:1–2].

Micah is an example of a spoiled brat. He is a mama's boy. He knew that his mother had been saving some money, and he decided to steal it. His mother, not knowing who stole the money, pronounced a curse on the thief. So he confessed to being the thief, and instead of his mama turning him across her knee and applying the board of education to the seat of knowledge, she congratulated him. She said, "Blessed be thou of the Lord, my son."

And when he had restored the eleven hundred shekels of silver to his mother, his mother said, I had wholly dedicated the silver unto the Lord from my hand for my son, to make a graven image and a molten image: now therefore I will restore it unto thee [Jud. 17:3].

When Micah returned the money to his mother, she told him that she had dedicated that money to the Lord to make a graven image and a molten image. You see, they have gone off into idolatry! So she turns around and gives it back to him. You know, there are a lot of Christians today that are just that inconsistent. She was dedicating the money to the Lord but using it to make an idol! Many groups take up an offering and say it is for the

Lord, then use most of it for the church social on Friday night. They say the money is dedicated to the Lord, but actually it is honoring the god of pleasure.

And the man Micah had an house of gods, and made an ephod, and teraphim, and consecrated one of his sons, who became his priest.

In those days there was no king in Israel, but every man did that which was right in his own eyes [Jud. 17:5–6].

Micah had a house of gods. His mother provided the silver for the idols, and Micah provided a shrine for them. He also made an ephod and teraphim to complete the furnishings of the shrine. Then, to top it all off, he consecrated one of his sons to be his priest. They had come to the place where "every man did that which was right in his own eyes."

And there was a young man out of Beth-lehem-judah of the family of Judah, who was a Levite, and he sojourned there.

And the man departed out of the city from Beth-lehem-judah to sojourn where he could find a place: and he came to mount Ephraim to the house of Micah, as he journeyed.

And Micah said unto him, Whence comest thou? And he said unto him, I am a Levite of Beth-lehem-judah, and I go to sojourn where I may find a place.

And Micah said unto him, Dwell with me, and be unto me a father and a priest, and I will give thee ten shekels of silver by the year, and a suit of apparel, and thy victuals. So the Levite went in [Jud. 17:7–10].

It must have bothered Micah a little that he had made his son a priest. So, when this unemployed itinerant preacher came by, Micah hired him. This Levite from Beth-lehem-judah became his private family priest. Here is a priest who is like a hired preacher who becomes a messenger boy of a church board or of a little group. God have mercy on the church that has this kind of a preacher. This Levite has now become a priest and has a house full of idols.

And the Levite was content to dwell with the man; and the young man was unto him as one of his sons.

And Micah consecrated the Levite; and the young man became his priest, and was in the house of Micah.

Then said Micah, Now know I that the Lord will do me good, seeing I have a Levite to my priest [Jud. 17:11–13].

This chapter is certainly a revelation of the low spiritual ebb to which the nation Israel had come. Here is a man who thinks just because he has a Levite for his preacher that that is all he needs. How tragic is that kind of thinking. Yet Micah expected the blessing of God upon him. And how many people are like that today?

IDOLATRY IN DAN

The Danites had been assigned territory that was occupied by the mighty Philistines. They felt that they needed more room in which to live. There was no king in Israel. It was a time of utter confusion. There was no leadership.

In those days there was no king in Israel: and in those days the tribe of the Danites sought them an inheritance to dwell in; for unto that day all their inheritance had not fallen unto them among the tribes of Israel [Jud. 18:1].

You will recall in the Book of Joshua that none of the tribes took possession of all the land that was coming to them. That certainly was true of the tribe of Dan way in the north. The Danites had a real problem. In fact, it was so bad they took to the hills.

And the children of Dan sent of their family five men from their coasts, men of valour, from Zorah, and from Eshtaol, to spy out the land, and to search it; and they said unto them, Go, search the land: who when they came to mount Ephraim, to the house of Micah, they lodged there [Jud. 18:2].

These men went out to see what territory the tribe of Dan could take in order to extend and expand the borders of their tribe. During their travels they came to the house of Micah.

When they were by the house of Micah, they knew the voice of the young man the Levite: and they turned in thither, and said unto him, Who brought thee hither? and what makest thou in this place? and what hast thou here?

And he said unto them, Thus and thus dealeth Micah with me, and hath hired me, and I am his priest [Jud. 18:3–4].

This man is nothing but a hired preacher. (God have mercy on the church that has a hired preacher who chooses to be a messenger boy for a little group rather than to preach and teach the Word of God, without fear, without favoritism, and without compromise.) This Levite has compromised. This is a period of compromise, corruption, and confusion, which are the marks of apostasy at any time. We are in a state of apostasy today. The church has compromised. It is in a state of corruption and confusion. Our problem is that it is not returning to its authority, which is the Word of God, and the Lord Jesus Christ who is revealed in the Word of God.

And they said unto him, Ask counsel, we pray thee, of God, that we may know whether our way which we go shall be prosperous.

And the priest said unto them, Go in peace: before the LORD is your way wherein ye go [Jud. 18:5–6].

This is the sweet talk of a hired preacher who says what people want to hear. The five men left and thought what the Levite told them was great.

And they said, Arise, that we may go up against them: for we have seen the land, and, behold, it is very good: and are ye still? be not slothful to go, and to enter to possess the land.

When ye go, ye shall come unto a people secure, and to a large land: for God hath given it into your hands; a place where there is no want of any thing that is in the earth.

And there went from thence of the family of the Danites, out of Zorah and out of Eshtaol, six hundred men appointed with weapons of war [Jud. 18:9–11].

A good report is brought back by the spies who suggest that the Danites should possess Laish. So a party of six hundred warriors is formed, and they take with them their families and possessions. On the way back to Laish, they stop by Micah's house and rob him of his idols and his priest. Then the Danites capture Laish, burn it, rebuild it, and live in it. They rename the city Dan.

And the children of Dan set up the graven image: and Jonathan, the son of Gershom, the son of Manasseh, he and his sons were priests to the tribe of Dan until the day of the captivity of the land.

And they set them up Micah's graven image, which he made, all the time that the house of God was in Shiloh [Jud. 18:30–31].

Here is a picture of real apostasy, friend. Who is Jonathan? He happens to be the grandson of Moses! These people had gone a long way from God. Remember that Moses had said, speaking for the Lord, "Thou shalt have no other gods before me. Thou shalt not make unto thee any graven image, or any likeness of any thing that is in heaven above, or that is in the earth beneath, or that is in the water under the earth" (Exod. 20:3–4). And here is Moses' grandson, a priest with an idol! This is tragic.

When I was a young man studying for the ministry, I was shocked to learn some of the things that were going on within the organized church. Because I had not been brought up in the church, it was a new world and a new life for me. I was deeply impressed with the life and ministry of Dwight L. Moody and considered him a real saint of God—which he *was,* by the way. Then a man who knew him and knew his family told me, "One of his sons holds an office in the most liberal organization in this country." During those early days nothing hurt me as that did. I just couldn't understand how a son of a man like Moody could depart from the Gospel of Jesus Christ and from the integrity and inerrancy of the Word of God!

My friend, apostasy is an *awful* thing. And a nation's problems begin with religious apostasy. This is what happened to the nation of Israel. Here we see Moses' grandson serving as priest with Micah's graven image!

CHAPTER 19

***THEME:** Moral awfulness—the home*

As we have seen in the preceding section, the downfall of a people begins with religious apostasy. From there it moves on to the second stage, which is moral awfulness. This is graphically illustrated in the frightful episode which concludes the Book of Judges. It centers about the tribe of Benjamin. This tribe engaged in gross immorality which led to civil war. It began with the men of Benjamin abusing and finally murdering a Levite's concubine. The other tribes try to exterminate the tribe of Benjamin. This period ends in total national corruption and confusion and with this the Book of Judges concludes: "In those days there was no king in Israel: every man did that which was right in his own eyes" (Jud. 21:25).

And it came to pass in those days, when there was no king in Israel, that there was a certain Levite sojourning on the side of mount Ephraim, who took to him a concubine out of Beth-lehem-judah.

And his concubine played the whore against him, and went away from him unto her father's house to Beth-lehem-judah, and was there four whole months [Jud. 19:1–2].

These two verses give us another insight into the life of the children of Israel of that day, and it is a good illustration of Romans chapters 1–3. Can you imagine a Levite marrying a woman like that? Well, he did, and she played the harlot, left him, and went back to her father's house. This Levite followed her, was warmly received by her father, and stayed several days. Then the Levite and his concubine left and headed northward. They stayed one night in Gibeah, a city of the Benjamites. An old man who was also from mount Ephraim and was sojourning in Gibeah offered them hospitality. That night, while they were being entertained by their host, some men of the city demanded (as was done in Sodom before its destruction) the Levite for their homosexual gratification. Believing it would mean final death for him, he gave them instead his concubine. They abused her all night and absolutely caused her death by raping her. This horrible act sounds like something that could have happened in our country—does it not? In fact, the parallel to our contemporary society is quite striking as you read through this section.

The Levite was really wrought up by this crime, and what he did reveals how low they were in that day. He took her and cut her up in pieces, then sent a piece to each tribe with a message of what had taken place!

The reaction of the rest of the nation to this outrage is recorded in the next two chapters.

CHAPTERS 20–21

***THEME:** Political anarchy—the state*

Following religious apostasy, then moral awfulness, the next step downward in the life of Israel (and of every nation) is political anarchy. We see this in the last two chapters of the Book of Judges.

When the tribes of Israel received a part of this dismembered woman with the message of what had taken place in Gibeah, they were incensed against the tribe of Benjamin. They believed the law should be enforced. In that respect they had not sunk as low as we have today in our philosophy that lawlessness should be permitted and we should have as little law as possible. They gave Benjamin an opportunity to deliver up the offenders, but instead Benjamin declared war against the other eleven tribes! So the tribes assembled together and came against Benjamin.

Then all the children of Israel went out, and the congregation was gathered together as one man, from Dan even to Beer-sheba, with the land of Gilead, unto the LORD in Mizpeh.

And the chief of all the people, even of all the tribes of Israel, presented them-

selves in the assembly of the people of God, four hundred thousand footmen that drew sword [Jud. 20:1–2].

Apparently the tribe of Benjamin had a tremendous army. We are given an interesting sidelight here:

Among all this people there were seven hundred chosen men lefthanded; every one could sling stones at an hair breadth, and not miss [Jud. 20:16].

I heard a liberal speak for fifteen minutes one time on the fact that David could not have been accurate enough to hit Goliath on the forehead. Consider this verse. These men were as accurate in that day with their slings as we are today with our missiles. If they could get in the range of a slingshot, it would be fatal for anyone. These left-handed men could split a hair!

This same liberal said that the reason David picked up five stones was so that he would have a reserve supply in case he missed with the first stone. Well, that liberal was wrong. Goliath had four sons in the army of the Philistines, and David had a stone for each one of them. David knew how accurate he was.

Now the men of Benjamin were overcome by sheer numbers. In fact, the tribe of Benjamin was almost destroyed.

And there fell of Benjamin eighteen thousand men; all these were men of valour.

And they turned and fled toward the wilderness unto the rock of Rimmon: and they gleaned of them in the highways five thousand men; and pursued hard after them unto Gidom, and slew two thousand men of them.

So that all which fell that day of Benjamin were twenty and five thousand men that drew the sword; all these were men of valour [Jud. 20:44–46].

The people in the tribe of Benjamin were judged because of their gross immorality. What a tragic thing it was for so many to die. This was the favorite tribe. Benjamin, you will recall, was the youngest son of old Jacob, and a favorite son. Benjamin was the one for whom Judah was willing to lay down his life. He occupied a place next to Judah.

Unfortunately gross immorality had taken place and had set tribe against tribe and class against class. Then what happened? It led to political anarchy. First there was religious apostasy in the temple, then moral awfulness in the home, and finally political anarchy in the state. These are the steps that any nation takes that goes down.

The final chapter in the Book of Judges deals with the mourning for Israel's lost tribe and the provision the people made for its future.

The slaughter of the Benjamites caused Israel to be faced with a new problem. Almost the entire tribe of Benjamin had been destroyed and the other tribes vowed not to let their daughters marry any of the few remaining Benjamites. Exactly *how* was the tribe of Benjamin going to be preserved? Before the war, the Israelites had made another vow. They said that any who refused to come to Mizpeh and fight would be put to death. They found out that the men of Jabesh-gilead had not responded to the appeal, and so the command went out for twelve thousand men of Israel to kill the males of Jabesh-gilead, marry the women, and bring the virgins back to the camp at Shiloh. These virgins then became wives to four hundred Benjamites. A means was also found to get wives for the remaining Benjamites and to rebuild the cities that had been destroyed in the fighting.

This period ends in total national corruption and confusion. The final verse concludes the sordid story of the Book of Judges:

In those days there was no king in Israel: every man did that which was right in his own eyes [Jud. 21:25].

Here in this twentieth century the heads of state would do well to study the Book of Judges. Back in 1928, when the depression first began, a brief editorial appeared in the staid *Wall Street Journal*, which went something like this:

> What America needs today is not Government controls, industrial expansion, or a bumper corn crop; American needs to return to the day when grandpa took the team out of the field in the early afternoon on Wednesday in order to hitch them to the old spring wagon into which grandma put all of the children after she washed their faces shining clean; and they drove off to prayer meeting in the little white church at the crossroads underneath the oak trees, where everyone believed the Bible, trusted Christ, and loved one another.

Where did our trouble begin? Because our trouble is primarily spiritual, it actually goes back to the church. The church went into apostasy. Then our problems centered in the home with the drug problem and the generation gap. Trouble has now moved into political circles, and we have anarchy. People say, "If we could just change this or that and put in this party or that party, everything would be fine." All of this is perfect nonsense. What we need today is to get back to a spiritual foundation. That is where we went off the track, and that is where our troubles began. We have seen in the Book of Judges the philosophy of history, and the hoop of history is still rolling. Frankly, I am disturbed because it has never changed. We today are in the midst of political anarchy. God have mercy on America!

BIBLIOGRAPHY

(Recommended for Further Study)

Davis, John J. *Conquest and Crisis—Studies in Joshua, Judges, and Ruth.* Grand Rapids, Michigan: Baker Book House, 1969.

Enns, Paul P. *Joshua.* Grand Rapids, Michigan: Zondervan Publishing House, 1981.

Enns, Paul P. *Judges.* Grand Rapids, Michigan: Zondervan Publishing House, 1982.

Epp, Theodore H. *Joshua—Victorious by Faith.* Lincoln, Nebraska: Back to the Bible Broadcast, 1968. (Devotional.)

Gaebelein, Arno C. *The Annotated Bible,* Vol. 2. Neptune, New Jersey: Loizeaux Brothers, 1917.

Grant, F. W. *Numerical Bible,* Vol. 2. Neptune, New Jersey: Loizeaux Brothers, 1891.

Gray, James M. *Synthetic Bible Studies,* Westwood, New Jersey: Fleming H. Revell Co., 1906.

Ironside, H. A. *Addresses on the Book of Joshua.* Neptune, New Jersey: Loizeaux Brothers, 1950.

Jamieson, Robert; Fausset, A. R.; and Brown, D. *Commentary on the Bible.* 3 Vols. Grand Rapids, Michigan: Wm. B. Eerdmans Publishing Co., 1945.

Jensen, Irving L. *Joshua, Rest—Land Won.* Chicago, Illinois: Moody Press, 1966.

Jensen, Irving L. *Joshua, A Self-Study Guide.* Chicago, Illinois: Moody Press, 1968.

Jensen, Irving L. *Judges & Ruth, A Self-Study Guide.* Chicago, Illinois: Moody Press, 1968.

Lewis, Arthur. *Judges and Ruth.* Chicago, Illinois: Moody Press, 1979.

McGee, J. Vernon. *Ruth, The Romance of Redemption.* Pasadena, California: Thru the Bible Books, 1943.

Mackintosh, C. H. *The Mackintosh Treasury: Miscellaneous Writings.* Neptune, New Jersey: Loizeaux, n.d.

Meyer, F. B. *Joshua, and the Land of Promise.* Fort Washington, Pennsylvania: Christian Literature Crusade, n.d. (A rich devotional study.)

Pink, Arthur W. *Gleanings in Joshua.* Chicago, Illinois: Moody Press, 1964.

Redpath, Alan. *Victorious Christian Living.* Westwood, New Jersey: Fleming H. Revell Co., 1955. (Devotional studies in Joshua.)

Ridout, Samuel. *Lectures on the Books of Judges & Ruth.* Neptune, New Jersey: Loizeaux Brothers, n.d. (Excellent.)

The Book of RUTH

INTRODUCTION

Ruth is the story of a little foreign girl who came out of paganism and idolatry in the land of Moab. She came from a people who were in many senses an outcast people, and she came into a knowledge of the Lord God of Israel, as Boaz said, "Under whose wings thou art come to trust (Ruth 2:12).

Ruth has only four brief chapters, but it is a mighty midget with a mighty message. In fact, it has several messages. It gives a genealogy that leads to the Lord Jesus Christ, and it explains His coming from the line of David. There are commentators who take the position that the primary purpose of the Book of Ruth is to give the genealogy. While I agree that this is an important purpose of the book, I do not believe it is the primary purpose. Keil and Delitzsch make this statement: "The last words of verse 17, 'he is the father of Jesse, the father of David,' show the object which the author had in view in writing down these events, or composing the book itself. This conjecture is raised into a certainty by the genealogy which follows, and with which the book closes." The Book of Ruth is very important in connection with the coming of Jesus Christ into this world. Without this little book, we could not connect the house of David with the tribe of Judah. It is an important link in the chain of Scripture that begins with Genesis and goes right down to that stable in Bethlehem and to the cross, to the crown, and to the throne of David on which our Lord will someday be seated. This is a very definite reason Ruth is included in the canon of Scripture.

However, the primary purpose of the book of Ruth is the presentation of an important phase in the doctrine of redemption. Redemption is possible only through a Kinsman-Redeemer. God could not redeem apart from a Mediator. Since only God could redeem, it was necessary for Him to become that person. Boaz furnishes the only figure for the Kinsman-Redeemer aspect of redemption which is so essential for any proper theory of the Atonement. This little Book of Ruth comes down to our level and tells the commonplace story of a couple who love each other. They were ordinary folk, average folk, and their love story is a mirror in which we can see the divine love of a Savior for you and me. As we proceed into the Book of Ruth, we see this wonderful love story unfold before us.

OUTLINE

Ruth is a very brief book, just four chapters, and there are many ways of dividing it. Some outlines are excellent, but the one we shall follow seems to satisfy the content of the book more than any other. It is the geographical division.

I. In the Land of Moab, Chapter 1

II. In the Fields of Boaz, Chapter 2

III. On the Threshingfloor of Boaz, Chapter 3

IV. In the Heart and Home of Boaz, Chapter 4

CHAPTER 1

***THEME:** In the land of Moab*

Now it came to pass in the days when the judges ruled, that there was a famine in the land. And a certain man of Beth-lehem-judah went to sojourn in the country of Moab, he, and his wife, and his two sons [Ruth 1:1].

This verse that opens the Book of Ruth covers a great deal. In fact, it sounds like modern newspaper reporting. When I was in college I had a job working on a newspaper, the *Memphis Commercial Appeal*. As a cub reporter, I went out with some of the other reporters. Also I got acquainted with the city editor, who was a very nice man, and he attempted to help me all he could. Well, I tried to write up a story of an incident we witnessed one night in Memphis and presented it to the city editor. He read it, just pushed it aside, and said he couldn't use it. Then he told me that there are two things which are always important to get into the first sentence of any article that's newsworthy: the time and the place. In fact, he said, "Get as much in the first sentence as you possibly can." The next time you're reading an important article on the front page of your paper, notice how much information is included in that opening sentence. Sometimes the first sentence is an entire paragraph, and it just about tells the whole story right there. It tells you *what* the incident is, *where* it took place, *when* it took place, and generally *how* it took place.

Now the Holy Spirit of God is a very wonderful reporter. And so in this very first verse He gives the time and the place. The time: "when the judges ruled." Those were dark days. In one sense, they were the darkest days in the history of the nation Israel. You will recall that the Israelites had been in Egyptian captivity, and God had redeemed them by blood and by power, and had brought them through the wilderness. Then He brought them into the Promised Land. And what great promise there was. You would think that this new generation, whose fathers had known the rigors of slavery in Egypt, would serve God in a very wonderful way. But, you know, they didn't.

The Book of Judges tells a sorry and sordid story of a departure from God, of how a people began by serving the living and true God, then turned from Him to idolatry and moral corruption, then how they cried to Him when the enemy oppressed them, and how He raised up judges to deliver them.

I agree with those who are saying right now that America must have revival or she will probably have revolution. Frankly, if you want to see a sweeping revival in this country, don't pray for revival—pray that God will put the church through the fire, and I'll guarantee that will bring revival. It has always brought revival among God's people in the past, and it did in the nation Israel. When they got far from God, judgment came—He sent them into slavery, or an enemy came and defeated them. Then in their suffering they cried out to God. And God was so gracious. He always raised up judges to deliver them.

The Book of Ruth fits into this period of the judges. The incidents that are recorded here take place on this black background of the judges, a time when a man like Samson was a public figure. Today when scandals have shaken our own country, think of the scandal of a Samson! During the period of compromise, corruption, and confusion, this lovely story takes place. It is light in the midst of darkness. This is the way God writes, is it not? He writes the story of salvation on the black background of sin, and He put this lovely little story on the black background of the time of the judges. This is the picture that we have before us. It is "in the days when the judges ruled."

Not only that, but we're told that the place was Beth-lehem-judah. Now that indeed is very interesting. Beth-lehem-judah has real meaning for a child of God today. And, frankly, Jesus Christ would never have been born in Bethlehem if the incidents recorded in the Book of Ruth hadn't first taken place in Bethlehem. As you sing "O Little Town of Bethlehem," remember that the Christmas story began way back in the incidents which transpired in the little Book of Ruth. These are the incidents that will concern us as we move into this very wonderful portion of Scripture.

The meaning of the name *Beth-lehem-judah* is interesting. Actually, the names in the Bible have a real meaning. *Beth-lehem* means "house of bread," and *Judah* means "praise." That's a wonderful place to live—don't you agree—in the house of bread and praise? The story of Ruth begins and ends there. And that's the place where Jesus was born. Because the names in the Bible, and especially in the Old Testament, have specific meanings, we miss a great deal by not having a translation of the names. I wish we did. At least we have in the notes of certain Bibles an explanation of the meanings of some of the names. It adds a wealth of meaning to the Word of God, as it does in this instance.

"And a certain man of Beth-lehem-judah went to sojourn in the country of Moab, he, and his wife, and his two sons." He lives in the house of bread and praise, but he goes to sojourn in the country of Moab. There's something in the Word of God about Moab that's quite interesting. It's almost humorous. In Psalm 108:9 it says, "Moab is my washpot." Now that's what God says of Moab. You see, these were an outcast people. They had a very sordid and sorry beginning, and Moab just doesn't stand out very well in the Word of God. One way to paraphrase what God says about Moab might be to say, "Moab is my garbage can."

Now will you look at this for just a moment. Here's a family—a certain man, his wife, and his two sons—that goes over to the land of Moab. They leave the house of bread and the house of praise and they go over to eat out of a garbage can. Did you ever hear that story before? I'm sure you immediately will be reminded of the parable that our Lord gave about a prodigal son. He left the father's house in which there was plenty, and he went over to the foreign country, where he longed to fill his stomach with the pods that the swine were eating. I do not think our Lord made up that story. In fact, I do not think He made up parables. I think every parable He gave was a true incident. Probably there were many sons in that day to whom His parable could have applied. And from that day to the present that story has been repeated in literally millions of lives. I talked to a young man here in Southern California not too long ago who had run away from his home in the East. That was his story. He accepted the Lord out here, and we called his father right from my study. How his father rejoiced! That story, my friend, has been lived by many sons.

But here it's the story of a prodigal family. When famine came to the land, they left. They got frightened. Well, their father Abraham got frightened also, and when a famine came to that land during his lifetime, he ran off to Egypt. And now here's another famine. This is one of thirteen that are mentioned in the Bible. Every time a famine is mentioned in the Word of God, it's a judgment from God. This is not only the time of the judges with dark days, but these are the darkest of the dark days when this incident took place. They didn't believe God could take care of them in the house of bread and of praise, so they ran off to the land of Moab.

Now I would like you to get acquainted with this family. It is an interesting family.

And the name of the man was Elimelech, and the name of his wife Naomi, and the name of his two sons Mahlon and Chilion, Ephrathites of Beth-lehem-judah. And they came into the country of Moab, and continued there [Ruth 1:2].

The name of the man is Elimelech. His name means "my God is King" or "the King is my God." Here is a man who has a name that's really meaningful. Just think of the testimony he gave where he worked. When they called him, they didn't say, "Elimelech," in English. They said, "My God is King," or, "God is my King." My, that's a wonderful name to have, isn't it? Why, his very name is a testimony. It's mighty bad, though, to have that name and run off to the land of Moab. He doesn't act as if God is his King.

The name of his wife is Naomi. Now if you were to look up her name in a good Bible dictionary, you'd find that her name means "pleasant." Well, I'd like to give her a really good name. I think her name really was Merry Sunshine. She was a wonderful person. She was the type of individual who always had a very happy outlook upon life. There are many Christians like that today. They always see the bright side. They always register that, and they live above their circumstances instead of being under their circumstances. Some people are always complaining, always finding fault, but not Naomi, not Merry Sunshine.

Elimelech and Naomi have two sons. Their names are Mahlon and Chilion. The name Mahlon means "unhealthy," and Chilion means "puny." She had two sickly boys. And I imagine Naomi had quite a testimony in Bethlehem because of that. Many people said, "I just don't see how Merry Sunshine can be so radiant and so joyful when she has the burden of those two unhealthy boys." Well, that's her story. And we're told that she and her husband were Ephrathites of Beth-lehem-judah.

"And they came into the country of Moab, and continued there." They not only went to Moab, they made their home there. Now although the prodigal son got into the pigpen, finally he said, "I will arise and go to my father" (Luke 15:18). Sometimes a prodigal stays in the pigpen a long time, and this family, unfortunately, stayed too long. And do you know what always happens to a Christian family—or to an individual who is God's child—which runs off to the far country? They always get a whipping in the far country. You know, that father who received his prodigal son when he came home, could have said to the servant, "Go get me my razor strap. I'm going to whip this boy within an inch of his life. He ran off and spent my money and disgraced my name. I'll teach him." But he didn't do that. He threw his arms around the boy. He told the servant to go kill the fatted calf and to bring the best robe for his son. You see, many Christians today think that God is a very stern, harsh Father and that if you come back to Him, He won't receive you, but He'll punish you. He won't whip you, friend. You'll get your whipping in the far country. That's where the prodigal son got his, and I'll tell you, he got a good one. And this family here is going to be taken to the woodshed. They're going to get a whipping in the far country.

But they are, I think, a fine family. "My God is King" is the father, the head of the family. And there's Merry Sunshine, the wife and mother, and then there are the two sickly boys, Mahlon and Chilion. They go to the land of Moab, and they go to eat out of the garbage can, and they continue living there.

Notice what happens.

And Elimelech Naomi's husband died; and she was left, and her two sons [Ruth 1:3].

I told you they were going to have trouble in the far country, and they did. It always happens. John says, "There is a sin unto death" (1 John 5:16). I do not know what the sin unto death is for you. For Ananias and Sapphira it was a lie to the Holy Spirit. I don't think that's a sin unto death today. If it were, we'd be very busy conducting funerals in the church. But I don't think it's the same for every Christian. When you get away from God, that's when trouble comes.

Now the husband died. Notice what happened after he died.

And they took them wives of the women of Moab; the name of the one was Orpah, and the name of the other Ruth: and they dwelled there about ten years [Ruth 1:4].

Now the very minute that they did that they broke the Mosaic Law. You see, having gotten out of fellowship with God and going to the far country, the next step is always in apostasy; it's to continue on in sin, and even to multiply it. And that's what they did. They broke the Mosaic Law and took wives of the women of Moab.

Orpah means "deer" or "fawn." It means she was the athletic type. And you wonder why an athletic type of girl married one of these sickly boys. But she did. After meeting Orpah, we come to the one we're really interested in: Ruth. And I could give you about ten different meanings for the name *Ruth.* It means "beauty"; it means "personality." And she had this characteristic—she was beautiful but she was not dumb. She is a remarkable person, and I hope that you're going to fall in love with her because she happens to be one of the ancestors of Jesus Christ. In other words, in His humanity, He had the blood of Ruth flowing through His veins. We're going to get acquainted with her. She married Mahlon in the land of Moab. There is a word I'd like to use to describe her, but Hollywood and the high-pressure publicity of our day have spoiled it. It would be "glamour." Certainly, in the best sense of the word, that would apply to Ruth. And why she ever married this sickly boy is difficult to understand at first, but I think we will understand it later on.

Now this prodigal family is in the far country. Trouble has already come to them, and more trouble is going to come to this mother and wife. She has lost her husband, and her two sons have married women of Moab.

And Mahlon and Chilion died also both of them; and the woman was left of her two sons and her husband [Ruth 1:5].

Now I was expecting that, by the way. I didn't think that they'd make it through another hard winter, and they didn't. And these two boys, Unhealthy and Puny, died. Now she has lost her entire family, and all she has left are two little daughters-in-law, foreign girls. That's all she has. I tell you, trouble did come. And the prodigal family, like the prodigal son, got their whipping in the far country.

Then she arose with her daughters in law, that she might return from the country of Moab: for she had heard in the country of Moab how the Lord had visited his people in giving them bread [Ruth 1:6].

The famine was over back in the Promised Land, and there was bread again in Bethlehem, the house of bread and praise. And so now she wants to return home. It's interesting. The prodigal family and the prodigal son will long for the father's house. And if they don't long for the father's house, they just don't happen to be the children of the father. The prodigal son will never be happy in the pigpen. He just wasn't made for a pigpen. He hasn't the nature of a pig. He has the nature of the father, and he will eventually say, "I will arise and go to my father." Now the pigs love pigpens. There is a story that Peter gives to us in 2 Peter 2:22, which I call the parable of the prodigal pig. ". . . The sow that was washed [has returned] to her wallowing in the mire." You see, one of the little pigs got all cleaned up and told the prodigal son, "You seem to be sold on going home, and I want to go with you." And so the pig went home with the prodigal son, but he didn't like it up there—clean sheets on the bed and a clean tablecloth—ugh! He told the prodigal son, "Why don't we put the food in the trough and all of us jump in and have a big time? And why do we have to have clean sheets? I like mud better." And finally the little pig said he'd arise and go to his father. And you know where his old man was—down there in the pigpen. And the prodigal pig went back to the pigpen; he always will. And the prodigal son will always go home, friends. You can depend on that. But today it's confusing. On the freeways of life there are prodigal sons going to pigpens and prodigal pigs going up to the father's house, and they ought not to be. Sometimes they get into the church, and they start causing trouble. Like a pig when he gets into the father's house, he starts causing trouble in the church. He's a troublemaker, but eventually he'll end up back in the pigpen. You just have to wait, you see.

So eventually this family must go home. Finally Naomi says she's going back to Bethlehem-judah.

> **Wherefore she went forth out of the place where she was, and her two daughters in law with her; and they went on the way to return unto the land of Judah [Ruth 1:7].**

Now Naomi is going to talk to her daughters-in-law just like a Dutch uncle. She's going to tell them what the situation is going to be when they get to Bethlehem. You see, the Moabites and the Israelites just didn't have anything to do with each other. The Israelites had no dealings with the Moabites, just like later on they didn't have any dealings with the Samaritans. Now here Naomi tells them that because they're Moabites it's going to cost them something to go up with her to Bethlehem. They'd never be able to marry again, and these were young women. It would mean perpetual widowhood and poverty for them because she had lost all of her property.

> **And Naomi said unto her two daughters in law, Go, return each to her mother's house: the LORD deal kindly with you, as ye have dealt with the dead, and with me [Ruth 1:8].**

Now she had a wonderful word for them. They'd been good daughters-in-law. And you know, it's difficult for a mother to feel that any girl is worthy of her son. But here's one who could say of these foreign girls that they had made good wives. But she encourages them to return and go back to their own mothers and not to go up with her because of what it would cost them. And she says,

> **The LORD grant you that ye may find rest, each of you in the house of her husband. Then she kissed them; and they lifted up their voice, and wept [Ruth 1:9].**

This is truly a womanly scene. Naomi tells them that if they stay in the land of Moab, they can remarry among their own people; but if they were to go up with her, they wouldn't have a chance. Here are these three women standing in the crossroads in the land of Moab. When I visited the land of Moab, I thought of these three women. Around any bend of the road there in that wild country, on those roads that twist and turn, you might be able to see these three, Ruth and Naomi and Orpah. There they stand, and they're weeping. They have their handkerchiefs out, and I call this the meeting of the handkerchief brigade. They're all weeping.

> **And they said unto her, Surely we will return with thee unto thy people [Ruth 1:10].**

Now their first decision was, "We'll go with you."

> **And Naomi said, Turn again, my daughters: why will ye go with me? Are there yet any more sons in my womb, that they may be your husbands? [Ruth 1:11].**

You see, the Mosaic Law said that when a man died, the nearest of kin was to marry his wife, and if there were a brother he was the one to marry her. This was a very strange law indeed, and we'll see it later on here in the Book of Ruth because this is the story of the kinsman-redeemer. So here Naomi just talks turkey to them. She tells them how it is. "If you go with me, you can never get married. My people couldn't identify themselves with you. It'd be too costly. You'll really be outcasts because we don't have any dealings with the Moabites."

Turn again, my daughters, go your way; for I am too old to have a husband. If I should say, I have hope, if I should have an husband also to-night, and should also bear sons [Ruth 1:12].

And so Naomi urged them to stay in their own land. She made it very plain. She said, "Even if I had more sons, which I never will, but if I did, would you wait for them to grow up? Why, you'd be robbing the cradle. You wouldn't want to do that."

Would ye tarry for them till they were grown? would ye stay for them from having husbands? nay, my daughters; for it grieveth me much for your sakes that the hand of the LORD is gone out against me [Ruth 1:13].

You see, God had judged Naomi's family, and she told them they'd have to bear that. She didn't want them to go with her for that reason.

Now here we go again.

And they lifted up their voice, and wept again: and Orpah kissed her mother in law; but Ruth clave unto her [Ruth 1:14].

Now we come to the parting of the ways. As I said, you might come around the curve in any road in Moab and see these three women. And had you and I gone by in that day and seen these three women in eastern garb weeping there, we would have thought that nothing of importance was taking place. But, my friend, I'll tell you how important it is: the decision made that day will determine whether Jesus Christ will be born in Bethlehem or not. And if the right decision is not made, you might as well send word to the wise men not to come, because He won't be born there. It may not look important to us, but a tremendous decision was being made. We find that Orpah kissed Naomi, but Ruth clung to her. Orpah turned back, and that's exactly what Naomi said.

And she said, Behold, thy sister in law is gone back unto her people, and unto her gods: return thou after thy sister in law [Ruth 1:15].

Orpah made the decision to go back. Her decision for God had not been real, you see. She goes back to idolatry. And when she goes back, she walks off the pages of Scripture into silence and into oblivion. We never hear of her again. But Ruth made a decision for God, and when she made this decision, it was for time and eternity. And you'll find her mentioned in the very first chapter of the New Testament. She's in the genealogy that led to Christ. Naomi wants to test her to see if she's genuine or not. She told her to go back to her gods, to go back with her sister-in-law.

And Ruth said, Entreat me not to leave thee, or to return from following after thee: for whither thou goest, I will go; and where thou lodgest, I will lodge: thy people shall be my people, and thy God my God [Ruth 1:16].

She made an important decision there. It's a sevenfold decision, and it's a decision for God. And this is what I believe is genuine repentance, friend. This is the kind of repentance that means something. That's exactly what the New Testament says. 2 Corinthians 7:10 says, "For godly sorrow worketh repentance to salvation not to be repented of: but the sorrow of the world worketh death." Ruth made this decision. She continues,

Where thou diest, will I die, and there will I be buried: the LORD do so to me, and more also, if aught but death part thee and me [Ruth 1:17].

Now that's Ruth's sevenfold decision, and it's a real decision for God. I want you to notice this because this is very important in this day when believers make a great deal of their dedication to God, and they promise God a great deal, but they don't carry through with it. I believe God holds us to it. What we need today are folk who make *real* decisions for God. The decision of Ruth was that kind of decision.

First of all, Ruth said, "Whither thou goest, I will go." In other words, she's saying to Naomi, "I made a decision to go with you, and I'm going with you. I'm not using this just as a passport to get into Palestine." And the second phase of her decision is, "And where thou lodgest, I will lodge." In other words, she would not only go with Naomi, but she'd also identify herself with her. "I accept your poverty." She bears the same name now, as she had married Merry Sunshine's son, and she will stick right with Naomi. Her third statement, "Thy people shall be my people—I'm forsaking my people, idolators, and I'm identifying myself with God's people." And, friend, you can't make a decision for God unless you identify yourself with God's people. It'd just be impossible to do otherwise, you see. And Ruth knew that. She said, "You say I'll be an outcast. All right, I'll be an outcast, but thy people will be my people." And then the fourth, "Thy God my God." Now I can explain why this girl Ruth decided to marry that unhealthy boy that moved into the neighborhood who'd come from the house of bread and praise over in the Promised Land. The reason, I think, is evident. For the first time she heard of the living and true God. She met a family that knew the living and true God, and she married into that family because she had come to know the living and the true God. "Thy God will be my God." What a decision she had made! And not only that but, "Where thou diest, will I die." That is more meaningful to Ruth than it would be for you and me today. What she's saying is this, "The hope of Israel is my hope." You see, the Israelite believed that someday he would be raised from the dead to live in that land. That was the hope of Abraham. He never believed that he was going to heaven. He believed he would be raised from the dead right down here, and that's the reason he bought the cave of Machpelah and buried Sarah there, and he himself was buried there. Isaac had that same hope, and even old Jacob, who died down in the land of Egypt, said he wanted to be buried back up there where his fathers were buried. This was because they had a hope of the resurrection of the dead. They were seeking "a city . . . whose builder and maker is God" (Heb. 11:10), which will be a reality on this earth someday. That's the Old Testament hope. When the Lord Jesus said to His disciples in the upper room in John 14:2, ". . . I go to prepare a place for you" *away* from this earth, that was brand new, you see. God's promise to Abraham was to give him an eternal home on this earth. And Ruth said not only that where Naomi died she would die, but also, "And there will I be buried." You see, her hope is in that land—just as the hope of Abraham, Isaac, and Jacob had been. She had now the Old Testament hope. Then the seventh part of her decision is this, ". . . The LORD do so to me, and more also, if aught but death part thee and me." What a decision she'd made! She said, "I didn't make this for just a day or for an hour. I made this decision for time and for eternity."

What we see in Ruth is genuine and real repentance. We hear a great deal today about repentance, and the average notion is that repentance means shedding a few tears. You will recall that 2 Corinthians 7:10 says, "For godly sorrow worketh repentance to salvation." Note that repentance is not salvation; it *leads* to salvation. ". . . But the sorrow of the world worketh death." What is the sorrow of the world? Well, it's to shed tears. The worldling can shed tears. Now look yonder at the crossroads again with these three women there. Orpah shed just as many tears as Ruth did. Her handkerchief was just as damp as Ruth's was. What's the difference between these two women? The difference is quite obvious. Orpah shed a great many tears, but hers were not tears of real repentance. What is real repentance? The Greek word used in 2 Corinthians 7:10 is *metanoia*. It means "to change your mind." It means to be going in one direction, then to change your mind, turn around, and go in the other direction. A lot of people come to a place where they're under conviction, and they intend to change—or at least they say they do—and they shed a few tears, but they keep right on going the same way. And that's exactly what Orpah did. She shed the tears right along with Ruth, but she didn't turn around and go to Bethlehem and make a stand for God. No, she went back to idolatry. And a lot of folk are like that today —they just shed tears. Tears are not repentance, friend, although they may be a byproduct of repentance.

My dad used to tell about a steamboat which plied on the Mississippi River years ago when he was a boy. He said it had a little, bitty boiler and a great big whistle. When this boat was moving upstream and blew its whistle, it would start drifting downstream, because it didn't have enough steam to do both. There are a lot of folk like that today. They have a great big whistle and a little, bitty boiler. They have never come to a saving knowledge of Christ. Oh, they'll shed a lot of tears over their sins—they blow their whistle —and they're very emotional. They love to give testimonies full of emotion, but their lives don't measure up. I know several men who can make people weep when they get up and give their testimonies. They have tears in their voice, but I wouldn't trust those men at all. I don't think they're born-again men at all, just emotional. They are like Orpah.

During my ministry I have learned to put less confidence in tears than I formerly did. I found out that these sob-sisters today can shed tears, but they don't really make a decision. Sometimes a person can be dry-eyed and make a decision for Christ, and it's genuine and real. Years ago when I was pastor in Pasadena, two couples came forward on Easter Sunday morning. One couple blubbered all over the place. They cried and wept so that we couldn't make any sense out of what they were saying. But they made a big impression on the officers who thought this couple was really genuinely saved. They were not. I pulled them out of two cults, and the pastor who followed me told me he did the same thing. The other couple was dry-eyed. Because they didn't shed a tear, one of the elders called me aside and asked, "Do you think they're converted?" Well, that's been at least twenty-five years ago, and every now and then I see that couple, and they're still standing for the Lord. Let me just ask you a personal question: did you really make a decision for Christ, or did you just shed a few tears? Tears themselves are meaningless, and the sorrow of this world worketh death, friend, and that kind of repentance is no good. But repentance that is genuine is not to be repented of. It will lead to salvation, and you'll be genuinely converted—as was Ruth.

Ruth makes a real decision for God. She says, "I accept the poverty. I accept being an outcast. I also accept the fact that I will remain a widow the rest of my life." She was willing to accept all of that in order to take a stand for God. She makes her decision to go back to Bethlehem with Naomi.

Now Merry Sunshine knew Ruth—

When she saw that she was stedfastly minded to go with her, then she left speaking unto her [Ruth 1:18].

She knew that when this girl made a decision, it was a real decision, it would stick; so she didn't need to say anything else to Ruth.

And so we follow them.

So they two went until they came to Beth-lehem. And it came to pass, when they were come to Beth-lehem, that all the city was moved about them, and they said, Is this Naomi? [Ruth 1:19].

Now they have returned. The prodigal family is coming home, but it's not a family now. Actually, it's just this widow Merry Sunshine, who doesn't look like Merry Sunshine, and a little foreign girl by the name of Ruth. And the people of the city ask, "Is this Naomi? Is this Merry Sunshine?"

And she said unto them, Call me not Naomi, call me Mara: for the Almighty hath dealt very bitterly with me.

I went out full, and the Lord hath brought me home again empty [Ruth 1:20–21a].

Now I do not know too much about mathematics, but I do know this: it's a long way between being full and being empty. Having zero and having everything is just about as far apart as you can put figures—or put anything. On one hand, empty; on the other hand, full. She went out full; she comes back empty. Friend, may I say this, if you're a child of God, you have been blessed with all spiritual blessings in the heavenlies, and you have everything in Christ. When you go out from His presence and lose your fellowship, you're going to find out something. You're going to find out that you get your whipping in the far country and you're going to come home empty, and I mean *empty*. But, thank God, when you come home that way, just like the prodigal son did, you'll find the Father waiting to receive you with outstretched arms. He'll bless you in a way that He's never blessed you before. He'll be very good to you. That's the thing that happened to the prodigal son. A robe was given to him, a fatted calf was killed for a banquet—all of this for the boy who returned home.

Now Naomi had told her friends to call her Mara, Gloomy Gus. She says,

why then call ye me Naomi, seeing the Lord hath testified against me, and the Almighty hath afflicted me? [Ruth 1:21b].

You'd think maybe they would change her name to Gloomy Gus, but they didn't. And the Spirit of God leaves it that way also. "So *Naomi* [not *Mara*] returned." The Spirit of God says that she's going to be Merry Sunshine again.

So Naomi returned, and Ruth the Moabitess, her daughter in law, with her, which returned out of the country of Moab: and they came to Beth-lehem in the beginning of barley harvest [Ruth 1:22].

This is a good time to arrive in Bethlehem. We have left the land of Moab, and in the next chapter we'll be going into the fields of Boaz near Bethlehem.

CHAPTER 2

***THEME:** In the field of Boaz*

> **And Naomi had a kinsman of her husband's, a mighty man of wealth, of the family of Elimelech; and his name was Boaz [Ruth 2:1].**

Here we have Boaz introduced to us, and he is actually the hero of our story. He will be the one who will set before us the type of the kinsman-redeemer—but that's a little later. Notice that immediately he's identified as a kinsman of her husband. That is important to note. "And Naomi had a kinsman." I can't pass that by without saying that Boaz is a picture and a type of the Lord Jesus Christ. And it can be said of you and of me that we have a Kinsman also, one who was made like we are, yet sinless—"holy, harmless, undefiled, separate from sinners" (Heb. 7:26). He is the one who is able to save us to the uttermost. The name *Boaz*, by the way, means "strength." He was a mighty man of wealth. And I'm told that you can also translate it "a mighty man of war." And it could be said "mighty man of law" also. All three were true of Boaz. He's a mighty man of war; he's a mighty man of wealth; and he is a mighty man of the Law. He is the one we're introduced to now. He was of the family of Elimelech.

> **And Ruth the Moabitess said unto Naomi, Let me now go to the field, and glean ears of corn after him in whose sight I shall find grace. And she said unto her, Go my daughter [Ruth 2:2].**

We find here one of three very strange laws; that is, they are strange to us because we haven't anything in our legal system today that corresponds to them. To glean grain or other produce was part of the Mosaic system. This was God's way of taking care of the poor, and Ruth and Naomi are very poor. The very fact that Ruth says she wants to go and glean is indicative of their poverty.

Now we want to look at this strange law. It is stated in several places. For instance, we have it in Leviticus 19:9–10: "And when ye reap the harvest of your land, thou shalt not wholly reap the corners of thy field, neither shalt thou gather the gleanings of thy harvest. And thou shalt not glean thy vineyard, neither shalt thou gather every grape of thy vineyard; thou shalt leave them for the poor and stranger: I am the LORD your God." You see, God told His people that they had to take care of the poor, and do it in this very unusual way. God didn't put them on relief. He didn't have an anti-poverty program that just gave them money. God did it, I think, in a very sensible way. They had to go and glean. The law is directed, you see, to the landowner. It is stated again in Leviticus 23:22: "And when ye reap the harvest of your land, thou shalt not make clean riddance of the corners of thy field when thou reapest, neither shalt thou gather any gleaning of thy harvest: thou shalt leave them unto the poor, and to the stranger: I am the LORD your God." And then the final reference is in Deuteronomy 24:19: "When thou cuttest down thine harvest in thy field, and hast forgot a sheaf in the field, thou shalt not go again to fetch it: it shall be for the stranger, for the fatherless, and for the widow. . . ." It was God's way of taking care of the poor people of that day. He didn't put them on relief; He didn't get them in a bread line; He didn't make them recipients of charity. He gave them something to do. They had to work for what they got. They could go into the fields and glean, and they would have to do it by hand. It's not like it is today in our country. Doing it by hand is not very efficient. The harvesters leave a great deal of the grain in the field, up to thirty percent. Once they'd gone through the field God wouldn't let them go back over it the second time. He said, "After you've gone over it the first time, then the poor can come in and glean." I think God's method is a good one. Of course, it's not up-to-date to fit into our modern, political economy, but God's method certainly worked in Ruth's day when thirty percent of the grain was left in the field. They tell me that there is a McCormick reaper now out in Kansas that cuts the grain and at the same time threshes it and sacks it up. If it drops just one little grain of oats or wheat, there's an arm that reaches down, picks it up and puts it in the sack. They don't miss a thing today! This was God's marvelous provision for the poor in a day when the poor were not even considered at all. And, friends, God is concerned for the poor. The Word of God has been the only thing that has given the poor man a chance. You go throughout the world and check that out for yourself. A great many of us today in this country are enjoying the benefits of those in the past who have labored, and we have entered into their labors. We are greatly blessed as a people. But many of you can remember when we were poor. I was a very poor boy myself, and you may have that background also. We owe a great deal to the Word of God, because it is only the Word of God that has ever given the poor man a square deal. The politicians won't, I can assure you of that. They are only after votes; they're not after the poor man's welfare. But God is, and this was God's marvelous arrangement.

And so Ruth acts upon this law which seems so strange to us today. She came under both categories, the stranger and the poor. She asked Naomi to let her go and glean, and Naomi told her to go.

And she went, and came, and gleaned in the field after the reapers: and her hap was to light on a part of the field belonging unto Boaz, who was of the kindred of Elimelech [Ruth 2:3].

And if you'd seen Ruth going out that day down the road from Bethlehem, you would have seen a girl who had no idea into which field she should go. How is she going to find her way into the field of Boaz? It's going to be very important that she get in that field. If she doesn't, then you can tell the wise men that there's no use coming to Bethlehem. Jesus won't be born there. And you can tell the shepherds to stay with their flocks on the hillside because He won't be born in Bethlehem. You see, it's important that she go into the right field. How is she going to find the right field?

When I was in Bethlehem, I took a walk myself. I may not have walked down the exact road that Ruth did, but it couldn't have been very far from it. And I thought of her as I walked. I think we've located the fields of Boaz. They're right down at the foot of the hill from Bethlehem. Bethlehem was a typical city in Palestine of that day. All of them were built upon a hill, and this little town of Bethlehem was no exception. Evidently down at the foot of the hill in a very fertile valley were the fields of Boaz. When Ruth went out of Bethlehem that day, she had no notion where to go. Now Scripture says, "Her *hap* was to light on a part of the field belonging unto Boaz. . . ." Well, the word *hap* is an old Anglo-Saxon word, coming from the same stem as *perhaps* or *happens*. Her "hap" was just a happenstance, as we call it today. From her viewpoint, it was just by chance. Actually, it was just that. Now this brings us again to the question: How did she find her way into the field of Boaz when it was so very important that she go into the right field? Did God put up a stop and go sign, a red and green light, or point an arrow into the right field? He did not. Well then, did a voice speak out of heaven? No, no voice spoke out of heaven. Well, she must have had a vision, someone thinks. But she didn't have a vision. Well, how in the world is this girl going to get into the right field? Let's ask Ruth. I would say to her, "Ruth, I'm sure that you had some pretty definite leading about the field of Boaz." And she'd say, "No, I didn't. You'd better go back and read the book of Ruth again. It says that my *hap* was to light on his field. I just happened to go in there." May I say to you, from the human viewpoint, it was just happenstance. From God's viewpoint, it's something else. He's going to lead her into the right field. But He's not going to lead her in the way a lot of people talk about it today.

Some folks talk about God's will as if they'd just had a Western Union telegram from Him or a Special Delivery air mail letter from heaven. My friend, God doesn't lead that way today, and I don't think He has ever led very many that way. Back in the Old Testament He led some in a very direct manner, but Ruth was not one of them. It seems to me that Ruth's decision was more important than some other decisions that were made. God said to Jonah, "Arise, go to Nineveh" (Jonah 1:2). And He told Jeremiah and Ezekiel to speak out. But I want to say this to you: what He told these men to do is not nearly as important as Ruth's getting into the right field, because Jesus' birth in Bethlehem is dependent upon her going into the right field. Now God is going to overrule in all of this, and God is going to guide in the background. That's the wonderful thing about the Lord's will. I'm not sure that it's necessary for God to give you and me a road map. Sometimes I wish He would. And I hear some people talk today as if they *have* a road map. They say, "The Lord's will was for me to do this, and I knew this was the Lord's will." I wish I could be that clear, that sure.

Years ago, when I was pastor in Cleburne, Texas, I received two calls from other churches, one to the east of Texas and the other to the west in California. And I didn't know which to take. I'm being honest with you. I actually got down on the floor and cried out to God to show me which call to accept. He didn't. I had no vision. But then I heard Dr. Harry Ironside make the statement that of the decisions he had to make in his life, eighty percent (I think this is the figure he gave) were made without knowing at the time they were God's will. He did not know until sometime later on. After hearing that, I went back home and told my wife that the atmosphere had all cleared, that I felt we were to go to California. I wasn't sure, but I felt that was the way I was to move.

As far as God's will for your life is concerned, if you think that He's going to put up a green light for you at every corner or an arrow pointing or a voice out of heaven, you're just wrong. He doesn't do it that way. And when I hear people say that, I just know there's something radically wrong with them, or they're trying to kid somebody. But wait just a minute—Dr. Ironside said that afterward he knew whether it had been God's will or not. And I think that sometimes God does let us go down the wrong road. "But," somebody is going to say, "you could make a pretty bad decision." You sure can. But the interesting thing is that if you have two ways before you and you take the wrong way, there's nothing in the world that'll keep you from coming back and starting over again. And you can be sure of one thing: If you had two ways to choose from and chose the wrong way first, then you *know* which is the right way. It's amazing today how many people interpret God's will as being the easy way. Well, it's not always the easy way. It certainly wasn't for Ruth.

If you'd asked Ruth if she knew she was going into the right field, she would have said, "I don't know what you're talking about." And had you asked her why she chose the field she did, I think she would have said to you, "I prayed about it. Before I left home this morning, I asked God to lead me. I really didn't know which road to take, but I got down here and looked into one field with nice grain but there weren't many poor people gleaning in it, so I was pretty sure that whoever owned that was a skinflint. But over on the other side of the road, my, there were a lot of poor people gleaning. And I knew that man must be a generous man, and I needed to find that kind of field because I'm a Moabitess, a foreigner, an outcast, and I didn't want to be put out; so that's why I chose this one." And I suppose that when she'd gone a distance down the road, and probably hesitated a minute, that the angels on the battlement of heaven looked over and held their breath. They said, "My, I hope she goes into the right field." She went into the right field. And I think that all heaven heaved a sigh of relief when they saw her going into the fields of Boaz. God is overruling. For Ruth there was the element of uncertainty, but on the other side there was the providential dealing of Almighty God.

One of the glorious things, as we go through this world today, is to know that our times are in His hands; to know that He is ordering the events of this universe; and to know that God has said that nothing can come to a child of His without His permission. You must remember that there was a hedge around Job, and even Satan couldn't touch him until God gave permission. God will not give permission unless it serves some lofty and worthy purpose. It did serve a lofty and worthy purpose in the life of Job. And I'm sure that Ruth did not realize the significance of the decision she was making. She just went in, and I think she prayed and had a reasonable basis for it. For the child of God today who is frustrated because he's looking for some sign, some experience, some light, some voice, some vision, some dream, he must realize that God is not speaking to us in that way today. God today is speaking to us through His Word. And the child of God who walks in fellowship with God, with no unconfessed sin in his life, and has not grieved the Holy Spirit, can commit his life to God. And when he gets to a place where he isn't clear just what God's will is for him, he can make a decision and move into the situation. Now maybe he makes a wrong decision, but God has permitted it for a purpose. As I look back on my life, there is one instance where I expected God to open up a door for me, and He didn't open up that door. In fact He slammed the door, as it were, in my face, and I felt very bad about it. But I thank God that He did it, because now I can look back and see that it was best. It's like what Joseph said to his brethren when they came to him after the death of old Jacob, their father. He said in Genesis 50:20, "But as for you, ye thought evil against me; but God meant it unto good." How wonderful that is, and may it be an encouragement to you today. Perhaps you are actually biting your fingernails and are wondering why you don't get clear leading. You know Christians who act like they have a hotline to heaven. Now it's wonderful that all of us have access to God, but I'm not sure that He always talks right back to us. So let's be very careful today about the way we banter about the statement, "I know this is the Lord's will." We just can't always be sure. But we can commit our way to Him, have no unconfessed sin in our lives, not grieve the Holy Spirit, and be in the center of the Lord's will as best we know. Yes, my friend, you can commit yourself to Him in a wonderful way. And even if you got into the same predicament that Joseph did, or even that Job did, say with him, "Though he slay me, yet will I trust in him" (Job 13:15). My friend, that's the glorious truth that brings a joy and an expectancy to life. The providence of God makes every day a thrill for the child of God. I'm glad that He didn't give me a blueprint because, frankly, I like to take a trip over a new road, going into an area I've never been before. I did that one autumn when we were in the Ozarks. My, how that road twisted and turned. And every twist and turn was a thrill—the autumn leaves were a riot of color. Nature seemed lavish, covering every hillside with polychrome pictures. And I'm so glad that God didn't send me pictures of it all ahead of time. What a thrill life can become for us!

And, behold, Boaz came from Bethlehem, and said unto the reapers, The Lord be with you. And they answered him, The Lord bless thee [Ruth 2:4].

Now for some unexplained reason, Boaz was detained from getting to his fields early in the morning. He was a prosperous man, and maybe he didn't have to be there early. But I judge by the character of the man that he was on top of every situation, and he probably had business that morning in Bethlehem. Perhaps he had to wait until the First National Bank of Bethlehem opened so he could get the payroll for his workers. But whatever the reason may have been, he didn't get out into his field until a little later.

Notice what he did when he got out there. He said to the reapers, "The Lord be with you." That's capital speaking. And they responded, "The Lord bless thee," and that's labor answering. Say, that doesn't sound like some of the labor leaders and capitalists of our day, does it? It doesn't sound like the steel workers or the steel owners either. Unfortunately, capital and labor both are very far from God today. Now, frankly, I am a poor preacher, and I'm not a capitalist. My dad was a working man. I remember him in overalls most of the time because he was a hard worker. I just can't sanction godless capitalism today. From listening to them, I get the impression that most of the labor leaders are very godless. I don't take sides today. I just wish that we could get something of real Christianity, the real born-again type, into this area. It would certainly help the relationship. You'd hear language like this. Capital: "The Lord be with you." And then labor answering: "The Lord bless thee." My, what a marvelous capital/labor relationship existed there in the fields of Boaz!

Then said Boaz unto his servant that was set over the reapers, Whose damsel is this? [Ruth 2:5].

Now we have really come to the part of our story that is exciting. This little foreign girl by the name of Ruth, willing to accept poverty and ostracism and perpetual widowhood, is out in the field gleaning. By chance, she has gone into the fields of Boaz, the most acceptable bachelor in Bethlehem. I suppose that the mothers of marriageable daughters in Bethlehem had given many a tea or invited him over for a meal. They say the way to a man's heart is through his stomach, and I imagine many had tried that route. But somehow or other he hadn't been interested in the local girls. But then one day he goes into his fields and he sees for the first time this little widow from Moab. And I tell you, he falls for her! Now our King James translation here is rather stilted. Don't misunderstand me—I still feel that the King James translation is our best for public use. Although the American Standard Version of 1901 is probably more accurate, it's very hard to improve on this King James. But there are places where I think we can bring it up to date, and this is such a place. What Boaz said here is not quite, "Whose damsel is this?" May I just give you several very free translations? He says, "Well, where in the world has she been that I haven't met her before?" That's very free, as you can see. Or let me give it another way. Perhaps as accurate Hebrew as you can possibly get, could not be translated, but would sound like a Hebrew wolf whistle. He fell for this girl. This is love at first sight.

And maybe you're wondering if I believe in love at first sight. May I say to you, I believe in it very strongly. I proposed to my wife on the second date we had. The reason I didn't propose to her on the first date was because I didn't want her to think I was in any hurry. Now don't get any ideas if you're a young person. It was a year before we got married. We wanted to make sure. Yes, I believe in love at first sight, but I think love ought to be tested by quite a bit of time before marriage takes place.

Boaz had a case of love at first sight. This man really fell for Ruth, and this is romance in the fields of Boaz if you please.

And the servant that was set over the reapers answered and said, It is the Moabitish damsel that came back with Naomi out of the country of Moab [Ruth 2:6].

His foreman tells Boaz who she is and implies, "Why, you certainly wouldn't want to know her. She just came in the fields here." And I think he's halfway apologizing and assuring Boaz that he had nothing to do with her coming into the field. He explains:

And she said, I pray you, let me glean and gather after the reapers among the sheaves: so she came, and hath continued even from the morning until now, that she tarried a little in the house [Ruth 2:7].

Although it's very clear to us that Boaz has fallen for this little foreign girl, his superintendent didn't see that at first, and he seems quite apologetic. "This Moabitish woman came out here and asked to glean, and I couldn't turn her down. After all, the Mosaic system permits her to come in here and glean since she's poor and a stranger." But he didn't need to be apologetic, because Boaz has fallen in love with this girl. And this reveals a great deal about Ruth, of course. It reveals that she certainly lived up to her name. As you'll remember, we did not attempt to translate Ruth into any English word because I do not think there is any one word that will quite describe her. *Ruth* means "beauty, personality," and we suggested the word *glamour*, but that word has been absolutely ruined by Hollywood and by cheap literature today so that I just don't know what word to use. But this scene reveals something of the attractiveness of this woman. What all the other girls and beauties of Bethlehem had not been able to accomplish, this girl did—and she didn't even try at all. She had already taken her position as an outcast, and she did not expect any attention at all. You'll notice her surprise when she finds out that she has attracted the attention of this man.

Now after his superintendent has apologetically given him the information he wanted, notice the reaction of Boaz. He turns and addresses Ruth.

Then said Boaz unto Ruth, Hearest thou not, my daughter? Go not to glean in another field, neither go from hence, but abide here fast by my maidens [Ruth 2:8].

Now let me pause and say that this is strange language. Here is a man that honestly would not want the poor in his fields. The Mosaic Law said he had to permit it. And I think Boaz was generous, but he just didn't put up a sign and say to the poor, "Come in and glean." And he didn't invite them in. But here is an occasion when he goes out of his way to urge Ruth not to go into any other field to glean. "I want you to glean in my field." Well now, is he interested or *is* he interested? Also, he adds,

Let thine eyes be on the field that they do reap, and go thou after them: have I not charged the young men that they shall not touch thee? and when thou art athirst, go unto the vessels, and drink of that which the young men have drawn [Ruth 2:9].

There are two things here that are very important. He not only invites her to stay in the field, but he also puts around her his cloak of protection. He says, "I have now given orders that you can come into this field, and that you will not be hurt or harmed in any way." Frankly, in that day it was very dangerous for a woman in Ruth's position—a widow, a woman from Moab. She was likely to have insult upon insult heaped upon her. And not only that but she would not be safe. And Boaz, recognizing that, immediately puts his cloak of protection around her.

It was almost as unsafe on the roads of Bethlehem in that day as it would be today on the streets of our modern cities. One of my missionary friends from Africa put it like this, "It is safer on the jungle trail in Africa, where I minister, than it is on the streets of Los Angeles." Now that's what civilization has risen to, and especially this new civilization with its liberal approach to crime. It's the cry-baby type that says that the poor criminal is to be brought back into society and is to be reclaimed. May I say to you, the whole point (and we need to get back to it) is to punish the criminal. That was the purpose of putting one into prison. It wasn't intended to do anything else but to punish him. And how much reclaiming are they doing today? May I say to you, that type of thinking is almost a farce today. God knows this because He knows the human family, and He knows you and me. He knows that you and I today have an old nature, and until you and I come to Jesus Christ, we can't be reclaimed, my friend.

Now will you notice Ruth's reaction to this very noble and generous gesture on the part of Boaz.

Then she fell on her face, and bowed herself to the ground, and said unto him, Why have I found grace in thine eyes, that thou shouldest take knowledge of me, seeing I am a stranger? [Ruth 2:10].

When I first wrote my book, *Ruth, the Romance of Redemption,* I assumed and took the position that here Ruth was actually being either naive or a coquette, that she was playing it rather cleverly by asking, "Why have I found grace in thine eyes, that thou shouldest take knowledge of me, seeing I am a stranger?" Now, frankly, I can't hold that position any longer. She is not being that at all. You see, she had been properly warned and made aware of her situation if she returned to Bethlehem with Naomi. And that's the reason the other woman of Moab, Orpah, didn't come. Orpah just wouldn't make the sacrifice. She was not willing to be a perpetual widow and be poverty-stricken the rest of her life, and be ostracized besides. Therefore, she remained in the land of Moab. But Ruth came, realizing all of that. When she went out into the fields of Boaz, she never dreamed that anyone would ever take any notice of her. In fact, she expected that they would all turn their backs upon her, because the Jews at this time didn't have dealings with the Moabites. As we'll see later on, even the Mosaic Law shut a Moabite out from the congregation of the Lord. The Moabites had a very bad beginning that's not very pretty to recount. And for that reason they are given this very low position. But this little Book of Ruth reveals something that is quite interesting: racial barriers *were* broken down, and God is concerned and loves even those who have upon them a stigma and a judgment.

Such is the picture of you and me today. ". . . While we were yet sinners, Christ died for us" (Rom. 5:8). And Paul says you just don't find love like that in this world today. Only God has a real concern for people. You just don't find love anywhere else like the love God shows for sinners. But here is an exhibition of it, and that's the reason Ruth says, "Why have I found grace in thine eyes?" She's absolutely startled. She's a stranger, an outcast. And I think it's an honest, sincere question she's raising. She can't understand this breaking over of a racial barrier. Here is an interest that she did not expect.

Now I can answer Ruth's question very easily. If she would just go home and look in a mirror, she'd see the reason. She's beautiful. She's lovely. She's attractive. She has everything that is desirable in a woman and a wife, and for that reason this man has fallen in love with her. I can answer her question.

But there is a question I cannot answer: Why have I found grace in the eyes of God? Now don't tell me to go home and look in the mirror, because I've done that. Frankly, friend, the image is something that's not quite attractive. I don't see the answer in the mirror. But God has extended grace toward us. And there are those who consider the theme of the Book of Ruth to be just that. The grace of God is exhibited here in the grace that was manifested to this woman. And I must concur to the extent that this is certainly a marvelous example of grace. You and I both can ask Ruth's question as we come to God: Why have I found grace in Thine eyes? We cannot find the answer within ourselves; we're not lovely; we're not beautiful to Him; we are not attractive; we do not have those qualities that God adores and that He rewards and respects. We're sinners, and we're in rebellion against God. And yet, in spite of all that, God loves us! That is one of the great truths of the Word of God. He *demonstrated* that love, because "while we were yet sinners, Christ died for us." He extended His grace to us. And, friend, that's the basis upon which He saves us today. He hasn't any other reason for saving us.

And Boaz answered and said unto her, It hath fully been shewed me, all that thou hast done unto thy mother in law since the death of thine husband: and how thou hast left thy father and thy mother, and the land of thy nativity, and art come unto a people which thou knewest not heretofore [Ruth 2:11].

Probably the reason Boaz had not met Ruth when she accompanied Naomi back to the land, was that he was away on one of those innumerable campaigns that were carried on during the times of the judges. You'll recall that Boaz could be described not only as a mighty man of wealth but also as a mighty man of the Law and a mighty man of war. Undoubtedly he was a soldier. So he evidently was out of town and, when he returned, he heard this buzzing about a widow who had come back with Naomi.

The things they were saying about her were quite good. Now Bethlehem was evidently given over to gossip, as most places are, and they were gossiping about this foreign girl, but what they were saying was good, which was unusual. They were amazed at her. They said, "Imagine! This little foreign girl has come back, and she's true to her mother-in-law. She didn't desert her when she got here. She doesn't chase around after the men, and she is a wonderful person." Boaz just couldn't believe that in addition to all he had heard about her character she was as attractive as she was. But now when he sees her and finds out that all of these qualities are wrapped up in one person, I'll tell you, that's the reason that he has fallen for her. Just listen to him as he realizes the tremendous sacrifice she has made.

The LORD recompense thy work, and a full reward be given thee of the LORD God of Israel, under whose wings thou art come to trust [Ruth 2:12].

She had come to trust the Lord God. This is the reason she had left the land of Moab and made that radical decision. She had said that the God of Naomi would be her God. She had turned from idolatry to the living and true God. This woman has come to trust God; she was one of His children. Therefore this is the wonderful testimony that she had there in the land of Israel. And Boaz says, "May a full reward be given to you. May you be recompensed for this decision." And if Boaz has anything to do with it, he's going to see that she gets a full reward, and he begins immediately to work toward that end. He's in love with her, friend, and he is going to redeem her. She needs to be redeemed.

Then she said, Let me find favour in thy sight, my lord; for that thou hast comforted me, and for that thou hast spoken friendly unto thine handmaid, though I be not like unto one of thine handmaidens [Ruth 2:13].

Ruth's reaction here is interesting. She hadn't expected any comfort. She hadn't expected to to spoken to in a friendly manner. And the reason she didn't expect any of this was that she was not like one of his handmaidens. And that was probably the reason he *did* notice her—she wasn't like the other girls. You know, today we're living in a society that talks a great deal about being an individual and having your own thoughts. Some time ago I had a bull session with a group of college students. They wanted to have it, and I met with them. That's the age when tremendous things are taking place in their own hearts. They are in rebellion because they're pulling loose from old ties. God made us that way purposely, by the way, but we won't go into that. These young people were talking about being individuals, making their own decisions, and being different. And do you know what? Every one of them looked alike. They wore their hair alike, they wore the same type of clothing, and they expressed themselves in the same way. I couldn't help but just sit there and laugh. They wondered why I was enjoying it so. It's interesting to hear people talk about how they want to be different, and yet they want to be exactly like the crowd. But, you see, Ruth was different. And that's the reason Boaz had fallen in love with her. Some of us should want to be a little different —not necessarily in dress—but we need to be different in other ways. If you're a child of God you *are* different. Talk about doing your own thinking—it's the child of God who thinks differently from the crowd. He has to. Christians are a minority group.

But now let's look in on Boaz and Ruth again. My, he has invited her to lunch! Can you imagine that? We think of those days as being more or less uncivilized. They were not in the jet set back in that day. But he meets her about ten o'clock in the morning, invites her to lunch, and she has lunch with him the same day. My friend, you can't improve on that, can you, even in our day?

And Boaz said unto her, At mealtime come thou hither, and eat of the bread, and dip thy morsel in the vinegar. And she sat beside the reapers: and he reached her parched corn, and she did eat, and was sufficed, and left [Ruth 2:14].

I want to ask again: Is Boaz interested in her? My, I'll tell you, he has fallen in love with this girl, and he'll make every effort now to make her his wife. We'll find that there was a big hurdle in the way.

And when she was risen up to glean, Boaz commanded his young men, say-

ing, Let her glean even among the sheaves, and reproach her not:

And let fall also some of the handfuls of purpose for her, and leave them, that she may glean them, and rebuke her not [Ruth 2:15–16].

He even says to his workmen, "I want you to show her every courtesy and consideration. Now you let her glean even among the sheaves." You know, the poor would be very apt to try to get up to where the grain was good, and you can well understand that the owner of the field would have to keep them behind his reapers. But Boaz said, "You let her come up and glean right where you're reaping." And Boaz was a man of the Law. Because he knew what it said, he instructed his men not to go back and pick up a sheaf if they happened to drop one. Now he's even going one step further. He says, "When you see that Ruth is gleaning immediately behind you, when nobody is looking, you just drop a sheaf back there and go on. When she gets up to it, she'll call. 'Yoo-hoo, you dropped a sheaf.' You just tell her you're sorry but you can't go back and get it, and for her to keep it."

So she gleaned in the field until even, and beat out that she had gleaned: and it was about an ephah of barley [Ruth 2:17].

An ephah was a bushel. The value of it would be a pretty good day's wage, especially for this little widow.

And she took it up, and went into the city: and her mother in law saw what she had gleaned: and she brought forth, and gave to her that she had reserved after she was sufficed.

And her mother in law said unto her, Where hast thou gleaned to-day? and where wroughtest thou? blessed be he that did take knowledge of thee. And she shewed her mother in law with whom she had wrought, and said, The man's name with whom I wrought to-day is Boaz [Ruth 2:18–19].

When Ruth brought in this tremendous amount of grain, Naomi said, "My, I've never seen anything quite like this! Where have you been today? Somebody has shown undue consideration for you." And so Ruth just tells the whole story to Naomi. And up to this point, actually, Ruth still doesn't know exactly who Boaz is, but Naomi does.

And Naomi said unto her daughter in law, Blessed be he of the LORD, who hath not left off his kindness to the living and to the dead. And Naomi said unto her, The man is near of kin unto us, one of our next kinsmen [Ruth 2:20].

The Hebrew *goel*, or "kinsman-redeemer," is the second law that is so strange to us because we do not have anything that corresponds to it. But it was God's provision for taking care of His people. You see, God gave the Law for a land and for a people. The Mosaic system was a marvelous system for that day and for that land.

Ruth certainly went into the right field, for this man was a near kinsman. And here in the Book of Ruth we see the law of the kinsman-redeemer in operation. Now you do not always see the Mosaic system in operation in Israel, but this little book highlights for us the law of the kinsman-redeemer, as well as the other two laws which we've mentioned that are very strange to us. One of them is the basis on which God took care of the poor. It was an unusual way. God would permit them to go into the fields and the vineyards and glean after the owner had sent his reapers and gatherers through one time. It was a marvelous way because a great deal was left. I had the privilege several years ago of holding meetings up in Turlock, California, right after the grape gathering had taken place. The owner of a very large vineyard found out that I liked grapes, and he told me just to go out into his vineyard and help myself; so the pastor and I went out there. He told us they had already gathered the grapes, and that we were welcome to whatever was left. Friends, if I'd had a ten-ton truck, I'm sure I could have filled it up with the grapes that were left there! We would look up under the vine and, my, some of the biggest, finest-looking, luscious bunches could be found. I told the pastor, "You and I are gleaning, and I think we fulfill our rightful place because we're poor preachers, and we're exercising that which is part of the Mosaic system." God's way of taking care of the poor preserved their dignity by giving them an opportunity to work for what they received.

Now here in our story of Ruth we encounter the law of the kinsman-redeemer. It is stated for us in Leviticus 25, and it actually operates in three different areas. It operates in relation to the land and in relation to individuals and in relation to widows.

Now Boaz was related to Naomi's husband, this man whose name was Elimelech (which means, "My God is King"). I take it that Elimelech's and Boaz's fathers were brothers, which made them cousins, and therefore we could also say that Boaz was cousin to Ruth's first husband. So Naomi tells Ruth that Boaz is one of their next kinsmen.

Now there's an emphasis upon this Hebrew *goel*. What does that mean? Well, let's look at this law in relationship to the land. "The land shall not be sold for ever: for the land is mine; for ye are strangers and sojourners with me. And in all the land of your possession ye shall grant a redemption for the land" (Lev. 25:23–24). Now how would God do this? "If thy brother be waxen poor, and hath sold away some of his possession, and if any of his kin come to redeem it, then shall he redeem that which his brother sold" (Lev. 25:25). This is the law of the kinsman-redeemer in relationship to land. Now let's see that in operation. When these people came into the land, God gave them the Promised Land; it was theirs. But they occupied it only as they were faithful to God. When they were unfaithful, God put them out of the land. He said, "The land is Mine, but I give it to you as a permanent, perpetual possession." He gave them title to it, and they still have title to it, by the way. God put them in the land according to tribes. A certain tribe had a certain section of the land. You may have maps in the back of your Bible, which show the division of the land among the tribes of Israel. And each family within each tribe had a particular plot of land. He could never leave it. But suppose he becomes poor. Perhaps he's had two or three years of crop failure. (Famine did come, because of their unfaithfulness to God.) And a man has to get rid of his land. Now he has a rich neighbor who sees the opportunity to take a mortgage. Well, all he can take is up to a fifty-year mortgage, because in the Year of Jubilee every mortgage is cancelled, and the land returns to its original owner. This law kept the land in a family. But it's a long way between jubilees. A man may be middle-aged at one jubilee, and in another fifty years he'll be gone. So if he had sold his property he would not get it back in his lifetime, but his son would get it. Now suppose he has a rich relative, a cousin for example, and that rich cousin is moved toward him, and wants to help him. Well, that rich cousin can come right in and pay the mortgage off, and restore it to the owner even before the Year of Jubilee. And I assume that in the Year of Jubilee whoever did the redeeming was also remunerated for whatever he'd put into the land. That was God's method. It would be wonderful to have a rich uncle, wouldn't it? It'd be wonderful to have that kind of a redeemer.

Now this applied not only to property but also to persons. "And if a sojourner or stranger wax rich by thee, and thy brother that dwelleth by him wax poor, and sell himself unto the stranger or sojourner by thee, or to the stock of the stranger's family: After that he is sold he may be redeemed again; one of this brethren may redeem him" (Lev. 25:47–48). Now a man may have been in very unfortunate circumstances. He not only lost his property, but perhaps due to drought and famine in the land, his children are hungry and he sells himself into slavery in order to feed his family. This poor fellow will be in slavery until the Year of Jubilee. If that year is forty-nine years away, that's going to be a long time to be in slavery. He may live and die in slavery. But suppose again that he has a rich relative, and one day he sees that rich uncle coming down the road, taking his checkbook out of his pocket. He says, "Look, I don't want my nephew to be in slavery," and he pays off the price of this man's slavery. He has redeemed him, you see, and the man can go free.

The kinsman-redeemer is a picture of the Lord Jesus Christ. He is our Kinsman-Redeemer. And that's the reason the word *redemption* is used in the New Testament rather than *atonement*. Atonement covered up sins, that's all. But redemption, friend, means to pay a price so that the one who is redeemed may go scot-free. Now Christ not only died to redeem our persons, He died also to redeem this earth. You and I live on an earth that someday is going to be delivered from the bondage of corruption, and there'll be a new heaven and a new earth. That is part of His redemption.

The only biblical example of a kinsman-redeemer is that of Boaz, which is the reason I wrote on the Book of Ruth. It reveals the love side of redemption. Here is a man who is a kinsman-redeemer, but he doesn't have to act in that capacity. We'll find out there's another kinsman who was actually a nearer relative than Boaz, and he had the opportunity to take action, but he turned it down. He did not care for Ruth but, you see, Boaz loved her. That made the difference. Now God didn't have to redeem us. We were lost *sinners*. If He did not redeem us, He could still be a just and holy God. But He loved us. You see, salvation by redemption is a love story. And now we have it told here in simple language illustrated by this little foreign girl from Moab and Boaz in the land of Israel.

And Ruth the Moabitess said, He said unto me also, Thou shalt keep fast by my young men, until they have ended all my harvest.

And Naomi said unto Ruth her daughter in law, It is good, my daughter, that thou go out with his maidens, that they meet thee not in any other field.

So she kept fast by the maidens of Boaz to glean unto the end of barley harvest and of wheat harvest; and dwelt with her mother in law [Ruth 2:21–23].

That took about six weeks. For six weeks, every afternoon, you'd see coming into Bethlehem—not wise men, not yet; not shepherds, not yet; not Joseph and Mary yet—Boaz and Ruth. Boaz is in love with Ruth. I think he looked like a dying calf in a thunderstorm. And the little town of Bethlehem is gossiping, good gossip, "Our most eligible bachelor has fallen." And I'm sure that Naomi with whom Ruth lived could look out the window and see them coming in every afternoon. She knows something needs to be done about this, because actually Ruth is in a most unique position. Boaz is in love with her, and he wants to redeem her.

It's wonderful to have a Savior who loves us, who came to this earth in order that He might redeem us.

CHAPTER 3

***THEME:** On the threshing floor of Boaz*

In this chapter we're on the threshing floor of Boaz. It's obvious that Ruth was not claiming what she had a right to, and so Naomi takes over. As we shall see, she is a regular matchmaker. Ruth stands in a most unusual position. And to understand what is taking place in this chapter, it's necessary, I think, to understand the third of the Mosaic laws that we encounter here—which is so strange to us. We have seen two of them already, and now we're introduced to the third. Also we must understand the threshing floor of that day and the significance of it. To understand that is essential.

Now if you think the laws we've looked at so far were unusual, you just look at this one: "If brethren dwell together, and one of them die, and have no child, the wife of the dead shall not marry without unto a stranger: her husband's brother shall go in unto her, and take her to him to wife, and perform the duty of an husband's brother unto her. And it shall be, that the firstborn which she beareth shall succeed in the name of his brother which is dead, that his name be not put out of Israel. And if the man like not to take his brother's wife, then let his brother's wife go up to the gate unto the elders, and say, My husband's brother refuseth to raise up unto his brother a name in Israel, he will not perform the duty of my husband's brother. Then the elders of his city shall call him, and speak unto him: and if he stand to it, and say, I like not to take her; Then shall his brother's wife come unto him in the presence of the elders, and loose his shoe from off his foot, and spit in his face, and shall answer and say, So shall it be done unto that man that will not build up his brother's house" (Deut. 25:5–9). Now I think you'll agree, friend, that this is an unusual law! As far as I know, the little Book of Ruth gives the only illustration of it in Scripture, but it must have been enforced many times because it was put in force when a man died childless.

Now here's the situation. Suppose there is a man living in the hill country of Ephraim, known today as Samaria. Suppose he has several sons. One evening one of the boys gets down the lantern, polishes it up, trims the wick, and that night when it gets dark he lights the lantern, and he starts down the road whistling. One of the brothers says to the others, "I wonder where in the world he's going." The others say they don't know. So late that night they hear him coming down the road whistling again. He comes in, and he doesn't say anything. They don't ask anything, but they're wondering. The second night he does the same thing and, believe me, they're curious by now. So they make a few inquiries the next day. The third night when the boy takes off and then returns, his brothers are waiting for him. They say to him, "Where have you been?" "Oh," he says, "I've been down the road." And they say, "We understand that there's a new neighbor moved in down there." He says, "Yes, there is." And one of the brothers says to him, "We understand that they have a daughter." And he says, "Yes." They ask, "Is it true that you've been down there to see her?" And he says, "Well, I've been trying to put the good neighbor policy into practice so I've been down there visiting them, yes." Well, they say, "We'd like to ask specifically, have you been to see the girl?" So he says, "Well, to answer specifically, I have." Then they say, "We want to be personal. Are you interested?" And he says, "Yes, I am, to be very honest." And they say, "Well, we've taken a good look at the girl, and we don't like her. We feel like we ought to have a family huddle because if anything happens to you, it means that one of us will have to marry the girl." According to the Mosaic Law she could claim one of them, you see, if she'd had no children. That was the provision. And the boy says, "Well, I'm going to marry her because I asked her tonight to marry me and she has agreed to it." "Well," they say, "we feel like you ought to go through the clinic. We hope you're healthy, because we're just not going to marry her. We're not interested in her." Now suppose this boy goes ahead and marries the girl, then he takes sick and dies, or he's gored by a boar, or a tree falls on him, or he drowns in the Jordan River, or he's killed in battle. What about that? Well, she is a widow now, and she can go immediately and claim one of these brothers. And, believe me, he's going to have difficulty turning her down. Now suppose he just stands to it and says, "I warned my brother. I told him not to marry this girl, and I just don't want to marry her." Then she can bring him into court. If he refuses to take her to wife even in court, she can step up to him, take off his shoe, and spit in his face! Friends, that meant he was disgraced, and a man is not apt to go that far.

So you can see, here is an unusual law which puts a childless widow in a most unique position. It changes her position altogether. She now can claim one of the brothers. In fact, that's her duty to her dead husband. Well, frankly, I can well understand that this is something that tied the families together in that day. It made every member of the family interested in who brother Isaac was going out to see since the other brothers were always involved in a situation like that.

This law was God's provision. And there were two objectives He had in mind that are obvious here, and there may be others. The first is that He wanted to protect womanhood. You can understand that if her husband died and left her with a farm and a vineyard and a flock of sheep, she would have difficulty. So she could claim immediately a brother or the nearest kinsman, and he'd have to make this decision. The Law was to protect womanhood. Now I've heard the criticism made that the Bible is a man's book. Well, my friend, when anybody makes that statement, it is evident he hasn't read the Book very carefully. Sometimes you wonder if the man has a chance—he doesn't have a chance here, that's for sure.

Now the second reason for this law is that God wanted to protect land rights. God not only gave to the nation Israel the land of Palestine, He not only gave to each tribe a particular section of that land, but He also gave to each individual family a particular parcel of land. Each family had their own land. As we have seen, a family could lose their land. But in the Year of Jubilee it would automatically return to the original owner. However, a widow might go out and marry some stranger who would gain ownership to the property. And so, you see, God protected that property. The nearest of kin had to be the one to marry her in order to make it possible to retain the title of the property in the nation and in the tribe and in the family. Now it seems to us like a very strange law, but apparently it was one that worked in the land of Israel.

In the case of Ruth, she's a widow without any children, and the property which belonged to her husband has been lost because she and Naomi are poverty-stricken. She has a perfect right to claim Boaz since he is a near kinsman. And as Naomi has already indicated, he is a kinsman-redeemer. The fact of the matter is, this man Boaz is sweating it out. His hands are tied. He cannot claim her for his wife. It's Ruth's move. She has to claim him as her husband. A little later on we'll find out that there happens to be another kinsman who is actually nearer than Boaz, and Ruth could claim *him* if she wanted to. Boaz doesn't know which one she'll claim. Therefore, Boaz must wait until Ruth makes the move. Because Ruth is not making the move, Naomi takes charge and tells Ruth, "You've got to let this man know that you want him as a kinsman-redeemer."

Now we're going to see a very strange

procedure. In order to understand it, it is necessary to understand the threshing floor of that day. You see, God made a wonderful provision for these people. Since they were an agricultural people, a great many of the laws pertain to agriculture. The Mosaic system was not only for the people of Israel, but also it was for that land. It was adapted in a very particular and peculiar way to the land which we know as Palestine. Therefore, we find here a law that relates to the threshing floor and the practices of the day. Customarily a threshing floor was located on top of a hill to catch any wind that was blowing in order to blow away the chaff. It was in the opposite position from a winepress which was located at the bottom of a hill, because it was easier to carry the grapes downhill than to lug them uphill. The winepress, you'll remember, was the place where Gideon was, as he was threshing grain. The reason he was down there threshing was because he was hiding it from the Midianites who had impoverished Israel. The angel of the Lord appeared to him—don't tell me God doesn't have a sense of humor—and addressed him, "Thou mighty man of valour" (Jud. 6:12). And there's Gideon down at the winepress, scared to death, when he should be up on top of the hill. You can imagine his frustration as he pitches that grain up into the air, and with no wind blowing down there at the bottom of the hill, the chaff and grain come back down around his neck. I think he was very discouraged. Then when the angel of the Lord appeared to him and said, "Thou mighty man of valour," I think Gideon looked around to see to whom He was talking. When he didn't see anybody else he turned to the angel of the Lord and said, "Who? Me? You don't mean to tell me that you think that I'm a mighty man of valour. I'm one of the biggest cowards you've ever seen." Friend, that's what he was. But thank God, He can use a coward who is dedicated to Him. And when this man was dedicated to the Lord, he could overcome the Midianites with only three hundred men. What an encouragement that ought to be to many of us today. Although the story of Ruth also takes place during the era of the judges, apparently it was at a time when Israel had returned to the Lord. Remember that while Naomi was still in Moab, she had heard that the famine (which was God's judgment) was over. Israel had probably returned to an era of tranquility, and the threshing floor was in its proper place at the top of a hill.

But now let's look at the threshing floor. The clay soil was packed to a hard smooth surface, and ordinarily it was circular with rocks placed around it. When I was in that land, I saw several places, especially in Samaria, where they had these threshing floors. The people were cutting the grain, not threshing it, when we were there in the spring; so we didn't see the threshing floor in operation. But there it was on top of a hill. They still do it the same way. After the grain was all cut, it was taken to the threshing floor. In the late afternoon a breeze would come up. It would blow until sundown and sometimes until midnight. Now as long as the breeze would blow they would thresh. Sheaves of grain were spread on the floor and trampled by oxen drawing a sled. Then the people took a flail and threw the grain up into the air so that the chaff would be blown away and the good grain would come down on the threshing floor. As long as the wind would blow, they would be there on the threshing floor. When the wind died down—whether it be at sundown, nine o'clock, midnight, or whatever time it was—they held a great religious feast. And at this season of the year all the families came up and camped around the threshing floor, which meant there were many people present. After the feast was over, the men would sleep around the grain. Since the threshing floor was circular, they would put their heads toward the grain and their feet would stick out like spokes. They slept that way to protect the grain from marauders or thieves who might break through and steal.

It was a time of feasting and thanking God for an abundant harvest. Several of the feast days of Israel—the feast of firstfruits and even Pentecost—were identified with that threshing floor. They would sing psalms praising God for a bountiful harvest. You can imagine them up there on that hill at night, looking out into the heavens and singing many of the psalms. When reading the psalms, note in particular how many of them deal with this particular religious feast.

With an understanding of the law of the kinsman-redeemer as it applied to the widow, and with the scene of the threshing floor in mind, let us move on.

> **Then Naomi her mother in law said unto her, My daughter, shall I not seek rest for thee, that it may be well with thee? [Ruth 3:1].**

All during the harvest season Naomi had been watching out the window each afternoon and had seen Ruth and Boaz coming into Bethlehem. It had been about six weeks. Now the barley was gathered, and the wheat was gathered. Naomi notices that Ruth is very modest and is not making any claim upon this man at all. She also notices the obvious, that he is in love with her. And so Naomi asks Ruth if she should seek rest for her. And the rest, of course, is marriage. "Shall I seek a marriage for you?" You remember that at the very beginning she urged each of her daughters-in-law to stay in the land of Moab and find rest in her husband's house. So now she says she will seek rest for Ruth.

And now is not Boaz of our kindred, with whose maidens thou wast? Behold, he winnoweth barley to night in the threshingfloor [Ruth 3:2].

She says, "This man Boaz is your kinsman-redeemer. You have a right to claim him. In fact, Ruth, you must claim him as your kinsman-redeemer. I want you to go up to the threshing floor tonight and let him know."

Wash thy self therefore, and anoint thee, and put thy raiment upon thee, and get thee down to the floor: but make not thyself known unto the man, until he shall have done eating and drinking [Ruth 3:3].

She tells Ruth to wait until the religious feast is over. Naomi says, "Now, Ruth, it's up to you to claim this man as your kinsman-redeemer." Ruth has been doing nothing in the way of claiming him, so Naomi is going to give her some very definite instructions. She tells her to do four things. I have felt that here is a picture of the sinner who comes to Jesus Christ. These are four steps that are essential for the sinner. The first one is this: Wash thyself. If you and I are going to come to Christ, we're told that it's "not by works of righteousness which we have done, but according to his mercy he saved us, by the washing of regeneration, and renewing of the Holy Ghost" (Titus 3:5). That's the reason our Lord said what He did to Nicodemus. "You may think you're a fine, religious man, and you are, but you need a bath—a spiritual bath. You need the washing of regeneration." And our Lord said to Nicodemus, ". . . Ye must be born again" (John 3:7). And, friend, if you are ever going to be fit for heaven, you must be born again. You must experience the new birth. Someone asked John Wesley why it was that he always preached on "ye must be born again" (for that was his favorite text). "Well," he said, "I'll tell you. The reason that I preach on 'ye must be born again' is because ye must be born again." You cannot get into heaven, friend, you cannot be saved until you have become a new creature in Christ Jesus. You and I are not fit for heaven until we have been born again, regenerated by the Holy Spirit. So Naomi tells Ruth, "You've been working hard out in the field. Wash thyself therefore." Now that's the first step that she is to take.

Now the second thing that Naomi tells Ruth to do is to anoint herself. After Ruth's first husband died, I suppose she put on widow's weeds and made no attempt to make herself attractive. But now Naomi realizes somebody is interested in Ruth, and so she tells her to get out that little bottle of perfume that she'd packed away and to use it generously. I can even suggest to you the name of the perfume that she used—"Midnight in Moab." And I want to tell you, that was an exotic perfume! And so Naomi says, "Anoint thee."

Now that corresponds also to our Christian experience. When you and I become children of God, we are babes, I grant that. But also we are brought to a full-grown status where we can understand divine truth. And there is something said to the believer about the anointing that he has. You and I have an anointing of the Holy Spirit. John tells us in 1 John 2:20, "But ye have an unction [anointing] from the Holy One, and ye know all things." That is, the Spirit of God is the one who can teach us all truth, and all of us need the teaching of the Spirit of God. That's the only way in the world we can ever understand the Word of God, friend. The Spirit of God must teach us. And that's one of the neglected facts today. Right now in theological circles they are fighting like mad over the doctrine of inspiration. Now knowing that the Bible is inspired of God is very important. But you can believe in the plenary, verbal inspiration of the Scripture and still be ignorant of the Word of God. Why? You must recognize that you cannot bring to this Book human intellect alone and expect to understand it. You may understand facts; you may learn certain intellectual things; but only the Spirit of God can teach you spiritual things. Paul says in 1 Corinthians 2:9–10, "But as it is written, Eye hath not seen, nor ear heard, neither have entered into the heart of man, the things which God hath prepared for them that love him. But God hath revealed them unto us by his Spirit. . . ." The Spirit of God is able to teach us and is able to lead us and guide us into all truth. How important it is to have the Spirit of God as our teacher. "But God hath revealed them unto us by his Spirit: for the Spirit searcheth all things, yea, the deep things of God." We need to recognize that when we are born again we are given an anointing of the Spirit of God. It's mentioned again in 1 John 2:27. "But the anointing which ye have received of him abideth in you, and ye need not that any man teach you: but as the same anointing teacheth you of all things, and is truth, and is no lie, and even as it hath taught you, ye shall abide in him." This doesn't mean that you dispense with human learning or human teachers. You and I today are the beneficiaries of that which has been bequeathed to us by the godly men of the past whom the Spirit of God has taught. And God gives teachers to the church today. But not even the teachers nor all the wealth of material from the past can enlighten you unless the Spirit of God is your teacher. And so Ruth's second step was important. She was to wash herself and then to *anoint* herself.

Then the third thing: "Put thy raiment upon thee." And I think Naomi said to her, "Ruth, remember that little party dress that you used to wear when you and my son would go out together? You looked so pretty in it. And if Boaz fell in love with you when you were wearing those black, ugly widow's weeds, say, what'll he think when he sees you in this little party dress? So you put on that dress now that you put away and never intended to wear again."

This is the third step for the believer. When you and I come to Christ and accept Him as Savior, we are told that He becomes our righteousness. He not only subtracts our sin, He not only regenerates us and makes us a child of God, but He makes over to us His own righteousness. Actually, it's spoken of as a *robe* of righteousness. In Romans 3:22 it is described in a very wonderful way: "Even the righteousness of God which is by faith of Jesus Christ unto all and upon all them that believe: for there is no difference." Paul speaks of it as a garment that comes down over the sinner, covering him, so that God sees us in Christ, and His righteousness becomes our righteousness. We stand complete in Him—"accepted in the beloved" (Eph. 1:6). This is the robe of righteousness that we have today.

A book came out several years ago called *The Robe*. And there was an intelligent, dynamic young lady who was a member of my church. She came up to me one Sunday evening and said, "I've been reading a book, and it's a thriller." I asked her what it was. She said it was *The Robe*. I was a little discouraged when she said that. She asked if I'd read it, and I said, "Not exactly. I have the book, and I've looked through it, but I have not read it in any detail. In fact, I haven't cared to." And she looked at me in great amazement. She said, "Do you mean to tell me that you're not interested in what happened to that robe?" And I said, "Frankly, no. That seamless robe which Christ wore doesn't have a romantic history. The soldiers shot craps to see who would get it, and the fellow who won it must have been some big, burly Roman soldier. That's a semi-tropical country, and I happen to know it can get very hot there; he probably sweated out that robe in just a few weeks and then dropped it in some corner. Then a little servant maid came along, picked it up, held her nose, and dropped it in the trash can." This young lady was certainly shocked when I said that. She said, "That's terrible! According to the story, that robe had such a romantic history." I replied, "That robe had no romantic history at all. But there is one that does, and that's the robe of righteousness which Christ puts over the sinner who will trust Him."

And you and I cannot stand sufficient in ourselves; we stand complete in Him. Romans 4:25 tells us that it was Christ "who was delivered for our offences, and was raised again for our justification," in order that we might have a righteousness to stand before God. "For he hath made him to be sin for us . . . that we might be made the righteousness of God in him" (2 Cor. 5:21). And you and I stand clothed in that robe of righteousness, and that one really has a romantic history.

Now the fourth thing Naomi tells Ruth to do is to get down to the threshing floor and let Boaz know that she wants to claim him as her kinsman-redeemer.

And it shall be, when he lieth down, that thou shalt mark the place where he shall lie, and thou shalt go in, and uncover his feet, and lay thee down; and he will tell thee what thou shalt do [Ruth 3:4].

And, friend, that's a very important step for you and me. That is a step that every sinner must take. Even in the church today are many folk who have joined the church, but they really never have received Jesus Christ. They never have gone down to the threshing floor and claimed Him as their Kinsman-Redeemer. And I'd like to ask: Have you really claimed

Jesus Christ as your Savior? My friend, you do have to *claim* Him. The language of Scripture says to believe *upon* or believe *into* the Lord Jesus Christ. It must be an active faith, not a faith that stands on the sidelines and nods its head. It's an active faith that claims Him as Kinsman-Redeemer. He is our Savior. Oh, what a gift! ". . .The gift of God is eternal life through Jesus Christ our Lord" (Rom. 6:23).

Under the Mosaic Law, Ruth is not only entitled to and has a right to claim Boaz as her kinsman-redeemer, but she *must* claim him. And not only that, it's obvious that Boaz wants to be her kinsman-redeemer. The incident that is taking place makes possible the coming of Jesus Christ to this earth to be born in Bethlehem, for these events before us in the Book of Ruth are taking place in Bethlehem. This girl is going to obey her mother-in-law, and there's nothing wrong with what she is being instructed to do, as we shall see. She was asked to claim him; she had not claimed him.

Many people will tell you they believe in the facts concerning the coming of Christ into the world, but they've never yet accepted Christ.

Several years ago after speaking at a State Christian Endeavor convention in Fresno, California, as I walked across the auditorium with my coat slung over my shoulder, I saw a little delegation of college fellows approaching me. I recognized one of them as one of the officers of a Christian group at Fresno State College where I'd previously spoken. He said to me, "Dr. McGee, we have a young fellow here that we would like to have you talk to." And I said, "Well, fine. What about? What's the background?" And he said, "Well, this fellow agreed to come to the service tonight, and we'd hoped he would accept Christ, but he didn't, and so we just wish you'd talk with him." So I said to him, "Do you believe the Bible?" He said, "Yes." I was amazed. I had a notion he'd be the kind of college boy who'd want to argue about it. So I said, "Do you believe the story about the flood? That's sort of ridiculous about the flood, isn't it?" He said that it wasn't ridiculous to him. I said, "What about Jonah and the fish? Isn't that ridiculous?" He said, "No, not to me." And I said, "Well, do you believe it?" He said, "Yes." Well, I thought I'd have a boy who'd want to argue—they generally do—and I was prepared for it. Then I said to him, "Do you believe that Jesus Christ came into this world 1900 years ago as the Son of God and that He was virgin born?" He said, "Yes." "Do you believe He performed miracles?" He said, "Yes." "Do you believe He died on the cross for our sins?" And he said, "Yes." So I asked, "Do you believe He rose again bodily?" He said, "Yes." "Do you believe that He ascended into heaven?" He said, "Yes." Well, my gracious, the fellow believed everything that I asked him. And what do you do then? My course in personal evangelism never told me what to do next, so I just stood there, not actually knowing what step to take. Finally I just blurted out to him, "Young man, don't you want to take Christ as your Savior?" And he blurted right back and said, "Yes, I do." Well, the thing that had happened was that everybody, including myself, had wanted to argue with him about the Bible, but nobody ever stopped and said to him, "Get down to the threshing floor and accept Christ as your Savior." And this young man in a very wonderful way accepted Christ as his Savior. We got down on our knees in that great auditorium which was almost empty now, and he accepted the Lord as his Savior. All he needed was just to get down to the threshing floor! And, frankly, I think there are a lot of folk like that today. Perhaps you are like that. You could be a church member, but really, have you ever gotten down to the threshing floor and personally, privately accepted Christ, claimed Him as *your* Savior from sin? When you trust Him, you will know what it is to pass from darkness to light.

Well, now, that's what Naomi tells Ruth to do.

And it shall be, when he lieth down, that thou shalt mark the place where he shall lie, and thou shalt go in, and uncover his feet, and lay thee down; and he will tell thee what thou shalt do.

And she said unto her, All that thou sayest unto me I will do.

And she went down unto the floor, and did according to all that her mother in law bade her [Ruth 3:4–6].

Now let me say that there is nothing questionable about the thing that Naomi is asking her to do. To begin with, Naomi would never have asked her to do it had it been improper. There have been those, however, who have criticized this, not understanding the threshing floor or this peculiar law. You see, she must claim him as a kinsman-redeemer. That's one thing. But this threshing floor was a public place. The harvesters were there with their families. Naomi is saying to Ruth, "Once they've finished the threshing for the evening and have had their dinner, and a time for praise to God, a religious service, then he will lie down. He'll put his head toward the grain and his feet out. Now you go and put your feet toward his feet and pull his cloak up over your feet, and then he'll let you know what to do." All of it would be out in the public. The idea that something immoral is to take place is due to our ignorance of the threshing floor during the harvest season.

And when Boaz had eaten and drunk, and his heart was merry, he went to lie down at the end of the heap of corn: and she came softly, and uncovered his feet, and laid her down.

And it came to pass at midnight, that the man was afraid, and turned himself: and, behold, a woman lay at his feet [Ruth 3:7–8].

You see, he got cold—the cloak had been pulled off him. He sat up, reached down, and felt around down there, and lo, a woman was there.

And he said, Who art thou? And she answered, I am Ruth thine handmaid: spread therefore thy skirt over thine handmaid; for thou art a near kinsman [Ruth 3:9].

Personally, friend, I think this is one of the loveliest things that we have in the Word of God. Do you know what she is saying to him? She is saying, "I want you as my kinsman-redeemer, and I want to tell you so." That really changed the thinking of this man. I imagine he had been down in the dumps a little, but now he's a shouting Methodist. Listen.

And he said, Blessed be thou of the Lord, my daughter: for thou hast shewed more kindness in the latter end than at the beginning, inasmuch as thou followedst not young men, whether poor or rich [Ruth 3:10].

In other words, he said, "When you came here, it was obvious you were not husband-hunting." She had taken a very quiet, retired place. But now she is claiming Boaz as her kinsman-redeemer and, believe me, he is not reluctant to act in that capacity. And she's doing it in such a lovely fashion. She could have taken him into court. According to the Mosaic Law, you see, she could have called the elders of the city together and told Boaz outright, "I claim you as my kinsman-redeemer," and it would have been a legal matter. But Naomi suggested this way of doing it. She said, "There will be no question about the legality because this man obviously wants to be your kinsman-redeemer. All you have to do is to let him know that you're willing to claim him, that you want him as your kinsman-redeemer." And so she goes down to the threshing floor and in this very quiet, modest way lets him know she wants him as her kinsman-redeemer. Boaz immediately wants to claim her as his wife, because that's what he's been waiting to hear. This man really goes into action now because the way is clear and he is free to move; she has claimed him.

Thank God we have a Savior, and our relationship to Him is a love story. He loved us and He gave Himself for us in order that He might redeem us. What a wonderful, warm experience it is to know that we have a Savior who died for us, who loves us and lives for us today.

Now notice what Boaz says.

And now, my daughter, fear not; I will do to thee all that thou requirest: for all the city of my people doth know that thou art a virtuous woman [Ruth 3:11].

And I'd have you note the reputation of this foreign girl who, under ordinary circumstances, would have been an outcast in Bethlehem, an outcast because the Mosaic Law shut out a Moabite. She'd been told that a Moabite and an Ammonite could not enter into the congregation of the Lord. She'd been coached by Naomi before they came to Bethlehem that there would be no possibility of her ever getting married, and Ruth had accepted her status. I imagine that the town gossips had looked her over very carefully at the beginning. I do not know what all they had said, but I'm sure that among other things they'd said, "My, this is certainly a pretty girl who has come back with Naomi. Certainly she will be trying to get some of our young men." But she made no attempt to do this. Instead she developed this wonderful reputation in the town of Bethlehem.

Boaz continues.

And now it is true that I am thy near kinsman: howbeit there is a kinsman nearer than I [Ruth 3:12].

How did he know about this? Well, he had already investigated. You see, Boaz was ready to move the minute Ruth gave him the green light. That was all he was waiting on.

The fact that there was another kinsman nearer than he was had tied his hands.

Now this other kinsman could quite possibly be a richer man than Boaz. Suppose Boaz had said to Ruth, back during the six weeks of harvest, "Ruth, I want to be your kinsman-redeemer." And suppose she had said, "Well, I thank you very much, but I don't want you. I am claiming this other man when the time comes. He is a wealthier man, and I want to claim him as my kinsman-redeemer." Poor Boaz would have really been in a bad spot. He had to wait until she gave the indication that she wanted him. Now the minute she lets him know, he tells her, "The problem is there happens to be another kinsman closer than I am, and he has priority." In other words, he'll have to be dealt with first. And this other kinsman, I would assume, was a brother of Elimelech, an uncle of Ruth's first husband, whereas Boaz was probably a cousin of her first husband. And so he says, "I want to be your kinsman-redeemer, but first I'll have to see how this other man feels about you."

Tarry this night, and it shall be in the morning, that if he will perform unto thee the part of a kinsman, well; let him do the kinsman's part: but if he will not do the part of a kinsman to thee, then will I do the part of a kinsman to thee, as the Lord liveth: lie down until the morning [Ruth 3:13].

In other words, Boaz is not sure what he will do if the other man wants to act as kinsman, but he has a plan that he's going to follow which he hopes will eliminate the other kinsman. And he emphasizes again and again this word *kinsman.* In the Hebrew it is *goel,* the kinsman-redeemer. He is the one to redeem Ruth's property, because she would inherit what her husband had; and he's the one to redeem her, you see. He has top priority. And Boaz tells Ruth to stay through the night. He did not want her to return to Bethlehem when it was dark—in that day the highways were no more safe than they are today. When we read about the period of the judges, we learn that people did not travel the main highways because they were not safe. Instead they'd take off across the fields. So what Boaz is doing is protecting this girl.

And she lay at his feet until the morning: and she rose up before one could know another. And he said, Let it not be known that a woman came into the floor [Ruth 3:14].

Now the reason for that, again, is obvious. He did not want this other kinsman to know, because if he had any ideas about claiming Ruth as his wife, this would be something that would cause him to eliminate Boaz immediately. Boaz wants to handle this case himself, and he moves into the situation.

Also he said, Bring the veil that thou hast upon thee, and hold it. And when she held it, he measured six measures of barley, and laid it on her: and she went into the city [Ruth 3:15].

In other words, he makes her a very generous gift.

And when she came to her mother in law, she said, Who art thou, my daughter? And she told her all that the man had done to her [Ruth 3:16].

Other commentators, after whom I have read, seem to misinterpret her question. When Naomi asked, "Who art thou, my daughter?" they say since it was dark when she came up to the door Naomi wasn't sure who it was. Well, she at least knew that she was "my daughter." Of course she knew it was Ruth. We need to understand the context here. When Naomi sent her, I think Ruth was reluctant to go. I imagine she had said, "Oh, I don't want to claim him. You told me that if I came back here no one would be interested in me. I'm a Moabite, an outcast. I don't want to go down and claim Boaz." And Naomi said, "Look. I know He's interested in you, and I know he's in love with you, and I know he wants to marry you. Therefore, you do what I say." I think she almost had to push Ruth out of the house. So when Ruth returns the next morning, Naomi says, "Who art thou, my daughter?" Now let me put it in good ol' American: "Are you Mrs. Boaz or not?" In other words, "Was I right?" And, of course, she was right.

And she said, These six measures of barley gave he me; for he said to me, Go not empty unto thy mother in law.

Then said she, Sit still, my daughter, until thou know how the matter will fall: for the man will not be in rest, until he have finished the thing this day [Ruth 3:17–18].

Ruth, you can just sit down there in the rocking chair and wait. From here on Boaz will be the man of action. He will take care of this case. You can rest in him. The work of redemption is going to be his work.

Friend, it's wonderful to have a Savior in whom you can rest, and know that He's your Redeemer. Oh, what a gift He is today! He has performed all the work of redemption. You and I are invited to enter into the rest of redemption because it is finished. You'll remember in His great high priestly prayer, He said to the Father, ". . . I have finished the work which thou gavest me to do" (John 17:4). Now that work was the work of redemption upon the cross. And when He was hanging there upon the cross, you will recall that He said, "It is finished" (John 19:30). And when He cried, "It is finished," then your redemption and my redemption was finished. He paid the penalty for your sin and my sin to such an extent that you cannot lift a little finger to add to your salvation. He has done it all.

Jesus paid it all,
All to Him I owe;
Sin had left a crimson stain,
He washed it white as snow.
—H. M. Hall

The work of redemption is *His* work, and you and I are to enter into that perfect work of redemption which He accomplished for us. And there is a wonderful peace that will come to the heart that will trust Him, recognizing that He has completed it all. Frankly, God doesn't need your little effort and my little effort. God is not receiving anything from us toward our salvation. First of all, you and I haven't anything to offer. You and I are bankrupt. You and I have to come to Him to receive everything. I understand that that is the offense of the cross which Paul talks about in Galatians, because there are many people today who like to talk about their character, their family, or their church membership. They feel that church membership is synonymous with salvation, that if you're a member of a church in good and regular standing it means God has accepted you. There is nothing farther from the truth than that. God is not receiving your effort and my effort today. The work of redemption is His work in its entirety. He was lifted up upon the cross as the Son of Man. "And as Moses lifted up the serpent in the wilderness, even so must the Son of man be lifted up: That whosoever believeth in him should not perish, but have eternal life" (John 3:14–15). It is on the basis of His work upon the cross for you and me that God saves us. And that is the reason He came to this earth over 1900 years ago as a man. The writer to the Hebrews says, ". . . A body hast thou prepared me" (Heb. 10:5). Sacrifice and offering God did not want. All of the animal sacrifices in the Old Testament were merely pointing to the coming of Christ, given to prepare people for the coming of the Savior into the world. It's our acceptance and our reception of Him that saves us. He is the Savior. Actually even our faith doesn't save us. It is Christ who saves us. Spurgeon said, "It is not thy hold on Christ that saves thee; it is Christ. It is not thy joy in Christ that saves thee; it is Christ. It's not even thy faith in Christ, though that be the instrument; it is Christ's blood and merit." You see, faith merely enables us to lay hold of the salvation Christ has purchased for us. Now today you either trust Him or you don't trust Him. There's no such thing as middle ground today. You're either resting in Him or you are trying to earn your own salvation.

And so Ruth 3 concludes with Naomi saying to Ruth, "The man will not be in rest, until he have finished the thing this day." And she said to Ruth, "Sit still, my daughter." There's nothing more for you to do. When you claimed him as your redeemer, that's all he asked you to do. The work of redemption is his work.

CHAPTER 4

***THEME:** In the heart and home of Boaz*

Ruth has come all the way from the land of Moab into the heart and home of Boaz. And we who were at one time strangers, far from God, without hope in the world, now have been made nigh by the blood of Christ. We today are in the family of God; we are in His heart. And one of these days we are going to be in His home. What a glorious, wonderful prospect we have of someday being with Him!

In this chapter we will see the work of Boaz. He has had to stand aside with his arms folded, but now he is free to move because Ruth has claimed him as her kinsman-redeemer. And I say this reverently to you, my friend: Christ, like Boaz, is not free to move in your behalf until you claim Him as your Kinsman-Redeemer. Christ died on the cross for you; He went through hell for you; and He even today stands at the door of your heart and knocks, saying, "Behold, I stand at the door, and knock: if any man hear my voice, and open the door, I will come in to him, and will sup with him, and he with me" (Rev. 3:20). But He won't crash the door. You will have to invite Him in. God offers the gift of eternal life in Christ Jesus, but you have to reach out your hand and take it by faith. By faith you receive Christ.

Boaz is ready to act in the capacity of kinsman-redeemer. Ruth is to wait and let him be the one to make all the arrangements. He is the one now who will step out into the open and claim her, actually jeopardizing everything that he has and everything that he is. But he wants her; he loves her. This is the great message of this book: redemption is a romance; because God loves us He redeemed us.

Then went Boaz up to the gate, and sat him down there: and, behold, the kinsman of whom Boaz spake came by; unto whom he said, Ho, such a one! turn aside, sit down here. And he turned aside, and sat down [Ruth 4:1].

"Boaz went up to the gate." Why did he go there? Well, simply because the gate served as the courthouse. That's where court convened. In our American way of life, in the past at least, the custom was to build the courthouse in the center of town, put a square around it, and actually build the town around it. In the state of Texas where I was born that was done in nearly all of the county seats.

In the days of Boaz it was different. You see, many of the towns were walled in order to protect the citizens from any marauder or enemy that would attack from the outside. The cities were very compact—streets were narrow, and houses were crowded close together. You can see that today in Bethlehem and in Jerusalem. Most of the old cities over there reveal this. Bethlehem in Ruth's day was that kind of place, so that the gate was the place where everybody came in or went out. Like the courthouse in the old days, especially on a Saturday, if you wanted to see anybody in the county, you'd just go to the courthouse square, and the chances were you would see him. Well, here in the Old Testament times they went to the gate. Now Boaz went to the gate for two reasons. It was where court convened, and he was going to take this other kinsman to court. The second reason is that he knows the other man will come in or out of that gate sooner or later that day. So he went to the gate, sat down, and waited there for him. Now I do not know how long he waited—it probably seemed a long time to Boaz—but finally the man he wanted to see came by. Now this man was a kinsman to Ruth and was nearer than Boaz. I do not know the relationship. In these early days they did not express relationships specifically. You just couldn't narrow it down to a second cousin or a kissing cousin. A man was either kin to you or he wasn't kin to you. And the same word would be used for a brother or an uncle or some other relationship. I assume that this other man was a brother of Elimelech, Naomi's husband, which made him an uncle of Ruth's first husband. So when Boaz sees him, he says, "Ho, such a one!" Now the question arises, didn't he know him by name? And I think the answer is yes, he knew him by name. We've all done something similar, I'm sure. Even though we know the person's name, just on the spur of the moment, we may address him without using his name. And Boaz, in the excitement of the situation, fails to call him by name. I'm confident Boaz knew him. They both lived there in Bethlehem, and they were related apparently by blood. So this other kinsman came and sat down. He responded to what was almost a command from Boaz. And I think that his reaction would have been simply this: "What in the world has happened to Boaz? Here it is the harvesting season and we're all busy in the fields, and he is detaining me. He must have something very important to discuss. This is really unusual." So the kinsman, if for no other reason than that of curiosity, wants to know what it is that's on the mind of Boaz.

And he took ten men of the elders of the city, and said, Sit ye down here. And they sat down [Ruth 4:2].

These ten men were elders, we're told, and they were the ones who constituted the judges. This is the courthouse, and court's in session. You will find way back in the Book of Genesis, that the men who came to the city of Sodom found Lot was sitting at the gate. Lot had become a petty judge there in the city of Sodom. Even that far back the city gate served as the courthouse, and the men who sat in the gate were the judges. Now Boaz has called the court into session, and they're ready to hear the case. And Boaz is ready to state it, by the way. Notice the strategy of this man. It's quite remarkable.

And he said unto the kinsman, Naomi, that is come again out of the country of Moab, selleth a parcel of land, which was our brother Elimelech's [Ruth 4:3].

Now notice the approach Boaz makes. Although he is primarily interested in Ruth, he doesn't even mention her at first. And does this verse mean that Boaz was Elimelech's brother also? Not in the Hebrew. "Our brother Elimelech" would mean "our near relative." Apparently there was a difference between these two men's relationships to Elimelech, or one kinsman wouldn't have been nearer than the other. He had to be nearer than Boaz was. In his approach, Boaz says that there's a piece of property involved. We have already seen that there was a law pertaining to property which involved the kinsman-redeemer. This law could be put into effect when a person's property fell into the hands of others through varied circumstances. In the case of Naomi, she and her family had left during a famine. When she came back, she had nothing. She could not retrieve her property. She would have to wait until the Year of Jubilee, and I assume that was a long way off. But now what is going to happen? Will a kinsman-redeemer come forward? Boaz is calling this other kinsman's attention, not to the person of Ruth, but to the property that belonged to Elimelech. He wants to know whether this other kinsman will redeem that property. I think that it's a logical step. Property had to be redeemed before a person could be redeemed.

Now Boaz says,

And I thought to advertise thee, saying, Buy it before the inhabitants, and before the elders of my people. If thou wilt redeem it, redeem it: but if thou wilt not redeem it, then tell me, that I may know: for there is none to redeem it beside thee; and I am after thee. And he said, I will redeem it [Ruth 4:4].

In other words, Boaz gives this man the priority that belongs to him. And the question is: Does this man want to be the redeemer? Will he redeem this property in order that it might be given to Naomi before the Year of Jubilee? Now the very interesting thing is that this other kinsman responds in the affirmative. He says, "I will redeem it." Apparently he was a generous men, and he was willing to perform the part of a kinsman in this connection. And I take it that if a man refused to be a kinsman, it brought upon him a certain amount of criticism, in fact, it brought a degree of disgrace. And I think that when this man agreed to redeem the property, Boaz's heart must have gone way down into his sock. But he would not give up. He had prepared for this eventuality, and he was ready now to reveal his hand, and to show that there was more to this case than just a piece of property.

Then said Boaz, What day thou buyest the field of the hand of Naomi, thou must buy it also of Ruth the Moabitess, the wife of the dead, to raise up the name of the dead upon his inheritance [Ruth 4:5].

It's as if Boaz said, "Well, I forgot to tell you that there is in connection with this property a little hurdle that you'll have to get over. You see, there is now a woman by the name of Ruth. She's a Moabitess, and she's connected with the property because she happened to marry a son of Elimelech. And now that both he and Elimelech are dead, she'll be the one to inherit this land. So the day that you redeem this property, you've also got to redeem this woman; that is, you'll have to step in and marry Ruth, because she's tied to this property." And I think Boaz made the problem very clear. And you'll notice he let the man know the nationality of the woman involved. "She is a *Moabitess.*" Now the Mosaic Law says very specifically in Deuteronomy 23:3, "An Ammonite or Moabite shall not enter into the congregation of the LORD." It would mean that if this man brought Ruth into the congregation of the Lord, it would jeopardize his own property. Now Boaz will not mind doing that. To tell the truth, Boaz will be delighted to do that. He loves her, and he is willing to make whatever sacrifice is involved. But this other man doesn't even know her. All he knows is that she is a woman of Moab. Regardless of what he may have heard, he certainly is not interested in marrying her, and he makes that very clear.

And the kinsman said, I cannot redeem it for myself, lest I mar mine own inheritance: redeem thou my right to thyself; for I cannot redeem it [Ruth 4:6].

Now I assume that this other kinsman was already married. It's quite possible that he had grown children the age of Boaz, and that his children were married. His property already would be allotted to his children. To marry this woman of Moab would jeopardize everything that he owned. He would be risking everything by marrying Ruth and bringing her into the congregation of the Lord. Very candidly, this other kinsman probably was right in what he said, that he could not redeem the property and Ruth because his own inheritance would be marred. Then he tells Boaz, "You go ahead and take my right of redemption to yourself if this is what you want to do."

Now I have attempted to lift out of this little book some of the great spiritual lessons that are here—and there are many. The kinsman-redeemer is one of the most marvelous pictures that we have of our Lord Jesus Christ who redeemed us. In other words, as we said at the very beginning, this story is a picture of our redemption. This is the way *our* Kinsman-Redeemer has acted in our behalf.

Also we have a marvelous picture in this other kinsman. What does he represent? I personally think that he represents the Mosaic Law. To begin with, he's nameless. The Law could not redeem us. It was *impossible* for the Law to redeem us. That's made very clear in the New Testament. "Therefore by the deeds of the law there shall no flesh be justified in his sight: for by the law is the knowledge of sin" (Rom. 3:20). The Law was never given to be a redeemer. The Law was given to reveal man's true condition. Paul calls it a ministration of condemnation (2 Cor. 3:9) and a ministration of death (2 Cor. 3:7). The Law was never a savior. The Law actually condemned us rather than saved us. It was given as an attempt to control the old nature. There was really never anyone who got saved by keeping the precepts of the Law. It was only as they brought the sacrifice that pointed to Christ that they were ever made acceptable to God. And that's the reason the great Day of Atonement was so important. It covered the sins of ignorance for everyone in Israel. On that day their attention was called to the fact that they needed a Savior even to deliver them from the Law. Like the other kinsman, the Law was unable to save. The other kinsman said it would mar his own inheritance. And the Law would have to lower its standards if it saved you or me, friend. I hear a great many people who talk rather foolishly about keeping the Law. They say, "I live by the Ten Commandments," or "I live by the Sermon on the Mount." Well, do you? There are those that say, "That's my religion." If that is your religion, I have a question for you: How are you getting along? Are you keeping it? "Oh," somebody says, "I'm trying mighty hard." A very prominent businessman told me that years ago in Nashville, Tennessee. Well, you can't find anywhere in the Sermon on the Mount or in the Ten Commandments or in the Mosaic system where it says you are to *try*. God says, "*Do* these things." He didn't say anything in the world about trying. You can't come half way. This other kinsman, who symbolizes the Law, said, "I cannot redeem." The Law cannot redeem you. You have to have somebody who will love you, friend, and somebody to pay the penalty of your sins. That's the only way you'll ever get saved. You cannot measure up to God's standard. You and I are way short of God's standard. We need today a Kinsman-Redeemer who loves us and who was not only willing to risk everything, but who actually gave His life. When He took our place, He paid an awful penalty. He died upon the cross for our sins.

In order to make a contract or agreement binding, it was necessary to follow an unusual procedure.

Now this was the manner in former time in Israel concerning redeeming and concerning changing, for to confirm all things; a man plucked off his shoe, and gave it to his neighbour: and this was a testimony in Israel [Ruth 4:7].

You'll recall that when we looked at this law back in Deuteronomy 25, it said that the woman was to take off his shoe and spit in his face. Well, I'm glad Boaz didn't spit in his face here, but he did take off the shoe. And we see that Boaz has taken the place of Ruth in this entire transaction; he is acting for her. On her behalf he takes off the shoe of the other man, and this girl is now to become his wife. Now I have given names to nearly everyone in this little Book of Ruth, and I have a name for this other kinsman. He's Old Barefoot. He lost his shoe. You know, only the Gospel has ever put shoes on our feet. "And your feet shod with the preparation of the gospel of peace" (Eph. 6:15). The old Law, my friend, is barefoot. It cannot save you at all.

Therefore the kinsman said unto Boaz, Buy it for thee. So he drew off his shoe.

And Boaz said unto the elders, and unto all the people, Ye are witnesses this day, that I have bought all that was Elimelech's, and all that was Chilion's and Mahlon's, of the hand of Naomi.

Moreover Ruth the Moabitess, the wife of Mahlon, have I purchased to be my wife, to raise up the name of the dead upon his inheritance, that the name of the dead be not cut off from among his brethren, and from the gate of his place: ye are witnesses this day [Ruth 4:8–10].

First he redeems the property, you see. Then he is also the redeemer for Ruth. He acts the part of a kinsman and makes her his wife. He does it because he's in love with her. Since Boaz depicts the Lord Jesus Christ, our Kinsman-Redeemer, it is very important to see that He has acted in our behalf. Now Boaz calls the people to witness the fact that he not only has redeemed the property, but he has also redeemed Ruth, the widow of Mahlon.

And all the people that were in the gate, and the elders, said, We are witnesses. The LORD make the woman that is come into thine house like Rachel and like Leah, which two did build the house of Israel: and do thou worthily in Ephratah, and be famous in Beth-lehem [Ruth 4:11].

These people of Bethlehem are rejoicing in this because—as we've been told twice—this girl, though a foreigner, an outsider, has made a wonderful name for herself in Bethlehem. It was obvious that she, as a Moabite, had made a tremendous sacrifice to trust God as her Savior. And she didn't spend her time running around chasing every man in the community, and Boaz had noted that, you remember.

The impression you get from some girls today is that they start out as soon as they are able, and they chase the boys until finally they run one down and marry him. And then we wonder why those marriages don't work out. I risk being thought archaic for saying this, but I believe it is still the prerogative of the man to do the chasing. The man is always the deliverer, and the woman is the receiver. God made them that way. And that's why He says to the man, "Husbands, love your wives" (Eph. 5:25). He didn't turn that around and instruct the wife to love the husband. Somebody asks, "Well, isn't she supposed to?" Of course she is, but she's a responder. She is to *respond* to him. If he loves her, then she will love him. If he treats her harshly and cruelly, she will become cold and indifferent, and love will die. In the majority of cases—and over the years I have counselled literally hundreds of cases that have to do with marriage problems—the man is to blame. You see, he is the one who is responsible because he is to be the leader.

As a man chooses a woman for his bride, and as Boaz claimed Ruth, so Christ came to this earth for His bride. He is the one who demonstrated His love by dying for us. And we are the responder—we are to respond to His love. We are to receive Him as Savior, then come to know Him. Oh, friend, that should be the ambition of every Christian—to *know* Him! It is sad that a great many people make a trip to Bethlehem once a year and look in a manger. He's not there, friend. Although he did come as a baby, He hasn't been a baby for a long time. Then at Easter they go look in an empty tomb, and He's not there either. He's the Man in the glory today. And Paul could write that his ambition was, "That I may know him, and the power of his resurrection, and the fellowship of his sufferings" (Phil. 3:10). That was the goal of this man. Oh, that we might know Him, our Kinsman-Redeemer, and love Him because He first loved us.

And now all the people of Bethlehem are joyful over the events that are taking place in the life of Boaz. And they continue to express this.

And let thy house be like the house of Pharez, whom Tamar bare unto Judah, of the seed which the LORD shall give thee of this young woman.

So Boaz took Ruth, and she was his wife: and when he went in unto her,

the LORD gave her conception, and she bare a son.

And the women said unto Naomi, Blessed be the LORD, which hath not left thee this day without a kinsman, that his name may be famous in Israel [Ruth 4:12–14].

The women said this to Naomi because, you see, Naomi needed a kinsman to carry on the line of Elimelech. Now it will be carried on through Boaz.

We have a Kinsman today, and that's the most wonderful news we can have, friend. Look today at this poor, sin-stained world. It is puzzled, not knowing where to turn. And look at the faces. I've looked into the faces of literally thousands of people in downtown Los Angeles and elsewhere. If they are happy, their faces don't reveal it. The children appear happy but not the older folk. Their lives seem almost aimless, without hope, without God in the world. They need a Kinsman. It's tragic to see people celebrate Christmas or Easter or anything that relates to Christ without knowing He is their Kinsman and without having received Him as their Kinsman-Redeemer.

And he shall be unto thee a restorer of thy life, and a nourisher of thine old age: for thy daughter in law, which loveth thee, which is better to thee than seven sons, hath born him.

And Naomi took the child, and laid it in her bosom, and became nurse unto it [Ruth 4:15–16].

This child, you see, is Naomi's grandson. And how precious he is to her.

And the women her neighbours gave it a name, saying, There is a son born to Naomi; and they called his name Obed: he is the father of Jesse, the father of David [Ruth 4:17].

Naomi's neighbors, seeing her great love for the child, named him Obed, meaning "servant" or "worshiper." Although he was of no blood kin to Naomi, he was legally her grandson. Undoubtedly, he became a little servant to Naomi in her old age and took the place left vacant by the death of her husband and two sons. Her estate, of course, would go to this son of Boaz and Ruth.

He is a worshiper of the living and the true God.

Now we're given Obed's genealogy. Obed is the father of Jesse. And who is Jesse? He is the father of David.

Now these are the generations of Pharez: Pharez begat Hezron, And Hezron begat Ram, and Ram begat Amminadab, And Amminadab begat Nahshon, and Nahshon began Salmon, And Salmon begat Boaz, and Boaz begat Obed, And Obed begat Jesse, and Jesse begat David [Ruth 4:18–22].

In one sense this genealogy that concludes the Book of Ruth is just about as important as any portion of the Old Testament. Do you know why? Because this little book and this genealogy are what connect the family of David with the tribe of Judah. Without it we would have no written record of the connection. This makes the little Book of Ruth very important, as you can see, because it fits into God's plan and into God's scheme.

As a fitting climax for the little Book of Ruth, let us look further at the kinsman-redeemer as he pictures the Lord Jesus Christ. In what sense did our Lord fulfill that which the kinsman-redeemer represents? There were several requirements a man had to meet in order to qualify as a kinsman-redeemer. We shall look at several of them.

First of all, he must be a *near kinsman.* Second, he must be *willing* to redeem. The third requirement is that the kinsman-redeemer must be *able* to redeem. And the fourth, the kinsman-redeemer must be *free* himself. And finally, the redeemer must have the *price* of redemption. He must be able to pay in legal tender that which is acceptable.

Now Boaz was able to meet all of these conditions as the kinsman-redeemer of Ruth. And the Lord Jesus Christ as our Kinsman-Redeemer, and the Kinsman-Redeemer of the world, meets all these requirements also.

First of all, let's consider that the kinsman-redeemer must be a near kinsman. That seems to be obvious and needs no proof. In fact, that is the reason Boaz could act. He said, "I am your near kinsman." Presented to us from beginning to end is the fact that Boaz was related to the family of Elimelech. And the Lord Jesus Christ is our Kinsman-Redeemer. He is a near kinsman. He is the one who took upon Himself our humanity. "Forasmuch then as the children are partakers of flesh and blood, he also himself likewise took part of the same; that through death he might destroy him that had the power of death, that is, the devil; And deliver them who through fear of death were all their lifetime subject to bondage. For verily he took not on him the nature of angels; but he took on him the seed of Abraham" (Heb. 2:14–16). The Lord Jesus Christ came into our human family, "he took on him the seed of Abraham," we're told here. We are also told that He ". . . can have compassion on the ignorant, and on them that are out of the way; for that he himself also is compassed with infirmity" (Heb. 5:2). He knew what it was to be a man. "But when the fulness of the time was come, God sent forth his Son, made of a woman, made under the law, To redeem them that were under the law, that we might receive the adoption of sons" (Gal. 4:4–5). He was born of a woman, born under the Law. You see, He came down and took upon Himself our humanity, and He became a man. And it was for the joy that was set before Him that He came down to this earth and entered into the human family. That, my friend, is one of the greatest encouragements that I could have today. If you could persuade me that God had not become man (you cannot persuade me of that, by the way, but if you could), then, I say it reverently and with some thought, I'd turn my back on God. However, you cannot persuade me of this, and I'll not turn my back on Him, because 2000 years ago He came down and took upon Himself my humanity. And He suffered down here; He bled and died. He is able to help me today because He knows me and He knows you. He knows you better than your friends know you, than your relatives know you, than your wife or husband knows you. He knows you better than you know yourself. He knows you today, and He can help you today because of that. Because God became man and took my humanity upon Himself, then, although there are many experiences in this life I cannot explain, and I do not know why certain things happen today, I accept them. Since He became a man, and since He found it necessary to come down to this earth to suffer and to bleed and to die for the sins of the world—which is in the plan and program of God—I know that life has some high and holy purpose. I'm going to get up and brush myself off when I fall again, and I'm going to continue right on through life because I know that we're pressing ". . . toward the mark for the prize of the high calling of God in Christ Jesus" (Phil. 3:14).

Christ's humanity has been expressed in a lovely little poem by Jean Ingelow:

O, God, O Kinsman loved, but not enough!
O Man, with eyes majestic after death,
Whose feet have toiled along our pathways rough,
Whose lips drawn human breath!

By that one likeness which is ours and Thine,
By that one nature which doth hold us kin;
By that high heaven where sinless Thou dost shine,
To draw us sinners in.

Anselm, one of the great saints during the period of the Middle Ages, in his book, *Cur Deus Homo*, that is, *Why God Became Man*, reduces to one well-defined point the problem of why God became a man. That point is defined by one word: *redemption*. The Lord Jesus Christ took upon Himself our humanity and our flesh that He might be our Kinsman-Redeemer. He qualifies as our Kinsman-Redeemer on this first point: He is our near Kinsman!

Not only must a kinsman-redeemer be a near kinsman, but he must also be *willing* to redeem. You will recall that Naomi's other kinsman was not willing to redeem. He very frankly told Boaz, "I'll mar my own inheritance. I cannot redeem it. You redeem my right for yourself." And Boaz was willing—not only willing—he *wanted* to redeem it, because he loved Ruth. And you and I today have a Kinsman who loves us. Why? There's no explanation in us. Paul said in Romans 3:24: "Being justified freely by his grace through the redemption that is in Christ Jesus." "Freely" means without a cause. He didn't find any cause in us at all. But He loves us, and He's a willing Redeemer. The writer to the Hebrews says, "Looking unto Jesus the author and finisher of our faith; who for the joy that was set before him endured the cross, despising the shame, and is set down at the right hand of the throne of God" (Heb. 12:2). And so we find that the Lord Jesus, as our Kinsman-Redeemer, was willing to redeem us. He wanted to redeem us and He loves us today. He was a willing sacrifice.

It has been suggested by some, and wrongly so, that because Jesus was a willing sacrifice, He was a suicide like Socrates. That's a blasphemous statement, but some of the liberals have made it, as they have made other blasphemous statements. Although His death was not a suicide, He certainly was willing to die—you see, He loved us!

Many years ago down in Houston, Texas, when a boarding house caught on fire, a woman broke through the lines and went into that house. It collapsed, and she was burned to death. The headlines read: "Poor Wretch Dies: Suicide." Later the newspaper corrected it, and printed an apology. Do you know why? It was because when workmen were digging around in the rubble, they found in a back room, a little iron bed, and in that little iron bed was a baby, *her* baby. She entered that burning building to save her baby. She wasn't a suicide. She loved that baby and wanted to save her child. The Lord Jesus was a willing Redeemer, friend, very willing, and it was because He loved us.

Third, a kinsman-redeemer must be *able* to redeem. I am sure that Naomi had some poor kinfolk there in Bethlehem—we all have poor kinfolk, haven't we? It might have been that one night after Naomi had come back from Moab that these poor kinfolk came over, they all got out their handkerchiefs and they wept. They said, "Naomi, we feel sorry for you, but we can't help you. In fact, we're in pretty bad shape ourselves. We can't even help ourselves." It's *nice* to have folk sympathize with you, but it's *wonderful* to have a kinsman who is able to write a check that doesn't bounce, and to have that kinsman come along and say, "I'll redeem you." Well, you and I have a Kinsman-Redeemer. One of the things that is said about Him is that He is able to redeem. Have you ever noticed the many times in the New Testament that it says the Lord Jesus is able? He is able. "Wherefore he is able also to save them to the uttermost that come unto God by him, seeing he ever liveth to make intercession for them" (Heb. 7:25). He is our great Kinsman-Redeemer with the ability to save. That, of course, was true of Boaz. He was called a mighty man of wealth. There was never any question about his ability. And, friend, there's never a question about whether the Lord Jesus can redeem. Job could say, "For I know that my redeemer liveth, and that he shall stand at the latter day upon the earth" (Job 19:25). I can say today that I know that my Redeemer liveth, because He is right now at God's right hand, and He stood one day upon this earth. In fact, He hung one day upon a cross that He might redeem us from sin. He is able to save. And we're told today that God has highly exalted Him and given Him a name above every name, and that some day every tongue must confess and every knee must bow to Him (Phil. 2:9–11). He is able to save. And may I say, He is able to save *you*. The question is: Has He saved you? He wants to, and He will if you'll come to Him.

BIBLIOGRAPHY

(Recommended for Further Study)

Barber, Cyril J. *Ruth.* Chicago, Illinois: Moody Press, 1983.

Davis, John J. *Conquest and Crisis—Studies in Joshua, Judges, and Ruth.* Grand Rapids, Michigan: Baker Book House, 1969.

Enns, Paul P. *Ruth.* Grand Rapids, Michigan: Zondervan Publishing House, 1981.

Gaebelein, Arno C. *The Annotated Bible.* Vol. 2. Neptune, New Jersey: Loizeaux Brothers, 1917.

Grant, F. W. *Numerical Bible.* Vol. 2. Neptune, New Jersey: Loizeaux Brothers, 1891.

Gray, James M. *Synthetic Bible Studies.* Westwood, New Jersey: Fleming H. Revell Co., 1906.

Jensen, Irving L. *Judges & Ruth, A Self-Study Guide.* Chicago, Illinois: Moody Press, 1968.

McGee, J. Vernon. *Ruth, The Romance of Redemption.* Pasadena, California: Thru the Bible Books, 1943

Mackintosh, C. H. *The Mackintosh Treasury: Miscellaneous Writings.* Neptune, New Jersey: Loizeaux, n.d.

Ridout, Samuel. *Lectures on the Books of Judges and Ruth.* Neptune, New Jersey: Loizeaux Brothers, n.d.

The Book of

1 SAMUEL

INTRODUCTION

The two Books of Samuel are classified as one book in the Jewish canon and should be considered as such. In the Latin Vulgate they are the first of four Books of Kings. Our title identifies the name of Samuel with these first two historical books. This is not because he is the writer, although we do believe that he is the writer of a good portion of it. It is because his story occurs first, and he figures prominently as the one who poured the anointing oil on both Saul and David. Samuel, then, is considered the writer of 1 Samuel up to the twenty-fifth chapter, which records his death. Apparently, Nathan and Gad completed the writing of these books. We learn this from 1 Samuel 10:25 and 1 Chronicles 29:29.

The Books of Samuel contain many familiar features. We read of the rise of the kingdom of Israel. There is also the story of Hannah and her little boy Samuel. Recorded in these books is the story of David and Goliath and the unusual and touching friendship of David and Jonathan. We have the account of King Saul's visit to the witch of En-dor, and 2 Samuel 7—one of the great chapters of the Word of God—gives us God's covenant with David. Finally, we have the record of David's great sin with Bathsheba and of the rebellion of his son Absalom.

In the Book of Judges we find that God used little people, many of whom had some serious fault or defect. Their stories are a great encouragement to those of us today who are little people. However, in 1 and 2 Samuel we meet some really outstanding folk: Hannah, Eli, Samuel, Saul, Jonathan, and David. We will become acquainted with each of them as we go through these books.

There are three subjects that may be considered themes of the Books of 1 and 2 Samuel. Prayer is the first. First Samuel opens with prayer, and 2 Samuel closes with prayer. And there's a great deal of prayer in between. A second theme is the rise of the kingdom. We have recorded in these books the change in the government of Israel from a theocracy to a kingdom. Of great significance is God's covenant with David given to us in 2 Samuel 7. We will comment further on the kingdom in a moment. The third theme is the rise of the office of prophet. When Israel was a theocracy, God moved through the priesthood. However, when the priests failed and a king was anointed, God set the priests aside and raised up the prophets as His messengers. We will find that for the nation of Israel this resulted in deterioration rather than improvement.

The rise of the kingdom is of particular importance. First and Second Samuel record the origin of this kingdom, which continues as a very important subject throughout both the Old and New Testaments. The first message of the New Testament was the message of John the Baptist: ". . . Repent ye: for the kingdom of heaven is at hand" (Matt. 3:2). The kingdom of which he spoke is the kingdom of the Old Testament, the kingdom that begins in the Books of Samuel. This kingdom we find has a very historical basis, an earthly origin, and geographical borders. This kingdom has a king, and its subjects are real people.

God's chosen form of government is a kingdom ruled by a king. Yet to change the form of our government today would not solve our problems. It is not the *form* that is bad—it is the *people* connected with it. But a kingdom is God's ideal, and He intends to put His King on the throne of this earth someday. When Jesus Christ, the Prince of Peace, rules this world it will be very unlike the job men are doing today. There will be no need for a poverty program, an ecological program, or for moral reforms. Rather, there will be righteousness and peace covering this earth like the waters cover the sea.

In these books the coming millennial kingdom is foreshadowed in several respects; and in the setting up of the kingdom of Israel we observe three things that our world needs: (1) a king with power who exercises that power in righteousness; (2) a king who will rule in full dependence upon God; and (3) a king who will rule in full obedience to God. The Lord Jesus Christ, the coming King of Kings, is the very One the world so desperately needs today.

OUTLINE

I. Samuel, God's Prophet, Chapters 1–8

A. Birth of Samuel, Chapters 1–2
   1. Hannah's Prayer and Answer, Chapter 1
   2. Hannah's Prophetic Prayer; Boy Samuel in Temple, Chapter 2

B. Call of Samuel, Chapter 3

C. Last Judge and First Prophet (Prophetic Office), Chapters 4–8
   1. Ark Captured by Philistines; Word of God to Samuel Fulfilled; Eli Dies and His Sons Slain, Chapter 4
   2. God Judged Philistines because of Ark; Ark Returned to Beth-shemesh, Chapters 5–6
   3. Samuel Leads in Revival (Put away Idols and Turn to Jehovah); Victory at Eben-ezer, Chapter 7
   4. Israel Rejects God and Demands a King; Samuel Warns Nation but Promises a King, Chapter 8

II. Saul, Satan's Man, Chapters 9–15

A. Saul Received, Chapters 9–10
   1. Saul Chosen as King, Chapter 9
   2. Saul Anointed as King, Chapter 10

B. Saul Reigning, Chapters 11–12
   1. Saul's Victory over Ammonites, Chapter 11
   2. Transfer of Authority from Samuel to Saul, Chapter 12

C. Saul Rejected, Chapters 13–15
   1. Saul's Rebellion against God, Chapter 13
   2. Jonathan Responsible for Victory over Philistines; Saul Takes Credit, Chapter 14
   3. Saul's Glaring Rebellion and Disobedience Regarding Agag, Chapter 15

III. David, God's Man; Saul, Satan's Man, Chapters 16–31

A. David Anointed, Chapter 16

B. David Trained, Chapters 17–18
   1. David Slays Goliath, Giant of Gath, Chapter 17
   2. Jonathan and David Make Covenant; Saul Gives Daughter Michal to David, Chapter 18

C. David Disciplined, Chapters 19–30
   1. Saul Attempts to Kill David Again, Chapter 19
   2. Jonathan Helps David Escape, Chapter 20
   3. David Escapes to Nob and Gath, Chapter 21
   4. David Gathers His Men; Saul Slays Priests of God, Chapter 22
   5. David Fights Philistines; Saul Pursues David; Jonathan and David Make Covenant, Chapter 23
   6. David Spares Saul's Life at En-gedi, Chapter 24
   7. Samuel Dies; David and Abigail, Chapter 25
   8. David Again Spares Saul's Life in Wilderness of Ziph, Chapter 26
   9. David Retreats to Land of Philistia (Ziklag), Chapter 27
   10. Saul Consults Witch of En-dor, Chapter 28
   11. Philistines Do Not Trust David in Battle, Chapter 29
   12. David Fights Amalekites for Destroying Ziklag, Chapter 30

D. Saul Mortally Wounded in Battle, Attempts Suicide, Chapter 31

CHAPTER 1

***THEME:** Birth of Samuel; Samuel taken to Eli*

This first Book of Samuel opens with the cry of a godly woman. While the people cry for a king, Hannah cries for a child. God builds the throne on a woman's cry. When woman takes her exalted place, God builds her a throne.

Eli, the high priest, thinks Hannah is drunk as she prays before the tabernacle in Shiloh. When he discovers her true anxiety for a child, he blesses her. Samuel is born to Hannah and she brings him to Eli in fulfillment of her vow.

Now there was a certain man of Ramathaim-zophim, of mount Ephraim, and his name was Elkanah, the son of Jeroham, the son of Elihu, the son of Tohu, the son of Zuph, an Ephrathite:

And he had two wives; the name of the one was Hannah, and the name of the other Peninnah: and Peninnah had children, but Hannah had no children [1 Sam. 1:1–2].

Elkanah had two wives. Perhaps you are thinking that God approved of this. No, my friend, as you read this record you will find that God did not approve of his having two wives. The fact that certain things are recorded in Scripture does not mean that God sanctions them. He is merely giving you the facts concerning history, persons, and events. For example, you will find that the lie of Satan is recorded in Scripture, but that does not mean God approves it! God showed His disapproval when Abraham took the maid Hagar as his second wife. In fact, the fruits of his sin are still in existence. Ishmael, Abraham's son by Hagar, became the head of the Arab nation, and the Jews and Arabs are still at odds today. Because Elkanah had two wives, there was trouble in the family. This is evidence that God is not blessing them at this particular time.

And this man went up out of his city yearly to worship and to sacrifice unto the LORD of hosts in Shiloh. And the two sons of Eli, Hophni and Phinehas, the priests of the LORD, were there [1 Sam. 1:3].

This verse disturbed me for a long time. Why in the world did Samuel have to tell us that the sons of Eli were at the tabernacle? Later on we will find out. Going to worship God at the tabernacle was not all that you might suppose it to be. Actually it was a dangerous place to be, because these sons of Eli were "sons of Belial," or sons of the devil, if you please.

Some churches are the worst places you can be in and the most dangerous places for you. I have heard people say concerning the Upper Room, "How wonderful to have been there with Jesus!" Would it? Do you know who was in the Upper Room! Satan! He was not invited, but he was there. The record tells us that Satan entered into Judas. The Upper Room was the most dangerous place to be in Jerusalem that night. So, going to worship God had its difficulties in Samuel's day. Evil was present there in the persons of Eli's sons. It is interesting that this is mentioned at this juncture in 1 Samuel.

And when the time was that Elkanah offered, he gave to Peninnah his wife, and to all her sons and her daughters, portions:

But unto Hannah he gave a worthy portion; for he loved Hannah: but the LORD had shut up her womb [1 Sam. 1:4–5].

Elkanah gave more to Hannah than he did to his other wife and all of their children. Why? He loved Hannah.

And her adversary also provoked her sore, for to make her fret, because the LORD had shut up her womb [1 Sam. 1:6].

Who was Hannah's adversary? It was Peninnah, Elkanah's other wife. They were not on speaking terms, and it was not a very pleasant home. Who told you that God approves of a man having two wives? They were having family trouble, and they did not have a counselor to whom they could go for help. Hannah was probably one of the most miserable persons in the world at this time, but she went to God in prayer.

And as he did so year by year, when she went up to the house of the LORD, so she provoked her; therefore she wept, and did not eat.

Then said Elkanah her husband to her, Hannah, why weepest thou? and why eatest thou not? and why is thy heart

grieved? am not I better to thee than ten sons?

So Hannah rose up after they had eaten in Shiloh, and after they had drunk. Now Eli the priest sat upon a seat by a post of the temple of the LORD.

And she was in bitterness of soul, and prayed unto the LORD, and wept sore.

And she vowed a vow, and said, O LORD of hosts, if thou wilt indeed look on the affliction of thine handmaid, and remember me, and not forget thine handmaid, but wilt give unto thine handmaid a man child, then I will give him unto the LORD all the days of his life, and there shall no razor come upon his head [1 Sam. 1:7–11].

The expression "she was in bitterness of soul" describes her deep disappointment at not having a son. So she prayed for a son and promised God two things if her desire was granted: (1) He would be a priest in the Levitical service all the days of his life, and (2) she would make him a Nazarite unto God—that is, he would be separated unto the service of God.

And it came to pass, as she continued praying before the LORD, that Eli marked her mouth.

Now Hannah, she spake in her heart; only her lips moved, but her voice was not heard: therefore Eli thought she had been drunken [1 Sam. 1:12–13].

Eli was the high priest, and he saw this distraught woman come to the tabernacle and pray. He watched her mouth, saw her lips move, but could not hear any sound. Neither, apparently, could he read her lips. Notice his reaction, which is an insight into the conditions of that day. The sons of Eli drank and caroused there. Eli knew it but had shut his eyes to it—he was an indulgent father. When Hannah prayed with such zeal in her heart, Eli thought she was drunk. Do you know why? Others who were drunk had come to the house of the Lord. This place of worship wasn't really the best place to come in that day.

And Eli said unto her, How long wilt thou be drunken? put away thy wine from thee.

And Hannah answered and said, No, my lord, I am a woman of a sorrowful spirit: I have drunk neither wine nor strong drink, but have poured out my soul before the LORD [1 Sam. 1:14–15].

We don't see much praying like Hannah's today. Would people think *you* were drunk by the way you pray? Our prayers are very dignified. Hannah, not wanting Eli to have the wrong impression, said:

Count not thine handmaid for a daughter of Belial: for out of the abundance of my complaint and grief have I spoken hitherto.

Then Eli answered and said, Go in peace: and the God of Israel grant thee thy petition that thou hast asked of him.

And she said, Let thine handmaid find grace in thy sight. So the woman went her way, and did eat, and her countenance was no more sad [1 Sam. 1:16–18].

Eli realized his mistake and gave a prophetic blessing. That Hannah's "countenance was no more sad" indicates her confidence that God had heard and would answer her prayer.

SAMUEL'S BIRTH

Wherefore it came to pass, when the time was come about after Hannah had conceived, that she bare a son, and called his name Samuel, saying, Because I have asked him of the LORD [1 Sam. 1:20].

The name *Samuel* means "heard of God." As I have said previously, this Book of 1 Samuel opens with the cry of a godly woman. While the people are crying for a king, Hannah is crying out for a child. God builds the throne on a woman's cry. When a woman takes her exalted place, God builds her a throne.

What a contrast that is to our contemporary society. For the past few months we have heard nothing on the news but abortion, abortion, abortion. Here is Hannah who wants a child, and some women today do not want their children. Of course there are times when abortion is essential for the mother's life or even for the sake of the child, but that should be determined by expert, scientific consultation. However, the issue today is that people want to sin, but they do not want to pay the consequences for their sin. My position is that when people sin they should bear the fruit of their sin. If a child is conceived, that child should be born and should be the responsibility of those who brought him into the world. People are trying hard to get away from the fruit of sin. We need to understand this principle: "Be not deceived; God is not mocked: for whatsoever a man soweth, that shall he also reap" (Gal. 6:7). We are living in a day of abortion. Hannah lived in a day when she wanted a son, and she dedicated that son unto the Lord. On her cry, God built a kingdom. What a tremendous tribute and wonderful monument to this woman's cry!

SAMUEL TAKEN TO ELI

And when she had weaned him, she took him up with her, with three bullocks, and one ephah of flour, and a bottle of wine, and brought him unto the house of the LORD in Shiloh: and the child was young.

And they slew a bullock, and brought the child to Eli.

And she said, Oh my lord, as thy soul liveth, my lord, I am the woman that stood by thee here, praying unto the LORD.

For this child I prayed; and the LORD hath given me my petition which I asked of him:

Therefore also I have lent him to the LORD; as long as he liveth he shall be lent to the LORD. And he worshipped the LORD there [1 Sam. 1:24–28].

When Hannah took her offering to the Lord, she kept her vow to God. She said, "I have promised to bring this little one to the Lord, and here he is." *Lent* is definitely a poor word to describe Hannah's gift of Samuel to the Lord. Her decision to give him completely over to the service of the Lord is irrevocable.

CHAPTER 2

THEME: *Hannah's prophetic prayer; Eli's evil sons; the boy Samuel in the tabernacle; Eli's sons judged*

Hannah's prayer of thanksgiving is prophetic, as she mentions the Messiah for the first time.

Eli's sons are evil and unfit for the priest's office. An unnamed prophet warns Eli that his line will be cut off as high priest and God will raise up a faithful priest.

HANNAH'S PROPHETIC PRAYER

This is one of the great prayers of Scripture.

And Hannah prayed, and said, My heart rejoiceth in the LORD, mine horn is exalted in the LORD: my mouth is enlarged over mine enemies; because I rejoice in thy salvation [1 Sam. 2:1].

A "horn" speaks of strength, something to hold on to. Hannah says "her strength," but she means her strength in the Lord. She is rejoicing over the fact that God has given her a son. She is victorious over those who ridiculed her for being barren, and she is rejoicing in her salvation. There has been a present deliverance.

Salvation comes in three tenses. (1) *We have been saved.* "Verily, verily, I say unto you, He that heareth my word, and believeth on him that sent me, hath [right now] everlasting life, and shall not come into condemnation; but is passed from death unto life" (John 5:24). That means that God has delivered us from the guilt of sin by the death of Christ. That is *justification*, and it is past tense. (2) God has also delivered us from what the old theologians called "the pollution of sin," which is present deliverance. *We are being saved.* It is a deliverance from the weaknesses of the flesh, the sins of the flesh, the faults of the mind, and the actions of the will. This is the present deliverance that Hannah is talking about. It is *sanctification* and is in the present tense. (3) Finally there is the deliverance from death in the future—not physical, but spiritual death. "Beloved, now are we the sons of God, and it doth not yet appear what we shall be: but we know that, when he shall appear, we shall be like him; for we shall see him as he is" (1 John 3:2). This is a future deliverance. *We shall be saved*. That will be *glorification*, which is future tense. We have been saved, we are being saved, and we will be saved. Hannah was rejoicing in her salvation.

You remember that Jonah said, "Salvation is of the LORD" (Jonah 2:9). The psalmist repeats again and again that salvation is of the Lord. The great truth of salvation is that it is by the grace of God. That is, we have been justified freely by His grace. The word *freely* means "without a cause." God found nothing in us to merit salvation. He found the explanation in Himself—He loves us.

There is none holy as the LORD: for there is none beside thee: neither is there any rock like our God [1 Sam. 2:2].

The Lord is spoken of as a "rock" in the Old Testament. In the New Testament the Lord Jesus Christ is called the "chief corner stone" (1 Pet. 2:6). In Matthew 16:18 Christ spoke of Himself when He said, ". . . upon this rock I will build my church." That Rock upon which Hannah rested is the same Rock upon which we rest today. There is no Rock like our God.

Talk no more so exceeding proudly; let not arrogancy come out of your mouth: for the LORD is a God of knowledge, and by him actions are weighed [1 Sam. 2:3].

When we come to God in prayer, we need to be very careful, friends, that we do not let our pride cause us to stumble. We need to recognize our weakness, our insufficiency, and our inability, and the fact that we really have no claim on God. Sometimes we hear people ask, "Why didn't God hear my prayer?" To be quite frank, why should He? What claim do you have on Him? If you have accepted Jesus Christ as Savior, you have a wonderful claim on God, and you can come to Him in the name of Jesus Christ. As His children we have Jesus' right and claim. However, we must remember that our prayers must be in accordance with His will.

The bows of the mighty men are broken, and they that stumbled are girded with strength.

They that were full have hired out themselves for bread; and they that were hungry ceased: so that the barren hath born seven; and she that hath many children is waxed feeble.

The LORD killeth, and maketh alive: he bringeth down to the grave, and bringeth up [1 Sam. 2:4–6].

The whole thought in this passage is that God gives life. As Job said, ". . . the LORD gave, and the LORD hath taken away; blessed be the name of the LORD" (Job 1:21). Only God has the power to give life, and only He has the right to take it away. Until you and I have the power to give life, we have no right to take life away. So far only God has that power. Believe me, God will take the blame (if that is what you want to call it) for the deaths of Ananias and Sapphira in Acts 5. He does not apologize for the fact that He intends to judge the wicked. They will go down into death and be separated from God. God does not apologize for what He does. Why? Because this is His universe; we are His creatures; He is running the universe His way.

Not long ago I talked to a young university student who had received Christ as Savior but who was still unwilling to accept many things. I said to him, "If you do not like the way God has worked out His plan of salvation, and you don't like the things He is doing, you can go off somewhere and make your own universe, set up your own rules, and run it your own way. But as long as you are in God's universe, you are going to have to do things His way." It is a most wonderful thing that you and I can bow to Him and come under His blessing if we are willing to do things His way.

The LORD maketh poor, and maketh rich: he bringeth low, and lifteth up [1 Sam. 2:7].

This verse brings up a question that many of us have: "Why are some people rich and some people poor?" I cannot understand why God has permitted some folks to be wealthy and others to be needy. I think I could distribute the wealth a little bit better than He has done it, I will be frank with you. But, you know, He did not leave that to me. That is His business and He will be able to explain it some day. I am going to wait for the explanation, because I know He has the answer.

He raiseth up the poor out of the dust, and lifteth up the beggar from the dunghill, to set them among princes, and to make them inherit the throne of glory: for the pillars of the earth are the LORD'S, and he hath set the world upon them.

He will keep the feet of his saints, and the wicked shall be silent in darkness;

for by strength shall no man prevail [1 Sam. 2:8–9].

Man, by his own effort, power, and strength, can never accomplish anything for God. Christians today need to recognize that fact. It is only what you and I do by the power of the Holy Spirit that will count. We need to learn to be dependent upon Him and rest in Him.

The adversaries of the LORD shall be broken to pieces; out of heaven shall he thunder upon them: the LORD shall judge the ends of the earth; and he shall give strength unto his king, and exalt the horn of his anointed [1 Sam. 2:10].

This is one of the great verses of Scripture and the first one to use the name *Messiah*—the word *anointed* is the Hebrew word *Messiah*. It is translated *Christos* in the Greek New Testament and comes to us as "Christ" in English. It is the title of the Lord Jesus. God is getting ready to set up a kingdom in Israel. Since Israel has rejected the theocracy, God is going to appoint them a king.

And Elkanah went to Ramah to his house. And the child did minister unto the LORD before Eli the priest [1 Sam. 2:11].

It may sound as though Samuel was being left in a place of protection and shelter. The tabernacle should have been a place like that, but unfortunately it was not.

ELI'S EVIL SONS

Now the sons of Eli were sons of Belial; they knew not the LORD [1 Sam. 2:12].

Eli's boys were "sons of Belial," meaning sons of the devil. They were not saved. Here they were, sons of the high priest, hanging around the tabernacle and actually ministering there!

There are many folk who send a son to a Christian school and feel very comfortable about it. I don't want you to misunderstand what I am saying—I thank God for Christian schools. The problem is that since the boy is in a good place, they quit praying for him. That boy may be in the most dangerous place imaginable. Other parents feel secure in the fact that their son is in a fine church. My friend, that's where the devil goes—to those wonderful places! Remember that the devil was in the Upper Room where Christ celebrated the Last Supper with His disciples. That room was the most dangerous place in Jerusalem that night because the devil was present. We need to remember that the boy who goes to a good church or a good school still needs prayer. He may be in a dangerous place.

This little fellow Samuel is in a dangerous place, and his mother is going to continue to pray for him, you may be sure of that.

And the priests' custom with the people was, that, when any man offered sacrifice, the priest's servant came, while the flesh was in seething, with a fleshhook of three teeth in his hand;

And he struck it into the pan, or kettle, or caldron, or pot; all that the fleshhook brought up the priest took for himself. So they did in Shiloh, unto all the Israelites that came thither.

Also before they burnt the fat, the priest's servant came, and said to the man that sacrificed, Give flesh to roast for the priest; for he will not have sodden flesh of thee, but raw.

And if any man said unto him, Let them not fail to burn the fat presently, and then take as much as thy soul desireth; then he would answer him, Nay; but thou shalt give it me now: and if not, I will take it by force [1 Sam. 2:13–16].

They were totally dishonest in the Lord's work. They were running one of the first religious rackets.

Wherefore the sin of the young men was very great before the LORD: for men abhorred the offering of the LORD [1 Sam. 2:17].

Their dishonesty caused many people to turn from God. The Israelites saw what Eli's sons were doing at the tabernacle and, instead of being drawn closer to the Lord, they were driven away. Friends, we need to be careful about how we live our lives and how we run our churches. This idea of shutting our eyes to sin in the church and trying to cover it up just drives people away from God. That is one of the protests of our young people today. Recently I have had the privilege of seeing over one hundred of these young people turn to Christ. I have talked with them and have seen them in action. They are against the organized church because of the hypocrisy that is in it. That disturbs me because I know it is there—just as it was in the tabernacle in Eli's day.

THE BOY SAMUEL IN THE TABERNACLE

But Samuel ministered before the LORD, being a child, girded with a linen ephod.

Moreover his mother made him a little coat, and brought it to him from year to year, when she came up with her husband to offer the yearly sacrifice [1 Sam. 2:18–19].

While Samuel is growing up under the influence of Eli's dishonest sons, his mother does not forget him. Hannah loves her little boy. She had promised to give him to the Lord, and she kept her word. And every year she makes a coat for him and gives it to him. There is nothing quite as tender and loving as this type of thing. I think one of the greatest joys that Mrs. McGee and I have is in selecting clothes, a little suit or something, for our grandson. Nothing is as satisfying as that. My heart goes out to Hannah as we see her here.

And Eli blessed Elkanah and his wife, and said, The LORD give thee seed of this woman for the loan which is lent to the LORD. And they went unto their own home.

And the LORD visited Hannah, so that she conceived, and bare three sons and two daughters. And the child Samuel grew before the LORD [1 Sam. 2:20–21].

God was good to Hannah. She had five other children, but she never forgot Samuel during all those years. Every year she made him a little coat. And, in spite of the bad environment of the tabernacle, Samuel grew before the Lord.

ELI'S SONS JUDGED

Now Eli was very old, and heard all that his sons did unto all Israel; and how they lay with the women that assembled at the door of the tabernacle of the congregation [1 Sam. 2:22].

Eli was an indulgent father who shut his eyes to the sins of his sons. Notice their awful, gross immorality "and how they lay with the women that assembled at the door of the tabernacle of the congregation"! There is a great deal of talk today about what is called the "new morality." I think Eli's sons beat the crowd today in the new morality. Actually, it was not even new in their day; it goes back to the time of the Flood.

And he said unto them, Why do ye such things? for I hear of your evil dealings by all this people [1 Sam. 2:23].

The actions of Eli's sons were an open scandal in Israel, and all Eli did was give his boys a gentle slap on the wrist!

Nay, my sons; for it is no good report that I hear: ye make the LORD's people to transgress [1 Sam. 2:24].

The people were doing what the priests were doing. Eli's sons were leading the Israelites into sin. Instead of taking positive steps to correct the situation, Eli gently rebukes them. He was an indulgent father.

If one man sin against another, the judge shall judge him: but if a man sin against the LORD, who shall entreat for him? Notwithstanding they hearkened not unto the voice of their father, because the LORD would slay them.

And the child Samuel grew on, and was in favour both with the LORD, and also with men [1 Sam. 2:25–26].

Even in this bad environment, Samuel is growing in favor with God and man. He is dedicated to God and backed by his mother's interest and prayer. God is going to use him.

And there came a man of God unto Eli, and said unto him, Thus saith the LORD, Did I plainly appear unto the house of thy father, when they were in Egypt in Pharaoh's house?

And did I choose him out of all the tribes of Israel to be my priest, to offer upon mine altar, to burn incense, to wear an ephod before me? and did I give unto the house of thy father all the offerings made by fire of the children of Israel?

Wherefore kick ye at my sacrifice and at mine offering, which I have commanded in my habitation; and honourest thy sons above me, to make yourselves fat with the chiefest of all the offerings of Israel my people? [1 Sam. 2:27–29].

God sent a prophet to old Eli who told him that God was through with him as the high priest. No longer would God move through the priest. Instead, God was now raising up a priest-prophet. It was going to be Samuel. He would minister for the Lord, and his office would be that of a prophet.

Wherefore the LORD God of Israel saith, I said indeed that thy house, and the house of thy father, should walk before me for ever: but now the LORD saith, Be it far from me; for them that honour me I will honour, and they that despise me shall be lightly esteemed [1 Sam. 2:30].

Let's be very careful in our lives to honor God. Psalm 107:1–2 says, "O give thanks unto the LORD, for he is good: for his mercy endureth for ever. Let the redeemed of the LORD say so, whom he hath redeemed from the hand of the enemy." The redeemed of the Lord need to say so today.

Behold, the days come, that I will cut off thine arm, and the arm of thy father's house, that there shall not be an old man in thine house.

And thou shalt see an enemy in my habitation, in all the wealth which God shall give Israel: and there shall not be an old man in thine house for ever.

And the man of thine, whom I shall not cut off from mine altar, shall be to consume thine eyes, and to grieve thine heart: and all the increase of thine house shall die in the flower of their age.

And this shall be a sign unto thee, that shall come upon thy two sons, on Hophni and Phinehas; in one day they shall die both of them [1 Sam. 2:31–34].

All of the prophecies mentioned in these verses came to pass. As we move through the Word of God, we shall see these things happen.

And I will raise me up a faithful priest, that shall do according to that which is in mine heart and in my mind: and I will build him a sure house; and he shall walk before mine anointed for ever [1 Sam. 2:35].

Who is this verse talking about? It is the Lord Jesus Christ. In Hannah's prayer, you remember, He is mentioned as the King, the Messiah, who is to come. He has been mentioned by Moses as a prophet and now in 1 Samuel is mentioned as a priest. The Lord Jesus Christ is Prophet, Priest, and King. He is the only One who ever fulfilled all of these offices.

CHAPTER 3

THEME: *Call of Samuel*

The story of God's calling of Samuel is ordinarily reserved for children. Let's bring it out of the nursery into the adult department. Not only is it a beautiful story, but it marks one of the great transitional periods in Scripture: the change from theocracy to monarchy, from priest to king. There is a total of four calls to Samuel: the first and second calls were to salvation (v. 7); the last two calls were to service (v. 10). As *Alice in Wonderland*, ostensibly written by Carroll for Alice Liddell (a friend's child), was a philosophical indictment against the social order of his day, so the story of Samuel's call is much more than a delightful story for children. It initiates a drastic change in the form of government. The period of the judges is over, and no longer will God move through the priest. He is now raising up a priest-prophet. Samuel will minister for the Lord, but his office will be that of a prophet. It is he who will pour the anointing oil on both kings, Saul and David. God will never speak directly to a king but will speak only through a prophet.

And the child Samuel ministered unto the LORD before Eli. And the word of the LORD was precious in those days; there was no open vision [1 Sam. 3:1].

I want you to note the word *child*. Samuel was not a wee child. The historian Josephus says he was twelve years old. He probably was a teen-ager. Samuel was a young man, and he ministered unto the Lord before Eli. A four-year-old child would not be serving the Lord in the tabernacle.

This verse tells us that "the word of the Lord was precious." That means it was scarce. God was not revealing Himself at this particular time. He is just beginning to move when He calls Samuel to be a prophet. God is moving from the use of the judge and priest to the use of the prophet. The prophet becomes the spokesman to and for the king.

And it came to pass at that time, when Eli was laid down in his place, and his eyes began to wax dim, that he could not see;

And ere the lamp of God went out in the temple of the LORD, where the ark of God was, and Samuel was laid down to sleep [1 Sam. 3:2–3].

It was the duty of the priests to take care of the lamp in the tabernacle. They were to put oil in it and see that it was kept burning. Eli was old, his eyesight dim, and the lamp was about to go out.

That the LORD called Samuel: and he answered, Here am I.

And he ran unto Eli, and said, Here am I; for thou calledst me. And he said, I called not; lie down again. And he went and lay down [1 Sam. 3:4–5].

Eli thought that Samuel was dreaming and told him to go back to bed.

And the LORD called yet again, Samuel. And Samuel arose and went to Eli, and said, Here am I; for thou didst call me. And he answered, I called not, my son; lie down again [1 Sam. 3:6].

We need to note here that God's first two calls to Samuel were calls to salvation.

Now Samuel did not yet know the LORD, neither was the word of the LORD yet revealed unto him [1 Sam. 3:7].

Samuel did not know the Lord. God was calling him to salvation. What is the age of accountability? Whatever it is, Samuel had reached it, and God is now going to hold him responsible. In the Book of Numbers a man was not able to go to war until he was twenty. The Levites did not begin their service until they were twenty-five years old, and the priests began to serve at age thirty. When Israel turned back to wander in the wilderness because of unbelief, only those who were under twenty years of age were allowed to live and go into the Promised Land. I do not know exactly how old Samuel was, but we can be certain he was not a toddler. Is twenty the age of accountability? I do not know. I am merely suggesting that it is much older than many people think.

The question has always been, "Would God have called Samuel a fifth, sixth, seventh, or fiftieth time?" I do believe with all my heart that there is a *time* to be saved. It has been expressed like this:

There is a time, I know not when;
A place, I know not where;
Which marks the destiny of men
To heaven or despair.
How long may men go on in sin?
How long will God forbear?
Where does hope end, and where begins
The confines of despair?

One answer from those skies is sent:
"Ye who from God depart,
While it is called today, repent,
And harden not your heart."

—Author unknown

Apparently there will come a day when one is not able to turn to God.

When Hermann Goering was placed in prison at the time of his trial, and later when he was to be executed, the prison chaplain had a long interview with him. The chaplain emphasized the necessity of preparing himself to meet God. In the course of the conversation, Goering ridiculed certain Bible truths and refused to accept the fact that Christ died for sinners. His was a conscious denial of the power of the blood. "Death is death," was the substance of his last words. As the chaplain reminded him of the hope of his little daughter meeting him in heaven, he replied, "She believes in her manner, I in mine." The chaplain was very discouraged when he left. Less than an hour later he heard that Hermann Goering had committed suicide. God called this man, and he refused the call.

God may call many times, but there apparently comes a day when man's heart is hardened. Proverbs 29:1 says, "He, that being often reproved hardeneth his neck, shall suddenly be destroyed, and that without remedy." Now I do not believe you can commit an unpardonable sin—that is, that you can do something today which cannot be forgiven by God tomorrow. But, does God withdraw His grace? No, He will never do that. But men can resist and rebel and reject until their conscience becomes seared with a hot iron. Men like Cain, Balaam, Samson, Korah, and Ahab all reached a day when they turned their backs against God. Acts 24:25 says of Felix, the Roman procurator before whom Paul was arraigned, "And as he reasoned of righteousness, temperance, and judgment to come, Felix trembled, and answered, Go thy way for this time; when I have a convenient season, I will call for thee." King Agrippa said to Paul, "Almost thou persuadest me to be a Christian" (Acts 26:28). Christ saved one thief that men need not despair, but He saved only one that men would not presume (Luke 23:39–43).

And the LORD called Samuel again the third time. And he arose and went to Eli, and said, Here am I; for thou didst call me. And Eli perceived that the LORD had called the child.

Therefore Eli said unto Samuel, Go, lie down: and it shall be, if he call thee, that thou shalt say, Speak, LORD; for thy servant heareth. So Samuel went and lay down in his place.

And the LORD came, and stood, and called as at other times, Samuel, Samuel. Then Samuel answered, Speak; for thy servant heareth [1 Sam. 3:8–10].

These verses contain the third and fourth calls to Samuel, the calls to service.

And the LORD said to Samuel, Behold, I will do a thing in Israel, at which both the ears of every one that heareth it shall tingle.

In that day I will perform against Eli all things which I have spoken concerning his house: when I begin, I will also make an end [1 Sam. 3:11–12].

When God says something, it is the same as done. In the Old Testament we have what has been called "prophetic tense." It is a past tense, but it speaks of the future. God speaks of things that have not yet happened as if they had already taken place. When God says something is going to happen, it *is* going to happen. God speaks to Samuel in these verses and tells him that He is about to move against the house of Eli.

Now this boy Samuel is loyal to Eli to the very end. He did not attempt to undermine him. He went to Eli and told him everything God had said to him. I want to say that if you are in God's service today and serving under some other man, be loyal to him. Don't tell me that you can be loyal to Christ and be disloyal to God's man who is above you. Oh, how loyalty is needed today!

And the LORD appeared again in Shiloh: for the LORD revealed himself to Samuel in Shiloh by the word of the LORD [1 Sam. 3:21].

How did God reveal Himself? By the Word. God today is also revealing Himself through His Word. He is illuminating by His Spirit the pages of Scripture. That is how you and I come to know Him, and to know Him is life eternal.

CHAPTER 4

***THEME:** God's judgment on Eli and his sons fulfilled*

Israel, without consulting Samuel, went out to battle against the Philistines, which led to defeat. Then they brought the ark of the covenant into battle, thinking its presence would bring victory. This reveals the superstitious paganism of the people who thought there was some merit in an object. The ark was captured, the two sons of Eli were slain, and Eli died upon hearing the news.

THE ARK IS CAPTURED BY THE PHILISTINES

This chapter is a dark picture indeed. We see the spiritual condition of Israel at this particular time. God is going to bring to a conclusion the thing He said He would do to the house of Eli.

And the word of Samuel came to all Israel. Now Israel went out against the Philistines to battle, and pitched beside Eben-ezer: and the Philistines pitched in Aphek.

And the Philistines put themselves in array against Israel: and when they joined battle, Israel was smitten before the Philistines: and they slew of the army in the field about four thousand men.

And when the people were come into the camp, the elders of Israel said, Wherefore hath the LORD smitten us to-day before the Philistines? Let us fetch the ark of the covenant of the LORD out of Shiloh unto us, that, when it cometh among us, it may save us out of the hand of our enemies [1 Sam. 4:1–3].

This section of Scripture gives us a revelation of Israel's superstition and just how far they are from God. It shows us how strong their self-sufficiency and selfishness are. With no thought of seeking God's direction, they go out to battle against the Philistines. What happens? They are defeated. What is lacking? They think perhaps they should have taken the ark with them into battle. Knowing the history of the ark—that as it had been carried down into the Jordan River, the water had been cut off so that Israel could cross over —they took the ark of the covenant into battle. The thought was that its presence would bring victory. My friend, this reveals the superstition and paganism of these people who thought there was some merit in the object. The merit was not in that box because God was not in that box. You cannot get God into a box! The merit was in the presence and person of God.

In church work today many people are equally as superstitious. They think that God, as it were, is in a box. They say, "Look at this method. It is a nice little package deal. It is success in a box. This method will solve our problem." So many people are moving in that direction today. My friend, that is not being spiritual. That is being superstitious. The merit is in Christ. Success is determined by whether or not we are with Him. That is all important.

So the people sent to Shiloh, that they might bring from thence the ark of the covenant of the LORD of hosts, which dwelleth between the cherubims: and the two sons of Eli, Hophni and Phinehas, were there with the ark of the covenant of God.

And when the ark of the covenant of the LORD came into the camp, all Israel shouted with a great shout, so that the earth rang again [1 Sam. 4:4–5].

Israel is going into battle. They send to Shiloh for the ark of the covenant. Because Hophni and Phinehas are "paid preachers," they are going to do what they are told to do. When the ark is brought into the camp, the Israelites have a great rally. They think they are getting somewhere spiritually, but this is nothing in the world but idolatry. They are worshiping a box—not God. Let us be careful in the ceremonies and rituals of our church. Are we worshiping a church? Are we worshiping a man? Are we worshiping a method? Are we worshiping a particular place? Or are we really worshiping the living and true God today?

And when the Philistines heard the noise of the shout, they said, What meaneth the noise of this great shout in the camp of the Hebrews? And they understood that the ark of the LORD was come into the camp.

And the Philistines were afraid, for they said, God is come into the camp. And they said, Woe unto us! for there hath not been such a thing heretofore.

Woe unto us! who shall deliver us out of the hand of these mighty Gods? these are the Gods that smote the Egyptians with all the plagues in the wilderness [1 Sam. 4:6–8].

The Philistines understand that the ark of the covenant has come into the camp of the Israelites. They are afraid for they say, "God is come into the camp." To them the ark is an idol. This shows that the Philistines are both superstitious and ignorant. Although they have heard of His power, they are certainly ignorant of the living and true God.

ELI DIES AND THE GLORY OF GOD DEPARTS FROM ISRAEL

The Philistines and the Israelites fight, and Israel loses the battle. There is a great slaughter of the Israelites, the ark of God is captured, and Eli's sons, Hophni and Phinehas, are slain.

And there ran a man of Benjamin out of the army, and came to Shiloh the same day with his clothes rent, and with earth upon his head.

And when he came, lo, Eli sat upon a seat by the wayside watching: for his heart trembled for the ark of God. And when the man came into the city, and told it, all the city cried out [1 Sam. 4:12–13].

Old Eli, with all his faults, was God's high priest, and he had a real concern for the things of God.

And when Eli heard the noise of the crying, he said, What meaneth the noise of this tumult? And the man came in hastily, and told Eli.

Now Eli was ninety and eight years old; and his eyes were dim, that he could not see.

And the man said unto Eli, I am he that came out of the army, and I fled to-day out of the army. And he said, What is there done, my son? [1 Sam. 4:14–16].

When news of Israel's terrible defeat reached the city, a great wail arose. Eli, old and blind, asks the reason for it.

And the messenger answered and said, Israel is fled before the Philistines, and there hath been also a great slaughter among the people, and thy two sons also, Hophni and Phinehas, are dead, and the ark of God is taken.

And it came to pass, when he made mention of the ark of God, that he fell from off the seat backward by the side of the gate, and his neck brake, and he died: for he was an old man,and heavy. And he had judged Israel forty years [1 Sam. 4:17–18].

This man maintains his composure when he is told about the death of his sons, but when he learns that the ark of God has been captured, he falls backward and dies. He was a big fat fellow. Perhaps he suffered a heart attack. Although he was a weak, indulgent father, I believe he was God's man.

Eli's death brings Samuel into the position of being God's spokesman.

CHAPTERS 5–6

***THEME:** Judgment of God upon Philistines*

Chapters 5 and 6 describe the experience of the Philistines with the captured ark of the covenant in their possession. They learned there was no merit in the ark—it was by no means a good-luck charm. Because of it ". . . the hand of the LORD was heavy upon them" (1 Sam. 5:6). Their idol Dagon was toppled and broken; the men developed a strange illness and many died. Deadly destruction followed the ark wherever it was taken. The Philistines, fearing for their lives, returned the ark to Israel, carried on a cart to a field of Beth-shemesh.

And the Philistines took the ark of God, and brought it from Eben-ezer unto Ashdod.

When the Philistines took the ark of God, they brought it into the house of Dagon, and set it by Dagon.

And when they of Ashdod arose early on the morrow, behold, Dagon was fallen upon his face to the earth before the ark of the LORD. And they took Dagon, and set him in his place again.

And when they arose early on the morrow morning, behold, Dagon was fallen upon his face to the ground before the ark of the LORD; and the head of Dagon and both the palms of his hands were cut off upon the threshold; only the stump of Dagon was left to him [1 Sam. 5:1–4].

When the Philistines captured the ark, they thought they had something good in their hands; but, every time they set it up in the house of their god Dagon, the idol would fall over. Now I want to submit something to you that I don't think you will find in any commentary. When the presence of the ark of the Lord in the house of Dagon caused the idol to fall over and nothing was left but the stump, I believe this reveals God's sense of humor. God was revealing to the Philistines that their god was powerless in His presence. I think this shows that the Lord has a real sense of humor in doing this sort of thing, because it really annoyed the Philistines. They soon saw that there was no merit in their having the ark. In fact, it was a very real danger to them.

But the hand of the LORD was heavy upon them of Ashdod, and he destroyed them, and smote them with emerods, even Ashdod and the coasts thereof.

And when the men of Ashdod saw that it was so, they said, The ark of the God of Israel shall not abide with us: for his hand is sore upon us, and upon Dagon our god [1 Sam. 5:6–7].

Thinking these calamities might be coincidental, they send the ark to another city of the Philistines.

They sent therefore and gathered all the lords of the Philistines unto them, and said, What shall we do with the ark of the God of Israel? And they answered, Let the ark of the God of Israel be carried about unto Gath. And they carried the ark of the God of Israel about thither.

And it was so, that, after they had carried it about, the hand of the LORD was against the city with a very great destruction: and he smote the men of the city, both small and great, and they had emerods in their secret parts.

Therefore they sent the ark of God to Ekron. And it came to pass, as the ark of God came to Ekron, that the Ekronites cried out, saying, They have brought about the ark of the God of Israel to us, to slay us and our people [1 Sam. 5:8–10].

I do not mean to be irreverent but everyone was passing the buck. Finally there was a meeting of the lords of the Philistines and they decided to send the ark back to Israel. God had sent judgment upon the Philistines. The Philistines had one question, "What shall we do with Israel's ark?"

And the ark of the LORD was in the country of the Philistines seven months [1 Sam. 6:1].

Again, I do not want to be irreverent, but having the ark was like having a hot potato. Whenever the ark was put near the idol of Dagon, it fell over. All that was left was a stump, and that is not a very satisfactory object to worship; an idol is bad enough! So the people of Gath had it and they didn't want it; so they sent it to Ekron and they, too, wanted to get rid of it.

And the Philistines called for the priests and the diviners, saying, What shall we do to the ark of the LORD? tell us wherewith we shall send it to his place.

And they said, If ye send away the ark of the God of Israel, send it not empty; but in any wise return him a trespass offering: then ye shall be healed, and it shall be known to you why his hand is not removed from you.

Then said they, What shall be the trespass offering which we shall return to him? They answered, Five golden emerods, and five golden mice, according to the number of the lords of the Philistines: for one plague was on you all, and on your lords [1 Sam. 6:2–4].

The Philistines wanted to get rid of the ark, but they were not sure how to go about it. Therefore they consulted with the priests and diviners who told them not to send the ark of the God of Israel away empty. They were to send an offering, and that offering speaks of the vileness of the Philistine worship. Many people wonder why God put the Philistines out of His land. The Promised Land was right at the crossroads of the world, and those who occupied it would influence the people of the world. God put them out because of the vileness of their worship. They had turned completely from God. Here again God is giving them an opportunity to turn to Him.

The Philistine offering consisted of five golden emerods (hemorrhoids, possibly, tumors or boils) and five golden mice.

And they laid the ark of the LORD upon the cart, and the coffer with the mice of gold and the images of their emerods [1 Sam. 6:11].

Notice that when the Philistines returned the ark to Israel, they put it on a cart. Nothing is going to happen to them for putting it on a cart. Do you know why? Very candidly, they did not know any better. God is not going to hold them responsible for this act. But Israel knew better, and we will see that God judged the Israelites because of the way they handled the ark. Why the difference? They knew better, friend.

And the kine took the straight way to the way of Beth-shemesh, and went along the highway, lowing as they went, and turned not aside to the right hand or to the left; and the lords of the Philistines went after them unto the border of Beth-shemesh [1 Sam. 6:12].

The cows which were hitched to the cart were obviously going against their natural instinct by leaving their calves at home. This was convincing proof to the Philistines that their troubles had been caused by an act of God.

And they of Beth-shemesh were reaping their wheat harvest in the valley: and they lifted up their eyes, and saw the ark, and rejoiced to see it.

And the cart came into the field of Joshua, a Beth-shemite, and stood there, where there was a great stone: and they clave the wood of the cart, and offered the kine a burnt offering unto the LORD.

And the Levites took down the ark of the LORD, and the coffer that was with it, wherein the jewels of gold were, and put them on the great stone: and the men of Beth-shemesh offered burnt offerings and sacrificed sacrifices the same day unto the LORD [1 Sam. 6:13–15].

The Israelites will not accept anything, you see, for themselves from the Philistines. They are, of course, to be commended for that.

And when the five lords of the Philistines had seen it, they returned to Ekron the same day [1 Sam. 6:16].

The Philistines see that the ark is received back, and they are glad to get it off their hands.

Now we will see that, when the ark was returned to the Israelites, they immediately had problems with it.

And he smote the men of Beth-shemesh, because they had looked into the ark of the LORD, even he smote of the people fifty thousand and threescore and ten men: and the people lamented, because the LORD had smitten many of the people with a great slaughter [1 Sam. 6:19].

The men of Beth-shemesh do that which God had strictly forbidden. That ark belonged in the Holy of Holies in the tabernacle. It was to be seen only by the high priest—even he was permitted to enter before it only once a year. When the ark was transported, as it was on the wilderness march, it was carefully and reverently covered. The Philistines did not know these things, but the Israelites did know.

And the men of Beth-shemesh said, Who is able to stand before this holy LORD God? and to whom shall he go up from us? [1 Sam. 6:20].

It is not that they looked in the ark and saw something that they should not have seen. That is not the point. The ark was a box. That is all it ever was. The point is that it was at the ark in the Holy of Holies that God met with His people. He is not meeting with them now. They have turned from Him. Their rebellion and blasphemy are revealed in their disobedience. Because of this, God brings judgment upon them.

And they sent messengers to the inhabitants of Kirjath-jearim, saying, The Philistines have brought again the ark of the LORD; come ye down, and fetch it up to you [1 Sam. 6:21].

Now in a superstitious way they want to get rid of the ark. They send messengers to Kirjath-jearim saying, "You come and get it." In other words, Israel is not ready to receive the ark. God's people are not prepared to return to Him.

CHAPTER 7

***THEME:** Samuel leads in revival; victory at Eben-ezer*

After twenty years, Israel is prepared to receive the ark. Israel turns from Baalim and Ashtaroth to serve the Lord.

SAMUEL LEADS IN REVIVAL

And the men of Kirjath-jearim came, and fetched up the ark of the LORD, and brought it into the house of Abinadab in the hill, and sanctified Eleazar his son to keep the ark of the LORD.

And it came to pass, while the ark abode in Kirjath-jearim, that the time was long; for it was twenty years: and all the house of Israel lamented after the LORD [1 Sam. 7:1–2].

After twenty years the Israelites begin to turn to God and away from Baalim and Ashtaroth. They have come to the place where they want God.

In this day in which we are living there is a renewed interest in the Word of God. I rejoice in this, because it is my firm conviction that God's people must get back to the Bible. I believe that all sixty-six books—all the way from Genesis to Revelation—are the Word of God. I believe in the Bible's integrity and inerrancy and in the fact that we need to get back to its teachings. We have been a long time getting back to God's Word. Progress has been slow. How many more years will it take? Many people today are getting very tired of listening to politicians who make promises, promises, promises, and then don't fulfill them. I want to say in their behalf that they *cannot* fulfill them—yet they promise. We also have all kinds of new nostrums coming from college professors and leaders in every field. There is only one thing wrong: they won't work. Maybe in desperation America will turn to God. That is what happened to Israel after twenty years.

And Samuel spake unto all the house of Israel, saying, If ye do return unto the LORD with all your hearts, then put away the strange gods and Ashtaroth from among you, and prepare your hearts unto the LORD, and serve him only: and he will deliver you out of the hand of the Philistines.

Then the children of Israel did put away Baalim and Ashtaroth, and served the LORD only [1 Sam. 7:3–4].

This is actually the beginning of Samuel's great ministry. Israel was deep in idolatry. They had turned from the living and true God. They had been defeated in so many battles that it had become old hat to them, and they were extremely discouraged. They were beginning to lament after the Lord. We, too, need to get back to the Lord. There is a hunger in the hearts of many people who are saying, "We are tired of eating the husks that pigs eat in the far country. We want to get back to the Father's house." Well, they have to come through the door of the Word of God.

And Samuel said, Gather all Israel to Mizpeh, and I will pray for you unto the LORD.

And they gathered together to Mizpeh, and drew water, and poured it out before the LORD, and fasted on that day, and said there, We have sinned against the LORD. And Samuel judged the children of Israel in Mizpeh [1 Sam. 7:5–6].

Samuel is not only the prophet of Israel, he is also the judge of the nation. Here we find Israel turning from false gods to the true God. This man Samuel is praying for them, and they confess their sins. This is the way back for God's people. I do not think there is another way back. I hear about all kinds of methods today that will be blessed by God. Let me put it right down in bold letters and tell it like it is. What God's people need to do is to go to God and *confess* their *sins*. They need to see themselves in the light of the Word of God. If we really see ourselves, we see that we have come short of the glory of God (Rom. 3:23); and then we can be assured that the blood of Jesus Christ, God's Son, will keep on cleansing us from all sin (1 John 1:9).

VICTORY AT EBEN-EZER

And the children of Israel said to Samuel, Cease not to cry unto the LORD our God for us, that he will save us out of the hand of the Philistines.

And Samuel took a sucking lamb, and offered it for a burnt offering wholly unto the LORD: and Samuel cried unto the LORD for Israel; and the LORD heard him.

And as Samuel was offering up the burnt offering, the Philistines drew

near to battle against Israel: but the LORD thundered with a great thunder on that day upon the Philistines, and discomfited them; and they were smitten before Israel.

And the men of Israel went out of Mizpeh, and pursued the Philistines, and smote them, until they came under Beth-car [1 Sam. 7:8–11].

God gave Israel a great victory, and it was the first one they had had for a long time. These people had lapsed into idolatry; they had been in sullen rebellion. When they began to turn to God, Samuel exacted a confession of sin and a promise to return to God. As a result God gave them a signal victory over the Philistines.

Then Samuel took a stone, and set it between Mizpeh and Shen, and called the name of it Eben-ezer, saying, Hitherto hath the LORD helped us [1 Sam. 7:12].

The name *Eben-ezer* means "stone of help." "Hitherto hath the Lord helped us." It was also a stone of remembrance, looking back to the past. It was a stone of recognition, a stone for the present. It was a stone of revelation, a stone for the future. "Hitherto [up to this point, up to the present time] God has helped us."

It is customary for us to look back over the past. Remember what the Lord said through Paul to the Philippians: "Being confident of this very thing, that he which hath begun a good work in you will perform it until the day of Jesus Christ" (Phil. 1:6). Friend, has God brought you to this point? Is He leading you today? Is He guiding you? If He has, you can say, "Hitherto has the Lord helped me." Since He has helped you up to this moment, He will continue to do that.

God has given us memories so that we can have roses in December. As memory plays on the keyboard of the past, I am sure that all of us can say, "Hitherto hath the Lord helped us." Joshua could say, ". . . as for me and my house, we will serve the LORD" (Josh. 24:15). David could say, "O give thanks unto the LORD, for he is good: for his mercy endureth for ever. Let the redeemed of the LORD say so, whom he hath redeemed from the hand of the enemy" (Ps. 107:1–2). I personally want to say that oh, the Lord is good! He is the One who has helped us and will help us.

A businessman said sometime ago, "You know, the use of time might be likened to the terminology of banking. Yesterday is a canceled check; tomorrow is a promissory note, but today is cash. Spend it wisely." Do you recognize God in your life? That is what Samuel meant by that Eben-ezer stone. It was a stone of revelation. It not only meant "hitherto," it also meant "henceforth." "The LORD is my shepherd," said David; then looking into the future, "I shall not want" (Ps. 23:1). Someone once said, "I am very interested in the future because I expect to spend the rest of my life there, and I want to be reasonably sure of what kind of a future it is going to be." "And we know that all things work together for good to them that love God, to them who are the called according to his purpose" (Rom. 8:28). Dr. R. A. Torrey always said that Romans 8:28 was a soft pillow for a tired heart. We all need an Eben-ezer stone. I trust that you have one in your life.

So the Philistines were subdued, and they came no more into the coast of Israel: and the hand of the LORD was against the Philistines all the days of Samuel [1 Sam. 7:13].

I think it can be said that from this time on the Philistines were never again as dominant and formidable a foe as they had been before the battle. This was a significant battle, and a stone now stands in memory of it. The stone was about three or four miles north by northwest of Jerusalem, in sight of the city.

And Samuel judged Israel all the days of his life.

And he went from year to year in circuit to Beth-el, and Gilgal, and Mizpeh, and judged Israel in all those places.

And his return was to Ramah; for there was his house; and there he judged Israel; and there he built an altar unto the LORD [1 Sam. 7:15–17].

This is the story. Samuel is a prophet and a judge of Israel. He is a circuit judge. He goes from Beth-el to Gilgal to Mizpeh and back to Ramah, all areas north of Jerusalem. He "judged Israel in all those places."

CHAPTER 8

***THEME:** Israel rejects God and demands a king*

Hosea 13:11 can be written over the remainder of 1 and 2 Samuel: "I gave thee a king in mine anger, and took him away in my wrath."

Samuel was a great judge and a man of God. He was brought up in the tabernacle where he saw the wickedness of Eli's sons and how God judged them. Yet notice what Samuel does.

And it came to pass, when Samuel was old, that he made his sons judges over Israel [1 Sam. 8:1].

Samuel made his own sons judges to succeed him, although they were unworthy and incompetent for the job. This act was a mistake. Samuel was a great judge, a wonderful prophet, and a great man of God—but he was a failure as a father just as Eli had been.

Now the name of his firstborn was Joel; and the name of his second, Abiah: they were judges in Beer-sheba.

And his sons walked not in his ways, but turned aside after lucre, and took bribes, and perverted judgment [1 Sam. 8:2–3].

These were Samuel's sons. They were totally dishonest. Strange, isn't it? Today we see so much of that. Many pastors have said to me, "Why is it that you can have a godly family in your church and the son or daughter can become a dissolute vagrant or go on drugs?" Many times there is no explanation for it. Well, Samuel was a great man, God's man, and look what his sons did.

Then all the elders of Israel gathered themselves together, and came to Samuel unto Ramah,

And said unto him, Behold, thou art old, and thy sons walk not in thy ways: now make us a king to judge us like all the nations [1 Sam. 8:4–5].

The people of Israel ask for a king. They are influenced, of course, by the surrounding nations. They give as their reason Samuel's advanced age and the waywardness of his sons.

But the thing displeased Samuel, when they said, Give us a king to judge us. And Samuel prayed unto the LORD.

And the LORD said unto Samuel, Hearken unto the voice of the people in all that they say unto thee: for they have not rejected thee, but they have rejected me, that I should not reign over them [1 Sam. 8:6–7].

The fact that Samuel had made his sons judges gives these people an excuse to ask for a king. Undoubtedly this was a heartbreak to Samuel. God comforts him with the assurance that Israel's rejection is not of him but of God himself. Samuel's sons are the excuse, but rejection of God's sovereignty is the real reason.

Then Samuel warns Israel what it will be like to have a king. He tells them that a king will reign over them, take their sons for soldiers, their daughters for cooks and maidservants, and part of their fields, vineyards, oliveyards, and animals for himself. He warns them that eventually they will cry out in their distress and that in that day the Lord will not hear them.

Nevertheless the people refused to obey the voice of Samuel; and they said, Nay; but we will have a king over us;

That we also may be like all the nations; and that our king may judge us, and go out before us, and fight our battles.

And Samuel heard all the words of the people, and he rehearsed them in the ears of the LORD.

And the LORD said to Samuel, Hearken unto their voice, and make them a king. And Samuel said unto the men of Israel, Go ye every man unto his city [1 Sam. 8:19–22].

The children of Israel are going to have their way. God is going to give them a king. What was true of Israel in the days of Moses is still true. "And he gave them their request; but sent leanness into their soul" (Ps. 106:15). God will grant Israel's desire for a king, but it will not be to their advantage. God's guidance of the nation will be indirectly through the prophet. As we shall see, God will not speak directly to the king, but still through the prophet who will convey God's word to the king. The king will accept it or reject it as he chooses.

CHAPTERS 9–10

***THEME:** Saul is chosen as king; Saul is anointed as king*

SAUL IS CHOSEN AS KING

Chapter 9 begins the second major section of the book of 1 Samuel. The first section dealt with Samuel; now the emphasis shifts to Saul. Saul is one of those strange individuals whom we encounter in the Word of God. Like Balaam, it is difficult to interpret him. Both in the Old and New Testaments there are several strange characters who move across the pages of Scripture in semidarkness. They come out, as it were, into the light but, like the groundhog, they see their shadow and move back into the darkness again.

Saul is not a king when we first meet him. In fact, I do not think he ever was a king in the true sense of the word.

> **Now there was a man of Benjamin, whose name was Kish, the son of Abiel, the son of Zeror, the son of Bechorath, the son of Aphiah, a Benjamite, a mighty man of power [1 Sam. 9:1].**

Kish was Saul's father, and he belonged to the tribe of Benjamin. Recalling the history of the twelve sons of Jacob in Genesis, the tribe originated with the youngest son, Benjamin, a favorite of his father. His mother had died at his birth and, as she was passing, she named him Benoni, "son of my sorrow." But when Jacob looked at the little fellow, he said, "No, he is going to be the son of my right hand," and he named him Benjamin. The boy was the favorite son and was protected by his brothers. Then in the Book of Judges, the tribe was decimated because of an episode of gross sin that took place in the tribe. It is from this tribe, Benjamin, that the first king comes.

> **And he had a son, whose name was Saul, a choice young man, and a goodly: and there was not among the children of Israel a goodlier person than he: from his shoulders and upward he was higher than any of the people [1 Sam. 9:2].**

This boy Saul was handsome. Physically he looked like a king, but he was an actor that played a part. He was not a king at heart. The people, however, were choosing their king by his outward appearance and not according to his character.

It is this emphasis on "outward appearance" that places our nation in such a dangerous position today. The most dangerous enemy we have is the television. The man that will ultimately control this country is the man who has a good television appearance. Why? Because we choose men by the way they look and the way they talk rather than by their character. If only we had an X-ray—instead of the television—that would reveal the true character of a man!

The children of Israel wanted a king, and they liked Saul. He was handsome. He was tall. He was fine looking. There wasn't a more kingly-looking man in the nation. He could have been both a television and a movie star. He looked the part and could play the part; the trouble was he was not a king at heart.

> **And the asses of Kish Saul's father were lost. And Kish said to Saul his son, Take now one of the servants with thee, and arise, go seek the asses [1 Sam. 9:3].**

I know that the Lord has a sense of humor. You just cannot miss it because it is in too many places in the Word of God. Saul is out looking for the asses of his father, and the asses of Israel are looking for a king. They are bound to get together, friend, and they do. The Lord must smile when a thing like this takes place. What a commentary on the human race!

> **And when they were come to the land of Zuph, Saul said to his servant that was with him, Come, and let us return; lest my father leave caring for the asses, and take thought for us [1 Sam. 9:5].**

Saul and his servant had looked all around for his father's animals and could not find them. Finally Saul said, "Let's go home because we are going to get lost too, and they will have to send out a search party for us."

> **And he said unto him, Behold now, there is in this city a man of God, and he is an honourable man; all that he saith cometh surely to pass: now let us go thither; peradventure he can shew us our way that we should go.**
>
> **Then said Saul to his servant, But, behold, if we go, what shall we bring the man? for the bread is spent in our vessels, and there is not a present to bring to the man of God: what have we?**

And the servant answered Saul again, and said, Behold, I have here at hand the fourth part of a shekel of silver: that will I give to the man of God, to tell us our way [1 Sam. 9:6–8].

Here is a little explanation inserted by the Spirit of God which is helpful:

(Beforetime in Israel, when a man went to inquire of God, thus he spake, Come, and let us go to the seer: for he that is now called a Prophet was beforetime called a Seer.) [1 Sam. 9:9].

There is a change of names. Men who dealt in necromancy and spiritism were called "seers." God wanted a different name for His man, and so he is called a "prophet." This actually makes Samuel the first of the order of prophets. Although Moses is called a prophet, Samuel is the first of the order of prophets. Samuel, of course, is the man Saul and his servant are talking about.

And they went up into the city: and when they were come into the city, behold, Samuel came out against them, for to go up to the high place [1 Sam. 9:14].

This does not mean that Samuel opposed Saul and his servant; it simply means that he met them on the way.

Now the LORD had told Samuel in his ear a day before Saul came, saying [1 Sam. 9:15].

The question is often asked, "Just how did God communicate in the Old Testament when it says, 'The Lord spake'?" I think that when it says the Lord spake, He spoke. That is the way communication came. It came by words. It is the words of Scripture that are inspired, not the thoughts. We are given an inkling of how God communicated when it says, "Now the Lord had told Samuel in his ear. . . ." What I hear in my ears are *words*. That is the only thing that makes sense and that, of course, is what Samuel heard.

To-morrow about this time I will send thee a man out of the land of Benjamin, and thou shalt anoint him to be captain over my people Israel, that he may save my people out of the hand of the Philistines: for I have looked upon my people, because their cry is come unto me [1 Sam. 9:16].

Many times God answers our request when it is not the best thing for us. When we keep crying to the Lord for whatever it is we want, finally He does for us what He did for Israel —He grants our request. When the children of Israel were in the wilderness, they cried for meat. God gave them meat, but He sent "leanness unto their souls." That is why prayer should be made in the name of Christ, which means that it must be according to His will and for His glory. All requests should hinge on that very important matter.

And when Samuel saw Saul, the LORD said unto him, Behold the man whom I spake to thee of! this same shall reign over my people [1 Sam. 9:17].

God granted their request and gave them a king. Saul was a man that impressed even Samuel. We will find out that Samuel regarded him highly and regretted the fact that he did not make good.

Then Saul drew near to Samuel in the gate, and said, Tell me, I pray thee, where the seer's house is.

And Samuel answered Saul, and said, I am the seer: go up before me unto the high place; for ye shall eat with me to-day, and to-morrow I will let thee go, and will tell thee all that is in thine heart.

And as for thine asses that were lost three days ago, set not thy mind on them; for they are found. And on whom is all the desire of Israel? Is it not on thee, and on all thy father's house? [1 Sam. 9:18–20].

Saul was actually not God's choice. That is, He gave Israel the sort of man He knew they wanted. As Saul moved among the people, they saw that he was tall, handsome, and looked like a king. When they asked for a king, God granted their request.

And Saul answered and said, Am not I a Benjamite, of the smallest of the tribes of Israel? and my family the least of all the families of the tribe of Benjamin? wherefore then speakest thou so to me? [1 Sam. 9:21].

Saul sounds a great deal like Gideon in this verse. He sounds very humble. Gideon said, ". . . Oh my Lord, wherewith shall I save Israel? behold, my family is poor in Manasseh, and I am the least in my father's house" (Jud. 6:15). Gideon was saying, "You can't get any smaller than I am." Gideon was telling the truth. He was a coward and frightened to death. Israel was at war and badly outnumbered. Saul had no reason to be afraid. Israel was not at war. He had been out looking for his father's longeared donkeys that had already been found. His mission was accomplished. The point is that there was nothing to prompt a speech like he gave. I personally feel that his was a false humility. I think Saul felt very much like he was the one who could be king.

And Samuel took Saul and his servant, and brought them into the parlour, and made them sit in the chiefest place among them that were bidden, which were about thirty persons [1 Sam. 9:22].

Apparently Samuel called a small group of leaders together.

And Samuel said unto the cook, Bring the portion which I gave thee, of which I said unto thee, Set it by thee.

And the cook took up the shoulder, and that which was upon it, and set it before Saul. And Samuel said, Behold that which is left! set it before thee, and eat: for unto this time hath it been kept for thee since I said, I have invited the people. So Saul did eat with Samuel that day.

And when they were come down from the high place into the city, Samuel communed with Saul upon the top of the house.

And they arose early: and it came to pass about the spring of the day, that Samuel called Saul to the top of the house, saying, Up, that I may send thee away. And Saul arose, and they went out both of them, he and Samuel, abroad.

And as they were going down to the end of the city, Samuel said to Saul, Bid the servant pass on before us, (and he passed on,) but stand thou still a while, that I may shew thee the word of God [1 Sam. 9:23–27].

We have here the formality they went through. Saul ate with Samuel that day, and they had a conference.

SAUL IS ANOINTED AS KING

Then Samuel took a vial of oil, and poured it upon his head, and kissed him, and said, Is it not because the LORD hath anointed thee to be captain over his inheritance? [1 Sam. 10:1].

Samuel anoints Saul as king and then kisses him, which was probably an act demonstrating his personal affection for Saul.

When thou art departed from me to day, then thou shalt find two men by Rachel's sepulchre in the border of Benjamin at Zelzah; and they will say unto thee, The asses which thou wentest to seek are found: and, lo, thy father hath left the care of the asses, and sorroweth for you, saying, What shall I do for my son? [1 Sam. 10:2].

As far as Kish is concerned, his son Saul is lost. But Saul is engaged in serious business. Samuel has anointed him king near the tomb of Rachel, which is in the territory of Benjamin near Bethlehem.

After that thou shalt come to the hill of God, where is the garrison of the Philistines: and it shall come to pass, when thou art come thither to the city, that thou shalt meet a company of prophets coming down from the high place with a psaltery, and a tabret, and a pipe, and a harp, before them; and they shall prophesy [1 Sam. 10:5].

This is what Saul is to encounter on his way back home.

And the spirit of the LORD will come upon thee, and thou shalt prophesy with them, and shalt be turned into another man [1 Sam. 10:6].

Here again we have a question: Was Saul converted? Is this verse the proof of his conversion? Certainly it is not a final proof.

I do not believe that he was converted. If I sound like I am prejudiced against Saul, I will tell you why. It is not because of the material we have already covered concerning him but what is coming that makes me believe that Saul was not genuine, and certainly not genuinely converted at all.

Someone is bound to say, "But the Spirit of God came upon Saul and he was a different man." Yes, but it does not say that he became a *new* man. After all, didn't the Spirit of God come upon Balaam? And we have no proof that he was converted. What about Judas? Christ sent out twelve disciples, and we are told that all of them performed miracles. Did Judas perform miracles? Certainly he did. Would you say that Judas was converted? So let us withhold making a final decision about

Saul—although I seem to have already made one.

And it was so, that when he had turned his back to go from Samuel, God gave him another heart: and all those signs came to pass that day [1 Sam. 10:9].

When Saul left Samuel, I think Samuel watched him walk away and said, "My, he is a fine fellow." But even a prophet can be wrong. The prophet Nathan was wrong when he told David to build God a house. God had to intervene, and Nathan had to correct himself. Samuel was wrong about Saul. As he looked at this young man Saul, he saw a big, husky, fine-looking fellow. He would have been able to play in the line of any professional football team. But he was no king at all.

And when they came thither to the hill, behold, a company of prophets met him; and the spirit of God came upon him, and he prophesied among them.

And it came to pass, when all that knew him beforetime saw that, behold, he prophesied among the prophets, then the people said one to another, What is this that is come unto the son of Kish? Is Saul also among the prophets? [1 Sam. 10:10–11].

The Spirit of God came upon Saul and he prophesied. Everyone who had known him before knew that something had happened to him. They asked, "Is Saul also among the prophets?" God was giving Saul an opportunity. God never withheld anything from him, and yet he failed.

And Saul said unto his uncle, He told us plainly that the asses were found. But of the matter of the kingdom, whereof Samuel spake, he told him not [1 Sam. 10:16].

He kept quiet about that.

And Samuel called the people together unto the LORD to Mizpeh;

And said unto the children of Israel, Thus saith the LORD God of Israel, I brought up Israel out of Egypt, and delivered you out of the hand of the Egyptians, and out of the hand of all kingdoms, and of them that oppressed you:

And ye have this day rejected your God, who himself saved you out of all your adversities and your tribulations; and ye have said unto him, Nay, but set a king over us. Now therefore present yourselves before the LORD by your tribes, and by your thousands [1 Sam. 10:17–19].

When the children of Israel asked for a king and took Saul, it meant they were turning their backs upon God. We need to note that their reception of Saul as king meant their rejection of God.

When he had caused the tribe of Benjamin to come near by their families, the family of Matri was taken, and Saul the son of Kish was taken: and when they sought him, he could not be found.

Therefore they inquired of the LORD further, if the man should yet come thither. And the LORD answered, Behold, he hath hid himself among the stuff [1 Sam. 10:21–22].

When the time came for Samuel to introduce Saul to the crowd as their king, he could not find him. This great big fellow, Saul, acted just like a little child. He ran and hid, and they had to find him and bring him out. Again, in my judgment, this is an evidence of false modesty. The anointing oil has been poured upon him, and if he is given an opportunity to be king and serve God, then let him step out in the open and act like a king.

And Samuel said to all the people, See ye him whom the LORD hath chosen, that there is none like him among all the people? And all the people shouted, and said, God save the king [1 Sam. 10:24].

And God save the people also! This was the first time this cry "God save the king!" was uttered. As you know, it is still used in modern England.

Then Samuel told the people the manner of the kingdom, and wrote it in a book, and laid it up before the LORD. And Samuel sent all the people away, every man to his house [1 Sam. 10:25].

"Then Samuel told" the children of Israel about "the manner of the kingdom, and wrote it in a book." On the basis of this we believe that Samuel wrote the first part of the book of 1 Samuel.

CHAPTERS 11–12

***THEME:** Saul's victory over the Ammonites; transfer of authority from Samuel to Saul*

SAUL'S VICTORY OVER THE AMMONITES

In the previous chapter I said some rather harsh things about King Saul, although I did not seem to have sufficient grounds at the time. I had only a strong suspicion that he was not genuine. I felt that he would have made a good actor but not a good king, even though he had a good beginning.

Then Nahash the Ammonite came up, and encamped against Jabesh-gilead: and all the men of Jabesh said unto Nahash, Make a covenant with us, and we will serve thee.

And Nahash the Ammonite answered them, On this condition will I make a covenant with you, that I may thrust out all your right eyes, and lay it for a reproach upon all Israel.

And the elders of Jabesh said unto him, Give us seven days' respite, that we may send messengers unto all the coasts of Israel: and then, if there be no man to save us, we will come out to thee [1 Sam. 11:1–3].

This was a very strong, ugly demand made by Nahash on the men of Jabesh. They needed deliverance.

Then came the messengers to Gibeah of Saul, and told the tidings in the ears of the people: and all the people lifted up their voices, and wept.

And, behold, Saul came after the herd out of the field; and Saul said, What aileth the people that they weep? And they told him the tidings of the men of Jabesh.

And the spirit of God came upon Saul when he heard those tidings, and his anger was kindled greatly.

And he took a yoke of oxen, and hewed them in pieces, and sent them throughout all the coasts of Israel by the hands of messengers, saying, Whosoever cometh not forth after Saul and after Samuel, so shall it be done unto his oxen. And the fear of the LORD fell on the people, and they came out with one consent [1 Sam. 11:4–7].

Notice how Saul identifies himself with Samuel. I do not think at this particular time that Saul's name could have stood alone. When Saul asked the people to come and linked his name with Samuel's name, however, the people came. They also came because of two main fears. They were afraid of Saul and also fearful of what the Ammonites might do to them.

And it was so on the morrow, that Saul put the people in three companies; and they came into the midst of the host in the morning watch, and slew the Ammonites until the heat of the day: and it came to pass, that they which remained were scattered, so that two of them were not left together [1 Sam. 11:11].

Saul divided his men into three companies. Then the Israelites went after the Ammonites and slew and scattered them so badly that not two of them were left together. Each Ammonite that survived fled by himself.

And the people said unto Samuel, Who is he that said, Shall Saul reign over us? bring the men, that we may put them to death [1 Sam. 11:12].

Some of the Israelites opposed the idea of having Saul as their king. Samuel ignored that opposition until the nation was united in favor of Saul. Saul's leadership in dealing with the Ammonites took care of the resistance.

And Saul said, There shall not a man be put to death this day: for to-day the LORD hath wrought salvation in Israel.

Then said Samuel to the people, Come, and let us go to Gilgal, and renew the kingdom there.

And all the people went to Gilgal; and there they made Saul king before the LORD in Gilgal; and there they sacrificed sacrifices of peace offerings before the LORD; and there Saul and all the men of Israel rejoiced greatly [1 Sam. 11:13–15].

Now all of Israel accepts Saul as king.

You may be saying, "Well, now, preacher, you see that you were wrong. You were prejudiced against King Saul, and look, he is making good!" Yes, he certainly started off like a great king, but let's keep reading. It is too bad that his story doesn't end here.

TRANSFER OF AUTHORITY FROM SAMUEL TO SAUL

Chapter 12 begins with the swan song of Samuel.

And Samuel said unto all Israel, Behold, I have hearkened unto your voice in all that ye said unto me, and have made a king over you [1 Sam. 12:1].

This is Samuel's swan song, his final speech. He was a remarkable man, and he was now succeeded by Saul. Although Israel's choice was a king rather than God, He would still bless the people if they would obey. That is evident. Saul was king, and God would give him every opportunity.

And now, behold, the king walketh before you: and I am old and grayheaded; and, behold, my sons are with you: and I have walked before you from my childhood unto this day [1 Sam. 12:2].

Samuel was brought up in the tabernacle. His life was spent in a "fish bowl"—he was always in public view. Probably no man ever had quite the public life that Samuel had. Many times in our age a man moves into public life and the people accept him. Then suddenly someone finds out about his black past, and the hero comes falling to the ground. Such was not the case with Samuel. He was brought as a little boy, by his mother, to the tabernacle. He lived his entire life before the people. Then he put in this sad note of a fond father, "My sons are with you." In other words, "Why didn't you accept them?" Samuel tried to put them in position but God would not have them. They were boys who were not acceptable to Him.

Behold, here I am: witness against me before the LORD, and before his anointed: whose ox have I taken? or whose ass have I taken? or whom have I defrauded? whom have I oppressed? or of whose hand have I received any bribe to blind mine eyes therewith? and I will restore it you [1 Sam. 12:3].

This is quite a statement for a man to make who had been before the public eye for so many years, and who had been a judge. He had had many opportunities to become rich but had not yielded to the temptation. Samuel is one of the outstanding men of the Word of God—yet he was a failure as a father. Many public men are like that. Many popular Christian leaders have had children who were failures. It is difficult to understand, but that is the way the human family has been moving down through the centuries and millenniums of the past.

Samuel said that if he had done any of the things he had mentioned to any of the people, he would restore it. It would have been easy for some men who had been miffed at one of Samuel's decisions to step out and say, "Well, you certainly were not fair with me." But nobody stepped out.

And he said unto them, The LORD is witness against you, and his anointed is witness this day, that ye have not found aught in my hand. And they answered, He is witness [1 Sam. 12:5].

Samuel's life could stand public inspection. It could be put under the hot spotlight of public opinion. He was truly a man of God.

Samuel continues by rehearsing Israel's history. Many men whom God made great used this method. Moses used it, Joshua used it, Gideon used it, and now Samuel uses it. In the New Testament we see that Stephen, when he appeared before the Sanhedrin, also rehearsed the history of Israel. Samuel is reminding his people of God's faithfulness and mercy to them. When their apostasy led to servitude and they cried to the Lord in their distress, He graciously heard and sent a deliverer. He is saying, as he did at Mizpeh, "Hitherto hath the LORD helped us."

Then he moves to their present state and condition.

Now therefore behold the king whom ye have chosen, and whom ye have desired! and, behold, the LORD hath set a king over you [1 Sam. 12:13].

Samuel makes it quite clear that Saul was the people's choice. Many people believe that the voice of the majority, the choice of the people, is the voice of God. The Bible contradicts this thinking. Generally the minority are closer to determining the will of God. The people wanted Saul. God was the One who chose David. What a difference when God makes the choice!

If ye will fear the LORD, and serve him, and obey his voice, and not rebel against the commandment of the LORD, then shall both ye and also the king that reigneth over you continue following the LORD your God [1 Sam. 12:14].

Just because Saul is the people's choice, God will not reject him. God is going to give him an opportunity.

But if ye will not obey the voice of the LORD, but rebel against the commandment of the LORD, then shall the hand of the LORD be against you, as it was against your fathers [1 Sam. 12:15].

Samuel is telling it like it is. If the people will serve God, He will bless them. If they do not serve Him, judgment will come.

Now God will respond to this in a dramatic and miraculous way.

Now therefore stand and see this great thing, which the LORD will do before your eyes.

Is it not wheat harvest to-day? I will call unto the LORD, and he shall send thunder and rain; that ye may perceive and see that your wickedness is great, which ye have done in the sight of the LORD, in asking you a king.

So Samuel called unto the LORD; and the LORD sent thunder and rain that day: and all the people greatly feared the LORD and Samuel [1 Sam. 12:16–18].

Elijah was not the first man that could "preach up a storm"—he brought in a thunderstorm, but Samuel did it before Elijah did. And this is God's seal, I think, upon Samuel's life. The thunder and rain were God's great "amen" on Samuel's career as God's spokesman.

And all the people said unto Samuel, Pray for thy servants unto the LORD thy God, that we die not; for we have added unto all our sins this evil, to ask us a king [1 Sam. 12:19].

It was sin for these people to ask for a king. They were rejecting God by wanting a king to rule over them like the other nations.

And Samuel said unto the people, Fear not: ye have done all this wickedness: yet turn not aside from following the LORD, but serve the LORD with all your heart [1 Sam. 12:20].

Friend, don't let past sins and mistakes spoil your life. Regardless of who you are or what you have done, if you will turn to the Lord for salvation and forgiveness, God will accept and richly bless you. Don't let the past destroy the future and ruin the present for you. Move out for God today, my Christian friend.

And turn ye not aside: for then should ye go after vain things, which cannot profit nor deliver; for they are vain [1 Sam. 12:21].

Hold to the Lord alone. Let the gimmicks alone. Today the church is experimenting with methods. The church does not seem to realize that only God can bless. We need to hold on to the Lord and His Word. I don't think the Bible needs defending. It needs explaining; it needs to be proclaimed. We need the exclamation point and the declaration mark more than we need a question mark.

For the LORD will not forsake his people for his great name's sake: because it hath pleased the LORD to make you his people [1 Sam. 12:22].

This is a glorious verse. Have you taken the name of the Lord? Is He your Savior? Are you resting in Him? He will not forsake you. The Lord says through the writer of Hebrews, "Let your conversation be without covetousness; and be content with such things as ye have: for he hath said, I will never leave thee, nor forsake thee" (Heb. 13:5). How wonderful is our God! It has pleased Him to make us His people.

Why did God choose the nation Israel? When you are looking for the answer, look to God and not to the people. God did it and that is enough. Perhaps God chose you, and some of your friends are wondering why. The important thing is that God chose us and that is enough. Thank God for that. He could have passed me by, but I rejoice in the fact that He did not. This is a tremendous message Samuel is giving the Israelites! Aren't you glad that you are on the Lord's side? Isn't it wonderful that you and the Lord are friends? Isn't it great that He is your Savior? He is for you and not against you. He wants to help you. He is a mighty Helper, friend, as well as a Savior. And He saves to the uttermost.

Moreover as for me, God forbid that I should sin against the LORD in ceasing to pray for you: but I will teach you the good and the right way [1 Sam. 12:23].

I have found in my radio ministry that many people have a gift. It is a gift of prayer, and I believe it is from God. There are some people in Southern California on beds of sickness and pain—some who will never leave their beds —who have a ministry of prayer. I wouldn't take anything for their prayers. I need their prayers.

Now that I am retired I have more opportunity to move out across the country. I am enjoying my greatest ministry today, and it is largely because of the prayers of God's people. For example, in Chicago a man shook hands with me and said, "You know, I have been praying for you for years." When I hear something like this, I feel like weeping and getting down on my knees before Him. It is a privilege to pray for others.

Samuel said, "God forbid that I should sin against the LORD in ceasing to pray for you." Each one of us has a prayer responsibility. I feel the necessity to pray for a certain group of ministers in this country, most of whom are my friends. I have been in their churches, and I know something about their problems. I pray for them regularly. I also have a responsibility to pray for my family. If I don't pray for them, who will? I have a responsibility to pray for my radio ministry. You too have a responsibility, Christian friend. We ought to pray for one another. There are many needy people. God forbid that we should sin against the Lord in ceasing to pray for one another.

Only fear the LORD, and serve him in truth with all your heart; for consider how great things he hath done for you.

But if ye shall still do wickedly, ye shall be consumed, both ye and your king [1 Sam. 12:24–25].

The last time I went to a football game it was at the Rose Bowl in Pasadena, California. It was a long time ago. I sat next to a man who was rooting for the other team, and I want to tell you he was a nut. His team would make an inch on the field and he would jump to his feet. You would think he was having a conniption fit of some kind. My, how he carried on. He irritated me because I was rooting for the other side. But as I looked at him, I could not help wishing that I had that kind of enthusiasm for the things of God. My friend, we need to serve Him with all of our hearts!

What a message there is for you and me in this swan song of Samuel the prophet.

CHAPTER 13

THEME: *Saul rebels against God*

The real nature of Saul begins to show. His son Jonathan got the victory at Michmash, but Saul blew the trumpet and took credit for it. In presumption, Saul intruded into the priest's office. Samuel rebuked and rejected Saul. The disarmament of Israel is revealed.

In this chapter I think I will be able to sustain the thesis that I presented in chapter 9 relative to King Saul. Saul's outward veneer made him look like a king, but underneath he was no king at all. He was nothing but a paper-doll king.

Saul reigned one year; and when he had reigned two years over Israel,

Saul chose him three thousand men of Israel; whereof two thousand were with Saul in Michmash and in mount Beth-el, and a thousand were with Jonathan in Gibeah of Benjamin: and the rest of the people he sent every man to his tent.

And Jonathan smote the garrison of the Philistines that was in Geba, and the Philistines heard of it. And Saul blew the trumpet throughout all the land, saying, Let the Hebrews hear.

And all Israel heard say that Saul had smitten a garrison of the Philistines, and that Israel also was had in abomination with the Philistines. And the people were called together after Saul to Gilgal [1 Sam. 13:1–4].

The true character of Saul is beginning to emerge. When we get a good view of him, we are going to see that he is a phony. We read in these verses that Jonathan "smote the garrison of the Philistines." Who got credit for the victory? It was Saul. Jonathan appears to be a capable military leader. Later on we will find that he gains another great victory by using very interesting strategy. But in this particular battle Jonathan did the fighting, and Saul blew the trumpet. Saul took the credit for winning. Saul believed in the motto: "He who tooteth not his own horn, said horn will go untooted." Saul blew his own horn. He did not give his son credit for winning the battle. He called all of Israel together and gave a phony report. The army knew Saul's report was not true and so did the followers of Jonathan. Folks are beginning to suspect that there is a weakness in Saul's army and that it is his Achilles' heel. Is he humble? I said at the beginning that Saul had a case of false humility, and this fact is coming to light now.

And the Philistines gathered themselves together to fight with Israel, thirty thousand chariots, and six thousand horsemen, and people as the sand which is on the sea shore in multitude: and they came up, and pitched in Michmash, eastward from Beth-aven.

When the men of Israel saw that they were in a strait, (for the people were distressed,) then the people did hide themselves in caves, and in thickets, and in rocks, and in high places, and in pits [1 Sam. 13:5–6].

Apparently the Philistines recovered from their losses and came with force against the Israelites.

And he tarried seven days, according to the set time that Samuel had appointed: but Samuel came not to Gilgal; and the people were scattered from him.

And Saul said, Bring hither a burnt offering to me, and peace offerings. And he offered the burnt offering [1 Sam. 13:8–9].

Here is another revelation concerning Saul. He presumed that because of his position as king he could offer a burnt offering. Later on we will find that another king by the name of Uzziah also presumed he could perform a priestly duty. God judged him severely—he became a leper (2 Chron. 26). Saul ignored God's explicit instructions that only a priest from the tribe of Levi could offer a burnt offering.

And it came to pass, that as soon as he had made an end of offering the burnt offering, behold, Samuel came; and Saul went out to meet him, that he might salute him.

And Samuel said, What hast thou done? And Saul said, Because I saw that the people were scattered from me, and that thou camest not within the days appointed, and that the Philistines gathered themselves together at Michmash [1 Sam. 13:10–11].

Saul was not willing to wait for Samuel. He was impatient and presumptuous. He thought he had three good reasons for not waiting for Samuel to appear: (1) The people were scattered; (2) the Philistines were coming against him; and (3) Samuel was a little late in arriving. Saul was rationalizing, of course. He was blaming everything and everyone else.

Therefore said I, The Philistines will come down now upon me to Gilgal, and I have not made supplication unto the Lord: I forced myself therefore, and offered a burnt offering [1 Sam. 13:12].

Saul "forced" himself to offer an offering and make supplication unto the Lord. May I say that he was lying. He was being falsely pious. This is the real Saul emerging.

And Samuel said to Saul, Thou hast done foolishly: thou hast not kept the commandment of the Lord thy God, which he commanded thee: for now would the Lord have established thy kingdom upon Israel for ever.

But now thy kingdom shall not continue: the Lord hath sought him a man after his own heart, and the Lord hath commanded him to be captain over his people, because thou hast not kept that which the Lord commanded thee [1 Sam. 13:13–14].

Saul was told in the beginning that if he obeyed God, he would be blessed, but if he disobeyed, there would be judgment. The ruler *must* obey the Lord. And what the world needs today is a ruler who is being ruled by the Lord. Our problems stem from the fact that we don't have that kind of ruler. Of course we will not get one until the Lord Jesus comes back to earth; that is God's ultimate goal for this earth. Saul has disobeyed, so God has another man to be king. He is going to bring him on the scene a little later. Even Samuel, at this time, does not know who he is.

And Samuel arose, and gat him up from Gilgal unto Gibeah of Benjamin. And Saul numbered the people that were present with him, about six hundred men.

And Saul, and Jonathan his son, and the people that were present with them, abode in Gibeah of Benjamin: but the Philistines encamped in Michmash.

And the spoilers came out of the camp of the Philistines in three companies: one company turned unto the way that leadeth to Ophrah, unto the land of Shual [1 Sam. 13:15–17].

The battle is about to begin. We will see here the real danger of disarmament.

There are people today who are trying to disarm America. They think that if you destroy all of the ammunition somehow or other war will be eliminated. Others believe that if a gun law is passed and honest people are disarmed, this will stop the crooks. You cannot disarm the crooks, friend. All you do is lay honest people open to violation by the unlawful ones. This is idealistic, foolish thinking.

Now there was no smith found throughout all the land of Israel: for the Philistines said, Lest the Hebrews make them swords or spears:

But all the Israelites went down to the Philistines, to sharpen every man his share, and his coulter, and his axe, and his mattock.

Yet they had a file for the mattocks, and for the coulters, and for the forks, and for the axes, and to sharpen the goads [1 Sam. 13:19–21].

The Philistines had disarmed the Israelites. The Israelites were permitted, however, some farm implements. But in order to sharpen them, they had to go down to the Philistines. In this way the enemy was able to keep an accurate count of what the Israelites had in the way of weapons.

So it came to pass in the day of battle, that there was neither sword nor spear found in the hand of any of the people that were with Saul and Jonathan: but with Saul and with Jonathan his son was there found.

And the garrison of the Philistines went out to the passage of Michmash [1 Sam. 13:22–23].

Only two men, Saul and Jonathan, had swords. I suppose the other men in the army carried mattocks, axes, clubs, and similar instruments. This was the way Saul's army was equipped to fight!

CHAPTER 14

THEME: *Jonathan's victory over the Philistines; Saul's hasty order is overridden*

JONATHAN'S VICTORY OVER THE PHILISTINES

Once again Jonathan gains a great victory, but Saul takes the credit for it and reveals his jealousy. He actually would have destroyed his own son!

Chapter 14 gives us the strategy of battle that Jonathan used against the Philistines. It is said that this is the chapter which the British General Allenby read the night before he made his successful attack upon the Turks in World War I. To me this is an interesting sidelight. I am unable to give you the details of the strategy of this battle since I am not well acquainted with the geography of the region—on a trip to Palestine I wanted to go there, but our time was limited—neither am I a military man. I am sure that when General Allenby read this chapter, it was a thrilling revelation to him to see how Jonathan executed his military tactics. General Allenby was a Christian who knew his Bible.

Apparently Jonathan's strategy was to take his men through a narrow pass. Here, with the few weapons they had to fight with, Jonathan's army had a distinct advantage. A similar battle took place at Thermopylae, a mountain pass in eastern Greece, where the Greeks, although greatly outnumbered, were able to hold off the Persian army. In Israel's case, this strategy certainly worked to their advantage since Israel was hopelessly outnumbered and almost unarmed.

We will pass over the details of this battle

and look instead at the great spiritual lesson that is here.

And Saul said unto Ahiah, Bring hither the ark of God. For the ark of God was at that time with the children of Israel [1 Sam. 14:18].

Saul should not have taken the ark to the battlefield. As we have seen before in the days of Samuel, the children of Israel used the ark in a superstitious manner, thinking it would help them win their battles. Apparently Saul has the same reason.

So the LORD saved Israel that day: and the battle passed over unto Beth-aven [1 Sam. 14:23].

In spite of Saul's action in bringing out the ark, Jonathan's strategy won the battle on the human side. God is with this young man—it is too bad that he did not live long. God saved Israel that day.

SAUL'S HASTY ORDER IS OVERRIDDEN

And the men of Israel were distressed that day: for Saul had adjured the people, saying, Cursed be the man that eateth any food until evening, that I may be avenged on mine enemies. So none of the people tasted any food.

And all they of the land came to a wood; and there was honey upon the ground.

And when the people were come into the wood, behold, the honey dropped; but no man put his hand to his mouth: for the people feared the oath.

But Jonathan heard not when his father charged the people with the oath: wherefore he put forth the end of the rod that was in his hand, and dipped it in an honeycomb, and put his hand to his mouth; and his eyes were enlightened [1 Sam. 14:24–27].

It is interesting to note that Jonathan did not know about his father's strange order that no man was to eat until the battle was won. Actually Jonathan had already won the battle. Now we are beginning to see the real nature of Saul. Jonathan gained the victory, and Saul takes credit for it. He is not willing to give the credit to his son. His "modesty" is gone, and his jealousy is revealed.

Then answered one of the people, and said, Thy father straitly charged the people with an oath, saying, Cursed be the man that eateth any food this day. And the people were faint.

Then said Jonathan, My father hath troubled the land: see, I pray you, how mine eyes have been enlightened, because I tasted a little of this honey.

How much more, if haply the people had eaten freely today of the spoil of their enemies which they found? for had there not been now a much greater slaughter among the Philistines? [1 Sam. 14:28–30].

It was a foolish command that Saul had given. The men were weary. They had fought a battle and won. They needed something to eat. Saul said, "I will not let anyone eat anything until I am avenged of my enemies." His modesty was absolutely gone.

And Saul built an altar unto the LORD: the same was the first altar that he built unto the LORD [1 Sam. 14:35].

He actually built an altar to the Lord and offered sacrifices!

And Saul said, Let us go down after the Philistines by night, and spoil them until the morning light, and let us not leave a man of them. And they said, Do whatsoever seemeth good unto thee. Then said the priest, Let us draw near hither unto God.

And Saul asked counsel of God, Shall I go down after the Philistines? wilt thou deliver them into the hand of Israel? But he answered him not that day [1 Sam. 14:36–37].

God is not using this man at all.

And Saul said, Draw ye near hither, all the chief of the people: and know and see wherein this sin hath been this day.

For, as the LORD liveth, which saveth Israel, though it be in Jonathan my son, he shall surely die. But there was not a man among all the people that answered him [1 Sam. 15:38–39].

Saul, you see, is not willing to take the blame himself. He says that someone else has sinned. The army stood silently. They knew the victory was Jonathan's. And now Saul was saying, "The reason God did not answer me was because someone did not obey me and broke the oath." The army knew that Jonathan had tasted the honey, and they knew that Saul was putting up a tremendous front at this time. They stood in silence because he was the king.

Then said he unto all Israel, Be ye on one side, and I and Jonathan my son will be on the other side. And the people said unto Saul, Do what seemeth good unto thee [1 Sam. 14:40].

The army is not saying much.

Therefore Saul said unto the LORD God of Israel, Give a perfect lot. And Saul and Jonathan were taken: but the people escaped [1 Sam. 14:41].

Saul believed Jonathan was guilty.

And Saul said, Cast lots between me and Jonathan my son. And Jonathan was taken.

Then Saul said to Jonathan, Tell me what thou hast done. And Jonathan told him, and said, I did but taste a little honey with the end of the rod that was in mine hand, and, lo, I must die [1 Sam. 14:42–43].

Jonathan was guilty—guilty of doing what Saul had not wanted him to do. Saul had said, "Cursed be the man that eateth any food this day." But was this something to die for?

And Saul answered, God do so and more also: for thou shalt surely die, Jonathan.

And the people said unto Saul, Shall Jonathan die, who hath wrought this great salvation in Israel? God forbid: as the LORD liveth, there shall not one hair of his head fall to the ground; for he hath wrought with God this day. So the people rescued Jonathan, that he died not [1 Sam. 14:44–45].

Saul would actually destroy his own son if he stood in his way. Why? Because Saul is jealous of Jonathan. He wants all of the glory for himself. The army had remained silent through all of Saul's rantings and ravings, but when Jonathan's life was at stake, they no longer kept quiet.

We are now seeing the true character of Saul. Later on we will see how he will act in direct disobedience to God. He is going to do something that will bring tragedy to the nation Israel. Had not God intervened, it would have meant the extermination of the nation. Saul is revealing that he is not God's man at all. He is actually Satan's man. We will see in the next chapter that Saul is not obeying God any longer—he is following his own devices. Finally the Spirit of God will no longer speak to him. God will no longer give him leading, and he will turn from God to the demonic world. Then we will study that remarkable incident when Saul actually consults the witch of En-dor. It is a section with a great lesson for us in these days in which we are seeing the manifestation of demonism, the occult, the worship of Satan, and astrology. God help America today because there are many Sauls abroad!

CHAPTER 15

THEME: *Saul's rebellion concerning Agag; Samuel rebukes Saul*

SAUL'S REBELLION CONCERNING AGAG

Saul's rebellion against the command of God is revealed in this chapter. Also we see his facade in wanting Samuel's help in covering up his sin before the people. Saul is rejected now as king, with no hope of recovery. We see Samuel's love for Saul as he mourns for him.

Why the extreme surgery in slaying the Amalekites and Agag? The answer is found in the Book of Esther. Haman, who almost succeeded in destroying the entire Jewish race, was an Amalekite. God knew the true character of this people which was first revealed in their unprovoked and malicious attack upon Israel in the wilderness (Exod. 17:8–16).

As we continue our study in the life of Saul, we find that he is indeed Satan's man. I trust we have not done him an injustice by identifying him as such. Personally I do not believe that he was ever saved, and I believe there was something of the hypocrite in the man —he pretended to be God's man, but he never was. Also he tried to cover up his rebellion and disobedience regarding Agag.

Samuel also said unto Saul, The LORD sent me to anoint thee to be king over his people, over Israel: now therefore hearken thou unto the voice of the words of the LORD.

Thus saith the LORD of hosts, I remember that which Amalek did to Israel, how he laid wait for him in the way, when he came up from Egypt.

Now go and smite Amalek, and utterly destroy all that they have, and spare them not; but slay both man and woman, infant and suckling, ox and sheep, camel and ass [1 Sam. 15:1–3].

These instructions may seem extreme to you if you are not familiar with the history of Amalek. Moses, who was there when it happened, rehearsed the episode for the younger generation in Deuteronomy 25:17–19: "Remember what Amalek did unto thee by the way, when ye were come forth out of Egypt; How he met thee by the way, and smote the hindmost of thee, even all that were feeble behind thee, when thou wast faint and weary; and he feared not God. Therefore it shall be, when the LORD thy God hath given thee rest from all thine enemies round about, in the land which the LORD thy God giveth thee for an inheritance to possess it, that thou shalt blot out the remembrance of Amalek from under heaven; thou shalt not forget it."

If these people had been permitted to live, they would probably have caused more trouble in the future than is imaginable. Apparently Saul spared some of these people, and when we come to the Book of Esther, we will get acquainted with one of them, Haman. He tried to exterminate the Hebrew nation and would have succeeded had not God intervened. When we get God's perspective we understand His immediate action. Very candidly, since you and I are not God and are not obligated to make God's decisions, we cannot pass judgment upon Him.

And Saul gathered the people together, and numbered them in Telaim, two hundred thousand footmen, and ten thousand men of Judah.

And Saul came to a city of Amalek, and laid wait in the valley.

And Saul said unto the Kenites, Go, depart, get you down from among the Amalekites, lest I destroy you with them: for ye shewed kindness to all the children of Israel, when they came up out of Egypt. So the Kenites departed from among the Amalekites [1 Sam. 15:4–6].

We find here that Saul gathered the people together and numbered them. Then he came to a city of Amalek and warned the Kenites to leave the Amalekites before they were destroyed. The Kenites, you recall, were descendants of Moses' father-in-law. We saw references to them in Judges 1:16 and 4:11–17. This was an act of mercy that no pagan nation would have practiced in that day.

And Saul smote the Amalekites from Havilah until thou comest to Shur, that is over against Egypt [1 Sam. 15:7].

Now up to this point Saul is being obedient.

And he took Agag the king of the Amalekites alive, and utterly destroyed all the people with the edge of the sword.

But Saul and the people spared Agag, and the best of the sheep, and of the oxen, and of the fatlings, and the lambs, and all that was good, and would not utterly destroy them: but every thing that was vile and refuse, that they destroyed utterly [1 Sam. 15:8–9].

He thought, *what a shame to destroy everything*! So he saved Agag, who was the ruler of the Amalekites. Saul had no right to spare him any more than he had the right to spare the humblest peasant among these people. This nation was wholly given to evil, and the king, above all others, should have been destroyed and judged at this time. Neither had Saul the right to save from destruction the best of the cattle. It would appear that he made his attack for the purpose of obtaining booty and spoil, and God had forbidden that. The Israelites were bringing judgment upon the Amalekites for Almighty God in this particular case.

Then came the word of the LORD unto Samuel, saying,

It repenteth me that I have set up Saul to be king: for he is turned back from following me, and hath not performed my commandments. And it grieved

Samuel; and he cried unto the LORD all night [1 Sam. 15:10–11].

Not only did the people choose Saul, Samuel chose him also. Samuel loved Saul. He wanted him to make good as king. I think he wanted Saul, even more than David, to be successful. Now, however, God has rejected Saul, and Samuel, who is obedient to God, must execute God's orders. Saul has not been obedient and judgment is coming.

SAMUEL REBUKES SAUL

And when Samuel rose early to meet Saul in the morning, it was told Samuel, saying, Saul came to Carmel, and, behold, he set him up a place, and is gone about, and passed on, and gone down to Gilgal.

And Samuel came to Saul: and Saul said unto him, Blessed be thou of the LORD: I have performed the commandment of the LORD [1 Sam. 15:12–13].

Saul says that he had been obedient, but notice Samuel's retort to this.

And Samuel said, What meaneth then this bleating of the sheep in mine ears, and the lowing of the oxen which I hear?

And Saul said, They have brought them from the Amalekites: for the people spared the best of the sheep and of the oxen, to sacrifice unto the LORD thy God; and the rest we have utterly destroyed [1 Sam. 15:14–15].

Listen to Saul as he begins to use double-talk and subterfuge in an attempt to camouflage his conduct. He had a very pious reason for sparing some of the animals. He wanted to have excellent animals to sacrifice to the Lord! This was, of course, an attempt to cover up his disobedience with pious pretense.

You can find that same kind of hypocrisy in our contemporary culture. I become rather amused when it is reported that the liquor interests donate money for beautiful gardens and scenic spots for people to visit and enjoy. They always like to make it known—and the media is apparently delighted to report—how much the liquor interests pay in taxes each year. Of course, anyone knows that the alcoholics are costing our government more than any taxes the liquor interests pay. There is the tendency to cover our evil businesses with good works. Many of God's people try to turn their disobedience into some pious project. I am not sure but what we are all guilty of that sort of thing.

When I came out of seminary and entered the ministry, I drove an old, beat-up jalopy, an old Chevrolet. As a young preacher I was satisfied with it. I was not married, and I enjoyed driving it around, although my congregation was embarrassed by it. In fact, they felt it was sort of a joke. Then I met a young lady, and I began to pray that the Lord would give me a new car. I told Him I needed a new car so that I could be more efficient in my visitation. To be honest, "more efficient visitation" did not enter into it at all. I wanted a nice car to impress this young lady! It is so easy for human beings, believers and nonbelievers, to rationalize.

When Saul's disobedience was discovered, you will notice, he tried to blame the *people* for what happened. He said, "The people spared the best of the sheep and of the oxen." However the record states that it was "Saul and the people." He was the king and the one who was responsible.

And Saul said unto Samuel, Yea, I have obeyed the voice of the LORD, and have gone the way which the LORD sent me, and have brought Agag the king of Amalek, and have utterly destroyed the Amalekites.

But the people took of the spoil, sheep and oxen, the chief of the things which should have been utterly destroyed, to sacrifice unto the LORD thy God in Gilgal [1 Sam. 15:20–21].

Saul says that he obeyed the voice of the Lord. Notice he does not say, "*My* God," or "*our* God," but "*thy* God." He does not take any responsibility at all for sparing the animals, yet he is the one to blame.

And Samuel said, Hath the LORD as great delight in burnt offerings and sacrifices, as in obeying the voice of the LORD? Behold, to obey is better than sacrifice, and to hearken than the fat of rams.

For rebellion is as the sin of witchcraft, and stubbornness is as iniquity and idolatry. Because thou hast rejected the word of the LORD, he hath also rejected thee from being king [1 Sam. 15:22–23].

This is one of those remarkable passages of Scripture. This is God's rejection of Saul as king on the basis of his rebellion and disobedience to God. This is an important message for all of us who claim to be children of God.

There is a great deal of this informal and friendly approach to the Lord Jesus Christ today. There are so many little songs that go something like this: "Jesus is a friend of mine." We need to be careful how we use an approach like this to Him. When you say that Jesus is a friend of yours, what do you mean? Actually, you are trying to bring Him down to your level. If I would say that the president of the United States is a friend of mine, I would be bringing him down to my level. But suppose that the president announced that Vernon McGee is his friend. That would bring me up to his level. When we begin to talk about Jesus as "a friend of mine," we are not being Scriptural. The Lord said, "*Ye* are *my* friends, if ye do whatsoever I command you" (John 15:14). Are you obedient unto Him? How dare any of us call Him friend if we are not obeying Him? To disobey Him is worse than witchcraft. It is rebellion against God. When you meet a person who is totally disobedient to the Lord, you almost have to conclude that he does not belong to the Lord at all. Now I am not saying that works enter into salvation. I *am* saying that if you are a child of God, if you come to the place where you know Him, you will obey him. He also said, "If ye love me, keep my commandments" (John 14:15). I am of the opinion that if you would say to the Lord, "I don't love you," He would say, "Forget about My commandments." The important thing is to be rightly related to the Lord Jesus Christ. To be a child of God is to know Him personally. That is what makes Christianity different from any religion in the world. You can be a Buddhist without knowing Buddha. You can be a follower of Confucius without knowing him. You can be a member of any other religion without knowing the founder, but you cannot be a Christian, friend, without knowing the Lord Jesus Christ. And to know Him is life eternal.

And Saul said unto Samuel, I have sinned: for I have transgressed the commandment of the Lord, and thy words: because I feared the people, and obeyed their voice [1 Sam. 15:24].

Notice the low motivation of this man. He said he was afraid of the people and so he obeyed their wishes. He wanted to please everyone. Many folks are like Saul. Lots of preachers try to please everybody. I heard about a prominent minister lately who has begun to compromise, and he says he is doing it because he wants to get along with everyone. That was Saul's approach. It is true that he confesses that he has transgressed, but his penitence is not genuine.

Now therefore, I pray thee, pardon my sin, and turn again with me, that I may worship the Lord.

And Samuel said unto Saul, I will not return with thee: for thou hast rejected the word of the Lord, and the Lord hath rejected thee from being king over Israel.

And as Samuel turned about to go away, he laid hold upon the skirt of his mantle, and it rent.

And Samuel said unto him, The Lord hath rent the kingdom of Israel from thee this day, and hath given it to a neighbour of thine, that is better than thou.

And also the Strength of Israel will not lie nor repent: for he is not a man, that he should repent [1 Sam. 15:25–29].

God made Saul king, and now He is taking the kingdom away from him because of his sin. It looks as if God has changed His mind when in reality He has not at all. It is not God who has changed, but Saul. Saul has sinned and so God must deal with him accordingly.

Then he said, I have sinned: yet honour me now, I pray thee, before the elders of my people, and before Israel, and turn again with me, that I may worship the Lord thy God [1 Sam. 15:30].

I do not believe Saul's repentance is genuine. Look how he is covering up his sin. He says to Samuel, "Let us go through the forms of worship together and not let the people know that I have been rejected." He wanted to repent, but not have to pay the penalty for his disobedience. He was a hypocrite right to the end.

Then said Samuel, Bring ye hither to me Agag the king of the Amalekites. And Agag came unto him delicately. And Agag said, Surely the bitterness of death is past.

And Samuel said, As thy sword hath made women childless, so shall thy mother be childless among women. And Samuel hewed Agag in pieces before the Lord in Gilgal [1 Sam. 15:32–33].

Agag came "delicately" unto Samuel because he knew he was in trouble. And Samuel killed Agag. Now that may be strong medicine for some folk today, but my friend, our God is a God of Judgment and He is going to judge wrong and evil. I am glad that God is going to judge. I don't know about you, but I thank God that no one is getting away with evil today. There may be those, even in high places, who think they are getting away with their sin, and dishonesty, and murder, and adultery, but they are not. God is going to judge them. No one is going to get away with sin, and we need to make that very clear today. So Samuel executed the judgment of God upon this vile, wicked ruler, Agag.

Then Samuel went to Ramah; and Saul went up to his house to Gibeah of Saul. And Samuel came no more to see Saul until the day of his death: nevertheless Samuel mourned for Saul: and the LORD repented that he had made Saul king over Israel [1 Sam. 15:34–35].

When the Bible says that God repented, it means that His actions look as though He changed His mind. He has not. God said all along that if Saul did not make good, He would remove him. Saul sinned, and so God removed him from his position as king. God still hates sin and will judge it. Saul was the choice of the people, and he failed. Yet Samuel mourned for him. I think Samuel loved Saul a great deal more than he loved David. He hated to see this man fail and turn aside. That is why his words to Saul were so strong and harsh; they came from a person who loved him. The words of Samuel were also coming from the heart of God.

My friend, God's love will not deter Him from judging sinners. He can love them and still execute judgment. Our God is holy and righteous and just, as well as loving.

CHAPTER 16

***THEME:** David anointed*

God chooses David as king to succeed Saul and sends Samuel to Bethlehem to anoint him as king. Because Saul is forsaken of God, David is brought into court to play upon his harp to soothe the evil spirit of Saul.

Chapter 16 brings us to a new subject. We will see David in contrast to Saul. David is God's man, and Saul is Satan's man. In chapter 15 we saw God's rejection of Saul. God gave Saul not just one opportunity but several opportunities to see if he would obey Him. Saul revealed that he was totally disobedient unto God. He should have made good, but he did not. The Lord did not need to wait to see the results of Saul's kingship. He already knew. But Saul needed to know. Samuel needed to know because he loved Saul. The people needed to know because they had chosen Saul.

Today you and I need to know if we are genuine children of God. For this reason we will be tested. We need the help of the Spirit of God because we are told in Hebrews 12:6, "For whom the Lord loveth he chasteneth, and scourgeth every son whom he receiveth." The Lord tests those whom He loves. This was God's method in Saul's day, and it is His method today. "Blessed is the man that endureth temptation: for when he is tried, he shall receive the crown of life, which the Lord hath promised to them that love him" (James 1:12).

Again, why extreme surgery in slaying the Amalekites and Agag? Amalek was a son of Esau. The Amalekites fought the children of Israel when they were trying to get into the Promised Land. God said He would have war with Amalek from generation to generation and would finally judge them. The Amalekites had five hundred years to change their ways. Because they had definitely turned their backs upon God, He judged them.

Now we come to the place where God chooses David to succeed Saul as king. God is sending Samuel to Bethlehem to anoint David king. David was God's choice. Although God had trouble with him, God has trouble with all of us, doesn't He?

And the LORD said unto Samuel, How long wilt thou mourn for Saul, seeing I have rejected him from reigning over

Israel? fill thine horn with oil, and go, I will send thee to Jesse the Beth-lehemite: for I have provided me a king among his sons [1 Sam. 16:1].

Believe me, Saul had Samuel on his side. Samuel loved him and hated to see God set him aside. It hurt Samuel to give Saul the ultimatum that he had been rejected and dismissed as king. Samuel's sorrow makes it all the more impressive.

And Samuel said, How can I go? if Saul hear it, he will kill me. And the LORD said, Take an heifer with thee, and say, I am come to sacrifice to the LORD.

And call Jesse to the sacrifice, and I will shew thee what thou shalt do: and thou shalt anoint unto me him whom I name unto thee [1 Sam. 16:2–3].

Samuel is afraid to go to Jesse because Saul is in no mood for opposition. He is desperate. As we move into this story, however, we find that it is God who makes the choice. He tells Samuel exactly what to do, but He does not give him any advance information. His lack of knowledge will protect him. So Samuel goes to Bethlehem and to the house of Jesse. He asks Jesse and his sons to come for a sacrifice.

And it came to pass, when they were come, that he looked on Eliab, and said, Surely the LORD's anointed is before him.

But the LORD said unto Samuel, Look not on his countenance, or on the height of his stature; because I have refused him: for the LORD seeth not as man seeth; for man looketh on the outward appearance, but the LORD looketh on the heart [1 Sam. 16:6–7].

All through this section we are given excellent spiritual principles. In chapter 15 Samuel said to Saul, "To obey is better than sacrifice, and to hearken than the fat of rams" (1 Sam. 15:22). You and I demonstrate whether or not we are children of the Lord Jesus Christ by our love for Him. It is not what we say in a testimony; it is whether or not we are obeying Him. The Christian life is one of reality. It is not a life of "put-on" and pretense.

When God looks at us, friend, He looks at us from the inside. He is an interior decorator. He always checks the interior. Samuel looks at this well-built, handsome young man and feels this must be God's choice for the next king of Israel. But God says to Samuel, "I don't want you to look at his outward appearance. Don't judge a man by his looks. Let me select the man this time. I will choose the king." God sees the heart, and thank God for that. We are so apt to judge folk, even in Christian circles, by their looks, by their pocketbook, by their status symbol—the Cadillac they drive, by the home they live in, or by the position they occupy. God never judges anyone on that basis. He is telling Samuel not to pay any attention to the outward appearance. God is going to look at the heart.

So Jesse had his sons pass before Samuel one by one. Samuel made it clear to Jesse why he had come, and Jesse had seven of his sons pass before Samuel.

Again, Jesse made seven of his sons to pass before Samuel. And Samuel said unto Jesse, The LORD hath not chosen these.

And Samuel said unto Jesse, Are here all thy children? And he said, There remaineth yet the youngest, and, behold, he keepeth the sheep. And Samuel said unto Jesse, Send and fetch him: for we will not sit down till he come hither [1 Sam. 16:10–11].

Surely even the father of David would never have chosen him above the other seven brothers. To begin with, David was only a boy. It is believed that he was about sixteen years old —possibly younger. He was a shepherd. He was out with the sheep. He didn't really know very much. Jesse certainly would not have chosen him above his brethren to be a king. In fact, he had ignored him entirely. He was so sure one of his other sons would be selected that he did not even invite David to the sacrifice. When Samuel found out that David was tending sheep, he said in substance, "This is important business, and I'm not about to sit down and eat until I have accomplished my mission."

And he sent, and brought him in. Now he was ruddy, and withal of a beautiful countenance, and goodly to look to. And the LORD said, Arise, anoint him: for this is he [1 Sam. 16:12].

When this verse says that David was "ruddy," it means that he had red hair—and he had a temper to match his red hair, a hot temper. But in addition to the fact that he was redheaded, he was a fine-looking fellow. He had a "beautiful countenance." God does not despise that which is beautiful. God can use beauty. He is the Creator of beauty. No one who lives on this earth can ignore the beauty in the many scenic spots in every state and country. And a sunset in any place is a thing of glory. God majors in beauty.

I resent the fact that the non-Christian world gets everything that is worthwhile and beautiful. Why is not beauty and talent dedicated to God today?

Well, David was a handsome young man, but God did not choose him for that reason. God knew his heart. He was God's choice. God knows what you and I do not know about him. Although David failed, down underneath was a faith that never failed. David loved and trusted God. He wanted to walk with Him. God took him to the woodshed and punished him within an inch of his life, and David never whimpered or cried aloud. He wanted that fellowship with God, and God loved him. He was a man after God's own heart.

Then Samuel took the horn of oil, and anointed him in the midst of his brethren: and the spirit of the LORD came upon David from that day forward. So Samuel rose up, and went to Ramah [1 Sam. 16:13].

Samuel anointed David king, and the Spirit of the Lord came upon him. At this time the Spirit of the Lord departed from Saul.

But the spirit of the LORD departed from Saul, and an evil spirit from the LORD troubled him.

And Saul's servants said unto him, Behold now, an evil spirit from God troubleth thee.

Let our lord now command thy servants, which are before thee, to seek out a man, who is a cunning player on an harp: and it shall come to pass, when the evil spirit from God is upon thee, that he shall play with his hand, and thou shalt be well [1 Sam. 16: 14–16].

I believe Saul was completely taken over by Satan. His servants noted that he had this mental malady, this spiritual sickness. It is said that music has power to tame the savage beast. Saul's servants suggested a contest to find out who was the best musician. David was a musician.

And Saul said unto his servants, Provide me now a man that can play well, and bring him to me.

Then answered one of the servants, and said, Behold, I have seen a son of Jesse the Beth-lehemite, that is cunning in playing, and a mighty valiant man, and a man of war, and prudent in matters, and a comely person, and the LORD is with him.

Wherefore Saul sent messengers unto Jesse, and said, Send me David thy son, which is with the sheep.

And Jesse took an ass laden with bread, and a bottle of wine, and a kid, and sent them by David his son unto Saul.

And David came to Saul, and stood before him: and he loved him greatly; and he became his armour-bearer.

And Saul sent to Jesse, saying, Let David, I pray thee, stand before me; for he hath found favour in my sight.

And it came to pass, when the evil spirit from God was upon Saul, that David took an harp, and played with his hand: so Saul was refreshed, and was well, and the evil spirit departed from him [1 Sam. 16:17–23].

David was an unusual person in many ways. David is brought into the palace. God looks at the inner man when He chooses someone for a particular office or task. Saul is now forsaken of God, and David is brought into court to play upon his harp. Although it is not yet known, Israel has a new king.

CHAPTERS 17–18

***THEME:** God trains David*

Chapter 17 is one of the most familiar in the Bible. This wonderful episode of David and Goliath reveals more than human bravery. It reveals that, even as a boy, David had a heart for God. He didn't volunteer to fight the giant because his people were being shamed, but because Goliath was defying the armies of the living God! As he faced his formidable foe, he testified to his faith in God: "Thou comest to me with a sword, and with a spear, and with a shield: but I come to thee in the name of the LORD of hosts, the God of the armies of Israel, whom thou hast defied" (1 Sam. 17:45).

DAVID SLAYS GOLIATH, GIANT OF GATH

Now the Philistines gathered together their armies to battle, and were gathered together at Shochoh, which belongeth to Judah, and pitched between Shochoh and Azekah, in Ephes-dammim.

And Saul and the men of Israel were gathered together and pitched by the valley of Elah, and set the battle in array against the Philistines [1 Sam. 17:1–2].

Israel is at war again with the Philistines, their perennial and perpetual enemy.

And the Philistines stood on a mountain on the one side, and Israel stood on a mountain on the other side: and there was a valley between them [1 Sam. 17:3].

These two armies were at a standstill. They were poised to enter the battle and did not want to fight. It was similar to Israel's present conflict. At the Suez Canal Israel is on one side and Egypt is on the other. Well, here are the Philistines on one mountain; Israel is on the other mountain, with a valley between. The Philistines are the aggressors.

And there went out a champion out of the camp of the Philistines, named Goliath, of Gath, whose height was six cubits and a span.

And he had an helmet of brass upon his head, and he was armed with a coat of mail; and the weight of the coat was five thousand shekels of brass [1 Sam. 17:4–5].

If a cubit is eighteen inches, Goliath was a pretty tall man. Since one span is about nine inches, Goliath was about nine feet, nine inches tall. He was a big boy. He could have played center or forward on any basketball team. Certainly these soldiers wanted to put the decision of the battle in the hands of Goliath and one Israelite.

And the staff of his spear was like a weaver's beam; and his spear's head weighed six hundred shekels of iron: and one bearing a shield went before him.

And he stood and cried unto the armies of Israel, and said unto them, Why are ye come out to set your battle in array? am not I a Philistine, and ye servants to Saul? choose you a man for you, and let him come down to me [1 Sam. 17:7–8].

Every day Goliath challenged the Israelites to send out a man to fight him but, after forty days, no one had accepted. David came on the scene because he had brought food to his brothers who were serving in the army. David was alarmed that no one would accept the challenge. His brothers tried to send him home, but David would not go. When Saul heard that David would go against Goliath, he tried to put his armor on him. David, however, was just a boy. He said, "I can't fight with these because I haven't tested them. I will just have to fight with the equipment I'm used to." What a lesson there is for us in this. Let's not try to be something we are not, or try to do something we are really not called to do. If God has called you to use a slingshot, friend, don't try to use a sword. If God has called you to speak, then speak. If God has called you to do something else, well, do that. If God has called you to sing, sing. But if He has not called you to sing, for goodness sake, don't do it. Too many people are trying to use a sword when the slingshot is really more their size.

And he took his staff in his hand, and chose him five smooth stones out of the brook, and put them in a shepherd's bag which he had, even in a scrip; and his sling was in his hand: and he drew near to the Philistine [1 Sam. 17:40].

Some people believe that David chose five smooth stones so that if he missed his first shot, he could use one or all of the others. David did not intend to miss, friend. Then why did he select five stones? The answer is found in 2 Samuel 21:22: "These four were born to the giant in Gath, and fell by the hand of David, and by the hand of his servants." Goliath had four sons, and David was sure they would come out when he killed their father. This is why David picked up five stones. That was the number he needed.

Then said David to the Philistine, Thou comest to me with a sword, and with a spear, and with a shield: but I come to thee in the name of the LORD of hosts, the God of the armies of Israel, whom thou hast defied.

This day will the LORD deliver thee into mine hand; and I will smite thee, and take thine head from thee; and I will give the carcases of the host of the Philistines this day unto the fowls of the air, and to the wild beasts of the earth; that all the earth may know that there is a God in Israel.

And all this assembly shall know that the LORD saveth not with sword and spear: for the battle is the LORD's, and he will give you into our hands [1 Sam. 17:45–47].

You know the rest of the story. It is so familiar. God gave David the victory, and he killed Goliath. The battle was the Lord's, and the giant was delivered into David's hands.

There are many great spiritual lessons in this chapter. For example, the giant represents the world; Saul, I think, represents Satan; and David represents the believer in the Lord Jesus Christ. We are admonished, "Love not the world, neither the things that are in the world. If any man love the world, the love of the Father is not in him" (1 John 2:15). We are *in* the world but not *of* it. What a difference there is between David and Samson. Samson treated the Philistines as friends—he even married one of them. David treated Goliath as an enemy. The world system, the *Kosmos*—which includes all governments, educational programs, and entertainments—is the enemy of the believer today. The interesting thing is that David's faith enabled him to go out to meet the giant and defeat him. "For whatsoever is born of God overcometh the world: and this is the victory that overcometh the world, even our faith" (1 John 5:4). It is the same lesson Joshua learned at Jericho: he found out that the battle is the Lord's. David also learned that he could not use the weapons of this world to fight the battle. He had to use his own weapons, his own methods—those in which God had schooled him. The believer today needs to recognize that the world can be overcome only by his faith and confidence in God.

DAVID AND JONATHAN MAKE A COVENANT

And it came to pass, when he had made an end of speaking unto Saul, that the soul of Jonathan was knit with the soul of David, and Jonathan loved him as his own soul [1 Sam. 18:1].

David was speaking to Saul. Saul had called David after the battle because he wanted to give him recognition for his deed. (I think Saul felt that he gave him too much recognition in light of what happened later.) As Jonathan, Saul's son, stood there listening as David and his father talked, "the soul of Jonathan was knit with the soul of David." The relationship of these two men was quite wonderful. We often speak about the love of a man for a woman —and that is wonderful—but nothing is as fine and noble as the love of two men for each other. They see in each other a mirror of themselves and are drawn together. Two men can be real friends. They can enjoy athletics and recreation together. They can work together and have a social life together. Jonathan was an outstanding man, as we have seen, and he loved David for his courage and his confidence in God.

And Saul took him that day, and would let him go no more home to his father's house [1 Sam. 18:2].

David now becomes a public figure, and he will occupy that position for the rest of his life.

Then Jonathan and David made a covenant, because he loved him as his own soul [1 Sam. 18:3].

The covenant that these two men made was that they would stick together. It is difficult to find another friendship equal to what these men had. There is nothing quite like it.

And Jonathan stripped himself of the robe that was upon him, and gave it to David, and his garments, even to his sword, and to his bow, and to his girdle [1 Sam. 18:4].

David was a peasant boy, and he did not have the clothes befitting his new public life. Jonathan shared his wardrobe with David. It was a very generous thing to do.

And David went out whithersoever Saul sent him, and behaved himself wisely: and Saul set him over the men of war, and he was accepted in the sight of all the people, and also in the sight of Saul's servants [1 Sam. 18:5].

David had that charisma that we hear so much about, which made him accepted by the public. David was actually a great man. God looked on his heart, the people are looking at the outside, and David looked good both on the inside and on the outside. Of course David was not sinless, as we shall see, but he had a real heart for God, and people loved him for it.

And it came to pass as they came, when David was returned from the slaughter of the Philistine, that the women came out of all cities of Israel, singing and dancing, to meet king Saul, with tabrets, with joy, and with instruments of music.

And the women answered one another as they played, and said, Saul hath slain his thousands, and David his ten thousands.

And Saul was very wroth, and the saying displeased him; and he said, They have ascribed unto David ten thousands, and to me they have ascribed but thousands: and what can he have more but the kingdom?

And Saul eyed David from that day and forward [1 Sam. 18:6–9].

Saul did not like the new song that the women were singing. Saul became jealous of David because of the people's applause and acceptance of him. As the story progresses, Saul will attempt to remove him from the limelight by actually destroying him. As David becomes the favorite of the people, he begins to see that Saul is not as friendly as he once was.

And it came to pass on the morrow, that the evil spirit from God came upon Saul, and he prophesied in the midst of the house: and David played with his hand, as at other times: and there was a javelin in Saul's hand [1 Sam. 18:10].

This is quite a dramatic scene. As David is playing on a harp, and Saul is sitting over there playing with a javelin, David may have guessed what he had in mind. He may have hit a sour note or two, I don't know, but suddenly Saul threw the javelin.

And Saul cast the javelin; for he said, I will smite David even to the wall with it. And David avoided out of his presence twice [1 Sam. 18:11].

Saul wanted to get rid of David permanently. David dodged the javelin and then departed. He took French leave—got out of the palace and the area as quickly as he could.

Wherefore when Saul saw that he behaved himself very wisely, he was afraid of him.

But all Israel and Judah loved David, because he went out and came in before them [1 Sam. 18:15–16].

DAVID MARRIES MICHAL, SAUL'S DAUGHTER

David is now the one who is being accepted by the nation. Saul has been wondering how he can trap him and finally decides upon a clever method. He promises David his daughter Merab for his wife on the condition that he continue to war with the Philistines, hoping he will be killed in battle. Then he fails to keep faith with David and gives Merab to another. Now we will see that he wants to give his younger daughter to David. Why? That would put David in the family where Saul could get to him any time he wanted to. I do not believe David ever loved Michal. We blame David for having several marriages, but he certainly got off to a bad start with this girl.

And Michal Saul's daughter loved David: and they told Saul, and the thing pleased him [1 Sam. 18:20].

It says here that Michal loved David, but it was not that marital love that is needed to make a success of marriage. In the beginning it was that love of the hero and his popularity. The day will come when she will ridicule him and despise him for his enthusiasm for God.

CHAPTERS 19–20

***THEME:** Saul attempts to kill David again; Jonathan helps David escape*

This chapter begins a section which I have labeled "David Disciplined." Saul personally attempts to kill David, then he openly gives orders that David be slain. Although several times King Saul briefly repents of his murderous intent, David's life is in jeopardy until Saul's death. During these days of exile—possibly a period of ten years—David is hunted like a wild animal. He is a nomad, a vagabond. Living in caves in the wilderness, he endures many hardships and privations. However, he is being tested and trained in God's school. He takes the full course and graduates *magna cum laude*. He becomes Israel's greatest king—in fact, the world's greatest king—and a man after God's own heart. Many of the wonderful Psalms of David are written during this rough and rugged period.

SAUL ATTEMPTS TO KILL DAVID AGAIN

And Saul spake to Jonathan his son, and to all his servants, that they should kill David.

But Jonathan Saul's son delighted much in David: and Jonathan told David, saying, Saul my father seeketh to kill thee: now therefore, I pray thee, take heed to thyself until the morning, and abide in a secret place, and hide thyself [1 Sam. 19:1–2].

Jonathan told David to get out of the palace, because his life was in danger there, and hide himself. Saul was now openly trying to take David's life. His friend, Jonathan, wants to help him.

And I will go out and stand beside my father in the field where thou art, and I will commune with my father of thee; and what I see, that I will tell thee.

And Jonathan spake good of David unto Saul his father, and said unto him, Let not the king sin against his servant, against David; because he hath not sinned against thee, and because his works have been to thee-ward very good [1 Sam. 19:3–4].

Jonathan has a plan. He is going to try and talk to his father. Saul and Jonathan go out into the field and Jonathan says, "David has actually helped you. He is one of your followers. He is a wonderful citizen of your kingdom. You should not try to kill him."

For he did put his life in his hand, and slew the Philistine, and the LORD wrought a great salvation for all Israel: thou sawest it, and didst rejoice: wherefore then wilt thou sin against innocent blood, to slay David without a cause?

And Saul hearkened unto the voice of Jonathan: and Saul sware, As the LORD liveth, he shall not be slain.

And Jonathan called David, and Jonathan shewed him all those things. And Jonathan brought David to Saul, and he was in his presence, as in times past [1 Sam. 19:5–7].

Saul listened to his son, and David came back to the palace. David was wary, however, because he knew his life was in danger.

And there was war again: and David went out, and fought with the Philistines, and slew them with a great slaughter; and they fled from him [1 Sam. 19:8].

Notice Saul's reaction to David's success.

And the evil spirit from the LORD was upon Saul, as he sat in his house with his javelin in his hand: and David played with his hand.

And Saul sought to smite David even to the wall with the javelin; but he slipped away out of Saul's presence, and he smote the javelin into the wall: and David fled, and escaped that night [1 Sam. 19:9–10].

An evil spirit comes upon Saul again, and he wants to kill David. It is a very dramatic scene. David is playing his harp, and Saul is fingering his javelin. David senses his murderous mood. Saul throws that javelin with the intent of pinning him to the wall. David knows that he is no longer safe in the palace even though he is married to Saul's daughter.

Saul also sent messengers unto David's house, to watch him, and to slay him in the morning: and Michal David's wife

told him, saying, If thou save not thy life to-night, to-morrow thou shalt be slain.

So Michal let David down through a window: and he went, and fled, and escaped.

And Michal took an image, and laid it in the bed, and put a pillow of goats' hair for his bolster, and covered it with a cloth [1 Sam. 19:11–13].

Here in the beginning Michal was on David's side. She told David that if he did not escape that very night he would be slain the next day. She knew her father meant business. So David fled from the palace, and Michal fixed up the bed to make it look like he was still in it.

And when Saul sent messengers to take David, she said, He is sick.

And Saul sent the messengers again to see David, saying, Bring him up to me in the bed, that I may slay him.

And when the messengers were come in, behold, there was an image in the bed, with a pillow of goat's hair for his bolster.

And Saul said unto Michal, Why hast thou deceived me so, and sent away mine enemy, that he is escaped? And Michal answered Saul, He said unto me, Let me go; why should I kill thee? [1 Sam. 19:14–17].

When Saul found out that he had been deceived, he demanded an explanation from his daughter. She placated him by saying that David would have killed her if she had failed to help him.

So David fled, and escaped, and came to Samuel to Ramah, and told him all that Saul had done to him. And he and Samuel went and dwelt in Naioth [1 Sam. 19:18].

Because Samuel had anointed David as king, his life too is in danger. Saul is now openly attempting to slay David. From now on David will live like a hunted animal. What will the future hold for David at this particular time? He will be on the run until the death of Saul.

JONATHAN HELPS DAVID ESCAPE

Saul knew his daughter Michal had deceived him concerning David. He knew Jonathan and David were good friends. Therefore Jonathan had to be wary, careful, and very secretive about communicating with David. That is why he used the method of shooting arrows.

And David fled from Naioth in Ramah, and came and said before Jonathan, What have I done? what is mine iniquity? and what is my sin before thy father, that he seeketh my life? [1 Sam. 20:1].

David asked the question, "What have I done?" He had never hurt Saul. In fact, he had actually helped him. But Saul was never a king. God knew he was not a king, and he was not God's choice. The people had wanted a king and they wanted Saul to be that king. God granted their request but, as it was during the time of Moses, He sent leanness to their souls. In the wilderness the children of Israel wanted meat, and He fattened them up with quail. He gave them what they wanted, but it was evident that they were not trusting God. If they had trusted the Lord, they would have been satisfied with manna and would not have cried out for meat, and they would have found joy and peace in their lives.

Many Christians today are way ahead of the Lord, begging Him for this, that, and the other thing. They are not willing to rest quietly and let God work things out in their lives. Many times when He grants our requests, we say, "Isn't it wonderful that He answered my prayer?" Not always. Sometimes we beg Him for something and, after He gives it to us, we realize it is the worst thing that could have happened to us. A wealthy man in Florida told me how he lost his son. He said, "The biggest mistake I ever made was to give him everything he wanted." Sometimes when we keep after God, He sends us what we are begging for, but the result is leanness to our souls. That was true of the children of Israel who wanted Saul as their king. He certainly is causing a problem for the nation.

David is puzzled. He cannot understand why Saul is after him.

And he said unto him, God forbid; thou shalt not die: behold, my father will do nothing either great or small, but that he will shew it me: and why should my father hide this thing from me? it is not so [1 Sam. 20:2].

Jonathan tells David that if his father makes a move to slay him, he will know about it.

And David sware moreover, and said, Thy father certainly knoweth that I

have found grace in thine eyes; and he saith, Let not Jonathan know this, lest he be grieved: but truly as the LORD liveth, and as thy soul liveth, there is but a step between me and death [1 Sam. 20:3].

What a statement!—"there is but a step between me and death." It was not only that way in David's day, it is also that way today. Whether we drive the freeways of the city or the highways of the country, you and I are within a step of death. Isaiah said that there is only a heartbeat between you and death. Death can come at any time. That is the reason we ought to be ready at any moment to move out into eternity and into the presence of God. How many folks have made every arrangement for this life but none for the next life! Are you a saved individual—that is, are you trusting Christ as Savior—so that if you should die at this moment you would go into the presence of God? Let me caution you not to put off accepting Christ as your Lord and Savior any longer.

Then said Jonathan unto David, Whatsoever thy soul desireth, I will even do it for thee [1 Sam. 20:4].

Jonathan was a *real* friend to David. It is wonderful to have a friend like that. Proverbs 18:24 says, "A man that hath friends must shew himself friendly: and there is a friend that sticketh closer than a brother." A brother may sometime let you down, but a real friend never will. A friend, we are told, is one who is born for adversity. A man proves he is your friend when you are in trouble. When David was in trouble, Jonathan proved to be his friend. He would do anything to protect David.

And David said unto Jonathan, Behold, to-morrow is the new moon, and I should not fail to sit with the king at meat: but let me go, that I may hide myself in the field unto the third day at even [1 Sam. 20:5].

David was expected to be at the palace at mealtime, but he was afraid to go. Instead he is asking Jonathan's permission to disappear for three days.

If thy father at all miss me, then say, David earnestly asked leave of me that he might run to Beth-lehem his city: for there is a yearly sacrifice there for all the family.

If he say thus, It is well; thy servant shall have peace: but if he be very wroth, then be sure that evil is determined by him [1 Sam. 20:6–7].

This was the way that David was going to find out the true feelings of Saul.

And Jonathan said, Far be it from thee: for if I knew certainly that evil were determined by my father to come upon thee, then would not I tell it thee?

Then said David to Jonathan, Who shall tell me? or what if thy father answer thee roughly?

And Jonathan said unto David, Come, and let us go out into the field. And they went out both of them into the field.

And Jonathan said unto David, O LORD God of Israel, when I have sounded my father about to-morrow any time, or the third day, and, behold, if there be good toward David, and I then send not unto thee, and shew it thee;

The LORD do so and much more to Jonathan: but if it please my father to do thee evil, then I will shew it thee, and send thee away, that thou mayest go in peace: and the LORD be with thee, as he hath been with my father.

And thou shalt not only while yet I live shew me the kindness of the LORD, that I die not:

But also thou shalt not cut off thy kindness from my house for ever: no, not when the LORD hath cut off the enemies of David every one from the face of the earth.

So Jonathan made a covenant with the house of David, saying, Let the LORD even require it at the hand of David's enemies.

And Jonathan caused David to swear again, because he loved him: for he loved him as he loved his own soul [1 Sam. 20:9–17].

Jonathan realized that David, his brother-in-law, would probably succeed Saul upon the throne. So he requested that when David came into power his own relationship with David's house might not be forgotten.

Plans were made so that these two friends could communicate. Jonathan would be watched to see if they made contact, so they had to be extremely careful. The plan called for Jonathan to shoot with his bow and arrows. No suspicion would be aroused if he went out often for archery because he was a warrior. David would be hiding in the field. Jonathan would go into the field with his armor-bearer and shoot an arrow. If he shot the arrow way beyond David, it meant that evil was determined against him and he should flee. If he shot the arrow closer to David, in front of him instead of beyond him, he would know it was safe to return.

On the third day Jonathan went out into the field with his bow. There would be no way for Saul to know that his son was about to deliver a message to David. The word about Saul was not favorable. Saul had made it very clear that he wanted to slay David. The arrow went flying through the air and landed way on the other side of him. That meant he was to flee. Jonathan instructed his armor-bearer to pick up the arrows he had shot and then take his artillery into the city. When the boy is gone, David and Jonathan meet and talk.

And Jonathan said to David, Go in peace, forasmuch as we have sworn both of us in the name of the LORD, saying, The LORD be between me and thee, and between my seed and thy seed for ever. And he arose and departed: and Jonathan went into the city [1 Sam. 20:42].

David is in danger from here on. He is going to flee, but the interesting thing is the covenant that David and Jonathan make. We will find that Jonathan kept his part of the covenant. He was faithful and true to David to the very end of his life. David was also faithful and true to Jonathan and his descendants.

Later on, both Saul and Jonathan are slain by the Philistines, and David comes to the throne. The safe thing for him to have done would have been to exterminate every member of the house of Saul. That means that if Jonathan had a son he should have been killed. The fact of the matter is that Jonathan did have a son. We are going to meet him a little later on in the story. His name was Mephibosheth, and he was crippled. When Saul and Jonathan were slain, a servant took the boy and hid him. But David is going to make good his covenant. David found the boy, took him to the palace, put him at his table, fed him, and cared for him. Why? He is making good his covenant with Jonathan because his friend showed him grace.

I will have occasion later on to go into more detail concerning this subject, but right now let me call your attention to the wonderful meaning of this story. David showed kindness to Mephibosheth for the sake of Jonathan. God has shown kindness to you and me for the sake of the Lord Jesus Christ. It is not because of who we are or what we have done that He saved us. Our salvation comes because of who Christ is and what He has done for us. "For God so loved the world, that he gave his only begotten Son, that whosoever believeth in him should not perish, but have everlasting life" (John 3:16). Because His Son died for us, God extends favor to us for Jesus' sake.

After David and Jonathan talked, Jonathan returned to the palace. I think he was a very sad man because he knew that his father was determined to slay his beloved friend.

CHAPTERS 21–22

THEME: *David involves the priests; David gathers his mighty men; Saul slays the priests of God*

DAVID INVOLVES THE PRIESTS

Then came David to Nob to Ahimelech the priest: and Ahimelech was afraid at the meeting of David, and said unto him, Why art thou alone, and no man with thee? [1 Sam. 21:1].

David is very much alone as he flees from Saul. His young men are with him, of course, so he is not alone in that respect. He is alone in that no one in his party is wearing the livery of King Saul.

And David said unto Ahimelech the priest, The king hath commanded me a business, and hath said unto me, Let no man know any thing of the business whereabout I send thee, and what I have commanded thee: and I have appointed my servants to such and such a place.

Now therefore what is under thine hand? give me five loaves of bread in mine hand, or what there is present.

And the priest answered David, and said, There is no common bread under mine hand, but there is hallowed bread; if the young men have kept themselves at least from women [1 Sam. 21:2–4].

The thought in this portion of Scripture is simply that the only bread available was on the table of showbread, which was not to be eaten except by the priest and only at a certain time—which was at the changing of the bread each Sabbath day.

And David answered the priest, and said unto him, Of a truth women have been kept from us about these three days, since I came out, and the vessels of the young men are holy, and the bread is in a manner common, yea, though it were sanctified this day in the vessel.

So the priest gave him hallowed bread: for there was no bread there but the shewbread, that was taken from before the LORD, to put hot bread in the day when it was taken away [1 Sam. 21: 5–6].

Although Israel had a God-given religion, and this bread was dedicated for religious purposes, there were some hungry men present who needed food. That bread would have become commonplace if it could not have been used to feed hungry mouths. That is what David was saying.

In giving David and his men the bread, the priest was breaking the letter of the Law but not the spirit of the Law. You will recall that the Pharisees challenged the Lord Jesus Christ about breaking the Law (which He did not do). The Lord refuted their accusations by referring to this incident in the life of David. Mark 2:23–28 tells us, "And it came to pass, that he went through the corn fields on the sabbath day; and his disciples began, as they went, to pluck the ears of corn. And the Pharisees said unto him, Behold, why do they on the sabbath day that which is not lawful? And he said unto them, Have ye never read what David did, when he had need, and was an hungered, he, and they that were with him? How he went into the house of God in the days of Abiathar the high priest, and did eat the shewbread, which is not lawful to eat but for the priests, and gave also to them which were with him? And he said unto them, The sabbath was made for man, and not man for the sabbath: therefore the Son of man is Lord also of the sabbath."

What the Lord was saying in His day was, "If David could do it, and it was all right, there is One here greater than David, and He can do it also." David ate the showbread because he had *need.* Christ is saying that human need supersedes all ritual and ceremonial laws.

Now a certain man of the servants of Saul was there that day, detained before the LORD; and his name was Doeg, an Edomite, the chiefest of the herdmen that belonged to Saul [1 Sam. 21:7].

There is a "Judas Iscariot" in the crowd that day at the tabernacle. His name is Doeg, and he is an Edomite. He is in Saul's service, and he is going to betray David and the high priest. David has a great deal to say about this man in Psalm 52.

And David said unto Ahimelech, And is there not here under thine hand spear or sword? for I have neither brought my sword nor my weapons with me, be-

cause the king's business required haste [1 Sam. 21:8].

Now I would like to call your attention to the way that last clause is misquoted. I have heard it said that certain things should be done for the Lord and done quickly because "the King's business requires haste." To begin with, let's understand what David is actually saying. He does not have a sword or a spear because he had to leave in a hurry. Also David is *not* on a mission for his king—he is misrepresenting here.

I am here to say that the King's business does not require haste. Have you ever noticed how patiently God works? He is going to work that way in the life of David. David is going to be schooled and trained in the caves of the earth. That is God's method. God is in no hurry. Moses was in a hurry, and he wanted to deliver the children of Israel forty years before God was ready. Moses was not ready either. God put him out in the desert and trained him and schooled him for forty years until he was ready. God brought His Son into the world thirty-three years before He went to the cross! The thing that marks the work of God is not haste but the fact that He works slowly and patiently. Oh my, how impatient we become! I am sure my wife would say, "Yes, and you are not the one to talk to people about patience because you are a very impatient man." That is true, I am impatient. I am trying, now that I am retired, to learn the art of waiting before the Lord. That is something we all need to learn. David needed to learn it too. God has had to train His men like that. God has had to teach patience to every man He has ever used. God moves and works slowly. If you want to see the way He moves, look how long it takes Him to make a diamond or a redwood tree. God's work does not require haste, friends. That is not God's method.

David is saying something in this chapter that is not true, as the context reveals. David was not on a mission for the king, and "the king's business requires haste" is in no way applicable to Christian work.

And the priest said, The sword of Goliath the Philistine, whom thou slewest in the valley of Elah, behold, it is here wrapped in a cloth behind the ephod: if thou wilt take that, take it: for there is no other save that here. And David said, There is none like that; give it me [1 Sam. 21:9].

It is interesting that David could use the slingshot when he was a youngster, but he has been in the king's palace a long time. Perhaps he has lost his cunning with the slingshot. Now he needs a sword and he uses Goliath's sword because it is available.

And David arose, and fled that day for fear of Saul, and went to Achish the king of Gath [1 Sam. 21:10].

David got as far away from Saul as he possibly could and went to Achish. When he arrived among these foreigners, he found he was in danger. They were enemies of Israel; so David had to pretend that he was a madman. He had to put on an act. Shakespeare's Hamlet had to do the same thing to keep from being slain.

Have I need of mad men, that ye have brought this fellow to play the mad man in my presence? shall this fellow come into my house? [1 Sam. 21:15].

David's act was good and the king of Achish believed it. David would not be in danger there.

DAVID GATHERS HIS MIGHTY MEN

Chapter 22 begins that period in David's life when he hides in the caves and dens of the earth. He is learning that the King's business does not require haste. God is schooling and training him as He has His other men. During these years when he hides from the presence of Saul who seeks to kill him, he is hunted and hounded. He is driven from pillar to post. He is forced to hide in the forests and caves of the earth to escape the king's wrath. During this time David describes himself in the following ways: (1) I am hunted like a partridge (1 Sam. 26:20); (2) I am like a pelican of the wilderness (Ps. 102:6); (3) I am like an owl of the desert (Ps. 102:6); (4) My soul is among lions (Ps. 57:4); and (5) They have prepared a net for my steps (Ps. 57:6).

David becomes weary during these years of running away from Saul. When Saul presses him hard, he withdraws to the cave of Adullam which is a rocky mountain fastness, southwest of Jerusalem, in a valley between Philistia and Hebron.

David therefore departed thence, and escaped to the cave Adullam: and when his brethren and all his father's house heard it, they went down thither to him.

And every one that was in distress, and every one that was in debt, and every

one that was discontented, gathered themselves unto him; and he became a captain over them: and there were with him about four hundred men [1 Sam. 22:1–2].

A marvelous comparison can be made between David and David's greater Son, the Lord Jesus Christ, during this period of his rejection which covered about ten years. This time in David's life compares to the present state of our Lord. You and I are living in the days of *His* rejection. The world has rejected Christ just as David was rejected and hunted like an animal. Saul, his enemy, was abroad; and our enemy, Satan, is abroad today. We are admonished in 1 Peter 5:8, "Be sober, be vigilant; because your adversary the devil, as a roaring lion, walketh about, seeking whom he may devour." David could say that his "soul was among lions," and we can say the same today. It is during these days that the Lord Jesus Christ is calling out of this world a people for His name. He is calling those who are in distress, those who are in debt, and those who are discontented.

These three classes of men existed in David's day. There were those who were in distress. They were persecuted and oppressed by Saul. David was a long time in breaking with Saul. There were many who were loyal to Saul, but they were finally forced to flee because their lives became endangered. Many fled to David and joined up with him.

If you have felt the whiplash of injustice in the world, if you have felt its unfairness, if you are oppressed and have no place to turn, look to the Lord Jesus Christ. Many people today are trying to find a way out of their troubles and are turning to all kinds of nostrums—some to drugs, some to drink, and some to suicide. There is One who is calling all of us today. "For the Son of man is come to seek and to save that which was lost" (Luke 19:10). He wants to help you. He can help you. "For in that he himself hath suffered being tempted, he is able to succour them that are tempted" (Heb. 2:18). Are you tested and tempted? Are you in distress? You need a Savior, and He is calling out those who will come to Him this day.

There were others who came to David during this time of rejection who were in debt. Debt is a cancer that destroys under any circumstance. In that day when a man got into debt he could lose his property and he could be sold into slavery. Men should have been protected, but they were not. This man Saul was permitting men to become slaves—he was not enforcing the Mosaic Law.

Sin has made us debtors to God. Remember that in the prayer Christ taught His disciples, it says, "Forgive us our debts." God alone can forgive us. Forgiveness always rests upon the payment of a debt, and those who were in debt had to flee. David, actually, did not pay the debt, but Christ did. He paid the debt of sin by dying on the cross. He set us free. That is what the Lord Jesus Christ did for you and for me. If you realize you are a debtor to God and have no means to pay, He will pay that debt for you. You can flee to Him. What a wonderful privilege that is!

The discontented also came to David. This means that they were bitter of soul. The circumstances and experiences of life had soured them. In the past few years I have noticed a restlessness sweeping our land and the world. In some areas it has become a great flood. Masses of people march in the street and protest about this, that, and the other thing. There is an undercurrent of dissatisfaction and discontentment. My friend, life will make you bitter unless you see the hand of God, as did Joseph whose story is told in the final chapters of Genesis.

There is One to whom you can go today. He is the Lord Jesus Christ, the rejected King. He is fairer than ten thousand, and He says, "Come unto me, all ye that labour and are heavy laden, and I will give you rest" (Matt. 11:28). He also says, ". . . If any man thirst, let him come unto me, and drink" (John 7:37). As David in exile receives these four hundred distressed, debtridden, and discontented men, what a picture he is of the Lord Jesus Christ in this age of His rejection as He is calling out of this world a people to His name.

And David went thence to Mizpeh of Moab: and he said unto the king of Moab, Let my father and my mother, I pray thee, come forth, and be with you, till I know what God will do for me.

And he brought them before the king of Moab: and they dwelt with him all the while that David was in the hold [1 Sam. 22:3–4].

Fleeing to Moab is what another Bethlehem family had done several generations before David. Elimelech, you recall, had taken his family to Moab during a period of famine in Israel. Because of this, Ruth the Moabitess is in the Bible story. The father of David would be the grandson of Ruth the Moabitess, which is undoubtedly the reason the king of Moab grants the couple asylum in Moab. The very fact that David leaves the land of Israel and goes to Moab means he is really a frightened man. Personally, I do not think he should have left Israel, as God would have protected him if he had stayed. His faith wavered a bit as had Abraham's when he went down to Egypt.

SAUL SLAYS THE PRIESTS OF GOD

And the prophet Gad said unto David, Abide not in the hold; depart, and get thee into the land of Judah. Then David departed, and came into the forest of Hareth.

When Saul heard that David was discovered, and the men that were with him, (now Saul abode in Gibeah under a tree in Ramah, having his spear in his hand, and all his servants were standing about him;)

Then Saul said unto his servants that stood about him, Hear now, ye Benjamites; will the son of Jesse give every one of you fields and vineyards, and make you all captains of thousands, and captains of hundreds;

That all of you have conspired against me, and there is none that sheweth me that my son hath made a league with the son of Jesse, and there is none of you that is sorry for me, or sheweth unto me that my son hath stirred up my servant against me, to lie in wait, as at this day? [1 Sam. 22:5–8].

It sounds like Saul is developing some paranoiac tendencies. He has developed a persecution complex. Maybe he is entitled to this complex, because he has discovered that his own son has not been loyal to him. He is wondering why these men in his cabinet have not revealed this fact to him—as apparently they had not. There is one man, however, who knows where David has fled and he tells Saul what he knows. We have met him before. He was at the tabernacle when David and his men ate the showbread.

Then answered Doeg the Edomite, which was set over the servants of Saul, and said, I saw the son of Jesse coming to Nob, to Ahimelech the son of Ahitub.

And he inquired of the LORD for him, and gave him victuals, and gave him the sword of Goliath the Philistine [1 Sam. 22:9–10].

After Doeg gives Saul his information, Saul decides to go after Ahimelech the priest.

Then the king sent to call Ahimelech the priest, the son of Ahitub, and all his father's house, the priests that were in Nob: and they came all of them to the king.

And Saul said, Hear now, thou son of Ahitub. And he answered, Here I am, my lord.

And Saul said unto him, Why have ye conspired against me, thou and the son of Jesse, in that thou hast given him bread, and a sword, and hast inquired of God for him, that he should rise against me, to lie in wait, as at this day?

Then Ahimelech answered the king, and said, And who is so faithful among all thy servants as David, which is the king's son in law, and goeth at thy bidding, and is honourable in thine house? [1 Sam. 22:11–14].

Saul sent for Ahimelech the priest and the other priests who were in Nob. Saul demanded that Ahimelech explain why he had helped David escape. The priest gave the king a truthful answer. He had the highest motives and was totally unaware that David was not being honest with him. Later on David felt very bad that he had deceived Ahimelech into thinking he was on a mission for Saul.

Did I then begin to inquire of God for him? be it far from me: let not the king impute any thing unto his servant, nor to all the house of my father: for thy servant knew nothing of all this, less or more.

And the king said, Thou shalt surely die, Ahimelech, thou, and all thy father's house.

And the king said unto the footmen that stood about him, Turn, and slay the priests of the LORD; because their hand also is with David, and because they knew when he fled, and did not shew it to me. But the servants of the king would not put forth their hand to fall upon the priests of the LORD [1 Sam. 22:15–17].

In his anger, Saul did not listen to reason but commanded his servants to slay the priests. They hesitated to carry out his order. But Saul had gone so far in his rebellion and sin that he would not stop at anything. So he commanded Doeg to do his dirty work for him.

And the king said to Doeg, Turn thou, and fall upon the priests. And Doeg the Edomite turned, and he fell upon the priests, and slew on that day fourscore and five persons that did wear a linen ephod [1 Sam. 22:18].

This was a serious and awful crime that Saul committed. If God had not rejected him before this, He certainly would have rejected him at this point.

And Nob, the city of the priests, smote he with the edge of the sword, both men and women, children and sucklings, and oxen, and asses, and sheep, with the edge of the sword [1 Sam. 22:19].

The bitterness and vengeance of this man Saul was terrible. Bitterness is something that we need to beware of today. We are warned about it in Hebrews 12:15 which says, "Looking diligently lest any man fail of the grace of God; lest any root of bitterness springing up trouble you, and thereby many be defiled." When bitterness gets into the hearts of God's people, it is a vicious and an awful thing. I have seen it in churches. I have seen officers of the church use their positions, not to bring glory to Christ, but to vent their spleens, bitterness, vengeance, and hatred against someone else. It is a terrible thing when bitterness takes over, and this is what happened in Saul's case. He was definitely Satan's man. You and I cannot be too sure about a person's salvation—even when he is active in the Lord's service—when you see him motivated by a vicious bitterness of heart and soul. It is indeed difficult to cull out the tares from the wheat at a time like that. Such was the case here.

CHAPTERS 23–24

***THEME:** God's protection and care of David in exile*

David continues to flee with his six hundred men. Jonathan contacts David and "strengthens his hand in God." David spares Saul's life at En-gedi.

DAVID FIGHTS THE PHILISTINES

Then they told David, saying, Behold, the Philistines fight against Keilah, and they rob the threshingfloors.

Therefore David inquired of the LORD, saying, Shall I go and smite these Philistines? And the LORD said unto David, Go, and smite the Philistines, and save Keilah.

And David's men said unto him, Behold, we be afraid here in Judah: how much more then if we come to Keilah against the armies of the Philistines?

Then David inquired of the LORD yet again. And the LORD answered him and said, Arise, go down to Keilah; for I will deliver the Philistines into thine hand.

So David and his men went to Keilah, and fought with the Philistines, and brought away their cattle, and smote them with a great slaughter. So David saved the inhabitants of Keilah [1 Sam. 23:1–5].

The Philistines, the perpetual enemies of Israel, were robbing the people of Keilah of their grain supply. Notice that David seeks God's will before he attempts to deliver Keilah. David is acting to protect these people, God's people, although he continues to flee from Saul.

When Saul learns that David and his men are contained in a walled city, he rushes his army down to capture them. Again David inquires of the Lord what his course of action should be. The Lord warns him to flee because the men of Keilah will not protect him from Saul—in spite of the fact that he has been their deliverer.

Then David and his men, which were about six hundred, arose and departed out of Keilah, and went whithersoever they could go. And it was told Saul that

David was escaped from Keilah; and he forbare to go forth [1 Sam. 23:13].

That is, David's men scattered—they didn't move out as an organized army.

SAUL PURSUES DAVID, AND JONATHAN AND DAVID MAKE A COVENANT

And David abode in the wilderness in strong holds, and remained in a mountain in the wilderness of Ziph. And Saul sought him every day, but God delivered him not into his hand.

And David saw that Saul was come out to seek his life: and David was in the wilderness of Ziph in a wood.

And Jonathan Saul's son arose, and went to David into the wood, and strengthened his hand in God [1 Sam. 23:14–16].

Notice how faithful and true Jonathan is to his friend David and the things he says to encourage him.

And he said unto him, Fear not: for the hand of Saul my father shall not find thee; and thou shalt be king over Israel, and I shall be next unto thee; and that also Saul my father knoweth.

And they two made a covenant before the LORD: and David abode in the wood, and Jonathan went to his house [1 Sam. 23:17–18].

In essence Jonathan is telling David that Saul knows what is going to happen but is fighting it. Saul is, of course, going against God's will. He is in complete rebellion against God. Jonathan, however, is willing to execute God's will. Jonathan's actions reveal that he is a great man. His attitude reminds me of John the Baptist who said of the Lord Jesus Christ, "He must increase, but I must decrease" (John 3:30).

Then came up the Ziphites to Saul to Gibeah, saying, Doth not David hide himself with us in strong holds in the wood, in the hill of Hachilah, which is on the south of Jeshimon? [1 Sam. 23:19].

Saul is determined to ferret out David and is aided by the Ziphites who promise to deliver David to him.

And Saul went on this side of the mountain, and David and his men on that side of the mountain: and David made haste to get away for fear of Saul; for Saul and his men compassed David and his men round about to take them [1 Sam. 23:26].

Saul has David surrounded at this point and would surely have captured him if Saul had not been called home to fight off an invasion of the Philistines. This reveals God's perfect timing which again saves David's life.

DAVID SPARES SAUL'S LIFE AT EN-GEDI

In chapter 24 David is still on the run. He is being hounded continually by Saul. I think this period of testing in David's life changed him from an innocent shepherd boy to a rugged man who became God's man and ruled over his people.

And it came to pass, when Saul was returned from following the Philistines, that it was told him, saying, Behold, David is in the wilderness of En-gedi.

Then Saul took three thousand chosen men out of all Israel, and went to seek David and his men upon the rocks of the wild goats [1 Sam. 24:1–2].

David had gone to a rugged place to hide. Saul went looking for David with an army of three thousand men while David had only six hundred men. Saul's army greatly outnumbered David's, but David made up for this imbalance by using strategy. Also, he knew the area and his men were rugged men, indeed.

And he came to the sheepcotes by the way, where was a cave; and Saul went in to cover his feet: and David and his men remained in the sides of the cave [1 Sam. 24:3].

Saul entered the very cave in which David was hiding and went to sleep. Saul's men were on guard, of course, but they were outside the cave, not inside. They permitted the king to have privacy in order that he might have a good nap. So this is the situation: David and his men, and Saul, are inside the cave. Saul's soldiers are outside the cave.

And the men of David said unto him, Behold the day of which the LORD said unto thee, Behold, I will deliver thine enemy into thine hand, that thou mayest do to him as it shall seem good unto thee. Then David arose, and cut off the skirt of Saul's robe privily [1 Sam. 24:4].

David quietly slipped up to the sleeping king and trimmed off the lower part of his garment.

And it came to pass afterward, that David's heart smote him, because he had cut off Saul's skirt [1 Sam. 24:5].

Right away David regretted his act because it would be a source of embarrassment to Saul. Imagine what would happen when Saul awakened, stood up, and found out he was wearing a mini-skirt!

And he said unto his men, The LORD forbid that I should do this thing unto my master, the LORD's anointed, to stretch forth mine hand against him, seeing he is the anointed of the LORD [1 Sam. 24:6].

David respected the *office* of king, although he may not have respected the man.

May I interject a thought at this particular point. I personally do not feel that the president of the United States, regardless of his party or character, should be made the subject of a cartoon or the object of ridicule. In a democracy, of course, he can be criticized, but to make our president a subject of ridicule, as do some cartoonists and some comedians, is entirely wrong. Now this is just my personal opinion, but I think that we ought to have more respect for the office than we do. We live in a country that has its faults, but it has been a great country for most of us, and its offices and officers should be respected.

It is interesting to note that although David is being hunted by Saul, David will not lay a hand on him. Why? Because Saul is God's anointed. David is going to let God deal with the king. My, if we could only come to the place where we would let God handle our enemies! As a rule *we* want to take care of them, but God can do a much better job. We are told in Romans 12:19, "Dearly beloved, avenge not yourselves, but rather give place unto wrath: for it is written, Vengeance is mine; I will repay, saith the Lord." When we take things in our own hands, we are no longer walking by faith. We are not trusting God. What we are really saying is, "Lord, we cannot trust You to handle this the way we want it handled, so we are going to do it ourselves." David, however, is going to let God handle Saul.

David is sorry he has cut off Saul's skirt. His conscience disturbs him because he has made the king an object of ridicule.

So David stayed his servants with these words, and suffered them not to rise against Saul. But Saul rose up out of the cave, and went on his way [1 Sam. 24:7].

Several of David's men had no use for Saul and would have killed him in a minute, but David would not permit it.

David also arose afterward, and went out of the cave, and cried after Saul, saying, My lord the king. And when Saul looked behind him, David stooped with his face to the earth, and bowed himself [1 Sam. 24:8].

Notice once again that although David may not respect Saul personally, he does have respect for Saul's office.

And David said to Saul, Wherefore hearest thou men's words, saying, Behold, David seeketh thy hurt?

Behold, this day thine eyes have seen how that the LORD had delivered thee to-day into mine hand in the cave: and some bade me kill thee: but mine eye spared thee; and I said, I will not put forth mine hand against my lord; for he is the LORD's anointed [1 Sam. 24:9–10].

David had demonstrated to Saul that he was not seeking his life. Saul had been told, and wrongly so, that David was out to get him. Nothing could have been further from the truth. I think David was very much misunderstood, maligned, and misrepresented by both friend and enemy. David's act of mercy in sparing Saul's life should have made it abundantly clear that he was not seeking the king's life.

As David continues to reason with him, Saul actually weeps.

And it came to pass, when David had made an end of speaking these words unto Saul, that Saul said, Is this thy voice, my son David? And Saul lifted up his voice, and wept.

And he said to David, Thou art more righteous than I: for thou hast rewarded me good, whereas I have rewarded thee evil [1 Sam. 24:16–17].

Now notice Saul's amazing Statement.

And now, behold, I know well that thou shalt surely be king, and that the kingdom of Israel shall be established in thine hand [1 Sam. 24:20].

This is an amazing confession coming from Saul. Saul realizes that what David has said is true and is greatly moved by the fact that he has spared his life. Then Saul acknowledges the fact that one day David will be king.

Swear now therefore unto me by the LORD, that thou wilt not cut off my seed after me, and that thou wilt not destroy my name out of my father's house.

And David sware unto Saul. And Saul went home; but David and his men gat them up unto the hold [1 Sam. 24:21–22].

After their conversation Saul returns home, but David and his men go to their stronghold. David still does not trust Saul. David goes farther and farther into the wilderness to hide, because he knows there will come a day when Saul will come after him again. I am of the opinion that Saul is actually demon-possessed at this time. We are told that an evil spirit had come upon him.

CHAPTER 25

***THEME:** Samuel dies; David meets Abigail*

In this chapter Samuel dies in his retirement. David encounters Nabal and Abigail. David in anger is prevented from the rash act of murdering Nabal and his servants by the presence and diplomacy of Abigail, Nabal's beautiful wife. Nabal dies after a night of drunkenness, and David takes Abigail to wife. She was a good influence in his life.

SAMUEL DIES

And Samuel died; and all the Israelites were gathered together, and lamented him, and buried him in his house at Ramah. And David arose, and went down to the wilderness of Paran [1 Sam. 25:1].

Scripture is quite brief concerning Samuel's death. It simply says that "all the Israelites were gathered together and lamented him." Samuel had been a great man of God; there is no question about that. He was outstanding. He was the bridge between the judges and the kings. He was the last of the judges and the first in the office of prophets. There were, of course, many prophets before Samuel, but he represented the office that continued on through the Old Testament and into the New Testament.

Samuel was also a force for good and probably prevented the full force of Saul's bitterness and hatred from being vented upon David. Samuel was a buffer between David and Saul. When Samuel died, David went a great distance into the wilderness—he went farther away from Saul than Elijah ever did from Jezebel.

DAVID AND ABIGAIL

As someone has said, "To be great is to be misunderstood." This certainly applies to David. He was great, and he was misunderstood. Because the world does not know David, it misjudges him. When the name of David is mentioned, immediately there is called to mind his sins of murder and adultery. There are those who inquire, "How could David commit such sin, and yet the Scriptures say that he was a man after God's own heart?" We will have an occasion to answer that question. But instead of questioning God's choice, we ought to investigate David's character. We will find that only those who are small will be critical of David. He is one of the outstanding characters in Scripture. To know him is to love him. I know of no man who presents such nobility of character.

David had a checkered career. He was born a peasant boy in Bethlehem, a son of Jesse of the tribe of Judah. He was brought up a little shepherd boy among seven fine-looking brothers who were older than he. He was passed by. Then one day his life changed. God had not passed him by. God knew his heart.

God does not look on the outward side of a man. God knew David's heart. He was anointed Israel's future king by Samuel. He slew the giant Goliath. As a musician he is called the "sweet psalmist of Israel." He penned the most beautiful poetry written in any language or sung in any tongue. If you have any doubt about it, have you anything to compare with Psalm 23? David married the princess Michal, the daughter of Saul. He was loved by Jonathan, the son of Saul. Never did a man have a friend like Jonathan. David became an outlaw. He gathered together a band of men during this time, and they lived in mountain strongholds. He pretended he was mad, like Hamlet, on one occasion. He finally became king of Judah and then of the entire nation of Israel. We are going to see that his own son led a rebellion against him, and once again he was forced to flee. He lived to see Solomon, his son, anointed king.

Instead of looking at David and Bathsheba and seeing David's sin, I want you to look at something else. Let's forget for the moment Goliath and David's heroic accomplishment and Jonathan's loyal friendship. Instead I want you to see the very simple story of life in this chapter. It reveals the innermost recesses of his soul. It is a story about David and Abigail, and it reveals how human David really was.

And there was a man in Maon, whose possessions were in Carmel; and the man was very great, and he had three thousand sheep, and a thousand goats: and he was shearing his sheep in Carmel.

Now the name of the man was Nabal; and the name of his wife Abigail: and she was a woman of good understanding, and of a beautiful countenance: but the man was churlish and evil in his doings; and he was of the house of Caleb [1 Sam. 25:2–3].

It seems that not all of Caleb's offspring turned out well, as we can see from this man Nabal. The name *Nabal* means "fool." I don't know how he got that name, but he certainly lived up to it. But then, aren't we all born fools? The Scriptures say that man is born like a wild ass's colt (Job 11:12). Look at your own life for a moment. Have you ever done anything foolish? I think all of us have done foolish things that we would rather not think about.

Nabal was a fool, but he was a rich man. He had neither honor nor honesty. He was a drunken beast. But he had a beautiful and intelligent wife. That is a rare combination in a woman but a pleasing one. The question is—how did this man get such a jewel for a wife? Dr. McConkey called the story of Nabal and Abigail "Beauty and the Beast." Frankly, I think her parents made the match. They were impressed by this man's wealth, and it was a case of beauty being sold for gold—traffic in a human soul. Perhaps you are saying, "That's terrible." It is terrible, but it happens all the time in our contemporary culture. How often it happens we do not know. It *is* an awful thing.

And David heard in the wilderness that Nabal did shear his sheep.

And David sent out ten young men, and David said unto the young men, Get you up to Carmel, and go to Nabal, and greet him in my name [1 Sam. 25:4–5].

David had been protecting Nabal's property. He had quite an army with him, and he could have robbed this man and taken his sheep for food, but he did not. Instead he kept thieves and marauders from getting the sheep. He did many things to assist Nabal. Now that David needs food, he sends his young men to ask for help.

And when David's young men came, they spake to Nabal according to all those words in the name of David, and ceased.

And Nabal answered David's servants, and said, Who is David? and who is the son of Jesse? there be many servants now a days that break away every man from his master [1 Sam. 25:9–10].

Nabal is saying that David has betrayed Saul and that he is disloyal.

Shall I then take my bread, and my water, and my flesh that I have killed for my shearers, and give it unto men, whom I know not whence they be?

So David's young men turned their way, and went again, and came and told him all those sayings [1 Sam. 25:11–12].

I told you at the beginning that David is redheaded and hot-headed. He is angry now.

And David said unto his men, Gird ye on every man his sword. And they girded on every man his sword; and David also girded on his sword: and there went up after David about four hundred men; and two hundred abode by the stuff [1 Sam. 25:13].

Someone in Nabal's household learned of this and informed Abigail.

But one of the young men told Abigail, Nabal's wife, saying, Behold, David sent messengers out of the wilderness to salute our master; and he railed on them [1 Sam. 25:14].

When Abigail heard what had happened between her husband and David's young men, she knew what David would do. So she got together a great deal of food.

Then Abigail made haste, and took two hundred loaves, and two bottles of wine, and five sheep ready dressed, and five measures of parched corn, and an hundred clusters of raisins, and two hundred cakes of figs, and laid them on asses.

And she said unto her servants, Go on before me; behold, I come after you. But she told not her husband Nabal.

And it was so, as she rode on the ass, that she came down by the covert of the hill, and, behold, David and his men came down against her; and she met them [1 Sam. 25:18–20].

Abigail went out to meet David with food before he could get to Nabal because David would have killed him.

Now David had said, Surely in vain have I kept all that this fellow hath in the wilderness, so that nothing was missed of all that pertained unto him: and he hath requited me evil for good [1 Sam. 25:21].

David's intention was to kill every man that belonged to Nabal.

And when Abigail saw David, she hasted, and lighted off the ass, and fell before David on her face, and bowed herself to the ground,

And fell at his feet, and said, Upon me, my lord, upon me let this iniquity be: and let thine handmaid, I pray thee, speak in thine audience, and hear the words of thine handmaid [1 Sam. 25:23–24].

Around the hill David came, riding at full tilt, flushed with anger, and probably saying to himself, "I'll get that fellow. He can't treat me that way." Then he looks down the road and sees a woman coming on a little donkey. He sees all the foodstuff, and his men are hungry. He halts his band of men before this beautiful woman. For the first time David, God's anointed, is face to face with a noble woman who means well by him. She bows before David. She gets right down in the dust and asks David to take his revenge upon her because she is Nabal's wife. She is wise in what she does because David is not about to do anything to a beautiful woman with an appeal like she made! Then she apologizes for the fact that her husband is a fool and a brute.

Let not my lord, I pray thee, regard this man of Belial, even Nabal: for as his name is, so is he; Nabal is his name, and folly is with him: but I thine handmaid saw not the young men of my lord, whom thou didst send [1 Sam. 25:25].

A "man of Belial" is a worthless person.

Now therefore, my lord, as the LORD liveth, and as thy soul liveth, seeing the LORD hath withholden thee from coming to shed blood, and from avenging thyself with thine own hand, now let thine enemies, and they that seek evil to my lord, be as Nabal.

And now this blessing which thine handmaid hath brought unto my lord, let it even be given unto the young men that follow my lord.

I pray thee, forgive the trespass of thine handmaid: for the LORD will certainly make my lord a sure house; because my lord fighteth the battles of the LORD, and evil hath not been found in thee all thy days [1 Sam. 25:26–28].

This was just the beginning of David's career. Sin came into his life later on, but up to this point David's life was as clean as a hound's tooth. He has lived for God, and he is attempting to please God. Abigail admires him for it.

Yet a man is risen to pursue thee, and to seek thy soul: but the soul of my lord shall be bound in the bundle of life with the LORD thy God; and the souls of thine enemies, them shall he sling out, as out of the middle of a sling [1 Sam. 25:29].

Although she does not mention him by name, Abigail is speaking about Saul as the one who is pursuing David. Then she says one of the most remarkable things about David, "But the soul of my lord shall be bound in the bundle of life with the LORD thy God."

Friend, that is exactly the position of the believer in Christ Jesus. John, in his first epistle, calls Christ "Eternal Life." He says, "For the life was manifested, and we have seen it, and bear witness, and shew unto you that eternal life, which was with the Father, and was manifested unto us" (1 John 1:2). When you and I trust Him as Savior, the Holy Spirit baptizes us into the body of believers. Paul says, "For by one Spirit are we all baptized into one body, whether we be Jews or Gentiles, whether we be bond or free; and have been all made to drink into one Spirit" (1 Cor. 12:13). You and I are brought into the body of believers—the body of Christ—by our faith in Christ. We are said to be *in* Christ. And there is no condemnation to those who are in Christ. So we are bound in the bundle of life with the Lord Jesus Christ.

Then Abigail said, "The souls of thine enemies God shall sling out." David knew all about slingshots, and what he had done to Goliath was well known in Israel.

Then Abigail continues.

And it shall come to pass, when the LORD shall have done to my lord according to all the good that he hath spoken concerning thee, and shall have appointed thee ruler over Israel;

That this shall be no grief unto thee, nor offence of heart unto my lord, either that thou hast shed blood causeless, or that my lord hath avenged himself: but when the LORD shall have dealt well with my lord, then remember thine handmaid [1 Sam. 25:30–31].

Abigail is saying to David, "Don't hold what my husband has done against us. You are going to be king." I can just see David sitting astride his horse, looking down at this woman who is actually down in the dust. She is a beautiful and and noble woman.

And David said to Abigail, Blessed be the LORD God of Israel, which sent thee this day to meet me:

And blessed be thy advice, and blessed be thou, which hast kept me this day from coming to shed blood, and from avenging myself with mine own hand [1 Sam. 25:32–33].

David was thankful to this woman for her wisdom in keeping him from an act that would have caused him regret.

So David received of her hand that which she had brought him, and said unto her, Go up in peace to thine house; see, I have hearkened to thy voice, and have accepted thy person [1 Sam. 25:35].

David accepted Abigail's food, advice, and person.

And Abigail came to Nabal; and, behold, he held a feast in his house, like the feast of a king; and Nabal's heart was merry within him, for he was very drunken: wherefore she told him nothing, less or more, until the morning light.

But it came to pass in the morning, when the wine was gone out of Nabal, and his wife had told him these things, that his heart died within him, and he became as a stone.

And it came to pass about ten days after, that the LORD smote Nabal, and he died [1 Sam. 25:36–38].

Nabal had a big party that night—he was a swinger. He had sobered up the next morning, and Abigail told him what had transpired the day before with David. Then "his heart died within him, and he became as a stone." He not only had a headache, he had a heartache too. What happened to him? Did he have a heart attack? It is well that God moved Abigail to intervene. David's hands would have been red with blood, and God didn't want them that way.

Now what is David going to do? There is a beautiful widow who lives in the desert of Paran. She is, actually, the only woman who has been a blessing to him.

And when David heard that Nabal was dead, he said, Blessed be the LORD, that hath pleaded the cause of my reproach from the hand of Nabal, and hath kept his servant from evil: for the LORD hath returned the wickedness of Nabal upon his own head. And David sent and communed with Abigail, to take her to him to wife [1 Sam. 25:39].

When David heard that Nabal was dead, he wanted Abigail for his wife. When she had intercepted David on the road, she had said, "When the LORD shall have dealt well with my lord, then remember thine handmaid." Well, David could not forget her. Do you know why? She had appealed to the best in him. She had advised him, and he knew her advice was right. He knew he loved her, and I think it was love at first sight.

David also recognized the hand of God. God can use beauty. That day on the road, as he thanked her for her good advice, two great souls stood in the presence of each other. Now that Nabal was dead, David asked her to become his wife, and she did. This marks the beginning of another phase of David's life.

Now something else took place of which God did not approve.

David also took Ahinoam of Jezreel; and they were also both of them his wives.

But Saul had given Michal his daughter, David's wife, to Phalti the son of Laish, which was of Gallim [1 Sam. 25:43–44].

Sin entered into his life, friend. He was a rugged man and he lived a rugged life, but one day he became a murderer. Since God called him a man after His own heart, does that mean He approved of his life? No. We will see that when David longed to build God a magnificent temple, God had to tell him "no." God would not permit him to build the temple because of the sin in his life.

CHAPTERS 26–27

***THEME:** David again spares Saul's life; David retreats to the land of Philistia*

David again spares Saul's life in the wilderness of Ziph. Note the contrast between Saul and David. Obviously Saul knows that David is God's choice, but he seeks to slay him. David recognizes that Saul is the anointed king, and he spares him.

DAVID AGAIN SPARES SAUL'S LIFE

And the Ziphites came unto Saul to Gibeah, saying, Doth not David hide himself in the hill of Hachilah, which is before Jeshimon?

Then Saul arose, and sent down to the wilderness of Ziph, having three thousand chosen men of Israel with him, to seek David in the wilderness of Ziph [1 Sam. 26:1–2].

Here goes Saul on another campaign, another crusade, to try to destroy David. This is what happened. David fled into the wilderness, and Saul went after him. David was a great soldier and he knew the terrain, which made him an expert general. He also had loyal men who were willing to die for him and with him. Saul did not know the terrain. Added to that, his followers were not as loyal as they could be, and Saul certainly suspected them.

David therefore sent out spies, and understood that Saul was come in very deed [1 Sam. 26:4].

David could not believe that Saul would come into territory that was unfamiliar to him. It was a military blunder of such proportions that David sent spies out to see if Saul really was in the area. His scouts reported that Saul was indeed in the wilderness.

And David arose, and came to the place where Saul had pitched: and David beheld the place where Saul lay, and Abner the son of Ner, the captain of his host: and Saul lay in the trench, and the people pitched round about him [1 Sam. 26:5].

David was in a position to observe where Saul and his men were, while he and his men were able to hide in the wilderness.

Then answered David and said to Ahimelech the Hittite, and to Abishai the son of Zeruiah, brother to Joab, saying, Who will go down with me to Saul to the camp? And Abishai said, I will go down with thee.

So David and Abishai came to the people by night: and, behold, Saul lay sleeping within the trench, and his spear stuck in the ground at his bolster: but Abner and the people lay round about him [1 Sam. 26:6–7].

David and Abishai went into Saul's camp and looked around. Saul was sleeping in a trench, surrounded by his men. At the head of his bed he had stuck his spear in the ground.

Then said Abishai to David, God hath delivered thine enemy into thine hand this day: now therefore let me smite him, I pray thee, with the spear even to the earth at once, and I will not smite him the second time [1 Sam. 26:8].

Abishai was saying to David, "If you just let me at him, I will strike him once. One blow is all I need, and you will be rid of your enemy."

And David said to Abishai, Destroy him not: for who can stretch forth his hand against the LORD's anointed, and be guiltless? [1 Sam. 26:9].

Once again David has the opportunity to kill Saul, but he refuses. He will not raise his hand against the Lord's anointed.

David said furthermore, As the LORD liveth, the LORD shall smite him; or his day shall come to die; or he shall descend into battle, and perish [1 Sam. 26:10].

David says, "God will have to take care of him." David is acting upon the principle found in Hebrews 10:30, ". . . Vengeance belongeth unto me, I will recompense, saith the Lord."

The LORD forbid that I should stretch forth mine hand against the LORD's anointed: but, I pray thee, take thou now the spear that is at his bolster, and the cruse of water, and let us go.

So David took the spear and the cruse of water from Saul's bolster; and they gat them away, and no man saw it, nor knew it, neither awaked: for they were all asleep; because a deep sleep from the LORD was fallen upon them [1 Sam. 26:11–12].

What David did was not difficult. He took Saul's spear and cruse of water, and no one wakened because the Lord had caused a deep sleep to fall upon Saul and his men.

Then David went over to the other side, and stood on the top of an hill afar off; a great space being between them [1 Sam. 26:13].

Now David withdrew from Saul's camp, but he did not go back to his men. Instead he went way over on the other side of Saul's camp and stood on the top of a hill. It was a place where he could easily escape if anyone came after him.

And David cried to the people, and to Abner the son of Ner, saying, Answerest thou not, Abner? Then Abner answered and said, "Who art thou that criest to the king?

And David said to Abner, Art not thou a valiant man? and who is like to thee in Israel? wherefore then hast thou not kept thy lord the king? for there came one of the people in to destroy the king thy lord.

This thing is not good that thou hast done. As the LORD liveth, ye are worthy to die, because ye have not kept your master, the LORD's anointed. And now see where the king's spear is, and the cruse of water that was at his bolster.

And Saul knew David's voice, and said, Is this thy voice, my son David? And David said, It is my voice, my lord, O king [1 Sam. 26:14–17].

Frankly, I think David is being sarcastic with Abner, who is Saul's captain and should have been protecting him. David is ridiculing Abner. David is telling him that the king could have been destroyed. About this time the king and his men begin to wake up, and they wonder what has happened. Then David says, "Where is Saul's spear and cruse of water? They are gone." David probably held them up and said, "Look, I've got them. I could have slain Saul, but I did not." And that is the important thing: David did not slay the king. He had a wonderful attitude about the whole thing. God was going to handle this affair as far as David was concerned. It may be easy for us to criticize David, but do we today let God handle our enemies? We try to take things in our own hands and try to answer our accusers and deal with them ourselves. God says, "Let Me handle the situation, and you walk by faith. Trust Me." We are going to find out that David trusted the Lord, and He took care of Saul in time.

Then Saul said to David, Blessed be thou, my son David: thou shalt both do great things, and also shalt still prevail. So David went on his way, and Saul returned to his place [1 Sam. 26:25].

Although again Saul admitted he was wrong and gave up his pursuit of David, David knew it was only a temporary respite.

We find that David's heart is becoming very discouraged. He is weary of this continual running away and hiding in the dens of the earth.

DAVID RETREATS TO THE LAND OF PHILISTIA

And David said in his heart, I shall now perish one day by the hand of Saul: there is nothing better for me than that I should speedily escape into the land of the Philistines; and Saul shall despair of me, to seek me any more in any coast of Israel: so shall I escape out of his hand [1 Sam. 27:1].

This is obviously a departure from the high plain of faith that characterizes the life of David. It is a period of just letting down. We find that the same thing happened to Abraham. It happened to Isaac, and it happened to Jacob. In fact, it seems that most of God's men have had this low period in their lives.

There is a message for you and me in this chapter. Perhaps this very day you are faced with problems. Perhaps you have been in a dark valley for a long time, and you wonder if you will ever come through it. There seems to be no solution to your problems. Well, if it is any comfort to you, there are many others who have been in the same valley—it is a well-worn route. This man David walked that path long before you and I got here. This is one of the reasons David has been such a help to me in my own Christian life. I can certainly sympathize with him. It looks as though he may spend the rest of his life running and will finally be slain by Saul.

And David arose, and he passed over with the six hundred men that were with him unto Achish, the son of Maoch, king of Gath.

And David dwelt with Achish at Gath, he and his men, every man with his household, even David with his two wives, Ahinoam the Jezreelitess, and Abigail the Carmelitess, Nabal's wife.

And it was told Saul that David was fled to Gath: and he sought no more again for him.

And David said unto Achish, If I have now found grace in thine eyes, let them give me a place in some town in the country, that I may dwell there: for why should thy servant dwell in the royal city with thee?

Then Achish gave him Ziklag that day: wherefore Ziklag pertaineth unto the kings of Judah unto this day [1 Sam. 27:2–6].

Here is David—discouraged, despondent—doing something he should not have done. He leaves the land of Israel and goes to live among the Philistines. There is nothing in this chapter that would reveal that David is a man of God.

CHAPTER 28

***THEME:** Saul consults the witch of En-dor*

Saul's interview with the witch of En-dor poses and provokes many questions. The primary one relates to Samuel. Did she bring Samuel back from the dead? Several explanations have been forthcoming: (1) Some expositors dismiss it as a fraud, taking the position that the witch was a ventriloquist; (2) others maintain that an overwhelming desire to communicate with dead loved ones makes the bereaved victims of deceit; and (3) a third group believe that the witch actually brought Samuel back from the dead. This is untenable, and it is inconsistent with the rest of Scripture.

THE PHILISTINES PLAN AN ATTACK, AND SAUL CONSULTS THE WITCH OF EN-DOR

And it came to pass in those days, that the Philistines gathered their armies together for warfare, to fight with Israel. And Achish said unto David, Know thou assuredly, that thou shalt go out with me to battle, thou and thy men.

And David said to Achish, Surely thou shalt know what thy servant can do. And Achish said to David, Therefore

will I make thee keeper of mine head for ever.

Now Samuel was dead, and all Israel had lamented him, and buried him in Ramah, even in his own city. And Saul had put away those that had familiar spirits, and the wizards, out of the land.

And the Philistines gathered themselves together, and came and pitched in Shunem: and Saul gathered all Israel together, and they pitched in Gilboa [1 Sam. 28:1–4].

Once again the Philistines were gathering their armies together to fight Israel. David gave no distinct promise that he would help them in their war with the Israelites—he certainly would avoid it if he could. Saul gathered his troops together at Gilboa.

And when Saul saw the host of the Philistines, he was afraid, and his heart greatly trembled.

And when Saul inquired of the LORD, the LORD answered him not, neither by dreams, nor by Urim, nor by prophets.

Then said Saul unto his servants, Seek me a woman that hath a familiar spirit, that I may go to her, and inquire of her. And his servants said to him, Behold, there is a woman that hath a familiar spirit at En-dor [1 Sam. 28:5–7].

Since God was not speaking to Saul, he turned to Satan in desperation. The witch of En-dor was probably a ventriloquist. I think she was partly phony and partly given over to spiritism.

I would like to dwell on the subject of spiritism for a moment. We are living in a day of frills and thrills in religion. One of the avenues which thrill-seekers are exploring is modern spiritism, or ancient necromancy. Of course, the strongest argument they have is the witch of En-dor. They say she brought Samuel back from the dead. The question is, "Did Samuel really come back from the dead and communicate with Saul?" If so, it is the only instance of such a thing in the Scripture.

Before answering this question, I want you to look at some important background material. Scripture positively condemns the practice of necromancy. This is what Deuteronomy 18:9–14 says about the subject: "When thou art come into the land which the LORD thy God giveth thee, thou shalt not learn to do after the abominations of those nations. There shall not be found among you any one that maketh his son or his daughter to pass through the fire, or that useth divination, or an observer of times, or an enchanter, or a witch, or a charmer, or a consulter with familiar spirits, or a wizard, or a necromancer. For all that do these things are an abomination unto the LORD: and because of these abominations the LORD thy God doth drive them out from before thee. Thou shalt be perfect with the LORD thy God. For these nations, which thou shalt possess, hearkened unto observers of times, and unto diviners: but as for thee, the LORD thy God hath not suffered thee so to do." We are living in a day when there is a great deal of practice in the areas just mentioned.

In *Time* magazine, several years ago, two fortunetellers were listed. According to the magazine, most of the Hollywood stars consulted them in order to find out what the future held for them. We are seeing a revival of this today, but it has been going on a long time. Back in 1947 *The Guardian*, a publication of the Church of England, ran this article: "In spite of the large amount of fraud, fake, deceit, and thought-reading, conscious or unconscious, that the investigator of psychic research has to contend with, there remains a nucleus of genuine matter that cannot be explained with our present knowledge except by accepting the hypothesis that human personalities exist through death, and that certain persons have the power and gift of contacting them. Churches have nothing to fear from genuine psychic phenomena." It is amazing that since then there has been a growing interest in this matter of looking at the stars. The so-called science of ESP has also been growing. Many people have purchased horoscopes. Millions of dollars are going into the pockets of astrologers annually.

May I say to you that the Word of God absolutely condemns this sort of thing, and God has judged nations in the past because of it. He even put His own people out of the land for turning from Him to these different abominations. My friend, these are the dangerous practices of the hour. The Scriptures warn us of the danger and predict that there will be an outbreak of it.

You will find in the account of Lazarus, the beggar, and the rich man (Luke 16:19–31) that the rich man was strictly forbidden to return to the living. He was told that he could not. Paul was caught up to heaven and *silenced*—he could not tell what he had seen (2 Cor. 12:2–4). In 2 Thessalonians 2:9 Paul says,

"Even him, whose coming is after the working of Satan with all power and signs and lying wonders." Paul, writing to a younger preacher, says, "Now the Spirit speaketh expressly, that in the latter times some shall depart from the faith, giving heed to seducing spirits, and doctrines of devils" (1 Tim. 4:1). We are seeing an increasing number of churches (they are *called* churches) where Satan is actually worshiped. This is something that the Word of God says will increase in the last days.

Now we find Saul going to the witch of En-dor.

And Saul disguised himself, and put on other raiment, and he went, and two men with him, and they came to the woman by night: and he said, I pray thee, divine unto me by the familiar spirit, and bring me him up, whom I shall name unto thee.

And the woman said unto him, Behold, thou knowest what Saul hath done, how he hath cut off those that have familiar spirits, and the wizards, out of the land: wherefore then layest thou a snare for my life, to cause me to die?

And Saul sware to her by the LORD, saying, As the LORD liveth, there shall no punishment happen to thee for this thing.

Then said the woman, Whom shall I bring up unto thee? And he said, Bring me up Samuel.

And when the woman saw Samuel, she cried with a loud voice: and the woman spake to Saul, saying, Why hast thou deceived me? for thou art Saul.

And the king said unto her, Be not afraid: for what sawest thou? And the woman said unto Saul, I saw gods ascending out of the earth [1 Sam. 28:8–13].

Notice that this frightens the old witch. She sees supernatural creatures coming out of the ground.

And he said unto her, What form is he of? And she said, An old man cometh up; and he is covered with a mantle. And Saul perceived that it was Samuel, and he stooped with his face to the ground, and bowed himself [1 Sam. 28:14].

If you read the account carefully, you will realize that Saul did not see Samuel. It was the witch, who may never have seen Samuel alive, who said she saw an old man covered with a mantle. Of course they jumped to the conclusion it was Samuel. When they did, he answered as Samuel—because demons can impersonate. Saul has laid himself wide open for Satan, and Satan has moved in.

And Samuel said to Saul, Why hast thou disquieted me, to bring me up? And Saul answered, I am sore distressed; for the Philistines make war against me, and God is departed from me, and answereth me no more, neither by prophets, nor by dreams: therefore I have called thee, that thou mayest make known unto me what I shall do [1 Sam. 28:15].

Saul is abandoned by God, and he is desperately afraid of the advancing Philistines.

Then said Samuel, Wherefore then dost thou ask of me, seeing the LORD is departed from thee, and is become thine enemy?

And the LORD hath done to him, as he spake by me: for the LORD hath rent the kingdom out of thine hand, and given it to thy neighbour, even to David:

Because thou obeyedst not the voice of the LORD, nor executedst his fierce wrath upon Amalek, therefore hath the LORD done this thing unto thee this day.

Moreover the LORD will also deliver Israel with thee into the hand of the Philistines: and to-morrow shalt thou and thy sons be with me: the LORD also shall deliver the host of Israel into the hand of the Philistines [1 Sam. 28:16–19].

It is interesting to note that nothing new is added. Saul does not get any new information. Samuel, before his death, had already pronounced the death, the destruction, and the rejection of Saul. Certainly Saul did not gain any comfort, any direction, or any new information from his excursion into the spirit world.

This reminds me of an account related by one of the friends of Job. By the way he introduces it, you would think that he had been given some tremendous revelation. Listen to him: "Now a thing was secretly brought to me, and mine ear received a little thereof.

In thoughts from the visions of the night, when deep sleep falleth on men, fear came upon me, and trembling, which made all my bones to shake. Then a spirit passed before my face; the hair of my flesh stood up: it stood still, but I could not discern the form thereof: an image was before mine eyes, there was silence, and I heard a voice, saying, Shall mortal man be more just than God? shall a man be more pure than his maker?" (Job 4:12–17). After this man had this tremendous experience and went through these gyrations, what came out of it that was new? Nothing! "Shall mortal man be more just than God? shall a man be more pure than his maker?" That is a self-evident truth. The spirit revealed nothing new!

It is obvious from the account of the witch of En-dor that God was not in it. To begin with, God would not call Samuel up—Saul makes it clear that God was no longer speaking to him. Was Satan able to call up Samuel? That, of course, is the question.

In Scripture we need to understand that only Christ ever communicated with the dead. He alone can speak to the dead. This man Saul had been abandoned by God. As far as he is concerned, heaven is silent. And so Saul turns to hell. Now did Samuel appear to Saul? Several explanations have been offered. There are those who dismiss the entire incident as a fraud. They do not believe anything about it was genuine. They say the witch was a ventriloquist and put on the whole show. I think she was a fraud, too, but because she was as frightened as Saul at what happened, we can't rule out the supernatural.

Houdini, in his day, said he could duplicate 95 percent of the so-called supernatural things that spiritualism claimed it could and did do. Granted that 99 percent of it is fraud, what about the rest of it? I believe that what happened at En-dor was supernatural, but I do not believe God had a thing to do with it. There is, of course, another explanation for what happened, and that is the desire of loved ones to communicate with those that have gone before. Both Sir Oliver Lodge and Sir Conan Doyle lost sons in war and wanted to see them. I believe even these men were taken in by spiritualism. Also, many others are deceived because of their strong desire to see their loved ones who are dead.

Kipling wrote a poem that I think is the answer to this.

The road to En-dor is easy to tread
For Mother or yearning Wife.
There, it is sure, we shall meet our Dead
As they were even in life.
Earth has not dreamed of the blessing in store
For desolate hearts on the road to En-dor.

Whispers shall comfort us out of the dark—
Hands—ah, God!—that we knew!
Visions and voices—look and hark!—
Shall prove that our tale is true,
And that those who have passed to the further shore
May be hailed—at a price—on the road to En-dor. . .

Oh, the road to En-dor is the oldest road
And the craziest road of all!
Straight it runs to the Witch's abode,
As it did in the days of Saul,
And nothing is changed of the sorrow in store
For such as go down the road to En-dor!

—Rudyard Kipling

There are those who say that the witch actually brought Samuel from the dead. I say to you that such an explanation is neither tenable nor consistent with the rest of Scripture. We are told in 1 Chronicles 10:13, "So Saul died for his transgression which he committed against the LORD, even against the word of the LORD, which he kept not, and also for asking counsel of one that had a familiar spirit, to inquire of it." God condemned the thing that Saul did.

There are those who use 1 Samuel 28:12 to prove that God caused Samuel to appear. "And when the woman saw Samuel, she cried with a loud voice: and the woman spake to Saul, saying, Why hast thou deceived me? for thou art Saul." I do not hold with this theory. I believe it was an impersonation by a false spirit rather than Samuel who appeared. God no longer spoke to Saul. Worse still, Saul no longer spoke to God. The dead cannot communicate with the living. This was satanic from beginning to end.

When I say that the dead cannot communicate with the living, there is one exception. Do you want to hear a voice from the dead? Well, listen to this: "And when I saw him, I fell at his feet as dead. And he laid his right hand upon me, saying unto me, Fear not; I am the first and the last: I am he that liveth, and was dead; and, behold, I am alive for evermore, Amen; and have the keys of hell and of death" (Rev. 1:17–18). It is the Lord Jesus

Christ who holds the keys of the grave and of death. He has come back from the dead.

I have a question for you: Why do you want to traffic with a witch or a spirit who you think can give you inside information? If that one is actually in touch with the spirit world, the information comes from hell, not from heaven—for hell is speaking to this earth as well as heaven. Any communication coming that route which looks supernatural (and it may be supernatural) comes from the pit of hell. Why not listen to the Man who went down through the doorway of death and came back? He is the only One who made a two-way thoroughfare of it. He says, "I was dead. I am alive forevermore, and I have the keys of death and of the grave." If you want any information, go to Him. If you want help, go to Him. If you want salvation, go to Him. He went down through the portal of death for you and for me, and He came out in mighty power which He makes available to His own.

CHAPTERS 29–30

***THEME:** David's life among the Philistines*

As we saw in chapter 27, David had become so discouraged and despondent because of Saul's determination to kill him that he left the land of Israel. God had not told him to leave any more than He had told Abraham to leave the land. On the part of both these men it was a lapse of faith. So David stepped out of the land and moved over into the country of Philistia.

The Philistines were definitely the enemies of his people. David spent some time there and became a good friend of the king of Gath, who was one of the lords of the Philistines. Then when war broke out between the Israelites and the Philistines, David found himself in an awkward spot. Since he had become friends with at least one of the lords of the Philistines, he felt he should be his ally. But God intervened and prevented David from attacking his own people. This was a narrow escape for him. Had God not intervened, David would have done something that he would have regretted the rest of his life.

Christian friend, we do not realize how many times God intervenes in our lives. We sometimes overstep the boundaries God has set, and we are not where we should be, or we are not doing what we should be doing. When we make errors in judgment, many times God graciously intervenes to keep us from committing a terrible sin that we would regret the rest of our lives. I am sure you can look back upon your life and recall many such occasions.

Now the Philistines gathered together all their armies to Aphek: and the Israelites pitched by a fountain which is in Jezreel.

And the lords of the Philistines passed on by hundreds, and by thousands: but David and his men passed on in the rereward with Achish [1 Sam. 29:1–2].

When war was about to break out, David and his men marched with the Philistines. All the lords of the Philistines knew David, and when they saw him marching with them, they did not like it—and rightly so. I am sure that if you saw a person who had been your enemy suddenly turn and be on your side, you would want to make sure that he was not going to come up from the rear and attack you. That sometimes happens even among Christian brethren today. When a formerly unfriendly person suddenly becomes friendly, you wonder if he is really your friend or whether he has some ulterior motive in mind.

PHILISTINES DISTRUST DAVID TO BATTLE ISRAEL

Then said the princes of the Philistines, What do these Hebrews here? And Achish said unto the princes of the Philistines, Is not this David, the servant of Saul the king of Israel, which hath been with me these days, or these years, and I have found no fault in him since he fell unto me unto this day? [1 Sam. 29:3].

This Philistine lord, Achish, could find no fault with him because David had been a loyal fellow. He had never attempted to undermine him—David was not that kind of a man. I think one of the tragedies in our Christian circles is men who attempt to undermine other Christians.

And the princes of the Philistines were wroth with him; and the princes of the Philistines said unto him, Make this fellow return, that he may go again to his place which thou hast appointed him, and let him not go down with us to battle, lest in the battle he be an adversary to us: for wherewith should he reconcile himself unto his master? should it not be with the heads of these men? [1 Sam. 29:4].

This is the way the Philistine lords reasoned, and there is a certain amount of logic in it. It could have been that David wanted to make peace with Saul, and what better way to do it than to turn and fight against the Philistines during the battle with Israel? That would certainly reconcile him to Saul. Since these men did not know David, they cannot be blamed for the position that they took.

Is not this David, of whom they sang one to another in dances, saying, Saul slew his thousands, and David his ten thousands? [1 Sam. 29:5].

These Philistine lords had heard about David; they knew he could be a formidable foe. So I believe their position was a reasonable and logical one. Achish, however, had full confidence in David.

Then Achish called David, and said unto him, Surely, as the LORD liveth, thou hast been upright, and thy going out and thy coming in with me in the host is good in my sight: for I have not found evil in thee since the day of thy coming unto me unto this day: nevertheless the lords favour thee not.

Wherefore now return, and go in peace, that thou displease not the lords of the Philistines [1 Sam. 29:6–7].

Achish is outvoted and outnumbered. The others will not have David, although Achish has confidence in him. In order to have harmony in their midst, Achish asks David to leave. This, my friend, is nothing but the providence of almighty God. It delivers David from fighting his own people.

And David said unto Achish, But what have I done? and what hast thou found in thy servant so long as I have been with thee unto this day, that I may not go fight against the enemies of my lord the king? [1 Sam. 29:8].

Although King Saul was David's enemy at the time, David would never turn against his own people. However, David's lapse of faith in stepping out of the land meant he was also stepping out of the will of God. This opened the way for sin to come into his life. The interesting thing is, Christian friend, that when a child of God steps out of the will of God, he will not lose his salvation, but he will have trouble.

In California, after World War II, a man came to see me. He was a young man when he was discharged from the service and was out of the will of God. While in this condition, he married an unsaved girl. His life had been a living hell from that day until the day I talked to him. His only solution to the problem was to get a divorce. I told him, "Don't get a divorce. Let her go if she wants to leave you, but stick it out, brother. This is what happened to you when you stepped out of God's will." You see, the child of God will not lose his salvation when he steps out of God's will, but he may get something he will wish he did not have. You will always get into trouble when you step out of the will of God. David stepped out of God's will and was about to commit an awful sin when God intervened.

So David and his men rose up early to depart in the morning, to return into the land of the Philistines. And the Philistines went up to Jezreel [1 Sam. 29:11].

Jezreel is in the north. If you have a good map, you ought to take a look at the geography at this point. It will make clearer a great deal of what is happening. Jezreel is near the Valley of Esdraelon. In fact, I would say it is part of it. It is here that the Scriptures tell us the last great War of Armageddon will be fought. It is being used as a wonderful fertile valley today.

As the Philistines go on up to Jezreel, David and his men start back home to Ziklag. It will not be a joyful homecoming, as we shall see.

DAVID FIGHTS AMALEKITES FOR DESTROYING ZIKLAG

While David and his men were away from home, an enemy from the south, the Amalekites, invaded the Philistine country and destroyed Ziklag. You will note by your map that Ziklag is way down in the south —even south of Beer-sheba—in the Philistine country.

And it came to pass, when David and his men were come to Ziklag on the third day, that the Amalekites had invaded the south, and Ziklag, and smitten Ziklag, and burned it with fire;

And had taken the women captives, that were therein: they slew not any, either great or small, but carried them away, and went on their way.

So David and his men came to the city, and, behold, it was burned with fire; and their wives, and their sons, and their daughters, were taken captives [1 Sam. 30:1–3].

Can you appreciate the position of David and his six hundred followers? They had returned to Ziklag, the city which had become their home, expecting to be reunited with their families. They returned to find it burned with fire and deserted. David and his men were distraught. They had lost their wives and children! As far as they knew, their loved ones had been slain.

Then David and the people that were with him lifted up their voice and wept, until they had no more power to weep.

And David's two wives were taken captives, Ahinoam the Jezreelitess, and Abigail the wife of Nabal the Carmelite [1 Sam. 30:4–5].

This came as a great blow and a sorrow to David. Among the missing loved ones was his wife Abigail. You remember that Abigail had been married to a very rich man whose name was Nabal (meaning "fool"). After he had died, David had taken her to wife. She was the good part of David's life, and she was the only woman who was a blessing to him.

And David was greatly distressed; for the people spake of stoning him, because the soul of all the people was grieved, every man for his sons and for his daughters: but David encouraged himself in the Lord his God [1 Sam. 30:6].

David was greatly distressed, not only because he lost his loved ones, but because his men spoke of stoning him. Because David was the leader, they blamed him for leaving Ziklag and going with the Philistines. David had made a blunder, a great blunder.

Most folk think of David as the shepherd boy who slew Goliath. Also they remember the black side of his life, the great sin he committed with Bathsheba. What they don't realize is that David was very much a human being like the rest of us. He made many blunders just like we do. He made a mistake when he left Israel to live among the Philistines. Now his men are ready to stone him "because the soul of all the people was grieved, every man for his sons and for his daughters." Notice they do not seem to be grieving for their wives. Do you know why? They think their wives have been slain but that their children are still alive. As the common colloquialism says it, David was between a rock and a hard place. He was between the devil and the deep blue sea. He was in a bad spot. He has lost his loved ones. His own followers, under this great emotional strain of having lost their loved ones, want to stone him. "But David encouraged himself in the Lord his God." This is one of the most wonderful statements ever made.

Friend, there are times in our lives when the circumstances will not produce any joy or happiness. There are times when we find ourselves in dark places, like David. We look about, and the situation looks hopeless. What should we do? Be discouraged? Give up? Say we are through? Friend, if we are children of God, we will encourage ourselves in the Lord. We will turn to Him at times like this. Sometimes the Lord puts us in such a spot so we will turn to Him. He wants to make Himself real to us. It was during times like these that David wrote some of his most helpful psalms. When troubles come, you can thumb your way through the Psalms and find where David is encouraging himself in the Lord. Several times he says, "The Lord is good . . . Let the redeemed of the Lord say so." David found this to be true.

And David said to Abiathar the priest, Ahimelech's son, I pray thee, bring me hither the ephod. And Abiathar brought thither the ephod to David [1 Sam. 30:7].

The ephod was a portion of the high priest's garments which speaks of prayer. This garment went over the garment that the regular priest wore. The ephod set the high priest apart. It was the garment he wore when he went in to the golden altar of prayer. It had two stones, one on each shoulder, on which were engraved the names of the twelve tribes of Israel: six on one shoulder and six on the other. In other words, the high priest came to the altar of prayer bearing Israel on his shoulders. This is a picture of Christ, our Great

High Priest, who carries us on His shoulders. Do you remember His story of that little sheep which got lost? What did the shepherd do? He put that lamb on his shoulders and brought him back. I do not know who you are or where you are, my friend, but I do know that the Lord is prepared to come and get you, put you on His shoulders, and bring you back to the fold. "Wherefore he is able also to save them to the uttermost that come unto God by him, seeing he ever liveth to make intercession for them" (Heb. 7:25).

And David inquired at the LORD, saying, Shall I pursue after this troop? shall I overtake them? And he answered him, Pursue: for thou shalt surely overtake them, and without fail recover all [1 Sam. 30:8].

With the ephod, the garment of prayer, David went to God for direction. He talked to his High Priest, the One who was his Shepherd. David appealed to his Lord, and the Lord encouraged him to go after the enemy.

So David went, he and the six hundred men that were with him, and came to the brook Besor, where those that were left behind stayed.

But David pursued, he and four hundred men: for two hundred abode behind, which were so faint that they could not go over the brook Besor [1 Sam. 30:9–10].

All provisions had been taken, and these men were absolutely faint. Two hundred of them could not make the trip because they had marched double time.

And they found an Egyptian in the field, and brought him to David, and gave him bread, and he did eat; and they made him drink water [1 Sam. 30:11].

On their way after the enemy, they found an Egyptian in the field. He was sick and told David he was the servant of one of the Amalekite leaders. When he got sick, they left him to die. David had overtaken this man, but he has yet to overtake the enemy. He wants to know where they are. The Egyptian servant says he will tell David what he wants to know if David promises not to return him to his master. David assures him that he will not be sent back to his master. The Egyptian tells David what had happened at the burning of Ziklag, then leads him to the Amalekites.

David makes a surprise attack upon the Amalekites as they are in revelry, enjoying the victory and the spoils they have taken.

And when he had brought him down, behold, they were spread abroad upon all the earth, eating and drinking, and dancing, because of all the great spoil that they had taken out of the land of the Philistines, and out of the land of Judah.

And David smote them from the twilight even unto the evening of the next day: and there escaped not a man of them, save four hundred young men, which rode upon camels, and fled [1 Sam. 30:16–17].

Only four hundred of the young men had transportation and were able to get away from David and his men. When the battle was over, David returned to Ziklag, along with the wives and children and all the flocks and herds that had been captured.

There was an argument among David's men as to whether the men who had not participated in the battle were entitled to any of the spoils. David put down a principle here, revealing his fairness which made him the kind of man God could use. The two hundred men who were not able to make the trip and do battle were to share equally in the booty. That revealed justice on the part of David.

CHAPTER 31

***THEME:** Saul and Jonathan die in battle*

We have now come to the final chapter of 1 Samuel. The Philistines are fighting against Israel. Thank the Lord that David is not engaged in this battle. As you recall, the providence of God intervened to keep him out of it. Because the Philistines did not trust him to fight with them, he had withdrawn and returned to Ziklag. There he found his city looted and burned and the women and children taken captive. While David and his men are hunting down the Amalekites, Israel is fleeing before the Philistines. They are being defeated in this battle because they are out of the will of God. As we have seen, when the Philistines came against Saul and he asked God for direction, God was silent. That is the reason Saul resorted to the witch of En-dor. Because of his rebellion and sinfulness, God did not answer him and is not protecting him now.

Now the Philistines fought against Israel: and the men of Israel fled from before the Philistines, and fell down slain in mount Gilboa [1 Sam. 31:1].

The battle goes against Israel from the very first.

And the Philistines followed hard upon Saul and upon his sons; and the Philistines slew Jonathan, and Abinadab, and Melchi-shua, Saul's sons.

And the battle went sore against Saul, and the archers hit him; and he was sore wounded of the archers [1 Sam. 31:2–3].

It is the beginning of the end for Saul. First he was hit in battle by an archer. Apparently it was someone who did not recognize that he had hit the king. It was, shall we say, a real bull's-eye. It is also tragic that Jonathan was slain in this battle. This is remarkable because on another occasion when Jonathan was fighting the Philistines, he slew 250 of the enemy at one time. This shows how hopelessly outnumbered Israel was at this time. This could well have been a battle in which David and Jonathan would have been on opposite sides, but God had intervened.

So we find that Saul is wounded.

Then said Saul unto his armour-bearer, Draw thy sword, and thrust me through therewith; lest these uncircumcised come and thrust me through, and abuse me. But his armour-bearer would not; for he was sore afraid. Therefore Saul took a sword, and fell upon it [1 Sam. 31:4].

When Saul saw that he was mortally wounded, he felt that the enemy would come and abuse him and taunt him. I think he was right. As we have seen, Saul was a proud, egotistical man, and he did not feel that such an end was becoming to him. His armorbearer was afraid to lay a hand on the king when Saul asked him to thrust him through with a sword. So Saul took a sword and fell upon it. It looks as if Saul was a suicide case. Was it really a suicide?

And when his armour-bearer saw that Saul was dead, he fell likewise upon his sword, and died with him.

So Saul died, and his three sons, and his armour-bearer, and all his men, that same day together.

And when the men of Israel that were on the other side of the valley, and they that were on the other side Jordan, saw that the men of Israel fled, and that Saul and his sons were dead, they forsook the cities, and fled; and the Philistines came and dwelt in them.

And it came to pass on the morrow, when the Philistines came to strip the slain, that they found Saul and his three sons fallen in mount Gilboa.

And they cut off his head, and stripped off his armour, and sent into the land of the Philistines round about, to publish it in the house of their idols, and among the people [1 Sam. 31:5–9].

We begin to see now, with Saul's armor being sent around, why he tried to get David to wear it when he fought Goliath. Had David won the battle wearing Saul's armor, the king would have gotten the credit for the victory. A case in point involves one of his sons. When Jonathan won a victory, instead of giving him credit for it, Saul blew the trumpet in the land and took the credit himself.

And they put his armour in the house of Ashtaroth: and they fastened his body to the wall of Beth-shan.

And when the inhabitants of Jabesh-gilead heard of that which the Philistines had done to Saul;

All the valiant men arose, and went all night, and took the body of Saul and the bodies of his sons from the wall of Beth-shan, and came to Jabesh, and burnt them there.

And they took their bones, and buried them under a tree at Jabesh, and fasted seven days [1 Sam. 31:10–13].

This concludes the book of 1 Samuel. Someone says, "Well, there wasn't such a mystery about the death of Saul after all." We are not through with this story yet. We will pick it up again in the book of 2 Samuel. We are going to find that Saul spared the Amalekites, and Samuel rebuked him for it. He told Saul, "To obey is better than sacrifice and to hearken than the fat of rams." God wanted obedience, and Saul's heart never bowed to almighty God. It is interesting that Saul spared the Amalekites, and we are going to find that it may have been the Amalekites who actually killed Saul. "But," someone says, "we have already read the record that says the Philistines killed Saul. An archer shot him, and he was mortally wounded. He tried to get his armor-bearer to kill him, but the man would not. Finally, Saul fell on his own sword. Isn't that the explanation? Isn't it a closed case? Wasn't it all wrapped up by the Beth-shan police department?" I don't think so. Second Samuel is going to give us some more information.

(For Bibliography to 1 Samuel, see Bibliography at the end of 2 Samuel.)

The Book of

2 SAMUEL

(For introductory material to 2 Samuel, see the Book of 1 Samuel.)

OUTLINE

I. Triumphs of David, Chapters 1–10

A. David Mourns the Death of Saul and Jonathan, Chapter 1
B. David Made King over Judah, Chapter 2
C. Civil War—Abner Joins with David but Is Murdered by Joab, Chapter 3
D. Ish-bosheth, Son of Saul, Killed, Chapter 4
E. David Made King over All Israel; Moves His Capital to Jerusalem, Chapter 5
F. David's Wrong and Right Attempts to Bring the Ark to Jerusalem, Chapter 6
G. God's Covenant to Build the House of David, Chapter 7
H. David Consolidates His Kingdom, Chapter 8
I. David Befriends Mephibosheth, Chapter 9
J. David Wars against Ammon and Syria, Chapter 10

II. Troubles of David, Chapters 11–24

A. David's Two Great Sins, Chapter 11
B. Nathan Faces David with His Sins; David Repents, Chapter 12
C. David's Daughter Tamar Raped by Amnon, David's Son; Amnon is Murdered by Absalom, David's Son, Chapter 13
D. David Permits Absalom to Return with Half-hearted Forgiveness, Chapter 14
E. Absalom Rebels against David, Chapter 15
F. Ziba, Mephibosheth's Servant, Deceives David; Shimei Curses David, Chapter 16
G. Absalom's Advisers (Ahithophel and Hushai) Disagree on Attack against David, Chapter 17
H. Absalom is Slain and David Mourns, Chapter 18
I. David Restored to Throne, Chapter 19
J. Sheba Revolts against David, Chapter 20
K. Three-Year Famine; Gibeonites Take Vengeance on House of Saul; War with Philistines, Chapter 21
L. David's Song of Deliverance (Psalm 18), Chapter 22
M. David's Last Words; David's Mighty Men, Chapter 23
N. David's Sin in Taking Census; Chooses Punishment and Buys Threshingfloor of Araunah, Chapter 24

CHAPTER 1

THEME: *David mourns the deaths of Saul and Jonathan*

In this chapter David mourns the deaths of Saul and Jonathan. The question of who killed Saul may not be answered completely in this chapter, but another suspect is added. A young Amalekite, who came out of the camp of Israel, reported to David the death of Saul and claimed credit for slaying him. David executed the young man for the crime. David's grief over the deaths of Saul and Jonathan is touching, poetic, and dramatic. It is a striking lamentation.

Here we are introduced to another suspect in the death of Saul.

Now it came to pass after the death of Saul, when David was returned from the slaughter of the Amalekites, and David had abode two days in Ziklag;

It came even to pass on the third day, that, behold, a man came out of the camp from Saul with his clothes rent, and earth upon his head: and so it was, when he came to David, that he fell to the earth, and did obeisance [2 Sam. 1:1–2].

This was a dark day in the history of Israel. War and defeat had come to these people because they were out of the will of God. There is a lesson for us in this. At the end of World War II we thought we had brought peace to the world, and we expected to rest on our laurels from then on and to enjoy life in sin, far from God. That, I am sure, is one of the reasons the world has not had a day of peace since the end of World War II. It has been continual war for us ever since. There will be turmoil and warfare for a nation, a people, or an individual who is out of the will of God. "There is no peace, saith my God, to the wicked" (Isa. 57:21). Isaiah said that three times. I wonder if that might not be applicable to us today.

As I have said, it was a dark day for Israel. You can see their position. King Saul was dead. Jonathan and his three sons were dead. Israel had lost the battle. The Philistines had taken all the northern area around Galilee, and now they had gained ground in the south.

David did not know what had happened in the battle. He and his men had been recovering their own loved ones from the Amalekite marauders. They had been back in Ziklag for two days without hearing a word. Finally, a man all disheveled, covered with mud and dirt and wearing torn clothes, stumbled into David's camp. He said he had come from the war. He told David that the Philistines had won the war and that Saul was dead. Then he told David what had happened.

And David said unto him, From whence comest thou? And he said unto him, Out of the camp of Israel am I escaped.

And David said unto him, How went the matter? I pray thee, tell me. And he answered, That the people are fled from the battle, and many of the people also are fallen and dead; and Saul and Jonathan his son are dead also.

And David said unto the young man that told him, How knowest thou that Saul and Jonathan his son be dead?

And the young man that told him said, As I happened by chance upon mount Gilboa, behold, Saul leaned upon his spear; and, lo, the chariots and horsemen followed hard after him.

And when he looked behind him, he saw me, and called unto me. And I answered, Here am I.

And he said unto me, Who art thou? And I answered him, I am an Amalekite.

He said unto me again, Stand, I pray thee, upon me, and slay me: for anguish is come upon me, because my life is yet whole in me.

So I stood upon him, and slew him, because I was sure that he could not live after that he was fallen: and I took the crown that was upon his head, and the bracelet that was on his arm, and have brought them hither unto my lord [2 Sam. 1:3–10].

Is this Amalekite speaking the truth? Or did he come upon the body of Saul and, finding him dead, take the crown and bracelet and bring them to David? I am of the opinion that when this Amalekite found Saul, after he had fallen on his sword, he was still alive. When this Amalekite came by, Saul asked him to finish the job. The interesting thing is that this young man confessed to David what he had done, and it sounds as though he expected

David to give him a medal for his deed and put him on a life pension.

Then David took hold on his clothes, and rent them; and likewise all the men that were with him:

And they mourned, and wept, and fasted until even, for Saul, and for Jonathan his son, and for the people of the LORD, and for the house of Israel; because they were fallen by the sword.

And David said unto the young man that told him, Whence art thou? And he answered, I am the son of a stranger, an Amalekite.

And David said unto him, How wast thou not afraid to stretch forth thine hand to destroy the LORD's anointed? [2 Sam. 1:11–14].

If this man did slay Saul, it was because Saul had disobeyed God when he refused to slay all of the Amalekites back in the Book of 1 Samuel. Had Saul obeyed God, this man would not have been alive to kill him, and perhaps Saul would have survived. David asked this young man how it was that he was unafraid to touch the Lord's anointed. David, you remember, would not take Saul's life even though he had opportunity. It is well sometimes to see things from God's viewpoint. As long as Saul was king, David would not touch him. No one else had better touch him either because God is the one who put the crown on his head, and God should be the one to take it off when the time comes.

There is danger in interfering with God's work. I could tell you some very interesting stories about folk who have attempted to interfere with God's work, God's program, and God's man. God moves in and judges. He has always done it. That is why David said to this young Amalekite, "Weren't you afraid to stretch forth your hand to destroy the Lord's anointed?"

And David called one of the young men, and said, Go near, and fall upon him. And he smote him that he died [2 Sam. 1:15].

David judged the Amalekite for touching the Lord's anointed.

And David said unto him, Thy blood be upon thy head; for thy mouth hath testified against thee, saying, I have slain the LORD's anointed [2 Sam. 1:16].

If this man made up his story and confession, it certainly was a fatal thing to do. David told him, "If you have lied to me, then your blood is upon you, because you confessed that you killed the Lord's anointed." I believe the young man really did kill Saul. He did what David would never have done, and David judged him for it.

And David lamented with this lamentation over Saul and over Jonathan his son [2 Sam. 1:17].

David's grief for Saul and Jonathan is revealed here, and it is genuine.

(Also he bade them teach the children of Judah the use of the bow: behold, it is written in the book of Jasher.) [2 Sam. 1:18].

Saul had taught Israel something. He made a contribution. You see, the Israelites had no iron weapons of war, so Saul taught them to be bowmen. The bow and arrow was a formidable weapon. Many of our ancestors would testify to that. The Indians used the bow and arrow to hold back their enemies and win many battles.

The beauty of Israel is slain upon thy high places: how are the mighty fallen! [2 Sam. 1:19].

His lamentation is written in the poetic form which came so naturally to the "sweet psalmist of Israel."

Tell it not in Gath, publish it not in the streets of Askelon; lest the daughters of the Philistines rejoice, lest the daughters of the uncircumcised triumph [2 Sam. 1:20].

"Tell it not in Gath"—Gath was the capital of the Philistines. "Publish it not in the streets of Askelon." Ashkelon is in the Gaza strip and is one of the five cities of the Philistines.

Ye mountains of Gilboa, let there be no dew, neither let there be rain, upon you, nor fields of offerings: for there the shield of the mighty is vilely cast away, the shield of Saul, as though he had not been anointed with oil.

From the blood of the slain, from the fat of the mighty, the bow of Jonathan turned not back, and the sword of Saul returned not empty [2 Sam. 1:21–22].

No one could say that either Saul or Jonathan was a coward.

Saul and Jonathan were lovely and pleasant in their lives, and in their death they were not divided: they were swifter than eagles, they were stronger than lions.

Ye daughters of Israel, weep over Saul, who clothed you in scarlet, with other delights, who put on ornaments of gold upon your apparel [2 Sam. 1:23–24].

Saul had brought prosperity to the land.

How are the mighty fallen in the midst of the battle! O Jonathan, thou wast slain in thine high places [2 Sam. 1:25].

David and Jonathan were bosom friends. They loved each other. David's grief is sincere.

I am distressed for thee, my brother Jonathan; very pleasant hast thou been unto me: thy love to me was wonderful, passing the love of women [2 Sam. 1:26].

It is interesting that David says, "passing the love of women," because he was married to Jonathan's sister. Later we will find that she betrays David. I think Michal loved him as a hero in the beginning, but the day came when she despised him.

David was not very successful in his love affairs. Abigail is the only noble woman that I have found in his retinue. I disagree with those who think Bathsheba was outstanding. I do not think she was. Although his relations with her were absolutely David's sin, and God judged him for it, why was she parading around on the roof like that? David had his problems with women, but he could say of Jonathan that he was a man who was true and loyal to him unto death. It is interesting to note that the men who were David's followers were loyal to him through thick and thin. He had that charisma which caused his men to stick with him. David was that type of man.

How are the mighty fallen, and the weapons of war perished! [2 Sam. 1:27].

This is a tremendous tribute to Jonathan in particular. David's grief over the deaths of Saul and Jonathan is touching. It is one of the most striking lamentations in the Word of God.

We are going to see in the next chapter that David is made king over Judah. We will also meet Abner, who was Saul's captain. Now, not all of Saul's sons had been killed, though all of them that fought in the battle were killed. But Saul had a younger son named Ish-bosheth. Abner made him king over the eleven remaining tribes and, of course, civil war broke out. David defeated Abner and the army, and after a long civil war had weakened the nation, David finally became king of all twelve tribes. He made Hebron his home at first. Later he moved to Mt. Zion in Jerusalem, which was the place that he loved above all others.

We are coming to a section that is historical. Although many people find it uninteresting, we are going to find some of the most thrilling accounts in the entire Word of God in this section. Also we will find some marvelous spiritual lessons there.

CHAPTERS 2–3

***THEME:** David made king over Judah*

David, by God's direction, goes up to Hebron where he is made king over the tribe of Judah. Abner, the captain of Saul's army, makes Saul's son Ish-bosheth the king over the other eleven tribes of Israel. Civil war ensues.

And it came to pass after this, that David inquired of the LORD, saying, Shall I go up into any of the cities of Judah? And the LORD said unto him, Go up. And David said, Whither shall I go up? And he said, Unto Hebron [2 Sam. 2:1].

"After this" refers to the time after the deaths of Saul and Jonathan and the period of mourning for them. Now that Saul is out of the picture, David wants to know what to do. He asks the Lord, "Shall I go up into any of the cities of Judah?" Why did he ask that question? He is in Philistine country. Saul is dead, and David is to be the next king. What should his next move be? He waited until he received his instructions from the Lord. David had learned that he must wait on the Lord for direction.

God told him to go up to Hebron. Hebron is located in the south of the land, not too far from the Philistine border. God is telling him to move cautiously. He is not to go up and arbitrarily take over Israel, but to move up into the land to make himself available.

So David went up thither, and his two wives also, Ahinoam the Jezreelitess, and Abigail Nabal's wife the Carmelite [2 Sam. 2:2].

When David headed for Hebron, he took with him the two women who were his wives at this time. Perhaps you are asking, "Does God approve of a man having two wives?" No. This matter will cause David a great deal of trouble—and later he will have other wives.

And his men that were with him did David bring up, every man with his household: and they dwelt in the cities of Hebron [2 Sam. 2:3].

David's loyal followers came with him and settled their families in the cities of Hebron.

And the men of Judah came, and there they anointed David king over the house of Judah. And they told David, saying, That the men of Jabesh-gilead were they that buried Saul [2 Sam. 2:4].

Now that David has made himself available, the men of his own tribe come to anoint him king over Judah.

And David sent messengers unto the men of Jabesh-gilead, and said unto them, Blessed be ye of the LORD, that ye have shewed this kindness unto your lord, even unto Saul, and have buried him [2 Sam. 2:5].

David does a very wise thing. The men who buried Saul were devoted to him, and now David thanks them for it. David has a great respect for the anointed of the Lord—he had two opportunities to slay him and make himself king, but he did not do it. David's good points are often passed over, because his sin seems to obscure them. It is like a cloud that covers the sky and shuts out the sunshine of his life. In many respects David was a wonderful man. Afterward he paid for his great sin every day of his life.

David complimented the men of Jabesh-gilead.

And now the LORD shew kindness and truth unto you: and I also will requite you this kindness, because ye have done this thing.

Therefore now let your hands be strengthened, and be ye valiant: for your master Saul is dead, and also the house of Judah have anointed me king over them [2 Sam. 2:6–7].

Then he asked for their support and devotion to him as king, even as they had given it to Saul. Notice that he is moving in a diplomatic and commendable manner at this time. We should recognize the fact that both Saul and Jonathan had sons, and one of them would have been the normal one to come to the throne had not God intervened. Abner, who had been captain of Saul's hosts, moved immediately to make one of them king. Notice what he did.

But Abner the son of Ner, captain of Saul's host, took Ish-bosheth the son of Saul, and brought him over to Mahanaim;

And made him king over Gilead, and over the Ashurites, and over Jezreel, and over Ephraim, and over Benjamin, and over all Israel [2 Sam. 2:8–9].

Here is the beginning of the division of the kingdom which will come after the reign of Solomon when Jeroboam leads a rebellion. This is the first fracture. At first David is made king over the southern kingdom of Judah, but the northern tribes make Ish-bosheth, a son of Saul, their king.

Ish-bosheth Saul's son was forty years old when he began to reign over Israel, and reigned two years. But the house of Judah followed David.

And the time that David was king in Hebron over the house of Judah was seven years and six months [2 Sam. 2:10–11].

This was an interval of civil war: war between the northern kingdom and David's kingdom, Judah, in the south. It depleted the resources and energy of the nation. It was indeed a tragic thing.

And Abner the son of Ner, and the servants of Ish-bosheth the son of Saul, went out from Mahanaim to Gibeon.

And Joab the son of Zeruiah, and the servants of David, went out, and met

together by the pool of Gibeon: and they sat down, the one on the one side of the pool, and the other on the other side of the pool [2 Sam. 2:12–13].

Abner and Joab were attempting to negotiate a solution to prevent civil war. But as you well know (and certainly we in this country ought to know by now), when you have folk on one side who are determined on one course and people on the other side who are determined on another course, negotiation is practically valueless. It is generally an exercise in futility, and that is what happens here.

And Abner said to Joab, Let the young men now arise, and play before us. And Joab said, Let them arise.

Then there arose and went over by number twelve of Benjamin, which pertained to Ish-bosheth the son of Saul, and twelve of the servants of David.

And they caught every one his fellow by the head, and thrust his sword in his fellow's side; so they fell down together: wherefore that place was called Helkath-hazzurim, which is in Gibeon [2 Sam. 2:14–16].

Abner said, "Let the young men come together in battle." Joab agreed. This was the way they were going to settle the issue.

And there was a very sore battle that day; and Abner was beaten, and the men of Israel, before the servants of David [2 Sam. 2:17].

David is a veteran of many campaigns now. He is not the innocent little shepherd we met at first. He has spent time hiding in the caves and dens of the earth, and he has collected men of war around him. He is rugged and adept at this type of warfare. So his men are able to win a victory over Abner and his "host," an army of superior numbers.

Now I want to call your attention to something that took place which will play a prominent part later on. Abner was followed by Asahel. Asahel was a brother of Joab, who was David's captain. Abner was Saul's captain.

And there were three sons of Zeruiah there, Joab, and Abishai, and Asahel: and Asahel was as light of foot as a wild roe [2 Sam. 2:18].

Zeruiah, by the way, was a sister of David. She had three outstanding sons.

And Asahel pursued after Abner; and in going he turned not to the right hand nor to the left from following Abner [2 Sam. 2:19].

Asahel took out after Abner. He is not a match for him at all, and Abner warns him.

And Abner said again to Asahel, Turn thee aside from following me: wherefore should I smite thee to the ground? how then should I hold up my face to Joab thy brother?

Howbeit he refused to turn aside: wherefore Abner with the hinder end of the spear smote him under the fifth rib, that the spear came out behind him; and he fell down there, and died in the same place: and it came to pass, that as many as came to the place where Asahel fell down and died stood still [2 Sam. 2:22–23].

Abner warned him to stop his pursuit. Asahel refused, and finally Abner turned around and drove a spear through him. Abner killed the brother of Joab. That means that in Joab's heart there will be bitterness, hatred, and the desire to get revenge. His revenge will come later, as we shall see.

And they took up Asahel, and buried him in the sepulchre of his father, which was in Beth-lehem. And Joab and his men went all night, and they came to Hebron at break of day [2 Sam. 2:32].

Asahel's funeral closes this chapter. After the funeral Joab and his men "went all night" and came to Hebron at the break of day. They reported to David all that had taken place.

CIVIL WAR CONTINUES

Chapter 3 continues the account of the long civil war that weakened the nation. Gradually David gained in strength. Abner, after a falling-out with Ish-bosheth, deserted to David. Joab, David's captain suspected Abner and, seeking revenge for his brother Asahel's death, murdered him.

Now there was long war between the house of Saul and the house of David: but David waxed stronger and stronger, and the house of Saul waxed weaker and weaker [2 Sam. 3:1].

The condition of the land is one of internal strife. There is civil war. The nation's energies are being depleted, and their resources are being exhausted. David has been in Hebron for seven and one-half years.

And unto David were sons born in Hebron: and his firstborn was Amnon, of Ahinoam the Jezreelitess;

And his second, Chileab, of Abigail the wife of Nabal the Carmelite; and the third, Absalom the son of Maacah the daughter of Talmai king of Geshur;

And the fourth, Adonijah the son of Haggith; and the fifth, Shephatiah the son of Abital;

And the sixth, Ithream, by Eglah David's wife. These were born to David in Hebron [2 Sam. 3:2–5].

You can see that David had more than two wives. He had others, and this will cause a great problem for David. God did not approve, and David did not get by with this. Among the list of David's sons is one by the name of Absalom. I am sure you are familiar with his story. Later on we will see him lead a rebellion against David. This is the son that David apparently wanted to follow him as king, but he was brutally killed by Joab in battle. It broke David's heart when he was slain. Who is the mother of Absalom? Maacah who was the daughter of Talmai, king of Geshur. Who was the king of Geshur? If you go back to 1 Samuel 27:8, you will find that David and his men invaded the Geshurites, and the Gezrites, and the Amalekites. I believe David was wrong in doing this. He slew these people, including the king of Geshur, and apparently took his daughter captive. She eventually became his wife. They had a son, and it was this young man who led the rebellion against David. My friend, God saw to it that David did not get away with his sin. It is important for us to note this.

ABNER JOINS WITH DAVID

This chapter tells us about a long period of civil war that in many ways is uninteresting as far as you and I are concerned. Abner, who had been the chief captain of Saul's army, had pushed Ish-bosheth, Saul's son, onto the throne. Being an older man who had had such a high position, he was not apt to listen to the young king. He did something he should not have done.

And Saul had a concubine, whose name was Rizpah, the daughter of Aiah: and Ish-bosheth said to Abner, Wherefore hast thou gone in unto my father's concubine?

Then was Abner very wroth for the words of Ish-bosheth, and said, Am I a dog's head, which against Judah do shew kindness this day unto the house of Saul thy father, to his brethren, and to his friends, and have not delivered thee into the hand of David, that thou chargest me to-day with a fault concerning this woman? [2 Sam. 3:7–8].

It was the exclusive right of the man who was the successor to the throne to cohabit with the deceased king's concubines. Abner infringed on the rights of Ish-bosheth and became angry when the king rebuked him for taking Rizpah, one of Saul's concubines, into his own harem. Candidly, the young king was justified in rebuking Abner, but Abner became so enraged that he immediately began to make overtures to David.

So do God to Abner, and more also, except, as the LORD hath sworn to David, even so I do to him;

To translate the kingdom from the house of Saul, and to set up the throne of David over Israel and over Judah, from Dan even to Beer-sheba.

And he could not answer Abner a word again, because he feared him [2 Sam. 3:9–11].

In other words, Abner made known his intention of abandoning the house of Saul and allying himself with David. He was going to help David become king over the twelve tribes. Now Ish-bosheth did not say a word to Abner. He was a son of Saul, but he had no army and no training whatsoever. He was not a warrier like his brother Jonathan. He had been brought up in the king's palace. And he feared Abner.

And Abner sent messengers to David on his behalf, saying, Whose is the land? saying also, Make thy league with me, and, behold, my hand shall be with thee, to bring about all Israel unto thee.

And he said, Well; I will make a league with thee: but one thing I require of thee, that is, Thou shalt not see my face, except thou first bring Michal Saul's daughter, when thou comest to see my face [2 Sam. 3:12–13].

David told Abner he could come only if he brought Saul's daughter, Michal, with him. You remember that Michal was David's first wife. Saul had taken her away from David. Believe me, David had a checkered career. This is the reason he suffered—he let sin enter his life. But above it all was a faith in God that never failed. He wanted more than all else to have a wonderful relationship with God.

And Ish-bosheth sent, and took her from her husband, even from Phaltiel the son of Laish.

And her husband went with her along weeping behind her to Bahurim. Then said Abner unto him, Go, return. And he returned [2 Sam. 3:15–16].

Abner's overture was accepted by David. We will find now that David will become king of all twelve tribes because of Abner's treachery.

JOAB MURDERS ABNER

All of this time Joab has not forgotten that Abner had slain his brother.

And when Abner was returned to Hebron, Joab took him aside in the gate to speak with him quietly, and smote him there under the fifth rib, that he died, for the blood of Asahel his brother [2 Sam. 3:27].

So Joab avenged his brother's death. When David heard that Joab had murdered Abner, he did not approve of it at all. In fact, he accused Joab of doing a very terrible thing. Concerning Abner's death he said a very interesting thing.

And the king lamented over Abner, and said, Died Abner as a fool dieth? [2 Sam. 3:33].

Why did David say that? It certainly is a strange epitaph to give a person. Abner was in Hebron. Hebron was one of the cities of refuge where a murderer was safe. In that city Joab could not have touched him. But Joab quietly took Abner aside and said to him, "Come out here. I want to talk with you. You are the captain on one side, and I am the captain on the other side. It would be nice if we could get together." So Abner stepped outside the city of refuge, and Joab killed him. That is why David said Abner died as a fool dies. He was a fool to leave Hebron.

Isn't that a message for us today? There is a refuge for every sinner in Christ. Regardless of how high a man's IQ is or what his position in life might be, if he is outside the place of refuge, he is lost. If the truth were told at many funerals today, the preachers would have to say about the departed person, "A fool has just died. He would not turn to Jesus Christ who is the place of refuge." Are you resting in Christ?

CHAPTERS 4–5

***THEME:** David is made king of all Israel*

ISH-BOSHETH, THE SON OF SAUL, IS KILLED

Troubled times for the nation Israel continue in this chapter. Internal strife and civil war followed the deaths of Saul and Jonathan. It was a time of great heartache and heartbreak for God's people.

This section of the Word of God is usually passed over. I am confident, however, that it has been given to us for at least two reasons: (1) To show us the family of the Lord Jesus Christ and to give us His genealogy; and (2) to give us an example. Paul tells us, "Now all these things happened unto them for ensamples: and they are written for our admonition . . ." (1 Cor. 10:11). It has been given to us that it might minister to us in a spiritual way.

We have already seen that there had been a rebellion against David who had been made king of the tribe of Judah. He had moved to Hebron which was situated just at the edge of the kingdom in the south. Abner had led a rebellion by putting Ish-bosheth, Saul's son, on the throne. But because Ish-bosheth reprimanded and rebuked him for taking one of Saul's concubines into his own harem, Abner left the house of Saul and allied himself with David. This was a mistake, because Joab was waiting to kill Abner in revenge for the slaying of his brother Asahel.

Now that Ish-bosheth has lost Abner, his military captain, his army is weak. He knows he cannot maintain his kingdom against David without an army. Abner has been murdered. What is he going to do?

And when Saul's son heard that Abner was dead in Hebron, his hands were feeble, and all the Israelites were troubled.

And Saul's son had two men that were captains of bands: the name of the one was Baanah, and the name of the other Rechab, the sons of Rimmon a Beerothite, of the children of Benjamin: (for Beeroth also was reckoned to Benjamin:

And the Beerothites fled to Gittaim, and were sojourners there until this day.) [2 Sam. 4:1–3].

The Beerothites were ejected by Saul and they fled to Gittaim. Beeroth, their town, passed into the possession of Benjamin.

And Jonathan, Saul's son, had a son that was lame of his feet. He was five years old when the tidings came of Saul and Jonathan out of Jezreel, and his nurse took him up, and fled: and it came to pass, as she made haste to flee, that he fell, and became lame. And his name was Mephibosheth [2 Sam. 4:4].

Mephibosheth is an unusual name, but please remember it. The story about Mephibosheth and David is one of the most beautiful stories ever told. This boy was Jonathan's son. As long as he lived, he was a constant danger to David because he had throne rights. Since he was Jonathan's son, however, David would never harm a hair of his head. Later on David will go looking for family members of Saul and Jonathan, not to slay them, but to show them kindness.

And the sons of Rimmon the Beerothite, Rechab and Baanah, went, and came about the heat of the day to the house of Ish-bosheth, who lay on a bed at noon.

And they came thither into the midst of the house, as though they would have fetched wheat; and they smote him under the fifth rib: and Rechab and Baanah his brother escaped [2 Sam. 4:5–6].

These two underlings, Rechab and Baanah, were petty officers under Abner in the army of Saul. When they discovered that Abner was dead—and they recognized the strength and power of David—they conspired to put Ish-bosheth, the son of Saul, to death. When Ish-bosheth was in bed, they slipped in upon him and slew him. It was a bloody, ugly thing that they did. It was also a mistake, by the way. By killing this man they expected to make peace with David. In fact, they thought David would reward them for their act.

For when they came into the house, he lay on his bed in his bedchamber, and they smote him, and slew him, and beheaded him, and took his head, and gat them away through the plain all night.

And they brought the head of Ish-bosheth unto David to Hebron, and said to the king, Behold the head of Ish-bosheth the son of Saul thine enemy, which sought thy life; and the LORD hath avenged my lord the king this day of Saul, and of his seed [2 Sam. 4:7–8].

They took the head of Ish-bosheth (imagine that!) to David. David was not about to accept it. David would never approve a thing like that.

And David commanded his young men, and they slew them, and cut off their hands and their feet, and hanged them up over the pool in Hebron. But they took the head of Ish-bosheth, and buried it in the sepulchre of Abner in Hebron [2 Sam. 4:12].

Rechab and Baanah were murderers—murderers of a king. David executed them summarily for their dastardly deed.

The eleven tribes in the north recognize that they no longer have any leadership and that it is foolish to carry on rebellion against David at this time. So they attempt to make overtures of peace.

DAVID IS MADE KING OVER ALL OF ISRAEL

Then came all the tribes of Israel to David unto Hebron, and spake, saying, Behold, we are thy bone and thy flesh [2 Sam. 5:1].

The tribes sent representatives to David. They said, "Behold we are thy bone and thy flesh." That was true. This civil war was terrible, especially because the tribes were fighting each other.

Personally, I think the worst war that this country fought was the Civil War. Looking back at it, that war seemed almost unnecessary. Certainly slavery is wrong, but it should have been abolished by means other than war. The hotheads and the protesters in that day were the ones who got the country in trouble. That is the reason I am opposed to all hotheaded protesters—regardless of what side they are on. They are typical of the crowd that got this nation into the trouble during the Civil War. Men like General Grant, Abraham Lincoln, and Robert E. Lee simply found themselves in an awkward situation. In the city of Atlanta you can still see the scars of the Civil War.

The nation of Israel, after more than seven years of civil war, is reunited under David. Now it enters the greatest period it has ever enjoyed. This period foreshadows the day when Christ will come and rule.

Also in time past, when Saul was king over us, thou wast he that leddest out and broughtest in Israel: and the LORD said to thee, Thou shalt feed my people Israel, and thou shalt be a captain over Israel [2 Sam. 5:2].

The tribes are rather late in acknowledging David as the legitimate and God-appointed ruler over them. They should have recognized him long before this, but they did not.

So all the elders of Israel came to the king to Hebron; and king David made a league with them in Hebron before the LORD: and they anointed David king over Israel.

David was thirty years old when he began to reign, and he reigned forty years.

In Hebron he reigned over Judah seven years and six months: and in Jerusalem he reigned thirty and three years over all Israel and Judah [2 Sam. 5:3–5].

Israel is about to enter its greatest period of prosperity and expansion. David is thirty years old when he begins to reign—still a young man. He had reigned over the single tribe of Judah for seven years and six months in Hebron. He will reign thirty-three years in Jerusalem over all Israel, all twelve tribes. David will reign for a total of forty years and six months.

DAVID MOVES HIS CAPITAL TO JERUSALEM

Notice the first move that David makes to consolidate the kingdom: he moved the capital of Israel from Hebron to Jerusalem.

And the king and his men went to Jerusalem unto the Jebusites, the inhabitants of the land: which spake unto David, saying, Except thou take away the blind and the lame, thou shalt not come in hither: thinking, David cannot come in hither.

Nevertheless David took the strong hold of Zion: the same is the city of David [2 Sam. 5:6–7].

Once again, here are men who underestimated David. He was a great military leader, political leader, and king, and most and best of all he was a man of God.

Now Zion was David's favorite spot. Mark that in your Bible. I have marked it in mine. If you have ever been to that land, you will recognize that it is the high point of the city. Actually, in David's day, Jerusalem was down near the Kidron valley. The walls that surrounded the city in that day have been excavated down in that area. The present city of Jerusalem is nearer Mount Zion, where the palace of David was built. Later on, below Mount Zion, the temple was erected. David chose all of this. Jerusalem was David's city. In many of his psalms he speaks of Mount Zion and Jerusalem. Frankly, it would not be my favorite city. I agree with David on many things, but not on Jerusalem. Pilate hated that city. He went there only during the feast days. That is why he was in Jerusalem when Jesus was arrested; he was there for the Passover. He was there to keep order and, when the Passover was over, he retired to Caesarea, which was located on the Mediterranean. I think I would prefer Caesarea to Jerusalem, too. As far as the Bible is concerned, however, Jerusalem is to be the great capital of this earth. I am delighted to know that I will not be living there throughout eternity. I am going to be in the New Jerusalem, which has a much greater vantage point than the earthly Jerusalem.

We need to note here that "David took the strong hold of Zion." He took the top of the hill and not the city proper. From that vantage point he was able to take this city of the Jebusites. The Jebusites found themselves overwhelmed before they even knew that there was a battle going on.

And David said on that day, Whosoever getteth up to the gutter, and smiteth the Jebusites, and the lame and the blind, that are hated of David's soul, he shall be chief and captain. Wherefore they said, The blind and the lame shall not come into the house [2 Sam. 5:8].

This verse is a source of controversy. Some Bible commentators hold that this is David's retort to the taunt of the Jebusites. Others believe it has a deeper meaning. Since Scripture gives us no explanation, we cannot know the exact meaning.

So David dwelt in the fort, and called it the city of David. And David built round about from Millo and inward [2 Sam. 5:9].

David first captured Mount Zion and established it as his fort; then he took the city.

And David went on, and grew great, and the LORD God of hosts was with him.

And Hiram king of Tyre sent messengers to David, and cedar trees, and carpenters, and masons: and they built David an house.

And David perceived that the LORD had established him king over Israel, and that he had exalted his kingdom for his people Israel's sake [2 Sam. 5:10–12].

He grew great, and God was with him. Hiram, the king of Tyre, recognized that David was an outstanding man, and so he worked out an arrangement with David whereby he supplied materials and workmen to build a palace.

And David took him more concubines and wives out of Jerusalem, after he was come from Hebron: and there were yet sons and daughters born to David [2 Sam. 5:13].

That is the record of the facts. God did not put His stamp of approval upon what David did. We will find that God definitely disapproves of polygamy. In David's son Solomon it resulted in the splitting of the kingdom and finally brought on the Babylonian captivity. Why? Because David and Solomon were kings and in places of leadership. Their actions were wrong. Who says they were wrong? God says they were wrong! After all, it is His universe, and He makes the rules. Although you may not like them, God's rules are good. God not only created us, but He laid down rules and regulations for our lives which would bring to the human family the ultimate in happiness and blessing.

And these be the names of those that were born unto him in Jerusalem; Shammuah, and Shobab, and Nathan, and Solomon,

Ibhar also, and Elishua, and Nepheg, and Japhia,

And Elishama, and Eliada, and Eliphalet [2 Sam. 5:14–16].

I know nothing about the first two boys mentioned in these verses, but I do know something about Nathan and Solomon. From the line of Nathan came Mary the mother of Jesus. From Solomon came Joseph, Mary's husband. The Lord Jesus Christ received the blood line and the legal title to the throne of David through Nathan and Solomon. That is the reason this information is recorded for us here.

WAR WITH THE PHILISTINES

But when the Philistines heard that they had anointed David king over Israel, all the Philistines came up to seek David; and David heard of it, and went down to the hold.

The Philistines also came and spread themselves in the valley of Rephaim [2 Sam. 5:17–18].

When David was escaping from Saul and went to live in the Philistine country, at least Achish considered David their man. Now that David has returned to his own nation and has been anointed king over all Israel, the Philistines are out to get him.

And David inquired of the LORD, saying, Shall I go up to the Philistines? wilt thou deliver them into mine hand?

And the LORD said unto David, Go up: for I will doubtless deliver the Philistines into thine hand.

And David came to Baal-perazim, and David smote them there, and said, The LORD hath broken forth upon mine enemies before me, as the breach of waters. Therefore he called the name of that place Baal-perazim.

And there they left their images, and David and his men burned them [2 Sam. 5:19–21].

Some time after this defeat, the Philistines returned. Again God delivered them into David's hand. Throughout David's reign there never was any peace with this enemy.

CHAPTER 6

THEME: *David's wrong and right attempts to bring the ark to Jerusalem*

In this chapter David does a right thing in a wrong way. He tried to bring up the ark to Zion on a cart, although God had given explicit directions for moving it. The Kohathites of the tribe of Levi were to carry the ark on their shoulders (Num. 7:9). Uzzah was smitten dead because he should have known better than to touch it. "Hands off" was made abundantly clear in God's instructions concerning the ark. David then brought the ark up in a right way. Michal rebukes David for his enthusiasm and devotion to God in bringing up the ark.

This chapter can be labeled, "Doing a Right Thing in a Wrong Way." I suppose this would be another way of putting the negative in that ancient epigram, "The end justifies the means." There have been many organizations and individuals who have used that as their philosophy of life. I do not mean to suggest that this was David's philosophy of life—it was not—but as far as this particular incident in chapter 6 is concerned, it was certainly true. I believe this is a page from one of the greatest days in the life of David.

Suppose you wanted to choose the greatest day in the life of David. What day would you choose? Would it be the day that Samuel poured the anointing oil on him as a young shepherd boy? How about the day that he slew the giant Goliath? Certainly his first romance with Michal, Saul's daughter, who was given to him in marriage, deserves consideration. Perhaps you might choose the day David escaped from Saul. Then again you might choose the day Saul died, because that meant that David would ascend the throne. You might think it was the day that he was made king of all Israel and the crown was placed upon his head. You might even want to suggest it was the day his son Absalom rebelled against him and was slain. Or perhaps you might choose the day his son Solomon was anointed king. All of these were great days in the life of a great man.

However, I believe there are two events that stand out above all others in the life of David: the day that David brought the ark of God to Jerusalem (recorded in ch. 6) and the day David purposed in his heart to build God a house (recorded in ch. 7). These are probably the two greatest days in David's life.

Now the ark of the covenant denoted the presence of God among His people. If you are not acquainted with the floor plan of the tabernacle, I would like to recommend my book about the tabernacle entitled *God's Portrait of Christ*. I emphasize these articles of furniture and their location in the tabernacle and then in the temple. In the outer court was the burnt altar and the brazen laver. Sin was dealt with there. Then there was the Holy Place which contained three articles of furniture, all of which spoke of worship and the person of Christ: the golden lampstand, the golden altar, and the table of showbread. Then inside the Holy of Holies was the ark and over it the mercy seat. This was where God met with His people. The ark is possibly the best picture of Christ we have in the Old Testament. It is the only picture, actually, that God ever painted.

Personally I do not care for the paintings of Christ, especially the way the artists of the Middle Ages pictured Him. No one knows how the Lord Jesus looked. There are those who say He was a white man, some say He was a black man, and others say He was a swarthy man with a dark complexion. Probably His skin was bronze, but we don't know because we have not been told. There is a picture of Him, however, in the tabernacle and especially in the ark, which was just a box made of acacia wood, of precise dimensions, and overlaid with gold inside and outside. Bezaleel was given a special ministry by the Spirit of God that he might make the ark. The ark, denoting the presence of God, became a hindrance to Israel because they looked upon it in a superstitious way. They thought there was some merit in that box, and there was not. It was just a symbol, a picture of the Lord Jesus Christ. It was made of gold, which speaks of His deity, and of wood, which speaks of His humanity. It was not two boxes; it was one box. It was a wooden box; it was a gold box. It was both. As such, it was a marvelous example of the hypostatical union of Jesus Christ. He is the God-man, or as one of the oldest creeds says: He is very man of very man, and He is very God of very God.

You will recall that during the time of Samuel the Philistines captured the ark and became very superstitious about it. They sent it back to Israel on a wagon and left it in the field of Abinadab. It stayed in that area for seventy years. When David captured Jerusalem, he wanted to move the ark up there because he felt that was the proper place for it, and apparently it was the place which God had chosen. One of the things the king was told was, "Three times a year shall all thy males appear before the LORD thy God in the place which he shall choose . . ." (Deut. 16:16). When David took Jerusalem, he made it the capital—and in Kirjath-jearim, eight miles west of Jerusalem, was the ark.

David had a passion and love for God that is seldom found today. I do not go along with these folks who are everlastingly criticizing David. I only wish in my own heart that I had that love and passion for God that he had. Listen to what he says in Psalm 9:1: "I will praise thee, O LORD, with my whole heart. . . ." David expressed his devotion from the depths of his heart in a most wonderful way. In Psalm 108:1 he declared, "O God, my heart is fixed; I will sing and give praise, even with my glory." Then in Psalm 103:1 he says, "Bless the LORD, O my soul: and all that is within me, bless his holy name." What a passion and love for God this man had! That is why he wanted to bring the ark of God to Jerusalem. We will see in this chapter that he will attempt to do it, but he goes about it in the wrong way.

The ark is mentioned fifteen times in the first seventeen verses. After you read this section (and I hope that you will read it carefully), you realize that the subject is the ark of the Lord. It seemed to be a rather important subject to David and to the Lord.

At least eleven of the psalms were composed around the great event of bringing the ark to Jerusalem. You can be sure of one thing: David did not have some peculiar superstition about the ark. He knew where the Lord was, and he knew He was not in that box. In Psalm 123:1 David says, "Unto thee lift I up mine eyes, O thou that dwellest in the heavens." David knew where God was, but he knew that the approach to God was made through the ark which spoke of a mediator between God and man.

This has been a rather lengthy introduction, because I believe this is an important chapter. Now notice what David wants to do.

Again, David gathered together all the chosen men of Israel, thirty thousand. And David arose, and went with all the people that were with him from Baale of Judah, to bring up from thence the ark of God, whose name is called by the name of the LORD of hosts that dwelleth between the cherubims.

And they set the ark of God upon a new cart, and brought it out of the house of Abinadab that was in Gibeah: and Uzzah and Ahio, the sons of Abinadab, drave the new cart [2 Sam. 6:1–3].

This is where David made his mistake. God had given specific instructions about moving the tabernacle and its furniture, but David did not follow those instructions. Someone might say, "Well, the Philistines didn't either, and they got away with it." They got away with it because they were ignorant. Light creates responsibility. If men have the light of the gospel, they are held responsible for rejecting it. I am not going to argue with you about the heathen in Africa, but I would like to argue with you about the heathen in my town and your town because they can hear the gospel, and their responsibility is great. If you turn your back on Jesus Christ, my friend, you can argue about the heathen all you want to, but you are lost and doomed and judged and are bound for eternal hell. That is the teaching of the Word of God. You may not like it; and, if you don't, you ought to move out of this universe into another one. This is God's universe and these are His rules.

So David goes to bring up the ark to Jerusalem, but he does it in the wrong way. The ark was constructed with rings on the four corners. Staves were put through those rings, and the ark was carried on the shoulders of the Levites. On the wilderness march the Kohathites put that ark on their shoulders and carried it. David simply did not follow God's instructions.

Friend, in just such a way God wants the gospel to go out today. I sometimes wonder why He doesn't get a better instrument than I am and why He doesn't write the gospel in the skies. But Jesus Christ has to be carried through this world on the shoulders of those who are His own. That is God's way of doing it today. That was God's way of doing it in David's day. David was wrong, so wrong. He is going to get into trouble, just as God's people today get in trouble when they do wrong.

And David and all the house of Israel played before the LORD on all manner of instruments made of fir wood, even on harps, and on psalteries, and on timbrels, and on cornets, and on cymbals [2 Sam. 6:5].

David was a musician. He believed in having lots of music, and he is going to bring the ark to Jerusalem with a great deal of it.

And when they came to Nachon's threshingfloor, Uzzah put forth his hand to the ark of God, and took hold of it; for the oxen shook it.

And the anger of the LORD was kindled against Uzzah; and God smote him there for his error; and there he died by the ark of God [2 Sam. 6:6–7].

This is a pretty serious situation. The ark was on the cart, and the oxen were shaking the cart. When Uzzah tried to steady the ark with his hand, the Lord smote him and he died. Some might say that it was a small breach of conduct for such extreme punishment. Uzzah's death so affected David that he stopped the procession and left the ark in the house of Obed-edom the Gittite. David was shaken and angry with the Lord. The Lord was angry, too. God was angry because David was moving the ark in the wrong way.

And David was displeased, because the LORD had made a breach upon Uzzah: and he called the name of the place Perez-uzzah to this day.

And David was afraid of the LORD that day, and said, How shall the ark of the LORD come to me? [2 Sam. 6:8–9].

You and I would do well, friend, to be afraid of the Lord. Psalm 111:10 tells us that "The fear of the LORD is the beginning of wisdom. . . ." Many people need to recognize that fact today. God is going to judge. I do not know about you, but I am a little weary of hearing all this love, love, lovey-dovey stuff. Sure, God is love. Certainly God loves you, but you can go on in sin, you can turn your back on Him, and you are lost. There is no way out of it. There is no other alternative. John 14:6 says, ". . . I am the way, the truth, and the life: no man cometh unto the Father, but by me." Jesus Christ spoke those words, and they are truth. We should fear Him and do as He tells us to do. David was afraid of the Lord that day, and he finally asked, "How shall the ark of the LORD come to me?"

So David would not remove the ark of the LORD unto him into the city of David: but David carried it aside into the house of Obed-edom the Gittite.

And the ark of the LORD continued in the house of Obed-edom the Gittite three months: and the LORD blessed Obed-edom, and all his household.

And it was told king David, saying, The LORD hath blessed the house of Obed-edom, and all that pertaineth unto him, because of the ark of God. So David went and brought up the ark of God from the house of Obed-edom into the city of David with gladness [2 Sam. 6:10–12].

He was determined to bring the ark to the city of David. Has he learned his lesson? How is he going to bring it up now? On the shoulders of the priests.

And it was so, that when they that bare the ark of the LORD had gone six paces, he sacrificed oxen and fatlings.

And David danced before the LORD with all his might; and David was girded with a linen ephod [2 Sam. 6:13–14].

I know there are going to be many arched eyebrows at the fact that David danced, but God is the One who put it in His Word. David danced by himself. It had nothing in the world to do with sex. Any kind of a dance today (and I do not care how you try to cover it up with culture and refinement) is a sex dance. David's dance was one of worship. Now if you could have a worshipful dance, I would be all for it, but I don't think you can, my friend. I do not find people in love with God like this man David was. David is rejoicing before God. Personally, I would like to see more people rejoicing and praising God today. I am concerned when I see believers with long faces. God doesn't like it, my friend. We are to come into His presence with joy. David did, you may be sure of that.

So David and all the house of Israel brought up the ark of the LORD with shouting, and with the sound of the trumpet.

And as the ark of the LORD came into the city of David, Michal Saul's daughter looked through a window, and saw king David leaping and dancing before the LORD; and she despised him in her heart [2 Sam. 6:15–16].

Michal did not like to see anyone who was in love with God like that, and she despised David for it. Remember, Michal is David's wife. Her attitude is a very serious thing as far as her relationship with David is concerned.

And they brought in the ark of the LORD, and set it in his place, in the midst of the tabernacle that David had pitched for it: and David offered burnt offerings and peace offerings before the LORD [2 Sam. 6:17].

Those burnt offerings speak of the person of Christ. The peace offerings speak of the peace that He made by the blood of His cross and of the relationship—the wonderful relationship—which was between God and David.

My friend, let's push aside the extraneous arguments we hear about David's dancing before the Lord and about Uzzah being smitten dead. The record is here in the Word of God; let's accept it as it is written. The important thing is to see the lesson that is here for us. What about your relationship to God? Let me give a personal testimony at this point. Driving down to the office this morning, feeling rather weary since I have just returned from a trip, I thanked God that He had brought me to another day. I thanked Him that I've confessed all my sins and am in a right relationship with Him. And I told Him that I love Him. How He deserves our love and adoration! The important thing to see in this chapter is David's relationship with God. Here is a man who is in love with his God. He is rightly related to Him and thrilled to be able to serve Him. Oh, that you and I might have the same *joy* of the Lord in our lives!

Then David returned to bless his household. And Michal the daughter of Saul came out to meet David, and said, How glorious was the king of Israel to-day, who uncovered himself to-day in the eyes of the handmaids of his servants, as one of the vain fellows shamelessly uncovereth himself! [2 Sam. 6:20].

David "uncovered himself" in the sense that he took off his royal garments which set him apart as the king. He mingled and mixed with the people, and thanked God, and rejoiced in the fact that the ark was being brought to the city of David. Michal did not like that. She liked dignity and reverence in worship. I am always afraid of these super-duper pious folks who talk everlastingly about dedication and piety. Watch those folks, my friend. They are dangerous. I fear them like David did. What a man of God he was!

And David said unto Michal, It was before the LORD, which chose me before thy father, and before all his house, to appoint me ruler over the people of the LORD, over Israel: therefore will I play before the LORD [2 Sam. 6:21].

David is saying, "Because God chose me, I will rejoice." My, I wish folk had a better time when they went to church. They would enjoy the services more.

And I will yet be more vile than thus, and will be base in mine own sight: and of the maidservants which thou hast spoken of, of them shall I be had in honour [2 Sam. 6:22].

When he says he will make himself "more vile," he means that he will come down to the level of the most humble worshiper. He doesn't mind being informal in his worship of God.

Because of her attitude, David "put her aside." That is, he became permanently estranged from her, and she was childless. Obviously, Michal did not share David's love and enthusiasm for God.

CHAPTER 7

***THEME:** God's covenant to build the house of David*

God's covenant with David makes this one of the great chapters of the Bible. The message of the Bible from this point on rests upon this promise that God makes to David. David desired deeply to build a temple to house the ark of God, and Nathan the prophet concurred with him in the plan. God appeared to Nathan to correct him, for God would not let David build the temple because he was "a bloody man." However, God gave him credit for his desire, and in turn He promised to build David a house. God promised a king and a kingdom to come in the line of David. He was referring not only to Solomon but to Christ, great David's greater Son, and His eternal Kingdom. God confirmed this promise with an oath (Ps. 89:34–37). David understood that a King was coming in his line who would be more than a man.

Frankly, it is very difficult to understand the prophets from this point on without knowing about this covenant. One of the reasons many people find themselves so hopelessly confused in the study of prophecy is because they do not pay attention to a chapter like this. Second Samuel 7 is by far the most significant chapter thus far in the Old Testament. The New Testament opens with: "The book of the generation of Jesus Christ, the son of David. . . ." That is important because the promises God made to David are to be fulfilled in prophecy.

When the angel Gabriel appeared to Mary, he said, ". . . Fear not, Mary: for thou hast found favour with God. And, behold, thou shalt conceive in thy womb, and bring forth a son, and shall call his name JESUS. He shall be great, and shall be called the Son of the Highest: and the Lord God shall give unto him the throne of his father *David*" (Luke 1:30–32). You see, God is fulfilling His promise to David.

Peter began in 2 Samuel 7 when he preached on the day of Pentecost: "Men and brethren, let me freely speak unto you of the patriarch David, that he is both dead and buried, and his sepulchre is with us unto this day. Therefore being a prophet, and knowing that God had sworn with an oath to him, that of the fruit of his loins, according to the flesh, he would raise up Christ to sit on his throne" (Acts 2:29–30; see also Acts 2:25–31, 34–36). Peter is making reference to that which God promised to David.

Paul, in the Book of Romans, says, "Paul, a servant of Jesus Christ, called to be an apostle, separated unto the gospel of God, (Which he had promised afore by his prophets in the holy scriptures,) Concerning his Son Jesus Christ our Lord, which was made of the seed of David according to the flesh" (Rom. 1:1–3).

The New Testament closes with the Lord Jesus Christ saying, "I Jesus have sent mine angel to testify unto you these things in the churches. I am the root and the offspring of David, and the bright and morning star" (Rev. 22:16). These are only a few of the fifty-nine references to David in the New Testament.

The Old Testament prophets based their message of the kingdom on the promise God gave to David in 2 Samuel 7. You will find that each of the Old Testament prophets goes back to David and God's promises to him concerning the kingdom. After all, what is the kingdom of heaven but the kingdom that God vouchsafed to David? For example, listen to Jeremiah 23:5, "Behold, the days come, saith the LORD, that I will raise unto David a righteous Branch, and a King shall reign and prosper, and shall execute judgment and justice in the earth." The kingdom became the theme song of the prophets.

DAVID'S DESIRE TO BUILD THE TEMPLE

And it came to pass, when the king sat in his house, and the LORD had given him rest round about from all his enemies;

That the king said unto Nathan the prophet, See now, I dwell in an house of cedar, but the ark of God dwelleth within curtains.

And Nathan said to the king, Go, do all that is in thine heart; for the LORD is with thee [2 Sam. 7:1–3].

Let us look at the background of these verses. We have seen that David took Jerusalem and made it his capital. Then Hiram, the king of Tyre, built David a palace on Mount Zion. Finally David brought the ark up to the city of Jerusalem. One night when David was in his palace, he began to think about the ark. I think it must have been a rainy night in Jerusalem. The first night I ever spent in that city, it rained, and I thought, *It must have been a rainy night when David awakened and heard the pitter-patter of rain on that lovely palace that his friend Hiram had built for him.* Then he thought of God's ark in a tent. Perhaps he could even hear the flapping of the tent, and he thought, *I want to build God a house.*

David called in Nathan, his prophet, and divulged to him the desires of his heart. He said, "I dwell in a house of cedar, but the ark of God dwelleth within curtains." Nathan told David to go ahead with his plans. And here is a case where a prophet was wrong, and I mean *wrong.* Nathan said, "Go, do all that is in thine heart; for the LORD is with thee." I would have said the same thing. The fact of the matter is, if someone came to me and said, "Dr. McGee, we want to underwrite your radio ministry on a certain station," I'll be frank with you, I would not say, "Well, let me go and pray about this and see whether this is what ought to be done." I would say, "Yes, this is what we want." But my decision might not be the will of God. I understand how Nathan felt. David's plans sounded good. Nathan could not think of anything better than building a house for God. But he was wrong. David, as we have indicated before, was a bloody man. Long before he committed his great sin, he was a bloody man. God said, "You cannot build me a temple." It was in the heart of David, however, and God gives him credit for it. I think we make a mistake by calling it Solomon's temple, because it was David who gathered all of the materials and made all of the arrangements with the contractor. Solomon just carried out the plans. The only temple Solomon ever had was on the side of his head. It should be called David's temple.

And it came to pass that night, that the word of the LORD came unto Nathan, saying,

Go and tell my servant David, Thus saith the LORD, Shalt thou build me an house for me to dwell in?

Whereas I have not dwelt in any house since the time that I brought up the children of Israel out of Egypt, even to this day, but have walked in a tent and in a tabernacle [2 Sam. 7:4–6].

God had to correct Nathan. God said to him, "You are going to have to correct the word you gave to David. You go tell David that I appreciate the fact that he wants to build Me a house. I never asked him to do it. I never asked any of My people to build Me a house." God had met with His people in a tent. In other words, God identified Himself with His people. That is why 1900 years ago Jesus Christ came to earth and took upon Himself our humanity. John says, "And the Word was made flesh, and dwelt among us, (and we beheld his glory, the glory as of the only begotten of the Father,) full of grace and truth" (John 1:14). That word *dwelt* means "pitched His tent" here among us. Instead of meeting man in a flimsy tent made of linen, God met man in a flimsy tent made of flesh. He came to earth and identified Himself with us. God has always identified Himself with His people.

In all the places wherein I have walked with all the children of Israel spake I a word with any of the tribes of Israel, whom I commanded to feed my people Israel, saying, Why build ye not me an house of cedar? [2 Sam. 7:7].

In other words, building the temple was David's idea—not God's commandment. God gives him credit for building the temple.

Now therefore so shalt thou say unto my servant David, Thus saith the LORD of hosts, I took thee from the sheepcote, from following the sheep, to be ruler over my people, over Israel [2 Sam. 7:8].

God says, "You were a little shepherd boy when I chose you. And I've made you ruler over My people."

And I was with thee whithersoever thou wentest, and have cut off all thine enemies out of thy sight, and have made thee a great name, like unto the name of the great men that are in the earth [2 Sam. 7:9].

In God's book David ranks as one of the greatest men who has lived on this earth. Compare David with any man who has ever ruled, and he is outstanding. If I understand the prophets correctly, it is God's intention, when David is raised from the dead in the resurrection, to let him rule on this earth as regent to the Lord Jesus Christ during the Millenniun.

Moreover I will appoint a place for my people Israel, and will plant them, that they may dwell in a place of their own, and move no more; neither shall the children of wickedness afflict them any more, as beforetime [2 Sam. 7:10].

This is what God is *going to do.* Notice the "I will's" of God. (1) "I will appoint a place for my people Israel; (2) I will plant them, that they may dwell in a place of their own, and move no more." Friend, that was a long time ago—actually, God said this over three thousand years ago, and it has not yet come to pass. But God is going to make good His promise.

And as since the time that I commanded judges to be over my people Israel, and have caused thee to rest from all thine enemies. Also the LORD telleth thee that he will make thee an house [2 Sam. 7:11].

God says to Nathan, "You go tell David that *I* will make *him* a house." David said, "I want to build God a house." God says, "David, you can't do it. Your hands are bloody. You can't build Me a house, but I know the desire is in your heart. I will give you credit for building Me a house, and I will build *you* a house." Isn't that just like the Lord? You can't outdo the Lord, friend.

One of the reasons so many of us are so poor today is because we do so little for the Lord. We never get in a position where He can do much for us. We can learn a lesson from David. David wanted to do something great for God, and God did something far greater for him.

And when thy days be fulfilled, and thou shalt sleep with thy fathers, I will set up thy seed after thee, which shall proceed out of thy bowels, and I will establish his kingdom [2 Sam. 7:12].

This is tremendous! We have read from the New Testament that the Lord Jesus Christ was made of the seed of David (Rom. 1:3). God said to David, "I am going to set up thy seed after thee, and He will establish the kingdom." God was not talking about Solomon. God was referring to the Lord Jesus Christ.

He shall build an house for my name, and I will stablish the throne of his kingdom for ever [2 Sam. 7:13].

Solomon is the subject here; he is the next in line. The kingdom, however, goes beyond Solomon and looks on to the future. "I will stablish the throne of his kingdom forever." This speaks of the throne of David. The Lord Jesus Christ will one day sit on the throne of David. That was the angel Gabriel's message to Mary. He said, "He shall be great, and shall be called the Son of the Highest: and the Lord God shall give unto him the throne of his father David" (Luke 1:32).

I will be his father, and he shall be my son. If he commit iniquity, I will chasten him with the rod of men, and with the stripes of the children of men [2 Sam. 7:14].

Listen again to God's "I will." In a unique way God says, "I will be his father." At His resurrection the Lord Jesus Christ said to Mary Magdalene, "Touch me not; for I am not yet ascended to my Father: but go to my brethren, and say unto them, I ascend unto my Father, and your Father; and to my God, and your God" (John 20:17). God is the Father of Jesus Christ because of His position in the Trinity. God is my Father by regeneration—"But as many as received him, to them gave he power to become the sons of God, even to them that believe on his name" (John 1:12). When I received Christ as my Savior, He gave me the right (the *exousia*) to become His son. That right is given to those who do neither more nor less than simply believe in His name. God says, "I will be his father, and he shall be my son."

The last part of verse 14 is a very strange statement. "If he commit iniquity, I will chasten him with the rod of men, and with the stripes of the children of men." Bishop Horsley gives an interesting translation of this: "When guilt is laid upon him, I will chasten him with the rod of men." That is exactly what God is saying now. God says, "When guilt is laid upon Him, I am going to be His Father, and He will be my Son." That is the unique relationship between God the Father and God the Son. But "if he commit iniquity," that is, when iniquity is laid upon Him—when your sin and my sin were put upon Him—it is with His stripes that we are healed. He died on the cross for you and me. He was delivered for our offenses. That is the reason He died on the cross. "Who his own self bare our sins in his own body on the tree, that we, being dead to sins, should live unto righteousness: by whose stripes ye were healed" (1 Pet. 2:24)—healed from sin. Isaiah the prophet says concerning Christ, "Yet it pleased the LORD to bruise him; he hath put him to grief . . ." (Isa. 53:10). The One coming in David's line would bear the sins of the world. Isaiah continues to speak of the Lord Jesus when he says, "Surely he hath borne our griefs, and carried our sorrows: yet we did esteem him stricken, smitten of God, and afflicted. But he was wounded for our transgressions, he was bruised for our iniquities: the chastisement of our peace was upon him; and with his stripes we are healed. All we like sheep have gone astray; we have turned every one to his own way; and the LORD hath laid on him the iniquity of us all" (Isa. 53:4–6). "With his stripes we are healed." Healed of what? We are healed of sin. Sin is the awful disease that afflicts mankind, my beloved. That is why God says, "I will chasten him with the rod of men, and with the stripes of the children of men."

But my mercy shall not depart away from him, as I took it from Saul, whom I put away before thee [2 Sam. 7:15].

In other words, though the line of David sinned grievously, God would carry through to the end His purpose with David and his line. And God did just that. He brought the Lord Jesus Christ into the world.

And thine house and thy kingdom shall be established for ever before thee: thy throne shall be established for ever [2 Sam. 7:16].

God considered this important because Psalm 89:34–37 says, "My covenant will I not break, nor alter the thing that is gone out of my lips. Once have I sworn by my holiness that I will not lie unto David. His seed shall endure for ever, and his throne as the sun before me. It shall be established for ever as the moon, and as a faithful witness in heaven. Selah." "Established for ever as the moon." Scientists are saying, after studying the rocks brought back from the moon, that the universe is probably from three to five billion years old—that's a long time. God said He would establish David's throne just as He established the moon. God made a covenant with David, and He will not break it.

According to all these words, and according to all this vision, so did Nathan speak unto David [2 Sam. 7:17].

DAVID'S PRAYER

Then went king David in, and sat before the LORD, and he said, Who am I, O Lord GOD? and what is my house, that thou hast brought me hitherto?

And this was yet a small thing in thy sight, O Lord GOD; but thou hast spoken also of thy servant's house for a great while to come. And is this the manner of man, O Lord GOD? [2 Sam. 7:18–19].

Once again consider Bishop Horsley's translation of this verse: "O Lord God, thou hast spoken of your servant's house for a great while to come, and hast regarded me in the arrangement about the man that is to be from above, O God Jehovah." That is a remarkable statement. They were looking for One to come. He was to be of the seed of the woman. He was to be from Abraham; He was to come from the tribe of Judah; now we are told that He will be in the family of David. David is overwhelmed by the fact that Jesus Christ will be in his line.

And what can David say more unto thee? for thou, Lord GOD, knowest thy servant [2 Sam. 7:20].

Have you ever poured out your heart to God until you didn't have anything left to say? That was David's state. He had poured out his heart and was empty; he was just sitting there before Him. I like to pray while I am driving alone in my car. I tell Him everything in my heart until I can't even think of anything else to say. How wonderful He is. How wonderful is our God.

For thy word's sake, and according to thine own heart, hast thou done all these great things, to make thy servant know them [2 Sam. 7:21].

Did God do all of this for David because he was a nice boy? He wasn't a nice boy, friend, as we are going to see. Neither did God save you or me because we were nice girls or boys. He saved us because of His marvelous, infinite grace. He does so many special things for us, not because of our goodness, but because of *His* goodness. He is wonderful. We are not. We ought to praise His name. David is overwhelmed by what God has told him. It is no wonder that he could sing those beautiful psalms.

Wherefore thou art great, O LORD God: for there is none like thee, neither is there any God beside thee, according to all that we have heard with our ears [2 Sam. 7:22].

Doesn't this verse do you good just to read it? My, what a privilege to have a God like this!

And now, O LORD God, the word that thou hast spoken concerning thy ser-

vant, and concerning his house, establish it for ever, and do as thou hast said [2 Sam. 7:25].

Did you know that this became David's salvation? Listen to what he says in 2 Samuel 23:5, "Although my house be not so with God; yet he hath made with me an everlasting covenant, ordered in all things, and sure: for this is all my salvation, and all my desire, although he make it not to grow." David rested upon what God had promised.

God has also made a promise to you. It is recorded in John 3:16. It says, "For God so loved the world, that he gave his only begotten Son, that whosoever believeth in him should not perish, but have everlasting life." Will you believe God? David believed God. Also we have seen that Abraham believed God. Moses believed God. Joshua believed God. And He wants *you* to believe God. Whatever your name is, He is saying to you today, "Believe Me. I'll save you if you will trust Christ as your Savior." That is His covenant with you and with me.

CHAPTERS 8–10

***THEME:** David consolidates, and enlarges his kingdom*

Now that David has established Jerusalem as his capital and has brought the ark of God there, he consolidates his kingdom and befriends the only living son of Jonathan, Mephibosheth. Also he gains victories over the old enemies of Israel and enlarges Israel's borders.

DAVID CONSOLIDATES HIS KINGDOM

And after this it came to pass, that David smote the Philistines, and subdued them: and David took Metheg-ammah out of the hand of the Philistines [2 Sam. 8:1].

The "after this" refers to the time after God made His covenant with David. David is now being fully established in the kingdom, and we find that he has a great victory over the Philistines. They were the perpetual and inveterate enemies of Israel. David drives them back, not only out of the land of Israel, but even beyond their own borders. The Philistines inhabited a great section of that land especially in the southern part.

In recounting David's conquest of the king of Zobah, it is said:

And David took from him a thousand chariots, and seven hundred horsemen, and twenty thousand footmen: and David hocked all the chariot horses, but reserved of them for an hundred chariots [2 Sam. 8:4].

Hadadezer, the king of Zobah, had a kingdom that went as far as the river Euphrates. We are told that David took a thousand chariots from him. David got rid of all but a few of the horses. In the Book of Deuteronomy God made a rule for the kings that they were not to multiply horses or wives. Although David multiplied wives (Solomon multiplied both horses and wives), he is apparently trying to follow the Lord's instructions in this matter concerning the horses.

There is a great deal of detail in this chapter. If you like to explore new areas and new lands, you will enjoy studying this chapter and tracing on a map the different areas in which David moved. He enlarged the borders of Israel. He extended them to the south in the land of the Philistines, and to the east in the land of the Moabites. He established garrisons in Syria and Edom. So we find that Syria, Moab, Ammon, the Philistines, and the Amalekites all became subject to David and apparently paid tribute.

And David gat him a name when he returned from smiting of the Syrians in the valley of salt, being eighteen thousand men.

And he put garrisons in Edom; throughout all Edom put he garrisons, and all they of Edom became David's servants. And the LORD preserved David whithersoever he went [2 Sam. 8:13–14].

In the southwest, the southeast, and now to the north, David was able to push back the borders of Israel and enlarge the kingdom. There is no use to say that the borders were enlarged in the west because the border in the west was the Mediterranean Sea.

And David reigned over all Israel; and David executed judgment and justice unto all his people [2 Sam. 8:15].

David was noted for his judgment and justice to his people. There has been a tremendous expansion and extension of the kingdom. David has brought the kingdom to its zenith and made it a world power corresponding to other kingdoms of that day.

DAVID BEFRIENDS MEPHIBOSHETH

This chapter records one of the most beautiful stories in the Scriptures. It is a story that reveals what a great man David really was. We usually think of David in connection with the sin he committed, and that is probably a natural thing to do. Suppose I had a large white screen before me. On that screen is one little black spot—some ink got on the screen. As I look at it, what is the most impressive thing about it? There is a vast area of white, but that one little black spot stands out. Or suppose you ride down the highway, as I have done in west Texas, and you see a couple of thousand sheep in a field. All of the sheep are white but one. Which sheep do you really see? So it is in the life of David. We always concentrate on his big sin, and it was big. The trouble is that we give sparse attention to the noble life and exploits of David. Someone has said, "There is so much good in the worst of us, and so much bad in the best of us, that it behooves most of us not to talk about the rest of us." Maybe we ought to reevaluate our viewpoint of David. There are so many bright spots in the long life of David, from that young shepherd boy who slew a giant, to an old man wise in experience who could write, "The LORD is my shepherd, I shall not want." In this chapter we shall see the gracious side of David's character.

Chapter 9 records the story of Mephibosheth. He is the son of Jonathan and the grandson of Saul. It is important at this point to recall some of the background of Saul. He had been the pitiless foe and bitter enemy of David. At the death of Saul, David began to marshal his forces. According to oriental custom of that day, a new king would naturally put to death all contenders to the throne of a former dynasty. Any claimant would be removed by execution. That would protect the new king from any threat. According to the code of that day, David would have been justified in putting to death any of the offspring of Saul. When Saul and Jonathan had been killed in the same battle, a little son of Jonathan's was hidden lest David find him and kill him. The name of this boy was Mephibosheth. David could more firmly establish his throne by slaying this boy and thus remove the last vestige of danger.

And David said, Is there yet any that is left of the house of Saul, that I may shew him kindness for Jonathan's sake?

And there was of the house of Saul a servant whose name was Ziba. And when they had called him unto David, the king said unto him, Art thou Ziba? And he said, Thy servant is he.

And the king said, Is there not yet any of the house of Saul, that I may shew the kindness of God unto him? And Ziba said unto the king, Jonathan hath yet a son, which is lame on his feet.

And the king said unto him, Where is he? And Ziba said unto the king, Behold, he is in the house of Machir, the son of Ammiel, in Lo-debar [2 Sam. 9:1–4].

Ziba, a servant of Saul, betrayed the hiding place of Mephibosheth, and David could have easily killed him.

Then king David sent, and fetched him out of the house of Machir, the son of Ammiel, from Lo-debar.

Now when Mephibosheth, the son of Jonathan, the son of Saul, was come unto David, he fell on his face, and did reverence. And David said, Mephibosheth. And he answered, Behold thy servant! [2 Samuel 9:5–6].

When Mephibosheth is brought before David, he falls on his face before him, expecting to be executed. Instead, David speaks kindly to him, calling him by his name.

And David said unto him, Fear not: for I surely shew thee kindness for Jonathan thy father's sake, and will restore thee all the land of Saul thy father; and thou shalt eat bread at my table continually [2 Sam. 9:7].

David quickly puts him at ease and explains the reason he has sent for him. He restores his inheritance to him and gives him a permanent place at the king's table—honoring him as one of his own sons!

And he bowed himself, and said, What is thy servant, that thou shouldest look upon such a dead dog as I am? [2 Sam. 9:8].

Notice the reaction of Mephibosheth to all of this. Had there been another king on the throne, he would have been slain. It would have been an entirely different story. Realizing this, Mephibosheth counts himself as "a dead dog." But David does not call him that. He says, "You are no dead dog. You are Mephibosheth, the son of Jonathan. I intend to show kindness to you."

Then the king called to Ziba, Saul's servant, and said unto him, I have given unto thy master's son all that pertained to Saul and to all his house.

Thou therefore, and thy sons, and thy servants, shall till the land for him, and thou shalt bring in the fruits, that thy master's son may have food to eat: but Mephibosheth thy master's son shall eat bread alway at my table. Now Ziba had fifteen sons and twenty servants [2 Sam. 9:9–10].

That is quite a household! So this property and land of Saul's was turned over to Mephibosheth. It rightfully belonged to him, and David sees to it that he gets it.

Then said Ziba unto the king, According to all that my lord the king hath commanded his servant, so shall thy servant do. As for Mephibosheth, said the king, he shall eat at my table, as one of the king's sons.

And Mephibosheth had a young son, whose name was Micha. And all that dwelt in the house of Ziba were servants unto Mephibosheth.

So Mephibosheth dwelt in Jerusalem: for he did eat continually at the king's table; and was lame on both his feet [2 Sam. 9:11–13].

What David did for Mephibosheth was wonderful, but there are some other impressive lessons with great spiritual truths which I don't want you to miss.

1. *A child of God recognizes that he is also a cripple in God's sight.* We are told in Romans 3:15–16: "Their feet are swift to shed blood: Destruction and misery are in their ways." That is the report from God's clinic on the human race. Our feet lead us astray. "All we like sheep have gone astray; we have turned every one to his own way; and the LORD hath laid on him the iniquity of us all" (Isa. 53:6). Then the writer of the Book of Proverbs says, "There is a way that seemeth right unto a man, but the end thereof are the ways of death" (Prov. 16:25). Our feet get us into trouble. The way that the soul and the feet are so closely connected in Scripture is quite interesting. I do not mean to make a bad pun; I am not talking about the sole of the foot.

Remembering that David for the rest of his life had a crippled boy who ate at his table, listen to the words of Psalm 56:13, "For thou hast delivered my soul from death: wilt not thou deliver my feet from failing, that I may walk before God in the light of the living?" Psalm 73:2 says, "But as for me, my feet were almost gone; my steps had well nigh slipped." David knew what it was to have lame feet! In Psalm 116:8 he says, "For thou hast delivered my soul from death, mine eyes from tears, and my feet from falling." My friend, all of us are actually cripples before God.

Modern philosophy and humanism present another picture of man. I once heard a liberal say that Christ came to reveal the splendors of the human soul! God says, "The heart is deceitful above all things, and desperately wicked: who can know it?" (Jer. 17:9). Out of the heart proceed evil thoughts, and it is a mess of bad things. You cannot expect any good from human nature. Paul could say, "For I know that in me (that is, in my flesh,) dwelleth no good thing: for to will is present with me; but how to perform that which is good I find not" (Rom. 7:18). Paul had no confidence in the flesh. The Law is condemnation. John 14:6 says, "Jesus saith unto him, I am the way, the truth, and the life: no man cometh unto the Father, but by me." When we come that way, He will receive us.

2. *David extended kindness to Mephibosheth for the sake of Jonathan.* This is another facet of this amazing incident. You see, David did not know the boy. He did what he did for the sake of Jonathan whom he loved. When David looked upon this boy, he did not see a cripple; he saw Jonathan. He had made a covenant with Jonathan. The kindness, mercy, and grace extended to a helpless person were for the sake of another.

We have seen how much Jonathan meant to David. When the news of his death reached him, he said: "How are the mighty fallen in the midst of the battle! O Jonathan, thou wast slain in thine high places. I am distressed for thee, my brother Jonathan: very pleasant hast thou been unto me: thy love to me was wonderful, passing the love of women" (2 Sam. 1:25–26). Now God has saved you and me because of Another—the Lord Jesus Christ. When we accept Jesus Christ as Savior, Ephesians 1:6 tells us that we are "accepted in the beloved." When God sees you and me in Christ, He accepts us and saves us.

3. *David said nothing about the lame feet of Mephibosheth.* There is no record that David ever mentioned it or made an allusion to it. He never said to him, "It is too bad that you are crippled." He treated him like a prince. He sat at the king's table, and his feet were covered with a linen cloth. My friend, God forgets our sin because it is blotted out by the blood of the Lord Jesus Christ. That is the *only* way God can forgive our sins. The writer of Hebrews put it this way: "And their sins and iniquities will I remember no more" (Heb. 10:17).

4. *Mephibosheth said nothing about his lame feet.* What do you think David and Mephibosheth talked about when they sat at the table? They talked about another person. Do you know who it was? It was Jonathan. David loved Jonathan. Mephibosheth loved Jonathan—he was his father. Jonathan was the subject of conversation.

What should you and I talk about? Some Christians take a keen delight in talking about the old days when they lived in sin. It is too bad that when we get together we don't talk about Another. The Lord Jesus Christ should be the main subject of our conversation.

5. *Others said nothing about Mephibosheth's lame feet.* There was a large company that ate at the king's table. One day they saw David bringing this crippled boy to the table. The gossips did not say, "Did you hear how it happened?" Instead they listened to the king. They heard David praise Mephibosheth. They had no time to indulge in cheap talk. Their hearts went out in love to this boy. You see, love "beareth all things, believeth all things, hopeth all things, endureth all things." Love "never fails" (1 Cor. 13:7–8).

As far as I can tell, David was never able to make this boy walk. If you see that you cannot walk well-pleasing to God, turn to the Lord Jesus Christ. Christ said to the man with palsy, whose friends had let him down through the roof, ". . . Son, be of good cheer; thy sins be forgiven thee. . . . Arise, and walk" (Matt. 9:2–5). The apostle Paul urges: "I therefore, the prisoner of the Lord, beseech you that ye walk worthy of the vocation wherewith ye are called, With all lowliness and meekness, with longsuffering, forbearing one another in love" (Eph. 4:1–2). If you are failing in your walk, turn to Christ for help.

Christ is sending out an invitation today into the highways and byways and out into the streets of your town. He is saying, "Come to my table of salvation just as you are, crippled, and I will feed you." He says, "Come unto me, all ye that labour and are heavy laden, and I will give you rest" (Matt. 11:28). He also says, ". . . If any man thirst, let him come unto me, and drink" (John 7:37).

What a wonderful picture of God's love is presented in this chapter!

DAVID WARS AGAINST AMMON AND SYRIA

And it came to pass after this, that the king of the children of Ammon died, and Hanun his son reigned in his stead. Then said David, I will shew kindness unto Hanun the son of Nahash, as his father shewed kindness unto me. And David sent to comfort him by the hand of his servants for his father. And David's servants came into the land of the children of Ammon.

And the princes of the children of Ammon said unto Hanun their lord, Thinkest thou that David doth honour thy father, that he hath sent comforters unto thee? hath not David rather sent his servants unto thee, to search the city, and to spy it out, and to overthrow it? [2 Sam. 10:1–3].

You can see that these people had no confidence at all in David. They believed that he intended to attack them. His friendly gesture was completely misunderstood.

Wherefore Hanun took David's servants, and shaved off the one half of their beards, and cut off their garments in the middle, even to their buttocks, and sent them away [2 Sam. 10:4].

My friend, that was an insult! I can't think of a way to more thoroughly humiliate David's ambassadors than this. Some commentators believe that this was Hanun's challenge to war—whereas David had meant it as a gesture of goodwill and peace.

When they told it unto David, he sent to meet them, because the men were greatly ashamed: and the king said,

Tarry at Jericho until your beards be grown, and then return.

And when the children of Ammon saw that they stank before David, the children of Ammon sent and hired the Syrians of Beth-rehob, and the Syrians of Zoba, twenty thousand footmen, and of king Maacah a thousand men, and of Ish-tob twelve thousand men [2 Sam. 10:5–6].

The Ammonites see that they have made themselves odious to David and prepare for war. They hire mercenaries from Syria—at considerable cost, we learn from the account in 1 Chronicles 19:6–7.

And when David heard of it, he sent Joab, and all the host of the mighty men.

And the children of Ammon came out, and put the battle in array at the entering in of the gate: and the Syrians of Zoba, and of Rehob, and Ish-tob, and Maacah, were by themselves in the field.

When Joab saw that the front of the battle was against him before and behind, he chose of all the choice men of Israel, and put them in array against the Syrians:

And the rest of the people he delivered into the hand of Abishai his brother, that he might put them in array against the children of Ammon [2 Sam. 10:7–10].

The Israelites were now veterans in warfare. Joab, apparently, is throwing his best forces between the approaching Syrian mercenaries and the forces of the Ammonites to prevent their joining together.

And the Syrians fled before Israel; and David slew the men of seven hundred chariots of the Syrians, and forty thousand horsemen, and smote Shobach the captain of their host, who died there.

And when all the kings that were servants to Hadarezer saw that they were smitten before Israel, they made peace with Israel, and served them. So the Syrians feared to help the children of Ammon any more [2 Sam. 10:18–19].

It was a tremendous victory for Israel. This establishes David, without doubt, as the great ruler of that day.

CHAPTER 11

***THEME:** David's two great sins*

We have now come to the second and last section of the Book of 2 Samuel, which I have labeled "The Troubles of David." We have seen the "Triumphs of David" in the first section. Under the blessing of God, David has become one of the great kings of the earth. However, the sin recorded in this chapter places David under the *judgment* of God. From here on David will have trouble. His life will be a series of heartbreaks.

This sin causes the enemies of God to blaspheme—until this day. Leering and suggestive, they exclaim, "This is the 'man after God's own heart'!"

The sin of David stands out like a tar-baby in a field of snow, like a blackberry in a bowl of cream. It may cause us to miss the greatness of the man. Remember that sin was the exception in David's life—not the pattern of it.

The Word of God does not play down the sin of David; it does not whitewash the man. God doesn't say it is not sin. God is going to call it sin, and David will be punished for it.

And it came to pass, after the year was expired, at the time when kings go forth to battle, that David sent Joab, and his servants with him, and all Israel; and they destroyed the children of Ammon, and besieged Rabbah. But David tarried still at Jerusalem [2 Sam. 11:1].

It was the time of the year when kings went forth to war. In other words, in that day the nations had an "open season" on each other like we do today on birds and animals. At a certain season you can shoot them; at other seasons you cannot. But, after all, isn't that true even in modern warfare today? During the monsoons in Vietnam, the war came to a standstill because they got bogged down in the swamps, and the rain kept the planes out of the air. After the monsoons let up, the war was on again. The approach to war in David's day may have been a great deal more modern than we think. The unfortunate thing about the two world wars is that the greatest suffering was caused by the winter weather rather than by the enemy, but they attempted to carry on the fighting. At least in David's day there was a season for warfare. Maybe they were a little more civilized than we are. At least they recognized a time when they could enjoy comparative peace.

Now David sent Joab and the army to fight the children of Ammon. David did not go with them. Instead he tarried at Jerusalem. That was unlike David. Why did he stay? I have only a suggestion to make. After David built his palace he found it very comfortable. It was quite different from the cave of Adullam where he had spent his youth. His palace was a place of luxury and comfort. Also David loved Mount Zion and wanted to stay around that place. Prosperity is one of the things that has trapped so many men and women. Our great comfort has become a curse in our nation. David tarried in Jerusalem. That was his first mistake. He should have gone to war with his men.

And it came to pass in an eveningtide, that David arose from off his bed, and walked upon the roof of the king's house: and from the roof he saw a woman washing herself; and the woman was very beautiful to look upon [2 Sam. 11:2].

In that day the roof was the place where people spent their evenings. They had no front porches or patios in the rear of their homes. Even today the old city of Jerusalem is very compact, and the flat roof is the place where the family gathers. David went up to the roof of his palace and walked back and forth, apparently a little nervous. I suppose he had a great many problems on his mind. His men were in the field fighting and it may be that his conscience was bothering him. As he walked, he looked around and saw this woman bathing on the roof of her home. Although it was David's sin—God put the blame right on David—it seems that Bathsheba was a contributing factor. She could have been a little bit more modest.

At the risk of sounding like a prude, let me say we are living in a day when women's dress has become a great temptation to men. I wonder how many women, even Christian women, realize what they are doing when they wear certain types of apparel. I have attended services in many churches in which the soloist would get up and carry you to the gates of heaven. Then I have seen her sit down and carry you to the gates of hell. It is my opinion that this woman Bathsheba was partially guilty. What was she doing bathing in public? When I say "public," certainly David was able to see her from his palace. I wonder if she thought there was a chance that David might see her, and she was purposely bathing on the roof.

And David sent and inquired after the woman. And one said, Is not this Bathsheba, the daughter of Eliam, the wife of Uriah the Hittite? [2 Sam. 11:3].

Uriah was actually a foreigner.

And David sent messengers, and took her; and she came in unto him, and he lay with her; for she was purified from her uncleanness: and she returned unto her house [2 Sam. 11:4].

This is the ugly story, and it is put in plain and simple language so that we cannot miss the point. If David had been out in the field with his men, this would never have happened. If Bathsheba had taken her bath inside her house, this would not have happened.

And the woman conceived, and sent and told David, and said, I am with child [2 Sam. 11:5].

David has a real problem. What is he going to do? Uriah, Bathsheba's husband, is one of David's mighty men. He is one of David's loyal followers.

And David sent to Joab, saying, Send me Uriah the Hittite. And Joab sent Uriah to David.

And when Uriah was come unto him, David demanded of him how Joab did, and how the people did, and how the war prospered [2 Sam. 11:6–7].

David pretended that he had brought Uriah back from the war for consultation to find out how the war was going.

And David said to Uriah, Go down to thy house, and wash thy feet. And Uriah departed out of the king's house, and there followed him a mess of meat from the king [2 Sam. 11:8].

David is doing everything he can, in this particular instance, to try and absolve himself of any guilt.

But Uriah slept at the door of the king's house with all the servants of his lord, and went not down to his house [2 Sam. 11:9].

Uriah slept at the door of the king's house. At a time of war this man would not go to his own home. This really surprised David. Also it was a rebuke to David who was enjoying the luxury of his palace.

And when they had told David, saying, Uriah went not down unto his house, David said unto Uriah, Camest thou not from the journey? why then didst thou not go down unto thine house? [2 Sam. 11:10].

You can see that David is trying to get Uriah in the position where David will not be blamed for the pregnancy.

And Uriah said unto David, The ark, and Israel, and Judah, abide in tents; and my lord Joab, and the servants of my lord, are encamped in the open fields; shall I then go into mine house, to eat and to drink, and to lie with my wife? as thou livest, and as thy soul liveth, I will not do this thing [2 Sam. 11:11].

Uriah was a great man. Although he was a foreigner, he was loyal to Israel. That made David's double sin all the greater. Uriah said, "The army and my commander are out in the field. They are in danger. I am not about to come back home and enjoy luxury and comfort."

And David said to Uriah, Tarry here to-day also, and to-morrow I will let thee depart. So Uriah abode in Jerusalem that day, and the morrow.

And when David had called him, he did eat and drink before him; and he made him drunk: and at even he went out to lie on his bed with the servants of his lord, but went not down to his house [2 Sam. 11:12–13].

Now David tries something else to trick Uriah into going home. David gets Uriah drunk! Yet the man still did not go home.

And it came to pass in the morning, that David wrote a letter to Joab, and sent it by the hand of Uriah.

And he wrote in the letter, saying, Set ye Uriah in the forefront of the hottest battle, and retire ye from him, that he may be smitten, and die [2 Sam. 11:14–15].

In my judgment this is the worst part of David's sin. He deliberately plotted the murder of Uriah. This is inexcusable. The Word of God records what David did. God did not cover it up; He brought it right out in the open. These are the facts. David is guilty.

And it came to pass, when Joab observed the city, that he assigned Uriah unto a place where he knew that valiant men were.

And the men of the city went out, and fought with Joab: and there fell some of the people of the servants of David; and Uriah the Hittite died also [2 Sam. 11:16–17].

This chills your blood, does it not?

Then Joab sent and told David all the things concerning the war;

And charged the messenger, saying, When thou hast made an end of telling the matters of the war unto the king,

And if so be that the king's wrath arise, and he say unto thee, Wherefore approached ye so nigh unto the city when ye did fight? knew ye not that they would shoot from the wall? [2 Sam. 11:18–20].

Joab's anticipation of David's reaction may be a cover-up to hide from the messenger the true significance of the message.

Who smote Abimelech the son of Jerubbesheth? did not a woman cast a piece of a millstone upon him from the wall, that he died in Thebez? why went ye nigh the wall? then say thou, Thy servant Uriah the Hittite is dead also.

So the messenger went, and came and shewed David all that Joab had sent him for.

And the messenger said unto David, Surely the men prevailed against us,

and came out unto us into the field, and we were upon them even unto the entering of the gate.

And the shooters shot from off the wall upon thy servants; and some of the king's servants be dead, and thy servant Uriah the Hittite is dead also.

Then David said unto the messenger, Thus shalt thou say unto Joab, Let not this thing displease thee, for the sword devoureth one as well as another: make thy battle more strong against the city, and overthrow it: and encourage thou him [2 Sam. 11:21–25].

This is very pious talk from David. Aren't you ashamed of him? He is a real sinner, friend. He has done an awful thing. What should be done to him? We shall see that God is going to punish him.

And when the wife of Uriah heard that Uriah her husband was dead, she mourned for her husband.

And when the mourning was past, David sent and fetched her to his house, and she became his wife, and bare him a son. But the thing that David had done displeased the LORD [2 Sam. 11:26–27].

"The thing that David had done *displeased* the LORD"—don't miss that. David did not get by with his sin. Up to this point in his life David has had many triumphs, but from now on, to his dying day, he will have trouble.

May I say to you, Christian friend, that you can sin. Someone asked me, "Can a Christian get drunk?" I replied, "Yes, a Christian can get drunk." This person was shocked, but then he asked, "Can he get by with it?" That is where the rub comes. The man of the world can get by with it; the Lord does not whip the devil's children. But He sure takes His own children to the woodshed. Will you take it from one who has been to the woodshed? I happen to know that you cannot get by with sin. David did not get by with it. The thing he did displeased the Lord. When a thing displeases the Lord, friend, He is going to do something about it.

David thinks he has gotten by with his sin, although there are a few people who know the facts. Joab, David's captain, knows the facts. A few of David's intimate counselors in Jerusalem who brought Bathsheba to the palace know the facts. Beyond that, no one knows, and the lips of these men are closed. They would not dare talk. David, however, wonders as he sits on his throne and looks around him. When David held court, there were probably two hundred people around him, and he undoubtedly looked into each face and silently asked himself, *Do they know*? After a time David probably sat back in satisfaction and said to himself, *Well, I got by with it. Nobody knows*.

My friend, whether it was known in Jerusalem or not, David's secret sin and our secret sins are open before God. Someone has put it this way, "Secret sin on earth is open scandal in heaven." God knows all about what we do.

CHAPTER 12

THEME: *Nathan faces David with his sins; David repents*

NATHAN FACES DAVID WITH HIS SINS

The critics who say that God allowed David to get by with his great sin apparently haven't read the whole story. Friend, we need to keep on reading. When Nathan confronts David with his sin, David repents. In spite of that, Nathan pronounces God's judgment upon David. David must learn that a man reaps what he sows.

God's man may get in sin, but he will not stay in sin. That is what distinguishes God's man from the man of the world. A sheep may fall in the mud, but he will struggle out of it as soon as he can. A pig will stay in the mud and enjoy it.

God has said that men, like pieces of pottery, can be marred. One flaw can ruin a valuable piece of pottery. A valuable article is put on sale because the merchant sees a flaw in it. I am a great one for sales as I go about the country. When I see that a sale is on, I rush down to the store. Usually I find that first-grade merchandise has become second-grade merchandise because of a flaw. It is marked down because of a little defect. Now David will have to be marked down because of his sin. In chapter 11 we saw David's sin in all of its blackness and ugliness. The Word of God does not soft-pedal it. The Word of God does not whitewash David's actions. His sin is as black as ink, and as dark as night, and as low as the underside of Satan and the bottomless pit, and as deep as hell. David *sinned.*

What David did displeased the Lord, and God is going to do something about it. You see, God did something about man's sin. He gave Jesus Christ to die on the cross and pay the penalty—sin is that heinous. It is God who says that sin is so black that it required the death of His Son. If you turn your back on God, you are lost. However, if you are God's man and you drop into sin, God is going to deal with you.

In chapter 11 we left David sitting on his throne in smug complacency. He thought he had gotten away with his sin, but he was wrong. David is going to live to regret that he ever committed that awful sin.

The first verse introduces us to Nathan who is one of the bravest men in Scripture. David could have merely lifted his scepter and without a word could have condemned Nathan to execution for his audacity. This, however, did not stop Nathan.

And the LORD sent Nathan unto David. And he came unto him, and said unto him, There were two men in one city; the one rich, and the other poor [2 Sam. 12:1].

Nathan is going to tell David a story. It is a story that will reveal David as though he were looking in a mirror. The Word of God is a mirror that reveals us as we really are. Nathan is going to hold up a mirror so that David can get a good look at himself. There was probably a lull in state business when Nathan came. Since Nathan was God's prophet, David said to him, "Do you have anything from the Lord for me?" He did. He told David a story about two men in one city. One man was rich and the other man was poor—a typical city with its ghetto and its rich estates.

The rich man had exceeding many flocks and herds:

But the poor man had nothing, save one little ewe lamb, which he had bought and nourished up: and it grew up together with him, and with his children; it did eat of his own meat, and drank of his own cup, and lay in his bosom, and was unto him as a daughter [2 Sam. 12:2–3].

The story of the rich man and the poor man sounds very familiar. The rich man had many flocks and herds. The poor man had one little lamb. It was a pet and dearly loved by the family. They fed it—it was probably a fat little fellow. It was all the poor man had. What a contrast. This has been the continual war between the rich and the poor. I personally think the outstanding problem today is not the racial problem, but the conflict between capital and labor, the rich and the poor.

And there came a traveller unto the rich man, and he spared to take of his own flock and of his own herd, to dress for the wayfaring man that was come unto him; but took the poor man's lamb, and dressed it for the man that was come to him [2 Sam. 12:4].

Nathan is telling a story that is quite familiar, is it not? The poor man had nothing but the little ewe lamb; the rich man had everything—yet he was a skinflint. I do not often discuss politics, but I would like to put down a principle in this world of sin today. I recognize that political parties say they have the solutions for the problems of the world because they want their candidates to be elected to office. I have no confidence in men. I do not believe that any politician today is going to champion the poor. This never has been done, and it never will be done. Let us not kid ourselves about that. It is quite interesting about the government poverty programs. Do they tax the rich? No! Taxes go up for the rest of us. I tell you, they are surely taking my little ewe lamb, friends.

And David's anger was greatly kindled against the man; and he said to Nathan, As the LORD liveth, the man that hath done this thing shall surely die [2 Sam. 12:5].

David thought Nathan had brought before him a case for someone in the kingdom and was asking for David to rule upon it. David had a sense of right and wrong. He also had a sense of justice. He is redheaded and hotheaded. When he heard Nathan's story, he probably sprang to his feet and demanded, "Where is this man? We will arrest him. We will execute him!"

It is interesting how easily you can see the sin in somebody else, but you cannot see it in your own life. That was David's problem.

And he shall restore the lamb fourfold, because he did this thing, and because he had no pity [2 Sam. 12:6].

David sounds like a preacher, doesn't he? It is so easy to preach to the other person, tell him his faults, analyze him, and tell him what to do. Most of us are amateur psychologists who put other people on our own little critical couches and give them a working over. That is David. David says, "Wherever that man is, we are going to see that justice is done."

And Nathan said to David, Thou art the man. Thus saith the LORD God of Israel, I anointed thee king over Israel, and I delivered thee out of the hand of Saul;

And I gave thee thy master's house, and thy master's wives into thy bosom, and gave thee the house of Israel and of Judah; and if that had been too little, I would moreover have given unto thee such and such things [2 Sam. 12:7–8].

It took courage for Nathan to say this to David. In my judgment he is the bravest man in the Bible. I know of no one who can be compared to him. He said, "David, you are the guilty one." What is David going to do? He is going to do something unusual, I can assure you of that. Dr. Margoliouth has said this: "When has this been done—before or since? Mary, Queen of Scots, would declare that she was above the law; Charles I would have thrown over Bathsheba; James II would have hired witnesses to swear away her character; Mohammed would have produced a revelation authorizing both crimes; Charles II would have publicly abrogated the seventh commandment; Queen Elizabeth would have suspended Nathan." Years ago, the Duke of Windsor would have given up his throne for her. We have had some presidents who would have repealed the Ten Commandments and appointed Nathan to the Supreme Court. David did not do any of these things. His actions will reveal his greatness.

God would have given David anything his heart wanted, but David longed for something that was not his. The new morality today says it was not sin. God still says this is sin, and the man after God's own heart cannot get by with it.

Wherefore hast thou despised the commandment of the LORD, to do evil in his sight? thou hast killed Uriah the Hittite with the sword, and hast taken his wife to be thy wife, and hast slain him with the sword of the children of Ammon [2 Sam. 12:9].

Nathan spells out the sins in no uncertain terms.

Don't you imagine, friends, that the court was shocked when they heard what Nathan said to David? There were undoubtedly many present who did not know what had happened. They hear Nathan accuse David of the most brutal crime written in the books. David has done the things that God said, "Thou shalt not do."

Is he going to get by with it?

Now therefore the sword shall never depart from thine house; because thou hast despised me, and hast taken the wife of Uriah the Hittite to be thy wife [2 Sam. 12:10].

May I say, Christian friend, that when the question arises, "Can a Christian sin?" the answer is yes. But when you sin, you despise God. God says that that is what you do. When David took Uriah's wife to be his wife, he was despising God.

Thus saith the LORD, Behold, I will raise up evil against thee out of thine own house, and I will take thy wives before thine eyes, and give them unto thy neighbour, and he shall lie with thy wives in the sight of this sun [2 Sam. 12:11].

Evil is going to arise against David out of his own house. And friends, in the next chapter a scandal breaks out among David's children that is an awful thing. It becomes a heartbreak to this man. But you will never find him whimpering or crying out to God about it, because David knew that God was putting the lash on his back. All that David wanted was what is written in Psalm 42:1, "As the hart panteth after the water brooks, so panteth my soul after thee, O God."

For thou didst it secretly: but I will do this thing before all Israel, and before the sun [2 Sam. 12:12].

DAVID REPENTS

And David said unto Nathan, I have sinned against the LORD. And Nathan said unto David, The LORD also hath put away thy sin; thou shalt not die [2 Sam. 12:13].

David should have died for this crime. God spared David's life and put away his sin, but David's baby died. God is not going to let David get by with his sin.

Howbeit, because by this deed thou hast given great occasion to the enemies of the LORD to blaspheme, the child also that is born unto thee shall surely die [2 Sam. 12:14].

And friends, the enemies of the Lord still blaspheme God because of what David did. When I was a pastor in downtown Los Angeles, there were many times when some unbeliever or skeptic came to me and said, "How could God choose a man like David?" They would actually leer at me while waiting for my reply. The enemy is still blaspheming. God is going to take David to the woodshed.

And Nathan departed unto his house. And the LORD struck the child that Uriah's wife bare unto David, and it was very sick.

David therefore besought God for the child; and David fasted, and went in, and lay all night upon the earth.

And the elders of his house arose, and went to him, to raise him up from the earth: but he would not, neither did he eat bread with them [2 Sam. 12:15–17].

David went before God and pleaded for Him to spare the little fellow's life. Finally they brought word to David that the child was dead.

But when David saw that his servants whispered, David perceived that the child was dead: therefore David said unto his servants, Is the child dead? And they said, He is dead.

Then David arose from the earth, and washed, and anointed himself, and changed his apparel, and came into the house of the LORD, and worshipped: then he came to his own house; and when he required, they set bread before him, and he did eat [2 Sam. 12:19–20].

David's servants are astounded. When the child was alive, David was in sackcloth and ashes. When the child died, he should have been beside himself with grief. Instead, he got up, took a shower, and changed his clothes, *then went to the house of God to worship.* His servants ask for an explanation.

And he said, While the child was yet alive, I fasted and wept: for I said, Who can tell whether GOD will be gracious to me, that the child may live?

But now he is dead, wherefore should I fast? can I bring him back again? I shall go to him, but he shall not return to me [2 Sam. 12:22–23].

David knew that the little baby was saved. He said, "I will go to him someday." David knew that when death came to him, he would be reunited with his son.

A child dying in infancy goes to be with the Lord. Matthew 18:10 says, "Take heed that ye despise not one of these little ones; for I say unto you, That in heaven their angels do always behold the face of my Father which is in heaven." The word *angels* in this verse should be translated "spirits." When a little baby dies today, that baby goes immediately to be with the Lord. That is the teaching of the Word of God. I don't know about you, but this means a great deal to me because I have a little one up there, and I am looking forward to one day being with her.

David could rejoice when his infant son died because he knew that one day he would see him again. That was not the case when his son Absalom died many years later. Absalom was a heartbreak to David. When he died, David wept and mourned. Why? David was not sure Absalom was saved.

THE BIRTH OF SOLOMON

And David comforted Bath-sheba his wife, and went in unto her, and lay with her: and she bare a son, and he called his name Solomon: and the LORD loved him.

And he sent by the hand of Nathan the prophet; and he called his name Jedidiah, because of the LORD [2 Sam. 12:24–25].

The name *Jedidiah* means "beloved of the Lord." This name was given by God through Nathan to Solomon.

DAVID AND JOAB TAKE RABBAH

And Joab fought against Rabbah of the children of Ammon, and took the royal city.

And Joab sent messengers to David, and said, I have fought against Rabbah, and have taken the city of waters.

Now therefore gather the rest of the people together, and encamp against

the city, and take it: lest I take the city, and it be called after my name.

And David gathered all the people together, and went to Rabbah, and fought against it, and took it [2 Sam. 12:26–29].

David is now back out in the field where he should have been all along. David's kingdom continues to be extended and expanded, and David becomes a great ruler of that day. What about his sin? Did he get by with it? In the next chapter we will find out that David's son Amnon committed an awful crime. He raped his half sister, a daughter of David. Absalom, a full brother of the girl who was raped, killed Amnon. Say, that was a scandal! Can you imagine how that news spread over Israel? The people said, "Look at the king ruling over us. He cannot even rule his own household!" Poor David.

Before we get through with the life of David, I feel like saying to the Lord, "You have whipped him enough. Why don't you take the lash off his back now?" But, you know, David never said that. David went into the presence of the Lord and cried: "Have mercy upon me, O God, according to thy lovingkindness: according unto the multitude of thy tender mercies blot out my transgressions. Wash me throughly from mine iniquity, and cleanse me from my sin. Restore unto me the joy of thy salvation; and uphold me with thy free spirit" (Ps. 51:1–2, 12). David wanted to be brought back into fellowship with his God.

CHAPTERS 13–14

THEME: *Crimes of David's sons—Amnon and Absalom*

There is that old bromide which says, "If you are going to dance, you are going to have to pay the fiddler." If you are going to indulge in sin, you will have to suffer the consequences. The Lord gives it to us straight in Galatians 6:7: "Be not deceived; God is not mocked: for whatsoever a man soweth, that shall he also reap." You are not going to get by with sin. Galatians 6:8 goes on to say, "For he that soweth to his flesh shall of the flesh reap corruption; but he that soweth to the Spirit shall of the Spirit reap life everlasting." There is no question that David had sown to the flesh. Don't think for one minute that now he can walk away from his sin, make a sweet little confession, and that is it. I have heard people say, "Well, the blood of Christ covers it." It certainly does, and you don't lose your salvation, brother. But I want to tell you that sin causes a festering sore that has to be lanced.

This brings us to chapter 13. David has made his confession of sin. God has told him, "Your sin has caused My enemies to blaspheme Me. I won't give you up, but you are not going to get by with it." Thank God that He will not give us up, but the chickens do come home to roost.

DAVID'S DAUGHTER RAPED BY HIS SON

And it came to pass after this, that Absalom the son of David had a fair sister, whose name was Tamar; and Amnon the son of David loved her [2 Sam. 13:1].

Although Absalom and Tamar had the same mother and father, Tamar was Amnon's half sister. David was their father, but they had different mothers.

And Amnon was so vexed, that he fell sick for his sister Tamar; for she was a virgin; and Amnon thought it hard for him to do any thing to her.

But Amnon had a friend, whose name was Jonadab, the son of Shimeah David's brother: and Jonadab was a very subtil man.

And he said unto him, Why art thou, being the king's son, lean from day to day? wilt thou not tell me? And Amnon said unto him, I love Tamar, my brother Absalom's sister [2 Sam. 13:2–4].

Amnon was not eating. He was so madly in love with Tamar that he had lost his appetite. His friend could see that he was not eating, but he also recognized the problem since Tamar was Absalom's sister and Amnon was afraid of Absalom.

And Jonadab said unto him, Lay thee down on thy bed, and make thyself sick: and when thy father cometh to see thee, say unto him, I pray thee, let my sister Tamar come, and give me meat, and dress the meat in my sight, that I may see it, and eat it at her hand.

So Amnon lay down, and made himself sick: and when the king was come to see him, Amnon said unto the king, I pray thee, let Tamar my sister come, and make me a couple of cakes in my sight, that I may eat at her hand.

Then David sent home to Tamar, saying, Go now to thy brother Amnon's house, and dress him meat [2 Sam. 13:5–7].

There is no use to read the next few verses which contain the sordid details of what happened next. Amnon raped Tamar. Then we are told that he hated her.

Then Amnon hated her exceedingly; so that the hatred wherewith he hated her was greater than the love wherewith he had loved her. And Amnon said unto her, Arise, be gone [2 Sam. 13:15].

This awful thing had taken place in the house of David. When Amnon was through with her, he flung her out.

And Tamar put ashes on her head, and rent her garment of divers colours that was on her, and laid her hand on her head, and went on crying [2 Sam. 13:19].

Tamar was thrown out of the house, and now she is in sackcloth and ashes.

And Absalom her brother said unto her, Hath Amnon thy brother been with thee? but hold now thy peace, my sister: he is thy brother; regard not this thing. So Tamar remained desolate in her brother Absalom's house.

But when king David heard of all these things, he was very wroth [2 Sam. 13: 20–21].

David is angry about what happened but does nothing about it. David was like many other men in Scripture: he was an indulgent father who raised a bunch of kids who were bad. That has happened again and again. It started with old Eli, God's high priest. His sons were not only immoral, they were godless and had a religious racket going. Then we come to Samuel. Since he was raised in the same atmosphere as Eli's sons, you would think Samuel would be more of a disciplinarian and that he would have maintained some authority and control over his sons. But his sons turned out to be corrupt and dishonest. Next we come to David. He knew Samuel, and he knew Samuel's sons. You would think he would have been more strict with his children, but he was not. He too was an indulgent father. He was angry about what Amnon did to his sister Tamar. But, after all, what kind of an example has David set for his boys? The chickens are beginning to come home to roost.

Perhaps you think I am a square because I say some old-fashioned things, but I am convinced that the main problem today in Christian homes is the lack of example and discipline on the part of the parents. My friend, if you are a Christian and you have a naughty little boy in your home, don't spend your time lecturing him. You are not going to get anywhere that way. Give him an example and discipline—and start soon, because the day will come when he will walk out.

Another strike against David is the fact that he had multiple wives and many children. As a king with many heavy responsibilities, how much time do you think he spent in rearing his children? The problem with many of us who have been in Christian work is that we probably have neglected our families for the sake of the work. We have excused our neglect on the basis that we were doing Christian work. I must confess that if I could go back and do one thing over again, it would be to spend more time with my daughter when she was growing up. I now have grandchildren, and they are wonderful. I am enjoying them more than I enjoyed my daughter when she was a child. Do you know why? I was too busy when she was small. Now I am not so busy and I can spend time with my grandchildren.

Christian parents need to realize that they need to spend time training their children. Don't get the impression that you are raising a little angel. There are many parents who treat a child as if he were a cross between an orchid and a piece of Dresden china. They believe that if they apply the board of education to the seat of knowledge they will break him in pieces or he will come apart. Proverbs 23:13 says, "Withhold not correction from the child: for if thou beatest him with the rod, he shall not die."

David did nothing about the problem created by Amnon. So what happened?

And Absalom spake unto his brother Amnon neither good nor bad: for Absalom hated Amnon, because he had forced his sister Tamar [2 Sam. 13:22].

This is David's home, friends. This is David's life at home. He did not get by with sin. God says that we will not get by with sin either. Absalom is marking time. He is waiting for the day when he can get even with Amnon. And that day will come.

AMNON MURDERED BY ABSALOM

I am not going into detail at this point, but the day came when Absalom killed Amnon. Absalom waited for two years before making his move. He invited the king's sons to a feast in connection with sheep-shearing time. Since Absalom had shown no signs of wanting revenge, David let Amnon go and attend the party.

Now Absalom had commanded his servants, saying, Mark ye now when Amnon's heart is merry with wine, and when I say unto you, Smite Amnon; then kill him, fear not: have not I commanded you? be courageous, and be valiant [2 Sam. 13:28].

When the day came that Amnon's "heart was merry with wine," Absalom had him killed.

The first message David received was that all his sons were dead. Then Jonadab told him that only Amnon was slain.

Now therefore let not my lord the king take the thing to his heart, to think that all the king's sons are dead: for Amnon only is dead.

But Absalom fled. And the young man that kept the watch lifted up his eyes, and looked, and, behold, there came much people by the way of the hill side behind him.

And Jonadab said unto the king, Behold, the king's sons come: as thy servant said, so it is [2 Sam. 13:33–35].

Since Absalom actually plotted Amnon's murder, he has to flee.

And it came to pass, as soon as he had made an end of speaking, that, behold, the king's sons came, and lifted up their voice and wept: and the king also and all his servants wept very sore.

But Absalom fled, and went to Talmai, the son of Ammihud, king of Geshur. And David mourned for his son every day [2 Sam. 13:36–37].

Absalom's mother was a daughter of the king of Geshur, and this is one reason why Absalom fled to him. As I have pointed out before, David made a mistake in marrying this foreign woman. Remember that he had married this woman during his lapse of faith when he withdrew from the land. She bore the king two very attractive children. One was Absalom and the other was Tamar. Apparently David did not discipline this wild boy, who was the son of a pagan and a Bedouin. In a way, Absalom seems to be justified in what he did, since David did not take matters into his own hands when Amnon sinned.

So Absalom fled, and went to Geshur, and was there three years.

And the soul of king David longed to go forth unto Absalom: for he was comforted concerning Amnon, seeing he was dead [2 Sam. 13:38–39].

After Absalom took Amnon's life, he fled. David wanted to bring him back, but he did not. David mourned for him and that is all he did. He mourned for him and wished for his return. Absalom, I believe, was more like David than any of his other sons. I think it was David's intention that Absalom succeed him as the next king of Israel. That ambition also lurked in the mind of Absalom, as we shall see.

DAVID PERMITS ABSALOM TO RETURN

Now Joab the son of Zeruiah perceived that the king's heart was toward Absalom.

And Joab sent to Tekoah, and fetched thence a wise woman, and said unto her, I pray thee, feign thyself to be a mourner, and put on now mourning apparel, and anoint not thyself with oil, but be as a woman that had a long time mourned for the dead:

And come to the king, and speak on this manner unto him. So Joab put the words in her mouth [2 Sam. 14:1–3].

Joab grew up in the vicinity of Tekoah and may have known this woman from earlier days.

And when the woman of Tekoah spake to the king, she fell on her face to the ground, and did obeisance, and said, Help, O king.

And the king said unto her, What aileth thee? And she answered, I am indeed a widow woman, and mine husband is dead.

And thy handmaid had two sons, and they two strove together in the field, and there was none to part them, but the one smote the other, and slew him. And, behold, the whole family is risen against thine handmaid, and they said, Deliver him that smote his brother, that we may kill him, for the life of his brother whom he slew; and we will destroy the heir also: and so they shall quench my coal which is left, and shall not leave to my husband neither name nor remainder upon the earth [2 Sam. 14:4–7].

Joab got her to play upon the feelings of David by telling him her sad story. Just as David had used deception, he was now being deceived.

Then said she, I pray thee, let the king remember the LORD thy God, that thou wouldest not suffer the revengers of blood to destroy any more, lest they destroy my son. And he said, As the LORD liveth, there shall not one hair of thy son fall to the earth [2 Sam. 14:11].

David grants her imaginary son a full pardon. Then she makes the application to David and Absalom.

And the woman said, Wherefore then hast thou thought such a thing against the people of God? for the king doth speak this thing as one which is faulty, in that the king doth not fetch home again his banished [2 Sam. 14:13].

The widow of Tekoah was putting David in the place of her imaginary prosecutors. What her prosecutors could do to her remaining son, David was doing to God's people by punishing Absalom for the crime he had committed. She is representing the people of Israel as the widowed mother. She claims to be speaking in the name of all Israel, and possibly she does express their feelings. Absalom was very popular with the people, and they probably felt that Amnon got what he deserved.

The final outcome of the incident is that in a half-hearted way David is willing for Absalom to return.

And the king said unto Joab, Behold now, I have done this thing: go therefore, bring the young man Absalom again.

And Joab fell to the ground on his face, and bowed himself, and thanked the king: and Joab said, To-day thy servant knoweth that I have found grace in thy sight, my lord, O king, in that the king hath fulfilled the request of his servant.

So Joab arose and went to Geshur, and brought Absalom to Jerusalem.

And the king said, Let him turn to his own house, and let him not see my face. So Absalom returned to his own house, and saw not the king's face [2 Sam. 14:21–24].

It is unfortunate that David did not want to see his son. It actually set the stage for Absalom's rebellion which takes place in chapter 15. Absalom was a bad boy, but he was a good politician. We shall see this in the next chapter.

Absalom's high-handed action of setting Joab's standing grain on fire to force Joab to come to him is another revelation of Absalom's personality.

And Absalom answered Joab, Behold, I sent unto thee, saying, Come hither, that I may send thee to the king, to say, Wherefore am I come from Geshur? it had been good for me to have been there still: now therefore let me see the king's face; and if there be any iniquity in me, let him kill me.

So Joab came to the king, and told him: and when he had called for Absalom, he came to the king, and bowed himself on his face to the ground before the king: and the king kissed Absalom [2 Sam. 14:32–33].

Absalom's prank succeeded in persuading Joab to bring him to his father for reconciliation. Although David's kiss was a sign of complete reconciliation and restoration of Absalom's position as the king's son, it was given reluctantly. The fact that his father did not give him instant, wholehearted forgiveness rankled in his soul.

God had not forgiven David half heartedly. God did not say, "Well, I forgive you, but we will not have fellowship any more. I will not restore to you the joy of your salvation." When God forgives, He forgives completely. You and I are admonished: "And be ye kind one to another, tenderhearted, forgiving one another, even as God for Christ's sake hath forgiven you" (Eph. 4:32). Has God forgiven us? Yes! How are we to forgive others? The same way that God does. David should have forgiven Absalom. He is setting the stage for rebellion.

Oh, my friend, our God is a God who forgives. Galatians 6:1 tells us, "Brethren, if a man be overtaken in a fault, ye which are spiritual, restore such an one in the spirit of meekness; considering thyself, lest thou also be tempted." It appears that many of us don't read that verse correctly. We think it says, "If any man be overtaken in a fault, take a baseball bat and hit him over the head!" We are reluctant to forgive, and we can be very mean at times, very unloving, and critical. There are times when the truth should be spoken, but when forgiveness is asked for, it should be extended immediately.

David made a blunder in not forgiving his son as God had forgiven David. He will live to regret it.

CHAPTERS 15–16

THEME: *Absalom rebels against David*

ABSALOM REBELS AGAINST DAVID

David, after committing his terrible sin, found that trouble came to him thick and fast. The same way that he had sinned, members of his family sinned, and David is not through with the effects of it yet. God really took David to the woodshed.

In this chapter Absalom leads a rebellion against David. In a very subtle way Absalom begins to steal the hearts of the children of Israel. He is an attractive young fellow—probably like David in many ways. He is the heir apparent to the throne; that is, David would like for him to succeed him. We find now that Absalom is back in Jerusalem, beginning to move secretly to plot David's overthrow. This is a dastardly deed, but the chickens are coming home to roost for David. Actually, a formidable revolution will break out which will cause David to flee from Jerusalem.

And it came to pass after this, that Absalom prepared him chariots and horses, and fifty men to run before him.

And Absalom rose up early, and stood beside the way of the gate: and it was so, that when any man that had a controversy came to the king for judgment, then Absalom called unto him, and said, Of what city art thou? And he said, Thy servant is of one of the tribes of Israel [2 Sam. 15:1–2].

Absalom stationed himself at the busiest gate of the city. When men with complaints came to the gate requiring justice, he listened to them with a great show of sympathy.

And Absalom said unto him, See, thy matters are good and right; but there is no man deputed of the king to hear thee.

Absalom said moreover, Oh that I were made judge in the land, that every man which hath any suit or cause might come unto me, and I would do him justice! [2 Sam. 15:3–4].

Absalom was a bad boy but a good politician; he was clever and crooked, subtle and sly.

And it was so, that when any man came nigh to him to do him obeisance, he put forth his hand, and took him, and kissed him.

And on this manner did Absalom to all Israel that came to the king for judgment: so Absalom stole the hearts of the men of Israel [2 Sam. 15:5–6].

Absalom is a true politician, isn't he? This is the way many men get elected to office today.

They have no qualifications other than the fact that they are good at handshaking and backslapping. There are many preachers who use this method today. They cannot preach, and they cannot teach, but they sure can slap backs. Unfortunately that is exactly what appeals to us. As far as I can tell from the Word of God, that is the way that the Antichrist will come to power. He is going to be the greatest little backslapper that the world has ever seen. Now Absalom was a good backslapper. He stood at the gate and said, "Oh, if I were only a judge. Then you would get *justice*!" You can understand the appeal that that kind of statement would make. Absalom was saying, "If you vote me into office, I can solve all of your problems. I will be able to take care of all the foreign and domestic affairs." That is what the politicians tell us today. Unfortunately, we listen to them, believe them, and vote for them. Then when they get into office, they do not produce.

Absalom, of course, is preparing for a rebellion against David, his father. This rebellion within the house of David is a terrible thing.

And it came to pass after forty years, that Absalom said unto the king, I pray thee, let me go and pay my vow, which I have vowed unto the LORD, in Hebron.

For thy servant vowed a vow while I abode at Geshur in Syria, saying, If the LORD shall bring me again indeed to Jerusalem, then I will serve the LORD [2 Sam. 15:7–8].

His request seems a little unusual—he says he wants to go south to Hebron to pay a vow he made in exile, yet he was in Syria in the north while he was in exile. However, David does not question it.

And the king said unto him, Go in peace. So he arose, and went to Hebron.

But Absalom sent spies throughout all the tribes of Israel, saying, As soon as ye hear the sound of the trumpet, then ye shall say, Absalom reigneth in Hebron [2 Sam. 15:9–10].

You will recall that Hebron is where David began his reign. He was king over Judah for seven years in Hebron. Absalom, obviously, did not go to Hebron to pay a vow. He went there to begin his rebellion.

And with Absalom went two hundred men out of Jerusalem, that were called; and they went in their simplicity, and they knew not any thing [2 Sam. 15:11].

In other words, these men went along with Absalom, but they did not know that the rebellion was prepared against David.

And Absalom sent for Ahithophel the Gilonite, David's counsellor, from his city, even from Giloh, while he offered sacrifices. And the conspiracy was strong; for the people increased continually with Absalom [2 Sam. 15:12].

This is a rebellion that gains momentum. It begins to snowball as it goes along, and soon there is a great company standing with Absalom. Even Ahithophel, David's counselor, is a partner to all of this. Before David actually realizes what is happening, the rebellion surfaces.

DAVID FLEES

And there came a messenger to David, saying, The hearts of the men of Israel are after Absalom.

And David said unto all his servants that were with him at Jerusalem, Arise, and let us flee; for we shall not else escape from Absalom: make speed to depart, lest he overtake us suddenly, and bring evil upon us, and smite the city with the edge of the sword [2 Sam. 15:13–14].

David is going to flee from Jerusalem. The question arises, "Why did he flee?" David loved the city of Jerusalem. Why didn't he make a stand in this city? I am confident that David knew God was punishing him for his sin. I know this is true on the basis of 2 Samuel 15:25–26 where we are told, "And the king said unto Zadok, Carry back the ark of God into the city: if I shall find favour in the eyes of the LORD, he will bring me again, and shew me both it, and his habitation: But if he thus say, I have no delight in thee; behold, here am I, let him do to me as seemeth good unto him." David knew what was happening to him. He knew that judgment was coming from God.

You recall in Samuel 13 that Amnon committed a crime against Tamar. David was disgraced by the awful thing that happened. This scandal had taken place in Jerusalem. You will also recall that David's great sin involving Uriah and Bathsheba—when David should have been out fighting with his army —took place in Jerusalem. David is leaving Jerusalem this time because he knows that

God is punishing him, and he does not want to see the city he built and loved become the scene of battle. In 2 Samuel 15:30 we are told, "And David went up by the ascent of mount Olivet, and wept as he went up, and had his head covered, and he went barefoot: and all the people that was with him covered every man his head, and they went up, weeping as they went up." David loved Jerusalem. He did not want it to be a place of battle; yet this city was to be destroyed more than any other city because of its rebellion and sin.

Also David fled from Jerusalem because he was not ready to press the issue with Absalom. We will see in the next chapters that it was in David's heart to spare the life of his son. He did not want harm to come to him. I think David loved Absalom above every person on earth. Leaving Jerusalem puts David's life in grave danger, but that is nothing new for him. He had been in great danger many times. He has more concern about his relationship with God and with his son than he has about his life.

With this background, let us look at the rebellion that is taking place.

Then said the king to Ittai the Gittite, Wherefore goest thou also with us? return to thy place, and abide with the king: for thou art a stranger, and also an exile.

Whereas thou camest but yesterday, should I this day make thee go up and down with us? seeing I go whither I may, return thou, and take back thy brethren: mercy and truth be with thee [2 Sam. 15:19–20].

Ittai is a native of Gath in Philistia, probably a general in his own country since David later makes him a joint commander with Joab and Abishai. He feels such loyalty to David that he and his entire family insist upon going into exile with him.

And Ittai answered the king, and said, As the LORD liveth, and as my lord the king liveth, surely in what place my lord the king shall be, whether in death or life, even there also will thy servant be.

And David said to Ittai, Go and pass over. And Ittai the Gittite passed over, and all his men, and all the little ones that were with him.

And all the country wept with a loud voice, and all the people passed over: the king also himself passed over the brook Kidron, and all the people passed over, toward the way of the wilderness [2 Sam. 15:21–23].

David had many loyal followers. There were many men willing to lay down their lives for him.

THE ARK IS RETURNED TO JERUSALEM

And lo Zadok also, and all the Levites were with him, bearing the ark of the covenant of God: and they set down the ark of God; and Abiathar went up, until all the people had done passing out of the city.

And the king said unto Zadok, Carry back the ark of God into the city: if I shall find favour in the eyes of the LORD, he will bring me again, and shew me both it, and his habitation [2 Sam. 15:24–25].

David sent the ark of the covenant of God back to Jerusalem where it belonged. He recognized that what was happening to him was the judgment of God. As he left the city, he went over the Mount of Olives, weeping as he went.

And one told David, saying, Ahithophel is among the conspirators with Absalom. And David said, O LORD, I pray thee, turn the counsel of Ahithophel into foolishness [2 Sam. 15:31].

Ahithophel had been a highly esteemed counselor of David. When he defected to Absalom's side, David prayed that his counsel to Absalom would be foolish, and God answered this prayer, by the way. Notice that David didn't ask for judgment upon Absalom.

HUSHAI IS SENT BACK

And it came to pass, that when David was come to the top of the mount, where he worshipped God, behold, Hushai the Archite came to meet him with his coat rent, and earth upon his head:

Unto whom David said, If thou passest on with me, then thou shalt be a burden unto me [2 Sam. 15:32–33].

He may have been elderly and would require more care.

But if thou return to the city, and say unto Absalom, I will be thy servant, O

king; as I have been thy father's servant hitherto, so will I now also be thy servant: then mayest thou for me defeat the counsel of Ahithophel.

And hast thou not there with thee Zadok and Abiathar the priests? therefore it shall be, that what thing soever thou shalt hear out of the king's house, thou shalt tell it to Zadok and Abiathar the priests.

Behold, they have there with them their two sons, Ahimaaz Zadok's son, and Jonathan Abiathar's son; and by them ye shall send unto me every thing that ye can hear.

So Hushai David's friend came into the city, and Absalom came into Jerusalem [2 Sam. 15:34–37].

When David heard of Ahithophel's defection to Absalom, he induced Hushai to go over to Absalom to defeat the counsels of this now dangerous enemy. Hushai was David's friend and would risk being a spy for him.

ZIBA, MEPHIBOSHETH'S SERVANT, DECEIVES DAVID

And when David was a little past the top of the hill, behold, Ziba the servant of Mephibosheth met him, with a couple of asses saddled, and upon them two hundred loaves of bread, and an hundred bunches of raisins, and an hundred of summer fruits, and a bottle of wine.

And the king said unto Ziba, What meanest thou by these? And Ziba said, The asses be for the king's household to ride on; and the bread and summer fruit for the young men to eat; and the wine, that such as be faint in the wilderness may drink [2 Sam. 16:1–2].

You recall that Mephibosheth was Jonathan's lame son. Because of David's great love for Jonathan, he cared for Mephibosheth.

Ziba, a servant of Mephibosheth, thought that the internal struggle within the house of David would give the house of Saul a chance to regain the throne—Mephibosheth was the sole heir to the throne. By telling his fictitious story, Ziba hoped to get something out of the estate of Mephibosheth. David, not having opportunity to check the facts, impetuously grants Ziba lands that had been Mephibosheth's.

SHIMEI CURSES DAVID

And when king David came to Bahurim, behold, thence came out a man of the family of the house of Saul, whose name was Shimei, the son of Gera: he came forth, and cursed still as he came.

And he cast stones at David, and at all the servants of king David: and all the people and all the mighty men were on his right hand and on his left.

And thus said Shimei when he cursed, Come out, come out, thou bloody man, and thou man of Belial:

The LORD hath returned upon thee all the blood of the house of Saul, in whose stead thou hast reigned; and the LORD hath delivered the kingdom into the hand of Absalom thy son: and, behold, thou art taken in thy mischief, because thou art a bloody man [2 Sam. 16:5–8].

What Shimei said to David had some truth in it. David was a bloody man, and judgment was coming upon him—there was no question about that.

Then said Abishai the son of Zeruiah unto the king, Why should this dead dog curse my lord the king? let me go over, I pray thee, and take off his head [2 Sam. 16:9].

Abishai, one of David's men, was all for silencing this man permanently.

Notice David's reaction to what Shimei said.

And the king said, What have I to do with you, ye sons of Zeruiah? so let him curse, because the LORD hath said unto him, Curse David. Who shall then say, Wherefore hast thou done so?

And David said to Abishai, and to all his servants, Behold, my son, which came forth of my bowels, seeketh my life: how much more now may this Benjamite do it? let him alone, and let him curse; for the LORD hath bidden him [2 Sam. 16:10–11].

David was saying, "I don't mind this outsider cursing me. I do not want to take revenge on him. The thing that is happening to me is the judgment of God. What disturbs me is that it is my own boy, Absalom, who is leading the rebellion against me."

We have been with David as he escaped from Jerusalem; now we go back to Jerusalem with Hushai as he offers his services to Absalom.

And Absalom, and all the people the men of Israel, came to Jerusalem, and Ahithophel with him.

And it came to pass, when Hushai the Archite, David's friend, was come unto Absalom, that Hushai said unto Absalom, God save the king, God save the king.

And Absalom said to Hushai, Is this thy kindness to thy friend? why wentest thou not with thy friend? [2 Sam. 16:15–17].

Absalom is surprised that this trusted friend of his father's did not go with him into exile.

And Hushai said unto Absalom, Nay; but whom the LORD, and this people, and all the men of Israel, choose, his will I be, and with him will I abide.

And again, whom should I serve? should I not serve in the presence of his son? as I have served in thy father's presence, so will I be in thy presence [2 Sam. 16:18–19].

Hushai is saying that the man whom God and the people choose will be his man, although he is secretly planning to be a spy for David.

Then said Absalom to Ahithophel, Give counsel among you what we shall do.

And Ahithophel said unto Absalom, Go in unto thy father's concubines, which he hath left to keep the house; and all Israel shall hear that thou art abhorred of thy father: then shall the hands of all that are with thee be strong.

So they spread Absalom a tent upon the top of the house; and Absalom went in unto his father's concubines in the sight of all Israel [2 Sam. 16:20–22].

Ahithophel advises Absalom to do an abominable thing, but it has great significance for Israel. Absalom's act was a coarse and rude declaration that David's rights had ended and that everything he owned now belonged to his son.

And the counsel of Ahithophel, which he counselled in those days, was as if a man had inquired at the oracle of God: so was all the counsel of Ahithophel both with David and with Absalom [2 Sam. 16:23].

The word of Ahithophel was obeyed without question—just as if it had been the command of God.

The act of Absalom fulfilled what the Lord had spoken to David: "Thus saith the LORD, Behold, I will raise up evil against thee out of thine own house, and I will take thy wives before thine eyes, and give them unto thy neighbour, and he shall lie with thy wives in the sight of this sun. For thou didst it secretly: but I will do this thing before all Israel, and before the sun" (2 Sam. 12:11–12).

We now find David back out in the dens and caves of the earth. What is he going to do? Absalom is going to try to win a victory over David's forces. David, however, is an old veteran and knows how to fight. Absalom is doing a very dangerous thing by going against his father. The tragic thing is that David loves him and wants to save him.

These were difficult days for David. I am sure by now that your heart goes out in sympathy to him. But David does not whimper or cry aloud. He says in substance, "Just as long as I know that things are right with God, I will bear these burdens that come upon me."

David was a great man, friend. He had committed awful sin, but he is like a wonderful piece of statuary with just one flaw in it. That is the way many Christians are today. Did you ever meet one who didn't have a flaw? We all have flaws in our lives. Thank God that He will not throw us overboard because of the flaws.

CHAPTERS 17–18

THEME: *Civil war between Absalom and David*

In chapter 17, Absalom hears the counsel of Ahithophel and Hushai, David's friend. When Absalom accepts Hushai's argument that David and his men are veterans in the field of battle and that Absalom needs reinforcements, David is able to escape and prepare for battle. In chapter 18 the two sides engage in civil war. The battle ends with Absalom's death. The chapter concludes with the touching grief of David over his slain son.

THE CONFLICTING COUNSEL OF AHITHOPHEL AND HUSHAI

As we have been following the different experiences of David, we saw first his triumphs, and now we are seeing his troubles. In fact, he is really in trouble right now. David's own son Absalom, whom I believe he loved above everything else in this world, is leading a rebellion against him. This was a heartbreak to the king. David withdrew from Jerusalem because he did not want it to become the scene of a battle and possibly be destroyed. Instead, David left his beloved city. He sent Hushai back to Absalom so that he might give him counsel that would be to David's advantage. Ahithophel, who had once been an advisor to David, had defected to Absalom. In chapter 17 these two advisors are giving Absalom contradictory counsel about whether or not to attack his father at this time.

Moreover Ahithophel said unto Absalom, Let me now choose out twelve thousand men, and I will arise and pursue after David this night:

And I will come upon him while he is weary and weak handed, and will make him afraid: and all the people that are with him shall flee; and I will smite the king only [2 Sam. 17:1–2].

In other words, if David could be destroyed, the rebellion would be broken and Absalom would be made king. Ahithophel's advice, of course, would be disastrous for David if it were followed. Ahithophel outlines his plan:

And I will bring back all the people unto thee: the man whom thou seekest is as if all returned: so all the people shall be in peace.

And the saying pleased Absalom well, and all the elders of Israel [2 Sam. 17:3–4].

Even Absalom agreed to this heartless plan.

Then said Absalom, Call now Hushai the Archite also, and let us hear likewise what he saith.

And when Hushai was come to Absalom, Absalom spake unto him, saying, Ahithophel hath spoken after this manner: shall we do after his saying? if not; speak thou [2 Sam. 17:5–6].

It was a good thing that Hushai was present, because he offers an altogether different strategy. He gives Absalom advice that is very good—but it is favorable to David. David is in a very vulnerable position and desperately needs time.

And Hushai said unto Absalom, The counsel that Ahithophel hath given is not good at this time.

For, said Hushai, thou knowest thy father and his men, that they be mighty men, and they be chafed in their minds, as a bear robbed of her whelps in the field: and thy father is a man of war, and will not lodge with the people.

Behold, he is hid now in some pit, or in some other place: and it will come to pass, when some of them be overthrown at the first, that whosoever heareth it will say, There is a slaughter among the people that follow Absalom.

And he also that is valiant, whose heart is as the heart of a lion, shall utterly melt: for all Israel knoweth that thy father is a mighty man, and they which be with him are valiant men [2 Sam. 17:7–10].

Hushai is giving Absalom good advice even though it is for David's benefit. His advice is simply this: "You must recognize, Absalom, that you are not a man of war. Your father is a man of war. He is acquainted with the field. He is a veteran. He is rugged. He has his mighty men with him. David and his men are chafed by what has happened. They are licking their wounds right now and are like a mother bear who has been robbed of her whelps—that mama bear is really going to fight and will become twice as dangerous as she would be otherwise. You would be very foolish to attack David now. But suppose you did attack him. David has been pursued before—he is an expert at evading capture. Saul hunted him for years. David would not be among the people. He would know where to hide. He would know how to escape. Suppose you went into his host and did not find David. Soon word would circulate that you were losing the battle, and you would find that the people who had temporarily joined you in your cause would not stay with you."

Now that Hushai has pointed out errors in judgment in Ahithophel's counsel, he outlines another strategy.

> **Therefore I counsel that all Israel be generally gathered unto thee, from Dan even to Beer-sheba, as the sand that is by the sea for multitude; and that thou go to battle in thine own person.**
>
> **So shall we come upon him in some place where he shall be found, and we will light upon him as the dew falleth on the ground: and of him and of all the men that are with him there shall not be left so much as one [2 Sam. 17:11–12].**

He is saying to Absalom, "The important thing is that you are not prepared to go into battle. Ahithophel is not prepared for battle. Just taking a few thousand men with you will not enable you to overcome David. What you need to do is to gather all Israel together, and you yourself lead the forces into battle. That is what is expected of a king. That is the way your father came to the throne. He was, first of all, a great general. We will have to overwhelm him and his men by sheer numbers." Hushai's advice was good all right, but it was not for Absalom's benefit. It was given for David's benefit. It would give David time to reconnoiter.

Now what did Absalom and the men of Israel think of Hushai's counsel?

> **And Absalom and all the men of Israel said, The counsel of Hushai the Archite is better than the counsel of Ahithophel. For the LORD had appointed to defeat the good counsel of Ahithophel, to the intent that the LORD might bring evil upon Absalom [2 Sam. 17:14].**

Absalom and his advisors felt that Hushai's advice was better. Very candidly, friend, Hushai's counsel was certainly better than that of Ahithophel from David's standpoint. God was at work in David's behalf.

WARNING IS SENT TO DAVID

While they are attempting to gather together the nation and unite them under Absalom, Hushai gets a warning to David. He is to escape over Jordan quickly. In the next few verses we see the movement of the spy system. When the message reached David, he responded quickly.

> **Then David arose, and all the people that were with him, and they passed over Jordan: by the morning light there lacked not one of them that was not gone over Jordan [2 Sam. 17:22].**

AHITHOPHEL'S SUICIDE

Because Ahithophel was a proud man and a highly respected advisor, when he saw that his counsel was not followed, he considered his career over. The record says that he put his house in order, then hanged himself.

ABSALOM PURSUES DAVID

Absalom now has gotten together a great army from all the tribes of Israel, and they pursue David.

> **Then David came to Mahanaim. And Absalom passed over Jordan, he and all the men of Israel with him.**
>
> **And Absalom made Amasa captain of the host instead of Joab: which Amasa was a man's son, whose name was Ithra an Israelite, that went in to Abigail the daughter of Nahash, sister to Zeruiah Joab's mother.**
>
> **So Israel and Absalom pitched in the land of Gilead [2 Sam. 17:24–26].**

David spent a great deal of his life running from somebody. In this instance, of course, it is indirectly because of his own sin.

David is actually in a very difficult position. He had fled Jerusalem without any preparation whatsoever. Those who were loyal to him had fled with him.

> **And it came to pass, when David was come to Mahanaim, that Shobi the son of Nahash of Rabbah of the children of Ammon, and Machir the son of Ammiel of Lodebar, and Barzillai the Gileadite of Rogelim,**
>
> **Brought beds, and basins, and earthen vessels, and wheat, and barley, and**

flour, and parched corn, and beans, and lentiles, and parched pulse,

And honey, and butter, and sheep, and cheese of kine, for David, and for the people that were with him, to eat: for they said, The people is hungry, and weary, and thirsty, in the wilderness [2 Sam. 17:27–29].

David finds that he has many allies in the people round about. They know David and the warrior that he is. The rulers of these kingdoms probably have very little confidence in Absalom, knowing he is deceitful and tricky. He would not be dependable. They do, however, have confidence in David. Therefore, they bring supplies to David and his men to ease their hardship.

Absalom's delay enables David to get supplies from his allies and ready his troops for combat.

CIVIL WAR

And David numbered the people that were with him, and set captains of thousands and captains of hundreds over them.

And David sent forth a third part of the people under the hand of Joab, and a third part under the hand of Abishai the son of Zeruiah, Joab's brother, and a third part under the hand of Ittai the Gittite. And the king said unto the people, I will surely go forth with you myself also [2 Sam. 18:1–2].

David wanted to go into battle with his men.

But the people answered, Thou shalt not go forth: for if we flee away, they will not care for us; neither if half of us die, will they care for us: but now thou art worth ten thousand of us: therefore now it is better that thou succour us out of the city [2 Sam. 18:3].

The army refused to let David go into battle.

And the king said unto them, What seemeth you best I will do. And the king stood by the gate side, and all the people came out by hundreds and by thousands.

And the king commanded Joab and Abishai and Ittai, saying, Deal gently for my sake with the young man, even with Absalom. And all the people heard when the king gave all the captains charge concerning Absalom [2 Sam. 18:4–5].

This is one of the saddest chapters in David's life. While the chapter of David's sin is the most sordid chapter, this is the saddest because it records the death of his son Absalom. Because they have urged him not to go with them to battle, David takes his place at the side of the gate as the army marches out. It marches out under three leaders: Joab, Abishai, and Ittai. As each of these three captains comes by, David charges him to deal gently with his son. All the army heard him give this order. I think some smiled, but others felt a bit resentful. Absalom would always be a troublemaker, and they would like to eliminate him. David, however, loved his son and did not want him to die. He said to his commanders, "Deal gently with my boy Absalom." David's men heard what he said.

So the people went out into the field against Israel: and the battle was in the wood of Ephraim;

Where the people of Israel were slain before the servants of David, and there was there a great slaughter that day of twenty thousand men [2 Sam. 18:6–7].

This was a civil war. It was a terrible thing. We had a civil war in the United States, and we know the sadness of brother fighting brother. David was a strategist and a general, and Absalom did not have anyone in his group who could match David's ability or the ability of David's three captains. Therefore, the children of Israel lost the battle.

For the battle was there scattered over the face of all the country: and the wood devoured more people that day than the sword devoured [2 Sam. 18:8].

The troops of Absalom became entangled in the woods of Ephraim when they attempted to flee from David's army. They became bottled in; the forest became the cause of death for many of them rather than the sword. They had picked the wrong place to battle with David.

ABSALOM SLAIN BY JOAB

And Absalom met the servants of David. And Absalom rode upon a mule, and the mule went under the thick boughs of a great oak, and his head caught hold of the oak, and he was taken up between the heaven and the

earth; and the mule that was under him went away.

And a certain man saw it, and told Joab, and said, Behold, I saw Absalom hanged in an oak [2 Sam. 18:9–10].

Apparently Absalom's head got caught in the forks of an oak tree while he was riding his mule through the woods. He was fleeing, by the way; and, when he got caught in the tree, the mule kept right on going, leaving Absalom in quite a predicament. Under other circumstances this incident could be rather humorous. In this case it is not.

And Joab said unto the man that told him, And, behold, thou sawest him, and why didst thou not smite him there to the ground? and I would have given thee ten shekels of silver, and a girdle [2 Sam. 18:11].

This man is shocked that Joab would want the prince, the son of David, killed.

And the man said unto Joab, Though I should receive a thousand shekels of silver in mine hand, yet would I not put forth mine hand against the king's son: for in our hearing the king charged thee and Abishai and Ittai, saying, Beware that none touch the young man Absalom.

Otherwise I should have wrought falsehood against mine own life: for there is no matter hid from the king, and thou thyself wouldest have set thyself against me [2 Sam. 18:12–13].

The soldier said, "The king told us not to touch his son, and if I had done anything to him, you would have punished me yourself." But Joab did not have time to argue with him. He had a matter of business to take care of immediately.

Then said Joab, I may not tarry thus with thee. And he took three darts in his hand, and thrust them through the heart of Absalom, while he was yet alive in the midst of the oak.

And ten young men that bare Joab's armour compassed about and smote Absalom, and slew him.

And Joab blew the trumpet, and the people returned from pursuing after Israel: for Joab held back the people.

And they took Absalom, and cast him into a great pit in the wood, and laid a very great heap of stones upon him: and all Israel fled every one to his tent [2 Sam. 18:14–17].

When Absalom was dead, the rebellion was over. Joab had no right to kill Absalom, especially after David had given the command that he was not to be touched. However, he is weary of all the trouble Absalom has caused, and he knows that the death of this boy will end the rebellion.

Then said Ahimaaz the son of Zadok, Let me now run, and bear the king tidings, how that the LORD hath avenged him of his enemies.

And Joab said unto him, Thou shalt not bear tidings this day, but thou shalt bear tidings another day: but this day thou shalt bear no tidings, because the king's son is dead.

Then said Joab to Cushi, Go tell the king what thou hast seen. And Cushi bowed himself unto Joab, and ran.

Then said Ahimaaz the son of Zadok yet again to Joab, But howsoever, let me, I pray thee, also run after Cushi. And Joab said, Wherefore wilt thou run, my son, seeing that thou hast no tidings ready? [2 Sam. 18:19–22].

Joab was reluctant to let Ahimaaz bear the news of Absalom's death to David because he did not have all the necessary information to give the king.

DAVID MOURNS FOR ABSALOM

But howsoever, said he, let me run. And he said unto him, Run. Then Ahimaaz ran by the way of the plain, and overran Cushi.

And David sat between the two gates: and the watchman went up to the roof over the gate unto the wall, and lifted up his eyes, and looked, and behold a man running alone [2 Sam. 18:23–24].

This, now, is one of the most touching scenes in the Word of God. David is sitting in the gate of the city, anxiously waiting for word to be brought to him.

And the watchman cried, and told the king. And the king said, If he be alone, there is tidings in his mouth. And he came apace, and drew near.

And the watchman saw another man running: and the watchman called unto

the porter, and said, Behold another man running alone. And the king said, He also bringeth tidings.

And the watchman said, Me thinketh the running of the foremost is like the running of Ahimaaz the son of Zadok. And the king said, He is a good man, and cometh with good tidings.

And Ahimaaz called, and said unto the king, All is well. And he fell down to the earth upon his face before the king, and said, Blessed be the LORD thy God, which hath delivered up the men that lifted up their hand against my lord the king.

And the king said, Is the young man Absalom safe? And Ahimaaz answered, When Joab sent the king's servant, and me thy servant, I saw a great tumult, but I knew not what it was [2 Sam. 18:25–29].

David has but one question to ask Ahimaaz, "Is the young man Absalom safe?" But Ahimaaz did not have all of the necessary information to tell the king. He did not know that Absalom was dead. And, friend, there are many messengers running about today telling the human family that God says all is well—but all is *not* well. Man is a sinner. He needs a Savior. Man needs to know that the Son of God died on the cross for him. Man needs to be born again. Ahimaaz did not have the message that David should have received.

And, behold, Cushi came; and Cushi said, Tidings, my lord the king: for the LORD hath avenged thee this day of all them that rose up against thee [2 Sam. 18:31].

Notice that David's first question is about Absalom. His chief concern is not for who won the battle but for the safety of Absalom.

And the king said unto Cushi, Is the young man Absalom safe? And Cushi answered, The enemies of my lord the king, and all that rise against thee to do thee hurt, be as that young man is [2 Sam. 18:32].

Cushi has the correct information. He is gently telling David that Absalom is dead. Then follows David's mourning for his son. It is the most touching expression of grief in the Bible or in any other literature. It is at this point one feels like saying, "Lord, you have whipped David enough for his sin. Let up on your son David."

And the king was much moved, and went up to the chamber over the gate, and wept: and as he went, thus he said, O my son Absalom, my son, my son Absalom! would God I had died for thee, O Absalom, my son, my son! [2 Sam. 18:33].

CHAPTER 19

THEME: *David is restored to the throne*

JOAB REPROVES DAVID

The news of Absalom's death was a real heartbreak to David. He had a tender love for his son, and he was extremely grieved when the boy died. Why? There are several reasons. First of all, I do not think that David was sure about the salvation of Absalom. You will recall that when David's first son by Bathsheba was born, he became very sick, and David fasted and prayed for him. When David heard that the little boy was dead, he arose, bathed, went to the house of God to worship, and then was ready for a good dinner. His servants could not understand his action. He made it very clear to them when he said, "I am going to him some day. He will not return to me, but it will be a great day when I go to him." He knew where the little fellow was. When Absalom died, however, David's heart broke. Why? He was not sure of the young man's salvation; he was not sure where his son was. Frankly, I believe that David felt his son was not saved, and that is why he was so stricken with grief. Also, even though David was a great king, he was a poor father; I am sure David realized this. He never quite succeeded in being the father he should have been, and Absalom was evidence of this failure.

David also recognized that trouble had

come upon him because of the sin he had committed. God had told him that strife would never depart from his house because of it. That is exactly what happened, and from the time of Absalom's death I believe David was a broken man. I think part of his grief was due to his disappointment. He had really hoped that Absalom would succeed him to the throne. He did not like the idea of Absalom rebelling against him, but he did want him to be the next king.

David's grief was such that even Joab was disturbed by it and rebuked David for it.

And it was told Joab, Behold, the king weepeth and mourneth for Absalom.

And the victory that day was turned into mourning unto all the people: for the people heard say that day how the king was grieved for his son [2 Sam. 19:1–2].

It should have been a great day of victory and a day of rejoicing because the enemy was defeated. For David, however, it was not a victory at all. Instead, it was a time of grief and sorrow beyond expression.

And the people gat them by stealth that day into the city, as people being ashamed steal away when they flee in battle [2 Sam. 19:3].

David's army should have been rejoicing because they had won the battle. Instead they left the battlefield after the victory and retreated to Jerusalem as if they had been defeated. Why? Because Absalom was slain and it had broken the heart of David.

But the king covered his face, and the king cried with a loud voice, O my son Absalom, O Absalom, my son, my son! [2 Sam. 19:4].

My, how David loved this boy! What a tender expression this is. David had been such a poor father—he had handled things so badly—but he loved his son and was broken by his death.

Now Joab was responsible for Absalom's death. I am not sure that David ever really comprehended just how his son died. I am sure that he heard quite a few stories relating how it occurred, but David probably did not want to pursue it too far.

And Joab came into the house to the king, and said, Thou hast shamed this day the faces of all thy servants, which this day have saved thy life, and the lives of thy sons and of thy daughters, and the lives of thy wives, and the lives of thy concubines;

In that thou lovest thine enemies, and hatest thy friends. For thou hast declared this day, that thou regardest neither princes nor servants: for this day I perceive, that if Absalom had lived, and all we had died this day, then it had pleased thee well [2 Sam. 19:5–6].

Of course Joab is pushing this situation to the opposite extreme, but certainly David would have preferred others dying rather than Absalom; that is quite evident. Joab rebukes David because he is so grieved about the death of his son who had become his enemy and would have killed David given the opportunity.

DAVID IS RESTORED TO THE THRONE

Then the king arose, and sat in the gate. And they told unto all the people, saying, Behold, the king doth sit in the gate. And all the people came before the king: for Israel had fled every man to his tent [2 Sam. 19:8].

The people needed some rallying point now. Everyone was depressed. It was a bad state of affairs: the man who had led the rebellion had been slain but, instead of rejoicing, the people witnessed the greatest grief that David ever expressed. However, after Joab talked to the king, David went up to the gate to let his men know that he deeply appreciated their loyalty to him.

And all the people were at strife throughout all the tribes of Israel, saying, The king saved us out of the hand of our enemies, and he delivered us out of the hand of the Philistines; and now he is fled out of the land for Absalom.

And Absalom, whom we anointed over us, is dead in battle. Now therefore why speak ye not a word of bringing the king back? [2 Sam. 19:9–10].

What happened was simply this: there were those who had gone over to Absalom's side and now that he was dead, they didn't know what to do. They decided that the best thing was to bring the king back.

And king David sent to Zadok and to Abiathar the priests, saying, Speak unto the elders of Judah, saying, Why are ye the last to bring the king back to his house? seeing the speech of all Is-

rael is come to the king, even to his house [2 Sam. 19:11].

Apparently, even in the tribe of Judah, there had been a great defection to Absalom's side. Now David rebukes them for their action.

Ye are my brethren, ye are my bones and my flesh: wherefore then are ye the last to bring back the king?

And say ye to Amasa, Art thou not of my bone, and of my flesh? God do so to me, and more also, if thou be not captain of the host before me continually in the room of Joab.

And he bowed the heart of all the men of Judah, even as the heart of one man; so that they sent this word unto the king, Return thou, and all thy servants [2 Sam. 19:12–14].

It was a unanimous desire to return David to his throne.

So the king returned, and came to Jordan. And Judah came to Gilgal, to go to meet the king, to conduct the king over Jordan.

And Shimei the son of Gera, a Benjamite, which was of Bahurim, hasted and came down with the men of Judah to meet king David.

And there were a thousand men of Benjamin with him, and Ziba the servant of the house of Saul, and his fifteen sons and his twenty servants with him; and they went over Jordan before the king [2 Sam. 19:15–17].

Shimei had cursed David when he went out. Now he wants to be the first one to welcome the king back.

And there went over a ferry boat to carry over the king's household, and to do what he thought good. And Shimei the son of Gera fell down before the king, as he was come over Jordan;

And said unto the king, Let not my lord impute iniquity unto me, neither do thou remember that which thy servant did perversely the day that my lord the king went out of Jerusalem, that the king should take it to his heart.

For thy servant doth know that I have sinned: therefore, behold, I am come the first this day of all the house of Joseph to go down to meet my lord the king.

But Abishai the son of Zeruiah answered and said, Shall not Shimei be put to death for this, because he cursed the LORD's anointed? [2 Sam. 19:18–21].

David was a generous fellow. He was a man who could forgive.

And David said, What have I to do with you, ye sons of Zeruiah, that ye should this day be adversaries unto me? shall there any man be put to death this day in Israel? for do not I know that I am this day king over Israel? [2 Sam. 19:22].

David is saying, "Why should I pay attention to this fellow? I know I am the king of Israel." David is satisfied that God has restored him to this position. "Why should I worry about a little fellow like Shimei? Why should I put him to death? What he thinks doesn't amount to anything." There are many Christians today who let little things bother them. They let little people bother them, and they should not. Is God blessing you, my friend? Perhaps you are a discouraged pastor. Are you having trouble with your board of deacons? Are you having problems with a troublemaker? My friend, forget it. You are serving God. God is on your side. Live above that small irritation and serve the Lord—and make sure that is what you are doing. Forget about the other things; we need to live above them.

Therefore the king said unto Shimei, Thou shalt not die. And the king sware unto him [2 Sam. 19:23].

David's final decision concerning Shimei was that he did not intend to punish him. In fact, David did not intend to deal with this man in any way.

And Mephibosheth the son of Saul came down to meet the king, and had neither dressed his feet, nor trimmed his beard, nor washed his clothes, from the day the king departed until the day he came again in peace [2 Sam. 19:24].

Mephibosheth, in deep appreciation to David, would not join in the rebellion. He remained loyal to David, and during all this time he fasted and prayed for the king. It is wonderful to have friends like that, is it not?

And it came to pass, when he was come to Jerusalem to meet the king, that the

king said unto him, Wherefore wentest not thou with me, Mephibosheth?

And he answered, My lord, O king, my servant deceived me: for thy servant said, I will saddle me an ass, that I may ride thereon, and go to the king; because thy servant is lame.

And he hath slandered thy servant unto my lord the king; but my lord the king is as an angel of God: do therefore what is good in thine eyes.

For all of my father's house were but dead men before my lord the king: yet didst thou set thy servant among them that did eat at thine own table. What right therefore have I yet to cry any more unto the king? [2 Sam. 19:25–28].

Mephibosheth tells David, "If you think I have betrayed you, then do to me as you please. I have no right to ask any other favor of you at all."

And the king said unto him, Why speakest thou any more of thy matters? I have said, Thou and Ziba divide the land.

And Mephibosheth said unto the king, Yea, let him take all, forasmuch as my lord the king is come again in peace unto his own house [2 Sam. 19:29–30].

This, I feel, proves Mephibosheth's sincerity.

And Barzillai the Gileadite came down from Rogelim, and went over Jordan with the king, to conduct him over Jordan.

Now Barzillai was a very aged man, even fourscore years old: and he had provided the king of sustenance while he lay at Mahanaim; for he was a very great man [2 Sam. 19:31–32].

Barzillai the Gileadite was a patriarch from another nation who had been generous to David and had given him sustenance during the rebellion. Now David wanted this man to go back to Jerusalem with him so he could reward him for his generosity.

And the king said unto Barzillai, Come thou over with me, and I will feed thee with me in Jerusalem.

And Barzillai said unto the king, How long have I to live, that I should go up with the king unto Jerusalem? [2 Sam. 19:33–34].

Barzillai said to David, "I have not many more years. I have had my threescore and ten, and ten more. I know my days are numbered, and I would just as soon stay home. I appreciate your generous offer of going and living in a palace, but I have reached the age where things like that do not tempt me at all."

I am this day fourscore years old: and can I discern between good and evil? can thy servant taste what I eat or what I drink? can I hear any more the voice of singing men and singing women? wherefore then should thy servant be yet a burden unto my lord the king? [2 Sam. 19:35].

Barzillai continues, "I am an old man. I can't hear the music anymore. Food does not taste like it once did. I don't want to come and mar the party. I don't want to be the one to slow down the king and his enjoyment."

Thy servant will go a little way over Jordan with the king: and why should the king recompense it me with such a reward? [2 Sam. 19:36].

Barzillai helped David because he knew David was God's man. He had confidence in the king. This was his motivation to assist David.

It is too bad that David had not been a little more forgiving with his own son. When Absalom sinned and came back, it might have been different if he had completely forgiven the boy. If he had received him like the father received the Prodigal Son by putting his arms around him, placing a robe on him, and killing the calf for a feast, I believe David would have spared himself the awful rebellion which took place.

CHAPTERS 20–22

***THEME:** Revolt, vengeance, and famine within the kingdom: war with the Philistines outside the kingdom*

Chapter 20 is the record of another revolt against David. After all the troubles that have come to David, you would think the Lord would let up on him; but, as He promised, the sword will not depart from the house of David. Through all of this we do not hear a whimper from David. He recognizes it as the just punishment of his sin.

Seemingly as a result of the petty jealousy of the men of Israel—because they had not been consulted in returning David to the throne—another revolt errupts, led by Sheba of the tribe of Benjamin.

SHEBA LEADS A REVOLT

And there happened to be there a man of Belial, whose name was Sheba, the son of Bichri, a Benjamite: and he blew a trumpet, and said, We have no part in David, neither have we inheritance in the son of Jesse: every man to his tents, O Israel [2 Sam. 20:1].

Sheba is called "a man of Belial," which means he is a rabble-rouser.

So every man of Israel went up from after David, and followed Sheba the son of Bichri: but the men of Judah clave unto their king, from Jordan even to Jerusalem [2 Sam. 20:2].

It is amazing how faithless and undependable the children of Israel were. Some people might say, "Well, that was a crude day before man was developed and civilized." I would like to ask those people a question. Do you think things are any better today? It is interesting that the president of this country, or any public official, can make some little statement that should not have been said and, when a poll is taken, they find out that his popularity has so diminished that he cannot be elected to office again. This can happen to any officeholder regardless of his party affiliation. That proves just how fickle the mob can be; it shows how fickle all of us are. God knows our hearts. Jeremiah 17:9 says, "The heart is deceitful above all things, and desperately wicked: who can know it?" Whose heart is this verse speaking about? The heart of a brutal dictator? No. It is speaking about your heart and mine. Wicked things are in the human heart. The apostle Paul could say in Romans 7:18, "For I know that in me (that is, in my flesh,) dwelleth no good thing: for to will is present with me; but how to perform that which is good I find not."

The ten tribes of Israel followed Sheba in his rebellion.

And David came to his house at Jerusalem; and the king took the ten women his concubines, whom he had left to keep the house, and put them in ward, and fed them, but went not in unto them. So they were shut up unto the day of their death, living in widowhood [2 Sam. 20:3].

These are the women, you remember, that Absalom had taken.

Then said the king to Amasa, Assemble me the men of Judah within three days, and be thou here present [2 Sam. 20:4].

Amasa, you may recall, was the captain of the rebel forces under Absalom. According to 2 Samuel 17:25 and 1 Chronicles 2:17, Amasa is the son of Abigail, a sister of David. This would make him a cousin of Absalom. After the defeat of the rebels under Amasa and the death of Absalom, David made Amasa captain of his army in the place of Joab.

So Amasa went to assemble the men of Judah: but he tarried longer than the set time which he had appointed him.

And David said to Abishai, Now shall Sheba the son of Bichri do us more harm than did Absalom: take thou thy lord's servants, and pursue after him, lest he get him fenced cities, and escape us.

And there went out after him Joab's men, and the Cherethites, and the Pelethites, and all the mighty men: and they went out of Jerusalem, to pursue after Sheba the son of Bichri [2 Sam. 20:5–7].

In other words, this man Amasa is not moving. So Joab leads the army in pursuit of the rebel, Sheba. Also Joab brutally slays Amasa, apparently believing he also is a traitor to David.

The chapter concludes with Joab continuing after the rebel, Sheba. When Sheba sought refuge in the city of Abel, and the army was preparing to attack the city to get him, a wise woman intervened. Sheba is slain by the people of Abel. This, of course, ends the rebellion. However, it does not end the troubles of David, as we shall see.

Through all of these trials David is not crying aloud, nor is he whimpering. He knows that the Lord is dealing with him in the woodshed. Don't think that David got by with his sin, friend. He was severely punished. However, David loved God. Underneath the faith that failed was a faith that never failed. That's David, God's man, a man after God's own heart.

FAMINE FOR THREE YEARS

Chapter 21 opens with a period of famine in the land of Israel.

Then there was a famine in the days of David three years, year after year; and David inquired of the Lord. And the Lord answered, It is for Saul, and for his bloody house, because he slew the Gibeonites [2 Sam. 21:1].

The reason God gives for the famine is rather strange, but in it there is a lesson for us.

THE GIBEONITES TAKE VENGEANCE ON THE HOUSE OF SAUL

And the king called the Gibeonites, and said unto them; (now the Gibeonites were not of the children of Israel, but of the remnant of the Amorites; and the children of Israel had sworn unto them: and Saul sought to slay them in his zeal to the children of Israel and Judah.)

Wherefore David said unto the Gibeonites, What shall I do for you? and wherewith shall I make the atonement, that ye may bless the inheritance of the Lord?

And the Gibeonites said unto him, We will have no silver nor gold of Saul, nor of his house; neither for us shalt thou kill any man in Israel. And he said, What ye shall say, that will I do for you.

And they answered the king, The man that consumed us, and that devised against us that we should be destroyed from remaining in any of the coasts of Israel,

Let seven men of his sons be delivered unto us, and we will hang them up unto the Lord in Gibeah of Saul, whom the Lord did choose. And the king said, I will give them.

But the king spared Mephibosheth, the son of Jonathan the son of Saul, because of the Lord's oath that was between them, between David and Jonathan the son of Saul [2 Sam. 21:2–7].

This is quite a remarkable passage of Scripture. To understand it we must go back to the days of Joshua when the Gibeonites deceived him and Joshua made a treaty with them (Josh. 9). Israel had been told by God not to make a treaty with anyone.

A treaty in that day (which some folk consider "uncivilized") was inviolate. When a treaty was made, the terms of the treaty were kept. Treaties were more than a scrap of paper. They were not made to be broken. In our day this matter of nations sitting around the conference table trying to make a treaty is almost laughable, because who will keep it? The average person has a right to be cynical about the way nations attempt to get along with each other. But when a nation is obeying God, its word is as good as its bond. Joshua made a treaty with the Gibeonites; but Saul came along and broke it. David attempted to make amends for Saul's actions, and he succeeded.

But the other side of the coin is interesting. God did not forget that Saul, representing Israel, had broken the treaty with the Gibeonites. Because the Israelites are His people, they are not going to get by with it. The three years of famine came upon them as a judgment. Now let me make this kind of an application to this incident, which I think is valid. You and I live in a day when it cannot be said that any particular nation is a Christian nation or a nation in obedience to God. But God does deal with nations; he does judge nations. God holds nations responsible—it does not make any difference what nation it is. God judged Egypt. God judged Babylon. God judged Assyria, Greece, and Rome; and God will judge America. I am of the opinion (and will you follow me now very carefully) that we are in the process of dissolution as a nation. There are several evidences of God's judgment upon us. Let me mention several things.

Since World War II it has been our intention to be a peacemaking nation yet to live in sin. Believe me, friend, after World War II Americans started plunging into sin. Also, we could not quit fighting. There has not been a moment since World War II that our troops have not been fighting somewhere. If it isn't Korea, it is Vietnam. If it isn't Vietnam, it is in Europe or on some other continent. We are talking peace today as we have never talked it before; yet there is no peace. Isaiah 57:21 says, "There is no peace, saith my God, to the wicked."

Another indication of this dissolution is that we have no great statesmen today. I recognize that there are quite a few of our boys in Washington who think that they are clever—and this type of thinking is not confined to any one party. Apparently they all feel that they could solve the problems of the world. Actually, it is rather pitiful to see this nation without great leaders. This is another evidence of God's judgment. Do you remember what God said in Isaiah 3:12? "As for my people, children are their oppressors, and women rule over them. O my people, they which lead thee cause thee to err, and destroy the way of thy paths." We see a continual movement in this direction in our own nation.

Right here in Southern California we have become the center of pornography. Also many of the "cults" and the "isms" originate in Southern California. Not long ago God gave us quite a shaking. I am of the opinion that the earthquake was a judgment of God. Now I know that there is a scientific explanation for the earthquake. Beneath us is the San Andreas fault, and we have several other faults. In fact, we have a whole lot of faults out here! I believe God is beginning to judge America. America is guilty of lawlessness and gross immorality, and God judges nations for that. If there is one thing 2 Samuel 21 reveals, it is the fact that God judges nations.

WAR WITH THE PHILISTINES

Next we find that David is engaged in continual warfare with the Philistines.

Moreover the Philistines had yet war again with Israel; and David went down, and his servants with him, and fought against the Philistines: and David waxed faint.

And Ishbi-benob, which was of the sons of the giant, the weight of whose spear weighed three hundred shekels of brass in weight, he being girded with a new sword, thought to have slain David.

But Abishai the son of Zeruiah succoured him, and smote the Philistine, and killed him. Then the men of David sware unto him, saying, Thou shalt go no more out with us to battle, that thou quench not the light of Israel [2 Sam. 21:15–17].

David is a great man, and his men know that there is no one to take his place. Now David is getting to be an old man, when he goes out to battle, he finds he does not have the stamina he used to have. He is easily overcome—that is an unusual experience for David! The leaders of Israel see that David is too old to engage in battle, and they tell him so. They tell him that he is needed more at home than on the battlefield.

A great battle took place, and God gave the victory to Israel.

These four were born to the giant in Gath, and fell by the hand of David, and by the hand of his servants [2 Sam. 21:22].

The giant spoken of in this verse was Goliath. You will recall that when David went out to meet Goliath he took five smooth stones. I have heard it described vividly that because David thought he might miss the first shot, he had some stones in reserve. Those who teach the story that way say that the lesson for us is that we, too, should have a reserve. However, the explanation is that Goliath had four sons. They were part of the Philistine army. David knew that when he slew the giant the four sons might want to come out and fight him. Although David did not have this experience at that time, of course the sons would want revenge. If Abishai had not come to David's aid in this his final battle with the Philistines, one of Goliath's sons, Ishbi-benob, would have had his revenge.

However, when David was a young man fighting Goliath, he had four other stones and was ready to take on Goliath's four sons. He was deadly accurate with the slingshot. He probably practiced several hours each day. I imagine he could put a stone in the hollow of a tree that was not big enough even for a squirrel to crawl into.

This chapter concludes David's career as a warrior. In a marvelous way, God has delivered David from all his enemies.

DAVID'S SONG OF DELIVERANCE

In chapter 22 we have the song David sings after God has delivered him from his enemies. It is the same as Psalm 18.

And David spake unto the LORD the words of this song in the day that the LORD had delivered him out of the

hand of all his enemies, and out of the hand of Saul [2 Sam. 22:1].

This is a song that David composed, apparently, at the end of his life. As he looked back over his life, he could see how the hand of God had moved and brought him to the place of old age. I believe he composed Psalm 23 about the same time, because at this time of his life he could say, "The LORD is my Shepherd; I *shall* not want." Paul put it this way, "Being confident of this very thing, that he which hath begun a good work in you will perform it until the day of Jesus Christ" (Phil. 1:6). God has brought you up to this moment, friend; why in the world do you think He is going to let you down now? God's loving care for David in the past gives him confidence in the future.

And he said, The LORD is my rock, and my fortress, and my deliverer;

The God of my rock; in him will I trust: he is my shield, and the horn of my salvation, my high tower, and my refuge, my saviour; thou savest me from violence [2 Sam. 22:2–3].

"The LORD is my rock." A rock is a place upon which to rest. Christ is the rock of our salvation—He is the foundation. We rest on Him. "And my fortress." That is for protection in life. "And my deliverer." He will deliver us in the time of temptation. "The God of my rock." The Lord is not only my rock, but He is the God of my rock, that is, of my faith. He is the object of my faith. "In him will I trust: he is my shield." He protects me from the enemy. "And the horn of my salvation." He is the One in whom I rest for salvation. He is "my high tower." That is where I go to view the land. He is my vision. "My refuge, my saviour." He is the One "who savest me from violence."

We are living in a day when we do not have anything that corresponds to genius in the way of writing. There is no great vision today. In our scientific age everything is run by computers. Everything is already taped. We know that two plus two equals four, but we don't seem to produce anything really original. How monotonous life is when God is left out of it. In contrast, David recognized God in all the experiences of his life, and his poetic expression of gratitude is a masterpiece of literature.

Thou hast also given me the shield of thy salvation: and thy gentleness hath made me great [2 Sam. 22:36].

David was a rough and rugged man. He was hotheaded. But God is gentle, and David's love for and association with God had quieted him. It had made David a gracious man: "Thy gentleness hath made me great." You and I need to associate more with God. My, how men need God in this hour in which we are now living!

This is a great psalm. David's psalms are wonderful. They open the heart. They open up the mind. They open up life. They let you live, friend. We hear so much about people wanting to "live." We have comforts and gadgets galore today. Many young people are growing up in homes of affluence where they have every comfort. Many leave all of that and go out and live as vagrants. They say it is because they want to *live.* Well, my friend, "things" won't enable you to live. Running off and throwing away all the bands and cords with which God has bound us will not enable us to live either. It is only when we come into a right relationship with God that we are enabled to really live.

Second Samuel 22 is a great psalm, one which David composed as he looked back over his life. Also, when we come to Psalm 23, you will find that I take the position it was not written by a little immature boy. Psalm 23 was not written by a college student who didn't really know what life was all about. Neither was it written by a middle-aged man who had ambition to get to the top in business or politics. It was not written by someone who wanted to become famous. Psalm 23 was written by an old king who looked back upon his life and could trace the hand of God moving in it. David was a man who had tasted everything. There was nothing that the world afforded that David had not tasted, my friend. David's conclusion was that the most wonderful thing of all was, "The LORD is my shepherd."

This beautiful song of praise is not only great literature, it opens new vistas for us and lets us see something that is much more glorious than a sunset or the rising of the moon. It speaks of the marvelous relationship one man had with the almighty God. How we need that today!

CHAPTER 23

***THEME:** David's last words; David's mighty men*

DAVID'S LAST WORDS

Now these be the last words of David. David the son of Jesse said, and the man who was raised up on high, the anointed of the God of Jacob, and the sweet psalmist of Israel, said [2 Sam. 23:1].

David was "the son of Jesse." Jesse was a peasant, a farmer in Bethlehem—David was never ashamed of that. God lifted David "up on high"; He placed him with the great men of the world. David was the "anointed of the God of Jacob." The same God who took that clever, conniving fellow Jacob and made him *Israel*, a prince with God, is the same God who took David and put him on the throne. He is the same God who saved me and the same God who saved you. He is gracious, good, and loving. Oh, my friend, how wonderful is our God!

David was also "the sweet psalmist of Israel." He was a musician: he wrote music, he played music, and he loved to hear music. I share David's love for music although I have no talent for reproducing music in any form. But I appreciate *good* music. I don't care for what we call "rock" music—in fact, to me it is not even music. I deeply regret that this type of music is being brought into the church. Good music, elevating music, music that thrills the soul has always contributed something beautiful to man's worship of his God.

The spirit of the LORD spake by me, and his word was in my tongue [2 Sam. 23:2].

The Spirit of God came upon David, and that is the way he wrote his psalms. Peter tells us that that is the way men wrote the Old Testament. "Knowing this first, that no prophecy of the scripture is of any private interpretation. For the prophecy came not in old time by the will of man: but holy men of God spake as they were moved by the Holy Ghost" (2 Pet. 1:20–21).

The God of Israel said, the Rock of Israel spake to me, He that ruleth over men must be just, ruling in the fear of God [2 Sam. 23:3].

It is obvious that the decisions made in our government today—regardless of the party—are not made "in the fear of God." They are made in fear of the voters. There is little effort being made to please God in our government. I wish it could be said that the United States of America is a Christian nation. It is not.

I was rather amused by the comments being made by some men who were out of work because of a decision made in Washington by the Senate. Each man who was out of work said, "I voted for that man because he said he was going to vote for this project, and he voted against it." Well, all the politician wanted was to be elected to office. He didn't care anything about the men and their project. We need men who will rule in the fear of God and, until we get them, we are going to have corruption in high places.

And he shall be as the light of the morning, when the sun riseth, even a morning without clouds; as the tender grass springing out of the earth by clear shining after rain [2 Sam. 23:4].

This is one of the more remarkable statements David ever made. You will recall that I said 2 Samuel 7 was one of the great chapters of the Bible. In that chapter God made a covenant with David. The Davidic covenant, upon which the future kingdom of Christ was to be founded, provided for David the promise of posterity in his house, a royal throne of authority, and a kingdom on earth established forever. God promised that the Messiah would come through the Davidic line. He is the same One promised to Eve in the Garden of Eden. He is the same One promised to Abraham, Isaac, and Jacob. He is the One whom Moses talked about. Joshua also spoke of Him. Now God's covenant with David concerns Him.

Although my house be not so with God; yet he hath made with me an everlasting covenant, ordered in all things, and sure: for this is all my salvation, and all my desire, although he make it not to grow [2 Sam. 23:5].

What David is saying is simply this: "My house is not worthy of this. We did not receive this by merit. It did not come because of who I am." If David had gotten his just deserts, God would never have made a covenant with him. Neither would God have saved you or me if it had been on the basis of merit. And yet

He made an everlasting covenant with David. God has made a covenant with us, too. It is recorded in John 3:16: "For God so loved the world, that he gave his only begotten Son, that whosoever believeth in him should not perish, but have everlasting life." Now I hold on to that. God has made that covenant. I never asked Him to make it. He did not make it because of who we are. He did not wait for you or me to make a suggestion. He did it 1900 years ago. He said, "Here it is; take it or leave it." I take it, by the way. I rest upon that. David said that his covenant was "ordered in all things, and sure." Friend, you can depend upon God. David says, "This is all my salvation." Well, God's covenant with me is my salvation. It is what I desire, friend. It should be the desire of every believer's heart, "although he made it not to grow."

DAVID'S MIGHTY MEN

Next we are given a catalog of David's mighty men.

These be the names of the mighty men whom David had: The Tachmonite that sat in the seat, chief among the captains; the same was Adino the Eznite: he lift up his spear against eight hundred, whom he slew at one time [2 Sam. 23:8].

These men, you will recall, came to David during the time that he was in exile. When David was being driven by Saul, he was an outcast, hunted like a partridge. He had to hide in the dens of the earth. It was during this time that those who were in distress came to him. They were persecuted and oppressed by Saul, and they fled to David. Others also came to him: those who had gotten into debt and could not pay, those who were discontented, and those who were bitter of soul. In this same way men come to Christ. They are in distress. According to their letters, many young rebels were once in distress. They write to me and tell me about their experiences with the Lord. They came to Christ with debts of sin, and He cancelled those debts. Are you discontented with life? If you are living a fulfilling life and doing all right, I guess I don't have any message for you at all. But if you are discontented down deep in your soul, and you want to be saved and have fellowship with God, come to Christ. He will remove your guilt and give you satisfaction in your life.

These men who came to David were outstanding men in many ways. They did many remarkable things. Let us look at a few of them.

And after him was Shammah the son of Agee the Hararite. And the Philistines were gathered together into a troop, where was a piece of ground full of lentiles: and the people fled from the Philistines.

But he stood in the midst of the ground, and defended it, and slew the Philistines: and the LORD wrought a great victory [2 Sam. 23:11–12].

Defending a patch of lentils may not seem very important, but Israel needed the food. It was the custom of the Philistines to wait until an Israelite's crop was ready to harvest, then they would come ravaging, plundering, and robbing. This year, as usual, everyone ran when they came—except one man, Shammah. He stopped, drew his sword, and defended it. One man against a troop of Philistines! "And the LORD wrought a great victory."

And three of the thirty chief went down, and came to David in the harvest time unto the cave of Adullam: and the troop of the Philistines pitched in the valley of Rephaim.

And David was then in an hold, and the garrison of the Philistines was then in Beth-lehem.

And David longed, and said, Oh that one would give me drink of the water of the well of Beth-lehem, which is by the gate [2 Sam. 23:13–15].

David was brought up in Bethlehem, and he thought about the refreshing water from the well there. I know how David felt. I was raised in a little town in Texas. My dad built our house and dug our well. The water was "gyp" water. A few years ago I went back to that place. I could hardly wait to get a drink of that water. I lay down on the ground by the faucet by the well and lapped up that water. My, it was delicious! I was raised on it. It took me back to my boyhood. Now David longed for water from the well at Bethlehem. He never gave a command to anybody to go and get him water, but three of his mighty men broke through the Philistine lines to get it for him. That is the way they became mighty men.

I think of the command that the Lord Jesus gave in Matthew 28:19–20 to go into all the world and preach the Gospel. Then I think back in the past to the men who broke through the enemy lines and took the Gospel to those who needed to hear. Think of the pioneer missionaries—I don't like to mention just one man, but think of men like the apostle Paul or Martin Luther. A great company of missionaries followed after them, and they have been breaking through the enemy lines ever since and getting out the Word of God. These are mighty men of David's greater Son, the Lord Jesus Christ.

Here is another of David's mighty men.

And Benaiah the son of Jehoiada, the son of a valiant man, of Kabzeel, who had done many acts, he slew two lion-like men of Moab: he went down also and slew a lion in the midst of a pit in time of snow:

And he slew an Egyptian, a goodly man: and the Egyptian had a spear in his hand; but he went down to him with a staff, and plucked the spear out of the Egyptian's hand, and slew him with his own spear.

These things did Benaiah the son of Jehoiada, and had the name among three mighty men [2 Sam. 23:20–22].

I love this one. This fellow slew a lion. That is not an easy thing to do, and he did it when there was snow on the ground. I know a lot of people who won't even come to church when there is a little rain on the sidewalk. May I say to you, they could not have much fellowship with a man like Benaiah. He was out there when there was snow on the ground. He was a tremendous man.

Uriah the Hittite: thirty and seven in all [2 Sam. 23:39].

Uriah the Hittite was one of David's mighty men. This is the man he sent to the front lines to be killed. This is the blot on the escutcheon of David.

CHAPTER 24

THEME: *David's sin in taking a census*

David commits another sin in taking a census. By now he should trust God instead of numbers. God again punishes David but permits him to choose his punishment. David casts himself upon the mercy of God. God sends a pestilence. David buys Araunah's threshing floor on which to rear an altar to God. David's refusal to accept it as a gift reveals his deep dedication and devotion to God. This spot became the place where Solomon erected the temple. Although the Mosque of Omar stands there today, Israel will sometime in the future build again a temple to the Lord God of Israel on that spot.

THE CENSUS

Actually, there are many who would not label this a sin. I call this another sin in the life of David. In God's sight, David's numbering the people was just as bad as his other sins. When you are guilty of breaking one part of the Law, you are guilty of all. His actions evidenced a lack of trust in God.

And again the anger of the LORD was kindled against Israel, and he moved David against them to say, Go, number Israel and Judah.

For the king said to Joab the captain of the host, which was with him, Go now through all the tribes of Israel, from Dan even to Beer-sheba, and number ye the people, that I may know the number of the people [2 Sam. 24:1–2].

At the beginning God had instructed David to number the people. God wanted it done in order to encourage David and to strengthen him. God wanted him to know that there was a great army behind him.

Friend, faith is not a leap in the dark. It is not a gamble. Faith is not even a "hope so." Faith is a sure thing. God never asks you to believe something that is not true. Faith rests upon a rock, a sure foundation. The Lord Jesus Christ is the foundation. Faith, therefore, is not just leaping out into space.

However, there is a time in your life, my friend, when you need to live and move by faith and to recognize that you cannot live by your own effort or by numbers. Unfortunately, the church today has not learned to trust God. As a result, at the congregational meetings the spiritual victories are never mentioned. The things that are mentioned are how much we have in the treasury, how many we baptized this year, and how many members we took in. If the figures look pretty good, we consider that it is a great spiritual victory. Actually, it might have been the worst thing in the world that could have happened in that church.

David sins in numbering the people at this time. Why? He now is an old king. David knows that God has put a foundation beneath him, and he knows that he can overcome the enemy. He does not need to number the people at all. I sometimes think that the curse of the church today is to have a fellow in it who is always figuring up something, always putting it down in black and white, but knows nothing about the spiritual victory that should be taking place. That is what David does here.

And David's heart smote him after that he had numbered the people. And David said unto the LORD, I have sinned greatly in that I have done: and now, I beseech thee, O LORD, take away the iniquity of thy servant; for I have done very foolishly.

For when David was up in the morning, the word of the LORD came unto the prophet Gad, David's seer, saying,

Go and say unto David, Thus saith the LORD, I offer thee three things; choose thee one of them, that I may do it unto thee.

So Gad came to David, and told him, and said unto him, Shall seven years of famine come unto thee in thy land? or wilt thou flee three months before thine enemies, while they pursue thee? or that there be three days' pestilence in thy land? now advise, and see what answer I shall return to him that sent me [2 Sam. 24:10–13].

God gives David a choice of punishment. David's answer to the Lord is remarkable. It reveals that he is a man who knows how to trust God. I have said it before, and I will say it again: David failed, it is true; he committed sin, but down beneath the faith that failed was a faith that never failed. Basically David did trust God, as his answer to Gad reveals.

And David said unto Gad, I am in a great strait: let us fall now into the hand of the LORD; for his mercies are great: and let me not fall into the hand of man [2 Sam. 24:14].

God gave David a choice of three punishments. He told David to choose one of them. David did not choose any of them. Instead he told the Lord that he did not want to fall into the hands of a man. That is one of the things that I have always prayed in my ministry: "O God, never put me in a position where I am subject to a man, or men." Fortunately, as I look back on my ministry, God never put me in the position where I had to lick shoe leather. I feel sorry today for some men in the ministry who have to go around licking shoe leather in order to continue. God have mercy on them! David did not want to be subject to man. He was willing to fall into the hands of God because he knew how to trust God. How wonderful it is when you see David doing this. The Lord decided to send a pestilence upon Israel. David knew he would be all right in the hands of God. This is the way you and I should feel when God punishes us.

My friend, those whom the Lord loves, He disciplines. From experience I can tell you that there is a tenderness in His discipline, there is a comfort in it all, and there is a blessing in it. He alone can wipe away the tears. He alone can bind up the broken-hearted. He alone can heal the wounds that are in the heart. The doctor can sew you up when you have been in an accident, but in great emotional accidents only the Lord Jesus can bind you up and put you together again. How we need Him today in our lives!

DAVID BUYS THE THRESHINGFLOOR OF ARAUNAH

Now we come to the last part of this book. David wants to build a temple for the Lord.

And Gad came that day to David, and said unto him, Go up, rear an altar unto the LORD in the threshingfloor of Araunah the Jebusite [2 Sam. 24:18].

Notice that Araunah was a Jebusite, not an Israelite.

And David, according to the saying of Gad, went up as the LORD commanded.

And Araunah looked, and saw the king and his servants coming on toward him: and Araunah went out, and bowed himself before the king on his face upon the ground.

And Araunah said, Wherefore is my lord the king come to his servant? And David said, To buy the threshingfloor of thee, to build an altar unto the LORD, that the plague may be stayed from the people [2 Sam. 24:19–21].

David explains his reason for wanting the threshingfloor.

And Araunah said unto David, Let my lord the king take and offer up what seemeth good unto him: behold, here be oxen for burnt sacrifice, and threshing instruments and other instruments of the oxen for wood.

All these things did Araunah, as a king, give unto the king. And Araunah said unto the king, The LORD thy God accept thee.

And the king said unto Araunah, Nay; but I will surely buy it of thee at a price: neither will I offer burnt offerings unto the LORD my God of that which doth cost me nothing. So David bought the threshingfloor and the oxen for fifty shekels of silver [2 Sam. 24:22–24].

It is a noble thing that David does. Oh, that God's people would learn this lesson! Some folk feel that we should not mention finances in God's work today. I recognize that there is an overemphasis on money, but consider what David did. Araunah wanted to *give* David the threshingfloor. David said, "You can't give it to me. I am going to pay for it." Why? David continued, "Neither will I offer burnt offerings unto the LORD my God of that which doth cost me nothing." God have mercy on folk today who are taking a spiritual free ride. My friend, pay your way, and God will honor and bless you. This action of David's is heart-searching. Are we attempting to give to God that which costs us nothing? God forgive us for being niggardly with Him. May we give as David gave—David, the man after God's own heart.

BIBLIOGRAPHY

(Recommended for Further Study)

Crockett, William Day. *A Harmony of the Books of Samuel, Kings and Chronicles.* Grand Rapids, Michigan: Baker Book House, 1959.

Darby, J. N. *Synposis of the Books of the Bible.* Addison, Illinois: Bible Truth Publishers, n.d.

David, John J. and Whitcomb, John C., Jr. *A History of Israel.* Grand Rapids, Michigan: Baker Book House, 1970. (Excellent.)

Epp, Theodore H. *David.* Lincoln, Nebraska: Back to the Bible Broadcast, 1965.

Gaebelein, Arno C. *The Annotated Bible.* Neptune, New Jersey: Loizeaux Brothers, 1917.

Gray, James M. *Synthetic Bible Studies.* Westwood, New Jersey: Fleming H. Revell Co., 1906.

Jensen, Irving L. *I and II Samuel.* Chicago, Illinois: Moody Press, 1968. (A self-study guide.)

Laney, J. Carl. *I & II Samuel.* Chicago, Illinois: Moody Press, 1982.

Kelly, William. *Lectures on the Earlier Historical Books of the Old Testament.* Addison, Illinois: Bible Truth Publishers, 1874.

Knapp, Christopher. *The Kings of Israel and Judah.* Neptune, New Jersey: Loizeaux Brothers, 1908. (Very fine.)

Meyer, F. B. *David: Shepherd, Psalmist, King.* Fort Washington, Pennsylvania: Christian Literature Crusade, n.d. (Devotional.)

Meyer, F. B. *Samuel the Prophet.* Fort Washington, Pennsylvania: Christian Literature Crusade, n.d. (Devotional.)

Sauer, Erich. *The Dawn of World Redemption.* Grand Rapids, Michigan: Wm. B.

Eerdmans Publishing Co., 1951. (An excellent Old Testament survey.)

Scroggie, W. Graham. *The Unfolding Drama of Redemption*. Grand Rapids, Michigan: Zondervan Publishing House, 1970. (An excellent survey and outline of the Old Testament.)

Unger, Merrill F. *Unger's Commentary on the Old Testament*. Vol. 1. Chicago, Illinois: Moody Press, 1981. (A fine summary of each paragraph. Highly recommended.)

Wood, Leon, J. *Israel's United Monarchy*. Grand Rapids, Michigan: Baker Book House, 1980. (Excellent.)

Wood, Leon, J. *The Prophets of Israel*. Grand Rapids, Michigan: Baker Book House, 1979. (Excellent.)

The Book of

1 KINGS

INTRODUCTION

First and Second Kings is the second in a series of three double books: 1 and 2 Samuel, 1 and 2 Kings, and 1 and 2 Chronicles. Originally, the double books were single books—one book of Samuel, one of Kings, and one of Chronicles. The Septuagint translators were the ones who made the divisions, and they did so more or less for the convenience of the reader. I think that it probably was a very wise decision.

Although the writer is unknown, 1 and 2 Kings were written while the first temple was still standing (1 Kings 8:8). Jeremiah is considered to be the traditional writer, while modern scholarship assigns the authorship to "the prophets."

The theme of these two Books of Kings is found in this expression that occurs nine times in 1 Kings: "as David his father." In other words, we are following the line of David, and each king was measured by the standard set by David. Very frankly, it was a human standard, and it was not the highest standard in the world. But we find that king after king failed to attain even to it. Thank God there were those who did measure up to it. However, we will find that this section of Scripture is a sorry and sordid section. It is history, and it reveals the decline and fall of the kingdom: first the kingdom was divided, and then each kingdom fell.

There are key verses that summarize the thrust of these two books. The first key verses describe the decline and fall of the northern kingdom: "For the children of Israel walked in all the sins of Jeroboam which he did; they departed not from them; Until the LORD removed Israel out of his sight, as he had said by all his servants the prophets. So was Israel carried away out of their own land to Assyria unto this day" (2 Kings 17:22–23).

The second key verse describes the fall of the southern kingdom: "And the king of Babylon smote them, and slew them at Riblah in the land of Hamath. So Judah was carried away out of their land" (2 Kings 25:21).

In 1 Kings we have the record of the *division* of the kingdom and 2 Kings records the *collapse* of the kingdom. Considering the two books as a unit, they open with King David, and they close with the king of Babylon. They are the book of man's rule over God's kingdom—and the results are not good, of course. The throne on earth must be in tune with the throne in heaven, if blessings are to come and benefits are to accrue to God's people. Yet man's plan cannot overthrow God's purposes, as we shall see.

First and Second Kings are actually a continuation of the narrative that was begun in 1 and 2 Samuel. These four books can be considered as a whole since they trace the history of the nation from the time of its greatest extension, influence, and prosperity under David and Solomon to the division, then captivity and exile of both kingdoms.

The moral teaching of these books is to show man his inability to rule himself and the world. In these four historical books we get a very graphic view of the rise and fall of the kingdom of Israel.

OUTLINE FOR 1 AND 2 KINGS

I. Death of David, 1 Kings 1–2

II. Glory of Solomon's Reign, 1 Kings 3–11

A. Solomon's Prayer for Wisdom, Chapters 3–4
B. Building of Temple, Chapters 5–8
C. Fame of Solomon, Chapters 9–10
D. Shame and Death of Solomon, Chapter 11

III. Division of the Kingdom (See Chronological table of the Kings of the Divided Kingdom), 1 Kings 12–2 Kings 16

IV. Captivity of Israel by Assyria, 2 Kings 17

V. Decline and Captivity of Judah by Babylon, 2 Kings 18–25

CHAPTER 1

***THEME:** Adonijah's abortive coup; Solomon anointed king*

The Books of Kings continue the narrative that was begun in the Books of Samuel. In this first chapter David is a senile old man. One of his sons, Adonijah, attempts to seize the throne. David, aroused by Nathan and Bathsheba, orders another son, Solomon, anointed as king of Israel. This is a tremendous chapter that opens 1 Kings.

DAVID'S DECLINING STRENGTH AND ADONIJAH'S PLOT

We begin on a sad note.

Now king David was old and stricken in years; and they covered him with clothes, but he gat no heat [1 Kings 1:1].

David is now an old man. It is difficult to conceive of him as an old man. We always think of David as a shepherd boy. It is hard to picture him as an old, senile man who needs nursing care.

His son Adonijah takes advantage of him in this condition. He attempts to put himself on the throne and make himself king. Of course, that is not going to fit in with God's plan. A great deal of intrigue goes on—intrigue is one of the things that characterizes the reign of David.

Let us find out who Adonijah is. First Kings is the first time that he is mentioned in any prominent connection.

Then Adonijah the son of Haggith exalted himself, saying, I will be king: and he prepared him chariots and horsemen, and fifty men to run before him.

And his father had not displeased him at any time in saying, Why hast thou done so? and he also was a very goodly man; and his mother bare him after Absalom [1 Kings 1:5–6].

Adonijah was David's fourth son, born to him in Hebron (2 Sam. 3:4). His mother was Haggith, one of David's wives, of whom we know nothing except that her name means "festive."

"Adonijah the son of Haggith exalted himself." That word *exalted* is interesting because there is a verse of Scripture that you can put right down over it: "For whosoever exalteth himself shall be abased; and he that humbleth himself shall be exalted" (Luke 14:11). "He that exalteth himself shall be abased" is going to be true of Adonijah. He certainly exalted himself.

The Scriptures tell us many things about Adonijah. He was a very proud young man with a high regard for himself. He was conceited, and you can detect in him some of the traits of his half brother Absalom who had led a rebellion against David. Adonijah, had something not been done, would also have led a rebellion against his father. David never had a reputation of disciplining his family. He had a disorganized family life; organized chaos reigned in David's palace, and Adonijah took full advantage of the situation. David never rebuked him. When he did wrong, I think David just smiled over his boy as an old indulgent man would do.

And he conferred with Joab the son of Zeruiah, and with Abiathar the priest: and they following Adonijah helped him [1 Kings 1:7].

Joab, who had been loyal to David for many years, now gives his allegiance to Adonijah. You can see his position; he is feathering his nest and preparing for the future. David is old, and in a short time he will be gone. Joab wants to be on the winning side. The only one on the scene who is making any move toward the throne is Adonijah. Joab has had tremendous influence in the palace and court of David. He has been David's right-hand man from the very beginning, and I am confident that he was loyal to David. I do not believe he would have permitted Adonijah to touch a hair of David's head, but he does want someone to come to the throne at this time. No other son of David seems to be a likely candidate. That is interesting because it implies that Joab would not have chosen Solomon to be king. In my judgment, David's choice was Absalom, not Solomon, and now he will probably smile when Adonijah makes his move for the throne, because he was very much like Absalom.

Now we find that Adonijah made a banquet. That is always a good way to get some support for any project. If you want to do something, have a church banquet, and you will receive a lot of support.

And Adonijah slew sheep and oxen and fat cattle by the stone of Zoheleth,

which is by En-rogel, and called all his brethren the king's sons, and all the men of Judah the king's servants [1 Kings 1:9].

Adonijah's intention was to announce at the banquet that he was king. By right of primogeniture he probably had a claim upon the throne. We are told that he was older than Solomon; according to the rules and regulations of the day, the oldest son was always the crown prince and was the successor. Absalom, of course, was dead, which put Adonijah next in line.

It was a bold move to send invitations to the king's sons, especially in light of the fact that Solomon did not receive an invitation; he was left out.

But Nathan the prophet, and Benaiah, and the mighty men, and Solomon his brother, he called not [1 Kings 1:10].

Adonijah knew that Nathan would be on Bathsheba's side. Nathan was the one who guided David during that awful period of David's great sin. Bathsheba, of course, was Solomon's mother. Now Nathan goes to her.

THE PLAN OF NATHAN AND BATHSHEBA

Wherefore Nathan spake unto Bath-sheba the mother of Solomon, saying, Hast thou not heard that Adonijah the son of Haggith doth reign, and David our lord knoweth it not? [1 Kings 1:11].

Adonijah was beginning to move behind David's back—he was not consulting the king at all. Now Nathan begins to move.

Go and get thee in unto king David, and say unto him, Didst not thou, my lord, O king, swear unto thine handmaid, saying, Assuredly Solomon thy son shall reign after me, and he shall sit upon my throne? why then doth Adonijah reign? [1 Kings 1:13].

David had made a promise to Bathsheba. When their second son was born (their first son had died), David promised her that he would be the next king. That son is Solomon. Now David was making no move to put him on the throne. I do not think David was enthusiastic about making him the king.

Behold, while thou yet talkest there with the king, I also will come in after thee, and confirm thy words [1 Kings 1:14].

Nathan is saying, "We had better alert David to what is taking place. You tell David what is happening, and I will enforce your words." Nathan wanted to wake up this senile king to what was going on right under his nose.

And Bath-sheba went in unto the king into the chamber: and the king was very old; and Abishag the Shunammite ministered unto the king.

And Bath-sheba bowed, and did obeisance unto the king. And the king said, What wouldest thou? [1 Kings 1:15–16].

It seems as though David had not seen Bathsheba for a long time.

And she said unto him, My lord, thou swarest by the LORD thy God unto thine handmaid, saying, Assuredly Solomon thy son shall reign after me, and he shall sit upon my throne.

And now, behold, Adonijah reigneth; and now, my lord the king, thou knowest it not:

And he hath slain oxen and fat cattle and sheep in abundance, and hath called all the sons of the king, and Abiathar the priest, and Joab the captain of the host: but Solomon thy servant hath he not called.

And thou, my lord, O king, the eyes of all Israel are upon thee, that thou shouldest tell them who shall sit on the throne of my lord the king after him [1Kings 1:17–20].

David had made no move to pick a successor from his several sons. Probably Adonijah was a very attractive, handsome, capable boy, and there were many people who wanted him for their next king.

Otherwise it shall come to pass, when my lord the king shall sleep with his fathers, that I and my son Solomon shall be counted offenders.

And, lo, while she yet talked with the king, Nathan the prophet also came in.

And they told the king, saying, Behold Nathan the prophet. And when he was come in before the king, he bowed himself before the king with his face to the ground.

And Nathan said, My lord, O king, hast thou said, Adonijah shall reign after

me, and he shall sit upon my throne? [1 Kings 1:21–24].

Nathan and Bathsheba wanted to know if David had chosen Adonijah to reign after him. David, of course, knew nothing about it.

Then king David answered and said, Call me Bath-sheba. And she came into the king's presence, and stood before the king.

And the king sware, and said, As the LORD liveth, that hath redeemed my soul out of all distress,

Even as I sware unto thee by the LORD God of Israel, saying, Assuredly Solomon thy son shall reign after me, and he shall sit upon my throne in my stead; even so will I certainly do this day [1 Kings 1:28–30].

When David spoke to Bathsheba about Solomon, notice that he said, "your son," and not "our son." David was not too enthusiastic about this boy. I don't think they had too much in common, as we shall soon see.

Then Bath-sheba bowed with her face to the earth, and did reverence to the king, and said, Let my lord king David live for ever.

And king David said, Call me Zadok the priest, and Nathan the prophet, and Benaiah the son of Jehoiada. And they came before the king.

The king also said unto them, Take with you the servants of your lord, and cause Solomon my son to ride upon mine own mule, and bring him down to Gihon [1 Kings 1:31–33].

The mule was the animal kings rode upon, while the horse was the animal of warfare. You will find in the Book of Revelation that the riding of the four horses speaks of turmoil and warfare. Also the Lord Jesus Christ will come again to his earth riding on a white horse, which speaks of warfare. He will come to put down rebellion on the earth; and before Him every knee shall bow. When the Lord came to earth the first time, He did not come to make war; He came to offer Himself as Israel's Messiah, and as such He rode a little donkey into Jerusalem. That is the animal upon which kings ride. Now David's own royal mount, a mule, is to be brought out, and Solomon is to be put upon it.

SOLOMON IS ANOINTED AS KING

So Zadok the priest, and Nathan the prophet, and Benaiah the son of Jehoiada, and the Cherethites, and the Pelethites, went down, and caused Solomon to ride upon king David's mule, and brought him to Gihon.

And Zadok the priest took an horn of oil out of the tabernacle, and anointed Solomon. And they blew the trumpet; and all the people said, God save king Solomon [1 Kings 1:38–39].

Now there is no question as to whom David has chosen to be his successor. Solomon is to be the next king.

And all the people came up after him, and the people piped with pipes, and rejoiced with great joy, so that the earth rent with the sound of them.

And Adonijah and all the guests that were with him heard it as they had made an end of eating. And when Joab heard the sound of the trumpet, he said, Wherefore is this noise of the city being in an uproar? [1 Kings 1:40–41].

The messenger who brought the details to Adonijah concluded with this:

And moreover the king's servants came to bless our lord king David, saying, God make the name of Solomon better than thy name, and make his throne greater than thy throne. And the king bowed himself upon the bed.

And also thus said the king, Blessed be the LORD God of Israel, which hath given one to sit on my throne this day, mine eyes even seeing it [1 Kings 1:47–48].

David put his seal of approval upon Solomon as king. David was an old man, and soon he would sleep with his fathers.

And all the guests that were with Adonijah were afraid, and rose up, and went every man his way.

And Adonijah feared because of Solomon, and arose, and went, and caught hold on the horns of the altar [1 Kings 1:49–50].

Adonijah's supporters were afraid and got out of there in a hurry. They knew they would be regarded as traitors. Adonijah, fearing for his life, ran to the tabernacle and caught hold of the horns of the altar for sanctuary.

And it was told Solomon, saying, Behold, Adonijah feareth king Solomon: for, lo, he hath caught hold on the horns of the altar, saying, Let king Solomon swear unto me today that he will not slay his servant with the sword.

And Solomon said, If he will shew himself a worthy man, there shall not an hair of him fall to the earth: but if wickedness shall be found in him, he shall die [1 Kings 1:51–52].

Solomon is being very fair with Adonijah. If Adonijah shows himself to be a loyal subject, then nothing will happen to him.

So king Solomon sent, and they brought him down from the altar. And he came and bowed himself to king Solomon: and Solomon said unto him, Go to thine house [1 Kings 1:53].

Adonijah, brought into the king's presence, submitted himself to the new king. Then Solomon dismissed him in peace.

CHAPTER 2

***THEME:** David's deathbed charge to Solomon and the beginning of Solomon's reign*

This chapter records David's final instructions to Solomon before his death and Solomon's wise execution of David's wishes.

DAVID'S CHARGE TO SOLOMON

Now the days of David drew nigh that he should die; and he charged Solomon his son, saying,

I go the way of all the earth: be thou strong therefore, and shew thyself a man [1 Kings 2:1–2].

First of all David said, "I go the way of all the earth." This is the way of man. In Romans 5:12 the apostle Paul says, "Wherefore, as by one man sin entered into the world, and death by sin; and so death passed upon all men, for that all have sinned." By man came death, and death is passed on to all men because all have sinned. The sin of Adam has been passed down to you and me; if the Lord tarries, we will go through the doorway of death. Why? Because this is the way of all the earth, the conclusion of this life's journey. It is not a very attractive subject. We don't like to think about death today because it is something a little too depressing for the human race.

In Psalm 23:4 David says, "Yea, though I walk through the valley of the shadow of death, I will fear no evil: for thou art with me; thy rod and thy staff they comfort me." David is not speaking about the fact that he has come to his deathbed. As someone has said, "The moment that gives you life begins also to take it away from you." David is likening life to a walk through a valley. At birth you start down through the valley, and the farther you walk the narrower it gets. At the end of the valley is death. All of us are walking through that valley today. You may be in robust health today, but you can be dead before the sun goes down.

Next David says to Solomon, "Be thou strong therefore, and show thyself a man." The Lord Jesus Christ put it like this to the crowd who had come out to see John the Baptist: "But what went ye out for to see? A man clothed in soft raiment? behold, they that wear soft clothing are in kings' houses" (Matt. 11:8). John the Baptist had been brought up in the wilderness. He was rugged. Our Lord was a rugged man also. I don't like the paintings I see of Him because they make Him almost effeminate, although some of the more recent pictures have tried to make Him look more masculine. May I say to you that if you could have seen Him when He walked upon this earth, you would have seen a rugged man. He had calluses on His hands—He was a carpenter. He was God, but He was a real man. He was very man of very man and very God of very God.

Solomon was not quite like his father. David was a man. Solomon was not much of a man. David was rugged. Solomon had been brought up in the palaces—in fact, he had been brought up in the women's palaces. Why did Solomon have a thousand women around him? My friend, the answer is quite obvious. All Solomon knew about was women. He was a sissy if there ever was one. I don't think he and David had much in common. So David says to him, "I have made you king. I want you to play the man. I don't think you are one, but do the best that you can." This is the injunction David gave to this boy who had been brought up with soft clothing. Solomon was not like David. He was not like John the Baptist. He was not like our Lord, either. But now he is the king of Israel.

And keep the charge of the LORD thy God, to walk in his ways, to keep his statutes, and his commandments, and his judgments, and his testimonies, as it is written in the law of Moses, that thou mayest prosper in all that thou doest, and whithersoever thou turnest thyself:

That the LORD may continue his word which he spake concerning me, saying, If thy children take heed to their way, to walk before me in truth with all their heart and with all their soul, there shall not fail thee (said he) a man on the throne of Israel [1 Kings 2:3–4].

David urges Solomon to stay close to the Lord and to the Word of God. His advice to this young man is very important.

There is very little attention ever given to David's legacy to Solomon, but I believe that what David left to him enabled him to become one of the great kings of the earth. In fact, Solomon is probably one of the best known kings who has ever lived.

Eason, in his *New Bible Survey* (Zondervan), enumerates David's legacy to Solomon:

1. *He transferred the leadership of the nation from the house of Saul and the tribe of Benjamin to Judah and established the royal house of David.* This becomes all-important as we shall see when we get to the New Testament. The Gospel of Matthew opens with the statement, "The book of the generation of Jesus Christ, the son of David, the son of Abraham" (Matt. 1:1). Then in Luke 1:31–32 the angel Gabriel said to Mary, "And, behold, thou shalt conceive in thy womb, and bring forth a son, and shalt call his name JESUS. He shall be great, and shall be called the Son of the Highest: and the Lord God shall give unto him the throne of his father David." Only a descendant of David is to occupy the throne of Israel.

2. *He established Jerusalem as the Holy City and as the religious center and national capital for all Jews.* This has continued down to this day. When Israel took the city of Jerusalem from the Arabs in the Six Day War of 1967, they declared that they had no intention of giving it up because it is a legacy that goes back to David. Jerusalem was David's favorite city, and he made it the capital for the nation of Israel. Solomon beautified the city by building the temple and making it the religious center of Israel. We should note, however, that it was David who made the preparations for the temple.

3. *He stamped out idolatry, practically speaking, and made the worship of Jehovah universal in the land.* This was his most important contribution.

4. He made conquests of many nations which paid tribute to Israel and its king. *He extended the borders of the country to Egypt on the south, and to the River Euphrates on the north and east.* David is actually the one who extended Israel's borders farther than they had ever been extended before or since. The peace during the reign of Solomon was possible because David had subdued Israel's enemies.

5. Although an Oriental monarch with a sizable harem, *David's foreign marriages were largely political and relatively free from religious and moral corruption.* Having a harem was the custom of that day, but God did not approve of David's many wives, and it was largely due to them that he was in hot water all of the time. The many sons that were born to him by these women caused constant dissension inside the palace. It was something that caused David woe and sorrow all of his life. It was Solomon, and not David, who was influenced by a foreign wife. It is true that David committed an awful sin, but it occurred *before* his marriage to Bathsheba. There was not even a breath of scandal after that.

6. David was a poet and musician who endeared himself to the people as the *"sweet psalmist of Israel"* and gave to us at least seventy-three psalms.

7. *David planned the temple,* which was to exalt the religious life of the nation and the worship of Jehovah, although he was not permitted to build the Lord's house.

8. Although there was still rivalry of a sort between the ten tribes of the north and Judah and Benjamin in the south—and had been

since the death of Saul and his son—David had no serious difficulty in *uniting all tribes under his rule* and making Jerusalem the national capital.

9. At the time of David's death, Israel was second to none in *power and military prowess*, and the people had a large measure of peace and freedom, as every man "sat under his own vine and fig tree." The peace that Solomon enjoyed during his reign was a peace that had been made by David during his reign.

And, behold, thou hast with thee Shimei the son of Gera, a Benjamite of Bahurim, which cursed me with a grievous curse in the day when I went to Mahanaim: but he came down to meet me at Jordan, and I sware to him by the LORD, saying, I will not put thee to death with the sword.

Now therefore hold him not guiltless: for thou art a wise man, and knowest what thou oughtest to do unto him; but his hoar head bring thou down to the grave with blood [1 Kings 2:8–9].

David is revealing here what seems like a vengeful spirit, but it actually is not. Although Shimei had demonstrated that he was a traitor, because David had made an oath not to touch him, Shimei was still alive. David was a man of his word. Now, however, he tells Solomon to keep his watchful eye on him and if he reveals any of his treachery, Solomon is to deal with him accordingly. The time does come, by the way, when Solomon deals with Shimei, but only after he disobeys and reveals that he is indeed a traitor.

DAVID'S DEATH

So David slept with his fathers, and was buried in the city of David.

And the days that David reigned over Israel were forty years: seven years reigned he in Hebron, and thirty and three years reigned he in Jerusalem.

Then sat Solomon upon the throne of David his father; and his kingdom was established greatly [1 Kings 2:10–12].

There is a note of sadness in the death of David. He had been a great man of God. Do you recall the first son of David and Bathsheba? He died when he was just a few days old. David said of him, "He will never come to me, but I will go to him." Now David has gone to be with that child.

Solomon, now that his father is gone, comes to the throne. At the change of any dynasty or ruler there is always a time of turmoil and great change.

SOLOMON'S ACCESSION TO THE THRONE

And Adonijah the son of Haggith came to Bath-sheba the mother of Solomon. And she said, Comest thou peaceably? And he said, Peaceably.

He said moreover, I have somewhat to say unto thee. And she said, Say on [1 Kings 2:13–14].

Even though Solomon is now on the throne, Adonijah has not given up the idea about wanting to be king. He comes to Bathsheba still harboring this thought. She does not have much confidence in him and inquires about his mission. He says that it is a peaceful one. She says, "Say on"—in other words, "I'm listening."

And he said, Thou knowest that the kingdom was mine, and that all Israel set their faces on me, that I should reign: howbeit the kingdom is turned about, and is become my brother's: for it was his from the LORD [1 Kings 2:15].

He is saying that he was more popular than Solomon and the people wanted him as king.

And now I ask one petition of thee, deny me not. And she said unto him, Say on.

And he said, Speak, I pray thee, unto Solomon the king, (for he will not say thee nay,) that he give me Abishag the Shunammite to wife [1 Kings 2:16–17].

He is saying, "Since the kingdom has been taken away from me, I have only one small request. I would like Abishag for my wife." Abishag, you recall, nursed David during his last days.

And Bath-sheba said, Well; I will speak for thee unto the king.

Bath-sheba therefore went unto king Solomon, to speak unto him for Adonijah. And the king rose up to meet her, and bowed himself unto her, and sat down on his throne, and caused a seat to be set for the king's mother; and she sat on his right hand.

Then she said, I desire one small petition of thee; I pray thee, say me not

nay. And the king said unto her, Ask on, my mother: for I will not say thee nay.

And she said, Let Abishag the Shunammite be given to Adonijah thy brother to wife [1 Kings 2:18–21].

This was an audacious request, but Adonijah knew that Solomon would not deny his mother anything. That is the reason he went to Bathsheba instead of going directly to Solomon.

And king Solomon answered and said unto his mother, And why dost thou ask Abishag the Shunammite for Adonijah? ask for him the kingdom also; for he is mine elder brother; even for him, and for Abiathar the priest, and for Joab the son of Zeruiah.

Then king Solomon sware by the LORD, saying, God do so to me, and more also, if Adonijah have not spoken this word against his own life [1 Kings 2:22–23].

What Adonijah was actually doing was making a move toward the throne. He was doing a dangerous thing, but he was being very clever about it all. Adonijah was Solomon's elder brother, and Solomon, of course, had been aware of his brother's move to seize the throne before David named a successor. Although Bathsheba, in her simplicity, felt that Adonijah's request for Abishag was reasonable, Solomon's keen mind instantly penetrated the plot.

Now therefore, as the LORD liveth, which hath established me, and set me on the throne of David my father, and who hath made me an house, as he promised, Adonijah shall be put to death this day.

And king Solomon sent by the hand of Benaiah the son of Jehoiada; and he fell upon him that he died [1 Kings 2:24–25].

Adonijah's death was a brutal thing, of course, but his death eliminated a contender for the throne. It was necessary to execute him in order to establish Solomon on the throne. As long as Adonijah lived, he would continue to connive and plot in an attempt to seize the throne.

Now, having removed Adonijah, Solomon realized it would be necessary to remove from positions of influence those who had supported him.

And unto Abiathar the priest said the king, Get thee to Anathoth, unto thine own fields; for thou art worthy of death: but I will not at this time put thee to death, because thou barest the ark of the LORD GOD before David my father, and because thou hast been afflicted in all wherein my father was afflicted.

So Solomon thrust out Abiathar from being priest unto the LORD; that he might fulfil the word of the LORD, which he spake concerning the house of Eli in Shiloh [1 Kings 2:26–27].

Abiathar, a descendant of Aaron, was removed from his priestly office and sent home in disgrace because he had participated in Adonijah's rebellion. The only reason he was not executed was because of his faithfulness to David during Absalom's rebellion. This ended the line of Eli.

Then tidings came to Joab: for Joab had turned after Adonijah, though he turned not after Absalom. And Joab fled unto the tabernacle of the LORD, and caught hold on the horns of the altar.

And it was told king Solomon that Joab was fled unto the tabernacle of the LORD; and, behold, he is by the altar. Then Solomon sent Benaiah the son of Jehoiada, saying, Go, fall upon him.

And Benaiah came to the tabernacle of the LORD, and said unto him, Thus saith the king, Come forth. And he said, Nay; but I will die here. And Benaiah brought the king word again, saying, Thus said Joab, and thus he answered me [1 Kings 2:28–30].

When Joab heard what happened to Abiathar and Adonijah, he took off for the tall timber. He ran to the tabernacle of the Lord and caught hold of the horns of the altar for sanctuary. Solomon chose Benaiah, the son of Jehoiada, to be Joab's executioner. He went after Joab and asked him to come outside the tabernacle. Joab refused, saying, "I'll die here if I have to die."

And the king said unto him, Do as he hath said, and fall upon him, and bury him; that thou mayest take away the innocent blood, which Joab shed, from me, and from the house of my father.

And the LORD shall return his blood upon his own head, who fell upon two men more righteous and better than he, and slew them with the sword, my father David not knowing thereof, to wit, Abner the son of Ner, captain of the host of Israel, and Amasa the son of Jether, captain of the host of Judah [1 Kings 2:31–32].

Joab had been a bloody man.

Their blood shall therefore return upon the head of Joab, and upon the head of his seed for ever: but upon David, and upon his seed, and upon his house, and upon his throne, shall there be peace for ever from the LORD.

So Benaiah the son of Jehoiada went up, and fell upon him, and slew him: and he was buried in his own house in the wilderness [1 Kings 2:33–34].

He was executed because of his part in a rebellion against Solomon.

Shimei was another traitor. David would not touch him because he had given his word that he would not. Solomon now puts restrictions on him.

And the king sent and called for Shimei, and said unto him, Build thee an house in Jerusalem, and dwell there, and go not forth thence any whither [1 Kings 2:36].

Solomon wanted Shimei to be where he could keep his eye on him. Wherever Shimei went, he sowed seeds of rebellion. Solomon wanted to watch his every move.

For it shall be, that on the day thou goest out, and passest over the brook Kidron, thou shalt know for certain that thou shalt surely die: thy blood shall be upon thine own head.

And Shimei said unto the king, The saying is good: as my lord the king hath said, so will thy servant do. And Shimei dwelt in Jerusalem many days [1 Kings 2:37–38].

Solomon commanded Shimei to build a home in Jerusalem and to remain within the city limits. He was forbidden to return and live with his own tribe. Shimei promised to be obedient to Solomon's terms.

And it came to pass at the end of three years, that two of the servants of Shimei ran away unto Achish son of Maachah king of Gath. And they told Shimei, saying, Behold, thy servants be in Gath.

And Shimei arose, and saddled his ass, and went to Gath to Achish to seek his servants: and Shimei went, and brought his servants from Gath [2 Kings 2:39–40].

Shimei went outside the city limits. He did this in direct disobedience to Solomon's orders. Solomon was told what Shimei had done; so the king sent for him.

Why then hast thou not kept the oath of the LORD, and the commandment that I have charged thee with?

The king said moreover to Shimei, Thou knowest all the wickedness which thine heart is privy to, that thou didst to David my father: therefore the LORD shall return thy wickedness upon thine own head;

And king Solomon shall be blessed, and the throne of David shall be established before the LORD for ever.

So the king commanded Benaiah the son of Jehoiada; which went out, and fell upon him, that he died. And the kingdom was established in the hand of Solomon [1 Kings 2:43–46].

With Shimei's death Solomon had completed the charge made to him by David his father. Solomon had removed most of the contenders to the throne. Now he could reign in peace.

CHAPTERS 3–4

***THEME:** Solomon's prayer for wisdom and God's answer*

In the chapters before us God appears to Solomon in a dream saying, "Ask what I shall give thee." Solomon asks for wisdom to govern Israel. His unselfish request so pleases God that He promises him much more than he asked for. In addition to wisdom, He gives him riches and honor. Solomon's decision in the case of two mothers claiming one child demonstrates that God had truly given him a wise and understanding heart.

And Solomon made affinity with Pharaoh king of Egypt, and took Pharaoh's daughter, and brought her into the city of David, until he had made an end of building his own house, and the house of the LORD, and the wall of Jerusalem round about.

Only the people sacrificed in high places, because there was no house built unto the name of the LORD, until those days [1 Kings 3:1–2].

One of the first things Solomon did after he became king was to marry a daughter of Pharaoh, king of Egypt. His marriage formed an alliance with Egypt. Solomon's marriages with heathen women were terrible mistakes and finally became his undoing. Remember that Solomon was brought up in a court of women. He was not acquainted with life as was David, his father. I do not believe that Solomon ever had the spiritual capacity for God that David had nor the longing for God in his life. Solomon did, however, recognize his shortcomings. After he married Pharaoh's daughter (and we only wish he had done this before), he went to the Lord and asked for wisdom.

After David's reign there was a period of relaxation. The people began to offer sacrifices in high places which was actually heathen, pagan worship. It was a return to idolatry.

SOLOMON'S SACRIFICE AND PRAYER FOR WISDOM

And Solomon loved the LORD, walking in the statutes of David his father: only he sacrificed and burnt incense in high places.

And the king went to Gibeon to sacrifice there; for that was the great high place: a thousand burnt offerings did Solomon offer upon that altar [1 Kings 3:3–4].

Solomon was perfectly willing to offer sacrifices on heathen altars—something that David never would have done. Although Solomon loved the Lord, he was not the kind of a man David was. Solomon was walking in the statutes of David, but he had that little flaw that we have already seen makes second-rate material.

In Gibeon the LORD appeared to Solomon in a dream by night: and God said, Ask what I shall give thee [1 Kings 3:5].

The Lord appeared to Solomon in a dream by night. Again, I must repeat that God today is not appearing to men in dreams. If you have had a dream, do not try to say that the Lord appeared to you. Just remember what you had for supper, and you will find out why you had the dream. God speaks to us today in His Word. Solomon did not have all of God's Word in his day, so God appeared to him in a dream and said, "Ask what you will. I will grant it to you." What is Solomon going to ask for? He has the choice of asking for anything he wants. The fact that he is going to make a wise choice indicates that he had a certain amount of human wisdom before God gave him His wisdom.

When the Lord told Solomon He would grant any wish, I think He recognized that Solomon had many deficiencies and was wholly and totally inadequate. But, my friend, who is adequate for these things? Who is adequate for living the Christian life? Not one of us. The fact of the matter is that we cannot live the Christian life, and God has never asked us to live it. He has asked that *He* might live that life through us. Now He is wanting to do something through Solomon. This king could have asked for riches or power. Instead, recognizing his deficiency, notice what he asks for.

And Solomon said, Thou hast shewed unto thy servant David my father great mercy, according as he walked before thee in truth, and in righteousness, and in uprightness of heart with thee; and thou hast kept for him this great kindness, that thou hast given him a son to sit on his throne, as it is this day [1 Kings 3:6].

Solomon realized that he was attempting to fill not the shoes but the throne of David. He recognized that he was totally inadequate for the job.

And now, O LORD my God, thou hast made thy servant king instead of David my father: and I am but a little child: I know not how to go out or come in.

And thy servant is in the midst of thy people which thou hast chosen, a great people, that cannot be numbered nor counted for multitude [1 Kings 3:7–8].

He considered himself "a little child" in experience. He felt incapable of governing this great nation. There are so many folk today attempting to serve God who do not seem to recognize their inadequacies. All of us are wholly inadequate to serve God. We should recognize that fact so that we are in a position where God can help us.

Give therefore thy servant an understanding heart to judge thy people, that I may discern between good and bad: for who is able to judge this thy so great a people? [1 Kings 3:9].

Solomon asked for an understanding heart to judge God's people. I want to consider this for just a moment. We always say that Solomon prayed for wisdom. That is certainly true, but what kind of wisdom did he pray for? He prayed for political wisdom. He wanted the ability to be a statesman. He wanted to know how to judge and rule over these people and make great national decisions. He did not pray for spiritual discernment. This is something that needs to be made very clear. In the books Solomon wrote, Proverbs and Ecclesiastes, we will find wisdom that will guide us in this world—Proverbs is a fine book to give to young men starting out on their own. Although in the Song of Solomon he does reveal spiritual discernment, in his old age his heathen wives turned away his heart from the Lord. Solomon did not pray for spiritual discernment. Solomon prayed for political wisdom, and this God gave him throughout his life.

SOLOMON'S PRAYER IS ANSWERED

And the speech pleased the LORD, that Solomon had asked this thing.

And God said unto him, Because thou hast asked this thing, and hast not asked for thyself long life; neither hast asked riches for thyself, nor hast asked the life of thine enemies; but hast asked for thyself understanding to discern judgment [1 Kings 3:10–11].

Solomon wanted to make wise decisions. In the sickening scene in every government today we see a group of men clamoring for positions. They want to be elected to an office. All of them are telling us how great they are and what marvelous abilities they have. They assure us that they are able to solve the problems. By now, friend, some of us have come to the conclusion that these boys are just kidding us. They don't have the solution and they don't have the wisdom. If only some men would come on the scene and say, "I don't have the wisdom; I recognize my inadequacies. But I am going to depend on God to lead and guide me." Something like that would be so startling it would probably rock the world. That is what Solomon said, and God commended him for it. It was a great step.

Behold, I have done according to thy words: lo, I have given thee a wise and an understanding heart; so that there was none like thee before thee, neither after thee shall any arise like unto thee [1 Kings 3:12].

Solomon does stand out as being a wise ruler. When you read the Books of Proverbs and Ecclesiastes, you will find human wisdom on the highest plane. I do not mean that these books are not inspired of God. It is obvious that God through Solomon is giving the highest of human wisdom, making it clear in both books that mere human wisdom is totally inadequate to meet the issues of life.

And I have also given thee that which thou hast not asked, both riches, and honour: so that there shall not be any among the kings like unto thee all thy days.

And if thou wilt walk in my ways, to keep my statutes and my commandments, as thy father David did walk, then I will lengthen thy days [1 Kings 3:13–14].

The standard, as we have indicated before, is David. That is a human standard and is not very high. But, frankly, few of the kings even came up to that standard.

And Solomon awoke; and, behold, it was a dream. And he came to Jerusalem, and stood before the ark of the covenant of the LORD, and offered up burnt offerings, and offered peace of-

ferings, and made a feast to all his servants [1 Kings 3:15].

The burnt offerings and peace offerings point to the Lord Jesus Christ. The burnt offering speaks of who He is. The peace offering speaks of the fact that He made peace by shedding His blood on the cross. Because of who He is, He is able to bring us into a right relationship with God. The shedding of His blood makes it possible to remove the guilt of our sins.

In the last part of this chapter we have a demonstration of Solomon's wisdom. He gives a clever solution to a real problem. There were two women. They were harlots, and they had one child between them. Each woman claimed the child as her own. They brought the matter to Solomon. How would you solve the problem? How would you find out who the real mother was? I suppose today some scientific method of determining the mother would be pursued, but Solomon had no such recourse. Solomon said to the women, "Since both of you claim the child, we will cut the baby in half, and each of you may have half of the child." The one who was not the mother, who had no love for the child and apparently had it in for the real mother, replied, "Sure, go ahead and cut the child in half." The real mother, however, said, "Oh, no, no. Don't do that. Give her the child." Solomon knew that the woman who was willing to give the child up in order to save its life was the real mother.

And all Israel heard of the judgment which the king had judged; and they feared the king: for they saw that the wisdom of God was in him, to do judgment [1 Kings 3:28].

This is only one example of the many wise decisions Solomon was able to make during his reign.

SOLOMON'S ELEVEN PRINCES

In chapter 4 Solomon brings the kingdom to its zenith. The things that marked his kingdom were peace and prosperity. Peace is what we would like to have, is it not? I think we could call Solomon the prince of peace while David was a man of war. But the peace that Solomon and those in his kingdom enjoyed was made possible by David, the man of war.

This has a spiritual application for us. We like to feel that God forgives sin because He is sentimental. God does not forgive sin on a low plane like that. A battle has been fought, my friend, and a great sacrifice has been made. Blood has been shed that we might have forgiveness of sin. The Lord Jesus Christ made peace by the blood of His cross. It is only through His blood that we can enter into peace.

So king Solomon was king over all Israel.

And these were the princes which he had; Azariah the son of Zadok the priest,

Elihoreph and Ahiah, the sons of Shisha, scribes; Jehoshaphat the son of Ahilud, the recorder.

And Benaiah the son of Jehoiada was over the host: and Zadok and Abiathar were the priests:

And Azariah the son of Nathan was over the officers; and Zabud the son of Nathan was principal officer, and the king's friend:

And Ahishar was over the household: and Adoniram the son of Abda was over the tribute [1 Kings 4:1–6].

In the first few verses of this chapter a list of Solomon's princes is given. Some of them apparently were the sons of the sons of David, which would mean that they were Solomon's nephews. Azariah is mentioned in verse 5. This man was either a son of Nathan, David's son, or a son of Nathan, the prophet.

SOLOMON'S TWELVE OFFICERS

And Solomon had twelve officers over all Israel, which provided victuals for the king and his household: each man his month in a year made provision [1 Kings 4:7].

Solomon had twelve officers. Each officer came from a tribe of Israel. They were in charge of providing the needs of the king and his household. This was Solomon's method of taxation.

THE GREATNESS OF THE KINGDOM

Judah and Israel were many, as the sand which is by the sea in multitude, eating and drinking, and making merry.

And Solomon reigned over all kingdoms from the river unto the land of the Philistines, and unto the border of

Egypt: they brought presents, and served Solomon all the days of his life [1 Kings 4:20–21].

This was a time of great prosperity and peace. The wars were over. There was plenty for everyone. And this, my friend, is just a little adumbration, a little preview, of the kingdom that is coming on this earth—the millennial kingdom.

And Judah and Israel dwelt safely, every man under his vine and under his fig tree, from Dan even to Beer-sheba, all the days of Solomon [1 Kings 4:25].

There are several things we need to note here. This was a time of security and safety, something which we do not have in this world today. "There is no peace, saith my God, to the wicked" (Isa. 57:21). But peace is coming on the earth when the Prince of Peace comes. In Solomon's day every man dwelt under his own vine and fig tree. That tells us that one man was not living in a mansion and another in a hovel. Each man had his vine and fig tree; he was living comfortably on his own property. It was so from Dan to Beer-sheba—that is, from the northern border to the southern border—all the days of Solomon.

And Solomon had forty thousand stalls of horses for his chariots, and twelve thousand horsemen [1 Kings 4:26].

I want to call attention to this verse. The horse was the animal of war, and God had forbidden the multiplication of horses. God gave a specific law that a king was not to multiply horses or wives: "But he shall not multiply horses to himself, nor cause the people to return to Egypt, to the end that he should multiply horses: forasmuch as the LORD hath said unto you, Ye shall henceforth return no more that way" (Deut. 17:16). Solomon multiplied both horses and wives. He had stables all over the land of Israel. I visited the ruins at Megiddo; that is, the mound that overlooks the valley of Esdraelon where we believe that the great issue will be finally settled in the last days at the battle, or war, of Armageddon. It is a tremendous view, by the way. But the thing that impressed me was the ruins there of Solomon's stables, stalls, and the troughs where his horses ate. These stables would accommodate at least 450 horses. Second Chronicles 9:25 says he had 4,000 stalls for horses! Solomon certainly multiplied horses, contrary to the wisdom of God.

SOLOMON'S GREAT WISDOM AND RENOWN

Now we are told something of the wisdom of Solomon.

And God gave Solomon wisdom and understanding exceeding much, and largeness of heart, even as the sand that is on the sea shore.

And Solomon's wisdom excelled the wisdom of all the children of the east country, and all the wisdom of Egypt [1 Kings 4:29–30].

The east is where the wise men came from.

For he was wiser than all men; than Ethan the Ezrahite, and Heman, and Chalcol, and Darda, the sons of Mahol: and his fame was in all nations round about [1 Kings 4:31].

Four outstanding wise men are mentioned in this verse.

And he spake three thousand proverbs: and his songs were a thousand and five.

And he spake of trees, from the cedar tree that is in Lebanon even unto the hyssop that springeth out of the wall: he spake also of beasts, and of fowl, and of creeping things, and of fishes [1 Kings 4:32–33].

We are told that Solomon spoke three thousand proverbs. We have only a few hundred recorded in the Bible. His songs were a thousand and five. Believe me, he was a song writer. We have only one of his songs, The Song of Solomon. Solomon was a dendrologist—"He spake of trees, from the cedar tree that is in Lebanon even unto the hyssop that springeth out of the wall." The hyssop is a humble little plant that grows on rocks. Solomon was also a zoologist—"he spake also of beasts"—and an ornithologist since he spoke of birds. He was an entomologist: he spoke of creeping things, or insects. He was an ichthyologist: he spoke of fishes. He spoke of these things because he had studied them and was an authority in these particular realms. This, apparently, is the beginning of the sciences. Solomon was interested in these things.

And there came of all people to hear the wisdom of Solomon, from all kings of the earth, which had heard of his wisdom [1 Kings 4:34].

Solomon gained a worldwide reputation for his wisdom, and many came to hear him. We have a few of the proverbs that he wrote recorded in the Book of Proverbs. As I have said before, these proverbs are extremely helpful to any young person entering adult life. There are certain proverbs that can guide a young man in life and business. You see, God is very practical with us. He gets right down to the nitty-gritty, where you and I walk in and out of the marts of trade, where we enter into the courts of the land and into social gatherings. Certain guiding principles of life are given to us in Proverbs. I am not saying that a young man can become a Christian by following the proverbs of Solomon, but he certainly will have a marvelous guide for his life.

CHAPTERS 5–6

***THEME:** Preparation and construction of the temple*

In chapter 5 Solomon works out a business deal with King Hiram of Tyre for cedar and workmen. Also out of Israel he raises a levy of thirty thousand workmen.

Chapter 6 details the construction of this costly and ornate temple which took seven years to complete.

And Hiram king of Tyre sent his servants unto Solomon; for he had heard that they had anointed him king in the room of his father: for Hiram was ever a lover of David [1 Kings 5:1].

Whatever King Hiram of Tyre is going to do will not be because of Solomon but because of his love, esteem, and respect for King David.

And Solomon sent to Hiram, saying,

Thou knowest how that David my father could not build an house unto the name of the Lord his God for the wars which were about him on every side, until the Lord put them under the soles of his feet.

But now the Lord my God hath given me rest on every side, so that there is neither adversary nor evil occurrent [1 Kings 5:2–4].

Friend, only God can give peace, whether it is world peace or peace in the human heart. God alone can give the rest today that the human heart needs. That is why our Lord, when they rejected Him as king, could send out His personal, private, individual invitation, "Come unto me, all ye that labour and are heavy laden"—that is, burdened with sin—"and I will give you rest" (Matt. 11:28). Only Christ can give that kind of rest. Now God had given Solomon rest from warfare. There was peace on every side.

And, behold, I purpose to build an house unto the name of the Lord my God, as the Lord spake unto David my father, saying, Thy son, whom I will set upon thy throne in thy room, he shall build an house unto my name [1 Kings 5:5].

Although the building of the temple all stems from David, he was not permitted to build it because he was a man of war.

Perhaps we should consider some of the background relative to the building of the temple. Man has been a builder from the beginning. In Genesis 4:17 we are told that Cain ". . . builded a city, and called the name of the city, after the name of his son, Enoch." The face of the earth is scarred by great mounds that hide the ruins of great cities and splendid buildings of the past. The spade of the archaeologist has penetrated into the depths, and you can judge each civilization by the height of the buildings. There are those who say that the cave men of the Stone Age (if they ever existed) were barbarians and uncivilized. They were not builders but sought refuge in caves. The Egyptians, the Assyrians, the Babylonians, the Greeks, and the Romans are all counted as civilized, and it is evidenced in their architecture. Modern man claims a high degree of culture because he has built subdivisions, shopping centers, apartment buildings, and tall office buildings. Today man is building his own cave in which to live and work—like a gopher. The rest of the time he crawls on the freeway like a worm. As long as he can push a button and turn a switch, he says he is living. That is modern man.

The first buildings of impressive design were the temples. All pagan peoples had temples. Some temples were crude; others, such as the Parthenon in Greece, were the highest expression of beauty. All of this building stems from the Tower of Babel, which was a monument to man's gargantuan resistance to God. Pagan temples have always been the highest architectural expression, but the pagans who have attended, both civilized and uncivilized, have been on the lowest spiritual level. These temples have been elaborate, large, ornate, rich, and impressive. The temples of the kings on the River Nile, Asshur of Nineveh, Marduk of Babylon, the ziggurats in the Tigris-Euphrates Valley, Baal of the Phoenicians, Athena of the Greeks and in Athens the Parthenon, Jupiter of the Romans, the Aztec temples of Mexico—all of them are manifestations of rebellion against God. ". . . When they knew God, they glorified him not as God, neither were thankful; but became vain in their imaginations. . . ." What did they do? They built temples, changing ". . . the glory of the uncorruptible God into an image made like to corruptible man, and to birds, and fourfooted beasts, and creeping things" (Rom. 1:21, 23). Each made a house for his god to live in. They put their gods in a box like a jack-in-the-box.

The temple Solomon built, however, was never considered in Scripture as a house in which God would live. In the Book of 2 Chronicles at the dedication of the temple, Solomon made it quite clear that God did not dwell in that place. "But will God in very deed dwell with men on the earth? behold, heaven and the heaven of heavens cannot contain thee; how much less this house which I have built!" (2 Chron. 6:18). If you think that the temple was built as a house in which God would dwell, you have missed the entire point. It was an approach for man to God and an access to God through sacrifices.

Notice now the conception of the temple, then its construction and character. It is rather important.

The building of the temple was first in David's mind, although God would not let him build it. First Chronicles 28:1–3 tells us part of the story: "And David assembled all the princes of Israel, the princes of the tribes, and the captains of the companies that ministered to the king by course, and the captains over the thousands, and captains over the hundreds, and the stewards over all the substance and possession of the king, and of his sons, with the officers, and with the mighty men, and with all the valiant men, unto Jerusalem. Then David the king stood up upon his feet, and said, Hear me, my brethren, and my people: As for me, I had in mine heart to build an house of rest for the ark of the covenant of the LORD, and for the footstool of our God, and had made ready for the building: But God said unto me, Thou shalt not build an house for my name, because thou hast been a man of war, and hast shed blood." The temple was not a dwelling place for God; it was to be His footstool.

It was in David's heart to build the temple. The pattern for the building was given to David, not Solomon. First Chronicles 28:19 tells us, "All this, said David, the LORD made me understand in writing by his hand upon me, even all the works of this pattern." In other words, David was given the blueprint of the temple even though God did not permit him to build it. David gave this pattern or blueprint to Solomon. "Take heed now; for the LORD hath chosen thee to build an house for the sanctuary: be strong, and do it. Then David gave to Solomon his son the pattern of the porch, and of the houses thereof, and of the treasuries thereof, and of the upper chambers thereof, and of the inner parlours thereof, and of the place of the mercy seat, and the pattern of all that he had by the spirit, of the courts of the house of the LORD, and of all the chambers round about, of the treasuries of the house of God, and of the treasuries of the dedicated things" (1 Chron. 28:10–12). David also gathered the material: "Now I have prepared with all my might for the house of my God the gold for things to be made of gold, and the silver for things of silver, and the brass for things of brass, the iron for things of iron, and wood for things of wood; onyx stones, and stones to be set, glistering stones, and of divers colours, and all manner of precious stones, and marble stones in abundance" (1 Chron. 29:2). The conception of the temple, you see, was in the heart of David. Solomon merely executed the construction of it.

Now with all David's accumulation of material at hand, Solomon contracts with Hiram king of Tyre for cedar and fir timber for the actual construction of the edifice.

And Hiram sent to Solomon, saying, I have considered the things which thou sentest to me for: and I will do all thy

desire concerning timber of cedar, and concerning timber of fir.

My servants shall bring them down from Lebanon unto the sea: and I will convey them by sea in floats unto the place that thou shalt appoint me, and will cause them to be discharged there, and thou shalt receive them: and thou shalt accomplish my desire, in giving food for my household [1 Kings 5:8–9].

In addition to the workmen from Tyre, Solomon employed a large work force of Israelites.

And king Solomon raised a levy out of all Israel: and the levy was thirty thousand men.

And he sent them to Lebanon, ten thousand a month by courses: a month they were in Lebanon, and two months at home: and Adoniram was over the levy [1 Kings 5:13–14].

This was a tremendous enterprise. After Solomon had built the temple, he went on to build other things. He had a building project that was too big, and he overtaxed his people.

Chapter 6 brings us to the actual construction of the temple. You will notice that the temple is twice as large as the tabernacle was. It was more ornate, elaborate, and costly. The simplicity of the tabernacle was lost, and there appears to be a spiritual deterioration, as we shall see.

And the house which king Solomon built for the LORD, the length thereof was threescore cubits, and the breadth thereof twenty cubits, and the height thereof thirty cubits [1 Kings 6:2].

Although the temple was twice as large as the tabernacle, it may be smaller than we realize. The tabernacle was 30 x 10 cubits "and the height thereof 30 cubits." The temple was three times higher than the tabernacle, which had been nothing in the world but a tent.

Even though the temple was small, it was like a jewel. Now a diamond is not as big as a straw stack, but it is much more valuable. That was true of the temple Solomon built.

And the porch before the temple of the house, twenty cubits was the length thereof, according to the breadth of the house; and ten cubits was the breadth thereof before the house.

And for the house he made windows of narrow lights.

And against the wall of the house he built chambers round about, against the walls of the house round about, both of the temple and of the oracle: and he made chambers round about:

The nethermost chamber was five cubits broad, and the middle was six cubits broad, and the third was seven cubits broad: for without in the wall of the house he made narrowed rests round about, that the beams should not be fastened in the walls of the house.

And the house, when it was in building, was built of stone made ready before it was brought thither: so that there was neither hammer nor axe nor any tool of iron heard in the house, while it was in building [1 Kings 6:3–7].

Let me say a word about the construction of the temple. As we have seen, it was only twice as large as the tabernacle. It was surrounded on three sides by a three-story building. This was the place where the priests lived during their course of service. In the front there was a portico that was 10 x 20 x 120 cubits—half as long as a football field. The brazen altar was 20 x 20 x 10 cubits, while the altar of the tabernacle was 5 x 5 x 3 cubits. There were ten lampstands to replace the one of the tabernacle. There were ten tables of showbread rather than one. There was a multiplication of some of the articles of furniture.

There were 30,000 Israelites used in the construction; they were drafted for the work. There were 150,000 extra workers and 3,300 overseers used in the construction of the building. Hiram, king of Tyre, furnished the material and the artifices. The temple was completed in seven years and six months. The temple was made of stone, and the sound of a hammer was not heard during the building. The cost of the building is estimated around five million dollars. It was like a jewel box. There were two pillars in it which were very impressive. Later on we will see what they mean.

I have mentioned these details by way of comparison. The temple was inferior to the tabernacle, not only in innate quality, but in that which the temple characterizes.

First of all, it was complicated. The simplicity of the tabernacle was lost. In the New Testament the temple is bypassed and the tabernacle is used for the typology. Why? Well, the temple had become very complicated. This has an application for us. We are living in a day when the emphasis is put on methods rather than on the Word of God. The church is filled with new programs and new methods.

When I first began my ministry I pastored in a little white church on a red clay hill in Georgia, surrounded by a cotton patch. We just had a back room that served as Sunday school. We didn't have very good facilities. We did have central heating, however, as a great big old potbellied stove sat right in the middle of the church. I went by that church a short time ago. The city of Atlanta has grown all around it now. The church now has a big Christian education department and all of the latest equipment. I asked a member of the church, one who had been saved during my ministry, "Does anybody ever get saved here today?" He said, "No. Nobody has been saved." May I say to you that there is a girl out on the mission field who was saved when it was a little old simple church. Although it was very simple, people got saved. I don't like all of the methods employed today. I think we need to get back to the Word of God.

The second thing I want you to notice is that Solomon made windows of narrow lights. There had been no windows in the tabernacle. Now Solomon's windows did not let in much light, but they did let in a little. The people no longer depended upon divine light as they had in the tabernacle. They depended on the natural light which came from outside.

The third indication of inferiority is that the cherubim were made of olive wood. They were ten cubits high—very impressive—but they were no longer made of solid gold. The fourth thing is that the temple was more ornate and gaudy than the tabernacle, and there was more ceremony and ritual connected with it.

This is the temple that was destroyed by Nebuchadnezzar. The temple put up by Zerubbabel was destroyed in turn and then supplanted by Herod's temple in Christ's day. The temple actually pointed to the Lord Jesus Christ. In John 2:19 Jesus said, "Destroy this temple, and in three days I will raise it up." He wasn't talking about Herod's temple; He was talking about His body: "Then said the Jews, Forty and six years was this temple in building, and wilt thou rear it up in three days? But he spake of the temple of his body" (John 2:20–21). The temple is equated with the body of Christ.

Because this chapter is largely a record of building detail, I have not quoted much of it. However, you will find it very interesting to read. As you read of the magnificence of the temple, keep in mind that it was conceived in the mind and heart of David, as he wanted a suitable place to house the ark of the covenant. (He had no idea, of course, of building a dwelling place for God; he said it was only a footstool for Him.) Its purpose was to provide access to God by sacrifice. Also notice how complicated it is in comparison to the tabernacle. After I had written a book on the tabernacle, I was going to follow it with a book on the temple. After a great deal of study, I threw up my hands in despair. It is much too complicated to illustrate or set before us the wonderful person of the Lord Jesus Christ. However, God honored it with His presence, and the place was filled with the Shekinah glory, as we shall see in the following chapter.

CHAPTER 7

THEME: *Solomon's building projects*

In chapter 7 we learn that not only did Solomon build the temple, but he built his own palace, the house of the forest of Lebanon, and a palace for the daughter of Pharaoh. Also in this chapter we have details concerning the construction of the porch of the temple, the molten sea for the temple, the ten lavers of brass and the ten golden lampstands for the temple.

But Solomon was building his own house thirteen years, and he finished all his house [1 Kings 7:1].

It took seven years to build the temple, but it took almost twice that long to build his own house. It must have been a very elaborate palace.

He built also the house of the forest of Lebanon; the length thereof was an hundred cubits, and the breadth thereof fifty cubits, and the height thereof thirty cubits, upon four rows of cedar pillars, with cedar beams upon the pillars [1 Kings 7:2].

Solomon also built the house of the forest of Lebanon. That was his lodge, his second house. Perhaps that is where he went on vacation. We are told that the "length thereof was an hundred cubits," which is half the length of a football field. The breadth was fifty cubits, which is seventy-five feet. The height of it was thirty cubits; that is forty-five feet. It was built "upon four rows of cedar pillars, with cedar beams upon the pillars." Hiram, king of Tyre, furnished the stone and the cedars, which were the cedars of Lebanon. There are very few of those tall, graceful cedars left today. All of that country, including Palestine, has been denuded. Apparently at one time it was heavily timbered.

And his house where he dwelt had another court within the porch, which was of the like work. Solomon made also an house for Pharaoh's daughter, whom he had taken to wife, like unto this porch [1 Kings 7:8].

"Of the like work" indicates it was also very ornate and elaborate. He built a house for Pharaoh's daughter—he seems to have put her in a favored position. He could not build each wife such a palace. If he had, he would have built a thousand palaces! That would have been a staggering building program, like a government housing development.

HIRAM, THE ARTISAN

And king Solomon sent and fetched Hiram out of Tyre.

He was a widow's son of the tribe of Naphtali, and his father was a man of Tyre, a worker in brass: and he was filled with wisdom, and understanding, and cunning to work all works in brass. And he came to king Solomon, and wrought all his work [1 Kings 7:13–14].

This man is Hiram, the artisan, and not Hiram, the king. He was a skilled worker in brass. He was the one who made all of the delicate pieces of statuary and the items that were made out of iron, brass, and gold. His work was highly ornamented, which is what Solomon wanted. Elaborate ornamentation is evidence of the affluent period and time of peace in which he lived. It is during an era of peace and prosperity that the arts develop. During Solomon's reign there was peace and plenty.

Now we are given more detail relative to the temple.

And he set up the pillars in the porch of the temple: and he set up the right pillar, and called the name thereof Jachin: and he set up the left pillar, and called the name thereof Boaz [1 Kings 7:21].

Jachin means "God shall establish," *Boaz* means "in it is strength." You will find that there are psalms which include these two concepts of strength and beauty. For example, Psalm 96:6 says, "Honour and majesty are before him: strength and beauty are in his sanctuary." Strength speaks of salvation—God is able to deliver those who are His. Beauty speaks of the beauty of worship. We are to worship God in the beauty of holiness. These two pillars were prominent in the temple. Spiritually, these two pillars should be in the life of anyone who is going to worship God. If you are going to worship God, you must have experienced the power of God in delivering you from sin. Then you can worship Him in the beauty of holiness. I see nothing wrong in having a beautiful sanctuary; I think it is quite proper. A beautiful sanctuary may be conducive to worship, but it does not always inspire worship and certainly is no substitute for worship. We worship Him in the beauty of holiness. That is, when we come into the presence of God, sense His presence, and realize our inadequacies, then we can see *Him* in all of His beauty and glory. This was Isaiah's experience when he went into the temple and saw a vision of God seated upon a throne, high, and holy, and lifted up. When Isaiah saw himself in the light of the presence of God, he saw his own uncleanness. "Then said I, Woe is me! for I am undone; because I am a man of unclean lips, and I dwell in the midst of a people of unclean lips: for mine eyes have seen the King, the LORD of hosts" (Isa. 6:5). The pillars Jachin and Boaz speak of that which worship really is—a redeemed soul who comes into the presence of a holy God.

Realizing that I am no authority in the realm of music, I still insist that music which does not lift you into the presence of God is not music for the church. There is a great deal of music in the church which definitely does not prepare anyone for worship. I have discovered in my ministry and conference work that many times a musical number given by the choir or a soloist before the message is absolutely devastating and destructive to the giving out of the Word of God. We need to recognize that the worship of God is based on the fact that He is high, holy, and lifted up.

Solomon also greatly enlarged the laver in the temple.

And he made a molten sea, ten cubits from the one brim to the other: it was round all about, and his height was five cubits: and a line of thirty cubits did compass it round about [1 Kings 7:23].

This huge laver was supported on twelve oxen cast in brass, three oxen looking in each direction. The brim of it was ornate with lilies. The laver was for the priests to wash in. While there was only one simple laver in the tabernacle, here we have multiplication and beautification in Solomon's temple.

Then made he ten lavers of brass: one laver contained forty baths: and every laver was four cubits: and upon every one of the ten bases one laver [1 Kings 7:38].

The purpose of these ten lavers was to cleanse such things as they offered for the burnt offering.

It takes more than size and beauty to bring cleansing to the heart. There are many churches today that conduct beautiful services, yet they do not cleanse the congregation nor bring them into the presence of God. They do not refresh the soul nor bring peace and joy to the heart. All the lavers in the world cannot cleanse one from sin. It is the water in the laver that cleanses. The water represents the Word of God. To wash in the Word of God is to apply the Word to the life.

And Solomon made all the vessels that pertained unto the house of the LORD: the altar of gold, and the table of gold, whereupon the shewbread was.

And the candlesticks of pure gold, five on the right side, and five on the left, before the oracle, with the flowers, and the lamps, and the tongs of gold [1 Kings 7:48–49].

In the tabernacle there was one lampstand which spoke of Christ. In the temple there were ten. Again there is multiplication that has an application for us. In our contemporary society there is danger in becoming overly familiar with the Lord Jesus Christ. For example, the other day I listened to a message given on the radio in which the speaker mentioned the name of Jesus over fifty times before he was halfway through his message. To keep mentioning His name over and over is like multiplying lampstands. Also I heard a man say the other day that he was going to come into the presence of Jesus and sit down and talk with Him. Maybe he will; I don't know. But the Bible does not suggest such familiarity with the glorified Christ. A man who was very familiar with Him when He was here on earth—who rebuked Him and made suggestions to Him, and reclined on His bosom in the upper room—was John. He was very familiar with Him in the days of His flesh. But John writes of his reaction when he sees the glorified Christ in these terms: "And when I saw him, I fell at his feet as dead . . ." (Rev. 1:17). I think that is where you and I are going to be when we come into Christ's presence. My friend, let's not keep multiplying lampstands, becoming overly familiar with Him. He is the One whom we *worship* and adore. He is the One before whom we fall down upon our faces.

So was ended all the work that king Solomon made for the house of the LORD. And Solomon brought in the things which David his father had dedicated; even the silver, and the gold, and the vessels, did he put among the treasures of the house of the LORD [1 Kings 7:51].

CHAPTER 8

***THEME:** Dedication of the finished temple*

In the chapter before us the ark of the covenant is brought into the completed temple, the Shekinah glory fills the house of the Lord, and Solomon gives his message and prayer of dedication.

> **Then Solomon assembled the elders of Israel, and all the heads of the tribes, the chief of the fathers of the children of Israel, unto king Solomon in Jerusalem, that they might bring up the ark of the covenant of the LORD out of the city of David, which is Zion [1 Kings 8:1].**

When the ark is brought from the tabernacle and installed in the place prepared for it in the holy of holies, the glory of the Lord fills the temple.

> **And it came to pass, when the priests were come out of the holy place, that the cloud filled the house of the LORD.**
>
> **So that the priests could not stand to minister because of the cloud: for the glory of the LORD had filled the house of the LORD [1 Kings 8:10–11].**

In Solomon's message of dedication he gives proper credit to David.

> **And it was in the heart of David my father to build an house for the name of the LORD God of Israel.**
>
> **And the LORD said unto David my father, Whereas it was in thine heart to build an house unto my name, thou didst well that it was in thine heart.**
>
> **Nevertheless thou shalt not build the house; but thy son that shall come forth out of thy loins, he shall build the house unto my name.**
>
> **And the LORD hath performed his word that he spake, and I am risen up in the room of David my father, and sit on the throne of Israel, as the LORD promised, and have built an house for the name of the LORD God of Israel [1 Kings 8: 17–20].**

The desire for a permanent structure to house the ark of God originated in the heart of David, as we have seen in 2 Samuel 7. Solomon merely executed David's plans. I think it should be called David's temple rather than Solomon's temple.

In Solomon's prayer of dedication he says that this temple is to be a place for the name of God, and a place where God's people are to approach Him. It is not a pagan temple in which there is an idol—nor in which God lives. Solomon understands that the temple is, as David had said, the footstool of God.

> **But will God indeed dwell on the earth? behold, the heaven and heaven of heavens cannot contain thee; how much less this house that I have builded? [1 Kings 8:27].**

It was merely a place for man to come and bow before Him and offer his sacrifices before Him. It served as an approach to God. It is a pagan notion to think that God can dwell in a house down here. Solomon said, "The heaven and heaven of heavens cannot contain thee." God is omnipresent—He is everywhere. He is also transcendent, above His creation.

Now here is a section that is quite interesting. It looks forward to the day when Israel would sin against God and be sent into captivity.

> **If they sin against thee, (for there is no man that sinneth not,) and thou be angry with them, and deliver them to the enemy, so that they carry them away captives unto the land of the enemy, far or near [1 Kings 8:46].**

This, by the way, is God's estimate of you and me—"there is no man that sinneth not." Don't tell me that *you* don't sin. God says you do.

> **Yet if they shall bethink themselves in the land whither they were carried captives, and repent, and make supplication unto thee in the land of them that carried them captives, saying, We have sinned, and have done perversely, we have committed wickedness.**
>
> **And so return unto thee with all their heart, and with all their soul, in the land of their enemies, which led them away captive, and pray unto thee toward their land, which thou gavest unto their fathers, the city which thou hast chosen, and the house which I have built for thy name [1 Kings 8:47–48].**

This is what they are to do when their temple is destroyed and they are captives in a strange land. This is exactly what Daniel will do over in Babylon. He will open his window toward Jerusalem and pray toward that temple, confessing the sins of his people and his own sins.

Then hear thou their prayer and their supplication in heaven thy dwelling place, and maintain their cause.

And forgive thy people that have sinned against thee, and all their transgressions wherein they have transgressed against thee, and give them compassion before them who carried them captive, that they may have compassion on them [1 Kings 8:49–50].

As we shall see, God will answer this prayer.

And it was so, that when Solomon had made an end of praying all this prayer and supplication unto the LORD, he arose from before the altar of the LORD, from kneeling on his knees with his hands spread up to heaven [1 Kings 8:54].

There has always been a question about the proper posture of prayer. Should you stand, kneel, get down on all fours, or prostrate yourself before the Lord on the ground? Solomon knelt when he prayed. Although no particular posture is essential—you can pray in most any position—this is where the posture of kneeling is mentioned. I think it was Victor Hugo who said that the soul is on its knees many times regardless of the posture of the body. It is the posture of the heart that is important.

And Solomon offered a sacrifice of peace offerings, which he offered unto the LORD, two and twenty thousand oxen, and an hundred and twenty thousand sheep. So the king and all the children of Israel dedicated the house of the LORD.

The same day did the king hallow the middle of the court that was before the house of the LORD: for there he offered burnt offerings, and meat offerings, and the fat of the peace offerings: because the brasen altar that was before the LORD was too little to receive the burnt offerings, and meat offerings, and the fat of the peace offerings.

And at that time Solomon held a feast, and all Israel with him, a great congregation, from the entering in of Hamath unto the river of Egypt, before the LORD our God, seven days and seven days, even fourteen days [1 Kings 8:63–65].

Obviously, the altars in the temple could not accommodate all the animal sacrifices mentioned in this passage. Therefore temporary altars were erected to handle the large number of animals which were sacrificed at this time. I think that these altars reached all the way up north to Hamath and all the way south to the river of Egypt. After the animals were offered, they were taken off the altars and divided among the people. It was a time of great celebration and picnicking, you might say.

On the eighth day he sent the people away: and they blessed the king, and went unto their tents joyful and glad of heart for all the goodness that the LORD had done for David his servant, and for Israel his people [1 Kings 8:66].

CHAPTERS 9–10

***THEME:** The fame of Solomon; the visit of the queen of Sheba*

God appears to Solomon a second time to encourage him, and He sets up David as a standard of measurement for him. The remainder of these two chapters gives proof of Solomon's greatness and of the prosperity of his reign.

GOD APPEARS TO SOLOMON A SECOND TIME

And it came to pass, when Solomon had finished the building of the house of the LORD, and the king's house, and all Solomon's desire which he was pleased to do.

That the LORD appeared to Solomon the second time, as he had appeared unto him at Gibeon.

And the LORD said unto him, I have heard thy prayer and thy supplication, that thou hast made before me: I have hallowed this house, which thou hast built, to put my name there for ever; and mine eyes and mine heart shall be there perpetually [1 Kings 9:1–3].

God is saying to Solomon, "I will meet with you here at the temple. This is the place for you to come, for the people to come, and for the world to come. This is the meeting place."

And if thou wilt walk before me, as David thy father walked, in integrity of heart, and in uprightness, to do according to all that I have commanded thee, and wilt keep my statutes and my judgments [1 Kings 9:4].

Now God charges Solomon, "And if thou wilt walk before me, as David thy father walked . . . Then I will establish the throne of thy kingdom upon Israel for ever." David is a human standard, not a high standard according to God's standards. David had a tremendous capacity for God. He loved God but he failed, fumbled, faltered, and fell. But he got up and came to God in confession. He wanted to have fellowship with God. God told Solomon that He wanted him to walk before Him as David his father had done—in integrity of heart.

Integrity of heart is important for us today because there is so much subterfuge and hypocrisy in Christian circles. I spoke at a church banquet some time ago where there were over one thousand people present. One of the politicians of that area got up and said a few words. You would have thought he was the most pious fellow in that crowd. But he managed to leave before the message. Do you know why? He did not want to hear it. He was not interested in God's Word. There is so much of that kind of hypocrisy today. One sees dishonesty and hypocrisy revealed on Sunday morning. Here comes a man out of the business world. He has been careless in his life; he has not been a good example in his home. Yet he walks into church with a Bible under his arm and talks about God and God's will, using all sorts of pious expressions. Whom is he attempting to fool? Does he think he is fooling God?

My friend, we don't fool God. We might as well tell Him the facts because He already knows them. David walked before God in integrity of heart. When he sinned, he confessed it and asked for cleansing. Although his faith failed for a moment, beneath the faith that failed was a faith that never failed. Imperfect though he was, God set him up as a standard: "walk before me, as David thy father walked."

Then I will establish the throne of thy kingdom upon Israel for ever, as I promised to David thy father, saying, There shall not fail thee a man upon the throne of Israel [1 Kings 9:5].

As long as Israel had a king, he was in the line of David. And there is One today in David's line whose nail-pierced hands hold the sceptre of this universe.

But if ye shall at all turn from following me, ye or your children, and will not keep my commandments and my statutes which I have set before you, but go and serve other gods, and worship them:

Then will I cut off Israel out of the land which I have given them; and this house, which I have hallowed for my name, will I cast out of my sight; and Israel shall be a proverb and a byword among all people [1 Kings 9:6–7].

The Jews are certainly a proverb and a byword today. This has come to pass literally.

And at this house, which is high, every one that passeth by it shall be aston-

ished, and shall hiss; and they shall say, Why hath the LORD done thus unto this land, and to this house?

And they shall answer, Because they forsook the LORD their God, who brought forth their fathers out of the land of Egypt, and have taken hold upon other gods, and have worshipped them, and served them: therefore hath the LORD brought upon them all this evil [1 Kings 9:8–9].

This also has come to pass literally. If you go to the spot where the temple once stood, you will see that it has been destroyed. The Mosque of Omar now stands there. Why is the land of Israel like it is? Why is the Mosque of Omar there? Israel forsook God, friend. That is the answer.

SOLOMON'S FAME

Next we are told that Solomon and Hiram had a little difficulty.

And it came to pass at the end of twenty years, when Solomon had built the two houses, the house of the LORD, and the king's house,

(Now Hiram the king of Tyre had furnished Solomon with cedar trees and fir trees, and with gold, according to all his desire,) that then king Solomon gave Hiram twenty cities in the land of Galilee.

And Hiram came out from Tyre to see the cities which Solomon had given him; and they pleased him not [1 Kings 9:10–12].

When Hiram saw the twenty cities, he felt that he had not been given full payment for all that he had done for Solomon in the building of the temple. Actually there was a misunderstanding, and this is the thing that caused a breach between these two men.

And he said, What cities are these which thou hast given me, my brother? And he called them the land of Cabul unto this day.

And Hiram sent to the king sixscore talents of gold [1 Kings 9:13–14].

This last sentence should read "Hiram *had* sent . . ."—explaining that the cities were in payment for the gold he had furnished (the timber, stone, and labor had been paid for in corn, wine, and oil).

And this is the reason of the levy which king Solomon raised; for to build the house of the LORD, and his own house, and Millo, and the wall of Jerusalem, and Hazor, and Megiddo, and Gezer.

And Solomon built Gezer, and Beth-horon the nether,

And Baalath, and Tadmor in the wilderness, in the land,

And all the cities of store that Solomon had, and cities for his chariots, and cities for his horsemen, and that which Solomon desired to build in Jerusalem, and in Lebanon, and in all the land of his dominion [1 Kings 9:15, 17–19].

This passage describes the extension of Solomon's kingdom and his tremendous building program.

And king Solomon made a navy of ships in Ezion-geber, which is beside Eloth, on the shore of the Red sea, in the land of Edom.

And Hiram sent in the navy his servants, shipmen that had knowledge of the sea, with the servants of Solomon.

And they came to Ophir, and fetched from thence gold, four hundred and twenty talents, and brought it to king Solomon [1 Kings 9:26–28].

Solomon just about cornered the gold market in that day. He also had quite a navy. Ezion-geber was situated on the eastern arm of the Red Sea. This was Solomon's seaport. It was situated near Israeli Eilat. It is thought that his navy extended its navigation as far away as Ophir in southwestern Arabia.

SOLOMON IS VISITED BY THE QUEEN OF SHEBA

The visit of the queen of Sheba reveals that Solomon had succeeded in witnessing for God to the world of that day. Solomon's fame had spread, and obviously multitudes were coming to Jerusalem to worship the living and true God. In the present dispensation, the church is to go to the world, but the commission to go into all the world was not given to the nation Israel. As Israel was true to God, she was a witness to the world, and the world came to Jerusalem to worship.

In chapter 10 we have a great illustration of the influence of Solomon in that day. The visit of this queen shows the effect of the reign of

Solomon, as God's representative, upon the nations of the world.

And when the queen of Sheba heard of the fame of Solomon concerning the name of the LORD, she came to prove him with hard questions [1 Kings 10:1].

The queen of Sheba came to Solomon because of what she had heard. She had heard of a temple where man could approach God—she wanted to know about that. She had heard of Solomon's wisdom; so she came to test him with difficult questions.

And she came to Jerusalem with a very great train, with camels that bare spices, and very much gold, and precious stones: and when she was come to Solomon, she communed with him of all that was in her heart.

And Solomon told her all her questions: there was not any thing hid from the king, which he told her not.

And when the queen of Sheba had seen all Solomon's wisdom, and the house that he had built,

And the meat of his table, and the sitting of his servants, and the attendance of his ministers, and their apparel, and his cupbearers, and his ascent by which he went up unto the house of the LORD; there was no more spirit in her [1 Kings 10:2–5].

Now the phrase, "and his ascent by which he went up unto the house of the LORD," should be translated, "and his burnt offering by which he went up unto the house of the LORD." She witnesses that Solomon approached God by a burnt offering. This is the offering that speaks more fully of Christ and His substitutionary death than all the others. Hebrews 9:22 says, "And almost all things are by the law purged with blood; and without shedding of blood is no remission." The burnt offering was a testimony to the queen of Sheba.

She was also impressed with the wisdom of Solomon and with his building program: the palace, the temple and the other buildings. All around were bounty, luxury, and temporal prosperity. For a brief moment in time, God's people were faithful and true witnesses of Him.

And so the queen responds to all that she has seen and heard:

And she said to the king, It was a true report that I heard in mine own land of thy acts and of thy wisdom.

Howbeit I believed not the words, until I came, and mine eyes had seen it: and, behold, the half was not told me: thy wisdom and prosperity exceedeth the fame which I heard [1 Kings 10:6–7].

She had not believed half of what she had been told and came to find that the half had not been told her. And I don't think the half has been told today concerning our Lord.

Happy are thy men, happy are these thy servants, which stand continually before thee, and that hear thy wisdom.

Blessed be the LORD thy God, which delighted in thee, to set thee on the throne of Israel: because the LORD loved Israel for ever, therefore made he thee king, to do judgment and justice [1 Kings 10:8–9].

This now is her testimony, and I think it reveals that she has come to know the living and true God.

And she gave the king an hundred and twenty talents of gold, and of spices very great store, and precious stones: there came no more such abundance of spices as these which the queen of Sheba gave to king Solomon [1 Kings 10:10].

She brought a great amount of wealth and gave it to Solomon.

And the navy also of Hiram, that brought gold from Ophir, brought in from Ophir great plenty of almug trees, and precious stones.

And the king made of the almug trees pillars for the house of the LORD, and for the king's house, harps also and psalteries for singers: there came no such almug trees, nor were seen unto this day [1 Kings 10:11–12].

Hiram was king of Tyre—of the Phoenicians who were a seagoing people. We see here that Solomon continued his building program. He made pillars for the house of the Lord and for the king's house, also harps and psalteries for singers.

And king Solomon gave unto the queen of Sheba all her desire, whatsoever she asked, beside that which Solomon gave her of his royal bounty. So she turned and went to her own country, she and her servants [1 Kings 10:13].

The story of the queen of Sheba is one example of the many who came to know God at this time. Similarly, the Book of Acts records only certain conversions such as those of the Ethiopian eunuch, Saul of Tarsus and Cornelius. Yet we know that literally thousands came to know Christ during that period. And there were thousands who came to know God through the temple in Jerusalem and the witness of the people of Solomon's day.

Now we are told something of the gold that came to Solomon:

Now the weight of gold that came to Solomon in one year was six hundred threescore and six talents of gold,

Beside that he had of the merchantmen, and of the traffic of the spice merchants, and of all the kings of Arabia, and of the governors of the country.

And king Solomon made two hundred targets of beaten gold: six hundred shekels of gold went to one target [1 Kings 10:14–16].

I cannot comprehend it when it says there were six hundred threescore and six talents of gold that came to him every year—he simply cornered the gold market. The kingdom had reached its zenith. Actually, David brought it to this position, but now Solomon is the one who is able to move in and enjoy the peace, the plenty, and the prosperity.

For the king had at sea a navy of Tharshish with the navy of Hiram: once in three years came the navy of Tharshish, bringing gold, and silver, ivory, and apes, and peacocks [1 Kings 10:22].

All of these are luxury items: apes for entertainment (these were Solomon's zoo); peacocks for beauty; and gold, silver, and ivory for magnificent decorations. There is a frivolous and tragic note here which is symptomatic of the condition of Solomon's kingdom. He is called to give a witness to the world—the world is coming to his door—and what does he do? He spends his time and energy with apes and peacocks simply to satisfy a whim.

So king Solomon exceeded all the kings of the earth for riches and for wisdom.

And all the earth sought to Solomon, to hear his wisdom, which God had put in his heart [1 Kings 10:23–24].

It was during this period that the kingdom reached its zenith and was characterized by very faithful witnessing. We have seen that illustrated in the life of the queen of Sheba, and now we are told that many others came to Jerusalem also. There was a real witness given to the world by Solomon—a witness for God.

And they brought every man his present, vessels of silver, and vessels of gold, and garments, and armour, and spices, horses, and mules, a rate year by year [1 Kings 10:25].

Frankly, the presents from these visitors enabled Solomon to build up a kingdom that was noted for its riches. Later, of course, that made Israel the subject of spoil by other nations when the kingdom was divided and weakened.

And Solomon gathered together chariots and horsemen: and he had a thousand and four hundred chariots, and twelve thousand horsemen, whom he bestowed in the cities for chariots, and with the king at Jerusalem [1 Kings 10:26].

Solomon, as he gathered horses and horsemen, expanded in a department in which God had forbidden him to expand. Solomon's stables would make these modern race tracks look like a tenant farmer's barn in Georgia.

And the king made silver to be in Jerusalem as stones, and cedars made he to be as the sycomore trees that are in the vale, for abundance.

And Solomon had horses brought out of Egypt, and linen yarn: the king's merchants received the linen yarn at a price.

And a chariot came up and went out of Egypt for six hundred shekels of silver, and an horse for an hundred and fifty: and so for all the kings of the Hittites, and for the kings of Syria, did they bring them out by their means [1 Kings 10:27–29].

Solomon really built up tremendous wealth in the kingdom. At that time he actually cornered the market on gold, silver, and precious stones.

My friend, what are you busy doing today? Are you getting out the Word of God or are you in the business of gathering a bunch of apes? Do you pay more for entertainment than you do for the Word of God? How about the peacocks for beauty? More money is spent today on beauty preparations than is given to the Lord's work. What about gold, silver, and precious stones? Are you so busy making money that you have no time left for the Lord? Oh, my friend, we are called to witness to the world. God have mercy on us for going into the business of apes and peacocks. How frivolous!

CHAPTER 11

***THEME:** The shame and death of Solomon*

Solomon is the most colossal failure in the pages of Scripture. ". . . For unto whomsoever much is given, of him shall be much required . . ." (Luke 12:48). He had the greatest opportunity of any man who ever lived. He began by failing to remove false religion (1 Kings 3:3). What was at first only a spot is now a plague of leprosy. He had a harem of one thousand wives, pagan women, who turned his heart away from the Lord. For this reason God stirred up enemies against Solomon and allowed Jeroboam to rise to prominence and finally split the kingdom.

SOLOMON FORSAKES GOD

But king Solomon loved many strange women, together with the daughter of Pharaoh, women of the Moabites, Ammonites, Edomites, Zidonians, and Hittites [1 Kings 11:1].

As far as women were concerned, Solomon was patterning his life after his father David. It is too bad he did not pattern his life after other areas of David's life, but he did not. Remember that Solomon had been brought up in the king's palace. He was sort of an effeminate fellow, unaccustomed to the rough and rugged life that David had known. Solomon began to gather women, just as someone else might have a hobby of gathering antique automobiles. He collected women of all nationalities.

Now these women turned the head of Solomon, causing him to go into idolatry and to permit it in the land. He violated God's prescribed law at this particular point.

Of the nations concerning which the LORD said unto the children of Israel, Ye shall not go in to them, neither shall they come in unto you: for surely they will turn away your heart after their gods: Solomon clave unto these in love [1 Kings 11:2].

I think this is the one place in Scripture where the word *love* can be changed to *sex*. That was Solomon's motive. He had been raised in the women's palace and had never known anything rough or manly. When he became an adult, Solomon spent his time gathering women. He was accustomed to their company. He was a dandy. He was like many men we have in our society today. God is going to deal with him in this connection. The Lord did not approve of what Solomon did, for the Scripture says:

And the LORD was angry with Solomon, because his heart was turned from the LORD God of Israel, which had appeared unto him twice,

And had commanded him concerning this thing, that he should not go after other gods: but he kept not that which the LORD commanded.

Wherefore the LORD said unto Solomon, Forasmuch as this is done of thee, and thou hast not kept my covenant and my statutes, which I have commanded thee, I will surely rend the kingdom from thee, and will give it to thy servant.

Notwithstanding in thy days I will not do it for David thy father's sake: but I will rend it out of the hand of thy son.

Howbeit I will not rend away all the kingdom; but will give one tribe to thy son for David my servant's sake, and for Jerusalem's sake which I have chosen [1 Kings 11:9–13].

"The LORD was angry with Solomon." Let's be fair with the Word of God. There are those who say, "Oh, look, God permitted Solomon to have a thousand wives." The record gives us the number accurately; that is history. But God's attitude toward it is also revealed: "the LORD was angry with Solomon."

The Lord said that he would not rend away all of the kingdom from Solomon. One tribe would be left for Solomon's son. That one tribe, I would say, was Benjamin. Solomon was a member of the tribe of Judah; naturally that tribe would also stand with him. So Benjamin and Judah were in the division that will go with the family of David. The other ten tribes in the north will follow Jeroboam.

SOLOMON IS CHASTENED

Now we come to the time at the end of Solomon's reign. God begins to stir up trouble for this man. "There is no peace, saith my God, to the wicked" (Isa. 57:21). Solomon had enjoyed peace. Now for the first time during his reign there was to be warfare.

And the LORD stirred up an adversary unto Solomon, Hadad the Edomite: he was of the king's seed in Edom [1 Kings 11:14].

Next we are introduced to Jeroboam.

And Jeroboam the son of Nebat, an Ephrathite of Zereda, Solomon's servant, whose mother's name was Zeruah, a widow woman, even he lifted up his hand against the king.

And this was the cause that he lifted up his hand against the king: Solomon built Millo, and repaired the breaches of the city of David his father.

And the man Jeroboam was a mighty man of valour: and Solomon seeing the young man that he was industrious, he made him ruler over all the charge of the house of Joseph [1 Kings 11:26–28].

Although Jeroboam was the son of a servant, Solomon recognized that he was a young man of considerable ability and talent. Solomon, therefore, elevated him to a high position and made him overseer of his public works.

And it came to pass at that time when Jeroboam went out of Jerusalem, that the prophet Ahijah the Shilonite found him in the way; and he had clad himself with a new garment; and they two were alone in the field:

And Ahijah caught the new garment that was on him, and rent it in twelve pieces:

And he said to Jeroboam, Take thee ten pieces: for thus saith the LORD, the God of Israel, Behold, I will rend the kingdom out of the hand of Solomon, and will give ten tribes to thee:

(But he shall have one tribe for my servant David's sake, and for Jerusalem's sake, the city which I have chosen out of all the tribes of Israel:) [1 Kings 11:29–32].

Ahijah the prophet took Jeroboam's new garment and tore it into twelve pieces. He gave ten pieces to Jeroboam and said to him, "God is going to give you ten tribes. The kingdom is going to be divided."

Why would God divide Israel into two kingdoms?

Because that they have forsaken me, and have worshipped Ashtoreth the goddess of the Zidonians, Chemosh the god of the Moabites, and Milcom the god of the children of Ammon, and have not walked in my ways, to do that which is right in mine eyes, and to keep my statutes and my judgments, as did David his father [1 Kings 11:33].

The prophet continues with his message. For David's sake, God will not take the kingdom out of the hand of Solomon, but He will take it out of the hand of Solomon's son and give ten tribes to Jeroboam.

After these things, Jeroboam is forced to flee for his life.

Solomon sought therefore to kill Jeroboam. And Jeroboam arose, and fled into Egypt, unto Shishak king of Egypt, and was in Egypt until the death of Solomon [1 Kings 11:40].

SOLOMON'S DEATH

And the rest of the acts of Solomon, and all that he did, and his wisdom, are they not written in the book of the acts of Solomon?

And the time that Solomon reigned in Jerusalem over all Israel was forty years.

And Solomon slept with his fathers, and was buried in the city of David his father: and Rehoboam his son reigned in his stead [1 Kings 11:41–43].

We will see more of the acts of Solomon and his wisdom in 1 and 2 Chronicles. He was a colorful ruler in the sense that he accumulated so much of this world's goods. Everything in the kingdom denoted wealth, affluence, and prosperity. In the New Testament our Lord refers to the glory that was Solomon's. There was indeed an earthly glory in his kingdom.

CHAPTERS 12–14

***THEME:** Division of the kingdom under Rehoboam and Jeroboam*

In chapter 12 Rehoboam, son of Solomon, succeeds to the throne. Jeroboam returns from Egypt and leads ten tribes in demanding a reduction in taxes. Rehoboam under the influence of the young men of his kingdom, having rejected the counsel of the old men who were Solomon's advisors, turns down the request of the ten northern tribes. Instead of reducing taxes, he threatens to raise them. Therefore, Jeroboam leads the ten tribes in revolt.

Jeroboam divides the nation religiously as well as politically by setting up a golden calf in Beth-el and one in the tribe of Dan. The northern tribes go into idolatry.

REHOBOAM'S ACCESSION AND FOOLISHNESS

Solomon dies, and his son Rehoboam comes to the throne.

> **And Rehoboam went to Shechem: for all Israel were come to Shechem to make him king.**
>
> **And it came to pass, when Jeroboam the son of Nebat, who was yet in Egypt, heard of it, (for he was fled from the presence of king Solomon, and Jeroboam dwelt in Egypt:)**
>
> **That they sent and called him. And Jeroboam and all the congregation of Israel came, and spake unto Rehoboam, saying,**
>
> **Thy father made our yoke grievous: now therefore make thou the grievous service of thy father, and his heavy yoke which he put upon us, lighter, and we will serve thee.**
>
> **And he said unto them, Depart yet for three days, then come again to me. And the people departed [1 Kings 12:1–5].**

Solomon had carried on a tremendous building program at great cost. After his death the people asked for their taxes to be lowered. We hear about the government costing so much today. If you want to know *why* it costs so much, go to the capital of any state, or go to any county seat or to our capital in Washington, D.C., and you will see why taxes are like they are. Believe me, government is a fat calf. It is really spending money and putting up many buildings. Spending requires increased taxation; this is something that is always going to cause trouble. Our problem today is one of taxation—our government costs too much. We are seeing the increase in buildings to house more committees and more workers. Before long there will probably be more people working for the government than are working in all other jobs put together. This is the movement today; there was the same problem during the days of Solomon. He kept building and in order to do it, he had to increase the taxes.

Rehoboam was asked by the people to reduce taxes. This young ruler had an opportunity to move in and make himself popular by reducing taxes. If he had done that, the people would have followed him. Where is the man today who has the nerve, after being elected to office, to fire about half of the government workers? If someone would do that and cut down taxes, he would make himself popular. Leaders are afraid to take the first step.

Rehoboam called a meeting of his wise men (only they were very unwise).

> **And king Rehoboam consulted with the old men, that stood before Solomon his father while he yet lived, and said, How do ye advise that I may answer this people?**
>
> **And they spake unto him, saying, If thou wilt be a servant unto this people this day, and wilt serve them, and answer them, and speak good words to them, then they will be thy servants for ever [1 Kings 12:6–7].**

Rehoboam first turned to the wise men in the kingdom who had counseled Solomon his father. Their advice was good, but Rehoboam did not follow it.

But he forsook the counsel of the old men, which they had given him, and consulted with the young men that were grown up with him, and which stood before him:

And he said unto them, What counsel give ye that we may answer this people, who have spoken to me, saying, Make the yoke which thy father did put upon us lighter?

And the young men that were grown up with him spake unto him, saying, Thus shalt thou speak unto this people that spake unto thee, saying, Thy father made our yoke heavy, but make thou it lighter unto us; thus shalt thou say unto them, My little finger shall be thicker than my father's loins.

And now whereas my father did lade you with a heavy yoke, I will add to your yoke: my father hath chastised you with whips, but I will chastise you with scorpions [1 Kings 12:8–11].

Then he asked the young men who had grown up with him what they would advise. They too gave him advice, but it was foolish.

So Jeroboam and all the people came to Rehoboam the third day, as the king had appointed, saying, Come to me again the third day.

And the king answered the people roughly, and forsook the old men's counsel that they gave him;

And spake to them after the counsel of the young men, saying, My father made your yoke heavy, and I will add to your yoke: my father also chastised you with whips, but I will chastise you with scorpions.

Wherefore the king hearkened not unto the people; for the cause was from the LORD, that he might perform his saying, which the LORD spake by Ahijah the Shilonite unto Jeroboam the son of Nebat [1 Kings 12:12–15].

Rehoboam heeded what the young men told him rather than what the wise older men said. He told the people, "Instead of decreasing the taxes, I intend to increase them. Instead of being less severe with the people, I intend to be more severe."

JEROBOAM BECOMES ISRAEL'S KING AND THE KINGDOM IS DIVIDED

So when all Israel saw that the king hearkened not unto them, the people answered the king, saying, What portion have we in David? neither have we inheritance in the son of Jesse: to your tents, O Israel: now see to thine own house, David. So Israel departed unto their tents [1 Kings 12:16].

This is rebellion. This is the splitting up of the kingdom, and it will result, of course, in civil war.

Then king Rehoboam sent Adoram, who was over the tribute; and all Israel stoned him with stones, that he died. Therefore king Rehoboam made speed to get him up to his chariot, to flee to Jerusalem [1 Kings 12:18].

All Israel stoned Adoram. That is the way they got rid of the tax collector. And when Rehoboam heard what had happened, he fled to Jerusalem.

So Israel rebelled against the house of David unto this day [1 Kings 12:19].

Israel rebelled against the house of David until the time 1 Kings was written. It was a rebellion that continued on until they returned from the Babylonian captivity. Rehoboam's unwise decision in not listening to the people enabled Jeroboam to take the ten northern tribes and build a northern kingdom.

JEROBOAM'S IDOLATRY

Then Jeroboam built Shechem in mount Ephraim, and dwelt therein; and went out from thence, and built Penuel.

And Jeroboam said in his heart, Now shall the kingdom return to the house of David:

If this people go up to do sacrifice in the house of the LORD at Jerusalem, then shall the heart of this people turn again unto their lord, even unto Rehoboam king of Judah, and they shall kill me, and go again to Rehoboam king of Judah.

Whereupon the king took counsel, and made two calves of gold, and said unto

them, It is too much for you to go up to Jerusalem: behold thy gods, O Israel, which brought thee up out of the land of Egypt.

And he set the one in Beth-el, and the other put he in Dan.

And this thing became a sin: for the people went to worship before the one, even unto Dan [1 Kings 12:25–30].

Jeroboam put a golden calf in Beth-el and one in Dan. He put them there for the people to worship so that they would not go to Jerusalem to worship in the temple. This marks the division of the kingdom into the northern and southern kingdoms.

We will now follow the account of the divided kingdom and will find that the method used in 1 and 2 Kings is to record some history about Israel and then some history about Judah. The record goes back and forth. We will be looking at both kingdoms as we go along, but the kingdom of Judah will last longer than the kingdom of Israel. Also, almost all of the prophets, except the post-captivity prophets, prophesied during this period (see Chronological Table of the Kings of the Divided Kingdom, p. 331). The Table shows which kings of Judah and Israel were contemporary—that is, those who ruled at the same time—and which prophets prophesied during each reign.

This brings us to the end of 1 Kings 12. Rehoboam is the king of the southern kingdom following in the Davidic line. Jeroboam is the king of the northern kingdom. He has introduced idolatry into the north by building two golden calves and placing them in Beth-el and Dan so that the people would no longer go to Jerusalem to worship. There is a division —soon civil war will break out. It will continue until the northern kingdom goes into captivity. And we will find that eventually the southern kingdom will also go into captivity. This is a sad period in the life of the nation of Israel. It contains many lessons for us and for our government.

In chapter 13 we see God's judgment against the false altar of Jeroboam and the strange incident of the man of God who was deceived by a fellow prophet.

The kingdom has now been divided following the rebellion led by Jeroboam who took the ten northern tribes and formed the kingdom of Israel. Rehoboam, a man who certainly did not have the wisdom nor the diplomacy of his father Solomon, was actually responsible for the splitting of the kingdom. The northern kingdom will eventually go into captivity in Assyria and the southern kingdom into Babylon.

There can be a great deal of confusion as we go through this section and read of king after king. You may wonder whether this king belongs to the northern kingdom or the southern kingdom, and whether he is good or bad. The chronological chart of the kings will give you that information.

When I was a freshman in college, I took a Bible course that was puerile—it was a weak cup of tea. There were certain questions that were always asked in that class. One of the questions was, "Name the kings of Israel and Judah and briefly describe the reign of each." Well, some freshman in years gone by had made a profound discovery. He found out that if he memorized the names of the kings and wrote after each one—"a bad King"—he could make 95% on the test. What freshman would want to make a better mark than that? So that is what all the freshmen did.

You are going to find that in the northern kingdom every king was bad. There wasn't a good one in the lot. There were only eight kings in the southern kingdom—over a two-hundred-year period—who could be called good. The rest of them were bad kings. This is a dark blot in the history of Israel. Yet, I think you would find a similar record in other lands. If you want to bring all of this down to today, how many good presidents have we had? Party allegiances aside, I believe that history will have to record that we did not do so well either. We have probably had a better percentage of good leaders than Israel, but our batting average hasn't been very good.

The thing that makes Israel's record so bleak is that these people had light from heaven. They had a revelation from God, and their responsibility was greater. But I also feel that the responsibility of our nation is greater than that of other nations because we have, in certain respects, more light from heaven than other nations. Unfortunately our political affairs are a black spot in the life of our nation.

I would like to look back to Solomon for a moment to see why the kingdom was rent. Here is what happened. Solomon was given a special dispensation of wisdom from God to administer the kingdom. Yet that wisdom, apparently, did not enter into his own personal life: Solomon obviously did not have spiritual wisdom or discernment. He did understand certain basic principles and concepts which enabled him to be a very wise ruler, but which did not enter into his personal, private, and certainly not his spiritual life. You begin to see early in his career that he never really broke with false religion. At the beginning, when he came to the throne, there was idolatry, and he closed his eyes to it—he took no particular, definite, positive stand against it. Then he began to engage in that which was the mark of prosperity. He sent ships out to bring back apes and peacocks. There's nothing particularly wrong with apes and peacocks, but such an obsession is wrong if you have been called to glorify God—to witness and live for Him. Solomon had a definite weakness.

The Book of Proverbs reveals the wisdom of Solomon, but the Book of Ecclesiastes reveals his foolishness. You will not find any failure of Solomon's or his father David's in the Book of Chronicles. The two Books of Chronicles cover the same ground as the Books of Kings with one difference: in Kings you have man's viewpoint; you have the history given. Chronicles gives God's viewpoint. God forgave David; and, when God forgave him, He blotted out his sin. Written from God's viewpoint, the sin is not mentioned in Chronicles, but God put it in Kings for men to see. Likewise God forgave Solomon his failure, and his sin is not recorded in Chronicles. In Kings we do see Solomon's weakness—he began to multiply wives. God never approved of polygamy; His wrath was against it.

The interesting thing is that immorality and false religion always go together. John made it very clear for the Christian when he said, "If we say that we have fellowship with him, and walk in darkness, we lie, and do not the truth" (1 John 1:6). Don't kid yourself—you cannot serve God and have fellowship with Him if you live in sin. You can fool the people around you. Unfortunately, we have Christian leaders today who live in sin. They have been proven immoral, and yet people go ahead and support them—I have never quite understood why. But they are not fooling God, and they certainly are not having fellowship with Him.

Solomon was a man who was a great failure. There are two men in the Scripture who had tremendous potential and opportunity: one was Samson, and the other one was Solomon. Both of these men failed God in a tragic way. In Ecclesiastes Solomon said, "Therefore I hated life; because the work that is wrought under the sun is grievous unto me: for all is vanity and vexation of spirit" (Eccl. 2:17). The glory of Solomon was a passing glory. Our Lord could say that Solomon in all his glory is not arrayed like that little flower by the side of the road that you passed unnoticed. May I say to you that the wealth and achievements of this world are also a passing glory.

I have given this background of Solomon at this point—I guess I have more or less preached his funeral service—because now we are seeing a kingdom divided, and it is divided because of the sin of Solomon.

THE PROPHECY AGAINST JEROBOAM'S FALSE ALTAR

We are going to move rather rapidly through this section—it is history. We will be following the course of the two kingdoms, one following after the other or sometimes together or overlapping.

We find that Jeroboam, who came to the throne in the northern kingdom, was given an opportunity to really serve God. Yet his fear was that the tribes in the north would go back to Jerusalem to worship. That might reunite the kingdom, and he wanted to keep it separate. So Jeroboam set up two golden calves for the people to worship, one in Samaria and one in Beth-el.

And, behold, there came a man of God out of Judah by the word of the Lord unto Beth-el, and Jeroboam stood by the altar to burn incense.

And he cried against the altar in the word of the Lord, and said, O altar, altar, thus saith the Lord; Behold, a child shall be born unto the house of David, Josiah by name; and upon thee shall he offer the priests of the high places that burn incense upon thee, and men's bones shall be burnt upon thee [1 Kings 13:1–2].

Let me pause here a moment. It is interesting to note *when* Josiah reigned. It was almost three hundred years later, but the prophet of God marks him out now. He was a good king and he reigned thirty-one years. Josiah led in one of the five great revivals that took place during the period of the kings. We will consider those revivals in Chronicles. These revivals are not mentioned in Kings but in Chronicles, which gives God's viewpoint. Revival is always from God's viewpoint. Man is interested in numbers, but it is impossible for him to determine the real converts. God knows the hearts and knows whether a spiritual movement has taken place or not.

The prophet of God prophesied against the altar, saying that God was going to raise up a man who would destroy such altars. Josiah was the one who would be raised up to accomplish that task.

And he gave a sign the same day, saying, This is the sign which the LORD hath spoken; Behold, the altar shall be rent, and the ashes that are upon it shall be poured out.

And it came to pass, when king Jeroboam heard the saying of the man of God, which had cried against the altar in Beth-el, that he put forth his hand from the altar, saying, Lay hold on him. And his hand, which he put forth against him, dried up, so that he could not pull it in again to him [1 Kings 13:3–4].

Jeroboam was by the altar when the man of God prophesied. He was making a sacrifice to a golden calf. When the man of God was finished speaking, Jeroboam put out his hand against him. In effect, the king was saying, "Lay hold on him. He is to be slain." When the king pointed to the man of God, his hand dried up; that is, it withered and became paralyzed.

The altar also was rent, and the ashes poured out from the altar, according to the sign which the man of God had given by the word of the LORD.

And the king answered and said unto the man of God, Entreat now the face of the LORD thy God, and pray for me, that my hand may be restored me again. And the man of God besought the LORD, and the king's hand was restored him again, and became as it was before.

And the king said unto the man of God, Come home with me, and refresh thyself, and I will give thee a reward [1 Kings 13:5–7].

The king changes his tune very definitely and begs the man of God to ask the Lord that his arm might be restored. The king's hand is restored to him, and in appreciation he offers to take the man of God home with him and reward him.

And the man of God said unto the king, If thou wilt give me half thine house, I will not go in with thee, neither will I eat bread nor drink water in this place:

For so was it charged me by the word of the LORD, saying, Eat no bread, nor drink water, nor turn again by the same way that thou camest.

So he went another way, and returned not by the way that he came to Beth-el [1 Kings 13:8–10].

The man of God, however, will not compromise with evil and idolatry. This is quite remarkable.

This is the place to say that there is a lot of double-talk and subterfuge in supposedly fundamentalist Christian circles. I have recently read a statement issued by a certain seminary that claims to be fundamental, and is trying to build a reputation as a conservative school. I have never before read such double-talk in any statement. It claims a super piety and a super intellectualism that is nothing in the world but a denial of the things of God. There is such compromise today in Christian circles! I don't mean that we are to become ugly and cantankerous, or to not speak to certain individuals or have fellowship with them. That is not the point. But what we do need is to have a clear-cut, honest statement of where we stand theologically.

My Christian friend, many believers are supporting organizations that they are not sure are sound. If you don't know whether or not a ministry is giving out the Word of God, you ought to check into it. It is important, and God will hold you responsible for how you invest your money. These are evil days in which we live. They were evil days during the time of Jeroboam, and this prophet was not about to stay and have lunch with the king. He refused to become involved with him.

However, in the next several verses we find that he was deceived by another prophet into disobeying the Lord and suffered the sad consequences. Although he was wary of association with an idolatrous king, he was deceived by a man who claimed to have counter directions from God. My friend, when the church of God today gets involved in the things of the world and makes all kinds of compromises, it is a stench in the nostrils of Almighty God. We are living in days that are much like Jeroboam's, and we need to exercise the same caution and discernment that was needed then by God's man.

You would think that the experience Jeroboam had with the man of God would have changed him. His hand had been withered and healed. Do you think he changed?

After this thing Jeroboam returned not from his evil way, but made again of the lowest of the people priests of the high places: whosoever would, he consecrated him, and he became one of the priests of the high places.

And this thing became sin unto the house of Jeroboam, even to cut it off, and to destroy it from off the face of the earth [1 Kings 13:33–34].

Chapter 14 describes the reigns of Jeroboam and Rehoboam and sets the pace for the sordid record of the kings of the divided kingdom. There was not one good king in the northern kingdom of Israel—all nineteen of them were bad kings. In the southern kingdom there were twenty kings, of which twelve of them were bad. Only eight of them could be labeled good kings. And of the eight, only five were outstanding. (See Chronological Table of the Kings of the Divided Kingdom on p. 331.)

The chapter opens with Jeroboam sending his wife to inquire of Ahijah the prophet because their son is very sick. The Lord's reply through Ahijah is that the child will die, and in addition He gives a further prophecy regarding His judgment on Jeroboam's family.

GOD'S JUDGMENT ON JEROBOAM

Go, tell Jeroboam, Thus saith the LORD God of Israel, Forasmuch as I exalted thee from among the people, and made thee prince over my people Israel,

And rent the kingdom away from the house of David, and gave it thee: and yet thou hast not been as my servant David, who kept my commandments, and who followed me with all his heart, to do that only which was right in mine eyes [1 Kings 14:7–8].

David is the standard, you see, for the kings of both the northern and southern kingdoms from now on. Jeroboam fell far short of the man David was, and God will set him aside.

And the rest of the acts of Jeroboam, how he warred, and how he reigned, behold, they are written in the book of the chronicles of the kings of Israel.

And the days which Jeroboam reigned were two and twenty years: and he slept with his fathers, and Nadab his son reigned in his stead [1 Kings 14:19–20].

JUDAH'S APOSTASY UNDER REHOBOAM

You would think things would be better in the southern kingdom with Rehoboam, but they weren't.

And it came to pass in the fifth year of king Rehoboam, that Shishak king of Egypt came up against Jerusalem:

And he took away the treasures of the house of the LORD, and the treasures of the king's house; he even took away all: and he took away all the shields of gold which Solomon had made.

And king Rehoboam made in their stead brasen shields, and committed them unto the hands of the chief of the guard, which kept the door of the king's house [1 Kings 14:25–27].

Old Rehoboam is now beginning to go down, but he is keeping up a front. When the golden shields are taken by the king of Egypt, he substitutes brass shields.

Next we are told that there was civil war.

And there was war between Rehoboam and Jeroboam all their days [1 Kings 14:30].

Finally, we have the death of Rehoboam.

And Rehoboam slept with his fathers, and was buried with his fathers in the city of David. And his mother's name was Naamah an Ammonitess. And Abijam his son reigned in his stead [1 Kings 14:31].

CHAPTERS 15–16

***THEME:** Kings of the divided kingdom*

In chapter 15 two of Judah's kings are mentioned: Abijam, a sinful king, and Asa, a good king. Also the reigns of two of Israel's kings are given to us: Nadab, the son of Jeroboam, who walked in the sins of his father, and Baasha, who murdered him and reigned in his stead.

Chapter 16 continues with the history of Baasha, then four other kings of Israel—each more wicked than his successor: Elah, Zimri, Omri, and Ahab who compounded his wickedness by marrying the infamous Jezebel.

REHOBOAM IS SUCCEEDED BY ABIJAM

I feel that we need a double portion of the Spirit of God as we go through this section. In the last part of chapter 14 we were told that Rehoboam, a son of Solomon, reigned over the southern kingdom of Judah and Benjamin. Jeroboam reigned over Israel in the north. He is the one who led a rebellion of the ten northern tribes. Civil war continued between the two kingdoms. It was a bitter war with brother fighting brother—there is nothing quite as bad as that.

We have also noted that so far none of the kings have been good. In fact, there is never a good king in Israel, and only eight good kings in the southern kingdom of Judah in the line of David.

We find that after the death of Rehoboam, his son Abijam (also called Abijah) comes to the throne:

> **Now in the eighteenth year of king Jeroboam the son of Nebat reigned Abijam over Judah.**
>
> **Three years reigned he in Jerusalem. And his mother's name was Maachah, the daughter of Abishalom [1 Kings 15:1–2].**

There is something quite interesting that you will find all through this section: every time a king is mentioned his mother is also mentioned. That is unusual. We are generally told who a man's father was and whom he succeeded, but in this portion the mother's name is given again and again. Why? It is because each mother had a great deal to do with influencing the life of her son. My position here is that the reason God recorded the name of the mother along with each king's name (and these are bad kings) is because she is partially responsible for the way he turned out. Also when the king was a good king, the mother was partially responsible. She must accept responsibility for him.

You and I are living in a time when a lot of condemnation and judgment are brought against young people who become vagrants and are dissolute. I recognize that trouble can arise out of a Christian home, but generally the background of a young person has something to do with the way he or she turns out. Ordinarily these troubled young people have a mother who is partially responsible for the way they act and live—you cannot escape it, friend. Now I know that this cuts very deep and very hard, but we need to recognize that a mother has had a great opportunity to influence her little one, and if a little one has grown up to feel neglected, unwanted, and unloved, maybe the mother ought to stop and think. Instead of trying to be president of the missionary society, to sing in the choir, and to do everything else in the church, a mother would be doing more for the Lord if she would stay home some evening, take the little one up in her arms and love him and let him know how much she really appreciates him. This is something that is being neglected in our day. The biggest problem that most young couples have today is finding a baby sitter. May I say to you that we need a few more "mother sitters" who take time to train little Willie and little Susie. My friend, it takes a lot of time and love to rear a child—this is something that is very important.

I have taken some extra time on this subject because, candidly, it will occur again and again. Every time we have a bad king, his mamma's name is given—I think God is trying to tell us something. If he was a good king, his mother's name is also given; she will get credit for that. I just would not want to be the mother of some of the rascals we are going to find here in Scripture. It would disturb me a great deal to have a son like most of these kings.

> **And he walked in all the sins of his father, which he had done before him: and his heart was not perfect with the LORD his God, as the heart of David his father [1 Kings 15:3].**

Abijam walked in all the sins of his father—he followed his father's pattern. Papa was to blame, also, for the way his son turned out; papa set the example. Abijam was not brought up in a very good home. He was a rotten, corrupt king, and his father and mother are responsible to a certain degree. We are told also that "his heart was not perfect with the LORD his God, as the heart of David his father." David had become the standard for these kings. It is true that David was a human standard, but it was a standard that God accepted.

Nevertheless for David's sake did the LORD his God give him a lamp in Jerusalem, to set up his son after him, and to establish Jerusalem [1 Kings 15:4].

The line of David, friend, never ends until you come to the Lord Jesus Christ. It ended there—you cannot follow the line of David after Christ. God says, "I won't let the lamp go out until the fulfillment of the covenant I made with David." There will come One to sit on his throne who will rule the world—that One is the Lord Jesus Christ.

Because David did that which was right in the eyes of the LORD, and turned not aside from any thing that he commanded him all the days of his life, save only in the matter of Uriah the Hittite [1 Kings 15:5].

Why did God accept David as the standard? Because of his sin? No! That was a black spot on David's record. Although little man is in no position to sit in judgment upon God, we do it nonetheless. But if you are going to judge God about His relationship with David, understand what God really said about David. God listed David's assets and liabilities in this verse: David did not turn aside from anything that He commanded except in the matter of Uriah the Hittite. That was the black spot on David's record. In every other matter he obeyed God. David did not live in sin. The king of Babylon did. What David did one time, the king of Babylon did every day. It was the weekend practice of the king of Egypt to do the thing David did one time. The whole thought is expressed by our Lord in the parable of the Prodigal Son. Friend, the son can get in the pigpen—we need to recognize that. God's child can get in the pigpen, but by the same token the child of God will not stay in the pigpen. Why won't he? The reason is obvious: he is a son of the father; he is not a pig. Pigs live in pigpens. Sons want to live in the father's house. My friend, if you want to live in a pigpen, that is where you belong! And that tells who you are. However, if you are in the pigpen but you have a desire in your heart to cry out to God for forgiveness, He will hear you. When you turn back to Him, He will receive you. David did a wrong thing, but David confessed his sin. However, obedience to God was the norm for David. I think it behooves us to be very careful about criticizing David—he was a great man. We are not worthy (at least I am not) to tie the strings of his shoes. He was a great man of God and became the earthly standard for the kings.

And there was war between Rehoboam and Jeroboam all the days of his life [1 Kings 15:6].

This was a time of civil strife. It was a time of brother fighting against brother, and it seriously weakened the kingdom.

ABIJAM IS SUCCEEDED BY ASA

Now the rest of the acts of Abijam, and all that he did, are they not written in the book of the chronicles of the kings of Judah? And there was war between Abijam and Jeroboam.

And Abijam slept with his fathers; and they buried him in the city of David: and Asa his son reigned in his stead [1 Kings 15:7–8].

Abijam did nothing outstanding during his reign—all was evil. He was a bad king. So he died and was buried with his fathers.

Abijam was succeeded by his son Asa. Now we come to the first good king, and we feel like saying, "Hallelujah, we've found a good king!"

And in the twentieth year of Jeroboam king of Israel reigned Asa over Judah.

And forty and one years reigned he in Jerusalem. And his mother's name was Maachah, the daughter of Abishalom.

And Asa did that which was right in the eyes of the LORD, as did David his father [1 Kings 15:9–11].

You can see that there is an overlapping here of two years. Asa reigned during the last two years of Jeroboam's reign. Asa reigned for forty-one years. He had one of the longest reigns of any king. In fact, the only two kings who reigned longer than Asa were Azariah (or Uzziah) and Manasseh.

Asa's mother's name was Maachah. Isn't that interesting? Asa was a good king, and she gets credit here for the way Asa turned out. Again David is the standard of right and wrong for a king—Asa measured up to David.

Now what did he do?

And he took away the sodomites out of the land, and removed all the idols that his fathers had made [1 Kings 15:12].

Asa did not go for the idea that we should be soft on homosexuals. He was opposed to homosexuality. It is not a mark of being civilized when any nation drops to the low level that we have today. God gives up any people who have a permissive society, openly allowing homosexuality. It is a mark of gross degradation—we are going down as a nation. Someone needs to speak out against this today. We need to recognize it as a sin—it is as corrupt, depraved, and degraded as any sin a person can commit. Man cannot sink any lower than this. When a person sinks this low, God gives him up. Our society is moving in that direction. Asa dealt with the problem, and he is called a good king. God has not changed His mind on this issue at all.

WAR WITH BAASHA

And there was war between Asa and Baasha king of Israel all their days [1 Kings 15:16].

Asa made war against Baasha, king of Israel. It was continual civil war.

We are told that Asa did other things also. He had to appease a kingdom that was arising in the north and becoming dominant—that kingdom was Syria.

Then Asa took all the silver and the gold that were left in the treasures of the house of the LORD, and the treasures of the king's house, and delivered them into the hand of his servants: and king Asa sent them to Ben-hadad, the son of Tabrimon, the son of Hezion, king of Syria, that dwelt at Damascus, saying,

There is a league between me and thee, and between my father and thy father: behold, I have sent unto thee a present of silver and gold; come and break thy league with Baasha king of Israel, that he may depart from me [1 Kings 15:18–19].

Asa sent Ben-hadad presents of gold and silver in order to appease him. To keep him from invading his kingdom, Asa made a league with him. This is probably the one thing he did that was wrong.

Then king Asa made a proclamation throughout all Judah: none was exempted: and they took away the stones of Ramah, and the timber thereof, wherewith Baasha had builded; and king Asa built with them Geba of Benjamin, and Mizpah [1 Kings 15:22].

Asa did all of this for protection, of course.

ASA IS SUCCEEDED BY JEHOSHAPHAT

The rest of all the acts of Asa, and all his might, and all that he did, and the cities which he built, are they not written in the book of the chronicles of the kings of Judah? Nevertheless in the time of his old age he was diseased in his feet.

And Asa slept with his fathers, and was buried with his fathers in the city of David his father: and Jehoshaphat his son reigned in his stead [1 Kings 15: 23–24].

As we shall see, Jehoshaphat was another good king.

NADAB IS SLAIN AND SUCCEEDED BY BAASHA

Now we come back to Nadab, the son of Jeroboam:

And Nadab the son of Jeroboam began to reign over Israel in the second year of Asa king of Judah, and reigned over Israel two years.

And he did evil in the sight of the LORD, and walked in the way of his father, and in his sin wherewith he made Israel to sin [1 Kings 15:25–26].

Nadab began to reign in the second year of the reign of Asa, king of Judah. Nadab ruled for two years over Israel. We will find in this succession of bad kings that there was a great deal of sin and political intrigue in the northern kingdom.

And Baasha the son of Ahijah, of the house of Issachar, conspired against him; and Baasha smote him at Gibbethon, which belonged to the Philistines; for Nadab and all Israel laid siege to Gibbethon [1 Kings 15:27].

You would think that somewhere along the line there would be peace, but there was not. There was war between Asa and Baasha all their days. The continual civil war depleted the energy and resources of both the kingdoms. It also made both kingdoms subject to the powers round about them. They were invaded again and again by Egypt in the south, by Syria, and finally by Assyria in the north. These people simply would not change their ways.

BAASHA'S DEATH, AND THE REIGNS OF ELAH AND ZIMRI

Baasha reigned longer than any other king in the north up to this point. He reigned for twenty-four years. But we are told that this man is to be put down because he did evil. The word of the Lord against Baasha came through Jehu:

Behold, I will take away the posterity of Baasha, and the posterity of his house; and will make thy house like the house of Jeroboam the son of Nebat.

Him that dieth of Baasha in the city shall the dogs eat; and him that dieth of his in the fields shall the fowls of the air eat [1 Kings 16:3–4].

This was a sad period in the life of the king. Because Baasha chose to share in the sins of the house of Jeroboam, he would also share in the severe penalty, even to the point of being devoured by dogs.

So Baasha slept with his fathers, and was buried in Tirzah: and Elah his son reigned in his stead.

And also by the hand of the prophet Jehu the son of Hanani came the word of the LORD against Baasha, and against his house, even for all the evil that he did in the sight of the LORD, in provoking him to anger with the work of his hands, in being like the house of Jeroboam; and because he killed him.

In the twenty and sixth year of Asa king of Judah began Elah the son of Baasha to reign over Israel in Tirzah, two years [1 Kings 16:6–8].

Elah had not reigned but two years until Zimri his captain conspired and led a rebellion against him:

And his servant Zimri, captain of half his chariots, conspired against him, as he was in Tirzah, drinking himself drunk in the house of Arza steward of his house in Tirzah.

And Zimri went in and smote him, and killed him, in the twenty and seventh year of Asa king of Judah, and reigned in his stead [1 Kings 16:9–10].

When Elah got drunk, Zimri went in and killed him. It seems that because of the conspirators in the northern kingdom no man was really safe. After Zimri killed Elah, he began to reign.

However, Zimri did not last very long either—only seven days.

In the twenty and seventh year of Asa king of Judah did Zimri reign seven days in Tirzah. And the people were encamped against Gibbethon, which belonged to the Philistines [1 Kings 16:15].

Another conspiracy and another rebellion got rid of Zimri.

And Omri went up from Gibbethon, and all Israel with him, and they besieged Tirzah.

And it came to pass, when Zimri saw that the city was taken, that he went into the palace of the king's house, and burnt the king's house over him with fire, and died [1 Kings 15:17–18].

These were dark days for the kingdom, and there are darker days yet to come.

TIBNI AND OMRI ARE RIVAL KINGS OF ISRAEL

After Omri's conspiracy succeeded in establishing him as king, another problem arose. A rival of Omri's also claimed to be king—his name was Tibni.

Then were the people of Israel divided into two parts: half of the people followed Tibni the son of Ginath, to make him king; and half followed Omri.

But the people that followed Omri prevailed against the people that followed Tibni the son of Ginath: so Tibni died, and Omri reigned [1 Kings 16:21–22].

Omri put Tibni to death, and then Omri reigned. He ruled for twelve years. He was a bad king and exceeded the other kings in his evil deeds.

But Omri wrought evil in the eyes of the LORD, and did worse than all that were before him [1 Kings 16:25].

ACCESSION OF AHAB; HIS MARRIAGE TO JEZEBEL

So Omri slept with his fathers, and was buried in Samaria: and Ahab his son reigned in his stead.

And Ahab the son of Omri did evil in the sight of the LORD above all that were before him [1 Kings 16:28,30].

Omri is succeeded by his son Ahab. Omri had been the most corrupt ruler up to that time, but his son Ahab exceeded him in evil.

And it came to pass, as if it had been a light thing for him to walk in the sins of Jeroboam the son of Nebat, that he took to wife Jezebel the daughter of Ethbaal king of the Zidonians, and went and served Baal, and worshipped him [1 Kings 16:31].

Ahab was evil, and he had a wife that helped him with his evil ways. She was a real helpmeet in the area of evil. What Ahab didn't think of, Jezebel did. What she didn't think of nobody else could—she was a mean woman. The combination of Ahab and Jezebel was the worst possible. You can be sure that Mr. and Mrs. Haman were bad. Herod and Herodias were evil enough. And we know of Ptolemy Dionysius and Cleopatra—they were quite a couple. Philip I of Spain and Bloody Mary also did pretty well together. These are four of the most infamous couples in history. In particular there were also several couples where the wife was dominant in diabolical designs. For example, there was Catherine deMedici and Henry II of France; Lucrezia Borgia (she was the daughter of a pope) and Alfonso; Macbeth and Lady Macbeth; Louis XV and Marie Antoinette of France; and finally, coming down to our day, Julius and Ethel Rosenberg. All of these are couples who stand out on the pages of history as being evil, but none can exceed Ahab and Jezebel—they head the list.

Jezebel was the daughter of a king who was also a priest of Baal and who murdered his brother. It is interesting to note that the name *Jezebel* means "unmarried" or "without cohabitation." In other words, the marriage of Ahab and Jezebel was not a romance—it was not a love match. Rather than a true marriage, it was just a wedding. Apparently there had never been a real meeting of these two people in a love relationship. She was a masculine woman with strong intellectual powers and a fierce passion for evil. She was strong-willed and possessed a dominant personality, but she had no moral sense. She was hardened into insensibility. She was unscrupulous and the most wicked person in history —bar none.

In the Book of Revelation, our Lord gave a message to the church of Thyatira: "Notwithstanding I have a few things against thee, because thou sufferest that woman Jezebel, which calleth herself a prophetess, to teach and to seduce my servants to commit fornication, and to eat things sacrificed unto idols" (Rev. 2:20). Jezebel was a dominating and domineering woman. Christ gave this message to Thyatira because it was a period without natural affection—it was a picture of Jezebel.

How did Jezebel and Ahab ever get together? I think it was quite easy. For years I went to young people's conferences. It was quite interesting how there could be a boy who was a bad apple and a girl who was a bad egg, and for some strange reason the bad apple and the bad egg always got together and started dating. It always happened that way, and that is the way it was with Ahab and Jezebel.

Something else happened during this period which reveals how ominous and critical those days were:

And he reared up an altar for Baal in the house of Baal, which he had built in Samaria.

And Ahab made a grove; and Ahab did more to provoke the LORD God of Israel to anger than all the kings of Israel that were before him.

In his days did Hiel the Beth-elite build Jericho: he laid the foundation thereof in Abiram his firstborn, and set up the gates thereof in his youngest son Segub, according to the word of the LORD, which he spake by Joshua the son of Nun [1 Kings 16:32–34].

At the time of the destruction of Jericho, Joshua said, ". . . Cursed be the man before the LORD, that riseth up and buildeth this city Jericho . . ." (Josh. 6:26). It had not been rebuilt until the time of Ahab and Jezebel, and the curse that was pronounced by Joshua came upon the builder, Hiel.

CHAPTER 17

***THEME:** Three years of drought as announced by Elijah*

God had to have His man present at the time when Ahab and Jezebel sat on the throne of Israel. It would have to be someone who would have the courage to stand up against them. God had that man ready. He was Elijah the prophet, one of the greatest men who ever walked across the pages of Scripture. Also he is probably the man who will return to the earth to witness in the last days—it is predicted that he will return.

ELIJAH ANNOUNCES THE DROUGHT

Elijah is introduced to us in a most dramatic way. He strides into the court of Ahab and Jezebel and makes a very brave announcement.

And Elijah the Tishbite, who was of the inhabitants of Gilead, said unto Ahab, As the LORD God of Israel liveth, before whom I stand, there shall not be dew nor rain these years, but according to my word [1 Kings 17:1].

Elijah walked into the court of Ahab and Jezebel and gave them the latest weather report. He said it was not going to rain except by his word and he was leaving town—he had no intention of saying the word. Then he walked out of the court just as dramatically as he had walked in. I think Ahab and Jezebel were taken aback because they never dreamed anyone could speak out so boldly. They will find out that Elijah has a habit of speaking out. You get the impression that Elijah was a rugged individual, and he was. But there's something else that should be said here about him—God had to train this man. God has always had a method of training the men He uses by taking them to the desert. You will recall that that is where He trained Moses. God took Abraham out of Ur of the Chaldees and placed him in a land with rugged terrain. God did the same for John the Baptist, and the apostle Paul spent at least two full years out in the Arabian desert. This is God's method of training His men. Now He is going to take out this man Elijah and teach him several things he needs to learn.

GOD FEEDS ELIJAH AT CHERITH AND ZAREPHATH

And the word of the LORD came unto him, saying,

Get thee hence, and turn thee eastward, and hide thyself by the brook Cherith, that is before Jordan [1 Kings 17:2–3].

God was telling Elijah to get as far out in the country as he could. So he went out into the desert and came to a little stream.

And it shall be, that thou shalt drink of the brook; and I have commanded the ravens to feed thee there [1 Kings 17:4].

God used two methods of caring for Elijah out in the desert. One was the brook which was a natural means. He was to drink the water. The other was a supernatural means—the ravens were to come and feed him. Well, Elijah stayed there for awhile, and then the brook began to dry up.

And it came to pass after a while, that the brook dried up, because there had been no rain in the land [1 Kings 17:7].

Here is this man out in the wilderness, and he goes to the brook every morning and notices that it is going down a little bit more each day. All he had to do was put a peg in the water to note how much it went down each day. Then he could figure out how many days it would be before he starved to death or died of thirst. Having the mathematical measurement, anyone with common sense would know that on a certain day the end would come.

This is the sin of statistics. Today the condition of a church is often determined by statistics. If you go to a church meeting and observe that the offering has been good, new members have been received, and there is increased attendance, the church is considered a howling success—and that may not be the true picture at all.

I once heard the story of a preacher who got up at a church business meeting and said, "We are going to call on the treasurer to give a report so that we can know the status quo of our church." One of the members got up and said, "Mr. Preacher, we don't know what the status quo means." The preacher replied, "The 'status quo' means the mess we are in." Interestingly enough, the true status quo of many churches and other organizations often reveals the mess they are in, although the statistics may look healthy.

Now Elijah could have figured very closely the time he was going to die—he could have done it mathematically. But, you see, the cold figures of mathematics do not take into account the spiritual fire that is there. You cannot put the condition of the church in the form of a bank statement. You cannot measure it on a computer. Even a revival is not determined by numbers. When Elijah looked at that little brook which was getting smaller and smaller he learned a spiritual lesson. He saw that his life was a dried-up brook. He was nothing—he was just a brook, a channel, through which living water *could* flow. The Lord Jesus Christ says, ". . . Whosoever drinketh of this water shall thirst again: But whosoever drinketh of the water that I shall give him shall never thirst; but the water that I shall give him shall be in him a well of water springing up into everlasting life" (John 4: 13–14). Sometimes we sing the song, "Make Me A Blessing," and I think that half of the folk don't know the meaning of the words. Why, it means that you are an empty brook and that you do not have any water of life. It is only as the water of life, the Word of God, flows through you that you can be a channel of blessing. Elijah had to learn that ". . . God hath chosen the foolish things of the world to confound the wise; and God hath chosen the weak things of the world to confound the things which are mighty" (1 Cor. 1:27). God was telling Elijah, "You are not a big, strong, rugged individual. You are no stronger or better than that dried-up brook. You will have no strength until the water of life flows through you."

It is said of Hudson Taylor that when he prepared young missionaries for service in his mission, he insisted, "Remember that when you come out here you are *nothing*. It is only what God can and will do through you that will be worth anything." One young missionary replied, "It is hard for me to believe that I am just nothing." And Hudson Taylor said to him, "Take it by faith because it is true—you are nothing." You and I are just dried-up brooks unless the Word of God is flowing through us.

And then God transferred Elijah:

And the word of the Lord came unto him, saying,

Arise, get thee to Zarephath, which belongeth to Zidon, and dwell there: behold, I have commanded a widow woman there to sustain thee.

So he arose and went to Zarephath. And when he came to the gate of the city, behold, the widow woman was there gathering of sticks: and he called to her, and said, Fetch me, I pray thee, a little water in a vessel, that I may drink.

And as she was going to fetch it, he called to her, and said, Bring me, I pray thee, a morsel of bread in thine hand.

And she said, As the Lord thy God liveth, I have not a cake, but an handful of meal in a barrel, and a little oil in a cruse: and, behold, I am gathering two sticks, that I may go in and dress it for me and my son, that we may eat it, and die [1 Kings 17:8–12].

After the widow told her story, Elijah told her to go into her house and make the cake. He assured her that she was not going to die.

And Elijah said unto her, Fear not; go and do as thou hast said: but make me thereof a little cake first, and bring it unto me, and after make for thee and for thy son.

For thus saith the Lord God of Israel. The barrel of meal shall not waste, neither shall the cruse of oil fail, until the day that the Lord sendeth rain upon the earth [1 Kings 17:13–14].

You know, Elijah and that widow stuck their heads down in that empty flour barrel every day and sang the doxology—and God sustained them out of an empty flour barrel. That barrel was as fertile as the plains of Canada or the corn fields of Iowa. Here is another lesson Elijah needed to learn.

It is a lesson you and I need to learn: we are nothing but empty flour barrels. I hear so much today about consecration—we are to "give our talents to the Lord." My friend, you and I have nothing to offer God. There was a wedding in Cana of Galilee: what was the most important thing at that wedding? Was it the bride's dress? No! It was that there were some empty water crocks there. The Lord filled them with water, and He was able to serve the guests a delicious refreshment. That was the important thing at the wedding. My friend, we are nothing but empty flour barrels and empty water crocks. We are nothing until the water of life and the bread of life have been put into us. And since we do not recognize this, we are having spiritual floor shows in many of our churches today. They have become religious nightclubs, and there is no more spiritual life in them than there is in a

Rose Bowl game in Pasadena, California. There is more enthusiasm and a larger crowd at many activities outside the church than there is at most church meetings. In fact, many church meetings are pretty sad and silly, if you ask me. We need to remember that we are empty flour barrels.

THE WIDOW'S SON IS RAISED BY ELIJAH

And it came to pass after these things, that the son of the woman, the mistress of the house, fell sick; and his sickness was so sore, that there was no breath left in him [1 Kings 17:17].

The widow's son died. And what did Elijah do?

And he said unto her, Give me thy son. And he took him out of her bosom, and carried him up into a loft, where he abode, and laid him upon his own bed.

And he cried unto the Lord, and said, O Lord my God, hast thou also brought evil upon the widow with whom I sojourn, by slaying her son?

And he stretched himself upon the child three times, and cried unto the Lord, and said, O Lord my God, I pray thee, let this child's soul come into him again.

And the Lord heard the voice of Elijah; and the soul of the child came into him again, and he revived [1 Kings 17:19–22].

Elijah made contact with the boy's body three times. This is the great principle of resurrection—it involves contact with life. Today Christianity needs to be in contact with Jesus Christ. When it is not, it is as dead as a dodo bird. We need to recognize that this is one of the great miracles of Scripture: "and the soul of the child came into him again, and he revived." You and I are dead bodies. We are lost sinners—dead in trespasses and sins. If we have trusted Christ, then we can say that we were crucified with Him nineteen hundred years ago; He died, and we died with Him. He was raised, and we were raised with Him. We are joined to the living Christ today—if we are not joined to Him, we are nothing. The apostle Paul expressed it this way: "I am crucified with Christ: nevertheless I live; yet not I, but Christ liveth in me: and the life which I now live in the flesh I live by the faith of the Son of God, who loved me, and gave himself for me" (Gal. 2:20).

Elijah had to learn that he was a dried-up brook, an empty flour barrel, a dead body. When Elijah recognized this, then God could use him. Martin Luther once said that God creates out of nothing. Until a man recognizes that he is nothing, God can do nothing with him. That is the problem with many of us today: we are too strong, we have too much ability, and God cannot use us.

CHAPTER 18

***THEME:** Elijah versus the prophets of Baal*

This is one of the most spectacular chapters in the Scriptures. Elijah challenges the prophets of Baal to a contest to determine who is really God. The prophets of Baal—all 450 of them—are about an even match for this one man Elijah. He is a great man!

ELIJAH AND OBADIAH

And it came to pass after many days, that the word of the Lord came to Elijah in the third year, saying, Go, shew thyself unto Ahab; and I will send rain upon the earth.

And Elijah went to shew himself unto Ahab. And there was a sore famine in Samaria [1 Kings 18:1–2].

God is ready to use Elijah. This man can now step out with boldness—he has learned that he is nothing and God is everything. He goes out to meet Ahab, and he is prepared.

And Ahab called Obadiah, which was the governor of his house. (Now Obadiah feared the Lord greatly:

For it was so, when Jezebel cut off the prophets of the LORD, that Obadiah took an hundred prophets, and hid them by fifty in a cave, and fed them with bread and water.)

And Ahab said unto Obadiah, Go into the land, unto all fountains of water, and unto all brooks: peradventure we may find grass to save the horses and mules alive, that we lose not all the beasts.

So they divided the land between them to pass throughout it: Ahab went one way by himself, and Obadiah went another way by himself [1 Kings 18:3–6].

The famine was now in the acute stage. Much of the vegetation had dried up and the cattle could no longer find places to graze. So Ahab and his servant, Obadiah, set out in search of possible pasture land. Ahab went one direction and Obadiah went another. Now Obadiah was the governor of Ahab's palace. He was a God-fearing man, and he had hidden one hundred prophets of God from Jezebel's wrath.

And as Obadiah was in the way, behold, Elijah met him: and he knew him, and fell on his face, and said, Art thou that my lord Elijah?

And he answered him, I am: go, tell thy lord, Behold, Elijah is here [1 Kings 18:7–8].

While Obadiah was looking for grazing sites, he met Elijah. Elijah told him to tell the king, "Behold, Elijah is here." My, how we need a voice like Elijah's today. I believe he is coming back in the last days after the church leaves the earth. This earth will need a strong voice then, and it will have one in Elijah.

And he said, What have I sinned, that thou wouldest deliver thy servant into the hand of Ahab, to slay me?

As the LORD thy God liveth, there is no nation or kingdom, whither my lord hath not sent to seek thee: and when they said, He is not there; he took an oath of the kingdom and nation, that they found thee not.

And now thou sayest, Go, tell thy lord, Behold, Elijah is here.

And it shall come to pass, as soon as I am gone from thee, that the spirit of the LORD shall carry thee whither I know not; and so when I come and tell Ahab, and he cannot find thee, he shall slay me: but I thy servant fear the LORD from my youth.

Was it not told my lord what I did when Jezebel slew the prophets of the LORD, how I hid an hundred men of the LORD's prophets by fifty in a cave, and fed them with bread and water? [1 Kings 18:9–13].

Obadiah does not want to deliver Elijah's message as he is afraid that Elijah will disappear before Ahab sees him. Obadiah is fearful for his own life, and he makes it very clear that he does not want to do what Elijah has asked.

And now thou sayest, Go, tell thy lord, Behold, Elijah is here: and he shall slay me.

And Elijah said, As the LORD of hosts liveth, before whom I stand, I will surely shew myself unto him today.

So Obadiah went to meet Ahab, and told him: and Ahab went to meet Elijah [1 Kings 18:14–16].

We have read the message three times now: "Behold, Elijah is here." With Elijah's assurances that he will certainly meet Ahab, Obadiah goes to the king. And you know what this man said? He said, "Behold, Elijah is here." And that will be the message again some day.

ELIJAH'S CHALLENGE TO AHAB

And it came to pass, when Ahab saw Elijah, that Ahab said unto him, Art thou he that troubleth Israel?

And he answered, I have not troubled Israel; but thou, and thy father's house, in that ye have forsaken the commandments of the LORD, and thou hast followed Baalim [1 Kings 18: 17–18].

Elijah said to Ahab, "I am not the one who is troubling Israel—*you* are!" Elijah's kind of preaching cannot be misunderstood. It is not double-talk; it is telling it like it is.

Before we go any further, I want to say that the liberal is always blaming the fundamentalist for causing division in the church. But who *really* caused it? The church held very fundamental beliefs at one time. Who brought bifurcation into the church? Who was it that led the church away from its foundation? The liberal did. I have been accused of leaving my former denomination, but I did not—my denomination left me. I still have the same beliefs that I had at the beginning. Unfortunately, my denomination has departed from those historic beliefs.

It has always been the custom of the liberal to blame any trouble in the church on the fundamentalist. The liberal is never to blame.

In the same way Ahab blames Elijah for the problem in the land. He accuses Elijah of stirring things up. The Word of God will always stir up things. The interesting thing is that rats will always scurry to a dark corner when the light is turned on.

Then Elijah challenged Ahab to a contest between himself and the prophets of Baal.

Now therefore send, and gather to me all Israel unto mount Carmel, and the prophets of Baal four hundred and fifty, and the prophets of the groves four hundred, which eat at Jezebel's table [1 Kings 18:19].

The contest was actually one between the Lord and Satan—between the worship of the living God and the worship of Baal. Outwardly it was a battle of Ahab and Jezebel with the 450 prophets against Elijah. Elijah, however, was worth a whole army.

THE LORD VERSUS BAAL AT MOUNT CARMEL

So Ahab sent unto all the children of Israel, and gathered the prophets together unto mount Carmel.

And Elijah came unto all the people, and said, How long halt ye between two opinions? if the LORD be God, follow him: but if Baal, then follow him. And the people answered him not a word [1 Kings 18:20–21].

The people of Israel have assembled at Carmel. It is going to be quite a contest. Elijah knew what was in the hearts of the people. They were pretending to worship the living and true God, but they were also worshiping Baal. The reason the people did not answer Elijah is that they were guilty of sin. It is that type of double-talk—a two-faced way of life—that today has become so abhorrent and is a stench in the nostrils of God. The double standard of many Christians has turned off many people as far as the church is concerned. If the average unsaved man knew the church as I know it today, I have my doubts that he would ever darken the door of a church. If there ever was a place where things should be made clear and plain, simple and forthright, it is in the church. Unfortunately, that is where there is more double-talk and beating around the bush than any place else.

Then said Elijah unto the people, I, even I only, remain a prophet of the LORD; but Baal's prophets are four hundred and fifty men [1 Kings 18:22].

Elijah had what I am pleased to call an Elijah complex—some of us develop that even today. Many times in my ministry I feel that I am the only one left. Then I find out that there is a preacher in a hollow in Tennessee, or on the side of a hill in Georgia, or down around a lake in Florida, or up in the mountains of California, or in the suburban areas of Chicago who is standing for God and paying a bigger price than I have ever paid. Then I just get rid of my Elijah complex and thank God that there are men standing for God and His Word in these days in which we are living. Now I recognize that there are many big-name preachers that you hear about but who are not actually standing for God. Instead they are pussy-footing around. They are trying to compromise. I heard one preacher give a certain message in one part of the country and then turn around in another part of the country and practically reverse his message. There is something wrong when you can't give the same message everywhere. There is something wrong with the message or with the man who gives it.

Elijah says to the people of Israel, "I am the only one who is standing for God." Now he was wrong—there were seven thousand people hiding in the hills who had not bowed the knee to Baal. I never cared too much for that crowd, but at least they did not worship Baal. Elijah did not even know about them. If Elijah had been on the radio in those days, he never would have received a letter from any of those folk. It is too bad that they did not encourage him a little bit, but they did not.

Elijah continues his message to the people and his challenge to the prophets of Baal:

Let them therefore give us two bullocks; and let them choose one bullock for themselves, and cut it in pieces, and lay it on wood, and put no fire under: and I will dress the other bullock, and lay it on wood, and put no fire under:

And call ye on the name of your gods, and I will call on the name of the LORD: and the God that answereth by fire, let him be God. And all the people an-

swered and said, It is well spoken [1 Kings 18:23–24].

In other words, Elijah said, "Let us taste of the Lord and see whether He is good or not. If Baal is God, then let us worship him. And if he is not, then let's kick him out. If the Lord God is the living God, we want to know." My friend, today God wants you to know Him. Although you may have doubts, if you're sincere and really want to know Him, He will reveal Himself to you—because God *wants* you to know. Faith is not groping in the dark: our faith rests upon facts. Your salvation depends on your believing those facts and trusting Christ.

Notice what is going to take place. I think this is one of the most dramatic scenes in Scripture.

And Elijah said unto the prophets of Baal, Choose you one bullock for yourselves, and dress it first; for ye are many; and call on the name of your gods, but put no fire under.

And they took the bullock which was given them, and they dressed it, and called on the name of Baal from morning even until noon, saying, O Baal, hear us. But there was no voice, nor any that answered. And they leaped upon the altar which was made.

And it came to pass at noon, that Elijah mocked them, and said, Cry aloud: for he is a god; either he is talking, or he is pursuing, or he is in a journey, or peradventure he sleepeth, and must be awakened.

And they cried aloud, and cut themselves after their manner with knives and lancets, till the blood gushed out upon them [1 Kings 18:25–28].

The prophets of Baal put on quite a performance. Elijah just sits there and watches them at first with a good deal of cynicism. They begin to call upon Baal. Nothing happens. They jump on the altar—and that doesn't help. They become fanatics. They display a lot of emotion. Their actions become almost hysterical. Finally, they begin to cut themselves, and the blood gushes out. They are sure this will stir Baal to action. Old Elijah says to them, "Say, it may be that he has gone on vacation and you will have to wait until he comes back. Or maybe he is taking his afternoon siesta and you are going to have to yell louder to wake him up." Elijah has a big time during their performance. And all the while the people of Israel are watching.

It is Martin Luther, by the way, who is credited with the statement, "One with God is a majority," and he knew the accuracy of that statement by experience. Elijah also learned this truth through experience in his day when there had been a wholesale departure of the northern kingdom from God. Under Ahab and Jezebel there was almost total apostasy—Elijah pretty much stood alone. It is true that there were seven thousand people who had not bowed to Baal, but they had retreated to the mountains. Not one of them stood with Elijah. He was not aware that they even existed until God told him. Elijah took a stand against calf worship. You might say he took a stand against new morality and rock music in the church. He took exception to many of the things that were going on and refused to compromise with the prophets of Baal. When they wrote a new "Confession of Faith" and rejected the authority of the Word of God, he was opposed to them.

It was Dr. Wilfred Funk who said that the most bitter word in the English language is "alone." Elijah stood alone. He did not voice public opinion, friend. He was no echo—he was no parrot. He was not promoting anyone else. He was no politician. He was more concerned about pleasing God than courting the popularity of the crowd. He sought divine approval rather than public applause. He was not a clown in a public parade. He was a fool for God's sake. He was a solo voice in the wilderness of the world. He carried on an all-out war against Satan and his hosts. He stood alone, arrayed against the prophets of Baal. Elijah chose Mount Carmel to take a dramatic stand for God.

Several years ago I stood in what is probably the exact area where Elijah and the prophets of Baal held their contest. Mount Carmel overlooks the Bay of Haifa and the blue Mediterranean Sea. It is a long ridge; and way out yonder to the east is Megiddo in the valley of Esdraelon. In this dramatic spot the lone, majestic figure of Elijah stood apart. He was detached. I think he looked bored after a few minutes of the performance by Baal's prophets. Then that ironic smile crossed his face and you could hear the acid sarcasm in his voice. He used the rapier of ridicule. He taunted and jeered at these prophets. And finally, with wilting scorn, he waved them aside.

And it came to pass, when midday was past, and they prophesied until the time

of the offering of the evening sacrifice, that there was neither voice, nor any to answer, nor any that regarded.

And Elijah said unto all the people, Come near unto me. And all the people came near unto him. And he repaired the altar of the LORD that was broken down [1 Kings 18:29–30].

Elijah is now going to have to depend on God. The altar of the Lord has been broken, and Elijah spends some time cementing it together. That was a dramatic move, friend.

What is it that has caused division in our country today? I recognize that there are many explanations being offered, but a departure from God is basic to the divisions in this nation. There was a time that there was a measure of unity, and it was a unity based on the fact that there is a living God—that is written in our constitution—and we are responsible to Him. There was a time when this nation believed that the Bible was an authority. Who divided this country? Those, my friend, who began to cut up the Word of God. That is what caused the division. It is hypocrisy today when so many are saying, "Let's get together." Get together on what, my friend? You cannot get together on nothing. It is like the story that is told about a man who was walking through the jungle in Africa, and he met an elephant. The elephant said to him, "Where are you going?" The man replied, "I am not going anywhere." The elephant said, "I'm not going anywhere either. Let's go together." That is the only way you are going to get together with today's crowd: you will have to agree on *nothing*. If you do that, you can all get together. My friend, you can't get together unless you've got something to gather around that will hold you together.

The altar was the place of unity. Elijah put it back together.

And Elijah took twelve stones, according to the number of the tribes of the sons of Jacob, unto whom the word of the LORD came, saying, Israel shall be thy name:

And with the stones he built an altar in the name of the LORD: and he made a trench about the altar, as great as would contain two measures of seed.

And he put the wood in order, and cut the bullock in pieces, and laid him on the wood, and said, Fill four barrels with water, and pour it on the burnt sacrifice, and on the wood [1 Kings 18:31–33].

Notice that Israel was *one* nation. It was not Israel and Judah, or Samaria and Jerusalem, but all twelve tribes as the one nation, Israel. So Elijah built an altar in the name of the Lord. Then he made a trench around the altar, put the wood in order, and cut the bullock in pieces. Finally he ordered that four barrels be filled with water and poured on the sacrifice and on the wood. Now it was a long way down to the water supply. As I stood on Mount Carmel, I wondered how long it took those who were bringing the water to get four barrels up the side of that mountain. It was a long route, but Elijah was in no hurry.

And he said, Do it the second time. And they did it the second time. And he said, Do it the third time. And they did it the third time.

And the water ran round about the altar; and he filled the trench also with water [1 Kings 18:34–35].

They fetched the water once, and Elijah said, "Go down and fill it again." And that was not enough. He said, "Do it the third time," and they did it the third time. I think if you could have seen Elijah that day there would have been a wry smile on his face. Do you know what that wry smile was about? Why did he pour water on that altar? My friend, only God can do the impossible. A little water won't keep the fire from falling, so he did not mind pouring the water over everything. He could have poured water for the next twenty-four hours, and the fire still would have fallen. Elijah is learning to depend on God—we have seen that. Remember, as he stood at that little brook and watched it dry up, he knew he was nothing in the world but a channel through which water could flow. He had also looked down in an empty flour barrel and sung the doxology. God fed Elijah, the widow, and her son out of that empty flour barrel for the period of the drought. And then he found out he was a dead body. He had learned that if anything was going to be done, God has to do it. He just stood up there that day, a wry smile on his face—I think Elijah had a sense of humor. And I know God has a sense of humor. Under his breath Elijah probably said, "Lord, if You don't do it, it won't be done."

And it came to pass at the time of the offering of the evening sacrifice, that Elijah the prophet came near, and said,

LORD God of Abraham, Isaac, and of Israel, let it be known this day that thou art God in Israel, and that I am thy servant, and that I have done all these things at thy word [1 Kings 18:36].

Friend, I wish we recognized the fact that if God doesn't do it, it's not going to be done. Do you understand Elijah's prayer? This is one of the great prayers of Scripture—it's not long, but it is great. He said, "LORD God of Abraham, Isaac, and of Israel . . . ." You will notice that Elijah used the term *Israel,* not *Jacob.* Why *Israel?* Well, Israel is the name that was given not to twelve tribes, but to *one nation.* Also in his prayer Elijah said, "Let it be known this day that thou art God in Israel, and that I am thy servant, and that I have done all these things at thy word." You and I need to be sure that what we are doing is according to the will of God. Don't do something that you want to do and then ask God to bless it. God doesn't move that way. You have to go His route if you want to receive the blessing. We have no right to demand anything of God. It is true that He demands a great deal of us, but we are not to demand anything of Him. He is not a Western Union boy. He will not come at your command. We are to pray according to His will.

Hear me, O LORD, hear me, that this people may know that thou art the LORD God, and that thou hast turned their heart back again [1 Kings 18:37].

Elijah is praying for the glory of God in this verse. That is what moves the arm of God. And do you know what happened?

Then the fire of the LORD fell, and consumed the burnt sacrifice, and the wood, and the stones, and the dust, and licked up the water that was in the trench.

And when all the people saw it, they fell on their faces: and they said, The LORD, he is the God; the LORD, he is the God.

And Elijah said unto them, Take the prophets of Baal; let not one of them escape. And they took them: and Elijah brought them down to the brook Kishon, and slew them there [1 Kings 18:38–40].

That was a pretty brutal thing to do, wasn't it? But it sure got rid of the apostasy and the heresy.

ELIJAH'S PRAYER FOR RAIN

And Elijah said unto Ahab, Get thee up, eat and drink; for there is a sound of abundance of rain [1 Kings 18:41].

When the people turned to God, the rain came and the blessings came.

So Ahab went up to eat and to drink. And Elijah went up to the top of Carmel; and he cast himself down upon the earth, and put his face between his knees.

And said to his servant, Go up now, look toward the sea. And he went up, and looked, and said, There is nothing. And he said, Go again seven times.

And it came to pass at the seventh time, that he said, Behold, there ariseth a little cloud out of the sea, like a man's hand. And he said, Go up, say unto Ahab, Prepare thy chariot, and get thee down, that the rain stop thee not.

And it came to pass in the mean while, that the heaven was black with clouds and wind, and there was a great rain. And Ahab rode, and went to Jezreel [1 Kings 18:42–45].

Elijah was a great man! And so that the people might realize that the drought was not just an accident of nature but was a disciplinary measure, it ended the same way that it had begun—by the command of God's man, Elijah. Elijah said that rain was coming, but at first nothing could be seen but blue water and blue sky. When his servant looked for the seventh time, however, a cloud as small as a man's hand could be seen. The cloud rapidly increased in size until the heavens were black and rain flooded the parched earth.

And the hand of the LORD was on Elijah; and he girded up his loins, and ran before Ahab to the entrance of Jezreel [1 Kings 18:46].

Elijah had told Ahab to hurry home because the creek would soon rise and he would not be able to cross it. But then Elijah began to run. Why? Because he is a man of like passion as we are. He is very much a human being, and we are going to see just how human he is.

CHAPTER 19

THEME: *Elijah under a juniper tree*

Ahab reports to Jezebel that Elijah had slain all her prophets of Baal. She vows to kill Elijah. He beats a cowardly retreat to Beer-sheba, where he leaves his servant and continues on into the wilderness to crawl under a juniper tree, where he requests that he might die. Evidently Elijah is suffering from nervous exhaustion. He is physically and mentally depleted. God gives him nourishing food and plenty of sleep. Then He treats him to a spectacular display: strong wind, earthquake, and fire. Elijah loves all of this. Then comes the still, small voice. Although this is contrary to Elijah's personality, God is in the still, small voice. He sends him back to the scene of action and danger. On the way, Elijah calls Elisha to be his successor.

ELIJAH RUNS FROM JEZEBEL

It is difficult to believe that Elijah is the same man who defied 450 prophets of Baal on the top of Mount Carmel. He seems to be a different man, but there is an explanation for his condition.

And Ahab told Jezebel all that Elijah had done, and withal how he had slain all the prophets with the sword.

Then Jezebel sent a messenger unto Elijah, saying, So let the gods do to me, and more also, if I make not thy life as the life of one of them by to-morrow about this time.

And when he saw that, he arose, and went for his life, and came to Beer-sheba, which belongeth to Judah, and left his servant there [1 Kings 19:1–3].

That was a threatening message Jezebel sent to Elijah. Being before the public defying the false worship in his nation had drained a great deal of his energy and strength. He did a strange thing when he heard Jezebel's message threatening to kill him. Like Simon Peter when he took his eyes off the Lord, looked at those waves, and began to sink, Elijah lost his courage. He began to run. He went to Beer-sheba which is way down south. And friend, take it from someone who has been there, it is way down in the desert. Anyone who got as far away as Beer-sheba could consider himself safe from a ruler in the northern kingdom. But Elijah, when he reached this place in the desert, left his servant there and continued on another day's journey.

But he himself went a day's journey into the wilderness, and came and sat down under a juniper tree: and he requested for himself that he might die; and said, It is enough; now, O LORD, take away my life; for I am not better than my fathers [1 Kings 19:4].

You must admit that this is quite a change for the man who stood on top of Mount Carmel and defied the prophets of Baal. Now he is hiding under a juniper tree way down at the other end of the land, hiding from a woman, Jezebel. Ahab had not made any effort to arrest him or destroy him, but Jezebel hated Elijah, and she was not going to let him live if she could help it.

I think we need to note that Elijah had gone through a traumatic experience when he stood before that altar, prayed to God, and fire from heaven fell. Then there was the execution of the prophets of Baal. Next there was a tremendous rain storm, which was a great victory for Elijah. When Ahab went back and reported to Jezebel all that had happened, she sent a telegram to Elijah saying, "I want you to know that I intend to get you!" She is the most wicked woman in the Bible. Elijah got his eyes off the Lord and ran to an area that was beyond the farthest outpost of civilization. When he got to Beer-sheba, he just kept going. Finally he felt that he was out of her reach. Frankly, when I see him crawling underneath that juniper tree, I am ashamed of him. I am sure that some very pious Christian would have given Elijah a fine little lecture on how to be cheerful and optimistic and smile in his situation. They would tell him that Romans 8:28 was still in the Bible. May I say to you, I don't think you could have gotten Elijah to smile while he was under that tree.

I heard an English divine who preached a sermon some time ago on the subject, "Brief, Bright, and Brotherly." Elijah did not feel that way underneath that juniper tree. You can criticize Elijah, you can find fault with him, you can denounce him, and you can say that he is not trusting God as he should. Some might even say he is a disgrace to the Lord. What has happened to our prophet? Is this the man who defied the prophets of Baal? Is this the man who said, "If the LORD be God, follow Him"? What disease has smitten him? What is the diagnosis? Could you give us the etiology of it?

Let me suggest several things. There was a physical cause for the way he acted. He was overworked. He was overwrought. He was overworried. He was physically exhausted. I think he could have dropped in his tracks after that experience at Mount Carmel. He was worn out after the arduous task of standing for God in the face of such opposition.

The sin of the ministry is not finances, although many people think it is. Unfortunately, there are some preachers who are running a religious racket, but money is not the problem with the average preacher. When I was ordained, I was warned about the three sins of the ministry: pride, being boring, and laziness. I am confident that some folk are never going to get under a juniper tree. Do you know why? They are too lazy. Although there were seven thousand believers who had not bowed a knee to Baal, they were not under the juniper tree. They were hiding in caves up in the hills. They would never have been able to stand the lofty heights of Mount Carmel, and they did not see the fire come down from heaven. Elijah stood alone. He was a prodigal of his own physical strength. Some dear saint, I am sure, whispered in his ear, "You are doing too much. Take it easy." Elijah would never have run away from Jezebel if he had not been exhausted. I think we need men today who are willing to *work* for God. I hear a lot of talk about folks being dedicated, but they are as lazy and careless in the Lord's work as they possibly can be. This could never be said of Elijah. He was under the juniper tree because he was exhausted.

There is also a psychological factor involved in this situation. This is the day of hypertension, frustration, sterility, frigidity, nervous debilitation, disappointment, discouragement, despondency, let-down, run-down, and breakdown. Perhaps you have misunderstood Elijah. He was rough and rugged. He was a blood-and-thunder man. But that rugged exterior concealed a sensitive soul. He was ruled by his emotions, and he could go from elation to dejection. He possessed the finer sensibilities—he had artistic taste and aesthetic taste. His nature was emotional, and he did things that were emotional. Perhaps he suffered, as the psychologists say, from manic-depressive psychosis. A woman is probably the most delicate of God's creatures, and a woman is emotional. She has a finer sensibility than a man. Elijah had that kind of a nature. Did you ever notice that God put a badger skin around all of the beauty, wealth, and workmanship of the tabernacle? A badger skin was the exterior of something fine and beautiful. The exterior of Elijah was like that. Now he is crying out for God to take his life. He is in bad shape.

And as he lay and slept under a juniper tree, behold, then an angel touched him, and said unto him. Arise and eat.

And he looked, and, behold, there was a cake baken on the coals, and a cruse of water at his head. And he did eat and drink, and laid him down again.

And the angel of the LORD came again the second time, and touched him, and said, Arise and eat; because the journey is too great for thee [1 Kings 19:5–7].

Elijah needed rest. The Lord knew that, so He put him to sleep. Elijah slept like a baby. He also needed some good food—I don't think he had been eating regularly. He awoke to find some bread being baked. Do you know who I think baked that bread? I believe it was the same One who prepared that breakfast on the shore of Galilee one morning after the Resurrection. It was our Lord who comforted Elijah, fed him, and then put him back to sleep. He fed him, the second time, and told Elijah, "The journey is too great for you." This was something that Elijah had learned.

My friend, today may be a very happy day for you. You may think that you are sufficient for the battle of life. But I want to tell you that the journey through life is too great for you. You are going to need a Savior. You are going to need a helper. Elijah, as rugged as he was, needed Him.

ELIJAH AT MOUNT HOREB

And he arose, and did eat and drink, and went in the strength of that meat forty days and forty nights unto Horeb the mount of God [1 Kings 19:8].

Strengthened by the food provided by God, Elijah continued to run. He went clear to Mount Horeb, the mount on which the law had been given to Moses.

And he came thither unto a cave, and lodged there; and, behold, the word of the LORD came to him, and he said unto him, What dost thou here, Elijah?

And he said, I have been very jealous for the LORD God of hosts: for the chil-

dren of Israel have forsaken thy covenant, thrown down thine altars, and slain thy prophets with the sword; and I, even I only, am left; and they seek my life, to take it away [1 Kings 19:9–10].

The Lord is dealing with Elijah. He is overwrought and needs real psychological help. I have been asked if I believe in going to a psychologist. I think there are times when a person needs to consult a psychologist. Most of us, however, could solve our problems if we crawled on the couch of the Lord Jesus Christ and told Him everything. We wouldn't have to be running around telling everybody else about our troubles and problems if we would just talk them over with Him. We ought to tell Him everything.

And he said, Go forth, and stand upon the mount before the LORD. And, behold, the LORD passed by, and a great and strong wind rent the mountains, and brake in pieces the rocks before the LORD; but the LORD was not in the wind: and after the wind an earthquake; but the LORD was not in the earthquake [1 Kings 19:11].

First of all there was a great and strong wind that split the mountains and broke the rocks. Oh, did he love a good wind storm! Then the mountain rolled and shook under his feet. He loved it—he was that type of man.

And after the earthquake a fire; but the LORD was not in the fire: and after the fire a still small voice [1 Kings 19:12].

After the earthquake there was a fire. After all, he was the man who brought fire down from heaven on Mount Carmel. He liked that too. But wait a minute. God was not in the strong wind, nor the earthquake, nor the fire. After the fire came a still, small voice. If there was one thing that Elijah did not like, it was a still, small voice. I am sure Elijah did not have that kind of a voice, but he had to learn that God moves in a quiet way—how wonderful it is to see God moving in this way. He was teaching Elijah a great lesson. The battle was not actually won on top of Mount Carmel by fire coming down from heaven. God moves in mysterious and unostentatious ways His wonders to perform. God moves in a quiet way. God uses little things to accomplish His purpose. As someone has said, "Great doors are swung on little hinges." God uses small things to open mighty doors. That is what Elijah had to learn.

And it was so, when Elijah heard it that he wrapped his face in his mantle, and went out, and stood in the entering in of the cave. And, behold, there came a voice unto him, and said, What doest thou here, Elijah?

And he said, I have been very jealous for the LORD God of hosts: because the children of Israel have forsaken thy covenant, thrown down thine altars, and slain thy prophets with the sword; and I, even I only, am left; and they seek my life, to take it away [1 Kings 19:13–14].

Many of us can identify with Elijah. Sometimes with our families or in our communities we are surrounded by unbelievers, and we get the feeling that we are the only ones on earth standing for Christ.

And the LORD said unto him, Go, return on thy way to the wilderness of Damascus: and when thou comest, anoint Hazael to be king over Syria:

And Jehu the son of Nimshi shalt thou anoint to be king over Israel: and Elisha the son of Shaphat of Abel-meholah shalt thou anoint to be prophet in thy room.

And it shall come to pass, that him that escapeth the sword of Hazael shall Jehu slay: and him that escapeth from the sword of Jehu shall Elisha slay [1 Kings 19:15–17].

God is saying to Elijah, "Go back to the north country; I have more work for you to do." He is to anoint Hazael to be king over Syria and Jehu to be king over Israel. Then God tells Elijah about his successor, Elisha.

Yet I have left me seven thousand in Israel, all the knees which have not bowed unto Baal, and every mouth which hath not kissed him [1 Kings 19:18].

Finally, He told Elijah that there was a remnant of seven thousand people who have not bowed to Baal. God always has a remnant, my friend. He had one in Elijah's day, and He has one today. I have been very unkind in my references to the remnant. But they were standing for God. They had not bowed the knee to Baal. They were not out in the open like Elijah; they were the silent ones, but they were true to the God of Israel.

ELISHA'S CALL

God now is preparing to take Elijah home, and He will raise up Elisha to take his place.

So he departed thence, and found Elisha the son of Shaphat, who was plowing with twelve yoke of oxen before him, and he with the twelfth: and Elijah passed by him, and cast his mantle upon him.

And he left the oxen, and ran after Elijah, and said, Let me, I pray thee, kiss my father and my mother, and then I will follow thee. And he said unto him, Go back again: for what have I done to thee?

And he returned back from him, and took a yoke of oxen, and slew them, and boiled their flesh with the instruments of the oxen, and gave unto the people, and they did eat. Then he arose, and went after Elijah, and ministered unto him [1 Kings 19:19–21].

Elisha now becomes the pupil of Elijah. He is being trained to take over his ministry, as we shall see.

CHAPTER 20

THEME: *Israel is attacked by Syria*

Remember that this event occurs during the time the kingdom of Israel is divided. The ten northern tribes bear the name of Israel. Because of the repeated sin of both king and people, God is permitting their enemies to attack them. However, again God is gracious and gives them opportunity to repent and return to Him. In this chapter God delivers Israel, though pitifully outnumbered, from the mighty army of Syria.

AHAB'S FIRST SYRIAN CAMPAIGN AND HIS VICTORY

And Ben-hadad the king of Syria gathered all his host together: and there were thirty and two kings with him, and horses, and chariots: and he went up and besieged Samaria, and warred against it [1 Kings 20:1].

God is now permitting the enemy to come in from the outside. Up to this time God had not permitted it at all. We are told, however, that God promised victory even to Ahab.

And, behold, there came a prophet unto Ahab king of Israel, saying, Thus saith the LORD, Hast thou seen all this great multitude? behold, I will deliver it into thine hand this day; and thou shalt know that I am the LORD.

And Ahab said, By whom? And he said, Thus saith the LORD, Even by the young men of the princes of the provinces. Then he said, Who shall order the battle? And he answered, Thou [1 Kings 20:13–14].

The promise of God's deliverance in this situation was not based upon Ahab's fidelity but on God's love for His people. God gave this man an opportunity to change. We hear a great deal today about lost opportunities and about opportunity knocking only once at the door of every man. I think opportunity stands at the door and keeps knocking. Now Ahab was promised a victory, and God gave him a great victory over the Syrians.

And they slew every one his man: and the Syrians fled; and Israel pursued them: and Ben-hadad the king of Syria escaped on an horse with the horsemen.

And the king of Israel went out, and smote the horses and chariots, and slew the Syrians with a great slaughter [1 Kings 20:20–21].

AHAB'S SECOND SYRIAN CAMPAIGN AND HIS REBUKE FOR SPARING BEN-HADAD'S LIFE

And the prophet came to the king of Israel, and said unto him, Go, strengthen thyself, and mark, and see what thou dost: for at the return of the year the king of Syria will come up against thee [1 Kings 20:22].

God was telling Ahab, "I have given you a victory now, but you be careful that you don't return to the worship of Baal. I have demonstrated that I am your God—the living God. The king of Syria is going to come against you again at the return of the year." It was not the end of the struggle; Ben-hadad was going to renew his effort to defeat Israel. This is a very vivid picture:

And the children of Israel were numbered, and were all present, and went against them: and the children of Israel pitched before them like two little flocks of kids; but the Syrians filled the country.

And there came a man of God, and spake unto the king of Israel, and said, Thus saith the LORD, Because the Syrians have said, The LORD is God of the hills, but he is not God of the valleys. Therefore will I deliver all this great multitude into thine hand, and ye shall know that I am the LORD [1 Kings 20:27–28].

Once again God gave Ahab victory over the enemy, but unfortunately, Ahab made the mistake of sparing Ben-hadad's life.

And Ben-hadad said unto him, The cities, which my father took from thy father, I will restore; and thou shalt make streets for thee in Damascus, as my father made in Samaria. Then said Ahab, I will send thee away with this covenant. So he made a covenant with him, and sent him away [1 Kings 20:34].

Ahab was told to eliminate the enemy, but he did not obey. There can be no compromise, friend, with sin. God never permits that, and that is exactly what Ahab had done.

And he said unto him, Thus saith the LORD, Because thou hast let go out of thy hand a man whom I appointed to utter destruction, therefore thy life shall go for his life, and thy people for his people [1 Kings 20:42].

Why is it today that judges are so lenient with criminals? It is because they have a guilt complex themselves, my friend. They feel guilty themselves, and they know they are sinners. It is almost like pointing the finger at themselves to convict someone else. It is very hard for one sinner to judge another sinner. This was the case with Ahab—that is why he spared Ben-hadad's life.

CHAPTER 21

***THEME:** Ahab and Naboth's vineyard*

The chapter before us is a page out of the lives of the wicked king and queen of Israel, Ahab and Jezebel, which reveals their covetous and ruthless characters.

NABOTH'S VINEYARD IS COVETED BY AHAB

And it came to pass after these things, that Naboth the Jezreelite had a vineyard, which was in Jezreel, hard by the palace of Ahab king of Samaria [1 Kings 21:1].

A few years ago I was in Samaria, and I must confess that it is one of the most beautiful spots in the land of Palestine. You can stand on the hill of Samaria where Ahab and Jezebel's palace stood (Omri built it), and you can see Jerusalem to the south, the valley of Esdraelon and the Sea of Galilee to the north, the Jordan river on the east, and the Mediterranean Sea on the west. It is a beautiful view on all four sides. There are not many places like that. If I were living in that land, that would be the spot where I would like to have my home.

And Ahab spake unto Naboth, saying, Give me thy vineyard, that I may have it for a garden of herbs, because it is near unto my house: and I will give thee for it a better vineyard than it; or, if it seem good to thee, I will give thee the worth of it in money.

And Naboth said to Ahab, The LORD forbid it me, that I should give the inheritance of my fathers unto thee [1 Kings 21:2–3].

Naboth had a vineyard in this area. And as I stood on that beautiful hill, I wondered what side it was on. We do know it was nearby. And with as lovely a palace as Ahab had, you would think he would be satisfied. But, no, he wants that vineyard. Naboth does not want to sell it for the very simple reason that the vineyard is his patrimony. It is what God had given to his ancestors, and it had been passed down from father to son. But now here is a king who wants it, and it takes a pretty brave man to turn him down.

And Ahab came into his house heavy and displeased because of the word which Naboth the Jezreelite had spoken to him: for he had said, I will not give thee the inheritance of my fathers. And he laid him down upon his bed, and turned away his face, and would eat no bread [1 Kings 21:4].

Ahab doesn't get his way, so he goes home and pouts like a little boy. Ahab, wicked as he is, is like a spoiled brat and won't eat now because he cannot have what he wants—he can't have that vineyard!

JEZEBEL'S MURDEROUS PLOT TO OBTAIN NABOTH'S VINEYARD

Ahab did not have any ideas about how to get Naboth's vineyard, but Jezebel did. I can assure you that she is going to work out something that will enable her husband to get it.

But Jezebel his wife came to him, and said unto him, Why is thy spirit so sad, that thou eatest no bread?

And he said unto her, Because I spake unto Naboth the Jezreelite, and said unto him, Give me thy vineyard for money; or else, if it please thee, I will give thee another vineyard for it: and he answered, I will not give thee my vineyard.

And Jezebel his wife said unto him, Dost thou now govern the kingdom of Israel? arise, and eat bread, and let thine heart be merry: I will give thee the vineyard of Naboth the Jezreelite [1 Kings 21:5–7].

Jezebel was absolutely masculine in her manner—she was a dominant and domineering woman. I would have been afraid of her myself, I must confess. She is a wicked woman, and she *is* going to get the vineyard. She contrives a nice little plot and arranges to have two lawless men witness against Naboth. They say that he blasphemed God and the king. Naboth is then carried out of the city and stoned to death. Can you think of anything more unjust than this? Well, it has happened many times in the history of the world. Many times the man on top who has everything has taken advantage of the little man.

Naboth was stoned to death. Did Ahab get by with it? My friend, you don't get by with sin. I don't care who you are—the day will come when you are going to have to settle up. And the day came when Ahab had to settle up.

And it came to pass, when Jezebel heard that Naboth was stoned, and was dead, that Jezebel said to Ahab, Arise, take possession of the vineyard of Naboth the Jezreelite, which he refused to give thee for money: for Naboth is not alive, but dead.

And it came to pass, when Ahab heard that Naboth was dead, that Ahab rose up to go down to the vineyard of Naboth the Jezreelite, to take possession of it [1 Kings 21:15–16].

So Jezebel came in and announced to her husband Ahab, "Naboth is dead, and you can have the vineyard." It looks like Ahab has gotten by with this wickedness, doesn't it? No, God has a man there. Thank God that there is a man around who will declare the Word of God!

AHAB'S AND JEZEBEL'S DOOM IS PREDICTED

And the word of the LORD came to Elijah the Tishbite, saying,

Arise, go down to meet Ahab king of Israel, which is in Samaria: behold, he is in the vineyard of Naboth, whither he is gone down to possess it.

And thou shalt speak unto him, saying, Thus saith the LORD, Hast thou killed, and also taken possession? And thou shalt speak unto him, saying, Thus saith the LORD, In the place where dogs licked the blood of Naboth shall dogs lick thy blood, even thine [1 Kings 21:17–19].

Remember that God has said, "Be not deceived; God is not mocked: for whatsoever a man soweth, that shall he also reap"

(Gal. 6:7). If you and I could speak with men from the past—whether they were God's men or Satan's—they would tell us that this is an immutable law of God; it cannot be changed.

Jacob found out the truth of this law. Pharaoh of Egypt, who killed the little Hebrew boys, thought he got by with his crime, but one day he found that *his* firstborn was dead. David committed an awful sin, but he did not get by with it. The same thing he did came back to him. Saul of Tarsus was a leader in the stoning of Stephen, but there came a day in Asia Minor, at Antioch of Pisidia, when he was stoned and left for dead. The fact of the matter is that he was dead, and God raised him from the dead.

Now here is the judgment that is pronounced on Ahab and Jezebel:

> **Behold, I will bring evil upon thee, and will take away thy posterity, and will cut off from Ahab him that pisseth against the wall, and him that is shut up and left in Israel,**
>
> **And will make thine house like the house of Jeroboam the son of Nebat, and like the house of Baasha the son of Ahijah, for the provocation wherewith thou hast provoked me to anger, and made Israel to sin [1 Kings 21:21–22].**

God says to Ahab, "I'm removing your house. Your line will not reign here." Now God is not through:

> **And of Jezebel also spake the LORD, saying, The dogs shall eat Jezebel by the wall of Jezreel [1 Kings 21:23].**

Both of these judgments very definitely come to pass.

CHAPTER 22

***THEME:** Ahab and the prophet Micaiah*

Now in chapter 22 we will see the fulfillment of the Lord's judgment against Ahab. While we have been following the career of this king of the northern kingdom, down in the south Jehoshaphat has come to the throne. He is a good king, but now he is going to make an alliance with Ahab.

> **And they continued three years without war between Syria and Israel.**
>
> **And it came to pass in the third year, that Jehoshaphat the king of Judah came down to the king of Israel [1 Kings 22:1–2].**

What has happened that would cause a good king like Jehoshaphat to make an alliance with a king as wicked as Ahab? Why would he fraternize with his natural enemy? It's an abnormal alliance, an unnatural confederacy. At this point it seems strange, but we will find out later that Jehoram, the son of Jehoshaphat, had married Athaliah, the daughter of Ahab and Jezebel. This was a case of the "sons of God marrying the daughters of men"; that is, a boy with a godly heritage married a girl with a very wicked one. And the wicked influence prevailed. When the believer and the unbeliever get married, my friend, you can always be sure that the believer is going to have trouble. When you marry a child of the devil, your father-in-law sees to it that you have trouble.

> **And the king of Israel said unto his servants, Know ye that Ramoth in Gilead is ours, and we be still, and take it not out of the hand of the king of Syria?**
>
> **And he said unto Jehoshaphat, Wilt thou go with me to battle to Ramoth-gilead? And Jehoshaphat said to the king of Israel, I am as thou art, my people as thy people, my horses as thy horses [1 Kings 22:3–4].**

Ramoth-gilead was one of the chief cities of the tribe of Gad, and it had been lost to Syria. The best thing to do would have been to leave things as they were—status quo. At least Jehoshaphat should have stayed out of it. He should have followed the advice given to him by the prophet of the Lord. It was too bad that the devil's man and God's man made an alliance. This was not Jehoshaphat's fight anyway. Gilead did not belong to him—it belonged to Ahab, and it was Ahab's quarrel, not his.

AHAB IS PROMISED VICTORY BY HIS LYING PROPHETS

And Jehoshaphat said unto the king of Israel, Inquire, I pray thee, at the word of the LORD today [1 Kings 22:5].

Jehoshaphat is God's man. He wants to know what the will of God is.

Then the king of Israel gathered the prophets together, about four hundred men, and said unto them, Shall I go against Ramoth-gilead to battle, or shall I forbear? And they said, Go up; for the LORD shall deliver it into the hand of the king.

And Jehoshaphat said, Is there not here a prophet of the LORD besides, that we might inquire of him? [1 Kings 22:6–7].

Jehoshaphat wants to know the mind of the Lord, and he suspects that they are not getting it through these false prophets. He has a real spiritual discernment, and so he asks, "Is there not here a prophet of the LORD besides, that we might inquire of him?"

And the king of Israel said unto Jehoshaphat, There is yet one man, Micaiah the son of Imlah, by whom we may inquire of the LORD: but I hate him; for he doth not prophesy good concerning me, but evil. And Jehoshaphat said, Let not the king say so [1 Kings 22:8].

Ahab then introduces Micaiah, the after-dinner speaker. And he does so in a most unusual way—he says, "I hate him." Then Jehoshaphat says to Ahab, "You really don't mean that you hate a man of God." Someone has said that a man is not really known by his friends. Rather, he is known by his enemies. Every man ought to make sure that he has the right enemies. The best compliment that could be paid to Micaiah was for Ahab to say, "I hate him."

In the Lord's work I have always prided myself on the fact that I had the right enemies. I like the enemies I have because they do not stand for the Word of God. It is well to have the right enemies as well as the right friends. I can truthfully say that I thank God for my friends. I can also thank God for my enemies.

A toastmaster once said about a preacher he was introducing, "He doesn't have an enemy." God have mercy on him! You only had to listen to him for three minutes, and you could see why he had no enemies. He was Mr. Milquetoast—he didn't stand for anything. Micaiah actually was the best friend Ahab ever had. Ahab just did not know it. Micaiah could say as Paul did, "Am I therefore become your enemy, because I tell you the truth?" (Gal. 4:16).

Then the king of Israel called an officer, and said, Hasten hither Micaiah the son of Imlah [1 Kings 22:9].

They brought Micaiah in. After all, he was very close at hand: Ahab was keeping him in prison. This is another of these great dramatic scenes:

And the king of Israel and Jehoshaphat the king of Judah sat each on his throne, having put on their robes, in a void place in the entrance of the gate of Samaria; and all the prophets prophesied before them.

And Zedekiah the son of Chenaanah made him horns of iron: and he said, Thus saith the LORD, With these shalt thou push the Syrians, until thou have consumed them.

And all the prophets prophesied so, saying, Go up to Ramoth-gilead, and prosper: for the LORD shall deliver it into the king's hand [1 Kings 22:10–12].

You can just imagine those four hundred prophets running around saying to Ahab, "Go up against the king of Syria." One of the prophets was especially dramatic. Zedekiah ran around with iron horns, pushing at everyone with them, saying, "This is the way you are going to do it." What a scene—two kings on their thrones and all those prophets running about crying, "Go up and fight. You will win."

DEFEAT IS PROPHESIED BY MICAIAH

And the messenger that was gone to call Micaiah spake unto him, saying, Behold now, the words of the prophets declare good unto the king with one mouth: let thy word, I pray thee, be like the word of one of them, and speak that which is good [1 Kings 22:13].

The messenger that brought forth Micaiah said, "I'd just like to put a bug in your ear: all of the prophets are prophesying something good. They are telling the king to fight because he will win. That is what he wants to hear. You should join with them. Then you could get back into the king's favor. Here's your chance, Micaiah." And, I suppose, this guard thought he was helping Micaiah.

And Micaiah said, As the LORD liveth, what the LORD saith unto me, that will I speak [1 Kings 22:14].

Micaiah's answer was not only dramatic, it was humorous. He said, "Whatever the Lord tells me to say, that is what I am going to say. I will tell it like it is." Then Micaiah came in and sized up the situation. He saw the two kings on their thrones and all of the false prophets of Baal running around the room. They were all saying nice things to Ahab. They had all read the book, *How to Win Friends and Influence People*. Micaiah had not read that book. Neither had he read *The Power of Positive Thinking*. In fact, he was pretty negative. There is a lot of power in negative thinking, friend. We need more of it today.

So he came to the king. And the king said unto him, Micaiah, shall we go against Ramoth-gilead to battle, or shall we forbear? And he answered him, Go, and prosper: for the LORD shall deliver it into the hand of the king [1 Kings 22:15].

Notice what Micaiah says to the kings. To him it is a humorous scene, so he joins in just for fun. I think he was as sarcastic as any man could be—just as sarcastic as Elijah could be. They were cut out of the same piece of cloth, by the way. Micaiah said, "Go, and prosper: for the LORD shall deliver it into the hand of the king." Immediately the king saw that he was being ridiculed.

And the king said unto him, How many times shall I adjure thee that thou tell me nothing but that which is true in the name of the LORD? [1 Kings 22:16].

The king said to Micaiah, "I know you are kidding me because you have never been on the side of the false prophets."

Suddenly Micaiah becomes very serious and solemn.

And he said, I saw all Israel scattered upon the hills, as sheep that have not a shepherd: and the LORD said, These have no master: let them return every man to his house in peace.

And the king of Israel said unto Jehoshaphat, Did I not tell thee that he would prophesy no good concerning me, but evil? [1 Kings 22:17–18].

And the king of Israel says to Jehoshaphat, "I told you so—I told you he would say nothing but evil about me."

Then Micaiah said, "I'm not through. I have something else to say to you that you ought to hear." And he gives a parable. You could call it a parable that is the *reductio ad absurdum*. It is a preposterous parable, a parable by contrast. (You will not find parables like this until you come to our Lord's teaching as recorded by Luke. Take, for example, the parable of the unjust judge: God is not an unjust judge.)

Notice what Micaiah says here:

And he said, Hear thou therefore the word of the LORD: I saw the LORD sitting on his throne, and all the host of heaven standing by him on his right hand and on his left.

And the LORD said, Who shall persuade Ahab, that he may go up and fall at Ramoth-gilead? And one said on this manner, and another said on that manner [1 Kings 22:19–20].

Isn't that ridiculous? Can you imagine God calling a meeting of the board of directors or of the church board to ask them what He should do in a case like this? God already knows what He is going to do, and He does not need any advice.

And there came forth a spirit, and stood before the LORD, and said, I will persuade him.

And the LORD said unto him, Wherewith? And he said, I will go forth, and I will be a lying spirit in the mouth of all his prophets. And he said, Thou shalt persuade him, and prevail also: go forth, and do so [1 Kings 22:21–22].

Imagine this! God says, "My, you smart little fellow! I wish I had thought of that."

Now therefore, behold, the LORD hath put a lying spirit in the mouth of all these thy prophets, and the LORD hath spoken evil concerning thee [1 Kings 22:23].

This was the nicest way Micaiah could call these prophets a bunch of liars.

But Zedekiah the son of Chenaanah went near, and smote Micaiah on the cheek, and said, Which way went the

Spirit of the LORD from me to speak unto thee?

And Micaiah said, Behold, thou shalt see in that day, when thou shalt go into an inner chamber to hide thyself.

And the king of Israel said, Take Micaiah, and carry him back unto Amon the governor of the city, and to Joash the king's son:

And say, Thus saith the king, Put this fellow in the prison, and feed him with bread of affliction and with water of affliction, until I come in peace [1 Kings 22:24–27].

Zedekiah, the false prophet, struck Micaiah on the cheek. This was an extreme insult. In response to the insult Micaiah said by implication that the day would come when the false prophets would hide themselves in terror. That time would come when Ahab was dead and Israel was defeated. Then Zedekiah would know what the truth was.

And Micaiah said, If thou return at all in peace, the LORD hath not spoken by me. And he said, Hearken, O people, every one of you [1 Kings 22:28].

Micaiah told Ahab that he was not coming back. If he did, then the Lord had not spoken by him. Then Micaiah said, "In view of the fact that you won't be coming back, Ahab, I want the people to witness that what I have spoken is the truth."

AHAB'S DEFEAT AND DEATH

Israel went to battle. They listened to the false prophets, and what happened? Israel lost the battle. And Ahab proved he was a deceiver all the way through. You see, the only man in the battle who had on king's robes was Jehoshaphat, which made him a marked man, because Ahab had disguised himself. You might say that Ahab set Jehoshaphat up as a clay pigeon to be slain in the battle. It was not Jehoshaphat's fight at all, but he almost didn't come out of it alive.

But the king of Syria commanded his thirty and two captains that had rule over his chariots, saying, Fight neither with small nor great, save only with the king of Israel.

And it came to pass, when the captains of the chariots saw Jehoshaphat, that they said, Surely it is the king of Israel. And they turned aside to fight against him: and Jehoshaphat cried out.

And it came to pass, when the captains of the chariots perceived that it was not the king of Israel, that they turned back from pursuing him [1 Kings 22:31–33].

Poor Jehoshaphat almost lost his life in the battle because of Ahab's deception.

And a certain man drew a bow at a venture, and smote the king of Israel between the joints of the harness: wherefore he said unto the driver of his chariot, Turn thine hand, and carry me out of the host; for I am wounded.

And the battle increased that day: and the king was stayed up in his chariot against the Syrians, and died at even: and the blood ran out of the wound into the midst of the chariot [1 Kings 22:34–35].

Ahab was not slain by a soldier that aimed at him. The king was not a target, and the soldier did not shoot at Ahab—yet that arrow found him. You might say it was the first guided missile. I imagine that he was just an ordinary soldier with one last arrow left in his quiver. He pulled it out, put it in his bow, and simply let it go. He didn't know where it was going. Ahab's death would have to be listed as accidental, but in God's record it was providential: that arrow was aimed.

And you know, God still uses a very crude form of weapon—He's still back in the bow and arrow days. In Psalm 64:7, we read: "But God shall shoot at them with an arrow; suddenly shall they be wounded." There are those today who think they have escaped the hand of God. But I want to tell you that God has an arrow with your name on it; it will find you one of these days. No matter how much you try to deceive and cover up, that arrow will find you. That is what happened to Ahab.

So the king died, and was brought to Samaria; and they buried the king in Samaria.

And one washed the chariot in the pool of Samaria; and the dogs licked up his blood; and they washed his armour; according unto the word of the LORD which he spake [1 Kings 22:37–38].

That which God had predicted through Elijah came to pass: Ahab died, and his blood was licked up by dogs in the same place that

Naboth had died. Of course, Ahab had tried to stay away from that place, but his chariot was brought into Naboth's vineyard, and the blood was washed out of it. The dogs were right there to lick it up. The prophecy was literally fulfilled. Whatever a man sows, my friend, he will reap. Why? Because God is not mocked. You cannot get by with sin; no one gets by with it. God sees to that; He is still on the throne.

Now we turn briefly to the reign of Jehoshaphat, and we find that he made a big mistake.

And he walked in all the ways of Asa his father; he turned not aside from it, doing that which was right in the eyes of the LORD: nevertheless the high places were not taken away; for the people offered and burnt incense yet in the high places [1 Kings 22:43].

This was a token of compromise that God could not nor did He bless in the life of Jehoshaphat. It is quite obvious here that this man is a compromiser, and yet he is rated as a good king because he did serve God in his own personal life.

And Jehoshaphat made peace with the king of Israel [1 Kings 22:44].

This was a mistake also—he should not have done this. We read in 2 Chronicles that Jehu the prophet met Jehoshaphat as he returned from his visit with Ahab: "And Jehu the son of Hanani the seer went out to meet him, and said to king Jehoshaphat, Shouldest thou help the ungodly, and love them that hate the LORD? therefore is wrath upon thee from before the LORD. Nevertheless there are good things found in thee, in that thou hast taken away the groves out of the land, and hast prepared thine heart to seek God" (2 Chron. 19:2–3). Now the groves were a place of great immorality, but the high places where sacrifices offered to Baal were not taken away. Jehoshaphat had compromised.

Jehoshaphat made ships of Tharshish to go to Ophir for gold: but they went not; for the ships were broken at Eziongeber.

Then said Ahaziah the son of Ahab unto Jehoshaphat, Let my servants go with thy servants in the ships. But Jehoshaphat would not [1 Kings 22:48–49].

The son of Ahab who had come to the throne in the northern kingdom wanted Jehoshaphat to join him in a business deal—it would be a peaceful mission this time—but Jehoshaphat would not compromise again. He had learned his lesson. He said, "No, thank you. I don't care for this kind of an arrangement at all."

And Jehoshaphat slept with his fathers, and was buried with his fathers in the city of David his father: and Jehoram his son reigned in his stead [1 Kings 22:50].

Jehoshaphat died and was succeeded by his son Jehoram.

Ahaziah the son of Ahab began to reign over Israel in Samaria the seventeenth year of Jehoshaphat king of Judah, and reigned two years over Israel.

And he did evil in the sight of the LORD, and walked in the way of his father, and in the way of his mother, and in the way of Jeroboam the son of Nebat, who made Israel to sin:

For he served Baal, and worshipped him, and provoked to anger the LORD God of Israel, according to all that his father had done. [1 Kings 22:51–53].

Ahaziah, the son of Ahab, began to reign over Israel in Samaria. He reigned for two years and followed in the footsteps of Ahab and Jezebel.

(For Bibliography to 1 Kings, see Bibliography at the end of 2 Kings.)

The Book of
2 KINGS

For introductory material and outline, see the Book of 1 Kings.

CHAPTER 1

***THEME:** Fire from heaven protects Elijah from Ahaziah*

First Kings 22:51 tells us that "Ahaziah the son of Ahab began to reign over Israel in Samaria. . . ." We pick up the story in 2 Kings at this point. In fact, there does not seem to be a proper division between 1 and 2 Kings. Ahaziah's reign in Israel is begun in 1 Kings and concluded in 2 Kings.

The king and the prophet take the place of the priest as God's instruments of communication.

In 2 Kings, the first chapter, Ahaziah, king of Israel and son of Ahab and Jezebel, fell down through a lattice and seriously injured himself.

> **Then Moab rebelled against Israel after the death of Ahab.**
>
> **And Ahaziah fell down through a lattice in his upper chamber that was in Samaria, and was sick: and he sent messengers, and said unto them, Go, inquire of Baal-zebub the god of Ekron whether I shall recover of this disease [2 Kings 1:1–2].**

I would be inclined to say he fell because he was drunk. This is only a guess. Then instead of going to the Lord God for help, Ahaziah—greatly influenced by his mother Jezebel—went to inquire of Baal-zebub, the god of Ekron. Ahaziah's request for an oracle was a direct challenge to the Lord God of Israel. He wanted to know if he would recover from the effects of the accident.

> **But the angel of the LORD said to Elijah the Tishbite, Arise, go up to meet the messengers of the king of Samaria, and say unto them, Is it not because there is not a God in Israel, that ye go to inquire of Baal-zebub the god of Ekron?**
>
> **Now therefore thus saith the LORD, Thou shalt not come down from that bed on which thou art gone up, but shalt surely die. And Elijah departed [2 Kings 1:3–4].**

This was one of Elijah's last missions. He went to meet the messengers and gave them this challenge. "Is it not because there is not a God in Israel, that ye go to enquire of Baal-zebub the God of Ekron?" Then he gave them God's unwelcome prognosis: Ahaziah would not recover; he would die. The messengers went back and reported to the king what Elijah had said.

ELIJAH IS PROTECTED BY GOD

> **And he said unto them, What manner of man was he which came up to meet you, and told you these words?**
>
> **And they answered him, He was an hairy man, and girt with a girdle of leather about his loins. And he said, It is Elijah the Tishbite [2 Kings 1:7–8].**

This furnishes us an interesting description of the physical appearance of Elijah.

> **Then the king sent unto him a captain of fifty with his fifty. And he went up to him: and, behold, he sat on the top of an hill. And he spake unto him, Thou man of God, the king hath said, Come down.**
>
> **And Elijah answered and said to the captain of fifty, If I be a man of God, then let fire come down from heaven, and consume thee and thy fifty. And there came down fire from heaven, and consumed him and his fifty [2 Kings 1:9–10].**

Remember that Ahaziah the king was the son of Jezebel, the woman who had tried to kill

Elijah. Apparently there was still a price on his head.

Elijah is quite a man, is he not? He simply did not fit in with the compromises of court life in that day.

There is much talk today about the fact that we should learn to communicate and learn to get along with everybody. May I say to you that this is *not* God's method. The compromise of the church and its leaders has not caused the world to listen to the church. As a matter of fact, the world is not listening at all. They pass the church right by. Why? The world will not listen until the church declares the Word of God. If the church preached God's Word, there would be communication.

Elijah managed to communicate. He was heard. People listened to him. He was a pretty rough type of an individual. The king sent another captain with fifty men, and he also ordered Elijah to come down from the top of the hill. What came down was fire from heaven which consumed the captain and his men.

And he sent again a captain of the third fifty with his fifty. And the third captain of fifty went up, and came and fell on his knees before Elijah, and besought him, and said unto him, O man of God, I pray thee, let my life, and the life of these fifty thy servants, be precious in thy sight [2 Kings 1:13].

This man asks for mercy, and God will extend mercy to him.

And the angel of the LORD said unto Elijah, Go down with him: be not afraid of him. And he arose, and went down with him unto the king.

And he said unto him, Thus saith the LORD, Forasmuch as thou hast sent messengers to inquire of Baal-zebub the god of Ekron, is it not because there is no God in Israel to inquire of his word? therefore thou shalt not come down off that bed on which thou art gone up, but shalt surely die [2 Kings 1:15–16].

Elijah boldly repeated God's pronouncement.

So he died according to the word of the LORD which Elijah had spoken. And Jehoram reigned in his stead in the second year of Jehoram the son of Jehoshaphat king of Judah; because he had no son.

Now the rest of the acts of Ahaziah which he did, are they not written in the book of the chronicles of the kings of Israel? [2 Kings 1:17–18].

This ends the line of Omri and Ahab.

CHAPTER 2

THEME: *The translation of Elijah*

This chapter brings us to the conclusion of Elijah's life. He is translated into heaven in a chariot of fire. Then Elisha comes into prominence. The chapter closes with the incident of irreverent hoodlums being attacked by bears.

ELIJAH'S DEPARTURE

And it came to pass, when the LORD would take up Elijah into heaven by a whirlwind, that Elijah went with Elisha from Gilgal.

And Elijah said unto Elisha, Tarry here, I pray thee; for the LORD hath sent me to Beth-el. And Elisha said unto him, As the LORD liveth, and as thy soul liveth, I will not leave thee. So they went down to Beth-el.

And the sons of the prophets that were at Beth-el came forth to Elisha, and said unto him, Knowest thou that the LORD will take away thy master from thy head today? And he said, Yea, I know it; hold ye your peace.

And Elijah said unto him, Elisha, tarry here, I pray thee; for the LORD hath sent me to Jericho. And he said, As the LORD liveth, and as thy soul liveth, I will not leave thee. So they came to Jericho [2 Kings 2:1–4].

Elijah is trying to get Elisha to stay back. Elisha will not leave Elijah because he knows that Elijah is going to leave the earth that day. Elisha wants to be present when the Lord takes him home.

And the sons of the prophets that were at Jericho came to Elisha, and said unto him, Knowest thou that the LORD will take away thy master from thy head today? And he answered, Yea, I know it; hold ye your peace [2 Kings 2:5].

The interesting thing is that people, then as well as today, were turning to all kinds of people and places for information. This is the day when the fortunetellers and those who deal with the zodiac and the occult are handing out many suggestions. People are turning everywhere except to God. You won't get any information from these areas that you cannot get from God. The sons of the prophets had information that Elijah was going to leave, but Elisha already knew it. They could not tell him anything new.

And Elijah said unto him, Tarry, I pray thee, here; for the LORD hath sent me to Jordan. And he said, As the LORD liveth, and as thy soul liveth, I will not leave thee. And they two went on.

And fifty men of the sons of the prophets went, and stood to view afar off: and they two stood by Jordan.

And Elijah took his mantle, and wrapped it together, and smote the waters, and they were divided hither and thither, so that they two went over on dry ground [2 Kings 2:6–8].

The Lord had parted the River Jordan for Joshua and the people of Israel at least five hundred years before this; now He repeats the miracle for Elijah and Elisha.

And it came to pass, when they were gone over, that Elijah said unto Elisha, Ask what I shall do for thee, before I be taken away from thee. And Elisha said, I pray thee, let a double portion of thy spirit be upon me.

And he said, Thou hast asked a hard thing: nevertheless, if thou see me when I am taken from thee, it shall be so unto thee; but if not, it shall not be so [2 Kings 2:9–10].

Now don't miss that. Elisha actually was a greater prophet than Elijah. He had a double portion of the Spirit of God upon him.

And it came to pass, as they still went on, and talked, that, behold, there appeared a chariot of fire, and horses of fire, and parted them both asunder; and Elijah went up by a whirlwind into heaven [2 Kings 2:11].

This is a spectacular conclusion of a spectacular life!

ELISHA RECEIVES A DOUBLE PORTION OF ELIJAH'S SPIRIT

And Elisha saw it, and he cried, My father, my father, the chariot of Israel, and the horsemen thereof. And he saw him no more: and he took hold of his own clothes, and rent them in two pieces.

He took up also the mantle of Elijah that fell from him, and went back, and stood by the bank of Jordan;

And he took the mantle of Elijah that fell from him, and smote the waters, and said, Where is the LORD God of Elijah? and when he also had smitten the waters, they parted hither and thither: and Elisha went over [2 Kings 2:12–14].

This man Elisha is taking Elijah's place, and he demonstrates his faith. He takes Elijah's robe and smites the waters just as Elijah had done. The power is not in the robe nor in Elijah; the power is in God, and Elisha knows that. Elisha had the faith Elijah had, and it is faith in the *God* of Elijah. He asks the question, "Where is the LORD God of Elijah?"

This is the important question today. Instead of looking to men or women, methods or some nostrum for help, as many people do, why not look to the Lord God of Israel? He is the *living* God, He is the God and Father of the Lord Jesus Christ. Look to Him, my friend.

Elisha took Elijah's mantle, smote the waters, and they parted. He crossed over the river to begin a new phase in his life.

ELISHA SUCCEEDS ELIJAH

And when the sons of the prophets which were to view at Jericho saw him, they said, The spirit of Elijah doth rest on Elisha. And they came to meet him,

and bowed themselves to the ground before him.

And they said unto him, Behold now, there be with thy servants fifty strong men; let them go, we pray thee, and seek thy master: lest peradventure the spirit of the LORD hath taken him up, and cast him upon some mountain, or into some valley. And he said, Ye shall not send [2 Kings 2:15–16].

The sons of the prophets (the theological students of that day) were still watching and they saw Elisha part the waters and return across the Jordan River. They doubted that Elijah had really gone up. They suspected that the Lord had dumped him in some abandoned area. What a peculiar idea they had of God!

And when they urged him till he was ashamed, he said, Send. They sent therefore fifty men; and they sought three days, but found him not.

And when they came again to him, (for he tarried at Jericho,) he said unto them, Did I not say unto you, Go not? [2 Kings 2:17–18].

Elijah was indeed gone, and there was no need to investigate. Elisha said, "I told you so!"

Then the men of the city of Jericho came to Elisha with a problem.

And the men of the city said unto Elisha, Behold, I pray thee, the situation of this city is pleasant, as my lord seeth: but the water is naught, and the ground barren.

And he said, Bring me a new cruse, and put salt therein. And they brought it to him.

And he went forth unto the spring of the waters, and cast the salt in there, and said, Thus saith the LORD, I have healed these waters; there shall not be from thence any more death or barren land.

So the waters were healed unto this day, according to the saying of Elisha which he spake [2 Kings 2:19–22].

Elisha made the bitter waters sweet. This was his *second* miracle. Today you can see those waters in the valley at Jericho. I did not drink the water when I visited there because water out in the open in that land is apt to be contaminated. I am told, however, by those who were brave enough to drink it, that the water was sweet and delicious to drink.

Next followed an incident which has been criticized as much as anything in the Scriptures. This incident is pointed out with glee by the enemies of the Word of God who bemoan the brutal slaying of these poor little children.

First, let's look at the background. Elisha was returning from Elijah's translation when this event took place. The word had gone before him concerning what had taken place. As he went up to Beth-el, "little children" mocked him. Elisha cursed them in the name of the Lord, and two female bears came out of the woods and "tare forty and two children."

Not only the critics but also many sincere believers have been stumped by this portion of Scripture. The scorner says, "You don't mean to tell me that God would destroy little children like that?" What is recorded here seems to contradict other portions of Scripture.

First of all we need to recognize that when we come into the world our human minds are more or less neutral. They are neutral on practically every subject but one, and that is an innate streak of rebellion against God. Man has an inborn bias against God. Man, first of all, is skeptical about the Bible. Man will believe anybody or anything except God. If you don't believe this statement, notice how people fall for the "scientific approach." Let a man on television put on a white coat and pince-nez glasses, make a statement about mouthwash, deodorant, or toothpaste, and everybody runs and buys it because it is "scientific." Well, my friend, that reveals the nature of man.

If a man is an honest doubter, he will find there is an answer to all the problems and questions that concern the Word of God. That does not mean that I can answer all of the problems, because I cannot. This is one question, however, that I can answer, and I want to spend a little time with it.

Now Elijah was succeeded by Elisha. In many respects Elisha was greater than Elijah. This will undoubtedly be a surprise to many people who consider Elijah one of the greatest prophets, and possibly one of the witnesses who will one day return to earth during the tribulation (Rev. 11:3–7). If you want to measure these two men by the miracles they performed, Elisha performed the most miracles. Elijah was the man for the public. Elisha was the one who ministered personally to individuals. Because his ministry was largely in this area, it was not quite as exciting and dramatic as Elijah's ministry. He was a gentle man in contrast to Elijah.

Elisha was a young man at the beginning of his ministry. On this occasion he was returning from beyond Jordan where Elijah had been caught up in a chariot of fire and taken to heaven. News of this event had spread like wildfire over the countryside. Many people knew about it as Elisha returned to Beth-el. Probably the news media of the day carried the news about Elijah. I guess the *Beth-el Bugle* had a headline about the prophet and the chariot of fire. The *Bugle* would not confirm the story but they did report that there were those who had seen the event take place.

Beth-el means "house of God." It was first mentioned by Abraham, then by Jacob. Beth-el, however, did not continue to live up to its name. At the time of the division of the kingdom, Jeroboam, you will recall, placed one of the golden calves in Beth-el for the people to worship so that they would not continue to go to Jerusalem to worship. There was also a school for false prophets at Beth-el. It was, of course, an imitation of the school of prophets in Judah. It was in this atmosphere that the children of Beth-el were educated. They were godless. They had no training. They had no discipline at home. I think Beth-el was a great deal like Los Angeles, where I live. How ironical it is: *Los Angeles* means "the city of angels," and we have everything else but angels here.

Now Elisha is on his way to Beth-el.

And he went up from thence unto Beth-el: and as he was going up by the way, there came forth little children out of the city, and mocked him, and said unto him, Go up, thou bald head; go up, thou bald head [2 Kings 2:23].

Then "little children" came out of the city. The accepted opinion is that these were precious little children. All of us are moved by children. I have a little grandson, and he has grandpa wrapped around his finger. These little ones really get to you. When you read this portion of Scripture, it touches your heart. If these "children" were beginners, primaries, juniors, or even junior high young people, I would have to admit that Elisha was rather cruel because what happened would be contrary to the teaching of the rest of Scripture.

The Lord Jesus said, ". . . Suffer little children, and forbid them not, to come unto me: for of such is the kingdom of heaven" (Matt. 19:14). As you read the Bible, you will discover God's tender care of the little ones.

Remember that at Kadesh-Barnea the people of Israel refused to go into the land, and they gave the following excuse: "And wherefore hath the LORD brought us unto this land, to fall by the sword, that our wives and our children should be a prey? were it not better for us to return into Egypt?" (Num. 14:3). They felt that their little ones would be in danger. But God said to them in essence, "You should have trusted Me. You thought that I would not take care of your little ones. Well, although you will die in the wilderness, your little ones, who you thought were in danger, are going to inherit the land and dwell in it."

"Little children" is *naar* or *nahar* in Hebrew. It is used of Isaac when he was twenty-eight, of Joseph when he was thirty-nine, also for the Sodomites who attacked the home of Lot. You will find it used in other places in Scripture, and it does not refer to little children as we think of them. For example, 1 Kings 12:8 says, "But he forsook the counsel of the old men, which they had given him, and consulted with the young men that were grown up with him, and which stood before him." This verse is speaking about the time Rehoboam forsook the wisdom of the older men, the wise men, and consulted with the younger men who had grown up with him. The word translated "young men" is the same word translated "little children" in 2 Kings 2:23. I am sure no one believes that Rehoboam was consulting with little juniors, or that he went to nursery school and talked things over with the little ones. They were young men. When Samuel came to anoint as king one of the sons of Jesse, you will remember that his sons were grown. As they passed by Samuel one by one, he said to Jesse, "Are these all thy children?" Well, the word *children* is the same word used in 2 Kings 2:23. It is used to describe Jesse's grown sons. The youngest son, David, was not even there. The hoodlums who were taunting Elisha were young men, not little children. You will find this word used in many places in Scripture, and in every other place it is translated "young men." This was a crowd of young fellows.

They were students of the false prophets. They were a gang that mocked and ridiculed Elisha. They said, "Go up, thou bald head." What did they mean by that? They were telling him to do the same thing Elijah had done. They were saying, "Why don't you take off like Elijah did?" They were ridiculing the truth in Scripture that God will take a people out of this world.

This is the same attitude, Peter says, that will appear on the earth again in the last days. This incident in 2 Kings is given to us to let us know that God intends to judge those who ridicule the second coming of Christ. Second Peter 3:3–4 says, "Knowing this first, that there shall come in the last days scoffers, walking after their own lusts, and saying, Where is the promise of his coming? for since the fathers fell asleep, all things continue as they were from the beginning of the creation." During the last days on earth there will be those who will ridicule believers about the coming of Christ. They will say something like, "Well, what is the matter? You haven't gone up yet. You are still hanging around. I thought you were going to leave us." This is the type of thing scoffers will say to believers. Many are already saying, "Where is the sign of His coming?" For this reason we ought to be careful today in the way that we teach the second coming of Christ. We should not go out on a limb. We should not become fanatics on the subject. We should handle it with care, even in a manner in which the Word of God handles it. So 2 Kings is just a little picture of the judgment that will come upon those who will ridicule Christ's return to earth. It is a fearful judgment.

And he turned back, and looked on them, and cursed them in the name of the Lord. And there came forth two she bears out of the wood, and tare forty and two children of them [2 Kings 2:24].

It is an awful thing for a preacher to deny the deity of Christ and the work He did at His first coming. It is a terrible thing to deny and ridicule the second coming of Christ. This brings a very severe judgment.

Notice that they called Elisha "bald head." We do know something about this man: he had a bald head.

There is a great deal about judgment in the Word of God. We need, therefore, to get our facts squared away. When you understand what we are talking about in this section, there is nothing here that is out of line with the rest of Scripture. He pronounced a curse upon them. Elisha sounds like Elijah here. He also sounds like the Lord Jesus Christ who said, "Woe unto thee, Chorazin! woe unto thee, Bethsaida! for if the mighty works, which were done in you, had been done in Tyre and Sidon, they would have repented long ago in sackcloth and ashes" (Matt. 11:21). He went on to say, "And thou, Capernaum, which art exalted unto heaven, shalt be brought down to hell . . ." (Matt. 11:23). That is judgment, friends.

We are living in a day when there is a great deal of pussy-footing in our legal system. The lack of the enforcement of law on the part of some judges is a scandal; it is responsible for the lawlessness on every hand. It is responsible for the shooting down of policemen. It is not safe to walk our streets any more. The minds of people in this country have been brainwashed. When are we going to wake up? When gangs of young hoodlums terrorize our neighborhoods, there should be punishment. I personally heard a leading attorney recently tell a small group, privately, that these young lawbreakers should be taken out and publicly whipped, as they used to do in the early days. He said if that were done it would break up a lot of the lawlessness. May I say to you that after the bears did their work, nobody else around Beth-el ridiculed Elisha—you may be sure of that.

CHAPTERS 3–4

THEME: *Miracles of Elisha*

Now Jehoram the son of Ahab began to reign over Israel in Samaria the eighteenth year of Jehoshaphat king of Judah, and reigned twelve years [2 Kings 3:1].

Jehoram was the son of Ahab and Jezebel and successor of his brother Ahaziah, who died without having any children.

And he wrought evil in the sight of the LORD; but not like his father, and like his mother: for he put away the image of Baal that his father had made.

Nevertheless he cleaved unto the sins of Jeroboam the son of Nebat, which made Israel to sin; he departed not therefrom [2 Kings 3:2–3].

He did not sin as Ahab had sinned, but he did cleave "unto the sins of Jeroboam" which was calf-worship.

And Mesha king of Moab was a sheepmaster, and rendered unto the king of Israel an hundred thousand lambs, and an hundred thousand rams, with the wool.

But it came to pass, when Ahab was dead, that the king of Moab rebelled against the king of Israel [2 Kings 3:4–5].

Moab was in subjection to Israel and paid tribute. When Ahab died, Moab attempted to regain her freedom, refusing to pay the tribute. Jehoram, therefore, gathered his troops together and made an alliance with Jehoshaphat to join forces with him to bring Moab back into subjection. When they were unable to find water for their troops, their campaign not only was halted, but they were in danger of being conquered by the Moabites. King Jehoshaphat, being a God-fearing man, suggested they call a prophet of God to give them direction. (We could wish he had asked for God's guidance before he formed this alliance with Israel's godless king.) Elisha's response is interesting and reveals his contempt for Jehoram.

And Elisha said unto the king of Israel, What have I to do with thee? get thee to the prophets of thy father, and to the prophets of thy mother. And the king of Israel said unto him, Nay: for the LORD hath called these three kings together, to deliver them into the hand of Moab.

And Elisha said, As the LORD of hosts liveth, before whom I stand, surely, were it not that I regard the presence of Jehoshaphat the king of Judah, I would not look toward thee, nor see thee [2 Kings 3:13–14].

WATER AND VICTORY

Then God promises that there will be victory—they will be given water and they will completely subjugate Moab.

Notice the remarkable way God accomplishes this.

And he said, Thus saith the LORD, Make this valley full of ditches [2 Kings 3:16].

The ditches are pits to retain the water that is coming.

And it came to pass in the morning, when the meat offering was offered, that, behold, there came water by the way of Edom, and the country was filled with water [2 Kings 3:20].

The Moabite troops which are mustered to defend their country against Israel now look out toward the advancing armies.

And they rose up early in the morning, and the sun shone upon the water, and the Moabites saw the water on the other side as red as blood:

And they said, This is blood: the kings are surely slain, and they have smitten one another: now therefore, Moab, to the spoil [2 Kings 3:22–23].

Thinking that the confederate kings had come to blows and the troops had destroyed each other, the Moabites forget about warfare and each man takes off to get his share of the spoil. This, of course, gives Israel a distinct advantage.

And when the king of Moab saw that the battle was too sore for him, he took with him seven hundred men that drew swords, to break through even unto the king of Edom: but they could not.

Then he took his eldest son that should have reigned in his stead, and offered

him for a burnt offering upon the wall. And there was great indignation against Israel: and they departed from him, and returned to their own land [2 Kings 3:26–27].

Human sacrifice was widely practiced by the Moabites. Undoubtedly he offered the sacrifice to his god Chemosh, hoping that by offering his heir, Chemosh would save him from the enemy. However, it was a signal victory for Israel, and certainly must have impressed them with the power and graciousness of the Lord God of Israel.

Chapter 4 contains five miracles performed by Elisha. While there is a similarity between the miracles of Elisha and Elijah, the miracles performed by Elisha are more extensive.

INCREASE OF THE WIDOW'S OIL

Now there cried a certain woman of the wives of the sons of the prophets unto Elisha, saying, Thy servant my husband is dead; and thou knowest that thy servant did fear the LORD: and the creditor is come to take unto him my two sons to be bondmen [2 Kings 4:1].

Elisha apparently had known her husband. She reminds him that her husband was a true believer. When he died he left an unpaid debt which the creditor had now come to collect. If a borrower did not have personal property as security, his own person and that of his dependents would serve as security. Therefore the creditor could legally take the widow's sons as payment.

And Elisha said unto her, What shall I do for thee? tell me, what hast thou in the house? And she said, Thine handmaid hath not any thing in the house, save a pot of oil [2 Kings 4:2].

Elisha recognizes his responsibility to help this little family. The Mosaic Law insists that widows and fatherless children be cared for.

Then he said, Go, borrow thee vessels abroad of all thy neighbours, even empty vessels; borrow not a few.

And when thou art come in, thou shalt shut the door upon thee and upon thy sons, and shalt pour out into all those vessels, and thou shalt set aside that which is full.

So she went from him, and shut the door upon her and upon her sons, who brought the vessels to her; and she poured out [2 Kings 4:3–5].

They had a regular oil well going in that house!

And it came to pass, when the vessels were full, that she said unto her son, Bring me yet a vessel. And he said unto her, There is not a vessel more. And the oil stayed.

Then she came and told the man of God. And he said, Go, sell the oil, and pay thy debt, and live thou and thy children of the rest [2 Kings 4:6–7].

This is actually a greater miracle than the widow of Zarephath's unfailing cruse of oil in Elijah's day.

A SON FOR THE "GREAT WOMAN" OF SHUNEM

This gracious woman, living in Shunem, entertained Elisha whenever he passed through her town.

And she said unto her husband, Behold now, I perceive that this is an holy man of God, which passeth by us continually.

Let us make a little chamber, I pray thee, on the wall; and let us set for him there a bed, and a table, and a stool, and a candlestick: and it shall be, when he cometh to us, that he shall turn in thither [2 Kings 4:9–10].

Since then, there have been many believers who have in their homes what they call the "prophet's chamber." As I have traveled about from place to place, holding Bible conferences, I've stayed in many prophet's chambers. I could tell you about people all across this country today, wonderful Christian folk, who have a room where preachers and missionaries are entertained and feel at home. You do not know what that means in the lives of many of God's people today.

Now Elisha appreciated this home that was always open to him. Lying on the bed one day, he determined to somehow reward this thoughtful woman for her kindness. Elisha summons his servant Gehazi:

And he said, What then is to be done for her? and Gehazi answered, Verily she hath no child, and her husband is old.

And he said, Call her. And when he had called her, she stood in the door.

And he said, About this season, according to the time of life, thou shalt embrace a son. And she said, Nay, my lord, thou man of God, do not lie unto thine handmaid.

And the woman conceived, and bare a son at that season that Elisha had said unto her, according to the time of life [2 Kings 4:14–17].

LIFE RESTORED TO THE SHUNAMMITE'S SON

Years later when her son was a grown child, he died. Elisha restored him to life, using the same method that Elijah had used (1 Kings 17); that is, personal contact with the dead child which brought life. The great principle here is that when we are dead in trespasses and sins, personal contact with Jesus Christ brings life. In Him we have life. He *is* life.

POISONOUS POTTAGE

The fourth miracle in this chapter concerns food for the sons of the prophets, who were actually students—theological students. This was during a time of famine and one of the boys went out to gather any wild fruits or vegetables that he could find. They concocted a stew of what they found.

So they poured out for the men to eat. And it came to pass, as they were eating of the pottage, that they cried out, and said, O thou man of God, there is death in the pot. And they could not eat thereof.

But he said, Then bring meal. And he cast it into the pot; and he said, Pour out for the people, that they may eat. And there was no harm in the pot [2 Kings 4:40–41].

Elisha, you see, makes it harmless.

ONE HUNDRED MEN FED MIRACULOUSLY

A man, attempting to be faithful to the Mosaic Law, brought the firstfruits of his harvest to the sons of the prophets since Jeroboam had driven the Levitical priests from the country. Because it was a small amount, the servant balked at inviting one hundred men to dinner!

And his servitor said, What, should I set this before an hundred men? He said again, Give the people, that they may eat: for thus saith the LORD, They shall eat, and shall leave thereof.

So he set it before them, and they did eat, and left thereof, according to the word of the LORD [2 Kings 4:43–44].

This reminds us of the times our Lord fed crowds of four thousand and five thousand with a few loaves and fish.

CHAPTER 5

***THEME:** Naaman the Syrian*

THE HEALING OF NAAMAN

Chapter 5 is one of the most interesting chapters in the life of Elisha the prophet. It reveals that he was probably as rugged as Elijah and that he had a good sense of humor. I believe the Lord has a sense of humor and likes to use men who have a sense of humor. You cannot help but smile when you read this episode although it deals with a man in a very desperate situation.

Now Naaman, captain of the host of the king of Syria, was a great man with his master, and honourable, because by him the LORD had given deliverance unto Syria: he was also a mighty man in valour, but he was a leper [2 Kings 5:1].

This first verse gives us a thumbnail sketch of Naaman. He was captain of the host of Syria. Although he was a pagan, he was both a great man and an honorable man. By him the Lord had given Syria deliverance—this is a remarkable thing. I am sure that you will agree that he was a man the Lord had used. You will find that the Lord uses men in this world who are not Christian. That may seem strange to you, but you don't have to read very far in the Word of God to find that He used men like

Pharaoh, Nebuchadnezzar, Cyrus, and Alexander the Great. Here we are told He used Naaman. We are also told that Naaman was a mighty man of valor. All of these things mentioned count in the high court of heaven. God does not despise these things. This heathen man was used of God: "By him the LORD had given deliverance unto Syria." Even though we find all of these fine things are said of him, we have this to add, ". . . but he was a leper." There are many folks in the world today about whom nice things can be said although they are not Christians. You can say that they are fine men and women and have done fine things. But you have to conclude it all by saying that they are sinners—"For all have sinned, and come short of the glory of God" (Rom. 3:23). No matter how nice people might be, they are all sinners in God's sight.

Lepers were not excluded from society in pagan nations. It is interesting that God gave Israel a law about segregating lepers because it kept the disease from spreading. Today lepers are put in a colony and kept separate from society. God put these instructions in His Book centuries before any pagan nation realized they were necessary. This is something for you to think about, friend. It is not until you come into what we would call a "civilized day" that men decided to separate lepers from the rest of society.

Leprosy in Scripture is a type of sin. One reason is that it was incurable by human means. Only God can cure sin and save a sinner. Naaman had many fine points, but he was a sinner. He tried to cover up his leprosy, but he could not cure it. Many people today whitewash sin. What they need is to be washed white, and only Christ can do that.

And the Syrians had gone out by companies, and had brought away captive out of the land of Israel a little maid; and she waited on Naaman's wife [2 Kings 5:2].

This is one of those unknown, unnamed characters in the Bible. She was a young maid, a little Hebrew girl, and a great person. To me she is as great as Queen Esther, Ruth the Moabite girl, Bathsheba, Sarah, Rebecca, and Rachel. This little maid "waited on Naaman's wife."

And she said unto her mistress, Would God my lord were with the prophet that is in Samaria! for he would recover him of his leprosy [2 Kings 5:3].

This little Hebrew maid was in no position to give orders, but one day she uttered a sigh and said, "Oh, that my master would go down and see the prophet in Samaria. He would recover him of his leprosy"—Elisha, you see, had quite a reputation. Well, someone—probably his wife—heard what she said, and it reached the ears of the king of Syria.

And one went in, and told his lord, saying, Thus and thus said the maid that is of the land of Israel [2 Kings 5:4].

The king of Syria was delighted to hear that something could be done for this very valuable man, and he immediately sent him to the king of Israel with a letter of introduction and a very handsome reward.

And the king of Syria said, Go to, go, and I will send a letter unto the king of Israel. And he departed, and took with him ten talents of silver, and six thousand pieces of gold, and ten changes of raiment.

And he brought the letter to the king of Israel, saying, Now when this letter is come unto thee, behold, I have therewith sent Naaman my servant to thee, that thou mayest recover him of his leprosy.

And it came to pass, when the king of Israel had read the letter, that he rent his clothes, and said, Am I God, to kill and to make alive, that this man doth send unto me to recover a man of his leprosy? wherefore consider, I pray you, and see how he seeketh a quarrel against me [2 Kings 5:5–7].

This letter from the king of Syria requesting that the captain of his army be healed of leprosy greatly disturbed the king of Israel. He exclaimed, "I am not God. I cannot heal him!" The message had been sent to the wrong person. The king of Israel read the message, but it should have gone to Elisha. I always feel like anyone who claims to have a gift of healing is almost being blasphemous, friend. The king of Israel said, "I don't claim to be able to heal anyone." Elisha did not claim to be a healer either, but he was in contact with the Great Physician. The king of Israel, however, came to the conclusion that the king of Syria was trying to start a quarrel with him—why else would he send the captain of his army with this impossible request?

And it was so, when Elisha the man of God had heard that the king of Israel had rent his clothes, that he sent to the king, saying, Wherefore hast thou rent thy clothes? let him come now to me, and he shall know that there is a prophet in Israel [2 Kings 5:8].

Elisha said, "Send Naaman down to me."

So Naaman came with his horses and with his chariot, and stood at the door of the house of Elisha.

And Elisha sent a messenger unto him, saying, Go and wash in Jordan seven times, and thy flesh shall come again to thee, and thou shalt be clean [2 Kings 5:9–10].

Naaman was from a great kingdom in the north. In fact, his nation was at that time bearing down upon the nation Israel. Syria had already gained victories over Israel, and Naaman expected the red carpet to be rolled out for him. And what happened?

Elisha told him to go and wash in the Jordan River seven times! Of course this hurt the pride of Naaman. Elisha actually received this man rudely. In fact, Elisha did not receive him at all—he did not even go to the door to receive him. You would think the prophet would bow and scrape to this great captain of the hosts of Syria. Instead, Elisha sent his servant to tell Naaman to go and wash seven times in the Jordan River. Do you think Naaman is going to accept this advice?

But Naaman was wroth, and went away, and said, Behold, I thought, He will surely come out to me, and stand, and call on the name of the LORD his God, and strike his hand over the place, and recover the leper [2 Kings 5:11].

Naaman was upset because he was a very proud man. He had never received treatment like this before. The Lord is not only going to heal his leprosy, He is also going to heal him of pride. When God saves you, He generally takes out of your life that thing which offends. Pride just happens to be one of the things God hates.

We hear a great deal about the fact that "God is love," but God also hates. You cannot love without hating. You cannot love the good without hating the evil. If you love your children, you would hate a mad dog that would come into the yard to bite your little ones. You would want to kill that mad dog. It is true that God loves man, and in unmistakable language God declares that He hates the pride in man's heart. Proverbs 6:16–19 lists seven things that God hates. First on His list are these: "A proud look, a lying tongue, and hands that shed innocent blood." Do you see what is number one on God's hate parade? It is a *proud look*. God says he hates that. He hates that as much as He hates murder. James 4:6 says, "But he giveth more grace. Wherefore he saith, God resisteth the proud, but giveth grace unto the humble." Pride is the undoing of man. It is a great sin. In Proverbs 16:18 we read, "Pride goeth before destruction, and an haughty spirit before a fall." Proverbs 11:2 says, "When pride cometh, then cometh shame: but with the lowly is wisdom." Finally, Proverbs 29:23 says, "A man's pride shall bring him low: but honour shall uphold the humble in spirit." Why does God hate pride? The definition of pride is "excessive self-esteem." It is inordinate self-esteem. It is more than reasonable delight in one's position and achievement. Paul put it like this, "For I say, through the grace given unto me, to every man that is among you, not to think of himself more highly than he ought to think; but to think soberly, according as God hath dealt to every man the measure of faith" (Rom. 12:4). Pride is placing an excessive price on self. It is demanding more than you are worth. Have you ever heard it said, "I wish I could buy that man for what he is worth and sell him for what he thinks he is worth?" Pride is the difference between what you are and what you think you are. It was the pride of Satan that brought him down. That was his sin. Pride was also the sin of Edom. Of Edom God said, "Though thou exalt thyself as the eagle, and though thou set thy nest among the stars, thence will I bring thee down, saith the LORD" (Obad. 4).

Man's pride runs counter to God's plan; and, whenever they meet, there is friction. There is no compromise. It is always a head-on collision. You see, God's plan of salvation is the supreme answer to man's pride. God lays man low. God takes *nothing* from man. Paul could say of himself when he met Jesus Christ, "But what things were gain to me, those I counted loss for Christ" (Phil. 3:7). Paul gave up religion. Paul gave up everything he had been; he rated it as dung—he said, "I just flushed it down." Christ and pride do not go together. You cannot be proud and at the same time trust Christ as your Savior. If you trust Him, my friend, you will lay all of your pride in the dust.

The story of Naaman is the finest example

that we have of a man being shorn of his pride. He was a great man, to be sure. God listed all the things that marked him out as a man of character and ability. But he was a leper. He was a sinner. God not only healed him of leprosy, He healed him of his pride. Believe me, Elisha insulted him. Naaman thought Elisha would come out to him, stand, and call on the name of the Lord his God, strike his hand over the place, and recover the leper. You know, that is religion. It is as if Naaman were saying, "Oh, if only I could have gotten into a healing line, and had him put his hand on me, and call upon God and pray. If only he had poured a little oil on me. That would be great." That is religion, friend. When God heals a person, it is by faith. He lays your pride in the ground. You do not go to a man for healing; you go to God, the Great Physician.

Are not Abana and Pharpar, rivers of Damascus, better than all the waters of Israel? may I not wash in them, and be clean? So he turned and went away in a rage [2 Kings 5:12].

This is one place where I agree with Naaman. I saw those beautiful rivers in Lebanon. I went up to the city of Byblos from Beirut, and I stopped at a place called, "Calling Cards of the Great Men of the Earth," because it is a place where many notable men have left inscriptions on the side of a cliff. I walked along a river there about half a mile and looked at the beautiful clear water rippling over the rocks. The Jordan is a muddy little stream, friend. It is not nearly as pretty as some of the streams in Lebanon. I rather agree with Naaman. He said, "Why in the world should I go and dip in the Jordan? Why not dip in a stream with clean water?"

This has an application for us. A lot of folks hate to come to the cross of Christ. It is a place of ignominy. It is a place of shame. People don't want to come to the cross. Instead they want to do something great. That is what Naaman wanted to do. Oh, the pride of Naaman! He said the rivers of Damascus were better, and they were. He was disgusted with the impudence and impertinence of the prophet to tell him to wash in the Jordan. But, my friend, you will have to come to the cross of Christ. You do not come to Jesus and stand before Him as a proud man. You cannot say that you have something you are resting on when you come to Him. You come, "just as I am without one plea, but that Thy blood was shed for me," and shed for every person. All you have to do is accept His work on the cross.

And his servants came near, and spake unto him, and said, My father, if the prophet had bid thee do some great thing, wouldest thou not have done it? how much rather then, when he saith to thee, Wash, and be clean? [2 Kings 5:13].

As Naaman was riding away in a rage, his servants attempted to reason with him, "If the prophet had asked you to do something great, you would have done it." How many people today would like to do some great thing for salvation? You don't have to do anything; He has already done it for us. All we have to do is receive it. We come as beggars. Naaman would have to come that way also.

Then went he down, and dipped himself seven times in Jordan, according to the saying of the man of God: and his flesh came again like unto the flesh of a little child, and he was clean [2 Kings 5:14].

Naaman went down to the Jordan and dipped in the water seven times according to Elisha's instructions. I would give almost anything in the world if I could have been there and watched him. I think every time he went down into the water he would come up and look at himself. He probably said, "This is absurd. I am not getting clean—I am not getting rid of my leprosy!" Then he went down into the water again. But he did dip himself in the Jordan seven times, and he was healed.

GEHAZI'S SIN AND THE PENALTY

And he returned to the man of God, he and all his company, and came, and stood before him: and he said, Behold, now I know that there is no God in all the earth, but in Israel: now therefore, I pray thee, take a blessing of thy servant.

But he said, As the LORD liveth, before whom I stand, I will receive none. And he urged him to take it; but he refused.

And Naaman said, Shall there not then, I pray thee, be given to thy servant two mules' burden of earth? for thy servant will henceforth offer neither burnt offering nor sacrifice unto other gods, but unto the LORD.

In this thing the LORD pardon thy servant, that when my master goeth into the house of Rimmon to worship there, and he leaneth on my hand, and I bow myself in the house of Rimmon: when I bow down myself in the house of Rimmon, the LORD pardon thy servant in this thing.

And he said unto him, Go in peace. So he departed from him a little way [2 Kings 5:15–19].

Now, deeply grateful for his healing, Naaman is pressing Elisha to accept these rich gifts he has brought as a token of his appreciation. But Elisha will not accept payment for what God has done.

Now Elisha had a servant named Gehazi. He hated to see that handsome reward slip by, so he took out after Naaman.

So Gehazi followed after Naaman. And when Naaman saw him running after him, he lighted down from the chariot to meet him, and said, Is all well?

And he said, All is well. My master hath sent me, saying, Behold even now there be come to me from mount Ephraim two young men of the sons of the prophets: give them, I pray thee, a talent of silver, and two changes of garments.

And Naaman said, Be content, take two talents. And he urged him, and bound two talents of silver in two bags, with two changes of garments, and laid them upon two of his servants; and they bare them before him [2 Kings 5:21–23].

Why did Gehazi take the offering from Naaman? Greed!

And when he came to the tower, he took them from their hand, and bestowed them in the house: and he let the men go, and they departed.

But he went in, and stood before his master. And Elisha said unto him, Whence comest thou, Gehazi? And he said, Thy servant went no whither [2 Kings 5:24–25].

Gehazi allowed the servants to carry the gifts as far as the tower; then he took them himself and sent the servants back to Naaman so that Elisha would not see them. With the gifts safely stowed away, Gehazi rushes back to his job, acting as if nothing had happened.

And he said unto him, Went not mine heart with thee, when the man turned again from his chariot to meet thee? Is it a time to receive money, and to receive garments, and oliveyards, and vineyards, and sheep, and oxen, and menservants, and maidservants?

The leprosy therefore of Naaman shall cleave unto thee, and unto thy seed for ever. And he went out from his presence a leper as white as snow [2 Kings 5:26–27].

The great sin of Naaman was pride. The great sin of Gehazi was greed. My beloved, greed is leprosy of the soul.

CHAPTER 6

***THEME:** The floating ax head and danger at Dothan*

In chapter 6 we will see two more thrilling experiences that Elisha had. Elisha was an outstanding prophet, although he was different from Elijah. Elijah's ministry was public; Elisha's ministry was more private (we have just seen how he dealt with Naaman, the captain of the Syrian host). Elijah was spectacular—he brought down fire and rain from heaven. Elisha was a quiet man; he shunned the spotlight. However, both prophets were God's men at God's time.

THE AX HEAD

Our attention will center now on Elisha. I do not think that any miracle so reveals the character of a person and a prophet as the miracle of the floating ax head.

And the sons of the prophets said unto Elisha, Behold now, the place where we dwell with thee is too strait for us [2 Kings 6:1].

Now this reveals something of the popularity of Elisha. He taught in a theological seminary, the school of the prophets. The school grew, and they needed larger quarters. This was due to the presence and the popularity of Elisha. The strength, I feel, and the value of any school is the character and the ability of those who teach. It is not the methods but the men that are important, especially in a Christian school.

Now notice what they did. In order to enlarge the school they said,

Let us go, we pray thee, unto Jordan, and take thence every man a beam, and let us make us a place there, where we may dwell. And he answered, Go ye [2 Kings 6:2].

The students built their own school. That would be an unusual thing in our day. Today everything has to be given to the students in order to get them through school and, if it doesn't suit them, they rebel. But these students went out to work, and Elisha encouraged them in it.

And one said, Be content, I pray thee, and go with thy servants. And he answered, I will go [2 Kings 6:3].

This is a refreshing and thrilling verse. It is an insight into the winsome character of Elisha. It reveals that he was popular with the students. By the way, do students ordinarily want to take their teacher with them beyond the boundary of the campus? They'd like to leave him there. But these asked Elisha to go with them.

So he went with them. And when they came to Jordan, they cut down wood [2 Kings 6:4].

Now a small tragedy takes place. I say "small" because the ordinary person would call this a trivial incident.

But as one was felling a beam, the axe head fell into the water: and he cried, and said, Alas, master! for it was borrowed [2 Kings 6:5].

There is something here that is quite interesting. It reveals that God is concerned about the small events in our lives. You remember that Paul said to the Philippians, "Pray about everything," and he did not mean to leave anything out.

The loss of an ax head may seem insignificant to us, but to this poor student it is not so small. The fact of the matter is, it is pretty big. In our day of gadgets when we can go down to the hardware store and get an ax head of about fifteen different shapes, this does not seem important. But in that day it was of tremendous importance because any kind of iron tool or weapon was scarce. And if you want to know something about that period, notice just one verse from 1 Samuel: "So it came to pass in the day of battle, that there was neither sword nor spear found in the hand of any of the people that were with Saul and Jonathan: but with Saul and with Jonathan his son was there found" (1 Sam. 13:22). Two swords for an entire army! It lets you know something of the scarcity of weapons and of tools in that day. So you can understand that the loss of an ax head was very important to this young man—and, of course, he had borrowed it.

Most commentators, I have discovered, romp all over this student. They give him a demerit for carelessness and a demerit for the fact that he borrowed something. Well, if this man were guilty, why did not Elisha, his teacher, rebuke him? Elisha did not. Elisha absolved him from all charges. He was not careless, but actually was very careful. Obviously there was a danger of an ax head coming off, and it happened often enough so that God included it in the Mosaic Law: "And this is the case of the slayer, which shall flee thither, that he may live: Whoso killeth his neighbour ignorantly, whom he hated not in time past; As when a man goeth into the wood with his neighbour to hew wood, and his hand fetcheth a stroke with the axe to cut down the tree, and the head slippeth from the helve and lighteth upon his neighbour, that he die; he shall flee unto one of those cities, and live" (Deut. 19:4–5).

God made this law because it evidently was something that occurred quite frequently. Now this man revealed his carefulness by cutting the wood so that there was nobody out in front of him. He was standing so that if the ax head came off it would go into the Jordan River. He was aiming it in a safe direction.

The second fault they find with him is that he borrowed it. Well, I think that I am qualified to speak for this fellow here. He was a poor seminary student, and he could not afford an ax in that day—no more than I could have owned a Cadillac when I was in seminary. He just could not have done it. He had to borrow it. I do not think that this poor fellow should be criticized on these two points.

In fact, I have a question to ask. Who

loaned this student an old ax with a head that would come off? That's the fellow I would like to talk to. I imagine that fellow is the same one who today gives secondhand clothes and old Christmas cards to missionaries and thinks he is serving the Lord.

Now this boy was distressed, and he could not reimburse the owner. He would have to face him without the ax and he didn't know what to do. Now notice Elisha's concern. "And the man of God said, Where fell it?" Let's stop there for just a moment because there have been those who have said, "Why did Elisha ask that question if he was a prophet? He would have known where the ax head fell." He knew, and he knew something else also. He knew that he needed to test that young man. By the Spirit of God he needed to test him. Notice that this young man knew exactly where that ax head went into the water. Don't tell me he was careless. Elisha is not doing it only for a test but for another reason. The Spirit of God knew that in the twentieth century there would be critics of this miracle, and, as they've explained away every other miracle, they would say, "Well, after all, the water was clear, and anybody could see where it was." The question Elisha asked precludes anyone saying that the water was clear. And if you know anything about the Jordan River, you know it was muddy. I have heard many romantic, wonderful things about that river, but to me it was the most disappointing thing that I saw. You talk about polluted water! You talk about a muddy little stream! You talk about a dirty thing! That's the Jordan River. Because it was muddy, Elisha said, "Where did it fall?" The young man knew right where it was, but he could not get it out because he could not see it. The water was *not* clear. Now notice what took place.

And the man of God said, Where fell it? And he shewed him the place. And he cut down a stick, and cast it in thither; and the iron did swim [2 Kings 6:6].

This was a miracle, and I do not think that you can explain it away. This is one miracle—not sensational, not as spectacular as going to heaven in a chariot of fire—that is great in its simplicity. It is a miracle when iron swims. It is contrary to all known physical laws. I recognize that since the day that the first iron ship was launched, ships of iron and steel now float on the seven seas. And that's no miracle. But, my friend, it was a miracle for an ax head on the bottom of the Jordan River to float to the top like a cork! I know it is not startling, not sensational; it's simple. This is Elisha's method. Elijah would have never done it this way. In fact, I don't think Elijah would have bothered with a thing like that. He would have said, "Son, forget it." But not Elisha.

An ax head, dormant on the bottom of the muddy Jordan, is raised, resurrected, if you please, restored to the owner, replaced on the handle, and it becomes useful again, utilitarian and functional. That's really a greater miracle than these others because there is a tremendous spiritual message here for us today. Man today is like that ax head. He has slipped off the handle. He has fallen. He is totally depraved.

So Elisha cut down a stick. He cast it into the waters of death. That stick is the cross of Christ. Our Lord came down to that cross, and He went down into the waters of death for you and me. "Who his own self bare our sins in his own body on the tree, that we, being dead to sins, should live unto righteousness: by whose stripes ye were healed" (1 Pet. 2:24).

Man today can rise from the waters of death and judgment through Christ. He can be placed back on the handle of God's plan and purpose for him, and he can be geared into God's program. Paul testifies, "I can do all things through Christ which strengtheneth me" (Phil. 4:13). And further, ". . . this one thing I do, forgetting those things which are behind, and reaching forth unto those things which are before, I press toward the mark for the prize of the high calling of God in Christ Jesus" (Phil. 3:13–14). It is no longer necessary for any person to live an aimless and useless life. Having no purpose in life is the thing that is driving literally thousands of people to suicide. This past week a half dozen college students committed suicide, and the whole explanation was, "It isn't worth living." My friend, of course it's not worth living when you are an old ax head down at the bottom of the muddy Jordan. It is not until Christ lifts you by His cross (His death for you and me) and places us back in His plan and purpose that life becomes worthwhile. A young man (not yet twenty-one years old) said to me, "My life is a failure." I said to him, "Your life hasn't even begun, and you are talking about being a failure!" How we need God today! The greatest miracle today, friend, is not to go to the moon. It is not even to go to heaven in a chariot of fire. Rather it is to go to the highest heaven when we are still sinners and have trusted Christ. That's the greatest miracle there is—to be lifted out of the muck and mire of this world and to be given meaning for our lives and enabled to live for God.

Therefore said he, Take it up to thee. And he put out his hand, and took it [2 Kings 6:7].

All you have to do is reach out the hand of faith today and take it, for He died for you. He rose again in order that He might lift you up. All you have to do from your position is to reach out the hand of faith and trust Him.

DANGER AT DOTHAN

The next episode begins with a very familiar ring. It sounds like a page out of the morning newspaper: "Then the king of Syria warred against Israel." They have been at it for a long time; actually, it was an old conflict even at that time. The present conflict between Israel and the Arab world has a definite Bible background.

Now notice the situation.

Then the king of Syria warred against Israel, and took counsel with his servants, saying, In such and such a place shall be my camp.

And the man of God sent unto the king of Israel, saying, Beware that thou pass not such a place; for thither the Syrians are come down.

And the king of Israel sent to the place which the man of God told him and warned him of, and saved himself there, not once nor twice.

Therefore the heart of the king of Syria was sore troubled for this thing; and he called his servants, and said unto them, Will ye not shew me which of us is for the king of Israel? [2 Kings 6:8–11].

The king of Syria was disturbed because every plan he made and every place he went was discovered by the king of Israel. He came to the conclusion that there was a spy in his camp. He called together his military and attempted to ferret out the traitor. "Which one of you is for the king of Israel?" Honestly there was no one—all of them were loyal to him.

And one of his servants said, None, my lord, O king: but Elisha, the prophet that is in Israel, telleth the king of Israel the words that thou speakest in thy bedchamber [2 Kings 6:12].

The prophet Elisha had "bugged" even the bedroom of the king of Syria and knew everything he said. And the way he "bugged" them in that day was that the Lord revealed this to him.

So the king of Syria decided to eliminate Elisha. He first sent out those to spy out where he was and they located him in Dothan. Dothan is a place north of Jerusalem about sixty miles. It means "two wells" and was a place where there was good pasture, a place where flocks were brought. At the present time and for several years Dr. Joseph Free, of Wheaton College, has been carrying on an excavation in that place. I am told that there is really not much to see there because it never was a very prominent place. But it was the headquarters of Elisha at this particular time. The king of Syria sends in the military, and they entirely surround the place. The servant of Elisha goes out in the morning, I suppose to get water out of one of those wells (which are still there today); he looks around and sees that the city of Dothan is surrounded by the hosts of Syria. You can be sure of one thing, he is alarmed. He comes back and reports to Elisha, and he says to him, "Alas, my master! What shall we do? The city is surrounded. We might just as well give up. It looks hopeless for us! What can we do under these circumstances?"

And he answered, Fear not: for they that be with us are more than they that be with them [2 Kings 6:16].

And I want to tell you, that seemed rather unrealistic because here were the hosts of Syria outside, and Elisha was very much alone with his servant—and that servant was frightened to death. So Elisha prayed, and his prayer is interesting.

And Elisha prayed, and said, LORD, I pray thee, open his eyes, that he may see. And the LORD opened the eyes of the young man; and he saw: and, behold, the mountain was full of horses and chariots of fire round about Elisha [2 Kings 6:17].

The question now arises: Is this the stated policy of God in dealing with His own?

Well, I have discovered that a great many Christians today have become great escape artists. They are sort of spiritual Houdinis. They can tell you about miraculous instances of God delivering them and leading them. But many other saints have to bow their heads in shame and say, "I've had no such experience, and I have had no such leading from God. It must mean that either I am out of touch with Him, or He is not for me at all." My friend, let's go back to Dothan. The answer, I believe, is here. Dothan is mentioned only two times in the Bible, and I think for a definite reason.

Another man approaches Dothan, a young man. In fact, he is a boy seventeen years of age, and danger and destiny await him there. Actually he is walking like a helpless and unsuspecting animal into a trap, and I feel like warning him, "Don't go to Dothan!" But that foolish "Houdini" Christian I referred to is apt to say," You don't need to worry, preacher. No harm is going to come to him. He's not going to be hurt at Dothan. He will be home next week because God will deliver him. After all, there are chariots of fire around Dothan, and he will be delivered." But is he? Joseph's brothers conspire against him. They want to murder him and, after they cool off just a little, the wiser of the brothers recommends that he be sold into slavery. My friend, that was worse than death in that day. It was a living hell to be sold into slavery, yet that is what is happening to this boy, seventeen years of age—and he happens to be God's man! Where are the chariots of fire? Just because you cannot see the chariots of fire does not mean they are not there. They are there. I see more evidences of the hand of God in the life of Joseph than I see in the life of Elisha who performed miracles, yet God never appeared to Joseph, never performed a miracle for him. But I see that God used this seeming disaster, and Joseph recognized it later on at the end of his life. He could say to his brothers, ". . . ye thought evil against me; but God meant it unto good . ." (Gen. 50:20). And at Dothan the chariots of fire are there, but they are going to be used in a different way.

SYRIAN SOLDIERS ARE BLINDED

And when they came down to him, Elisha prayed unto the LORD and said, Smite this people, I pray thee, with blindness. And he smote them with blindness according to the word of Elisha [2 Kings 6:18].

Elisha did a very unusual thing. He asked God to smite the hosts of the Syrians with blindness, and God did just that. Then Elisha led them all the way into Samaria and told them that he was leading them where Elisha was! When they got to Samaria, he turned them over to the king of Samaria. The king wanted to slay them, but Elisha said, "Don't do that. Feed them and send them home."

And he prepared great provision for them: and when they had eaten and drunk, he sent them away, and they went to their master. So the bands of Syria came no more into the land of Israel [2 Kings 6:23].

Both the power and graciousness of Israel's God, as represented by Elisha, must have really shaken the Syrian king. He abandoned his war against Israel. However, at a later date Ben-hadad (this, by the way, is a title rather than a proper name) again besieged Samaria, as we shall see in the next episode.

BEN-HADAD BESIEGES SAMARIA

And it came to pass after this, that Ben-hadad king of Syria gathered all his host, and went up, and besieged Samaria.

And there was a great famine in Samaria: and, behold, they besieged it, until an ass's head was sold for fourscore pieces of silver, and the fourth part of a cab of dove's dung for five pieces of silver [2 Kings 6:24–25].

The famine was so severe that a donkey's head (imagine how little meat there would be on that, and it could only be boiled, I guess, and made into soup or stew!) was sold for a ridiculous price. They were really having inflation!

The next few verses reveal the horrible fact that they were actually eating their children because of the desperate shortage of food.

Then he said, God do so and more also to me, if the head of Elisha the son of Shaphat shall stand on him this day [2 Kings 6:31].

We don't know why the king considered Elisha as responsible for the horrors of the siege. Probably he thought it was in Elisha's power to provide food in a miraculous way and was going to execute him because he did not.

The episode is continued without a break in the next chapter. This is another thrilling incident in the life of this man Elisha.

CHAPTER 7

THEME: *Elisha's promise of plenty is fulfilled*

Chapter 7 continues the narrative of chapter 6. Holding Elisha responsible for the siege, the king of Israel sends an executioner to slay him. However, God forewarns Elisha and gives him the good news that the famine will end on the following day.

Then Elisha said, Hear ye the word of the LORD; Thus saith the LORD, Tomorrow about this time shall a measure of fine flour be sold for a shekel, and two measures of barley for a shekel, in the gate of Samaria [2 Kings 7:1].

A measure of fine flour actually means about four pecks, which would be about a bushel. One shekel would probably be worth about sixty-five cents. That means the inflation would be over. They would be having a real discount sale on flour. How could such a thing come to pass? How could food be brought into the city when the Syrian host was camped outside the walls allowing no one in or out? Apparently the king believed Elisha's audacious prophecy because he spared his life at this time. However, his right-hand man scoffed at the idea.

Then a lord on whose hand the king leaned answered the man of God, and said, Behold, if the LORD would make windows in heaven, might this thing be? And he said, Behold, thou shalt see it with thine eyes, but shalt not eat thereof [2 Kings 7:2].

This prediction was literally fulfilled the next day.

Now the scene shifts to a pathetic group of hopeless men outside the city gates.

And there were four leprous men at the entering in of the gate: and they said one to another, Why sit we here until we die?

If we say, We will enter into the city, then the famine is in the city, and we shall die there: and if we sit still here, we die also. Now therefore come, and let us fall unto the host of the Syrians: if they save us alive, we shall live; and if they kill us, we shall but die.

And they rose up in the twilight, to go unto the camp of the Syrians: and when they were come to the uttermost part of the camp of Syria, behold, there was no man there [2 Kings 7:3–5].

Because they were lepers, they were excluded from society and were dependent upon relatives or friends bringing them food. Now that everyone inside the city was starving, of course, there was no surplus for them.

As we have said, leprosy is a type of sin. The application for us is that before we came to Christ we were in a predicament equally as desperate. We were like the lepers, sitting among the dead, having no hope and without God in the world.

The lepers, realizing they had nothing to lose, decided to throw themselves upon the mercy of the enemy. When they reached the camp of the Syrians, they found it deserted. What had happened to that great host—probably a hundred thousand or more?

For the LORD had made the host of the Syrians to hear a noise of chariots, and a noise of horses, even the noise of a great host: and they said one to another, Lo, the king of Israel hath hired against us the kings of the Hittites, and the kings of the Egyptians, to come upon us.

Wherefore they arose and fled in the twilight, and left their tents, and their horses, and their asses, even the camp as it was, and fled for their life [2 Kings 7:6–7].

The sound of an approaching army had put them in panic. The Syrians did not march in an orderly way. When they took off, it was every man for himself. They were traveling at night and they were traveling fast.

And when these lepers came to the uttermost part of the camp, they went into one tent, and did eat and drink, and carried thence silver, and gold, and raiment, and went and hid it; and came again, and entered into another tent, and carried thence also, and went and hid it [2 Kings 7:8].

In that day, the army carried with it all the food they would need. This was a long campaign—they were besieging Samaria,the city there on the hill. In their scramble to get away, they had left everything, all the supplies they had. After the Syrian army had fled, the lepers went into the camp and gorged themselves on gourmet food for as long as they could eat. Then they found and hid more gold and silver than they would ever need.

Then they said one to another, We do not well: this day is a day of good tidings, and we hold our peace: if we tarry till the morning light, some mischief will come upon us: now therefore come, that we may go and tell the king's household [2 Kings 7:9].

Now the excitement is over, and they begin to come to themselves. "Here we are gorging ourselves when the people in the city are starving. We've got to go tell them the good news!"

There is a great spiritual lesson for us here. At this moment you and I are enjoying the Word of God. Today is a day of good tidings, and we sit here and enjoy it. What about getting the Word out to others? What are you doing to share the Word of God with those who are starving spiritually? You ought to be busy getting the Word of God out to needy hearts. One man told me, "I can't speak, I can't teach, I can't sing, I can't do much of anything except make money." Believe me, God has given him a talent for making money. He simply cannot lose money. Everything he touches turns to gold. I believe his ability is a gift from God, and he certainly is using it to get the Word of God out. God expects each of us to use the talents He has given us to publish the good tidings which are the Word of God. We must not hold our peace in this desperate hour!

After the lepers told the king the good news, the children of Israel went into the abandoned Syrian camp and found enough food to feed an army of several thousand. There was an abundance of food. The super markets in Samaria had a big sale; you could buy food cheap. You did not have to buy animal heads for food anymore. You could buy filet mignon instead! The prophecy of Elisha was literally fulfilled.

CHAPTERS 8–10

***THEME:** Judgment of the wicked*

The people of Israel soon forgot God's marvelous deliverance and returned to their sin. So again they suffer the judgment of a famine.

ELISHA'S PREDICTION OF FAMINE

Then spake Elisha unto the woman, whose son he had restored to life, saying, Arise, and go thou and thine household, and sojourn wheresoever thou canst sojourn: for the LORD hath called for a famine; and it shall also come upon the land seven years.

And the woman arose, and did after the saying of the man of God: and she went with her household, and sojourned in the land of the Philistines seven years [2 Kings 8:1–2].

Elisha told the Shunammite woman to leave the land and go to another place because there was going to be a seven-year famine in the land. She believed and obeyed Elisha. She took her household into the land of the Philistines and lived there during the period of the famine. The famine, once again, was a judgment of God upon the northern kingdom.

Frankly I believe that the different tragedies that have struck our land in recent years have been a warning to our nation. The earthquakes, hurricanes, storms, and other tragedies that have swept across our land have, I think, been warnings from God to stop and think and change our ways.

THE SHUNAMMITE'S LAND RESTORED

And it came to pass at the seven years' end, that the woman returned out of the land of the Philistines: and she went forth to cry unto the king for her house and for her land.

And the king talked with Gehazi the servant of the man of God, saying, Tell me, I pray thee, all the great things that Elisha hath done.

And it came to pass, as he was telling the king how he had restored a dead body to life, that, behold, the woman, whose son he had restored to life, cried to the king for her house and for her land. And Gehazi said, My lord, O king, this is the woman, and this is her son, whom Elisha restored to life.

And when the king asked the woman, she told him. So the king appointed unto her a certain officer, saying, Restore all that was hers, and all the fruits of the field since the day that she left the land, even until now [2 Kings 8:3–6].

When the famine was over and the Shunammite woman returned to her former home, she apparently found others living on her land. At the same time, in God's providence, the king was inquiring about some of the lesser known acts of the prophet Elisha, and Gehazi was telling him about Elisha raising the Shunammite woman's son from the dead. The king made a ruling that her property was to be restored to her as well as all the fruit of the land.

ELISHA PREDICTS HAZAEL'S TREASON

Here is another incident in the life of Elisha that is quite remarkable. You will recall that the king of Syria had attempted to capture Elisha and slay him. But now the king is an old man, and he is sick.

And Elisha came to Damascus; and Ben-hadad the king of Syria was sick; and it was told him, saying, The man of God is come hither [2 Kings 8:7].

The king thought that Elisha would restore him to health. In view of the fact that his own life might hang in the hands of Elisha, of course the king would not touch one hair of his head.

And the king said unto Hazael, Take a present in thine hand, and go, meet the man of God, and inquire of the LORD by him, saying, Shall I recover of this disease? [2 Kings 8:8].

Hazael went to meet Elisha. He is the captain of Ben-hadad's hosts. There is a reference to him in 1 Kings 19:15 which says, "And the LORD said unto him [Elijah], Go, return on thy way to the wilderness of Damascus: and when thou comest, anoint Hazael to be king over Syria." So Hazael had been anointed king many years earlier; he is just waiting around for old Ben-hadad to die. You can well understand that it would be very difficult for the king's successor—whether it be a son, a general, or someone else—to shed very many tears at his funeral because it was his funeral that would bring his successor to power. So Hazael went out to meet Elisha, but I don't think he went with a great deal of enthusiasm. He took an impressive gift to Elisha, which was from the king.

So Hazael went to meet him, and took a present with him, even of every good thing of Damascus, forty camels' burden, and came and stood before him, and said, Thy son Ben-hadad king of Syria hath sent me to thee, saying, Shall I recover of this disease?

And Elisha said unto him, Go, say unto him, Thou mayest certainly recover: howbeit the LORD hath shewed me that he shall surely die [2 Kings 8:9–10].

Notice the message that Elisha gave: "You will surely live, but you won't live." That sounds like double-talk. Can't you just see Hazael when he hears that the king is going to die? A smirk comes over his face, and then a smile because he is going to be king.

And he settled his countenance stedfastly, until he was ashamed: and the man of God wept [2 Kings 8:11].

Elisha's knowing eyes bored into him until Hazael felt embarrassed. Then Elisha began to weep.

And Hazael said, Why weepeth my lord? And he answered, Because I know the evil that thou wilt do unto the children of Israel: their strong holds wilt thou set on fire, and their young men wilt thou slay with the sword, and wilt dash their children, and rip up their women with child [2 Kings 8:12].

Hazael is amazed, "Why weepeth my lord? Why are you weeping about this man who sought your life?" Elisha was not weeping for the king. Elisha loved his people. He loved his God. He loved the service God had given to him—he was a prophet. The heartbreak because of Ben-hadad had been bad enough, but Hazael is going to bring even more heartbreak to the people. Although Elijah had anointed Hazael king, and Hazael professes that he isn't going to do evil, Elisha knows better.

And Hazael said, But what, is thy servant a dog, that he should do this great thing? And Elisha answered, The LORD hath shewed me that thou shalt be king over Syria [2 Kings 8:13].

I don't know whether or not he was a dog, but he *did* it.

So he departed from Elisha, and came to his master; who said to him, What said Elisha to thee? And he answered, He told me that thou shouldest surely recover.

And it came to pass on the morrow, that he took a thick cloth, and dipped it in water, and spread it on his face, so that he died: and Hazael reigned in his stead [2 Kings 8:14–15].

This is what Elisha foresaw. In substance he had said, "Of course the king will be glad to hear he is going to recover, and that's what you are going to tell him, but you won't let him recover.

The rest of this chapter will be less confusing if you follow along carefully the Chronological Table of the Kings on page 331.

And in the fifth year of Joram the son of Ahab king of Israel, Jehoshaphat being then king of Judah, Jehoram the son of Jehoshaphat king of Judah began to reign.

Thirty and two years old was he when he began to reign; and he reigned eight years in Jerusalem.

And he walked in the way of the kings of Israel, as did the house of Ahab: for the daughter of Ahab was his wife: and he did evil in the sight of the LORD [2 Kings 8:16–18].

Now you can see *why* God doesn't go for mixed marriages. Although Jehoram was the son of the God-fearing king Jehoshaphat, he married the daughter of Ahab and Jezebel, and under her evil influence, "he walked in the ways of the kings of Israel."

Now we begin to see that Israel is going downhill as a great nation. Both Edom and Libnah revolted against them. Then Jehoram died, and Ahaziah became the new king of Judah. He joined forces with Joram, king of Israel, to war against the Syrians. Joram was wounded and went back to Jezreel to be healed from the wounds which he suffered at the hands of the Syrians.

And king Joram went back to be healed in Jezreel of the wounds which the Syrians had given him at Ramah, when he fought against Hazael king of Syria. And Ahaziah the son of Jehoram king of Judah went down to see Joram the son of Ahab in Jezreel, because he was sick [2 Kings 8:29].

In the next chapter we shall see what happened to him while he was in Jezreel recovering from his wounds.

JEHU IS ANOINTED KING OVER ISRAEL

As we begin this chapter, we need to keep in mind that Ahaziah, the king of Judah, went up to visit Joram at Jezreel because Joram was wounded in battle and was in Jezreel recovering. Apparently he was a very sick man.

And Elisha the prophet called one of the children of the prophets, and said unto him, Gird up thy loins, and take this box of oil in thine hand, and go to Ramoth-gilead:

And when thou comest thither, look out there Jehu the son of Jehoshaphat the son of Nimshi, and go in, and make him arise up from among his brethren, and carry him to an inner chamber;

Then take the box of oil, and pour it on his head, and say, Thus saith the LORD, I have anointed thee king over Israel. Then open the door, and flee, and tarry not.

So the young man, even the young man the prophet, went to Ramoth-gilead [2 Kings 9:1–4].

The young prophet did the thing Elisha commanded him to do. You will notice that Elisha is not spectacular in what he does. You would think he would not have sent a young prophet to anoint a king but that Elisha would have done it himself. Samuel, you remember, had anointed Saul as king, and he also came to David and anointed him king. You would naturally think that Elisha would want to be the one to anoint the king, but he did not. He sent a young prophet to anoint Jehu king, and he did it secretly and privately. This is probably the reason he sent a young man to do it—no one would suspect the motives of a young prophet.

So Jehu was anointed king. He was one of the bloodiest rascals you will meet on the pages of Scripture, and yet he did the will of God in many respects. God said that He would cut off from Ahab every male member and none would be left in Israel.

And I will make the house of Ahab like the house of Jeroboam the son of Nebat, and like the house of Baasha the son of Ahijah:

And the dogs shall eat Jezebel in the portion of Jezreel, and there shall be none to bury her. And he opened the door, and fled [2 Kings 9:9–10].

Jezebel will not escape God's judgment for her wickedness.

Then Jehu came forth to the servants of his lord: and one said unto him, Is all well? wherefore came this mad fellow to thee? And he said unto them, Ye know the man, and his communication.

And they said, It is false; tell us now. And he said, Thus and thus spake he to me, saying, Thus saith the LORD, I have anointed thee king over Israel.

Then they hasted, and took every man his garment, and put it under him on the top of the stairs, and blew with trumpets, saying, Jehu is king [2 Kings 9:11–13].

When it was known that Jehu had been anointed king, it put everyone in a flurry, and they began to move. They blew the trumpets and said, "Jehu is king." Joram is sick in Jezreel and Ahaziah is there visiting him. What is going to happen in Jezreel now?

JEHU EXECUTES JORAM

Now Joram down there in Jezreel doesn't know that God has removed him from his throne and has anointed Jehu king over Israel. As Joram and Ahaziah, king of Judah, are there visiting, the watchman reports that a company of horsemen is coming. Joram sends a messenger to meet them with the question: "Is it peace"—are you bringing good news or bad? Instead of answering his question, Jehu tells him to fall in line behind him. Now the second watchman reports to Joram.

And the watchman told, saying, He came even unto them, and cometh not again: and the driving is like the driving of Jehu the son of Nimshi; for he driveth furiously [2 Kings 9:20].

The messengers who were sent out to meet Jehu never came back to report to the king because Jehu is coming to exterminate this king. So Joram and Ahaziah themselves ride out to meet Jehu.

And it came to pass, when Joram saw Jehu, that he said, Is it peace, Jehu? And he answered, What peace, so long as the whoredoms of thy mother Jezebel and her witchcrafts are so many? [2 Kings 9:22].

Obviously no loyal subject would dare make such a statement about the queen mother. Joram instantly recognizes that Jehu is leading a revolt.

And Joram turned his hands, and fled, and said to Ahaziah, There is treachery, O Ahaziah.

And Jehu drew a bow with his full strength, and smote Jehoram between his arms, and the arrow went out at his heart, and he sunk down in his chariot [2 Kings 9:23–24].

As Joram was trying to escape, Jehu drew his bow and put an arrow through his heart. Notice that Joram is called Jehoram in this instance. Both names have the same meaning in Hebrew and are used interchangeably for both the king of Israel and the king of Judah.

JEHU EXECUTES AHAZIAH

Jehu had come to Jezreel to exterminate Joram. Ahaziah, as we have already seen, was visiting Joram. He was keeping bad company, by the way, with those of the house of Ahab. Ahaziah was in the wrong place at the wrong time!

But when Ahaziah the king of Judah saw this, he fled by the way of the garden house. And Jehu followed after him, and said, Smite him also in the chariot. And they did so at the going up to Gur, which is by Ibleam. And he fled to Megiddo, and died there [2 Kings 9:27].

Jehu's followers pursued and mortally wounded Ahaziah.

And his servants carried him in a chariot to Jerusalem, and buried him in his sepulchre with his fathers in the city of David [2 Kings 9:28].

JEHU EXECUTES JEZEBEL

And when Jehu was come to Jezreel, Jezebel heard of it; and she painted her

face, and tired her head, and looked out at a window [2 Kings 9:30].

Now we come to the slaying of Jezebel, the queen mother, which was indeed a frightful thing. She was a bloody, mean, terrible woman. She was a member of a royal family, the beautiful daughter of Ethbaal, king of Zidon. Probably she had been one of the most beautiful women of her day and of all history. As a young woman I think Jezebel could compare with Helen of Troy, Salome, Cleopatra, and Catherine de' Medici. When Ahab and Jezebel married, it was the society event of the year. The best people of the two kingdoms were there. There was a surplus of royalty gathered. It was respectful and dignified—even Elijah could not find fault with the event. The common people of both realms celebrated. It should also be added that the demons of hell joined the festivities. They laughed with glee, and the devil was glad. However, crepe was on the gate of heaven and the angels wept. Instead of wedding bells, it was a funeral dirge. That was heaven's view of this marriage. The world saw things differently, as it always does. Why is the world optimistic and heaven pessimistic? God looks on the heart. Man has only a limited view of things.

Jezebel is one of the most remarkable women in history. She was capable, she was influential, and she had a dominant personality. Her evil influence was felt in three kingdoms and extended beyond her lifetime. Her notorious life became a proverb. She poured a stream of poison into history. Scripture never mentions her again until you come to the Book of Revelation at the conclusion of the Bible.

Her name is suggestive. It means "unmarried, chaste." You have here a veiled suggestion of an abnormality and a perversion. She was probably cold and sexless, yet she was beautiful and alluring. Strong men yielded to her seductive charms. No one resisted her, not even Ahab. She dominated him and ruled the northern kingdom.

She introduced the worship of Baal. She imported 450 prophets of Baal and 400 prophets of Astarte. She was reckless, violent, rapacious, and ferocious. She killed God's prophets. God's people went underground. She engineered the marriage of her daughter to the house of David. During her long reign as the consort of Ahab, her will was supreme; no person dared to oppose her—except Elijah. She is the Lady Macbeth of Shakespeare and the Clytemnestra of Greek tragedy. Her crimes were many. Blood flowed freely from her influence. None resisted her. For a time it seemed as if God was in hiding and doing nothing.

Finally Jezebel commited her crowning crime. She arranged the death of Naboth so that Ahab might possess his vineyard. Her deed was high-handed, cold-blooded murder. It was a dastardly deed, and heaven could no longer remain silent. God's patience was exhausted, and He sent Elijah to announce His judgment. The day of reckoning came. First Ahab was killed, and the dogs licked up his blood just as the prophet had said they would. Now it is Jezebel's turn. She will be trodden underfoot, and the dogs will eat her to the point that there will not even be enough left for a decent burial. Fourteen years had elapsed since the death of Ahab and undoubtedly Jezebel did not believe that God's word would ever be fulfilled in her case. She was unmoved. She defied God. She stayed on in Jezreel, thinking perhaps that the death of Ahab was just a coincidence. She felt that she could get by and nothing would happen to her. But, you know, there is a law of God written in neon lights in every sphere on the crossroads of life: "Be not deceived; God is not mocked: for whatsoever a man soweth, that shall he also reap" (Gal. 6:7). ". . . For with the same measure that ye mete withal it shall be measured to you again" (Luke 6:38).

This is one of the most sordid and sadistic chapters in history. It is gruesome, it is ghastly, and it is a gory sight. Added to that, it is grizzly. It is one of the most revolting and repulsive scenes on the pages of Scripture. Jezebel is the queen mother. She has been living in luxury in the palace at Jezreel. The terrible prophecy of that horrible man Elijah has not been fulfilled. Suddenly out of the north came a swift chariot. It was Jehu driving furiously. He had just slain two kings, the king of Judah and the king of Israel—her own son, Joram. What does she do? She paints her eyes and arranges her hair, and looks out of a window. This proud queen still thinks she can seduce her captor—captivate him with her charms. She had a grandson twenty-three years old. She is no longer young; she is an old woman. No secret formulas for lotions, powders, sprays, and creams can make this faded queen look attractive. As she looks from an upstairs window at Jehu, she begins with flattery.

And as Jehu entered in at the gate, she said, Had Zimri peace, who slew his master? [2 Kings 9:31].

Her inference is, "Can't we get together and talk this over? Come up and see me sometime."

And he lifted up his face to the window, and said, Who is on my side? who? And there looked out to him two or three eunuchs.

And he said, Throw her down. So they threw her down: and some of her blood was sprinkled on the wall, and on the horses: and he trode her under foot [2 Kings 9:32–33].

Jehu is unmoved and untouched by Jezebel's words. He is without pity or mercy. Jezebel did not awe Jehu. She had no appeal for him. He did not even respect her. He said, "Throw her down!" And the eunuchs threw her down and she broke open like a ripe watermelon. This is the most frightful, terrible, and vivid picture in all of the annals of tragedy. Hammond says that history presents no parallel to such an indignity. It is truly unprecedented. A queen mother was customarily treated with respect.

And when he was come in, he did eat and drink, and said, Go, see now this cursed woman, and bury her: for she is a king's daughter [2 Kings 9:34].

How could Jehu enjoy a hearty meal after he had done this awful thing? As someone has said, he was "a fiend in human form." He was a rough soldier with no courtesy and certainly no chivalry. All he had was crude ambition. He did not shrink from any crime. He was depraved and degraded.

And they went to bury her: but they found no more of her than the skull, and the feet, and the palms of her hands.

Wherefore they came again, and told him. And he said, This is the word of the LORD, which he spake by his servant Elijah the Tishbite, saying, In the portion of Jezreel shall dogs eat the flesh of Jezebel:

And the carcase of Jezebel shall be as dung upon the face of the field in the portion of Jezreel; so that they shall not say, This is Jezebel [2 Kings 9: 35–37].

When Jehu sent servants out to bury Jezebel, the dogs had already devoured her. The dogs had a big gourmet meal. But, my friend, there was no laughter in heaven because of this. There was no mourning, either. Perhaps in heaven it was being said—as the Book of Revelation tells us that it will be said in the future—"For true and righteous are his judgments: for he hath judged the great whore, which did corrupt the earth with her fornication, and hath avenged the blood of his servants at her hand" (Rev. 19:2). The horrible death of Jezebel illustrates again the truth of Galatians 6:7: "Be not deceived; God is not mocked: for whatsoever a man soweth, that shall he also reap."

Chapter 10 continues the judgment on the house of Ahab through the murderous heart of Jehu.

AHAB'S HOUSE IS JUDGED

And Ahab had seventy sons in Samaria. And Jehu wrote letters, and sent to Samaria, unto the rulers of Jezreel, to the elders, and to them that brought up Ahab's children, saying,

Now as soon as this letter cometh to you, seeing your master's sons are with you, and there are with you chariots and horses, a fenced city also, and armour;

Look even out the best and meetest of your master's sons, and set him on his father's throne, and fight for your master's house [2 Kings 10:1–3].

Jehu is giving the sons of Ahab the privilege of fighting for the throne of Israel. Not one of the seventy sons is willing to tackle Jehu.

Then the elders of Israel—to save their own necks—prove their allegiance to Jehu by slaying these seventy sons of Ahab.

So Jehu slew all that remained of the house of Ahab in Jezreel, and all his great men, and his kinsfolks, and his priests, until he left him none remaining [2 Kings 10:11].

JEHU MASSACRES THE ROYAL PRINCES OF JUDAH

And he arose and departed, and came to Samaria. And as he was at the shearing house in the way,

Jehu met with the brethren of Ahaziah king of Judah, and said, Who are ye? And they answered, We are the brethren of Ahaziah: and we go down to salute the children of the king and the children of the queen.

And he said, Take them alive. And they took them alive, and slew them at the pit of the shearing house, even two and forty men; neither left he any of them [2 Kings 10:12–14].

After dealing with the house of Ahab, Jehu was on his way to assume the throne in Samaria. He met forty-two sons (or nephews) of Ahaziah, the king of Judah. He slew them also. It is interesting to note, however, that one of them was spared, and he was a descendant of the house of Saul.

And when he was departed thence, he lighted on Jehonadab the son of Rechab coming to meet him: and he saluted him, and said to him, Is thine heart right, as my heart is with thy heart? And Jehonadab answered, It is. If it be, give me thine hand. And he gave him his hand; and he took him up to him into the chariot [2 Kings 10:15].

Jehu, still on his way to Samaria, met Jehonadab, the Rechabite. The question he put to him was, "Are you friend or foe?" Jehonadab was the founder of the very strict sect of Rechabites mentioned by Jeremiah. He was undoubtedly a man of influence. Apparently he heartily approved of Jehu's anti-Ahab policy and was willing to lend his support by being seen in Jehu's chariot.

JEHU EXTERMINATES BAAL'S WORSHIPERS

And Jehu gathered all the people together, and said unto them, Ahab served Baal a little; but Jehu shall serve him much.

Now therefore call unto me all the prophets of Baal, all his servants, and all his priests; let none be wanting: for I have a great sacrifice to do to Baal; whosoever shall be wanting, he shall not live. But Jehu did it in subtilty, to the intent that he might destroy the worshippers of Baal [2 Kings 10:18–19].

The next thing Jehu did was to bring together all of the prophets of Baal by issuing a false statement that he would offer a great sacrifice to Baal. Jehu had no intention of worshiping Baal. When all the prophets came together, he slew them. His sacrifice to Baal was a trap and the prophets fell right into it.

JEHU FOLLOWS THE SINS OF JEROBOAM

While it is true that Jehu slew the prophets of Baal, he did not turn to the prophets of God.

Howbeit from the sins of Jeroboam the son of Nebat, who made Israel to sin, Jehu departed not from after them, to wit, the golden calves that were in Beth-el, and that were in Dan [2 Kings 10:29].

Jehu went back to the calf worship that Jeroboam had established. He did not worship Baal, nor the gods of the Zidonians, but he engaged in the calf worship that apparently came out of the land of Egypt.

Jehu did not turn to the Lord, but because he was zealous for the Lord, God gave him an earthly reward—that is, He extended the reign of his house for four generations.

And the LORD said unto Jehu, Because thou hast done well in executing that which is right in mine eyes, and hast done unto the house of Ahab according to all that was in mine heart, thy children of the fourth generation shall sit on the throne of Israel [2 Kings 10:30].

Although Jehu was a very brutal man, God makes the wrath of man to praise Him!

ISRAEL IS SMITTEN BY HAZAEL OF SYRIA

In those days the LORD began to cut Israel short: and Hazael smote them in all the coasts of Israel [2 Kings 10:32].

What is happening here? The northern kingdom is getting ready to go into captivity. From now on there will be decline which will ultimately end in disaster. They will be carried away into captivity by Assyria.

The chapter concludes with the death of Jehu who had been king of Israel for twenty-eight years.

CHAPTERS 11–12

THEME: *Joash, the boy king*

The story of Ahab and Jezebel is not a pretty section, and you probably thought we were through with them, but we are not. While it is true that Jehu had eliminated all the line of Ahab in the northern kingdom of Israel, a daughter of Ahab and Jezebel had married into the southern kingdom of Judah and was at this time the queen mother. Believe me, she took after mama and papa and was the meanest of them all. Her name is Athaliah, and she is going to perform an unbelievably terrible act.

ATHALIAH MURDERS HER GRANDCHILDREN

And when Athaliah the mother of Ahaziah saw that her son was dead, she arose and destroyed all the seed royal [2 Kings 11:1].

As long as Ahaziah had lived Athaliah actually had been the queen because she controlled her son. She was very much like Jezebel. Now that Ahaziah was dead, a grandson would come to the throne and Athaliah did not want that. She was afraid that she would not be able to control him, and she would lose her position. So what did she do? She slew all the line of David that she could get her hands on. Talk about a bloodthirsty act! She tried to exterminate the line of David. This was another attempt of Satan to destroy the line that is leading to the Lord Jesus Christ. Satan attempted to wipe out the line of David so that the Savior would not be born. Down through the ages the devil has tried to eliminate the Jews. In Egypt the Lord preserved Moses, and the Jews were not slain but allowed to leave Egypt. Haman, in the Book of Esther, attempted to exterminate the Jews but was foiled. Satan was behind each of these attempts. Now here is this woman Athaliah attempting to exterminate the line of David.

Although she thought she had killed all of them, she missed one, as we are told here.

But Jehosheba, the daughter of king Joram, sister of Ahaziah, took Joash the son of Ahaziah, and stole him from among the king's sons which were slain; and they hid him, even him and his nurse, in the bedchamber from Athaliah, so that he was not slain.

And he was with her hid in the house of the LORD six years. And Athaliah did reign over the land [2 Kings 11:2–3].

She came to the throne after her son was killed and for years she was ruling alone—that was the way she wanted it. But all the while this little boy Joash was growing up.

JOASH COMES TO THE THRONE OF JUDAH

And the seventh year Jehoiada sent and fetched the rulers over hundreds, with the captains and the guard, and brought them to him into the house of the LORD, and made a covenant with them, and took an oath of them in the house of the LORD, and shewed them the king's son [2 Kings 11:4].

When Joash (sometimes called Jehoash) was about seven years old, Jehoiada sent for the rulers, the captains, and the guard. He revealed to them that the king had a son. When they discovered that there was a son in the line of David it brought encouragement, joy, and hope to their hearts. They had had enough of this woman Athaliah anyway, and they jumped at the chance to dethrone her.

And he commanded them, saying, This is the thing that ye shall do; A third part of you that enter in on the sabbath shall even be keepers of the watch of the king's house;

And a third part shall be at the gate of Sur; and a third part at the gate behind the guard: so shall ye keep the watch of the house, that it be not broken down.

And two parts of all you that go forth on the sabbath, even they shall keep the watch of the house of the LORD about the king [2 Kings 11:5–7].

They were to "compass the king round about, every man with his weapons in his hand." Extra precautions were taken to preserve the life of this little fellow because his life would not have been worth a plugged nickel if Athaliah had been able to get to him. She would have slain him without a qualm although he was her grandson! This woman was as heartless as Jezebel. So the young boy was well protected until the time he could be brought before the people.

And the guard stood, every man with his weapons in his hand, round about the king, from the right corner of the temple to the left corner of the temple, along by the altar and the temple.

And he brought forth the king's son, and put the crown upon him, and gave him the testimony; and they made him king, and anointed him; and they clapped their hands, and said, God save the king [2 Kings 11:11–12].

This was a great day for the southern kingdom to crown a king in the line of David. Things had looked very discouraging there for a time.

ATHALIAH IS SLAIN

And when Athaliah heard the noise of the guard and of the people, she came to the people into the temple of the LORD [2 Kings 11:13].

Of course Athaliah had not been invited to the coronation of the king. She evidently was in the palace of David on Mount Zion, which was situated right above the temple area. When she heard the clamor and noise in the temple area, she went there to see what was going on.

And when she looked, behold, the king stood by a pillar, as the manner was, and the princes and the trumpeters by the king, and all the people of the land rejoiced, and blew with trumpets: and Athaliah rent her clothes, and cried, Treason, Treason [2 Kings 11:14].

This, of course, was Athaliah's idea of treason.

But Jehoiada the priest commanded the captains of the hundreds, the officers of the host, and said unto them, Have her forth without the ranges: and him that followeth her kill with the sword. For the priest had said, Let her not be slain in the house of the LORD

And they laid hands on her; and she went by the way by the which the horses came into the king's house: and there was she slain [2 Kings 11:15–16].

Athaliah tried to flee. There was no way in the world for her to have her trial transferred to another district where she could be expected to receive a fair trial. They just executed her as she fled and saved an appeal to the supreme court. They got rid of her, which was, in my opinion, the proper thing to do at that time.

REVIVAL

The removal of Athaliah took a dark cloud off the southern kingdom. There was a new king, but naturally this little boy had to have counselors to rule in his stead because he was so young. One of them was Jehoiada who had engineered bringing Joash to the throne and executing Athaliah.

And Jehoiada made a covenant between the LORD and the king and the people, that they should be the LORD's people; between the king also and the people [2 Kings 11:17].

This is the beginning of a return to God. Jehoiada the priest now leads in a movement to return to the worship of Jehovah. The worship of Baal was prevalent; it had penetrated even into Judah. Probably the people were still going to the temple of the Lord, but they were worshiping Baal at the same time.

The same thing is going on today. Many people are religious on Sunday and then live for the devil the rest of the week. There are many church members doing that today, and they wonder why the church is dead! The explanation is not found in a building; it is found in people. That is where the deadness lies at the present time.

And all the people of the land went into the house of Baal, and brake it down; his altars and his images brake they in pieces thoroughly, and slew Mattan the priest of Baal before the altars. And the priest appointed officers over the house of the LORD [2 Kings 11:18].

This is the beginning of a great spiritual movement that is nothing short of a revival.

And he took the rulers over hundreds, and the captains, and the guard, and all the people of the land; and they brought down the king from the house of the LORD, and came by the way of the gate of the guard to the king's house. And he sat on the throne of the kings.

And all the people of the land rejoiced, and the city was in quiet: and they slew Athaliah with the sword beside the king's house.

Seven years old was Jehoash when he began to reign [2 Kings 11:19–21].

What a day of rejoicing this was to have a descendant of David back on the throne and the wicked foreign usurper and her temple of Baal gone from the land!

THE REIGN OF JEHOASH (JOASH)

In the twelfth chapter we have the reign of Jehoash, and we will see that it is Jehoiada the high priest who is engineering it. This is the beginning of a great spiritual movement that I would call revival.

At this juncture I would like to have a roll call of kings. There was a total of nineteen kings who reigned over the northern kingdom of Israel. There was a total of twenty kings who reigned over the southern kingdom of Judah. Among the nineteen kings who ruled over Israel, not one of them could be labeled a righteous king. Actually the only thing you could say about them was that every one of them was a *bad* king—there was not a good one in the lot. In the southern kingdom of Judah there were twenty kings, and only ten of them could be considered good. Five of the kings were exceptional, and during their reigns there were five periods of reformation and revival. All of the reformation and blessing was incubated in the nest of spiritual revival. These brief periods of respite kept the fires burning on the altars that were all but extinguished at other times. Five times revival flared up and swept through the nation—not a fire of destruction but of construction and instruction. God visited His people with the heaven-sent times of refreshing. There was a turning to the Word of God and a return to the worship of God. There was power and prosperity.

When a revival comes, my friend, there will be new joy in the church. There will be renewed power in the church. There will be a new love. First, however, there must be a return to the Bible. A return to the Word of God has brought about every great spiritual revival. I personally believe that we can have a true revival today. Years ago Dr. Griffith Thomas said, "I cannot see anywhere in Scripture that revival of the true church is contrary to the will of God." Dr. R. A. Torrey also said, "There is no such teaching in Scripture that revival is contrary to the will of God." Dr. James M. Gray said, "We recall nothing in the epistles justifying the conclusion that the experiences of the early church may not be repeated today." My friend, let's do our part in getting out the Word of God so that God will be able to do a real work of grace in our time.

In chapter 12 we see Joash (also called Jehoash) as an adult.

In the seventh year of Jehu Jehoash began to reign; and forty years reigned he in Jerusalem. And his mother's name was Zibiah of Beer-sheba [2 Kings 12:1].

Joash (or Jehoash) began his reign as a child of seven and continued until he was forty-seven years old. His mother was Zibiah of Beersheba. Remember how the mother's names are often given because mothers have a tremendous influence on their sons.

And Jehoash did that which was right in the sight of the LORD all his days wherein Jehoiada the priest instructed him [2 Kings 12:2].

Joash was taught in the Word of God. My friend, what we need today are not empty-headed politicians who are everlastingly coming up with nostrums and criticizing all other parties and politicians, thinking only *they* have the answer. May I say to you, we need men today who are instructed in the Word of God and who *know* God today. We need a spiritual renewing in this land, and it can only come through the Word of God.

But the high places were not taken away: the people still sacrificed and burnt incense in the high places [2 Kings 12:3].

"Revival" did not mean that everyone had turned to God. Many were still sacrificing and offering incense in the high places. Even among the priests there were those who were not revived.

And Jehoash said to the priests, All the money of the dedicated things that is brought into the house of the LORD, even the money of every one that passeth the account, the money that every man is set at, and all the money that cometh into any man's heart to bring into the house of the LORD,

Let the priests take it to them, every man of his acquaintance: and let them repair the breaches of the house, wheresoever any breach shall be found [2 Kings 12:4–5].

The temple was in disrepair. It needed to be repaired. The priests took the money that was supposed to be used to repair the breaches of the temple and used it for other things.

But it was so, that in the three and twentieth year of king Jehoash the priests had not repaired the breaches of the house.

Then king Jehoash called for Jehoiada the priest, and the other priests, and said unto them, Why repair ye not the breaches of the house? now therefore receive no more money of your acquaintance, but deliver it for the breaches of the house.

And the priests consented to receive no more money of the people, neither to repair the breaches of the house [2 Kings 12:6–8].

It is the same old story today. I think, very candidly, that you can test Christians and churches by their use or abuse of money. Many people in churches say, "Let's make So-and-So the treasurer or put him on the board of deacons because he is a good business man." May I say to you that you had better find out whether or not he is a spiritual man. That is the important thing.

What did they do? They had to prepare a locked box so that the money would be safe and the priests could not get their hands on it.

But Jehoiada the priest took a chest, and bored a hole in the lid of it, and set it beside the altar, on the right side as one cometh into the house of the LORD: and the priests that kept the door put therein all the money that was brought into the house of the LORD [2 Kings 12:9].

I think this box was a good idea. Anyone can juggle figures, and I have seen officers who handle the money do just that—it is an absolute disgrace. "Joash's chest" is used today by many organizations to raise money. I wonder sometimes if people who use it recognize its background. The chest was secured so that some deacons and preachers and other religious racketeers could not get their hands on the offerings. This was a good idea that you might want to use sometime.

TEMPLE TREASURES BUY OFF HAZAEL

Although there had been a great spiritual movement in the land, the nation was beginning to go downhill.

Then Hazael king of Syria went up, and fought against Gath, and took it: and Hazael set his face to go up to Jerusalem.

And Jehoash king of Judah took all the hallowed things that Jehoshaphat, and Jehoram, and Ahaziah, his fathers, kings of Judah, had dedicated, and his own hallowed things, and all the gold that was found in the treasures of the house of the LORD, and in the king's house, and sent it to Hazael king of Syria: and he went away from Jerusalem [2 Kings 12:17–18].

In other words, Joash was buying time. He was trying to buy off Hazael, king of Syria.

And the rest of the acts of Joash, and all that he did, are they not written in the book of the chronicles of the kings of Judah?

And his servants arose, and made a conspiracy, and slew Joash in the house of Millo, which goeth down to Silla [2 Kings 12:19–20].

We will talk more about revival when we get to the two Books of Chronicles. Joash was just forty-seven years old when he died. His servants killed him, and he was buried with his fathers in the city of David. Joash had been a good king. We will find that his son Amaziah will also be a good king.

CHRONOLOGICAL TABLE OF THE KINGS OF THE DIVIDED KINGDOM

JUDAH

King	Reign		Character	Prophet
1. Rehoboam	931–913 B.C.	(17 yrs.)	Bad	Shemaiah
2. Abijah	913–911	(3 yrs.)	Bad	
3. Asa	911–870	(41 yrs.)	Good	
4. Jehoshaphat	870–848*	(25 yrs.)	Good	
5. Jehoram	848–841*	(8 yrs.)	Bad	
6. Ahaziah	841	(1 yr.)	Bad	
7. Athaliah	841–835	(6 yrs.)	Bad	
8. Joash	835–796	(40 yrs.)	Good	Joel
9. Amaziah	796–767	(29 yrs.)	Good	
10. Azariah (or Uzziah)	767–740*	(52 yrs.)	Good	Isaiah
11. Jotham	740–732*	(16 yrs.)	Good	Micah
12. Ahaz	732–716	(16 yrs.)	Bad	
13. Hezekiah	716–687	(29 yrs.)	Good	
14. Manasseh	687–642*	(55 yrs.)	Bad	Nahum
15. Amon	642–640	(2 yrs.)	Bad	Habakkuk
16. Josiah	640–608	(31 yrs.)	Good	Zephaniah
17. Jehoahaz	608	(3 mo.)	Bad	Jeremiah
18. Jehoiakim	608–597	(11 yrs.)	Bad	
19. Jehoiachin	597	(3 mo.)	Bad	
20. Zedekiah	597–586	(11 yrs.)	Bad	

(Destruction of Jerusalem and captivity of Judah)

*Co-regency

ISRAEL

King	Reign		Character	Prophet
1. Jeroboam I	931–910 B.C.	(22 yrs.)	Bad	Ahijah
2. Nadab	910–909	(2 yrs.)	Bad	
3. Baasha	909–886	(24 yrs.)	Bad	
4. Elah	886–885	(2 yrs.)	Bad	
5. Zimri	885	(7 days)	Bad	
6. Omri	885–874*	(12 yrs.)	Bad	Elijah
7. Ahab	874–853	(22 yrs.)	Bad	Micaiah
8. Ahaziah	853–852	(2 yrs.)	Bad	
9. Joram	852–841	(12 yrs.)	Bad	Elisha
10. Jehu	841–814	(28 yrs.)	Bad	
11. Jehoahaz	814–798	(17 yrs.)	Bad	
12. Jehoash	798–782	(16 yrs.)	Bad	Jonah
13. Jeroboam II	782–753*	(41 yrs.)	Bad	Amos, Hosea
14. Zechariah	753–752	(6 mo.)	Bad	
15. Shallum	752	(1 mo.)	Bad	
16. Menahem	752–742	(10 yrs.)	Bad	
17. Pekahiah	742–740	(2 yrs.)	Bad	
18. Pekah	740–732*	(20 yrs.)	Bad	
19. Hoshea	732–721	(9 yrs.)	Bad	

(Capture of Samaria and captivity of Israel)

*Co-regency

CHAPTER 13

THEME: *The final acts of Elisha*

Friend, this is a rugged portion of Scripture; yet it can minister to our hearts. This is an especially good section for the rulers of nations. We are following both kingdoms of Israel and Judah. In the north the ten tribes constitute the northern kingdom, and in the south the tribes of Judah and Benjamin constitute the southern kingdom. In the south the line of David is reigning. That is the line that will be followed right on into the New Testament to the birth of the Lord Jesus Christ. As we have seen, the line of David was almost eliminated by Athaliah, the daughter of Ahab and Jezebel, who married into the family of David.

JEHOAHAZ REIGNS OVER ISRAEL

In chapter 13 we find that Jehoahaz, the son of Jehu, reigned over Israel for seventeen years. He followed in the sinful steps of Jeroboam. Actually, there is nothing very sensational or interesting about his reign. Many people feel that sin brings excitement into life. There is nothing quite as boring as sin after a while. The man who starts drinking reaches the day when he is a drunkard; and, at that point, he is as boring as anyone can possibly be. And his life loses its purpose. The same thing is true of any individual who indulges in sin. This period of history is very boring. There is excitement only when God is moving. How we need Him today on the scene!

In the three and twentieth year of Joash the son of Ahaziah king of Judah Jehoahaz the son of Jehu began to reign over Israel in Samaria, and reigned seventeen years.

And he did that which was evil in the sight of the LORD, and followed the sins of Jeroboam the son of Nebat, which made Israel to sin; he departed not therefrom [2 Kings 13:1–2].

Jeroboam is the one who instituted calf-worship in Israel. He led Israel away from the worship of the true God and led them into sin. When Ahab and Jezebel came to the throne, they went way beyond that. They began an active worship of Baal, which actually was demonism. Now Jehoahaz, like his father Jehu, does not go into Baal worship, nor sink into the depths of sin like Ahab and Jezebel did. He does go as far as Jeroboam did, however, and that is bad enough.

REPENTANCE OF JEHOAHAZ

Because of Israel's sin, God allowed the king of Syria to come against Israel.

And the anger of the LORD was kindled against Israel, and he delivered them into the hand of Hazael king of Syria, and into the hand of Ben-hadad the son of Hazael, all their days.

And Jehoahaz besought the LORD, and the LORD hearkened unto him: for he saw the oppression of Israel, because the king of Syria oppressed them [2 Kings 13:3–4].

This man knew he was in danger and in trouble. So in fear he turns to the Lord.

(And the LORD gave Israel a saviour, so that they went out from under the hand of the Syrians: and the children of Israel dwelt in their tents, as beforetime [2 Kings 13:5].

Notice how gracious God is. The minute the king called upon Him, He heard and answered prayer! He delivered the people from Syria's oppression. My friend, you and I today do not realize how good God is and how good He is to you and me today. Oh, how wonderful He is!

Nevertheless they departed not from the sins of the house of Jeroboam, who made Israel sin, but walked therein: and there remained the grove also in Samaria.)

Neither did he leave of the people to Jehoahaz but fifty horsemen, and ten chariots, and ten thousand footmen; for the king of Syria had destroyed them, and had made them like the dust by threshing [2 Kings 13:6–7].

We see the goodness of the Lord in the life of Jehoahaz. The king called upon God and He answered. But the king and his people went on in sin, and they continued their idol worship. The king of Syria so destroyed the defense of Jehoahaz that he was never able to properly defend his kingdom again.

Now the rest of the acts of Jehoahaz, and all that he did, and his might, are they not written in the book of the chronicles of the kings of Israel?

And Jehoahaz slept with his fathers; and they buried him in Samaria: and Joash his son reigned in his stead [2 Kings 13:8–9].

Here we have the record of the death of Jehoahaz. This is the record of man: The king is dead, long live the king.

JEHOASH REIGNS OVER ISRAEL

Another king comes to the throne of the northern kingdom.

In the thirty and seventh year of Joash king of Judah began Jehoash the son of Jehoahaz to reign over Israel in Samaria, and reigned sixteen years [2 Kings 13:10].

Now we come to a very confusing period because the names of the kings in both kingdoms are similar, if not identical. It is difficult to know who is reigning, where he is reigning, and the circumstances of the reign. I am not so sure but what the Lord left it that way for a definite reason.

And he did that which was evil in the sight of the LORD; he departed not from all the sins of Jeroboam the son of Nebat, who made Israel sin: but he walked therein [2 Kings 13:11].

Jeroboam was the standard. When a king reached his level of sin, God always judged.

ELISHA'S DEATH: HIS PROPHECY IS FULFILLED

It was at this time that Elisha fell sick; it was the illness that brought death to him.

Now Elisha was fallen sick of his sickness whereof he died. And Joash the king of Israel came down unto him, and wept over his face, and said, O my father, my father, the chariot of Israel, and the horsemen thereof [2 Kings 13:14].

Elisha had been a tower of strength to the northern kingdom in a way that Elijah had not been. (When the news of Elijah's translation reached the palace, I imagine there was a celebration party!) However, Elisha had been a tremendous help to the king, and he was heartbroken when the prophet became ill.

And Elisha said unto him, Take bow and arrows. And he took unto him bow and arrows [2 Kings 13:15].

When the king visits him, Elisha does not just accept his sympathy and flowers. He is still a prophet of God, and he is giving God's message to him.

And he said to the king of Israel, Put thine hand upon the bow. And he put his hand upon it: and Elisha put his hands upon the king's hands.

And he said, Open the window eastward. And he opened it. Then Elisha said, Shoot. And he shot. And he said, The arrow of the LORD's deliverance, and the arrow of deliverance from Syria: for thou shalt smite the Syrians in Aphek, till thou have consumed them [2 Kings 13:16–17].

Well, Joash is not noted for his faith. Although he is weeping over the prophet who is dying, he is not a man of great faith, and he doesn't believe God is going to give him the victory over Syria.

And he said, Take the arrows. And he took them. And he said unto the king of Israel, Smite upon the ground. And he smote thrice, and stayed.

And the man of God was wroth with him, and said, Thou shouldest have smitten five or six times; then hadst thou smitten Syria till thou hadst consumed it: whereas now thou shalt smite Syria but thrice [2 Kings 13:18–19].

Because he didn't have the faith that God would give him deliverance, discouragement caused him to quit.

Many wonderful projects for God never come to fruition, are never executed, because a child of God meets opposition or discouragement. He gives up, and says, "The project is not in God's will." That is the attitude of Joash—he smote only three times. He is saying by this, "I don't think God will see me through." Today I see so much soft "faith." Folk sit on the sidelines and engage in wishful thinking. They say, "Oh, I want to do something for God." And the next time I see them, they are still sitting there. God expects you to get on the move for Him. If you believe God can use you, then get busy! Elisha gives us a very practical lesson here.

THE MIRACLE AT HIS TOMB

And Elisha died, and they buried him. And the bands of the Moabites invaded the land at the coming in of the year.

And it came to pass, as they were burying a man, that, behold, they spied a band of men; and they cast the man into the sepulchre of Elisha: and when the man was let down, and touched the bones of Elisha, he revived, and stood up on his feet [2 Kings 13:20–21].

Even in death Elisha was a miracle-working individual. What a tremendous tower of strength he had been in that nation.

But Hazael king of Syria oppressed Israel all the days of Jehoahaz.

And the LORD was gracious unto them, and had compassion on them, and had respect unto them, because of his covenant with Abraham, Isaac, and Jacob, and would not destroy them, neither cast he them from his presence as yet [2 Kings 13:22–23].

While God is punishing Israel with the word of Hazael, He does not allow the oppression to go too far.

So Hazael king of Syria died; and Ben-hadad his son reigned in his stead.

And Jehoash the son of Jehoahaz took again out of the hand of Ben-hadad the son of Hazael the cities, which he had taken out of the hand of Jehoahaz his father by war. Three times did Joash beat him, and recovered the cities of Israel [2 Kings 13:24–25].

In other words, as his faith, so was it done unto him—*three* times God gave him victory.

CHAPTERS 14–16

***THEME:** Good and bad kings of Israel and Judah*

AMAZIAH'S REIGN OVER JUDAH

Now we come to the reign of Amaziah over Judah. As was indicated before, Amaziah was a good king. He reigned for twenty-nine years.

In the second year of Joash son of Jehoahaz king of Israel reigned Amaziah the son of Joash king of Judah [2 Kings 14:1].

The fact that there are two kings by the same name is certainly confusing. The chronological table will help clear up the confusion.

He was twenty and five years old when he began to reign, and reigned twenty and nine years in Jerusalem. And his mother's name was Jehoaddan of Jerusalem [2 Kings 14:2].

Amaziah's mother was Jehoaddan. The mothers of these kings will receive the credit if their sons are good kings and the blame if they are bad kings. Amaziah was a good king so he must have had a wonderful mother.

And he did that which was right in the sight of the LORD, yet not like David his father: he did according to all things as Joash his father did [2 Kings 14:3].

Amaziah, the son of Joash, succeeded to the throne of Judah, and we are told that he did that which was right in the sight of the Lord although he failed to measure up to David's standard.

We also find that the civil war between the two kingdoms continued during this particular period.

Now they made a conspiracy against him in Jerusalem: and he fled to Lachish; but they sent after him to Lachish, and slew him there.

And they brought him on horses: and he was buried at Jerusalem with his fathers in the city of David.

And all the people of Judah took Azariah, which was sixteen years old, and made him king instead of his father Amaziah.

He built Elath, and restored it to Judah, after that the king slept with his fathers [2 Kings 14:19–22].

Amaziah fled to the city of Lachish, where there was a fortress which offered refuge, to avoid capture by conspirators.

JEROBOAM II REIGNS OVER ISRAEL

In the fifteenth year of Amaziah the son of Joash king of Judah Jeroboam the son of Joash king of Israel began to reign in Samaria, and reigned forty and one years.

And he did that which was evil in the sight of the LORD: he departed not from all the sins of Jeroboam the son of Nebat, who made Israel to sin.

He restored the coast of Israel from the entering of Hamath unto the sea of the plain, according to the word of the LORD God of Israel, which he spake by the hand of his servant Jonah, the son of Amittai, the prophet, which was of Gath-hepher [2 Kings 14:23–25].

Jeroboam did evil in the sight of the Lord. He did, however, restore the border of Israel, according to Jonah, the son of Amittai, the prophet. This is an historical reference to Jonah who wrote the Book of Jonah. This confirms the fact that Jonah was a real person and prophet in Israel. Finally Jeroboam II died and Zachariah came to the throne. We are moving toward the end of this nation.

AZARIAH (UZZIAH) REIGNS OVER JUDAH

In the twenty and seventh year of Jeroboam king of Israel began Azariah son of Amaziah king of Judah to reign.

Sixteen years old was he when he began to reign, and he reigned two and fifty years in Jerusalem. And his mother's name was Jecholiah of Jerusalem.

And he did that which was right in the sight of the LORD, according to all that his father Amaziah had done;

Save that the high places were not removed: the people sacrificed and burnt incense still on the high places [2 Kings 15:1–4].

In many ways Azariah (Uzziah) was a good king. However, he did something that he should not have done: he intruded into the priest's office. For this he was smitten with leprosy (2 Chron. 26:15–21). It broke Isaiah's heart when he died because Isaiah was afraid Azariah's successors would lead the nation back into idolatry. Azariah's fears were well-grounded, for his grandson did just that. We will spend more time on the reign of Uzziah when we come to Chronicles and Isaiah.

In Israel Zachariah, the last of the line of Jehu, was slain by Shallum after he had reigned for only six months. Shallum did not do very well, either. He reigned for only one month and was overthrown and slain by Menahem. Menahem reigned for ten years and did evil as had Jeroboam.

At this time Pul, king of Assyria, came against Israel, and Menahem paid one thousand talents of silver to preserve his kingdom. It was a dark period for the nation. At his death, his son Pekahiah succeeded him to the throne but reigned only two years, when Pekah, his captain, conspired and slew him.

During the reign of Pekah, Tiglath-pileser, king of Assyria, came against Israel and took captive the tribe of Naphtali. Pekah was slain by Hoshea. Jotham reigned in Judah, and was recognized as a good king.

JOTHAM REIGNS OVER JUDAH

Now we return to the kings of Judah and the son of Azariah (Uzziah).

Five and twenty years old was he when he began to reign, and he reigned sixteen years in Jerusalem. And his mother's name was Jerusha, the daughter of Zadok [2 Kings 15:33].

He is rated as a good king, and the Lord records the name of his mother.

And he did that which was right in the sight of the LORD: he did according to all that his father Uzziah had done.

Howbeit the high places were not removed: the people sacrificed and burned incense still in the high places. He built the higher gate of the house of the LORD [2 Kings 15:34–35].

He also tolerated the idolatry which would eventually send his people into captivity.

As we begin chapter 16, let me say that if you enjoy history, you will find this section intensely interesting. If you are looking for spiritual lessons, you will find some very practical things in this section. Much of this part of God's Word is extremely helpful. Remember, all of these things happened as examples for us.

AHAZ REIGNS OVER JUDAH

Twenty years old was Ahaz when he began to reign, and reigned sixteen years in Jerusalem, and did not that which was right in the sight of the LORD his God, like David his father.

But he walked in the way of the kings of Israel, yea, and made his son to pass through the fire, according to the abominations of the heathen, whom the LORD cast out from before the children of Israel [2 Kings 16:2–3].

Pekah reigned twenty years before he was murdered. In the seventeenth year of Pekah's reign in Israel, Ahaz began his reign as king of Judah. Ahaz was not a good king.

And he sacrificed and burnt incense in the high places, and on the hills, and under every green tree [2 Kings 16:4].

He walked in the wicked ways of the kings of Israel. He did the terrible thing of offering children as sacrifices to heathen gods—probably to Merodach (Marduk) or to Baal. This practice was about as low as a person could sink spiritually, and this is the thing Ahaz did. We are told that he "sacrificed and burnt incense in the high places, and on the hills, and under every green tree." In other words, Ahaz went the whole route into idolatry and pagan and heathen worship.

Then Rezin king of Syria and Pekah son of Remaliah king of Israel came up to Jerusalem to war: and they besieged Ahaz, but could not overcome him [2 Kings 16:5].

In the prophecy of Isaiah, chapter 7, there is an extended section on this. It is a very important section, because in it is the prophecy of the virgin birth of Jesus Christ. Isaiah is prophesying to this man Ahaz who will not listen to God. So Isaiah challenges him to trust God. Then Ahaz appeals to Assyria for help. This opens the door for Assyria to come down and ultimately take the northern kingdom into captivity.

At that time Rezin king of Syria recovered Elath to Syria, and drave the Jews from Elath: and the Syrians came to Elath, and dwelt there unto this day [2 Kings 16:6].

"Unto this day" means, of course, up to the time that this record was written.

In this verse the word *Jew* is used for the first time in the Bible. There are those who hold that *Jew* applies only to those of the tribe of Judah. However, notice that here it refers to folk in the northern kingdom of Israel—in fact, up on the border of Syria. As we shall see, all twelve tribes were given that name.

> **So Ahaz sent messengers to Tiglath-pileser king of Assyria, saying, I am thy servant and thy son: come up, and save me out of the hand of the king of Syria, and out of the hand of the king of Israel, which rise up against me.**
>
> **And Ahaz took the silver and gold that was found in the house of the LORD, and in the treasures of the king's house, and sent it for a present to the king of Assyria [2 Kings 16:7–8].**

And so the Assyrians are bribed. They come to Ahaz' aid first by attacking Damascus in Syria and then by taking the city.

> **And king Ahaz went to Damascus to meet Tiglath-pileser king of Assyria, and saw an altar that was at Damascus: and king Ahaz sent to Urijah the priest the fashion of the altar, and the pattern of it, according to all the workmanship thereof [2 Kings 16:10].**

He wanted this altar copied and erected in the temple of God. All the while Isaiah was prophesying to him and against him for what he was doing.

> **And king Ahaz cut off the borders of the bases, and removed the laver from off them; and took down the sea from off the brasen oxen that were under it, and put it upon a pavement of stones [2 Kings 16:17].**

Ahaz is showing his utter disrespect for the temple of the true and living God.

> **And the covert for the sabbath that they had built in the house, and the king's entry without, turned he from the house of the LORD for the king of Assyria.**
>
> **Now the rest of the acts of Ahaz which he did, are they not written in the book of the chronicles of the kings of Judah?**
>
> **And Ahaz slept with his fathers, and was buried with his fathers in the city of David: and Hezekiah his son reigned in his stead [2 Kings 16:18–20].**

Ahaz mutilated the house of God and seems to have stripped it of its elaborate ornamentation.

The chapter concludes with the death of Ahaz and the record of the fact that his son Hezekiah reigned after him. It is an amazing thing that a godless man like Ahaz would have a son like Hezekiah, the story of whose reign we shall see in a following chapter.

CHAPTER 17

***THEME:** Israel goes into captivity*

These are the reasons God permitted Israel to go into captivity:

1. *Disobeyed God* (v. 13)—"Yet the LORD testified against Israel, and against Judah, by all the prophets, and by all the seers, saying, Turn ye from your evil ways, and keep my commandments and my statutes, according to all the law which I commanded your fathers, and which I sent to you by my servants the prophets."

2. *Doubted God* (v. 14, see also 2 Chron. 36:15–16)—"Notwithstanding they would not hear, but hardened their necks, like to the neck of their fathers, that did not believe in the LORD their God."

3. *Defied God* (v. 15) in that they refused to observe the sabbatic year for 490 years—"To fulfil the word of the LORD by the mouth of Jeremiah, until the land had enjoyed her sabbaths: for as long as she lay desolate she kept sabbath, to fulfil threescore and ten years" (2 Chron. 36:21).

The story of this nation is the story of every individual.

HOSHEA'S REIGN

In chapter 17 we come to the end of the line as far as Israel is concerned. The ten northern tribes are carried into captivity by Assyria.

In the twelfth year of Ahaz king of Judah began Hoshea the son of Elah to reign in Samaria over Israel nine years.

And he did that which was evil in the sight of the LORD, but not as the kings of Israel that were before him [2 Kings 17:1–2].

He is not as bad as Ahab (and Jezebel), nor as bad as Ahaziah, but he is bad enough.

Against him came up Shalmaneser king of Assyria; and Hoshea became his servant, and gave him presents.

And the king of Assyria found conspiracy in Hoshea: for he had sent messengers to So king of Egypt, and brought no present to the king of Assyria, as he had done year by year: therefore the king of Assyria shut him up, and bound him in prison.

Then the king of Assyria came up throughout all the land, and went up to Samaria, and besieged it three years [2 Kings 17:3–5].

We are introduced to Shalmaneser, king of Assyria. He captured the northern kingdom and exacted tribute from them. When he discovered that king Hoshea had formed a conspiracy against him and was not paying his tribute, he besieged Samaria. Samaria was the city that Omri, the father of Ahab, had built. Ahab built a palace there. It was one of the most beautiful spots in the land. Now the king of Assyria besieged it.

ISRAEL'S CAPTIVITY

In the ninth year of Hoshea the king of Assyria took Samaria, and carried Israel away into Assyria, and placed them in Halah and in Habor by the river of Gozan, and in the cities of the Medes [2 Kings 17:6].

There are those who say that the ten tribes are lost; that is, the tribes have popped up in Great Britain from where they spread to the United States. This is a nice theory which ministers to the pride of many folk who would like to believe that they are members of the lost tribes, but this idea of ten lost tribes is entirely man-made. You will not find it in the Word of God. For example, in the New Testament James wrote in his epistle, "James, a servant of God and of the Lord Jesus Christ, to the twelve tribes which are scattered abroad, greeting" (James 1:1). Apparently James did not think the tribes were lost. The folk who hold this theory believe the ten tribes were lost when they went into Assyrian captivity. When the Jews returned to their land, you will find that some out of all the tribes came back. Actually, a small percentage of the people returned. Several million Jews went into captivity and only about 65,000 returned to Palestine.

SINS WHICH CAUSED ISRAEL'S CAPTIVITY

For so it was, that the children of Israel had sinned against the LORD their God, which had brought them up out of the land of Egypt, from under the hand of Pharaoh king of Egypt, and had feared other gods,

And walked in the statutes of the heathen, whom the LORD cast out from before the children of Israel, and of the kings of Israel, which they had made [2 Kings 17:7–8].

The Lord had been very patient with these people. Over a period of over two hundred years (after the division of the kingdom) the Lord had given them every opportunity and ample time to return to Him. But they did not. They continually went off into idolatry. The Word of God is very clear that he sent them into captivity because they insisted on worshiping other gods.

And the children of Israel did secretly those things that were not right against the LORD their God, and they built them high places in all their cities, from the tower of the watchmen to the fenced city.

And they set them up images and groves in every high hill, and under every green tree [2 Kings 17:9–10].

On top of the hills and under the trees pagan worship was carried on. Israel indulged in this gross immorality and licentiousness.

And there they burnt incense in all the high places, as did the heathen whom the LORD carried away before them; and wrought wicked things to provoke the LORD to anger:

For they served idols, whereof the LORD had said unto them, Ye shall not do this thing [2 Kings 17:11–12].

God had put the heathen out of the land for their immorality and idolatry. Do you think that God would permit His own people to stay in the land and do the same things? Well, He would not. He allowed Assyria to come and carry them away into captivity.

Yet the LORD testified against Israel, and against Judah, by all the prophets, and by all the seers, saying, Turn ye from your evil ways, and keep my commandments and my statutes, according to all the law which I commanded your fathers, and which I sent to you by my servants the prophets [2 Kings 17:13].

God had sent the prophets Ahijah, Elijah, Micaiah, Elisha, Jonah, Amos, and Hosea to these people in the northern kingdom of Israel. To the southern kingdom of Judah he had sent the prophets Shemaiah, Joel, Isaiah and Micah. Later on He will be sending Nahum, Habakkuk, Zephaniah, and Jeremiah. Every prophet warned the people of both kingdoms what would take place if they did not return to God and forsake their evil ways.

Notwithstanding they would not hear, but hardened their necks, like to the neck of their fathers, that did not believe in the LORD their God [2 Kings 17:14].

What was the basic sin? They were guilty of unbelief. The great sin of mankind is our refusal to believe God. You and I are living in a contemporary culture that has ruled God out. He has no place in our educational system. He is not appealed to by our government officials. Unfortunately, neither is He appealed to by many of our churches today. As a result, God will judge us as He judged His own people long ago.

And they rejected his statutes, and his covenant that he made with their fathers, and his testimonies which he testified against them; and they followed vanity, and became vain, and went after the heathen that were round about them, concerning whom the LORD had charged them, that they should not do like them [2 Kings 17:15].

The northern kingdom was taken into captivity. What about the southern kingdom?

Also Judah kept not the commandments of the LORD their God, but walked in the statutes of Israel which they made [2 Kings 17:19].

Judah will not profit from Israel's experience, as we shall see.

And the LORD rejected all the seed of Israel, and afflicted them, and delivered them into the hand of spoilers, until he had cast them out of his sight.

For he rent Israel from the house of David; and they made Jeroboam the son of Nebat king: and Jeroboam drave Israel from following the LORD, and made them sin a great sin [2 Kings 17:20–21].

You will recall that Jeroboam instituted calf-worship in Israel.

For the children of Israel walked in all the sins of Jeroboam which he did; they departed not from them;

Until the LORD removed Israel out of his sight, as he had said by all his servants the prophets. So was Israel carried away out of their own land to Assyria unto this day [2 Kings 17: 22–23].

"Unto this day" means, of course, the day 2 Kings was written.

ISRAEL'S CITIES REPOPULATED WITH FOREIGNERS

When the king of Assyria took the northern kingdom captive, he brought in other people to inhabit the land. The area of the northern kingdom was called Samaria. The Samaritans of the New Testament are the descendants of the colonists brought in by the king of Assyria. This is their beginning.

Wherefore they spake to the king of Assyria, saying, The nations which thou hast removed, and placed in the cities of Samaria, know not the manner of the God of the land: therefore he hath sent lions among them, and, behold, they slay them, because they know not the manner of the God of the land.

Then the king of Assyria commanded, saying, Carry thither one of the priests whom ye brought from thence; and let them go and dwell there, and let him teach them the manner of the God of the land.

Then one of the priests whom they had carried away from Samaria came and dwelt in Beth-el, and taught them how they should fear the LORD.

Howbeit every nation made gods of their own, and put them in the houses of the high places which the Samaritans had made, every nation in their cities wherein they dwelt [2 Kings 17: 26–29].

This brings us to the end of the northern kingdom. The land has become a mixture of peoples, and there is a great deal of intermarriage. The ten tribes will never again form the northern kingdom. They are scattered now, but they are not lost.

CHAPTER 18

***THEME:** Revival and testing under Hezekiah*

Now we come to King Hezekiah. This section is so remarkable that it is not only recorded here in 2 Kings, but also in 2 Chronicles, and in the historical section of the prophecy of Isaiah.

We have just seen that the northern kingdom of Israel was taken into captivity by Assyria. God gives three reasons why this happened: Israel disobeyed God, they doubted God, and they defied God. During the same period the southern kingdom of Judah had a very wonderful king. From this point on we shall be following only the history of the southern kingdom since the northern kingdom is out of the picture. The reason God did not send Judah into captivity at this time is because Judah did have a few good kings who were responsible for a time of revival.

Hezekiah was one of these. In fact, he was the best king who reigned in the land after David.

Now it came to pass in the third year of Hoshea son of Elah king of Israel, that Hezekiah the son of Ahaz king of Judah began to reign.

Twenty and five years old was he when he began to reign; and he reigned twenty and nine years in Jerusalem. His mother's name also was Abi, the daughter of Zachariah.

And he did that which was right in the sight of the LORD, according to all that David his father did [2 Kings 18:1–3].

Ahaz, the father of Hezekiah, was a very wicked king; yet he had this wonderful son. This leads us to believe that the mother of Hezekiah was a very fine mother and a godly woman. We are told here that her name was Abi.

JUDAH'S REVIVAL UNDER HEZEKIAH

He removed the high places, and brake the images, and cut down the groves, and brake in pieces the brasen serpent that Moses had made: for unto those days the children of Israel did burn incense to it: and he called it Nehushtan [2 Kings 18:4].

Hezekiah was a remarkable man. He led his people in a revival and began by attempting to remove idolatry from the land.

This verse mentions the brazen serpent that Moses put up in the wilderness (see Num. 21:1–9). What happened to that serpent that Moses had made? Well, it had been kept. Naturally it would be a tremendous memento, and it was kept in the temple. Then the day came when the children of Israel began to worship it! Instead of looking at it in faith as their fathers had, when they had been bitten by poisonous serpents in the wilderness as a judgment from God for rebellion, they began to worship it. Now it was a stumbling block. They had forgotten the meaning of it. The serpent pointed to Christ according to John 3:14–15 which says, "And as Moses lifted up the serpent in the wilderness, even so must the Son of man be lifted up: That whosoever believeth in him should not perish, but have eternal life." The brazen serpent was a symbol that was fulfilled by Christ. These people had turned the thing all around and had begun to worship the serpent instead of God.

As I have studied the seven churches of Asia Minor, I have noted that in the city of

Pergamos (more correctly, Pergamum), the serpent was worshiped. It seems the children of Israel were doing the same thing. They burned incense to the brazen serpent and called it Nehushtan. Now Hezekiah broke it in pieces. It was time to get rid of it.

There is a great spiritual lesson in this. There are certain organizations, certain movements, and certain methods that God has used in the past. Unfortunately, folk did not know when God was through with them, and they refused to disband them. I could name half a dozen organizations that I am confident God raised up and which served a great purpose, but which went to seed. They continued operating for no other reason than to perpetuate jobs for those they employed. They became Nehushtan. They became brazen serpents that at one time had served a purpose and were mightily used by God. Then the day came when God was through with them.

I have been in churches where people have been using the same methods for years and years. They say, "This is the way we have always done it." It may be that it is time to change some of those methods—there is no monotony with God. Do you realize that Paul never gave an invitation for people to come forward after a service? Apparently Dwight L. Moody began that practice. Now most evangelists think they have to give an invitation for people to come forward, and I have seen it actually become a stumbling block. God led Moody to do it, but He may not lead *you* to do it. Although I was pastor in a downtown Los Angeles church and there were many converts who responded to the invitation at the Sunday services, my most solid converts were those who were saved in the Bible study on Thursday night when no invitation was given. What God leads someone else to do, He may not lead you to do. You can certainly begin worshiping the equivalent of a brazen serpent and call it Nehushtan.

I have spent some time on this subject because I think it is important. Thank God that Hezekiah got rid of the serpent. I am of the opinion that many of the long-faced saints really criticized Hezekiah. They probably said, "He has gotten rid of our marvelous, wonderful, brazen serpent." Well, thank God he broke it to pieces, friend. If you have a few little idols lying around your church or in your life, I suggest you get rid of them. Maybe there is some method or some particular way you have of doing things that you ought to change.

He trusted in the LORD God of Israel; so that after him was none like him among all the kings of Judah, nor any that were before him.

For he clave to the LORD, and departed not from following him, but kept his commandments, which the LORD commanded Moses [2 Kings 18:5–6].

If there was none after Hezekiah to compare to him, and none before him, then we must conclude that he was outstanding. He is on a par with David. He was a great king who was mightily used of God. That is the reason that his life is given to us in three books of the Old Testament: 2 Kings, 2 Chronicles, and Isaiah.

THE FIRST INVASION OF JUDAH

And the LORD was with him; and he prospered whithersoever he went forth: and he rebelled against the king of Assyria, and served him not.

He smote the Philistines, even unto Gaza, and the borders thereof, from the tower of the watchmen to the fenced city.

And it came to pass in the fourth year of king Hezekiah, which was the seventh year of Hoshea son of Elah king of Israel, that Shalmaneser king of Assyria came up against Samaria, and besieged it.

And at the end of three years they took it: even in the sixth year of Hezekiah, that is the ninth year of Hoshea king of Israel, Samaria was taken [2 Kings 18:7–10].

Hezekiah was a courageous king. Under his command Judah rebelled against Assyria and defeated the Philistines. During the sixth year of Hezekiah's reign, Shalmaneser, king of Assyria, took Samaria. The northern kingdom was defeated. Now there was nothing, not even a barbed-wire fence, between Assyria and Judah. King Hezekiah was in a bad spot.

And the king of Assyria did carry away Israel unto Assyria, and put them in Halah and in Habor by the river of Gozan, and in the cities of the Medes:

Because they obeyed not the voice of the LORD their God, but transgressed his covenant, and all that Moses the servant of the LORD commanded, and

would not hear them, nor do them [2 Kings 18:11–12].

This is a review of Israel's captivity.

Now in the fourteenth year of king Hezekiah did Sennacherib king of Assyria come up against all the fenced cities of Judah, and took them.

And Hezekiah king of Judah sent to the king of Assyria to Lachish, saying, I have offended; return from me: that which thou puttest on me will I bear. And the king of Assyria appointed unto Hezekiah king of Judah three hundred talents of silver and thirty talents of gold [2 Kings 18:13–14].

Hezekiah tried to rebel against Assyria, but he was not successful. Because he did not succeed, he will have to pay.

At that time did Hezekiah cut off the gold from the doors of the temple of the LORD, and from the pillars which Hezekiah king of Judah had overlaid, and gave it to the king of Assyria [2 Kings 18:16].

THE SECOND INVASION OF JUDAH BY SENNACHERIB

And the king of Assyria sent Tartan and Rabsaris and Rab-shakeh from Lachish to king Hezekiah with a great host against Jerusalem. And they went up and came to Jerusalem. And when they were come up, they came and stood by the conduit of the upper pool, which is in the highway of the fuller's field [2 Kings 18:17].

Sennacherib threatens Jerusalem with a great army.

And when they had called to the king, there came out to them Eliakim the son of Hilkiah, which was over the household, and Shebna the scribe, and Joah the son of Asaph the recorder.

And Rab-shakeh said unto them, Speak ye now to Hezekiah, Thus saith the great king, the king of Assyria, What confidence is this wherein thou trustest? [2 Kings 18:18–19].

Rab-shakeh attempts to frighten them by suggesting two things.

Thou sayest, (but they are but vain words). I have counsel and strength for the war. Now on whom dost thou trust, that thou rebellest against me?

Now, behold, thou trustest upon the staff of this bruised reed, even upon Egypt, on which if a man lean, it will go into his hand, and pierce it: so is Pharaoh king of Egypt unto all that trust on him [2 Kings 18:20–21].

Knowing that Hezekiah is expecting aid from Egypt, Rab-shakeh ridicules Egypt as a bruised reed that would snap and pierce his hand the moment he put any weight on it. He says, "You won't get any help from Egypt!"

Now he attempts to knock out the second prop.

But if ye say unto me, We trust in the LORD our God: is not that he, whose high places and whose altars Hezekiah hath taken away, and hath said to Judah and Jerusalem, Ye shall worship before this altar in Jerusalem? [2 Kings 18:22].

When Hezekiah took away the high places, Sennacherib thought he was taking down the altars to the living and true God. He did not understand that Hezekiah was cleansing the land of pagan altars and idols and that his action was obedience, not sacrilege. The Jews were to worship God at the one altar in Jerusalem, and they approached Him only through a bloody sacrifice. It looked to Sennacherib, however, as if Hezekiah had thrown over his God just when he needed Him most.

Now therefore, I pray thee, give pledges to my lord the king of Assyria, and I will deliver thee two thousand horses, if thou be able on thy part to set riders upon them [2 Kings 18:23].

This is an insult and a strong expression of contempt for the military power of Judah.

Then said Eliakim the son of Hilkiah, and Shebna, and Joah, unto Rab-shakeh, Speak, I pray thee, to thy servants in the Syrian language; for we understand it: and talk not with us in the Jews' language in the ears of the people that are on the wall [2 Kings 18:26].

The Jews were lined up on the wall of the city of Jerusalem hearing all that was going on. The officials of Judah say; "Speak to us in the Syrian language; we can understand it." Old Rab-shakeh said, "Not on your life—this is going on television!" He was really demoralizing the troops.

Then Rab-shakeh stood and cried with a loud voice in the Jews' language, and spake, saying, Hear the word of the great king, the king of Assyria:

Thus saith the king, Let not Hezekiah deceive you: for he shall not be able to deliver you out of his hand [2 Kings 18:28–29].

He is getting through to the people, brainwashing them with propaganda.

Neither let Hezekiah make you trust in the LORD, saying, The LORD will surely deliver us, and this city shall not be delivered into the hand of the king of Assyria.

Hearken not to Hezekiah: for thus saith the king of Assyria, Make an agreement with me by a present, and come out to me, and then eat ye every man of his own vine, and every one of his fig tree, and drink ye every one the waters of his cistern:

Until I come and take you away to a land like your own land, a land of corn and wine, a land of bread and vineyards, a land of oil olive and of honey, that ye may live, and not die: and hearken not unto Hezekiah, when he persuadeth you, saying, The LORD will deliver us [2 Kings 18:30–32].

He is attempting to persuade the Jews to surrender. He repeats that neither Hezekiah nor God can help them. He promises that their lives will be spared only through surrender. He is saying, "Make terms with me and I'll leave you in peace to enjoy your own homes for a time." Then he adds, "Even if we transplant you, it will be to a beautiful land like your own."

Hath any of the gods of the nations delivered at all his land out of the hand of the king of Assyria?

Where are the gods of Hamath, and of Arpad? where are the gods of Sepharvaim, Hena, and Ivah? have they delivered Samaria out of mine hand?

Who are they among all the gods of the countries, that have delivered their country out of mine hand, that the LORD should deliver Jerusalem out of mine hand? [2 Kings 18:33–35].

To Rab-shakeh this seemed a crushing and unanswerable argument. It was true that no god had ever delivered his people out of the king of Assyria's power. Of course he did not know that the gods of the other countries were "no gods," while the living God was "the Lord of the whole earth."

But the people held their peace, and answered him not a word: for the king's commandment was, saying, Answer him not [2 Kings 18:36].

Whatever impression his arguments may have made on the hearts of those who heard, no one said a word.

CHAPTER 19

***THEME:** Hezekiah's recourse to God and Isaiah's prophecy*

As we have seen, Hezekiah came to the throne at a troubled, disturbed, and uncertain time in the land. The northern kingdom had been taken into captivity by Assyria. Now the Assyrian army has come to the gates of Jerusalem. This is enough to frighten Hezekiah, but added to this, Rab-shakeh, who is the henchman of the king of Assyria, is outside the gate sending out taunts and insults. He is boasting about the great things Assyria is going to do to Jerusalem, and he ridicules the idea that God can deliver them. Poor Hezekiah wilts under all of this, which is natural because Hezekiah is just learning to turn to the Lord and trust Him.

HEZEKIAH SEEKS HELP FROM GOD

And it came to pass, when king Hezekiah heard it, that he rent his clothes, and covered himself with sackcloth, and went into the house of the LORD [2 Kings 19:1].

Tearing his clothes and wearing sackcloth indicate Hezekiah's deep distress and heavy afflictions. Notice that he goes into the house of the Lord. That is a good place to go when you are in mental turmoil. It is time to turn to God.

And he sent Eliakim, which was over the household, and Shebna the scribe, and the elders of the priests, covered with sackcloth, to Isaiah the prophet the son of Amoz [2 Kings 19:2].

I wonder if you have noted the parallel to the days in which we are living. We think of our nation as being Christian and sophisticated and of Hezekiah's nation as being uncivilized and halfway pagan. Well, in our disturbed condition have you heard of any of our politicians, educators, leaders, or military men turning to God and appealing to Him for deliverance? No! Instead the nation looks to the "expert" and listens to the man who has a high I.Q. to give the best advice. We have listened to men like that, friend, since I was a young man, and that is a long span now. We get farther and farther into the night. Our problems are mounting. Our difficulties are overwhelming today. Nowhere, not even in the church, do you hear anyone appeal to God. Our only chance is to turn to God in this dark and late hour in the history of our nation. We are a young nation, but we are already old and on the way out. History tells us that the life of most nations is around two hundred years. Instead of turning to God, it is always, "Let's get together. Let's try a new approach. Let's get a new method. Let's work on this problem from a different angle. Let's get an authority in psychology, or medicine, or government, or education, and they will show us the way out." My friend, all of these experts have moved us farther into the night, and we are in trouble. We need God. No nation ever needed God as this nation needs God right now. Thank God Hezekiah had enough sense to call upon God in his hour of need! He sent a delegation to God's prophet, Isaiah.

And they said unto him, Thus saith Hezekiah, This day is a day of trouble, and of rebuke, and blasphemy: for the children are come to the birth, and there is not strength to bring forth.

It may be the LORD thy God will hear all the words of Rab-shakeh, whom the king of Assyria his master hath sent to reproach the living God; and will reprove the words which the LORD thy God hath heard: wherefore lift up thy prayer for the remnant that are left.

So the servants of king Hezekiah came to Isaiah [2 Kings 19:3–5].

Notice Hezekiah says, "It may be the LORD *thy* God will hear all the words of Rab-shakeh . . ." He does not say "*our* God," he says "*thy* God." Poor Hezekiah—maybe he is not very well acquainted with God, but he has enough sense to appeal to Him at a time like this. As a matter of fact, he has no other place to go at this moment.

And Isaiah said unto them, Thus shall ye say to your master, Thus saith the LORD, Be not afraid of the words which thou hast heard, with which the servants of the king of Assyria have blasphemed me.

Behold, I will send a blast upon him, and he shall hear a rumour, and shall return to his own land; and I will cause him to fall by the sword in his own land [2 Kings 19:6–7].

This prophecy was fulfilled literally. Notice the encouragement that Isaiah gives to the king. He says, "Don't worry about this man. He is not going to come into your city. He is just a blowhard. He is boasting and blaspheming, but God has heard him and will deal with him. There is no need for you to worry."

Oh, if we would only learn to let God deal with our enemies. The trouble is that *we* deal with them, and when we do that we move ourselves from the place of faith and trust in God so that God does not move in our behalf. The result is that we come out on the short end of the deal. The Lord can handle enemies much better than we can, just as He did in this case.

THE THREATENING LETTER

So Rab-shakeh returned, and found the king of Assyria warring against Libnah: for he had heard that he was departed from Lachish.

And when he heard say of Tirhakah king of Ethiopia, Behold, he is come out to fight against thee: he sent messengers again unto Hezekiah, saying [2 Kings 19:8–9].

Rab-shakeh returned to his master and found him carrying on a war with Libnah. And a threatening move of the king of Ethiopia kept him from returning to attack Jerusalem immediately. So he sends this letter of warning to Hezekiah.

Thus shall ye speak to Hezekiah king of Judah, saying, Let not thy God in whom thou trustest deceive thee, saying, Jerusalem shall not be delivered into the hand of the king of Assyria.

Behold, thou hast heard what the kings of Assyria have done to all lands, by destroying them utterly: and shalt thou be delivered?

Have the gods of the nations delivered them which my fathers have destroyed; as Gozan, and Haran, and Rezeph, and the children of Eden which were in Thelasar?

Where is the king of Hamath, and the king of Arpad, and the king of the city of Sepharvaim, of Hena, and Ivah? [2 Kings 19:10–13].

It was a disturbing message. The king of Assyria had swept aside everything in his path. How did Hezekiah think he could escape?

And Hezekiah received the letter of the hand of the messengers, and read it: and Hezekiah went up into the house of the LORD, and spread it before the LORD [2 Kings 19:14].

My friend, we need to spread our disturbing letters before the Lord just as Hezekiah did. Since my radio program has been on the air, I have received some wonderful letters, but I have received some of the other kind too. I learned a long time ago to turn them over to the Lord, and let Him work the problem out. He is a specialist at this sort of thing. Hezekiah did a wise thing when he spread the letter out before the Lord.

HEZEKIAH'S PRAYER

And Hezekiah prayed before the LORD, and said, O LORD God of Israel, which dwellest between the cherubims, thou art the God, even thou alone, of all the kingdoms of the earth; thou hast made heaven and earth.

LORD, bow down thine ear, and hear: open, LORD, thine eyes, and see: and hear the words of Sennacherib, which hath sent him to reproach the living God [2 Kings 19:15–16].

Notice how Hezekiah approaches God. Martin Luther prayed like that. My how these men could lay hold of God! Luther would cry out to God, "Lord, are you hearing me? Lord, hear me. Lord, let your ear be open to my prayer." Do you ever feel that God is not listening to you? This is the way Hezekiah felt.

Of a truth, LORD, the kings of Assyria have destroyed the nations and their lands,

And have cast their gods into the fire: for they were no gods, but the work of men's hands, wood and stone: therefore they have destroyed them [2 Kings 19:17–18].

What this man Rab-shakeh says is true. He is not boasting when he says that Assyria has swept everything before them and has cast each nation's gods into the fire.

Now therefore, O LORD our God, I beseech thee, save thou us out of his hand, that all the kingdoms of the earth may know that thou art the LORD God, even thou only [2 Kings 19:19].

GOD'S ANSWER

Now God will answer his prayer through Isaiah the prophet.

Then Isaiah the son of Amoz sent to Hezekiah, saying, Thus saith the LORD God of Israel, That which thou hast prayed to me against Sennacherib king of Assyria I have heard [2 Kings 19:20].

God says, "I was listening when you were praying to Me."

This is the word that the LORD hath spoken concerning him; The virgin the daughter of Zion hath despised thee, and laughed thee to scorn; the daughter of Jerusalem hath shaken her head at thee.

Whom hast thou reproached and blasphemed? and against whom hast thou exalted thy voice, and lifted up thine eyes on high? even against the Holy One of Israel [2 Kings 19:21–22].

God intends to destroy the arm of Assyria.

By thy messengers thou hast reproached the Lord, and hast said, With the multitude of my chariots I am come up to the height of the mountains, to

the sides of Lebanon, and will cut down the tall cedar trees thereof, and the choice fir trees thereof: and I will enter into the lodgings of his borders, and into the forest of his Carmel.

I have digged and drunk strange waters, and with the sole of my feet have I dried up all the rivers of besieged places [2 Kings 19:23–24].

God here repeats the boast of the king of Assyria that mountains do not stop him, deserts do not stop him—he digs wells for water. Rivers do not stop him—he will find ways of drying them up.

Now God addresses the proud Assyrian king. He says that the rise and fall of nations is *His* doing. As Isaiah had written earlier, God calls Assyria the "rod of mine anger" and the "staff . . . mine indignation" (see Isa. 10:5).

Hast thou not heard long ago how I have done it, and of ancient times that I have formed it? now have I brought it to pass, that thou shouldest be to lay waste fenced cities into ruinous heaps.

Therefore their inhabitants were of small power, they were dismayed and confounded; they were as the grass of the field, and as the green herb, as the grass on the house tops, and as corn blasted before it be grown up [2 Kings 19:25–26].

That is, Assyria's victims were unable to make an effectual resistance because it was God who had put a fear in their hearts.

But I know thy abode, and thy going out, and thy coming in, and thy rage against me.

Because thy rage against me and thy tumult is come up into mine ears, therefore I will put my hook in thy nose, and my bridle in thy lips, and I will turn thee back by the way by which thou camest [2 Kings 19:27–28].

God says, "You have come into My land; you have made your boast. Now I am going to put My hook in your nose, pull you right out of My land, and send you home."

And this shall be a sign unto thee, Ye shall eat this year such things as grow of themselves, and in the second year that which springeth of the same; and in the third year sow ye, and reap, and plant vineyards, and eat the fruits thereof [2 Kings 19:29].

The Lord now addresses Hezekiah. Apparently the presence of the Assyrian army had prevented the farmers around Jerusalem from sowing their land. God promised that there would be enough volunteer growth to feed them, and even in the third year they would be able to sow their crops and reap them in peace. Sennacherib and his army would not be around to destroy their crops.

And the remnant that is escaped of the house of Judah shall yet again take root downward, and bear fruit upward.

For out of Jerusalem shall go forth a remnant, and they that escape out of mount Zion: the zeal of the Lord of hosts shall do this.

Therefore thus saith the Lord concerning the king of Assyria, He shall not come into this city, nor shoot an arrow there, nor come before it with shield, nor cast a bank against it [2 Kings 19:30–32].

Isaiah is making a very bold statement, but it is the Word of the Lord. I am sure the people of Jerusalem are wondering if Isaiah is a true prophet. When Isaiah had made the prophecy that "a virgin shall conceive and bear a son," the people probably said, "My, that is a great prophecy. When will it take place?" Well, it wouldn't take place for seven hundred years, and none of them would be around to see its fulfillment. But now Isaiah is making a prophecy in a local situation, and they will see its fulfillment within days.

Here is the Assyrian army camped outside the gates of Jerusalem. This great army had swept everything before them. They were feared and dreaded in the ancient world. Now God says through Isaiah that they will not besiege the city of Jerusalem and that they will not even shoot an arrow into the city!

Now, you think that over for a moment. There are 185,000 soldiers around the walls of Jerusalem. Out of that number you would certainly find some trigger-happy soldier with a bow and arrow who would shoot at least one arrow over the wall. My friend, if he does that, Isaiah is not a true prophet of God. God says that not an arrow is going to fall in that city, and He says it by the mouth of Isaiah. That is the way the people of his day would know that he is a true prophet of God.

God says, "I'm going to save this city, and I will save it for two reasons."

For I will defend this city, to save it, for mine own sake, and for my servant David's sake [2 Kings 19:34].

He will do it for His name's sake—God does many things for His name's sake—and for David's sake. You see, God loved David. He did many things for David's sake.

And, my friend, David had a greater Son, a virgin-born Son, the Lord Jesus Christ. He will save sinners who trust Him—for Christ's sake. And when a believer prays to the Father in Jesus' name, the Father answers for Christ's sake.

And it came to pass that night, that the angel of the LORD went out, and smote in the camp of the Assyrians an hundred fourscore and five thousand: and when they arose early in the morning, behold, they were all dead corpses [2 Kings 19:35].

I love the way this translation reads, ". . . and when they arose early in the morning, behold, they were all dead corpses." Friend, the Assyrians did not wake in the morning. Why not? They were dead. Of course it means that when the folk inside the city awoke in the morning, they found about 185,000 dead bodies outside the city walls.

SENNACHERIB IS ASSASSINATED BY HIS SONS

So Sennacherib king of Assyria departed, and went and returned, and dwelt at Nineveh.

And it came to pass, as he was worshipping in the house of Nisroch his god, that Adrammelech and Sharezer his sons smote him with the sword: and they escaped into the land of Armenia. And Esarhaddon his son reigned in his stead [2 Kings 19:36–37].

Sennacherib was slain by his sons. It is interesting that the prophecy concerning Assyria was literally fulfilled in that day.

CHAPTER 20

***THEME:** Hezekiah's illness and healing*

This chapter is very meaningful to me because I have had an experience with illness and healing that is somewhat like Hezekiah's experience.

Keep in mind that Hezekiah was an outstanding king. There was none like him after David. "He did that which was right in the sight of the LORD, according to all that David his father did"—this is God's testimony concerning him.

HEZEKIAH'S ILLNESS

In those days was Hezekiah sick unto death. And the prophet Isaiah the son of Amoz came to him, and said unto him, Thus saith the LORD, Set thine house in order; for thou shalt die, and not live [2 Kings 20:1].

Hezekiah's illness is recorded three times in Scripture (2 Kings 20; 2 Chron. 32; and Isa. 38), and each account adds a little something to the total picture. It must have been a difficult task for Isaiah to deliver a death sentence to Hezekiah, the king. Very candidly, however, the sentence of death rests upon each one of us although we do not know the day or hour. The Scripture says, "And as it is appointed unto men once to die, but after this the judgment" (Heb. 9:27). This is a divine date. If each one of us knew the exact time we would die, would it not change our way of living? Even many Christians say, "Death is way off yonder in the future. I won't worry about it now." Well, we may not worry about it, but we ought to live knowing that death will be the ultimate goal.

Many years ago when a fine young minister was told by his doctor that he had a recurrence of cancer and his days were limited, he sent out a letter to some of his friends. I was privileged to be included in that list and I was shaken when I read his letter. Let me give you an excerpt from it: "One thing I have discovered in the last few days. When a Christian is suddenly confronted with the sentence of death, he surely begins to give a proper evaluation of material things: my fishing gear, and books, and orchard are not nearly so valuable as they were a week ago." With that in mind, let us look at Hezekiah's experience.

Then he turned his face to the wall, and prayed unto the LORD, saying,

I beseech thee, O LORD, remember now how I have walked before thee in truth and with a perfect heart, and have done that which is good in thy sight. And Hezekiah wept sore [2 Kings 20:2–3].

Hezekiah turned his face to the wall and prayed to the Lord. I think I understand his position. Suppose you were told that you had cancer and neither you nor the doctor knew what the outcome would be. All of my life in the ministry I have visited people with cancer. I could understand how they could have cancer, but I never could understand how I could have it. It rocked me when the doctor told me I had cancer—I could not believe it. When I had to accept the fact, I was not given any assurance at all that I would live—nor have I any assurance today. I just know that I have cancer. May I say to you, it gives you a different set of values.

My life is a little different today. Many people have wondered about my conduct in certain areas. They ask, "Why did you resign as pastor of a church when you were still active?" I have no ambition in the ministry. God gave me the privilege of being pastor of a great church in its heyday and of conducting the largest midweek service in that day and generation. I considered that a privilege. But now my ambition is to live in such a way that I will please the Lord. It has caused me to change in many different ways. Someone said to me the other day, "You are trying to kill yourself in carrying on your radio ministry and holding conferences." You know, I am afraid if I don't, I am going to displease Him.

When I was taken to the hospital, I had no idea what the outcome of my illness would be. The nurse had to help me get into bed because I was so weak. I was not physically weak—I was frightened; I am a coward. She asked, "Are you sick?" I replied, "No. I am scared to death!" She was a Christian nurse, and she smiled at that. I asked her to leave me alone for awhile, and I turned my face to the wall, just as Hezekiah did, and I cried out to God. I told Him that I did not want to die—and I *didn't* want to die.

When we are ill I believe we should go to God in prayer and ask others to pray for us. I believe in faith healing—not in faith healers—I know God can heal. Well, an acquaintance wrote me a letter in which she said, "I am not going to pray that you get well because I know that you are ready to go and be with the Lord. I am praying that He will take you home." I got an answer back to her in a hurry. I said, "Now look here. You let the Lord handle this. Don't try and tell Him how I feel. I don't want to die. I want to live. I want to live as long as I can."

When I turned my face to the wall there in the hospital, I promised Him, "Lord, if you will raise me up, I will teach your Word everywhere I can go." That is what I have been trying to do. I don't want to let Him down because I don't want Him to say, "Well, look here, preacher, I will have to call you home because you are not doing what you said you would do." Friend, we have a different outlook on life when we are in a position like this. The doctor, a wonderful Christian man, has told me that he cannot help me, but my recovery has come from the hand of God. Of course, I told him that I wanted to know why he sends me a bill if God is the One doing the work. It is wonderful, friend, to be in a position where you have to trust the Lord. I have no other alternative. Where in the world am I going to go if I don't go to the Lord? I am trusting the Lord and I am not being pious when I say that—it was forced on me.

Now Hezekiah was in that same position. Only God could help him. When he turned his face to the wall, he reminded the Lord that he had walked before Him in truth and with a perfect heart, and he had done that which was good in His sight.

And it came to pass, afore Isaiah was gone out into the middle court, that the word of the LORD came to him, saying,

Turn again, and tell Hezekiah the captain of my people, Thus saith the LORD, the God of David thy father, I have heard thy prayer, I have seen thy tears: behold, I will heal thee: on the third day thou shalt go up unto the house of the LORD [2 Kings 20:4–5].

The Lord had seen Hezekiah's tears. I am sure he has seen my tears, too, and yours.

And I will add unto thy days fifteen years; and I will deliver thee and this city out of the hand of the king of Assyria; and I will defend this city for mine own sake, and for my servant David's sake [2 Kings 20:6].

This is great news that the Lord will heal him and extend his life fifteen more years!

HEZEKIAH'S RECOVERY

And Isaiah said, Take a lump of figs. And they took and laid it on the boil, and he recovered [2 Kings 20:7].

God used natural means to raise up Hezekiah, but He also used supernatural means. This is wonderful. It is what James is saying, "Is any sick among you? let him call for the elders of the church; and let them pray over him, anointing him with oil in the name of the Lord" (James 5:14).

There are two ways a person can be anointed with oil. One is ceremonial, and the other is medicinal. A great many people seem to have missed it, but James is talking about a medicinal anointing. God is saying through James that we should be very practical. The doctor should be called, but the elders of the church should also be called to pray. And the prayer will raise up the one who is sick.

In Hezekiah's case they put figs on the "boil"—which may well have been cancer. God said, "I am going to add fifteen years to your life, but you had better put figs on that boil." Friend, my recommendation is not to be fanatical, but be sensible. If you have cancer, then face up to it. I wanted to know the facts and so did Hezekiah. Believe me, God laid it out before him, and God spared his life for fifteen more years.

And Hezekiah said unto Isaiah, What shall be the sign that the LORD will heal me, and that I shall go up into the house of the LORD the third day? [2 Kings 20:8].

Hezekiah asked for a sign to show that his life would be extended. The Lord has given me no sign whatsoever that my life will be lengthened. That, of course, is up to my heavenly Father, but I want Him to leave me here as long as He possibly can. If He has another plan, I will have to accept it.

It is not always God's will to extend our lives. I notice in the early church that James was a martyr—he was executed by Herod. Peter, on the other hand, was delivered from prison. I do not know why one man was delivered and the other man became a martyr. All of that is in the providence of God. It is His will that we want. Let's pray, "Oh God, bend me and reconcile me to your will—whatever it is." But I am going to let God know how I feel about it. I used to visit a dear lady who was in such pain that she knew she would not get well. She said, "Dr. McGee, don't pray for me to get well. Just pray that the Lord will take me." That is what the Lord did, by the way. But I do not pray that way unless the person wants me to do so.

And Isaiah said, This sign shalt thou have of the LORD, that the LORD will do the thing that he hath spoken: shall the shadow go forward ten degrees, or go back ten degrees?

And Hezekiah answered, It is a light thing for the shadow to go down ten degrees: nay, but let the shadow return backward ten degrees.

And Isaiah the prophet cried unto the LORD: and he brought the shadow ten degrees backward, by which it had gone down in the dial of Ahaz [2 Kings 20:9–11].

HEZEKIAH'S FOOLISHNESS

Now we come to a phase in Hezekiah's life that blanches my soul.

At that time Berodach-baladan, the son of Baladan, king of Babylon, sent letters and a present unto Hezekiah: for he had heard that Hezekiah had been sick [2 Kings 20:12].

He sends a get-well card and a gift.

And Hezekiah hearkened unto them, and shewed them all the house of his precious things, the silver, and the gold, and the spices, and the precious ointment, and all the house of his armour, and all that was found in his treasures: there was nothing in his house, nor in all his dominion, that Hezekiah shewed them not [2 Kings 20:13].

Hezekiah did a foolish thing. He let the ambassadors from Babylon see the treasure that Solomon had gathered. The wealth of the world was there, which was not general knowledge. Hezekiah was big-hearted—Babylon had sent him a get-well card, and so he gives these men from Babylon a guided tour of his kingdom.

Then came Isaiah the prophet unto king Hezekiah, and said unto him, What said these men? and from whence came they unto thee? And Hezekiah said, They are come from a far country, even from Babylon.

And he said, What have they seen in thine house? And Hezekiah answered, All the things that are in mine house have they seen: there is nothing among my treasures that I have not shewed them [2 Kings 20:14–15].

He rolled out the red carpet and showed them everything.

And Isaiah said unto Hezekiah, Hear the word of the LORD.

Behold, the days come, that all that is in thine house, and that which thy fathers have laid up in store unto this day, shall be carried into Babylon: nothing shall be left, saith the LORD [2 Kings 20:16–17].

These ambassadors made an inventory of all the riches and took it back to Babylon with them to wait for the proper time when they needed gold. When they wanted to get the treasure, they knew where to come.

And of thy sons that shall issue from thee, which thou shalt beget, shall they take away; and they shall be eunuchs in the palace of the king of Babylon [2 Kings 20:18].

This is what is going to happen to Hezekiah's offspring.

Then said Hezekiah unto Isaiah, Good is the word of the LORD which thou hast spoken. And he said, Is it not good, if peace and truth be in my days? [2 Kings 20:19].

I don't like Hezekiah's reply to Isaiah. It was not a confession of sin at all. Rather, he wanted peace in his day and showed little concern for his offspring upon whom the coming catastrophe would fall.

HEZEKIAH'S DEATH

And the rest of the acts of Hezekiah, and all his might, and how he made a pool, and a conduit, and brought water into the city, are they not written in the book of the chronicles of the kings of Judah?

And Hezekiah slept with his fathers: and Manasseh his son reigned in his stead [2 Kings 20:20–21].

This may seem like an awful thing for me to say, but Hezekiah should have died when the time came for him to die. Three things took place after God extended his life that were foolish acts: he showed his treasures to Babylon, which will cause great trouble in the future; he begat a son, Manasseh, who was the most wicked of any king; he revealed an arrogance, almost an impudence, in his later years. His heart became filled with pride. Second Chronicles 32:25 tells us, "But Hezekiah rendered not again according to the benefit done unto him; for his heart was lifted up: therefore there was wrath upon him, and upon Judah and Jerusalem." You see, it might have been better if Hezekiah had died at God's appointed time.

That is why I want to be very careful. The Lord has spared me and I do not want to do anything to disgrace Him. My friend, this is a wonderful chapter. We have a wonderful heavenly Father.

CHAPTER 21

***THEME:** Manasseh's evil reign*

Chapter 21 is quite a let-down after chapter 20, and yet there is a tremendous message here for us. Hezekiah was the best king since David—there was none to compare with him. He was like David in another way: neither of these men were good fathers. Hezekiah fathered a son who was the worst king that ever reigned in the southern kingdom. It is a heartbreak when you read about Manasseh, Hezekiah's son, turning out the way he did. Now I cannot confirm the statement I am about to make, but I believe that the shekinah glory—the visible presence of God—returned to heaven during the reign of Manasseh. As far as we can determine, the shekinah glory was present during the reign of Hezekiah, and I can't see any events that happened after the reign of Manasseh that would have caused the shekinah glory to leave. When God's presence left the temple, it was a desolate place, forsaken of God. As we look at the life of this man Manasseh, we will see his total abhorrence for the temple and all the things of God.

MANASSEH'S SINS

Manasseh was twelve years old when he began to reign, and reigned fifty and five years in Jerusalem. And his mother's name was Hephzibah [2 Kings 21:1].

Manasseh began his reign as a twelve-year-old boy. He was a rascal, but someone says, "He is young. He will outgrow it." Well, he did not outgrow it. He got worse and worse and worse. He reigned for fifty-five years. God gave him ample opportunity to change his ways. In 2 Chronicles we find that he did finally repent. God is always patient and long-suffering. He is not willing that any should perish.

Manasseh's mother's name is mentioned. Her name was Hephzibah. She will have to accept the responsibility for her son. If there is any credit, she will receive that, too. She may have been a wonderful mother. I don't know how Hephzibah raised this boy, but Manasseh was as wicked as he could be, and the damage he did to his country was irreparable.

And he did that which was evil in the sight of the LORD, after the abominations of the heathen, whom the LORD cast out before the children of Israel [2 Kings 21:2].

Manasseh was as bad as any of the pagans that God put out of the land when he brought His people into the land.

For he built up again the high places which Hezekiah his father had destroyed; and he reared up altars for Baal, and made a grove, as did Ahab king of Israel; and worshipped all the host of heaven, and served them [2 Kings 21:3].

Hezekiah, you recall, had destroyed the pagan places of worship, and a partial revival took place under his influence. All of his work came to naught because Manasseh raised up altars for Baal, and he worshiped all the host of heaven and served them—which means he worshiped the sun, moon, and stars, and all the hosts of heaven that the Greeks named Apollo and Diana, etc. Manasseh was a wicked man.

Someone says, "My, but we have come a long way today." No, we haven't. We are seeing a strong resurgence of astrology, and multitudes of "civilized" folk live by the horoscope. Many people still worship the host of heaven today.

And he built altars in the house of the LORD, of which the LORD said, In Jerusalem will I put my name.

And he built altars for all the host of heaven in the two courts of the house of the LORD [2 Kings 21:4–5].

Manasseh defied Almighty God. He put up pagan altars in the house of the Lord where God had said, "Here is where I will set *My* name."

And he made his son pass through the fire, and observed times, and used enchantments, and dealt with familiar spirits and wizards: he wrought much wickedness in the sight of the LORD, to provoke him to anger [2 Kings 21:6].

He even made his own son pass through the fire or into the fire. This was actually a human sacrifice. An image was heated until it was red hot and then a baby was placed in it as an offering! It was a horrible, sadistic, satanic form of idolatrous worship.

And he set a graven image of the grove that he had made in the house, of which the LORD said to David, and to Solomon his son, In this house, and in Jerusalem, which I have chosen out of all tribes of Israel, will I put my name for ever:

Neither will I make the feet of Israel move any more out of the land which I gave their fathers; only if they will observe to do according to all that I have commanded them, and according to all the law that my servant Moses commanded them [2 Kings 21:7–8].

These people did not know it at the time, but they were getting ready to travel. They were headed for Babylonian captivity, because the land was theirs on one condition: obedience.

But they hearkened not: and Manasseh seduced them to do more evil than did the nations whom the LORD destroyed before the children of Israel [2 Kings 21:9].

Not only was Manasseh as bad as the heathen, he was *worse.* I have news for him: God will not tolerate the Israelites' wickedness. He will put them out of the land.

And the LORD spake by his servants the prophets, saying,

Because Manasseh king of Judah hath done these abominations, and hath done wickedly above all that the Amorites did, which were before him, and hath made Judah also to sin with his idols:

Therefore thus saith the LORD God of Israel, Behold, I am bringing such evil upon Jerusalem and Judah, that whosoever heareth of it, both his ears shall tingle.

And I will stretch over Jerusalem the line of Samaria, and the plummet of the house of Ahab: and I will wipe Jerusalem as a man wipeth a dish, wiping it, and turning it upside down [2 Kings 21:10–13].

Just as God had judged Samaria and all Israel, God is now going to judge Jerusalem and all Judah. God said he will "wipe Jerusalem as a man wipes a dish"—God is going to do some dishwashing. Jerusalem is His land—His dish—the Israelites have made it filthy; so He is going to wipe them out of it.

You may be very clever and sophisticated and think you don't need God, but you are walking on His earth, breathing His air, using His sunshine, and drinking His water. He even gave you the body that you have. Every now and then He washes His dishes. Nations down through the centuries lie along the highway of time in rubble and ruin. Do you know why? They did the same thing that our nation is doing today: living without God, feeling no need of God. God said that He was going to wipe Jerusalem as a man wipes a dish, and He did just that.

And I will forsake the remnant of mine inheritance, and deliver them into the hand of their enemies; and they shall become a prey and a spoil to all their enemies [2 Kings 21:14].

God says that He is going to take His finger out of the dike and let the enemy come in like a flood.

Moreover Manasseh shed innocent blood very much, till he had filled Jerusalem from one end to another; beside his sin wherewith he made Judah to sin, in doing that which was evil in the sight of the LORD [2 Kings 21:16].

When a man or a nation goes into sin, they don't sin in just one respect; they sin in many respects. Now we have not only forgotten God, we have become an immoral nation. Lawlessness and murder are the order of the day. Some companies have moved away from large cities, trying to get away from lawlessness. Well, we cannot get away from it until this nation returns to God. That is the first step.

Now the rest of the acts of Manasseh, and all that he did, and his sin that he sinned, are they not written in the book of the chronicles of the kings of Judah?

And Manasseh slept with his fathers, and was buried in the garden of his own house, in the garden of Uzza: and Amon his son reigned in his stead [2 Kings 21:17–18].

This is the story of Manasseh. There is not much to say except that he was evil and corrupt, and he died.

AMON'S BRIEF REIGN

Amon was twenty and two years old when he began to reign, and he reigned

two years in Jerusalem. And his mother's name was Meshullemeth, the daughter of Haruz of Jotbah.

And he did that which was evil in the sight of the LORD, as his father Manasseh did.

And he walked in all the way that his father walked in, and served the idols that his father served, and worshipped them:

And he forsook the LORD God of his fathers, and walked not in the way of the LORD [2 Kings 21:19–22].

Amon is a bad one, too—he walked in his father's footsteps. He forsook the Lord. Therefore, the Lord forsook him.

And the servants of Amon conspired against him, and slew the king in his own house [2 Kings 21:23].

Amon's wickedness led to revolution. Today we as a nation are on the way to revolution. It is unfortunate that our leaders seem to be interested only in getting elected. It seems that they are actually willing to sell their country in order to do that. We are living in dangerous days, friend.

JOSIAH REIGNS OVER JUDAH

And the people of the land slew all them that had conspired against king Amon; and the people of the land made Josiah his son king in his stead.

Now the rest of the acts of Amon which he did, are they not written in the book of the chronicles of the kings of Judah?

And he was buried in his sepulchre in the garden of Uzza: and Josiah his son reigned in his stead [2 Kings 21:24–26].

This section brings us to the last of the great kings. Josiah was not only a great king, but the greatest revival took place during the time of his reign.

CHAPTERS 22–23

***THEME:** Josiah's good reign*

In chapters 22 and 23 we find that Josiah, who begins to reign when he is eight years old and reigns for thirty-one years, is one of the best kings who reigned after Solomon. During his reign a great and needed revival comes to the nation. Hilkiah, the high priest, is his counselor, assistant, and adviser.

JOSIAH'S GOOD LIFE

Josiah was eight years old when he began to reign, and he reigned thirty and one years in Jerusalem. And his mother's name was Jedidah, the daughter of Adaiah of Boscath [2 Kings 22:1].

Notice how young these kings are when they begin to reign. Why are they so young? Well, papa got killed. God removed him.

And he did that which was right in the sight of the LORD, and walked in all the way of David his father, and turned not aside to the right hand or to the left [2 Kings 22:2].

The sun has come up again; the light is shining once more in the land. Josiah has come to the throne. He led a movement that resulted in the greatest revival these people ever had after David and Solomon.

It is my firm conviction today that the only thing that can save our nation is revival. It is either going to be revival or revolution. There is corruption in government on all levels. There is corruption in all organizations today. Immorality and lawlessness abound. Sex, liquor, drugs, filthy magazines, foul pictures, scandals, and riots reign. This nation is wallowing like a pig in a swine's sty. We are like the prodigal son in a far country in the pigpen with the pigs. Without revival, revolution stares us in the face. Socialism is creeping in today. Political parties are willing to sell the birthright of this nation in order to stay in power. The church today is under the blight of apostasy. Liberalism controls the organized church. There is a brazen denial of the Word of God even in so-called evangelical circles. The Word of God has been lost in the church, and there are atheists today in the pulpit.

The first thing Christians need to recognize is that revival is personal and individual. I don't think revival has ever begun as a mass movement. What we need today is not politicians calling other politicians crooks. We need politicians who will say, "I have been wrong. I am going to get right with God." It would be a strange thing, and I suppose it would frighten our nation, but it's what we need.

Josiah, the man at the top, did that which was right in the sight of the Lord. The revival began with him.

THE TEMPLE IS REPAIRED

And it came to pass in the eighteenth year of king Josiah, that the king sent Shaphan the son of Azaliah, the son of Meshullam, the scribe, to the house of the LORD, saying,

Go up to Hilkiah the high priest, that he may sum the silver which is brought into the house of the LORD, which the keepers of the door have gathered of the people [2 Kings 22:3–4].

The second thing that Josiah did was to repair the temple. Apparently, the temple was not in use when Josiah came to the throne. It had become sort of a warehouse, a storage area for odds and ends.

And let them deliver it into the hand of the doers of the work, that have the oversight of the house of the LORD: and let them give it to the doers of the work which is in the house of the LORD, to repair the breaches of the house.

Unto carpenters, and builders, and masons, and to buy timber and hewn stone to repair the house [2 Kings 22:5–6].

He tells the people to get busy and repair the temple.

The church today is very much like the temple in Josiah's day. It is in great need of repair. I am not speaking of church buildings—there are many beautiful church buildings. I stayed in a motel back east some time ago, and there was a church right across the street from my room. I was told that it cost one-half million dollars to build. The week I was there I noticed on Sunday morning, as I was leaving for my speaking appointment, that there were about twenty-five cars parked by the church for the Sunday morning service. There weren't any more than twenty-five cars for the evening service, and the rest of the week the church was dark. That place needs repairing, let me tell you!

Our conservative churches today are torn asunder by strife and bickering. They are huge and attractive. But is the Spirit of God there? The church is not witnessing. True believers should be out telling people about the Lord. You frighten Christians when you talk about witnessing for Christ. We do not need any more pious platitudes, saccharin sweetness, back-slapping, and hand-pumping. Let's let these service clubs do that. They are better at it than we are anyway. What we need today is to get the church straightened out on the inside.

THE BOOK OF THE LAW IS DISCOVERED

And Hilkiah the high priest said unto Shaphan the scribe, I have found the book of the law in the house of the LORD. And Hilkiah gave the book to Shaphan, and he read it [2 Kings 22:8].

The third thing that brought revival to the nation was a return to the Word of God. They had lost the Bible, and they had lost it in the church. But they found the Word of God and put it back into their lives. The Word of God is the only thing we have as a weapon, friend. It is God's Word that is alive, and powerful, and sharper than any two-edged sword (Heb. 4:12). There is no short cut, no easy route, no new method to revival. We have a flood of books today on Christian experience. I have looked over quite a few of these books and find them as dead as a doornail. What is the problem? They present a method instead of presenting the Word of God. They are not saying, "Let's get back to the Word of God." We don't need so-and-so's book; we need the Bible. We don't need the book of the month; we need the Book of the ages.

How many churches today in this land really rest upon the Word of God and preach it? Although there are still many faithful pastors, there are many who have departed from the faith. They have lost the Bible in church. Remember when Jesus was a boy, Mary and Joseph lost Him in the temple. Believe me, Jesus, as well as the Bible, is lost in the church today. Hilkiah, the high priest, found the Word of God. Did he find it out on the dump heap? No! He found it in the temple. It had been lost. A return to the Bible has to be the beginning of a revival.

I was with a fine young preacher not long

ago. He was questioning me about my method of study. I found out that he had read all the latest books. In fact, he rather embarrassed me when he asked, "Have you read so-and-so? Have you seen this book and the other book?" I said no to each one. He asked, "Have you quit reading books?" I said, "Well, I'm pretty much read up, and the new books coming out don't seem to interest me because they are presenting a method." He said, "What do you read then?" I told him that I read the Bible. Then I asked him the pointed question, "How much time do you spend each week in the Word of God?" His answer was amazing. He spent less than one hour a week studying God's Word! He had already told me about the problems he was having, and it was very easy to give him a remedy. He needed to get into the Word of God.

And Shaphan the scribe came to the king, and brought the king word again, and said, Thy servants have gathered the money that was found in the house, and have delivered it into the hand of them that do the work, that have the oversight of the house of the LORD.

And Shaphan the scribe shewed the king, saying, Hilkiah the priest hath delivered me a book. And Shaphan read it before the king [2 Kings 22:9–10].

Imagine this! Now Josiah is hearing the Word of God for the first time!

And it came to pass, when the king had heard the words of the book of the law, that he rent his clothes [2 Kings 22:11].

The fourth step toward revival is repentance. The reading of the Word of God brought repentance. When the king heard the Word of God, he tore his clothes as an expression of deep emotion. Why? Because the Word of God revealed their sin. Without the Word of God they did not realize how far they had strayed from God's law. A return to the Word of God brings revival. It wasn't like some of these nice little groups I often hear about today that are going to have a "revival" campaign. They have a banquet and call in all of the preachers. The object is to talk sweetly and optimistically and get everyone together. My friend, real revival does not come unless there is true repentance.

I heard of a man, a very fine Christian, who stood before a group of church officers and told them, "What this church needs is for this group of officers to get down on their faces before God and repent!" Do you know what they did? They got rid of him. They didn't want him around. Oh, if we would really come to the Word of God, it would bring conviction. There would be weeping and rending of clothes and a real revival.

Go ye, inquire of the LORD for me, and for the people, and for all Judah, concerning the words of this book that is found: for great is the wrath of the LORD that is kindled against us, because our fathers have not hearkened unto the words of this book, to do according unto all that which is written concerning us [2 Kings 22:13].

Josiah is frightened because he knows they deserve God's judgment.

The message God returns to Josiah through Huldah the prophetess reveals both God's justice and His grace.

Thus saith the LORD, Behold, I will bring evil upon this place, and upon the inhabitants thereof, even all the words of the book which the king of Judah hath read:

Because they have forsaken me, and have burned incense unto other gods, that they might provoke me to anger with all the works of their hands; therefore my wrath shall be kindled against this place, and shall not be quenched [2 Kings 22:16–17].

Now notice God's grace to Josiah.

Because thine heart was tender, and thou hast humbled thyself before the LORD, when thou heardest what I spake against this place, and against the inhabitants thereof, that they should become a desolation and a curse, and has rent thy clothes, and wept before me; I also have heard thee, saith the LORD.

Behold therefore, I will gather thee unto thy fathers, and thou shalt be gathered into thy grave in peace; and thine eyes shall not see all the evil which I will bring upon this place. And they brought the king word again [2 Kings 22:19–20].

JOSIAH'S FURTHER REFORMATIONS

And the king sent, and they gathered unto him all the elders of Judah and of Jerusalem.

And the king went up into the house of the LORD, and all the men of Judah and all the inhabitants of Jerusalem with him, and the priests, and the prophets, and all the people, both small and great: and he read in their ears all the words of the book of the covenant which was found in the house of the LORD.

And the king stood by a pillar, and made a covenant before the LORD, to walk after the LORD, and to keep his commandments and his testimonies and his statutes with all their heart and all their soul, to perform the words of this covenant that were written in this book. And all the people stood to the covenant [2 Kings 23:1–3].

The people said that not only would they read the Word of God, they would also walk it—they would live in the manner it prescribed.

We could have revival in many of our churches, but there must be a conviction of sin that only the Word of God can bring. When the Bible brings conviction to the heart, repentance must follow. To repent means to make things right, my friend. Repentance means to turn around and go in the opposite direction. If you are going the wrong way, you turn around and go the right way.

I heard of an evangelist who held meetings in upper New York state years ago. He preached for a week, and not one person made a move toward God. Then one night the leading deacon in the church came forward, shedding tears of repentance. That broke the meeting wide open because he was the one standing in the way of revival in that church. He apologized to someone he had wronged, and all during the night as he prayed, the Lord would convict him of something else—his life hadn't been right. He would go over and knock on the door of the person he had wronged, and say, "I'm here to make things right." That went on all night! Imagine getting folk out of bed in the middle of the night! By morning there was a revival going on in that town because one man repented.

Now Josiah as king has a tremendous influence. He will now put into operation a very bold plan. His repentance put him in first gear, and he started moving out.

First he put idolatry out of the temple of God.

And the king commanded Hilkiah the high priest, and the priests of the second order, and the keepers of the door, to bring forth out of the temple of the LORD all the vessels that were made for Baal, and for the grove, and for all the host of heaven: and he burned them without Jerusalem in the fields of Kidron, and carried the ashes of them unto Beth-el [2 Kings 23:4].

All of the things that pertain to the worship of false gods were burned in the fields of Kidron, outside of the city of Jerusalem. The ashes were then taken out of town so that the people could not even look to the ashes.

Then Josiah put away immorality.

And he brake down the houses of the sodomites, that were by the house of the LORD, where the women wove hangings for the grove [2 Kings 23:7].

Today the church is looking upon homosexuality as permissible behavior. God says in Romans 1:26 and 27 that He gave up a people because of this unnatural thing. I'm of the opinion that God will give this nation up if we continue smiling upon the unnatural sex orgies that are taking place in our land.

Josiah had the courage to condemn the sodomites. He not only condemned their actions, he put them out of the kingdom. Unnatural sex is wrong even if the church today condones it. I know that there are groups that say, "We ought to accept this sort of thing among consenting adults and even among consenting teenagers. It is perfectly all right." Who told them it was all right? Somebody says, "Well, I think it is all right." Well, my friend, that judgment is no bigger than your little mind—and you may have a Ph.D. Your little mind and my little mind are not big enough to make judgments like that. *God* has said that sodomy will bring down His wrath. It has in the past, and He has not changed. We have changed, but God has not changed. Josiah was a brave man, and he got rid of the sodomites.

Josiah also stopped the offering of human sacrifices—children—to Molech.

And he defiled Topheth, which is in the valley of the children of Hinnom, that no man might make his son or his daughter to pass through the fire to Molech [2 Kings 23:10].

Josiah also broke down images, altars, high places, and groves that kings before him had brought into the land. He even went beyond the borders of Judah—as far north as Beth-el. Second Chronicles 34:33 sums it up in one verse: "And Josiah took away all the abominations out of all the countries that pertained to the children of Israel, and made all that were present in Israel to serve, even to serve the LORD their God. And all his days they departed not from following the LORD, the God of their fathers."

It is interesting that at Beth-el he came upon the grave of the prophet who had predicted he would do these things (1 Kings 13:2).

Then he said, What title is that that I see? And the men of the city told him, It is the sepulchre of the man of God, which came from Judah, and proclaimed these things that thou hast done against the altar of Beth-el.

And he said, Let him alone; let no man move his bones. So they let his bones alone, with the bones of the prophet that came out of Samaria [2 Kings 23:17–18].

Now Josiah makes a tremendous positive move. He reinstitutes the Passover.

THE PASSOVER IS REINSTITUTED

And the king commanded all the people, saying, Keep the passover unto the LORD your God, as it is written in the book of this covenant.

Surely there was not holden such a passover from the days of the judges that judged Israel, nor in all the days of the kings of Israel, nor of the kings of Judah;

But in the eighteenth year of king Josiah, wherein this passover was holden to the LORD in Jerusalem [2 Kings 23:21–23].

The holding of the Passover is a wonderful thing. Apparently it had not been kept for a long time; they had passed it by. What does it mean? The Passover speaks of Christ. The people had forgotten all about Him. Paul says, ". . . For even Christ our passover is sacrificed for us" (1 Cor. 5:7). Today we are trying to have religion without Christ. The deity of Christ is ridiculed in seminaries and in pulpits. The value of Christ's death is rejected and spurned. The efficacy of Christ's blood is hooted down as something evil—even by some men in the pulpit.

My friend, the only thing that can save our nation is revival. Somebody asks, "Can it come?" Yes, I believe it can come. There is a "sound of going in the tops of the mulberry trees" today. A flood tide came in the sixteenth century, which was led by the reformers Luther, Calvin, and Zwingli. Wycliffe and John Knox in the fourteenth and fifteenth centuries were the reformers before the Reformation. In the seventeenth century came another spiritual awakening known as the Puritan Movement. In the eighteenth century, a time of darkness and deism, came another great spiritual awakening led by Wesley and Whitfield. In the nineteenth century there was a mighty turning to God in Oxford, and the missionary movement resulted. Toward the end of the century great revivals were led by Moody and Finney. In the twentieth century (hear me now very carefully) there has been no great world-sweeping, earth-shaking revival. There have been a few local revivals. The twentieth century is quickly drawing to an end. Look around you today. When we had a depression in this country, we did not turn to God as a nation. We were plunged into World War II and saw the spilling of American blood that had not been equaled. That experience apparently did not teach us a thing. There was no revival. Since then we have had the Korean and the Vietnam wars. Neither did they bring us back to God.

Many people seem to think that if they get out and protest, things will change. But what we need is some real deep conviction on the inside. We need to recognize our coldness and indifference. When was the last time you confessed your coldness and indifference to the Lord? Have you told Him today that you love Him? He is your Savior, my friend, and I am convinced that even in this dark hour, as has happened in the past, we can have a revival. The story of Josiah encourages me. It was in the darkest hour in the life of his nation that revival came.

JOSIAH'S DEATH

Now we come to a heartbreak in this story of Josiah. Great revival had come near the end of the kingdom of Judah. Soon his people will go into captivity. God moved in a mighty way to reveal the fact that He can send revival in the most difficult and dark days.

Now what ended the revival?

In his days Pharaoh-nechoh king of Egypt went up against the king of Assyria to the river Euphrates: and king Josiah went against him; and he slew

him at Megiddo, when he had seen him [2 Kings 23:29].

Josiah should have stayed home. He should have kept his nose out of it. This was not his fight, but he went out anyway. What happened? He was slain at Megiddo. (By the way, Megiddo in the great valley of Esdraelon is the place where the war of Armageddon is to be fought in the last days.) Josiah was a great man of God, but he was foolish. He entered a battle that was none of his concern.

This story might be a message for another nation I know about. I am afraid that we have meddled enough throughout the world today. We need to recognize that the *only* message that America has for the world is not democracy but the Word of God. We were blessed when we were sending out God's Word. Today we are sending out propaganda and we have become an immoral nation. God is not in the things we do as a nation, and we are no longer being blessed.

And his servants carried him in a chariot dead from Megiddo, and brought him to Jerusalem, and buried him in his own sepulchre. And the people of the land took Jehoahaz the son of Josiah, and anointed him, and made him king in his father's stead [2 Kings 23:30].

JEHOAHAZ REIGNS AND IS DETHRONED

Jehoahaz was twenty and three years old when he began to reign; and he reigned three months in Jerusalem. And his mother's name was Hamutal, the daughter of Jeremiah of Libnah.

And he did that which was evil in the sight of the Lord, according to all that his fathers had done.

And Pharaoh-nechoh put him in bands at Riblah in the land of Hamath, that he might not reign in Jerusalem; and put the land to a tribute of an hundred talents of silver, and a talent of gold [2 Kings 23:31–33].

You would think that Jehoahaz would follow in the righteous steps of his father, but he did not. Jehoahaz was an evil king. As a matter of fact, he hardly got the throne warm sitting on it—he lasted for only three months. Pharaoh didn't like the way he was reigning. He removed him from the throne and took him down to the land of Egypt, where he died.

JEHOIAKIM IS MADE KING

And Pharaoh-nechoh made Eliakim the son of Josiah king in the room of Josiah his father, and turned his name to Jehoiakim, and took Jehoahaz away: and he came to Egypt, and died there.

And he did that which was evil in the sight of the Lord, according to all that his fathers had done [2 Kings 23:34, 37].

Jehoiakim was another son of Josiah, and he reigned for eleven years. He also was an evil king. We go from bad to worse. Jehoahaz was bad; Jehoiakim was worse.

At this time the great power of Babylon is rising in the east on the Euphrates River. Babylon is displacing Assyria. Babylon, in fact, overcame Assyria. Babylon will also overcome Egypt and become the first great world power, as we will see in the Book of Daniel. It is at this point that we ought to read the Book of Jeremiah, because Jeremiah was the great prophet during this era. He was the one calling Israel back to God and warning them that if they do not turn to God they will be taken captive and sent to Babylon. Jeremiah's words seemed unbelievable to the people of Israel, because at this time Nebuchadnezzar king of Babylon was not a formidable foe. The false prophets were telling the nation that God simply could not get along without them. Jerusalem was the city of God; His holy temple was there; they were His chosen people. He couldn't get along without them. Well, they will find that He could get along without them. Actually, He didn't need that temple; it would soon be destroyed.

CHAPTERS 24–25

THEME: *The kingdom of Judah goes into captivity*

NEBUCHADNEZZAR COMES AGAINST JUDAH

In his days Nebuchadnezzar king of Babylon came up, and Jehoiakim became his servant three years: then he turned and rebelled against him [2 Kings 24:1].

Egypt's Pharaoh-nechoh had put Jehoiakim on the throne, but he lost all Egypt's Asiatic possessions to Babylon's Nebuchadnezzar. Now when Nebuchadnezzar comes against Judah, Jehoiakim knuckles under for three years, then rebels against him.

And the LORD sent against him bands of the Chaldees, and bands of the Syrians, and bands of the Moabites, and bands of the children of Ammon, and sent them against Judah to destroy it, according to the word of the LORD, which he spake by his servants the prophets.

Surely at the commandment of the LORD came this upon Judah, to remove them out of his sight, for the sins of Manasseh, according to all that he did [2 Kings 24:2–3].

As we have seen, Manasseh was an evil man. If the shekinah glory didn't depart during his reign, there was nothing worse afterward that would have caused it to depart. Because these people did not depart from the sins of Manasseh, they will be going into captivity.

And also for the innocent blood that he shed: for he filled Jerusalem with innocent blood; which the LORD would not pardon [2 Kings 24:4].

While it is true that God will pardon all sin, the sinner will have to come to Him in repentance. There are certain sins that are not pardonable. Although Christ died for all sins, they are not pardonable because men will not come to Christ in repentance. My friend, He is the only One in the world who can forgive your sin. He died for you and paid the penalty for your sins. Who else can forgive your sins? He alone is the way, the truth, and the life.

JEHOIAKIM DIES, AND JEHOIACHIN REIGNS

Now the rest of the acts of Jehoiakim, and all that he did, are they not written in the book of the chronicles of the kings of Judah?

So Jehoiakim slept with his fathers: and Jehoiachin his son reigned in his stead [2 Kings 24:5–6].

The names of father and son are so similar, it is easy to confuse them.

And the king of Egypt came not again any more out of his land: for the king of Babylon had taken from the river of Egypt unto the river Euphrates all that pertained to the king of Egypt [2 Kings 24:7].

This is the exact land that God had vouchsafed to Abraham and to those who came after him. Why was Babylon, instead of Israel, in control of this area now?

Jehoiachin was eighteen years old when he began to reign, and he reigned in Jerusalem three months. And his mother's name was Nehushta, the daughter of Elnathan of Jerusalem.

And he did that which was evil in the sight of the LORD, according to all that his father had done [2 Kings 24:8–9].

This is the reason. They have continued in sin and in their rebellion against God. Remember that God had given them the occupancy of the land on one condition: their obedience. Did they still own the land? Oh, yes. God had given them the land by an unconditional covenant. But their occupancy was conditional, and they failed to meet that condition.

JEHOIACHIN IS TAKEN CAPTIVE (FIRST DEPORTATION)

At that time the servants of Nebuchadnezzar king of Babylon came up against Jerusalem, and the city was besieged.

And Nebuchadnezzar king of Babylon came against the city, and his servants did besiege it.

And Jehoiachin the king of Judah went out to the king of Babylon, he, and his mother, and his servants, and his princes, and his officers: and the king of Babylon took him in the eighth year of his reign [2 Kings 24:10–12].

The king and all of the nobility were carried away in the first group that went into captivity. This took place about 605 B.C.

And he carried out thence all the treasures of the house of the LORD, and the treasures of the king's house, and cut in pieces all the vessels of gold which Solomon king of Israel had made in the temple of the LORD, as the LORD had said.

And he carried away all Jerusalem, and all the princes, and all the mighty men of valour, even ten thousand captives, and all the craftsmen and smiths: none remained, save the poorest sort of the people of the land.

And he carried away Jehoiachin to Babylon, and the king's mother, and the king's wives, and his officers, and the mighty of the land, those carried he into captivity from Jerusalem to Babylon [2 Kings 24:13–15].

This is a sad and sordid story.

ZEDEKIAH IS MADE KING BY NEBUCHADNEZZAR

And the king of Babylon made Mattaniah his father's brother king in his stead, and changed his name to Zedekiah.

Zedekiah was twenty and one years old when he began to reign, and he reigned eleven years in Jerusalem. And his mother's name was Hamutal, the daughter of Jeremiah of Libnah.

And he did that which was evil in the sight of the LORD, according to all that Jehoiakim had done [2 Kings 24:17–19].

Zedekiah was Jehoiachin's uncle. He did not improve the line of kings. You would think that the captivity would sober him. It did not at all. Trouble will do one of two things for an individual. It will either soften or harden you. It will either draw you to God or drive you away from God. You can never be the same after you experience trouble and suffering. The sun will soften wax, but the sun will harden clay. It is the same sun that softens one and hardens the other.

For through the anger of the LORD it came to pass in Jerusalem and Judah, until he had cast them out from his presence, that Zedekiah rebelled against the king of Babylon [2 Kings 24:20].

Once again the false prophets said, "Look, God is on our side." But God was not on Israel's side because Israel was not on God's side.

Presumption is something many people need to be careful about. I have heard people say, "I am doing this certain thing because I know it is God's will. He has revealed it to me." Then they go ahead and do whatever they had in mind, and they fail. God was not in it at all. I know missionaries who have gone to the field and come back to say, as one young man said to me, "I made a mistake in going out." "But," I said, "you told me you were in God's will. You were sure." He said, "I thought I was." Well, we had better not *think* so, we had better be sure when we begin to talk about God being on our side. Actually we should make sure not that God is on our side but that we are on His side.

This was Judah's problem. They were far from God, yet they felt that they were God's people and He would protect them.

In chapter 25 we see the final deportation of Judah. Nebuchadnezzar, king of Babylon, came three times against Jerusalem. He deported the royalty and the military and the skilled workmen, but he did not destroy the city until he came the third time.

We have seen that Nebuchadnezzar had made Zedekiah king of Judah, but after a few years Zedekiah rebelled, and now we see that Nebuchadnezzar comes the final time and makes an end of Judah.

THE SIEGE

And it came to pass in the ninth year of his reign, in the tenth month, in the tenth day of the month, that Nebuchadnezzar king of Babylon came, he, and all his host, against Jerusalem, and pitched against it: and they built forts against it round about.

And the city was besieged unto the eleventh year of king Zedekiah [2 Kings 25:1–2].

The exactness of the date indicates the extreme importance of this siege. It was the beginning of the end of Jerusalem.

And on the ninth day of the fourth month the famine prevailed in the city, and there was no bread for the people of the land [2 Kings 25:3].

The intensity of the suffering is described for us in Lamentations.

And the city was broken up, and all the men of war fled by night by the way of the gate between two walls, which is by the king's garden: (now the Chaldees were against the city round about:) and the king went the way toward the plain.

And the army of the Chaldees pursued after the king, and overtook him in the plains of Jericho: and all his army were scattered from him.

So they took the king, and brought him up to the king of Babylon to Riblah; and they gave judgment upon him [2 Kings 25:4–6].

The enemy broke into the city, and the king with his troops tried to escape. But they were captured. The prophet Jeremiah had predicted the fall of Jerusalem, and he was considered a traitor because he told the people the truth.

And they slew the sons of Zedekiah before his eyes, and put out the eyes of Zedekiah, and bound him with fetters of brass, and carried him to Babylon [2 Kings 25:7].

This man was deceived by false prophets but would not listen to God's prophet. Now he is carried away into captivity, blinded.

JERUSALEM IS BURNED

And he burnt the house of the LORD, and the king's house, and all the houses of Jerusalem, and every great man's house burnt he with fire [2 Kings 25:9].

Because of the rebellion of Jerusalem, Nebuchadnezzar burned and leveled it to such an extent that when Nehemiah came to the city seventy years after the Captivity and looked upon that place, it almost seemed hopeless. But he rallied the people, and the biggest thing he had to overcome was discouragement. The armies of Nebuchadnezzar had devastated the city. The false prophets had insisted that God would not let the city be destroyed. They were indeed *false* prophets.

There are people today who are giving this country a false message. They are saying that Americans belong to the ten "lost" tribes of Israel. They are saying that God is on our side, and He won't let us down. My friend, God does not *need* us. Where did that notion come from? God sent His chosen people into captivity. It was a sad day for them. And it ought to be a lesson for us in this day.

And all the army of the Chaldees, that were with the captain of the guard, brake down the walls of Jerusalem round about.

Now the rest of the people that were left in the city, and the fugitives that fell away to the king of Babylon, with the remnant of the multitude, did Nebuzar-adan the captain of the guard carry away.

But the captain of the guard left of the poor of the land to be vinedressers and husbandmen [2 Kings 25:10–12].

They left those who would be of no value to them. Also they wanted the land to continue to produce so they could exact tribute from it.

And the pillars of brass that were in the house of the LORD, and the bases, and the brasen sea that was in the house of the LORD, did the Chaldees break in pieces, and carried the brass of them to Babylon.

And the pots, and the shovels, and the snuffers, and the spoons, and all the vessels of brass wherewith they ministered, took they away [2 Kings 25: 13–14].

The army of Nebuchadnezzar really cleaned house. The temple was cleaned out before it was destroyed with fire. All that wealth was carried away into Babylon. We will have occasion, when we get to the Book of Daniel, to find that those vessels from the temple had been stored away and were brought out when Belshazzar had his great banquet. Jerusalem was plundered, burned, and left a pile of rubble.

Jerusalem has been destroyed about twenty-seven times. Each time the city has been rebuilt upon the rubble. The hill that is Jerusalem today is largely built upon the rubble of past cities. Many people, especially tour agents, say, "Go to Jerusalem and walk where Jesus walked." Well, my friend, you will not be walking where Jesus walked. The city that Jesus lived and walked in is buried under tons of rubble. At some spots you have to look down twenty feet, twenty-five feet, sometimes forty-five feet to see the city where Jesus lived.

GEDALIAH APPOINTED GOVERNOR

And Gedaliah sware to them, and to their men, and said unto them, Fear not to be the servants of the Chaldees: dwell in the land, and serve the king of Babylon; and it shall be well with you [2 Kings 25:24].

Nebuchadnezzar appointed Gedaliah to govern the people who were left in the land. They should have listened to him—and to the prophet Jeremiah—who urged them to settle down and accept this form of government. Instead of that, they assassinate the governor Gedaliah!

But it came to pass in the seventh month, that Ishmael the son of Nethaniah, the son of Elishama, of the seed royal, came, and ten men with him, and smote Gedaliah, that he died, and the Jews and the Chaldees that were with him at Mizpah.

And all the people, both small and great, and the captains of the armies, arose, and came to Egypt: for they were afraid of the Chaldees [2 Kings 25: 25–26].

A great company of them fled into Egypt and became colonists down there. By the way, Jeremiah went with this group—not willingly, but he was forced to go.

JEHOIACHIN RELEASED

And it came to pass in the seven and thirtieth year of the captivity of Jehoiachin king of Judah, in the twelfth month, on the seven and twentieth day of the month, that Evil-merodach king of Babylon in the year that he began to reign did lift up the head of Jehoiachin king of Judah out of prison;

And he spake kindly to him, and set his throne above the throne of the kings that were with him in Babylon;

And changed his prison garments: and he did eat bread continually before him all the days of his life.

And his allowance was a continual allowance given him of the king, a daily rate for every day, all the days of his life [2 Kings 25:27–30].

Evil-merodach extends amnesty as he comes to the throne of Babylon. Although other captured kings are in his court, Jehoiachin is given a position of honor among them. It is interesting that the period of the kings should conclude with kindness being shown to this last descendant of David who had grown old in a Babylonian prison.

BIBLIOGRAPHY

(Recommended for Further Study)

Crockett, William Day. *A Harmony of the Books of Samuel, Kings and Chronicles.* Grand Rapids, Michigan: Baker Book House, 1951.

Darby, J. N. *Synopsis of the Books of the Bible.* Addison, Illinois: Bible Truth Publishers, n.d.

Davis, John J. and Whitcomb, John C., Jr. *A History of Israel.* Grand Rapids, Michigan: Baker Book House, 1970. (Excellent.)

Epp, Theodore H. *David.* Lincoln, Nebraska: Back to the Bible Broadcast, 1965.

Epp, Theodore H. *Elijah—A Man of Like Nature.* Lincoln, Nebraska: Back to the Bible Broadcast, 1969.

Gaebelein, Arno C. *The Annotated Bible.* Neptune, New Jersey: Loizeaux Brothers, 1912-22.

Gray, James M. *Synthetic Bible Studies.* Old Tappan, New Jersey: Fleming H. Revell Co., 1906.

Jensen, Irving L. *I Kings and Chronicles.* Chicago, Illinois: Moody Press, 1968. (A self-study guide.)

Jensen, Irving L. *II Kings with Chronicles.* Chicago, Illinois: Moody Press, 1968. (A self-study guide.)

Kelly, William. *Lectures on the Earlier Historical Books of the Old Testament.* Addison, Illinois: Bible Truth Publishers, 1874.

Knapp, Christopher. *The Kings of Israel and Judah.* Neptune, New Jersey: Loizeaux Brothers, 1908. (Very fine.)

Krummacher, F. W. *Elijah the Tishbite.* Grand Rapids, Michigan: Baker Book House, n.d.

Krummacher, F. W. *Elisha.* Grand Rapids, Michigan: Baker Book House, n.d.

Mackintosh, C. H. *Miscellaneous Writings.* Neptune, New Jersey: Loizeaux Brothers, n.d.

McNeely, Richard J. *First and Second Kings.* Chicago, Illinois: Moody Press, 1978.

Meyer, F. B. *David: Shepherd, Psalmist, King.* Fort Washington, Pennsylvania: Christian Literature Crusade, n.d.

Meyer, F. B. *Elijah and the Secret of His Power.* Fort Washington, Pennsylvania: Christian Literature Crusade, n.d. (A rich devotional study.)

Pink, Arthur W. *Gleanings from Elisha.* Chicago, Illinois: Moody Press, 1972.

Sauer, Erich. *The Dawn of World Redemption.* Grand Rapids, Michigan: Wm. B. Eerdmans Publishing Co., 1951. (An excellent Old Testament survey.)

Scroggie, W. Graham. *The Unfolding Drama of Redemption.* Grand Rapids, Michigan: Zondervan Publishing House, 1970. (An excellent survey and outline of the Old Testament.)

Unger, Merrill F. *Unger's Commentary on the Old Testament.* Vol. 1. Chicago, Illinois: Moody Press, 1981. (A fine summary of each paragraph. Highly recommended.)

Wood, Leon J. *Israel's United Monarchy.* Grand Rapids, Michigan: Baker Book House, 1979. (Excellent.)

Wood, Leon J. *The Prophets of Israel.* Grand Rapids, Michigan: Baker Book House, 1977. (Excellent.)

Note: The dates listed are those of the first printings.

The Book of

1 CHRONICLES

INTRODUCTION

The two Books of Chronicles are very similar in many ways. They cover the same historical ground all the way from Saul to Zedekiah. Then are the Chronicles a duplication of Kings? Emphatically, no. Greek translators gave Chronicles the title, "Things Omitted," which is a good title, but not adequate. Chronicles include more than that which is omitted in the other historical books. Actually Chronicles is another instance of the law of recurrence or recapitulation. The policy of the Holy Spirit in giving the Word of God is to give a great expanse of truth, to cover a great deal of territory, then come back and select certain sections which He wants to enlarge upon. It is as if the Spirit of God takes up a telescope, looks out over the landscape for us, then takes a particular portion of it and puts it under the microscope and lets us look at it in detail. This is what is happening in 1 and 2 Chronicles.

We have seen the law of recurrence or recapitulation in operation before. In Genesis, the second chapter goes back over the seven days of creation, and lifts out one thing: the creation of man. For us, that is very important since we are members of Adam's race. Also the Book of Deuteronomy (*Deuteronomy* means a "second law") is more than a repetition of the Law. Rather it is an interpretation of the Law in the light of forty years' experience with it in the wilderness.

Now we will see in the Chronicles that God goes over the ground which He had covered in 1 and 2 Samuel and 1 and 2 Kings in order to add details and to emphasize things which He considers important. Let me give you some examples of this. The emphasis in 1 Chronicles is David, and the emphasis in 2 Chronicles is David's posterity. The northern kingdom is practically ignored when the division occurs between the northern and southern kingdoms. Chronicles does not record David's sin. Why? Well, God so completely forgave it that He does not even mention it again. When God forgives, He forgets. In Kings the history of the nation is given from the standpoint of the throne; in Chronicles it is given from the standpoint of the altar. In Kings the palace is the center; in Chronicles the temple is the center. Kings gives us the political history of the nation, while Chronicles gives the religious history. Chronicles is the interpretation of Kings. All through the Books of Kings we noted the phrase, "Is it not written in the book of the chronicles of the kings of Israel?" Chronicles, you see, is the interpretation of Kings. Also Kings gives us man's viewpoint while Chronicles gives us God's viewpoint.

Ezra is probably the writer of the Chronicles. There is a striking similarity in style and language to the Books of Ezra and Nehemiah. Evidently Chronicles was written during the Babylonian captivity. The two Books of Chronicles not only constituted one book in the original, but apparently also included Ezra and Nehemiah. This lends support to the Jewish tradition of the authorship of Ezra.

OUTLINE

I. Genealogies, Chapters 1–9

II. Saul's Reign, Chapter 10

III. David's Reign, Chapters 11–29

A. David's Mighty Men, Chapters 11–12
B. David and the Ark, Chapters 13–16
C. David and the Temple, Chapter 17
D. David's Wars, Chapters 18–20
E. David's Sin in Numbering People, Chapter 21
F. David's Preparation and Organization for Building the Temple, Chapters 22–29

CHAPTERS 1–9

***THEME:** Genealogies*

The first nine chapters contain the genealogies, and in many senses this is one of the most remarkable passages of the Word of God.

Notice how it begins:

> **Adam, Sheth, Enosh,**
> **Kenan, Mahalaleel, Jered,**
> **Henoch, Methuselah, Lamech,**
> **Noah, Shem, Ham, and Japheth**
> **[1 Chron. 1:1–4].**

These are the names of the men about whom we have read in the first eight chapters of Genesis.

As you read the genealogy, you will notice that the same policy is followed that was used in the Book of Genesis. That is, the rejected lines are mentioned first, then we are given the line that is to be followed through the Scriptures to the Lord Jesus Christ.

Notice that the sons of Japheth are listed, then the sons of Ham, and finally the sons of Shem. Only the line of Shem continues. It leads to Abraham. Then Abraham's posterity is recorded: Ishmael and his sons, also the sons of Abraham by Keturah, and finally Abraham's son Isaac. Then Isaac's line is followed—first listing the descendants of Esau. However, the line which leads to the Lord Jesus will continue through Isaac's other son, Jacob.

Chapter 2 begins the genealogy of Jacob, which continues through chapter 9. Coming to verse 15, we find the posterity of Jesse, and one of Jesse's sons was David. Now we will follow his line, because the Lord Jesus will be a "son" of David.

Chapter 3 records the family of David, and we find that David had some sons we had not known about before—they were not mentioned in the Books of Kings.

> **And these were born unto him in Jerusalem; Shimea, and Shobab, and Nathan, and Solomon, four, of Bath-shua the daughter of Ammiel [1 Chron. 3:5].**

Did you ever hear of Shimea and Shobab? We know Solomon, but who is Nathan? Well, if you go over to the genealogy of the Lord Jesus, which is recorded in the Gospel of Luke, you will find that the line goes through Nathan rather than through Solomon. Mary, the mother of Jesus, traced her ancestry through Nathan, while Joseph's genealogy is traced through Solomon. In Matthew we see that the Lord Jesus gets His legal title to the throne of David through Solomon, and in Luke we see that He gets His blood title to the throne of David through Nathan. This is very important, because in the ancestry of Solomon, Jeconiah (whom the Lord calls Coniah) appears, and the Lord declares that ". . . no man of his seed shall prosper, sitting upon the throne of David, and ruling any more in Judah" (Jer. 22:30). This one man produced a short circuit in the line leading to the Messiah, which is further proof that Joseph could not be the father of the Lord Jesus and that Jesus must be virgin born.

In chapter 4 the posterity of Judah through Caleb and Shelah is followed, also the tribe of Simeon.

Chapter 5 traces the tribe of Reuben to the captivity.

> **Now the sons of Reuben the firstborn of Israel, (for he was the firstborn; but, forasmuch as he defiled his father's bed, his birthright was given unto the sons of Joseph the son of Israel: and the genealogy is not to be reckoned after the birthright.**
>
> **For Judah prevailed above his brethren, and of him came the chief ruler; but the birthright was Joseph's:) [1 Chron. 5:1–2].**

This verse informs us that Reuben's lost birthright was given to Joseph, not to Judah. However, Judah prevailed, and the ruler came from Judah. The record of the tribes of Gad and the half tribe of Manasseh is given until their captivity. The final two verses give the reason for the captivity.

Chapter 6 traces the tribe of Levi (family of the high priests), through the sons Gershon, Kohath, and Merari.

Chapter 7 gives the genealogies of the tribes of Issachar, Benjamin, Naphtali, Manasseh, Ephraim, and Asher. All of these went into Assyrian captivity.

Chapter 8 traces the genealogy of the tribe of Benjamin, with special reference to Saul and Jonathan.

Chapter 9 opens with a tremendous statement relative to the preservation of the genealogies.

So all Israel were reckoned by genealogies; and, behold, they were written in the book of the kings of Israel and Judah, who were carried away to Babylon for their transgression [1 Chron. 9:1].

Apparently the genealogies of each tribe of Israel were on exhibit in the temple. They were registered until the people went away into captivity. However, the genealogies were preserved and brought back to Jerusalem. When the returning remnant rebuilt the temple, the genealogies were there. At the time the Lord Jesus was born, those genealogies were intact, and you may be sure that the enemies of Jesus went in and checked His genealogy. As we have said, the Gospel of Matthew carries Joseph's genealogy, from whom He gets the legal title to the throne, and the Gospel of Luke carries Mary's genealogy, from which He gets the blood title to the throne of David. As far as we know, there never was an attack made upon the genealogy of the Lord Jesus Christ. It was accurate, and it was available for all to see.

When the temple was destroyed by Titus the Roman in A.D. 70, apparently the genealogies were also destroyed. However, the important thing to note is that here in Chronicles the genealogies are traced to the time of the captivity. Then after the return of a remnant of Israel, the genealogies were continued until the time the Lord Jesus Christ came into the world. After His lifetime the record disappeared. Why? Well, God was interested in making it very clear to us that Jesus was "very man of very man." God wants us to know that Jesus Christ came in the line of Adam and that He is the last Adam—there won't be a third one. Jesus heads up the last family here on earth. There are only two families: the family of Adam and the family of God.

Adam's family is a lost family, and you and I were born into it. We were born sinners, alienated from God, with no capacity for God. This alienation is obvious as we look around the world today. The entire human family is in Adam's family—and "in Adam all die." It is a very dismal prospect that we have in Adam.

However, we have hope in Christ, the last Adam. He heads the other family, the family of God. He is called the second man because the Lord is going to make a whole lot of other men in this new family. And that genealogy goes right back to the One who is born of the Spirit. If you today can say, "I came to Christ and trusted Him. He is my Savior, and the Spirit of God has made Him real to me," then you belong to the last Adam's family. In this family there is *life*. The Lord Jesus said that is what He brought. In fact He said, "I am the life." He also said, "I am come that they might have life, and that they might have it more abundantly" (John 10:10). He makes life more than mere existence or an exciting trip on drugs or alcohol. The trip with Him will eventuate in a trip to heaven—into His very presence.

The remainder of chapter 9 is an emphasis upon the tribe of Levi.

Now the first inhabitants that dwelt in their possessions in their cities were, the Israelites, the priests, Levites, and the Nethinims [1 Chron. 9:2].

It means that the first *of* the Israelites was of the tribe of Levi—first the priests, those who had the service of God, then the Levites. You see, not all of the tribe of Levi served in the priesthood. The family of Aaron served as priests. The others were more or less custodians of the temple.

Then the Nethinims are mentioned. The word *Nethinims* means "servants." They could have been slaves. There is a question as to whether or not Israel had slaves. I think they did, but not of their own brethren. Essentially that is what the Gibeonites had become. They were used in the service of the temple—probably swept out the place, polished the brass, and things like that.

Let me point out another interesting verse from this chapter.

And these are the singers, chief of the fathers of the Levites, who remaining in the chambers were free: for they were employed in that work day and night [1 Chron. 9:33].

There was a great deal of singing going on, which was directed by certain Levites. (If I were an Israelite, I would certainly know I didn't belong to the tribe of Levi, because I can't sing.) In Israel music was developed to a very high degree. You may recall that David was very much interested in music. In fact, he was called the sweet psalmist of Israel, and the majority of the psalms came from his pen.

The chapter concludes with the genealogy of the family of Saul. It follows through Saul and his son Jonathan, which is quite remarkable.

Chapter 9 concludes the genealogy of

Chronicles. It is the longest genealogy in Scripture, and there is nothing like it in the literature or history of the world. It begins with Adam and goes to Jesus Christ. It begins with the first Adam and goes to the last Adam. It is the greatest genealogical table in existence. It tells us that all of us are in the same family. Of course no one can trace his genealogy back to Adam in our day, because the genealogies were destroyed when Titus the Roman burned the temple in A.D. 70. Nevertheless, we can tell the general route by which we came from Adam. Many of us go back through Japheth, some of us go back through Ham, some of us go back through Shem, but we all go back to Adam.

It is interesting and important to note the glaring omissions in the genealogies recorded here in Chronicles. For example, Cain and his family are not even mentioned. Didn't Adam have a son by the name of Cain? Yes, but he is not listed here because his line ended. It was destroyed in the Flood as recorded in Genesis 7. Also I think there are omissions in all of the genealogical tables—even in Genesis. This may throw light on the very important question of the age of man. How old is mankind? It is my personal opinion that mankind is older than 6000 years. I think he has been on this earth a long time. However, when God created him, he was Adam, a *man*, not a monkey!

Perhaps you have seen the satirical cartoon directed at the theory of evolution and man's vaunted civilization and so-called progress. It pictures a scene of devastation. All the atomic bombs have been exploded, and man has at last destroyed himself. The last vestige of life has disappeared—with two exceptions. There are two monkeys sitting on a tree which is stripped of all its leaves and most of its limbs. There they sit, surveying this scene of desolation. All human life has disappeared. The caption of the cartoon reads, "Now we're going to have to do it all over again!"

Of course the Scriptures assure us that mankind will not commit suicide. But what about man's progress? He has been on this earth a long time since the days of Adam.

Psychology attempts to tabulate and classify man according to his I.Q. It is a rather mechanical device, of course, and it classifies him mechanically according to his achievements and his aptitudes. On one end of the scale is "subnormal," on the other end is "supernormal" or "genius," and somewhere in between is "normal." However, God's tests are different. All must come under His classification. Do you know what God says? God says none of them are normal—". . . all have sinned, and come short of the glory of God" (Rom. 3:23).

There are three universal facts in relationship to man which are true without exception:

1. Adam and all his children must die. In the beginning, God said to Adam, "In the day that thou eatest thereof thou shalt surely die" (Gen. 2:17). However, God did not create man to die. Scripture tells us that ". . . by *man* came death, and death passed upon all men . . ." (Rom. 5:12, paraphrased). It also says, ". . . in Adam all die . . ." (1 Cor. 15:22). And, ". . . it is appointed unto men once to die . . ." (Heb. 9:27). This earth on which you and I live is nothing but a great big graveyard. David said on his deathbed, "I go the way of all the earth" (1 Kings 2:2). All the freeways today eventually lead to the cemetery. "Though I walk through the valley of the shadow of death" (Ps. 23:4) is the picture of man going through life. Like a monster, death stalks this earth.

There are three kinds of death: physical death, spiritual death, and eternal death. Adam did not die physically until about 900 years after he ate the prohibited fruit. But he died spiritually instantly. Death means separation. Physical death is separation of the spirit from the body. Spiritual death means the separation of man from God. And eternal death means the separation of man from God. Eternal death is separation from God eternally. That is what hell will be—a place where God never goes, my friend. There is no blessing, nor mercy, nor love of God there.

2. Another universal fact is that Adam and all his children are sinners. God says of us, "All have sinned." The proof of this statement is that all die—"in Adam all die." All sinned in Adam.

Abraham was a good man, but Abraham sinned—Ishmael is an evidence of that. Caleb was a good man and outstanding, but he had his concubine. And sin has driven contemporary man away from God. He is in open rebellion against God. He has gone out, as did Cain, from the presence of the Lord.

Chapter 59 of Isaiah is a chapter everyone ought to read. Let me quote just one verse: "But your iniquities have separated between you and your God, and your sins have hid his face from you, that he will not hear" (Isa. 59:2). Adam and his children are sinners, separated from God. Sin is a scourge, a sickness, a plague, which has infected the race. My friend, a heart condition is bad, but only a few of the human family have heart trouble. Cancer is terrible—I know it from personal experience—but a small percentage has cancer. However, *all* have sinned. Of course there is one grand exception to this: the Lord Jesus Christ didn't have to die because He did not sin. He challenged His enemies, "Which of you convinceth me of sin? . . ." (John 8:46). No one did. He said, "No man taketh it [my life] from me, but I lay it down of myself. I have power to lay it down, and I have power to take it again . . ." (John 10:18). The Lord Jesus is the exception to the universality of sin. However, He is the *only* exception. The rest of us have sinned.

3. The third universal fact is that Adam and all his children have obtained mercy. Enoch was saved. How? By faith. Noah was a good man, but he wasn't saved because of that. It was by *faith* that Noah prepared an ark to the saving of his house. Abraham was a good man, but he sinned. Abraham believed God, and *that* was counted unto him for righteousness. Actually that is the problem in the Near East today. Is it possible that Abraham's sin is the cause of continual fighting between Israel and the Arab countries? Absolutely. If he, through that little Egyptian maid Hagar, had not brought Ishmael into the world, the Arabs wouldn't be over there today. David also was a great man of God, but we all agree that David sinned. And, my, God was certainly merciful to him! God is rich in mercy. Paul said to the Ephesians, "But God, who is rich in mercy, for his great love wherewith he loved us, Even when we were dead in sins, hath quickened us together with Christ, (by grace ye are saved;)" (Eph 2:4–5). And Peter said, "Blessed be the God and Father of our Lord Jesus Christ, which according to his abundant mercy hath begotten us again unto a lively hope by the resurrection of Jesus Christ from the dead" (1 Pet. 1:3). Our God has made it possible for the children of Adam to obtain mercy.

Have you received mercy from the hand of God yet? It is there for you.

This glorious truth is only part of the message that we find here in the genealogies of the first nine chapters of 1 Chronicles. It is the genealogy of the family of Adam, and you and I are in it. We all belong to the same race. We are all fallen in nature. We are all on an equality; we are born equal in the sense that we all have sinned and come short of the glory of God. And salvation today is for all mankind.

CHAPTER 10

THEME: *Saul's Reign*

Here we can see the distinction that God is making between the Books of Samuel and Kings and the Books of Chronicles. In the Books of Samuel we find a great deal about King Saul. In fact, his entire history is given there. When we come to Chronicles and see God's viewpoint, we find only one chapter given. The rest of 1 Chronicles is all about David, and it goes on into 2 Chronicles with the history of David's family. David is the subject, not Saul. Down here from the human viewpoint Saul occupied a prominent place. That is why it is amazing here to find only one chapter devoted to Saul.

Now what is the subject of this chapter? Did the Lord pick out some outstanding performance of Saul? No. Works do not commend a person to God. The chapter is not about Saul's works. It is about his death and how he was slain.

I am of the opinion that a great many men and women who have occupied a large place in human history will not get much of a write-up in heaven. This is certainly true of Saul!

You will recall that when we were studying 1 and 2 Samuel, we attempted to determine who had slain Saul. Who was the one that was responsible for his murder? Or did he commit suicide? The record in those books goes something like this: Saul was mortally wounded in the battle with the Philistines. Then he told his armorbearer to kill him because he didn't want the disgrace of being killed by a Philistine. The armorbearer refused to take his sword to kill the king. So Saul fell on his own sword. Was Saul physically able to kill himself? Did he commit suicide? That has always been a question. Then a young man of the Amalekites told David that when he came upon the scene, Saul was still alive and that

Saul had asked him to kill him. The young Amalekite claimed that he was the one who had slain King Saul, and he brought Saul's crown and bracelet to David to prove his story. King David had the Amalekite slain, saying, ". . . Thy blood be upon thy head; for thy mouth hath testified against thee, saying, I have slain the LORD'S anointed" (2 Sam. 1:16). Now who is responsible for the death of King Saul? We almost need to call in the FBI. But actually it won't be necessary to call them into the case, because we will have a confession here from the one who is responsible for Saul's death.

Now the Philistines fought against Israel; and the men of Israel fled from before the Philistines, and fell down slain in mount Gilboa.

And the Philistines followed hard after Saul, and after his sons; and the Philistines slew Jonathan, and Abinadab, and Malchi-shua, the sons of Saul.

And the battle went sore against Saul, and the archers hit him, and he was wounded of the archers [1 Chron. 10: 1–3].

He was wounded by the Philistines, but he did not die from that wound.

Then said Saul to his armour-bearer, Draw thy sword, and thrust me through therewith; lest these uncircumcised come and abuse me. But his armour-bearer would not; for he was sore afraid. So Saul took a sword, and fell upon it.

And when his armour-bearer saw that Saul was dead, he fell likewise on the sword, and died.

So Saul died, and his three sons, and all his house died together.

And when all the men of Israel that were in the valley saw that they fled, and that Saul and his sons were dead, then they forsook their cities, and fled: and the Philistines came and dwelt in them [1 Chron. 10:4–7].

I assume from this record that when that Amalekite came along, Saul was already dead. The Amalekite knew that David and Saul had been enemies, so he went into the presence of David and took credit for the slaying of Saul. The motive which he had was the hope that David would bestow some honor upon him and give him some reward for the slaying of Saul. He didn't dream that David would react as he did. David executed him on his own confession—David said that he was condemned out of his own mouth. However, it appears that the young man was lying, and that he really did not slay the king.

And it came to pass on the morrow, when the Philistines came to strip the slain, that they found Saul and his sons fallen in mount Gilboa.

And when they had stripped him, they took his head, and his armour, and sent into the land of the Philistines round about, to carry tidings unto their idols, and to the people.

And they put his armour in the house of their gods, and fastened his head in the temple of Dagon [1 Chron. 10:8–10].

The Philistines did this terrible dishonor to Saul's body. The temple of Dagon was in Ashdod. You remember that Samson had pulled down the pillars in the temple of Dagon when they were making sport of him there. Now this is where the Philistines brought the head and the armor of Saul.

And when all Jabesh-gilead heard all that the Philistines had done to Saul,

They arose, all the valiant men, and took away the body of Saul, and the bodies of his sons, and brought them to Jabesh, and buried their bones under the oak in Jabesh, and fasted seven days [1 Chron. 10:11–12].

Does this close the case? No, we still haven't been told who really killed King Saul. But the final verses of this chapter will give us the confession we have been waiting for.

So Saul died for his transgression which he committed against the LORD, even against the word of the LORD, which he kept not, and also for asking counsel of one that had a familiar spirit, to inquire of it;

And inquired not of the LORD: therefore he slew him, and turned the kingdom unto David the son of Jesse [1 Chron. 10:13–14].

Now, who was it that slew Saul? It says that he inquired not of the Lord; therefore He slew him. Who is *he?* The Lord is the One who took his life. It is as Job said, ". . . the LORD gave, and the LORD hath taken away; blessed be the name of the LORD" (Job 1:21). The Lord takes the responsibility.

God says that He removed Saul. God executed him. Do you wish to find fault with the Lord? Can God be arrested for murder? My friend, God has taken many a person. By the way, that is the reason God says you and I are never to take a human life. The Lord gave and the Lord hath taken away. Until you and I can *give* life, we have no business in taking life. Only God can give life; so God can take away life, and for Him it is not murder. For you and me it is murder to take a life, and we must surrender our own lives when we do it. This is the reason David executed the Amalekite when he claimed he had murdered King Saul.

Why was Saul executed? He died "for his transgression which he committed against the LORD, even against the word of the LORD, which he kept not, and also for asking counsel of one that had a familiar spirit"—Saul turned to Satan for advice. For these reasons God took his life. In the New Testament we find that God took the lives of Ananias and Sapphira. A great many people give Simon Peter the credit (or the blame) for that. I believe that Simon Peter was the most surprised person there that day. God was the One responsible for their deaths. And Saul died because of his transgression. Many times God reaches in and takes a human life because of that.

I have lived long enough now so that I can look back and see that many times God has put a man aside. He can put a man on the shelf by putting him out of His service. He can remove him from an office. God moves in the affairs of men. God has not abdicated today. He is still running the universe. It is His universe and He will run it His way. If He wants to remove someone, that is His business, not yours or mine. He is not accountable to us, but we are accountable to Him. He is the One who calls the shots. He is the One who is the umpire, and He will make the decisions.

By the way, to whom are you listening today? Do you hear God's voice? Or are you listening to man's voice, even to Satan's voice? This is the sin that causes God to move into the affairs of men.

What a chapter this is! It throws heaven's light on a very moot subject.

CHAPTERS 11–12

***THEME:** David's Reign*

We have now come to the third major division of 1 Chronicles. The first nine chapters recorded the remarkable genealogies. The second division, only one chapter, was on the reign of King Saul.

From God's viewpoint Saul did not make anywhere near the splash that many of the people in his day thought he had. He did not impress God. The Lord records his death and the reason for it but gives us nothing about the accomplishments of Saul.

Now we come to the section which deals with the reign of King David. First we will see David's mighty men (chs. 11–12), then David and the ark (chs. 13–16), David and the temple (ch. 17), David's wars (chs. 18–20), David's sin in numbering the people (ch. 21), and David's preparation and organization for building the temple in chapters 22–29.

The remainder of this book is about David and David's reign. In fact, the genealogy that is given in the first chapters brings us up to David, and beyond into the family of David. The next book, 2 Chronicles, will follow the story of the line of David. There is practically no attention given to the northern kingdom after it rebelled and withdrew from the reign of David's family.

It is also well to note as we go along how God puts the emphasis on certain things in David's life and plays down others. You will notice that I called chapter 21 "David's Sin." It has nothing to do with his sin with Bathsheba, which is the sin which immediately comes to the minds of men when they speak of David. Rather, God records his sin in numbering the people. In God's sight this was the greatest sin.

I believe there is a tremendous lesson for us in this. Many Christians consider certain things as sin, and other things they don't consider sin at all. I believe that when we get into God's presence we will find that we have had some false notions in this connection. What they thought was a great sin may not have been one and, what they thought was slight and unimportant, God put down as sin.

In David's life everyone could point the finger at him relative to his sin with Bathsheba. And God punished him for that sin—it was a terrible sin. But God forgave him of that because he came in confession to the Lord. Although this matter of numbering the people may seem insignificant to us, we shall see that it was rather important as far as God was concerned—and we'll see why.

This should cause all of us to get a different perspective of what sin really is. We need to recognize sin not only in the sense of acts—things to do and not to do—but also sins of the thoughts and intents. We need to study the Word of God in order to understand *God's* perspective of sin.

Then all Israel gathered themselves to David unto Hebron, saying, Behold, we are thy bone and thy flesh [1 Chron. 11:1].

You will recall back in Samuel, which covered this period of history, we were told that for seven years David reigned over the two tribes in the south, Judah and Benjamin, and his capital was Hebron. That is all passed over in Chronicles. Why? Because God looks at Israel as one nation of twelve tribes. From God's perspective, David really became king when he became the king over all of Israel and all twelve of the tribes of Israel accepted him, and said, "We are thy bone and thy flesh."

And moreover in time past, even when Saul was king, thou wast he that leddest out and broughtest in Israel: and the Lord thy God said unto thee, Thou shalt feed my people Israel, and thou shalt be ruler over my people Israel [1 Chron. 11:2].

They were acknowledging the hand of God in this. David did not become king until the people accepted him as being God's choice, which was seven years after he began to reign over Judah and Benjamin.

Therefore came all the elders of Israel to the king to Hebron; and David made a covenant with them in Hebron before the Lord; and they anointed David king over Israel, according to the word of the Lord by Samuel [1 Chron. 11:3].

Now he is made king over all twelve tribes. From God's viewpoint, this is when David began his reign.

And David and all Israel went to Jerusalem, which is Jebus; where the Jebusites were, the inhabitants of the land [1 Chron. 11:4].

David had inspected that land. I think that he had been over that land with a fine-toothed comb and probably knew it better than the spies that had been sent in by Joshua. He knew a great deal about it, and Jerusalem was the city that he had chosen to become the capital. It was the place where the temple was to be built. It was David's choice, and it was the Lord's choice.

A great deal is said in the Word of God about the city of Jerusalem. Of course it is not the city of Jerusalem as we see it today. Many of you have visited Jerusalem or seen pictures of it. Excavations in recent years have revealed that the wall in early times went the opposite direction from the way it goes today. The city of David was down below, and they always looked up to the temple. Later on, when the walls were moved, and built up on Mount Zion and higher up, one looked down to the temple area. It is this way today. A great deal of the city of Jerusalem is above the temple area.

The temple area is located on Mount Moriah, which goes like a ridge right through Jerusalem today. And over there, outside the wall, on that ridge is where Golgotha is located, the place of the skull where Jesus was crucified. This is the place David chose.

And the inhabitants of Jebus said to David, Thou shalt not come hither. Nevertheless David took the castle of Zion, which is the city of David [1 Chron. 11:5].

David took the castle of Zion, and it was there that he built his palace. Mount Zion was very precious to David.

And David said, Whosoever smiteth the Jebusites first shall be chief and captain. So Joab the son of Zeruiah went first up, and was chief [1 Chron. 11:6].

Joab is the number one man in the service of David. He was an adviser to David, and he was the number one man who led the army. He belonged to the mighty men of David. You will recall that we were told something about his exploits when he first came to David, incidents of how he led the army and how he fought for David. This man became the captain. You might say that he was the one in charge of the Pentagon in David's day. He had command of all the brass—the army and navy, and whatever else they might have had. He had charge of it all.

And David dwelt in the castle; therefore they called it the city of David [1 Chron. 11:7].

The "city of David" is actually the Mount Zion area. Apparently it was here that David's palace was constructed. David loved Mount Zion.

And he built the city round about, even from Millo round about: and Joab repaired the rest of the city [1 Chron. 11:8].

Joab was not only in charge of David's military, he was in charge of the urban renewal program.

So David waxed greater and greater: for the LORD of hosts was with him [1 Chron 11:9].

David brought Israel up to the place where it was a great kingdom and had tremendous influence throughout the world. David laid the foundation on which Solomon was able to bring a witness to the world of that day.

DAVID'S MIGHTY MEN

David's mighty men are those who came to him during the time of his rejection. Now that he has been elevated to the place of kingship, these men are elevated also.

There is a corollary here that we cannot pass by. Today the Lord Jesus Christ is calling out a people to His name; they are His "mighty men." And these are the days of Christ's rejection. His own people said, "We will not have this man rule over us." He has not assumed His position on the throne as King of kings and Lord of lords. David also was a rejected man, although he had been anointed king of Israel. Saul was still reigning—God gave him every opportunity to make good, but he did not. During those years, David was fleeing for his life; it was the period of his rejection. And there came to him from every side men who put themselves under his command. They became David's mighty men. In our day, Christ is rejected by the world. I don't have to labor to make that point. If we can't see that, we can't see anything. You and I live in a world where the Lord Jesus Christ is rejected. But during this period He is calling out a people to His name. He is our Savior, our Lord and Master today, so we will have to wait until He comes to the place of Kingship. Then, we are told, we are to reign with Him.

Since our Lord is rejected, I don't know why in the world some believers attempt to become the most popular people in town. They cannot be. The Lord Jesus said that since the world hated Him, it would hate us also.

If you are popular with the world today, it is time to take a long look at yourself. The late Dr. Bob Schuller used to say, "I judge a man not by the friends he has but by the enemies he has. If you have the right kind of enemies, you are all right." My friend, if you are a true believer in the Lord Jesus Christ, then the devil's crowd will be your enemies. We are living in the period of Christ's rejection, and He is calling out His mighty men.

The three men who were singled out as being the mightiest were the men who brought water from the well of Bethlehem to David. This is a tremendous story.

Now three of the thirty captains went down to the rock to David, into the cave of Adullam; and the host of the Philistines encamped in the valley of Rephaim.

And David was then in the hold, and the Philistines' garrison was then at Bethlehem.

And David longed, and said, Oh that one would give me drink of the water of the well of Beth-lehem, that is at the gate!

And the three brake through the host of the Philistines, and drew water out of the well of Beth-lehem, that was by the gate, and took it, and brought it to David: but David would not drink of it, but poured it out to the LORD,

And said, My God forbid it me, that I should do this thing: shall I drink the blood of these men that have put their lives in jeopardy? for with the jeopardy of their lives they brought it. Therefore he would not drink it. These things did these three mightiest [1 Chron. 11: 15–19].

David had been brought up in Bethlehem. That was his hometown. There was a well at the entrance there and, many a time after he had been out with his sheep, he had come back thirsty and had stopped at that well to get a drink. Now the Philistines have him holed up and he cannot get to that well. He said, "I sure would like to have a drink from that well." It was just a wish, not a command. These three men broke through the lines of the Philistines and got the water and brought it to David. The interesting thing is that he would not drink it, but he poured it out as a drink offering to God.

There are some analogies we can make from this. Jesus was born at Bethlehem, and He is that Water from Bethlehem; He is the Water of Life. There are many of the mighty men of Jesus Christ who down through the centuries have taken this Water to a thirsty world. I think of Livingstone, Judson, Henry Martin, and other wonderful missionaries of the past. Then there are all the missionaries today. I have visited them in Mexico, South America, Africa, Asia, and Europe. These are the ones who have left everything to penetrate barriers in order to get the Word of God to a thirsty world. The Lord takes note of them, my friend. They are listed among the mighty men.

Notice how David's men responded when he merely expressed a wish—he would never have given such a command. Yet our Lord has *commanded* us to take the Water of Life to the whole world. And what have we done with it? Are you obeying His orders?

Notice what David did with the water that was brought to him at such tremendous risk. David was unselfish—no wonder his men loved him. They were willing to suffer for him because he was willing to suffer with them. He wouldn't take that drink because his men didn't have water, and he chose to take his place with them.

Psalm 22:14 tells us that when the Lord Jesus died on the cross He said, "I am poured out like water. . . ." He poured His life out like water on the ground. He took His place down here as one of us—". . . unto us a child is born, unto us a son is given . . ." (Isa. 9:6). He took our hell that we might share His heaven.

And, my friend, if we are to be rewarded by Him, we are to make a sacrifice for Him.

There is another incident in this chapter that I have always appreciated.

Benaiah the son of Jehoiada, the son of a valiant man of Kabzeel, who had done many acts; he slew two lionlike men of Moab: also he went down and slew a lion in a pit in a snowy day [1 Chron. 11:22].

I love that. He slew a lion. Did you notice when he did it? He did it on a snowy day. Our Lord took note of that. I also think the Lord takes note of faithful people who will come to church rain or shine.

Now in chapter 12 there is only one incident which I would like to call to your attention.

There were some men of the tribe of Gad who came to David during the time of his rejection. This is what is recorded of them:

These were of the sons of Gad, captains of the host: one of the least was over an hundred, and the greatest over a thousand.

These are they that went over Jordan in the first month, when it had overflown all his banks; and they put to flight all them of the valleys, both toward the east, and toward the west.

And there came of the children of Benjamin and Judah to the hold unto David.

And David went out to meet them, and answered and said unto them, If ye be come peaceably unto me to help me, mine heart shall be knit unto you: but if ye be come to betray me to mine enemies, seeing there is no wrong in mine hands, the God of our fathers look thereon, and rebuke it.

Then the spirit came upon Amasai, who was chief of the captains, and he said, Thine are we, David, and on thy side, thou son of Jesse: peace, peace be unto thee, and peace be to thine helpers; for thy God helpeth thee. Then David received them, and made them captains of the band [1 Chron. 12:14–18].

Here is a group of men who came to David. They swam the Jordan River at flood time. They were just about to give up and David went down to meet them. He didn't know whether they were friends or enemies and he said in effect, "If you mean to harm me, I'll destroy you." They said, "Oh no, David, we have come over to be on your side." They wanted to live for David. They wanted to be on his side and in his service.

Too many Christians who want to be in the service of the Lord think that it is just a matter of being busy. However, the point is: do you want to live for Christ? That is what these men from Gad were saying to David. "We want to be on your side, David. We want to yield ourselves to you and live for you."

We can carry this spiritual application a step further. Christ has brought you over "Jordan" by His death and resurrection, and He has blessed you with all spiritual blessings. But you have to return to the world to live the Christian life. The Lord Jesus prayed for His own, "I pray not that thou shouldest take them out of the world, but that thou shouldest keep them from the evil" (John 17:15). We are to live the Christian life here and now. My friend, the only place you ever will have an opportunity to live the Christian life is right down here on this earth. And to do this, you will have to yield to Christ. This idea today that living the Christian life is a cheap sort of thing, that it is compromise and hypocrisy, is dead wrong. You will have to swim the water. It will cost you something. You will have to go to the One who is greater than David—to the Lord Jesus—and surrender to Him. Oh, what joy it is to be in His service!

CHAPTERS 13–16

***THEME:** David and the ark*

In this section we see God's viewpoint of David's first attempt to bring the ark of the covenant to Jerusalem. During the period of the judges, you may recall, the ark had been captured in war by the Philistines. Because it had caused them no end of trouble, they placed it on a new cart and sent it back to Israel (1 Sam. 6). From that time to this, the ark had remained in the house of Abinadab at Kirjath-jearim. Now David makes an attempt to bring the ark to his capital, which is Jerusalem. God took note of this because it pleased Him that David was putting an emphasis on spiritual matters.

However, David starts off on the wrong foot, as we shall see.

And David consulted with the captains of thousands and hundreds, and with every leader [1 Chron. 13:1].

David now is Israel's new king. As he comes to the throne, he has tremendous plans, he has great vision, and he wants to bring the ark to Jerusalem. So he consults with "every leader." I feel that David made a mistake in consulting all these men. God was leading him and giving him direction; he didn't need human advice.

As I see it, there is a serious problem developing in many churches today because there are too many men who want to have their fingers in the pie. That is, they (especially the boards of churches) want to make the decisions. The problems arise because many of those men are not spiritually equipped to make decisions. Many times their wrong decisions hurt the cause of Christ.

It seems to me that David made a mistake by consulting with all of these leaders. He got into trouble by listening to everybody.

And David said unto all the congregation of Israel, If it seem good unto you, and that it be of the LORD our God, let us send abroad unto our brethren every where, that are left in all the land of Israel, and with them also to the priests and Levites which are in their cities and suburbs, that they may gather themselves unto us:

And let us bring again the ark of our God to us: for we inquired not at it in the days of Saul [1 Chron. 13:2–3].

This is a sidelight on the days of Saul. During that period the worship of God in the tabernacle was entirely omitted. As a result, the entire tabernacle organization was broken up. The Levites were scattered. Now word is sent out throughout the entire land that David wants to bring up the ark.

And all the congregation said that they would do so: for the thing was right in the eyes of all the people [1 Chron. 13:4].

The decision is unanimous. They all want the ark brought to Jerusalem.

So David gathered all Israel together, from Shihor of Egypt even unto the entering of Hemath, to bring the ark of

God from Kirjath-jearim [1 Chron. 13:5].

In 1 Samuel 7 we have the record of the ark being taken to Kirjath-jearim and left there because they had had a bad experience with it.

And David went up, and all Israel, to Baalah, that is to Kirjath-jearim, which belonged to Judah, to bring up thence the ark of God the LORD, that dwelleth between the cherubims, whose name is called on it [1 Chron. 13:6].

Of course, God did not *live* in the ark, nor between the cherubims, but that is the place He designated as His meeting place with the people of Israel. His presence was there.

Now they will make their big mistake. As someone has put it, this is doing a right thing in a wrong way. It was right to bring the ark up to Jerusalem, but the method of doing it was wrong.

And they carried the ark of God in a new cart out of the house of Abinadab: and Uzza and Ahio drove the cart [1 Chron. 13:7].

God had given explicit directions as to how the ark was to be carried. Other parts of the tabernacle could be transported on carts, but not the ark. Notice what God had said to Moses: "And when Aaron and his sons have made an end of covering the sanctuary, and all the vessels of the sanctuary, as the camp is to set forward; after that the sons of Kohath shall come to bear it: but they shall not touch any holy thing, lest they die. These things are the burden of the sons of Kohath in the tabernacle of the congregation" (Num. 4:15). The ark was never to be carried on a wagon. It was to be borne on the shoulders of the sons of Kohath. Why? Well, the ark speaks of Christ, and He is to be carried, even today, by individuals.

A lot of people would like to do it the easy way. My friend, it will require work to get out the Word of God. Many people complain about the expense. I deplore the expense myself, but I want to tell you that it will cost us to get out the Word of God. We can't put it on a wagon. We must carry it. Each one needs to shoulder his own pack. So let's get it out. Paul says, "For every man shall bear his own burden" (Gal. 6:5). That is another way of saying that each one must shoulder his own pack.

In other words, all of us have to put our shoulders to the wheel to get the Word of God out to a world that desperately needs it. God doesn't write the gospel in the sky; it has to be passed along by His children.

And David and all Israel played before God with all their might, and with singing, and with harps, and with psalteries, and with timbrels, and with cymbals, and with trumpets [1 Chron. 13:8].

David was a great musician, and this was an occasion of real joy. But it was all interrupted very suddenly.

And when they came unto the threshingfloor of Chidon, Uzza put forth his hand to hold the ark; for the oxen stumbled.

And the anger of the LORD was kindled against Uzza, and he smote him, because he put his hand to the ark: and there he died before God [1 Chron. 13:9–10].

Why? Because they were doing it wrong. They were not giving the right testimony. "But," you may say, "this was certainly a severe sort of thing—a man just put his hand on it!" Well, to begin with, the ark should not have been on that cart. And the ark did not need Uzza to steady it.

Today there are many folk who are putting their hands in the Lord's work where they should not be putting them. They are interfering with the Lord's work. I could tell you of many instances of men, probably meaning well, but not doing it God's way. As a result, blessing does not come. Just so in the case of the ark—the man who interfered was put out of the way.

And David was displeased, because the LORD had made a breach upon Uzza: wherefore that place is called Perez-uzza to this day [1 Chron. 13:11].

David was displeased by it, as much as you would be, and as much as the critic is today.

And David was afraid of God that day, saying, How shall I bring the ark of God home to me? [1 Chron. 13:12].

Oh, how often we attempt to do things our own way, and then when we fail, we blame it on God! We say, "How am I going to do this for the Lord?" Well, do it God's way. Turn it over to Him. That is what David finally had to do.

So David brought not the ark home to himself to the city of David, but carried it aside into the house of Obed-edom the Gittite.

And the ark of God remained with the family of Obed-edom in his house three months. And the LORD blessed the house of Obed-edom, and all that he had [1 Chron. 13:13–14].

This concludes the episode. The ark is not going to be brought up to Jerusalem at this time. God is blessing the family that has it now, but David is going to turn his attention to something else.

THE PROSPERITY OF KING DAVID

In chapter 14 we see that God is prospering David and that his fame is spreading.

Now Hiram king of Tyre sent messengers to David, and timber of cedars, with masons and carpenters, to build him an house [1 Chron. 14:1].

David and Hiram were great friends. We are told elsewhere that Hiram loved David. Here at the beginning of David's reign, Hiram wants to help him build his house, his palace.

And David perceived that the LORD had confirmed him king over Israel, for his kingdom was lifted up on high, because of his people Israel.

And David took more wives at Jerusalem: and David begat more sons and daughters [1 Chron. 14:2–3].

Now perhaps you are saying, "And God permitted this!" Yes, God permitted a multiplication of wives, but God did not approve of it. In fact, this will eventuate in God judging him, and it will bring sorrow to him for the rest of his life. It is wrong. This record is not given to us because God approved of it. But God wants us to know that this is exactly what happened. This is a historical record, and as we follow it we will discover God's attitude.

At one time, during the time of David's rejection, the Philistines thought he had become their man (1 Sam. 27). Now that he has returned to his own people and has been crowned as their king, the Philistines are out to get him.

And the Philistines came and spread themselves in the valley of Rephaim.

And David inquired of God, saying, Shall I go up against the Philistines? and wilt thou deliver them into mine hand? And the LORD said unto him, Go up; for I will deliver them into thine hand.

So they came up to Baal-perazim; and David smote them there. Then David said, God hath broken in upon mine enemies by mine hand like the breaking forth of waters: therefore they called the name of that place Baal-perazim.

And when they had left their gods there, David gave a commandment, and they were burned with fire [1 Chron. 14:9–12].

This was a great victory for David over the Philistines. And Israel hadn't had many victories over these people.

And the Philistines yet again spread themselves abroad in the valley.

Therefore David inquired again of God; and God said unto him, Go not up after them; turn away from them, and come upon them over against the mulberry trees [1 Chron. 14:13–14].

David could have said, "Well, here are the Philistines back again to fight against me. I had victory before, so I'll go out against them again." No, he inquired of God, and God said he shouldn't do it. He told David to retreat and to draw the Philistines to the mulberry trees. There David would have the advantage.

There are a great many Christians who actually tempt the Lord. They don't trust Him; they actually tempt Him. They enter into some sort of a business, or an agreement, or they try to do something and, as the saying goes, they bite off more than they can chew. They claim to be doing it because they "trust the Lord." Well, what makes them think the Lord told them to do it that way?

My friend, God expects you and me to use sanctified common sense. I have known folk who say they are acting on faith, when it is not faith but presumption. They call it trusting the Lord but, actually, they do these things when the Lord never indicated to them that they should.

God wants us to use sanctified common sense and to wait for His leading. Everything that is called faith is not actually faith. I have seen folk make shipwreck of faith in that way.

A dear lady came to the church where I served in Pasadena years ago. She said she was going to a faith healer and I advised her not to. I thought she should go to a doctor. She said, "Oh, Dr. McGee, you are so wrong. God is going to heal me. You think I ought not to go to this faith healer but I am going and I will be healed." She went and she was not healed. She couldn't understand it. She thought God was going to heal her. The whole affair made shipwreck of that woman's faith and she got to the place where she completely turned her back upon God. She said, "He let me down." No, He didn't. He doesn't want us to do something very foolish. He wants us to use good old sanctified common sense. She should have gone to a doctor. Her foolishness eventuated in her death.

My friend, of course we need to trust the Lord. But we need to make sure we are getting our directions from Him. Sometimes we are to go out and do battle, and sometimes we are to withdraw.

And it shall be, when thou shalt hear a sound of going in the tops of the mulberry trees, that then thou shalt go out to battle: for God is gone forth before thee to smite the host of the Philistines [1 Chron. 14:15].

A pastor friend of mine came to tell me about a church he was going to serve; and, because I knew things about the church, I advised him not to go. He asked, "Why?" I answered, "You had better wait until you hear the 'sound of going in the tops of the mulberry trees' before you go there." You see, there are times when you and I are simply to wait until there is no doubt that God is preparing the way for us. This talk of stepping out on faith may not be faith at all. It may be presumption. Instead of trusting God, we may be tempting God. We need to wait for the Lord to give the signal, for that sound in the tops of the mulberry trees. We need to be careful that what we call stepping out on faith isn't simply a foolish move. Sometimes we are tempting God instead of trusting Him.

David therefore did as God commanded him: and they smote the host of the Philistines from Gibeon even to Gazer.

And the fame of David went out into all lands; and the LORD brought the fear of him upon all nations [1 Chron. 14:16–17].

This is why I said that David was one of the great world leaders. His kingdom was one of the great world kingdoms at that particular time. God was with this man. That little nation in that insignificant land became a great world power. This should not strike us as strange. There have been other instances like it in the history of the world. Venice, the city of Venice, ruled the world at one time—and it was just a city. So it is not a surprise that a little nation like Israel could be a world power. We are told the reason for it. Verse 2 told us that David perceived that the Lord had confirmed him king over Israel, and verse 17 tells us that the Lord brought the fear of him upon all nations. It was God who brought David to world power.

As we have seen, chapters 13–16 are devoted to David and the ark—that is, of his bringing the ark up to Jerusalem to the place he had chosen. This is quite interesting in view of the fact that these chapters could be giving us a report of the business of the state, some of the many decisions that David made, treaties he signed with the surrounding nations, wars he fought, even accounts of state dinners and other state functions. It could be very much like a newscast we would see on television today. Instead these chapters tell us about the moving of the ark.

There is a lesson in this for us. It helps us to see what is the important matter in the sight of God. We get the news and a lot of propaganda on our newscasts. What do you think would be God's viewpoint of the news today? Would the emphasis be where we find it on CBS or NBC or XYZ? Where does God put the emphasis? We should learn from this attention to the moving of the ark that God is interested in the worship of His people. The ark was the very heart and center of the worship for Israel. This is where God puts the emphasis.

History itself should teach us that all too often we put the emphasis on passing things. Once there was a busy staff in the palace of Napoleon in Paris. Today it is a museum. There are no important decisions being made there today. We think of Versailles and how beautiful it is. How important it was in the past. Great decisions were made there, but now it is just a showcase. It is something for tourists to visit—that is all. It would have been well to have known what God thought was important during those years.

Another question arises. What happened to the tabernacle? My feeling is that it was worn out. After all, it was a tent, made largely of cloth. The golden boards, the brass pillars, and the silver bases were probably taken by the Philistines. There is no record of what happened to the tabernacle other than the ark. The important thing was the ark. Why? Because crowning the ark was the mercy seat. That is the place where God met the people of Israel.

The important thing for you and for me is to have a place where we can receive mercy from God. All of us need God's mercy. God is prepared today to extend mercy because He has a mercy seat for us. "My little children, these things write I unto you, that ye sin not. And if any man sin, we have an advocate with the Father, Jesus Christ the righteous: And he is the propitiation for our sins: and not for ours only, but also for the sins of the whole world" (1 John 2:1–2). That word *propitiation* means "mercy seat." Christ is the mercy seat for our sins. Now this is important to God. Actually, it is not what you and I hear on television that is really important, and it is not the decisions made in Washington (although I do not belittle them), but the important decisions are God's decisions.

As we have seen, David attempted to bring the ark to Jerusalem. Although that was the proper thing to do, he did it in the wrong way. Not only had David chosen Jerusalem as the place for the ark, but God had chosen that same place. So it was important that the ark be brought to Jerusalem. The problem was that David tried to do it in the wrong way. God had given instructions in the Book of Numbers that the ark was to be carried on the shoulders of the Kohathites of the tribe of Levi. There could not be an easier way or any kind of short-cut method used.

My friend, getting out the Word of God today is not easy. Too many people think that the work of the Lord should be some kind of picnic and something very delightful. It is delightful to know one is doing His will out of love for Him—that always makes it a thrilling experience—but it does not make it easy.

God's Word needs to be carried by God's people. "So then faith cometh by hearing, and hearing by the word of God" (Rom. 10:17). God blesses the proclamation of His Word. Paul goes on to say that they have to hear, but how are they going to hear without a preacher? Paul also tells us: "For the preaching of the cross is to them that perish foolishness; but unto us which are saved it is the power of God" (1 Cor. 1:18). God wants the human family to hear His Word through human means. He doesn't write it in the sky. He expects us to preach it, my friend.

As we look around us, we see a restlessness. The church, having departed from the Word of God, is in as much disarray as any other institution. The theology of both Roman Catholicism and Protestantism is a shambles, my friend. Why? Because both got away from the Word of God, and as a result they are not doing it God's way. My firm conviction is that the most important matter is to get the ark of God on the move, by which I mean get the gospel going out, get the Word of God moving out to the human family. Let's put the emphasis where God puts it.

Now here in chapter 15 David is going to move the ark in the right way.

And David made him houses in the city of David, and prepared a place for the ark of God, and pitched for it a tent [1 Chron. 15:1].

God considers the preparation of a place for the ark—not David's housing project—the important matter. "David made him houses in the city of David" *was* a housing project, and I'm sure that was considered important by a great many people.

Then David said, None ought to carry the ark of God but the Levites: for them hath the LORD chosen to carry the ark of God, and to minister unto him for ever [1 Chron. 15:2].

My question is: David, why didn't you do this the first time? Why did you have to go through that sad experience before you did it the right way?

Well, that's the way most of us learn. The old cliché is accurate: hindsight is better than foresight. It is easy for me to tell David he should have done it right in the first place, and then McGee turns right around, and the next step I take, I do it wrong. Then I have to learn to do it God's way. I have a notion that is the experience of most of us.

And David gathered all Israel together to Jerusalem, to bring up the ark of the LORD unto his place, which he had prepared for it [1 Chron. 15:3].

Do you remember that in days gone by when America faced a crisis our national leaders called for a day of prayer? We don't do that any more. Instead we get the brain trust together and expect them to solve the problems. We have seen that the decisions of the brain trust in the past have been as foolish as though they had been made by children; yet we don't change our method. That is the tragedy of America in this dark hour in which we are living.

David thought it was important to gather

all Israel together to bring up the ark of the Lord. And God thought it was important. This is the reason He recorded it in Chronicles, which is His viewpoint of this historical period.

Now David prepares to move the ark the right way.

And David assembled the children of Aaron, and the Levites [1 Chron. 15:4].

Then he gives the chief of each family and the number of men each would furnish.

And David called for Zadok and Abiathar the priests, and for the Levites, for Uriel, Asaiah, and Joel, Shemaiah, and Eliel, and Amminadab,

And said unto them, Ye are the chief of the fathers of the Levites: sanctify yourselves, both ye and your brethren, that ye may bring up the ark of the LORD God of Israel unto the place that I have prepared for it [1 Chron. 15:11–12].

David had prepared a place for the ark, but we are not told exactly where it was. Was it the threshing floor of Araunah? Later on he bought that place for the site on which the temple was to be built. This is on the ridge called Mount Moriah, the place where Abraham offered Isaac. The ridge goes right through Jerusalem; and Golgotha, the place on which Christ was crucified, is located on this same ridge. I am of the opinion that the place David prepared for the ark was on Mount Moriah.

For because ye did it not at the first, the LORD our God made a breach upon us, for that we sought him not after the due order [1 Chron. 15:13].

You will recall that David blamed God at first; he thought He was wrong in taking the life of Uzza, but then he discovered he himself was the one who was wrong, and he is confessing that.

So the priests and the Levites sanctified themselves to bring up the ark of the LORD God of Israel [1 Chron. 15:14].

Have you noticed the repetition of the expression "the ark of the Lord God of Israel"? We get the impression that the ark is very important to God.

And the children of the Levites bare the ark of God upon their shoulders with the staves thereon, as Moses commanded according to the word of the LORD [1 Chron. 15:15].

He is referring to God's explicit instructions in the fourth chapter of Numbers.

David, we know, was a musician, and he wanted music with all of this.

And David spake to the chief of the Levites to appoint their brethren to be the singers with instruments of music, psalteries and harps and cymbals, sounding, by lifting up the voice with joy [1 Chron. 15:16].

David wanted the brass band, the orchestra, and all the choirs. It was to be a great day when the ark of God was brought to Jerusalem. This was the high point of David's coming to Jerusalem. God does not even record David's coming to Jerusalem to capture it from the Jebusites, nor does He record the great building project that David launched. Got puts the emphasis upon the spiritual, and I hope we get the message.

So David, and the elders of Israel, and the captains over thousands, went to bring up the ark of the covenant of the LORD out of the house of Obed-edom with joy [1 Chron. 15:25].

Oh, this was a great day!

And it came to pass, when God helped the Levites that bare the ark of the covenant of the LORD, that they offered seven bullocks and seven rams [1 Chron. 15:26].

All of these sacrifices pointed to Christ.

And David was clothed with a robe of fine linen, and all the Levites that bare the ark, and the singers, and Chenaniah the master of the song with the singers: David also had upon him an ephod of linen.

Thus all Israel brought up the ark of the covenant of the LORD with shouting, and with sound of the cornet, and with trumpets, and with cymbals, making a noise with psalteries and harps [1 Chron. 15:27–28].

What a day this was!

I have always wanted a big orchestra, but I never did have it in any church I served. I guess the Lord just didn't want me to have one. I believe one of the reasons the church service is so dead and the reason the world passes it by is that there is no evidence of joy.

Look at people going to any church today and see if they look happy.

Look at a newscast of a crowd at a baseball game, and you don't see a sad face in the whole lot. Even those who are losing don't seem to be sad. They all seem to be having a good time. The tragedy of the hour is that God's people don't seem to be having a good time. We ought to be!

I think the world in that day heard about David bringing up the ark to Jerusalem. I think there were visitors from other countries who went home and said, "You should have been in Jerusalem with me. It was a great day, a great day!"

Have you noticed that there is nothing in the newscasts, nothing on the front pages of the newspapers, which is spiritual or which shows the joy of the Lord? They will publish a freak sort of thing, an oddball news item about religion, or something about some religious nut. Today that which is spiritual and joyful has disappeared from the life of America. That is when we as a nation have begun to die, by the way.

Now, however, we see that not everybody was in accord with David in this celebration.

And it came to pass, as the ark of the covenant of the Lord came to the city of David, that Michal the daughter of Saul looking out at a window saw king David dancing and playing: and she despised him in her heart [1 Chron. 15:29].

Michal was King Saul's daughter and the first wife of David. She looked at him showing his enthusiasm and joy in serving the Lord, and she thought in her heart, *He is a religious fanatic!*

Oh, how we need men like David in our day. It does not have to be fanaticism, but we do need the underlying river of joy flowing through the hearts and lives of God's people. That is the great message in chapter 15.

THE ARK IS SETTLED IN ITS PLACE

In chapter 16 we find that the ark is placed in the tent David had prepared for it, and David provides for its perpetual care.

So they brought the ark of God, and set it in the midst of the tent that David had pitched for it: and they offered burnt sacrifices and peace offerings before God.

And when David had made an end of offering the burnt offerings and the peace offerings, he blessed the people in the name of the Lord.

And he dealt to every one of Israel, both man and woman, to every one a loaf of bread, and a good piece of flesh, and a flagon of wine [1 Chron. 16:1–3].

It was an occasion of great joy on the part of the people of Israel.

Then "they offered burnt sacrifices." As we saw in our study of Leviticus, the burnt sacrifices typified what God sees in Christ. The burnt offering ascended to the presence of God. Also they offered "peace offerings" which speak of the fact that Christ made peace by the blood of His cross. Everything is right between God and us when we come God's way through Christ.

The exaltation of the Person of Christ and the fact that He shed His blood is the gospel right here in the Old Testament.

And he appointed certain of the Levites to minister before the ark of the Lord, and to record, and to thank and praise the Lord God of Israel [1 Chron. 16:4].

We need to get so involved in the Word of God that we become enthusiastic. Anyone who is enthusiastic and excited about a football game is called a *fan*, but a person who feels that way about religion is called a fanatic! Well, we don't need fanatics, but we do need believers who get involved in the Word of God to the extent that they feel like thanking and praising the Lord God!

David had this organized. Asaph was the chief, and next to him was Zechariah—then a whole list of them. My, what a group of musicians he had there.

Now we see David's glorious psalm of thanksgiving.

Then on that day David delivered first this psalm to thank the Lord into the hand of Asaph and his brethren [1 Chron. 16:7].

We'll see this psalm again because it is Psalm 105. "O give thanks unto the Lord; call upon his name: make known his deeds among the people. Sing unto him, sing psalms unto him: talk ye of all his wondrous works" (Ps. 105:1–2). My friend, we need to talk about God and get His Word out. Unfortunately, many Christians today know more about the things advertised on television than they do about the Word of God. Also there are preachers among us who know more about the baseball clubs than they know about the Bible. In this computerized age we all are being pressed into a little form. My Christian friend, for God's sake get into the Word of God and learn what liberty is in Christ!

Give thanks unto the LORD, call upon his name, make known his deeds among the people [1 Chron. 16:8].

God has been moving in the past, and He is still moving today. He is not through with this little world and I think that His hand can be seen in the affairs of the world today.

Sing unto him, sing psalms unto him, talk ye of all his wondrous works [1 Chron. 16:9].

Singing is an important way in which to praise God. Although I can't sing, I can make a "joyful noise unto the Lord." I don't attempt to sing in public, but when I get in the car by myself, I really let go with a song. It doesn't sound good even to me, but I like to praise God.

Glory ye in his holy name: let the heart of them rejoice that seek the LORD.

Seek the LORD and his strength, seek his face continually [1 Chron 16:10–11].

James 4:8 tells us, "Draw nigh to God, and he will draw nigh to you. . . ." All we must do for salvation is to come to Christ and trust Him as our Savior. God has promised that we shall be saved. However that doesn't insure fellowship with God. We have to follow through with "Seek the Lord and his strength, seek his face continually."

Do you seek His face continually? What is the first thing you think about when you wake up in the morning? When you go to bed at night, what is the last thing you think about? Do you think about God all during the day? Or do you just leave God behind when you go to work or go to school or go to a social gathering?

Remember his marvellous works that he hath done, his wonders, and the judgments of his mouth [1 Chron. 16:12].

We were in the Hawaiian Islands, and one evening there was a glorious sunset. I called attention to it and said, "My, look at what God has done." God does things in such a magnificent way. He had plenty of light, a great big sun, a lot of sky, and big mountains. He let that sun go down and put a lot of color in it just so we could enjoy it. David calls attention to God's wonderful creation. He calls attention to God's works.

O ye seed of Israel his servant, ye children of Jacob, his chosen ones.

He is the LORD our God; his judgments are in all the earth [1 Chron 16:13–14].

God made judgments in all the earth at that time. I think that He is making judgments today. His hands are moving in the affairs of men. Oh, I know that Satan is the god of this world. I know that God has given him a certain amount of rope in the present age and that he is going to be turned loose in the Great Tribulation Period. That does not mean that God is not in control. God is finally going to close in on Satan and all his works because He is the God of judgment.

Be ye mindful always of his covenant; the word which he commanded to a thousand generations;

Even of the covenant which he made with Abraham, and of his oath unto Isaac;

And hath confirmed the same to Jacob for a law, and to Israel for an everlasting covenant [1 Chron. 16:15–17].

There are many people who would like to minimize the covenant that God made with Abraham. Well, my friend, David doesn't minimize that covenant. David says, "Let's talk about it." God's covenants are still important today. God made a covenant with Abraham and He hasn't gone back on it. God promised Abraham that He would give to him and to his offspring the land we call the Holy Land, and God is going to do it. When they get that land given to them from the hand of God, they will not need to fear the Egyptians or the Arabs or the Russians. They won't need to fear anyone because every man is going to dwell under his own vine and under his own fig tree in peace. In other words, people will own their own property. All the land belongs to God, and God will give it to them in His time.

Just as God made a covenant with Abraham and with his offspring, so God has also made covenants with us. He has promised us all spiritual blessings in Christ Jesus.

It is apparent that David understood that God had made a covenant with him regarding the land.

Saying, Unto thee will I give the land of Canaan, the lot of your inheritance;

When ye were but few, even a few, and strangers in it.

And when they went from nation to nation, and from one kingdom to another people;

He suffered no man to do them wrong: yea, he reproved kings for their sakes,

Saying, Touch not mine anointed, and do my prophets no harm [1 Chron. 16:18–22].

God had His protecting hand on the patriarchs as they moved about. This has primary reference, I am sure, to Abraham, Isaac, and Jacob, but it has application for us as well. We need to be very careful about laying a hand or a *tongue* on God's anointed. Before you criticize your pastor, ask yourself if you are hurting or helping the work of God.

Sing unto the LORD, all the earth; shew forth from day to day his salvation.

Declare his glory among the heathen; his marvellous works among all nations.

For great is the LORD, and greatly to be praised: he also is to be feared above all gods [1 Chron. 16:23–25].

Today all creation is groaning in pain waiting for the redemption of the sons of God. There is a day coming when all creation will be released. Then, my friend, we shall hear music the like of which we have never heard before.

For all the gods of the people are idols: but the LORD made the heavens [1 Chron. 16:26].

The word *idol* is the Hebrew *elil*, meaning "a thing of naught." Idols are nothings. They are just a piece of wood, or stone, or metal. They can be animal, vegetable or mineral. In contrast, the Lord God is identified as the *Creator*.

Glory and honour are in his presence; strength and gladness are in his place.

Give unto the LORD, ye kindreds of the people, give unto the LORD glory and strength.

Give unto the LORD the glory due unto his name: bring an offering, and come before him: worship the LORD in the beauty of holiness [1 Chron. 16:27–29].

This does not simply mean to worship Him in a beautiful church. It means to worship Him in the beauty of holiness, all that He is in His person. Most of us don't even know what it is to worship God. Right now as we read this psalm, don't you really feel like just saying a little "Amen" or a "Glory to God" or a "Praise the Lord"—not as little Christian clichés but from the depth of your heart? How wonderful He is!

Fear before him, all the earth: the world also shall be stable, that it be not moved.

Let the heavens be glad, and let the earth rejoice: and let men say among the nations, The LORD reigneth [1 Chron. 16:30–31].

That day is coming!

Let the sea roar, and the fulness thereof: let the fields rejoice, and all that is therein.

Then shall the trees of the wood sing out at the presence of the LORD, because he cometh to judge the earth [1 Chron. 16:32–33].

The trees are going to sing. I'm waiting for that day. Someone asks, "How do you think they'll sing?" Well, I don't know. But when we get to that day, you and I will both know. It will be wonderful. It will all be to the praise of God.

O give thanks unto the LORD; for he is good: for his mercy endureth for ever [1 Chron. 16:34].

God is not short on mercy. Mercy is what I need. Mercy is what you need. He has plenty of it. Why don't you go to Him today? He has what you need.

And say ye, Save us, O God of our salvation, and gather us together, and deliver us from the heathen, that we may give thanks to thy holy name, and glory in thy praise.

Blessed be the LORD God of Israel for ever and ever. And all the people said, Amen, and praised the LORD.

So he left there before the ark of the covenant of the LORD Asaph and his brethren, to minister before the ark continually, as every day's work required:

And Obed-edom with their brethren, threescore and eight; Obed-edom also the son of Jeduthun and Hosah to be porters:

And Zadok the priest, and his brethren the priests, before the tabernacle of the LORD in the high place that was at Gibeon.

To offer burnt offerings unto the LORD upon the altar of the burnt offering continually morning and evening, and to do according to all that is written in the law of the LORD, which he commanded Israel [1 Chron. 16:35–40].

They kept the way open to God. Apparently there had not been a continuation of the sacrifices and of worship during the reign of Saul. David now organizes it. The ark is in Jerusalem, and he designates those who shall minister before the ark continually.

It is interesting that we are not told who was his secretary of state, or his secretary of the treasury, or his representative at the United Nations, but we are told who were the ones who took care of the ark and who worshiped before God and carried on the spiritual matters of his kingdom.

And with them Heman and Jeduthun, and the rest that were chosen, who were expressed by name, to give thanks to the LORD, because his mercy endureth for ever [1 Chron 16:41].

This is the reason we are to give thanks to God—"his mercy endureth forever."

And with them Heman and Jeduthun with trumpets and cymbals for those that should make a sound, and with musical instruments of God. And the sons of Jeduthun were porters.

And all the people departed every man to his house: and David returned to bless his house [1 Chron. 16:42–43].

CHAPTER 17

THEME: *David and the temple*

David's desire to build God a house so delighted the Lord that He repeats the entire episode as recorded in 2 Samuel 7.

Now it came to pass, as David sat in his house, that David said to Nathan the prophet, Lo, I dwell in an house of cedars, but the ark of the covenant of the LORD remaineth under curtains [1 Chron. 17:1].

I think it rained the night before, and as David heard the pitter-patter of the rain on his palace, he thought of the ark of God out there in a tent. Now David says to Nathan, "I want to build God a house."

Then Nathan said unto David, Do all that is in thine heart; for God is with thee [1 Chron. 17:2].

Nathan said what he thought was right. I am very sympathetic with Nathan. However, here is a case when a prophet of God was wrong. God will have to straighten him out.

And it came to pass the same night, that the word of God came to Nathan, saying,

Go and tell David my servant, Thus saith the LORD, Thou shalt not build me an house to dwell in:

For I have not dwelt in an house since the day that I brought up Israel unto this day; but have gone from tent to tent, and from one tabernacle to another [1 Chron. 17:3–5].

God always identifies Himself with His people, which is the reason He took upon Himself our humanity, my friend. Back in the Old Testament He met with His people in a tent because they lived in tents.

Wheresoever I have walked with all Israel, spake I a word to any of the judges of Israel, whom I commanded to feed my people, saying, Why have ye not built me an house of cedars? [1 Chron. 17:6].

Now when the people of Israel moved into the Promised Land and built permanent homes, there was no permanent temple built. And God says that He didn't say to them, "Why haven't you built Me a house of cedars?" But this desire has come into the heart of David.

Now therefore thus shalt thou say unto my servant David, Thus saith the LORD of hosts, I took thee from the sheepcote, even from following the sheep, that thou shouldest be ruler over my people Israel:

And I have been with thee whithersoever thou hast walked, and have cut off all thine enemies from before thee, and have made thee a name like the name of the great men that are in the earth [1 Chron. 17:7–8].

God told Nathan to deliver a message to David. God said to David, in effect, "I don't want you ever to forget your humble beginning. I went down and picked you up, a little shepherd boy, and I made you king over My people." God made David great like the great men in the earth. David stands as one of the great men of history.

Also I will ordain a place for my people Israel, and will plant them, and they shall dwell in their place, and shall be moved no more; neither shall the children of wickedness waste them any more, as at the beginning [1 Chron. 17:9].

God says the day will come when *He* will put Israel in that land, and then they will have peace. They will turn to Jehovah God in that day—they are still far from that. There is quite a division in Israel today as to whether or not they should even follow the orthodox viewpoint.

And since the time that I commanded judges to be over my people Israel. Moreover I will subdue all thine enemies. Furthermore I tell thee that the LORD will build thee an house [1 Chron. 17:10].

Isn't this just like our God? David had said, "I want to build God a house." God said, "David, you can't do it. You are a bloody man, and I can't let you build the temple. But I will build *you* a house." It was in David's heart to build God a house, and God gave him credit for it.

And it shall come to pass, when thy days be expired that thou must go to be with thy fathers, that I will raise up thy seed after thee, which shall be of thy sons; and I will establish his kingdom.

He shall build me an house, and I will stablish his throne for ever [1 Chron. 17:11–12].

Who is this One? Notice God's message to the virgin Mary: "And, behold, thou shalt conceive in thy womb, and bring forth a son, and shalt call his name JESUS. He shall be great, and shall be called the Son of the Highest: and the Lord God shall give unto him the throne of his father David: And he shall reign over the house of Jacob for ever; and of his kingdom there shall be no end" (Luke 1:31–33). The great covenant which God made with David is to be fulfilled in Jesus Christ.

I will be his father, and he shall be my son: and I will not take my mercy away from him, as I took it from him that was before thee:

But I will settle him in mine house and in my kingdom for ever: and his throne shall be established for evermore [1 Chron. 17:13–14].

God means this. God will build a kingdom on this earth, and Jesus Christ is coming to establish that kingdom.

According to all these words, and according to all this vision, so did Nathan speak unto David [1 Chron. 17:15].

As we have said, this entire incident was recorded in 2 Samuel 7. And here in Chronicles He goes over it again because He considers it important.

And David the king came and sat before the LORD, and said, Who am I, O LORD God, and what is mine house, that thou hast brought me hitherto? [1 Chron. 17:16].

Notice the reaction of David. "I just don't understand your goodness, your grace, and your mercy." My friend, I am another one who can say the same thing. Why has God been so good to me? Why has God been so good to you? Our God is not short on mercy, is He? Oh, to come to Him and have personal communication with Him—we have a communication from Him, His Word.

And yet this was a small thing in thine eyes, O God; for thou hast also spoken of thy servant's house for a great while to come, and hast regarded me accord-

ing to the estate of a man of high degree, O LORD God [1 Chron. 17:17].

That is a remarkable statement. They were looking for One to come. He was to be of the seed of the woman. He was to be from Abraham; He was to come from the tribe of Judah; now we are told that He will be in the family of David. David is overwhelmed by the fact that the Messiah will be in his line.

What can David speak more to thee for the honour of thy servant? for thou knowest thy servant [1 Chron. 17:18].

Have you ever poured out your heart to God until you didn't have anything left to say? This is David's state here. He had poured out his heart and is empty. He is just sitting there before God.

O LORD, for thy servant's sake, and according to thine own heart, hast thou done all this greatness, in making known all these great things [1 Chron. 17:19].

Did God do all of this for David because he was a nice boy? No, he wasn't always a nice boy. Neither did God save you and me because we were nice folk. He saved us because of His marvelous, infinite grace. He does so many special things for us, not because of our goodness, but because of *His* goodness. David is overwhelmed by what God has told him. It is no wonder he could sing those beautiful psalms.

O LORD, there is none like thee, neither is there any God beside thee, according to all that we have heard with our ears [1 Chron. 17:20].

My, what a privilege to have a God like this!

And what one nation in the earth is like thy people Israel, whom God went to redeem to be his own people, to make thee a name of greatness and terribleness, by driving out nations from before thy people, whom thou hast redeemed out of Egypt?

For thy people Israel didst thou make thine own people for ever; and thou, LORD, becamest their God [1 Chron. 17:21–22].

David reviews and marvels at God's grace to the nation Israel.

Therefore now, LORD, let the thing that thou hast spoken concerning thy servant and concerning his house be established for ever, and do as thou hast said.

Let it even be established, that thy name may be magnified for ever, saying, The LORD of hosts is the God of Israel, even a God to Israel: and let the house of David thy servant be established before thee [1 Chron. 17:23–24].

David believed and rested upon what God had promised.

For thou, O my God, hast told thy servant that thou wilt build him an house: therefore thy servant hath found in his heart to pray before thee.

And now, LORD, thou art God, and hast promised this goodness unto thy servant:

Now therefore let it please thee to bless the house of thy servant, that it may be before thee for ever: for thou blessest, O LORD, and it shall be blessed for ever [1 Chron 17:25–27].

CHAPTERS 18–20

THEME: *David's wars*

At this point somebody is going to say, "You have been emphasizing that Chronicles is God's viewpoint. How can wars be fitted into this interpretation?" Because that is a question in the minds, I am sure, of many folk, let me make some preliminary statements.

In the New Testament James, in a very practical manner, asked the question: "From where do wars come?" He not only asked the question, but he gives the answer: "From whence come wars and fightings among you? come they not hence, even of your lusts that war in your members? Ye lust, and have not: ye kill, and desire to have, and cannot obtain: ye fight and war, yet ye have not, because ye ask not" (James 4:1–2). In other words, the background of war is the sinful heart of man. It is very easy to protest wars, but we will never get rid of wars by protesting. Protesting may bring a single war to an end but another one is sure to start, because the basic problem is in the sinful heart of man.

The Lord Jesus came into our world and this is what He said, "When a strong man armed keepeth his palace, his goods are in peace: But when a stronger than he shall come upon him, and overcome him, he taketh from him all his armour wherein he trusted, and divideth his spoils" (Luke 11:21–22). Why did He say that? Because there are enemies abroad. We do not live in an ideal situation. The Millennium has not come yet—nor is man able to produce it. The Prince of Peace is the only One who will bring peace to this earth. Until He comes, we will do well to keep our powder dry.

Immediately after man sinned, God said to Satan, "And I will put enmity between thee and the woman, and between thy seed and her seed . . ." (Gen. 3:15). Friend, you cannot remove that.

There are going to be wars until sin is removed from this earth, until all wickedness is removed. Wars are the symptom. The disease is sin. It is sin that is the problem.

David is becoming a man whom God has blessed and as a result there are enemies round about. As long as he was a little petty king, a tribal king, they paid very little attention to him. God lets us know that He took note of the fact that even David's kingdom was in a world where there was war. Since you and I live in that kind of a world also, we do well to keep locks on our doors. Crime at home and abroad is the result of sin in the heart of man.

Now let's look at David's wars. The nations mentioned here were the perpetual enemies of Israel and always attacked when the nation was weak.

> **Now after this it came to pass, that David smote the Philistines, and subdued them, and took Gath and her towns out of the hand of the Philistines.**
>
> **And he smote Moab; and the Moabites became David's servants, and brought gifts.**
>
> **And David smote Hadarezer king of Zobah unto Hamath, as he went to stablish his dominion by the river Euphrates.**
>
> **And David took from him a thousand chariots, and seven thousand horsemen, and twenty thousand footmen: David also houghed all the chariot horses, but reserved of them an hundred chariots [1 Chron. 18:1–4].**

Why did David get rid of the horses? Because God had told His people that their king was not to multiply horses or wives. Later on, his son Solomon really went into the horse business, but David did not.

These were the spoils of war. I think by the time David died, Israel had cornered the gold market. The gold was there in Jerusalem.

> **And David took the shields of gold that were on the servants of Hadarezer, and brought them to Jerusalem.**
>
> **Likewise from Tibhath, and from Chun, cities of Hadarezer, brought David very much brass, wherewith Solomon made the brasen sea, and the pillars, and the vessels of brass [1 Chron. 18:7–8].**

You see, the materials out of which Solomon constructed the temple were accumulated by David.

Then we see that the king of Hamath sent gifts of appreciation to David for his victory over a mutual foe.

> **Them also king David dedicated unto the LORD, with the silver and the gold**

that he brought from all these nations; from Edom, and from Moab, and from the children of Ammon, and from the Philistines, and from Amalek [1 Chron. 18:11].

David is given the victory over all of these old enemies of Israel which had fought against them when they were weak. You see, in order to become a king over that land, there were enemies to be driven out.

The child of God in our day has enemies also. In Ephesians 6:11 we are told to "Put on the whole armour of God. . . ." Our enemy doesn't happen to be a flesh and blood enemy. Our enemy is a *spiritual* enemy. That is the point Paul is making in Ephesians 6:12: "For we wrestle not against flesh and blood, but against principalities, against powers, against the rulers of the darkness of this world, against spiritual wickedness in high places." This is the situation in which you and I find ourselves.

This idea that the Christian can sit down and twiddle his thumbs, that he can compromise with everything that comes along, is entirely wrong. As Christians, we need to stand for what is right. I once heard a country preacher down in Georgia say, "A lot of people, instead of standing on the promises, are sitting on the premises." Unfortunately, that is true. We have spiritual enemies that must be overcome.

WAR WITH AMMON AND SYRIA

Chapter 19 records an incident that reveals God has a sense of humor. It also suggests that David was a hotheaded fellow, but that he did try to live in peace.

Now it came to pass after this, that Nahash the king of the children of Ammon died, and his son reigned in his stead [1 Chron. 19:1].

Ammon was an enemy of Israel. David didn't want to make war. David is on the defensive as he was most of his life, as we have seen—God's man will usually find himself on the defensive.

As we mentioned in the previous chapter, we are told to put on the whole armor of God. What is it for? To march? No, we are to put it on to *stand*. That is the important thing. The tragedy of the hour is that so few of God's people will stand.

Wanting to repay an old kindness, David sent a message of comfort to Hanun upon the death of his father.

And David said, I will shew kindness unto Hanun the son of Nahash, because his father shewed kindness to me. And David sent messengers to comfort him concerning his father. So the servants of David came into the land of the children of Ammon to Hanun, to comfort him [1 Chron. 19:2].

Now notice what happened.

But the princes of the children of Ammon said to Hanun, Thinkest thou that David doth honour thy father, that he hath sent comforters unto thee? are not his servants come unto thee for to search, and to overthrow, and to spy out the land? [1 Chron 19:3].

This is a very serious charge made by these men—apparently young men—who are around the king. They say, "David is not your friend. He wasn't a friend of your father's. These men he has sent are spies!" Now notice what they did to David's ambassadors.

Wherefore Hanun took David's servants, and shaved them, and cut off their garments in the midst hard by their buttocks, and sent them away [1 Chron. 19:4].

They shaved them, which was a disgrace for a Jew—he was told not to even trim his beard. Then for their complete humiliation, they cut off their uniforms. You can imagine how these fellows felt. That was not a day of nudism, and they were greatly embarrassed. Of course it was an insult that could not be ignored, and David was a hotheaded fellow.

Then there went certain, and told David how the men were served. And he sent to meet them: for the men were greatly ashamed. And the king said, Tarry at Jericho until your beards be grown, and then return [1 Chron. 19:5].

Since these men were too humiliated to return to Jerusalem, David went down to Jericho to meet with them. David told them to stay in retirement until their beards were grown out again. And, of course, they would be given new uniforms.

Word got back to the people of Ammon what David had said when he heard how his ambassadors had been treated.

And when the children of Ammon saw that they had made themselves odious to David, Hanun and the children of Ammon sent a thousand talents of sil-

ver to hire them chariots and horsemen out of Mesopotamia, and out of Syria-maachah, and out of Zobah [1 Chron. 19:6].

Instead of David being the one who wanted to make war, this new king of the Ammonites wanted to. He wanted to demonstrate that he could overthrow David. I am sure this was in his mind when he humiliated David's ambassadors. So he hires an army from Syria to help him overcome David.

When David hears of this, he goes into action.

And when David heard of it, he sent Joab, and all the host of the mighty men.

And the children of Ammon came out, and put the battle in array before the gate of the city: and the kings that were come were by themselves in the field.

Now when Joab saw that the battle was set against him before and behind, he chose out of all the choice of Israel, and put them in array against the Syrians [1 Chron. 19:8–10].

The Syrians had the best army, so Joab chose the best of his forces to put them over against the Syrians. The Syrians were coming from the north and Ammon was coming from the south.

And the rest of the people he delivered unto the hand of Abishai his brother, and they set themselves in array against the children of Ammon.

And he said, If the Syrians be too strong for me, then thou shalt help me: but if the children of Ammon be too strong for thee, then I will help thee [1 Chron. 19:11–12].

His strategy was very good. He told his brother that he would come to his aid if he were to be overcome but his brother should come to his aid in case he were overcome. They were going to concentrate their forces at the place of the most heavy attack. That was good strategy. (It was the strategy which was used by both sides in the American Civil War, by the way.)

Be of good courage, and let us behave ourselves valiantly for our people, and for the cities of our God: and let the Lord do that which is good in his sight.

So Joab and the people that were with him drew nigh before the Syrians unto the battle; and they fled before him [1 Chron. 19:13–14].

Joab was a real army man, a real soldier. He would have been trained under David, and he and David were probably tops as far as military men were concerned.

And when the children of Ammon saw that the Syrians were fled, they likewise fled before Abishai his brother, and entered into the city. Then Joab came to Jerusalem [1 Chron. 19:15].

He came back to Jerusalem to report.

And when the Syrians saw that they were put to the worse before Israel, they sent messengers, and drew forth the Syrians that were beyond the river: and Shophach the captain of the host of Hadarezer went before them [1 Chron. 19:16].

They sent for reinforcements.

And it was told David; and he gathered all Israel, and passed over Jordan, and came upon them, and set the battle in array against them. So when David had put the battle in array against the Syrians, they fought with him.

But the Syrians fled before Israel: and David slew of the Syrians seven thousand men which fought in chariots, and forty thousand footmen, and killed Shophach the captain of the host.

And when the servants of Hadarezer saw that they were put to the worse before Israel, they made peace with David, and became his servants: neither would the Syrians help the children of Ammon any more [1 Chron. 19:17–19].

David did not want to go into battle. Remember we are getting God's viewpoint of the situation, and He makes it very clear that David wanted peace with the Ammonites. He didn't want to fight them. When he had seen an army prepared against him, he had sent Joab on the first campaign and the enemy had fled. But that didn't end the war. The enemy went out to get reinforcements, and with allies on their side they again gathered against Israel. This time David himself went out to lead the battle. May I say to you that when David led Israel into battle, he went into battle to win!

It is a tragedy for any nation to fight a war without the determination to win. How tragic that is. My friend, we are not to fight wars just to fight wars! Our nation has found itself in very tragic circumstances because we have fought wars we did not intend to win. If we had fought to win, we would have spared thousands of lives.

Some people will read this part of the history of Israel and say that God is a bloody God. No, friend, God is not bloody. He knows the way to save human lives. That way is to subdue the aggressor and win the war.

We live in a sinful world, my friends. It is a brutal world. It is a mean world. If you like to quote Browning, "God's in His heaven and all's right with the world," you are not quoting what Scripture teaches. We are getting God's viewpoint here. All is not right with the world.

We live in a day of permissiveness. This is the day of the foul-mouthed. We no longer have personal honesty or personal integrity or human sincerity. We need to face the fact that we are in a world of sin. Laws should be enforced, and criminals should be punished. God says that as long as we are in a world like this, a strong man armed will keep his house. We are getting God's viewpoint here, which is quite interesting.

WAR WITH AMMONITES AND PHILISTINES

Chapter 20 concludes this section on the wars of David.

The constant, persistent, enemies of Israel —and especially of David—were the Ammonites and the Philistines. There was no such thing as compromise between Israel and those enemies.

And it came to pass, that after the year was expired, at the time that kings go out to battle, Joab led forth the power of the army, and wasted the country of the children of Ammon, and came and besieged Rabbah. But David tarried at Jerusalem. And Joab smote Rabbah, and destroyed it [1 Chron. 20:1].

It looks as if Joab was the aggressor in this case. Although he may have been, we need to remember that David had made a friendly gesture to the young king of Ammon, but he was insulted and immediately the new king came against David in warfare. So this is just a continuation of that warfare.

There can be no compromise with the enemy. There can be no compromise with evil.

This idea today that right and wrong can walk together is all wrong. "Can two walk together, except they be agreed?" (Amos 3:3). My friend, if you are walking with evil, it is because you have compromised with it, you have agreed with the evil. This is something that the world is forgetting. It would be amusing if it were not so tragic that there are so many people who are horrified at war when it is across the ocean but are happy to tolerate lawlessness in our streets. They say we must learn to understand and to appreciate the lawbreakers. May I say that there is a hypocrisy in our contemporary culture that is sickening beyond degree. If it is evil across the ocean, it is evil here. Evil must be opposed. Lawlessness *must* be opposed. Right and wrong are in opposition. There cannot be an agreement between the two.

It is during this campaign that David stayed at Jerusalem, and this is the time that he committed his great sin with Bathsheba. Notice that God doesn't record that sin here. God has said that He forgives our sins and that He will remember our sins no more. He means that.

Now here is another persistent enemy of Israel: the Philistines.

And it came to pass after this, that there arose war at Gezer with the Philistines; at which time Sibbechai the Hushathite slew Sippai, that was of the children of the giant: and they were subdued.

And there was war again with the Philistines: and Elhanan the son of Jair slew Lahmi the brother of Goliath the Gittite, whose spear staff was like a weaver's beam.

And yet again there was war at Gath, where was a man of great stature, whose fingers and toes were four and twenty, six on each hand, and six on each foot: and he also was the son of the giant [1 Chron 20:4–6].

In this conflict with the Philistines, three men who were giants were slain by David and his men. David, of course, became famous as a young fellow for slaying the giant Goliath. The Philistines were the unrelenting enemy of Israel all during the life of David.

My friend, the believer has an unrelenting enemy also. We are fighting against spiritual wickedness in high places. If you are a child of God, you are also a soldier of God. That is the reason we are enjoined to "Put on the whole armour of God . . ." (Eph. 6:11). We are not to march against anyone; we are to *stand.* If you stand for the things of God, you are in a battle. You are in a war whether you like it or not. The wars may cease in Asia and in Africa and in Europe and in the western hemisphere, but there will still be war as long as there is evil in the world. As Paul said to the Ephesian believers, "Wherefore take unto you the whole armour of God, that ye may be able to withstand in the evil day, and having done all, to stand" (Eph. 6:13). This is the message in chapter 20 for you and for me.

CHAPTER 21

THEME: *David's sin in taking a census*

This chapter deals with the greatest sin that David committed, and it has nothing in the world to do with Bathsheba. It is the kind of sin about which folk say, "Well, I can't see why this is such a great sin." Everyone seems to think that the matter of Bathsheba is a terrible sin, and I'm in that number. I agree it was an awful sin. But in this chapter, as in all of Chronicles, we are given God's perspective. God does not record David's sin with Bathsheba in the Book of Chronicles, but He does record this sin of numbering the people because it is on the spiritual level. It won't affect David's salvation one whit, but it certainly is going to affect him and the nation of Israel in their personal relationship with God.

And Satan stood up against Israel, and provoked David to number Israel [1 Chron. 21:1].

Now we have found the real culprit. This was satanic. Satan was in back of this whole incident. This throws light upon David's great sin.

David's sin with Bathsheba was a personal sin, a sin of the flesh. In Psalm 51, he cried, "Have mercy upon me, O God, according to thy lovingkindness: according unto the multitude of thy tender mercies blot out my transgressions" (Ps. 51:1). He was referring to his sin with Bathsheba. But here "Satan stood up against Israel," and moved David to take this census.

And David said to Joab and to the rulers of the people, Go, number Israel from Beer-sheba even to Dan; and bring the number of them to me, that I may know it [1 Chron. 21:2].

You recall that Moses had taken a census of the people on two occasions. In the Book of Numbers we are told that he took a census at the beginning of the wilderness march and then again at the end of the wilderness march. There was nothing wrong with that. At least, God did not find fault with that. But here it is sin. There are those who say that the reason David did this was because he was proud. Well, let's read on.

And Joab answered, the LORD make his people an hundred times so many more as they be: but, my lord the king, are they not all my lord's servants? why then doth my lord require this thing? why will he be a cause of trespass to Israel? [1 Chron. 21:3].

Here is the first man to oppose the computer. David wanted statistics and there is a sin in statistics. Everything today is being computerized, including all of us, for that matter. Joab opposed getting these statistics because he felt that pride was involved in this. I am of the opinion that although pride did enter into it, pride is not the total explanation of the sin.

"Thus saith the LORD, Let not the wise man glory in his wisdom, neither let the mighty man glory in his might, let not the rich man glory in his riches: But let him that glorieth glory in this, that he understandeth and knoweth me, that I am the LORD which exercise lovingkindness, judgment, and righteousness, in the earth: for in these things I delight, saith the LORD" (Jer. 9:23–24). God was not pleased when David took a census because David was not delighting in the Lord; he was delighting in his own might. So the thing that motivated him to number the people was the awful sin of *unbelief*. David was trusting numbers instead of trusting God.

Nevertheless the king's word prevailed against Joab. Wherefore Joab departed, and went throughout all Israel, and came to Jerusalem.

And Joab gave the sum of the number of the people unto David. And all they of Israel were a thousand thousand and an hundred thousand men that drew sword: and Judah was four hundred threescore and ten thousand men that drew sword.

But Levi and Benjamin counted he not among them: for the king's word was abominable to Joab [1 Chron. 21:4–6].

In Israel he had 1,100,000 men, and in Judah he had 500,000 men. When Moses had taken the census, he had 603,000 men. David has a million more men than Moses had!

What a contrast this is to David, the shepherd boy, when he came into the camp and saw the great giant Goliath strutting up and down defying Israel. This little shepherd boy didn't want to take a census; he didn't number the army. He just said, "Let me go out after him." Why did he have the courage to do it? Well, he trusted the Lord. He went out with a sling and five stones! My friend, you don't feel the need of God when you have one million men. When you have only a slingshot and five stones, you know you need Him.

I'm afraid that our nation is in very much this same position today. "The greatest nation on earth"—how often we hear that phrase! I imagine the people in the Roman Empire heard that until they got tired of hearing it. They did the same in Babylon and in Greece and in Egypt. Those kingdoms are long gone as great world empires. Why? Because they trusted in armies. Don't misunderstand me. Every nation needs an army to defend itself in this evil world. We are not to be fools and fanatics who say we need no protection and no army. But that is not where our confidence should be!

Joab protests to David. He says, "David, all these men are yours. You don't need to number them. God has given you all these people, and they will be adequate with God." But David insisted on a census.

Today people think that with our atom bombs and hydrogen bombs we have no need for God. My friend, we do need God. People are trusting the wrong things in our day. David's great sin was unbelief.

I realize this fact does not register with many people. Just as today we point the finger at David for his sin with Bathsheba, so we would point our finger at a church member who would stagger into the church service while he was drunk. But you could walk into our Sunday morning church service in unbelief and no one would be the wiser. And if your unbelief was known, this would not be considered a serious matter. My friend, God is telling us here that he considers unbelief the most serious matter. Satan is always behind unbelief. He puts unbelief into our hearts and minds so that we will not trust God. He is always urging us to put our trust in men, in armies, in money, in anything but God. That is the sin of statistics.

May I say that a great many folk today trust mathematics and not the Maker. They trust the computer and not the Christ. They trust in numbers and not in the name of the Lord.

David learned his lesson. Listen to him: "It is better to trust in the LORD than to put confidence in man. It is better to trust in the LORD than to put confidence in princes" (Ps. 118:8–9). "In thee, O LORD, do I put my trust: let me never be put to confusion" (Ps. 71:1).

We need to ask ourselves these penetrating questions. Do we really trust God? Do we really believe God? "But without faith it is impossible to please him . . ." (Heb. 11:6). The Lord Jesus said that when the Holy Spirit would come into the world, He would convict the world of sin. What kind of sin? ". . . because they *believe not* on me" (John 16:9). Paul writes, ". . . for whatsoever is not of faith is sin" (Rom. 14:23). This is the sin of David, and it is real sin. David soon began to see what a terrible thing he had done.

DAVID CHOOSES HIS PUNISHMENT

And God was displeased with this thing; therefore he smote Israel.

And David said unto God, I have sinned greatly, because I have done this thing: but now, I beseech thee, do away the iniquity of thy servant; for I have done very foolishly [1 Chron. 21:7–8].

Now the Lord is going to put before David a choice of punishment.

And the LORD spake unto Gad, David's seer, saying,

Go and tell David, saying, Thus saith the LORD, I offer thee three things:

choose thee one of them, that I may do it unto thee.

So Gad came to David, and said unto him, Thus saith the LORD, Choose thee

Either three years' famine; or three months to be destroyed before thy foes, while that the sword of thine enemies overtaketh thee; or else three days the sword of the LORD, even the pestilence, in the land, and the angel of the LORD destroying throughout all the coasts of Israel. Now therefore advise thyself what word I shall bring again to him that sent me [1 Chron. 21:9–12].

Now listen to David. This is tremendous. I hope you agree with me by now that David was a great man. Oh, he was human like I am and you are. He stubbed his toe, he committed sins, he had his faults, but he never lost his salvation nor his desire for fellowship with God.

And David said unto Gad, I am in a great strait: let me fall now into the hand of the LORD; for very great are his mercies: but let me not fall into the hand of man [1 Chron. 21:13].

David knew his God. Here is a man who ordered the census because he was trusting in man. He sees now what he has done. I think David is an old man now, and he remembers that little shepherd boy who went out with his slingshot and five smooth stones. How he trusted God, and what a testimony he had then! David was as human as we are; we trust God for salvation, but we don't trust Him for the problems of life. David now looks about at his enemies. Their numbers are great; they are giant nations. David wonders if his army is big enough. He has forgotten for the moment that his God is big enough for all the giants and all the nations that are threatening him. So David takes a census.

How many times have you and I taken a census? We didn't really trust God, and we put our faith in something else.

But David knows his God. He says to Gad, "Don't let me fall into the hand of man. I want to fall into the hands of God." Why? Because David has learned that God is merciful. I am afraid that many of us have not learned that. God has ". . . not dealt with us after our sins; nor rewarded us according to our iniquities. For as the heaven is high above the earth, so great is his mercy toward them that fear him" (Ps. 103:10–11).

God is merciful in salvation. He holds out today salvation to a lost world. On what basis? Christ is the Mercy Seat. You recall that John puts it this way: "And he is the propitiation for our sins: and not for ours only, but also for the sins of the whole world" (1 John 2:2). What is propitiation? It is the Mercy Seat. He has an abundance of mercy. All you have to do if you want to be saved is to go into court with God, plead guilty, and then ask for mercy. He has plenty of mercy. That is the way He will save you. There is a pardon for you, and you must claim it.

Also there is the mercy of God in providence. I look back upon my life—oh, how good He has been! He is so merciful today, not only to me but to the whole unsaved world. Why didn't He come in judgment last night? Because He is merciful. He will come some day but He is long-suffering, He is merciful, He keeps giving time for repentance. He pities us like a father pities his children. His mercy will extend into the future. We can lean securely on His mercy. It will never cease. It is not just a momentary happy disposition with Him. It is not some development in His character. He didn't just read *How to Win Friends and Influence People* and then decide to be merciful. David could say, "O give thanks unto the LORD; for he is good: for his mercy endureth for ever" (Ps. 136:1). So David casts himself upon God's mercy.

So the LORD sent pestilence upon Israel: and there fell of Israel seventy thousand men.

And God sent an angel unto Jerusalem to destroy it: and as he was destroying, the LORD beheld, and he repented him of the evil, and said to the angel that destroyed, It is enough, stay now thine hand. And the angel of the LORD stood by the threshingfloor of Ornan the Jebusite.

And David lifted up his eyes, and saw the angel of the LORD stand between the earth and the heaven, having a drawn sword in his hand stretched out over Jerusalem. Then David and the elders of Israel, who were clothed in sackcloth, fell upon their faces.

And David said unto God, Is it not I that commanded the people to be numbered? even I it is that have sinned and done evil indeed; but as for these sheep, what have they done? let thine hand, I pray thee, O LORD my God, be on me, and on my father's house; but not on

thy people, that they should be plagued [1 Chron. 21:14–17].

Notice this marvelous prayer of David. He takes full responsibility for his sin. I would say that David has changed a great deal. The time when he committed the sin with Bathsheba he wasn't going to say a word about it. He even tried to push the blame for the death of Uriah the Hittite to someone else. David tried to cover up. Now it is different. He has learned his lesson. His soul stands absolutely naked before God. He tells the Lord, "I am responsible. I did this thing. Let the judgment fall upon me."

DAVID BUYS THE THRESHINGFLOOR OF ORNAN

Then the angel of the LORD commanded Gad to say to David, that David should go up, and set up an altar unto the LORD in the threshingfloor of Ornan the Jebusite [1 Chron. 21:18].

When I was in Jerusalem, I walked up and down the site of that threshingfloor. It is located on Mount Moriah, the place where the Mosque of Omar stands today. That is the old temple area. So here we learn that it was not actually David who chose that spot for the temple; God chose it. And David certainly concurred with Him.

And David went up at the saying of Gad, which he spake in the name of the LORD.

And Ornan turned back, and saw the angel; and his four sons with him hid themselves. Now Ornan was threshing wheat.

And as David came to Ornan, Ornan looked and saw David, and went out of the threshingfloor, and bowed himself to David with his face to the ground [1 Chron. 21:19–21].

Ornan was threshing wheat at his threshingfloor. It is interesting that I was there just at the beginning of harvest season. Every afternoon the wind would come up. I sat in our hotel room and I could look over this area, the temple area, the site of Ornan's threshingfloor. The wind really whistled through there, so much so that we had to close the doors to our room. In the days of David they would wait for that wind to come up, and then they would pitch the grain up into the air. The wind would blow away the chaff and the good grain would fall down upon the threshingfloor.

As I have mentioned before, Mount Moriah is the place where Abraham offered up Isaac. And at the other end of that same ridge is Golgotha, the place of the skull, where God offered up His Son. When I was there, I took a picture of the sheaf of rock which was taken out to make the roadway up to the Damascus gate. The wall of Jerusalem goes up over that ridge. It is very high. After taking that picture, I turned right around, walked ten steps, and took a picture of Golgotha—located on the same ridge, at the same elevation. It was a continuous ridge until they put the roadway through there. You see, God chose the site of Ornan's threshingfloor on Mount Moriah because that is the place where God told Abraham to offer his son, looking forward to the time of the temple sacrifices and finally to the sacrifice of the Lamb of God which takes away the sin of the world.

Then David said to Ornan, Grant me the place of this threshingfloor, that I may build an altar therein unto the LORD: thou shalt grant it me for the full price: that the plague may be stayed from the people.

And Ornan said unto David, Take it to thee, and let my lord the king do that which is good in his eyes: lo, I give thee the oxen also for burnt offerings, and the threshing instruments for wood, and the wheat for the meat offering: I give it all [1 Chron. 21:22–23].

This man Ornan was very generous. He offered the property, and the wheat that he was gathering in which David could use for a meal offering, also the wood and the oxen for a burnt offering. This man offered the whole thing to David. But now listen to David:

And king David said to Ornan, Nay; but I will verily buy it for the full price: for I will not take that which is thine for the LORD, nor offer burnt offerings without cost [1 Chron. 21:24].

David refused to offer to God that which cost him nothing.

So David gave to Ornan for the place six hundred shekels of gold by weight [1 Chron. 21:25].

David paid the full price for the threshingfloor.

And David built there an altar unto the LORD, and offered burnt offerings and peace offerings, and called upon the

Lord; and he answered him from heaven by fire upon the altar of burnt offering [1 Chron. 21:26].

David now makes a sacrifice to God. The fire from heaven indicated that God had accepted David's offering.

And the Lord commanded the angel; and he put up his sword again into the sheath thereof [1 Chron. 21:27].

The sword of judgment was sheathed. But at Golgotha, that sword pierced the side of the Lord Jesus Christ. As someone has said, "I got into the heart of God through a spear wound."

At that time when David saw that the Lord had answered him in the threshingfloor of Ornan the Jebusite, then he sacrificed there.

For the tabernacle of the Lord, which Moses made in the wilderness, and the altar of the burnt offering, were at that season in the high place at Gibeon.

But David could not go before it to inquire of God: for he was afraid because of the sword of the angel of the Lord [1 Chron. 21:28–30].

I want you to see something very important here. David put this altar in the place where the temple is to be built, and he offers a sacrifice. This is the place God met with His people. This is now become the place of sacrifice. You see, David understood what a lot of church members today do not understand. David put up this altar, and he offered on it a burnt offering. That burnt offering speaks of the Person of Christ. Then he offered a peace offering. This speaks of Christ as our Peace. Christ made peace by the blood of His cross. Jesus Christ is our Peace. He has sprinkled His own blood on the mercy seat for us. He is our great High Priest. He has ascended into heaven and stands at the right hand of the Father. There is no access to God except through the Lord Jesus Christ. David understood this, and he offered the burnt offering and the peace offering to God.

Now remember that there was a plague going on. David has seen the angel with a drawn sword in his hand stretched out over Jerusalem. David offers sacrifices to God and calls on the name of the Lord. What was he asking for? For mercy!

God is a God of mercy, of loving-kindness. But did you know that God doesn't save us by His mercy? God can't just be bighearted. He can't be a sentimental old gentleman. You see, there is a penalty that must be paid. Sin must be dealt with. God is also righteous and He cannot save us simply by His mercy, or by His love. God can't save you by love, friend. He loves you and He will extend mercy to you but He cannot save you that way. We are saved by *grace* through faith. What does that mean? That means that someone had to pay the penalty for our sins. God couldn't just open the back door of heaven and slip us in under cover of darkness. He cannot let down the bars of heaven. Sin must be dealt with. He cannot shut His eyes to sin in order to save us. We are guilty sinners before God, and the penalty must be paid. Jesus Christ came to pay our penalty. He is the propitiation, He is the mercy seat for you and me.

CHAPTERS 22–29

***THEME:** David's preparation and organization for building the temple*

From this point through to the end of 1 Chronicles, we have the organization, the gathering of the materials, and the enthusiasm of David for building the temple which God would not allow him to build.

Let me remind you again that Chronicles gives God's viewpoint, and to Him the temple is the most important project David had in mind. David had a housing project—we saw that. He built many houses in Jerusalem; it was a great urban development. However, the important thing was the building of the temple. Why? My friend, until an individual or a people are right with Almighty God, all these subsidiary subjects must sink into insignificance. When a right relationship with Him is established, then urban development is important. Then a poverty program is very much in order. It looked like David had a poverty program when, after he brought the ark to Jerusalem, he was handing out the groceries. Why? Well, because the spiritual part had been settled.

Today we hear so much about urban development and about poverty programs. The news media puts such emphasis on these things and makes people think that if these material things can be solved then the problems of the world would be solved. My friend, man is far from solving the problems of the world because he hasn't solved the major problem, which is his relationship with God. As a result, there is corruption in urban development; there is corruption in poverty programs.

The temple speaks of that which is spiritual, of a right relationship with God. From God's viewpoint that was the important thing that went on in David's kingdom—rather than the continual wars, the intrigue, the petty politics such as are considered newsworthy in our day.

It is interesting to apply this to more recent history. Great Britain was the nation which ruled the world for many years. There was the saying that the sun never set on the British Empire. Great Britain controlled more of the world than any other nation ever has. They were not perfect, and one can find much to criticize, but it still is true that Great Britain had a tremendous influence for good on the entire world.

The significant factors in her history did not take place at 10 Downing Street. They didn't take place in Parliament under the tower of Big Ben. Probably the most important thing was when a young fellow by the name of John Wesley went upstairs in Aldersgate. When I was there, I had to pause a moment and thank God for that man and his work, because we are still reaping the benefits from it. Down the street from Aldersgate is the place where Wesley began his preaching. There is a graveyard there; and, when the state church put him out, he stood on the tombstones and started preaching. The result was a spiritual movement of such magnitude that even Lloyd George said that John Wesley did more for the British Empire than any Englishman who ever lived.

Probably the newspapers and magazines didn't think Wesley was important; yet he was God's instrument for saving Great Britain from a revolution, and God enabled him to begin a movement which brought civilization throughout the world. We can belittle the colonial policy (and Great Britain bogged down under it with all the wrongs inherent in it), but the important thing is that this was a movement which sent missionaries throughout the world and brought a civilizing Christian influence throughout the world.

Even the most prejudiced person in the world surely must admit that those days were better than the godless age in which we are living—which is getting nowhere.

From God's viewpoint, David's preparations for the temple were more important than anything else David did.

Then David said, This is the house of the LORD God, and this is the altar of the burnt offering for Israel.

And David commanded to gather together the strangers that were in the land of Israel; and he set masons to hew wrought stones to build the house of God [1 Chron. 22:1–2].

David is determined that the temple is to be built there on the threshingfloor of Ornan.

And David prepared iron in abundance for the nails for the doors of the gates, and for the joinings; and brass in abundance without weight;

Also cedar trees in abundance: for the Zidonians and they of Tyre brought much cedar wood to David [1 Chron. 22:3–4].

The Zidonians were, of course, the inhabitants of Zidon (sometimes called Sidon). As we have seen, Hiram, king of Tyre and Sidon, was the one who provided the stone and timber for the construction of the temple.

And David said, Solomon my son is young and tender, and the house that is to be builded for the LORD must be exceeding magnifical, of fame and of glory throughout all countries: I will therefore now make preparation for it. So David prepared abundantly before his death [1 Chron. 22:5].

Notice the word *magnifical!* As we see it from God's viewpoint, David made abundant preparation for the temple. He knew that Solomon was young and inexperienced, and the temple of God must be exceedingly magnificent. This is my reason for saying it should be called David's temple rather than Solomon's temple.

Then he called for Solomon his son, and charged him to build an house for the LORD God of Israel.

And David said to Solomon, My son, as for me, it was in my mind to build an house unto the name of the LORD my God:

But the word of the LORD came to me, saying, Thou hast shed blood abundantly, and hast made great wars: thou shalt not build an house unto my name, because thou hast shed much blood upon the earth in my sight [1 Chron. 22:6–8].

Although the wars David fought were forced upon him—he was not the aggressor—God said that he was a bloody man. God is not for war—His name is not Mars. He is opposed to war. He wants peace, and His Son is the Prince of Peace who will bring peace to this earth. God would not allow David to build the temple because he was a man of war.

Behold, a son shall be born to thee, who shall be a man of rest; and I will give him rest from all his enemies round about: for his name shall be Solomon, and I will give peace and quietness unto Israel in his days [1 Chron. 22:9].

God said that Solomon would be a man of peace and rest because He would give peace to Israel in his days. But, as we shall see, the peace was not permanent.

However, there was One who stood before the people of Israel when the religious rulers rejected Him, and said, "Come unto me, all ye that labour and are heavy laden . . ." (Matt. 11:28). He didn't actually say, "I will give you rest," as our Authorized Version has it, but "I will rest you." He will do what Solomon was unable to do. He is great David's greater Son. It is He who can bring rest and peace, solace and quietness to the human soul. God is merciful because His Son died for you. Won't you accept His overture? He has moved heaven and hell to reach the door of your heart. He won't come any further, but He says, "Behold, I stand at the door, and knock: if any man hear my voice, and open the door, I will come in to him, and will sup with him, and he with me" (Rev. 3:20).

He shall build an house for my name; and he shall be my son, and I will be his father; and I will establish the throne of his kingdom over Israel for ever [1 Chron. 22:10].

As we have seen, the Lord Jesus Christ is the final fulfillment of this promise.

It is my personal feeling that David was not much interested in having Solomon become king. Solomon was a sissy. Solomon was brought up in the palace, in the women's court. He knew nothing of living and defending himself in the rugged terrain of that land as David his father had done. David and Solomon were far apart, and the explanation, of course, is their backgrounds. In effect, David says to Solomon, "You are going to build the temple. Oh, I want to encourage you and get you enthusiastic about it, because it is the desire of my heart to build a magnifical temple, and God won't let me do it because I am a bloody man."

My friend, let me pause here a moment to remind you that David did not get by with sin. He was not able to do the thing he wanted to do above everything else on this earth, which was to build a temple for God. There is many a man whom God has not permitted to reach the goal he wanted to reach, because of sin in his life. Sin drags us all down. It dragged David down.

Now, my son, the LORD be with thee; and prosper thou, and build the house of the LORD thy God, as he hath said of thee [1 Chron. 22:11].

How David was encouraging this boy—and he knew he needed encouraging! He has been brought up in the court of the women, and he's not a very aggressive fellow.

As we shall see, Solomon reaped the benefits of the reign of David. It can be said truly of him, as the Lord Jesus put it, ". . . other men laboured, and ye are entered into their labours" (John 4:38). Solomon entered into the labors of another, and that was his father David.

Only the LORD give thee wisdom and understanding, and give thee charge concerning Israel, that thou mayest keep the law of the LORD thy God [1 Chron. 22:12].

David is urging his son to follow in God's ways. I think David detected some of his weaknesses, and I am sure Bathsheba detected some of the weaknesses in Solomon. One of those traits was his weakness in the direction of women. This is David's advice to Solomon which we are reading. If you want to read his mother's advice to him, you will find it in the last chapter of Proverbs.

Then shalt thou prosper, if thou takest heed to fulfil the statutes and judgments which the LORD charged Moses with concerning Israel: be strong, and of good courage; dread not, nor be dismayed [1 Chron. 22:13].

David knew that Solomon would get discouraged. He knew that Solomon was a weakling. He tells him to be a man—be strong and courageous.

Now, behold, in my trouble I have prepared for the house of the LORD an hundred thousand talents of gold, and a thousand thousand talents of silver; and of brass and iron without weight; for it is in abundance: timber also and stone have I prepared; and thou mayest add thereto [1 Chron 22:14].

David told Solomon that he wouldn't have to stint in the building of this temple. He wouldn't have to cut any corners. There would be no shortage of materials. David said that in the days of his trouble, the days in which he had attempted to build up the kingdom with all the labor involved, he had carried on the work of gathering the materials for the temple of God.

God had taken note of that. God had seen what was in the heart of David. That is why David is called a man after God's own heart. God wanted this heart attitude, this emphasis on the spiritual values, above everything else.

My friend, what is really the goal of your life? What ambition do you have? We are told that today we have a generation of young people without any purpose or goal in life. They have been brought up in homes of affluence with no Christian direction. There has been no pointing to something that is worthwhile, something that is glorious and great. They haven't had that direction in their homes, neither have they had direction in their schools. The schools are not doing their job. I may sound like a heretic and a real revolutionary, but I don't think it would hurt to close up many of our schools today. I don't think they are serving their purpose until they give moral training and direction and discipline to our young people.

What is the purpose of living? Why are there so many suicides among our young people? Why are so many of them dissolute vagrants wandering aimlessly all over the world? My heart goes out to them because someone has failed. Papa and Mamma have failed. The schools have failed. The churches have failed.

May I say to you that David was giving his son some direction. He told him, "You have a worthy goal—build God a house." Let me pass on to you something that was given to me early in life. The catechism asks the question: "What is the chief end of man?" The answer is: "Man's chief end is to glorify God and enjoy Him forever."

Oh, I wish I could get you enthusiastic—not about baseball or football or any kind of ball, not in the things around you, not even in church work (that may sound revolutionary also)—but in the Lord Jesus Christ. I wish I could get you really interested in His person.

My friend, Jesus Christ has promised me and He has promised you that we shall be with Him forever. Since He is God, His way is going to prevail, not yours or mine. He has something glorious in view. I don't have it because I don't know what is out there, but I am interested in what He has for me. We should all be able to say with Paul, "I press toward the mark for the prize of the high calling of God in Christ Jesus" (Phil. 3:14). David is a man after God's own heart because he had something high and noble and lofty in his heart.

Moreover there are workmen with thee in abundance, hewers and workers of stone and timber, and all manner of

cunning men for every manner of work [1 Chron. 22:15].

You see, he had arranged with Hiram to take charge of all the building.

Of the gold, the silver, and the brass, and the iron, there is no number. Arise therefore, and be doing, and the LORD be with thee [1 Chron. 22:16].

Get busy, young man! Here is a goal that is worthwhile.

David also commanded all the princes of Israel to help Solomon his son, saying,

Is not the LORD your God with you? and hath he not given you rest on every side? for he hath given the inhabitants of the land into mine hand; and the land is subdued before the LORD, and before his people.

Now set your heart and your soul to seek the LORD your God; arise therefore, and build ye the sanctuary of the LORD God, to bring the ark of the covenant of the LORD, and the holy vessels of God, into the house that is to be built to the name of the LORD [1 Chron. 22:17–19].

David is commanding the leaders of Israel to become involved in this project also.

Now, my friend, whoever you are (and I am speaking to you as a Christian), you may have sunk down to a pretty low level in your living. It may be that all the church work you do is gossip, or all you do is find fault with the preacher. Maybe you are not guilty of these things, but instead of "standing on the promises, you are sitting on the premises"—you are doing nothing. I'd like to alert you, stick a pin in you, and say, wake up! Come alive and make a move toward Jesus Christ. Tell Him that you want to go along with Him, that you want a spiritual emphasis in your life. Do something *definite;* do something *positive.* Don't just sit there—do it right now. That is what David is saying to his boy Solomon. He really put a pin in him!

LEVITES ARE ORGANIZED TO SERVE AND SING

As we come to chapter 23, keep in mind that we are still in the section that is all about the temple. Again let me say that God considered this important, and here is the place He put the emphasis. David also considered it of utmost importance, and we see more of his zeal and enthusiasm for the worship of God in these arrangements he has made.

My friend, if you are a child of God, David is putting this challenge to you. Do *you* really put God first in your life? Is He a thrill to you? Do you rejoice in that relationship? Do you want to do something for God? Does He give direction and purpose to your life? Is it the desire of your heart to know Him and to serve Him?

Unfortunately, many of our churches feature activity without action. Like a merry-go-round, we get on and have a nice little ride, then we get off at the same place we got on. We are not going any place. David was on the move for God, and he is urging his son Solomon to get on the move and build this great temple.

So when David was old and full of days, he made Solomon his son king over Israel [1 Chron. 23:1].

David now makes Solomon king in his stead.

Perhaps you are asking, "What did David die of?" Well, he was full of days—that was his problem. And it is the problem many of us have.

And he gathered together all the princes of Israel, with the priests and the Levites.

Now the Levites were numbered from the age of thirty years and upward: and their number by their polls, man by man, was thirty and eight thousand [1 Chron. 23:2–3].

When the Levites were numbered, as they came out of Egypt, there were about eight thousand of them. Now there are thirty-eight thousand. They have increased in numbers, as God said they would.

Not only did David gather the materials for the construction of the temple, but he also organized the Levites to serve in the temple.

Of which, twenty and four thousand were to set forward the work of the house of the LORD; and six thousand were officers and judges:

Moreover four thousand were porters; and four thousand praised the LORD with the instruments which I made, said David, to praise therewith [1 Chron. 23:4–5].

David put a great emphasis on music. Think of it—four thousand praised the Lord with music!

You will recall that the Levites served in the tabernacle. The family of Aaron served as the priests, and the three families of Levites had their duties.

And David divided them into courses among the sons of Levi, namely, Gershon, Kohath, and Merari [1 Chron. 23:6].

The Gershonites, the Kohathites, and the Merarites all had very definite assignments in caring for the tabernacle. On the wilderness march they were responsible for moving the tabernacle. They took it down and they put it up. The Gershonites carried the curtains and the coverings. The Kohathites carried the articles of furniture. The Merarites carried the boards and the bars and the pillars. As we saw in the Book of Numbers, it was quite an undertaking to take down the tabernacle in the morning and reassemble it in the evening and restore the service of it.

And also unto the Levites; they shall no more carry the tabernacle, nor any vessels of it for the service thereof [1 Chron. 23:26].

The Levites' assignment to carry the tabernacle through the wilderness is over. Now they have a new ministry for the Lord.

Again, this is something that I wish we could learn. God has raised up many fine Christian organizations; then after they have served their purpose, there are folk who try to preserve them. Some of them are as dead as a dodo bird. They do not serve any good purpose. When God is through with a thing, He is through with it, my friend. It is time to get something new going. To the Levites, God is saying in effect, "We're not going to be trotting around in the wilderness any more. Now we will have a temple and your service is going to be different." Oh, my friend, let's keep step with God and do something that is alive and moving!

The Levites now have a new service. The staves are removed from the ark. It will not be moved again. It is to remain permanently in Jerusalem on the threshingfloor of Ornan. David has bought the place, and the temple will be erected there. In the temple there will be a great deal for the Levites to do; so David organizes them into shifts, selected by lot. They will serve for a period of time, then they will retire—have time off. This is the way David organized the service of the temple.

DIVISION OF THE SONS OF AARON

In chapter 24, David gives the divisions of the sons of Aaron into orders to serve in the temple.

Now these are the divisions of the sons of Aaron. The sons of Aaron; Nadab, and Abihu, Eleazer, and Ithamar.

But Nadab and Abihu died before their father, and had no children: therefore Eleazar and Ithamar executed the priest's office [1 Chron. 24: 1–2].

Aaron's sons were priests, and this record takes us back to the time they were in the wilderness. The tenth chapter of Leviticus records the sin of Nadab and Abihu and their resulting death.

And David distributed them, both Zadok of the sons of Eleazar, and Ahimelech of the sons of Ithamar, according to their offices in their service [1 Chron. 24:3].

This is a very highly organized procedure that David is putting into force. David not only bought the property where the temple is to stand, he gathered the building materials, and now he organizes the priests to serve. This is my reason for saying that the temple was David's temple, not Solomon's temple.

Thus were they divided by lot, one sort with another; for the governors of the sanctuary, and governors of the house of God, were of the sons of Eleazar, and of the sons of Ithamar [1 Chron. 24:5].

There were twenty-four orders. These sons were organized into orders. One group would come and do their work under the direction of one of the sons, then another group under the direction of another son would come and replace them. I think it must have been quite interesting to watch. Not long ago I had the privilege of watching the changing of the guard at Buckingham Palace in London. What a ceremony, what a show that is! I have a suspicion that the kings of the past would be surprised to see how it is being done today, and I'm not sure they would be in favor of it. I think they really overdo the pageantry. However, I imagine that when the Levites changed shifts for temple service it was done with precision and order.

The families of the Levites had grown so in number that it would be impossible for all of them to serve at once. As we have seen, from the time of Moses to the time of David, the

Levites had increased from about eight thousand to thirty-eight thousand. For this reason David divided them into orders.

In the next section, the sons of Kohath are divided, and following them, the sons of Merari were divided. David planned that each family would carry on the service of the temple.

SINGERS AND ORCHESTRA ARE ORGANIZED

In chapter 25, we find that David organized the singers in the same way.

Moreover David and the captains of the host separated to the service of the sons of Asaph, and of Heman, and of Jeduthun, who should prophesy with harps, with psalteries, and with cymbals: and the number of the workmen according to their service was:

Of the sons of Asaph; Zaccur, and Joseph, and Nethaniah, and Asarelah, the sons of Asaph under the hands of Asaph, which prophesied according to the order of the king [1 Chron. 25:1–2].

All of this was organized before the temple was built. You will find in the marvelous sixty-eighth Psalm, a song of David, these words: "Thy God hath commanded thy strength: strengthen, O God, that which thou hast wrought for us. Because of thy temple at Jerusalem shall kings bring presents unto thee" (Ps. 68:28–29). David is anticipating the time the temple will stand in Jerusalem as a testimony to the world. Long before the temple was built, the singers were gathering in Jerusalem to worship God, and this is one of the songs they sang. You see, David had brought up the ark to Jerusalem, and it was kept in a tent. Also there was an altar there on the threshingfloor of Ornan where David, you recall, had offered sacrifices—burnt sacrifices and peace offerings—unto God.

So the number of them, with their brethren that were instructed in the songs of the Lord, even all that were cunning, was two hundred fourscore and eight.

And they cast lots, ward against ward as well the small as the great, the teacher as the scholar [1 Chron. 25: 7–8].

They were divided by lot into twenty-four groups. This would mean that twice each month there would be a change in the service. Each of these would serve only two weeks out of the year. Then they would go back to the city from which they had come and there was service for them to perform in their hometowns. These priests and Levites served as instructors and in many ways throughout the land of Israel.

I believe all this organization was one of the greatest feats of David's reign. It is the thing which God noted and recorded here.

PORTERS AND GUARDS ARE ORGANIZED

Not only are the priests organized, but there are others. Who is going to sweep out the place? And who is going to guard it? In chapter 26 we see that David had all of this carefully planned.

Concerning the divisions of the porters: Of the Korhites was Meshelemiah the son of Kore, of the sons of Asaph [1 Chron. 26:1].

They were divided in much the same way. And while all these people are serving, there will need to be someone on guard duty. There will be guards placed to watch the gates and they will be on duty twenty-four hours a day.

And they cast lots, as well the small as the great, according to the house of their fathers, for every gate [1 Chron. 26:13].

Every gate was covered by guards.

TREASURERS APPOINTED

They will have to have a treasurer to keep track of the finances for the temple. He will have to make his report.

And of the Levites, Ahijah was over the treasures of the house of God, and over the treasures of the dedicated things [1 Chron. 26:20].

The treasurers were responsible for the vast store of dedicated things which had been accumulating.

Which Shelomith and his brethren were over all the treasures of the dedicated things, which David the king, and the chief fathers, the captains over thousands and hundreds, and the captains of the host, had dedicated.

Out of the spoils won in battles did they dedicate to maintain the house of the Lord.

And all that Samuel the seer, and Saul the son of Kish, and Abner the son of Ner, and Joab the son of Zeruiah, had dedicated; and whosoever had dedicated any thing, it was under the hand of Shelomith, and of his brethren [1 Chron. 26:26–28].

OFFICERS AND JUDGES APPOINTED

The Levites were to be the judges, you see. They also were to act in official capacities in many ways. It was God's original purpose that Israel be a theocracy with Him ruling, and with the tabernacle in the center of the community, and with the priesthood getting the decisions from God Himself. This changed because of the failure of the Levites. So God raised up judges. Then we saw the failure of the judges, and the people demanded a king. This is the reason David is now on the throne. Although Israel is now a monarchy, David is putting great emphasis upon bringing it back under God's control.

CAPTAINS AND PRINCES APPOINTED

Now the children of Israel after their number, to wit, the chief fathers and captains of thousands and hundreds, and their officers that served the king in any matter of the courses, which came in and went out month by month throughout all the months of the year, of every course were twenty and four thousand [1 Chron. 27:1].

Twelve captains were appointed, each man serving one month of the year over a course of twenty-four thousand.

Furthermore over the tribes of Israel: the ruler of the Reubenites was Eliezer the son of Zichri: of the Simeonites, Shephatiah the son of Maachah [1 Chron. 27:16].

And so on—one man from each of the twelve tribes so that there were twelve princes of the tribes of Israel.

Now notice this verse:

But David took not the number of them from twenty years old and under: because the LORD had said he would increase Israel like to the stars of the heavens [1 Chron. 27:23].

David took the census before because he didn't believe God; it was an act of unbelief. God told him, "Trust Me. I'll supply all the men you need for your army." Now David does not take a census. He rests upon God's promise.

Chapter 27 concludes with a list of officers which are in charge of King David's personal properties.

DAVID'S FINAL MESSAGE

In the last two chapters of 1 Chronicles, David calls together all the leaders in Israel. It is a great meeting, and it will be one of his last because he has come to the end of his life. He will have a message for Israel and a message for Solomon that the nation will hear. This is a wise move on David's part.

And David assembled all the princes of Israel, the princes of the tribes, and the captains of the companies that ministered to the king by course, and the captains over the thousands, and captains over the hundreds, and the stewards over all the substance and possession of the king, and of his sons, with the officers, and with the mighty men, and with all the valiant men, unto Jerusalem [1 Chron. 28:1].

These are the men who are responsible for the leadership of the nation.

Then David the king stood up upon his feet, and said, Hear me, my brethren, and my people: As for me, I had in mine heart to build an house of rest for the ark of the covenant of the LORD, and for the footstool of our God, and had made ready for the building [1 Chron. 28:2].

Despite his age, he forces himself to stand as he delivers this important and final message to his people.

But God said unto me, Thou shalt not build an house for my name, because thou hast been a man of war, and hast shed blood [1 Chron. 28:3].

David will not get away from this position of frank confession to the people. He gives the reason God will not allow him to build the temple: he has been a bloody man.

And of all my sons, (for the LORD hath given me many sons,) he hath chosen Solomon my son to sit upon the throne of the kingdom of the LORD over Israel [1 Chron. 28:5].

David makes it clear that God had chosen and commissioned Solomon. He turns over all the responsibility for Solomon to God. This gives the impression that Solomon was not David's choice.

And he said unto me, Solomon thy son, he shall build my house and my courts: for I have chosen him to be my son, and I will be his father [1 Chron. 28:6].

David's heart and soul were in the preparation for building the temple. God would not permit him to build it himself, and he acquiesced to the will of God. However, he made every preparation of material and workmen, and he encourages Solomon to build.

Now David gives the blueprint to Solomon.

Then David gave to Solomon his son the pattern of the porch, and of the houses thereof, and of the treasuries thereof, and of the upper chambers thereof, and of the inner parlours thereof, and of the place of the mercy seat.

And the pattern of all that he had by the spirit, of the courts of the house of the LORD, and of all the chambers round about, of the treasuries of the house of God, and of the treasuries of the dedicated things:

Also for the courses of the priests and the Levites, and for all the work of the service of the house of the LORD, and for all the vessels of service in the house of the LORD [1 Chron. 28:11–13].

Just as Moses had been given the blueprint for the tabernacle, it was David (not Solomon) who had been given the blueprint for the temple.

Many models of the temple have been made, and they are very impressive. Obviously, they are not as the temple really looked. However, in the new section of Jerusalem there is a new, exclusive hotel called the Holyland Hotel. On the grounds of that hotel is a model of the city of Jerusalem. This is not a little cheap thing that has been thrown together, or something made by a person who doesn't really know what he is doing. But it was made after years of research by Jews in that land. They have made a model of the entire city. I was thrilled to see how it looked. The fact of the matter is, I took pictures of it myself. They say that they have it looking as it did in the days of Herod. Well, the days of Herod are the days of Christ. It is the way it looked in the days of our Lord and in New Testament times. And, my friend, it just doesn't look like the models we have had in the past. I believe it is probably nearer to how it really looked than any other model which has been made before.

The model is built in the spacious gardens in the rear of the hotel. The scale is 1:50 (2 centimeters equal 1 meter; ¼ inch equals 1 foot). As you walk around it, it gives you a real conception of how Jerusalem looked (see reproductions on pages 408 and 422.

The model of the temple has a simplicity about it, and I believe that is how it actually was. Yet the details in Kings and Chronicles seem very complicated. It is not as simple as the tabernacle was, yet there is a simplicity about it. It was neither the architecture nor the size that was impressive, but the beauty and wealth that was bestowed upon it. Although the floorplan of Herod's temple was the same as God gave to David, it was not nearly as expensive as David's temple. Herod built the temple to gratify man, while David lavished the wealth of his kingdom upon it to glorify God.

David said to Solomon, "You don't need to stint. I have gathered enough material to make it magnificent." It was ornate, covered with gold and silver and precious stones.

It has always been my feeling that a church building should correspond to the neighborhood in which it is located. I do not like to see great cathedrals erected in poor communities and slum areas. In a rich neighborhood, you would want a building commensurate with the homes. However, today the emphasis should not be upon buildings because our bodies are the temple of God.

Of course David had no notion of making a temple for God to *live* in. God does not live in a box! Solomon in his prayer of dedication very frankly said, ". . . behold, the heaven and heaven of heavens cannot contain thee; how much less this house that I have builded?" (1 Kings 8:27). The whole created universe cannot contain God. How could a little house contain Him? The temple was to be a meeting place. God met with man there. And the temple was for the glory and honor of God. Today God does neither dwell nor meet you in a building. He dwells in individuals by the Holy Spirit.

David assigned the proportionate *weight* of gold or of silver that was to go into the articles of furniture and instruments of service.

He gave of gold by weight for things of gold, for all instruments of all manner of service; silver also for all instruments of silver by weight, for all instruments of every kind of service:

Even the weight for the candlesticks of gold, and for their lamps of gold, by weight for every candlestick, and for the lamps thereof: and for the candlesticks of silver by weight, both for the candlestick, and also for the lamps thereof, according to the use of every candlestick [1 Chron. 28:14–15].

The thought here is that there was to be no stinting. There was nothing parsimonious about the temple. It was a great expanse and expenditure of the wealth of the kingdom of David. Keep in mind that David did this in order to honor God.

All this, said David, the LORD made me understand in writing by his hand upon me, even all the works of this pattern [1 Chron. 28:19].

This is a remarkable verse. The pattern of the temple was from God just as much as the pattern of the tabernacle was from God.

God gave the pattern, the blueprint; God selected the site—the threshingfloor of Ornan; God inspired and encouraged David but would not allow him to do the actual building.

And David said to Solomon his son, Be strong and of good courage, and do it: fear not, nor be dismayed: for the LORD God, even my God, will be with thee; he will not fail thee, nor forsake thee, until thou hast finished all the work for the service of the house of the LORD [1 Chron. 28:20].

David is enthusiastic and excited about the temple, and he is doing all he can to stimulate Solomon. He wants Solomon to get busy on it.

And, behold, the courses of the priests and the Levites, even they shall be with thee for all the service of the house of God: and there shall be with thee for all manner of workmanship every willing skilful man, for any manner of service: also the princes and all the people will be wholly at thy commandment [1 Chron. 28:21].

You see, David had everyone in the kingdom —the priests, the workmen, the princes, the Levites—all stimulated and stirred up to do this. All Solomon had to do was to carry out his orders and follow the plans David had set up for him.

DAVID EXHORTS THE PEOPLE

As we come to chapter 29, we find that the emphasis shifts from the temple to the kingdom, although he had in mind to his dying day that the center of the kingdom would be the temple.

This is David's last message to his people. You will recall that when old Jacob was dying he called in his sons. When Moses reached the end of his life, he had a message for all twelve tribes. Now David has a message for his people as he comes to the end of his life.

Furthermore David the king said unto all the congregation, Solomon my son, whom alone God hath chosen, is yet young and tender, and the work is great: for the palace is not for man, but for the LORD God [1 Chron. 29:1].

When David says that Solomon is young and tender, he means that he is a sissy and inexperienced. Old David is a veteran. Although he is a gracious, generous man, he can be hard-boiled. Solomon is a novice.

Now I have prepared with all my might for the house of my God the gold for things to be made of gold, and the silver for things of silver, and the brass for things of brass, the iron for things of iron, and wood for things of wood; onyx stones, and stones to be set, glistering stones, and of divers colours, and all manner of precious stones, and marble stones in abundance.

Moreover, because I have set my affection to the house of my God, I have of mine own proper good, of gold and silver, which I have given to the house of my God, over and above all that I have prepared for the holy house [1 Chron. 29:2–3].

David says, "I have prepared with all my might for the house of my God." Oh, to have the heart of David, and put God first in our lives! These are gifts of his own individual property.

The gold for things of gold, and the silver for things of silver, and for all manner of work to be made by the hands of artificers. And who then is willing to consecrate his service this day unto the LORD? [1 Chron. 29:5].

David has set the example. There was no stinting or holding back in his giving. Then he put out the challenge to his people.

Then the chief of the fathers and princes of the tribes of Israel, and the captains of thousands and of hundreds,

with the rulers of the king's work, offered willingly [1 Chron. 29:6].

Now there is a response on the part of the people.

And gave for the service of the house of God of gold five thousand talents and ten thousand drams, and of silver ten thousand talents, and of brass eighteen thousand talents, and one hundred thousand talents of iron.

And they with whom precious stones were found gave them to the treasure of the house of the LORD, by the hand of Jehiel the Gershonite [1 Chron. 29: 7–8].

The people gave generously, and they gave with joy.

Then the people rejoiced, for that they offered willingly, because with perfect heart they offered willingly to the LORD: and David the king also rejoiced with great joy [1 Chron. 29:9].

It was a great thrill to David to see his people give so willingly toward the enrichment of the temple.

My friend, I used to see a motto that read: "Give till it hurts." That motto may be all right for the world, but it is not God's motto. If it hurts you to give, don't give! God wants you to give when it brings joy to your heart and life. Give hilariously, Paul said. This is what the people are doing here, and it was a time of great rejoicing.

Wherefore David blessed the LORD before all the congregation: and David said, Blessed be thou, LORD God of Israel our father, for ever and ever [1 Chron. 29:10].

Notice that David called God the father of the nation Israel. In the Old Testament He was not called the father of individuals. In fact, David never called Him Father. God called David His servant. That is very interesting. The Mosaic Law never made a son of God. Only faith in Jesus Christ can make us sons of God.

DAVID PRAYS

Now we have the great kingdom prayer of David.

Thine, O LORD, is the greatness, and the power, and the glory, and the victory, and the majesty: for all that is in the heaven and in the earth is thine; thine is the kingdom, O LORD, and thou art exalted as head above all [1 Chron. 29:11].

Do these words sound familiar to you? You will recall that when the disciples asked the Lord Jesus to teach them to pray, He gave them a model prayer. He took them right back here to David's prayer. "Thy kingdom come" was in the heart of David. These are words of brevity and simplicity, and they gather up the aspiration and hopes of centuries. This is one of the greatest prayers in the Scriptures and certainly in the Old Testament. It is all-comprehensive, majestic and filled with adoration, praise and thanksgiving. It repudiates all human merit and declares human dependence upon God. It reveals self-humiliation, confession, and dedication of self. It admits that all belongs to God. David recognized that the kingdom is God's. The Lord Jesus laid hold of this to teach His disciples.

The Scriptural concept of the kingdom is both an eternal kingdom and a temporal kingdom. It is a universal kingdom and a local kingdom. It is immediate, and it is mediated. Generally speaking, it is the reign of heaven over the earth.

When God created Adam, He gave him dominion. Now what does He mean by "the Kingdom"? It is the rule of God over the earth. It is a prayer for the recovery of the earth, to bring it back under the rule of God.

I hope you don't think that God is ruling the earth today. If He were, we would not have heartbreak, tears, disappointments, nor wars. This is the kingdom we should pray for. It will only come about in God's way. It will come through divine protocol, and the divine aspects will be adhered to. Man will not be able to build this kingdom here on this earth; only the Lord Jesus Christ can establish the kingdom. "*Thine* is the kingdom."

It is my personal feeling that the so-called Lord's Prayer is not for public praying. It is not just something to add to the ritual of a Sunday morning service. I believe it is good for private devotion. "Thine is the kingdom" ought to be the prayer of every believer. David was looking forward to the coming of the kingdom here upon this earth. That will be a glorious day!

But who am I, and what is my people, that we should be able to offer so willingly after this sort? for all things come of thee, and of thine own have we given thee [1 Chron. 29:14].

The very interesting thing is that you can't give God anything because it belongs to Him in the first place. But He can bless you when you give, and He will bless you. The reason some of us are so poor and narrow-minded and little is because we are not generous with God. God can only bless us when we open our hearts to Him.

> **O Lord our God, all this store that we have prepared to build thee an house for thine holy name cometh of thine hand, and is all thine own [1 Chron. 29:16].**

Oh, how we need to recognize this!

SOLOMON COMES TO THE THRONE

Now the people, having blessed God and having offered sacrifices to Him, make Solomon king.

> **And did eat and drink before the Lord on that day with great gladness. And they made Solomon the son of David king the second time, and anointed him unto the Lord to be the chief governor, and Zadok to be priest.**
>
> **Then Solomon sat on the throne of the Lord as king instead of David his father, and prospered; and all Israel obeyed him [1 Chron. 29:22–23].**

The kingdom was united behind Solomon, and he exercised royal authority before David's death.

DAVID DIES

Thus David the son of Jesse reigned over all Israel.

And the time that he reigned over Israel was forty years; seven years reigned he in Hebron, and thirty and three years reigned he in Jerusalem.

And he died in a good old age, full of days, riches, and honour: and Solomon his son reigned in his stead [1 Chron. 29:26–28].

This is the record that God has given. He wants you to know how He feels about David. Maybe you don't like David; God does. I am glad that the Lord loved David and dealt with him as He did, because David is so human. This encourages me. Vernon McGee is very human also, and I have found that God will deal with him just as graciously and just as severely as He dealt with David. The Lord is good. The Lord is wonderful! You and I cannot build Him a temple, but we can offer the temples of our bodies to Him. He doesn't get very much when He gets me, but He does have me. Oh, what joy it is to be committed to Him!

(For Bibliography to 1 Chronicles, see Bibliography at the end of 2 Chronicles.)

The Book of

2 CHRONICLES

INTRODUCTION

We have seen at the conclusion of 1 Chronicles that David had assembled all the material for the temple, had arranged for the manpower, had given encouragement to the leaders of the nation Israel and to the people, organized the service of the temple, provided all the money, and told Solomon to get busy. Now in 2 Chronicles Solomon is going to get busy.

We have seen that 1 Chronicles was actually all about David. It began with those long genealogies. There was a lot of begetting from Adam right on down to David. Why was the genealogy given? Because it led to David. Why David? Because David leads to Christ, and the New Testament opens with: "The book of the generation of Jesus Christ, the son of David . . ." (Matt. 1:1). That is the reason it is given.

I will mention again that in the Books of Chronicles we are getting God's viewpoint. In the Books of Samuel and the Books of Kings we were given man's viewpoint. This does not mean that those books were not inspired. They are inspired. But He gives first the human viewpoint, then the divine viewpoint. And the emphasis is on David. Where did David put the emphasis? He put it on the building of the temple of God.

In 2 Chronicles we will find two major themes. The first is the building of the temple. The second theme is revival. This book covers chronologically the same period as Kings but gives certain notable emphases.

The first nine chapters are given over to the reign of Solomon. Six of those chapters are concerning the building of the temple. It is pretty evident where God is putting the emphasis. The building of the temple was Solomon's greatest accomplishment. People always think of Solomon in regard to all the wives that he had. That is quite spectacular —no question about it—but it is not where God puts the emphasis. His having many wives wasn't in the will of God. That was contrary to the will of God, and that was a factor which brought about the division of the kingdom. Don't tell me he got by with it. He didn't. Sin always brings judgment. It doesn't matter who it is that commits the sin, it will bring judgment. The only way that anyone can get to heaven is to have a Savior, and that Savior is Jesus Christ.

So the first major theme of 2 Chronicles is Solomon's construction of the temple. That is important. God thought it was important and inspired the writer to devote six chapters to it.

From chapter 10 to the end of the book the kingdom is divided. We have seen from the Books of Kings that after the kingdom was divided there were many kings who ruled and that most of those kings were not very attractive. We have made the statement that there was not a single good king in Israel, the northern kingdom. So we find in Chronicles that there is no emphasis on the kingdom of Israel at all. The emphasis in this book is on the southern kingdom, Judah, and on David's line. That was a pretty bad lot, too. However, there were five of those kings who were outstanding: Asa, Jehoshaphat, Joash, Hezekiah, Josiah. These five kings were the means of bringing revival back to the nation. God puts the emphasis on revival, and we will spend a great deal of time talking about revival in this section.

Many years ago I belonged to a group of ministers who were praying for revival. I finally quit going because the attitude was that if we prayed hard enough, God would send revival.

May I say that God is sovereign. We are not going to *make* God do anything. God has a program and He is not about to change His program for you or for me. The important thing is for you and for me to get in step with God! I tell you, the *will* of God comes out of eternity, down through the centuries, and moves on through the centuries into eternity. God pity the little man who gets in front of that steam roller. It will go right over you, brother.

Someone will be sure to say he doesn't like that. May I remind you that we are the creatures. The creature does not try to get God to do something. It is God who is trying to get *us* to do something. That is the big problem. We tend to get things backwards. It is not God's duty to obey us. It is our duty to obey God. You may ask, "Well, doesn't God want to send revival?" Sure He does. And aren't we to meet His conditions? Yes, but I don't think they are meeting His conditions. It is interesting that the spiritual movement which has come about in our day did not come by these perspicuous theologians putting down conditions and the churches following them. The spiritual movement is not even in the church today. Most of the churches are as dead as dodo birds. The movement today is not among these brainy theologians. I get so tired and weary of reading their material today. Oh, they speak *ex cathedra:* they have all the answers! They have answers but no action—there's no spiritual movement.

Out of some of our seminaries today there is coming a great deal of material; these professors write with great authority. They have a lot of authority, but they haven't any action. (And I really don't think they have much authority.) May I say to you today, my friend, we need to learn to bow to the *will* of God and to come in very close to Him: cast ourselves upon Him. We're going to see that there are certain men—even kings—whom God used in a marvelous way, because they were willing to *take* orders and not *give* orders. I believe that the biggest hindrance to revival is the church leadership. They are the ones who are holding it back—and have been for years.

You may be saying, "Why, McGee, you sound like a revolutionary!" My friend, I have been a revolutionary ever since I entered the ministry, but nobody ever listened to me. I have said from the very beginning that we don't bring revival by listening to the theologians. We need to listen to the Word of God. And that is the reason I am trying to give out the Word of God. Now let me confess that I have had some ideas myself. But I am retired now, and I have discovered that the great ideas and the great programs that I had worked out were never used by God. I am beginning to suspect that revival could not come if God followed my plans either! It is ". . . Not by might, nor by power, but by my spirit, saith the LORD of hosts" (Zech. 4:6). It is not by brain nor by brawn, but by the Holy Spirit. It is hard to learn that, by the way.

The spotlight of this book is on the kings who followed in the line of David. Special prominence is given to the five kings in whose reigns were periods of revival, renewal, and reformation. The book concludes with the decree of Cyrus after the seventy years of captivity. No record is given of the period of the captivity. That was "time out" in God's program. Remember that this is the record from God's point of view.

OUTLINE

I. Solomon's Reign, Chapters 1–9

II. Division of the Kingdom and History of Judah, Chapters 10–36

Reformations Given Prominence:

A. Asa's, Chapters 14–16
B. Jehoshaphat's, Chapters 17–20
C. Joash's, Chapters 23–24
D. Hezekiah's, Chapters 29–32
E. Josiah's, Chapters 34–35

CHAPTER 1

THEME: *Solomon becomes king and prays for wisdom*

And Solomon the son of David was strengthened in his kingdom, and the Lord his God was with him, and magnified him exceedingly [2 Chron. 1:1].

You will remember that I made the point that Solomon was not David's choice. He was God's choice. I really do not think that David wanted Solomon to be the next king. I think it is obvious that his choice would have been the boy who rebelled against him, Absalom. He loved Absalom. It broke David's heart when Absalom was slain. It crushed him. You remember that when he sent out his army he gave specific instructions to each of his captains that Absalom was not to be hurt. David was willing to sacrifice everything for that boy. He loved him. I think that Absalom had a lot of David's temperament. I believe in some ways he was very much like David, but he was not *God's* choice. God had chosen Solomon, and God is going to bless Solomon. God chooses the weak things of this world, and God is going to use Solomon. The strength of God is revealed in weakness. David is gone now. He had been a great man but Solomon is young and tender, a weakling. God will use Solomon and will allow Solomon to do the actual building of the temple.

"Solomon the son of David was strengthened in his kingdom;" the kingdom will come to its zenith under Solomon. David put the foundation under the kingdom. "And the Lord his God was with him, and magnified him exceedingly." How gracious God is!

We will see that Solomon will disobey God. He will come to the place where God will repudiate him and tell him that He will divide the kingdom. Solomon was responsible for that division. The reason God did not divide the kingdom during the reign of Solomon was for the sake of David, not for the sake of Solomon.

…en Solomon spake unto all Israel, to … captains of thousands and of hun… ls, and to the judges, and to every … rnor in all Israel, the chief of the … ers [2 Chron. 1:2].

…ee, Solomon has a meeting of the leader… f Israel here.

…o Solomon, and all the congregation with him, went to the high place that was at Gibeon; for there was the tabernacle of the congregation of God, which Moses the servant of the Lord had made in the wilderness [2 Chron. 1:3].

The tabernacle was up there at Gibeon. We must remember that the ark was brought by David to Jerusalem, and it is there in a tent. But they couldn't come directly and immediately to God. This is tremendous! The way to God was through that tabernacle because the brazen altar was there, and that brazen altar speaks of the cross of Christ. They had to go there to approach God.

You and I must come before God in the same way. There is an idea today that anybody, under any circumstances, can just rush into the presence of God and that God has His listening-ear out. The Bible teaches that the Lord does not always hear prayers. Listen to the words of Peter: "For the eyes of the Lord are over the righteous, and his ears are open unto their prayers: but the face of the Lord is against them that do evil" (1 Pet. 3:12). God never said He would hear the prayers of those who do evil. I believe that the only prayer the sinner can pray to God is to go to Him and accept His mercy in Christ Jesus. If you wish to approach God, you must approach Him through the cross.

This is what Solomon does. He takes the leaders and they go to Gibeon where the tabernacle and the brazen altar are. He is being smart at the beginning of his reign.

But the ark of God had David brought up from Kirjath-jearim to the place which David had prepared for it: for he had pitched a tent for it at Jerusalem.

Moreover the brasen altar, that Bezaleel the son of Uri, the son of Hur, had made, he put before the tabernacle of the Lord; and Solomon and the congregation sought unto it [2 Chron. 1:4–5].

The way to God is through the brazen altar. They couldn't go to Him through the ark. In other words, you and I don't come immediately to God. The way of the cross leads home. There is no other way.

And Solomon went up thither to the brasen altar before the Lord, which was at the tabernacle of the congregation, and offered a thousand burnt offerings upon it [2 Chron. 1:6].

A model of the Temple reconstructed by Herod
(Holyland Hotel, Jerusalem; Photo by Ronald E. Pitkin).

They certainly are not stingy in their sacrifices. You will notice all the way through this period that there was an abundance of sacrifices during Solomon's reign.

In that night did God appear unto Solomon, and said unto him, Ask what I shall give thee.

And Solomon said unto God, Thou hast shewed great mercy unto David my father, and hast made me to reign in his stead.

Now, O LORD God, let thy promise unto David my father be established: for thou hast made me king over a people like the dust of the earth in multitude [2 Chron. 1:7–9].

God has made good a promise not only to David but to Abraham: "Your offspring will be like the dust"—you can't number them.

Give me now wisdom and knowledge, that I may go out and come in before this people: for who can judge this thy people, that is so great? [2 Chron. 1:10].

People commend Solomon and say that he was so smart to ask for wisdom. God gave him credit for asking that. But where did he get the idea? If we turn back to chapter 22 of 1 Chronicles, we read, "And David said to Solomon, My son, as for me, it was in my mind to build an house unto the name of the LORD my God: But the word of the LORD came to me, saying, Thou hast shed blood abundantly, and hast made great wars: thou shalt not build an house unto my name, because thou hast shed much blood upon the earth in my sight . . . Now, my son, the LORD be with thee; and prosper thou, and build the house of the LORD thy God, as he hath said of thee. Only the LORD give thee wisdom and understanding, and give thee charge concerning Israel, that thou mayest keep the law of the LORD thy God" (1 Chron. 22:7–8 and 11–12). At least Solomon was listening to his father. When David had said, "The Lord give thee wisdom and understanding," he remembered that. So when the Lord asked, "What do you want, Solomon?" he said, "I need wisdom and understanding." God gives him credit for it, though.

And God said to Solomon, Because this was in thine heart, and thou hast not asked riches, wealth, or honour, nor the life of thine enemies, neither yet hast asked long life; but hast asked wisdom and knowledge for thyself, that thou mayest judge my people, over whom I have made thee king:

Wisdom and knowledge is granted unto thee: and I will give thee riches, and wealth, and honour, such as none of the kings have had that have been before thee, neither shall there any after thee have the like [2 Chron. 1:11–12].

God grants his request for wisdom and gives him other blessings besides. I want you to notice, though, that the request was for wisdom to rule the people. Solomon did not ask for spiritual discernment. We will see that Solomon lacked spiritual discernment in his own life. Although he was given divine wisdom to rule, he did not seem to have wisdom to order his personal life.

And Solomon gathered chariots and horsemen: and he had a thousand and four hundred chariots, and twelve thousand horsemen, which he placed in the chariot cities, and with the king at Jerusalem.

And the king made silver and gold at Jerusalem as plenteous as stones, and cedar trees made he as the sycomore trees that are in the vale for abundance [2 Chron. 1:14–15].

The sycamore tree grows over there today, but you don't see many cedar trees. He made cedar trees as abundant as the sycamore, and silver and gold like the stones. If you have ever been in that land or even seen pictures of it, you know that there are rocks and stones everywhere. There are more rocks in that land than any place I have ever been. Imagine Solomon making silver and gold as commonplace as those stones!

And Solomon had horses brought out of Egypt, and linen yarn: the king's merchants received the linen yarn at a price.

And they fetched up, and brought forth out of Egypt a chariot for six hundred shekels of silver, and an horse for an hundred and fifty: and so brought they out horses for all the kings of the Hittites, and for the kings of Syria, by their means [2 Chron. 1:16–17].

You will notice that he is already getting into an area which was forbidden to him. God had told them when the day should come that they would have a king ". . . he shall not multiply horses to himself, nor cause the people to return to Egypt, to the end that he should multiply horses: forasmuch as the LORD hath said unto you, Ye shall henceforth return no more that way. Neither shall he multiply wives to himself, that his heart turn not away: neither shall he greatly multiply to himself silver and gold" (Deut. 17:16–17). Solomon is amassing horses and he is becoming personally wealthy. We will find that he will also multiply wives to himself.

CHAPTERS 2–4

***THEME:** Construction of the temple*

Solomon moves forward now according to the instructions that David his father had given him.

SOLOMON PREPARES TO BUILD

And Solomon determined to build an house for the name of the LORD, and an house for his kingdom.

And Solomon told out threescore and ten thousand men to bear burdens, and fourscore thousand to hew in the mountain, and three thousand and six hundred to oversee them [2 Chron. 2:1–2].

The blueprints are laid out, and Solomon begins the organization to build. Notice that building the temple is the part of Solomon's reign that God emphasizes.

And Solomon sent to Huram the king of Tyre, saying, As thou didst deal with David my father, and didst send him cedars to build him an house to dwell therein, even so deal with me [2 Chron. 2:3].

Hiram loved David, and David loved Hiram. On this basis Solomon appeals to him. I think Hiram had problems with Solomon, as we shall see. He had been very generous with David, but he finds Solomon a little difficult to deal with.

Behold, I build an house to the name of the LORD my God, to dedicate it to him, and to burn before him sweet incense, and for the continual shewbread, and for the burnt offerings morning and evening, on the sabbaths, and on the new moons, and on the solemn feasts of the LORD our God. This is an ordinance for ever to Israel [2 Chron. 2:4].

Notice that this is to be an ordinance *forever*. There have been criticisms of the restoration of temple sacrifices during the Millennium. Since the animal sacrifices pointed forward to the sacrifice of Christ on the cross, why would animal sacrifices be resumed during the Millennium? Because God ordained it; that is answer enough. They will be meaningful, of course, and will be a reminder of the sacrifice of the Lord Jesus Christ.

And the house which I build is great: for great is our God above all gods [2 Chron. 2:5].

In our day what makes a thing great? What makes a man great? What makes a nation great? What makes a church great? God, my friend. This is something else we are losing sight of.

But who is able to build him an house, seeing the heaven and heaven of heavens cannot contain him? who am I then, that I should build him an house, save only to burn sacrifice before him? [2 Chron. 2:6].

It was by a sacrifice that they approached God. And the only way you and I can come to God is through the sacrifice of the Lord Jesus Christ. The important thing to note here is that Solomon had no misgivings as to who God was, or whether God would occupy and live in that house.

I once read an article about a theologian who made the statement that what Solomon was attempting to do was build a little house to put God in a box and that the people had the idea that God should be put in a box—that He could be held there. May I say to you that Solomon had no conception like that at all; neither did the people. They were much farther advanced than a great many people are today, even in our churches. Many people call the church "God's house." Well, God doesn't occupy a house. He never did. The temple was a place to make sacrifices. It was a place of *approach* to God. And it had to be worthy of

Him. It was highly ornate, very beautiful. It was not very large compared to other buildings of that day. For instance, if you put the temple that Solomon built down beside the temple of Diana in Ephesus or the pyramids, it would be a pygmy. But it made up for its small size in its wealth—the tremendous amount of silver and gold that went into it.

Send me now therefore a man cunning to work in gold, and in silver, and in brass, and in iron, and in purple, and crimson, and blue, and that can skill to grave with the cunning men that are with me in Judah and in Jerusalem, whom David my father did provide [2 Chron. 2:7].

You see, they had to get the skilled workmen from the outside, because the Israelites were an agricultural people, as God intended them to be. It is interesting to see that when Jewish people return to Israel in our day, they return to the soil. I have traveled from one end of Israel to the other end, and from the Dead Sea to the Mediterranean Sea, and some of the finest farms I have ever seen are there. I do not believe there is land anywhere any richer than the Valley of Esdraelon where Megiddo is located. It certainly is rich country. In Solomon's day the nation Israel did not have artificers or artisans, and they had to call upon Hiram for those.

Send me also cedar trees, fir trees, and algum trees, out of Lebanon: for I know that thy servants can skill to cut timber in Lebanon; and, behold, my servants shall be with thy servants [2 Chron. 2:8].

In other words, Solomon's men would learn from them. These cedar trees are the famous cedars of Lebanon.

Even to prepare me timber in abundance: for the house which I am about to build shall be wonderful great [2 Chron. 2:9].

It won't be large, but it will be great.

And, behold, I will give to thy servants, the hewers that cut timber, twenty thousand measures of beaten wheat, and twenty thousand measures of barley, and twenty thousand baths of wine, and twenty thousand baths of oil [2 Chron. 2:10].

Later on we shall see there was a misunderstanding relative to this payment that Solomon was to make.

Then Huram the king of Tyre answered in writing, which he sent to Solomon, Because the LORD hath loved his people, he hath made thee king over them.

Huram said moreover, Blessed be the LORD God of Israel, that made heaven and earth, who hath given to David the king a wise son, endued with prudence and understanding, that might build an house for the LORD, and an house for his kingdom.

And now I have sent a cunning man, endued with understanding, of Huram my father's [2 Chron. 2:11–13].

Then he goes on to describe this one whom he is sending.

And Solomon numbered all the strangers that were in the land of Israel, after the numbering wherewith David his father had numbered them; and they were found an hundred and fifty thousand and six hundred.

And he set threescore and ten thousand of them to be bearers of burdens, and fourscore thousand to be hewers in the mountain, and three thousand and six hundred overseers to set the people awork [2 Chron. 2:17–18].

These are to be the helpers, you see. These are the men who will do the common labor.

SOLOMON BEGINS CONSTRUCTION OF THE TEMPLE

Then Solomon began to build the house of the LORD at Jerusalem in mount Moriah, where the LORD appeared unto David his father, in the place that David had prepared in the threshing-floor of Ornan the Jebusite [2 Chron. 3:1].

As we have seen, this threshing floor of Ornan is the site where centuries before Abraham had been told to offer Isaac. Then on that same ridge, right outside the city of Jerusalem, is located Golgotha, the place of the skull, where Jesus was crucified. David had bought this parcel of ground from Ornan. It is still the temple area today.

To those of us who are not in the construction business, the details of the blueprints and the building supplies are not particularly interesting. We will only cull out certain great truths which we do not find mentioned elsewhere.

Now these are the things wherein Solomon was instructed for the building of the house of God. The length by cubits after the first measure was threescore cubits, and the breadth twenty cubits [2 Chron. 3:3].

It is twice as large as the tabernacle was: 60 x 20 cubits. This translated into feet would be approximately 90 x 30 feet. These dimensions are for the temple proper; around it there are to be many other buildings. It was quite imposing when all the buildings were in place, but the temple proper was only twice as large as the tabernacle.

Now let me call your attention to certain things, some of which we have seen, and some we have not seen.

The wings of these cherubims spread themselves forth twenty cubits: and they stood on their feet, and their faces were inward [2 Chron. 3:13].

These are the cherubims that looked down on the mercy seat. You will recall that back in the tabernacle which Moses was instructed to build, God gave no measurement for the cherubim. They speak of Deity, and Deity cannot be measured. But here in the temple the measurement is given, and they are undoubtedly much larger than in the tabernacle. There is a note of deterioration here, as they are attempting to measure Deity, and that cannot be done.

Let me remind you that we are seeing the temple from God's viewpoint. What is it that God calls attention to which was not given from the human viewpoint in Kings? Well, it is the beauty of the veil.

And he made the veil of blue, and purple, and crimson, and fine linen, and wrought cherubims thereon [2 Chron. 3:14].

The veil speaks of the humanity of Christ. God calls attention to that. When Christ was crucified, the veil of the temple was torn in two, since the veil represented the humanity of Christ. The rending of that veil signified that a "new and living way" was opened for all believers into the very presence of God with no other sacrifice than Christ's. Here in Chronicles God calls attention to the beauty of the veil. It is as if He said, ". . . This is my beloved Son, in whom I am well pleased" (Matt. 3:17).

Something else we should notice is the pillars.

Also he made before the house two pillars of thirty and five cubits high, and the chapiter that was on the top of each of them was five cubits [2 Chron. 3:15].

This meant that these pillars went up very high (see model of the temple, pp. 408 and 422). Compared to the size of the building, they seem almost out of proportion. These pillars speak of strength and beauty.

Strength and beauty are two things which modern man thinks he has attained. We boast of our strength; yet we are powerless to maintain law and order. And as far as beauty is concerned, have you looked at modern art? My daughter majored in art, and she took me through a classroom to show me what they were doing. She would say, "Dad, isn't that beautiful?" Well, I didn't want to misrepresent how I felt—I couldn't say it was beautiful. I could say, "My, I haven't seen anything like that!" And believe me, I hadn't.

God is interested in strength and beauty, and those pillars of the temple were very impressive. In the next chapter He again mentions this matter of strength and beauty:

To wit, the two pillars, and the pommels, and the chapiters which were on the top of the two pillars, and the two wreaths to cover the two pommels of the chapiters which were on the top of the pillars [2 Chron. 4:12].

God is calling particular attention to it.

And he made chains, as in the oracle, and put them on the heads of the pillars; and made an hundred pomegranates, and put them on the chains [2 Chron. 3:16].

He mentions these chains. What do they represent? They speak of the unity of the nation. The chains picture the unity of the individuals that constitute the tribes, and the tribes in turn constitute the nation.

God is interested in absolute unity. This is something which God's people are losing sight of in our day. We are split and fragmented into thousands of different groups today. There are always new organizations coming into existence. I am not sure that all this is honoring to the Lord. You see, in the New Testament God has given a picture of unity that is even better than the chain. It is the body. He says His church is a body. In a body there can be many members, and some of the members are of honor and some of dishonor, but they are all in one body. That is the picture of the church.

Notice also the use of pomegranates—one hundred of them. Also we read:

And four hundred pomegranates on the two wreaths; two rows of pomegranates on each wreath, to cover the two pommels of the chapiters which were upon the pillars [2 Chron. 4:13].

Pomegranates speak of fruitfulness, and that is the emphasis here.

I didn't specifically mention the colors that are used here. Notice that the veil was of blue and purple and crimson and fine linen. Blue is the color of the heaven above. Purple is the color of royalty, and crimson speaks of redemption through the blood of Christ. White speaks of the holy walk. All these colors are important from God's point of view.

Chapter four gives details about the articles of furniture: the altar of brass, the huge laver, the ten smaller lavers, the candlesticks, the tables. Then there were pots and shovels and basins. The brazen altar was four times as large as the one in the tabernacle. There were additional lavers in the temple. There were other additions and changes.

The innovations and enlargements took away the simplicity of the tabernacle and the plain references to Christ. It is the tabernacle and not the temple which became the figure that was used in the Epistle to the Hebrews to depict the person and work of Christ.

CHAPTERS 5–6

THEME: *The completed temple*

Thus all the work that Solomon made for the house of the LORD was finished: and Solomon brought in all the things that David his father had dedicated; and the silver, and the gold, and all the instruments, put he among the treasures of the house of God.

Then Solomon assembled the elders of Israel, and all the heads of the tribes, the chief of the fathers of the children of Israel, unto Jerusalem, to bring up the ark of the covenant of the LORD out of the city of David, which is Zion [2 Chron. 5:1–2].

After the temple was completed, the ark was brought into the temple. Zion is right up on the hill not very far from the temple area. I have walked it several times, both up and down, because it is not too far.

We don't know the exact spot where David was keeping the ark, but it was in the city of David which is Mount Zion. That is not a very large area and it is not far from the temple area.

Also king Solomon, and all the congregation of Israel that were assembled unto him before the ark, sacrificed sheep and oxen, which could not be told nor numbered for multitude [2 Chron. 5:6].

The thought here is that there was no attempt to count them because they represent the sacrifice of Christ. And that is something which cannot be counted or measured.

And the priests brought in the ark of the covenant of the LORD unto his place, to the oracle of the house, into the most holy place, even under the wings of the cherubims:

For the cherubims spread forth their wings over the place of the ark, and the cherubims covered the ark and the staves thereof above.

And they drew out the staves of the ark, that the ends of the staves were seen from the ark before the oracle; but they were not seen without. And there it is unto this day [2 Chron. 5:7–9].

"Unto this day" refers, of course, to the time of the writing of Chronicles. The staves were drawn out.

The ark is to move no more. You will remember that the ark was constructed in the wilderness at Mount Sinai, and then the children of Israel spent forty years wandering in the wilderness. The ark was always carried before them as they traveled. It was the ark that went first through the Jordan River when they entered the Promised Land. After they had arrived in the land, the ark was still moved from place to place. Remember that once it was even captured by the Philistines, and then it was sent back by them.

The ark had been brought to Jerusalem by David, and he had kept it at Mount Zion until the time when the temple should be completed. That time has now come, and the ark is placed into the most holy place, and the staves are removed. It is to move no more. The males of the children of Israel are to appear at the tabernacle at three feasts of the year: Passover, Pentecost, and the Feast of Tabernacles. This means that from now on they will come to Jerusalem on those feast days and appear at the temple where the ark rests.

You will remember that the ark speaks of the Lord Jesus Christ, of His person. Above the ark was the mercy seat which speaks of His work of redemption, His shedding of blood, the fact that He is now our propitiation. All of that is permanent. ". . . but now once in the end of the world [lit., the end of the age] hath he appeared to put away sin by the sacrifice of himself" (Heb. 9:26). It is permanent, it is basic, it is established. Let me use the figure of speech here: the staves have been pulled out. There will be no other way of salvation. Peter could say to his people, "Neither is there salvation in any other; for there is none other name under heaven given among men, whereby we must be saved" (Acts 4:12). My friend, the staves have been pulled out. The ark is not on the move any more.

Also the withdrawing of the staves indicates rest. The Lord Jesus gives rest to those who come to Him. Also there is to be a *place* of rest. Our Lord spoke of that place when He said to His own men in the Upper Room, ". . . I go to prepare a place for you. And if I go and prepare a place for you, I will come again, and receive you unto myself; that where I am, there ye may be also" (John 14:2–3). The place is prepared, and one of these days we will go to that place.

One of the characteristics of that place is its permanence, the fact that it is a place of eternity. "And God shall wipe away all tears from their eyes; and there shall be no more death, neither sorrow, nor crying, neither shall there be any more pain: for the former things are passed away" (Rev. 21:4). This is the city of God. It is permanent, and ". . . the Lord God Almighty and the Lamb are the temple of it" (Rev. 21:22). My friend, the staves are already pulled out. How wonderful that we are not going to be on the march. We don't have to go looking for God. As Paul said to the Romans, we don't have to go to heaven to bring Christ down, nor do we have to go down to hell to bring Him up. He is right there for us. This is permanent; it is eternal. It will not be changed. He drew out the staves.

There was nothing in the ark save the two tables which Moses put therein at Horeb, when the LORD made a covenant with the children of Israel, when they came out of Egypt [2 Chron. 5:10].

Two things that had been placed in the ark by Moses are now missing: Aaron's rod and the pot of manna. The manna, you will recall from the account of Numbers 17, would disappear if the people didn't gather it. And if it was not eaten the same day, it would spoil. However a pot of manna was preserved in the ark as a memorial. Now it is gone. The manna was a symbol of Christ as the Bread of Life, who feeds those who are His own. Aaron's rod that budded (Exod. 16) is a symbol of Christ's resurrection. It has been actualized to us today by the historical fact that Jesus died (that's His humanity), was buried, then rose again the third day—that's not human; it reveals His deity. The priesthood of the Lord Jesus Christ rests upon His resurrection, just as Aaron's priesthood was confirmed by the budding of his rod, a type of resurrection.

And it came to pass, when the priests were come out of the holy place: (for all the priests that were present were sanctified, and did not then wait by course) [2 Chron 5:11].

You see, all the courses came up for this act of dedication. The singers were there, and the orchestra with cymbals and psalteries and harps, and 120 trumpet players!

It came even to pass, as the trumpeters and singers were as one, to make one sound to be heard in praising and thanking the LORD; and when they lifted up their voice with the trumpets and cymbals and instruments of music, and praised the LORD, saying, For he is good; for his mercy endureth for ever: that then the house was filled with a cloud, even the house of the LORD [2 Chron. 5:13].

This was a great occasion!

So that the priests could not stand to minister by reason of the cloud: for the

glory of the LORD had filled the house of God [2 Chron. 5:14].

Now as we come to chapter 6 we have the message of Solomon for this occasion and his prayer of dedication.

SOLOMON'S MESSAGE

This is a tremendous message that Solomon gives.

Then said Solomon, The LORD hath said that he would dwell in the thick darkness.

But I have built an house of habitation for thee, and a place for thy dwelling for ever.

And the king turned his face, and blessed the whole congregation of Israel: and all the congregation of Israel stood [2 Chron. 6:1–3].

Now Solomon addresses the people.

And he said, Blessed be the LORD God of Israel, who hath with his hands fulfilled that which he spake with his mouth to my father David, saying [2 Chron. 6:4].

David, you see, is the one responsible for the temple.

Since the day that I brought forth my people out of the land of Egypt I chose no city among all the tribes of Israel to build an house in, that my name might be there; neither chose I any man to be a ruler over my people Israel:

But I have chosen Jerusalem, that my name might be there; and have chosen David to be over my people Israel [2 Chron. 6:5–6].

In God's sovereign will He chose Jerusalem to be the center and the capital of this earth. It will be that some day. He chose Jerusalem for the place the temple would stand. He chose David to be the king, and now one in David's line. This is the arbitrary, the absolute will of God in making this choice.

Now, my friend, our choices are often quite different from God's choices. For example, I would not have chosen Jerusalem. I think the most beautiful spot in that land is at Samaria where Ahab and Jezebel lived. Many folk build on a hillside so they have a view of the valley, but in Samaria you can look in every direction. On the west you see the Mediterranean Sea. On the east you see the Jordan Valley and the Sea of Galilee. On the south you see Jerusalem, and when you look to the north you see Mount Hermon. That's quite a view! I would choose that place for the capital. But God did not consult me or my wishes. God chose Jerusalem. This is the sovereign will of God. God says, "I have chosen Jerusalem."

My friend, God has His will for you and for me. I actually believe that for a child of God He has a certain place, a certain house for you to live in. His will for you involves everything in your life. The great problem for you and me is to get in the will of God. We can stand off and argue all we want to about the free will of man and God's sovereignty, but it is a fruitless waste of time. I'll tell you something that is very profitable: it is to get to the place—in fact, on the *spot* that God has marked "X"—which He has chosen for you and for me. When you and I get on that spot, we will be in the right place. God's will is the important thing.

God chose Jerusalem; God chose this man David.

Now it was in the heart of David my father to build an house for the name of the LORD God of Israel [2 Chron. 6:7].

Solomon is saying that he has done what David wanted done; he is carrying out his wishes in building the temple.

The LORD therefore hath performed his word that he hath spoken: for I am risen up in the room of David my father, and am set on the throne of Israel, as the LORD promised, and have built the house for the name of the LORD God of Israel.

And in it have I put the ark, wherein is the covenant of the LORD, that he made with the children of Israel [2 Chron. 6:10–11].

This is all-important to see.

SOLOMON'S PRAYER

Now we have this wonderful prayer of dedication.

And he stood before the altar of the LORD in the presence of all the congregation of Israel, and spread forth his hands:

For Solomon had made a brasen scaffold, of five cubits long, and five cubits broad, and three cubits high, and had

set it in the midst of the court: and upon it he stood, and kneeled down upon his knees before all the congregation of Israel, and spread forth his hands toward heaven [2 Chron. 6: 12–13].

If you are wondering about the proper posture for prayer, Solomon kneeled down. On your knees is a fitting posture for a creature in the presence of his Creator.

Solomon begins with thanksgiving.

And said, O LORD God of Israel, there is no God like thee in the heaven, nor in the earth; which keepest covenant, and shewest mercy unto thy servants, that walk before thee with all their hearts:

Thou which hast kept with thy servant David my father that which thou hast promised him; and spakest with thy mouth, and hast fulfilled it with thine hand, as it is this day [2 Chron. 6:14–15].

He is thanking God because He is the Creator and because of His mercy and His faithfulness. In His grace He had moved into the heart of David, into the nation, and into the heart and life of Solomon.

In our day a great many Christians need an experience with God. It seems that they are satisfied to stand off and stiff-arm the Lord. They keep Him at a distance, yet they say, "Yes, I'm a Christian." My friend, let's have a close relationship with Him and real fellowship.

But will God in very deed dwell with men on the earth? behold, heaven and the heaven of heavens cannot contain thee; how much less this house which I have built! [2 Chron. 6:18].

This is an important verse, to which I have referred before. Certainly neither Solomon nor the nation Israel had any notion of "boxing God in" when they built a temple for Him. Rather the temple was to be a meeting place between God and man.

That thine eyes may be upon this house day and night, upon the place whereof thou hast said that thou wouldest put thy name there; to hearken unto the prayer which thy servant prayeth toward this place [2 Chron. 6:20].

You see, this temple was the place where man could meet God.

Hearken therefore unto the supplications of thy servant, and of thy people Israel, which they shall make toward this place: hear thou from thy dwelling place, even from heaven; and when thou hearest, forgive [2 Chron. 6:21].

The temple was to become the very center of the life of the nation Israel.

And if thy people Israel be put to the worse before the enemy, because they have sinned against thee; and shall return and confess thy name, and pray and make supplication before thee in this house;
Then hear thou from the heavens, and forgive the sin of thy people Israel, and bring them again unto the land which thou gavest to them and to their fathers [2 Chron. 6:24–25].

When they had sinned, they were to come back to that temple.

When the heaven is shut up, and there is no rain, because they have sinned against thee; yet if they pray toward this place, and confess thy name, and turn from their sin, when thou dost afflict them [2 Chron. 6:26].

When there is a drought in the land because of the sin of the people, what are they to do? Come back to God in prayer.

If there be dearth in the land, if there be pestilence, if there be blasting, or mildew, locusts, or caterpillars; if their enemies besiege them in the cities of their land; whatsoever sore or whatsoever sickness there be [2 Chron 6:28].

Whatever calamity might come to them, they were to return to the temple and pray to God.

Then hear thou from heaven thy dwelling place, and forgive, and render unto every man according unto all his ways, whose heart thou knowest; (for thou only knowest the hearts of the children of men:) [2 Chron. 6:30].

God knows us, my friend. That is the reason we ought to be doing business with Him.

Moreover concerning the stranger, which is not of thy people Israel, but is come from a far country for thy great name's sake, and thy mighty hand, and thy stretched out arm; if they come and pray in this house;

Then hear thou from the heavens, even from thy dwelling place, and do according to all that the stranger calleth to thee for; that all people of the earth may know thy name, and fear thee, as doth thy people Israel, and may know that this house which I have built is called by thy name [2 Chron. 6:32–33].

You see, this was a great missionary project. The temple was not only for Israel—the whole world was to come there. If a stranger or foreigner would come from a far country—from the end of the earth—he could meet God at the temple.

If they sin against thee, (for there is no man which sinneth not,) and thou be angry with them, and deliver them over before their enemies, and they carry them away captives unto a land far off or near [2 Chron 6:36].

In the country to which they are taken captive, they are to turn in the direction of the temple and lift their voices to God. This is what Daniel did, you recall. Daniel opened his windows toward Jerusalem (the temple by that time had been destroyed), kneeled, and prayed to God three times a day (Dan. 6:10). And God heard his prayer.

If they return to thee with all their heart and with all their soul in the land of their captivity, whither they have carried them captives, and pray toward their land, which thou gavest unto their fathers, and toward the city which thou hast chosen, and toward the house which I have built for thy name:

Then hear thou from the heavens, even from thy dwelling place, their prayer and their supplications, and maintain their cause, and forgive thy people which have sinned against thee.

Now, my God, let, I beseech thee, thine eyes be open, and let thine ears be attent unto the prayer that is made in this place [2 Chron. 6:38–40].

The temple was to be the meeting place.

Now therefore arise, O Lord God, into thy resting place, thou, and the ark of thy strength: let thy priests, O Lord God, be clothed with salvation, and let thy saints rejoice in goodness.

O Lord God, turn not away the face of thine anointed: remember the mercies of David thy servant [2 Chron. 6:41–42].

This is a glorious prayer. Notice that he makes it on the basis of the mercy God extended to David.

You and I are to pray because Christ has made a mercy seat for us by His shed blood. He made peace for us by the blood of His cross, and God is prepared to extend mercy to us.

CHAPTER 7

***THEME:** God's acceptance of the temple*

In the preceding chapter we have seen the dedication service of the temple. We have read Solomon's message and his great prayer of dedication. In this chapter we shall see God's response to it.

Now when Solomon had made an end of praying, the fire came down from heaven, and consumed the burnt offering and the sacrifices; and the glory of the Lord filled the house [2 Chron. 7:1].

This is what happened, you recall, when Moses finished the construction of the tabernacle in the wilderness. When he set it up, the glory of the Lord filled it (Exod. 40:34–35). God accepts this temple that Solomon has built.

Notice that fire from heaven consumes the sacrifice. This means that the judgment of God has fallen upon sin. God does not accept the temple because it is beautiful—and it is that. He does not accept it because of the lavish expenditure of wealth. The basis of His acceptance is the fact that it is pointing to Christ. It is *His* sacrifice, actually, that makes this acceptable to God. The glory of the Lord filled the temple, as we have seen in the final verses of chapter 5, and now also fire from heaven consumes the burnt offering.

These people had the visible presence of God. In the New Testament, in Paul's Epistle to the Romans, he answers the question: who are Israelites? He gives eight fingerprints of identification, one of which is that they had the *glory*. No other people have had the visible presence of God except the Israelites.

And the priests could not enter into the house of the LORD, because the glory of the LORD had filled the LORD'S house.

And when all the children of Israel saw how the fire came down, and the glory of the LORD upon the house, they bowed themselves with their faces to the ground upon the pavement, and worshipped, and praised the LORD, saying, For he is good; for his mercy endureth for ever [2 Chron. 7:2–3].

And, my friend, this is an expression that I trust will get into your vocabulary, and that you will say from time to time, "The LORD is good; His mercy endureth forever." You recall that the psalmist said, "The LORD is good. Let the redeemed of the LORD say so." If you and I are not "say-so Christians," nobody else will be. Nobody in politics will be saying how good God is; they will be telling us how great *they* are and what their party is doing for the country. Candidly, none of the politicians seem to be doing much good, by the way. But the *Lord* is good. Let the redeemed of the Lord *say so*.

Then the king and all the people offered sacrifices before the LORD.

And king Solomon offered a sacrifice of twenty and two thousand oxen, and an hundred and twenty thousand sheep: so the king and all the people dedicated the house of God [2 Chron. 7:4–5].

These verses have caused a great deal of criticism by the skeptics of the Bible. They love to criticize on the basis of three issues: (1) They say this offering and sacrifice was an extravagance; (2) they say it would have been physically impossible to offer that many sacrifices on the altar; and (3) they say there was no necessity for all this slaughter of animals. I'm sure the members of the Society for the Prevention of Cruelty to Animals would protest this.

Now let us look at these three issues from a biblical perspective. We need to look at things in the light of the Word of God. In the first place, although the temple was the center for all this activity, I do not think that every one of those animals was sacrificed on one altar. For this special occasion they probably had erected altars all over that temple area. It was not a physical impossibility.

Now why was there all of this expenditure? Well, it was necessary in order for each area to have its own sacrifice. It was as when the people of Israel came out of the land of Egypt and a lamb was slain for each home. There must have been literally thousands of lambs that were slain that night. It was not a needless waste for two reasons. The primary meaning of it is that it symbolizes the sacrifice of the Lord Jesus Christ. And, my friend, it was Simon Peter who said that His blood was precious. "Forasmuch as ye know that ye were not redeemed with corruptible things, as silver and gold, from your vain conversation received by tradition from your fathers; But with the precious blood of Christ, as of a lamb without blemish and without spot" (1 Pet. 1:18–19). This is not a great expenditure because it is pointing to Christ. The second reason that it was not a "needless waste" was that the meat was used for food afterward. Although the "burnt offerings" were totally consumed by fire, other offerings, such as the peace offering, were eaten. This dedication of the temple was a time of great feasting and great celebrating.

Let's be fair with the Bible, my friend.

I have observed the people who are always talking about the great extravagance of money spent for the Lord. It is an amazing fact that even Christian people are guilty of this kind of criticism. I knew a dear lady who was very much interested in Bible classes; she had one in her home. We had a Bible teacher come to our church. The people liked him, and they gave him a very generous offering. He stayed with us for about ten days and the church gave him $500.00 plus his expenses. This lady thought that was ridiculous; it was too great an expenditure. Also this lady was interested in music, and she was on the music committee of the town where she lived, and they brought a certain opera singer to town. He sang one night and they gave him $2,000.00. She thought that was wonderful. May I say to you, it is interesting that when something is being spent for the Lord it is just a waste, but when something is spent for the things of the world it is all right.

To anyone who thinks they were slaying too many animals for sacrifice, how many animals are slain in this country every day? There are thousands of animals slain every day in the packing houses of our country. No one raises a voice or does anything to protest that. After all, that is to satisfy *us*. But when something is done for the glory of God, there will always be people who will object. I don't know about you, but I'm on Solomon's side here. I think he did the right thing, because the sacrifices were pointing to the Lord Jesus Christ, and He shed His precious blood for me.

And the priests waited on their offices: the Levites also with instruments of music of the LORD, which David the king had made to praise the LORD, because his mercy endureth for ever, when David praised by their ministry; and the priests sounded trumpets before them, and all Israel stood [2 Chron. 7:6].

I wish I could get God's people to praise the Lord and to say that God is good and His mercy endures forever. Oh, how good God has been to me! Has He been good to you, friends? Well then, say so.

Moreover Solomon hallowed the middle of the court that was before the house of the LORD: for there he offered burnt offerings, and the fat of the peace offerings, because the brasen altar which Solomon had made was not able to receive the burnt offerings, and the meat offerings, and the fat.

Also at the same time Solomon kept the feast seven days, and all Israel with him, a very great congregation, from the entering in of Hamath unto the river of Egypt [2 Chron. 7:7–8].

From the entering of Hamath to the river of Egypt means from the extreme north to the extreme south of the land.

GOD'S SECOND APPEARANCE TO SOLOMON

And the LORD appeared to Solomon by night, and said unto him, I have heard thy prayer, and have chosen this place to myself for an house of sacrifice.

If I shut up heaven that there be no rain, or if I command the locusts to devour the land, or if I send pestilence among my people;

If my people, which are called by my name, shall humble themselves, and pray, and seek my face, and turn from their wicked ways; then will I hear from heaven, and will forgive their sin, and will heal their land [2 Chron. 7:12–14].

I am going to spend time on this last verse because it has been so often used out of context without regard to its primary meaning. It has been quoted as a promise to us from God that if we do certain things, He will do certain things. This verse has been tailored to fit into any local situation. I don't believe I have ever participated in an evangelistic campaign without someone at some time getting up and quoting this verse of Scripture and saying that he was resting on these promises. I believe that a careful consideration of this verse, its location and content and context, will prevent us from taking it like a capsule and swallowing it without some attention to its real meaning. We do violence to it by wresting it from its place. Just because it seems to fit into our plans and says what we want to say, we ignore its primary purpose and rob it of its vitality. It becomes, actually, a meaningless verse as it is being used in our day.

Now I want to speak very plainly to you. I am a dispensationalist. I think it is the only system that deals with the entire Bible consistently. It gives a literal meaning to the Word of God and gives it a real meaning. I am a graduate of a denominational seminary in which most of the Scripture was absolutely ignored because they had no interpretation for it. The way we were taught the Bible was sort of like going to a corncrib and taking out enough to feed the chickens—and the rest you didn't worry about. That was because they had no interpretation for it. The problem was that no one wanted to come back for more because if you went into more sections of Scripture than just those few they taught, you might get into trouble. Although the dispensational interpretation has its problems, it solves more problems than any other interpretation that I have heard.

Let me give you examples of the position I take. I recognize that the Sermon on the Mount looks forward to the time of the kingdom and it will be the law of the kingdom. However, I also believe that it has a message for us today. I think the way the Lord's Prayer is used in a great many churches by an affluent society is absolutely meaningless. In the Great Tribulation that prayer will really mean something to people. Although I am a dispensationalist, I am not a hyper-dispensationalist. I don't exclude the Sermon on the Mount. I preach on it. It shows that man comes short of God's standards. I find the Lord's Prayer helpful. I pray it. I have written a little book on it entitled, *Let Us Pray*. There is an *interpretation* of Scripture—that is one thing. Then there is an *application* of Scripture, which is something else. Remember the old adage that "all Scripture is written *for* us, but not all Scripture is written *to* us." The interpretation of a verse of Scripture will teach what it means in its setting and context. It may not be written *to* us at all. We can think of many commands given in the Old Testament which are not commands given to us. However, the application of all of Scripture is *for* us. God has something to teach us throughout the entire Scripture.

Now let's go back to 2 Chronicles 7:14. The setting is at the dedication of David's temple which Solomon had built. It is God's Word to Solomon concerning that land in that day. At the dedication Solomon prayed this great prayer which we have seen. Now He remembers the prayers of His people, and He says to Solomon, "If my people, which are called by my name. . . ." To whom is He talking? "My people, which are called by My name." That is Israel. God is talking to Solomon about Israel. Now, if these will humble themselves, if they will pray, if they will seek His face, if they will turn from their wicked ways, *then* God promises three things to Israel: He will hear their prayer, He will forgive them, He will heal their land. These were definite conditions that God put down for Israel, and their history demonstrates the accuracy and literalness of these specifics.

Now when you come to the New Testament, you find that John the Baptist says, ". . . Repent ye: for the kingdom of heaven is at hand" (Matt. 3:2). And the Lord Jesus Christ repeated that, calling upon the nation to meet these conditions—so that the promises of God could be fulfilled. It was a legitimate offer. In our day, the people of Israel have been scattered throughout the world. They cannot have peace in that land because they have not met those conditions. This is a *literal* interpretation.

Now there is an *application*. This verse has a message for me. I can't toss it aside just because God did not direct it to me. It contains a formula for this hour. "My people"—God has a people which we call the church or the body of Christ, those who have accepted the Savior, "Who gave himself for us, that he might redeem us from all iniquity, and purify unto himself a peculiar people, zealous of good works" (Titus 2:14). I guess one could say a lot of us are peculiar people, but this means a people for Himself. *"Shall humble themselves"*—the flesh is proud but we are admonished to be humble. "I therefore, the prisoner of the Lord, beseech you that ye walk worthy of the vocation wherewith ye are called, With all lowliness and meekness, with longsuffering, forbearing one another in love" (Eph. 4:1–2). We are told in Galatians 5:22–23 that longsuffering and meekness are fruits of the Spirit. Humbleness is commended for the believer today. *"And pray"*—certainly many, many times in the New Testament we are admonished to pray. The Lord Jesus told His disciples to watch and pray. The epistles contain numerous commands to pray. *"And seek My face"* is also a New Testament admonition: "If ye then be risen with Christ, seek those things which are above, where Christ sitteth on the right hand of God. Set your affection on things above, not on things on the earth" (Col. 3:1–2). *"And turn from their wicked ways."* This also applies to us. God has a great deal to say about repentance for believers. "As many as I love, I rebuke and chasten: be zealous therefore, and repent" (Rev. 3:19). Repentance is for the child of God.

Now how about God's part? God had promised that He would *hear*. "And whatsoever we ask, we receive of him, because we keep his commandments, and do those things that are pleasing in his sight" (1 John 3:22). He promised to *forgive:* "If we confess our sins, he is faithful and just to forgive us our sins, and to cleanse us from all unrighteousness" (1 John 1:9).

"And will heal their land." That does not apply to us. I can't find anywhere in the New Testament where the Lord has promised to heal a piece of real estate. If God has blessed you in a business way, that is extra—a blessing that He has not promised. Nowhere does God promise material blessing to us. We are blessed with all *spiritual* blessings in Christ Jesus. We were aliens, enemies of God, and now we have been made the sons of God. We have been redeemed by the blood of Christ, and He forgives us our sins. Heaven is our home, and the New Jerusalem is our goal. We have been delivered from hell. These are our blessings. Nowhere are we promised a land or healing in our land.

May I say to you that if you would wish to lift out verse 14 and apply the entire verse to your present situation, then you must take verse 15 along with it.

Now mine eyes shall be open, and mine ears attent unto the prayer that is made in this place [2 Chron. 7:15].

If you want to follow this particular injunction, then I suggest you board the next plane to Jerusalem and go to the temple site. You would find that the temple isn't even there—the Mosque of Omar is there now, but if you intend to follow this passage, you must go to Jerusalem because that is where "this place" is.

I don't know why folk will lift out of context one verse of Scripture and claim it for themselves. It was never intended that way. This promise was given to Israel at the dedication of the temple. Although it has application for us, it is better to go to the New Testament and find God's promises to us directly.

For now have I chosen and sanctified this house, that my name may be there for ever: and mine eyes and mine heart shall be there perpetually [2 Chron. 7:16].

I stayed for a week in a hotel overlooking the temple area. When I would get up in the morning, I would walk out to the window—actually a big glass door—and look at this temple area. I thought, *I am looking at a spot where God is also looking*. This is a spot that is very dear to Him.

And as for thee, if thou wilt walk before me, as David thy father walked, and do according to all that I have commanded thee, and shalt observe my statutes and my judgments:

Then will I stablish the throne of thy kingdom, according as I have covenanted with David thy father, saying, There shall not fail thee a man to be ruler in Israel (2 Chron. 7:17–18].

God has promised that in the Davidic line there would not be a time when there would not be a ruler. There is no ruler around on this earth today who can claim to be in David's line. But there is One sitting at God's right hand who is in David's line, and He has been told, ". . . Sit thou at my right hand, until I make thine enemies thy footstool" (Ps. 110:1; see also Heb. 10:12–13).

But if ye turn away, and forsake my statutes and my commandments, which I have set before you, and shall go and serve other gods, and worship them;

Then will I pluck them up by the roots out of my land which I have given them; and this house, which I have sanctified for my name, will I cast out of my sight, and will make it to be a proverb and a byword among all nations [2 Chron 7:19–20].

It certainly has become a byword today. It is no longer a sacred spot—the Mosque of Omar stands there.

And this house, which is high, shall be an astonishment to every one that passeth by it; so that he shall say, Why hath the LORD done thus unto this land, and unto this house? [2 Chron. 7:21].

That place today is where the Mosque of Omar stands. I stood there with several folk overlooking the temple area and one of them raised the question stated in this verse. "Why, this is where God's house was supposed to be, and look at it today. There is heathenism and paganism here as much as there is anywhere on the earth. You'd think that since this is God's spot He would not permit this kind of thing to happen." Well, my friend, this is exactly what God said *would* happen.

And it shall be answered, Because they forsook the LORD God of their fathers, which brought them forth out of the land of Egypt, and laid hold on other gods, and worshipped them, and served them: therefore hath he brought all this evil upon them [2 Chron. 7:22].

I was privileged to tell that individual that the Word of God says very clearly that this would happen because Israel had forsaken the Lord God. I could show him that God is true to His Word.

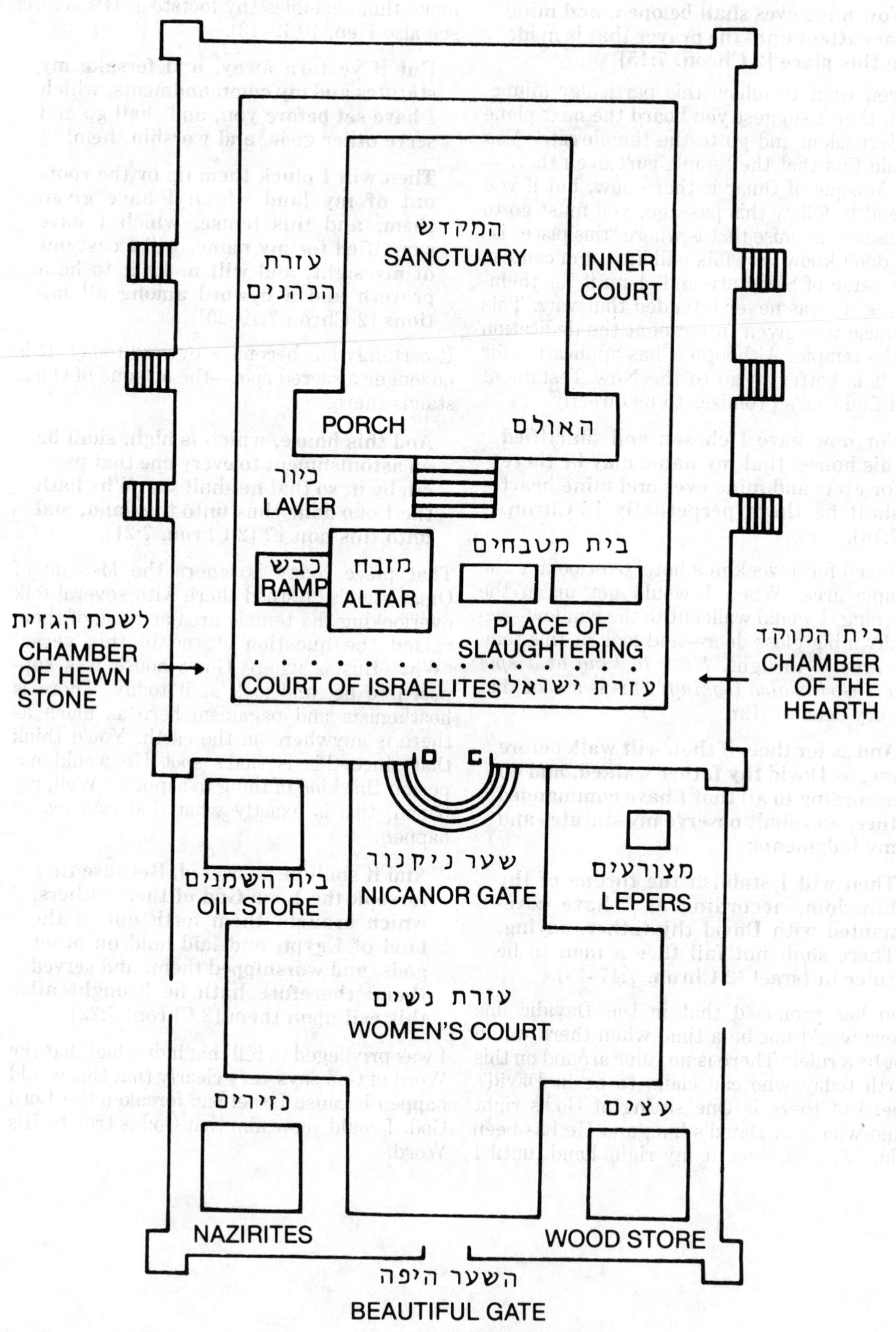
המקדש
SANCTUARY
עזרת
הכהנים
INNER
COURT
PORCH
האולם
כיור
LAVER
בית מטבחים
מזבח
כבש
RAMP
ALTAR
לשכת הגזית
CHAMBER
OF HEWN
STONE
PLACE OF
SLAUGHTERING
בית המוקד
CHAMBER
OF THE
HEARTH
COURT OF ISRAELITES
עזרת ישראל
שער ניקנור
בית השמנים
OIL STORE
NICANOR GATE
מצורעים
LEPERS
עזרת נשים
WOMEN'S COURT
נזירים
עצים
NAZIRITES
WOOD STORE
השער היפה
BEAUTIFUL GATE

FLOORPLAN OF THE TEMPLE

CHAPTERS 8–9

***THEME:** Accomplishments and fame of Solomon*

These next two chapters tell something of the experience and the work of Solomon and his testimony in other areas. This man became a very energetic ruler. He attempted to carry out all the plans and purposes and promises of David.

> **And it came to pass at the end of twenty years, wherein Solomon had built the house of the LORD, and his own house [2 Chron. 8:1].**

This building of the temple was a long project. It actually took half his reign to build it. This is the thing of which God took special note.

> **That the cities which Huram had restored to Solomon, Solomon built them, and caused the children of Israel to dwell there.**
>
> **And Solomon went to Hamath-zobah, and prevailed against it [2 Chron. 8:2–3].**

This is the only war that is recorded during the reign of Solomon, and it doesn't seem to be very significant at all.

> **But of the children of Israel did Solomon make no servants for his work; but they were men of war, and chief of his captains, and captains of his chariots and horsemen [2 Chron. 8:9].**

Solomon put his own people in the army and in places of leadership, while the menial tasks were assigned to descendants of the Canaanite tribes, the old possessors of the land, who had not been exterminated.

> **And these were the chief of king Solomon's officers, even two hundred and fifty, that bare rule over the people [2 Chron. 8:10].**

This is something that Solomon did which caused great difficulty later on. God notes it, but He does not commend it or bless it.

> **And Solomon brought up the daughter of Pharaoh out of the city of David unto the house that he had built for her: for he said, My wife shall not dwell in the house of David king of Israel, because the places are holy, whereunto the ark of the LORD hath come [2 Chron. 8:11].**

This is an interesting decision which Solomon made in reference to his wife, the daughter of Pharaoh. He built her a palace away from the city of David.

I notice that an interpretation that one gets in Israel today is that Solomon married these different women from various other countries for political advantage. Your father-in-law is not apt to make war against you. So this was one of the ways in which Solomon brought peace to the land. A man would not come up to fight against a country in which his daughter was the queen. I do not know whether this reason for Solomon's many wives is true or not. I have a notion that it is partly accurate. Under any circumstance, it was against God's command.

The remainder of the chapter tells more about the temple and that Solomon celebrated the feasts and appointed the priests and Levites to their courses just as David had planned it.

As we come to chapter 9, we see that it is the final chapter that concerns Solomon. We have seen that Solomon's most important accomplishment was the construction of the temple. Now what else in Solomon's life does God consider important enough to record a second time? It is very interesting to see that Solomon did succeed in doing what God had intended Israel to do—that is, be a witness to the world. We are told here how it was accomplished.

The way Israel was to witness was different from the way the church is to witness in our day. Israel faced in; the church faces out. Israel was to go up to Jerusalem to the temple and invite the world to come with her to worship. But the church is to begin at Jerusalem and go to the ends of the earth. In other words, the church is to take the gospel to the world, and Israel was to invite the world to come and share in the revelation of God in the temple. Israel was to bear witness to the living and true God as a nation in a world of polytheism, of many gods. And the church is to bear witness to a resurrection, and the living Savior, as individuals to all the nations in a world of atheism. Now, Israel fulfilled her God-given purpose to a certain extent, which is evidenced by the number of Gentiles who came to Jerusalem to worship and to know God through the service of the temple there. The measuring rod for the success of the church is the number of tribes and nations to whom we carry the gospel today.

Now it is the inclination of all of us who are in the church to disparage the efforts of Israel and at the same time to magnify the success of the church. Constantly we hear on every hand of the failure of the nation Israel. And at the same time the exaggerated report is given of the success of the gospel in faraway places. I remember after World War II we heard about a revival in China and then a revival in Germany. I checked with those who were in both places and they said there was no revival there. It is interesting that we always hear of revivals in faraway places.

The fact of the matter is that we are in an awful apostasy today. The days are getting darker. There are many wonderful churches and pastors who are still faithful today, but they know the difficulty of the hour in which we are living. Although there are still a few preachers and teachers who are sheltered in institutions who see the present-day situation as though they were looking through rose-colored glasses, anyone who is working out in the world knows that we are in an apostasy today.

On the other hand, Israel succeeded in a far greater measure than we often realize. We tend to measure their success by their final failure—the final apostasy of the nation which led to their captivity. There *was* a period when they did not fail God. A witness went forth from Jerusalem to the nations of the world. They were drawn to Jerusalem like a magnet. The high water mark was during the reign of Solomon. The nation reached a pinnacle at that time. Afterward there was deterioration, and decline set in like dry rot.

The Scriptures give us two isolated examples of the influence on the Gentiles during the reign of David and Solomon. Undoubtedly there were many others that we do not know about. Hiram, the king of Tyre and friend of David, came to know God. He made lavish gifts for the temple. He furnished material and workmen for the temple. Do you remember what he wrote to Solomon? ". . . Blessed be the LORD God of Israel, that made heaven and earth, who hath given to David the king a wise son . . ." (2 Chron. 2:12). Hiram was a son of Japheth. The story of the queen of Sheba is given to us to record that Israel reached the ends of the then-known world with a witness for God. She is a representative of the sons of Ham. It is her story that is given to us in this chapter.

May I remind you that in the New Testament, when we are told about the early church and its outreach into the world, we are also given just a few examples. There is the Ethiopian eunuch who is the son of Ham. There is Cornelius who is the son of Japheth. There is Saul of Tarsus who is the son of Shem.

VISIT OF THE QUEEN OF SHEBA

And when the queen of Sheba heard of the fame of Solomon, she came to prove Solomon with hard questions at Jerusalem, with a very great company, and camels that bare spices, and gold in abundance, and precious stones: and when she was come to Solomon, she communed with him of all that was in her heart.

And Solomon told her all her questions: and there was nothing hid from Solomon which he told her not [2 Chron. 9:1–2].

In other words, Solomon told her the secret of his kingdom. He told her that *God* had given him his wisdom. He told her that the temple was their approach to God because God had said it was there He would meet with His people.

And when the queen of Sheba had seen the wisdom of Solomon, and the house that he had built,

And the meat of his table, and the sitting of his servants, and the attendance of his ministers, and their apparel; his cupbearers also, and their apparel; and his ascent by which he went up into the house of the LORD; there was no more spirit in her [2 Chron. 9:3–4].

In 1 Kings 10:24 we are told, "And all the earth sought to Solomon, to hear his wisdom, which God had put in his heart." We are given just this one illustration of the queen of Sheba who came to see the wisdom of Solomon. You can see that the nation of Israel was successful in witnessing to the world.

"His ascent by which he went up into the house of the Lord" was the burnt offering which he made. That burnt offering speaks of Christ. No nation on earth had anything that would compare to an offering for sin. This was the thing which absolutely amazed her. This was the offering that was pointing to Christ. David had said and written so much about Christ that I don't think Solomon left her without an explanation of the One who was to come to take away sin.

And she said to the king, It was a true report which I heard in mine own land of thine acts, and of thy wisdom:

Howbeit I believed not their words, until I came, and mine eyes had seen it: and, behold, the one half of the greatness of thy wisdom was not told me: for thou exceedest the fame that I heard [2 Chron. 9:5–6].

This woman said, "When I heard about what God had done, I just didn't believe it." But she had faith enough so that when she heard about the greatness of Solomon, she made a long, arduous trip to see for herself. Believe me, it was a long, arduous trip in that day. She couldn't go out to the airport and take a plane which would bring her there in a couple of hours. It was probably a couple of months across a hot, burning desert. She came all the way in order that she might know something of the wisdom of this man and learn about his approach to God. That was the thing that left no spirit in her. She couldn't believe it until she had seen it. Now listen to her:

Happy are thy men, and happy are these thy servants, which stand continually before thee, and hear thy wisdom.

Blessed be the LORD thy God, which delighted in thee to set thee on his throne, to be king for the LORD thy God: because thy God loved Israel, to establish them for ever, therefore made he thee king over them, to do judgment and justice [2 Chron. 9:7–8].

This woman is now praising God! When our Lord spoke of her, He said, "The queen of the south shall rise up in the judgment with this generation, and shall condemn it: for she came from the uttermost parts of the earth to hear the wisdom of Solomon . . ." (Matt. 12:42). There is a Sheba in southwestern Arabia and in Africa. Since the Lord Jesus said that she came from the uttermost parts of the earth, I assume she came from Africa. But her entourage reveals the wealth and luxury of the orient. The wise men never made a greater impression than did this woman. She came with great pomp and ceremony befitting an oriental monarch. It seems that the burnt offering was what impressed her the most. This was the most complete and perfect picture of Christ that was given in the Old Testament. How well did Israel succeed in giving a witness to the Gentiles? Well, this woman came to know the living and true God.

Our Lord, you recall, one day spoke to a woman at a well and said: "Woman, believe me, the hour cometh, when ye shall neither in this mountain, nor yet at Jerusalem, worship the Father" (John 4:21). In Jesus' day, that "hour" was coming. And that hour did come so that today we are to take the Gospel to the ends of the earth. However, in Solomon's day, the world came to Jerusalem to hear the Gospel.

SOLOMON'S SPLENDOR

And king Solomon passed all the kings of the earth in riches and wisdom.

And all the kings of the earth sought the presence of Solomon, to hear his wisdom, that God had put in his heart [2 Chron. 9:22–23].

Solomon was bearing a witness to the world in his day.

And Solomon had four thousand stalls for horses and chariots, and twelve thousand horsemen; whom he bestowed in the chariot cities, and with the king at Jerusalem [2 Chron. 9:25].

This reveals the defect in this man's character. The king had been forbidden by the Mosaic Law to multiply horses and wives. Solomon multipled both. One of the most impressive things at Megiddo is the ruins of the stables that Solomon had there. And there are ruins of his stables in several other areas. He really multiplied horses!

And he reigned over all the kings from the river even unto the land of the Philistines, and to the border of Egypt.

And the king made silver in Jerusalem as stones, and cedar trees made he as the sycomore trees that are in the low plains in abundance.

And they brought unto Solomon horses out of Egypt, and out of all lands [2 Chron. 9:26–28].

Solomon was one of the great rulers of this world.

DEATH OF SOLOMON

Now the rest of the acts of Solomon, first and last, are they not written in the book of Nathan the prophet, and in the prophecy of Ahijah the Shilonite, and in the visions of Iddo the seer against Jeroboam the son of Nebat?

And Solomon reigned in Jerusalem over all Israel forty years.

And Solomon slept with his fathers, and he was buried in the city of David his father: and Rehoboam his son reigned in his stead [2 Chron. 9:29–31].

God had fulfilled His promise to Solomon. He had given him supernatural wisdom for which he had asked, and in addition He had given him riches and wealth and honor.

CHAPTERS 10–12

***THEME:** The division of the kingdom under Rehoboam*

We have come now to the second and final division of the Book of 2 Chronicles. The first nine chapters were devoted to the reign of Solomon. Now Solomon is dead, and his son Rehoboam comes to the throne. The stupidity of Rehoboam leads to the division of the kingdom. The northern kingdom, composed of ten tribes, becomes known as Israel. The southern kingdom of two tribes takes the name of Judah. God puts the emphasis on the kingdom of Judah because this is the line of David which leads to Christ. In this section of the nation's history are five periods of revival. These are enlarged upon in Chronicles, as we are seeing them from God's viewpoint.

REHOBOAM COMES TO THE THRONE

And Rehoboam went to Shechem: for to Shechem were all Israel come to make him king.

And it came to pass, when Jeroboam the son of Nebat, who was in Egypt, whither he had fled from the presence of Solomon the king, heard it, that Jeroboam returned out of Egypt [2 Chron. 10:1–2].

The Book of 2 Chronicles does not tell us this, but back in Kings we were told that this man Jeroboam had attempted to lead a rebellion even before the death of Solomon. He was forced to flee for his life and had gone down into the land of Egypt. He stayed there until the death of Solomon. Now he has returned with the intent of raising up a rebellion in the kingdom. If Rehoboam had been wise in his judgment and had been a little more mild and modest, he could have prevented the splitting of the kingdom; but he did not.

Now Jeroboam is back in the land, and we read:

And they sent and called him. So Jeroboam and all Israel came and spake to Rehoboam, saying,

Thy father made our yoke grievous: now therefore ease thou somewhat the grievous servitude of thy father, and his heavy yoke that he put upon us, and we will serve thee [2 Chron. 10:3–4].

Taxes were the cause of the dissension. Probably the single thing that has caused more revolution and rebellion has been this matter of taxes. It has been the downfall of many nations. It brought the Roman Empire to its knees, and excessive taxation to support the royalty was responsible for the French Revolution. Also it produced the American Revolution. Taxation without representation brought about the Boston Tea Party and the incidents which led to the revolution. If our taxes keep going up as they are, we may have another tea party, because high taxation will ultimately wreck any nation. Unfortunately, our representatives in the state and national government don't seem to think that it is a problem. Taxes were the problem in Rehoboam's time. Solomon had carried on a tremendous building program. It was very impressive. Not only had he built the temple, but we are told in Kings that he built all sorts of palaces and buildings. Such a big building program had to be paid for, and as a result there had been an enormous increase in taxes. This gave Jeroboam a lever whereby he could make a protest. He gathered with Israel and said to Rehoboam, "Now look here, your father made our yoke grievous." Actually, Jeroboam was very mild in his approach. He said to Rehoboam that if he would reduce the taxes, he would go along with him. If Rehoboam had done that, there would not have been a rebellion.

And he said unto them, Come again unto me after three days. And the people departed [2 Chron. 10:5].

What they had asked was really a fair thing. Rehoboam would have had an opportunity to look at the indebtedness and decide what was the wise thing to do. The wise thing would have been to reduce taxes.

And king Rehoboam took counsel with the old men that had stood before Solomon his father while he yet lived, saying, What counsel give ye me to return answer to this people?

And they spake unto him, saying, If thou be kind to this people, and please them, and speak good words to them, they will be thy servants for ever.

But he forsook the counsel which the old men gave him, and took counsel with the young men that were brought up with him, that stood before him [2 Chron. 10:6–8].

Rehoboam definitely showed poor judgment. He should have followed the wisdom of the older men who had been counselors during the reign of Solomon. They knew the situation. Unfortunately, he turned to the young men.

And the young men that were brought up with him spake unto him, saying, Thus shalt thou answer the people that spake unto thee, saying, Thy father made our yoke heavy, but make thou it somewhat lighter for us; thus shalt thou say unto them, My little finger shall be thicker than my father's loins.

For whereas my father put a heavy yoke upon you, I will put more to your yoke: my father chastised you with whips, but I will chastise you with scorpions [2 Chron. 10:10–11].

The young men advised, "Don't ease up. We want this picnic to continue. All of us have public jobs, and those of us who are not eating out of the public trough would like very much to get in the trough. Don't reduce the taxes. Increase them!" This was probably the most foolish thing that young Rehoboam could have done.

The older men conceded that Solomon did overtax the people. They advised that it was time to stop the building program. It was time to put a lid on all the government spending. The time had come to reduce taxes.

By the way, have you ever heard of any government which has reduced taxes? Our politicians go into office saying they will reduce taxes. I think in my lifetime I have voted for half a dozen presidents and every one of them was going to reduce taxes. I have been voting for governors and for mayors, and they all promise to reduce the taxes. Yet our taxes continue to increase.

Rehoboam will follow this policy also.

So Jeroboam and all the people came to Rehoboam on the third day, as the king bade, saying, Come again to me on the third day.

And the king answered them roughly; and king Rehoboam forsook the counsel of the old men,

And answered them after the advice of the young men, saying, My father made your yoke heavy, but I will add thereto: my father chastised you with whips, but I will chastise you with scorpions [2 Chron. 10:12–14].

Rehoboam delivers verbatim to the people the heartless and insensitive judgment of the young men.

So the king hearkened not unto the people: for the cause was of God, that the LORD might perform his word, which he spake by the hand of Ahijah the Shilonite to Jeroboam the son of Nebat [2 Chron. 10:15].

The prophecy to which this refers is given in 1 Kings 11:9–39.

And when all Israel saw that the king would not hearken unto them, the people answered the king, saying, What portion have we in David? and we have none inheritance in the son of Jesse: every man to your tents, O Israel: and now, David, see to thine own house. So all Israel went to their tents [2 Chron. 10:16].

Israel refers to the ten tribes. *Judah* refers to the two tribes of Judah and Benjamin. However, the name *Israel* sometimes will refer to the southern kingdom also because God regards them as one people.

But as for the children of Israel that dwelt in the cities of Judah, Rehoboam reigned over them.

Then king Rehoboam sent Hadoram that was over the tribute; and the children of Israel stoned him with stones,

that he died. But king Rehoboam made speed to get him up to his chariot, to flee to Jerusalem.

And Israel rebelled against the house of David unto this day [2 Chron. 10: 17–19].

King Rehoboam sent a tax gatherer to gather taxes and the people stoned him to death. Rehoboam just hadn't realized how incensed these people were. So Israel rebelled against the house of David. "Unto this day" means up to the time when 2 Chronicles was written.

EARLY DAYS OF REHOBOAM'S REIGN

When Rehoboam goes back to Jerusalem, he finds that his kingdom has really been cut down by quite a bit. Then he does another foolish thing.

And when Rehoboam was come to Jerusalem, he gathered of the house of Judah and Benjamin an hundred and fourscore thousand chosen men, which were warriors, to fight against Israel, that he might bring the kingdom again to Rehoboam [2 Chron. 11:1].

First Rehoboam lost part of his kingdom by his own folly. Now he is doing another foolish thing by attempting internal warfare. He wants a civil war in Israel.

But the word of the LORD came to Shemiah the man of God, saying,

Speak unto Rehoboam the son of Solomon, king of Judah, and to all Israel in Judah and Benjamin, saying,

Thus saith the LORD, Ye shall not go up, nor fight against your brethren: return every man to his house: for this thing is done of me. And they obeyed the words of the LORD, and returned from going against Jeroboam [2 Chron. 11:2–4].

God intervenes and prevents a civil war.

And he fortified the strong holds, and put captains in them, and store of victual, and of oil and wine.

And in every several city he put shields and spears, and made them exceeding strong, having Judah and Benjamin on his side [2 Chron. 11:11–12].

Now Rehoboam turns his attention to the building of fortifications to protect himself from the northern kingdom. That which had been part of the kingdom of David and Solomon is now lost to him and becomes his enemy because of his very foolish decision to listen to the young men rather than to the wise counselors of Solomon.

And the priests and the Levites that were in all Israel resorted to him out of all their coasts [2 Chron. 11:13].

You remember that the Levites had been given certain cities throughout Israel but that they had no territory as a tribe such as the other tribes had been given. Now the Levites leave all their cities in the northern kingdom, and all the priests and Levites move south to Judah and Jerusalem.

For the Levites left their suburbs and their possession, and came to Judah and Jerusalem: for Jeroboam and his sons had cast them off from executing the priest's office unto the LORD:

And he ordained him priests for the high places, and for the devils [demons], and for the calves which he had made [2 Chron. 11:14–15].

All the priests and Levites who lived up in the northern kingdom moved south so that they could continue to serve at the temple. Then Jeroboam institutes demon worship. The record in Kings gives us more detail: "If this people go up to do sacrifice in the house of the LORD at Jerusalem, then shall the heart of this people turn again unto their lord, even unto Rehoboam king of Judah, and they shall kill me, and go again to Rehoboam king of Judah. Whereupon the king took counsel, and made two calves of gold, and said unto them, It is too much for you to go up to Jerusalem: behold thy gods, O Israel, which brought thee up out of the land of Egypt. And he set the one in Beth-el, and the other put he in Dan" (1 Kings 12:27–29). The people worshiped the golden calves. Back of all this idolatry is Satan. This is Satan worship.

I had the privilege of visiting the places of the seven churches of Asia. You will recall that the Lord said to the church at Pergamos, "I know thy works and where thou dwellest, even where Satan's seat is . . ." (Rev. 2:13). That was a city given over to idolatry. Behind idolatry is Satan. Demonism manifests itself in many different ways.

And after them out of all the tribes of Israel such as set their hearts to seek the LORD God of Israel came to Jerusalem, to sacrifice unto the LORD God of their fathers.

So they strengthened the kingdom of Judah, and made Rehoboam the son of Solomon strong, three years: for three years they walked in the way of David and Solomon [2 Chron. 11:16–17].

There were some folk in the ten northern tribes who were still faithful to God, and they would come down to Jerusalem to worship.

Now we are told something of Rehoboam's personal life:

And Rehoboam loved Maachah the daughter of Absalom above all his wives and his concubines: (for he took eighteen wives, and threescore concubines; and begat twenty and eight sons, and threescore daughters.)

And Rehoboam made Abijah the son of Maachah the chief, to be ruler among his brethren: for he thought to make him king.

And he dealt wisely, and dispersed of all his children throughout all the countries of Judah and Benjamin, unto every fenced city: and he gave them victual in abundance. And he desired many wives [2 Chron. 11:21–23].

Because the record of his many wives appears in the Bible, a great many folk assume that God approves of polygamy. No. God records this to let us know that He does not approve of it. This man Rehoboam did wrong by not listening to the counselors of Solomon but listening to the young men instead. He was wrong in trying to start a civil war. He was wrong in having many wives. This is recorded because it is history; it is what he did. It is one of the many things for which God judged him.

REHOBOAM'S APOSTASY

In the life of Rehoboam one sin led to another. Now we see that he leads his people in apostasy.

And it came to pass, when Rehoboam had established the kingdom, and had strengthened himself, he forsook the law of the LORD, and all Israel with him [2 Chron. 12:1].

God did not approve of Rehoboam's conduct. People read the things these men did in the Old Testament, and they say, "Look what they did and they got by with it." That is often said about Abraham when he took Hagar and had the boy Ishmael. Friends, he didn't get by with it. Do you know who is the big problem in the Middle East today? The sons of Abraham—the Israelites and the Arabs. Who is the Arab? Well, I had an Arab guide take me down to the city of Jericho. I wanted someone who knew about the place, and this was a brilliant fellow who had worked with Sir Charles Marsdon and Miss Kathleen Kenyon in their excavations. He was very helpful to me. We were talking about the land, and I made the statement that God had given it to Abraham and to his offspring. This Arab smiled and looked me straight in the eye and said, "Dr. McGee, I am as much a son of Abraham as any Jew who is alive today." And he was right! He could trace his ancestry right back to Ishmael. He boasted of the fact that he was an Ismaelite, a son of Abraham. Did God approve when Abraham took Hagar? God records it as history. Then He lets you see the results. It certainly has never been a blessing. In fact, it has been a thorn in the flesh down through the centuries.

Now God records the apostasy of Jeroboam. Also He records the forsaking of the Law by Rehoboam and Israel. God condemns these things, but He records them as history.

INVASION BY EGYPT

Now God's judgment falls upon Rehoboam. For the first time He opens up that southern kingdom to the invasion of a major nation. You see, Rehoboam had forsaken the Word of God; he had led his people in apostasy. When he did this, God did something He had not done before. Previous to this, God had put a wall around His people, and the great nations of that day were not permitted to invade that territory.

And it came to pass, that in the fifth year of king Rehoboam Shishak king of Egypt came up against Jerusalem, because they had transgressed against the LORD,

With twelve hundred chariots, and threescore thousand horsemen: and the people were without number that came with him out of Egypt: the Lubims, the Sukkiims, and the Ethiopians [2 Chron. 12:2–3].

First, Shishak king of Egypt came up and carried away great booty. He lugged away a great deal of the gold and other wealth of that kingdom.

So Shishak king of Egypt came up against Jerusalem, and took away the treasures of the house of the LORD, and the treasures of the king's house; he

took all: he carried away also the shields of gold which Solomon had made.

Instead of which king Rehoboam made shields of brass, and committed them to the hands of the chief of the guard, that kept the entrance of the king's house.

And when the king entered into the house of the LORD, the guard came and fetched them, and brought them again into the guard chamber [2 Chron. 12: 9–11].

These, you recall, are the great shields of gold that David brought and that Solomon placed in the temple. After these had been captured as booty, Rehoboam substitutes something inferior. No longer do they have shields of gold; now they have shields of brass. The judgment of God is upon them because of their sins.

This was a humbling experience for Rehoboam. He had been brought up in the affluence of the reign of Solomon and had experienced the blessing that had come. He had known nothing but wealth and luxury and expected it to go on forever. He begins to realize there may be an end to the glory of the kingdom of Solomon.

And when he humbled himself, the wrath of the LORD turned from him, that he would not destroy him altogether; and also in Judah things went well [2 Chron. 12:12].

This reveals the amazing mercy of God. When this man humbles himself, God immediately withdraws judgment upon him and the people of Judah.

So king Rehoboam strengthened himself in Jerusalem, and reigned: for Rehoboam was one and forty years old when he began to reign, and he reigned seventeen years in Jerusalem, the city which the LORD had chosen out of all the tribes of Israel, to put his name there. And his mother's name was Naamah an Ammonitess [2 Chron. 12:13].

It is interesting to learn who was Rehoboam's mother. You recall that David had been very friendly with the Ammonites—although they had made war against him. Now we find that Rehoboam, his grandson, was the son of an Ammonite woman. She undoubtedly had something to do with the character of this man. As we saw in the Books of Kings, God always mentions the mother's name. Why? Because she bears part of the responsibility for her son. If he turns out well, she shares in the credit. If he turns out to be a wicked, evil king, she must take part of the blame.

And he did evil, because he prepared not his heart to seek the LORD,

Now the acts of Rehoboam, first and last, are they not written in the book of Shemaiah the prophet, and of Iddo the seer concerning genealogies? And there were wars between Rehoboam and Jeroboam continually.

And Rehoboam slept with his fathers, and was buried in the city of David: and Abijah his son reigned in his stead [2 Chron. 12:14–16].

CHAPTER 13

THEME: *Abijah reigns over Judah*

After Rehoboam's death, his son Abijah came to the throne. Although Abijah is not considered a good king, and the record in 1 Kings says that ". . . he walked in all the sins of his father . . . and his heart was not perfect with the LORD his God . . ." (1 Kings 15:3), yet here in Chronicles we read of an episode during which he honored the Lord.

And Abijah set the battle in array with an army of valiant men of war, even four hundred thousand chosen men: Jeroboam also set the battle in array against him with eight hundred thousand chosen men, being mighty men of valour.

And Abijah stood up upon mount Zemaraim, which is in mount Ephraim, and said, Hear me, thou Jeroboam, and all Israel:

Ought ye not to know that the LORD God of Israel gave the kingdom over Israel to David for ever, even to him and to his sons by a covenant of salt?

Yet Jeroboam the son of Nebat, the servant of Solomon the son of David, is risen up, and hath rebelled against his lord [2 Chron. 13:3–6].

As we have seen, there was a reason for that, a sufficient reason: the foolishness of Rehoboam.

And there are gathered unto him vain men, the children of Belial, and have strengthened themselves against Rehoboam the son of Solomon, when Rehoboam was young and tenderhearted, and could not withstand them [2 Chron. 13:7].

He was not only young and tenderhearted, but he was very foolish.

This is the plea on the part of Abijah to try to bring back the ten tribes, but there is no use now because Jeroboam has made himself king, and he is not about to make peace.

But Jeroboam caused an ambushment to come about behind them: so they were before Judah, and the ambushment was behind them.

And when Judah looked back, behold, the battle was before and behind: and they cried unto the LORD, and the priests sounded with the trumpets [2 Chron. 13:13–14].

They cry unto God for help. Now notice God's gracious response.

Then the men of Judah gave a shout: and as the men of Judah shouted, it came to pass, that God smote Jeroboam and all Israel before Abijah and Judah.

And the children of Israel fled before Judah: and God delivered them into their hand.

And Abijah and his people slew them with a great slaughter: so there fell down slain of Israel five hundred thousand chosen men [2 Chron. 13:15–17].

This is a great victory.

And Abijah pursued after Jeroboam, and took cities from him, Bethel with the towns thereof, and Jeshanah with the towns thereof, and Ephrain with the towns thereof.

Neither did Jeroboam recover strength again in the days of Abijah: and the LORD struck him, and he died [2 Chron. 13:19–20].

This is God's judgment upon Jeroboam for dividing the nation.

But Abijah waxed mighty, and married fourteen wives, and begat twenty and two sons, and sixteen daughters.

And the rest of the acts of Abijah, and his ways, and his sayings, are written in the story of the prophet Iddo [2 Chron. 13:21–22].

Abijah was no great king, but after him comes his son who will lead the first revival.

CHRONOLOGICAL TABLE OF THE KINGS OF THE DIVIDED KINGDOM

JUDAH

King	Reign		Character	Prophet
1. Rehoboam	931–913 B.C.	(17 yrs.)	Bad	Shemaiah
2. Abijah	913–911	(3 yrs.)	Bad	
3. Asa	911–870	(41 yrs.)	Good	
4. Jehoshaphat	870–848*	(25 yrs.)	Good	
5. Jehoram	848–841*	(8 yrs.)	Bad	
6. Ahaziah	841	(1 yr.)	Bad	
7. Athaliah	841–835	(6 yrs.)	Bad	
8. Joash	835–796	(40 yrs.)	Good	Joel
9. Amaziah	796–767	(29 yrs.)	Good	
10. Azariah (or Uzziah)	767–740*	(52 yrs.)	Good	Isaiah
11. Jotham	740–732*	(16 yrs.)	Good	Micah
12. Ahaz	732–716	(16 yrs.)	Bad	
13. Hezekiah	716–687	(29 yrs.)	Good	
14. Manasseh	687–642*	(55 yrs.)	Bad	Nahum
15. Amon	642–640	(2 yrs.)	Bad	Habakkuk
16. Josiah	640–608	(31 yrs.)	Good	Zephaniah
17. Jehoahaz	608	(3 mo.)	Bad	Jeremiah
18. Jehoiakim	608–597	(11 yrs.)	Bad	
19. Jehoiachin	597	(3 mo.)	Bad	
20. Zedekiah	597–586	(11 yrs.)	Bad	

(Destruction of Jerusalem and captivity of Judah)

*Co-regency

ISRAEL

King	Reign		Character	Prophet
1. Jeroboam I	931–910 B.C.	(22 yrs.)	Bad	Ahijah
2. Nadab	910–909	(2 yrs.)	Bad	
3. Baasha	909–886	(24 yrs.)	Bad	
4. Elah	886–885	(2 yrs.)	Bad	
5. Zimri	885	(7 days)	Bad	
6. Omri	885–874*	(12 yrs.)	Bad	
7. Ahab	874–853	(22 yrs.)	Bad	Elijah
8. Ahaziah	853–852	(2 yrs.)	Bad	Micaiah
9. Joram	852–841	(12 yrs.)	Bad	Elisha
10. Jehu	841–814	(28 yrs.)	Bad	
11. Jehoahaz	814–798	(17 yrs.)	Bad	
12. Jehoash	798–782	(16 yrs.)	Bad	Jonah
13. Jeroboam II	782–753*	(41 yrs.)	Bad	Amos, Hosea
14. Zechariah	753–752	(6 mo.)	Bad	
15. Shallum	752	(1 mo.)	Bad	
16. Menahem	752–742	(10 yrs.)	Bad	
17. Pekahiah	742–740	(2 yrs.)	Bad	
18. Pekah	740–732*	(20 yrs.)	Bad	
19. Hoshea	732–721	(9 yrs.)	Bad	

(Capture of Samaria and captivity of Israel)

*Co-regency

CHAPTERS 14–16

***THEME:** Revival under Asa, king of Judah*

During the reign of Asa we will come to the first revival. I believe that God has given us a lesson on revival in this book. The road to revival is a rocky, unpaved, uphill road. However, the road is well-marked, the road maps are clear, and there are certain bridges that must be crossed.

Asa is one of the five kings whom God used to bring revival to the southern kingdom. The northern kingdom never had a revival. They had nineteen kings, and all of them were bad. There's not one good one in the lot. Of the twenty kings over Judah, ten of them could be called good, and five of them were outstanding. These kings were Asa, Jehoshaphat, Joash, Hezekiah, and Josiah. During their reigns there was a period of reformation, which was incubated in a time of revival. There is a similarity among all of the kings, but there are also some striking differences.

So Abijah slept with his fathers, and they buried him in the city of David: and Asa his son reigned in his stead. In his days the land was quiet ten years [2 Chron. 14:1].

Asa is the first of the kings in whose reign there was a revival. Solomon was his great-grandfather, Rehoboam was his grandfather, and, of course, Abijah was his father.

And Asa did that which was good and right in the eyes of the LORD his God:

For he took away the altars of the strange gods, and the high places, and brake down the images, and cut down the groves:

And commanded Judah to seek the LORD God of their fathers, and to do the law and the commandment [2 Chron. 14: 2–4].

Here is the character of the man. He is absolutely outstanding.

Also he took away out of all the cities of Judah the high places and the images: and the kingdom was quiet before him.

And he built fenced cities in Judah: for the land had rest, and he had no war in those years; because the LORD had given him rest [2 Chron. 14:5–6].

He was also a man of peace. However, we find that Ethiopia made war against him.

And there came out against them Zerah the Ethiopian with an host of a thousand thousand, and three hundred chariots; and came unto Mareshah.

Then Asa went out against him, and they set the battle in array in the valley of Zephathah at Mareshah [2 Chron. 14:9–10].

Not only was Asa a man of peace, he was also a man of prayer. We have a glimpse into the private life of the king, and it is commendable.

And Asa cried unto the LORD his God, and said, LORD, it is nothing with thee to help, whether with many, or with them that have no power: help us, O LORD our God; for we rest on thee, and in thy name we go against this multitude. O LORD, thou art our God; let not man prevail against thee.

So the LORD smote the Ethiopians before Asa, and before Judah: and the Ethiopians fled [2 Chron. 14:11–12].

This is real praying. It is not flowery, but direct and right to the point. He says exactly what he means. Asa was a great man of prayer. The revival that came to the nation came because he was this kind of a king.

They smote also the tents of cattle, and carried away sheep and camels in abundance, and returned to Jerusalem [2 Chron. 14:15].

God gave Asa a great military victory.

ENCOURAGEMENT OF AZARIAH, THE PROPHET

On the road to revival there are three bridges which must be crossed. We come now to the first bridge, which is a knowledge of the Word of God.

And the spirit of God came upon Azariah the son of Oded:

And he went out to meet Asa, and said unto him, Hear ye me, Asa, and all Judah and Benjamin: The LORD is with you, while ye be with him; and if ye seek him, he will be found of you; but if ye forsake him, he will forsake you.

Now for a long season Israel hath been without the true God, and without a teaching priest, and without law [2 Chron. 15:1–3].

The tragedy of the hour in our day is that there is not enough Bible teaching in the church. I say this very kindly, but we do not need more preachers. You can buy them like bananas, by the dozen. Bible teachers are few and far between; yet they are needed. And they were needed in Asa's day. They did not have a teaching priest. They had priests and Levites—they were knee-deep in priests and Levites—but they did not have a teaching priest. Consequently they were without the Law, without the Word of God.

But when they in their trouble did turn unto the LORD God of Israel, and sought him, he was found of them [2 Chron. 15:4].

It's just that simple, and yet it is just that complicated.

My friend, if you mean business with God, God will mean business with you. I hear people say, "Oh, I try to study. I try to pray. I try to do this but I don't get anywhere." My friend, who are you kidding? May I say to you that when you say that, you make God a liar. I have news for you—God is no liar. God says, "If you seek Me, I am there." If you mean business with God, God will mean business with you. Oh, search your heart, my friend. If you really want to know God's Word, then God is ready to meet you any time you are ready.

And in those times there was no peace to him that went out, nor to him that came in, but great vexations were upon all the inhabitants of the countries.

And nation was destroyed of nation, and city of city: for God did vex them with all adversity.

Be ye strong therefore, and let not your hands be weak: for your work shall be rewarded [2 Chron. 15:5–7].

Asa is beginning to turn to God. This prophet encourages him in this, and he explains why they had had trouble and so many problems.

Now I strongly suspect that the prophet's message applies to us as well as to Judah. I'm not speaking *ex cathedra* but, in studying the Word of God and seeing how God dealt with these people here, I am wondering if the root of our national problems is not the same. We have all those smart boys in Washington, and they make stupid decisions. How can such smart boys make such stupid decisions? Why is it that we cannot have law and order? Why is it that we can't really have peace? Why is there such lawlessness today? Let me venture my opinion on the basis of the Word of God. It is because God has been left out. He is not in the government circles in Washington. They think they don't need God because they have the smart boys. My friend, in this hour in which we are living, our nation needs *God!*

And when Asa heard these words, and the prophecy of Oded the prophet, he took courage, and put away the abominable idols out of all the land of Judah and Benjamin, and out of the cities which he had taken from mount Ephraim, and renewed the altar of the LORD, that was before the porch of the LORD.

And he gathered all Judah and Benjamin, and the strangers with them out of Ephraim and Manasseh, and out of Simeon: for they fell to him out of Israel in abundance, when they saw that the LORD his God was with him [2 Chron. 15:8–9].

God always has a remnant that will turn to Him.

So they gathered themselves together at Jerusalem in the third month, in the fifteenth year of the reign of Asa.

And they offered unto the LORD the same time, of the spoil which they had brought, seven hundred oxen and seven thousand sheep.

And they entered into a covenant to seek the LORD God of their fathers with all their heart and with all their soul [2 Chron. 15:10–12].

You will notice that these people are crossing the first bridge. They are not trying to detour around it. They have come to a knowledge of God's Word. They are turning to God and seeking Him with all their heart and soul. This characterized every one of the revivals. There was a return to the Word of God.

I am bold enough to state dogmatically that there has never been a revival without a return to the Word of God. There is no detour around the Bible. There is no substitute for it. The great spiritual movement in the days of John Wesley, my friend, was built around the Word of God. Wesley read the Bible in three languages every morning! Dwight L. Moody and the great spiritual awakening in his day led to the great Bible institute movement, one of the greatest movements in the study of the Word. It is dying out in our day. Why? Because they are getting away from the Word of God. We need more than just a superficial familiarity with the Word of God. We need more than an artificial vocabulary of the right words. Revival does not depend on an activity, nor on a service, nor on a method. It requires a real knowledge and love of the Word of God.

In our contemporary society there are movements and there are evangelists whom God is using, but I am disturbed because they are not making the study of the Word of God paramount. I find it difficult to get these movements, and even some of our schools, interested in studying the entire Word of God. My friend, we cannot have a real revival unless it is based on a thorough knowledge of the Bible. I hope revival will come. I believe this is the first bridge on the route. We'll have to cross over this bridge first.

Now at this great assembly which Asa had called in Jerusalem, they entered into a covenant with God to seek Him with all their hearts.

That whosoever would not seek the LORD God of Israel should be put to death, whether small or great, whether man or woman.

And they sware unto the LORD with a loud voice, and with shouting, and with trumpets, and with cornets [2 Chron. 15:13–14].

This was making it very harsh; yet there was a ready response from the hearts of the people. This man Asa brought about many reforms at this time.

And all Judah rejoiced at the oath: for they had sworn with all their heart, and sought him with their whole desire; and he was found of them: and the LORD gave them rest round about [2 Chron. 15:15].

My friend, if you seek the Lord with your whole heart, He will be found of you.

We have seen that the first bridge to revival is a knowledge of the Word of God. Now we come to the second bridge which is scriptural separation. The word *separation* is one of the most abused words in Christian circles. Asa here is practicing scriptural separation:

And also concerning Maachah the mother of Asa the king, he removed her from being queen, because she had made an idol in a grove: and Asa cut down her idol, and stamped it, and burnt it at the brook Kidron [2 Chron. 15:16].

This is indeed interesting—his own mother was engaged in idolatry! Notice that she wasn't just a friend of people who were idolaters, but she herself was an idolater. This is the reason Asa removed her from the place of influence.

But the high places were not taken away out of Israel: nevertheless the heart of Asa was perfect all his days [2 Chron. 15:17].

Asa could have removed these high places, but he did not. He went only part way with God—and yet God used him. How gracious God is!

I am weary of folk who consider themselves separated and roundly criticize everyone else in the ministry whose methods are different from theirs. My friend, that is not scriptural separation at all. Separation is not an attempt to straighten out every individual and try to force men whom God is using to conform to your pattern. That is the narrowest form of bigotry. I feel that some folk ought to get separated from themselves—that would really be separation! If you want revival, the place to begin is with yourself. I suggest that you get in a room by yourself, draw a circle right around you, and say, "Lord, begin a revival, and let it start inside this circle."

ASA'S LAPSE OF FAITH

In the six and thirtieth year of the reign of Asa Baasha king of Israel came up against Judah, and built Ramah, to the intent that he might let none go out or come in to Asa king of Judah [2 Chron. 16:1].

We have read in several verses that people from the northern kingdom would move to Judah because they saw that there was a revival going on under Asa. Baasha wanted to keep his people in his own kingdom and didn't want them to be moving south to Judah.

Then Asa brought out silver and gold out of the treasures of the house of the LORD and of the king's house, and sent to Ben-hadad king of Syria, that dwelt at Damascus, saying,

There is a league between me and thee, as there was between my father and thy father: behold, I have sent thee silver and gold: go, break thy league with Baasha king of Israel, that he may depart from me [2 Chron. 16:2–3].

Israel became a formidable enemy to Asa and Judah. So what does Asa do? He turns to a former ally that he had, King Ben-hadad of Syria. And what did that indicate? It indicated a lack of faith in God.

And Ben-hadad hearkened unto king Asa, and sent the captains of his armies against the cities of Israel; and they smote Ijon, and Dan, and Abel-maim, and all the store cities of Naphtali [2 Chron. 16:4].

The king of Syria responded and sent in his troops.

And it came to pass, when Baasha heard it, that he left off building of Ramah, and let his work cease.

Then Asa the king took all Judah; and they carried away the stones of Ramah, and the timber thereof, wherewith Baasha was building; and he built therewith Geba and Mizpah [2 Chron. 16: 5–6].

The maneuver was successful, but now the Lord has something to say to Asa.

And at that time Hanani the seer came to Asa king of Judah, and said unto him, Because thou hast relied on the king of Syria, and not relied on the LORD thy God, therefore is the host of the king of Syria escaped out of thine hand.

Were not the Ethiopians and the Lubims a huge host, with very many chariots and horsemen? yet, because thou didst rely on the LORD, he delivered them into thine hand.

For the eyes of the LORD run to and fro throughout the whole earth, to shew himself strong in the behalf of them

whose heart is perfect toward him. Herein thou hast done foolishly: therefore from henceforth thou shalt have wars [2 Chron. 16:7–9].

Why did God send a prophet to Asa to rebuke him? Why does God judge Asa? It is for his lack of faith.

The third bridge we must cross for revival is faith in God—not faith in methods, nor in man, nor in a church, nor in a system, nor in an organization. Revival requires faith in God.

When Baasha came against Asa in civil war, Asa turned to Ben-hadad of Syria, the ancient enemy. Hanani reminded him that he had every evidence that God would deliver him. God had delivered into his hand the army of the Ethiopians and the Lubims. Yet at this crisis point Asa demonstrated a lack of faith.

We need to clearly understand that although there is one act of faith which saves us—that is justification is by faith; the moment we put our trust in Jesus Christ, we are saved—life does not end when we are saved. My friend, we are to *live* by faith. Paul wrote to the Roman believers, "For I am not ashamed of the gospel of Christ: for it is the power of God unto salvation to every one that believeth; to the Jew first, and also to the Greek." Then he uses one of the strangest expressions imaginable: "For therein is the righteousness of God revealed from faith to faith: as it is written, The just shall live by faith" (Rom. 1:16–17). What does it mean that therein is the righteousness of God revealed from faith to faith? It means we are *saved* by faith, and we are to *live* by faith.

Hanani said to Asa, "For the eyes of the LORD run to and fro throughout the whole earth, to shew himself strong in the behalf of them whose heart is perfect toward him." This means that God is looking for a man or a woman who will believe in Him. By the way, would you like to be that person who believes God? I don't mean you are to become a fanatic, but you can believe God on the good solid testimony of His Word. Do you know that you cannot possibly please God unless you believe Him? "But without faith it is impossible to please him . . ." (Heb. 11:6). The writer to the Hebrews also tells us that we are compassed about with a great cloud of witnesses. Because of this, ". . . let us lay aside every weight, and the sin which doth so easily beset us. . . ." What is the sin? Unbelief. ". . . and let us run with patience the race that is set before us" (Heb. 12:1). Let's not only be saved by faith, my friend, let's live by faith. Many folk claim to be Christians, yet they live like agnostics.

Then Asa was wroth with the seer, and put him in a prison house; for he was in a rage with him because of this thing. And Asa oppressed some of the people the same time [2 Chron. 16:10].

This is amazing! Asa will not accept the rebuke. Why? Because he didn't believe it. Neither did he have real faith and dependence on God.

Living without God means spiritual death for us. There could be no way in the world for us to be used of God.

Now we will see that God struck him with a disease.

And Asa in the thirty and ninth year of his reign was diseased in his feet, until his disease was exceeding great: yet in his disease he sought not to the LORD, but to the physicians [2 Chron. 16:12].

God struck him with a disease which was serious and then became critical. He turned to the physicians. There is nothing wrong in that. The point is that he didn't turn to God in all of this. It is just as important for a believer to go to God when he gets sick as it is to call the doctor. Not only do I believe that, but I am a walking proof that God is faithful. When it was discovered that I had cancer, I not only went to the doctor, I went to God in prayer. I didn't go to a so-called faith healer. I went to the Great Physician. When you get sick, there are two things you ought to do: you should call the doctor and you should call upon God. Probably the most practical writer in the New Testament said, "Is any sick among you? let him call for the elders of the church; and let them pray over him, anointing him with oil in the name of the Lord" (James 5:14). He said two things should be done. The first was prayer, turning to God, calling on the name of the Lord. The second was anointing the sick one with oil. Now that was not a ceremonial act, not a religious act; it was medicinal. He was saying they should call on the Lord and call the doctor. That is practical.

The difficulty with Asa was that he called the doctor, but he didn't call on the Lord. It is amazing and very sobering to see a man who had experienced revival but now is not walking with God and is not living by faith.

My friend, to live by faith is to have faith in God. It means we take our problems and our difficulties to the Lord and turn them over to

Him. It is a faith that accepts whatever answer He gives us because He hears and answers our prayers in His own way. He may not answer in our way, but He will answer according to His will. You can be sure of one thing: if you turn things over to Him, you will be in His will. If you are in His will, that is the very best answer you can get—lots better than what you may have asked for.

And Asa slept with his fathers, and died in the one and fortieth year of his reign.

And they buried him in his own sepulchres, which he had made for himself in the city of David, and laid him in the bed which was filled with sweet odours and divers kinds of spices prepared by the apothecaries' art: and they made a very great burning for him [2 Chron. 16:13–14].

They burned a lot of candles for him.

During Asa's reign Judah experienced a touch of revival. He went only part way with God, and yet God used him.

CHAPTERS 17–20

THEME: *Revival during Jehoshaphat's reign*

This section records the second great revival period. It was much greater than the revival of Asa. Jehoshaphat, the son of Asa, was a man marvelously used of God. Remember that Chronicles gives God's viewpoint of the period of the kings and records what God considers important during the reigns of these men.

And Jehoshaphat his son reigned in his stead, and strengthened himself against Israel [2 Chron. 17:1].

That is, he strengthened the kingdom of Judah against Israel, the northern kingdom.

And he placed forces in all the fenced cities of Judah, and set garrisons in the land of Judah, and in the cities of Ephraim, which Asa his father had taken [2 Chron. 17:2].

You recall in the previous chapter we are told of war between Judah and Israel. Jehoshaphat is taking precautions to protect his kingdom.

And the LORD was with Jehoshaphat, because he walked in the first ways of his father David, and sought not unto Baalim [2 Chron. 17:3].

Notice that it says he walked in the "first ways" of his father—not in the way David walked in his old age, but when he was a young king, trusting the Lord.

But sought to the LORD God of his father, and walked in his commandments, and not after the doings of Israel.

Therefore the LORD stablished the kingdom in his hand; and all Judah brought to Jehoshaphat presents; and he had riches and honour in abundance [2 Chron. 17:4–5].

In the Old Testament a sign of God's approval was material prosperity.

TEACHING THE WORD

And his heart was lifted up in the ways of the LORD: moreover he took away the high places and groves out of Judah.

Also in the third year of his reign he sent to his princes, even to Ben-hail, and to Obadiah, and to Zechariah, and to Nethaneel, and to Michaiah, to teach in the cities of Judah.

And with them he sent Levites, even Shemaiah, and Nethaniah, and Zebadiah, and Asahel, and Shemiramoth, and Jehonathan, and Adonijah, and Tobijah, and Tobadonijah, Levites; and with them Elishama and Jehoram, priests.

And they taught in Judah, and had the book of the law of the LORD with them, and went about throughout all the cities of Judah, and taught the people [2 Chron. 17:6–9].

Do you realize what Jehoshaphat did? He started a "Thru the Bible" program! Because I sign my name J. Vernon McGee, people ask me what the "J" stands for, and I generally give them some facetious answer. So I'll give you one: it stands for *Jehoshaphat* because he was the first one to start a "Thru the Bible" program. He sent out the Levites. Since they didn't have mechanical means of communication, they had to go out personally. Jehoshaphat sent them out by the hundreds and maybe even by the thousands. They spread throughout the entire kingdom teaching the Word of God. My friend, that is the way of revival.

Until the church gets back to the Word of God, there will be no real revival. All movements in or out of the church will come to naught unless they are anchored in the Word of God. There are wonderful things that are happening today. Some are inside the church; some are outside the organized church. If they are rooted in the Word of God, revival will be the result.

Now notice the reaction to the teaching of the Word of God.

And the fear of the LORD fell upon all the kingdoms of the lands that were round about Judah, so that they made no war against Jehoshaphat.

Also some of the Philistines brought Jehoshaphat presents, and tribute silver; and the Arabians brought him flocks, seven thousand and seven hundred rams, and seven thousand and seven hundred he goats.

And Jehoshaphat waxed great exceedingly: and he built in Judah castles, and cities of store [2 Chron. 17:10–12].

Jehoshaphat had to build great storage places to house all the gifts that were brought to him. You see, this man was marvelously used of God. When revival came to Judah, it had its effect upon all the nations around them. The revival spread. Even the Philistines, who were the inveterate enemies of David, became friendly and sent gifts and silver for tribute to him. It even penetrated among the Arabian people. The Arabs sent flocks of animals to him.

You will also notice that there was no war against him. Spiritual revival is a cure for war. If a nation wishes to have peace, it must turn to God. That is God's method and always has been. If a nation is constantly at war, it is because that nation has turned away from God.

And he had much business in the cities of Judah: and the men of war, mighty men of valour, were in Jerusalem [2 Chron. 17:13].

This was a time of peace, but Jehoshaphat kept an army for protection. The captains are listed in the next few verses. He is a great ruler. He has provided ample protection in case there should be an attack by the enemy, but God has given him peace.

These waited on the king, beside those whom the king put in the fenced cities throughout all Judah [2 Chron. 17:19].

Jehoshaphat is a great man by all measurements. But now we see him doing something that is almost unbelievable.

JEHOSHAPHAT'S ALLIANCE WITH AHAB

Now Jehoshaphat had riches and honour in abundance, and joined affinity with Ahab [2 Chron. 18:1].

Jehoshaphat teamed up with Ahab. He had fellowship with Ahab. I cannot think of two men more unlike than these two men.

And after certain years he went down to Ahab to Samaria. And Ahab killed sheep and oxen for him in abundance, and for the people that he had with him, and persuaded him to go up with him to Ramoth-gilead [2 Chron. 18:2].

This seems unbelievable. It is one of the strangest partnerships on record in the pages of Scripture, or anywhere else. It is almost like saying that you could have day and night at the same time or that you can have light and darkness at the same time. How these two ever came together is a mystery. They have nothing in common spiritually. Jehoshaphat is one of the most godly kings personally, and he has been used to bring revival to his nation. He loves God, and he loves the Word of God. He is what we would call a spiritually-minded man. On the other hand, Ahab is as godless as they come. He hates God. He has given himself over to idolatry and immorality. How can these two be buddy-buddy? How can they enjoy each other's company? What is it that they have in common? Well, let's do a little investigation here.

They had a threefold alliance and partnership. It is all based on material reasons, physical reasons. They had nothing in common spiritually.

1. There was a matrimonial alliance between the two. Jehoram, the son of Jehoshaphat, married Athaliah, the daughter of Ahab and Jezebel. This Athaliah was a bloody woman who walked in the ways of her parents. We have already seen that in the Books of Kings. I suppose these two men thought they could cement relations between Judah and Israel and bring about an undivided kingdom. They tried to do this by intermarrying. What they did was wrong.

This is also a significant spot in our contemporary culture. I may sound like an antiquated preacher to a lot of folk, but I must speak out on a subject which is clearly taught in the Word of God. Here in Southern California we lead the world in divorce rates. Although I am not an authority in this field, there is one area on which I can speak loud and clear: a believer and an unbeliever—a Christian and a non-Christian—should not get married under any circumstances. Here the son of Jehoshaphat, hot out of a revival, marries that cold-blooded daughter of Ahab and Jezebel. That brought tragedy. In fact, it almost exterminated the line of David.

There is more tragedy, more heartache and heartbreak, more broken lives, more maladjusted children over this one problem of broken homes than anything else I know about. It will not work for a professing Christian to marry one who is not a Christian. If two non-Christian people get married and one is converted after they have married, that is a different situation. The apostle Paul writes specifically about that situation. However, God has much to say against a Christian deliberately walking into the trap of marrying a non-Christian—and it is a *trap*.

2. Jehoshaphat and Ahab had a market alliance. We are told that Jehoshaphat joined himself with Ahaziah, the son of Ahab, when he became king of Israel, and they sent ships to Tarshish. This is recorded in 1 Kings 22 and also in 2 Chronicles 20. The ships were sent for commerce in grain and gold. There was a shipwreck, and the cargo was lost. God could not bless this alliance.

3. Jehoshaphat and Ahab had a military alliance. Ahab was having problems with Syria; so he asked Jehoshaphat to enter into an alliance with him and go with him up to Ramoth-gilead. He gave a big feast for Jehoshaphat with sheep and oxen in abundance. And so he persuaded Jehoshaphat. Notice that Jehoshaphat is now sitting ". . . in the seat of the scornful" (Ps. 1:1). What the armies of the northern kingdom could not accomplish against the southern kingdom of Judah, Ahab accomplished by involving Jehoshaphat in a war with Syria. It reminds one of Chamberlain at Munich with Hitler and Mussolini. It reminds one of Yalta with Roosevelt and Churchill. It reminds one of Marshall in London. I'm sure there are alliances being made today, alliances which should never be made at all and which God cannot bless.

And Ahab king of Israel said unto Jehoshaphat king of Judah, Wilt thou go with me to Ramoth-gilead? And he answered him, I am as thou art, and my people as thy people; and we will be with thee in the war [2 Chron. 18:3].

Jehoshaphat is in the family of Ahab now by this intermarrying of their children. So he is willing to make an alliance and says, "We are one. We are together." Now remember, God had given Jehoshaphat peace. Ahab is asking him to go to war. Jehoshaphat agrees. And yet he is disturbed. He has a mind for God, and this situation gives him a certain amount of anxiety.

And Jehoshaphat said unto the king of Israel, Inquire, I pray thee, at the word of the Lord to-day [2 Chron. 18:4].

Jehoshaphat says, "Let's find out what God has to say about this venture." So Ahab brings in his whole army of prophets.

Therefore the king of Israel gathered together of prophets four hundred men, and said unto them, Shall we go to Ramoth-gilead to battle, or shall I forbear? And they said, Go up; for God will deliver it into the king's hand [2 Chron. 18:5].

Who are these prophets? They are prophets of Baal!

Now Jehoshaphat has discernment enough to know there is something wrong here.

But Jehoshaphat said, Is there not here a prophet of the Lord besides, that we might inquire of him?

And the king of Israel said unto Jehoshaphat, There is yet one man, by whom we may inquire of the Lord: but I hate him; for he never prophesied good unto me, but always evil: the same is Micaiah the son of Imla. And Je-

hoshaphat said, Let not the king say so [2 Chron. 18:6–7].

Jehoshaphat says, "You don't really mean that you hate him because he gives you the Word of God!" So Ahab agreed to send for him.

There are a lot of folk in our day also who hate a man who gives out the Word of God. In the church which I served for many years was a sign on the pulpit which I saw every time I stood there to speak. It read: "Sir, we would see Jesus." I like that. But I always felt there ought to be another verse of Scripture on the congregation's side of the pulpit: "Am I therefore become your enemy, because I tell you the truth?" (Gal. 4:16).

Micaiah is one of the great men of the Bible, as we have seen in 1 Kings 22. He was a man of God who gave out the Word of God. He told Ahab the truth at the peril of his own life. This man is now called on the scene.

And the king of Israel and Jehoshaphat king of Judah sat either of them on his throne, clothed in their robes, and they sat in a void place at the entering in of the gate of Samaria; and all the prophets prophesied before them [2 Chron. 18:9].

You can imagine those four hundred prophets running around saying to Ahab, "Go up against the king of Syria." One of them was especially dramatic. Zedekiah ran around with iron horns, pushing at everyone with them, saying, "This is the way you are going to do it!" What a scene—two kings on their thrones and all those prophets running around crying, "Go up and fight. You'll win!"

And the messenger that went to call Micaiah spake to him, saying, Behold, the words of the prophets declare good to the king with one assent; let thy word therefore, I pray thee, be like one of theirs, and speak thou good [2 Chron. 18:12].

The messenger tries to tip off Micaiah as to the situation he will face and advises him to get in step with the rest of them. He says all the prophets agree that they should go up to war so the smart thing for Micaiah to do is to agree with them. Maybe he even brought along a copy of *How to Win Friends and Influence People.* He told him to be sure to say the right thing to get on the good side of the king.

And Micaiah said, As the LORD liveth, even what my God saith, that will I speak [2 Chron. 18:13].

Micaiah is not intimidated. He is going to say what God has for him to say. You can be sure of that.

And when he was come to the king, the king said unto him, Micaiah, shall we go to Ramoth-gilead to battle, or shall I forbear? And he said, Go ye up, and prosper, and they shall be delivered into your hand [2 Chron. 18:14].

Micaiah does have a sense of humor. I enjoy that. I often say—and I say it reverently—that God has a sense of humor and there is a great deal of humor in the Bible. This is one instance of that.

Remember the scene. The two kings are sitting on their thrones. Four hundred men are running around saying, "Go up, go up." Now with biting sarcasm Micaiah joins the parade, and says, "Go up, go up."

And the king said to him, How many times shall I adjure thee that thou say nothing but the truth to me in the name of the LORD? [2 Chron. 18:15].

Ahab says to him, "Stop kidding me. You can't fool me. I know you don't agree with them." You see, Ahab wanted the Word of God, but he didn't want it. He knew the difference between truth and falsehood, but he didn't want to obey the truth. There are a lot of folk like that today.

Now Micaiah becomes serious. Here is God's message: Not only will they lose the battle, but Ahab will be slain.

Then he said, I did see all Israel scattered upon the mountains, as sheep that have no shepherd: and the LORD said, These have no master; let them return therefore every man to his house in peace.

And the king of Israel said to Jehoshaphat, Did I not tell thee that he would not prophesy good unto me, but evil? [2 Chron. 18:16–17].

The king of Israel says to Jehoshaphat, "I told you so—I told you he would predict nothing but evil unto me!"

Now Micaiah really lets him have it. He is serious now, and he is sarcastic. Oh, with what biting irony he gives this parable to Ahab!

Again he said, Therefore hear the word of the LORD; I saw the LORD sitting upon his throne, and all the host of heaven standing on his right hand and on his left.

And the LORD said, Who shall entice Ahab king of Israel, that he may go up and fall at Ramoth-gilead? And one spake saying after this manner, and another saying after that manner [2 Chron. 18:18–19].

This is ridiculous! Can you imagine God calling a board of directors' meeting to find out what He should do? The Lord doesn't ask for advice, my friend. Oh, what biting sarcasm this is! There were all kinds of suggestions. Now there comes out a wee little spirit and says he has a good idea.

Then there came out a spirit, and stood before the LORD, and said, I will entice him. And the LORD said unto him, Wherewith?

And he said, I will go out, and be a lying spirit in the mouth of all his prophets. And the LORD said, Thou shalt entice him, and thou shalt also prevail: go out, and do even so [2 Chron. 18:20–21].

Micaiah's ridiculous parable is a subtle way of saying that all these prophets of Baal are a pack of liars!

Now therefore, behold, the LORD hath put a lying spirit in the mouth of these thy prophets, and the LORD hath spoken evil against thee [2 Chron. 18:22].

In other words, these prophets have not been telling you the truth. God is going to judge you.

Now Ahab is not about to pay any attention to what Micaiah says. He gives orders to put him in prison and keep him there.

Then the king of Israel said, Take ye Micaiah, and carry him back to Amon the governor of the city, and to Joash the king's son;

And say, Thus saith the king, Put this fellow in the prison, and feed him with bread of affliction and with water of affliction, until I return in peace [2 Chron. 18:25–26].

Old Micaiah has the parting shot. Listen to him:

And Micaiah said, If thou certainly return in peace, then hath not the LORD spoken by me. And he said, Hearken, all ye people [2 Chron. 18:27].

I love this! Before Micaiah was taken off, he said, "Look, if you come back, the Lord hasn't spoken by me. But you are not coming back." So he turns to the people, "He won't be here, but you will be here. Remember what I said!" This is tremendous!

So the king of Israel and Jehoshaphat the king of Judah went up to Ramoth-gilead.

And the king of Israel said unto Jehoshaphat, I will disguise myself, and will go to the battle; but put thou on thy robes. So the king of Israel disguised himself; and they went to the battle [2 Chron. 18:28–29].

Ahab proved he was a deceiver all the way through. You see, the only man in the battle who was wearing royal robes was Jehoshaphat, which made him a marked man. Clever old Ahab had disguised himself. You might say that Ahab set Jehoshaphat up as a clay pigeon to be slain in the battle. It was not Jehoshaphat's fight at all, but he almost got killed!

Now the king of Syria had commanded the captains of the chariots that were with him, saying, Fight ye not with small or great, save only with the king of Israel.

And it came to pass, when the captains of the chariots saw Jehoshaphat, that they said, It is the king of Israel. Therefore they compassed about him to fight: but Jehoshaphat cried out, and the LORD helped him; and God moved them to depart from him [2 Chron. 18:30–31].

The only reason he came out alive is because God intervened on his behalf.

Old Ahab is feeling very satisfied with himself. Because of his cleverness he expects to come through the battle unscathed. But notice what happens.

And a certain man drew a bow at a venture, and smote the king of Israel between the joints of the harness: therefore he said to his chariot man, Turn thine hand, that thou mayest carry me out of the host; for I am wounded [2 Chron. 18:33].

On the Syrian side there was a soldier who ended up with one arrow left in his quiver. "He drew his bow at a venture"—he wasn't aiming at anything. But that arrow had old Ahab's name on it, and it got him. What happened? He died, just as Micaiah said he would.

Jehoshaphat went back home a sadder and wiser man.

JEHOSHAPHAT REBUKED FOR HIS ALLIANCE

As Jehoshaphat returns home, he is met by a prophet with a message from God.

And Jehoshaphat the king of Judah returned to his house in peace to Jerusalem.

And Jehu the son of Hanani the seer went out to meet him, and said to king Jehoshaphat, Shouldest thou help the ungodly, and love them that hate the Lord? therefore is wrath upon thee from before the Lord [2 Chron. 19:1–2].

"Shouldest thou help the ungodly?" is a very good question. It is something our generation, which has gone lovey-dovey on everything, should think about. My friend, God never asks you to love one who is an enemy of God. It is one thing to love a sinner. It is another thing to love his sin. We need to distinguish between the two. We are to hate the sinner's sin. If the sinner will not change, but persists and insists on sticking with his sin, then he becomes identified with his sin. There is no alternative, my beloved. There are people who are actually God's enemies, they are enemies of the Word of God, and they are inveterate enemies of Christianity. Years ago a very pious fellow said to me, "I pray for Joe Stalin." Well, I didn't, and I make no apology for it. Stalin was brought up in a school in which he was given some Bible teaching. He had an opportunity to know God. Yet he turned into an avowed enemy of God. I do not believe God expected us to pray for him. I don't feel that this lovey-dovey hypocrisy is honoring to God. I have had folk tell me how much they love me. Several have been very extravagant in their statements, and they were the ones I found out who were not even my friends. God cannot honor this hypocritical position of running around mouthing that we love everybody when really there are only a very few people whom we do love. We are to love God's people; this is His command. And we are to love the sinner in the sense that we should try to bring him to Christ. However, this does not mean that we are to compromise with sin!

There is another tremendous lesson here that I don't want us to miss. God did not send Jehu to Jehoshaphat *before* he went up to join himself with Ahab and Jezebel. At that time He did not send him to give him a little message on separation. Jehoshaphat was a man of God. He made his mistakes. God allowed him to go through this experience with Ahab because God was going to teach him a lesson from this.

We have a great many people today who have made themselves to be like God's spiritual policemen. They like to tell everybody else how they should be separated and with whom they should associate and with whom they should not associate. God makes it very clear that we are not to judge others in questionable matters. Remember that people are not coming before us in judgment anyway. "Who art thou that judgest another man's servant? to his own master he standeth or falleth. Yea, he shall be holden up: for God is able to make him stand" (Rom. 14:4). We fall into the error of criticizing others because they are not as separated as we think they should be. You see, God is able to make him stand. If he has a personal faith in Jesus Christ, God will hold him. I would like to put it like this. I must give an account some day for my life to the Lord Jesus Christ. He is my Master. You are not. In the same way, I am not *your* master. The Lord Jesus Christ is your Master. You will give your account to Him. The fact that I will some day give an account to the Lord Jesus Christ keeps me plenty busy. I don't have time to sit in judgment on you, and I trust that you do not have the time to sit in judgment on me. It is not our business; it is *His* business. God will rebuke me if I do the wrong thing. That's what He did for Jehoshaphat. He taught him through this experience and Jehoshaphat learned his lesson.

Nevertheless there are good things found in thee, in that thou hast taken away the groves out of the land, and hast prepared thine heart to seek God [2 Chron. 19:3].

Jehoshaphat was a remarkable man, but the marriage of his son into the family of Ahab brought judgment from God upon him and his nation, as we shall see.

And Jehoshaphat dwelt at Jerusalem: and he went out again through the

people from Beer-sheba to mount Ephraim, and brought them back unto the LORD God of their fathers [2 Chron. 19:4].

Now we will see some of the reforms that Jehoshaphat engaged in here. He was a wonderful man.

And he set judges in the land throughout all the fenced cities of Judah, city by city,
And said to the judges, Take heed what ye do: for ye judge not for man, but for the LORD, who is with you in the judgment.
Wherefore now let the fear of the LORD be upon you; take heed and do it: for there is no iniquity with the LORD our God, nor respect of persons, nor taking of gifts [2 Chron. 19:5–7].

In my judgment, this is the entire difficulty with our legal system today. When a godless man sits on the judge's bench, he does not feel a responsibility to God. He is a dangerous judge, regardless of who he is. He is a dangerous judge because he is subject to all these vices. To begin with, he is apt to make a wrong judgment. Also he is apt to show respect of persons, and may be led to take a bribe.

Moreover in Jerusalem did Jehoshaphat set of the Levites, and of the priests, and of the chief of the fathers of Israel, for the judgment of the LORD, and for controversies, when they returned to Jerusalem.
And he charged them, saying, Thus shall ye do in the fear of the LORD, faithfully, and with a perfect heart [2 Chron. 19:8–9].

You see how Jehoshaphat organized everything in his kingdom around God.

INVASION BY ENEMY NATIONS

It came to pass after this also, that the children of Moab, and the children of Ammon, and with them other beside the Ammonites, came against Jehoshaphat to battle.

Then there came some that told Jehoshaphat, saying, There cometh a great multitude against thee from beyond the sea on this side Syria; and, behold, they be in Hazazon-tamar, which is En-gedi.
And Jehoshaphat feared, and set himself to seek the LORD, and proclaimed a fast throughout all Judah [2 Chron. 20:1–3].

You see, now this man has a normal reaction: he is afraid. He goes to God in prayer and sends word out to his people to join him in fasting and prayer.

And Judah gathered themselves together, to ask help of the LORD: even out of all the cities of Judah they came to seek the LORD.
And Jehoshaphat stood in the congregation of Judah and Jerusalem, in the house of the LORD, before the new court [2 Chron. 20:4–5].

JEHOSHAPHAT'S PRAYER

And said, O LORD God of our fathers, art not thou God in heaven? and rulest not thou over all the kingdoms of the heathen? and in thine hand is there not power and might, so that none is able to withstand thee?
Art not thou our God, who didst drive out the inhabitants of this land before thy people Israel, and gavest it to the seed of Abraham thy friend for ever? [2 Chron. 20:6–7].

Jehoshaphat is doing something that his father, Asa, did not do. Asa did not rest upon the experiences of the past, which would have given him faith. Jehoshaphat, knowing what God has promised in the past and what God has done in the past, now rests upon the promises of God. He goes over this entire situation in his prayer to God and then he concludes his prayer:

O our God, wilt thou not judge them? for we have no might against this great company that cometh against us; neither know we what to do: but our eyes are upon thee.
And all Judah stood before the LORD, with their little ones, their wives, and their children [2 Chron. 20:12–13].

What a scene! What a king! He casts himself entirely upon God in a helpless situation. What a wonderful thing it is.

GOD'S ANSWER

Then upon Jahaziel the son of Zechariah, the son of Benaiah, the son of

Jeiel, the son of Mattaniah, a Levite of the sons of Asaph, came the spirit of the LORD in the midst of the congregation [2 Chron. 20:14].

Notice how often genealogies are used in the Scripture to identify the prophets or some of the other men who are brought across the pages of the Bible. It is very important. I wonder if you know who your great-great-great-grandfather was. I haven't any idea who mine was. But these folk kept accurate genealogies.

Listen to the words of Jahaziel. He is God's spokesman now.

And he said, Hearken ye, all Judah, and ye inhabitants of Jerusalem, and thou king Jehoshaphat. Thus saith the LORD unto you, Be not afraid nor dismayed by reason of this great multitude; for the battle is not yours, but God's [2 Chron. 20:15].

I need to remind myself of this. It is easy for me to forget that the ministry God has given me is the Lord's. I go at it like it is mine; I begin to carry the burden and face the problems and worry about the difficulties. Every now and then I have to remind myself that this is *God's* work. And since it is His (I say this reverently), He will have to work out the problems. The secret of prayer is to go to God in faith. As the hymn has it, "Take your burden to the Lord, and leave it there." The trouble with me is that I don't leave it there. I spread my problems out before the Lord, then I sack them up, put them right back on my back, and go on carrying them.

Oh, how wonderful God is! He says, "Don't be afraid, Jehoshaphat. The battle is not yours—you couldn't fight it; it is Mine." I find myself—and I'm sure you do also—in situations from which I cannot extricate myself. God says, "Turn it over to Me. I'll take care of it." Oh, that you and I might learn to turn it over to Him as Jehoshaphat did!

And they rose early in the morning, and went forth into the wilderness of Tekoa: and as they went forth, Jehoshaphat stood and said, Hear me, O Judah, and ye inhabitants of Jerusalem; Believe in the LORD your God, so shall ye be established; believe his prophets, so shall ye prosper [2 Chron. 20:20].

Now they are going out to meet the advancing enemy. Jehoshaphat encourages his troops to put their trust in the Lord.

God is saying to you and me, "Believe in Me. Rest in Me and believe My Word." Don't listen to what Mr. Ph.D. has to say; listen to what *God* has to say. "Believe in the LORD your God, so shall ye be established; believe his prophets, so shall ye prosper."

And when he had consulted with the people, he appointed singers unto the LORD, and that should praise the beauty of holiness, as they went out before the army, and to say, Praise the LORD; for his mercy endureth for ever [2 Chron. 20:21].

This is an unusual way to organize an army! He didn't get out his atom bomb; he just organized a choir to go ahead and praise the Lord—for His mercy endureth forever.

This whole chapter is thrilling to read. Now notice what happened. The Lord gave them the victory. God won the battle for them.

And on the fourth day they assembled themselves in the valley of Berachah; for there they blessed the LORD: therefore the name of the same place was called, The valley of Berachah, unto this day [2 Chron. 20:26].

Berachah is a name which has been taken by several churches in this country. It is a good name for a church, by the way. It means "the place to bless the Lord" or "the place to praise the Lord." Every church ought to be a Berachah church.

Then they returned, every man of Judah and Jerusalem, and Jehoshaphat in the forefront of them, to go again to Jerusalem with joy; for the LORD had made them to rejoice over their enemies.

And they came to Jerusalem with psalteries and harps and trumpets unto the house of the LORD.

And the fear of God was on all the kingdoms of those countries, when they heard that the LORD fought against the enemies of Israel.

So the realm of Jehoshaphat was quiet: for his God gave him rest round about [2 Chron. 20:27–30].

It is God who gives rest and peace. Our nation hasn't learned that. We think if we make this kind of an alignment, this kind of treaty, we won't have to fight in war. Well, we have fought two world wars in order to bring peace in the world and all we have is war. Do you know why? Because God hasn't given us peace. Our world is not trusting the Prince of Peace. This is the reason.

The chapter ends with the market alliance Jehoshaphat had with the son of Ahab, to which we have already referred. God could not bless this alliance with the ungodly son of Ahab.

Although Jehoshaphat was a great king, he was not perfect. God says that he ". . . departed not from it, doing that which was right in the sight of the LORD" (see v. 32).

Howbeit the high places were not taken away: for as yet the people had not prepared their hearts unto the God of their fathers [2 Chron. 20:33].

Idolatry was the ultimate downfall of the nation.

CHAPTERS 21–22

THEME: *Lapse into apostasy and sin*

We come now to a section of the Word of God that in many senses is complicated. Sin is the reason for its complication because sin is always complicated. Let me illustrate this. If I say to you that I am holding in my hand a stick that is absolutely straight, you will know exactly how it looks because it can be straight in only one way. But suppose I say that I am holding a stick that is crooked. You would have no idea how it looks because a thing can be crooked in a million different ways. In just such a way, sin allures a great many folk because it is devious. It is enticing because it seems to be unusual and strange and it is complicated. We will see this in the life of Jehoram, who comes to the throne after the death of Jehoshaphat.

JEHORAM'S EVIL REIGN

Now Jehoshaphat slept with his fathers, and was buried with his fathers in the city of David. And Jehoram his son reigned in his stead [2 Chron. 21:1].

Jehoram happened to be the son who had married into the family of Ahab and Jezebel, and he learned to do evil from them. I think he was a very apt pupil, by the way.

And he had brethren the sons of Jehoshaphat, Azariah, and Jehiel, and Zechariah, and Azariah, and Michael, and Shephatiah: all these were the sons of Jehoshaphat king of Israel.

And their father gave them great gifts of silver, and of gold, and of precious things, with fenced cities in Judah: but the kingdom gave he to Jehoram; because he was the firstborn.

Now when Jehoram was risen up to the kingdom of his father, he strengthened himself, and slew all his brethren with the sword, and divers also of the princes of Israel [2 Chron. 21:2–4].

He eliminated all the competition by the most dastardly means imaginable. He slew all his brothers and others of the royal family. Why did he do this?

And he walked in the way of the kings of Israel, like as did the house of Ahab: for he had the daughter of Ahab to wife: and he wrought that which was evil in the eyes of the LORD [2 Chron. 21:6].

God does not bless mixed marriages, my friend.

Howbeit the LORD would not destroy the house of David, because of the covenant that he had made with David, and as he promised to give a light to him and to his sons for ever [2 Chron. 21:7].

This man was so wicked that God would have been justified in exterminating the line. But, you see, God is faithful to His promises. He would not destroy the line of David because He had made a covenant with David.

Now we find that judgment immediately begins to come upon him.

In his days the Edomites revolted from under the dominion of Judah, and made themselves a king.

Then Jehoram went forth with his princes, and all his chariots with him: and he rose up by night, and smote the Edomites which compassed him in, and the captains of the chariots.

So the Edomites revolted from under the hand of Judah unto this day. The same time also did Libnah revolt from under his hand; because he had forsaken the LORD God of his fathers [2 Chron. 21:8–10].

God makes it very clear why this judgment came upon Jehoram. The Word says that this judgment was from the hand of God. He can't have peace because he has forsaken the Lord God of his fathers.

I get just a little impatient with people who say the Bible doesn't teach God's judgment on sin. What they really mean is that they don't believe the Bible. If they would say that, I would not find fault with them. What they believe is their business. But when they try to tell me that the Bible doesn't teach God's judgment, when it is as clear as it possibly can be, I object. God says He judges sin, and a great many of us can testify to the fact in our own lives.

Moreover he made high places in the mountains of Judah, and caused the inhabitants of Jerusalem to commit fornication, and compelled Judah thereto [2 Chron. 21:11].

He actually pushed the people back into the idolatry from which his father, Jehoshaphat, had delivered them.

THE MESSAGE OF ELIJAH

Now God calls in an old friend whom you may have forgotten about. This is the man whom God always called in to deliver the difficult message. He was a troubleshooter, and he is the right man for the job. The man is Elijah.

And there came a writing to him from Elijah the prophet, saying, Thus saith the LORD God of David thy father, Because thou hast not walked in the ways of Jehoshaphat thy father, nor in the ways of Asa king of Judah [2 Chron. 21:12].

There are many people who speak of Elijah as one of the prophets who did not write. He is called one of the nonwriting prophets. Of course, this means that there is no book in the Bible named for him or written by him. Although he didn't write a book, he did write a message. And when this man Elijah wrote a message, it singed the paper! He began by citing the reason for this harsh message: "Because thou hast not walked in the ways of Jehoshaphat thy father, nor in the ways of Asa king of Judah . . ." Now let's read the message.

But hast walked in the way of the kings of Israel, and hast made Judah and the inhabitants of Jerusalem to go a-whoring, like to the whoredoms of the house of Ahab, and also hast slain thy brethren of thy father's house, which were better than thyself:

Behold, with a great plague will the LORD smite thy people, and thy children, and thy wives, and all thy goods:

And thou shalt have great sickness by disease of thy bowels, until thy bowels fall out by reason of the sickness day by day [2 Chron. 21:13–15].

Elijah would be the prophet who could deliver a message like this. It is a harsh message but one that God wanted delivered to this man Jehoram.

The contents of the message are not unusual. This is the kind of message you would expect Elijah to deliver. However, the circumstances are extraordinary. It raises three questions: who? when? where? Let's first consider the "who?"—who is Elijah? This message is directed to Jehoram, the son of Jehoshaphat. The record in Kings tells us that Elijah was translated in the eighteenth year of Jehoshaphat. He was not on earth during the reign of Jehoram, and the assumption is that he could not write this prophecy. Some Bible students conclude that this is another Elijah, that he is not Elijah the Tishbite. That reminds me of the argument as to whether or not Shakespeare wrote the works of Shakespeare. As you know, some believe the author was Francis Bacon or someone else. I like Mark Twain's comment. He said, "Shakespeare did not write Shakespeare, but it was written by another man by the same name!" I consider that a conclusive answer in Elijah's case also. If this had not been Elijah the Tishbite, God would have made that clear. There is no impossible barrier, unless you reject the supernatural. If you do that, you will reject not only this but a great deal of the Bible. Our old friend, Elijah the prophet, is the one who wrote the message.

Now the second question is "when?"—when

did Elijah write it? Did he write it after his translation? Grotius maintains that the postmark was Paradise. Well, we can dismiss that as pure speculation. There is a very simple explanation: he wrote it *before* his translation. You may say, "But that's supernatural." Exactly. That is the point I am trying to make. Prophecy is supernatural. A prediction projects into the future; that's what makes it prophecy. We have many incidents of this. Isaiah spoke of Cyrus of Persia two centuries before he was even born. Daniel wrote of Alexander the Great. Elisha predicted the reign of Hazael over Syria. Micah named the town of Bethlehem as being the place where the Messiah would be born. Only God can prophesy with such accuracy.

The final question is "where?"—where did Elijah write this prophecy? Elijah was a prophet to the northern kingdom. This is the only reference to Elijah in Chronicles, because Chronicles is giving God's viewpoint. Didn't God take delight in Elijah? Of course He did. Then why isn't Elijah mentioned in this book in more detail? It is not that God omitted Elijah and his work; God omits the whole history of the northern kingdom. Elijah was the prophet to the northern kingdom, and this is the only time Elijah spoke to a king in the south. He never spoke to Jehoshaphat for the simple reason that Jehoshaphat was a good king and did not need one of the scorching messages from Elijah. Now when Jehoram, his son, comes to the throne, there is a message waiting for him. Elijah had written it before he was translated. Elijah not only left his mantle with Elisha, he left this message for Jehoram. He said, "You'll be seeing him; I won't."

This would suggest that when Elijah was translated, his message was not finished. It makes me believe that this man Elijah is one of the two witnesses mentioned in Revelation, chapter 11. He is going to deliver a harsh message again in a day when men have turned from God. I think this makes for a very intriguing passage of Scripture, with an unsual message delivered at this time.

What we find here is that when Jehoram came to the throne, he found a message on the front steps of the palace. It was thrown there by God's paperboy.

JUDGMENT FALLS ON JEHORAM

Now we'll see the accuracy of Elijah's prediction.

Moreover the LORD stirred up against Jehoram the spirit of the Philistines, and of the Arabians, that were near the Ethiopians:

And they came up into Judah, and brake into it, and carried away all the substance that was found in the king's house, and his sons also, and his wives; so that there was never a son left him, save Jehoahaz, the youngest of his sons [2 Chron. 21:16–17].

All of these had been at peace with both Asa and Jehoshaphat. Now their spirit is stirred up. War is coming. Why? War is the result of sin. We sometimes think of war as being made out on the battlefield. War takes place right at home, friends. It begins in the sinfulness of the human heart.

And after all this the LORD smote him in his bowels with an incurable disease.

And it came to pass, that in process of time, after the end of two years, his bowels fell out by reason of his sickness: so he died of sore diseases. And his people made no burning for him, like the burning of his fathers.

Thirty and two years old was he when he began to reign, and he reigned in Jerusalem eight years, and departed without being desired. Howbeit they buried him in the city of David, but not in the sepulchres of the kings [2 Chron. 21:18–20].

It was good riddance of bad rubbish when he died. The place in which they buried him and the lack of respect at his burial show how this man was hated. We will see in the next chapters that his wife was one of the most hated women who ever reigned.

AHAZIAH'S WICKED REIGN

And the inhabitants of Jerusalem made Ahaziah his youngest son king in his stead: for the band of men that came with the Arabians to the camp had slain all the eldest. So Ahaziah the son of Jehoram king of Judah reigned [2 Chron. 22:1].

The names get confusing because sometimes different names are used for the same person. Ahaziah is the Jehoahaz of 2 Chronicles 21:17. He is the only son left. All the other sons of Jehoram were killed.

Forty and two years old was Ahaziah when he began to reign, and he reigned one year in Jerusalem. His mother's

name also was Athaliah the daughter of Omri.

He also walked in the ways of the house of Ahab: for his mother was his counsellor to do wickedly.

Wherefore he did evil in the sight of the LORD like the house of Ahab: for they were his counsellors after the death of his father to his destruction [2 Chron. 22:2–4].

Athaliah is really the queen on the throne. She is the power behind the throne. She is the daughter of Ahab and Jezebel, and the granddaughter of Omri. She never really gave up her position. Remember that she turned her husband, Jehoram, away from God. Now her son, Ahaziah, listens to her and aligns himself with the northern kingdom and with the house of Ahab—which was to his destruction. Justice with a vengeance will be wrought upon him.

He walked also after their counsel, and went with Jehoram the son of Ahab king of Israel to war against Hazael king of Syria at Ramoth-gilead: and the Syrians smote Joram [2 Chron. 22:5].

This gets confusing, too, because there was a Jehoram in both the northern and the southern kingdoms. It looks as though we have the same man back again, but Jehoram, king of Judah, is dead. His son, Ahaziah, is the king, and now he aligns himself with Jehoram, king of Israel. Jehoram was wounded in this battle with the Syrians.

And he returned to be healed in Jezreel because of the wounds which were given him at Ramah, when he fought with Hazael king of Syria. And Azariah the son of Jehoram king of Judah went down to see Jehoram the son of Ahab at Jezreel, because he was sick [2 Chron. 22:6].

Azariah, king of Judah, went to visit Jehoram, king of Israel, who was recovering at Jezreel, and he probably took him a basket of fruit or something.

And the destruction of Ahaziah was of God by coming to Joram: for when he was come, he went out with Jehoram against Jehu the son of Nimshi, whom the LORD had anointed to cut off the house of Ahab [2 Chron. 22:7].

The interesting thing is that Jehu didn't know that Ahaziah, this king from the southern kingdom, was up there. Notice what happened.

And it came to pass, that, when Jehu was executing judgment upon the house of Ahab, and found the princes of Judah, and the sons of the brethren of Ahaziah, that ministered to Ahaziah, he slew them [2 Chron. 22:8].

These "sons of the brethren of Ahaziah" were not the brothers of Ahaziah, since they had been slain by Arabian marauders (2 Chron. 21:17), but these were the sons of these brothers, and therefore Ahaziah's nephews. The "princes of Judah" were probably distant relatives who held important offices in the court. Jehu slew them all. Now he goes after Ahaziah, who had escaped, and he is found and slain.

And he sought Ahaziah: and they caught him, (for he was hid in Samaria,) and brought him to Jehu: and when they had slain him, they buried him: Because, said they, he is the son of Jehoshaphat, who sought the LORD with all his heart. So the house of Ahaziah had no power to keep still the kingdom [2 Chron. 22:9].

This is a bloody period. God records it to let us know that He judges sin. He wants us to know that man doesn't get by with sin. How complicated it is! I said before that the way of sin is crooked and complicated.

ATHALIAH'S BRUTAL REIGN

But when Athaliah the mother of Ahaziah saw that her son was dead, she arose and destroyed all the seed royal of the house of Judah [2 Chron. 22:10].

I'll be very frank with you. It takes a bloody person and a mean one to kill her own grandchildren! If you are a grandparent, you share my feeling about grandchildren. I know why they call them grandchildren—they are grand. The fact of the matter is, I think grandchildren are more wonderful than children. If I had known how wonderful they were, I'd have had my grandchildren before I had my children!

I do not understand how this bloody queen could slay her grandchildren, but that is what she did. She slew all but one—because she couldn't find him.

But Jehoshabeath, the daughter of the king, took Joash the son of Ahaziah, and stole him from among the king's

sons that were slain, and put him and his nurse in a bedchamber. So Jehoshabeath, the daughter of king Jehoram, the wife of Jehoiada the priest, (for she was the sister of Ahaziah,) hid him from Athaliah, so that she slew him not.

And he was with them hid in the house of God six years: and Athaliah reigned over the land [2 Chron. 22:11–12].

If this had not taken place, the line of David would have been cut off. And God's promise to David concerning the coming of the Messiah would never have taken place. This is how close it was.

You can see that Satan has made attempts again and again to try to destroy the line that would lead to Christ. You will recall how Satan tried to destroy the line that would lead to Christ when all the male babies were to be slain down in the land of Egypt. He tried to have all the Jews exterminated at the time of Haman. After Jesus was born, he worked through old Herod and tried to kill Jesus by killing all the baby boys around Bethlehem. Here is another instance when Satan had the line of David reduced so there was only one survivor.

This little fellow, Joash, was one year old when he was hidden. He was kept hidden away in the temple for six years. During that time the bloody queen ruled the land.

CHAPTERS 23–24

***THEME:** Revival during Joash's reign*

During the reign of Joash, the third period of revival came to the southern kingdom of Judah. Of course it was not much of a revival, and most of the credit for a return to God belongs to the priest Jehoiada.

JOASH IS MADE KING

And in the seventh year Jehoiada strengthened himself, and took the captains of hundreds, Azariah the son of Jeroham, and Ishmael the son of Jehohanan, and Azariah the son of Obed, and Maaseiah the son of Adaiah, and Elishaphat the son of Zichri, into covenant with him [2 Chron. 23:1].

The leadership of Judah was dissatisfied with the bloody queen Athaliah. So now Jehoiada, the priest, calls them to a meeting, a very private meeting, to let them know that there is a son of David who is still alive. They all pledge themselves to make this little fellow of the line of David their king.

They gathered Levites and the chiefs of Israel and laid careful plans to crown little Joash who was in the line of David. A third part of the group would act as porters at the doors of the temple on the sabbath. A third part would be at the king's house. A third part would be at the gate of the foundation. They would not permit anyone inside the temple except the priests and the Levites. The Levites around the little king would all be armed with weapons. Jehoiada gave out spears and bucklers and shields which were kept in the temple. All of these arrangements were carried out.

Then they brought out the king's son, and put upon him the crown, and gave him the testimony, and made him king. And Jehoiada and his sons anointed him, and said, God save the king [2 Chron. 23:11].

This was an exciting and thrilling coup, and little seven-year-old Joash, who is in the line of David, is now on the throne of Judah.

EXECUTION OF ATHALIAH

Athaliah thought that she had killed off all her offspring. Why had she done such a brutal act? She had a thirst for power. She wanted to be queen.

There are certain men and certain women in this world who will do anything for power. Every group or class of people has them. There are preachers who will do that, deacons will do it, politicians and dictators will do that. There are many members of the human family who will stoop to almost anything in order to have power. They are, like this queen, craving for power.

Now when Athaliah heard the noise of the people running and praising the king, she came to the people into the house of the LORD [2 Chron. 23:12].

I tell you, this woman Athaliah was taken by surprise.

And she looked, and, behold, the king stood at his pillar at the entering in, and the princes and the trumpets by the king: and all the people of the land rejoiced, and sounded with trumpets, also the singers with instruments of music, and such as taught to sing praise. Then Athaliah rent her clothes, and said, Treason, Treason [2 Chron. 23:13].

From her standpoint it was high treason!

Then Jehoiada the priest brought out the captains of hundreds that were set over the host, and said unto them, Have her forth of the ranges: and whoso followeth her, let him be slain with the sword. For the priest said, Slay her not in the house of the LORD.

So they laid hands on her; and when she was come to the entering of the horse gate by the king's house, they slew her there [2 Chron. 23:14–15].

REVIVAL THROUGH JEHOIADA

Joash is still a little fellow, only seven years old; so Jehoiada is his regent. Jehoiada is actually the one who will make the decisions until this boy comes of age. Jehoiada is God's priest, and he leads the nation back to the worship of God.

And Jehoiada made a covenant between him, and between all the people, and between the king, that they should be the LORD's people [2 Chron. 23:16].

Jehoiada broke down the altars of Baal and killed the priests of Baal. He revived worship of Jehovah by setting up the order of priests and Levites for the burnt offerings. Singing was restored as it had been ordained by David. Porters watched the gates so nothing unclean entered the temple.

And all the people of the land rejoiced: and the city was quiet, after that they had slain Athaliah with the sword [2 Chron. 23:21].

There is repetition over and over of the same theme. Sin always brings complications, trouble, heartbreak, the judgment of God. Revival restores peace and quiet to the land.

REIGN OF JOASH

Joash was seven years old when he began to reign, and he reigned forty years in Jerusalem. His mother's name also was Zibiah of Beer-sheba [2 Chron. 24:1].

Jehoiada, the priest, is the one who really guided and led this little fellow during the early part of his reign. However, his mother's name is given to us, and she must have been a good mother. She apparently agreed with the return to the Lord which was taking place. Her home was in Beer-sheba. When I was down there not long ago, I thought of the mother of Joash. Beer-sheba is also the town of Abraham.

And Joash did that which was right in the sight of the LORD all the days of Jehoiada the priest.

And Jehoiada took for him two wives; and he begat sons and daughters [2 Chron. 24:2–3].

Joash did what was right under the coaching of Jehoiada; then we have the strange statement that he took two wives for him. Of course this didn't happen when he was seven years old—remember that he reigned forty years. Is the implication that it was all right to have two wives? No. It was wrong. It is not recorded because God approved of it; it is recorded because that is what he did. Considering the background of that day, two wives was really a small number. This was extremely mild, especially for a king in that period.

And it came to pass after this, that Joash was minded to repair the house of the LORD [2 Chron. 24:4].

As Joash grew up, Jehoiada grew old—he was one hundred and thirty years old when he died. Apparently he lost his control over the other priests, and the temple was not restored. Although it is questionable to say that Joash led in the revival—there wasn't much of a revival under him—it *was* revival. And he was the one who planned and insisted on repairing the temple of God.

And he gathered together the priests and the Levites, and said to them, Go out unto the cities of Judah, and gather of all Israel money to repair the house

of your God from year to year, and see that ye hasten the matter. Howbeit the Levites hastened it not.

And the king called for Jehoiada the chief, and said unto him, Why hast thou not required of the Levites to bring in out of Judah and out of Jerusalem the collection, according to the commandment of Moses the servant of the LORD, and of the congregation of Israel, for the tabernacle of witness? [2 Chron. 24:5–6].

Apparently Jehoiada has grown old, and the priests are indifferent. They have fallen down on their job.

For the sons of Athaliah, that wicked woman, had broken up the house of God: and also all the dedicated things of the house of the LORD did they bestow upon Baalim [2 Chron. 24:7].

This tells us what had actually happened to the temple and who was responsible. God's temple was in a terribly disreputable condition. So Joash takes the matter in his own hands.

And at the king's commandment they made a chest, and set it without at the gate of the house of the LORD.

And they made a proclamation through Judah and Jerusalem, to bring in to the LORD the collection that Moses the servant of God laid upon Israel in the wilderness.

And all the princes and all the people rejoiced, and brought in, and cast into the chest, until they had made an end [2 Chron. 24:8–10].

"Until they had made an end" means that they got all they needed.

Now it came to pass, that at what time the chest was brought unto the king's office by the hand of the Levites, and when they saw that there was much money, the king's scribe and the high priest's officer came and emptied the chest, and took it, and carried it to his place again. Thus they did day by day, and gathered money in abundance [2 Chron. 24:11].

Joash couldn't trust the Levites going out and collecting the money, so he puts this chest there in the temple, and people put their contributions there.

By the way, many organizations since then have used this method. They put out what they call a "chest of Joash" and ask folk to put their offerings in it.

And the king and Jehoiada gave it to such as did the work of the service of the house of the LORD, and hired masons and carpenters to repair the house of the LORD, and also such as wrought iron and brass to mend the house of the LORD.

So the workmen wrought, and the work was perfected by them, and they set the house of God in his state, and strengthened it [2 Chron. 24:12–13].

As a result, the repair work of the temple was completed.

And when they had finished it, they brought the rest of the money before the king and Jehoiada, whereof were made vessels for the house of the LORD, even vessels to minister, and to offer withal, and spoons, and vessels of gold and silver. And they offered burnt offerings in the house of the LORD continually all the days of Jehoiada [2 Chron. 24:14].

There were sufficient funds to remake the vessels and implements to carry on the regular services in the temple.

But Jehoiada waxed old, and was full of days when he died; an hundred and thirty years old was he when he died [2 Chron. 24:15].

This gives the explanation of why the priests were negligent in carrying out the order of the king. Jehoiada was probably senile. He had experienced bringing up this boy, and I suppose he had liberties that no one else would have had with the king.

And they buried him in the city of David among the kings, because he had done good in Israel, both toward God, and toward his house [2 Chron. 24:16].

Jehoiada actually received royal honors in his death.

APOSTASY AFTER JEHOIADA

Now after the death of Jehoiada, a new era begins.

Now after the death of Jehoiada came the princes of Judah, and made obei-

sance to the king. Then the king hearkened unto them.

And they left the house of the LORD God of their fathers, and served groves and idols: and wrath came upon Judah and Jerusalem for this their trespass [2 Chron. 24:17–18].

You see, as long as Jehoiada lived, the princes did not dare go into idolatry. Jehoiada maintained a very strong influence. Joash is a young king and probably very lenient. These princes pledge allegiance to him, but they go out and worship idols again.

Yet he sent prophets to them, to bring them again unto the LORD; and they testified against them: but they would not give ear [2 Chron. 24:19].

In His mercy, God sends prophets to warn them, but they will not listen. So God sends a message by a man who is the son of Jehoiada.

And the spirit of God came upon Zechariah the son of Jehoiada the priest, which stood above the people, and said unto them, Thus saith God, Why transgress ye the commandments of the LORD, that ye cannot prosper? because ye have forsaken the LORD, he hath also forsaken you [2 Chron. 24:20].

Now notice the shocking thing that happens.

And they conspired against him, and stoned him with stones at the commandment of the king in the court of the house of the LORD [2 Chron. 24:21].

My thought is that Joash had been given wrong information about this man. He was the son of Jehoiada! You would think that Joash would never have done a thing like this, but it reveals the evil influence of the princes and the despicable deeds that they were engaged in. They put him to death.

Thus Joash the king remembered not the kindness which Jehoiada his father had done to him, but slew his son. And when he died, he said, The LORD look upon it, and require it [2 Chron. 24:22].

In other words, this dying man calls upon God to take vengeance upon the king for this.

JUDGMENT UPON JOASH

And it came to pass at the end of the year, that the host of Syria came up against him: and they came to Judah and Jerusalem, and destroyed all the princes of the people from among the people, and sent all the spoil of them unto the king of Damascus.

For the army of the Syrians came with a small company of men, and the LORD delivered a very great host into their hand, because they had forsaken the LORD God of their fathers. So they executed judgment against Joash [2 Chron. 24:23–24].

God judges them by defeat in battle. Although Joash had been a good king, he had ordered this heartless murder. God must judge him because he is the king and because of his influence upon the whole nation.

And when they were departed from him, (for they left him in great diseases,) his own servants conspired against him for the blood of the sons of Jehoiada the priest, and slew him on his bed, and he died: and they buried him in the city of David, but they buried him not in the sepulchres of the kings [2 Chron. 24:25].

Jehoiada the priest had been buried with honor; now Joash the king is buried with dishonor.

Now concerning his sons, and the greatness of the burdens laid upon him, and the repairing of the house of God, behold, they are written in the story of the book of the kings. And Amaziah his son reigned in his stead [2 Chron. 24:27].

So we see that Joash at the beginning led a revival under the influence of Jehoiada; but, after Jehoiada's death, he apparently lapsed into a state of apostasy.

CHAPTERS 25–28

***THEME:** The reigns of Amaziah, Uzziah, Jotham, and Ahaz*

AMAZIAH'S REIGN

Amaziah was twenty and five years old when he began to reign, and he reigned twenty and nine years in Jerusalem. And his mother's name was Jehoaddan of Jerusalem.

And he did that which was right in the sight of the LORD, but not with a perfect heart [2 Chron. 25:1–2].

I guess you could say he was a moderately good king.

Now it came to pass, when the kingdom was established to him, that he slew his servants that had killed the king his father [2 Chron. 25:3].

He executed the men who had murdered his father.

But he slew not their children, but did as it is written in the law in the book of Moses, where the LORD commanded, saying, The fathers shall not die for the children, neither shall the children die for the fathers, but every man shall die for his own sin [2 Chron. 25:4].

He obeyed the Mosaic Law in this respect.

This is an important principle. You will never be judged because of the sins of your mother or the sins of your father. You stand judged on the basis of your *own* sins. On the other hand you may have a very godly mother or father, but you will never go to heaven because of godly parents. You will go to heaven because of the faith that *you* must exercise in Christ. This is a tremendous principle that is put down here.

Moreover Amaziah gathered Judah together, and made them captains over thousands and captains over hundreds, according to the houses of their fathers, throughout all Judah and Benjamin: and he numbered them from twenty years old and above, and found them three hundred thousand choice men, able to go forth to war, that could handle spear and shield [2 Chron. 25:5].

He is getting ready for war. Also he hires an enemy—mercenary soldiers from Israel.

But there came a man of God to him, saying, O king, let not the army of Israel go with thee; for the LORD is not with Israel, to wit, with all the children of Ephraim.

But if thou wilt go, do it, be strong for the battle: God shall make thee fall before the enemy: for God hath power to help, and to cast down [2 Chron. 25:7–8].

He warns Amaziah to trust God. After all, he has the example of Jehoshaphat and Asa in the past. He should know that God would not want him to hire men of Israel.

And Amaziah said to the man of God, But what shall we do for the hundred talents which I have given to the army of Israel? And the man of God answered, The LORD is able to give thee much more than this.

Then Amaziah separated them, to wit, the army that was come to him out of Ephraim, to go home again: wherefore their anger was greatly kindled against Judah, and they returned home in great anger.

And Amaziah strengthened himself, and led forth his people, and went to the valley of salt, and smote of the children of Seir ten thousand [2 Chron. 25:9–11].

Amaziah obeyed what the man of God had told him. He separated the army of Israel from his own army and sent them back to Israel. Then God gave him a victory over the children of Seir. The battle was fought down by the Dead Sea.

Now it came to pass, after that Amaziah was come from the slaughter of the Edomites, that he brought the gods of the children of Seir, and set them up to be his gods, and bowed down himself before them, and burned incense unto them [2 Chron. 25:14].

It is amazing that this man would do a thing like this, but it reveals the iniquity that is in the human heart.

Wherefore the anger of the LORD was kindled against Amaziah, and he sent unto him a prophet, which said unto him, Why hast thou sought after the gods of the people, which could not

deliver their own people out of thine hand?

And it came to pass, as he talked with him, that the king said unto him, Art thou made of the king's counsel? forbear; why shouldest thou be smitten? Then the prophet forbare, and said, I know that God hath determined to destroy thee, because thou hast done this, and hast not hearkened unto my counsel [2 Chron. 25:15–16].

Now civil war breaks out again.

Then Amaziah king of Judah took advice, and sent to Joash, the son of Jehoahaz, the son of Jehu, king of Israel, saying, Come let us see one another in the face [2 Chron. 25:17].

Amaziah said, "Let's see each other eyeball to eyeball." He was challenging Israel to go to war. Joash replies to Amaziah with a little parable.

And Joash king of Israel sent to Amaziah king of Judah, saying, The thistle that was in Lebanon sent to the cedar that was in Lebanon, saying, Give thy daughter to my son to wife: and there passed by a wild beast that was in Lebanon, and trode down the thistle.

Thou sayest, Lo, thou hast smitten the Edomites; and thine heart lifteth thee up to boast: abide now at home; why shouldest thou meddle to thine hurt, that thou shouldest fall, even thou and Judah with thee? [2 Chron. 25:18–19].

In other words, the parable was an insulting way of saying, "If you stay home and mind your own business, you won't get hurt."

But Amaziah would not hear; for it came of God, that he might deliver them into the hand of their enemies, because they sought after the gods of Edom [2 Chron. 25:20].

Amaziah would not listen. Now God judges him.

And Joash the king of Israel took Amaziah king of Judah, the son of Joash, the son of Jehoahaz, at Beth-shemesh, and brought him to Jerusalem, and brake down the wall of Jerusalem from the gate of Ephraim to the corner gate, four hundred cubits.

And he took all the gold and the silver, and all the vessels that were found in the house of God with Obed-edom, and the treasures of the king's house, the hostages also, and returned to Samaria [2 Chron. 25:23–24].

Of course it was an easy victory for Israel. It was a fulfillment of the prophet's warning, "I know that God hath determined to destroy thee, because thou hast done this, and hast not hearkened unto my counsel."

Now after the time that Amaziah did turn away from following the LORD they made a conspiracy against him in Jerusalem; and he fled to Lachish: but they sent to Lachish after him, and slew him there.

And they brought him upon horses, and buried him with his fathers in the city of Judah [2 Chron. 25:27–28].

UZZIAH'S REIGN

Now the son of Amaziah, Uzziah, came to the throne when he was only a teenager.

Then all the people of Judah took Uzziah, who was sixteen years old, and made him king in the room of his father Amaziah.

He built Eloth, and restored it to Judah, after that the king slept with his fathers.

Sixteen years old was Uzziah when he began to reign, and he reigned fifty and two years in Jerusalem. His mother's name also was Jecoliah of Jerusalem [2 Chron. 26:1–3].

Uzziah was a good king but not an outstanding one. There was no revival during his reign. It was during this period, by the way, that Isaiah began his ministry. He was commissioned at the death of Uzziah, as Isaiah tells us in Isaiah 6:1. As we have seen, the northern kingdom did not have a good king, not one. In the southern kingdom there were a few good kings. Five of them could be considered exceptional because during their reign there was revival and reformation. Uzziah's reign did not produce revival, but he was a good king. The denominational seminary from which I graduated was quite liberal, but it did have a Bible course, although it was very fragmentary. One of the questions that had been asked from time immemorial was to name the kings of Israel and Judah and briefly describe the reign of each. Some ingenious freshman of days gone by had discovered that if you would write after each one of them, "A bad king," you couldn't make less than ninety five percent—and what freshman wants to make more than that? So what we all did was memorize the kings and write after each one of them, "A bad king." Now when we wrote, "Bad king" after Uzziah's name, we were wrong; Uzziah was not exceptional, but he was a good king.

And he did that which was right in the sight of the LORD, according to all that his father Amaziah did.

And he sought God in the days of Zechariah, who had understanding in the visions of God: and as long as he sought the LORD, God made him to prosper [2 Chron. 26:4–5].

UZZIAH'S SUCCESSES

And he went forth and warred against the Philistines, and brake down the wall of Gath, and the wall of Jabneh, and the wall of Ashdod, and built cities about Ashdod, and among the Philistines [2 Chron. 26:6].

Gath was one of the strongholds of the Philistines.

I visited Ashdod some time ago. It is experiencing a tremendous business boom today because they have made a harbor there. In the old days the ancient ships could come to Caesarea but not to Ashdod. Now there is a wonderful man-made harbor there, and I suppose it receives more of the goods that are being shipped in and out of Israel than any other port. It is the place where the oil pipe lines come from the Red Sea. The oil is piped, put into the tankers, and carried from there. There is building going on everywhere. Now this entire area is what Uzziah took. All of this was Philistine country. But that wasn't all:

And the Ammonites gave gifts to Uzziah: and his name spread abroad even to the entering in of Egypt; for he strengthened himself exceedingly.

Moreover Uzziah built towers in Jerusalem at the corner gate, and at the valley gate, and at the turning of the wall, and fortified them.

Also he built towers in the desert, and digged many wells: for he had much cattle, both in the low country, and in the plains: husbandmen also, and vine dressers in the mountains, and in Carmel: for he loved husbandry [2 Chron. 26:8–10].

We are told that he "loved husbandry"—he was a farmer at heart, a farmer and a rancher. Down in that area from Ashdod and Ashkelon and Gath, all the way down to Beer-sheba, is great pasture land. It is today a great place for raising cattle and sheep, which is what Uzziah did. Then on up toward Carmel is the valley of Esdraelon, and that is great fruit country, especially vineyards. We are told that King Uzziah loved that sort of thing.

Moreover Uzziah had an host of fighting men, that went out to war by bands, according to the number of their account by the hand of Jeiel the scribe and Maaseiah the ruler, under the hand of Hananiah, one of the king's captains.

The whole number of the chief of the fathers of the mighty men of valour were two thousand and six hundred.

And under their hand was an army, three hundred thousand and seven thousand and five hundred, that made war with mighty power, to help the king against the enemy [2 Chron. 26:11–13].

The southern kingdom of Judah was strong militarily at this time.

And Uzziah prepared for them throughout all the host shields, and spears, and helmets and habergeons, and bows, and slings to cast stones.

And he made in Jerusalem engines, invented by cunning men, to be on the towers and upon the bulwarks, to shoot arrows and great stones withal. And his name spread far abroad; for he was marvellously helped, till he was strong [2 Chron. 26:14–15].

In ancient warfare they had certain kinds of machines that would hurl rocks. Also they could fix bows that would shoot arrows without being pulled by human power. And they were able to build bows of tremendous size that would shoot arrows a great distance. It is interesting to note that this man Uzziah was responsible for this new method of warfare.

Now Uzziah—as we have seen with all the kings, even the good ones—has a chink in his armor. Each has a weakness; each has his Achilles' heel. That is man even today. Regardless of what man he is, there is a weak spot in him.

UZZIAH'S WEAKNESS

Sometimes success is the worst thing that can happen to any of us, because we become lifted up with pride. Pride was Uzziah's downfall.

But when he was strong, his heart was lifted up to his destruction: for he transgressed against the LORD his God, and went into the temple of the LORD to burn incense upon the altar of incense [2 Chron. 26:16].

He went into the temple of the Lord to burn incense upon the altar of incense. Wasn't that all right? No, it was all wrong for him. Why?

And Azariah the priest went in after him, and with him fourscore priests of the LORD, that were valiant men:

And they withstood Uzziah the king, and said unto him, It appertaineth not unto thee, Uzziah, to burn incense unto the LORD, but to the priests the sons of Aaron, that are consecrated to burn incense: go out of the sanctuary; for thou hast trespassed; neither shall it be for thine honour from the LORD God [2 Chron. 26:17–18].

The priests could actually resist the king in this matter. The king was usurping the priest's office; he was doing what was strictly forbidden for anyone to do except the sons of Aaron. Only the priests of the line of Aaron could enter into the holy place—the golden lampstand and the altar of incense were there.

Then Uzziah was wroth, and had a censer in his hand to burn incense: and while he was wroth with the priests, the leprosy even rose up in his forehead before the priests in the house of the LORD, from beside the incense altar [2 Chron. 26:19].

This was instant judgment from God upon Uzziah.

And Azariah the chief priest, and all the priests, looked upon him, and, behold, he was leprous in his forehead, and they thrust him out from thence; yea, himself hasted also to go out, because the LORD had smitten him.

And Uzziah the king was a leper unto the day of his death, and dwelt in a several house, being a leper; for he was cut off from the house of the LORD: and Jotham his son was over the king's house, judging the people of the land [2 Chron. 26:20–21].

The son of Uzziah had to take over the affairs of state, because Uzziah was in quarantine for the rest of his life.

Now the rest of the acts of Uzziah, first and last, did Isaiah the prophet, the son of Amoz, write [2 Chron. 26:22].

In the prophecy of Isaiah, we read that Isaiah began his ministry at the death of Uzziah (Is. 6:1).

So Uzziah slept with his fathers, and they buried him with his fathers in the field of the burial which belonged to the kings; for they said, He is a leper: and Jotham his son reigned in his stead [2 Chron. 26:23].

Uzziah's funeral could almost be called a happy funeral. Death for a Christian should not be a dread. Paul could say to the Thessalonian believers, "But I would not have you to be ignorant, brethren, concerning them which are asleep, that ye sorrow not, even as others which have no hope" (1 Thess. 4:13). Also to the Corinthian Christians he said, "O death, where is thy sting? O grave, where is thy victory?" (1 Cor. 15:55). Funerals are not always as sad as they seem. The funeral of Uzziah was not sad. Why not? He was a leper. Uzziah had been a good king, but God records his sin also. He had intruded into the priest's office. That was the spot on the apple. His sin was the sin of presumption. There are still people today who sin by presumption. They attempt to approach God by man's way and not by God's way. God has told us that we must come to Him in *His* way. The Lord Jesus Christ said, ". . . I am the way, the truth, and the life: no man cometh unto the Father, but by me" (John 14:6). Uzziah had tried to come to God in his own way, and he had become a leper. This was a terrible disease. It was an awful disease physically, it was an awful disease psychologically, and it was an awful disease in every way. It entailed a great deal of suffering. Death for Uzziah was a sweet release. Uzziah was God's man in spite of his sin, and God judged him for his sin. Remember that Paul wrote to the believers, "For if we would judge ourselves, we should not be judged" (1 Cor. 11:31). Uzziah was judged of God down here, but he went to Paradise as God's man.

There are multitudes of believers who are helpless and hopeless in a frail and feeble body. One of these days there will be a sweet release for them. What a wonderful and joyful thing it is to go into the presence of Christ! There is nothing to sorrow about in a case like that. I imagine Jotham was dry-eyed at the funeral of his father. I'm sure he loved his father, and he understood that his father was a saved man.

JOTHAM'S REIGN

Jotham is another king whom we would classify as a good king. Judah has had three good kings in a row—that was unusual.

> **Jotham was twenty and five years old when he began to reign, and he reigned sixteen years in Jerusalem. His mother's name also was Jerushah, the daughter of Zadok.**
>
> **And he did that which was right in the sight of the LORD, according to all that his father Uzziah did: howbeit he entered not into the temple of the LORD. And the people did yet corruptly [2 Chron. 27:1–2].**

Something very strange and interesting is said about this man: "he entered not into the temple of the LORD." There is a background for this. When his father went into the temple, he was made a leper. But, of course, he went the wrong way—he intruded into the holy place. This boy Jotham did what was right in the sight of the Lord, but he stayed away from the temple. You can't help but feel sympathetic toward him, but he set a very bad example for the nation. As a result "the people did yet corruptly." They did not turn to God. Here is a man with a tremendous opportunity to lead his people back to God, but he had this hang-up—perhaps a root of bitterness. His father was made a leper in the temple, and he didn't want to go into that temple.

There are a great many people today who do just that sort of thing. They are kept away from God's house by prejudice. I have seen a number of folk who have dropped out of God's service because of prejudice, or an unfortunate incident which had happened years before or had involved a loved one. When I was a young man, I got acquainted with the son of a great Baptist preacher from Texas. He was really living it up in Pasadena when I met him. We used to play handball and volleyball together back in those days. When I tried to talk with him, he said, "Now listen, don't talk to me about religion. I know as much about it as you do." Then he told me how a group of deacons of the church had mistreated his father. He said, "I will never again darken the door of a church." I think he was wrong and I told him that. But very candidly, there was a background for it. That is the way it was with Jotham. There was an understandable background for his action.

> **He built the high gate of the house of the LORD, and on the wall of Ophel he built much.**
>
> **Moreover he built cities in the mountains of Judah, and in the forests he built castles and towers [2 Chron. 27:3–4].**

In that day the land was wooded. Today the hills are bare, for the most part. However trees are being planted now so that more of the land is becoming wooded again. Back in those days it was a land flowing with milk and honey. Jotham built castles among the trees in the hills. He was a great builder. I guess he is the man who started building subdivisions.

> **He fought also with the king of the Ammonites, and prevailed against them. And the children of Ammon gave him the same year an hundred talents of silver, and ten thousand measures of wheat, and ten thousand of barley. So much did the children of Ammon pay unto him, both the second year, and the third.**
>
> **So Jotham became mighty, because he prepared his ways before the LORD his God [2 Chron. 27:5–6].**

He kept his nation strong militarily as his father had done.

> **He was five and twenty years old when he began to reign, and reigned sixteen years in Jerusalem.**
>
> **And Jotham slept with his fathers, and they buried him in the city of David: and Ahaz his son reigned in his stead [2 Chron. 27:8–9].**

Only one brief chapter is devoted to the reign of Jotham. Here is a young man who could have been a great king, but a prejudice prevented him from being a great king and doing great things for God.

AHAZ' REIGN

We knew that sooner or later Judah would get a bad king, and here he is. At this time the northern kingdom of Israel was on the verge of going into captivity, and the southern kingdom of Judah was brought very low by the sins of Ahaz, as we shall see.

Ahaz was twenty years old when he began to reign, and he reigned sixteen years in Jerusalem: but he did not that which was right in the sight of the LORD, like David his father:

For he walked in the ways of the kings of Israel, and made also molten images for Baalim [2 Chron. 28:1–2].

Ahaz was a bad king. He walked in the ways of the kings of Israel, and that meant evil ways. David was the human standard by which these kings were measured, and this man fell far short of that human standard. As a result we now begin to see the sad future of the southern kingdom. The northern kingdom will go into captivity to the Assyrians. God will give many warnings to the southern kingdom, but they, likewise, will follow into captivity—not to Assyria, but later on to Babylon.

Moreover he burnt incense in the valley of the son of Hinnom, and burnt his children in the fire, after the abominations of the heathen whom the LORD had cast out before the children of Israel [2 Chron. 28:3].

This means he offered his children on a red hot altar. Actually, it was an idol that was heated red-hot for human sacrifices.

He sacrificed also and burnt incense in the high places, and on the hills, and under every green tree [2 Chron. 28:4].

Ahaz went completely into idolatry and plunged the southern kingdom into idolatry.

INVASION BY SYRIA AND ISRAEL

Wherefore the LORD his God delivered him into the hand of the king of Syria; and they smote him, and carried away a great multitude of them captives, and brought them to Damascus. And he was also delivered into the hand of the king of Israel, who smote him with a great slaughter [2 Chron. 28:5].

As it were, God opens up the doors of His nation, His people, and permits the enemy to come in. Syria comes down, and for the first time the wall is breached into the southern kingdom. There are many who are taken captive. The sad part is that the northern kingdom had joined with Syria in making this attack, and so we find that many who were taken captive actually became captives of Israel, the northern kingdom. Israel took men of Judah into captivity.

For Pekah the son of Remaliah slew in Judah an hundred and twenty thousand in one day, which were all valiant men; because they had forsaken the LORD God of their fathers [2 Chron. 28:6].

God makes the reason crystal-clear.

And Zichri, a mighty man of Ephraim, slew Maaseiah the king's son, and Azrikam the governor of the house, and Elkanah that was next to the king.

And the children of Israel carried away captive of their brethren two hundred thousand, women, sons, and daughters, and took also away much spoil from them, and brought the spoil to Samaria [2 Chron. 28:7–8].

This is the very sad plight of the southern kingdom. God permitted this to happen because Ahaz and the people had plunged into idolatry with abandon.

Now God sends a prophet to Israel to speak to them because of their extreme cruelty to their brethren.

But a prophet of the LORD was there, whose name was Oded: and he went out before the host that came to Samaria, and said unto them, Behold, because the LORD God of your fathers was wroth with Judah, he hath delivered them into your hand, and ye have slain them in a rage that reacheth up unto heaven.

And now ye purpose to keep under the children of Judah and Jerusalem for bondmen and bondwomen unto you: but are there not with you, even with you, sins against the LORD your God? [2 Chron. 28:9–10].

God had expressly forbidden taking their brethren into slavery (Lev. 25:39–40).

Now hear me therefore, and deliver the captives again, which ye have taken captive of your brethren: for the fierce wrath of the LORD is upon you.

Then certain of the heads of the children of Ephraim, Azariah the son of Johanan, Berechiah the son of Meshillemoth, and Jehizkiah the son of Shallum, and Amasa the son of Hadlai,

stood up against them that came from the war [2 Chron. 28:11–12].

A group of leaders in the northern kingdom took their stand against enslaving their brethren from the southern kingdom.

And said unto them, Ye shall not bring in the captives hither: for whereas we have offended against the LORD already, ye intend to add more to our sins and to our trespass: for our trespass is great, and there is fierce wrath against Israel.

So the armed men left the captives and the spoil before the princes and all the congregation.

And the men which were expressed by name rose up, and took the captives, and with the spoil clothed all that were naked among them, and arrayed them, and shod them, and gave them to eat and to drink, and anointed them, and carried all the feeble of them upon asses, and brought them to Jericho, the city of palm trees, to their brethren: then they returned to Samaria [2 Chron. 28:13–15].

They were able to secure their release and return them to their homes.

The southern kingdom of Judah was in a really sad plight at this time. If it had not been for the fact that God intervened, they would have been almost eliminated as a nation. It did weaken them a great deal and laid them open to further invasion.

INVASION BY EDOM AND PHILISTIA

At that time did king Ahaz send unto the kings of Assyria to help him.

For again the Edomites had come and smitten Judah, and carried away captives.

The Philistines also had invaded the cities of the low country, and of the south of Judah, and had taken Beth-shemesh, and Ajalon, and Gederoth, and Shocho with the villages thereof, and Timnah with the villages thereof, Gimzo also and the villages thereof: and they dwelt there [2 Chron. 28: 16–18].

When God removed His protection, it was like opening the flood gates and letting the enemy come in. This was, of course, the result of the nation's sin. Wars are the direct result of sin. In the New Testament James asks the question, "From whence come wars and fightings among you?" The answer is, "come they not hence, even of your lusts that war in your members? Ye lust, and have not: ye kill, and desire to have . . ." (James 4:1–2). As long as there is sin in the heart of man, he cannot have peace. He can't have any kind of peace—peace with God, peace in his own heart, or peace with his fellowman. There must be a settling of the sin question in order to have peace. The experience of Judah illustrates this. Because of sin on the part of the people they will not have peace.

Ahaz made another big mistake. Instead of turning to God, he turned to Assyria for help.

And Tilgath-pilneser king of Assyria came unto him, and distressed him, but strengthened him not.

For Ahaz took away a portion out of the house of the LORD, and out of the house of the king, and of the princes, and gave it unto the king of Assyria: but he helped him not [2 Chron. 28: 20–21].

Ahaz put his trust in the king of Assyria. He sent him a generous gift from the wealth of the temple and of the palace. The king of Assyria accepted it, but he never did send any help to Ahaz. He didn't need to. He was a powerful king, and poor Ahaz was a very weak king. Ahaz had turned from God and trusted in Assyria, and Assyria let him down. Assyria did not make good on their treaty. You cannot expect nations to be true to their treaties. Why not? Very simply, as long as men are sinners, men will be liars, which means you cannot trust them. The Bible tells us we are not to put our trust in man. We are to put our trust in God.

And in the time of his distress did he trespass yet more against the LORD: this is that king Ahaz.

For he sacrificed unto the gods of Damascus, which smote him: and he said, Because the gods of the kings of Syria help them, therefore will I sacrifice to them, that they may help me. But they were the ruin of him, and of all Israel [2 Chron. 28:22–23].

Ahaz then cut up the vessels of the house of God, he shut up the doors of the temple, and he made heathen altars in every corner of Jerusalem.

> **And Ahaz slept with his fathers, and they buried him in the city, even in Jerusalem: but they brought him not into the sepulchres of the kings of Israel: and Hezekiah his son reigned in his stead [2 Chron. 28:27].**

So ends this very sad and sordid and sorry reign of Ahaz.

CHAPTERS 29–32

***THEME:** Revival during Hezekiah's reign*

We come now to the reign of Hezekiah and one of the periods of revival in the nation of Judah. You would think that after the reign of Ahaz there would be no hope for the nation. They were depleted of their resources, they had been defeated in war, they had been betrayed by Assyria, and you would think there would be no help for them from any quarter. However, Hezekiah came to the kingdom for such a time as this, because he is God's man.

> **Hezekiah began to reign when he was five and twenty years old, and he reigned nine and twenty years in Jerusalem. And his mother's name was Abijah, the daughter of Zechariah [2 Chron. 29:1].**

Both the mother and the grandfather are mentioned here, but there is no mention of his father, old Ahaz. Apparently Hezekiah had a godly mother and a godly grandfather, and they influenced this young man.

> **And he did that which was right in the sight of the LORD, according to all that David his father had done [2 Chron. 29:2].**

The Book of 2 Kings has a more succinct account of the revival under Hezekiah. "He removed the high places, and brake the images, and cut down the groves, and brake in pieces the brasen serpent that Moses had made: for unto those days the children of Israel did burn incense to it: and he called it Nehushtan. He trusted in the LORD God of Israel; so that after him was none like him among all the kings of Judah, nor any that were before him. For he clave to the LORD, and departed not from following him, but kept his commandments, which the LORD commanded Moses. And the LORD was with him; and he prospered whithersoever he went forth . . ." (2 Kings 18:4–7).

When you come down all the list of the twenty-one kings of Judah who followed David, there is none greater than Hezekiah. He is the outstanding one, a man who turned to God. I believe he led in one of the greatest revivals, and there were some great ones.

I mentioned that his revival is recorded in 2 Kings. Here in 2 Chronicles, which is written from God's point of view, four lengthy chapters are devoted to Hezekiah. Evidently God took great delight in Hezekiah. Also Isaiah the prophet has in the center of his book several chapters which are historical and not prophetic. They have to do with—yes, you guessed it—Hezekiah. Three times in the Word of God we are told about this man and the great return to God which he led.

In Chronicles we are told the positive things which he did to restore worship. In Kings we are told the negative things he had to do. He had to remove the high places and break the images and had to break in pieces the brazen serpent that Moses had made because the people were burning incense to it. He had to get rid of that stumbling block. He contemptuously called it "Nehushtan"—it was just a piece of brass. There had been one time when the people had looked at the serpent in faith, trusting the promise of God, then the brazen serpent had been the basis of physical salvation for those who were bitten by the poisonous snakes. Now it had become an object of worship. It had become an idol. It was a stumbling block to the people.

There are those today who worship the symbol of the cross. They feel that there is some merit in having a cross in their possession. My friends, there would be no merit in it at all. You can make an idol of anything—you can worship the spigot because it gives you water, you could worship the window because it brings you light, or you could worship the automobile because it transports you. A great many people today worship the television screen; they sit before it for hours each day. May I say to you, there is no merit in objects. The merit is in God, of course; this is written from God's viewpoint.

Now in Chronicles we are given the positive side of Hezekiah's reforms.

He in the first year of his reign, in the first month, opened the doors of the house of the LORD, and repaired them [2 Chron. 29:3].

Remember that Ahaz had nailed shut the doors of the temple. Nobody was using it. As soon as Hezekiah began to reign, he opened the doors of the temple. They were open for the first time in a long time. Now Hezekiah tells them to clean everything.

And he brought in the priests and the Levites, and gathered them together into the east street,

And said unto them, Hear me, ye Levites, sanctify now yourselves, and sanctify the house of the LORD God of your fathers, and carry forth the filthiness out of the holy place [2 Chron. 29:4–5].

Hezekiah says, "Sanctify now yourselves." There had to be a return to holy living, to honesty, and to integrity. There had to be a setting-apart for God. That was something that was needed. I think we need the same thing today. We have too much of this homogenized Christianity today—mixing good and bad together.

For our fathers have trespassed, and done that which was evil in the eyes of the LORD our God, and have forsaken him, and have turned away their faces from the habitation of the LORD, and turned their backs.

Also they have shut up the doors of the porch, and put out the lamps, and have not burned incense nor offered burnt offerings in the holy place unto the God of Israel [2 Chron. 29:6–7].

He places the blame where it belongs. They have brought disaster upon themselves because of their sins.

Wherefore the wrath of the LORD was upon Judah and Jerusalem, and he hath delivered them to trouble, to astonishment, and to hissing, as ye see with your eyes.

For, lo, our fathers have fallen by the sword, and our sons and our daughters and our wives are in captivity for this [2 Chron. 29:8–9].

Now he tells them what is upon his heart.

Now it is in mine heart to make a covenant with the LORD God of Israel, that his fierce wrath may turn away from us [2 Chron. 29:10].

TEMPLE WORSHIP RESTORED

Then Hezekiah the king rose early, and gathered the rulers of the city, and went up to the house of the LORD.

And they brought seven bullocks, and seven rams, and seven lambs, and seven he goats, for a sin offering for the kingdom, and for the sanctuary, and for Judah. And he commanded the priests the sons of Aaron to offer them on the altar of the LORD [2 Chron. 29:20–21].

Hezekiah set a good example. He took a public stand for God. I believe this is one of the things that is needed today. God's people need to take a public stand for God. We need to stand for God in our place of work and in our social gatherings.

The priests made an atonement for all Israel with the burnt offerings and sin offering. Music was again brought into the worship in the temple. There was singing and instrumental music as David had organized it. The whole congregation sang praises to God and worshiped Him.

And Hezekiah rejoiced, and all the people, that God had prepared the people: for the thing was done suddenly [2 Chron. 29:36].

FEAST OF PASSOVER RESTORED

And Hezekiah sent to all Israel and Judah, and wrote letters also to Ephraim and Manasseh, that they should come to the house of the LORD at Jerusalem, to keep the passover unto the LORD God of Israel [2 Chron. 30:1].

Here is another wonderful thing this man did. Remember that his father had carried on warfare against the northern kingdom, and many of those from Judah had been taken captive. You might think that Hezekiah would have come to the throne with a spirit of vengeance in his heart and with a spirit of getting even. But notice that after he had opened up the temple of God, restoring the worship of God and giving his own public testimony, he sends an invitation to the northern kingdom to come and worship God. What a wonderful, marvelous spirit this is!

> **For the king had taken counsel, and his princes, and all the congregation in Jerusalem, to keep the passover in the second month [2 Chron. 30:2].**

Authority for observing the Passover in the second month, instead of the first, is given in Numbers 9:10–11.

Although the invitation, which Hezekiah sent into the northern kingdom, was rejected and ridiculed by some, many responded and came to keep the Passover with their brethren.

> **Then they killed the passover on the fourteenth day of the second month: and the priests and the Levites were ashamed, and sanctified themselves, and brought in the burnt offerings into the house of the LORD.**
>
> **And they stood in their place after their manner, according to the law of Moses the man of God: the priests sprinkled the blood, which they received of the hand of the Levites.**
>
> **For there were many in the congregation that were not sanctified: therefore the Levites had the charge of the killing of the passovers for every one that was not clean, to sanctify them unto the LORD [2 Chron. 30:15–17].**

The people had come from all over Israel, and some of them were not sanctified.

> **For a multitude of the people, even many of Ephraim, and Manasseh, Issachar, and Zebulun, had not cleansed themselves, yet did they eat the passover otherwise than it was written. But Hezekiah prayed for them, saying, The good LORD pardon every one**
>
> **That prepareth his heart to seek God, the LORD God of his fathers, though he be not cleansed according to the purification of the sanctuary.**
>
> **And the LORD hearkened to Hezekiah, and healed the people [2 Chron. 30: 18–20].**

This, I think, is one of the loveliest things Hezekiah did. When he sent invitations to the people of Israel in the north, many came down out of the different tribes to Jerusalem to worship. But, you see, these people had been without the Word of God all their lives. They had been living in the northern kingdom, in the place of idolatry, and yet they had a hunger and a desire to serve God and to obey Him. When they came down for the feast, they were supposed to have been cleansed, to have prepared their hearts for the Passover, and they hadn't done that. They went ahead and ate the Passover without knowing that they should have been cleansed. When it was told to Hezekiah, he prayed for them: "The good Lord pardon every one." Isn't that a lovely thing which he did for them? It was ignorance on their part. Their hearts had been seeking the Lord, but they didn't understand that they had to be purified. The Lord listened to the prayer of Hezekiah and healed the people. This reveals that the form and the ceremony are not the important things. God is interested in the condition of the hearts of the people. What a wonderful, glorious lesson this is here.

> **And the children of Israel that were present at Jerusalem kept the feast of unleavened bread seven days with great gladness: and the Levites and the priests praised the LORD day by day, singing with loud instruments unto the LORD [2 Chron. 30:21].**

They were having such a wonderful time, that they decided to extend the feast for another week.

> **And the whole assembly took counsel to keep other seven days: and they kept other seven days with gladness [2 Chron. 30:23].**

This was a joyous return to the Lord and to His Word.

> **So there was great joy in Jerusalem: for since the time of Solomon the son of David king of Israel there was not the like in Jerusalem.**
>
> **Then the priests the Levites arose and blessed the people: and their voice was heard, and their prayer came up to his holy dwelling place, even unto heaven [2 Chron. 30:26–27].**

Now I want you to notice this man Hezekiah. His father old Ahaz, had made idolatry the state religion in Judah. Now Hezekiah begins to rid the land of idols.

Now when all this was finished, all Israel that were present went out to the cities of Judah, and brake the images in pieces, and cut down the groves, and threw down the high places and the altars out of all Judah and Benjamin, in Ephraim also and Manasseh, until they had utterly destroyed them all. Then all the children of Israel returned, every man to his possession, into their own cities [2 Chron. 31:1].

After this, there was a great period of reformation that took place. Hezekiah was the man who led in all of this.

And thus did Hezekiah throughout all Judah, and wrought that which was good and right and truth before the LORD his God.

And in every work that he began in the service of the house of God, and in the law, and in the commandments, to seek his God, he did it with all his heart, and prospered [2 Chron. 31:20–21].

Now let's look a little more closely at the life of Hezekiah. What kind of a man was he?

First of all, he was a man of faith. When I say *faith*, I mean more than what is generally thought of as faith.

A member of a certain "ism" told me that there were four things one had to do to be saved. So I asked him, "What do you think you have to do to be saved?" I won't mention all four things, but one of them was faith. I told him, "I don't agree with you on any of the four." He was a little shocked. He said, "Well, certainly you believe in faith, because I know you preach on that." I said, "But I don't mean *faith* in the same way that you mean *faith*. You are saying that if one believes hard enough he will be saved."

The modern conception of faith reminds me of the county fairs I used to go to when I was a boy. At each fair there was a gadget to test a man's strength. There was a weight on a pair of scales that looked like a giant thermometer. A man would come along and hit the thing with a sledge hammer, which would knock the weight up. A fellow would come along with his girl friend, and they would challenge him to try out his strength. He would take off his coat, spit on his hands, and swing that hammer with all his might to see if he could ring the bell up at the top. He would make the supreme effort. He would really try hard.

That's the way some folk think faith is. They say, "If I could only believe hard enough." My friend, faith is not a psychological response to anything. Faith is not in the feelings; it is an accomplished fact. Faith is that which is wrought in the soul by the Holy Spirit. It is a conviction that is born in the spirit of man.

After Peter made his great confession of faith in Jesus Christ, the Lord Jesus said, ". . . Blessed art thou, Simon Bar-jona: for flesh and blood hath not revealed it unto thee, but my Father which is in heaven" (Matt. 16:17). Faith is not self-meritorious. "For by grace are ye saved through faith . . ." (Eph. 2:8). Faith is only the instrument. Christ is the Savior and He is the object of faith.

Spurgeon said, "It is not thy hold on Christ that saves thee. It is Christ. It is not thy joy in Christ that saves thee. It is Christ. It is not even thy faith, though that be the instrument; it is Christ's blood and merit." There is no merit in faith. It is not a matter of believing enough. You could believe the wrong thing. There are many people who die as martyrs for fanatic beliefs. They can have ever so much faith, but it is in the wrong thing or the wrong person.

True faith "brings nothing so that it may take all." Faith says, "Lord, I believe; help Thou mine unbelief." Faith trusts God.

Now in the remainder of chapter 31, we see Hezekiah's further reforms. Also there will be reformation in your life when the Lord Jesus saves you, my friend. He is going to change your life.

Remember that when the man sick of the palsy was brought to Christ, Jesus told him his sins were forgiven. The crowd of scribes and Pharisees began to murmur, and call this a case of blasphemy. Jesus said, ". . . What reason ye in your hearts? Whether is easier, to say, Thy sins be forgiven thee; or to say, Rise up and walk?" They had no answer for Jesus. Obviously, it is just as easy to do the one as to do the other. It is also just as difficult to do the one as to do the other. Only God can do either one of them. Only God can forgive sin. Only God can make a person get up and walk. "But that ye may know that the Son of man hath power upon earth to forgive sins, (he said unto the sick of the palsy,) I say unto thee, Arise, and take up thy couch, and go into thine house" (Luke 5:22–24).

My friend, if Christ has forgiven your sin, you have taken up your bed and you have walked. You have walked away from your old life. You have walked away from your old sin.

You have been changed. If you have not walked away, you are still paralyzed with sin.

Hezekiah is a man of real faith in God, and it changed his life. And now he is changing the kingdom.

Hezekiah is not only a man of faith, he is a man of prayer. In chapter 32 it looks as if the Lord allowed Judah to pass from the sunlight of God's blessing to the darkness of disaster. Sennacherib came down from Assyria again, and he was ready to make an attack upon the city of Jerusalem. He began by terrifying the inhabitants.

After these things, and the establishment thereof, Sennacherib king of Assyria came, and entered into Judah, and encamped against the fenced cities, and thought to win them for himself [2 Chron. 32:1].

Hezekiah took steps to strengthen and fortify the city, but his confidence was in God. He encouraged his people to trust in Him.

Be strong and courageous, be not afraid nor dismayed for the king of Assyria, nor for all the multitude that is with him: for there be more with us than with him:

With him is an arm of flesh; but with us is the LORD our God to help us, and to fight our battles. And the people rested themselves upon the words of Hezekiah king of Judah [2 Chron. 32:7–8].

After this Sennacherib sent representatives to intimidate the people and break down their morale and shake their confidence in God.

Who was there among all the gods of those nations that my fathers utterly destroyed, that could deliver his people out of mine hand, that your God should be able to deliver you out of mine hand?

Now therefore let not Hezekiah deceive you, nor persuade you on this manner, neither yet believe him: for no god of any nation or kingdom was able to deliver his people out of mine hand, and out of the hand of my fathers: how much less shall your God deliver you out of mine hand? [2 Chron. 32:14–15].

Also Sennacherib sent letters to demoralize them.

He wrote also letters to rail on the LORD God of Israel, and to speak against him, saying, As the gods of the nations of other lands have not delivered their people out of mine hand, so shall not the God of Hezekiah deliver his people out of mine hand [2 Chron. 32:17].

The record in 2 Kings gives this in more detail. When Hezekiah received the letter, he went up into the house of the Lord, and spread the letter before Him. His wonderful prayer is recorded in 2 Kings 19:14–19. Hezekiah was a real man of prayer.

And for this cause Hezekiah the king, and the prophet Isaiah the son of Amoz, prayed and cried to heaven [2 Chron. 32:20].

Hezekiah depended upon the Lord for help, and He delivered the city in a miraculous way.

And the LORD sent an angel, which cut off all the mighty men of valour, and the leaders and captains in the camp of the king of Assyria. So he returned with shame of face to his own land. And when he was come into the house of his god, they that came forth of his own bowels slew him there with the sword.

Thus the LORD saved Hezekiah and the inhabitants of Jerusalem from the hand of Sennacherib the king of Assyria, and from the hand of all other, and guided them on every side [2 Chron. 32:21–22].

THE ILLNESS OF HEZEKIAH

In those days Hezekiah was sick to the death, and prayed unto the LORD: and he spake unto him, and he gave him a sign [2 Chron. 32:24].

In 2 Kings 20, the record tells us that Hezekiah turned his face to the wall and prayed and wept before the Lord.

I think I understand how he felt. It rocked me when the doctor told me I had cancer. I could not believe it. When I had to accept the fact, I was not given any assurance at all that I would live. When I was taken to the hospital, I had no idea what the outcome of my illness would be. The nurse had to help me get into bed because I was so weak. I was not physically weak, I was frightened—I am a coward! She asked, "Are you sick?" "No," I said, "I am scared to death!" She was a Christian nurse, and she smiled at that. I asked her to leave me alone for a while, and I turned my face to the wall, just as Hezekiah had done, and I cried out to God. I told Him that I did not want to die.

When we are sick, I believe we should go to God in prayer and ask others to pray for us. I believe in faith healing (but not in faith *healers*); I know God can heal. Well, an acquaintance wrote me a letter in which she said, "I am not going to pray that you get well because I know that you are ready to go and be with the Lord. I am praying that He will take you home." I got an answer back to her in a hurry. I wrote, "Now look here. You let the Lord handle this. Don't try and tell Him how I feel. I don't want to die. I want to live. I want to live as long as I can!"

Now Hezekiah was in that same position. Only God could help him. When he turned his face to the wall, he reminded the Lord that he had walked before Him in truth and with a perfect heart and he had done that which was good in His sight.

They put a poultice of figs on his "boil"—it could have been cancer. Whatever it was, God healed him and gave him fifteen more years.

But Hezekiah rendered not again according to the benefit done unto him; for his heart was lifted up: therefore there was wrath upon him, and upon Judah and Jerusalem.

Notwithstanding Hezekiah humbled himself for the pride of his heart, both he and the inhabitants of Jerusalem, so that the wrath of the LORD came not upon them in the days of Hezekiah [2 Chron. 32:25–26].

The kingdom of Judah had become very poor during the reign of Ahaz, but now it has again become wealthy.

And Hezekiah had exceeding much riches and honour: and he made himself treasuries for silver, and for gold, and for precious stones, and for spices, and for shields, and for all manner of pleasant jewels [2 Chron. 32:27].

When the ambassadors from Babylon had come, he very foolishly showed them the entire wealth of his kingdom (see 2 Kings 20: 12–19). Now, here is God's comment on this episode:

Howbeit in the business of the ambassadors of the princes of Babylon, who sent unto him to inquire of the wonder that was done in the land, God left him, to try him, that he might know all that was in his heart [2 Chron. 32:31].

This may seem like an awful thing for me to say, but Hezekiah should have died when the time came for him to die. Three things took place after God extended his life that were foolish acts: he showed his treasures to Babylon, which will cause great trouble in the future; he begat a son, Manasseh, who was the most wicked of any king; he revealed an arrogance, almost an impudence in his later years. His heart became filled with pride. Second Chronicles 32:25 tells us, "But Hezekiah rendered not again according to the benefit done unto him; for his heart was lifted up: therefore there was wrath upon him, and upon Judah and Jerusalem." You see, it might have been better if Hezekiah had died at God's appointed time.

That is why I want to be very careful. The Lord has spared me and I do not want to do anything to disgrace Him. My friend, this is a wonderful chapter. We have a wonderful heavenly Father.

DEATH OF HEZEKIAH

Now the rest of the acts of Hezekiah, and his goodness, behold, they are written in the vision of Isaiah the prophet, the son of Amoz, and in the book of the kings of Judah and Israel.

And Hezekiah slept with his fathers, and they buried him in the chiefest of the sepulchres of the sons of David: and all Judah and the inhabitants of Jerusalem did him honour at his death. And Manasseh his son reigned in his stead [2 Chron. 32:32–33].

Now I would like to talk a few moments on the subject of revival. I think it is very important for us to note that God is sovereign in this matter of revival. "The wind bloweth where it listeth, and thou hearest the sound thereof, but canst not tell whence it cometh, and whither it goeth: so is every one that is born of the Spirit" says our Lord in John 3:8. Only God can send a revival. God is sovereign in this through the working of the Holy Spirit.

God is not a Western Union boy or a bellboy. You can't just push a button and have Him come at your command. I hear some folks in their prayers command the Lord to do something. We *cannot* give commands to God, my friend. Remember the experience of Elijah on Mount Carmel. The prophets of Baal had screamed themselves hoarse and had yelled like fanatics, but they were not able to bring down fire upon the sacrifice. Then Elijah laid the stones in order and he put wood on there and put the sacrifice on it and poured water over it. Then he prayed to God. He was a man of like passions as we are. In effect he said to the Lord: "All we can do is just get the stones together and put a little order into them. We can put the wood here and the sacrifice on it, but You will need to send the fire." Elijah knew the fire must come from God. God responded at that time.

As I write this, there is a spiritual movement in our land. At first I thought it was confined to young people, but I find it also includes young married couples. Young couples are seeing their children growing away from them. They are coming to realize that they must have answers to some of the problems. One young father said to me, "I thought I could always solve my problems, but I need God." Today there is a turning to the Word of God, and I rejoice in it. I see it everywhere.

Very candidly, I never saw that in my ministry in the church. This movement is largely outside the church. I've seen it in meetings that we have had all over this country. Young people, and older ones too, are coming to the conferences. There seems to be a real interest in the Word of God.

There are pastors and some religious leaders who are trying to capitalize on this; so they feed these young people a bunch of garbage. They give them "hard rock" music in place of Bible study. They give them everything but the Word of God. You remember our Lord asked, "If a son shall ask bread of any of you that is a father, will he give him a stone? . . ." (Luke 11:11). And certainly don't give him "hard rock!" Give him the Word of God.

I find them listening to my Bible teaching program, and I have told them, "I'm old fashioned. I teach the Bible just as it is. Why do you listen to me?" One of them said, "Well, we listen to you because you tell it like it is." That's the only way I know how to tell it, and I've been telling it that way for years, but nobody listened. Now they are beginning to listen. Are we on the verge of a spiritual awakening? I am praying that the Lord will send it. I want to be very frank with you; if it comes, *He* will be the One who will send it. I'm just getting my raincoat out in case the showers of blessing come. I have never seen revival in my day, and I would really like to see one. Wouldn't you?

Let me present a challenge to you. Why don't you make an inventory of your own personal life? If you want God to move in on your life, ask yourself these questions:

1. Am I honest?
2. Am I truthful?
3. Am I faithful? Can I be depended upon?
4. Am I pure? Am I really pure in this dirty day of filthy pictures and filthy language?
5. Am I dedicated? Am I really a dedicated child of God? Dwight L. Moody heard a man say that the world has yet to see what God can do with a man who is fully yielded to Him. Moody's response was, "By the grace of God, I will be that man." I think Moody was that man and yet, Moody, on his deathbed said, "The world has yet to see what God can do with a man who is fully yielded to Him." Oh, my friend, let's get into the position where God can move through us to give the Water of Life to a thirsty world.

CHAPTER 33

***THEME:** Manasseh's evil reign*

As we have seen, Hezekiah had been sick unto death, but he had prayed to God and Isaiah had prayed with him. He had some sort of boil which may well have been a cancer. God healed him and extended his life for fifteen years. That was a gracious dispensation on the part of God in answer to prayer. But when one looks at this in the full light of the history that followed, one wonders if it was the best thing that could have taken place.

First of all, it was during that fifteen-year period after his life had been spared that Hezekiah displayed the wealth of his kingdom to the ambassadors from Babylon. This opened the door for Nebuchadnezzar to come years later and take the city. He knew exactly where the gold was, and he took it by force. That was the Fort Knox of Israel. No one is attacking Fort Knox today. They tell me that the security there is unbelievable, but the gold is leaking out. The nations of the world aren't able to get it by attack; so they are getting it in another way. Well, that gold in Israel tempted Babylon to come and take it. It had been a very foolish thing for Hezekiah to show that gold to them.

Secondly, you will notice here that Manasseh was twelve years old when he began to reign. This means that this boy was born during the fifteen-year period after God had extended the life of Hezekiah. Manasseh was the most wicked king of all. During his reign there was such godlessness that God had to intervene.

Manasseh was twelve years old when he began to reign, and he reigned fifty and five years in Jerusalem:

But did that which was evil in the sight of the LORD, like unto the abominations of the heathen, whom the LORD had cast out before the children of Israel [2 Chron. 33:1–2].

It's a strange thing, isn't it? Hezekiah was the best king and led the nation in a revival. His son comes to the throne and is the worst king. How can you explain that? I'll let you in on a secret: I cannot explain it.

Around me today things are happening like that which I cannot explain. Periodically I hear of a very fine Christian home with wonderful Christian parents in which a son or a daughter rebels against everything. When one looks at young vagrants across the entire land, one can conclude that they were neglected at home. They saw godless, materialistic parents who were fighting all the time, or they came from broken homes, homes that were centered merely on self and selfishness. I can understand why they rebelled against all that and just walked out. But why is it that a son or daughter will simply walk out of a lovely, Christian home and join the rebellious crowd? I really cannot explain it. I can give two possible reasons, and both of them are feeble.

The first reason is that young people are influenced by the other young people around them. All young people go through a period when they feel that their parents are stupid. I can remember after I had gone away to college I was almost ashamed to come home and to carry on a conversation with those at home. They just didn't know enough, you see. That is a period that youth go through.

I have heard other young people tell me the same thing. One young pastor told me how ashamed he was of his dad when he went off to college. But after he had been out in the big bad world and had faced some problems, he returned home for a visit. He realized that although his dad had been somewhat stupid, he had managed to make a good living and had provided a marvelous home for his family. He said that the thing which amazed him was how much his dad had learned in those few years he had been away from home! I think all young people go through such a period, and I can understand that young people are influenced by other young folk who have left home in rebellion. That is one explanation.

Also I have noted that young folk who rebel against a Christian home, especially if they have made a profession of faith, will return to the Lord in time. The king we are looking at here, Manasseh, is an illustration of this.

The reign of Manasseh was evil beyond imagination. It is my conviction that the Shekinah glory, which was the visible presence of God, left the temple. The prophet Ezekiel saw the vision of the Shekinah glory lifted up and removed from the Holy of Holies because of the sins of the people and their rebellion. It moved out to the walls of Jerusalem and waited there. The people did not turn back to God. Then the Shekinah glory withdrew to the Mount of Olives and lingered there. Still there was no movement of the people back to God. So the Shekinah glory was caught back up into heaven. *Ichabod*, which means "the glory has departed," was written over the threshold of the temple. Their house was indeed left unto them desolate.

I know that most expositors feel that the Shekinah glory left the temple during the captivity. I don't feel that is accurate. If the Shekinah glory did not leave during the reign of Manasseh, I cannot see any other period in Israel's history that would cause the glory, the presence of God, to leave. I believe this was the time.

Notice how long this man reigned. He reigned fifty-five years in Jerusalem. This man reigned much longer than others, longer than David, longer than Solomon, longer than his father. Why? Because God is merciful. God is longsuffering. He is not willing that any should perish. After all, God has plenty of time on His hands. He has eternity in back of Him and eternity in front of Him. He is in no hurry, friends. Don't think you are going to push God, or rush Him, or move Him. I hear people say to someone to pray. They say, "If you go right to God, He'll begin to move." Friends, He may and then again, He may not. He will take His time. God is in no hurry. He will give Manasseh ample opportunity to turn to Him.

We are getting God's viewpoint in Chronicles. In 2 Kings 21 we are told of the evils of Manasseh's reign, and here in Chronicles God repeats that he "did that which was evil in the sight of the LORD, like unto the abominations of the heathen, whom the LORD cast out before the children of Israel."

For he built again the high places which Hezekiah his father had broken down, and he reared up altars for Baalim, and made groves, and worshipped all the host of heaven, and served them [2 Chron. 33:3].

He went into idolatry in a big way. He was as bad as Ahab and Jezebel, and he worshiped Baal as they had done.

Also he built altars in the house of the LORD, whereof the LORD had said, In Jerusalem shall my name be for ever.

And he built altars for all the host of heaven in the two courts of the house of the LORD [2 Chron. 33:4–5].

He introduced right into the *temple* in Jerusalem the worship of the hosts of heaven: like the worship of Jupiter, the worship of Mercury, the worship of Venus, and the worship of all the stars. In other words, he established the horoscope there. You could have had your horoscope read in the temple in that day.

I'm sorry to say that some churches actually promote this same sort of thing. It is big business today. You can go to any dime store or magazine rack and buy a horoscope. Some folk say it is just innocent fun, but it is not that for a lot of people. They put more confidence in the horoscope than they put in God.

I recall an interview on television some time ago in which an outstanding entertainer made the statement that she had been looking at her horoscope and that she was a Virgo. The girl had been married five or six times and apparently had other affairs, and I would not think she was a Virgo by any manner of calculation! And she felt that when such-and-such a star crossed such-and-such a star, that would be a very important time for her. It is amazing that in our day intelligent people can place so much confidence in the stars.

Manasseh was very much interested in the horoscope. "And he built altars for all the host of heaven in the two courts of the house of the LORD." And he didn't stop with that.

And he caused his children to pass through the fire in the valley of the son of Hinnom: also he observed times, and used enchantments, and used witchcraft, and dealt with a familiar spirit, and with wizards: he wrought much evil in the sight of the LORD, to provoke him to anger [2 Chron. 33:6].

He went all the way into idolatry. We are not told how far he went in causing "his children to pass through the fire." There were degrees. He could have let them pass through the fire and only get well singed. Or he could put the baby right down in the arms of that red-hot idol. You just cannot think of anything as bad as that! This is idolatry, and Manasseh seems to have gone into it all the way.

Also Manasseh used enchantments and witchcraft and dealt with familiar spirits (lit., a divining demon present in the physical body of the conjurer). In our day along with the movement back to God we are seeing a return to satanic worship.

And he set a carved image, the idol which he had made, in the house of God, of which God had said to David and to Solomon his son, In this house, and in Jerusalem, which I have chosen before all the tribes of Israel, will I put my name for ever:

Neither will I any more remove the foot of Israel from out of the land which I have appointed for your fathers; so that they will take heed to do all that I have commanded them, according to the whole law and the statutes and the ordinances by the hand of Moses [2 Chron. 33:7–8].

God had promised that if these people would worship Him and be faithful to Him, He would bless them. Notice what Manasseh is doing to Judah.

So Manasseh made Judah and the inhabitants of Jerusalem to err, and to do worse than the heathen, whom the LORD had destroyed before the children of Israel.

And the LORD spake to Manasseh, and to his people: but they would not hearken [2 Chron. 33:9–10].

MANASSEH IS CAPTURED AND THEN RESTORED

You can be sure that when a man or a nation reaches this place, God will move.

Wherefore the LORD brought upon them the captains of the host of the king of Assyria, which took Manasseh among the thorns, and bound him with fetters, and carried him to Babylon [2 Chron. 33:11].

He was actually taken from his throne and carried captive to Babylon.

And when he was in affliction, he besought the LORD his God, and humbled himself greatly before the God of his fathers.

And prayed unto him: and he was entreated of him, and heard his supplication, and brought him again to Jerusalem into his kingdom. Then Manasseh knew that the LORD he was God [2 Chron. 33:12–13].

This man had a remarkable experience. I would have given him up, I'm sure, but God did not give him up. God sent trouble—and plenty of it—to him. He was carried away as a captive to Babylon. This should have been a warning to the nation that God was now getting ready to send them into captivity because of their continual sin. When Manasseh found himself in real trouble, he sincerely came back to God. God forgave him and restored him! Yet he was very much of a weakling, as such men generally are.

When he returned to Jerusalem, he took away the strange gods and the idols out of the house of the Lord, and he repaired the altar of the Lord and sacrificed there.

Nevertheless the people did sacrifice still in the high places, yet unto the LORD their God only [2 Chron. 33:17].

In other words, the people never did truly come back to God but still sacrificed in the high places.

Apparently Manasseh reigned all this time. When he was a helpless captive in Babylon, God heard his prayer. This reveals how gracious God is! Here was a son of godly parents who went into sin to the very limit and then came back to God. That should be an encouragement to parents who are reading this today. Maybe you have a son or a daughter who has gone the very limit, and you despair that your child will ever turn back to God. I would have given Manasseh up, but God didn't. God heard his prayer.

REIGN OF AMON

Amon was two and twenty years old when he began to reign, and reigned two years in Jerusalem [2 Chron. 33:21].

The evil which Manasseh had done had its effect on this young man, his son. I can understand why his son went off into evil as he did.

Friends of mine, folk of means, really lived it up until middle age. They were converted after their children were nearly grown. Then after they were converted, they had other children who are wonderful godly children. But the older children have gone the limit into sin.

But he did that which was evil in the sight of the LORD, as did Manasseh his father: for Amon sacrificed unto all the carved images which Manasseh his father had made, and served them;

And humbled not himself before the LORD, as Manasseh his father had humbled himself; but Amon trespassed more and more [2 Chron. 33:22–23].

Amon followed in the footsteps of his father in his early days.

CHAPTERS 34–35

THEME: *Revival during Josiah's reign*

We come now to the last great revival under Josiah. The hour is late. It is five minutes before 12:00 in the history of this nation, and yet God sends revival. This is the last revival to take place before the captivity. Judah has come to the end of the line, and it is amazing that a revival takes place. It follows after the reigns of Manasseh and Amon, two men who really plunged that nation into idolatry and sin. One would think there was no hope at all, but there is always hope. The Holy Spirit is still sovereign in this matter of revival.

I do not know whether we will have a revival in our day or not. Humanly speaking, the nation of Judah could not have revival, but the Spirit of God is sovereign, and God can move in. He can move in today. There is nothing in the Word of God that would preclude that possibility.

One man said to me, "The trouble with you men who believe in prophecy and emphasize the terrible days that are ahead is that you have no place for revival." I disagree with that. My feeling is that he doesn't have any place for revival. The reason I say that is because he and his group are trying to work it up themselves. My friend, you cannot work it up or pray it down. The Spirit of God is sovereign.

Our prayer today should be, "Lord, put me in the will of God." Our prime concern is to make sure that our own lives are right before God. We are not going to get God to do something when our lives are not right in His sight. We need to straighten out our own lives before God. We need to ask ourselves these questions: Am I honest? Am I truthful? Am I pure? There is no use talking about revival as long as we are not getting right in our hearts before God. When we are right with God, then we can look to the Spirit of God to move in a sovereign way, and then we can ask Him to move according to His will.

Now we will look here at Josiah and see that God marvelously used him.

REFORMATION UNDER JOSIAH

Josiah was eight years old when he began to reign, and he reigned in Jerusalem one and thirty years.

And he did that which was right in the sight of the LORD, and walked in the ways of David his father, and declined neither to the right hand, nor to the left [2 Chron. 34:1–2].

You hear people today asking what is right and what is wrong. And you hear some strange answers given. Josiah did that which was right *in the sight of the Lord*. It is what *God* says is right that is right and what *God* says is wrong that is wrong.

Remember that it was God who divided the light from the darkness. You and I cannot do that! We can go into a room and turn on the light switch, and the darkness disappears. We cannot divide it; we can't run a line down the middle and say, "On this side I will put light and on this side I will put darkness." God can do that, and God can say what is right and what is wrong.

For in the eighth year of his reign, while he was yet young, he began to seek after the God of David his father: and in the twelfth year he began to purge Judah and Jerusalem from the high places, and the groves, and the carved images, and the molten images [2 Chron. 34:3].

In the eighth year of his reign Josiah was sixteen years old, and he began to seek God. The spiritual movement today, and the turning to the Word of God, is largely among young people. Although it is not confined to them, they certainly are the majority. I meet these young folks in my conference travels and all around the world. They are interested in the Word of God. Josiah was only sixteen when he began to seek after God. He was twenty when he began his reforms in Judah. You see, revival will lead to reformation.

As I mentioned before, when your sins are forgiven, you will pick up your bed and walk. You will walk away from your sins if you are truly converted. If revival comes in our day, we will not have a divorce problem or a sex revolution. We will see a tremendous change take place. God can accomplish this, and He may do it. This section of the Word of God can be a great encouragement to us.

Josiah was a fearless reformer. After he had cleaned up his southern kingdom of Judah, he went into the tribes of Israel in the north.

Now in the eighteenth year of his reign, when he had purged the land, and the house, he sent Shaphan the son of Azaliah, and Maaseiah the governor of the city, and Joah the son of Joahaz the recorder, to repair the house of the LORD his God [2 Chron. 34:8].

When Josiah was twenty-six years old, he began the repair of the temple. It had fallen into disrepair under the reign of Manasseh, his grandfather, and Amon, his father.

And when they came to Hilkiah the high priest, they delivered the money that was brought into the house of God, which the Levites that kept the doors had gathered of the hand of Manasseh and Ephraim, and of all the remnant of Israel, and of all Judah and Benjamin; and they returned to Jerusalem [2 Chron. 34:9].

"Manasseh and Ephraim" are, of course, tribes of Israel. At this time the northern kingdom had been taken into Assyrian captivity; only a remnant was left in the land. These tribes, which we hear called "lost tribes," certainly were not lost in this day, as they were sending in money for the repair of the temple.

Now the temple was repaired, and they made an amazing discovery.

THE LAW OF MOSES IS FOUND

And when they brought out the money that was brought into the house of the LORD, Hilkiah the priest found a book of the law of the LORD given by Moses [2 Chron. 34:14].

You see, there weren't many copies in that day. There may have been a few others, but the Word of God had been lost.

And Hilkiah answered and said to Shaphan the scribe, I have found the book of the law in the house of the LORD. And Hilkiah delivered the book to Shaphan.

And Shaphan carried the book to the king, and brought the king word back again, saying, All that was committed to thy servants, they do it [2 Chron. 34:15–16].

You may be saying, "I can see that this is going to be right down your alley!" It sure is, although it is not my alley, but God's alley—His Word is very important to Him. Notice what happens.

Then Shaphan the scribe told the king, saying, Hilkiah the priest hath given me a book. And Shaphan read it before the king.

And it came to pass, when the king had heard the words of the law, that he rent his clothes [2 Chron. 34:18–19].

Renting (or tearing) his clothes indicated strong emotion. He was dismayed when he heard the Word of God for the first time, because he and his people had strayed so far from God's commands.

And the king commanded Hilkiah, and Ahikam the son of Shaphan, and Abdon the son of Micah, and Shaphan the scribe, and Asaiah a servant of the king's, saying,

Go, inquire of the LORD for me, and for them that are left in Israel and in Judah, concerning the words of the book that is found: for great is the wrath of the LORD that is poured out upon us, because our fathers have not kept the word of the LORD, to do after all that is written in this book [2 Chron. 34:20–21].

A return to the Word of God brings revival. Nothing else will bring revival. What is wrong in our day? Why don't we see revival? The reason is simple. The church has neglected the Word of God. Churches have tried every known gimmick and every kind of method. Nothing happens. Revival does not come that way. Revival comes when people return to the Word of God and find out what God has to say.

Josiah is a shaken man, and he wants to know what God is going to do.

And Hilkiah, and they that the king had appointed, went to Huldah the prophetess, the wife of Shallum the son of Tikvath, the son of Hasrah, keeper of the wardrobe; (now she dwelt in Jerusalem in the college:) and they spake to her to that effect.

And she answered them, Thus saith the LORD God of Israel, Tell ye the man that sent you to me [2 Chron. 34:22–23].

Now this is God's message to Josiah:

Thus saith the LORD, Behold, I will bring evil upon this place, and upon the inhabitants thereof, even all the curses that are written in the book which they have read before the king of Judah:

Because they have forsaken me, and have burned incense unto other gods, that they might provoke me to anger with all the works of their hands; therefore my wrath shall be poured out upon this place, and shall not be quenched [2 Chron. 34:24–25].

God will send judgment just as He promised. However, He has a personal word for Josiah.

And as for the king of Judah, who sent you to inquire of the LORD, so shall ye say unto him, Thus saith the LORD God of Israel concerning the words which thou hast heard;

Because thine heart was tender, and thou didst humble thyself before God, when thou heardest his words against this place, and against the inhabitants thereof, and humbledst thyself before me, and didst rend thy clothes, and weep before me; I have even heard thee also, saith the LORD.

Behold, I will gather thee to thy fathers, and thou shalt be gathered to thy grave in peace, neither shall thine eyes see all the evil that I will bring upon this place, and upon the inhabitants of the same. So they brought the king word again [2 Chron. 34:26–28].

God intends to judge these people, but He will not do it until Josiah is gone.

Then the king sent and gathered together all the elders of Judah and Jerusalem.

And the king went up into the house of the LORD, and all the men of Judah, and the inhabitants of Jerusalem, and the priests, and the Levites, and all the people, great and small: and he read in their ears all the words of the book of the covenant that was found in the house of the LORD.

And the king stood in his place, and made a covenant before the LORD, to walk after the LORD, and to keep his commandments, and his testimonies, and his statutes, with all his heart, and with all his soul, to perform the words of the covenant which are written in this book [2 Chron. 34:29–31].

My friend, let's be very candid and very matter-of-fact and very direct. I believe we could have a revival today, but first there must be a return to the Word of God to find out what God wants us to do. Then I believe there will be and there must be a total commitment to God on the part of God's people. There can be none of this halfhearted service which we see. There can be none of this business of trying to go with the world and trying to go with God. It is impossible to do both. There must be a clear-cut dedication of heart and life to God. When that takes place, the Spirit of God is free to move.

In chapter 35 we have a record of the Passover that was kept. This was a new experience for his generation, and it is interesting to note that Josiah carefully followed the procedure which is written in the Book of Moses.

So all the service of the LORD was prepared the same day, to keep the passover, and to offer burnt offerings upon the altar of the LORD, according to the commandment of king Josiah.

And the children of Israel that were present kept the passover at that time, and the feast of unleavened bread seven days.

And there was no passover like to that kept in Israel from the days of Samuel the prophet; neither did all the kings of Israel keep such a passover as Josiah kept, and the priests, and the Levites, and all Judah and Israel that were present, and the inhabitants of Jerusalem.

In the eighteenth year of the reign of Josiah was this passover kept [2 Chron. 35:16–19].

The Passover is symbolic of the death of Christ. The nation has returned to the knowledge that there must be a redemption made for sins. You see, they had learned about the Passover because they had discovered the book of the law of Moses. This was a tremendous occasion. God says, "There was no passover like to that kept in Israel from the days of Samuel the prophet."

Josiah was the man responsible for this great return to the Word of God. Now we come to the death of this man. Even godly men like this make mistakes—all human beings do.

DEATH OF JOSIAH

After all this, when Josiah had prepared the temple, Necho king of Egypt came up to fight against Charchemish

by Euphrates: and Josiah went out against him.

But he sent ambassadors to him, saying, What have I to do with thee, thou king of Judah? I come not against thee this day, but against the house wherewith I have war: for God commanded me to make haste: forbear thee from meddling with God, who is with me, that he destroy thee not [2 Chron. 35:20–21].

Josiah should have stayed at home. He had no business engaging in this war.

Nevertheless Josiah would not turn his face from him, but disguised himself, that he might fight with him, and hearkened not unto the words of Necho from the mouth of God, and came to fight in the valley of Megiddo [2 Chron. 35:22].

He refused to stay out of the fight. Now notice what happens.

And the archers shot at king Josiah; and the king said to his servants, Have me away; for I am sore wounded.

His servants therefore took him out of that chariot, and put him in the second chariot that he had; and they brought him to Jerusalem, and he died, and was buried in one of the sepulchres of his fathers. And all Judah and Jerusalem mourned for Josiah.

And Jeremiah lamented for Josiah: and all the singing men and the singing women spake of Josiah in their lamentations to this day, and made them an ordinance in Israel: and, behold, they are written in the lamentations [2 Chron. 35:23–25].

Josiah had been a good king and a great king. He had led a tremendous revival, a great turning to God. But his death ended the revival. Now God's judgment will fall upon the southern kingdom of Judah.

CHAPTER 36

***THEME:** The captivity of Judah*

The days were numbered for the southern kingdom of Judah. Josiah was the last good king of the nation. All the kings who followed him were bad. There was not a good one in the lot. Their evil reigns hastened the judgment of God upon the kingdom of Judah. We are given only a brief word about their attitude toward God and a statement of the main events that brought about the ruin of the nation.

REIGN OF JEHOAHAZ

Then the people of the land took Jehoahaz the son of Josiah, and made him king in his father's stead in Jerusalem.

Jehoahaz was twenty and three years old when he began to reign, and he reigned three months in Jerusalem.

And the king of Egypt put him down at Jerusalem, and condemned the land in an hundred talents of silver and a talent of gold [2 Chron. 36:1–3].

This son of Josiah was deposed by the king of Egypt. He was a rascal and was on the throne only three months. Things are beginning to move quickly now.

REIGN OF JEHOIAKIM

Jehoiakim was twenty and five years old when he began to reign, and he reigned eleven years in Jerusalem: and he did that which was evil in the sight of the LORD his God.

Against him came up Nebuchadnezzar king of Babylon, and bound him in fetters, to carry him to Babylon.

Nebuchadnezzar also carried of the vessels of the house of the LORD to Babylon, and put them in his temple at Babylon [2 Chron. 36:5–7].

During his reign the king of Babylon comes against the land.

REIGN OF JEHOIACHIN

Jehoiachin was eight years old when he began to reign, and he reigned three months and ten days in Jerusalem: and he did that which was evil in the sight of the LORD [2 Chron. 36:9].

He didn't last very long—he hardly got the throne warm.

REIGN OF ZEDEKIAH

Zedekiah is Judah's last king.

Zedekiah was one and twenty years old when he began to reign, and reigned eleven years in Jerusalem.

And he did that which was evil in the sight of the LORD his God, and humbled not himself before Jeremiah the prophet speaking from the mouth of the LORD.

And he also rebelled against king Nebuchadnezzar, who had made him swear by God: but he stiffened his neck, and hardened his heart from turning unto the LORD God of Israel.

Moreover all the chief of the priests, and the people, transgressed very much after all the abominations of the heathen; and polluted the house of the LORD which he had hallowed in Jerusalem [2 Chron. 36:11–14].

CAPTIVITY

Nebuchadnezzar now does more than knock at the door. He pushes over the wall and burns Jerusalem and takes Judah into captivity.

Here is God's explanation:

And the LORD God of their fathers sent to them by his messengers, rising up betimes, and sending; because he had compassion on his people, and on his dwelling place:

But they mocked the messengers of God, and despised his words, and misused his prophets, until the wrath of the LORD arose against his people, till there was no remedy.

Therefore he brought upon them the king of the Chaldees, who slew their young men with the sword in the house of their sanctuary, and had no compassion upon young man or maiden, old man, or him that stooped for age: he gave them all into his hand.

And all the vessels of the house of God, great and small, and the treasures of the house of the LORD, and the treasures of the king, and of his princes; all these he brought to Babylon.

And they burnt the house of God, and brake down the wall of Jerusalem, and burnt all the palaces thereof with fire, and destroyed all the goodly vessels thereof.

And them that had escaped from the sword carried he away to Babylon; where they were servants to him and his sons until the reign of the kingdom of Persia [2 Chron. 36:15–20].

Now the next verse cites another reason for God's judgment. This is most interesting.

To fulfil the word of the LORD by the mouth of Jeremiah, until the land had enjoyed her sabbaths: for as long as she lay desolate she kept sabbath, to fulfil threescore and ten years [2 Chron. 36:21].

You see, God accomplished a twofold purpose. God always has many things in mind in everything that He does. First of all, they had rejected the prophets. They were living on borrowed time; God would have been justified to have sent them into captivity one hundred years before this time.

It makes me wonder if our nation is not living on borrowed time. How much longer will God put up with our sins? For the nation of Judah, their time had come. There was no more remedy. There is a time when a nation reaches this point. I wonder how close our nation is to this time.

Secondly, for 490 years Israel had not observed the sabbatic years. They had been breaking God's law of the land, which He had given them even before they set foot upon it: "And the LORD spake unto Moses in mount Sinai, saying, Speak unto the children of Israel, and say unto them, When ye come into the land which I give you, then shall the land keep a sabbath unto the LORD. Six years thou shalt sow thy field, and six years thou shalt prune thy vineyard, and gather in the fruit thereof; But in the seventh year shall be a sabbath of rest unto the land, a sabbath for the LORD: thou shalt neither sow thy field, nor prune thy vineyard. That which groweth of its own accord of thy harvest thou shalt not reap, neither gather the grapes of thy vine undressed: for it is a year of rest unto the land" (Lev. 25:1–5). Because of their greed, they had not allowed the land to enjoy its sabbaths. In other words, they had not allowed it to remain fallow every seventh year as God had commanded. They thought they had gotten by with it. For 490 years they had been doing it, then God said, "I'll put you out of the land for seventy years so the land can enjoy its sabbaths." That is the reason the captivity lasted for seventy years. This is quite remarkable.

You see, my friend, God is not mocked. "Be not deceived; God is not mocked: for whatsoever a man soweth, that shall he also reap" (Gal. 6:7).

Notice that the seventy years in exile are passed over entirely. The people are out of the land and out of the will of God. God's clock is not spelled B-U-L-O-V-A or G-R-U-E-N; God's clock is spelled I-S-R-A-E-L, and it runs only while Israel is in the land.

We have seen in this book that although there was a general decline of the nation, there were five periods of revival, renewal, and reformation. There is a striking feature which characterizes each period:

Asa	Return and obedience to the Word of God
Jehoshaphat	Return and obedience to the Word of God
Joash	Return and obedience to the Word of God
Hezekiah	Return and obedience to the Word of God
Josiah	Return and obedience to the Word of God

In each instance, return to the Word of God led to the repentance of the people and the temporary reformation of the nation.

DECREE TO REBUILD THE TEMPLE

Second Chronicles concludes with a bright hope for the future.

Now in the first year of Cyrus king of Persia, that the word of the Lord spoken by the mouth of Jeremiah might be accomplished, the Lord stirred up the spirit of Cyrus king of Persia, that he made a proclamation throughout all his kingdom, and put it also in writing, saying,

Thus saith Cyrus king of Persia, All the kingdoms of the earth hath the Lord God of heaven given me; and he hath charged me to build him an house in Jerusalem, which is in Judah. Who is there among you of all his people? The Lord his God be with him, and let him go up [2 Chron. 36:22–23].

This is repeated in the introduction to the Book of Ezra which continues the historical record from this point. It is wonderful to see that although God had sent His people into captivity, He had not forgotten them. How gracious He is!

BIBLIOGRAPHY

(Recommended for Further Study)

Crockett, William Day. *A Harmony of the Books of Samuel, Kings, and Chronicles.* Grand Rapids, Michigan: Baker Book House, 1951.

Darby, J. N. *Synopsis of the Books of the Bible.* Addison, Illinois: Bible Truth Publishers, n.d.

Davis, John J. and Whitcomb, John C., Jr. *A History of Israel.* Grand Rapids, Michigan: Baker Book House, 1970. (Excellent.)

Epp, Theodore H. *David.* Lincoln, Nebraska: Back to the Bible Broadcast, 1965.

Gaebelein, Arno C. *The Annotated Bible.* Neptune, New Jersey: Loizeaux Brothers, 1912-22.

Gray, James M. *Synthetic Bible Studies.* Westwood, New Jersey: Fleming H. Revell Co., 1906.

Heading, John. *I & II Chronicles.* Kansas City, Missouri: Walterick Publishers, 1982.

Jensen, Irving L. *I Kings with Chronicles.* Chicago, Illinois: Moody Press, 1968. (A self-study guide.)

Jensen, Irving L. *II Kings with Chronicles*. Chicago, Illinois: Moody Press, 1968. (A self-study guide.)

Kelly, William. *Lectures on the Earlier Historical Books of the Old Testament*. Addison, Illinois: Bible Truth Publishers, 1874.

Knapp, Christopher, *The Kings of Israel and Judah*. Neptune, New Jersey: Loizeaux, 1908. (Very fine.)

Mackintosh, C. H. *Miscellaneous Writings*. Neptune, New Jersey: Loizeaux Brothers, n.d.

Meyer, F. B. *David: Shepherd, Psalmist, King*. Fort Washington, Pennsylvania: Christian Literature Crusade, n.d.

Sailhamer, John. *I & II Chronicles*. Chicago, Illinois: Moody Press, 1983.

Sauer, Erich. *The Dawn of World Redemption*. Grand Rapids, Michigan: William B. Eerdmans Publishing Co., 1951. (An excellent Old Testament survey.)

Scroggie, W. Graham. *The Unfolding Drama of Redemption*. Grand Rapids, Michigan: Zondervan Publishing House, 1970. (An excellent survey and outline of the Old Testament.)

Unger, Merrill F. *Unger's Commentary on the Old Testament*. Vol. 1. Chicago, Illinois: Moody Press, 1981. (A fine summary of each paragraph. Highly recommended.)

Wood, Leon J. *Israel's United Monarchy*. Grand Rapids, Michigan: Baker Book House, 1979. (Excellent.)

Wood, Leon J. *The Prophets of Israel*. Grand Rapids, Michigan: Baker Book House, 1977. (Excellent.)

The Book of
EZRA
INTRODUCTION

Ezra is the writer of this book. He is one of the characters who has not received proper recognition. He was a descendant of Hilkiah, the high priest (Ezra 7:1), who found a copy of the Law during the reign of Josiah (2 Chron. 34:14).

Ezra, as a priest, was unable to serve during the Captivity. There was no temple. It had been destroyed. He did, however, give his time to a study of the Word of God. Ezra 7:6 tells us that he was "a ready scribe in the law of Moses."

Ezra was also a great revivalist and reformer. The revival began with the reading of the Word of God by Ezra. We will see that in Nehemiah 8. Also, Ezra was probably the writer of 1 and 2 Chronicles and Psalm 119 (the longest chapter in the Bible).

Ezra organized the synagogue. He was the founder of the order of scribes. He helped settle the canon of Scripture and arranged the Psalms. Let us pay tribute to Ezra who was the first to begin a revival of Bible study. Is this not God's program for revival?

We have had no real revival in our day. Dwight L. Moody made this statement (and he saw a revival), "The next revival will be a revival of Bible study." Those who have tried to whip up revivals by organization, by methods, and by gimmicks have failed. Revival will come only as people come back to the Word of God.

The theme of the Book of Ezra is *The Word of the Lord*. There are *ten* direct references to God's Word in this little book: Ezra 1:1; 3:2; 6:14, 18; 7:6, 10, 14; 9:4; 10:3, 5. The place of the Word of God is seen in the total lives of these people: religious, social, business, and political.

The key to this book is found in Ezra 9:4 and 10:3: they "trembled at the words of the God of Israel."

Dr. James M. Gray made this statement concerning the Book of Ezra: "We already have seen that the Babylonian captivity did not bring the Jews to national repentance and so lead to national restoration. As the reading of Ezra will disclose, when Cyrus, king of Persia, gave permission to the captives to return to Jerusalem and rebuild the temple, scarcely fifty thousand Jews availed themselves of the privilege, a considerable portion of whom were priests and Levites of the humbler and poorer class."

The Book of Ezra is the last of the historical books, but they do not follow *ad seriatum* (one right after the other).

When we conclude 2 Chronicles, we see that the southern kingdom of Judah went into captivity for seventy years. We do not hear a word from them after they were captured until Ezra picks up their history. There are three *historical* books that are called "postcaptivity" books: Ezra, Nehemiah, and Esther. Also there are three *prophetical* "postcaptivity" books: Haggai, Zechariah, and Malachi.

Now Ezra and Nehemiah belong together. Ezra was a priest and Nehemiah was a layman. They worked together in such a way that God's will was accomplished in Jerusalem. Together they were instrumental in seeing that the walls, the city of Jerusalem, and the temple were rebuilt.

Haggai and Zechariah also worked together. They encouraged the people to build the temple. Haggai was a practical man, as we shall see when we get to his book. The reconstruction and refurbishing of the temple were his supreme passion. He was as simple and factual as $2+2=4$. He was neither romantic nor poetic, but he sure was practical. Zechariah, on the other hand, was a dreamer. Haggai had his feet on the ground and Zechariah had his head in the clouds. For example, Zechariah saw a woman going through the air in a bushel basket. My friend, that is poetical! Haggai would never have seen that. But the interesting thing is that Zechariah would never have concerned himself about the measurements of the temple and that you must have doors in it and a foundation under it. Haggai and Zechariah went together just like Ezra and Nehemiah. The practical man and the poet must walk together; God arranged it that way.

The Books of Haggai and Zechariah should be read and studied with the Book of Ezra, for all three books were written in the shadow of the rebuilt temple, and were given to encourage the people in building. "Then the prophets, Haggai the prophet, and Zechariah the son of Iddo, prophesied unto the Jews that were in Judah and Jerusalem in the name of the God of Israel, even unto them" (Ezra 5:1).

In the Book of Ezra there are two major divisions. There is the return of the captives from Babylon led by Zerubbabel in the first six chapters. About fifty thousand returned. Then there is the return led by Ezra in Chapters 7–10, and about two thousand people followed Ezra.

OUTLINE

I. Return from Babylon Led by Zerubbabel, Chapters 1–6
(About 50,000 returned)
A. Restoration of Temple by Decree of Cyrus, Chapter 1
B. Return under Zerubbabel, Chapter 2
C. Rebuilding of Temple, Chapter 3
D. Retardation of Rebuilding by Opposition, Chapter 4
(Decree of Artaxerxes)
E. Renewal of Rebuilding of Temple, Chapters 5–6
(Decree of Darius)

II. Return from Babylon Led by Ezra, Chapters 7–10
(About 2,000 returned)
A. Return under Ezra, Chapters 7–8
B. Reformation under Ezra, Chapters 9–10

CHAPTERS 1–2

THEME: *Decree and return of a remnant to Jerusalem*

DECREE OF CYRUS FOR THE TEMPLE RESTORATION

Now in the first year of Cyrus king of Persia, that the word of the LORD by the mouth of Jeremiah might be fulfilled, the LORD stirred up the spirit of Cyrus king of Persia, that he made a proclamation throughout all his kingdom, and put it also in writing, saying [Ezra 1:1].

Notice that right away Ezra puts an emphasis upon the Word of God.

Also, Cyrus, king of Persia, is mentioned. He was one of the most enlightened rulers of the ancient world. He was a subject of predictive prophecy. He was named before he was born—almost two hundred years before his coming as king of Persia. Isaiah 44:28 says, "That saith of Cyrus, He is my shepherd, and shall perform all my pleasure: even saying to Jerusalem, Thou shalt be built; and to the temple, Thy foundation shall be laid." Isaiah 45:1 continues, "Thus saith the LORD to his anointed, to Cyrus, whose right hand I have holden, to subdue nations before him; and I will loose the loins of kings, to open before him the two leaved gates; and the gates shall not be shut."

Cyrus is a type of Christ. Daniel was a prime minister in the court of Cyrus and evidently led him to a knowledge of the living and true God. Cyrus knew what he was doing when he made a decree proclaiming that the nation of Israel could return to their land. We are told that the will of the Lord was fulfilled in that act. Here is prophecy that was indeed fulfilled.

It was during the reign of Cyrus that Daniel gave some of his greatest prophecies, including the seventy weeks prophecy concerning Israel.

At least one-fourth of the Bible, when it was initially given, was prophetic. A large portion of it has already been fulfilled. Ezra 1:1 is one of those portions of Scripture that has been fulfilled. Over three hundred prophecies concerning the *first* coming of Christ have been literally fulfilled. There are those who say there are also over three hundred prophecies concerning the *second* coming of Christ, although I have never checked that out.

The birth of Christ was predicted in the Old Testament, and four things were said in connection with it:

1. He was to be born in Bethlehem (Mic. 5:2).
2. He was to be called a Nazarene (Jud. 13:5).
3. He was to be called out of Egypt (Hos. 11:1).
4. There would be weeping in Ramah, a little town near Jerusalem (Jer. 31:15). Matthew fits all of these pieces together and gives us the Christmas story. Fulfilled prophecy is what Matthew 2 is all about.

Ezra 1:1 is also fulfilled prophecy. The seventy years of captivity were over, the decree was given, and the children of Israel could return to their land. Very few returned, however.

Thus saith Cyrus king of Persia, the LORD God of heaven hath given me all the kingdoms of the earth; and he hath charged me to build him an house at Jerusalem, which is in Judah [Ezra 1:2].

The decree of Cyrus is very important. In the first place, Cyrus said that he had been given all the kingdoms of the earth. I can hear someone asking, "What about the United States of America?" May I say that the United States was not a very interesting place in that day. It was not a kingdom. Cyrus was talking about the kingdoms that existed during his day. Cyrus was the kingpin; "The LORD God of heaven hath given me"—he was the man at the top.

He realized that God had given him his position. I wonder today how many of the rulers of this world, in this so-called civilized age, recognize that they are ministers of God? They have been put into office by God whether they know it or not!

Now I want you to notice the expression, "The LORD God of heaven." It is a designation of God which is peculiar to Ezra, Nehemiah, and Daniel. You see, after the fall of Jerusalem and the destruction of Jerusalem God could no longer be identified with the temple as the One who dwelt between the cherubim. The glory had departed; "Ichabod" was written over the escutcheon of Israel. Ezekiel had the vision of the departure of the Shekinah glory. For this reason in the postcaptivity books He is "the LORD God of heaven."

Ezekiel saw the vision of God's glory departing from the temple at Jerusalem. It lifted from the temple and paused to see if the people of God would return to Him and turn away from their idolatry. They did not. It went over the city and the city walls and paused again. But the people did not turn to God. Then the Shekinah glory lifted to the top of the Mount of Olives and waited again. But there was no turning to God. So the glory was caught up to heaven and was not seen again.

One day there walked into the temple One who made a whip of cords, and He cleansed that temple (John 2). Although the Shekinah glory was not visible—He was veiled in human flesh—He was God. He had laid aside His glory when He came to earth, but He was very God of very God and He was very man of very man. Because His glory was veiled, He was rejected and crucified. Although man crucified Him, He is a king. In the Gospel of Matthew He was born a king, He lived like a king, He performed miracles as a king, He taught as a king, He was arrested as a king, tried as a king, and He died as a king. He was buried as a king. He arose as a king and went back to heaven as a king. He is coming again someday as a king. He is ". . . the King of kings and Lord of lords . . ." (1 Tim. 6:15). Today He is the Lord God of heaven. Don't go to Bethlehem to look for Him. He is in heaven. He is at God's right hand.

When the Shekinah glory was removed from the earth, God gave His people into the hands of the Gentiles and sent them into Babylonian captivity. He dissolved the theocracy of Israel and became the God of heaven. He is still that to His ancient people, and He will remain that until He returns to Jerusalem to establish His throne again as the Lord of the whole earth. Jerusalem will then be the city of the great King.

Now going back to the second verse of the Book of Ezra, notice that Cyrus very definitely said, "He hath charged me to build him an house at Jerusalem." The word *charged* means that God had "commanded" him to do this. This is remarkable when we remember that Cyrus was a Gentile world ruler at this time! Apparently Cyrus, through the ministry of Daniel the prophet, came to a knowledge of the living and true God.

Cyrus now gives permission for the Jews who had been in Babylonian captivity to return to Jerusalem.

Who is there among you of all his people? his God be with him, and let him go up to Jerusalem, which is in Judah, and build the house of the LORD God of Israel, (he is the God,) which is in Jerusalem [Ezra 1:3].

You'll notice that God has commanded Cyrus to do this, but Cyrus did not command the people to go to Jerusalem; he granted them permission to go up.

And whosoever remaineth in any place where he sojourneth, let the men of his place help him with silver, and with gold, and with goods, and with beasts, beside the freewill offering for the house of God that is in Jerusalem [Ezra 1:4].

Permission was granted to the people to return. Those who did not choose to return were to make an offering of gold and silver and other things of value that would assist those returning to execute this command to rebuild the temple at Jerusalem.

Then rose up the chief of the fathers of Judah and Benjamin, and the priests, and the Levites, with all them whose spirit God had raised, to go up to build the house of the LORD which is in Jerusalem.

And all they that were about them strengthened their hands with vessels of silver, with gold, with goods, and with beasts, and with precious things, beside all that was willingly offered [Ezra 1:5–6].

As I have indicated before, there was actually a very small percentage of the people who went up. I don't want to sit in judgment on them because they may have had a very good excuse for not going up. But, apparently, it was God's will for them to go up and some did not choose to go. They had settled down in Babylon. I am of the opinion many of them were settled and enjoying the comfort and affluent society of Babylon. Many of them had become prosperous, and so they chose not to go up. They at least felt that it was not God's will or the time for them to go up. It's not, therefore, for me to say that these people are out of the will of God. I do know that later on, when we get to the Book of Esther, we'll see the story of those who remained in the land; and it's not a very pretty story. At that time they were definitely out of the will of God. One thing that can be said in their favor is that there was, apparently, no spirit of enmity or of judgment between the two groups—those who returned and those who did not. Those who remained helped their brethren who went up. They provided the things that they needed.

This has an application and is quite interesting to me. I do not feel that everyone is called today to go as a foreign missionary. I'm confident I was never called to leave my land and to go to foreign people. And I can be very frank and tell you why God didn't call me to go. I said to a friend of mine, when we were visiting a mission field down in Mexico, and I said it again in South America when I was down there, "I can very easily see why God did not call me. I do not mean to be crude, but I do not have the intestinal fortitude to have stayed down here!" I don't think I could have endured the slow pace. I like to see action, and you don't see that on the mission field—things move slowly. God has some wonderful people on the mission field! However, because God didn't call me doesn't mean we're not to support those He did call. We should support those who are doing a good job and back them up with our prayers and our encouragement. This goes for those who are out on the front lines in this country giving out the Word of God. In warfare it is estimated that for every soldier out on the fighting front there have to be ten people behind him getting supplies to him—food, clothing, medical care, and ammunition. This is true in God's army today.

Now in Ezra's day the people who did not return felt a responsibility to become partners with their brethren who went back to Jerusalem. The group that returned was of the poorer class. There were "the chief of the fathers of Judah and Benjamin, and the priests, and the Levites." They were humble folk. The psalmist says, "The meek will he guide in judgment: and the meek will he teach his way" (Ps. 25:9). These are the ones who had the understanding of the times, and so they returned to their land.

Also Cyrus the king brought forth the vessels of the house of the LORD which Nebuchadnezzar had brought forth out of Jerusalem, and had put them in the house of his gods [Ezra 1:7].

How did Cyrus get "the vessels of the house of the LORD"? Well they were being used—desecrated—at Belshazzar's drunken feast the night that Babylon fell to the Medes and the Persians. Daniel records this: "Belshazzar, whiles he tasted the wine, commanded to bring the golden and silver vessels which his father Nebuchadnezzar had taken out of the temple which was in Jerusalem; that the king, and his princes, his wives, and his concubines, might drink therein. Then they brought the golden vessels that were taken out of the temple of the house of God which was at Jerusalem; and the king, and his princes, his wives, and his concubines, drank in them. They drank wine, and praised the gods of gold, and of silver, of brass, of iron, of wood, and of stone" (Dan. 5:2–4). That very night the city of Babylon was captured. The Persian kings had put away these vessels, and when Cyrus became king, they were there—God saw to this. Now these holy vessels ("holy" in the sense that they were for the use of God) are put back in the hands of the priests and Levites who are returning to Jerusalem.

Even those did Cyrus king of Persia bring forth by the hand of Mithredath the treasurer, and numbered them unto Sheshbazzar, the prince of Judah [Ezra 1:8].

As they were officially delivered to the Jews, we are given some details concerning them.

And this is the number of them: thirty chargers of gold, a thousand chargers of silver, nine and twenty knives,

Thirty basins of gold, silver basins of a second sort four hundred and ten, and other vessels a thousand.

All the vessels of gold and of silver were five thousand and four hundred. All these did Sheshbazzar bring up with them of the captivity that were brought up from Babylon unto Jerusalem [Ezra 1:9–11].

They represent tremendous wealth. These are sent back to Jerusalem.

RETURN UNDER ZERUBBABEL

Chapter 2 gives a list of those who returned to Jerusalem under the leadership of Zerubbabel.

Now these are the children of the province that went up out of the captivity, of those which had been carried away, whom Nebuchadnezzar the king of Babylon had carried away unto Babylon, and came again unto Jerusalem and Judah, every one unto his city;

Which came with Zerubbabel: Jeshua, Nehemiah, Seraiah, Reelaiah, Morde-

cai, Bilshan, Mizpar, Bigvai, Rehum, Baanah. The number of the men of the people of Israel [Ezra 2:1–2].

To attempt to read this list would be a real exercise in pronunciation. Hebrew names were difficult enough to pronounce before the Captivity. Then after the Captivity they really became difficult because there was the inclusion of that which was of the Persian and Babylonian languages.

Notice that in verse 2 a man named Nehemiah is mentioned. This is not the Nehemiah that wrote the book of the Bible bearing that name. Nehemiah, the writer, did not return to the land with the first group. Also a man named Mordecai is mentioned. He is not the same man who is mentioned in the Book of Esther.

As we read down the list, we see some very interesting names. For instance the "men of Anathoth."

The men of Anathoth, an hundred twenty and eight [Ezra 2:23].

That is quite a group from that little town who went back. I have seen this little town, and it is a place of interest because it is the town where Jeremiah purchased a field. You will remember that in Jeremiah's day the children of Israel were on the verge of being carried away into captivity. I would not call his purchase of some land at that time a good investment in real estate, would you? When Jeremiah bought this land, it did not look as though Israel had a future. But God had him buy the land as a sign that Judah would be restored. Jeremiah's act was one of faith. God promised that His people would return to the land, and they did. These men of Anathoth had a sealed, lawful claim to the land because Jeremiah had purchased it and given it to them. They were going back to claim their possession. You can read the story in Jeremiah 32.

There are many very beautiful spiritual lessons for us in this section. We can be partners in this enterprise—some rebuild the temple, some give out the Word of God, some go as missionaries, some support those who go. And something that is quite wonderful is that someday we are to be rewarded. Every man's work will be inspected with a reward in mind. We all will appear before the judgment seat of Christ. Every believer will appear before the judgment seat of Christ. "For we must all appear before the judgment seat of Christ; that every one may receive the things done in his body, according to that he hath done, whether it be good or bad" (2 Cor. 5:10). Added to that, "Every man's work shall be made manifest: for the day shall declare it, because it shall be revealed by fire; and the fire shall try every man's work of what sort it is. If any man's work abide which he hath built thereupon, he shall receive a reward. If any man's work shall be burned, he shall suffer loss: but he himself shall be saved; yet so as by fire" (1 Cor. 3:13–15). When I was in Corinth, I had pictures taken of me standing on the *bema*. Nobody judged me then; neither did I receive a reward. But one of these days I am going to stand before the judgment seat of Christ. I don't want Him to blame me. I don't want Him to say that everything I did was wood, hay, and stubble. I don't want my labors to go up in smoke. I want there to be a little gold among my works.

The singers: the children of Asaph, an hundred twenty and eight [Ezra 2:41].

There were 128 singers who went back to the land. The spirit of praise and rejoicing was in their hearts and lives. They had a lot to sing about. Interestingly enough, more singers returned to the land than did Levites (Ezra 2:40).

And of the children of the priests: the children of Habaiah, the children of Koz, the children of Barzillai; which took a wife of the daughters of Barzillai the Gileadite, and was called after their name:

These sought their register among those that were reckoned by genealogy, but they were not found: therefore were they, as polluted, put from the priesthood [Ezra 2:61–62].

Three families of the priests could not prove their relationship to the nation through genealogical records. Because they could not declare their pedigree, they were officially excluded. However, they were permitted to go with the Jews on their trip to the land.

Today the child of God ought to know that he is a son of God. The apostle Paul could say, "I know whom I have believed." We should have a "know-so" salvation, my friend—not a "think-so" or "hope-so." ". . . for I know whom I have believed, and am persuaded that he is able to keep that which I have committed unto him against that day" (2 Tim. 1:12).

The whole congregation together was

forty and two thousand three hundred and threescore,

Beside their servants and their maids, of whom there were seven thousand three hundred thirty and seven: and there were among them two hundred singing men and singing women [Ezra 2:64–65].

This passage of Scripture gives us the total number of people who returned to the land at this time under Zerubbabel:

Total congregation	42,360
Servants and maids	7,337
Singers (male and female)	200
Grand Total	49,897

CHAPTERS 3–4

THEME: *Temple rebuilding begun and halted*

This first group that returned to Jerusalem after the Captivity numbered only about fifty thousand. In the next delegation, led by Ezra, only about two thousand returned. There were others who came, which may have swelled the population to about sixty thousand—yet there were several million Israelites at this time. You can see that the great majority remained in the land of Babylon and in the other areas rather than return to the Promised Land.

And when the seventh month was come, and the children of Israel were in the cities, the people gathered themselves together as one man to Jerusalem [Ezra 3:1].

Obviously there is a time lapse between chapters 2 and 3 of Ezra. Ezra 2 concluded with the children of Israel returning to the land. They took an abundance of wealth with them to rebuild the temple and restore the land. During the lapse of time they built homes, because we find later that Haggai rebuked them for building their homes and neglecting the temple. The elapsed time could have been several weeks, several months, or as much as two years.

Then stood up Jeshua the son of Jozadak, and his brethren the priests, and Zerubbabel the son of Shealtiel, and his brethren, and builded the altar of the God of Israel, to offer burnt offerings thereon, as it is written in the law of Moses the man of God [Ezra 3:2].

The thing that most interests me is that they searched the Scriptures and they found what was written in the Law of Moses. When they found what was written, there was no controversy or difference of opinion. They not only returned to the land, they also returned to the Law of Moses. The Bible was their authority; therefore neither the ideas nor the opinions of individuals entered into their decision. Things were not done for the sake of expediency.

There is an application here for us. What men say and think is not important. The Scriptures are all-sufficient and contain all of the instruction that is needed for the guidance of those who would be faithful to God in any particular period of church history.

This is the reason I do not give talks on methods, or psychology, or sex. I preach and teach the Word of God. We need to look at the *total* Word of God, not just one or two familiar well-worn passages. I thank God for those familiar passages, but I think some of them have been worn out at the expense of other sections of the Word of God. When we look at the total Word of God, we won't need a book on how to be happy though married and books like that which are going around. The Word of God has the answers. Why not go back to the source?

And they set the altar upon his bases; for fear was upon them because of the people of those countries: and they offered burnt offerings thereon unto the LORD, even burnt offerings morning and evening [Ezra 3:3].

The altar erected was the altar of burnt offering. This altar, as we have already seen, speaks of the cross of Christ. The burnt sacrifice that was offered speaks of the person of Christ and His sacrifice for us. Christ offered Himself without spot to God. He died in the sinner's stead. What they were doing when they offered this sacrifice was meeting about the person of Christ and His atoning death.

That is the place of meeting today for believers.

Every believer should understand that those who have trusted Christ as Savior and have been baptized by the Holy Spirit into the body of believers (the church) are brothers. My brother is one with whom I can have fellowship. Fellowship is not a question of the color of a person's skin, or of his social status, or of his wealth. Fellowship has nothing to do with the fact that a person is a Baptist, a Methodist, a Presbyterian, a Nazarene, a Pentecostal, or a Roman Catholic. None of that makes any difference. Is he a believer in Jesus Christ? That is the important thing. If a person is a child of God, he and I can meet together and have fellowship. This is a very wonderful thing.

In these folk who had returned from captivity we find a marvelous unity—which should characterize all the children of God. The psalmist said, "Behold, how good and how pleasant it is for brethren to dwell together in unity!" (Ps. 133:1). These people who had come back to the land were poor, humble folk. They were not seeking position; they were just trying to do the will of God.

You and I are living at the end of an age, and it is becoming to those who really have an understanding of the times to be through with pretension. "The meek will he guide in judgment: and the meek will he teach his way" (Ps. 25:9). We need to be meek. In our churches and other organizations we are always trying to do something big. Oh, my friend, we don't need to do that. What we need is to meet around the person of Jesus Christ, as this returning remnant was doing.

They kept also the feast of tabernacles, as it is written, and offered the daily burnt offerings by number, according to the custom, as the duty of every day required;

And afterward offered the continual burnt offering, both of the new moons, and of all the set feasts of the LORD that were consecrated, and of every one that willingly offered a freewill offering unto the LORD [Ezra 3:4–5].

These folk have returned to the Word of God. They have put up the altar, and now they begin to build the foundations of the temple.

Now in the second year of their coming unto the house of God at Jerusalem, in the second month, began Zerubbabel the son of Shealtiel, and Jeshua the son of Jozadak, and the remnant of their brethren the priests and the Levites, and all they that were come out of the captivity unto Jerusalem; and appointed the Levites, from twenty years old and upward, to set forward the work of the house of the LORD.

Then stood Jeshua with his sons and his brethren, Kadmiel and his sons, the sons of Judah, together, to set forward the workmen in the house of God: the sons of Henadad, with their sons and their brethren the Levites.

And when the builders laid the foundation of the temple of the LORD, they set the priests in their apparel with trumpets, and the Levites the sons of Asaph with cymbals, to praise the LORD, after the ordinance of David king of Israel [Ezra 3:8–10].

So far these people have only built an altar and laid the foundation for the temple, but they are so thrilled and enthusiastic that they act as though the entire temple has been rebuilt. They had a dedication service, a time of praise, and sang praises to God. It was a thrilling experience for them.

If you are as old as I am, you can remember back in the 1920s when many churches were able to complete only the basements of their buildings. They would buy a lot, build a basement, cover the basement with tar paper, and that is where the congregation would meet. Then the Depression came, and many of those churches were never finished. The congregations continued to meet in the basements with the tar-paper roofs. These have largely disappeared today because in our affluent society we must have the very latest thing in modern architecture; we would never be satisfied with a basement.

However, these Jews were delighted and thrilled with the foundation they had built. So they held a praise service.

And they sang together by course in praising and giving thanks unto the LORD; because he is good, for his mercy endureth for ever toward Israel. And all the people shouted with a great shout, when they praised the LORD, because the foundation of the house of the LORD was laid [Ezra 3:11].

Now these were the younger folk who had never seen Solomon's temple.

But many of the priests and Levites and chief of the fathers, who were ancient men, that had seen the first house, when the foundation of this house was laid before their eyes, wept with a loud voice; and many shouted aloud for joy:

So that the people could not discern the noise of the shout of joy from the noise of the weeping of the people: for the people shouted with a loud shout, and the noise was heard afar off [Ezra 3: 12–13].

There were two groups present during the dedication service. There were the young people who had never seen the temple of old. This was something new to them. In all their youth and enthusiasm they were praising God, and the Lord blessed them. The other group was composed of the old-timers. They remembered Solomon's temple and how beautiful it was. I have a notion that some of them said to each other, "This second temple is nothing. If these young people could only have seen Solomon's temple!" What they were saying was not very encouraging to the younger group, but it was true. One of the problems God had to overcome was discouragement that came because of the older group talking the way they did. As a result we find that Haggai the prophet told the people, "The Lord says, 'Go ahead and build.' God is with you. He was not in that beautiful temple of Solomon's at the end—the glory had left it—but God is with you now. Go ahead and build!"

There are a lot of old-timers today who discourage the work of God. I feel that one of the reasons that this present spiritual movement is largely outside of the church today is because many old-timers are holding back. They only remember the old days, and they are not about to enter the new days. There is a danger of sitting in judgment upon this spiritual movement of today. I find myself critical of many facets of the program, and I am an old-timer. But let's withhold judgment for a time. Let's see what is going to happen. The Lord knows those who belong to Him. He is going to separate the wheat and the tares. That is His business, not ours. Let us thank God that there is a movement toward God today and rejoice in it. Let us not weep and criticize in this present hour.

I recall that when I was a student in seminary I was asked to hold some summertime meetings in Georgia. In those days it was customary to hold meetings, which they sometimes called protracted meetings. They asked me to preach, and I did. In spite of the preacher, the Lord blessed and people were saved.

I will never forget the last night of a particular meeting. Some of the young officers of the church were rejoicing with me at the way things had gone. An old-timer was sitting there listening to us. He had long whiskers, and he looked to me like Father Time. Finally he said, "You boys had a pretty good meeting, but I remember when. . . ." Then we heard all about "when." When he got through with his tales of the past, our meeting did not seem like anything at all. That was very discouraging; we all left a little depressed that night. Later I asked another member of the church who was almost as old as "Father Time" and she said, "The meeting he told you about wasn't all that great. You know, he is in his dotage, and the older he gets the bigger that meeting gets. It wasn't nearly as wonderful as he thought it was."

ARTAXERXES' DECREE HALTS REBUILDING

Opposition to the rebuilding program did not come from the inside but from the outside. This is a rather detailed section, and I am not going to spend much time in it except to call attention to what is taking place.

Now when the adversaries of Judah and Benjamin heard that the children of the captivity builded the temple unto the LORD God of Israel;

Then they came to Zerubbabel, and to the chief of the fathers, and said unto them, Let us build with you: for we seek your God, as ye do; and we do sacrifice unto him since the days of Esar-haddon king of Assur, which brought us up hither [Ezra 4:1–2].

I will have occasion later on to call attention to the fact that not only two tribes returned to the land (Judah and Benjamin), but all twelve tribes actually went back. These people are saying that they returned to the Promised Land during the days of Esar-haddon, king of Assur (Assyria). It was Assyria, you remember, which had taken the northern tribes captive. Some of these people apparently had trickled back into the land and had mixed with the Samaritans. As a result they wanted to join up with those who had come from Babylon. The enemies' first effort to hinder the work of rebuilding the temple is to offer to become allies.

That has always been the subtlety of Satan in his work through the liberal wing of the church. Liberalism divided the church and then said, "You fundamentalists are always fighting. Join with us." Because we did not join with them, they call us the troublemakers. Liberalism split the church in the beginning, and now they want us to come back on their terms.

Here the "adversaries of Judah and Benjamin" said, "We have been worshiping God here all along, and you folk have just gotten back. Let us join with you, and we'll worship Him together." That sounds very good on the surface, but they were not genuine, as we shall see.

But Zerubbabel, and Jeshua, and the rest of the chief of the fathers of Israel, said unto them, Ye have nothing to do with us to build an house unto our God; but we ourselves together will build unto the LORD God of Israel, as king Cyrus the king of Persia hath commanded us [Ezra 4:3].

The chief fathers of Israel were not very nice, were they? They absolutely rejected the enemies' offer to become allies. The Israelites do not seem to be interested in the ecumenical movement at all. In fact, they seem actually rude. But the very interesting thing is that they were right. The important thing is to be right. When the psychological approach comes in conflict with the Bible, the Bible must prevail for the child of God.

Then the people of the land weakened the hands of the people of Judah, and troubled them in building,

And hired counsellors against them, to frustrate their purpose, all the days of Cyrus king of Persia, even until the reign of Darius king of Persia [Ezra 4:4–5].

Now we can see that they were enemies, not friends. As soon as they were turned down, they began to actively oppose them.

And in the days of Artaxerxes wrote Bishlam, Mithredath, Tabeel, and the rest of their companions, unto Artaxerxes king of Persia; and the writing of the letter was written in the Syrian tongue, and interpreted in the Syrian tongue [Ezra 4:7].

They decided to compose a letter to the king of Persia with false accusations against the remnant that had returned to rebuild Jerusalem.

Here is a copy of the letter they sent:

This is the copy of the letter that they sent unto him, even unto Artaxerxes the king; Thy servants the men on this side the river, and at such a time.

Be it known unto the king, that the Jews which came up from thee to us are come unto Jerusalem, building the rebellious and the bad city, and have set up the walls thereof, and joined the foundations.

Be it known now unto the king, that, if this city be builded, and the walls set up again, then will they not pay toll, tribute, and custom, and so thou shalt endamage the revenue of the kings [Ezra 4:11–13].

Their argument is that Jerusalem was a rebellious city and that Artaxerxes will have trouble with it again if he allows the city to be rebuilt.

So the king of Persia took their advice. He searched the records to see if their accusation was accurate. In his letter of reply, he said:

And I commanded, and search hath been made, and it is found that this city of old time hath made insurrection against kings, and that rebellion and sedition have been made therein.

There have been mighty kings also over Jerusalem, which have ruled over all countries beyond the river; and toll, tribute, and custom, was paid unto them.

Give ye now commandment to cause these men to cease, and that this city be not builded, until another commandment shall be given from me.

Take heed now that ye fail not to do this: why should damage grow to the hurt of the kings? [Ezra 4:19–22].

When this letter comes back from the king of Persia, the so-called friends who wanted to cooperate with the building program hurriedly bring the letter to the building site.

Now when the copy of king Artaxerxes' letter was read before Rehum, and Shimshai the scribe, and their companions, they went up in haste to Jerusa-

lem unto the Jews, and made them to cease by force and power.

Then ceased the work of the house of God which is at Jerusalem. So it ceased unto the second year of the reign of Darius king of Persia [Ezra 4:23–24].

They were forced to halt the building program.

CHAPTERS 5–6

THEME: *Temple rebuilt, finished, and dedicated*

We have seen already that the rebuilding of the temple was stopped by the opposition of the enemy. They wrote a letter to Artaxerxes which gave a false impression of Jerusalem. They called it a rebellious and bad city. The king Artaxerxes did go back in the records and find out that there had been a rebellion on the part of these people, at the very end of the kingdom—the southern kingdom of Judah. Three times they had rebelled. And finally Nebuchadnezzar came and destroyed the city. But they did not investigate thoroughly. Although they found the rebellion to be true, they did not look for the decree that had been made to rebuild the city of Jerusalem.

This was a period of great discouragement. They not only stopped building; they were also tempted to walk away from the entire project. They felt this would be the best way to solve their problems.

There are many people who feel that if they could just change their location they could solve their problems. That is not always true. You cannot run away from your problems. Fortunately, this time the people did not run away. God raised up the prophets Haggai and Zechariah.

Candidly, we ought to study the books of Haggai and Zechariah (also Daniel and Esther) in connection with Ezra and Nehemiah. They belong in the same passage, and studying them together would be very profitable.

Then the prophets, Haggai the prophet, and Zechariah the son of Iddo, prophesied unto the Jews that were in Judah and Jerusalem in the name of the God of Israel, even unto them [Ezra 5:1].

These two prophets were called upon by God to encourage the people to resume rebuilding the temple. They knew, of course, that there had been a decree from Cyrus, king of Persia, which granted them permission to rebuild Jerusalem. And they knew it was God's will and God's time to rebuild the city. Haggai called them the Lord's messengers.

These two men were not alike. The only thing they had in common was that they were both prophets of God. Haggai had his feet on the ground. He was a solid, stable individual. He was a man upon whom you could rest. He wanted the facts. He carried a measuring rod along with him and measured everything. Everything had to be all wool, a yard wide, and warranted not to rip, tear, unravel, or become run down at the heel. That was Haggai. He got right down to the nitty-gritty. He spoke, we would say today, to the *conscience* of the nation. His messages were ones that went deep and hurt. His type was not popular—nor is it popular today.

Zechariah was an entirely different type of individual. He had his head in the clouds. He had tremendous visions and a message to match. He appealed to the emotions of the people. He spoke to their *hearts*. These two men together, Haggai and Zechariah, spoke to the conscience and heart of Israel. Apparently Haggai was considered the leader, but both of them encouraged the people to resume their building program. It would be very profitable at this juncture to read the Books of Haggai and Zechariah.

Then rose up Zerubbabel the son of Shealtiel, and Jeshua the son of Jozadak, and began to build the house of God which is at Jerusalem: and with them were the prophets of God helping them.

At the same time came to them Tatnai, governor on this side the river, and Shethar-boznai, and their companions, and said thus unto them, Who hath

commanded you to build this house, and to make up this wall? [Ezra 5:2–3].

When work was resumed, their enemies heard about it. We are told that Tatnai was a Persian governor of Samaria, and Shethar-Boznai was probably a high official. They come and challenge the workmen. They say, "What's the big idea? You were ordered to stop building!"

Now the answer they give them is really not an answer at all. To begin with, Tatnai and his crowd are enemies. They are men of the world, and the Jews are not about to cast their pearls before swine. Would they understand if they said that *God* told them to build? After all, "The secret of the LORD is with them that fear him . . ." (Ps. 25:14)—and with no one else. "The natural man receiveth not the things of the Spirit of God: for they are foolishness unto him . . ." (1 Cor. 2:14). They just answered ". . . a fool according to his folly . . ." (Prov. 26:4). In fact, they answered by asking a question.

Then said we unto them after this manner, What are the names of the men that make this building? [Ezra 5:4].

In other words, "We didn't see your names on the list that was given to us. If you were part and parcel of this, if you were part of the building crew, we would be glad to answer you. But since your names are not on the list, we will not answer you." I would call that a very nice way of saying, "It's none of your business. You have no right to ask that question of us."

Now that kind of reply could put these builders in a very difficult position, but notice what happens.

But the eye of their God was upon the elders of the Jews, that they could not cause them to cease, till the matter came to Darius: and then they returned answer by letter concerning this matter [Ezra 5:5].

The wonderful thing is that you can depend on God to keep His eye on those who are His own. So off goes another letter to the king—by this time Darius is the king. Apparently about seven years had gone by.

The copy of the letter that Tatnai, governor on this side the river, and Shethar-boznai, and his companions the Apharsachites, which were on this side the river, sent unto Darius the king:

They sent a letter unto him, wherein was written thus; Unto Darius the king, all peace [Ezra 5:6–7].

This is another letter the enemy gets off post-haste—I think he sends it special delivery.

Be it known unto the king, that we went into the province of Judea, to the house of the great God, which is builded with great stones, and timber is laid in the walls, and this work goeth fast on, and prospereth in their hands [Ezra 5:8].

As you can see, the thought in the letter is this: We didn't go up there specifically to spy this out—we are really not their enemies—we just happened to be in the neighborhood and stopped by for a little visit. And this is what we found.

Then asked we those elders, and said unto them thus, Who commanded you to build this house, and to make up these walls?

We asked their names also, to certify thee, that we might write the names of the men that were the chief of them [Ezra 5:9–10].

They were not told the names of the prophets, Haggai and Zechariah.

And thus they returned us answer, saying, We are the servants of the God of heaven and earth, and build the house that was builded these many years ago, which a great king of Israel builded and set up [Ezra 5:11].

They give them the history of the Captivity, which had occurred about seventy years before.

But after that our fathers had provoked the God of heaven unto wrath, he gave them into the hand of Nebuchadnezzar king of Babylon, the Chaldean, who destroyed this house, and carried the people away into Babylon.

But in the first year of Cyrus the king of Babylon the same king Cyrus made a decree to build this house of God [Ezra 5:12–13].

They gave them concrete evidence that King Cyrus had commanded them to rebuild the temple—he even sent the temple vessels back with them.

And the vessels also of gold and silver of the house of God, which Nebuchadnezzar took out of the temple that was in Jerusalem, and brought them into the temple of Babylon, those did Cyrus the king take out of the temple of Babylon, and they were delivered unto one, whose name was Sheshbazzar, whom he had made governor;

And said unto him, Take these vessels, go, carry them into the temple that is in Jerusalem, and let the house of God be builded in his place [Ezra 5:14–15].

The letter concludes with this request:

Now therefore, if it seem good to the king, let there be search made in the king's treasure house, which is there at Babylon, whether it be so, that a decree was made of Cyrus the king to build this house of God at Jerusalem, and let the king send his pleasure to us concerning this matter [Ezra 5:17].

These enemies did not believe that a decree had ever been made by Cyrus, but the letter is saying that the Jews' claim of such a decree is the basis on which they are rebuilding. So they ask that a search be made. They are certain that no such decree exists, but that these people are doing this on their own.

CYRUS' DECREE CONFIRMED

A great deal has been made concerning the *position* and the *condition* of God's people. These two things are quite different, by the way. Positionally, the Jews were in the place God wanted them to be—in the land. The decree for them to return to the land was made by Cyrus, who acknowledged that he was doing it at the command of God. So these people are in the position God wanted them to be in. However, their condition is not so good. They are discouraged. They would like to walk away from the whole business. So God raised up prophets to encourage them.

It seems that God's people today tend to get their position and condition mixed up. If you are in Christ today, you are safe. Your position is good. But how is your condition? Are you a discouraged saint? Are you anchored in Christ with a sure salvation, but you want to give up and quit? Do you want to walk away from it all? If that is how you feel, my friend, although your *position* is good, your *condition* is bad. That was the state of the Jews in the Book of Ezra.

Now the very interesting thing is that God is with His people, and His will is going to be done. We find now that a discovery was made. This is a case of the enemy getting his foot in his mouth. He should have kept quiet. Notice what happened.

Then Darius the king made a decree, and search was made in the house of the rolls, where the treasures were laid up in Babylon [Ezra 6:1].

They went down in a basement somewhere and dug up old archives which were covered with dust—

And there was found at Achmetha, in the palace that is in the province of the Medes, a roll, and therein was a record thus written:

In the first year of Cyrus the king the same Cyrus the king made a decree concerning the house of God at Jerusalem, Let the house be builded, the place where they offered sacrifices, and let the foundations thereof be strongly laid; the height thereof threescore cubits, and the breadth thereof threescore cubits [Ezra 6:2–3].

Also—

And also let the golden and silver vessels of the house of God, which Nebuchadnezzar took forth out of the temple which is at Jerusalem, and brought unto Babylon, be restored, and brought again unto the temple which is at Jerusalem, every one to his place, and place them in the house of God [Ezra 6:5].

It was all recorded there. All of this is unearthed by King Darius. He never would have known about this decree if the enemy had not mentioned it. This was a real blunder on the part of the enemies of the Jews.

Now this is the message that King Darius returns to Tatnai:

Now therefore, Tatnai, governor beyond the river, Shethar-boznai, and your companions the Apharsachites, which are beyond the river, be ye far from thence:

Let the work of this house of God alone; let the governor of the Jews and the elders of the Jews build this house of God in his place [Ezra 6:6–7].

Tatnai was a governor with an important job, and he thought he could stop the building of the temple in Jerusalem. But when the decree of Cyrus was located, the present King Darius realizes that it was a law of the Medes and Persians, and it could not be altered or changed. So he makes a further decree.

Moreover I make a decree what ye shall do to the elders of these Jews for the building of this house of God: that of the king's goods, even of the tribute beyond the river, forthwith expenses be given unto these men, that they be not hindered [Ezra 6:8].

He says, "Now, look, not only are you to stop hindering the work, you are to help it along. You are to keep the taxes that you gather over there on that side of the river—instead of sending them over here to Persia—you are to give the money to these folk for the rebuilding of the temple." God does make the wrath of man to praise Him!

And that which they have need of, both young bullocks, and rams, and lambs, for the burnt offerings of the God of heaven, wheat, salt, wine, and oil, according to the appointment of the priests which are at Jerusalem, let it be given them day by day without fail:

That they may offer sacrifices of sweet savours unto the God of heaven, and pray for the life of the king, and of his sons [Ezra 6:9–10].

What a decree this was!

Also, he decrees a severe penalty upon anyone who would hinder the work.

Also I have made a decree, that whosoever shall alter this word, let timber be pulled down from his house, and being set up, let him be hanged thereon; and let his house be made a dunghill for this [Ezra 6:11].

At this point you would find it thrilling to read the Books of Haggai and Zechariah. They are marvelous. We designate them as minor prophets, but they are batting in the major leagues!

And the elders of the Jews builded, and they prospered through the prophesying of Haggai the prophet and Zechariah the son of Iddo. And they builded, and finished it, according to the commandment of the God of Israel, and according to the commandment of Cyrus, and Darius, and Artaxerxes king of Persia [Ezra 6:14].

The temple is rebuilt under the inspiration of Haggai and Zechariah.

TEMPLE FINISHED AND DEDICATED

And this house was finished on the third day of the month of Adar, which was in the sixth year of the reign of Darius the king.

And the children of Israel, the priests, and the Levites, and the rest of the children of the captivity, kept the dedication of this house of God with joy [Ezra 6:15–16].

Notice that it says, "the children of Israel . . . and the rest of the children of the captivity." Who is meant? Of course it means what it says: the children of *Israel*—not only the children of Judah and Benjamin. These folk are of the ten tribes of Israel, which some people today call the ten *lost* tribes. My friend, they didn't get lost. They are here with their brethren keeping "the dedication of this house of God with joy."

And offered at the dedication of this house of God an hundred bullocks, two hundred rams, four hundred lambs; and for a sin offering for all Israel, twelve he goats, according to the number of the tribes of Israel [Ezra 6:17].

For whom was the sin offering? The language here is even more explicit. It was for "all Israel." Did only people from the tribes of Judah and Benjamin return to the land? No! There were people from all twelve tribes. There were "twelve he goats," according to the number of the tribes of Israel. Now don't tell me that ten tribes got lost and ended up in Great Britain, and a few of them came to America on the Mayflower. That simply is not true. The record here is quite clear that none of the tribes were lost. If *any* of them are lost, they are *all* lost because they were all together after the Captivity. This will be confirmed again later on.

PASSOVER KEPT

And the children of the captivity kept the passover upon the fourteenth day of the first month.

For the priests and the Levites were purified together, all of them were pure, and killed the passover for all the children of the captivity, and for their brethren the priests, and for themselves.

And the children of Israel, which were come again out of captivity, and all such as had separated themselves unto them from the filthiness of the heathen of the land, to seek the LORD God of Israel, did eat,

And kept the feast of unleavened bread seven days with joy: for the LORD had made them joyful, and turned the heart of the king of Assyria unto them, to strengthen their hands in the work of the house of God, the God of Israel [Ezra 6:19–22].

Just five weeks after the dedication of the temple the Passover was held. The Passover spoke of the death of Christ, our Passover who was offered for us. When they gathered around the Passover, they were gathering around the Person of the Lord Jesus Christ, according to the Word of God.

CHAPTERS 7–8

***THEME:** Return under Ezra*

Now we come to the second major division in the little Book of Ezra. The first six chapters told us about the return of the Jews from Babylon to Jerusalem under the leadership of Zerubbabel—about fifty thousand Jews left Babylon at that time. The Jews had gone into the Babylonian captivity because they continually turned to idolatry, and God gave them a gold cure in Babylon. Also the Jews had disobeyed the Mosaic Law in that they had not allowed the land to lie fallow every seventh year. They probably did not think it was too important. They thought they were getting by with breaking that law, but God said, "I'm going to put you out of the land for seventy years so that the land can catch up on the sabbaths it has missed." After the land had rested and renewed itself for seventy years, God allowed His people to return.

Then there was another wave of revival among the Jews who had been captives and were still living in Babylon. Ezra led a second group back to Jerusalem. Up to this point Ezra, although he is the writer of this book, has not figured in its history at all. In the final four chapters we meet the author. In chapters 7 and 8 we see the return of the Jews led by Ezra. In chapters 9 and 10 we see the reformation under Ezra. Revival led to reformation, and that is always the order. We will see that again when we study Nehemiah.

Ezra is one of the neglected characters of the Bible. I do not believe he has received proper recognition by Bible expositors, and certainly not from the church. I wonder if you have ever heard a sermon on the Book of Ezra. Have you ever heard this book taught? Well, it is one that is easily passed by. In the next few chapters we are going to meet Ezra and get acquainted with him.

Now after these things, in the reign of Artaxerxes king of Persia, Ezra the son of Seraiah, the son of Azariah, the son of Hilkiah,

The son of Shallum, the son of Zadok, the son of Ahitub,

The son of Amariah, the son of Azariah, the son of Meraioth,

The son of Zerahiah, the son of Uzzi, the son of Bukki,

The son of Abishua, the son of Phinehas, the son of Eleazar, the son of Aaron the chief priest [Ezra 7:1–5].

This is the Artaxerxes who gave Nehemiah permission to return to Jerusalem to rebuild the city, which marks the beginning of the great prophecy of the "Seventy Weeks" of Daniel. We will discuss him when we get to the Book of Nehemiah.

The man here who interests me is not the king, but Ezra himself. Who is he? Ezra was a lineal descendant of Phinehas, the grandson of Aaron. He belongs, therefore, to the priestly line. Had there been a temple in Jerusalem, he probably would have functioned in it as a priest—probably the high priest. But there was no temple; it had been burned and destroyed.

Apparently Ezra did not feel like returning to Jerusalem with the first delegation. There was no place for him in Jerusalem, and apparently he was ministering to those who remained in Babylon. Now a group of about two thousand Jews, led by Ezra, planned to go to Jerusalem. The temple had been rebuilt so that there was a place for him to minister. We are going to find that he was also a teacher of the Word of God.

Phinehas, the son of Eleazar, the grandson of Aaron, is mentioned in this passage. He first appears in Scripture at a time of licentious idolatry, where his zeal and action stopped the plague that was destroying Israel. You will recall that when Balaam the prophet was not allowed to curse Israel, he taught the king to foster intermarriage with them for the purpose of bringing the world, the flesh, and the devil into the midst of God's people. In Numbers 25:7–11 we are told that one of the Israelites took a Midianitish woman. When Jews married pagan people, they were drawn into the worship of their gods. Judgment fell upon Israel in the form of a plague. Phinehas stayed the plague by executing the man who had taken the Midianitish woman and executing her also. Two lives were sacrificed in order to save a multitude of lives. As a reward for his efforts, God promised Phinehas that the priesthood would remain in his family forever.

I would like to add a practical word which I consider a logical application of this section to our present condition. There are many judges today who feel that capital punishment is brutal, uncivilized, and should be abolished. The original purpose of capital punishment was the protection of other human lives. When a guilty person is not executed for his crime, then hundreds have to pay with their lives. Today we are not safe in our cities because there are no longer executions. Don't tell me that executions do not deter crime. I have discovered that when a traffic officer writes a ticket it will slow me down on a highway—don't tell me it does not slow *you* down! It is a deterrent to crime, and that is its purpose. That was the reason the Jew and his Midianitish woman were executed. Because of the death of this couple, multitudes in Israel were saved from the pollution that had broken out in that nation.

I remember hearing a whimsical story about the early days in the West when a man was asked to say something before he was hanged for a murder he had committed. This was the statement he made: "I want you to know that this is going to be a lesson to me." Well, my friend, that was not the purpose of his hanging. It was not to be a lesson to him. It was to protect the men, women, and children who were living in that day. Why don't we face up to the facts in life today? Why can't we see that we are sacrificing hundreds of lives to protect one criminal? God does not do it that way, because He wants to *save* human life; and He knows how bad the human heart can be. God says, "The heart is deceitful above all things, and desperately wicked . . ." (Jer. 17:9). There is a great lesson to be learned from the action of Phinehas, one of the ancestors of Ezra.

This Ezra went up from Babylon; and he was a ready scribe in the law of Moses, which the LORD God of Israel had given: and the king granted him all his request, according to the hand of the LORD his God upon him [Ezra 7:6].

Ezra "was a ready scribe in the law of Moses." Since he was not able to execute the office of priest, he spent his time studying the Word of God. Now he is going to be able to use what he has learned. You will find out that he is labeled "a ready scribe" again and again. Ezra 7:21 tells us that Ezra had a reputation down in Babylon, even with the king, as being a scribe of the words of the Lord God. He was a teacher of the Word of God.

And there went up some of the children of Israel, and of the priests, and the Levites, and the singers, and the porters, and the Nethinims, unto Jerusalem, in the seventh year of Artaxerxes the king [Ezra 7:7].

There was another revival among the Jews in Babylon, and this time about two thousand people wanted to return to the land.

And he came to Jerusalem in the fifth month, which was in the seventh year of the king.

For upon the first day of the first month began he to go up from Babylon, and on the first day of the fifth month came he to Jerusalem, according to the good hand of his God upon him [Ezra 7:8–9].

They returned to Jerusalem in the seventh year of Artaxerxes the king. It took them almost five months to make the trip. They could not go by jet stream; they had to go by foot, and it was a long, arduous trip in that day.

For Ezra had prepared his heart to seek the law of the LORD, and to do it, and to

teach in Israel statutes and judgments [Ezra 7:10].

Ezra had prepared his heart for the day that he would return to his land. He knew it was coming because he had faith in God. So he prepared his heart and studied the Law of Moses (the first five books of the Bible) and the Book of Joshua, which were in existence in that day. It is the belief of many that Ezra wrote 1 and 2 Chronicles. Ezra not only studied God's Word, he also did what it said. Oh, my, that is so important! It is one thing to *study* God's Word and another thing to *do* it. Ezra also wanted to *teach* the Word. He wanted God's people to know God's statutes and judgments.

Now this is the copy of the letter that the king Artaxerxes gave unto Ezra the priest, the scribe, even a scribe of the words of the commandments of the LORD, and of his statutes to Israel.

Artaxerxes, king of kings, unto Ezra the priest, a scribe of the law of the God of heaven, perfect peace, and at such a time.

I make a decree, that all they of the people of Israel, and of his priests and Levites, in my realm, which are minded of their own freewill to go up to Jerusalem, go with thee [Ezra 7:11–13].

Artaxerxes made a decree which allowed Ezra and his followers to return to their land. It was not a commandment that they go, but it was permission to return according to their own particular desires and according to the leading of the Lord.

Forasmuch as thou art sent of the king, and of his seven counsellors, to enquire concerning Judah and Jerusalem, according to the law of thy God which is in thine hand;

And to carry the silver and gold, which the king and his counsellors have freely offered unto the God of Israel, whose habitation is in Jerusalem [Ezra 7: 14–15].

Evidently Ezra had a real witness in the court, because the king and his counselors made this offering to "the God of Israel." Ezra was given the authority to appoint magistrates and judges. They got together all of this material, Ezra was given the king's decree, then preparation was made for them to leave. The decree reveals a tremendous reverence for God. Notice how it concludes:

And whosoever will not do the law of thy God, and the law of the king, let judgment be executed speedily upon him, whether it be unto death, or to banishment, or to confiscation of goods, or to imprisonment [Ezra 7:26].

This law, of course, was in reference to the Jews after they arrived in the land. In other words, if they return to their land, they must mean business as far as their relationship to God is concerned.

Notice now the thanksgiving of Ezra.

Blessed be the LORD God of our fathers, which hath put such a thing as this in the king's heart, to beautify the house of the LORD which is in Jerusalem [Ezra 7:27].

Not only was the temple to be rebuilt, it was also to be beautified. I think God's house ought to be made beautiful, as beautiful as it can possibly be according to the ability of the folk who are identified with it.

And hath extended mercy unto me before the king, and his counsellors, and before all the king's mighty princes. And I was strengthened as the hand of the LORD my God was upon me, and I gathered together out of Israel chief men to go up with me [Ezra 7:28].

Ezra led a fine delegation back to the land. It was not as large as the first delegation, but a great many of the leaders were in the second group.

Chapter 8 gives the list of Ezra's companions. Notice that Ezra made sure that the Levites went with them. The Nethinims, who were the servants, went along also.

Then we see something that reveals how human Ezra was.

Then I proclaimed a fast there, at the river of Ahava, that we might afflict ourselves before our God, to seek of him a right way for us, and for our little ones, and for all our substance [Ezra 8:21].

Ezra calls for a fast and a great prayer meeting at the river of Ahava. He wanted to know God's will.

For I was ashamed to require of the king a band of soldiers and horsemen to help us against the enemy in the way:

because we had spoken unto the king, saying, The hand of our God is upon all them for good that seek him; but his power and his wrath is against all them that forsake him.

So we fasted and besought our God for this: and he was entreated of us [Ezra 8:22–23].

He said, "You know, I went before the king and told him that the hand of our God was with us, that He will be against our enemies and will lead us back to our land." Then Ezra looked at the delegation gathered by the river ready to go on that long march. He looked at the families and the little ones, and he knew the dangers along the way. The normal thing would be to ask the king for a little help—for a few guards to ride along with them. Then the king would say, "I thought you were trusting the Lord."

Sometimes some of us become very eloquent about how we are trusting God and how wonderful He is, but when we get right down to the nitty-gritty, we don't really trust Him. Ezra is that kind of an individual. He surely is human. He says, "I was ashamed to go ask the king." What was the alternative? He called a prayer meeting and a fast. He said, "Oh, Lord, we just have to depend on You." You know, the Lord puts many of us in that position many, many times.

Then we departed from the river of Ahava on the twelfth day of the first month, to go unto Jerusalem: and the hand of our God was upon us, and he delivered us from the hand of the enemy, and of such as lay in wait by the way.

And we came to Jerusalem, and abode there three days [Ezra 8:31–32].

We find that the king sent a great deal of gold, silver, and vessels with this delegation. This wealth was put in the care of the priests, and they needed protection, you see. And God did watch over them, and they arrived safely at their destination. They stayed in Jerusalem three days and took the treasure into the temple—into the house of God.

Also the children of those that had been carried away, which were come out of the captivity, offered burnt offerings unto the God of Israel, twelve bullocks for all Israel, ninety and six rams, seventy and seven lambs, twelve he goats for a sin-offering: all this was a burnt offering unto the LORD [Ezra 8:35].

In this verse twelve "he goats" are mentioned again. Why? It was for *all* Israel for a sin offering. What a wonderful, glorious thing it was for these Jews to be back in Jerusalem offering their sacrifices to God!

CHAPTERS 9–10

THEME: *Revival under Ezra*

In chapter 9 we come to one of the great prayers in the Bible. In three of the post-captivity books there are three great ninth chapters which record prayers: Ezra 9, Nehemiah 9, and Daniel 9. Now here before us is the great prayer of Ezra. The occasion for it was a very sad thing which had taken place among God's people.

Now when these things were done, the princes came to me, saying, The people of Israel, and the priests, and the Levites, have not separated themselves from the people of the lands, doing according to their abominations, even of the Canaanites, the Hittites, the Perizzites, the Jebusites, the Ammonites, the Moabites, the Egyptians, and the Amorites [Ezra 9:1].

Note that the Egyptians are mentioned and so are other pagan peoples. The Hittites were a great people. Information on the Hittite nation was discovered after I was in school, and I have been interested in reading about them. Throughout Asia Minor, especially along the coast, great cities like Ephesus, Smyrna, and Troy were first established by the Hittites. They were indeed a great people, but they were heathen. The people of Israel had not separated themselves from these folk.

When the first delegation of Jews returned to the land, they met discouragement. We will learn more about this when we come to the prophecy of Haggai. We will see how he helped them overcome the hurdles of discouragement that were before them. Believe me, they ran a long line of hurdles, and through Haggai they were able to clear them. With the help of Nehemiah, the active layman, the walls and temple of Jerusalem were rebuilt; but there was discouragement on every hand. It is at times like this that you let down. It has happened to many Christians.

Someone has said that discouragement is the devil's greatest weapon. The Jews let down their guard and intermarried with the surrounding heathen and enemies of God and Israel. That in turn led to a practice of the abomination of the heathen. The lack of separation plunged them into immorality and idolatry. In some cases I don't think these people took the trouble to get married because the heathen of that day did not pay much attention to formality of marriage any more than the heathen in our contemporary society pay attention to it. We are told that we live in an advanced age. We have new freedom. We are a civilized people. My friend, we are not different from the pagan peoples of Ezra's day.

For they have taken of their daughters for themselves, and for their sons: so that the holy seed have mingled themselves with the people of those lands: yea, the hand of the princes and rulers hath been chief in this trespass [Ezra 9:2].

Even the leadership was involved in this. They were all the more guilty before God, because privilege always increases responsibility. The returned remnant is in a sad, sordid, and squalid condition. Now there are several things Ezra could have done in this situation. He could have broadcasted a program on patriotism, run up the Israeli flag, displayed the star of David, and held great rallies on patriotism. But he did not do that. He might have delivered a withering blow against the intermarriage and immorality and idolatry by making speeches, but Ezra did not do that either. Or he could have followed another procedure: he could have formed an organization and become involved in trying to recover these couples who had gone into this immorality. That, my friend, is how we do it today. But Ezra was not familiar with our modern way of doing things. But I want you to notice what he did. It is something that we don't see much of in our day.

And when I heard this thing, I rent my garment and my mantle, and plucked off the hair of my head and of my beard, and sat down astonied [Ezra 9:3].

Remember that Ezra did not arrive in his native land until about seventy-five years after the first delegation of fifty thousand led by Zerubbabel. When Ezra arrived with his delegation of two thousand, he found that the temple had been rebuilt, but not the walls of the city. And the population was in a sad, sordid condition. They had intermingled and intermarried with the heathen. Immorality and idolatry were running rampant. There was a lack of separation, and the Jews were a miserable and bedraggled lot. When all of this was brought to Ezra's attention, and he found that it was accurate, he was absolutely overwhelmed and chagrined that God's people would drop to such a low level.

Today we talk about the apostasy of the church—at least I do. But I wonder if we are as exercised about it as we should be. Since I have retired and am on the outside looking at the condition of the church from a different view, I must confess that I would like to wash my hands of it and say, "Well, it is no affair of mine." But it is an affair of mine. And, friends, it is so easy for you and me to point an accusing finger at that which is wrong, but notice what Ezra did. He was so overwhelmed by the sin of his people that he tore his clothes and tore out his hair. Instead of beginning a tirade against them (which would have been characteristic of many people today), notice the next step Ezra took.

Then were assembled unto me every one that trembled at the words of the God of Israel, because of the transgression of those that had been carried away; and I sat astonied until the evening sacrifice [Ezra 9:4].

"Then were assembled unto me every one that trembled at the words of God." I love that. Now let me pause here for just a moment. How many people really take the Word of God seriously? I think I know the fundamental church fairly well. I know many wonderful fundamentalists. They are the choicest people. They are my crowd, and I love them. However, there are many who profess to have a love for the Word of God, and they have notebooks and marked-up Bibles to prove it.

The interesting thing is that their own lives are marked up and fouled up, and they are doing nothing about it. They say that they believe the Word of God, but it has no effect upon their lives whatsoever. They do not tremble at the Bible. Like the man of the world, they say, "God is love." And He is—it is wonderful to know that God is love. But He is more than that. Our God is a holy God. He will punish sin, and that is the thing that is troubling Ezra.

Ezra sat astonished "until the evening sacrifice" because of the transgression of those who had been carried away. Ezra was shocked by this. Does this concern us? Really, today, how much are we involved? How much do we believe the Word of God? My Christian friend, it would pay you and me to go to a solitary place and ask ourselves these questions: "Do I *really* believe God's Word? Do I really obey it?" The Lord Jesus said, "If ye love me, keep my commandments" (John 14:15).

And at the evening sacrifice I arose up from my heaviness; and having rent my garment and my mantle, I fell upon my knees, and spread out my hands unto the Lord my God [Ezra 9:5].

What does it mean to spread out your hands to God? It means that you are not concealing anything. It means when you go to God in prayer, friend, that your mind and soul stand absolutely naked before Him. Ezra went to God with his hands outspread. He was holding nothing at all back from God. The apostle Paul put it this way, "I will therefore that men pray every where, lifting up holy hands, without wrath and doubting" (1 Tim. 2:8). We need to remember that in *our* prayer lives.

PRAYER OF EZRA

And said, O my God, I am ashamed and blush to lift up my face to thee, my God: for our iniquities are increased over our head, and our trespass is grown up into the heavens [Ezra 9:6].

Now notice what he is saying. He does not say, "For *their* iniquities are increased over *their* head, and *their* trespass is grown up unto the heavens." He says, "For *our* iniquities are increased over *our* head, and *our* trespass is grown up unto the heavens."

Today it is easy to divorce yourself from the church. The church is in a bad state. I'll grant you that. But, my friend, it is not *their* sin; it is *our* sin. If the church is in apostasy, my friend, then *we* are in apostasy. "Not my brother, not my sister, but it's me, O Lord, standin' in the need of prayer."

Since the days of our fathers have we been in a great trespass unto this day; and for our iniquities have we, our kings, and our priests, been delivered into the hand of the kings of the lands, to the sword, to captivity, and to a spoil, and to confusion of face, as it is this day [Ezra 9:7].

Listen to Ezra. This is a great prayer. He knew what it was to be a captive in a foreign land. He either had been born in captivity or had been taken captive as a little boy, and he knew what it meant. That is why he trembled when he recognized that God would judge him.

My friend, there are many people today being judged of God. I could give instance after instance. Several years ago a man came to me who was eaten up with venereal disease. He said, "I thought I got by with it. Now I am going to have to die from this dirty, filthy disease." And he did. Someone says, "Well, God should have extended mercy to him." Yes, God would have extended mercy to him, but the interesting thing is that this man was guilty. Our God is a holy God and He judges sin. It is too bad that more of us don't tremble at the Word of God.

And now for a little space grace hath been shewed from the Lord our God, to leave us a remnant to escape, and to give us a nail in his holy place, that our God may lighten our eyes, and give us a little reviving in our bondage [Ezra 9:8].

This is a great verse. Ezra says, "We have had just for a little space grace." The seventy years of captivity is over. God has permitted His people to return to their land, and off they go again, following the heathen—doing the very thing that had sent them into captivity in the first place.

Ezra says, "There is just a *remnant* of us." These Jews obeyed enough to return to the land—most of the Jews did not return to the land; those who did were just a remnant.

"To give us a nail in his holy place"—do you know what that "nail" is? That nail is Christ. "My anchor holds within the veil." Do you know why? Because I am nailed there. Christ was nailed on the cross down here that I might be nailed yonder at the throne of God for eternity. Consider what Isaiah 22:22–23 says, "And the key of the house of David will I lay upon his shoulder; so he shall open, and none shall shut; and he shall shut, and none shall open. And I will fasten him as a nail in a sure place; and he shall be for a glorious throne to his father's house." So believers are nailed up there, not on a cross, but in heaven for eternity. You see, a nail is fixed *in a sure place*. What a wonderful illustration this is. The Jews did not lose their salvation, but they sure lost a great deal else including the blessing of God and their reward. Many of us are saved today, but we will get no reward at all.

That He "may lighten our eyes, and give us a little reviving in our bondage." I think this is a true picture of revival. The term *revival* is not actually a Bible word. I have always used this word from the pulpit in the popular sense, which means a spiritual upsurge, with sinners converted en masse, and a new interest in the things of the Spirit. Technically, *revival* means "to recover life, or vigor; return to consciousness." It refers to that which has life, then ebbs down almost to death, has no vitality, and then is revived. Romans 14:9 speaks of Christ's resurrection this way: ". . . Christ both died, and rose, and revived . . ." Obviously the word *revival* must be confined to believers if we are going to be technical. It means that the believer is in a low spiritual condition and is brought back to vitality and power. So here in Ezra's day a real revival is going to take place.

Ezra's prayer continues.

For we were bondmen; yet our God hath not forsaken us in our bondage, but hath extended mercy unto us in the sight of the kings of Persia, to give us a reviving, to set up the house of our God, and to repair the desolations thereof, and to give us a wall in Judah and in Jerusalem [Ezra 9:9].

How wonderful God was to these people. They confessed their sin, and God is going to bless them.

And now, O our God, what shall we say after this? for we have forsaken thy commandments.

Which thou hast commanded by thy servants the prophets, saying, The land, unto which ye go to possess it, is an unclean land with the filthiness of the people of the lands, with their abominations, which have filled it from one end to another with their uncleanness.

Now therefore give not your daughters unto their sons, neither take their daughters unto your sons, nor seek their peace or their wealth for ever: that ye may be strong, and eat the good of the land, and leave it for an inheritance to your children for ever.

And after all that is come upon us for our evil deeds, and for our great trespass, seeing that thou our God hast punished us less than our iniquities deserve, and hast given us such deliverance as this [Ezra 9:10–13].

In other words, Ezra is saying, "We did not get all that was coming to us. We deserved more punishment for our sins than we received."

Should we again break thy commandments, and join in affinity with the people of these abominations? wouldest not thou be angry with us till thou hadst consumed us, so that there should be no remnant nor escaping?

O LORD God of Israel, thou art righteous: for we remain yet escaped, as it is this day: behold, we are before thee in our trespasses: for we cannot stand before thee because of this [Ezra 9:14–15].

Only the mercy of God, the confession of sin, the sacrifice of Christ, and the grace of God could make it possible for Him to save these people, restore and revive them. God is going to do all of these things because of the prayer of Ezra. The remnant that was there will cry out to God for mercy.

When we take that position, God is ready to hear.

REVIVAL UNDER EZRA

After this great prayer meeting, there began a movement of revival. And revival always leads to reformation. When there is true revival, you don't need a fingerprint expert to find the results.

Now when Ezra had prayed, and when he had confessed, weeping and casting himself down before the house of God, there assembled unto him out of Israel a very great congregation of men and women and children: for the people wept very sore [Ezra 10:1].

An intense conviction of sin came over God's people at this particular time, and it was certainly something that was needed.

And Shechaniah the son of Jehiel, one of the sons of Elam, answered and said unto Ezra, We have trespassed against our God, and have taken strange wives of the people of the land: yet now there is hope in Israel concerning this thing [Ezra 10:2].

This man Shechaniah apparently became the mouthpiece for this group of people who recognized their sin and wanted to confess. He came to Ezra and said, "We have trespassed against our God." That is a very candid acknowledgment. He continued,"We have taken strange wives of the people of the land." That, my friend, is nailing it down and dealing with specifics. What they had done was absolutely contrary to the Law of Moses. They had not consulted in this grave matter "that which was written." In other words, they had departed from the Word of God. Now he casts himself upon the mercy of God and says, "Yet now there is hope in Israel concerning this thing."

Now therefore let us make a covenant with our God to put away all the wives, and such as are born of them, according to the counsel of my lord, and of those that tremble at the commandment of our God; and let it be done according to the law [Ezra 10:3].

There were those who now joined in confession who likewise trembled at the commandment of God. That is, they not only read it and studied it; they let the Word of God have its way in their hearts. When the transgression was called to their attention, they confessed it. They did not attempt to rationalize, excuse, or cover over their sin. They came right out and confessed it. They did this according to the Word of God.

Arise; for this matter belongeth unto thee: we also will be with thee: be of good courage, and do it.

Then arose Ezra, and made the chief priests, the Levites, and all Israel, to swear that they should do according to this word. And they sware.

Then Ezra rose up from before the house of God, and went into the chamber of Johanan the son of Eliashib: and when he came thither, he did eat no bread, nor drink water: for he mourned because of the transgression of them that had been carried away [Ezra 10: 4–6].

Breaking the Law of God was a very serious thing. They went before Him with great travail of soul. What everyone went through is rather heart-rending, but the Word of God had been transgressed and the people had to repent.

Friend, that is where revival must begin. First, we must walk in the light of God's Word. When we come to the Word of God, it brings conviction to our hearts. We see that we are coming short of the glory of God. We realize that we are openly transgressing that which God has written. When we go to Him in confession, and there is real repentance, the result will be that God's children will be revived.

Today we are busy preaching repentance to a lost world. I am not sure that God is asking the lost world to repent. He is saying to the world, "Believe on the Lord Jesus Christ, and thou shalt be saved . . ." (Acts 16:31).

When you come to Christ as Savior, something else happens. It happened in Thessalonica. In 1 Thessalonians 1:9 Paul says, "For they themselves shew of us what manner of entering in we had unto you, and how ye turned to God from idols to serve the living and true God." "Turning to God" took priority over "turning from idols." Repentance does not precede faith. Faith goes before and repentance follows—it follows as surely as the night follows day. If it doesn't follow, the faith is not genuine—it isn't saving faith. Repentance is the thing that is so lacking in the church today. Have you ever noticed that in the Bible God asks the church to repent? In the seven letters to the seven churches of Asia Minor recorded in the Book of Revelation God asks all but two of them to repent. God was talking to believers, not to unsaved people.

Personally, I do not agree with these people who are constantly asking the mayor, or governor, or the president to declare a day of prayer. They say, "Let's have a national day of prayer. We need prayer." Oh, my friend, what are you talking about? I cannot believe that Ezra sent out word to the Hittites, the Perizzites, the Canaanites, the Jebusites, the Ammonites, the Moabites, the Egyptians, and the Amorites that they were invited to a great day of prayer. Let's face it—America is a pagan nation. Believers are a minority. This is a day when every minority is being heard except the Bible-believers. I think one could organize a rally of a host of people in our nation for a day of prayer. But what good would it do? God is saying to the lost, "Come to me and be saved through Jesus Christ." He is saying to His church, "Repent. Come back to Me. Come out of your coldness and indifference." The thing that we need today is revival, and a revival will not come without repentance among believers. In Ezra's day God's people were no longer indifferent, you see; but in our day there is indifference in the church.

Lyman Abbot made this statement years ago, "When I was a boy, I heard my father say that if by some miracle God would change every cold, indifferent Christian into ten blatant infidels, the church might well celebrate a day of thanksgiving and praise." The trouble with the church today is that it is filled with cold, indifferent church members—perhaps many of them are not even saved. If revival comes, friend, you are going to see this indifferent crowd either come over on the Lord's side or else they will make it very clear that they belong to the devil.

Ezra went to God in genuine repentance and others are following suit.

> **And they made proclamation throughout Judah and Jerusalem unto all the children of the captivity, that they should gather themselves together unto Jerusalem;**
>
> **And that whosoever would not come within three days, according to the counsel of the princes and the elders, all his substance should be forfeited, and himself separated from the congregation of those that had been carried away [Ezra 10:7–8].**

They were making a real line of separation. They are under the Mosaic Law. In the church today I don't believe you could force the issue as they are doing here. They are removing all of the chaff that they possibly can from the good wheat. It would take about "three days" to come from any section in that land, and this proclamation was directed to all those who had come out of the Babylonian captivity, who had returned to rebuild the city, the walls, and the temple. They were to come together for a time of spiritual refreshing, but repentance must precede it. Those who would not come because they felt that things were not being done the way they wanted them done, or had some other objection, were to be cast out of the congregation.

The church needs housecleaning today. I don't mean taking from the church roll the names of the members who *can't* be located either. What the average church needs to do is get rid of some of the members they *can* locate—those who need to repent but will *not* repent.

Bitterness today is like quinine in a barrel of water. It doesn't take much to make the water bitter. I remember when I was a boy my mother would always tell me when I cut up a chicken, "Be careful and don't break the gall bladder. You'll ruin the whole chicken if you do." She was right. You could spoil the entire fowl if you broke the gall bladder. God wants to get rid of that gall bladder of bitterness in His church. For instance, Hebrews 12:15 says, "Looking diligently lest any man fail of the grace of God; lest any root of bitterness springing up trouble you, and thereby many be defiled." Just a few complainers and critics in the church can absolutely stifle any spiritual movement. Oh, how many lives have been wrecked by bitterness!

> **Then all the men of Judah and Benjamin gathered themselves together unto Jerusalem within three days. It was the ninth month, on the twentieth day of the month; and all the people sat in the street of the house of God, trembling because of this matter, and for the great rain.**
>
> **And Ezra the priest stood up, and said unto them, Ye have transgressed, and have taken strange wives, to increase the trespass of Israel.**
>
> **Now therefore make confession unto the LORD God of your fathers, and do his pleasure: and separate yourselves from the people of the land, and from the strange wives [Ezra 10:9–11].**

In other words, don't just be a hearer of the Word of God but be a doer of the Word also.

We are hearing a great deal today about the need for action in the church, but what the church really needs is to get cleaned up. There needs to be confession. Even a lack of love needs to be confessed. "By this shall all men know that ye are my disciples, if ye have love one to another" (John 13:35).

> **Then all the congregation answered and said with a loud voice, As thou hast said, so must we do [Ezra 10:12].**

What Ezra asked these people to do was a bitter pill to swallow. I am confident that there was a great wrenching of the heart and a great agony of the soul as these people separated themselves from their loved ones.

It is interesting that while they were gathered together quite a rainstorm came up.

But the people are many, and it is a time of much rain, and we are not able to stand without, neither is this a work of one day or two: for we are many that have transgressed in this thing. [Ezra 10:13].

A rainstorm came up and everybody wanted to scatter. Now Ezra had a whole lot of sense. He said, "We don't want to stand out here in all of this rain, especially because of the women and children. Instead of doing this in a slipshod manner, what we want to do is come back another day and do this thing right."

Let now our rulers of all the congregation stand, and let all them which have taken strange wives in our cities come at appointed times, and with them the elders of every city, and the judges thereof, until the fierce wrath of our God for this matter be turned from us [Ezra 10:14].

Ezra wanted things to be done in an orderly way, and this is what they did.

And they gave their hands that they would put away their wives; and being guilty, they offered a ram of the flock for their trespass [Ezra 10:19].

The offering mentioned speaks of the fact that the people are united as one. They are united in this tremendous effort to set things right with God.

Following this verse is a list of those who agreed to put away their foreign wives. They entered into a solemn agreement and pledged to do it.

All these had taken strange wives: and some of them had wives by whom they had children [Ezra 10:44].

This verse tells a sad story, does it not? The sins of the fathers will be visited on the children. We see here just how thoroughly this separation was to be carried out. Ezra was God's man for the hour. For this generation, at least, he helped preserve the testimony of the Jews for the fulfillment of God's plan.

BIBLIOGRAPHY

(Recommended for Further Study)

Darby, J.N. *Synopsis of the Books of the Bible.* Addison, Illinois: Bible Truth Publishers, n.d.

Dennett, Edward. *Ezra and Nehemiah.* Addison, Illinois: Bible Truth Publishers, n.d.

Gaebelein, Arno C. *The Annotated Bible.* 1917. Reprint. Neptune, New Jersey: Loizeaux Brothers, 1970.

Gray, James M. *Synthetic Bible Studies.* Old Tappan, New Jersey: Fleming H. Revell Co., 1906.

Ironside, H.A. *Notes on the Book of Ezra.* Neptune, New Jersey: Loizeaux, n.d.

Jensen, Irving L. *Ezra, Nehemiah, Esther: A Self-Study Guide.* Chicago, Illinois: Moody Press, 1970.

Kelly, William. *Lectures on Ezra and Nehemiah.* Addison, Illinois: Bible Truth Publishers, n.d.

Laney, J. Carl. *Ezra & Nehemiah.* Chicago, Illinois: Moody Press, 1982.

Luck, G. Coleman. *Ezra and Nehemiah.* Chicago, Illinois: Moody Press, 1961.

Sauer, Erich. *The Dawn of World Redemption.* Grand Rapids, Michigan: Wm. B. Eerdmans Publishing Co., 1951. (An excellent Old Testament survey.)

Scroggie, W. Graham. *The Unfolding Drama of Redemption.* Grand Rapids, Michigan: Zondervan Publishing House, 1970. (An excellent survey and outline of the Old Testament.)

Unger, Merrill F. *Unger's Bible Handbook.* Chicago, Illinois: Moody Press, 1966. (A concise commentary on the entire Bible.)

Unger, Merrill F. *Unger's Commentary on the Old Testament.* Vol. 1. Chicago, Illinois: Moody Press, 1981. (A fine summary of each paragraph. Highly recommended.)

The Book of

NEHEMIAH

INTRODUCTION

The use of the first person pronoun in Nehemiah 1:1 gives the impression that Nehemiah was the writer. If Ezra was the writer, he was copying from the journal of Nehemiah. This book, as was true in the Book of Ezra, has copies of letters, decrees, registers, and other documents. The same man wrote both books. The writer perhaps was Ezra. The Books of Ezra and Nehemiah are one in the Hebrew canon. Nehemiah was a layman; Ezra was a priest. In the Book of Ezra the emphasis is upon the rebuilding of the temple; in the Book of Nehemiah the emphasis is upon the rebuilding of the walls of Jerusalem. In Ezra we have the religious aspect of the return; in Nehemiah we have the political aspect of the return. Ezra is a fine representative of the priest and scribe. Nehemiah is a noble representative of the businessman. Nehemiah had an important office in the court of the powerful Persian king, Artaxerxes, but his heart was with God's people and God's program in Jerusalem. The personal note is the main characteristic of the book. I find myself coming to this book again and again because of the kind of a book that it is.

Chronologically this is the last of the historical books. We have come to the end of the line as far as time is concerned. As far as the Jews are concerned, the Old Testament goes no further with their history. The Book of Ezra picks up the thread of the story about seventy years after 2 Chronicles. The seventy years of captivity are over and a remnant returns to the land of Israel. The return under Ezra took place about fifty years after the return of Zerubbabel. Nehemiah returned about fifteen years after Ezra. These figures are approximate and are given to show the stages in the history of Israel after the Captivity. This enables us to see how the "seventy weeks" of Daniel fit into the picture in a normal and reasonable way. The "seventy weeks" of Daniel begin with the Book of Nehemiah (not with Ezra) ". . . from the going forth of the commandment to restore and to build Jerusalem unto the Messiah the Prince shall be seven weeks, and threescore and two weeks. . . ." The background of the events in Nehemiah is ". . . the street shall be built again, and the wall, even in troublous times" (Dan. 9:25).

The following dates, suggested by Sir Robert Anderson, seem to be a satisfactory solution to the problem of the "seventy weeks" of Daniel:

Decree of Cyrus, 536 B.C.—Ezra 1:1–4.

Decree of Artaxerxes, 445 B.C. (twentieth year of his reign)—Nehemiah 2:1–8. "Seventy weeks" begin.

The first "seven weeks" end, 397 B.C.—Malachi. (For details see Sir Robert Anderson's *The Coming Prince*.)

The word *so* occurs thirty-two times. It denotes a man of action and few words. Mark this word in your Bible and notice how this ordinarily unimportant word stands out in this book.

The key verses for this book are: (1) "And it came to pass, when I heard these words, that I sat down and wept, and mourned certain days, and fasted, and prayed before the God of heaven" (Neh. 1:4) and (2) "And I sent messengers unto them, saying, I am doing a great work, so that I cannot come down: why should the work cease, whilst I leave it, and come down to you?" (Neh. 6:3).

OUTLINE

I. Rebuilding the Walls, Chapters 1–7

A. Nehemiah's Prayer for the Remnant at Jerusalem, Chapter 1

B. Nehemiah's Request of the King; Return to Jerusalem; Review of the Ruins of Jerusalem, Chapter 2:1–16

C. Nehemiah's Encouragement to Rebuild the Walls, Chapter 2:17–20

D. Rebuilding the Walls and the Gates, Chapter 3

E. Nehemiah's Response to Opposition, Chapters 4–6
(Wall completed, 6:15)

F. Nehemiah's Register of People, Chapter 7

II. Revival and Reform, Chapters 8–13

A. Great Bible Reading Led by Ezra, Chapter 8

B. Revival—the Result, Chapters 9–10

C. Reform—Another Result, Chapters 11–13

CHAPTER 1

***THEME:** Nehemiah's prayer for the remnant at Jerusalem*

God's chosen people were called to witness against idolatry, but too often they themselves succumbed and became idolaters. God sent them to Babylon, the fountainhead of idolatry, to take the "gold cure." They returned repudiating idolatry. Their restoration was incomplete, however. They were not free from this time on to the time of the Roman Empire. The New Testament opens with them under the rule of Rome.

Three men played important roles in the rebuilding of Jerusalem. There was Zerubbabel, the prince, who represented the political side. Then there was Ezra, the priest, and finally Nehemiah, the layman. The king, the priest, and the prophet actually failed to rebuild the walls of Jerusalem and cleanse the temple, so God raised up Nehemiah, whom we designate a layman. Frankly, it is an unfortunate distinction today to talk about the clergy and the laymen. One is half of the other. We need both.

I started out in the ministry wearing a Prince Albert coat, a winged collar, and a derby hat. One of my friends told me that when I stood behind the pulpit on Sunday morning in my white collar and white shirt, I looked like a mule looking over a whitewashed fence! Then one day, as a young preacher, the realization came to me that I was no different from the men sitting in the pews. I took off all of that garb and wore what the other men were wearing.

I was playing golf one day with some friends. One of the men invited a friend who was an officer in a church. He apparently did not know I was coming. When he saw me, he said, "Oh, my, Dr. McGee is here. Now we are going to have to watch our language." Well, do you know what I did? I called his hand in a hurry. I said, "Now listen, brother. I am no different than you are. If you want to cuss, you cuss. But let us understand one thing: whether I am here or not, *God* hears your language. It does not make any difference whether I hear what you say, or not." There is a false distinction being made today between the clergy and the laity. It is equally important that both of them be in fellowship with God.

It was a layman, though, who rebuilt the walls of Jerusalem and cleansed the temple. I believe that even in this day God can and will raise up a layman to do a great work and put His work on a sure foundation. And it needs rebuilding today. Candidly, I am looking to God to raise up a young man who will not be a product of our seminaries. I have no objection to seminary graduates, but from time to time God raises up men who do not have that background—men like Dwight L. Moody, Billy Sunday, and Billy Graham. We need men like Nehemiah.

Nehemiah believed in watching and working. He also believed in working and praying. Watch and pray, or work and pray, are the words that characterize this man. He had a good government job in Persia. He was cupbearer to the king. He was a good, moral, honest man. He could have remained in Persia, but if he had, he would not have been in the record of God. We would never have heard of him. I want you to notice some of the things that mark out this man as we get acquainted with him. Let me introduce you to Nehemiah, the loyal layman.

NEHEMIAH'S CONCERN FOR THE REMNANT AT JERUSALEM

The first seven chapters of this book deal with the *rebuilding* of the walls. The rest of the book deals with *revival* and *reform.* The first chapter begins with Nehemiah's prayer.

The words of Nehemiah the son of Hachaliah. And it came to pass in the month Chisleu, in the twentieth year, as I was in Shushan the palace,

That Hanani, one of my brethren, came, he and certain men of Judah; and I asked them concerning the Jews that had escaped, which were left of the captivity, and concerning Jerusalem [Neh. 1:1–2].

When Nehemiah speaks of "Jews that had escaped," he is referring to those Jews who had returned to the land. Nehemiah could have returned to the land, but for some reason he did not. He took a job instead. I am not going to criticize him because God uses men like this, and He used Nehemiah.

Notice that this man with an important position had a concern for God's work. He was deeply concerned about God's cause. One day while he was busy going back and forth in the palace, he saw one of his brethren who had just arrived from Jerusalem, who was probably bringing with him a message to the palace. Nehemiah stopped him and asked, "How are things going in the land?" This is the word he received:

And they said unto me, The remnant that are left of the captivity there in the province are in great affliction and reproach: the wall of Jerusalem also is broken down, and the gates thereof are burned with fire [Neh. 1:3].

That is not a very pretty picture. What a pitiful spectacle was God's cause and His people! The Jews were in disrepute because they had failed, and God could not afford to let that happen. Unfortunately, *we* cannot afford to let it happen today either. Nehemiah became extremely concerned about this report, and there are several things he could have said in reply. He could have said, "It's too bad, brethren. Sorry to hear it. I'll put you on my prayer list. God bless you." There are other pious platitudes and Christian clichés he could have given, but he probably did not know about them. The important thing is that Nehemiah was concerned.

NEHEMIAH'S PRAYER

And it came to pass, when I heard these words, that I sat down and wept, and mourned certain days, and fasted, and prayed before the God of heaven [Neh. 1:4].

There are several things I would like to call to your attention in this particular verse. Nehemiah was not indifferent to the sad plight of the people, and neither was he a carping critic. He could have said, "The people should have done this, or they should have done that." Nehemiah was concerned. Looking back at the Book of Ezra, do you remember *his* reaction to the condition of the people? He was a priest and he, too, was concerned. Now here is a layman who is concerned.

Today the cause of Christ is in jeopardy. I wonder if those who criticize and pretend to be interested are really concerned. If the thing you are criticizing doesn't break your heart, stop it! There is too much talk and not enough tears. You are not God's messenger if the message doesn't cause you personal anguish.

While I think that Ezra was an older man, I believe Nehemiah was a younger man. Ezra was probably a little boy at the time of the Captivity, but it is my opinion that Nehemiah had been born in captivity; as had many others. This is the reason, when we were studying Ezra, that I did not criticize these people for remaining in Babylon. Although they were out of the will of God, there were some very godly people who did not return to the land. The apostle Paul tells us in Romans 14:4, "Who art thou that judgest another man's servant? to his own master he standeth or falleth . . ." You and I have no right to judge these people. Always we ought to be careful in judging other believers when we do not know all of the circumstances.

He "sat down and wept"—Nehemiah was on state business, but that did not keep him from sitting down and weeping. Notice that he "mourned certain days, and fasted, and prayed." This was the resource and the recourse of these men. That is what Ezra did, and now also Nehemiah weeps and prays.

Once again I must call your attention to the expression "God of heaven." This expression occurs in the Books of Ezra, Nehemiah, and Daniel. It is a designation of God which is peculiar to these three books. After the fall of Jerusalem and the destruction of Jerusalem, God could no longer be identified with the temple as the One who dwelt between the cherubim. The glory had departed. "Ichabod" was written over the escutcheon of Israel. The Lord God had returned to heaven. For this reason in the postcaptivity books He is "the LORD God of heaven." He did not appear again until one time in Bethlehem when the angel said, "Glory to God in the highest" (Luke 2:14). Christ had come to earth veiled in human flesh. Someday He is coming again. The Lord Jesus Christ Himself said, "And then shall appear the sign of the Son of man in heaven: and then shall all the tribes of the earth mourn, and they shall see the Son of man coming in the clouds of heaven with power and great glory" (Matt. 24:30). I don't *know* what that sign is, but I rather suspect it is the Shekinah glory of God coming back. However, in Nehemiah's day He is the God of heaven, and Nehemiah addresses Him in this way.

This is a great prayer, and there will be another in chapter 9.

And said, I beseech thee, O LORD God of heaven, the great and terrible God, that keepeth covenant and mercy for them that love him and observe his commandments [Neh. 1:5].

Let's pause here just a moment and consider the word *terrible*. It is a word that has been greatly misunderstood and abused. Really and truly, preachers should not be called *Reverend* because it means "terrible." Well, perhaps I am wrong; maybe some of us should be called "The Terrible Mr. So-and-So." Seriously, *Reverend* is a word that should only be applied to God. Someone has expressed it this way:

"Call me Mister, call me friend,
A loving ear to all I lend,
But do not my soul with anguish rend,
PLEASE stop calling me Reverend."
—Author unknown

Reverend was a title given to ministers in the old days when they were held in high regard in the community. That is no longer true, of course. In fact, it is not even true in the church today. There are some people who claim their church is different, but in most churches there is a small group who try to crucify the preacher. However, in the old days when a preacher was called *Reverend*, it was a term of respect, although it was a misnomer. Today I can almost always detect an unsaved man by the way he addresses me. Years ago, when I used to go to a dry cleaning establishment, the young fellow who operated it always called me "Reverend." From the time I walked into his establishment until the time I walked out, he used that term at least twenty times. He really wore it out. He was an unsaved man. He paid little attention to what I was saying when I witnessed to him, but he liked to use the title of Reverend.

God is the reverend God, the One who incites terror. But He is also the God "who keepeth covenant and mercy for them that love him and observe his commandments." He is a God of judgment, but He is also a gracious God.

Let thine ear now be attentive, and thine eyes open, that thou mayest hear the prayer of thy servant, which I pray before thee now, day and night, for the children of Israel thy servants, and confess the sins of the children of Israel, which we have sinned against thee: both I and my father's house have sinned [Neh. 1:6].

Notice Nehemiah's wording in this prayer. Does he say, "I come to confess the sins which *they* have sinned?" No. He confessed the sins "which *we* have sinned against thee: both I and my father's house have sinned." Now this man nails it down: "I am a sinner. My father's house has sinned. The nation has sinned." How many times do we hear that kind of a confession of sin in our churches?

In his prayer Nehemiah made a confession: the failure of the Jews was because of sin. Nehemiah said, "Both I and my father's house have sinned." This man was no self-righteous Pharisaic onlooker.

We have dealt very corruptly against thee, and have not kept the commandments, nor the statutes, nor the judgments, which thou commandedst thy servant Moses [Neh. 1:7].

We can see from this verse that Nehemiah believed God's Word. He rested in it. And he knew God's Word. He was concerned because God's commandments were ignored.

Remember, I beseech thee, the word that thou commandedst thy servant Moses, saying, If ye transgress, I will scatter you abroad among the nations [Neh. 1:8].

Nehemiah not only believed God's Word, he also believed in the return of the Jews to Jerusalem. There are a lot of *preachers* who do not believe that today, which may be the reason God sometimes has to use laymen. God's truth cannot always penetrate those of us who are preachers, but He can sometimes reach a layman.

But if ye turn unto me, and keep my commandments, and do them; though there were of you cast out unto the uttermost part of the heaven, yet will I gather them from thence, and will bring them unto the place that I have chosen to set my name there. [Neh. 1:9].

Nehemiah said to the Lord, "You said that you would scatter us if we disobeyed you, and we have disobeyed. You also said that if we turned and came back to You, that even though we be 'cast out unto the uttermost part of the heaven,' You would bring us back to the land." Nehemiah believed that the Jews would return to the land. He counted on it and that is why he prayed this way.

Now these are thy servants and thy people, whom thou hast redeemed by thy great power, and by thy strong hand.

O LORD, I beseech thee, let now thine ear be attentive to the prayer of thy servant, and to the prayer of thy servants, who desire to fear thy name: and

prosper, I pray thee, thy servant this day, and grant him mercy in the sight of this man. For I was the king's cupbearer [Neh. 1:10–11].

Nehemiah is willing and wants to be used of God. But he is not running ahead of God; he prays about it. He says, "If you want to use me, I am making myself available." When Nehemiah spoke about the king in his prayer, he called him "this man." We will see him going to ask the king if he may return to the land. Nehemiah does not want to run ahead of God, and so he goes to Him first in prayer.

CHAPTER 2

***THEME:** Nehemiah's return to Jerusalem*

NEHEMIAH'S REQUEST TO RETURN TO JERUSALEM

In this chapter we see that Nehemiah requests permission from the king and returns to Jerusalem. He reviews the ruins of the city and encourages the people to build the walls.

And it came to pass in the month Nisan, in the twentieth year of Artaxerxes the king, that wine was before him: and I took up the wine, and gave it unto the king. Now I had not been beforetime sad in his presence [Neh. 2:1].

Notice it is at this particular point where the "seventy weeks" of Daniel begin: "in the twentieth year of Artaxerxes the king." This is an important date in prophecy.

This man Nehemiah is a delightful fellow, as we are going to see. I would have loved to have known him. He is the kind of a layman that you want to get acquainted with. He has a political job—that of cupbearer to the king. His function is to taste anything brought to the king. For example, if a glass of wine is brought to the king, Nehemiah tastes it first. If he suffers no ill effects, then the king will drink the wine. His job as cupbearer is dangerous, as you can see.

The job of cupbearer demanded that Nehemiah be in the king's presence much of the time. Naturally he would become a friend of the king. I think that many times when the king had to make a decision he would ask his cupbearer, "What do you think about this matter?" In time the cupbearer became sort of an advisor, a member of the king's cabinet. Probably because of his job Nehemiah stayed in the land of his captivity, hoping that someday he might be able to use his position to help his people. Maybe that is why he asked his brethren how things were in Jerusalem.

Nehemiah is preparing to make a request of the king, but he is not quite ready. On this particular day he does not feel well. Since he received the bad news about the Jews in the land, he has been fasting, mourning, and praying. I think his eyes were red. He did not look his usual happy self. Never before had he looked sad. Usually he was a bright, cheerful fellow. The king noticed that Nehemiah was not himself.

Wherefore the king said unto me, Why is thy countenance sad, seeing thou art not sick? this is nothing else but sorrow of heart. Then I was very sore afraid [Neh. 2:2].

Nehemiah did not know that his feelings showed. He had tried to conceal the way he felt but apparently was not able to. So the king asked him a point-blank question, "Why are you sad? You are not physically ill, so it must be sorrow of heart. Something is troubling you. Tell me what it is." At the king's question Nehemiah became very much afraid.

And said unto the king, Let the king live for ever: why should not my countenance be sad, when the city, the place of my fathers' sepulchres, lieth waste, and the gates thereof are consumed with fire? [Neh. 2:3].

Nehemiah said, "Let the king live for ever." The cupbearer could always say that wholeheartedly since he tasted what came before the king! He hoped the king would stay in good health, and he hoped he would also.

Then he blurted out what was troubling him, "Why shouldn't I be sad, O king, my master? The city of my fathers and the sepulchers where they are buried lie in waste and the gates are consumed with fire."

Then the king said unto me, For what dost thou make request? So I prayed to the God of heaven [Neh. 2:4].

This is the first verse in this book where the word *so* occurs, but it will occur thirty-two times. Nehemiah uses this word as a shortcut to get around a lot of protocol and flowery verbiage that does not mean anything. You will find that this man gets right to the point. He does not beat around the bush. He said, "So I prayed to the God of heaven"—right in the presence of the king. The king had said to Nehemiah, "You evidently want to make a request of me. What is it that you want to ask me?" So Nehemiah shot up a prayer to the God of heaven. It was a brief prayer and I think it was something like, "Oh Lord, help me say the right thing. I am in a very tight spot!"

And I said unto the king, If it please the king, and if thy servant have found favour in thy sight, that thou wouldest send me unto Judah, unto the city of my fathers' sepulchres, that I may build it [Neh. 2:5].

Nehemiah asked the king to grant him a leave of absence that he might go to Jerusalem to help rebuild it.

And the king said unto me, (the queen also sitting by him,) For how long shall thy journey be? and when wilt thou return? So it pleased the king to send me; and I set him a time [Neh. 2:6].

There is a reason for that parenthetical insertion: "(the queen also sitting by him,)." Not only was Nehemiah a young man, I think he was a handsome young man with a very good personality. I imagine there were times when court business could become quite boring. The king would become involved with some petty political matter and would have to settle it with a great deal of discussion. The queen would become bored and start a conversation with the cupbearer. She might have said, "Where did you go this weekend?" And Nehemiah would say that being a Jew he went to the synagogue on Saturday. Then on Sunday he took a little trip in a boat up the Euphrates River and did a little fishing. The queen and Nehemiah probably had many conversations along this line.

So when Nehemiah asked the king for permission to return to the land, the queen probably nudged the king in the ribs and said to him, "Let him go if that is what he wants to do." The king thought about it for a moment and then asked, "For how long shall thy journey be?" The king probably started to say, "This is a busy season. It is going to be difficult to get along without you, Nehemiah. I don't know if we can spare you or not." About that time the queen nudged him and said, "Let him go." Finally the king said, "How long will this take and when will you return?" Obviously the king liked Nehemiah, too, and he wanted him to come back. At this point Nehemiah could go into detail but he does not. He simply says, "*So* it pleased the king to send me; and I set him a time."

There is a lot of wasted verbiage today. The other day I listened to a television program concerning the work of one of our government committees which was hearing witnesses concerning a certain matter. A certain lawyer was speaking. I listened to him for fifteen minutes—and he could have put his entire testimony in two sentences. He certainly did string it out. He took advantage of the fact that he was appearing before this committee and that he was being televised. He used a great deal of excess verbiage. Nehemiah did not waste words. He got right to the point.

Moreover I said unto the king, If it please the king, let letters be given me to the governors beyond the river, that they may convey me over till I come into Judah [Neh. 2:7].

Nehemiah realized that his trip would be a difficult one through dangerous country. He asked the king for letters of introduction and explanation to the governors along his route so they would give him protection as he traveled through their lands.

And a letter unto Asaph the keeper of the king's forest, that he may give me timber to make beams for the gates of the palace which appertained to the house, and for the wall of the city, and for the house that I shall enter into. And the king granted me, according to the good hand of my God upon me [Neh. 2:8].

Now Nehemiah trusted the Lord, but as a government official he didn't mind asking the king for his official assistance and protection along the route.

NEHEMIAH'S REVIEW OF THE RUINS OF JERUSALEM

Then I came to the governors beyond the river, and gave them the king's letters. Now the king had sent captains of the army and horsemen with me [Neh. 2:9].

It looks as if half the army of Persia accompanied Nehemiah on his journey. God had opened the heart of the king to protect Nehemiah, and he knew that the hand of God was upon him. He went on his journey well protected. You remember that when Ezra had asked the king for permission to return to the land, he wanted to ask the king for protection; but he had been so eloquent in telling the king how God would take care of him and lead him that he was ashamed to ask for an escort. He was afraid the king would say, "Aren't you trusting the Lord?" Nehemiah, however, felt that he had the right to ask for protection because he was a government official.

Friend, God is not going to lead all of us alike. He led Ezra one way, and he led Nehemiah another way. He will lead you one way and He will lead me another way. I made a mistake at the beginning of my ministry by trying to imitate a certain preacher. He was highly successful and a great man of God. One day an elder of my church, who had known me ever since I was fourteen years old, said, "Vernon, I want to have lunch with you." I went to the bank where he was vice president, and from there we went to his club for lunch. All he said to me as we sat there was, "You know, we would rather have an original Vernon McGee than an imitation anybody else." That was all he said and that was all he needed to say. From that day to this I have not tried to imitate anyone. And Lord help the man who would try to imitate me! What a tragic thing it is for one man to try to duplicate another man. God will not lead us alike. Ezra went back to the land with no support whatsoever. Nehemiah returned to the land with half of the Persian army. God will use both ways.

When Sanballat the Horonite, and Tobiah the servant, the Ammonite, heard of it, it grieved them exceedingly that there was come a man to seek the welfare of the children of Israel [Neh. 2:10].

When Nehemiah reached his destination, there was already opposition. There are three fellows we are going to meet. There is Sanballat the Horonite, Tobiah the Ammonite, and Geshem the Arabian, whom we will meet later on. These three men were the enemies of God and His people. They had tried to hinder the building of the temple, and now they want to hinder the rebuilding of the wall. When Nehemiah came with a tremendous entourage of servants and soldiers, everybody in the country heard of it. They wanted to know who in the world he was. They were told that he was cupbearer to the king of Persia, and that he was coming to help the Jews. When that word got around, the enemy was grieved. They didn't like that.

It is always interesting to see how news is received. It usually depends upon who you are whether news is good or not. The gospel is not good news to its enemies. In fact, it is anything but good news.

So I came to Jerusalem, and was there three days [Neh. 2:11].

In this verse we note the word *so* again. At this point Nehemiah could have written two or three chapters about his journey to Jerusalem and the thrilling experiences he had on the way. Instead he simply says, "So I came to Jerusalem." Mark it down every time he uses the word *so*. He is cutting down on a great many words.

And I arose in the night, I and some few men with me; neither told I any man what my God had put in my heart to do at Jerusalem: neither was there any beast with me, save the beast that I rode upon [Neh. 2:12].

After arriving in Jerusalem Nehemiah did not want to stir up undue alarm, so he went out at night under the cover of darkness to make his inspection and see what the real condition was. He had no entourage of servants with him. It was no parade. He was a layman—this is the way a businessman would do it.

And I went out by night by the gate of the valley, even before the dragon well, and to the dung port, and viewed the walls of Jerusalem, which were broken down, and the gates thereof were consumed with fire.

Then I went on to the gate of the fountain, and to the king's pool: but there was no place for the beast that was under me to pass [Neh. 2:13–14].

There was so much debris that Nehemiah could not ride horseback through it. He had to dismount.

Then went I up in the night by the brook, and viewed the wall, and turned back, and entered by the gate of the valley, and so returned [Neh. 2:15].

Nehemiah had circled the entire city. He was finished with his inspection.

And the rulers knew not whither I went, or what I did; neither had I as yet told it to the Jews, nor to the priests, nor to the nobles, nor to the rulers, nor to the rest that did the work [Neh. 2:16].

Nehemiah used caution and good judgment in doing God's work. I love to see certain laymen today who are doing things for God. If I may be personal, we have here in California a group of men who comprise the "Thru the Bible Radio" Board. They meet regularly and they are always a great encouragement to me. I am no businessman and, very candidly, I need advice. It is marvelous what these men do. I just listen to them as they discuss certain things. Every once in a while one of them will take me to lunch and say, "Now look, here is something I think is important as far as the radio ministry is concerned." It is usually something I have never thought of before. Now this man Nehemiah intrigues me—I am anxious to follow his story through and see what action he will take.

NEHEMIAH'S ENCOURAGEMENT TO REBUILD THE WALLS

Now having made the proper survey and evaluation of the work to be done, he called a meeting.

Then said I unto them, Ye see the distress that we are in, how Jerusalem lieth waste, and the gates thereof are burned with fire: come, and let us build up the wall of Jerusalem, that we be no more a reproach.

Then I told them of the hand of my God which was good upon me; as also the king's words that he had spoken unto me. And they said, Let us rise up and build. So they strengthened their hands for this good work [Neh. 2:17–18].

Nehemiah called a meeting of the leaders in the surrounding area of Jerusalem. He told them how God had led. He told them about his leave of absence and why he had come to Jerusalem. He had already made his inspection. He knew what the situation was and he said to the group, "Let's do this job. God is with us." They all responded to his enthusiasm and said, "Let us rise up and build."

Nehemiah was a real leader, a God-inspired leader. The leaders responded to this man. Again here is his familiar word *so*. *"So* they strengthened their hands for this good work." He could have elaborated a great deal and told us how this group gathered together and responded to his leadership, but Nehemiah did not do that. He is a very modest layman who stays in the background.

But when Sanballat the Horonite, and Tobiah the servant, the Ammonite, and Geshem the Arabian, heard it, they laughed us to scorn, and despised us, and said, What is this thing that ye do? will ye rebel against the king? [Neh. 2:19].

Here is the enemy—three men. This is not a nice little trio to have around you, friends. I suppose that every man of God not only has wonderful men around him, but he also has a few men like Sanballat the Horonite, and Tobiah the servant, the Ammonite, and Geshem the Arabian. The enemy will use different methods to try to discourage you. Generally, ridicule is the first method the enemy tries.

When I was converted, I worked in a bank and I had gone the limit into sin, I must confess. I was in grave sin. I shall never forget the reaction when I made the announcement that I was resigning and that the Lord had called me into the ministry. I did not know anyone could be ridiculed like that. I remember how discouraged I was when I left that place. I felt like giving it all up and going back and saying, "Look fellows, I was kidding you. I just want to come back and be one of you again." But I soon found that I was frozen out. I had lost a lot of my so-called friends. It was during the days of prohibition, and they were only interested in drinking rot-gut liquor and running around. I went back to school and, oh, how discouraged I felt. The enemy started out by using ridicule. He doesn't do that to me anymore. That is the first phase of the devil's warfare against you, friends. He will have folks make fun of you as a Christian. At times you will find the going extremely rough. It was true of Nehemiah. The three leading enemies used the weapon of ridicule at first to deter the people from attempting the Herculean project of rebuilding the walls and gates.

Then answered I them, and said unto them, The God of heaven, he will prosper us; therefore we his servants will arise and build: but ye have no portion, nor right, nor memorial in Jerusalem [Neh. 2:20].

Notice what happened. I cannot help but love Nehemiah, and I hope you do too. He said, "Get out of my way. We are going to work. God is with us in this." How wonderful—and God was indeed with them.

CHAPTER 3

***THEME:** Rebuilding the walls and the gates*

This chapter brings us to the rebuilding of the walls and gates. It was one of the greatest building projects ever undertaken. What Nehemiah did was a tremendous thing. It was a wonderful way in which God was moving. You see, God had led Ezra and Zerubbabel back to the land to rebuild the temple. Their task was a different one from Nehemiah's. He was a layman, and his work was to rebuild the walls and gates of Jerusalem. God accomplishes His work in different ways with different men. God always moves like that, friend.

Many of us in the ministry started out trying to imitate someone. Well, it doesn't work. We just have to be ourselves. Have you ever noticed what God can do with one nose, two eyes, one mouth, and two ears? He can make a billion faces, and no two of them will be alike. He certainly can come up with a variety of faces. He also makes an infinite number of fingers and no two fingers are alike, and the fingerprints are all different. God does it like that because He wants each one of us to be himself.

The story of the rebuilding of the walls of Jerusalem is given to us in a most wonderful way. Ten gates tell us the story. It begins with the sheep gate and ends with the sheep gate. Sometimes the question is asked, "Were there other gates in the wall of Jerusalem?" I do not think there were at that time, although there could have been. These ten gates were selected to tell the story of the gospel. They give God's plan of salvation. I have written a booklet entitled *The Gospel in the Gates of Jerusalem,* which goes into more detail concerning these gates.

SHEEP GATE

Then Eliashib the high priest rose up with his brethren the priests, and they builded the sheep gate; they sanctified it, and set up the doors of it; even unto the tower of Meah they sanctified it, unto the tower of Hananeel [Neh. 3:1].

At the sheep gate is where it all began. This is the gate where the Lord Jesus entered into Jerusalem. We have on record one occasion when He came through this gate and came to the pool of Bethesda (John 5:2). Frankly, I think He used the sheep gate to enter Jerusalem every time until His triumphal entry—when He entered through the east gate. There are those who make the mistake of identifying the east gate with the golden gate. I have heard people say that because the east gate is sealed up today, it will not be opened until Jesus Christ comes through it. The east gate is *not* the golden gate; the golden gate is the gate that leads to the temple. That is the gate which will be opened for Him and which will lead Him right into the Holy of Holies.

The sheep gate is the gate through which the animals were brought for sacrifice. This is the gate our Lord used. I think He was acting out, as it were, a walking parable. He was illustrating what John the Baptist said about Him, ". . . Behold the Lamb of God, which taketh away the sin of the world" (John 1: 29b). He is the Lamb of God in His Person and in His work. He takes away the sin of the world. Therefore, the sheep gate symbolizes the cross of Christ. This is where you begin with God. The cross is the *only* place you can begin with God. God does not ask us for anything until we come to Christ and accept Him as Savior. God has only one thing to say to the world and that is, "What will you do with my Son, who died for you?" Not until you answer that question will He ask you about your life and your service. If you turn Him down and you do not want to accept His Son, then He does not ask you for anything. He doesn't want your good works, nor does He want your money. He does not want anything from you. Instead, He has something to give you. His Son *died* for you. It is the sheep gate which sets that concept before us. It all begins at the sheep gate.

And next unto him builded the men of Jericho. And next to them builded Zaccur the son of Imri [Neh. 3:2].

Jericho is the place of the curse, and its men worked right next to the sheep gate. That is interesting to me. The men of Jericho came up to Jerusalem from down in the Jordan valley. They built right next to the sheep gate. If you came around the Mount of Olives on the road to Jericho, you would be at the place where these men worked. The pinnacle of the temple and the temple area is at that spot.

Jericho is the city upon which a curse was pronounced. Joshua said, ". . . Cursed be the man before the LORD, that riseth up and buildeth this city Jericho . . ." (Josh. 6:26). In the days of Ahab there was a man who rebuilt this city, and the curse came upon him and his sons. It was the city of the curse.

You and I live in a world today that has been cursed by sin. I don't have to labor that point—all you have to do is look around you. Man has gotten this world in a mess! Man just does not seem able to solve his problems. There are non-Christian men in high places who are saying that the problems today are beyond the solution which man can offer. We live in a cursed world. Only Christ's death on the cross can remove the judgment of sin from your life and my life, because (Ezek. 18:4 tells us), ". . . the soul that sinneth, it shall die." My friend, that is a judgment on you. It is a judgment on me. Christ can bear that for you because of His death on the cross. If you have not trusted Him, you *can* trust Him now.

FISH GATE

Next we come to the fish gate.

But the fish gate did the sons of Hassenaah build, who also laid the beams thereof, and set up the doors thereof, the locks thereof, and the bars thereof [Neh. 3:3].

It was to this gate that fish were brought in from the Mediterranean Sea and the Jordan River. There were many fish eaters in those days. The fish gate was one place you would not have any problem locating, friends. Your nose would lead you right to it. Now, what does the fish gate symbolize? Well, the Lord Jesus said to the men who followed Him, ". . . I will make you fishers of men" (Matt. 4:19).

After the disciples learned the facts of the gospel, Jesus said to them, "And, behold, I send the promise of my Father upon you: but tarry ye in the city of Jerusalem, until ye be endued with power from on high" (Luke 24:49). That is, don't go yet. Wait until you are baptized by the Holy Spirit, indwelt by the Holy Spirit, regenerated by the Holy Spirit, and then filled by the Holy Spirit. On the day of Pentecost they were filled, and they became fishers of men. Today that is what God is saying to His own. He is not asking any unsaved man to be a fisher of men. How could He? An unsaved man would not know what God is talking about. But God is saying to His own, "I want you to fish for men."

I believe that we are to fish for men in different ways. I disagree with people who insist that those who fish must go from door to door. I don't think every person can do that. I think there are some people who are called to witness a little differently. For example, prayer evangelism is one way of effectively reaching people today. We all have different gifts; God made all of us differently. There are different ways to spread the gospel. However, I am of the opinion that all of us need to go through the fish gate one way or another. You should have a part in getting out the Word of God. Jesus says, "I want you to follow *Me*, and *I'll* make you a fisher of men."

When we come to Nehemiah 3:4, we begin a list of individuals who worked to rebuild the walls. It is wonderful that their names have been recorded in the Book of Life. To read this section is an exercise in pronunciation. Frankly, you cannot be dogmatic about the pronunciation of these names. You can follow a self-pronouncing Bible, but no one can guarantee its accuracy. However, these individuals are known to God. They helped build the walls of Jerusalem. Someday they are going to be rewarded for their labor.

And next unto them the Tekoites repaired; but their nobles put not their necks to the work of their Lord [Neh. 3:5].

These nobles thought they were too good to do this type of work—or perhaps they had some other excuse. You suspect that they had lily-white hands and would not think of lifting stones to repair the walls of Jerusalem. My friends, if you have seen the stones in the walls of Jerusalem, you marvel at the work which individuals must have put forth to build them, and maybe you have a little sympathy for the nobles of the Tekoites. They just would not put their necks to the work. It took a lot of manpower to move those stones. It took a lot of grunting and groaning to build those walls. This work created a lot of sore backs, sore hands, and sore feet. In fact, a person was sore all over from this hard labor. However the nobles were shirkers and fell down on the job.

It is interesting to note that the nobles were right next to the fish gate, which speaks of witnessing. These men were not witnesses for God at all. I don't know about you, but I would not want to be in that group. I would hate to have it reported in the eternal Word of God that I did not do what He called me to do. In our day I am afraid that there are many people in the church who are not doing what God has called them to do. I am talking about saved people, not the unsaved. These Christians are not doing anything. They are not serving God. In Proverbs 11:26 it says, "He that withholdeth corn, the people shall curse him. . . ." Corn represents the Word of God, and it is a terrible thing to hold back the Word of God from those who are hungry. Have you ever stopped to think about that? Read this verse carefully: "He that withholdeth corn, the people shall curse him. . . ." We are also told that there will be certain people in eternity that will rise up and call an individual blessed. I think there will be people in hell that will rise up and curse some folk who are in heaven because they withheld corn from them. Jesus said, "Follow me and I will make you fishers of men." If we are going to be in His will today, somewhere along the line we are going to have to become involved in a movement that is getting out the Word of God to hungry hearts. None of us can do it alone. It must be a team effort.

OLD GATE

Next we come to the third gate that is mentioned. It is the old gate.

Moreover the old gate repaired Jehoiada the son of Paseah, and Meshullam the son of Besodeiah; they laid the beams thereof, and set up the doors thereof, and the locks thereof, and the bars thereof [Neh. 3:6].

I asked a friend the first time we visited the city of Jerusalem and saw the gates, "Which one is the old gate? They all look old to me." The old gate was one that had been there from the very beginning. Jeremiah 6:16 tells us the message this gate has for us: "Thus saith the LORD. Stand ye in the ways, and see, and ask for the old paths, where is the good way, and walk therein, and ye shall find rest for your souls. . . ."

We are living in a day where people are interested in the thing that is new. They must have the latest model automobile, the latest fashion, and the latest thing for the house. One day a man whose fetish was to have the latest style in clothes said to me, "I notice that you are wearing a narrow lapel, and today it is the style to wear a wide lapel." The lapel on a coat does not make any difference to me, but it does make a great deal of difference to many people. Concerning my home, another man said to me, "You have an old place, don't you?" My home is about twenty-five years old, and I still think of it as new. In the south I lived in a house that was one hundred years old, but in Southern California my house is already old. We are living in a day when things are changing radically and rapidly. The conditions under which our grandfathers proposed to our grandmothers were vastly different from those under which young folks in this present day deal with the matter of marriage. Morality is changing. People talk about "new morality," but it was old even in the time of Noah.

It is this constant search for something new that is leading us to frustration. It is the thing that has taken many folks down the garden path to a dead end street with no purpose in life whatsoever. Jeremiah says that we need to ask for the "old paths," because there we will find rest for our souls. Instead of running to psychiatrists and trying this and that new method, what we really need to do is come to the One who says, "Come unto me, all ye that labour and are heavy laden, and I will rest you. Take my yoke upon you, and learn of me; for I am meek and lowly in heart: and ye shall find rest unto your souls. For my yoke is easy, and my burden is light" (Matt. 11:28–30). My friend, in Christ we find rest. The human heart needs something greater than this mechanical, electronic, push-button age in which we live. We need to get back to the old paths.

Next unto him repaired Uzziel the son of Harhaiah, of the goldsmiths [Neh. 3:8a].

Does this impress you as being unusual? The stones in the walls of Jerusalem, as I have said, were tremendous; their weight was enormous. Now goldsmiths were accustomed to sitting at benches and working with little pieces of gold. They were not used to working with large stones. Although it was hard work for them to rebuild the wall, they did it. God took note of that and recorded what the goldsmiths did. In our day there are folks who are making real sacrifices for God and it is difficult for them. Remember, my friend, God takes note of it.

Next unto him also repaired Hananiah the son of one of the apothecaries, and they fortified Jerusalem unto the broad wall [Neh. 3:8b].

An apothecary is a druggist. They are the pill-rollers. They don't make pills any larger than you can swallow; yet these folk were working with great big stones. These men were really rock-and-rollers now! God took note of them also and recorded it in His Word. I like to see people today who are really putting their necks to the work, those who have to grunt and groan in the Lord's work and are really doing something for Him.

I know several pastors, real men of God, who are killing themselves in the work of the Lord. I had a wonderful friend in Southern California who had a heart attack and died. He was a man of God, and he actually killed himself in the work of the Lord. I know of others today who are doing the same thing. I said to a pastor up north, "Look, brother, I know something about what you are going through. You are overworking. You are doing too much. You have to slow down." My friend, if you have a good pastor and he is working too hard, go to him and put your arms around him (I hope that won't give him a heart attack!), and tell him you are praying for him. He may be one of the goldsmiths or the pill-rollers. Tell him not to overwork. Men of God are needed today.

And next unto him repaired Shallum the son of Halohesh, the ruler of the half part of Jerusalem, he and his daughters [Neh. 3:12].

You ought to take note of this. We have the women's liberation movement today, and they had it in Jerusalem during Nehemiah's day. They said, "We are going out and help build the walls of Jerusalem. Men do it. We are going to do it too." Apparently Shallum the son of Halohesh did not have any sons, so his daughters went to work helping him build the walls of Jerusalem. God took note of it and recorded it.

VALLEY GATE

The valley gate repaired Hanun, and the inhabitants of Zanoah; they built it, and set up the doors thereof, the locks thereof, and the bars thereof, and a thousand cubits on the wall unto the dung gate [Neh. 3:13].

The valley gate is the one that led out of the city of Jerusalem down into the valley—it could have been on any side of the city, because you have to go down into a valley to get out of Jerusalem. This is the gate through which many of us are called to go.

When I think of this gate, I think of the valley of the shadow of death. All of us are walking in that valley. David spoke of it in Psalm 23. As you walk down that canyon, it keeps getting narrower and narrower until—if the Lord doesn't come—you will walk out right through that gate.

This gate also has a practical side. It is the gate of humility, the gate of humbleness. God sometimes has to lead us through trials and difficulties in order to teach us some lessons. We are told that faith develops in us different virtues, and one of them is lowliness of mind. In the Epistle to the Colossians it is called ". . . humbleness of mind . . ." (Col. 3:12). This is something that you cannot cultivate in your own human strength.

Humility has to come from the inside. It is the fruit of the Holy Spirit. I am reminded of the man who said to his friend, "I have been trying to be humble and at last I have succeeded." The friend said, "Well, I know you are *proud* of that." The man replied, "I sure am." Humility is not attained by human effort. We have to be humbled by the Spirit of God.

The story is told about a minister in Scotland who while in seminary was the leading student in his class. Once during his student days he was invited to preach in a certain church because of his fine scholastic record. Since he was a star pupil, he entered the pulpit with great pride. When he stood before the congregation to preach, it was confusion. He found out that it was easy to put a sermon on paper in his study, but to get up and deliver it was another thing. He became frightened. He forgot everything he knew. He left the pulpit at the close of the sermon in great shame and humility. A dear little Scottish lady had watched his every action and met him as he left the pulpit. She said, "Young man, if you had only gone into the pulpit as you came down, you would have come down as you went up." God has to put us in the school of humility. Humility is a fruit of the Spirit. The valley gate is one that many of us need to go through.

DUNG GATE

But the dung gate repaired Malchiah the son of Rechab, the ruler of part of Beth-haccerem; he built it, and set up the doors thereof, the locks thereof, and the bars thereof [Neh. 3:14].

This is an important gate for the health of the city, but not much is said about it. Today the dung gate leads to the wailing wall in Jerusalem, but in Nehemiah's day it was located at the southwest angle of Mount Zion. The dung gate was where the filth was carried out, where the garbage was taken away. In 2 Corinthians 7:1 Paul says, "Having therefore these promises, dearly beloved, let us cleanse ourselves from all filthiness of the flesh and spirit, perfecting holiness in the fear of God." Paul dealt with this subject in the Christian life as much as any other. You and I need to recognize that we need to confess our sins to God. Honest confession is the means by which we get out the garbage. "If we confess our sins, he is faithful and just to forgive us our sins, and to cleanse us from all unrighteousness" (1 John 1:9).

GATE OF THE FOUNTAIN

But the gate of the fountain repaired Shallun the son of Colhozeh, the ruler of part of Mizpah; he built it, and covered it, and set up the doors thereof, the locks thereof, and the bars thereof, and the wall of the pool of Siloah by the king's garden, and unto the stairs that go down from the city of David [Neh. 3:15].

I believe that the gate of the fountain refers to what our Lord meant when He said to the woman at the well, "But whosoever drinketh of the water that I shall give him shall never thirst; but the water that I shall give him shall be in him a well of water springing up into everlasting life" (John 4:14).

At the Feast of Tabernacles Christ stood up and said, "He that believeth on me, as the scripture hath said, out of his belly shall flow rivers of living water" (John 7:38). In the next verse John explains His statement: "(But this spake he of the Spirit, which they that believe on him should receive: for the Holy Ghost was not yet given; because that Jesus was not yet glorified.)" (John 7:39). In Romans 8:9 Paul says, "But ye are not in the flesh, but in the Spirit, if so be that the Spirit of God dwell in you. Now if any man have not the Spirit of Christ, he is none of his." The gate of the fountain, therefore, teaches the fact that every believer is indwelt by the Spirit of God, and that he needs an infilling of the Spirit. When a believer is filled with the Spirit, he is not just a well, but a fountain of living water which will gush out to be a blessing to other people. All of us should be a blessing to others in these days in which we live.

WATER GATE

As we read down through this chapter, we come to the seventh gate.

Moreover the Nethinims dwelt in Ophel, unto the place over against the water gate toward the east, and the tower that lieth out [Neh. 3:26].

The water gate was the gate used to bring water into the city. An aqueduct brought some water into the city but not all of it. The remainder was carried in through the water gate.

What does the water gate have to say to us? I believe it symbolizes the Word of God. When we get a little farther along in this book, we will see that it was here that Ezra put up a pulpit. When Ezra erected a pulpit at the water gate, he read from the Word. The place he chose was symbolic; it was no accident. The New Testament makes this clear when it speaks of the washing of water by the Word. The Lord Jesus Christ said, "Now ye are clean through the word which I have spoken unto you" (John 15:3). In His prayer in John 17:17 the Lord said, "Sanctify them through thy truth: thy word is truth." The water gate pictures the Word of God. We are washed by the water of the Word. It is through this gate that we are trying to spread the Word. We all need to be water boys, helping to bring the water to those who are thirsty.

The psalmist asked the question, "Wherewithal shall a young man cleanse his way?" How is he to get clean? "By taking heed thereto according to thy word" (Ps. 119:9). The startling thing about the water gate is that it was not repaired. Apparently when the other gates and walls were torn down, the water gate remained intact. That was unusual. It did not need any repairs at all. Does that tell you anything? The Word of God, friend, does not need any repairs. It is intact.

There are many people today who try to prove that the Bible is the Word of God. There are also those who try to prove that the Bible is *not* God's Word. My ministry at the beginning was an apologetic ministry. I tried to prove that the Bible was the Word of God. I learned, however, that I do not need to prove it; I am to give it out, and the Spirit of God takes care of that. I have already come to the definite, dogmatic conclusion that the Bible is indeed the Word of God. I don't *think* it is—I *know* it is. And I know what it can do for you today. Therefore it does not need my weak support. The Bible will take care of itself.

When I first became a pastor in downtown Los Angeles, California, the late Dr. Bob Shuler was still pastor of the Trinity Methodist Church. He said to me one day, "You don't need to defend the Word of God. It will take care of itself. It is like having a lion in a cage in your backyard. You don't need to have guards to protect the lion from the pussycats in the neighborhood. You just open the door and the lion will take care of himself. He will also take care of the pussycats." The Word of God is like that today. It needs to be given out. It does not need any repair, certainly not my weak repair. All the Lord asks me to do is to give it out.

HORSE GATE

From above the horse gate repaired the priests, every one over against his house [Neh. 3:28].

Now the horse was an animal ridden by a warrior. Zechariah 1:8 speaks of a man riding upon a red horse. Behind him there were red horses, speckled, and white. Revelation 6:4 says, "And there went out another horse that was red: and power was given to him that sat thereon to take peace from the earth, and that they should kill one another: and there was given unto him a great sword." These symbolic horses are powers making war.

The Lord Jesus rode into Jerusalem on a little donkey. He was not meek because He rode upon that animal; it was the animal ridden by kings. It was not considered a humble little animal in that day. Men only rode horses during a time of war. The horse was the symbol of war.

The horse gate speaks of the "soldier service" of the believer today. In Ephesians 2:6 Paul tells us that God has ". . . raised us up together, and made us sit together in the heavenlies in Christ Jesus." That great truth is in the first part of the book. In the second part of Ephesians we are told to ". . . walk worthy of the vocation wherewith ye are called" (Eph. 4:1). Our heads are up in the heavenlies, but our feet are down here on the ground where we have to walk. Not only that, in Ephesians 6:11 we are told to "put on the whole armour of God, that ye may be able to stand against the wiles of the devil." There is a real battle to be fought. It is a spiritual battle. Ephesians 6:12 continues: "For we wrestle not against flesh and blood, but against principalities, against powers, against the rulers of the darkness of this world, against spiritual wickedness in high places." We are not fighting against flesh and blood but against spiritual forces in this battle. As I write this, there is an increasing interest in the Word of God. There are also a great many adversaries. Paul said the same thing in his day: "For a great door and effectual is opened unto me, and there are many adversaries" (1 Cor. 16:9).

I never realized that certain folks were my enemies until I began to give out the Word of God. It is amazing that you can be attacked by certain men who ought to support God's Word. These men claim to be Christians, and you would think that, if they didn't have something good to say, they wouldn't say anything; but they have been very critical of my Bible teaching ministry. Because there are many adversaries, we need to put on the whole armor of God. And we are told to take the sword of the Spirit. The sword of the Spirit is the Word of God. That is the only weapon we want to use.

In 2 Timothy 2:3 Paul said to a young preacher, "Thou therefore endure hardness, as a good soldier of Jesus Christ." This verse speaks of the fact that as believers we are going to have battles to fight. If you are not in a battle today, apparently you are not standing for the Lord, because the battle is waxing hot in many places. If you take a stand for the Lord, somebody is going to try to cut you down. Many of God's children are having a real struggle in this hour in which we live.

EAST GATE

After them repaired Zadok the son of Immer over against his house. After him repaired also Shemaiah the son of

Shechaniah, the keeper of the east gate [Neh. 3:29].

The next gate we come to is the east gate, a gate that fills us with anticipation and excitement. Obviously, this gate was located on the east side of the city. It was the first one that was opened in the morning. The east gate in modern Jerusalem is sealed. There are those who seem to think that it is the gate through which the Lord Jesus Christ will come when He returns to earth. He may do that, but Scripture does not say that He will. Scripture indicates that He will enter through the golden gate, which is not in the wall of the city but in the temple.

Although the east gate is now sealed, it was the first gate opened each morning, because it was facing in the direction of the rising sun. All during the night the watchman was on the wall, walking up and down, making his rounds. Early in the morning he comes around to the east gate and watches the horizon for the first sign of daybreak. Perhaps there were people in the city who were disturbed that night, fearing there might have been an enemy out in the darkness, and they could not sleep. Maybe they paced up and down most of the night. Finally they ask, "Watchman, what of the night? Isn't it ever going to end?" The watchman replies, "Well, it is still dark out there, but the morning is coming." After a while there is that glimmer of light in the eastern horizon. Finally the watchman gives the signal and says, "It is light out here; I can see that there is no enemy. And the sun is coming up." What a sigh of relief goes up from that city!

We as believers ought to be gathered at the "east gate" because there is a glimmer of light on the horizon—the sun may be coming up before long. But before the sun comes up, the Bright and Morning Star will appear. "For the Lord himself shall descend from heaven with a shout, with the voice of the archangel, and with the trump of God: and the dead in Christ shall rise first: Then we which are alive and remain shall be caught up together with them in the clouds, to meet the Lord in the air: and so shall we ever be with the Lord" (1 Thess. 4:16–17). This event is what we call the Rapture. "Caught up" is a translation of the Greek *harpazō*, and one of the synonyms is the word *rapture*. When someone says that the Bible does not teach the Rapture, they are just arguing semantics. The Scripture says that He is going to take His own out of the world before the sun comes up. And there is a little glimmer of light today. I have no date to suggest concerning the time of the Rapture. Unfortunately, there are men today who are saying that between now and A.D. 2000 the Lord will come. I would like to know where they get that idea. They act as if they have a private line to heaven that the rest of us do not have access to. Scripture tells us, however, that our Lord is coming, and I believe that the next event is the Rapture of the church. We ought to be gathered at the east gate my friend, in this day when it is so dark. It is comforting to know that there is a little glimmer of light, and we have a hope.

After him repaired Hananiah the son of Shelemiah, and Hanun the sixth son of Zalaph, another piece. After him repaired Meshullam the son of Berechiah over against his chamber [Neh. 3:30].

This verse is interesting in that all this man Meshullam did was repair the part over against the chamber where he lived. My friend, you may not be able to witness to the *world;* you may not be able to reach your neighborhood; but you can reach your family. You can give the Word of God to your family. It is wonderful to have a saved family, and it is your responsibility to get God's Word to them. One man said to me concerning his family, "I feel I should get them saved." I disagree with that. His business was to see that they heard the gospel. Then their decision was between them and the Lord. Meshullam just repaired over against his chamber. Apparently that was all God expected him to do, and He recorded it.

GATE MIPHKAD

After him repaired Malchiah the goldsmith's son unto the place of the Nethinims, and of the merchants, over against the gate Miphkad, and to the going up of the corner [Neh. 3:31].

What is the gate Miphkad? *Miphkad* means "review" or "registry." When a stranger came to Jerusalem, he had to have a visa—not like those we have today, but he had to stop at this gate and register. It was also a gate of review. When the army had been out fighting a battle and returned, they passed through this gate. It was here that David reviewed his soldiers returning from battle. How he loved them, and how they loved him! Most of them would gladly have laid down their lives for him. When they passed through this arch, David was there to thank his battle-scarred men for their unselfish loyalty and daring.

As we saw in 1 Thessalonians 4, at the time of the Rapture we are going to be caught up to meet the Lord in the air. Some people say, "Oh, that is going to be wonderful." Well, it is. But did you know that after the Rapture we are going to appear before the judgment seat of Christ? "For we must all appear before the judgment seat of Christ; that every one may receive the things done in his body, according to that he hath done, whether it be good or bad" (2 Cor. 5:10).

This is not the same judgment as that at the Great White Throne mentioned in Revelation 20:11–15. Only believers will be present at the judgment seat of Christ, because this judgment does not concern salvation but reward. Believers will receive rewards for things done in the body. You will not be there if you are not saved. You will be rewarded according to what you have done, whether it be good or bad. And Paul says, on the basis of that, "Knowing therefore the terror of the Lord, we persuade men . . ." (2 Cor. 5:11). In effect, Paul says, "I want to keep busy because I am going to have to turn in a report about whether I am working eight hours a day, or if I am giving the Lord sixty minutes in every hour, twenty-four hours every day, seven days a week." Under the Law the Jews only gave God one day, but our Lord says that regardless of what we do, we are to do it unto Him. He does not care if we wash dishes or dig ditches. Someone has said, "You can dig a ditch so straight and true that even God can look it through." And He is going to "look it through" someday, my friend. He is going to take a close look at how you lived down here. That is the picture of the gate Miphkad. David knew his battle-scarred men and what they had done. Every once in a while he would call one out of the ranks and say, "I have a reward for you." There are going to be many unknown Christians who will be called out before the judgment seat of Christ and rewarded. We think of the preachers, the missionaries, the officers of the church, and the Sunday school teachers receiving great rewards, but I think that some of the greatest rewards will go to some of the unknown saints who live for God in this day. Miphkad can be a wonderful gate for you and me to come to someday. The prospect of it should cause us to examine our lives a little more closely.

And between the going up of the corner unto the sheep gate repaired the goldsmiths and the merchants [Neh. 3:32].

We have been through ten gates, and now we are back at the sheep gate. We have been all of the way around the walls of Jerusalem, and we are right back where we started. As you will recall, the sheep gate symbolizes the cross of Christ. We began with the cross of Christ and we end with the cross of Christ. It is Christ's cross that is all important.

As we stand at the sheep gate, I would like to tell you the story of the late Dr. MacKay, the great Scottish preacher who was holding meetings in London. After a service a young man came to him and said, "Dr. MacKay, I would like to speak to you for a moment." Dr. MacKay replied, "Well, I must take the train back to the place where I am staying, but you may walk with me to the train." On the way as they walked, the young man said, "What you say about trusting Christ is not clear to me." Dr. MacKay went over the plan of salvation once again, but the young man said, "I am sorry, but I cannot seem to feel that I understand savingly. It does not seem to get through." The preacher heard his train coming and he asked the young man if he had a Bible. He said, "No, I don't." Dr. MacKay said, "Here is my Bible. Take it and turn to Isaiah 53:6 and read that verse. When you come to the first 'all' you bend down low and go right in there. Then, when you get to the last 'all' stand up straight and you will come out right." So the young man took his Bible and Dr. MacKay rushed down to get his train.

The young man stood there holding the Bible, a little puzzled. He moved over under a street light and turned to Isaiah 53:6. *Now what did he say to do? He said at the first "all" to bend down low.* "All we like sheep have gone astray; we have turned every one to his own way. . . ." The young man thought, *That sure is a picture of me.* He continued to read the verse: ". . . and the LORD hath laid on him the iniquity of us all." He stood there puzzled. *Oh, yes, I am to stand up straight and come out. I see it now. I am to trust Christ. The Lord God has laid all of my sins on Jesus. Now I can stand up straight—He has forgiven me!*

The next evening Dr. Mackay arrived early and sat on the platform looking for the young man. The service started and he had not located him yet. He had his Bible and, after all, Dr. MacKay, being Scottish, was not about to part with that Bible. Finally he saw the young man come in, and Dr. MacKay went to meet him and get his Bible. He said, "Young man, did you do what I said?" The lad replied,

"Yes, I did. I read Isaiah 53:6. I bent down at the first 'all' and stood straight up at the last 'all.'" Dr. MacKay asked, "And what happened?" The lad replied, "I know now that Jesus is my Savior and I have trusted him."

My friend, we begin at the sheep gate, and we come out at the sheep gate. I think that throughout eternity we are going to talk about the sheep gate, where Jesus died over 1900 years ago for your sins and mine.

CHAPTER 4

THEME: *Nehemiah's response to opposition from without*

In the preceding chapter we saw that Nehemiah—an ingenious fellow—used a special strategy to get the wall around Jerusalem built. As we moved around the wall, we saw that different people were allocated a certain section of wall to repair so that the wall was going up all the way around the city at the same time. In this chapter we will see that they managed to build it about halfway up. The enemies found that the weapon of laughter did not stop the work, so now they are going to employ a new method to try to stop the building.

But it came to pass, that when Sanballat heard that we builded the wall, he was wroth, and took great indignation, and mocked the Jews [Neh. 4:1].

Laughing at them hadn't stopped them—the work progressed—so now the enemy will use the weapon of ridicule before others. They mock that which was precious to God but despised by Sanballat.

And he spake before his brethren and the army of Samaria, and said, What do these feeble Jews? will they fortify themselves? will they sacrifice? will they make an end in a day? will they revive the stones out of the heaps of the rubbish which are burned? [Neh. 4:2].

The questions which the enemy asked were pertinent questions. They were questions the children of Israel were asking themselves. They wondered if they would be able to complete the task. Ridicule is one method the enemy will use.

Now Tobiah the Ammonite was by him, and he said, Even that which they build, if a fox go up, he shall even break down their stone wall [Neh. 4:3].

Tobiah the Ammonite—he is a wisecracker—comes through with a sarcastic remark. It had a touch of humor in it, by the way. Now a fox is a very light-footed animal. A fox can walk over ground and not leave much of a track. A fox can run on a wall and not disturb a thing on it. What Tobiah is saying is that these feeble Jews are building a wall that even a light-footed fox would knock down. After all, some of the builders were goldsmiths, druggists, and women. My, how the enemy ridiculed them! Believe me, this was discouraging for these people who had been working so hard.

What is Nehemiah going to do? The resource and the recourse of this man is prayer. Notice what he does.

Hear, O our God; for we are despised: and turn their reproach upon their own head, and give them for a prey in the land of captivity:

And cover not their iniquity, and let not their sin be blotted out from before thee: for they have provoked thee to anger before the builders [Neh. 4:4–5].

These men who tried to hinder the building were God's enemies as well as the Jews' enemies. This is a prayer under the Law. Under the Law, the Jews had a perfect right to ask for justice. They were correct to ask that a righteous judgment be made. God intends to do that, friend; that has never changed.

However, the Lord Jesus Christ has reversed it for those of us who are believers today. Today we are told *not* to pray for revenge. We are definitely told in Ephesians 4:32, "And be ye kind one to another, tenderhearted, forgiving one another, even as God for Christ's sake hath forgiven you." In Romans 12:19 Paul wrote, "Dearly beloved, avenge not yourselves, but rather give place unto wrath: for it is written, Vengeance is mine; I will repay, saith the Lord." There are certain matters that we should turn over to the Lord and He will handle them. If we attempt to handle them, it means that we are not walking by faith.

There are certain things that I think *we* are to take care of. It is quite evident from Scripture that there are times when a rebuke should be given. We find that Paul told the Corinthians that they were to deal with the things in their church that were wrong. Paul told Timothy, "Preach the word; be instant in season, out of season; reprove, rebuke, exhort with all longsuffering and doctrine" (2 Tim. 4:2). *Reprove* means "to convict." *Rebuke* means "to threaten." *Exhort* means "to comfort." The child of God is to use the sword of the Lord, which is the Word of God. That sword needs to be pushed into that thing which is corrupt and wrong in our lives. It is also to be used to apply the balm of Gilead to a broken heart. There are times when a rebuke should be delivered. God help the preacher who is not faithful in that connection. We are living in a day when people grasp to themselves teachers with itching ears. They want a flowery message that just washes itself out into nothing. They don't want to hear a message that deals with their indifference and the sin in their lives. As a result, a great many churches—even some so-called Bible churches—have nothing to offer but that which is sweet. While it is true that there is a lot of Scripture that is sweet, there is some of God's Word that is bitter. Many people feel that the bitter side should not be heard.

Under Law, my friend, the people could pray that justice be brought to pass upon their enemies. We need to remember that those who are the enemies of the people of God are also the enemies of God Himself.

However, the life of God's people is not simply a life of prayer; it also is a walk and a warfare. So what did these people do?

So built we the wall; and all the wall was joined together unto the half thereof: for the people had a mind to work [Neh. 4:6].

Nehemiah ignored the sarcasm of the enemy, prayed to God, and continued to build. So the opposition of ridicule was overcome by the people.

But it came to pass, that when Sanballat, and Tobiah, and the Arabians, and the Ammonites, and the Ashdodites, heard that the walls of Jerusalem were made up, and that the breaches began to be stopped, then they were very wroth [Neh. 4:7].

When the enemy saw that laughing at them and ridiculing them are not going to stop the building of the wall, they begin to move in another direction. They are angry now.

And conspired all of them together to come and to fight against Jerusalem, and to hinder it.

Nevertheless we made our prayer unto our God, and set a watch against them day and night, because of them [Neh. 4:8–9].

Once again we see that prayer is Nehemiah's resource and recourse. His motto is now "pray and watch." "Nevertheless we made our prayer unto our God." It is fine to use pious platitudes when we back them up with something. I know many people who will say, "Let us pray about it." Have you ever heard someone say that? What I want to know is, what are you going to do after you pray? When I was a pastor, I asked a man to do something. He said, "Well, I will pray about it." I replied, "Wait a minute. If that is your way of saying no to me, say it right now to my face, and I will find someone else to do it. I don't think you need to pray about this matter. Either you can do it or you can't do it. Either you will or you won't. Which is it?" To tell the truth, he wouldn't do it. He was just putting me off, and our conversation enabled me to find someone else for the job. There are many people today who simply mouth pious platitudes.

Nehemiah could have uttered a pious platitude. He could have said, "We are trusting the Lord. We won't do anything." That is the easy way out. That is what many people are doing today. They say they are trusting the Lord, but what are they doing about it? If you really trust the Lord, you will be doing something. Nehemiah knew that the enemy was plotting to come against him, so he set a watch. This is what God expected him to do, of course.

Not only was there trouble without; there was trouble within.

And Judah said, The strength of the bearers of burdens is decayed, and there is much rubbish: so that we are not able to build the wall [Neh. 4:10].

This is the time to be careful, because the Devil can hurt you most severely from the inside. One of Satan's greatest weapons against God's people is discouragement.

I received a letter some time ago from a young missionary couple serving in the jungles of South America. It was their first term of service, and they were very discouraged. From their letter it sounded as though they were ready to come home. They said, "You do not know what it means to us to listen to your radio program late at night down here in this foreign land, among people whose language we do not yet understand." The Devil, of course, was using his weapon of discouragement.

We, too, were discouraged and were ready to take our program off that particular station in South America. Then the Lord undertook in a marvelous way, and we were able to continue broadcasting the program. We were so glad, because we know the Bible teaching is an encouragement to these young folk. Oh, how wonderful the Lord is to us, friend! The Devil uses discouragement in all our lives.

And our adversaries said, They shall not know, neither see, till we come in the midst among them, and slay them, and cause the work to cease.

And it came to pass, that when the Jews which dwelt by them came, they said unto us ten times, From all places whence ye shall return unto us they will be upon you [Neh. 4:11–12].

The enemy took advantage of the Jews' discouragement, and they planned a surprise attack. "We are going to take them when they are not looking for us."

What will be Nehemiah's strategy against a surprise attack?

Therefore set I in the lower places behind the wall, and on the higher places, I even set the people after their families, with their swords, their spears, and their bows [Neh. 4:13].

Nehemiah put every man in the position where he could defend his own family, which made him more comfortable when he was building, of course. With his family at home, some distance away from him, a builder did not know whether or not they were safe. So Nehemiah put them with their families and armed them well.

And I looked, and rose up, and said unto the nobles, and to the rulers, and to the rest of the people, Be not ye afraid of them: remember the Lord, which is great and terrible, and fight for your brethren, your sons, and your daughters, your wives, and your houses [Neh. 4:14].

"Remember the Lord" was to be their motto, their rallying cry. As you may remember in the Spanish-American War, our nation's battle cry was "Remember the Maine." In World War I it was "Remember the Lusitania." In World War II it was "Remember Pearl Harbor." Napoleon always reminded his soldiers of some past victory to stir them up to fight. When Paul the apostle wrote his swan song to a young preacher named Timothy, he gave him a rallying cry. The correct translation of 2 Timothy 2:8 is, "Remember Jesus Christ!" That is the rallying cry of believers today. "Remember the Lord" was the rallying cry for the Jews in Nehemiah's day.

And it came to pass, when our enemies heard that it was known unto us, and God had brought their counsel to nought, that we returned all of us to the wall, every one unto his work [Neh. 4:15].

The Jews could go back to work now. The enemy had retired. They found they could not surprise the Jews.

Nehemiah is an ingenious fellow. He still has more strategy. I like him—I wish I had him around today.

And it came to pass from that time forth, that the half of my servants wrought in the work, and the other half of them held both the spears, the shields, and the bows, and the habergeons; and the rulers were behind all the house of Judah.

They which builded on the wall, and they that bare burdens, with those that laded, every one with one of his hands wrought in the work, and with the other hand held a weapon [Neh. 4: 16–17].

I love this. Each builder had a trowel in one hand with which to build, and in the other hand he carried a sword with which to defend himself. These two weapons or instruments should be in the hands of believers today. The trowel represents the fact that believers should build themselves up in the most holy faith. That is for the inside.

I disagree with folks who say that when a

person is saved he should jump right in and start witnessing. I really don't think new converts ought to be used in a ministry. They first need to learn from experience that Jesus saves and keeps and satisfies. It is wonderful to hear that So-and-So was saved yesterday, or last week; but let us hear from him in a year or two years from today to see if he has been built up in the faith. You see, we need to be built up. The trowel needs to be in our hand. Also we need to hold the sword of the Spirit. That is also important. The sword of the Spirit is the Word of God with which we defend ourselves. We need the trowel in one hand and the sword in the other.

Spurgeon put out a magazine years ago called *The Sword and the Trowel*—I think it is still in existence. I was in Spurgeon's church some time ago and stood in his pulpit. What a great man of God he was, and an example of one who believed that you ought to hold the trowel in one hand and the sword in the other.

For the builders, every one had his sword girded by his side, and so builded. And he that sounded the trumpet was by me.

And I said unto the nobles, and to the rulers, and to the rest of the people, The work is great and large, and we are separated upon the wall, one far from another.

In what place therefore ye hear the sound of the trumpet, resort ye thither unto us: our God shall fight for us [Neh. 4:18–20].

Nehemiah said, "I will watch. When you hear the trumpet, come to that spot, and we will meet the enemy head on."

So we laboured in the work: and half of them held the spears from the rising of the morning till the stars appeared [Neh. 4:21].

I don't know what union these men belonged to, but they certainly worked longer than eight hours. They worked from the rising of the sun until the stars appeared in the sky. Believe me, they were tired and weary in the work of the Lord.

Likewise at the same time said I unto the people, Let every one with his servant lodge within Jerusalem, that in the night they may be a guard to us, and labour on the day [Neh. 4:22].

To men who had come from far away places, like Jericho, Nehemiah said, "Stay close by, because we want you to be ready to guard at night."

So neither I, nor my brethren, nor my servants, nor the men of the guard which followed me, none of us put off our clothes, saving that every one put them off for washing [Neh. 4:23].

I was just about ready to say to Nehemiah, "Boy, I'll bet you got dirty during all that time." But Nehemiah says, "Of course when we took a bath we took off our clothes." (You see, there is humor in the Bible, friend. Even in a crisis like this, the Lord inserted a little humor.) Otherwise they never removed their clothes—day or night. They were on guard all of the time. Oh, to be so clothed today with the armor of God!

There are trying times ahead. Real difficulty is going to arise which will cause Nehemiah to become angry and which almost disrupted the work of the Lord.

CHAPTER 5

***THEME:** Nehemiah's response to opposition from within*

While engaged in this important project of rebuilding the walls of Jerusalem, Nehemiah has been met by opposition in many forms. My, the Devil is subtle. First the enemy laughed at the Jews. Then the enemy ridiculed them. Finally there was open opposition. It was so intense that Nehemiah had his builders put a trowel in one hand and a sword in the other hand while they worked on the wall. Nehemiah and his associates worked so hard that they did not take their clothes off except to bathe.

Now we see opposition coming from within. This is where the Devil strikes his greatest blow. In the history of the church we have seen that when the Devil could not destroy the church by persecution, the next thing he did was to join it! The Devil had already caused discouragement among the Jews, and now he goes a step farther and causes conflict within.

And there was a great cry of the people and of their wives against their brethren the Jews.

For there were that said, We, our sons, and our daughters, are many: therefore we take up corn for them, that we may eat, and live.

Some also there were that said, We have mortgaged our lands, vineyards, and houses, that we might buy corn, because of the dearth.

There were also that said, We have borrowed money for the king's tribute, and that upon our lands and vineyards [Neh. 5:1–4].

Human nature really does not change. Even though we are living today in an electronic, mechanical, technological, and space age, problems are about the same as those during Nehemiah's day. I think that all of our technical devices merely multiply our problems and make them very thorny and difficult to solve. Because the Jews were so busy building the walls, they did not have the opportunity to carry on their personal business. They had to buy corn—food for their families, and in doing so they had to mortgage their property. Some of them had to mortgage their property in order to pay their taxes—taxes were high in that day. They were borrowing money from their own brethren.

Yet now our flesh is as the flesh of our brethren, our children as their children: and, lo, we bring into bondage our sons and our daughters to be servants, and some of our daughters are brought unto bondage already: neither is it in our power to redeem them; for other men have our lands and vineyards [Neh. 5:5].

For a long time this problem had been growing, but up to this time Nehemiah did not know about it. These folks wanted to build the walls of Jerusalem, so they very quietly mortgaged their property to their brethren. There were those who were in the lending business, you see.

The foes outside had not been able to harm as long as there was love and harmony within, but now there is conflict. This problem had also come into the early church, you remember. Ananias and Sapphira had conspired to deceive their brethren and were judged by God with sudden death. Their conspiracy had to do with money. I do not know why money is such a temptation, but it is.

I am well acquainted with a church that has been giving out a false financial statement for some time. The old bromide "figures don't lie, but liars will figure" is still true. There is a certain way that even a CPA can present a financial statement that looks good, but in reality the whole truth has not been told. That happens in many churches today. That is the way the Devil gets into churches. I have always noticed that he comes in this way. This is what Nehemiah had to deal with.

The Scripture gives us some advice in Philippians 1:27–28: "Only let your conversation be as it becometh the gospel of Christ: that whether I come and see you, or else be absent, I may hear of your affairs, that ye stand fast in one spirit, with one mind striving together for the faith of the gospel; And in nothing terrified by your adversaries: which is to them an evident token of perdition, but to you of salvation, and that of God." The word *conversation* in this passage means "your way of life." Paul says, "You let harmony be inside. Be honest in your dealings. Don't give false reports or belittle a brother. Tell the truth. When you tell the truth, it will produce harmony." Good old practical James had something to say about this subject, too, in James 3:16, which says, "For where envying and strife is, there is confusion and every evil work." That is what happened with Ananias and Sapphira. They lied about their dealings with the church and brought in confusion. In Nehemiah's day some Jews had borrowed money. When they couldn't pay back the money, they actually had to sell their sons and daughters into slavery. It was only for a certain period of time, but long enough to wreck their lives in some cases. Those who had borrowed money were charged interest. We always think of "usury" as excessive interest, but it really means regular interest. The interesting thing is, though it might be legitimate in the business world today to charge interest, it was not legal for the children of Israel to do it. God said that the Jews were not to charge their brethren interest.

Up to this point Nehemiah has kept his cool. He has been able to go right along with his people and be patient with them, but now Nehemiah is angry.

And I was very angry when I heard their cry and these words [Neh. 5:6].

Nehemiah was not just a little angry, he was *very* angry.

Then I consulted with myself, and I rebuked the nobles, and the rulers, and said unto them, Ye exact usury, every one of his brother. And I set a great assembly against them [Neh. 5:7].

"Then I consulted with myself"—this is something for him to decide; so he thinks the matter through.

And I said unto them, We after our ability have redeemed our brethren the Jews, which were sold unto the heathen; and will ye even sell your brethren? or shall they be sold unto us? Then held they their peace, and found nothing to answer [Neh. 5:8].

Nehemiah openly rebuked the nobles and the rulers for their actions. Nehemiah exposed those who had done wrong in the presence of the group, which is the right thing to do when such a thing occurs. Also, the church congregation should be warned if there are those in it who are not being honest in their dealings and are moving in an underhanded way. Evil should be brought out into the open.

Nehemiah exposed the underhanded dealings of his brethren. He was angry. Somebody says, "You should not get angry." Paul says, "Be ye angry, and sin not . . ." in Ephesians 4:26. It depends upon the *reason* for your anger. If you become angry because of your own personal welfare, it is wrong. If you become angry because God's program, God's glory, and God's name are being hurt, then you can "be angry and sin not." Nehemiah was not quiet about the sin he uncovered. He did not acquiesce. He was not passive. He spoke right out.

We ought to be stirred up to a righteous anger when we see something wrong in the church. We should not mollycoddle the wrongdoer and shut our eyes to his sin. Many people say, "We just don't want to disturb things." You don't? My friend, you had better do something because the Devil has moved in on you, and he will divide you. We need courage today. We need conviction. The church no longer has a good name in the world, and the world is passing it by. The spiritual movement that is emerging is largely outside the organized church. Christians have been playing church. The controlling group in the church has been having a good time, but they are not reaching the lost, and the world is passing by uninterested.

A preacher in the North said to me, "It makes me angry to think that you cannot reach out and touch the lost today because they know about the hypocrisy, the pious platitudes, and the dishonesty inside the church." But there are those in the world who are longing to know the truth. They want to know if we are being honest in what we have to say. Some of the brethren deal with wrongs in the church by sweeping them under the rug with the excuse that they want to maintain a "Christian" attitude by being sweet and nice. That's not acting like a Christian—it is acting like a *coward!*

Nehemiah brought the sin of his brethren right out into the open and nobody was able to answer him. They had to keep quiet while he was there, but they will cause all the trouble they can. They are also going to cause Nehemiah a lot of trouble when he goes back to the palace in Shushan. Nevertheless, he rebuilt the walls of Jerusalem, and he served God in his day and generation.

Also I said, it is not good that ye do: ought ye not to walk in the fear of our God because of the reproach of the heathen our enemies? [Neh. 5:9].

Christ is a reproach today in the world. Is He a reproach because of the conduct of the church? Because of the conduct of believers? Because of the conduct of you and me? This is a question we need to ask ourselves. Nehemiah said, "Look, you are causing the enemy to blaspheme because of what you are doing!"

I likewise, and my brethren and my servants, might exact of them money and corn: I pray you, let us leave off this usury [Neh. 5:10].

Nehemiah said, "I was in a position where I could have benefited financially." This was the real test of Nehemiah. He did not use his position for gain. In our society the grasping person is after the last farthing. Many a man is putting the dollar ahead of God. You can put a dime so close to your eye that you cannot see even the sun. There are many folks looking at the world like that.

Restore, I pray you, to them, even this day, their lands, their vineyards, their oliveyards, and their houses, also the hundredth part of the money, and of the corn, the wine, and the oil, that ye exact of them [Neh. 5:11].

Nehemiah appealed to the wealthy Jews to restore what they had collected and not to collect any more payments.

Then said they, We will restore them, and will require nothing of them; so will we do as thou sayest. Then I called the priests, and took an oath of them, that they should do according to this promise [Neh. 5:12].

I love this fellow Nehemiah. He says, "I don't believe your verbal promises. I want you to sign on the dotted line." Although they were *God's* people, He knew better than to take them at their word. They had to put their oath in writing.

I think one of the biggest mistakes I ever made in the ministry was to believe some Christians. I hate to say that, but I say it from experience. We should be able to trust the word of a Christian. An outstanding Christian businessman—whom I know to be honest—said to me, "McGee, I have gotten to the place where I don't even like to do business with Christians. I would much rather do business with the man in the world because I automatically watch him. But the Christian—I assume he will be honest, but that is not always the case."

Nehemiah was a practical man. He said, "All right, you have promised to return what you have taken. I don't believe you. Sign on the dotted line. That is what I want you to do."

Also I shook my lap, and said, So God shake out every man from his house, and from his labour, that performeth not this promise, even thus be he shaken out, and emptied. And all the congregation said, Amen, and praised the LORD. And the people did according to this promise [Neh. 5:13].

I think that if something as strong as this statement of Nehemiah's were read from the pulpit in our day, the congregation would say, "Amen." It takes just one bad apple to spoil the whole barrel of apples. One skunk in a field full of cats will give them all a bad name. It would be well to mark out the man who is causing trouble, to get the bad apple out of the barrel, and remove the skunk from the field of cats. This is what Nehemiah did. He actually pronounced a curse upon them. What a picturesque scene! What a dramatic scene! Nehemiah "shook out his lap." Remember that he was a government official and wore a uniform. He shook out his long robe in front of the crowd and said, "This is the way God will shake you out, and I will shake you out, if you don't make your promise good." That is the way to talk to people like this! To the Galatians (5:12) Paul could say, "I would they were even cut off which trouble you." He wished the legalizers would be absolutely *cut off* because of the damage they were doing to the Galatian believers. This is strong language!

Now we will be given a glimpse of the personal life of Nehemiah.

Moreover from the time that I was appointed to be their governor in the land of Judah, from the twentieth year even unto the two and thirtieth year of Artaxerxes the king, that is, twelve years, I and my brethren have not eaten the bread of the governor [Neh. 5:14].

He had a right to draw a salary, but he did not.

But the former governors that had been before me were chargeable unto the people, and had taken of them bread and wine, beside forty shekels of silver; yea, even their servants bare rule over the people: but so did not I, because of the fear of God [Neh. 5:15].

The governors before Nehemiah received their salaries, but Nehemiah chose not to accept a salary. I love this man!

Yea, also I continued in the work of this wall, neither bought we any land: and all my servants were gathered thither unto the work [Neh. 5:16].

Nehemiah did not go into the real estate business. He stayed out of land speculation. He gained no mortgages on land by lending money or grain. He did not take anything on the side.

Moreover there were at my table an hundred and fifty of the Jews and rulers, beside those that came unto us from among the heathen that are about us [Neh. 5:17].

He regularly entertained one hundred fifty table guests. He also entertained Jews from surrounding nations who had come to live in the city but had not yet found a place to live. Apparently he did all of this at his own expense. He was different from the other governors.

Now that which was prepared for me daily was one ox and six choice sheep; also fowls were prepared for me, and once in ten days store of all sorts of wine: yet for all this required not I the bread of the governor, because the bondage was heavy upon this people [Neh. 5:18].

He did not demand the governor's food allowance, because he had a heart for his hardworking brethren.

Think upon me, my God, for good, according to all that I have done for this people [Neh. 5:19].

He was a wonderful man. His concern was for his people, but they would forget him. It is a sad thing, but many a famous person has learned that the world forgets. People have short memories. But Nehemiah asked God to remember him. He said, "Think upon me, my God." How wonderful to know that, while God does not remember our sins, He will always remember our good works. And He even records them in a book!

CHAPTER 6

***THEME:** Wall finished in spite of crafty opposition*

We have seen that Nehemiah encountered just about every form of opposition imaginable in rebuilding the walls of Jerusalem. Satan has thrown in his pathway many things from his bag of tricks to cause him to stumble and fall and fail in his endeavor. Satan does the same thing to us today, only many times in our experience he succeeds and we fail. God does not want us to fail. In fact, He has made every arrangement so that we do not need to fail—yet we do. But Nehemiah did not fail.

In this chapter we find that the wall is about finished.

Now it came to pass, when Sanballat, and Tobiah, and Geshem the Arabian, and the rest of our enemies, heard that I had builded the wall, and that there was no breach left therein; (though at that time I had not set up the doors upon the gates;) [Neh. 6:1].

Notice the honesty of this man. He adds, "Though at that time I had not set up the doors upon the gates." Nehemiah is like Nathanael because there is no guile in him whatsoever—he is not being subtle or clever. Unfortunately, there are many people in their church work who don't tell you everything they should tell you about certain matters. Many times their reports are not full and complete. They are slanted. They are built up and filled in, and the entire truth is not told.

I have always appreciated honesty in my doctor. The first thing he told me when he suspected that I had cancer was, "Dr. McGee, I am going to tell you the truth because, if I don't, you won't have confidence in me." From that day to this, he has laid it on the line. When there didn't seem to be any hope for me, he told me the plain facts. He did not attempt to paint a rosy picture. He did not attempt to cover up. He told it like it was. I have always appreciated it. Honesty is something that is badly needed in business, in social gatherings, and in the church. Of course we should not be blunt or crude. If you are introduced to a lady, you don't have to tell her that she is beautiful if she is not. You can't kid her anyway—I think she knows. We simply need to be more honest in our dealings with one another.

Now when the enemy, Sanballat, Tobiah, Geshem, and others hear that the wall is completed, Nehemiah honestly admits the report is a bit exaggerated. The gates are not set up. The honesty of Nehemiah is a tremendous thing. He tells it like it is.

That Sanballat and Geshem sent unto me, saying, Come, let us meet together in some one of the villages in the plain of Ono. But they thought to do me mischief.

And I sent messengers unto them, saying, I am doing a great work, so that I cannot come down: why should the work cease, whilst I leave it, and come down to you? [Neh. 6:2–3].

The enemies now reverse their tactics. Since they could not stop the work, they now propose to get together with Nehemiah and work out a compromise. Their intention is not to promote the welfare of Nehemiah. This is the old satanic method of "When you can't fight them, join them." Today it is called the ecumenical movement.

The place they were going to meet was on the plain of Ono. Nehemiah properly turned down their invitation. He said, "Oh, no," to Ono because "they thought to do me mischief." They were plotting against him, probably planning to slay him. There was no use going into great detail with the enemy; he simply sent messengers to them, saying, "I am doing a great work, so that I cannot come down." The enemy wanted to compromise, but Nehemiah said, "No!"

There are those in the church today who want to compromise. They feel that you are bigoted and dogmatic if you don't meet with them and try to work out a compromise. I quit meeting with folks like that a long time ago. Today I meet only with those who want to meet around the person of Christ. You would be amazed at some of the churches in which I have held meetings. Although I am in total disagreement with the organizations and some of their doctrines, I will meet with anybody around the person of Christ, but I am not prepared to meet with the enemy at all.

Looking back a few years, I believe William Jennings Bryan made a big mistake in meeting Clarence Darrow in Cleveland, Tennessee, to debate the subject of evolution. I think Bryan walked all over Darrow. Any unbiased person who reads the debate will have to come to the conclusion that Bryan was on the winning side, but I believe that the very fact that he met with Darrow was wrong. It was really a losing battle, and it has certainly been demonstrated since then that it was. You cannot win over an enemy by meeting with him like that. That is my conviction.

Although I am an ordained minister, I don't belong to any denomination or organization. As a result, I can meet with any person or group who believes the Word of God, believes in the deity of Christ, and believes that He died for our sins—regardless of the label they use. It makes no difference to me. But I do not meet with the enemy. Nehemiah was doing a good work, and he did not have time to come down and waste his time with the enemy. God's people do not need to compromise. Nehemiah had an uncompromising attitude, and I admire him for it.

Yet they sent unto me four times after this sort: and I answered them after the same manner.

Then sent Sanballat his servant unto me in like manner the fifth time with an open letter in hand [Neh. 6:4–5].

The enemy was persistent. He always is. Did they really want to be friendly and compromise with Nehemiah? The fact of the matter is that Nehemiah's presence was desperately needed in Jerusalem in order to complete the building of the wall. The letter from the enemy was couched in polite language, but it was a hook with bait on it. Notice that it contained a threat.

Wherein was written, It is reported among the heathen, and Gashmu saith it, that thou and the Jews think to rebel: for which cause thou buildest the wall, that thou mayest be their king, according to these words [Neh. 6:6].

Old Gashmu is ever with us. He is the fellow who is the worst gossip of all. I have discovered that sometimes the worst gossip is a man and not a woman.

This letter—accusing Nehemiah of attempting to rebel against Persia and set up a separate state—was made public, either by being posted or by being read aloud. It was designed to discourage those who were working on the wall. It accused Nehemiah of wanting to become king.

And thou hast also appointed prophets to preach of thee at Jerusalem, saying, There is a king in Judah: and now shall it be reported to the king according to these words. Come now therefore, and let us take counsel together [Neh. 6:7].

Not only did they accuse him of claiming kingship. They also accused him of hiring prophets to support what he said! These were awful things to circulate about Nehemiah. The letter indicated that they wanted to find out if these things were really true because they were going to report it to the king. They are exerting pressure on Nehemiah to meet with them.

Then I sent unto him, saying, There are no such things done as thou sayest, but thou feignest them out of thine own heart [Neh. 6:8].

Nehemiah's reaction to the enemy was, "You actually did not hear the things you are accusing me of; you made them up yourself." This was a nice way of calling them liars.

For they all made us afraid, saying, Their hands shall be weakened from the work, that it be not done. Now therefore, O God, strengthen my hands [Neh. 6:9].

In facing this problem, Nehemiah went to the Lord. He said, "The enemy is doing this to weaken me and to hinder Your work. Strengthen my hands."

Afterward I came unto the house of Shemaiah the son of Delaiah the son of Mehetabeel, who was shut up; and he said, Let us meet together in the house of God, within the temple, and let us shut the doors of the temple: for they will come to slay thee; yea, in the night will they come to slay thee.

And I said, Should such a man as I flee? and who is there, that, being as I am, would go into the temple to save his life? I will not go in [Neh. 6:10–11].

Shemaiah, a false prophet, pretends to have a great interest in Nehemiah's safety. He says he wants to reveal a plot against the governor's life. The temple was the only place where Nehemiah would be safe. He is asking him to do a very cowardly thing. What he did not reckon on was Nehemiah's spiritual insight.

And, lo, I perceived that God had not sent him; but that he pronounced this prophecy against me: for Tobiah and Sanballat had hired him.

Therefore was he hired, that I should be afraid, and do so, and sin, and that they might have matter for an evil report, that they might reproach me.

My God, think thou upon Tobiah and Sanballat according to these their works, and on the prophetess Noadiah, and the rest of the prophets, that would have put me in fear [Neh. 6:12–14].

Nehemiah is in the thick of plots and schemes to destroy him. Well, he dealt with this crowd that pretended to be his friends, but he is still in a difficult spot. He is caught between a rock and a hard place. He turns around and finds himself in the middle of another plot, but he turns to God. The land was once again cursed with false prophets. It seems that they were the most determined enemies of God's servants.

So the wall was finished in the twenty and fifth day of the month Elul, in fifty and two days [Neh. 6:15].

Without fanfare of trumpets, great ceremony, or ribbon cutting, the wall is finished.

And it came to pass, that when all our enemies heard thereof, and all the heathen that were about us saw these things, they were much cast down in their own eyes: for they perceived that this work was wrought of our God [Neh. 6:16].

The work was finished in fifty-two days. Only God could have done this through them. But even though the wall is now completed, there is still danger.

Moreover in those days the nobles of Judah sent many letters unto Tobiah, and the letters of Tobiah came unto them.

For there were many in Judah sworn unto him, because he was the son in law of Shechaniah the son of Arah; and his son Johanan had taken the daughter of Meshullam the son of Berechiah.

Also they reported his good deeds before me, and uttered my words to him.

And Tobiah sent letters to put me in fear [Neh. 6:17–19].

The enemy still persists in his opposition by circulating letters to the nobles of Judah. Tobiah had evidently married a daughter of one of the nobles! All of this time there was this playing "footsie" with the enemies of God. Tobiah had a "telephone" right into the walls of Jerusalem so that everything Nehemiah did or said was reported to Tobiah. Also, "they reported his good deeds before me." That is, these kinfolk by marriage would come to Nehemiah and say, "Nehemiah, you are too hard on Tobiah! He is really a lovely gentleman." Then they would begin to tell of his good works. "And uttered my words to him"—they were acting as liaison officers, which means they were a bunch of tattletales. Everything Nehemiah would say, and all that went on in Jerusalem, was reported to Tobiah. And "Tobiah sent letters to put me in fear." Tobiah would respond with threatening letters.

CHAPTER 7

***THEME:** Nehemiah's register of the people*

As we begin this chapter, we see that the wall has been completed. Now the people begin to protect the city of Jerusalem. Many of the homes have already been built, but inside the city there is still much work to be done. They are still clearing out the debris. It is necessary to protect the city because the enemy that tried to thwart and hinder the rebuilding of the walls would now like to destroy the city.

Now it came to pass, when the wall was built, and I had set up the doors, and the porters and the singers and the Levites were appointed [Neh. 7:1].

After the wall was finished, Nehemiah set the doors at the different gates, and then he appointed these men to protect the city. The *porters* were the watchmen. They were the ones who took care of the wall. They were on guard duty all around the wall, letting those on the inside know what was going on outside. If an enemy or some danger approached, they would sound the alarm. They watched both day and night—it was a twenty-four-hour job. The standards for this job were high, but we will find that some of the rules that were set up were not enforced as they should have been. The guards of the wall were not to be indifferent to who came and went inside the city walls.

At this point I want to say something that I trust will not be misunderstood. We are told today that we are not to be indifferent to those who come and go in our fellowship, because we are not to fellowship with *all* who are professing Christians. Notice what Paul says in 1 Corinthians 5:11: "But now I have written unto you not to keep company, if any man that is called a brother be a fornicator, or covetous, or an idolater, or a railer, or a drunkard, or an extortioner; with such an one no not to eat." Today, although we are to give doctrine top priority—for instance, we cannot make those who deny the inerrancy of Scripture our brothers and fellowship with them in worship—Paul is not dealing with doctrine when he says we are not to keep company with one who is a fornicator. He is talking about that man or woman in the church who will not deal with that sin in his or her life. Fellowship has been based on doctrine. We break fellowship with those who do not agree with us on doctrinal issues. But Paul is stating here that *conduct* is a basis for breaking fellowship—as well as doctrine.

There was a preacher in Southern California who got into trouble on a morals charge. He moved to another area and the same thing happened. Yet the people in his new church had been warned about him. They had been willing to overlook his sin because his doctrine was right. His conduct about wrecked the church—in fact, it almost wrecked two churches. We seem to have a lopsided view. We emphasize doctrine, and that is as it should be; but what about morals? When Paul writes not to keep company with a brother who is a fornicator or covetous, he is not referring to doctrine. What about a man who is money hungry? What about a man who is not honest in his dealings? Are we to have fellowship with him?

Let us also understand that breaking fellowship with another believer on a point of doctrine does not mean that we are to sit in judgment upon him. To a young preacher Paul writes: "Nevertheless the foundation of God standeth sure, having this seal, the Lord knoweth them that are his. And, Let every one that nameth the name of Christ depart from iniquity" (2 Tim. 2:19). You don't know and I don't know who are really God's children, but God knows His own. You and I are not called upon to carry a crusade against them, because God will judge them. We are just to break fellowship with them; we are not to sit in judgment upon them. The point is that we as believers are to be on our guard. An apt motto for us is: Eternal vigilance is the price of liberty.

In addition to appointing porters to guard the city of Jerusalem, Nehemiah appointed singers. I am not in that group, I can assure you. In the next chapter we are going to find Nehemiah saying, "The joy of the LORD is your strength." The spirit of praise is the spirit of power. This means that we should be a rejoicing group of folk, but joy is often absent from the contemporary church. It is not made up of a happy group of people. Oh, they will laugh at a good story and enjoy a banquet, but Bible study is not a joy to them. If you could stand where I have stood for many years, you would see how apparent this is in the faces of the congregation. The troublemakers in the church are generally the ones who do not enjoy Bible study.

In Ephesians 5:18–19 Paul describes the mark of a Spirit-filled Christian when he says, "And be not drunk with wine, wherein is excess; but be filled with the Spirit; Speaking to yourselves in psalms and hymns and spiritual songs, singing and making melody in your heart to the Lord." Although I can speak, I can't sing. However, I can sing in my heart. If I have any music in me that is where it is—it has never come out. But my heart does sing at times, and I often long to be able to sing with my voice also.

The word *psalms* in this verse means "to praise." Oh, how sweet is the name of Jesus. The word *hymn* means "to ascribe perfection to Deity." Holy, holy, holy, is the Lord of hosts. This is what we are to sing about—how wonderful He is! This will bring joy into your life.

I was sitting in the study of a fellow pastor some time ago and noticed this motto on his wall: "Joy is the flag that is flown in the heart when the Master is in residence." When you are walking in the will of God, and you are in the center of His will, and you are having fellowship with Him, you will have joy in your life. How wonderful it is!

Having porters and singers made for a great city, but that is not all. Levites were also appointed. They were ministers. God calls ministers. Proverbs 18:16 says, "A man's gift maketh room for him, and bringeth him before great men." How true that is. If God has called you to be a minister, He will make room for you. That is, He will give you a place to serve.

That I gave my brother Hanani, and Hananiah the ruler of the palace, charge over Jerusalem: for he was a faithful man, and feared God above many [Neh. 7:2].

Hanani was not Nehemiah's blood brother. You will recall, at the beginning of the Book of Nehemiah, that while he was serving in the court of Artaxerxes one of his brethren from Jerusalem came and told him about the condition of the Remnant that had returned. He was one of Nehemiah's fellow-Israelites rather than a blood brother. Hanani apparently was one of the leaders in Jerusalem, and it had been he who informed Nehemiah as to the conditions in Jerusalem, as we read in chapter 1. So Nehemiah already knew this man. That is why he said, "I gave my brother Hanani, and Hananiah the ruler of the palace, charge over Jerusalem. . . ." Did Hanani receive this position because he was an educated man and had been to seminary? Is that the way your Bible reads? Well, mine does not read that way either. He was one of the men placed in charge over Jerusalem because he "was a faithful man, and feared God above many." He was "faithful," not "educated."

I wish I could get this point over to our seminary students today. Now don't misunderstand what I am about to say. We need an educated ministry. The desire for an educated ministry was the origin of our school system in the United States. Education is necessary, but it is possible to go to seed in that direction. There are many men in the ministry who lack character—yet they are *educated.* Someone has made the statement, "You can even educate a fool." That is true, and there are many educated fools in this world, not only in the ministry but everywhere else. But the thing that God wants is *faithfulness.* In 1 Corinthians 4:2 Paul says, "Moreover it is required in stewards, that a man be found faithful." Can your pastor depend on you? Can your fellow Christian depend on you? Are you faithful? Education is profitable *if* you are faithful. It is not worth anything if you are not faithful.

And I said unto them, Let not the gates of Jerusalem be opened until the sun be hot; and while they stand by, let them shut the doors, and bar them: and appoint watches of the inhabitants of Jerusalem, every one in his watch, and every one to be over against his house [Neh. 7:3].

Each entrance to the city was to be watched during the day. At night, when anything could happen, all were to maintain watchfulness. Each one was to watch at least his own household. So God holds *us* responsible for at least our own households. The Lord Jesus Christ said, "And what I say unto you I say unto all, Watch" (Mark. 13:37). That should be the attitude of each believer.

Now the city was large and great: but the people were few therein, and the houses were not builded [Neh. 7:4].

Not all of the building inside was completed at this time. It was possible that a man might become interested in building his own house and forget to watch. The whole spirit of building the walls and gates had been with the trowel in one hand and the sword in the other. My, how we need both of them in the Lord's work today!

The remainder of this chapter is a genealogical record.

And my God put into mine heart to gather together the nobles, and the rulers, and the people, that they might be reckoned by genealogy. And I found a register of the genealogy of them which came up at the first, and found written therein,

These are the children of the province, that went up out of the captivity, of those that had been carried away, whom Nebuchadnezzar the king of Babylon had carried away, and came again to Jerusalem and to Judah, every one unto his city;

Who came with Zerubbabel, Jeshua, Nehemiah, Azariah, Raamiah, Nahamani, Mordecai, Bilshan, Mispereth, Bigvai, Nehum, Baanah. The number, I say, of the men of the people of Israel was this [Neh. 7:5–7].

This is the same genealogy as found in Ezra, the second chapter. Why in the world would God waste so much printer's ink giving us the same genealogy again? I will tell you why. The Word of God says, ". . . the righteous shall be in everlasting remembrance" (Ps. 112:6). God says, "I know these folks and I want *you* to know that I know them." He has listed their names in one place, then made a carbon copy. I have been told that in some of the bureaus in Washington they make fifteen copies of everything, and God has His carbon copies also. It is as though God says, "You may not find these names interesting, but I do. These are My folk." This genealogy is just a leaf out of God's memorial book. There are quite a few genealogies found in Scripture. In Genesis 49 the twelve tribes are listed. In 2 Samuel 23 we find the list of David's mighty men. The first few chapters of 1 Chronicles are lists of names. Nehemiah 3 gives us another listing. Romans 16 is made up of a roster of names. Hebrews 11 also lists those who were faithful. These are just names to us, but God remembers each person and records his name in the Lamb's Book of Life.

The children of Azgad, two thousand three hundred twenty and two [Neh. 7:17].

Who in the world was Azgad? He was a man who was carried away in the Babylonian captivity. During the seventy years, plus a few more, his family had been multiplying. There were 2,322 descendants and each one of them could say, "I am related to Azgad." When one was challenged to prove he was an Israelite, he could say, "Azgad was my great-great-great-great-great grandfather. I know who I am."

There are people today who say, "Well, I *think* I am a child of God. I *hope* I am a child of God." My friend, you can *know* that you are a child of God. First John 5:12 says, "He that hath the Son hath life; and he that hath not the Son of God hath not life." If you have trusted the Lord Jesus Christ as your Savior, you have Him and you have life. If you don't believe what He says, then you are calling Him a liar. If you have put your faith in Christ, you have *life* on the authority of God's Word. And God has written it down. The son of Azgad could say, "I know who I am. Look here, my name is written down."

And these were they which went up also from Tel-melah, Tel-haresha, Cherub, Addon, and Immer: but they could not shew their father's house, nor their seed, whether they were of Israel [Neh. 7:61].

There were those who could not prove they were Israelites. They said, "We think we are Israelites. We hope we are. We try to be." Thinking, hoping, and trying to be Israelites did not make them such. It did not help them. They had to *know* who they were. When they could not show their genealogy, they were put out.

These sought their register among those that were reckoned by genealogy, but it was not found: therefore were they, as polluted, put from the priesthood [Neh. 7:64].

They could not declare their genealogy. You not only need to be saved, you need to *know* it, my friend.

And the Tirshatha said unto them, that they should not eat of the most holy things, till there stood up a priest with Urim and Thummim [Neh. 7:65].

The discerning of the priesthood in that day was by the Urim and the Thummim in the breastplate of the priest. It was the way in which the high priest ascertained God's will. It was God's provision in that day, but today we determine God's will through His Word. And it tells us how we can have eternal life.

So the priests, and the Levites, and the porters, and the singers, and some of the people, and the Nethinims, and all Israel, dwelt in their cities; and when the seventh month came, the children of Israel were in their cities [Neh. 7:73].

This is the last verse of the chapter. The children of Israel are back in the land now. Under the leadership of Nehemiah a tremendous work has been done. But his work is not finished. There is more to do.

CHAPTER 8

***THEME:** Great Bible reading led by Ezra*

In the previous chapter we saw that, after Nehemiah had made adequate preparations to guard the city, he appointed singers. He wanted Jerusalem to be filled with the joy of the Lord. Then he conducted a great Bible reading, which was essential to revival.

And all the people gathered themselves together as one man into the street that was before the water gate; and they spake unto Ezra the scribe to bring the book of the law of Moses, which the LORD had commanded to Israel [Neh. 8:1].

Ezra is called to bring forth the book of the Law of Moses. There is going to be a great Bible reading.

And Ezra the priest brought the law before the congregation both of men and women, and all that could hear with understanding, upon the first day of the seventh month [Neh. 8:2].

Notice that only those who could "hear with understanding" gathered. That means there must have been a nursery for the crying babies. Maybe Nehemiah took care of them, I don't know; but proper preparation was made so that those gathered would be able to concentrate on what was being read.

And he read therein before the street that was before the water gate from the morning until midday, before the men and the women, and those that could understand; and the ears of all the people were attentive unto the book of the law [Neh. 8:3].

I don't know where I could find a congregation who would listen to me read from the Bible from "morning until midday"—I always had trouble getting them to listen for forty-five minutes. Their impression of my sermons was similar to that of the two little old ladies who were walking out of church one Sunday morning. One of them said, "My, that preacher certainly preaches a long time." Her friend replied, "No, he really doesn't preach a long time, it just *seems* like a long time!" To most people forty-five minute sermons seem like a long time. These Israelites who gathered to hear God's Word read were really interested, however. They had been in captivity for seventy years and had never before heard the Word of God. It was a new experience for them.

And Ezra the scribe stood upon a pulpit of wood, which they had made for the purpose; and beside him stood Mattithiah, and Shema, and Anaiah, and Urijah, and Hilkiah, and Maaseiah, on his right hand; and on his left hand, Pedaiah, and Mishael, and Malchiah, and Hashum, and Hashbadana, Zechariah, and Meshullam [Neh. 8:4].

With Ezra stood these thirteen men.

And Ezra opened the book in the sight of all the people; (for he was above all the people;) and when he opened it, all the people stood up [Neh. 8:5].

When Ezra opened God's Word, everyone stood up, and they remained standing throughout the reading. While they listened from morn to midday they did not have soft–cushioned pews upon which to sit.

First of all there was praise to God.

And Ezra blessed the LORD, the great God. And all the people answered, Amen, Amen, with lifting up their hands: and they bowed their heads, and worshipped the LORD with their faces to the ground [Neh. 8:6].

This means that the people went down on all fours and touched the ground with their foreheads. That is the way they worshiped in that day. "And Ezra blessed the LORD, the great God."

Also Jeshua, and Bani, and Sherebiah, Jamin, Akkub, Shabbethai, Hodijah, Maaseiah, Kelita, Azariah, Jozabad, Hanan, Pelaiah, and the Levites, caused the people to understand the law: and the people stood in their place [Neh. 8:7].

Here is another list of very important individuals. These are the men who will explain God's Word to the assembled people.

So they read in the book in the law of God distinctly, and gave the sense, and caused them to understand the reading [Neh. 8:8].

This great assembly of all the people was gathered by the water gate inside the walls of Jerusalem. The men mentioned in verse 7 were stationed throughout the crowd. Ezra, the scribe, would read a certain portion of the Law and then he would stop while each of these men stationed out in the congregation would ask his group, "Did you understand what was read?" Probably most of them nodded in the affirmative. Maybe some of them raised their hands and said, "We do not quite understand what that means." So the man assigned to his group would explain that portion of the Law to them. Then Ezra would read another section of the Law. Then he would stop while the people would ask questions, and their teacher would answer them.

I wonder what would happen if we had a great Bible reading in our churches today. Someone could stand up and read God's Word. You could have people stationed throughout the congregation to explain any questions that might arise from what was read. Suppose the first chapter of Ephesians was read. You would not have to read very far before a real problem would appear. Ephesians 1:4 says, "According as he hath chosen us in him before the foundation of the world . . . ." This would raise questions right away. What does Paul mean? Is he teaching the doctrine of election? What is the doctrine of election? Perhaps a great Bible reading in our churches would lead to revival. This one in the Book of Nehemiah did.

The reading of the Law, and the asking and answering of questions caused the people to understand the Law. They stood in their places and, when something came up that they did not quite understand, they would have it clarified. I personally believe that the entire Bible should be taught in this way, and that every unclear verse should be explained. I do not agree with this business of taking a text and preaching the gospel from it. That is the reason there has been such a lack of interest in the Word of God. I am not sure but what it is handling the Bible deceitfully to take a text or a theme, then launch out into the deep with no thought of ever coming back to the Scriptures to explain them. I believe God intends for us to read the Bible and attempt to explain it as we go along.

There is another lesson in Nehemiah 8:8. There are many methods used in preaching. There is the psychological approach, and the scholarly approach, and many go off on other tangents. A dear saint said to a president of a seminary that she was listening to me teach the Bible by explaining it verse by verse. He replied in a very casual manner, "Well, that is one way of doing it, I guess, but it certainly is not the scholarly and proper way to preach." Well, that is the way the Lord is leading me to do it, and I believe it is the scriptural method. Here it is: "They read in the book of the law of God distinctly, and gave the sense, and caused them to understand the reading." We need to understand what God is saying in His Word.

I have occasion to speak in many places, and I have heard the Scriptures read in just about every way imaginable. Every now and then some brother gets up and reads the Word with great emphasis. He reads it as if it is the Word of *God*. But too often some fellow gets up and ducks his head as he reads so that nobody can hear him past the third pew. Or else he mumbles the words. Nehemiah 8:8 says that the law was read *distinctly*. That is how God wanted it done. Ezra and the other men did not have a course in homiletics or public speaking, but they *believed* it was the Word of God, and they *read* it like it was the Word of God. It is my understanding that this is the way God expects us to conduct a church service. I don't care how loud the soloist sings, or how sweetly the organist plays, or how flowery the message, if the Bible is not read distinctly, and the sense of it is not given so that the people understand, the service is of no avail whatsoever. God wants understanding to come from the reading of His Word.

And Nehemiah, which is the Tirshatha, and Ezra the priest the scribe, and the Levites that taught the people, said unto all the people, This day is holy unto the LORD your God; mourn not, nor weep. For all the people wept, when they heard the words of the law [Neh. 8:9].

Many of these people had never before heard the Word of God. The clear reading and teaching of the Law caused them to be convicted of sin. It caused a great emotional outburst and the tears of repentance to flow. Possibly it also caused them to weep for joy because they were so moved.

Then he said unto them, Go your way, eat the fat, and drink the sweet, and send portions unto them for whom nothing is prepared: for this day is holy unto our LORD: neither be ye sorry; for the joy of the LORD is your strength [Neh. 8:10].

This is social service for you. This is the social gospel. My friend, if the Word of God means something to you and you get something from it, it will make you want to go out and do something nice for someone. It will also make you want to do something for God.

They tell a whimsical story in California which is a switch from the boy scout doing his good deed by helping an old lady across the street. They say that in one of these retirement areas for senior citizens someone came up with a new type of vitamin which was so effective a little old lady helped two boy scouts across the street! My friend, I tell you, the Word of God is a vitamin that will make you do a good turn for someone.

"Send portions unto them for whom nothing is prepared." They were to do something for the poor. "Neither be ye sorry"—rather they were to rejoice because the joy of the Lord was to be their strength. In Philippians 4:13 Paul said to believers, "I can do all things through Christ which strengtheneth me." Then in Philippians 4:4 he said, "Rejoice in the Lord alway; and again I say, Rejoice." Paul was telling believers that the very source of power was "joy." The secret is prayer, but the source of power is joy. The Word of God should make you joyful. That is one reason why I feel there is something wrong if a church service does not make you happy and bless your heart.

For over a period of twenty-one years in downtown Los Angeles, California, we had the privilege of having what was said to be the largest midweek service in America. Anywhere from 1,500 to 2,500 people attended the class. After the service I followed the custom of going out on the front porch and shaking hands with the folk as they were leaving. I could always tell whether the Bible study had been a blessing or not. Sometimes folk would come out and sort of mumble as they shook my hand. I could tell right away that it had not been a blessing to them. Then others would be radiant as they shook my hand, and say, "Oh, I am rejoicing in the Lord." And I would know that the Bible study had accomplished its purpose.

The Word of God is supposed to bring you joy. That is one of the reasons John wrote his first epistle. In 1 John 1:4 he says, "And these things write we unto you, that your joy may be full." God doesn't want you to have a little fun; He wants you to have a whole lot of fun reading and studying His Word. Studying the Bible ought to bring joy into your life. If it doesn't, face up to it, friend; something is radically wrong with you. You ought to go to God in prayer and say, "Lord, I want your Word to bring joy into my life. Whatever cloud there is, I want it removed that I may experience the joy of the Lord when I study the Word." That will make church-going a really happy affair.

Have you ever seen a crowd going to a football game? My, it is like a holiday, with all of the rejoicing that goes on. Have you ever watched people coming into church on a Sunday morning? Boy, what a duty! What a burden! There are lots of folks with burdens, but the burdens should be lifted in the service. People should come out of the service with joy in their hearts.

And all the people went their way to eat, and to drink, and to send portions, and to make great mirth, because they had understood the words that were declared unto them [Neh. 8:12].

I hope this Bible study makes you happy. I read three letters recently. One was from a discouraged missionary to whom the Word of God is bringing joy. Another concerned a home which was about to fall apart. The Word of God brought joy. The third letter was from a man who had bitterness in his heart against me. He apparently was influenced by some people who are my enemies, but the Word of God began to work in his life. The Bible can have an effect on all of us if we will let it.

And on the second day were gathered together the chief of the fathers of all the people, the priests, and the Levites, unto Ezra the scribe, even to understand the words of the law [Neh. 8:13].

The initial study of God's Law caused many of the leaders to come to Ezra the following day for more instruction. During Bible conferences I am not much impressed when someone says to me on Sunday night, "This has been a great day. I have been greatly blessed." I look for them on Monday night, and if they don't come, I wonder if they were sincere on Sunday night.

And they found written in the law which the LORD had commanded by Moses, that the children of Israel should dwell in booths in the feast of the seventh month:

And that they should publish and proclaim in all their cities, and in Jerusalem, Go forth unto the mount, and fetch olive branches, and pine branches, and myrtle branches, and palm branches, and branches of thick trees, to make booths, as it is written.

So the people went forth, and brought them, and made themselves booths, every one upon the roof of his house, and in their courts, and in the courts of the house of God, and in the street of the water gate, and in the street of the gate of Ephraim [Neh. 8:14–16].

This is a celebration of the Feast of Tabernacles. The dwelling in booths was to be a reminder to them of the fatherly care and protection of God while Israel was journeying from Egypt to Canaan.

Here in Nehemiah's day they are obeying the Law that had been read to them. They had heard the Word of God and are doing what it commanded. My friend, it is one thing to read and study the Bible and have it bring joy to you, but that joy will end unless you obey what you have read and let it have its way with you.

In the following chapter we will see that the result of this great Bible reading was revival.

CHAPTERS 9–10

THEME: *Prayer and revival*

You will recall that while studying the Book of Ezra I mentioned that several books contain a great ninth chapter. Ezra chapter 9, Nehemiah chapter 9, and Daniel chapter 9—all have to do with the subject of revival.

Now let us be clear about what is meant by the word *revival.* It is a word that is greatly misunderstood. It means "to recover life and vigor." It also means "to return to consciousness." It refers to that which has life which ebbs away, sometimes even to death, where there is no vitality, and then it revives. Paul speaks about the resurrection of Christ in Romans 14:9. He says that Christ *revived.* "For to this end Christ both died, and rose, and revived, that he might be Lord both of the dead and living." This is a good use of the term *revival.*

Obviously our use of the word *revival* is confined to believers. It refers to believers in a poor spiritual state who were brought back to vitality and power. *Revival* is used that way in this chapter. However, I am sure that many of you have discovered that this term has been broadened in its meaning to refer to people coming to Christ. Actually one is dependent upon the other. You can never have a period of soul-winning unless God's people are revived.

In this chapter we will see a period of revival which followed the reading of the Word of God. This reading probably went on for quite a period—how long I do not know. Ezra the scribe read from the pulpit by the water gate, and the people wept and mourned. Having never heard it before, they were bound to show emotion at the reading of God's Word. It had a tremendous effect upon the people at the time, and it led them to do certain things. They recognized how far short they had fallen from the standard God had set for them. We also saw in the Book of Ezra that it had an effect on Ezra himself. We need to recognize that there cannot be any revival apart from the Word of God. As I have mentioned, Dwight L. Moody thought the next revival that would come after his day would be a revival of God's Word. I wish our contemporary evangelists would pay more attention to teaching the Bible rather than to methods, sentiment, emotional appeals, and the "bigness" which is not necessarily a token of revival.

Notice what God did for these people.

Now in the twenty and fourth day of this month the children of Israel were assembled with fasting, and with sackclothes, and earth upon them.

And the seed of Israel separated themselves from all strangers, and stood and confessed their sins, and the iniquities of their fathers [Neh. 9:1–2].

They confessed their sins—their own and the sins of their fathers.

And they stood up in their place, and read in the book of the law of the LORD their God one fourth part of the day; and another fourth part they confessed, and worshipped the LORD their God [Neh. 9:3].

The Word of God revealed to them their sinfulness. Fasting, sackcloth, and ashes demonstrated their sincerity. Confession and worship followed.

In this day the younger generation is very critical of my generation, and rightly so. If they are returning to God's Word, they will lose their critical attitude and start confessing how much *we* have failed; but they will first confess their own sins.

You and I are in no position to confess anything until we confess our own sins. If you don't feel that you have any sins to confess, my friend, you need to come to the Word of God. The children of Israel read the Law for one-fourth of the day; then they did something about what they had read—they confessed their sins. You cannot bring God down to your level. Many people try to do that. Neither can you reach that state of perfection that will raise you to God's level. If you say that you have, then you deceive yourself. *I* didn't say that; the *Bible* says it: "If we say that we have no sin, we deceive ourselves, and the truth is not in us. If we confess our sins, he is faithful and just to forgive us our sins, and to cleanse us from all unrighteousness" (1 John 1:8–9). If you read the Word of God, you will see that you are a sinner. When you recognize that fact, you will want to confess your sins.

Confession means to agree with God's Word instead of offering excuses or attempting to rationalize our actions. Confession is calling what we are doing or thinking exactly what it is: *sin.* When we do that we have confessed our sins, and God is faithful and just to forgive us. You will recall that in the Upper Room Jesus washed the feet of His disciples. That is what He is doing today at God's right hand in heaven. He cleanses us. You cannot walk down our streets today without your mind getting dirty, or your eyes getting dirty, or your ears getting dirty. Perhaps even your feet and hands get dirty. So we go to God in confession. After the Feast of the Passover Jesus rose from supper and began to wash the feet of His disciples. "Peter saith unto him, Thou shalt never wash my feet. Jesus answered him, If I wash thee not, thou hast no part with me" (John 13:8). There are many people attempting to serve God today who are not walking in the light of God's Word. "If we say that we have fellowship with him, and walk in darkness, we lie, and do not the truth: But if we walk in the light, as he is in the light, we have fellowship one with another, and the blood of Jesus Christ his Son cleanseth us from all sin" (1 John 1:6–7). It is not *how* you walk, but *where* you walk that is important. When you walk in the light of the Word of God, you will see that you fall short of His glory. When you see that, you will come to Him in confession. If you don't, He says to you, "If I wash you not, you have no part with me." That is, you will have no fellowship with Him. Therefore, the children of Israel spent one-fourth of the day reading the Bible and spent another fourth of the day confessing their sins.

After teaching the Epistle to the Romans, I received about a dozen letters from folks who confessed that they had been talking against me; and one person said that he had hated me at one time. These people did not need to confess their sins to me, although I do believe that if you have wronged someone, you should talk to them and get the matter straightened out. The point is that the Word of God had an effect on the lives of these people. If it has an effect on you, it will cause you to go to God in confession. This is the road to revival; there is no other road.

Now I believe that after the confession of sin was made (and I think it was private confession), these people straightened out the wrong they had done. On the day of Pentecost Peter did not bring in revival by getting up and confessing how he had denied the Lord Jesus. Dr. Luke and Paul both tell us that our Lord appeared to Simon Peter privately. It was a private matter that had to be taken care of by those involved. You don't take a bath in public; at least I hope you don't. And we are not to confess in public either. It should be a private affair. Simon Peter confessed privately, and I am sure he got things straightened out. Public confession is just a wave of hysteria; it is not revival. It certainly has not brought revival in our day. We need to recognize that we cannot disassociate ourselves from others. Notice that Nehemiah says that when they stood up *they* confessed and they said, "*We* have sinned." It is important to see that it was that kind of confession.

Revival begins as an individual affair. There are those who have thought that Charles Finney was on the fringe of fanaticism. I used to think that too, but, after reading what he has said, I have changed my mind. He said that a revival is not a miracle, but the conditions for revival must be met. You can draw a circle, get inside that circle, and say, "Lord, begin a revival in this circle," and that is where it will have to be. After all, Elijah was a one-man revival. And there have been other men who have met these conditions for revival.

These folk met the conditions for revival, and great blessing came.

Then stood up upon the stairs, of the Levites, Jeshua, and Bani, Kadmiel, Shebaniah, Bunni, Sherebiah, Bani, and Chenani, and cried with a loud voice unto the LORD their God.

Then the Levites, Jeshua, and Kadmiel, Bani, Hashabniah, Sherebiah, Hodijah, Shebaniah, and Pethahiah, said, Stand up and bless the LORD your God for ever and ever: and blessed be thy glorious name, which is exalted above all blessing and praise [Neh. 9:4–5].

This type of confession will not lead to some public demonstration where the individual gets up, calls attention to himself, and tells everyone what a sinner he is, which makes him very important in the eyes of folk, I have discovered. After hearing the Word of God, they made their confession; then they praised and exalted God. This is what *we* need to do. How we need to exalt God in our services and praise Him! A pastor was telling me that their midweek service got pretty boring, saying the same prayers every week; so one Wednesday he decided that, instead of making the same old requests, they would praise God! He said, "It almost brought revival." When we begin to praise and exalt the high and holy name of God, it will bring revival.

Thou, even thou, art LORD alone; thou hast made heaven, the heaven of heavens, with all their host, the earth, and all things that are therein, the seas, and all that is therein, and thou preservest them all; and the host of heaven worshippeth thee [Neh. 9:6].

Have you ever stood on the seashore and watched those great waves pound against the rocks? Has it caused you to worship God? Have you had this experience as you stood in a forest? I have walked in the northern woods of Canada—oh, how thrilling it was! The vaulted ceiling of those tall trees was my temple, and I worshiped God. He is the Creator. He made all of those trees. He made the universe.

Thou art the LORD the God, who didst choose Abram, and broughtest him forth out of Ur of the Chaldees, and gavest him the name of Abraham;

And foundest his heart faithful before thee, and madest a covenant with him to give the land of the Canaanites, the Hittites, the Amorites, and the Perizzites, and the Jebusites, and the Girgashites, to give it, I say, to his seed, and hast performed thy words; for thou art righteous:

And didst see the affliction of our fathers in Egypt, and heardest their cry by the Red sea;

And shewedst signs and wonders upon Pharaoh, and on all his servants, and on all the people of his land: for thou knewest that they dealt proudly against them. So didst thou get thee a name, as it is this day [Neh. 9:7–10].

The Israelites praised God because of the way He had led their fathers in the past. They glorified God concerning Abraham and how He preserved him in the land of Canaan. They praised God for the way He brought their nation out of the land of Egypt, led them by miracles through the wilderness, and protected and preserved them.

Have you ever thanked God that you live in this country? My grandfather on my father's side lived in Northern Ireland. He was Scottish and an Orangeman, but he lived in Northern Ireland. The people were fighting, so he moved to this country. I thank God for my grandfather, and I thank God that he came to this land. I don't want to live in Northern Ireland. I don't care how people feel about the old sod over there; I am thankful I am an American. And Nehemiah's people were glad they were Israelites.

They recognized that not only was God their Creator, He was their Redeemer. They were thanking God for the redemption that came to them when He led their people out of Egypt.

These are two things for which you and I are to thank God. He is the Creator; this is His universe. We thank Him for it. Also we ought to thank Him that He saved us; He redeemed us. By the way, have you told Him that you love Him? My, we need to do that! Don't wait until Sunday morning when you are in church to sing the doxology. Right where you are now you can praise God from whom all blessings flow. He is the Creator; He has given me everything that is material and physical. I thank Him for it. Also He has *saved* me, a sinner! How I thank Him for that. How wonderful He is.

Neither have our kings, our princes, our priests, nor our fathers, kept thy law, nor hearkened unto thy commandments and thy testimonies, wherewith thou didst testify against them.

For they have not served thee in their kingdom, and in thy great goodness that thou gavest them, and in the large and fat land which thou gavest before them, neither turned they from their wicked works [Neh. 9:34–35].

Look how God blessed the nation of Israel. Yet the kings, princes, priests, and fathers of the nation did not obey God's commandments. God has also blessed the United States. Our forefathers who founded this country certainly believed that the Bible was the Word of God, and they founded our nation on morality. We have much for which to thank God. But they sinned, and we continue to sin. How long will God's patience continue?

Behold, we are servants this day, and for the land that thou gavest unto our fathers to eat the fruit thereof and the good thereof, behold, we are servants in it [Neh. 9:36].

The Israelites recognized that the judgment of God was upon them. Will the judgment of God come upon our nation? I don't think we can escape it, my friend.

And it yieldeth much increase unto the kings whom thou hast set over us because of our sins: also they have dominion over our bodies, and over our cattle, at their pleasure, and we are in great distress.

And because of all this we make a sure covenant, and write it; and our princes, Levites, and priests, seal unto it [Neh. 9:37–38].

The terms of the covenant will be seen in the next chapter. And each leader of the nation was asked to put his personal seal on this covenant. The people had resolved to obey God's Word.

What kind of a covenant have you made with God? I have heard people say that they will not sign any pledge—not even to give a certain amount of money—because they might not be able to fulfill it. May I say to you, if you buy a house, or anything on which you are to make payments, they are certainly going to make you sign on the dotted line. I don't know why people can sign up for everything else in life, but they are afraid to sign up with God. My friend, if you mean it, sign up with Him. Oh, how many folk have failed Him, but He is gracious. If we mean business with Him, He means business with us.

In chapter 10 we read that the Israelites are making a covenant with God. They are signing on the dotted line. Have you ever made a covenant with Him? Have you ever promised the Lord anything? A covenant is a serious matter, but I believe the Lord likes to know that we really mean business with Him.

In this chapter we find that Nehemiah, the governor, and twenty-two priests are listed first. They sign the covenant. Individual Levites sign the names of their families on the covenant. Also, forty-four chiefs of the people are listed.

They clave to their brethren, their nobles, and entered into a curse, and into an oath, to walk in God's law, which was given by Moses the servant of God, and to observe and do all the commandments of the LORD our Lord, and his judgments and his statutes [Neh. 10:29].

Their covenant is to keep the Law, and they list specifically three items to which they covenant. Obviously, they list these because they had not been keeping these items of the Law.

And that we would not give our daughters unto the people of the land, nor take their daughters for our sons [Neh. 10:30].

This seems to have been a perpetual problem with Israel. They are now covenanting that there will be no intermarriage with the heathen.

And if the people of the land bring ware or any victuals on the sabbath day to sell, that we would not buy it of them on the sabbath, or on the holy day: and that we would leave the seventh year, and the exaction of every debt [Neh. 10:31].

The second thing to which they covenant is that there will be no trade on the sabbath day or on any of the holy days. Also, the seventh year, which was the year of release in the sabbatical system, is to be faithfully observed.

The final item to which they covenant is in reference to the firstfruits and provision for the sacrifices. Let me just lift out excerpts from the remainder of the covenant.

Also we made ordinances for us, to charge ourselves yearly with the third part of a shekel for the service of the house of our God:

For the shewbread, and for the continual meat offering, and for the continual burnt offering . . .

And we cast the lots among the priests, the Levites, and the people, for the wood offering, to bring it into the house of our God . . .

And to bring the firstfruits of our ground, and the firstfruits of all fruit of all trees, year by year, unto the house of the LORD:

Also the firstborn of our sons, and of our cattle . . .

And that we should bring the firstfruits of our dough, and our offerings, and the fruit of all manner of trees, of wine and of oil . . .

. . . and we will not forsake the house of our God [Neh. 10:32–39].

CHAPTERS 11–13

THEME: *Reform*

Chapter 11 contains another great list which continues into chapter 12. These people were willing to do whatever God wanted them to do. Note the few verses from this chapter.

> **And the rulers of the people dwelt at Jerusalem: the rest of the people also cast lots, to bring one of ten to dwell in Jerusalem the holy city, and nine parts to dwell in other cities [Neh. 11:1].**

The people cast lots. One out of every ten persons would stay in Jerusalem. The other nine would move to other cities. I guess the person who drew the shortest straw stayed in Jerusalem, and the other nine went out to make their homes in other places. This could be a situation in which there would be a lot of complaining. It would be a perfect opportunity for people to say, "Why did God let this happen to me? I would rather live in a small town or in the country."

> **And the people blessed all the men, that willingly offered themselves to dwell at Jerusalem [Neh. 11:2].**

There were many people who wanted to move out to the suburban areas even in that day. But for those who were willing to dwell in Jerusalem, they just thanked God for them. These folk are strangers to us, but God knew each one; and He records their names because they had willing hearts.

> **Now these are the chief of the province that dwelt in Jerusalem: but in the cities of Judah dwelt every one in his possession in their cities, to wit, Israel, the priests, and the Levites, and the Nethinims, and the children of Solomon's servants [Neh. 11:3].**

In the following verses are the names of those who were willing to live in Jerusalem. God takes note of the willing heart!

Chapter 12 continues the list begun in chapter 11. The people listed here are those who just praised God.

Years ago, when I was a pastor in Pasadena, California, I used to visit a lady who was going blind and was partially confined to a wheelchair. You would think this dear lady needed to be helped and comforted. To tell the truth, I don't think she did, but I needed help in those days. I was a young preacher, and I went by to listen to her. Do you know why? She would praise God. My, how she could praise the Lord! Chapter 12 lists those who praised God, and I imagine that her name is somewhere in the list—we don't have the latest list. God, I am sure, keeps a continuing record.

The bulk of this chapter is devoted to a dedication of the walls of Jerusalem. This was a thrilling occasion!

> **And at the dedication of the wall of Jerusalem they sought the Levites out of all their places, to bring them to Jerusalem, to keep the dedication with gladness, both with thanksgivings, and with singing, with cymbals, psalteries, and with harps.**
>
> **And the sons of the singers gathered themselves together, both out of the plain country round about Jerusalem, and from the villages of Netophathi [Neh. 12:27–28].**

They brought together all the musicians. They had a great music festival. Listed here are the names of those inscribed in the Lamb's Book of Life. They are meeting together to dedicate the walls of Jerusalem.

Nehemiah brought people from all over the land to this dedication because Jerusalem was the city where the temple was.

> **So stood the two companies of them that gave thanks in the house of God, and I, and the half of the rulers with me [Neh. 12:40].**

Next Nehemiah lists the priests. They were all there.

> **Also that day they offered great sacrifices, and rejoiced: for God had made them rejoice with great joy: the wives also and the children rejoiced: so that the joy of Jerusalem was heard even afar off [Neh. 12:43].**

The strangers, visitors, tourists, and others passing through that land who heard the great shout of praise and joy probably said, "What in the world is going on over there?" Undoubtedly they went to find out. What a testimony this was to the pagan world around them!

On one occasion when I was in Oakland,

California, I passed by a stadium where a baseball game was being played. Someone hit a home run, and a great shout went up from that place. It must have been an exciting game, and I wished that I was there watching it. That was a natural reaction, you see. I thought at the time, *My, if I could only get that kind of a shout to go up when I preach, the whole community would hear it, and I have a notion that many people would investigate to find out what caused it.*

One of the reasons people pass by the church today is because they think we are a dead and boring lot. And nine times out of ten they are correct. There ought to be more of the joy of the Lord in our services today—real joy. In the Epistle to the Philippians we will find that the very source of power is joy. And remember that Nehemiah said, "The joy of the LORD is your strength."

If you are a crybaby Christian, you are not going to have much of a testimony. A dear lady once told me, "My husband is unsaved, and, Dr. McGee, I just can't reach him." Then she began to blubber. She continued, "I speak to him at breakfast in the morning. I weep and tell him how much I love him and want him saved." Then again at supper she did the same thing. I got to thinking about that. Would you want to have breakfast and dinner with a weeping woman? I don't know about you, but I would not. It certainly would not help the digestion. I have a notion her husband was plenty sick of it. Later I told her, "I have a suggestion. Why don't you quit talking to your husband at breakfast and dinner." "Oh," she replied, "You mean I should quit witnessing?" I told her, "Yes, quit witnessing in the way you have been doing it, and start witnessing a new way. Start praying for him. Stop weeping before him—'the *joy* of the LORD is your strength.' "

In chapter 13 we see again the demonstration that eternal vigilance is the price of freedom. It is the price of Christian liberty and Christian freedom, too.

Somewhere between chapters 12 and 13 Nehemiah returned to his job in the palace at Shushan. Remember that he had only asked for a leave of absence. He had been back in Persia for awhile—maybe a year or two—when he asked for another leave of absence so that he could go to Jerusalem. He made a shocking discovery. The people were not keeping the separation that they should have.

On that day they read in the book of Moses in the audience of the people; and therein was found written, that the Ammonite and the Moabite should not come into the congregation of God for ever;

Because they met not the children of Israel with bread and with water, but hired Balaam against them, that he should curse them: howbeit our God turned the curse into a blessing.

Now it came to pass, when they had heard the law, that they separated from Israel all the mixed multitude [Neh. 13:1–3].

The story of Balaam can be found in Numbers 23–24. The Israelites read the account and decided that the thing to do was to obey the Word of God. They had intermarried with Ammonites and Moabites, which God had forbidden. The children of Israel realized they must put them out of the land.

And before this, Eliashib the priest, having the oversight of the chamber of the house of our God, was allied unto Tobiah [Neh. 13:4].

Oh, oh! Here was the high priest, through the marriage of his son or daughter, allied to the house of Tobiah. The high priest himself had disobeyed God in this important matter of separation. God had strictly forbidden intermarriage with the heathen. God, I think, had given them a very humorous illustration of it; in fact, a real cartoon, which was that they should never plow with an ox and an ass hitched together. You see, an ox is a clean beast and an ass is an unclean beast. They are not to be yoked together. The believer and the unbeliever should not be yoked together, either.

I know a man in business today who is paying an awful price for a partnership that he made before his eyes were opened to this principle. We should not be unequally yoked together in marriage or business.

And he had prepared for him a great chamber, where aforetime they laid the meat offerings, the frankincense, and the vessels, and the tithes of the corn, the new wine, and the oil, which was commanded to be given to the Levites, and the singers, and the porters; and the offerings of the priests [Neh. 13:5].

The priest had turned over the temple storage room to Tobiah. They no longer brought the offerings of the people to the storage place.

Instead they cleaned it out, put down a nice shag rug, some lovely furniture, a king-sized bed, and invited old Tobiah to come in. They told him he could have the room any time he wanted it.

But in all this time was not I at Jerusalem: for in the two and thirtieth year of Artaxerxes king of Babylon came I unto the king, and after certain days obtained I leave of the king:

And I came to Jerusalem, and understood of the evil that Eliashib did for Tobiah, in preparing him a chamber in the courts of the house of God.

And it grieved me sore: therefore I cast forth all the household stuff of Tobiah out of the chamber [Neh. 13:6–8].

All this happened while Nehemiah was away. I love this man Nehemiah. He said, "We are going to get rid of Tobiah. He is not going to be in the house of God!" Remember that our Lord commended the church at Ephesus when He said to them, ". . . thou hast tried them which say they are apostles, and are not, and hast found them liars" (Rev. 2:2). So Nehemiah went to the temple, got Tobiah's suitcase, and pitched it out of the window. He said to Tobiah, "You are not staying here any more. You will receive no more free rent."

Then I commanded, and they cleansed the chambers: and thither brought I again the vessels of the house of God, with the meat offering and the frankincense [Neh. 13:9].

Nehemiah had the chambers fumigated! Once again the rooms were put into order for their original purpose in the service of God. But Nehemiah did not stop there.

And I perceived that the portions of the Levites had not been given them: for the Levites and the singers, that did the work, were fled every one to his field [Neh. 13:10].

The Levites who served in the temple had not been properly supported; so they had to get a job working in the fields. God's service, therefore, had been neglected. I believe today that many ministers are being asked to do more work than they can handle. Many a minister is having to neglect the study of God's Word because his church wants him to be an administrator and practically everything else. He needs help with the responsibilities of the church so that he will be free to study and pray. I love Nehemiah—and I think now you will discover why. He said the preacher ought to have a raise. He tells them, "You are going to bring in the tithe that belongs here and see that these men are taken care of who are in the service of God." My! I love a layman like that—and God approved it, by the way.

Remember me, O my God, concerning this, and wipe not out my good deeds that I have done for the house of my God, and for the offices thereof [Neh. 13:14].

Nehemiah asked God to record what he had done, and the Lord did just that; here it is in His Word.

Nehemiah also found out that the people were doing something else—they were breaking the Sabbath day.

In those days saw I in Judah some treading wine presses on the sabbath, and bringing in sheaves, and lading asses; as also wine, grapes, and figs, and all manner of burdens, which they brought into Jerusalem on the sabbath day: and I testified against them in the day wherein they sold victuals.

There dwelt men of Tyre also therein, which brought fish, and all manner of ware, and sold on the sabbath unto the children of Judah, and in Jerusalem [Neh. 13:15–16].

They came in from the seacoast bringing fish.

Then I contended with the nobles of Judah, and said unto them, What evil thing is this that ye do, and profane the sabbath day? [Neh. 13:17].

The nobles are the ones who permitted this.

Did not your fathers thus, and did not our God bring all this evil upon us, and upon this city? yet ye bring more wrath upon Israel by profaning the sabbath [Neh. 13:18].

Nehemiah reminded the people of God's wrath which had previously been visited upon the nation for doing just what they were presently doing.

And it came to pass, that when the gates of Jerusalem began to be dark before the sabbath, I commanded that the gates should be shut, and charged that they should not be opened till after the sabbath: and some of my servants set I at the gates, that there should no

burden be brought in on the sabbath day.

So the merchants and sellers of all kind of ware lodged without Jerusalem once or twice.

Then I testified against them, and said unto them, Why lodge ye about the wall? if ye do so again, I will lay hands on you. From that time forth came they no more on the sabbath [Neh. 13:19–21].

Just before the Sabbath, at sunset, Nehemiah commanded that the gates be shut. The merchants came with their wares thinking they could sell them. Nehemiah crawled up on the wall to see if the merchants had come, and there they were waiting outside the gates. They came on the first Sabbath that the gates were closed, and they came on the second Sabbath and the gates were closed. Then Nehemiah told them, "If you come here again, I will come out after you." They knew he meant business, and they came no more.

Now another transgression comes to Nehemiah's attention.

In those days also saw I Jews that had married wives of Ashdod, of Ammon, and of Moab:

And their children spake half in the speech of Ashdod, and could not speak in the Jews' language, but according to the language of each people.

And I contended with them, and cursed them, and smote certain of them, and plucked off their hair, and made them swear by God, saying, Ye shall not give your daughters unto their sons, nor take their daughters unto your sons, or for yourselves [Neh. 13:23–25].

Nehemiah discovers Jews who had married women from heathen nations. Nehemiah "contended with them, and cursed them, and smote certain of them, and plucked off their hair!" When it says that he "cursed" them, it doesn't mean that he swore at them, but that he pronounced a curse upon them. And he made them swear that they would not continue to intermarry with foreigners. He was using extreme measures, but they were needed.

Revival, you see, will always lead to reformation. When there is a revival, everything that needs cleaning up will be cleaned up. The only way that our nation can solve the problems that it faces is by a revival among the people of God.

Nehemiah concludes by saying:

Remember them, O my God, because they have defiled the priesthood, and the covenant of the priesthood, and of the Levites.

Thus cleansed I them from all strangers, and appointed the wards of the priests and the Levites, every one in his business;

And for the wood offering, at times appointed, and for the firstfruits. Remember me, O my God, for good [Neh. 13:29–31].

These verses summarize Nehemiah's great contributions to the spiritual well-being of his people. All foreigners were removed from positions of honor and responsibility, and the priests and Levites were given back their proper occupations. The offerings for the temple were resumed. Nehemiah's final words are, "Remember me, O my God, for good." Our Lord wonderfully answered his prayer by recording his work in His Word, which is a permanent remembrance. God remembers him for good. And I remember Nehemiah for good. I hope you do, too. He was a great layman of God.

BIBLIOGRAPHY

(Recommended for Further Study)

Barber, Cyril J. *Nehemiah: The Dynamics of Effective Leadership.* Neptune, New Jersey: Loizeaux Brothers, 1976.

Campbell, Donald K. *Nehemiah: Man in Charge.* Wheaton, Illinois: Victor Books, 1979.

Darby, J. N. *Synopsis of the Books of the Bible.* Addison, Illinois: Bible Truth Publishers, n.d.

Dennett, Edward. *Ezra and Nehemiah.* Addison, Illinois: Bible Truth Publishers, n.d.

Gaebelein, Arno C. *The Annotated Bible.* 1917, Reprint. Neptune, New Jersey: Loizeaux Brothers, 1970.

Getz, Gene A. *Nehemiah: A Man of Prayer and Persistence.* Ventura, California: Regal Books, 1981. (Character studies on Abraham, Moses, Joshua, and David have also been published. Excellent for individual or group study.)

Gray, James M. *Synthetic Bible Studies.* Old Tappan, New Jersey: Fleming H. Revell Co., 1906.

Ironside, H. A. *Notes on the Book of Nehemiah.* Neptune, New Jersey: Loizeaux Brothers, 1925.

Jensen, Irving L. *Ezra, Nehemiah, Esther: A Self-Study Guide.* Chicago, Illinois: Moody Press, 1970.

Kelly, William. *Lectures on Ezra and Nehemiah.* Addison, Illinois: Bible Truth Publishers, n.d.

Luck, G. Coleman. *Ezra and Nehemiah.* Chicago, Illinois: Moody Press, 1961.

Sauer, Erich. *The Dawn of World Redemption.* Grand Rapids, Michigan: Wm. B. Eerdmans Publishing Co., 1951. (An excellent Old Testament survey.)

Scroggie, W. Graham. *The Unfolding Drama of Redemption.* Grand Rapids, Michigan: Zondervan Publishing House, 1970. (An excellent survey and outline of the Old Testament.)

Seume, Richard H. *Nehemiah: God's Builder.* Chicago, Illinois: Moody Press, 1978.

Unger, Merrill F. *Unger's Bible Handbook.* Chicago, Illinois: Moody Press, 1966.

Unger, Merrill F. *Unger's Commentary on the Old Testament.* Vol. 1. Chicago, Illinois: Moody Press, 1981. (A fine summary of each paragraph. Highly recommended.)

The Book of

ESTHER

INTRODUCTION

It is uncertain who wrote this book, but Mordecai could have been the writer (see Esth. 9:29).

"For if thou altogether holdest thy peace at this time, then shall there enlargement and deliverance arise to the Jews from another place; but thou and thy father's house shall be destroyed: and who knoweth whether thou art come to the kingdom for such a time as this?" (Esth. 4:14).

The Book of Esther in one sense is the most remarkable in the Bible, and that is because the name of God is not mentioned in this book at all. There is not even a divine title or pronoun that refers to God. Yet the heathen king is mentioned 192 times. Prayer is not mentioned—it wouldn't be, since God is omitted. The Book of Esther is never quoted in the New Testament. There's not even a casual reference to it. But the superstition of the heathen is mentioned, and lucky days, and we'll be introduced into a pagan, heathen court of a great world monarch who ruled over the then-known world. This is indeed an unusual book.

It is an unusual book for another reason: it is named for a woman. Actually, there are only two books in the Bible named for women. (Some want to include the epistles of John. I disagree with that, so don't submit that one to me.) Ruth and Esther are the two books named for women. I've written on both of these books: *Ruth, the Romance of Redemption* and *Esther, the Romance of Providence*. Redemption is a romance; it is a love story. We love Him because He first loved us, and He gave Himself for us because He loves us. The Book of Esther is the romance of providence. God directs this material universe in which we live today by His providence. In fact, it's the way He directs all of His creation.

Back in Deuteronomy, before God brought the Israelites into the Promised Land, He outlined their history for them. He told them about the Babylonian captivity, and He also told them that Rome would destroy the city of Jerusalem and the people would be taken into captivity. It actually happened that way. But in Deuteronomy 31:18 God says this: "And I will surely hide my face in that day for all the evils which they shall have wrought, in that they are turned unto other gods."

In the Book of Esther God has hidden His face from them. But we can say, "God standeth in the shadows keeping watch over His own." So the Book of Esther gives us a record of a group of people out of the will of God.

Now, when Cyrus made the decree—after the seventy years of Babylonian captivity—that the people might return to the land, not all of them returned. Less than sixty thousand returned, and we had the record of that in Ezra, Nehemiah, and in the two prophetic books of Haggai and Zechariah. But what about the largest segment that did not return to the land? (We have a similar condition today. We speak of the nation Israel. Well, there are probably two million who have returned there, but there are about sixteen million who are scattered throughout the world today. So that, actually, the majority are not in the land at all. That is evident, and I use it merely as a parallel to illustrate what it was in that day.) Several million of these people did not return to the land after the decree of Cyrus. They should have. God had commanded them to. Now they're out of the will of God. The question is, do we have any record of these people, this large number, that did not return to the land? Yes, and that record is in the Book of Esther. It is recorded here. In other words, we just have one page out of their history, one small item of their experience, and one scrap and shred of evidence in their voluminous record. And the little Book of Esther becomes all important for that reason.

In this we see God in a new way. Although they are not in His will, we see God directing them. How? By His providence.

What is providence? Well, all the great doctrines that we have today are taught in certain books of the Old Testament. You have redemption taught in the Book of Exodus, and the love side of redemption taught in the Book of Ruth. And the Book of Job teaches repentance. And resurrection is taught in the Book of Jonah. So the great doctrines of our Christian faith are taught in certain books of the Old Testament. Now, the Book of Esther illustrates providence. These people in a foreign land, out of the will of God, have not obeyed His orders because His orders were to return to the land of Israel. They remained. They disobeyed. They forgot God; they were far from Him. They did not call upon Him in time of trouble. When they first came into the land of their captivity, they could say, "How shall we sing the LORD's song in a strange land?" They couldn't sing; they sat down and wept when they remembered Zion. But now they've forgotten Zion. In fact, it's in rubble and ruins, and they don't want to go back there. They have made a covenant at the beginning, ". . . let my tongue cleave to the roof of my mouth; if I prefer not Jerusalem . . ." (Ps. 137:6). They've forgotten, and their tongue is silent in this book. They're not praising God at all, nor are they praying to Him. That makes this, you see, a very remarkable book. But what about God? Well, He hasn't forgotten them. How can God direct them if they've rejected Him? Well, God does it by His providence. And the Book of Esther teaches the providence of God. Now, what is providence? Will you forgive me if I'm theological for just a moment? If you want a definition, here's a theological definition: Providence is the means by which God directs all things; both animate and inanimate; seen and unseen; good and evil toward a worthy purpose, which means His will must finally prevail. Or as the psalmist said, ". . . his kingdom ruleth over all" (Ps. 103:19). In Ephesians 1:11 Paul tells us that God ". . . worketh all things after the counsel of his own will." Our God is running the universe today, friends, even though there are some who think that it has slipped out from under Him. Emerson was wrong when he said, "Things are in the saddle and ride mankind." Things are riding mankind all right, but they are not in the saddle. God is in the saddle.

There are three words we need to keep in mind before we can properly understand the providence of God in relationship to the material universe and to man in particular.

The first word is *creation.* We understand by "creation" that God, by His fiat word, spoke this universe into existence. Do you have a better explanation? If you do, I would like to hear it. Frankly, I become a little annoyed with some of the college teachers today who are not experts in the field of science but speak as though they were experts about how evolution formed man. Will you please tell me where all of the "goo" came from out of which the earth and man evolved? When did the earth begin? Did it begin out of nothing? Don't tell me that it has always existed, because if you do, then you have an infinite universe. If you have an infinite universe, then you have to have somebody who is infinite to run things. We are on the horns of a dilemma. There are only two explanations for the universe: One is *speculation*—evolution comes under that heading, and prior to evolution there were other theories—all of them have been or will be exploded. They are speculation.

The second explanation is *revelation.* The only way that you and I, certainly as Christians, will ever understand how this universe began is by faith. We understand that God brought this universe into existence, and the only way that you and I know this is by revelation. ". . . Faith cometh by hearing and hearing by the Word of God" (Rom. 10:17). Either you believe in creation or you believe in speculation. There's no third explanation for the universe. That's creation.

Then the second word is *preservation.* And that's a tremendous word. It is by God's preservation that the universe is held together. Hebrews 1:3 tells us that Christ "upholds all things by the word of his power." Colossians 1:17 says, "And he is before all things, and by him all things consist." What is the "stickum" that holds this universe together? What is it that makes it run just like clockwork today so that a man can be sent to the moon and it is possible to plot exactly where the moon will be? Scientists can send a little gadget out toward Mars and they know exactly where Mars will be. You think it is remarkable that man can do things like that, but I think it is remarkable that we have a universe that runs like clockwork today. Who runs it? The Lord Jesus Christ runs the universe. He upholds all things by the word of His power.

The third word is *providence.* This is the word we will consider in the Book of Esther. Providence is the way that God is directing the universe. He is moving it into tomorrow —He is moving it into the future by His providence. *Providence* means "to provide." God will provide. Remember what Abraham said on top of Mount Moriah, when he and his son Isaac had gone to this mountain to sacrifice to God. They had everything they needed except a sacrifice. "And Isaac spake unto Abraham his father, and said, My father: and he said, Here am I, my son. And he said, Behold the fire and the wood: but where is the lamb for a burnt offering? And Abraham said, My son, God will provide himself a lamb for a burnt offering: so they went both of them together" (Gen. 22:7–8). Nineteen hundred years later, God provided a Lamb on that same mountain ridge that goes through Jerusalem. On Golgotha the Lord Jesus Christ was crucified. He was the Lamb that God provided. He was ". . . the Lamb of God which taketh away the sin of the world" (John 1:29). God provides.

Providence means that the hand of God is in the glove of human events. When God is not at the steering wheel, He is the backseat driver. He is the coach who calls the signals from the bench. Providence is the unseen rudder on the ship of state. God is the pilot at the wheel during the night watch. As someone has said, "He makes great doors swing on little hinges." God brought together a little baby's cry and a woman's heart down by the River Nile when Pharaoh's daughter went to bathe. The Lord pinched little Moses and he let out a yell. The cry reached the heart of the princess, and God used it to change the destiny of a people. That was providence. That was the hand of God.

The Book of Esther provides us with the greatest illustrations of the providence of God. Although His name is never mentioned, we see His providence in each page of this wonderful little book.

OUTLINE

I. The Wife Who Refused to Obey Her Husband, Chapter 1

II. The Beauty Contest to Choose a Real Queen, Chapter 2

III. Haman and Anti-Semitism, Chapter 3

IV. For Such a Time as This, Chapter 4

V. The Scepter of Grace and the Nobility of Esther, Chapter 5

VI. When a King Could Not Sleep at Night, Chapter 6

VII. The Man Who Came to Dinner but Died on the Gallows, Chapter 7

VIII. The Message of Hope That Went out from the King, Chapter 8

IX. The Institution of the Feast of Purim, Chapters 9–10

CHAPTER 1

THEME: *The wife who refused to obey her husband*

This chapter out of the history of a pagan nation is inserted in the Word of God for a very definite purpose: to teach the providence of God. We shall see this as we turn the pages of this story. It begins with the law of a heathen kingdom and a difficulty—a matrimonial difficulty. It was a very personal affair that arose in the kingdom, but it had international repercussions.

Now it came to pass in the days of Ahasuerus, (this is Ahasuerus which reigned, from India even unto Ethiopia, over an hundred and seven and twenty provinces:) [Esth. 1:1].

First we should understand that *Ahasuerus* is not the name of the man, but the title. It means "high father" or "venerable king." As the word *Caesar* is a title and does not identify the man, so *Ahasuerus* does not identify this Persian king in secular history. There is quite a divergence of opinion concerning his identity.

The viewpoint that I hold is that Ahasuerus of the Book of Esther is Xerxes the Great of Persia, because he is the one who actually brought the kingdom to its zenith. Xerxes is the man who made the last great effort of the East to overcome the West, and it was a tremendous effort. A volume published by the British Museum in 1907 entitled *The Sculptures and Inscriptions of Darius the Great on the Rock of Behistun in Persia* establishes with the "Cyrus Cylinders" translation that Ahasuerus and Esther were the parents of the Cyrus of Isaiah 44:28; 45:1.

Xerxes reigned over a kingdom, a great empire, from India to Ethiopia. It extended through the Fertile Crescent which was the very heartland of the world.

That in those days, when the king Ahasuerus sat on the throne of his kingdom, which was in Shushan the palace,

In the third year of his reign, he made a feast unto all his princes and his servants; the power of Persia and Media, the nobles and princes of the provinces, being before him [Esth. 1:2–3].

This banquet would pale into insignificance anything that man might attempt in our day. There were 127 provinces in his kingdom, and out of each of these he brought a delegation (how many, I don't know), so that he had present probably one or two thousand people for this banquet. This is what we would call a very swanky affair. It cost millions of dollars. It was a banquet to end all banquets. It was a great event in the history of the world. How can God get in on a scene like this? Well, He will by His providence. "God stands in the shadows, keeping watch over His own."

When he shewed the riches of his glorious kingdom and the honour of his excellent majesty many days, even an hundred and fourscore days [Esth. 1:4].

For 181 days Ahasuerus boarded these fellows. He had a perpetual smorgasbord for six months! The father of Louis XV of France was talking with the preceptor and the exchequer of the kingdom about this banquet, and he said that he did not see how the king had the patience to have that kind of a banquet. The exchequer, who was handling the finances for Louis XV, said that he did not see how he financed it.

This banquet revealed the wealth, the luxury, and the regal character of this oriental court. As I have indicated the reason for it seems obvious. He had called in all of his princes and all of his rulers from every corner of his kingdom that he might win their wholehearted support for the military campaign to capture Greece and to make himself the supreme ruler of the world of that day. And, of course, he almost succeeded in that attempt. I am confident he would have succeeded had not God already predicted that the operation would eventuate in failure, that the power would move from the East to the West.

Xerxes wanted his princes and rulers to know that he was able to pay for the war he was contemplating. He displayed the wealth of his kingdom by giving this great pagan feast. The banquet was pagan from beginning to end. It was a godless thing. There are those who try to find spiritual lessons here. Very candidly, I see none whatsoever. What I do see is God's introducing us to a pagan court where decisions are made that affect the world. It looks as if God is left out, but God wants you to know that He is overruling these circumstances, and He is going to accomplish His own purpose.

And when these days were expired, the king made a feast unto all the people that were present in Shushan the palace, both unto great and small, seven days, in the court of the garden of the king's palace [Esth. 1:5].

Xerxes brought the banquet to a climax in the last seven days. Apparently he brought in a tremendous population of people for the final seven days in the court of the garden.

Where were white, green, and blue, hangings, fastened with cords of fine linen and purple to silver rings and pillars of marble: the beds were of gold and silver, upon a pavement of red, and blue, and white, and black, marble [Esth. 1:6].

The silver, the gold, the jewels, and the beautiful hangings tell us of the wealth of this kingdom. It is a gaudy display. The ruins of those palaces still testify to the richness of Persia. A few years ago this same kingdom of Persia celebrated its twenty-five hundredth anniversary in the same place. Television coverage and current magazines showed something of the tremendous wealth. The banquet cost millions of dollars. There was a great deal of criticism of it because of the poverty in that land. But the banquet Xerxes put on was costly beyond imagination. Judging from secular history, the purpose of Xerxes in giving this banquet was to win support for his forthcoming military campaign. He wanted everyone to know he could afford a war. He used a feast to convince his princes and rulers.

We have seen this method used on a comparably small scale in our day. Several years ago, when one of the great automobile concerns came out with a new model, they brought all of their dealers from over the world to Detroit for a convention. It was made up of drinking parties and banquets and was held with the idea of selling the dealers on the new model that was to come out. So it was with Xerxes, only he was bidding for their support in a new campaign. Human nature does not change. In the Medo-Persian Empire, Xerxes was getting ready to go to war, but first he put forth a great selling effort.

And they gave them drink in vessels of gold, (the vessels being diverse one from another,) and royal wine in abundance, according to the state of the king [Esth. 1:7].

This banquet, pagan from beginning to end, ended in a drunken orgy.

And the drinking was according to the law; none did compel: for so the king had appointed to all the officers of his house, that they should do according to every man's pleasure [Esth. 1:8].

This verse tells us that "the drinking was according to the law; none did compel." Even these pagan Oriental rulers, who had absolute sovereignty, never forced anyone to drink, although they themselves were given to it, as was this man Xerxes, as we shall see. But today we are more civilized and a man either has to drink or get out. Some businessmen tell me that it is almost impossible today to go to some business meetings and not participate in a cocktail party. One executive in a company told me that the president of the concern called him to his office and rebuked him because he had not participated in drinking at a company cocktail party. You would think that this president would want sober men for his executives. But, you see, we are civilized, and we compel people to drink.

Also Vashti the queen made a feast for the women in the royal house which belonged to king Ahasuerus [Esth. 1:9].

Vashti made a feast for the women's auxiliary. The men brought their wives, but they did not go to the same banquet in that day. It was a breach of social custom for men and women to attend the same feast. It was different from our present-day banquets. The women were kept in separate quarters. The banquet for the men was serious business, and apparently they did not mix sex and business. Xerxes was selling a war; so Vashti entertained the women at another banquet.

On the seventh day, when the heart of the king was merry with wine, he commanded Mehuman, Biztha, Harbona, Bigtha, and Abagtha, Zethar, and Carcas, the seven chamberlains that served in the presence of Ahasuerus the king [Esth. 1:10].

This verse tells us that the king got drunk. He overstepped himself. You did not have to drink at these banquets, but if you wanted to, you could have all you wanted. It seems that the king was not a teetotaler. The king was "high" on the seventh day. Here the question arises concerning not only this king but any king or ruler: Is he a fit ruler if he is engaged in drunkenness? We are told that the Oriental people today are asking if America with all of her drunkenness is in a position to be the leader of the nations of the world. This is a question that America must answer within the next few years. If it continues as it is today, drunkenness will ultimately destroy our land.

We find Xerxes under the influence of alcohol, doing something that he would never have done if he had been sober. He commanded his chamberlains who served in his presence to bring Vashti to the banquet.

To bring Vashti the queen before the king with the crown royal, to shew the people and the princes her beauty: for she was fair to look on [Esth. 1:11].

The king had displayed his wealth and his luxury, and he had demonstrated to them his ability to carry on the campaign he had in mind. Now, under the influence of alcohol, he does something that is contrary to the proprieties of that day. He will display Vashti, who is a beautiful woman to look at. He decides that he will bring her into the banquet court before that convention of men. He would never have done this had he not been drunk. It was a very ungentlemanly thing to do. In fact, it was positively crude. He wanted everyone to see Vashti, his treasure, his crowning jewel, as it were.

But the queen Vashti refused to come at the king's commandment by his chamberlains: therefore was the king very wroth, and his anger burned in him [Esth. 1:12].

The king said to his guests, "I have a real surprise for you. I want you to see my queen. She is going to stand before you with the crown royal upon her head. She is very beautiful." In a few minutes one of the chamberlains whispered in the king's ear, "She won't come." Don't tell me that women did not have rights in that day! Vashti turned down the king's request. Imagine having to get up and say, "I'm very sorry, gentlemen, but we will have to change the program of the evening. Our main attraction did not arrive. The queen will not be here this evening." That started the buzzing throughout the banquet. The guests began to say, "What kind of a king is he that he cannot even command the queen?"

Although I feel that Vashti was perfectly justified in refusing to come at the king's commandment, I think she should have thought the thing over. She should have considered the fact that her refusal might cause a scandal that would hurt her husband in his position. Under the circumstances she should have gone to the banquet. She should have obeyed the king.

Then the king said to the wise men, which knew the times, (for so was the king's manner toward all that knew law and judgment:

And the next unto him was Carshena, Shethar, Admatha, Tarshish, Meres, Marsena, and Memucan, the seven princes of Persia and Media, which saw the king's face, and which sat the first in the kingdom;)

What shall we do unto the queen Vashti according to law, because she hath not performed the commandment of the king Ahasuerus by the chamberlains? [Esth. 1:13–15].

This situation called for a crisis meeting of the cabinet. The men named in this passage were the princes who met with him privately and personally, just as the cabinet meets with the president of the United States. Now this whole thing might sound silly to us today, but in that day it was no incidental matter. The queen had refused to obey a commandment of the king. The cabinet had to take care of this crisis. Here they are preparing for a great campaign, and the queen will not do what the king asks her to do. What should be done with her? It seems that there was no law which they could exercise.

And Memucan answered before the king and the princes, Vashti the queen hath not done wrong to the king only, but also to all the princes, and to all the people that are in all the provinces of the king Ahasuerus [Esth. 1:16].

We've heard much about the fact that back in those days women were chattel. In many cases that was true, but apparently Vashti had a lot of freedom, and there was no law which could force her to obey the king's command to come to the banquet. The cabinet was going to have to come up with a severe and harsh law to take care of the situation. About this time a little fellow named Memucan speaks up. He's the spokesman, and a henpecked husband. How do I know he is henpecked? He is afraid that, when the deed of the queen comes to the attention of all women, they will look with contempt upon their husbands. Memucan is Mr. Milquetoast. If the queen gets away with this, he would not want to go home. I don't think he had much to say in his own home. I think his wife made most of the decisions. This, perhaps, is one of the reasons he spoke out at this cabinet meeting.

There are many men who take orders from others in their employment—they never get a chance to express themselves. Then they go home and their wives won't let them express themselves either. I have known such men who speak out when they serve on church boards. They talk and talk, but they make no contribution to the welfare and development of the church. They talk but have nothing to say. They make suggestions that have no merit. Memucan is this kind of a man.

> **For this deed of the queen shall come abroad unto all women, so that they shall despise their husbands in their eyes, when it shall be reported, The king Ahasuerus commanded Vashti the queen to be brought in before him, but she came not.**
>
> **Likewise shall the ladies of Persia and Media say this day unto all the king's princes, which have heard of the deed of the queen. Thus shall there arise too much contempt and wrath [Esth. 1: 17–18].**

This man, Memucan, is one of the princes, you see. He says, "I will have a fight over this matter when I go home." In fact, I think he came to the conclusion that if something was not done, he would not go home.

Perhaps you have heard of the henpecked husband who came to the office one morning and boasted, "Last night my wife was down on her knees to me." One of the fellows, knowing the situation, was a little skeptical. He said, "What were the circumstances, and what exactly did she say to you?" He looked a little embarrassed and admitted, "Well, she was down on her knees, looking under the bed, and she said, 'Come out from under there, you coward!' "

There is also the story about the man who told the people in his office that his wife said that he was a model husband. He told this to a hard-boiled secretary and she did not commend him. Instead she said, "Why don't you look up the word *model* in the dictionary, and you won't be so proud of it." He took her advice. A "model," he found out, was a small imitation of the real thing. That is what Memucan was. He was henpecked; he was Mr. Milquetoast. He said loud and clear, "Something must be done to protect our homes in this matter." And actually it was a real crisis because the king and queen set an example for the kingdom.

Notice Memucan's proposal.

> **If it please the king, let there go a royal commandment from him, and let it be written among the laws of the Persians and the Medes, that it be not altered, That Vashti come no more before king Ahasuerus; and let the king give her royal estate unto another that is better than she [Esth. 1:19].**

I trust that you realize the setting for the Book of Esther is a pagan court. A pagan law is being enacted which has nothing to do with the Mosaic Law, neither is it Christian by any means. It is a new law, but it is the law of the Medes and the Persians.

> **And when the king's decree which he shall make shall be published throughout all his empire, (for it is great,) all the wives shall give to their husbands honour, both to great and small.**
>
> **And the saying pleased the king and the princes; and the king did according to the word of Memucan:**
>
> **For he sent letters into all the king's provinces, into every province according to the writing thereof, and to every people after their language, that every man should bear rule in his own house, and that it should be published according to the language of every people [Esth. 1:20–22].**

The queen is set aside. No more is she to be the queen. It happened because she refused to obey the king. A decree went out. It declared that in the kingdom a wife was to honor her husband, and he was to rule. Apparently, this had not been true before in the empire of the Medes and Persians. Now it is law, and it cannot be altered or changed.

This law reveals the character of Xerxes as he stands in profane history. You will remember that he took his army, the largest that had ever been marshaled, as far as Thermopylae. Also he came with a fleet of three hundred ships which were destroyed at Salamis. This man, in a fit of madness, went down to the sea and beat the waves with a belt for destroying his fleet! Now a man who will do that evidently has something radically wrong with him. It seems that he was a man who suffered from some form of abnormality, as most of the world rulers have—and still do. Julius

Caesar, Napoleon, and Hitler were men of abnormal mental processes. Nebuchadnezzar, great man that he was, represented as the head of gold, suffered from a form of abnormality known as hysteria. We find him moving through these cycles in the Book of Daniel.

Any man today who even wants to be a world ruler ought to be examined by a psychiatrist! However, forms of abnormality have not kept men from achieving greatness in the history of the world. This is true of Xerxes. He was a man of tremendous ability. Yet in unreasoning anger he allowed this banishment of his lovely queen. It became the law of the Medes and Persians, an edict which could not be altered. Although later the king himself wanted to break the law, he could not. The law of the Medes and the Persians could not be broken.

CHAPTER 2

***THEME:** The beauty contest to choose the real queen*

After these things, when the wrath of king Ahasuerus was appeased, he remembered Vashti, and what she had done, and what was decreed against her [Esth. 2:1].

This verse begins, "After these things." After *what* things? Well, the things that had taken place in the first chapter, and the campaign to Greece where Xerxes was soundly defeated. After his defeat he returned in deep dejection to his palace. Added to his misery was the absence of his queen and the fact that the law of the Medes and Persians could not be altered—even by the king himself. Vashti could never again be his queen.

We must turn to secular history for the campaign of Xerxes against the Greeks, since the Bible gives us no record of this campaign. He led a great army against the Greeks. The secret of the strength of the Persians was in numbers, but the individual Persian soldier was not as well trained as the individual Greek soldier. The Greeks emphasized the individual, and as a result one Greek soldier could have taken care of ten Persians. So at the battle at Thermopylae, only a few men could get in the narrow pass. As a result, the Greeks won a signal victory over the Persian army. It was an unfortunate defeat for Xerxes, but God was overruling. The power was about to pass from Persia to Greece.

After his defeat and in his loneliness he paces up and down in the palace every day. He is thinking of Vashti, but the law that he has made concerning the queen cannot be changed. He has set aside this beautiful woman, and he can never have her again. The servants know his state of mind, and they are watching him. They know that something must be done.

Then said the king's servants that ministered unto him, Let there be fair young virgins sought for the king:

And let the king appoint officers in all the provinces of his kingdom, that they may gather together all the fair young virgins unto Shushan the palace, to the house of the women, unto the custody of Hege the king's chamberlain, keeper of the women; and let their things for purification be given them [Esth. 2: 2–3].

Members of the king's cabinet, occupying high positions, notice how moody and lonely the king is. They make a suggestion that there be conducted a beauty contest and that the entire kingdom be searched for women who were beautiful. They were to be brought in from near and far. I am sure that the number of women chosen was in the hundreds.

And let the maiden which pleaseth the king be queen instead of Vashti. And the thing pleased the king; and he did so [Esth. 2:4].

The king was to be the judge, the sole judge, of this contest.

Now in Shushan the palace there was a certain Jew, whose name was Mordecai, the son of Jair, the son of Shimei, the son of Kish, a Benjamite [Esth. 2:5].

The story in the Book of Esther to this point has just been the window dressing—the stage props. We have had a glimpse into a heathen court. We have been introduced to the happenings there for a very definite purpose. It explains the beauty contest and how Esther came to the throne. Because she became queen, she was able to intervene and intercede in behalf of her people. An entire people would have been exterminated at that time had she not been in that position on the throne. We will begin to see the hand of God moving in the palace.

Up to this point there has been nothing spiritual in the palace. It was as godless as anything could possibly be. Drunken orgies were often held, but God is going to overrule. We are going to see His providence. He is arranging the events so that at the proper time He will have someone to intervene in behalf of His people, the Jews.

Somebody is going to raise the question about this beauty contest and say, "It looks as if God approves of beauty contests." No, I don't think He does. But, my friend, when a child of God gets out of God's will, He permits many things to happen of which He does not approve. And He will overrule through these events. God's overruling power is one of the important lessons in this little Book of Esther. Many Christians today are living on the fringe of God's will. They are not really being directed by the will of God. They are not what we call *in* the will of God. Yet God directs them by His providence. Esther is an illustration of this.

Actually our story begins with "a certain Jew, whose name was Mordecai." He was of the tribe of Benjamin. The question that immediately arises is: What is he doing here? He belonged to the royal family of Israel. He was from the family of Saul.

Who had been carried away from Jerusalem with the captivity which had been carried away with Jeconiah king of Judah, whom Nebuchadnezzar the king of Babylon had carried away [Esth. 2:6].

God had permitted His people to return to their own land, as He had prophesied through Isaiah. Cyrus had given a decree to permit them to return, and those who were in the will of God did return to Palestine. However, very few returned to their homeland. The greater number of them had made a place for themselves in the land of their captivity—they had learned shopkeeping from the Gentiles—and elected to remain. They liked it. When they were free to go, they did not want to return to their homeland. Many of them, out of the will of God, chose to remain, and Mordecai happened to be one of them. He should have been back in the land of Israel but—of all places—notice where he is: in the palace. He has a political job.

You may remember that Joseph also had a political job in Egypt; yet he was in the will of God directly. Daniel in the court of Babylon was also in the will of God. But Mordecai is not in the direct will of God. You will see that the Book of Esther is the book of the providence of God. As I have said, a popular definition of providence is this: Providence is how God coaches the man on second base. And this man Mordecai is going to be brought "home," although he is out of the will of God, and although he is not looking to God for help. Even at a time when you would think he and his people would turn to God, they do not. There is no mention of God or of prayer in this book at all because these people are out of the will of God.

Both Mordecai and Esther come on the pages of Scripture in a poor light, although they are very high-type individuals, as we shall see later on in the story. Mordecai was taken captive, probably at a young age, in the second deportation of captives that left Jerusalem. That was during the reign of Jeconiah (better known as Jehoiachin). The first deportation that left Jerusalem was made up of the princes, the nobility, the upper class—Daniel was with that group. The second captivity took out those, shall we say, of the upper-middle class. This man Mordecai was in that group.

After the third deportation, when Jerusalem was finally destroyed, only the poorest class was left in the land. Mordecai had a young cousin whose parents may have been slain when Nebuchadnezzar took the city, for multitudes were slain.

And he brought up Hadassah, that is, Esther, his uncle's daughter: for she had neither father nor mother, and the maid was fair and beautiful; whom Mordecai, when her father and mother were dead, took for his own daughter [Esth. 2:7].

Esther's Hebrew name was *Hadassah*, which means "star." She certainly was a star and a very beautiful woman, according to Scripture. Mordecai adopted her as his own daughter. Her one great asset was beauty. When the announcement was made that there was to be a choice of another queen for Ahasuerus, immediately Mordecai became interested. His position in the palace no doubt gave him the opportunity to see the different girls that were brought from all over the kingdom to enter the contest. I am sure he compared them with Esther and decided that none of them were as beautiful as his adopted daughter.

So it came to pass, when the king's commandment and his decree was heard, and when many maidens were gathered together unto Shushan the palace, to the custody of Hegai, that Esther was brought also unto the king's house, to the custody of Hegai, keeper of the women.

And the maiden pleased him, and she obtained kindness of him; and he speedily gave her her things for purification, with such things as belonged to her, and seven maidens, which were meet to be given her, out of the king's house: and he preferred her and her maids unto the best place of the house of the women [Esth. 2:8–9].

You can see the providence of God moving into this situation. Mordecai took his young cousin Esther and entered her in the beauty contest. I must say that at this particular juncture I do not have much respect for this man. Before the story is over, I am going to change my mind, and I will eat my words, but right now I despise him for what he is doing. To begin with, he is disobeying God. God had told His people not to intermarry with the heathen. He is definitely breaking the Mosaic Law by entering this girl in the beauty contest on the chance that she might become the next queen. The girls who did not win the contest would automatically enter the harem of the king. If Esther lost, she would be forced to become a concubine. She would be exposed to an awful life, but Mordecai is willing to take that risk.

We can see God taking command of the situation. Esther was brought to the king's house. She pleased Hegai, the keeper of the women. She obtained kindness from him, and he gave her everything she needed to help make her even more beautiful.

Esther had not shewed her people nor her kindred: for Mordecai had charged her that she should not shew it [Esth. 2:10].

Remember that the Jews were a captive people and anti-Semitism always has been a curse in the nations of the world. And it had been in this nation. You cannot read the account of Nebuchadnezzar's destruction of Jerusalem without realizing his hatred for these people. It was he who brought them to Babylon, but he is no longer on the scene, and a new nation has charge of them. Yet the anti-Semitic feeling remains. Mordecai, being very sensitive to that, warns Esther not to reveal her nationality. This silence is tantamount to a denial of her religion, because religion is the thing that has identified these people down through the years. The moment Mordecai and Esther denied their nationality, that moment they denied their religion. By remaining in the land of captivity they were out of the will of God. It is of interest to note that today, when men and women are out of the will of God, they have very little to say about their faith in Christ.

And Mordecai walked every day before the court of the women's house, to know how Esther did, and what should become of her [Esth. 2:11].

When you are in the will of God, you can rest in the fact that God is causing all things to work together for good. Mordecai is not resting in God, because he is out of God's will. He is pacing up and down, nervously biting his fingernails, wondering how things will turn out. He wonders if he has not made a terrible blunder and mistake by entering Esther in this beauty contest. He is absolutely frightened at what he has done. He is worried sick. He cannot sleep at night. This is Mordecai's condition. When you are out of God's will, you are not apt to rest on your laurels and say everything will be all right. At this point he has not, nor can he, put it into God's hands. I am not sure that he knew anything about the providence of God. However, God is overruling in this.

May I remind you of my definition of providence? Providence is the way God leads the man who will not be led. We see God beginning to move at this particular point. It is no accident that Esther is given the most prominent place and that she is shown every favor and given every consideration. There are no accidents with God.

Notice the type of beautification that went on.

Now when every maid's turn was come to go in to king Ahasuerus, after that

she had been twelve months, according to the manner of women, (for so were the days of their purifications accomplished, to wit, six months with oil of myrrh, and six months with sweet odours, and with other things for the purifying of the women;) [Esth. 2:12].

May I say to you that if your wife takes a few hours in the beauty salon, you ought not to complain—these girls spent a whole year there! The first six months they went to the spa for reducing and oil treatments. Then the next six months they went to the perfumers. I suppose they even swam in cologne in that day in order to be prepared to go into the presence of the king. You can see the tremendous emphasis that was placed on the physical, and this is typical of a pagan culture. The farther away America gets from God the more counters we have in our department stores for beauty aids. Have you noticed that? And with the multiplicity of beautifying treatments, it is rather disappointing that we don't have more beauty than we do. But these girls went through an entire year of beauty-conditioning for the contest.

Women have not changed much over the years. A great deal of makeup was used to make the women in this contest beautiful. A lot of makeup is used today. I hope no one is going to take issue with me about the use of makeup or about whether Esther should have entered this contest. Very candidly, I don't think she should have entered the contest, and we are going to find out that she did not need makeup. There are many extremists on the subject of makeup. A dear lady once came to me when I was pastor in downtown Los Angeles, California. She thought that some of the girls were using too much makeup. She did not think a Christian ought to use it, and she put me out on a limb when she asked me what I thought about the subject. I said, "Well, it depends on the woman. Some women would be greatly improved if they used a little makeup, and I think we should all do the best we can with what God has given us." She took that personally, and I want to add that she had reason to. I felt like saying to her, "A little makeup, lady, would improve you a great deal."

In Esther's case God permitted all of this by His providence. Her entrance into the contest and her acceptance by the man in charge of the contestants were all ordered by God. Hegai, keeper of the women, thought Esther looked like a winner, so he put her up front. It was a step forward in God's program. It was not an accident. God's providence was overruling in her life.

Then thus came every maiden unto the king; whatsoever she desired was given her to go with her out of the house of the women unto the king's house.

In the evening she went, and on the morrow she returned into the second house of the women, to the custody of Shaashgaz, the king's chamberlain, which kept the concubines: she came in unto the king no more, except the king delighted in her, and that she were called by name [Esth. 2:13–14].

After one year of preparation, the time came for each maiden to go to the king's chambers. For her visit she could have anything she wanted in the line of clothes or jewelry. Soon it would be Esther's turn to go to the king. She was taking an awful chance. If she did not win, she would become one of the concubines of the king of Persia, which certainly would have been a horrible thing for this Jewish maiden. This is the reason Mordecai is biting his fingernails. He knows they are out of the will of God, and he knows the terrific chance this girl, whom he raised, is taking. But God is going to overrule.

Now when the turn of Esther, the daughter of Abihail the uncle of Mordecai, who had taken her for his daughter, was come to go in unto the king, she required nothing but what Hegai the king's chamberlain, the keeper of the women, appointed. And Esther obtained favour in the sight of all them that looked upon her [Esth. 2:15].

When it was Esther's turn to go to the king, it was decided that she was a natural beauty. It would have been like gilding a lily to send her to the beauty parlor. She was already beautiful and lovely. Everyone who saw her said, "There is the winner!" She stood out above everyone else. Is the hand of God moving? Yes! He is moving by His providence. He is going to put her on the throne next to the king, because, if she is not there, the whole nation of Israel is going to be destroyed. If that happens, God will be violating His Word, and God never does that.

So Esther was taken unto king Ahasuerus into his house royal in the tenth month, which is the month Tebeth, in the seventh year of his reign.

And the king loved Esther above all the women, and she obtained grace and favour in his sight more than all the virgins; so that he set the royal crown upon her head, and made her queen instead of Vashti [Esth. 2:16–17].

When the king saw Esther, he did not have to look any further for a queen. The contest was over as far as he was concerned. He had found the one to take Vashti's place, and Esther was made queen.

How did she become the winner? Was it by accident or chance? I don't think so. Her selection was by the providence of Almighty God. We will see in the next chapter that it was essential for God to go before and make arrangements to protect His people. He did this by making Esther queen. For this reason we were introduced to the pagan palace, the banquet, and the drunken orgy that took place. God wants us to see His overruling in the affairs of men and Satan. This should be a comfort to God's children in this hour in which we live.

We are told that the king loved Esther. I must confess that I am not impressed by it at all. Those of you who have read my book on Ruth know the emphasis put upon the romance of Boaz and Ruth, the loveliest love story, I think, that has ever been told. It is a picture of Christ's love for His church. But I have to say that I do not find that quality in the story of Ahasuerus and Esther. This is an old, disappointed king who almost had reached the end of the road. I am reminded of the story of a foreigner who came to this country. He asked, "What is this, these three R's that I keep hearing about in this country?" Some wiseacre gave him this answer, "At twenty it is Romance; at thirty it is Rent; and at fifty it is Rheumatism." Well, it was rheumatism with the king. This is an old king marrying a lovely young girl. He is an old pagan with no knowledge at all of what real love in God might mean to a couple. I must say that I cannot see anything here to wax eloquent about or to say that this is a picture —as some have done—of Christ and His church.

However, the event is of utmost importance. It is thrilling to see this girl, belonging to a captive people, suddenly become queen over one of the greatest gentile empires the world has ever seen. The wave of anti-Semitism that was imminent would have blotted out these people, and God's entire purpose with Israel would have been frustrated; but when danger strikes, Esther is in a unique position. God moved her into that place.

Then the king made a great feast unto all his princes and his servants, even Esther's feast; and he made a release to the provinces, and gave gifts, according to the state of the king [Esth. 2:18].

You will remember that this book opened with a feast. Now we have another feast, Esther's feast. Since the king has a lovely queen to take Vashti's place, he suspends taxes for one year. If such a thing were done in our day, it would rock the world! It is interesting to see that the king did have the authority to suspend taxes for a year. We all would rejoice if they would conduct some kind of contest in Washington, D.C., that would help reduce taxes!

And when the virgins were gathered together the second time, then Mordecai sat in the king's gate [Esth. 2:19].

Mordecai has a new position—not a job, a *position*. He is sitting in the king's gate. This means that he is a judge, for the courthouse of the ancient world was the gate of the city. Most of the cities were walled, and out through the gate all the citizens would pass sooner or later. Court convened at the city gate, not at the courthouse in the town square. You may recall that the city gate was the place Boaz went to have a legal matter settled. Also, it is said of Lot that he sat in the gate, which meant that he had gotten into politics in Sodom and had a judgeship.

Look at Mordecai. Isn't it interesting that when Esther becomes queen the next thing you know Mordecai is a judge, sitting in the gate? That is nepotism, or getting your kinfolk into office. I do not know whether Mordecai was made judge because of his ability or because Esther whispered in the ear of the king, "This man Mordecai has been just like a father to me. He is a man of remarkable ability, and I think you ought to give him a good position." And the king may have said, "Well, that is interesting. We've just had an opening for a judge here at the east gate, and I'll give him that position." This is a very human book, you see, and politics haven't changed one bit, have they?

Esther had not yet shewed her kindred nor her people; as Mordecai had charged her: for Esther did the commandment of Mordecai, like as when

she was brought up with him [Esth. 2:20].

This girl is a rather remarkable person. Even married to the king, she still takes instructions from the man who reared her. And I will say that I believe Mordecai is one of the outstanding men in Scripture to whom we have paid very little attention. He apparently was a man of remarkable ability.

At this point something takes place that seems extraneous, and yet it is upon this incident that the whole book hinges. As someone has said, "God swings big doors on little hinges." Again we see the providence of God; He is moving behind the scene here.

In those days, while Mordecai sat in the king's gate, two of the king's chamberlains, Bigthan and Teresh, of those which kept the door, were wroth, and sought to lay hand on king Ahasuerus.

And the thing was known to Mordecai, who told it unto Esther the queen; and Esther certified the king thereof in Mordecai's name.

And when inquisition was made of the matter, it was found out; therefore they were both hanged on a tree: and it was written in the book of the chronicles before the king [Esth. 2:21–23].

This is an interesting incident. Mordecai was sitting at the gate. Crowds were coming and going through the gate. He heard two men talking, and he heard them mention the name of the king. He cupped his ears so he could hear what they were talking about and discovered they were plotting to kill the king. So Mordecai immediately got word to Esther about the plot.

This is a very familiar picture: an Oriental potentate and fellows with long mustachios, hiding behind pillars, plotting against the king. Actually, intrigue in an Oriental court was common; there always seemed to be someone who was after the king's job. Mordecai's new position gained him a vantage point so that he was able to overhear the plot.

After Mordecai told Esther about the plan to kill the king, Esther told her husband. I suppose she said to the king, "You remember that I recommended Mordecai as a judge, and you can see that he is already doing an excellent job. He has discovered a plot against your life." The FBI investigated and found it to be true. These fellows were then arrested. They didn't have a long, drawn out trial that spent taxpayers' money. The king ordered them to be put to death, and they were executed by hanging. This was to discourage others who might attempt to plot against the king. Of course, they were very uncivilized in that day, but they did not go in for lawlessness and pampering criminals. This entire incident was written down in the chronicles of the king, in the minutes, if you please, of the kingdom of Persia.

It is interesting to see that something was omitted here. Mordecai was not rewarded or recognized for his service. I suppose he brooded over it many times, wondering why in the world he had been ignored. He wasn't even given a boy scout badge or a lifesaver button for saving the king's life. Certainly he deserved that much. Why was this incident passed by? God is overruling. By His providence, God is directing this entire affair.

CHAPTER 3

***THEME:** Haman and anti-Semitism*

This is a chapter in the life of the Jew that has been duplicated many, many times. When you read this chapter, you can almost substitute the name of Pharaoh instead of Haman, or you can substitute the name of Hitler or Nasser—in fact, there are many names that would fit in here. There never has been a time since Israel became a nation down in the land of Egypt to the present moment that there has not been a movement somewhere to exterminate them.

After these things did king Ahasuerus promote Haman the son of Hammedatha the Agagite, and advanced him, and set his seat above all the princes that were with him [Esth. 3:1].

Here we are introduced to a man by the name of Haman. He is one in the long line of those who have led in a campaign of anti-Semitism. He is promoted by the king to the position that would correspond to prime minister. He was an Agagite. If you turn back to 1 Samuel 15:8, you will find that Agagite was the royal family of the Amalekites. Saul should have obeyed God and destroyed the Agagites. If Saul had done what he had been commanded to do, his people would not have been in this situation, because the Agagites would have completely disappeared. God could see down through history and He knew what was coming. Saul's failure to exterminate the Agagites almost led to the extermination of his own people. But again, God is behind the scenes, keeping watch over His own.

No weapon is going to prosper against Israel. Many people thought that Hitler might become a world dictator but that sending our boys to Europe was premature. I think we should have provided equipment and arms and let Germany and Russia slug it out. When they got so weak they could no longer fight, then we could have stepped in. There are those who said we should not have entered the Vietnam War. I agree with that. I think this idea of always shipping our manpower abroad is entirely wrong. We thought we stopped Hitler, but it was God who stopped him. God is going to stop Haman, too. Now we are beginning to see why God has moved Esther to the throne. If she had not been there, this anti-Semite Haman would have exterminated the Jews. That certainly was his intention.

And all the king's servants, that were in the king's gate, bowed, and reverenced Haman: for the king had so commanded concerning him. But Mordecai bowed not, nor did him reverence [Esth. 3:2].

The king sent out word that he had a new prime minister. Everyone was to bow before him and recognize his position. Now we have seen already that Mordecai is a judge at the gate. He has a political job, which means that he is one of the officials of the kingdom, and he must bow to Haman. But we are told that he did not bow to Haman. Friends, I am prepared to change my mind about Mordecai. I feel like throwing my hat up in the air because he refuses to reverence Haman. I think all of the other flunkies in the king's service went down on all fours when Haman passed by—in that day they didn't just bend to the waist when they bowed.

I see now for the first time the hand of God beginning to move in the life of Mordecai. You may say, "But he is out of the will of God. How can God move in a case like that? He should have returned to his own land." Right! For reasons of his own he did not return but, being a Jew, his place was back in Palestine. It is clear that he is out of the will of God, but he is still recognizing God. Though he makes no appeal to Him anywhere in the Book of Esther, he does recognize God. Do you know how I have come to this conclusion? God's law to the Jews was explicit. They were not to bow to anything but God Himself. They were not to make an image or ever bow to an image. They were not to bow down to anything or anyone. And so when this man Haman comes by after his promotion, everybody who has a political job gets down on his face before him—except one man, Mordecai. Believe me, he is obvious when he is the only one left standing!

Mordecai and Esther were not faithful enough to return to Jerusalem, but they were willing to jeopardize their lives in order to save their people. Therefore, I'm sorry for what I said previously about Mordecai.

Then the king's servants, which were in the king's gate, said unto Mordecai,

Why transgressest thou the king's commandment?

Now it came to pass, when they spake daily unto him, and he hearkened not unto them, that they told Haman, to see whether Mordecai's matters would stand: for he had told them that he was a Jew [Esth. 3:3–4].

He was asked why he didn't bow, and for the first time Mordecai reveals that he is a Jew. Up to this time he has told no one. And you will remember that he had instructed Esther, when she entered the beauty contest, not to let anyone know her race. Even her husband did not know it. But now Mordecai tells them, "The reason I am not bowing to Haman is because I am a Jew." The minute he says that he is also telling them his religion. He worships only the true and living God; he bows to no idol, to no image, to no man. He had been taught in Deuteronomy 6:4, "Hear, O Israel: The LORD our God is one LORD." He was to declare to the world, the ancient world, the world of idolatry, the unity of the Godhead. Today in a world of atheism, we are to declare the Trinity—Father, Son, and Holy Spirit. Mordecai took a stand, and now the others know why. The Jew was known in the world of that day as a worshiper of the one and true God.

I feel like saying, "Hurrah for Mordecai!" I apologize for what I previously said about him. He is beginning now for the first time to take a stand for God, and it is going to cost him a great deal. I do not think he dreamed it would be so far-reaching as to touch all of his people, but he recognizes that it probably will cost him his job, and even his life.

And when Haman saw that Mordecai bowed not, nor did him reverence, then was Haman full of wrath.

And he thought scorn to lay hands on Mordecai alone; for they had shewed him the people of Mordecai: wherefore Haman sought to destroy all the Jews that were throughout the whole kingdom of Ahasuerus, even the people of Mordecai [Esth. 3:5–6].

In this passage Haman reveals that he is a small man. He should have ignored Mordecai. As Mordecai is beginning to stand out as a man of God, this man Haman begins to stand out in all of his ugliness as a man of Satan. The first thing we notice is his littleness. We are going to note all the way through the story that Haman is a little man. You will hear him later on crying on his wife's shoulder. He will say something like this, "I've got everything in the world I want; I can have anything in the kingdom, but that little Jew won't bow to me." It is a small man who will let that sort of thing bother him, and he is permitting it to disturb him a great deal.

Haman is going to attempt to do a terrible thing. He is going to try to destroy all the Jews that live in the kingdom of Ahasuerus. I am sure he knew nothing about God's promise to Abraham to bless those who blessed the Jews and curse those who cursed the Jews. But God makes good that promise. We have only to turn back the pages of history to find that the Jew has attended the funeral of every one of the nations that tried to exterminate him. Hitler tried to exterminate them. He thought he would get rid of them; yet today Hitler and his group are gone, but the Jew is still with us. Yes, God has promised to take care of His people. The fact that they have not been exterminated is in itself miraculous. God has indeed preserved them. And we will see Him do it in the book of Esther.

In the first month, that is, the month Nisan, in the twelfth year of king Ahasuerus, they cast Pur, that is, the lot, before Haman from day to day, and from month to month, to the twelfth month, that is, the month Adar [Esth. 3:7].

Each day Haman's irritation grows. Every time he goes through the gate everybody goes down on his face except that little Jew Mordecai, and it disturbs him. He resolves to do something about it. When Haman discovered that Mordecai's refusal to bow to him was based upon his religious convictions, he decided that a nationwide massacre of the Jews would solve his problem.

Haman had the magicians cast the lot called Pur to decide which day of the year the Jews would be destroyed. What the magicians and Haman did not realize was that God was the One who disposed the lot. God overruled in this situation. The lot fell in the last month of the year, which allowed time for Haman's plot to be discovered and stopped.

And Haman said unto king Ahasuerus, There is a certain people scattered abroad and dispersed among the people in all the provinces of thy kingdom; and their laws are diverse from all people; neither keep they the king's laws:

therefore it is not for the king's profit to suffer them.

If it pleases the king, let it be written that they may be destroyed: and I will pay ten thousand talents of silver to the hands of those that have the charge of the business, to bring it into the king's treasuries [Esth. 3:8–9].

Haman brought it to the attention of Xerxes that there were some people living in his kingdom who were different. They were unusual; they followed the Mosaic Law. They were a people who should be exterminated. He convinced the king that the Jews were defying the king's laws and that their liquidation would bring a lot of wealth into his treasuries from their confiscated property. You will remember that Xerxes had recently been engaged in war, a costly one. He needed money to pay for the bills incurred. Perhaps Haman's idea would bring in enough money to take care of the deficit. The king, of course, was interested in that plan. Most politicians are interested in ways to raise more money, and this seemed like a way out for the king.

Xerxes had so little regard for life, as most potentates of that day did, that he did not even inquire who the people Haman wanted to exterminate were. Haman doesn't know that Esther, the queen, happens to belong to that nationality. Xerxes himself does not know that his queen is Jewish and that he is signing away her life at this time.

And the king took his ring from his hand, and gave it unto Haman the son of Hammedatha the Agagite, the Jews' enemy [Esth. 3:10].

Xerxes took a ring off his finger and gave it to Haman. It was his signet ring. The signet on the ring was pressed down in soft wax and that became the signature of the king. An order that had that signet stamped on it became the law of the kingdom. So Xerxes carelessly takes off his ring, hands it to Haman, and says in effect, "I don't know who they are and I don't care who they are, but if you feel they ought to be exterminated, then you go ahead and take care of the matter." What little regard Xerxes had for human life! He had dissipated the wealth of his kingdom against Greece, and it is variously estimated how many men perished in that campaign. Some feel that as many as two million men died in that war. It didn't seem to bother him one bit that so many had given their lives for a mistake that he had made.

And the king said unto Haman, The silver is given to thee, the people also, to do with them as it seemeth good to thee.

Then were the king's scribes called on the thirteenth day of the first month, and there was written according to all that Haman had commanded unto the king's lieutenants, and to the governors that were over every province, and to the rulers of every people of every province according to the writing thereof, and to every people after their language; in the name of king Ahasuerus was it written, and sealed with the king's ring.

And the letters were sent by posts into all the king's provinces, to destroy, to kill, and to cause to perish, all Jews, both young and old, little children and women, in one day, even upon the thirteenth day of the twelfth month, which is the month Adar, and to take the spoil of them for a prey [Esth. 3:11–13].

This decree to destroy the Jews goes out as a law of the Medes and Persians. It took quite an effort to get this word out because, as you will recall, this empire stretched from India all the way across Asia down through the Fertile Crescent and Mediterranean Sea. It included some of Europe and all of Asia Minor and reached into Africa, through Egypt, and to Ethiopia. It was a vast kingdom. In it were people speaking many languages, a minimum of 127 languages. Also we have to take into account that there were tribes speaking various dialects in these provinces. This law had to be translated into these many tongues. This was quite a government project. The scribes had the job of translating and making enough copies of the law. This was a huge undertaking. When enough copies were made to cover the entire kingdom, they went out by camel and donkey, runner and messenger. On a certain day the Jews were going to be exterminated. This law was giving anti-Semitism full rein and permitting a great many people to do what apparently was in their hearts to do. On this designated day it would be *legal* to kill Jews.

This decree went out as a law of the Medes and Persians. We were told again and again at the very beginning of this book that a law once made was irrevocable. This law could not be changed; it could not be repealed. Another law, we will find out, was issued that counteracted it; yet this law had to stand on the books.

The copy of the writing for a commandment to be given in every province was published unto all people, that they should be ready against that day.

The posts went out, being hastened by the king's commandment, and the decree was given in Shushan the palace. And the king and Haman sat down to drink; but the city Shushan was perplexed [Esth. 3:14–15].

The city of Shushan was perplexed. The Jews were not traitors. They had committed no great crime. Why should extreme measures be used like this to try to exterminate them? Although they may not have liked the Jews and considered them foreigners with differing customs, the city's inhabitants did not want to exterminate them. They could not understand Xerxes' permitting a decree like this to go out. At the palace late that evening you could see the riders getting their orders. Literally hundreds of men must have been pressed into service because of the extent of the kingdom. You could see these different riders being given copies of the new decree that had become law. One company started riding the road to the south, one to the north, another to the west, and to the east. They rode all night. When they came to a little town, they would nail on the bulletin board of that town the decree for the people to read the next morning. Then the riders kept going. When their horses got tired, they were given fresh horses to carry on the job. All over the kingdom is spread the decree that the Jews are to perish. They are "hastened," we are told, by the king's commandment. Yes, the city "Shushan was perplexed," but it didn't bother the king. He and old Haman sat down together and had cocktails that evening. What the king did not realize was that the decree was going to touch his queen.

My friend, anti-Semitism is an awful thing—and it is with us today. Certainly no Christian should have any part in it.

Anti-Semitism had its origin down in the brickyards of Egypt, under the cruel hands of Pharaoh, where the Jews became a nation. From that time on, the great nations of the world have moved against them. It was the story of Assyria, and it was the story of Babylon that took them into captivity. In this Book of Esther we see how they fared in Persia. Rome also must plead guilty, and the Spanish Inquisition was largely leveled at the Jews. Then under Hitler in Germany it is estimated that six million Jews perished.

What is the reason for the thing that we call anti-Semitism? Let us analyze it briefly. There are *two* things that are behind it. The first reason is a natural one, and the second reason is supernatural.

The natural reason is simply this: They are unlovely. Now do not misunderstand me. There was a Christian Jew in Memphis who was a very personal friend of mine. He was a wonderful person. Let us face the facts. A godless person, Jew or Gentile, is unlovely. I know of no person more unlovely than a godless Gentile, nor do I know of a lovelier person than a Christian Jew. God saw us unlovely, undone, and unattractive; but by His sovereign grace He makes us new creatures in Christ. That same grace reached down and called the Jews a chosen people.

Then there is a supernatural reason why the Jews are hated. In the providence and design of God, those who have been the custodians of His written Word have been the people of the Jewish race. Our Bible has come to us through them. God chose them for that. They transmitted the Scriptures. Satan hates them because they have been the repository of the Scriptures and because the Lord Jesus Christ, after the flesh, came from them. Paul put it like this: "Whose are the fathers, and of whom as concerning the flesh Christ came . . ." (Rom. 9:5). There is no way of escaping it. And because of this, there is a supernatural hatred of Jews. This is certainly clear in the Bible. We know that God has chosen them as His people and as His nation. They are hated by Satan and, as a result, the nations of the world at times are fanned into fury against these people.

The law made by Xerxes could not be revoked. We have already seen one law that set aside Vashti the queen. That law could not be changed. Even the king could not change it. The law ordering the extermination of the Jews was signed by the king. It became the law of the Medes and Persians. There was no way it could be changed. How will God save His people? Another decree will have to be made. Somebody is going to have to intervene. God, by the way, has been preparing for this very thing.

When we first began the study of this little book, we talked about the providence of God. We looked at a scene at a pagan palace where a drunken orgy was taking place. Several thousand people were attending a banquet. A family scandal is revealed, and the queen, who refused to obey the king, is set aside. What does this have to do with God's saving His people? It has everything to do with it. God was moving, and He is going to continue to move in a mighty way. He has placed a person right next to the throne. She is going to be the means of saving the Jews. God moves in the affairs of men by His providence.

God's providence is illustrated in the story of the birth of Jesus Christ. Caesar Augustus signed a tax bill that decreed that all the world was to be taxed. When he signed that bill, he did not know that he was fulfilling prophecy. He did not know that the tax bill would cause a maiden in Nazareth to go to Bethlehem, where her first child would be born. I think Caesar Augustus would have laughed and said, "I don't know anything about babies, but I do know about taxes." Micah 5:2 foretold the birth of Christ in Bethlehem. Caesar signed a bill that caused Mary to be in Bethlehem at just the right time to give birth to the Lord Jesus Christ. God was in Caesar's palace. God was in the palace of Xerxes. "Standeth God in the shadows keeping watch over His own."

CHAPTER 4

***THEME:** For such a time as this*

The terrible decree is going out to every corner of the kingdom. Now notice Mordecai's reaction:

When Mordecai perceived all that was done, Mordecai rent his clothes, and put on sackcloth with ashes, and went out into the midst of the city, and cried with a loud and a bitter cry;

And came even before the king's gate: for none might enter into the king's gate clothed with sackcloth [Esth. 4: 1–2].

When Mordecai heard about the decree to annihilate the Jews, he put on sackcloth and ashes. My, what a performance! He *believed* the decree; he *knew* it could not be changed. I would guess that there were roughly fifteen million Jews at that time in the kingdom. It would have been a terrible slaughter, so unnecessary and uncalled for. Because one petty official would not bow down to Haman, an entire race was to be exterminated. This was satanic, of course.

And in every province, whithersoever the king's commandment and his decree came, there was great mourning among the Jews, and fasting, and weeping, and wailing; and many lay in sackcloth and ashes [Esth. 4:3].

Do you notice that there is no call to prayer? You see, these people are out of the will of God. The decree of Cyrus, prophesied by Isaiah, had permitted them to return to Israel, but they did not return. They are out of God's will, and consequently there is no call to prayer whatsoever. But they go through the remainder of the ritual: fasting, putting on of sackcloth and ashes, and great mourning.

They *believed* the decree that had gone out from Xerxes. It was the law of the Medes and the Persians, which was unalterable according to these historical books and also according to the Book of Daniel. And you remember that even Xerxes himself, when he had put aside his beautiful queen, could never take her again because the decree had been made that she was to come no more before the king. Even *he* could not change his own law after it had been made. And so when this decree of death came throughout the empire, the Jews believed it and mourned in sackcloth and ashes.

Conspicuously absent today (the church, I think, is responsible for it) is conviction concerning sin—not only in the hearts and lives of the unsaved, but in the hearts and lives of believers. The average believer says, "Yes, I trust Christ." But he has no real conviction of sin in his life at all. It is absent in contemporary church life. When is the last time that you heard a sinner, saved or lost, cry out to God for mercy? At the beginning of my ministry I saw a great many tears, I saw people cry out to God. I do not see that today. Even in evangelistic crusades there is a lot of "coming forward," but there is that lack of weeping over sin in the lives of folk. Why? They just don't believe God means it, my friend. They do not believe that God intends to enforce judgment against sin and the sinner who will hold to it and not turn to Christ.

Mordecai knew and believed the seriousness of the decree. He tore his clothes and put on sackcloth with ashes. He went out into the center of the city and cried with a loud and bitter cry. Jews all over the kingdom mourned, fasted, wept, and wailed. They all *believed* the seriousness of the decree.

So Esther's maids and her chamberlains came and told it her. Then was the queen exceedingly grieved; and she sent raiment to clothe Mordecai, and to take away his sackcloth from him: but he received it not [Esth. 4:4].

Queen Esther, feeling perfectly safe and secure as queen, was embarrassed by the conduct of Mordecai, her adoptive father. Here he was, out in the city, walking up and down, moaning, wailing, and groaning. So what does she do? She sends him a sporty new suit of clothes. They were gay, gaudy, expensive, and fine. The colors were probably bright. But, you see, all the bright colors and new clothes will not change the king's edict. Mordecai would not receive the clothes. They would not remove the stigma.

There is an application here. The covering of religion will not remove the fact that man is a guilty sinner before God. Neither will religion alter the fact that the wages of sin is death.

People deal with sin in many different ways. Some try the gaudy clothes method. They refuse to believe that man is a sinner. They reach out for any garment that might hide from them the reality of sin. Others put on the gaudy clothes of reformation. They say that sin is just a little mistake, and they try to cover it. They think sin can be reformed.

Someone has said that the modern pulpit has become a place where a mild-mannered man gets up before a group of mild-mannered people and urges them to be more mild-mannered. Friends, I cannot think of anything more insipid than that. No wonder the world has passed by the church. We don't need reforming; we need to be *regenerated.* We need to be born again.

Nicodemus, a ruler of the Jews, was religious, but our Lord said to him, ". . . Ye must be born again" (John 3:7). We need a new nature because we have a sinful nature, and that sinful nature is not going to heaven, my friend. You have to come to the Lord Jesus Christ and trust Him. He died on the cross for you. He took your place and has already paid the penalty of your sin. All you have to do is accept what has been done for you. If you go to heaven, it will be because you trusted the One who died for you.

There is another kind of gaudy clothes that people wear known as "education." They say that sin is selfishness. All you have to do is educate and train folk and they won't be selfish. I had a sister who was younger than I was. My Dad used to bring us a sack of gumdrops when he came home from work. He would tell me that I was to divide the candy with her. I always took the first piece, and she would protest because sometimes it worked out that I also took the last piece. That always gave me one more gumdrop than she had. So a rule had to be made that one time I would take the first piece of candy and the next time she would take the first piece. Sometimes I took the first piece when it was really my sister's turn. May I say that all of the instruction and education given to me never kept me from being selfish. And don't try to kid me, it hasn't helped *you,* either.

Many years ago, Dr. Shaler Matthews from the University of Chicago's School of Religion came up with this definition of sin: "Sin is the backward pull of an outworn good." Think that one over for awhile. If you take away all of the modifiers, you see that he is saying that sin is good! And that is what religion finally winds up telling you. May I say to you that you need a new garment. You need the righteousness of Christ. That is the *only* thing that will enable you to stand before God.

Now Mordecai was not about to accept any gaudy clothes from his daughter, the queen. When the clothes came back to her, she knew that something serious was going on. Esther knew that it was not something minor that caused her father to return the clothes.

Then called Esther for Hatach, one of the king's chamberlains, whom he had appointed to attend upon her, and gave him a commandment to Mordecai, to know what it was, and why it was [Esth. 4:5].

Esther wants some answers. She wants to know what has caused Mordecai to put on sackcloth and ashes.

So Hatach went forth to Mordecai unto the street of the city, which was before the king's gate [Esth. 4:6].

Of course as queen she could not have gone to him herself. So she sends a messenger.

And Mordecai told him of all that had happened unto him, and of the sum of the money that Haman had promised to pay to the king's treasuries for the Jews, to destroy them.

Also he gave him the copy of the writing of the decree that was given at Shushan to destroy them, to shew it unto Esther, and to declare it unto her, and to charge her that she should go in unto the king, to make supplication unto him, and to make request before him for her people.

And Hatach came and told Esther the words of Mordecai [Esth. 4:7–9].

Mordecai sent a message back to Queen Esther which said in effect, "The reason that I am in sackcloth and ashes is that our people, you and I, have come under an awful decree of death." Then he gave the messenger a copy of the decree so that Esther could read it for herself. I wish that folk who say that the Bible does not teach that man is a sinner would read what God's Word says. It is all there in black and white. If they will read it, they will see that God declares we are sinners and are under His sentence of death.

So the messenger returned to Esther with Mordecai's message and a copy of the king's decree.

Again Esther spake unto Hatach, and gave him commandment unto Mordecai [Esth. 4:10].

After Esther heard Mordecai's message and read the decree, she sent him another message.

All the king's servants, and the people of the king's provinces, do know, that whosoever, whether man or woman, shall come unto the king into the inner court, who is not called, there is one law of his to put him to death, except such to whom the king shall hold out the golden sceptre, that he may live: but I have not been called to come in unto the king these thirty days [Esth. 4:11].

In other words, "That's too bad. I am sorry to hear it. I didn't know about it before." And she adds, "But I have not been called into the king's presence now for thirty days. I do not know his attitude toward me—and you know what the law is." As was the case in every kingdom of that day, anyone who dared go into the presence of the king without being summoned would be summarily, automatically, put to death—unless the king extended his sceptre to him. Xerxes was noted for his fits of temper; he could have put his queen to death if she had gone in without being called. So she sent back word to Mordecai, "If I go in, it may mean death to me."

And they told to Mordecai Esther's words [Esth. 4:12].

Then Mordecai returned to her this memorable message:

Then Mordecai commanded to answer Esther, Think not with thyself that thou shalt escape in the king's house, more than all the Jews.

For if thou altogether holdest thy peace at this time, then shall there enlargement and deliverance arise to the Jews from another place; but thou and thy father's house shall be destroyed: and who knoweth whether thou art come to the kingdom for such a time as this? [Esth. 4:13–14].

We must remember that there had been another queen and a decree which had set her aside. Esther was probably taking warning from that, but, if she thinks the decree will protect her, she is wrong. The decree is that *all* of the Jews are to be slain, and she is Jewish. Mordecai puts it on the line: "Just because you happen to be the queen does not exempt you from the execution because it will reach every Jew in the kingdom, and it will also reach the queen." We will find out later that Xerxes did not know that she was a Jewess.

Mordecai went on to say that if Esther held her peace then deliverance would come from another source. Some day when I see Mordecai (and I *do* expect to see him), I would like to ask him what he had in mind when he said that deliverance would arise from another place. I have thought this over, and I ask you the question: "What other place was there to which they could turn?" Where could deliverance come to them except from God? He was their only hope at this time, and I am confident that Mordecai had that in mind. God would move in another direction. He must have known that deliverance would come because he was acquainted with the promises that God had made to Abraham.

So Mordecai challenges Esther. Xerxes was a world ruler. Would deliverance come from the north, east, south, or west? There was not a person on the topside of the earth who could have delivered her. So he said to Esther, "Who knoweth whether thou art come to the kingdom for such a time as this?" I think Mordecai now detects that the hand of God has been moving and that Esther is on the throne for a purpose.

We begin to see God by His providence moving now in the affairs of the nation. It is obvious that Esther did not accidentally win a beauty contest. She was not accidentally the one who became queen. She is there for a very definite purpose, and God has been arranging this all the time. He is prepared for this event. God knows what is coming. That is why, friends, we can trust Him. When we put our hand in His hand, He has the power to hold us. He knows what is going to happen tomorrow and next month and next year. He will care for us. All we have to do is trust Him.

Mordecai is becoming a noble man now in my estimation. He is revealing that he is taking a stand for God. He is willing to die for God. Watch Esther now. She is a queen, every inch a queen.

Then Esther bade them return Mordecai this answer,

Go, gather together all the Jews that are present in Shushan, and fast ye for me, and neither eat nor drink three days, night or day: I also and my maidens will fast likewise; and so will I go unto the king, which is not according to the law: and if I perish, I perish.

So Mordecai went his way, and did according to all that Esther had commanded him [Esth. 4:15–17].

These are the words of a noble woman. She tells Mordecai to gather all of the Jews in the city together to fast. She and her maidens would do the same. She would go to the king for help, and she was willing to perish if need be. Once again you will notice that nothing is said about prayer. Why doesn't she pray? Because she is out of the will of God. Why don't the Jews pray? They, too, are out of God's will. When Jonah was on the boat running away from God, nothing is said about prayer. He was out of the will of God. He shouldn't have been on that boat. It is hard to pray when you are out of God's will. It is possible that some of the Jews prayed, but it certainly is not mentioned.

Esther's decision to go before the king is a very brave act. But, beloved, there is One more noble. He vaulted the battlements of heaven, came down to earth, and took upon Himself our human flesh. He did not say, "If I perish, I perish." He said ". . . the Son of Man came to give his life a ransom for many" (Matt. 20:28).

CHAPTER 5

***THEME:** The sceptre of grace*

Now it came to pass on the third day, that Esther put on her royal apparel, and stood in the inner court of the king's house, over against the king's house: and the king sat upon his royal throne in the royal house, over against the gate of the house [Esth. 5:1].

The king was sitting on his royal throne opposite the entrance to the palace. Around him were his court attendants dressed in all of their finery. Imagine the color! In addition to that were the awnings, the tapestries, the gold and silver and marble of the throne room. The king was probably conducting state business when Esther stepped out from an alcove, or from behind a pillar, and stood there in her royal apparel. And I want to say, friends, that she was beautiful.

And it was so, when the king saw Esther the queen standing in the court, that she obtained favour in his sight: and the king held out to Esther the golden sceptre that was in his hand. So Esther drew near, and touched the top of the sceptre [Esth. 5:2].

Esther had prepared herself to appear before the king. You will remember that when she came the first time before the king and won the beauty contest that she required none of the fine clothing or elaborate accessories that the other girls had required. By her natural beauty she had won, and the king had fallen in love with her. But this time I am sure that she spent a great deal of time on her dress. We are told that "Esther put on her royal apparel," which means that she put on the finest that she had. It meant that she looked the best that she could. In fact, if I may use the common colloquialism of the street, she knocked the king's eye out! I tell you, she was lovely.

When she stepped into that royal court and waited—it was certainly a dramatic moment—the king looked at her. The question is: Will he raise the sceptre or will he not? And in that moment I am confident this Hebrew girl prayed, although there is no record of it. She must have recognized how helpless and hopeless she really was. And then the king held out the golden sceptre to her, and possibly smiled. Then she advanced and put her hand on the sceptre, which was the custom of the day.

What a picture we have here. In this book I have been emphasizing the law of the Medes and Persians and comparing their law to the Law of God. God's Law says, "The soul that sinneth, it shall die . . ." (Ezek. 18:20). And, friends, God has never changed that. It is as true now as it ever was. That is God's Law. It is immutable. He could not change that without changing His character.

There is another side to the story. We see that in holding out the sceptre to Queen Esther, the king was giving her her life. May I say to you, our God holds out the sceptre to mankind today. It is true that ". . . all have sinned, and come short of the glory of God" (Rom. 3:23). It is true that we are ". . . dead in trespasses and sins" (Eph. 2:1). It is true that ". . . the soul that sinneth, it shall die." (Ezek. 18:4). But, you see, our God had to overcome that tremendous law, and the only way in the world He could overcome it was for Him to come to this earth Himself, and take upon Himself our sins, and pay that penalty—for that law was not abrogated, and it is not abrogated today. When God saved you, my friend, it was because Somebody else paid the penalty for your sins. He died a substitutionary death upon that cross for you and me. As a result of that, God holds out to the earth the sceptre of grace, and He says to any individual, "You can come to Me. You can touch that sceptre of grace. You can receive salvation from Me."

Now Esther has come into the presence of the king, and he recognizes immediately that she would never have made this effort if an emergency had not arisen.

Then said the king unto her, What wilt thou, queen Esther? and what is thy request? it shall be even given thee to the half of the kingdom [Esth. 5:3].

He knows she did not come to him in this manner because of some petty problem. He knows she did not come to ask for money to buy a new hat or to suggest that they go out to dinner at the local restaurant. He knows something is troubling his queen. He sees that she is trembling and greatly distressed. He wants her to feel comfortable, and so he says, "It shall be given thee to the half of the kingdom." This is not an idle expression. To make her feel at ease, he hands her a blank check and invites her to fill in the amount.

And Esther answered, If it seem good unto the king, let the king and Haman come this day unto the banquet that I have prepared for him [Esth. 5:4].

Esther does not make her request known right away. She simply invites the king to lunch and asks him to bring Haman too. She wants Haman present when she lets the king know that the thing he has demanded is not only the death of the Jews but her death also.

What Esther did was an audacious and brave thing. She knew she was the only help for her people. After all, God had placed her in the position of being queen by His providence. I am sure that Esther would never have said that she was there by the will of God. In fact, she does not even mention the name of God. But she did go into the presence of the king knowing that it might mean her death. The die is cast.

My friend, we are all going to stand before the King of kings some day. Every believer will stand before Him to see whether or not he will receive a reward. This judgment will be at the Bema seat of Christ. There is another judgment where only the lost will appear. This will be at the Great White Throne, where they will be judged according to their works.

As the king held out the sceptre to Esther, and she stepped up and touched it, so God holds out the sceptre of grace to us today; and He asks us to come and touch it by faith, accepting what He has to offer. He is not gracious to us because we are beautiful. My mirror tells me I'm not beautiful, and both of us are ugly on the inside, too. Sin comes out of the human heart. We hear much about the fact that we should take care of all the pollution—and I am all for it—but I want to start where all the trouble begins, which is the human heart. He is holding out the sceptre of grace to all who will receive His Son, the Lord Jesus Christ.

Then the king said, Cause Haman to make haste, that he may do as Esther hath said. So the king and Haman came to the banquet that Esther had prepared [Esth. 5:5].

You can see the feeling of the king in this verse. He said, "You tell Haman that Esther has invited us to dinner and that he is to come that he may do as Esther has said." The king has been very generous to Haman. He has made him prime minister. He gave Haman his ring and let him send out the request that he wanted to slay the Jews. But when the comparison is made with Queen Esther, Haman must obey her. She is the queen. So this puts her in a very favorable light indeed. The king and Haman came to the banquet that Esther had prepared.

And the king said unto Esther at the banquet of wine, What is thy petition? and it shall be granted thee: and what is thy request? even to the half of the kingdom it shall be performed [Esth. 5:6].

At the banquet Esther is obviously nervous, and the king can see that there is something that is deeply troubling her. He asks her what her request is and offers her up to half of the kingdom. As we have seen, this idiomatic expression means she can have anything she wants. He sees that she is still anxious, so he hands her this blank check.

There is a lesson here. God, through the Lord Jesus Christ, has given us a blank check. Paul could say in Philippians 4:19: "But my God shall supply all your need according to his riches in glory by Christ Jesus." God has given us a blank check, but the amount is not filled in, even though He has signed it. How wonderful it is to have such a King. But He is more than a King. He is our Savior. He is the Savior of the world. He is holding out the sceptre of grace to a lost world.

Why is this cruel king being so gracious and patient with Esther? Proverbs 21:1 says, "The king's heart is in the hand of the LORD as the rivers of water: he turneth it whithersoever he will." In the story of Esther, the Lord is moving the king in a definite way.

Then answered Esther, and said, My petition and my request is:

If I have found favour in the sight of the king, and if it please the king to grant my petition, and to perform my request, let the king and Haman come to the banquet that I shall prepare for them, and I will do to–morrow as the king hath said [Esth. 5:7–8].

Esther still does not have the courage to express her request to the king, so she says, "I am having another banquet tomorrow. We have just had a smorgasbord today, but you come back tomorrow and I will prepare a real banquet. *Then* I will let you know what my request is." You can see the fear that is in the heart of this girl. There was nothing more for the king and Haman to do but to finish the meal and then depart.

Then went Haman forth that day joyful and with a glad heart: but when Haman saw Mordecai in the king's gate, that he stood not up, nor moved for him, he was full of indignation against Mordecai [Esth. 5:9].

Haman came out from the banquet very happy that he only had been the guest of the king and queen. His ego has been greatly expanded. He had made such a hit with the queen that she invited him back the next day for another banquet. This section illustrates that "Pride goeth before destruction, and an haughty spirit before a fall" (Prov. 16:18). The Greeks also have a proverb. It goes something like, "Whom the gods would destroy, they first make mad."

As Haman left the banquet, all the functionaries of the kingdom bow before him—except one, Mordecai, a judge, who stands erect. You would think that a man in Haman's position would ignore a little thing like Mordecai's refusal to bow to him. But he is not going to ignore it. He is full of indignation against Mordecai, but he restrains himself for the time being. He thinks, "I'll get even with you in a few days."

Nevertheless Haman refrained himself: and when he came home, he sent and called for his friends, and Zeresh his wife.

And Haman told them of the glory of his riches, and the multitude of his children, and all the things wherein the king had promoted him, and how he had advanced him above the princes and servants of the king [Esth. 5: 10–11].

Haman is certainly playing the fool. He wants to do a little bragging. As you may have noticed, when a man starts bragging, there are usually three areas he talks about. First he boasts about his riches, the money he makes. Then he talks about his fine children—or grandchildren (that's what I do). Then he will generally boast about his promotion and high position. Haman went all the way. He boasted in all three areas.

Haman said moreover, Yea, Esther the queen did let no man come in with the king unto the banquet that she had prepared but myself; and to-morrow am I invited unto her also with the king [Esth. 5:12].

There is another thing that men boast about. They like to boast about being great with the ladies. He had had lunch with the queen today, and tomorrow he was going to have dinner with her! Haman was very human as well as being a rascal and villain. He does not know what is in store for him. He would do well to turn down the queen's invitation, but this man will not do that.

Yet all this availeth me nothing, so long as I see Mordecai the Jew sitting at the king's gate [Esth. 5:13].

There is one little fly in the ointment. He cannot get over the fact that Mordecai won't bow to him. All of the things on the credit side of the ledger don't mean a thing when compared to the indignity given him by Mordecai. Someone has said that you can always tell the size of a man by the things that irritate him. If little things irritate him, he is a little man. If it takes big things to irritate him, he is a big man.

My friend, what bothers you? Do little things like that annoy you? Oh, don't let insignificant things mar your life. That is the mark of littleness. Yet most of us must confess that it is the small things, the "little foxes that spoil the vines" as far as our own lives are concerned.

Haman revealed himself to be a little man. After all, Mordecai was only a judge, a petty judge, in the kingdom. Haman was the prime minister. Ignore the fellow! Not Haman. "All this availeth me nothing, so long as I see Mordecai the Jew, sitting at the king's gate."

Then said Zeresh his wife and all his friends unto him, Let a gallows be made of fifty cubits high, and to-morrow speak thou unto the king that Mordecai may be hanged thereon: then go thou in merrily with the king unto the banquet. And the thing pleased Haman; and he caused the gallows to be made [Esth. 5:14].

Zeresh, his wife, and his friends suggested that he build a gallows for Mordecai. So late that evening they built a gallows fifty cubits (that's about seventy-five feet) high! Think of that! Remember that the meaning of the name *Mordecai*, is "little"—he was a short fellow. To erect a gallows seventy-five feet high on which to hang a short fellow reveals the resentment, the hatred, and the bitterness in his heart. However, with this happy solution Haman goes to bed.

CHAPTER 6

***THEME:** When a king could not sleep at night*

On that night could not the king sleep, and he commanded to bring the book of records of the chronicles; and they were read before the king [Esth. 6:11].

The fact that the king could not sleep seems to be a very small thing, but God uses small things. Also, I am of the opinion that the king had many sleepless nights. As Shakespeare said, "Uneasy lies the head that wears a crown." There were nights when I am sure the king felt that his life was in jeopardy. But this night that the king could not sleep was the most eventful night in the history of the empire because it is the turning point in the Book of Esther.

Have you noticed that God uses the little things to carry out His program? Years before in Egypt God brought together a woman's heart and a baby's cry when Pharaoh's daughter found the baby Moses in the Nile River. By this he changed the destiny of a nation. A supposedly unimportant thing occurred at the palace of Shushan—the king could not sleep. So he commanded his servants to bring the uninteresting records of the kingdom to him. They were read before the king. Evidently the reading of these records was conducive to sleep. They were the king's sleeping pill. The fatal hour had come, and now we are going to see the hand of God begin to move.

A servant was summoned who began to drone off this record, which is like a log or the minutes of the kingdom. I do not mean to be unlovely, but to me the most boring thing in the world is to listen to minutes. Have you ever heard any minutes that were interesting? I never have. I have been on all kinds of boards, and I've gotten off every board I could get off because I don't like to listen to the minutes. They are boring. On the nights that the king could not sleep, he would say, "Bring in the minutes. Let's read them again." Soon the king would drop off to sleep.

On this particular night the servants just happened to turn to a certain place in the minutes. Did I say *happened* to turn? Little things are beginning to pile up and reveal God's hand in the glove of human circumstances. God is moving. He is overruling. It was no accident that Esther became queen. It was no accident that she presented herself to the king and found favor in his sight. It was no accident that he accepted her invitation to a banquet. Now he is unable to sleep, and it is no accident that the servant began to read at a certain place.

And it was found written, that Mordecai had told of Bigthana and Teresh, two of the king's chamberlains, the keepers of the door, who sought to lay hand on the king Ahasuerus.

And the king said, What honour and dignity hath been done to Mordecai for this? Then said the king's servants that ministered unto him, There is nothing done for him [Esth. 6:2–3].

You talk about the Mafia; these two fellows belonged to the Mafia of that day. Mordecai overheard these two men plotting, the kind of plotting that we always think of in connection with the Persian Empire—shadowy figures behind pillars, plotting in low tones of putting a dagger in the king. Mordecai passed that word on to Queen Esther, and she notified the king. That incident was recorded in the chronicles of the kingdom. When the chamberlain read this, the king became alert for a moment. He rose up in bed and said, "By the way, you didn't read there—or I must have missed it—was this man Mordecai rewarded?" The chamberlain looked down and read the next set of minutes and replied, "No, he was never rewarded." The king said, "The man who saved my life must be rewarded!"

While all of this was going on in the palace, there is a knock at the outside door.

And the king said, Who is in the court? Now Haman was come into the outward court of the king's house, to speak unto the king to hang Mordecai on the gallows that he had prepared for him.

And the king's servants said unto him, Behold, Haman standeth in the court. And the king said, Let him come in.

So Haman came in. And the king said unto him, What shall be done unto the man whom the king delighteth to honour? Now Haman thought in his heart, To whom would the king delight to do honour more than to myself? [Esth. 6:4–6].

Just at the time the king discovered Mordecai had never been rewarded for saving his life, Haman was heard coming into the outer court. The king said, "Who is in the court?" It was Haman. He hadn't slept too well either. He had come to the king's house to get permission to hang Mordecai on the gallows that he had prepared for him. Apparently Haman had the privilege of coming into the king's presence at any time. When Haman came in, the king brought him into the conversation without giving him any background. He had come to ask for the life of Mordecai at the same moment the king is prepared to reward him!

These circumstances reveal the providence of God. In the shadows God is keeping watch over His own. Although these people are out of the will of God, in the land far away from where God wants them, they are still not out from under His direct leading. These providential dealings could not have been accidental.

When Haman walks into the king's presence, he is greeted with the question, "What shall be done unto the man whom the king delighteth to honour?" Haman thought the king was talking about him. After all, he had been made prime minister. He had been given the ring of the king—he had paid a certain sum of money, true, but he was able to get permission to exterminate the Jewish people *en toto*—and certainly there is no one else in the kingdom that he can think of that the king would delight to honor. But the king was thinking of Mordecai.

And Haman answered the king. For the man whom the king delighteth to honour,

Let the royal apparel be brought which the king useth to wear, and the horse that the king rideth upon, and the crown royal which is set upon his head:

And let this apparel and horse be delivered to the hand of one of the king's most noble princes, that they may array the man withal whom the king delighteth to honour, and bring him on horseback through the street of the city, and proclaim before him, Thus shall it be done to the man whom the king delighteth to honour [Esth. 5:7–9].

The true nature of Haman is revealed in his answer. I am sure you can see what is in his heart; Haman had his eye upon the throne. It was his intention, when the time was right, to eliminate the king. That is the story of the Persian monarchs anyway. It was difficult for a man to stay on the throne very long. Even in Israel's history, as recorded in 1 and 2 Kings, if it were not so tragic, it would be humorous to see how short a time some of the kings ruled. Some of them only made it through two months. When a king sat on his throne and looked around him, he didn't know who was his friend and who was his enemy. He couldn't imagine because he realized that any man who was lifted up would attempt to slay him in order that he might become king. Obviously this was in the heart of Haman.

Haman was thinking, "To whom would the king delight to do honor more than to myself? You let me have the apparel of the king, put the crown on my head, let me ride the king's horse, let it be announced by a herald when I go through the streets." What is he doing? Haman is preparing the people for the day when the crown and the royal apparel will be his. I am of the opinion that the king would suspect this type of thing, for he recognized that Haman was thinking of himself and certainly not of Mordecai.

Then the king said to Haman, Make haste, and take the apparel and the horse, as thou hast said, and do even so to Mordecai the Jew, that sitteth at the king's gate: let nothing fail of all that thou hast spoken [Esth. 6:10].

There was nothing that could have been asked of Haman that would have been more displeasing, more ignominious, or more distasteful than to put the royal garments on Mordecai, put him on the king's horse, and lead him through the streets proclaiming that this is the man that the king delighted to honor! To accord him this honor was mortification beyond words to Haman. He hated Mordecai.

Then took Haman the apparel and the horse, and arrayed Mordecai, and brought him on horseback through the street of the city, and proclaimed before him, Thus shall it be done unto the man whom the king delighteth to honour [Esth. 6:11].

Instead of leading Mordecai through the streets in honor, Haman had intended to hang him on the gallows. The humiliation of Haman at this point is absolutely unspeakable. You can imagine the feeling that he had as he led this horse, with the man who would not bow to him seated on it, through the street. He had a gallows at home, seventy-five feet high, on which to hang him!

And Mordecai came again to the king's gate. But Haman hasted to his house mourning, and having his head covered.

And Haman told Zeresh his wife and all his friends every thing that had befallen him. Then said his wise men and Zeresh his wife unto him, If Mordecai be of the seed of the Jews, before whom thou hast begun to fall, thou shalt not prevail against him, but shalt surely fall before him.

And while they were yet talking with him, came the king's chamberlains, and hasted to bring Haman unto the banquet that Esther had prepared [Esth. 6:12–14].

Finally the ordeal was over. Mordecai returned to the king's gate. But Haman hurried to his house, mourning, and having his head covered. Shame beyond shame. He told his wife and friends everything that had happened. Zeresh was a nice little wife, was she not? She suggested that the gallows be built, and now she is telling Haman, "I told you so. You're beginning to fall."

It is not exactly comforting to have your wife and friends suggest that probably tomorrow will be your last day! Things are happening thick and fast. Haman no sooner gets home and explains to his wife and his wise men what had happened than there is a knock at the door. The king's servants tell Haman to hurry up, the banquet is ready that he had promised to attend. He had looked forward to this dinner, you remember, and had boasted about the fact that he was the only one whom the queen had invited with the king to attend her banquet. He is going to be late for the dinner that he had been looking forward to, but the events were taking place so fast he couldn't keep up with them. Things are beginning to happen to his disadvantage. He has no control over circumstances. Do you know why? Because God is overruling everything and seeing to it that Haman's plot does not succeed.

CHAPTER 7

***THEME:** The man who came to dinner but died on the gallows*

So the king and Haman came to banquet with Esther the queen.

And the king said again unto Esther on the second day at the banquet of wine, What is thy petition, queen Esther? and it shall be granted thee: and what is thy request? and it shall be performed, even to the half of the kingdom [Esth. 7:1–2].

Haman went to the banquet with mingled feelings. He is thrilled that the queen has invited him to dinner, but he is still mortified at the honor given to Mordecai. I am of the opinion that at this moment Haman does not quite understand why Mordecai had been honored and he was passed by.

Now Esther has, if I may use the expression, screwed up her courage, after the second day, to tell the king the thing that is in her heart. She could not do it before, but now she is ready—even though she is nervous. Once again the king renews his overture to the queen. He says, "Queen Esther, what is your petition, and it shall be granted to you." Once again he offers her up to half the kingdom. This is the third time the king has asked the queen what is on her mind.

Then Esther the queen answered and said, If I have found favour in thy sight, O king, and if it please the king, let my life be given me at my petition, and my people at my request.

For we are sold, I and my people, to be destroyed, to be slain, and to perish. But if we had been sold for bondmen and bondwomen, I had held my tongue, although the enemy could not countervail the king's damage [Esth. 7:3–4].

When Esther spoke, it was a frightful thing that she revealed. Both the king and Haman were startled because neither of them knew her nationality. Her request was that her life and the lives of her people be spared. When

Mordecai had entered her in the beauty contest and also when she had become queen, he had instructed her not to tell her nationality, not to reveal to anyone that she was a Jewess. So she had kept this fact to herself all of this time.

Haman, as you remember, had gotten an edict from the king that all the Jews in the kingdom were to be destroyed. He did not know that the queen was a Jewess. She now identifies herself with her people. So far removed that she did not even want to be known as a Jewess, she now takes her place with her condemned people. For her to do this in that day was also to identify herself with her religion and with her God, because they both go together.

She said to the king, "Although the king would have suffered a great loss, I would have kept quiet if we were just going to be sold into slavery. But that isn't the problem—we are to be *slain* on a certain day!" She wanted him to know that the Jews had been betrayed and were to be destroyed as a people.

The king was absolutely amazed. Who would dare attempt to destroy the queen? And who would dare attempt to destroy her people? What she said was as shocking a statement as the king ever expected to hear. The queen and her people were going to perish.

Then the king Ahasuerus answered and said unto Esther the queen, Who is he, and where is he, that durst presume in his heart to do so? [Esth. 7:5].

The king is startled. He doesn't dream that there is any such thing taking place in his kingdom. He apparently does not recognize even yet who the people are to be slain. Frankly, this man had little regard for life. If you read the secular campaign of Xerxes which he made into Europe against Greece, you will find that he threw men about as if they all were expendable. He lost thousands and thousands of men in that campaign, and it did not disturb him one bit. Human life was very cheap in that day. The thing that now disturbs him is that they are the people of Esther. His queen is in mortal danger. So the king asks, "Who is he? Where is he? Who would presume to do such a thing?"

I still don't think it has yet dawned on Haman what is really taking place. He did not know that the decree to slay the nation Israel would affect the queen. He did not know she was Jewish. There he was at the banquet table, reclining on a couch—the prime minister, with the full confidence of the king.

Ahasuerus has asked who hatched this plot, and Esther now reveals her bravery. She is putting her life on the line by answering the king's question.

And Esther said, The adversary and enemy is this wicked Haman. Then Haman was afraid before the king and the queen [Esth. 7:6].

Haman has no answer for that. He is dumbfounded to learn that Esther is Jewish.

God is moving behind the scenes. God is watching over His own. No weapon formed against Israel will prosper. God is going to bless those who bless the Jews and curse those who curse the Jews. The providence of God is going to keep the children of Israel.

The king is so startled at the sudden turn of events that he leaves the banquet table and goes into the garden. After all, he is implicated to a certain extent. And so he leaves to think this matter over.

And the king arising from the banquet of wine in his wrath went into the palace garden: and Haman stood up to make request for his life to Esther the queen; for he saw that there was evil determined against him by the king [Esth. 7:7].

The king needed to think things through. He simply could not believe that Haman would do such a thing. But the queen had begged and pleaded for her life because of Haman. He believed his queen. The king needed time to cool off a little so that he could think clearly about Esther's plight and about Haman, his trusted adviser and prime minister.

While the king was walking in the garden, Haman stood up to make request for his life to Esther the queen. This man who was so glib in asking that others be put to death now becomes like a slave. He grovels at the feet of the queen. He realizes that the king is not going to let this thing pass and that evil is determined against him. He knows that the queen is his only hope. He is mad with fear, and so he gets down on his knees to plead for his life in a craven way.

Then the king returned out of the palace garden into the place of the banquet of wine; and Haman was fallen upon the bed whereon Esther was. Then said the king, Will he force the queen also before me in the house? As

the word went out of the king's mouth, they covered Haman's face [Esth. 7:8].

As Haman was begging for his life, he could see that he was getting nowhere. He knew he was going to be punished for the evil he had done, so in his madness he began to pull himself up on her couch. You will recall that it was the custom to recline on couches while dining. About this time the king returned and, seeing Haman and the queen, said, "Will he force the queen also before me in the house?" Haman, coward that he was, was clawing in terror at her couch. He was beside himself with fear. The king says in effect, "What in the world is this man trying to do there pawing at my queen?"

Notice that King Ahasuerus does not have to issue an order at all. He just came in from the garden, saw what was taking place, made the statement, and those who are standing by know what to do. It is interesting to note that the servants did not make a move until the king spoke. They were simply standing by, watching. You see, the queen had not yet called for any help. She was too frightened and filled with fear to call for help. But when the king spoke, these great big fellows stepped up and took Haman. They not only placed him under palace guard but also under house arrest.

And Harbonah, one of the chamberlains, said before the king, Behold also, the gallows fifty cubits high, which Haman had made for Mordecai, who had spoken good for the king, standeth in the house of Haman. Then the king said, Hang him thereon.

So they hanged Haman on the gallows that he had prepared for Mordecai. Then was the king's wrath pacified [Esth. 7:9–10].

The king did not waste any time. He was not only the arresting officer, he was also the supreme court. Haman died the same night on the very gallows he had built for Mordecai. This is a revelation of a great truth that runs all the way through the Word of God. Paul annunciated it for believers in Galatians 6:7, "Be not deceived; God is not mocked: for whatsoever a man soweth, that shall he also reap." Is it not interesting that the very gallows that Haman had prepared to hang an innocent man on is the gallows on which he is hanged?

Jacob had this experience. He deceived his father. Oh, he was a clever boy. He put on Esau's clothes. Old Isaac smelled them and said, "It smells just like my son Esau." They didn't have any of these lovely deodorants in that day, and I want to tell you, when Esau came in, even if you did not hear him, your senses told you he had arrived. And so Jacob put that goatskin on his hands, and blind old Isaac reached out and said, "It feels like him." Jacob thought he was clever. He is God's man, but God did not let him get by with it. One day when he was old and the father of twelve sons, they brought to him the coat of many colors, dipped in the blood of a goat, and they said, "Is this your son's coat?" Old Jacob broke down and wept. He too was deceived about his favorite son.

Paul knew a great deal about the operation of this law in his own experience. He is the man who apparently gave the orders for the stoning of Stephen—they put their clothes at his feet. He was in charge. But he did not get by with it. You may say, "Well, he was converted. He came to Christ and his sins were forgiven." Yes, they were forgiven, but chickens always come home to roost. Whatever a man sows, that is what comes up, friend. Paul had a harvest, and his seed did come up. On his first missionary journey he went into the Galatian country and came to Lystra, where they stoned him and left him for dead. Paul had experienced the truth of these words, "Whatsoever a man soweth, that shall he also reap." God is not mocked.

This man Haman is experiencing the same thing. He learned it the hard way. Here is a man who went to a banquet and found out it was a necktie party, and they hanged him. Psalm 37:35–36 says, "I have seen the wicked in great power, and spreading himself like a green bay tree. Yet he passed away, and, lo, he was not: yea, I sought him, but he could not be found." Listen to what the psalmist says. It is interesting. Little man, you can have your day. You can be a villain if you want to be one. You can run against God's plan and purpose for you, but you won't defeat God, because you are going to pass off the stage. That is what happened to Haman.

You and I stand guilty before God as sinners. We deserve exactly the condemnation of a Haman. You may say, "I never committed a crime like that." Who said you did? But you just happen to have the same kind of human nature that he had, which is in rebellion against God, which is opposed to God. And in that state, while you were dead in trespasses and sins, Christ died for you, took your place on the cross. My friend, if you will trust Him, He will be your *Savior*.

CHAPTER 8

THEME: *The message of hope that went out from the king*

Although Haman is dead, the threat of death still hangs over every Jew. The decree he sent forth that Jews may be slain on a certain day is still in effect. Because the decree is a law of the Medes and Persians it cannot be changed. That presents a real problem. What is the solution? This chapter will answer that question.

On that day did the king Ahasuerus give the house of Haman the Jews' enemy unto Esther the queen. And Mordecai came before the king: for Esther had told what he was unto her.

And the king took off his ring, which he had taken from Haman, and gave it unto Mordecai. And Esther set Mordecai over the house of Haman [Esth. 8:1–2].

For the first time Esther let it be known that Mordecai was her adoptive father—Mordecai, the man whose refusal to bow to Haman occasioned this terrible decree.

This passage indicates that the king was quite free with the use of his ring. It was a powerful and important ring. It could be pressed down into wax and make a law that would destroy a people. This was the ring he passed on to Haman when he was prime minister. It is the ring he now passes on to Mordecai. I feel that the ring is in good hands now, but the king certainly seems to be careless in passing it around.

And Esther spake yet again before the king, and fell down at his feet, and besought him with tears to put away the mischief of Haman the Agagite, and his device that he had devised against the Jews [Esth. 8:3].

Esther cried to the king for help, but nothing could be done to change the decree. It could not be changed in any shape or form. Even the king could not change the law.

Again the king is gracious and extends his sceptre.

Then the king held out the golden sceptre toward Esther. So Esther arose and stood before the king.

And said, If it please the king, and if I have found favour in his sight, and the thing seem right before the king, and I be pleasing in his eyes, let it be written to reverse the letters devised by Haman the son of Hammedatha the Agagite, which he wrote to destroy the Jews which are in all the king's provinces:

For how can I endure to see the evil that shall come unto my people? or how can I endure to see the destruction of my kindred? [Esth. 8:4–6].

Esther makes it quite plain to the king that the judgment against Haman is of no avail unless something is done to save her people. Something *must* be done to save them.

Then the king Ahasuerus said unto Esther the queen and to Mordecai the Jew, Behold, I have given Esther the house of Haman, and him they have hanged upon the gallows, because he laid his hand upon the Jews [Esth. 8:7].

It is true that the king gave to Esther and to Mordecai the house of Haman, but that did not spare the Jews at all. Things were still no better for the Jews than they were before Haman's death.

Write ye also for the Jews, as it liketh you, in the king's name, and seal it with the king's ring: for the writing which is written in the king's name, and sealed with the king's ring, may no man reverse [Esth. 8:8].

Mordecai now acts swiftly.

Then were the king's scribes called at that time in the third month, that is, the month Sivan, on the three and twentieth day thereof; and it was written according to all that Mordecai commanded unto the Jews, and to the lieutenants, and the deputies and rulers of the provinces which are from India unto Ethiopia, an hundred twenty and seven provinces, unto every province according to the writing thereof, and unto every people after their language, and to the Jews according to their writing, and according to their language [Esth. 8:9].

Again the scribes are called in to make copies of the new decree in every language in the kingdom.

And he wrote in the king Ahasuerus' name, and sealed it with the king's ring, and sent letters by posts on horseback, and riders on mules, camels, and young dromedaries.

Wherein the king granted the Jews which were in every city to gather themselves together, and to stand for their life, to destroy, to slay, and to cause to perish, all the power of the people and province that would assault them, both little ones and women, and to take the spoil of them for a prey.

Upon one day in all the provinces of king Ahasuerus, namely, upon the thirteenth day of the twelfth month, which is the month Adar [Esth. 8:10–12].

The original decree is not altered in any way. It cannot be. It stands. But now another decree is made and sent out just as the first one was. It is signed by the king. The entire power of the king, as evidenced in his army and his officers, is now on the side of the Jews. This changes the entire picture, you see. When this new decree comes to the Jews, their hearts are filled with joy and gladness.

As we read this record, we can see the picture. It must have been late in the evening that Queen Esther had gone into the presence of the king to plead for her people. Now the new decree is written and signed with the king's ring. The kingdom was polyglot—many languages were spoken. You can see that all the amanuenses were summoned to write the decree in the languages of the 127 provinces—and probably there were hundreds of copies for each language.

The kingdom employed all means of communication common to that day. Heralds were sent on horseback, on mules, on camels, and on dromedaries—across the Arabian Desert, up the Euphrates and Tigris rivers, down into India, and some into Africa. The heralds were riding in every direction getting this decree out as quickly as possible into every village and hamlet in the kingdom. This new decree provides a way of escape for the Jews. If they receive the message in time—and *believe* it—they can save their lives.

This is probably one of the most wonderful pictures of our salvation in Scripture. It is not an illustration that is used very much today, but it is a picture straight from God. "Now all these things happened unto them for ensamples: and they are written for our admonition, upon whom the ends of the world are come" (1 Cor. 10:11). God has sent out a decree. It says, ". . . the soul that sinneth, it shall die" (Ezek. 18:4). This does not only refer to certain people on skid row or some criminals; it refers to everyone. "For *all* have sinned, and come short of the glory of God" (Rom. 3:23, italics mine). "But we are *all* as an unclean thing, and all our righteousnesses are as filthy rags; and we all do fade as a leaf; and our iniquities, like the wind, have taken us away" (Isa. 64:6, italics mine). God cannot save us today by *perfection* because we cannot offer it. God cannot save us by *imperfection* because He cannot lower His standard. We belong to a lost race. That is the predicament of humanity. That is the problem of the human family. We like to think that the problem is somewhere else, in someone else's heart, but it is right in our own hearts. Out of the heart proceed all the evil things. The world is polluted. It is not only the rivers and the air; the human heart is polluted. God has to judge. Men are sinners and need a Savior. Many people don't like to hear that. Many churches today have become liberal, and liberalism is based on weakness. The men in the pulpit do not have the courage to stand up and tell people that they are sinners and need a Savior. Of course, it is an unpopular message. All of us would rather be flattered. But it is God's decree, and it stands unalterable. It means eternal death to ignore it.

But thank God, another decree has gone out from the throne of God. It is: ". . . be ye reconciled to God" (2 Cor. 5:20). We are ambassadors in this world today. An ambassador is the highest ranking representative appointed by a country to represent it in another country. The ambassador represents both a friendly country and a friendly potentate. Our God is friendly. You don't have to do anything to reconcile God. He has done it for you. Christ has died for you and for me. What can we add to what Christ has already done?

You cannot do anything to soften God's heart. His heart is already soft toward us because Jesus has already paid the penalty for our sin. Now we can say that ". . . If God be for us, who can be against us?" (Rom. 8:31). God is on our side, friend. The decree has come out, ". . . Believe on the Lord Jesus Christ, and thou shalt be saved. . ." (Acts 16:31). If you put your trust in Christ, you will be saved. That is the provision that King Ahasuerus made for the Jews. All they have to do is believe the new decree and act upon it. It will rescue them from certain death.

God has a way to save *sinners*. You are not

good enough to go to heaven, and you never will be. God has to work you over. You and I have to come to Him and accept the salvation that provides for us a robe of righteousness that is perfect. Christ gives us *His* righteousness! You cannot improve on that! God could not take us to heaven as we are; we have to be born again. This is what our Lord said to Nicodemus, a ruler of the Jews, ". . . ye must be born again" (John 3:7). In 1 Peter 1:23, God puts it this way, "Being born again, not of corruptible seed, but of incorruptible, by the word of God, which liveth and abideth for ever." It is because folk hear and believe the Word of God that they are born again and their lives are being changed.

I don't talk to people about "committing their lives to God" as if they had something to commit. Do you think He wants your old life? My friend, He wants to give you a new life. He wants to regenerate you. He wants to save you.

The Jews in Esther's day had to recognize that a decree had been made to destroy them. Also they had to believe that the king was on their side and had issued another decree to save them. We too must believe that the King of kings is on our side. I am an ambassador for Christ, and, therefore, on behalf of God I must say to you, ". . . be ye reconciled to God" (2 Cor. 5:20). He is reconciled to you.

So the second decree from the king went out.

The copy of the writing for a commandment to be given in every province was published unto all people, and that the Jews should be ready against that day to avenge themselves on their enemies.

So the posts that rode upon mules and camels went out, being hastened and pressed on by the king's commandment. And the decree was given at Shushan the palace [Esth. 8:13–14].

There was a need for haste, and there is a need for haste today. I am not trying to frighten you, but this may be the last time you will have an opportunity to accept Christ as Savior. *Now* is the accepted time to believe Christ. The only time God wants you to be in a hurry, friend, is to accept His Son.

And Mordecai went out from the presence of the king in royal apparel of blue and white, and with a great crown of gold, and with a garment of fine linen and purple: and the city of Shushan rejoiced and was glad [Esth. 8:15].

The royal apparel Mordecai is now wearing is certainly different from the sackcloth and ashes he wore only a short time before. His appearance in the city undoubtedly reinforced the joy produced by the king's new decree. Notice the contrast between the two decrees; Haman's decree produced sorrow, and the king's decree produced joy.

Salvation can bring real joy into your life. You can go to a nightclub and spend one hundred dollars, and I will grant you that you can have a good time. If you are an unsaved person, you will have a good time because you can watch the show, get drunk, and eat like a glutton. Yes, you'll have a good time that night, but you won't in the morning. You will feel bad, and in it all you will never know what real joy is. Only when you come to Christ will you experience real joy.

The Jews had light, and gladness, and joy, and honour [Esth. 8:16].

Light is what God offers you. Jesus is the Light of the world. He also is the gladness, and joy, and honor of the world. The thing that gives dignity to sinners is to receive the Savior, who is God manifest in the flesh, who died for them. That will lift sinners out of the muck and mire. It will enable a sinner to walk through this world with his head held high, rejoicing. My, how we need to rejoice! Are you joyful today, Christian friend, with that gladness that comes from deep down in your heart? If you are not filled with joy, come to Christ and He will give you something to be glad about.

And in every province, and in every city, whithersoever the king's commandment and his decree came, the Jews had joy and gladness, a feast and a good day. And many of the people of the land became Jews; for the fear of the Jews fell upon them [Esth. 8:17].

For fear of the Jews many of the people became Jews, that is, they accepted their religion. The nation Israel was a better witness to the world than we give it credit for.

CHAPTERS 9–10

THEME: *Institution of the Feast of Purim*

The day of the Jews' execution is at hand.

Now in the twelfth month, that is, the month Adar, on the thirteenth day of the same, when the king's commandment and his decree drew near to be put in execution, in the day that the enemies of the Jews hoped to have power over them, (though it was turned to the contrary, that the Jews had rule over them that hated them;)

The Jews gathered themselves together in their cities throughout all the provinces of the king Ahasuerus, to lay hand on such as sought their hurt: and no man could withstand them; for the fear of them fell upon all people [Esth. 9:1–2].

The Jews prepare themselves for the attack. The king's new decree is protecting them, so they get everything ready to defend themselves.

It is interesting to note that Herodotus, the Greek historian, records that Ahasuerus (Xerxes) returned home after his defeat in the Greek campaign, about 480 B.C., and that his wife, Amestris, was a cold and vindictive queen. That would be Esther, of course; and to an outsider it is understandable that she would appear vindictive and cold. After all, she stepped in and put an end to Haman's evil activities, and she was also able to save her people from their enemies at that particular time.

There are people who feel that it was brutal and cruel for a court of law to sentence many of Hitler's henchmen to prison, but those henchmen were rascals of the first order. Their treatment of the Jews in concentration camps was absolutely inhuman. To many people on the outside it did not look as though Hitler's men should be treated with such harshness, but those who knew the inside story knew that they got justice.

And all the rulers of the provinces, and the lieutenants, and the deputies, and officers of the king, helped the Jews; because the fear of Mordecai fell upon them.

For Mordecai was great in the king's house, and his fame went out throughout all the provinces: for this man Mordecai waxed greater and greater [Esth. 9:3–4].

Now Mordecai, one of their own, is by the side of the king. Haman, who would have put the Jews to death, is gone. The very throne that had once condemned the Jews now protects them.

The very throne of God protects us today. The apostle Paul says, "Who shall lay any thing to the charge of God's elect? It is God that justifieth. Who is he that condemneth? It is Christ that died, yea rather, that is risen again, who is even at the right hand of God, who also maketh intercession for us" (Rom. 8:33–34). Notice how He justifies: (1) Christ died; (2) He is risen again; (3) He is even at the right hand of God; and (4) He also makes intercession for us. These are the reasons no one can condemn a believer. How wonderful this is! Today there is a *Man* in the glory—He knows exactly how you feel, and He knows exactly how I feel. And in that position He is interceding for us. Things have changed for us sinners. "Seeing then that we have a great high priest, that is passed into the heavens, Jesus the Son of God, let us hold fast our profession. For we have not an high priest which cannot be touched with the feelings of our infirmities; but was in all points tempted like as we are, yet without sin. Let us therefore come boldly unto the throne of grace, that we may obtain mercy, and find grace to help in time of need" (Heb. 4:14–16).

I have a Savior who is despised by the world. A lot of dirty, blasphemous things are being said about Him. But, my friends, He is the *Man* in glory. He is the King of kings. He is the Lord of lords. He is the Lily of the Valley. He is the One altogether lovely. He is the Chief among ten thousand. And some day He is coming again. We ought to get in practice bending our knees to Him, adoring and praising Him. That is very important. He should become sweeter to us with each passing day. In fact, there is a song entitled "Sweeter As The Years Go By." That is the way it should be for each one of us. Do you rejoice more as a Christian today than you did one year ago? Or ten years ago? I thank God that I am a happier Christian today than I was ten years ago.

Now suppose that some Israelite living during the time of Queen Esther had said, "Well, I don't believe the new decree that has come from the king. I don't think the king is that good. I am going to protect myself the best way I can. I am going to make a little Maginot Line and hide in back of it. I will make a fortress and defend myself." But, my friend, it was death for the Jew who did not believe the king's decree.

Notice that the Jews had to have faith in the king's message. Like them, we must have faith in God's message, which is the gospel. The *gospel* means "good news." First Corinthians 15:3–4 gives us God's message in a nutshell: "For I delivered unto you first of all that which I also received, how that Christ died for our sins according to the scriptures; And that he was buried, and that he rose again the third day according to the scriptures." God has sent out a decree to a lost world. Men and women are saved by faith and not by the works of the law. John 1:12 says of the Lord Jesus, "But as many as received him, to them gave he power to become the sons of God, even to them that believe on his name." The main thrust of Peter's sermon on the day of Pentecost was: through Christ is the remission of sins (see Acts 2).

The gospel is what saves men today. The gospel is what Someone has done for us. It is not a request on God's part for you and me to do something. On the contrary, the gospel is what He has done for us. If we do not place our trust and faith in Christ, there is no hope for us at all. Now, you may break some bad habits, you may forsake evil, you may go to church, you may be baptized, and you may take part in the Lord's Supper; and you may still be miserable. The only way to have real peace is to take God at His Word and believe His message. When you believe it, there is salvation.

The Jews who did not believe the king's decree had no hope at all. But the Jews who accepted the king's decree were joyful and glad, we are told. Why? Their faith in the king's decree brought deliverance.

And Mordecai wrote these things, and sent letters unto all the Jews that were in all the provinces of the king Ahasuerus, both nigh and far [Esth. 9:20].

Many people have asked the question, "Who wrote the Book of Esther?" I believe this passage gives us at least a suggestion that Mordecai was the author.

Wherefore they called these days Purim after the name of Pur. Therefore for all the words of this letter, and of that which they had seen concerning this matter, and which had come unto them,

The Jews ordained, and took upon them, and upon their seed, and upon all such as joined themselves unto them, so as it should not fail, that they would keep these two days according to their writing, and according to their appointed time every year [Esth. 9:26–27].

In our day the Feast of Purim is commemorated by the orthodox Jews first in their synagogues. It is a celebration of gladness, and it is concluded by the reading of the Book of Esther. As they read it, they spit as the name of Haman is mentioned. I understand that they can use one or two expressions: "Let his name be blotted out," or "Let him be accursed." Then the following day they come together for a joyful service because it is a feast that celebrates the fact that God has delivered them (and they include subsequent deliverances such as that from the German atrocities) according to the promise that He made to Abraham. God had said, ". . . I will bless them that bless thee, and curse him that curseth thee . . ." (Gen. 12:3).

And that these days should be remembered and kept throughout every generation, every family, every province, and every city; and that these days of Purim should not fail from among the Jews, nor the memorial of them perish from their seed [Esth. 9:28].

The Book of Esther concludes with this interesting sidelight in chapter 10:

And the king Ahasuerus laid a tribute upon the land, and upon the isles of the sea.

And all the acts of his power and of his might, and the declaration of the greatness of Mordecai, whereunto the king advanced him, are they not written in the book of the chronicles of the kings of Media and Persia?

For Mordecai the Jew was next unto king Ahasuerus, and great among the Jews, and accepted of the multitude of his brethren, seeking the wealth of his people, and speaking peace to all his seed [Esth. 10:1–3].

You and I have a Savior who is going to bring real peace to this world someday.

It is interesting to note that there are three prayers the Jews pray at the time of the Feast of Purim. In the first prayer they thank Jehovah that they are counted worthy. In the second prayer they thank Him for preserving their ancestors. In the third prayer they thank Him that they have lived to enjoy another festival.

We as Christians see in the Passover Feast a spiritual meaning—". . . Christ our passover is sacrificed for us" (1 Cor. 5:7). He is the salvation of God for us. In the Feast of Purim we see the keeping power of God, His providence, His sovereignty. As the writer of the Proverbs puts it, "The lot is cast into the lap; but the whole disposing thereof is of the LORD" (Prov. 16:33). He will keep His nation Israel; He will keep His church; and He will keep the individuals who are His. He is able to save to the uttermost those who come unto God through Him.

It is a sad commentary on the present generation that most Christians know only a distant, providential oversight. They do not learn to walk with God in close fellowship, obeying God's Word.

> "He knows and loves and cares,
> Nothing this truth can dim:
> He gives the very best to those
> Who leave the choice to Him."

My friend, He wants to lead you by His eye. We need to move closer to Him today. Most believers know only of the distant providence of God which leads from way out yonder those who won't be led.

How many Christians today are walking in their own will! Things are going nicely. The sun is shining in the sky and the stones are removed from their pathway. They think they can work everything out by themselves; so they don't look to God. Then one day the winds begin to howl, the waves begin to roll, the way seems dark, and all of a sudden they cry out to Him, "Lord save me; I am perishing! Show me the way." Then if they get through that crisis, they say, "The Lord led me." My friend, only by God's providence did He lead you. You were actually not in the will of God.

So much is said today about the dedication of life and heart. I get so weary of hearing, "Come and dedicate your life to God." My friend, I am not asking you to do that. You can get down on your knees right now and dedicate your heart and life, and tomorrow you can be entirely out of God's will. At that point you revert to being moved again by the providence of God. Oh, He wants to lead you today—He wants to guide you *directly*. I don't care who you are, or where you are going, He will overrule you. You may be a Hitler, or a Stalin, or even a Judas Iscariot. God overruled Judas, and He will overrule you, friend. But you can know the luxury and joy of coming to Him—not just in one act—but moment by moment, day by day, seeking God's will for your life. You can begin to walk out—from wherever you are now—in the *will* of God. What joy there is in walking in His will!

However, if you slip out from under God's *direct* dealings, you have not slipped out from under His *providential* dealings. God ever stands in the shadows, keeping watch over His own.

BIBLIOGRAPHY

(Recommended for Further Study)

Darby, J. N. *Synopsis of the Books of the Bible*. Addison, Illinois: Bible Truth Publishers, n.d.

Gaebelein, Arno C. *The Annotated Bible*. 1917. Reprint. Neptune, New Jersey: Loizeaux Brothers, 1970.

Gray, James M. *Synthetic Bible Studies*. Old Tappan, New Jersey: Fleming H. Revell Co., 1906.

Ironside, H. A. *Notes on the Book of Esther*. Neptune, New Jersey: Loizeaux Brothers, 1921.

Jensen, Irving L. *Ezra, Nehemiah, Esther: A Self-Study Guide*. Chicago, Illinois: Moody Press, 1970.

McGee, J. Vernon. *Esther, the Romance of Providence*. Pasadena, California: Thru the Bible Books, 1951.

Sauer, Erich, *The Dawn of World Redemption*. Grand Rapids, Michigan: Wm. B. Eerdmans Publishing Co., 1951. (An excellent Old Testament survey.)

Scroggie, W. Graham. *The Unfolding Drama of Redemption*. Grand Rapids, Michigan: Zondervan Publishing House, 1970. (An excellent survey and outline of the Old Testament.)

Unger, Merrill F. *Unger's Bible Handbook*. Chicago, Illinois: Moody Press, 1966. (A concise commentary on the entire Bible.)

Unger, Merrill F. *Unger's Commentary on the Old Testament*. Vol. 1. Chicago, Illinois: Moody Press, 1981. (A fine summary of each paragraph. Highly recommended.)

Whitcomb, John C. *Esther: Triumph of God's Sovereignty*. Chicago, Illinois: Moody Press, 1979. (An excellent treatment.)

The Book of JOB

INTRODUCTION

Job is a very remarkable and marvelous book. It is the first of the poetical books which also include Psalms, Proverbs, Ecclesiastes, Song of Solomon, and Lamentations. The reference "poetical books" denotes *form* rather than imaginative or capricious content. Neither does the term *poetical* mean that it is rhythmic. Hebrew poetry is achieved by repeating an idea or "parallelism." The dialogue in the Book of Job is poetry. All the conversation is in poetic form. If you have ever read Homer's *Iliad* and *Odyssey*, you know that they are examples in secular literature of this Hebrew form.

The author of Job is unknown. It has been suggested that the writer was Moses. Other suggestions have included Ezra, Solomon, Job himself, and Elihu. Elihu, mentioned in this book, is one of the miserable comforters of Job. The idea that Elihu may be the author is based on Job 32:16–17: "When I had waited, (for they spake not, but stood still, and answered no more;) I said, I will answer also my part, I also will shew mine opinion."

This is not said in the context of conversation, but the author is expressing his own thoughts in first person. Then the conversation resumes, and it is Elihu who is speaking. This indicates that Elihu may be the author of the book.

Another interesting thing about this book is that we do not know the period in which Job lived. And we do not know where he lived. I know that it says he was in the land of Uz, but we honestly don't know where the land of Uz was located. We cannot fix it at any particular spot. It is interesting that the time and place, which are so essential to other books, are not given here.

I would suggest that Job was written during the patriarchal period. It is possible that Job knew Jacob. The fact that the Book of Job makes no reference to the Mosaic Law nor to any of the events recorded in the Book of Exodus would seem to indicate that it was written before Exodus.

Here are the arguments which lead us to place Job in the time of the patriarchs:

1. The length of Job's life span. "After this lived Job an hundred and forty years, and saw his sons, and his sons' sons, even four generations. So Job died, being old and full of days" (Job 42:16–17). We know that at the time of the patriarchs people had long life spans such as that of Job.

2. Job acted as the high priest in his family. Since there is no mention of the children of Israel or any other priesthood, evidently this took place before they came into existence.

3. Eliphaz was descended from Esau's eldest son. "These are the names of Esau's sons; Eliphaz the son of Adah the wife of Esau, Reuel the son of Bashemath the wife of Esau" (Gen. 36:10). This would make it seem that Job was a contemporary of Jacob.

This book is a great philosophical work. There are many problems that are raised and settled by this book:

1. The Book of Job raises the issue of why the righteous suffer. I really should say that it gives *one* of the reasons why the righteous suffer. I do not believe that this is the *primary* teaching of this book, although there are a great many Bible scholars who take that position.

2. Job was written to rebuke the slander of Satan against mankind.

3. Job was written to reveal Job to himself.

4. The Book of Job teaches patience. James says, ". . . Ye have heard of the patience of Job . . ." (James 5:11). Was Job patient? I'll be honest with you, it is difficult to see how this man was patient. We'll consider this when we get to the end of the book.

5. I think the *primary purpose* of the Book of Job is *to teach repentance.* If you want to disagree with this right now, just stay with us until we get to the end of the book and then draw your own conclusions.

You see, when men want to talk or write about repentance, they always pick a character who has had a sinful beginning. For example, they will point out Manasseh, the most ungodly king of Judah. We studied about him back in the historical books of the Old Testament, and we saw that he repented. May I say to you, that is the kind of repentance we like to think of.

There was Saul of Tarsus, the greatest enemy the Lord Jesus Christ ever had. He repented. There was St. Francis of Assisi, a dissipated nobleman of his day, and he repented. There was Jerry McAuley, the drunken bum on skid row in New York City, and he repented.

God didn't pick a man like that in order to teach repentance. He could have! But God selected the best man who ever lived in the time of the Old Testament, possibly the best man who ever lived with the exception of Jesus Christ. God chose this man and showed that he needed to repent. When we get to the end of this book, we find the words of Job himself. "I have heard of thee by the hearing of the ear: but now mine eye seeth thee. Wherefore I abhor myself, and repent in dust and ashes" (Job 42:5–6). This ought to teach every believer today—it should teach everyone who reads this—that no matter how good we think we are, we need to see ourselves as God sees us. All our righteousness is as filthy rags. We need to repent.

This is a great philosophical work and has been acclaimed so by many. Tennyson called this book "the greatest poem, whether of ancient or modern literature." Speaking of the Book of Job, Thomas Carlyle, the Scottish philosopher said, "I call that one of the grandest ever written with pen." Martin Luther said that this book is "more magnificent and sublime than any other book of Scripture." And Dr. Moorehead said, "The Book of Job is one of the noblest poems in existence."

The prose section of the Book of Job is a gigantic sweeping drama that encompasses earth and heaven. This does not mean it is fiction. Job is referred to as a historical character in the Scriptures (see Ezek. 14:14, 20; James 5:11), and Paul quotes from the Book of Job (1 Cor. 3:19).

Many writers have used Job as the basis for their plots, including H. G. Wells and Archibald MacLeish in his one-time Broadway hit, *J. B.* In his play MacLeish attempted to make an analogy between the Book of Job and modern man. Very candidly, I think he missed it, although he mentioned the human predicament today, and he knew about that. I don't think he quite knew about Job and the great purpose of that book. His play speaks of the despair and also the hope of modern man, but beyond that I think the analogy breaks down. The Book of Job reveals a man who was very conscious of God, but who could find nothing wrong with himself, one who was very egotistical about his own righteousness and maintained it in the face of those who were around him. Job felt that before God he was all right. In fact, he wanted to come into the presence of God to defend himself. When Job did that, he found that he needed to repent!

This is not a description of modern man by any means. The psychiatrists have told man today that his problem is that his mother didn't love him as she should have. In my opinion, the thing that is wrong with this generation is that mother didn't paddle as much as she should have. But we are told that mother and father have neglected the boy and the girl. Now I admit there may be some truth to that, and perhaps this is a part of the problem. However, we cannot shift the blame to others. Modern man refuses to take the blame for his deficiencies, inabilities, and sins. He tries to put the blame on somebody else. He will not accept responsibility for himself and his own actions.

Now, there is One who bore all of our sins. Until you and I recognize that *we* are sinners and need to turn to Him, my friend, we are only putting the blame on the wrong person. I think it is pretty low for any man to put the blame for his sins on his mother. That is a terrible thing, and yet that is what we find today.

Modern man is in a real predicament, and he is in great despair. He is blaming his sin on others, and he can find no place to go to find that comfort which he craves. Instead he has surrounded himself with materialism and secularism. I knew a man once who must have had twenty-five different buttons at the headboard of his bed. He could turn on lights all over the place, have a bell ring, open and close doors, and turn on outside lights—all from his bed. I had never seen anything like it. That to him was a great security. Many of us do that. We each have our own "security blanket," and we snuggle up to it.

However, the problem with modern man is that he doesn't have God in his consciousness. He doesn't know that there is a Savior to whom he can go. That is different from Job. Job was very conscious of God and trusted Him. The fact is that God will put Job through the mill, as we shall see, and will finally bring him into His very presence. God stripped Job of all his securities in order to bring him to Himself.

Modern man is being put through the mill even in an affluent society. Despite all his gadgets and comforts of life, he is adrift on a piece of driftwood out in the midst of a vast ocean, and he doesn't know where he is or where he is going. That is rather frightening. Actually, it is beginning to force some folk to think that somewhere there is a Someone. We have a song today that says to "put your hand in the hand of the Man from Galilee." Well, that is getting pretty close, but it still misses the point that modern man must come to Him as a *sinner* and must accept Him as Savior. People today talk about commitment. What *is* your commitment, by the way? You cannot just say, "Lord, Lord," and expect Him to be your Lord and Master. First He must be your *Savior*! He died for you. If you don't begin with Jesus Christ at the cross, you will not begin with Him anywhere.

I have spent time on this because I think it is important. Job had a consciousness of the presence of God all the way through his troubles. He was not adrift in the sense that modern man is adrift. What Job could not understand was why God permitted him to be put through the mill. Job did not recognize that he needed to repent—until God dealt with him.

OUTLINE

I. Drama (Prose), Chapters 1–2

- A. Scene I: Land of Uz. Job's Prosperity and Serenity, 1:1–5
- B. Scene II: Heaven. Satan's Slander of God and Job, 1:6–12
- C. Scene III: Land of Uz. Job's Loss of Children and Wealth, 1:13–22
- D. Scene IV: Heaven. God and Satan, 2:1–6
- E. Scene V: Land of Uz. Job's Loss of Health and Wife's Sympathy, 2:7–10

II. Dialogue (Poetry), Chapters 2:11–42:6

- A. Scene VI: City Dump, 2:11–37:24
  1. Job's Loss of Understanding from Friends, 2:11–13
  2. Job vs. Eliphaz, Bildad, Zophar, 3:1–32:1
  3. Job vs. Elihu, 32:2–37:24
- B. Scene VII: Jehovah vs. Job, 38:1–42:6

III. Epilogue (Prose), Chapter 42:7–17

Scene VIII: Land of Uz. Job's Blessings Doubled.

CHAPTER 1

THEME: *Drama in heaven and on earth*

LAND OF UZ

There was a man in the land of Uz, whose name was Job; and that man was perfect and upright, and one that feared God, and eschewed evil [Job 1:1].

The land of Uz was somewhere in the Middle East, but beyond that there is nothing specific known about it. The historian Josephus gives us a glimmer of light on its location. In Genesis 10:22–23 Uz is listed as a son of Aram, a son of Shem. In Genesis 22:20–21 Huz (or Uz) is the firstborn of Nahor who was Abraham's brother. Josephus tells us that Uz was the founder of the ancient city of Damascus. Damascus is, in fact, the oldest, continuously inhabited city in the world. So I think we can say that Job lived somewhere in the Syrian desert.

That same desert is the place where the Lord sent the apostle Paul for his "postgraduate studies." God schooled and disciplined many of His men out on that desert. My friend, *your* land of Uz and *my* land of Uz may be in different places geographically. It could be any place on this earth. That is not the important matter. The important thing is that there are certain lessons God wants us to learn in that place.

We are told that Job was *perfect*. What does it mean when it says he was perfect? It means he was perfect in his relation to God in the sense that he had offered the sacrifices (as we will see in v. 5). In those days the sacrifice was a burnt offering.

Then we read that he *feared God*. He had a high and holy concept of God and, as a result, he hated evil. You can see that he is different from modern man who is without any knowledge of God.

And there were born unto him seven sons and three daughters.

His substance also was seven thousand sheep, and three thousand camels, and five hundred yoke of oxen, and five hundred she asses, and a very great household; so that this man was the greatest of all the men of the east [Job 1:2–3].

He had a wonderful family of ten children. He was very wealthy, and they all just lived in luxury and ease. He had camels for transportation. He must have been in the trucking business of that day. He also had she asses for milk. That was considered a delicacy in that day. It's one delicacy that I'm willing to miss, by the way.

This man lived in the lap of luxury. The last part of verse 3 would indicate to us that he was Howard Hughes, John D. Rockefeller, Henry Ford, and the oil men of Texas all rolled into one.

And his sons went and feasted in their houses, every one his day; and sent and called for their three sisters to eat and to drink with them [Job 1:4].

They were living in the lap of luxury and certainly had it easy. But notice that in the midst of all that plenty and ease there was a fear in the heart of Job.

And it was so, when the days of their feasting were gone about, that Job sent and sanctified them, and rose up early in the morning, and offered burnt offerings according to the number of them all: for Job said, It may be that my sons have sinned, and cursed God in their hearts. Thus did Job continually [Job 1:5].

The thing that interests me is that he didn't feel that he needed an offering. He felt that he was right with God. But he thought that maybe these sons and daughters weren't as close to God as they should be, so he offered sacrifices for them. He was the high priest in his own family.

Now this is the end of scene one. It is a gorgeous scene of a wealthy man with a lovely family living with an abundance of everything. But he had one fear in his heart. It is a fear that a great many folk have today about their sons and daughters. He recognized that he couldn't cope with that problem himself, so he went to God.

My friend, there are a great many parents who are distraught today because they have a son or daughter who has left home and gotten into trouble, and is maybe even on drugs. Many of these parents have never been able to go to God themselves as Job did. As a result, they carry with them problems that they cannot solve. Job knew where to go with his fears. He offered a burnt offering for his children. That burnt offering speaks of Christ. This man is a man of God.

HEAVEN

Our next scene opens in heaven, and what a scene it is. Neither Job nor any of the other people in this book knew that this took place at all. But this scene will enable us today to understand and interpret some of the things which happen to God's people. I don't say that it is the total explanation, but it is a part of it.

Now there was a day when the sons of God came to present themselves before the LORD, and Satan came also among them [Job 1:6].

Now this is the scene in heaven. The sons of God, His created intelligences, come before Him. I must confess I know very little about them. I think they are numberless, as numberless as the sand on the seashore, which means you and I cannot count them. And they are not human beings; they do not belong to our race. Yet these are God's created intelligences, and they are responsible creatures. They must come to report to God as a matter of regular routine. That is something I suppose we would expect. But there is also something here that is rather shocking. We are told that "Satan came also among them." That is a surprise.

And the LORD said unto Satan, Whence comest thou? Then Satan answered the LORD, and said, From going to and fro in the earth, and from walking up and down in it [Job 1:7].

By the way, Satan must also make a report. That is amazing, isn't it? Do you think he came from hell? No, he didn't. Friends, hell hasn't been opened up yet. No one is in hell today. It will not be opened up until the Millennium takes place on this earth. Hell is the place prepared for the Devil and his angels, but they are not there yet. The fact of the matter is that Satan has as much access to this earth as you and I have, and more so.

This earth is the domain of Satan. He has not been in hell. He says that he has been going up and down—east, west, north, and south—on this earth. Remember that Scripture calls him ". . . the god of this world . . ." (2 Cor. 4:4) and ". . . the prince of the power of the air . . ." (Eph. 2:2). So that we know that he has great access and freedom on this earth today. We are warned by Peter, "Be sober, be vigilant; because your adversary the devil, as a roaring lion, walketh about, seeking whom he may devour" (1 Peter 5:8). My friend, this is a warning, and this is exactly what we are told here in the Book of Job. Satan himself said that he has the freedom to go up and down this earth.

You remember that when Satan tempted the Lord Jesus he offered to Him the kingdoms of this earth. The Lord Jesus never said, "You don't have them to offer." He simply refused the temptation. Apparently those kingdoms are accessible to Satan, and he has that kind of freedom.

When you look at this earth today, it does look like Satan is running things, does it not? God is overruling all things, but He has given Satan a period of freedom. We are told that this world in which you and I live is controlled by Satan. He must be overcome, and we can only overcome him by the blood of the Lamb. Now this is quite a revelation, isn't it? And it is contrary to modern thinking.

And the LORD said unto Satan, Hast thou considered my servant Job, that there is none like him in the earth, a perfect and an upright man, one that feareth God, and escheweth evil? [Job 1:8].

God gives a good report of Job. He says he is an outstanding man. It would seem that Satan has been trying to get at Job. I draw that conclusion from Satan's next statement.

Then Satan answered the LORD, and said, Doth Job fear God for nought?

Hast not thou made an hedge about him, and about his house, and about all that he hath on every side? thou hast blessed the work of his hands, and his substance is increased in the land [Job 1:9–10].

Apparently Satan had been trying to get through to Job and made the discovery that he couldn't get through to him because there was a hedge about him. He tells the Lord, "You have put a hedge around him, and I can't touch him."

I believe that there is a hedge about every believer today, and I do not think that Satan can touch you unless God permits it. And if God permits it, it will be for His purpose. That is what this book teaches us.

But put forth thine hand now, and touch all that he hath, and he will curse thee to thy face [Job 1:11].

Now Satan casts this slur upon Job. I think he despises mankind. He suggests that Job is really a timeserver to God. And Satan has no use for you or me. He says we are timeservants and that if God took down that hedge and took everything from us, we would curse God.

Mind you, there are a lot of people in the world who would curse God. There is no question about that. All one needs to do is listen to men on the street here in Southern California. I hear God cursed nearly every day.

One day I walked by a construction site where one of the foremen was attempting to make some sort of an adjustment. It didn't work and the piece fell down. My, he began to curse God. Now he may go to church on Sunday and carry a big Bible under his arm—I don't know about that. But I do know this, he cursed God. We hear that constantly today. Men are not rightly related to God, my friend.

This man Job had a hedge around him, and when Satan found he couldn't touch him, he said, "I'd like to get to him." Satan hates mankind. Why in the world anyone wants to serve Satan is more than I know, because he despises us. I wouldn't want a master like that. I want a master who would love me and be sympathetic toward me. And that is the kind of Master I do have.

And the Lord said unto Satan, Behold, all that he hath is in thy power; only upon himself put not forth thine hand. So Satan went forth from the presence of the Lord [Job 1:12].

We learn here that sometimes God permits Satan to take away from us those things that we lean on. I know that when our little security blanket is taken away from us we feel so helpless, incapable and lost in this world. Many of us cry out to God at such a time.

Notice that God is going to permit Satan to take all Job's possessions from him. Believe me, Satan would destroy us if he could. He has slandered both God and Job, inferring that God is not worthy to be served and loved for Himself alone, but that He must pay Job to love Him. Satan is the enemy of God and man.

BACK IN THE LAND OF UZ

And there was a day when his sons and his daughters were eating and drinking wine in their eldest brother's house [Job 1:13].

Job's children were having a high, old time, friends. They were going around from one brother's house to another, and it was a banquet every day. They were really living it up.

And there came a messenger unto Job, and said, The oxen were plowing, and the asses feeding beside them:

And the Sabeans fell upon them, and took them away; yea, they have slain the servants with the edge of the sword; and I only am escaped alone to tell thee [Job. 1:14–15].

Here Job has been having a rather nice life, and then suddenly things begin to happen. He didn't even know he had enemies like this, but now the Sabeans come in and take away his cattle.

While he was yet speaking, there came also another, and said, The fire of God is fallen from heaven, and hath burned up the sheep, and the servants, and consumed them; and I only am escaped alone to tell thee [Job 1:16].

"The fire of God." That is interesting. I kid a friend of mine who is an insurance agent. You know the policy always states they are not liable if your house is destroyed by "an act of God." We always blame God if something is destroyed. They were saying the same thing in that day. Why didn't he say, "The fire of Satan"? Who did it? Why, Satan did it! Why don't the insurance policies say, "If God permits Satan to destroy my house"?

While he was yet speaking, there came also another, and said, The Chaldeans made out three bands, and fell upon the camels, and have carried them away, yea, and slain the servants with the edge of the sword; and I only am escaped alone to tell thee [Job 1:17].

We talk about the crash of the stock market. I tell you, Job had real stock, and it was all taken away. Everything was wiped out.

While he was yet speaking, there came also another, and said, Thy sons and thy daughters were eating and drinking wine in their eldest brother's house:

And, behold, there came a great wind from the wilderness, and smote the four corners of the house, and it fell upon the young men, and they are dead; and I only am escaped alone to tell thee [Job. 1:18–19].

Here is a tragedy beyond tragedies. All of his children are slain. A real Texas-style tornado hit that house and all his children are killed. What would you do in a case like that? Notice what Job does:

Then Job arose, and rent his mantle, and shaved his head, and fell down upon the ground, and worshipped,

And said, Naked came I out of my mother's womb, and naked shall I return thither: the LORD gave, and the LORD hath taken away; blessed be the name of the LORD.

In all this Job sinned not, nor charged God foolishly [Job 1:20–22].

Watch this man and listen to his testimony. Here is a viewpoint of life and a philosophy of life that Christians need today toward material things. You and I came into this world with nothing. We were naked as jaybirds when we came into this world. And we are going to leave the world the same way. Remember the old bromide, "There are no pockets in a shroud"? My friend, you can't take anything with you.

The story is told that years ago all the relatives were standing outside the bedroom door of the patriarch of a very wealthy family. They were waiting for the old man to die and for the family lawyer to come out. When he came, he announced to them all that the father had died. Immediately one of the more greedy ones asked, "How much did he leave?" And the lawyer replied, "He left it all. He didn't take anything with him."

That is the way it will be with all of us. It makes no difference how many deeds you have or how strong your safety deposit box may be, what you accumulate or how much insurance you have. When you go and when I go, we're going just like we came into this world. It is very important for us to get this into our philosophy of life. You may be living today in an expensive home, or you may be living in a hovel. You may have a big bank account, or you may not have anything to count at all. You may have a safety deposit box filled with stocks and bonds, or you may not even have a safety deposit box. It makes no difference who you are. We're all going to leave the same way we came into this world. Whatever you have, you are simply a steward of it. Really, in the final analysis, it does not belong to you, does it?

This man Job falls down, and he worships God. Oh yes, he rent his mantle, he shaved his head, and you could have heard this man weeping half a mile away. He has lost everything, even his sons and his daughters. But he says, "The LORD gave, and the LORD hath taken away; blessed be the name of the LORD."

My friend, whatever you have, the Lord gave it to you. And He can take it away if He wishes. He is going to hold you and me responsible for how we use the things He permits us to have. That is the reason that in 2 Corinthians Paul calls us all "stewards." A steward handles what belongs to someone else. God is going to ask us how we used His material things. Everything down here is His, and you are just using them. When you leave, you won't be taking them with you.

Job understood this, and he did not lose his faith. He is still holding on to God. "In all this Job sinned not, nor charged God foolishly."

CHAPTER 2

***THEME:** Heaven, God, and Satan; land of Uz; down to the dump of the city*

HEAVEN, GOD, AND SATAN

Again there was a day when the sons of God came to present themselves before the LORD and Satan came also among them to present himself before the LORD [Job 2:1].

The created intelligences make their regular report again. Notice that they all had to report to God. You and I are going to have to report to God some day. Remember that the Christian is going to stand at the judgment seat of Christ (2 Cor. 5:10), and there we are going to report on our stewardship on earth. We are going to give an account to Him. (As believers we will not stand at the Great White Throne judgment of Revelation 20:11–15, which is where the unbeliever must give his account.) All the creatures of God must come to make their report to Him.

Remember, my friend, He is God. We are not operating freely today. We hear the cry all around us, "We want liberty." How much liberty do we have? A grasshopper can jump higher than a man can jump, size for size. If we could jump like a grasshopper, we could jump over the tallest building. God created us with certain limitations. We are creatures. He is the Creator. We must all answer to Him.

When these sons of God came to present themselves to Him, notice that Satan also had to come to give his report. He is not beyond the jurisdiction of God. Although God already knew what he would report, Satan had to appear before God and tell the Lord what he had been doing.

And the LORD said unto Satan, From whence comest thou? And Satan answered the LORD, and said, From going to and fro in the earth, and from walking up and down in it [Job 2:2].

In other words, Satan again reports that he has been down in his bailiwick. He was running this place down here. I believe he still runs it, friends. Just look around you and see who runs this world.

And the LORD said unto Satan, Hast thou considered my servant Job, that there is none like him in the earth, a perfect and an upright man, one that feareth God, and escheweth evil? and still he holdeth fast his integrity, although thou movedst me against him, to destroy him without cause [Job 2:3].

Now this shows us clearly that what the Lord allowed Satan to do with Job was done without a cause in Job. People are always saying, "Why does God let this happen to me?" Perhaps the answer from the Lord is, "There is no reason for it in you. I am not spanking you. I am not punishing you. I just want to bring you closer to Me." That is what He did with Job. It was without a cause in Job.

Sometimes we point our finger at some believer and say that God is whipping him, which may not be true at all. It may be that God is testing him in a way He cannot test you or me, because He couldn't trust us with that much trouble. Very frankly, I would never want to go through what Job had to suffer!

The Lord calls Satan's attention to Job again. "Job is still serving Me. You said that if I would permit you to take everything away from Job, he would turn his back on Me—but he hasn't done that. He has maintained his integrity."

And Satan answered the LORD, and said, Skin for skin, yea, all that a man hath will he give for his life.

But put forth thine hand now, and touch his bone and his flesh, and he will curse thee to thy face.

And the LORD said unto Satan, Behold, he is in thine hand; but save his life [Job 2:4–6].

You know, Satan is accurate about most of us. There is a chink in our armor. We have our Achilles' heel—that certain weakness. When we get right down to the bare bones, we all cave in. But God has given us a promise: "There hath no temptation taken you but such as is common to man: but God is faithful, who will not suffer you to be tempted above that ye are able; but will with the temptation also make a way to escape, that ye may be able to bear it" (1 Cor. 10:13). God will never allow us to be tempted beyond what we can stand. We need to recognize that.

My friend, wherever you are and whatever you are going through, God is able to sustain you. That is a great comfort. We do not know what a day may bring forth. It could be tragic beyond words or it could be a delightful, wonderful day. Whichever it is, God says, "I will enable you to get through it." God will see to it that our armor stands up. That is a wonderful thing to know.

Satan is a liar. Satan says that Job will give anything for his own body and that if he is allowed to touch his bone and flesh, Job will curse God.

LAND OF UZ

So went Satan forth from the presence of the LORD, and smote Job with sore boils from the sole of his foot unto his crown.

And he took him a potsherd to scrape himself withal; and he sat down among the ashes [Job 2:7–8].

This man is being tested in every part of his life. Satan is attempting to break him down, of course. He has lost his finances, he has lost his family, and now his physical body is being attacked.

There is seemingly no human explanation for the troubles of Job. It is not a punishment for his sins, and the whole thing would be senseless without proper insight. That is the reason God gives the explanation to us at the beginning of the book so *we* will be able to understand. What was happening to Job was for a lofty and worthy purpose. There was a good and sufficient reason in the internal counsels of God. When all the facts were in and all the facets considered, God had a purpose in it. It was discipline. We can say that it was good for Job.

When father whips little Willy, he says, "This hurts me more than it hurts you." Little Willy answers, "Yes, but not in the same place." This experience was for Job's ultimate good. Remember that God's ways are not our ways, "For as the heavens are higher than the earth, so are my ways higher than your ways, and my thoughts than your thoughts" (Isa. 55:9).

We try to deliver our children from suffering; we do all we can to prevent it. We give them everything we can afford to make life pleasant for them, and we spoil them. We have raised a spoiled generation.

A day came when Job realized that something good was coming out of his experience, but at first he did not understand at all. Not only was it for the good of Job, but it was for the glory of God. Remember that God's character had been impugned by Satan. I think all the created intelligences in heaven shuddered when they heard Satan cast that aspersion on God. His implication was: You're not worthy to be loved. You have to *pay* Job to love You and serve You. You have paid lovers.

How about it, friend? Are we just time-servers? Are we paid lovers? God is good and God is merciful to us. We rejoice in His goodness. But it is when we are under trial that we reveal our true metal. The fires always burn out the dross, you know, and testing reveals that which is genuine. We are to be lights in this world. Light is for the darkness, and God puts us in the darkness so that our lights will shine.

God has not promised an easy life to any of His children. On the contrary, we are told that the way will be rough. If we suffer with Him we will reign with Him. If there is no pain, there will be no pomp. If there is no suffering, no struggle, then there will be no sceptre either. It is difficult for us to bow under the awful hand of Almighty God. This is why Paul wrote, "Knowing therefore the terror of the Lord, we persuade men . . ." (2 Cor. 5:11).

What kind of trouble did Job have? We are told that he had sore boils and that he scraped himself with a potsherd, that is, a piece of broken pottery. There has been a great deal of speculation among Christian doctors about what Job's illness might have been. Dr. Cedric Harvey was an English doctor in London who suggested that Job was actually a victim of psychosomatic dermatitis. Now there is a good one for you. The Word of God says he was covered with boils, and this Christian doctor says he had psychosomatic dermatitis. That shows what becoming a doctor can do for you.

Psychosomatic dermatitis is a disease of the skin induced by anxiety. Well, I don't think that is the explanation of it, but the doctor couldn't be there to diagnose it personally anyway, so I can contradict him. Dr. Harvey has written about this in a medical magazine. He goes on to say that a study of the book points up Job's insomnia, terrifying dreams, general state of anxiety, all now generally accepted as symptoms of psychosomatic dermatitis. Remember this the next time you have to scratch yourself. At least you will know the name of your disease.

Dr. Charles J. Brim, a New York heart specialist, diagnosed Job's illness as pellagra, a vitamin deficiency disease. Now you can take your choice between these two diagnoses. As a matter of fact, it has even been suggested that he had cancer. I hope you won't mind if I just say he had boils. Whatever it was, this man was in real trouble.

Satan moved in on Job to take away from him all that any man rests upon in dignity in this life. Now we are introduced to his wife. Listen to her!

> **Then said his wife unto him, Dost thou still retain thine integrity? curse God, and die [Job 2:9].**

Satan wants to get him so beaten down that he doesn't even want to call himself a man.

His wife's suggestion to curse God and die is strange advice coming from a wife. Apparently she wanted to be a widow. However, it might be a tender suggestion, because she could see the suffering that he was going through. Satan removed everything else that Job had. Why didn't he remove his wife, too? I think the reason is that his wife wasn't any help to Job. It would seem that she actually would do the devil's bidding.

> **But he said unto her, Thou speakest as one of the foolish women speaketh. What? shall we receive good at the hand of God, and shall we not receive evil? In all this did not Job sin with his lips [Job 2:10].**

Job did maintain his integrity.

This is now the actual beginning of the book. We have shown how Job has been attacked and how he has maintained his integrity. Now the friends of Job come to visit and "comfort" him. Now his integrity will really be attacked. This is where the dialogue begins.

DOWN TO THE DUMP OF THE CITY

Now when Job's three friends heard of all this evil that was come upon him, they came every one from his own place; Eliphaz the Temanite, and Bildad the Shuhite, and Zophar the Naamathite: for they had made an appointment together to come to mourn with him and to comfort him [Job 2:11].

Now we are introduced to the three friends, and we need to get to know them. Eliphaz was a Temanite. Teman was a grandson of Esau according to Genesis 36: 10–11. Bildad was a Shuhite. Shuah was a son of Abraham according to Genesis 25:2. Zophar was a Naamathite. Naamah was in northern Arabia. These facts lead us to place the time of Job at the time of the patriarchs and it also gives to us the general location where Job lived, although we do not know the specific spot.

These men came to mourn with Job. Since I am going to say some very ugly things about his friends, I think I ought to say what I can that is good about them. They were real friends to Job until this happened to him. This experience alienated them from Job, and the reason it did was that they did not know God nor did they know why God does certain things.

This is a good reason why even today many of us should be very careful about trying to explain why certain things happen to other people. We have no right to say that God has let something happen to So-and-so for such-and-such a reason. We may think it is a good reason, but the problem is that we really don't *know* the reason.

These friends of Job were just as sure of their reasons as people are today. They thought they knew why certain things happen, but they were entirely wrong.

However, note that they were real friends to Job.

And when they lifted up their eyes afar off, and knew him not, they lifted up their voice, and wept: and they rent every one his mantle, and sprinkled dust upon their heads toward heaven.

So they sat down with him upon the ground seven days and seven nights, and none spake a word unto him: for they saw that his grief was very great [Job 2:12–13].

They had heard that their friend Job was in trouble, but they didn't dream it was as severe as it really was. The last time they had seen Job he was in a beautiful home with his fine sons and daughters around him. They had seen the wealth of Job spread there upon the landscape. Now they had come to visit him. They probably at least expected to find him in his luxurious home, but here they find him out at the dump heap of the town where they emptied the garbage, and he is scraping himself with an old broken piece of pottery. He doesn't have anything at all. *Everything* is gone. Poor Job.

These friends mourned and wept and howled. For seven days they just sat there and didn't say a word. They sat with Job for seven days and seven nights! I would say they were friends. As far as they knew how, they tried to comfort him by just sitting there with him for seven days. Although they mourned for him during this full time, they were in no position to comfort him for three reasons: (1) They did not understand God; (2) they did not understand Job; and (3) they did not understand themselves.

As they sit for seven days of mourning, Job is under their critical gaze, and they shake their heads in a knowing manner. They are all brilliant men. They are all philosophers, men who do a great deal of thinking. During all those seven days they are thinking, and they all come to one conclusion. They come to it from different angles, but the conclusion is the same: *Job must be an awful sinner for these things to happen to him. God must be punishing him. He had better get his life straightened out.* This is the conclusion of each of them.

Finally Job just can't stand it any longer. They are beginning to shake their heads in a knowing way with a smirk on their faces. They seem to say, "Aha, brother Job, it finally comes out. You've been living in sin, and you gave the impression that you were such a pious individual. Now we know that this has come to you because your sin is out at last." Well, Job just can't take that. He can take everything else that has happened to him but not a false accusation. So the dialogue begins. Job is the first to speak. Listen to the heartbreak of this man in the chapter that follows.

CHAPTER 3

***THEME:** Job's first discourse—his complaint*

We have seen that Job is being made a test case; he is a guinea pig. Satan has challenged God. He has said to God, "You have put a hedge around Job and have given him everything. But if those things are taken away from him, he will curse You to Your face!" Satan was casting a slur upon mankind and a blasphemy upon God. The intelligences of heaven must have cringed and certainly blushed when they heard this highest creature, whom God had created and who had fallen, cast such a slur upon the Almighty God.

God permitted Satan to get at this man Job. Satan began to move into this man's life. We have seen how he took one thing after another away from him in order to break him down. Before we go into the dialogues, I think we ought to pause and see the background of all this again.

You and I belong to a lost race. It is difficult to think that you and I are living down here among a bunch of liars and cut-throats and thieves and murderers. We say, "But *I'm* not like that." I'm afraid you are—all of us are. We belong to that kind of race. That is the reason God cannot take us to heaven as we are. After all, if God took the world to heaven as it is today, we wouldn't have anything but just the world all over again. I don't know how you feel about it, but I see no reason just to duplicate this all again. And God apparently sees no reason to do it either. Therefore He is not taking us to heaven as we are. That is the reason the Lord Jesus had to say to a refined, polished, religious Pharisee, ". . . Ye must be *born* again" (John 3:7). If it is any comfort to any of us, we are all in the same boat. We talk about "normal" behavior today. A psychologist is great at that. How in the world does he arrive at "normal" behavior? What he does is to plot a chart, and where the majority of people are, that is what he calls normal. At one end are the abnormal and the other end are the supernormal—there are a few who fall at either end of the chart. How does he know that the mass of people in the middle are normal? I don't think they are. God says we are *all* in sin.

This creature called man is frail, feeble, and faulty. It is easy to upset the equilibrium of any man. It can happen to any of us. It is easy to depart from the pattern and to tip the scale. Statistics reveal that one out of ten people spends time in a mental institution, and the number keeps increasing.

God has placed certain props about man to make man stand straight and upright. The Book of Ecclesiastes puts it like this: "Lo, this only have I found, that God hath made man upright; but they have sought out many inventions" (Eccl. 7:29). God has clothed man with an armor of protection, a security, if you please. God has given certain aids to all men, godly and ungodly alike. He makes it rain on the just and on the unjust. The wicked get just as much sunshine and air to breathe, and their health is just as good as those who are the godly, the believers in Christ. The Devil knows that if he can get to a man, remove the props, strip man of every vestige of aid, take away his security blanket, he can upset man and turn him upside down, destroy his morale, rearrange his thinking, brainwash him. Therefore, God has placed a hedge about a man to keep the Devil away. Sometimes Satan is permitted to crash the gate, and he will strip a man down to his naked soul. God permitted the Devil to brainwash Job.

The Book of Job presents the problem. It states the stripping of a man's soul. It does not give the solution, although answers are suggested. You must go to the New Testament for the real answer. It is sort of like the algebra book I had at school. The problems were in the front of the book and the answers were in the back. The Bible is like that. You get the problem here, but you must turn over to the New Testament to get the answer.

In many respects the Old Testament is a very unsatisfactory book. Nothing is actually solved in it. As someone has put it: The Old Testament is *expectation;* the New Testament is *realization.*

In chapters 1 and 2, the Devil has been brainwashing Job. He has stripped Job of every vestige of covering. We need to look at this because it will help us as we enter this dialogue that Job has with his friends.

1. Satan stripped Job of material substance. One of the basic needs of man is material substance. An animal is already born with a coat on. When you and I came into the world someone had to furnish us with a coat. Later on, we had to buy our own coat. We have to have food and clothing and shelter. Man needs flocks, herds, barns, and lands. He needs to have things about him. He needs a home.

Scripture tells us that God has given us all things richly to enjoy. God wants man to enjoy the things that He has put in this world. Although the curse of sin is on this world, God has provided for man in a very wonderful way.

Physical things can be spiritual blessings. Prosperity is a gift of God. There is nothing wrong in building bigger barns. The danger lies in *depending* on these things, leaning upon them as if that is all there is to life.

Actually, I think the prosperity and the affluence of the United States has been giving us a bad conscience for a long time. We have spent billions of dollars passing out crumbs to other countries in order that we might enjoy what we have. It has been to no avail because all we are doing is salving a bad conscience. Our gadgets and our conveniences and our comforts have created almost a prison for us. On holiday weekends I am amazed to see droves of people fleeing to the desert or to the seashore to get away from their electric blankets, their TV sets, their push-button kitchens. They want to rough it, they say. They feel as if they are in prison. The Christian today needs to get alone and take an inventory of himself: Am I trusting in *things* or am I trusting in God?

Job lost all. He went from prosperity to poverty. Job was moved, but he wasn't removed from the foundation.

2. God permitted Satan to take away Job's loved ones. You and I need loved ones to prop us up. I think the reason the Lord makes little babies so attractive is so that we will cuddle them and hug them. That is what they need. The biggest thrill I ever had in my life was to hold in my arms our first child, and the Lord took that child. The greatest thrill I have today is to hold our little grandsons. How wonderful it is. God has made us that way.

When the child grows older, he still goes to parents for love and sympathy. He hurts his little finger and runs to mama to kiss it. You know that doesn't do it a bit of good, but it sure helps him. Without this kind of love the child develops conflicts and complexes. I believe the psychologist is right about that.

Then the time comes for the little eaglet to be pushed out of the nest. The teenager becomes less dependent on the parent, and then one day the love is transferred to someone else. Finally the love passes on to his own children. But we always need loved ones.

Poor old Job lost all of his children in one day—seven sons and three daughters!

3. Health is a great factor in the well-being of man. I notice that when the paper lists suicides it often says, "So-and-so had been in ill health." There are countless numbers of saints who have been bed-ridden and laid aside from normal activity by ill health. Perhaps they have learned to trust God in a way that you and I have not. Satan was permitted to take away Job's health. That was a tremendous blow to him.

4. Then Job lost the love and sympathy of a companion. God gave Adam a helpmeet. A "helpmeet" means the "other half" of him, the responder, the other part of him. I think God has a rib for every man; that is, He has a wife for him. God has instituted marriage for the welfare and happiness of man. Many a man who stands at the forge of life today, faithful and strong, facing the battle and daily grind goes home and pillows his head on the breast or in the lap of a wife who understands him, and maybe he even sobs out his soul to her. How wonderful that is! Job had lost the sympathy and the compassion of his wife, as we have seen.

5. Job's friends came to mourn with him, but he found that they were just a mirage on the desert. When he saw them coming, he thought they were an oasis, but they were only a mirage, and he finally calls them "miserable comforters." We are going to see why.

Now what else can the devil do to Job? He has removed all his props. Now Satan will move in and destroy Job's whole set of values. This is the thing we need to watch as we study the dialogues that ensue.

6. Job loses his sense of worth and the dignity of his own personality. What shall a man give in exchange for his soul? God pity the young people today who throw away their lives for a pill or to please a group of evil-minded companions. *It is God who attaches real value to man.* The Lord Jesus said, ". . . Ye are of more value than many sparrows" (Luke 12:7). Yet He tells us that the Father knows all the sparrows and when they fall. Do you know what proves we are of more value? It is that Christ died for us. That tells us how much we are worth. We are worth the blood of Jesus Christ!

It was during the Dark Ages that Mueritus, a brilliant scholar, fell sick and was picked up on the highway. The doctors, thinking he was a bum, began talking about him in Latin. They said, "Shall we operate on this worthless creature?" Mueritus understood Latin very well. He raised up and answered them in Latin, "Do not call a creature worthless for whom Christ died." Remember that the Devil tries to cause us to lose our sense of worth and the dignity of our own personality.

7. Job will lose his sense of the justice of God, and he will become critical and cynical before it is over. In studying this book we need to realize that it is inspired just as all the Bible is inspired, but not all that the characters say is true. This is an illustration of what I mean: the Devil was not inspired to tell a lie to Eve when he said, ". . . Ye shall not surely die" (Gen. 3:4), but the record of his lying is inspired. Some folk believe that every statement they find in the Bible is true, but we need to notice carefully who is making the statement. In the Book of Job we will find these men saying things that are not true.

8. Job will also lose his sense of the love of God. The man who said, ". . . the LORD gave, and the LORD hath taken away; blessed be the name of the LORD" (Job 1:21), is the same man who later cried, "For the arrows of the Almighty are within me, the poison whereof drinketh up my spirit: the terrors of God do set themselves in array against me" (Job 6:4). Then in chapter 9 we hear his cry as, "Oh, that there were a daysman to stand between us." In other words, "Oh, that there were someone to take hold of the hand of God and take hold of my hand and bring us together!" We will need to go to the New Testament to find the answer to this cry of Job: "For there is one God, and one mediator between God and men, the man Christ Jesus" (1 Tim. 2:5). Thank God you and I have Someone who is our daysman!

I have spent time on this because it is very important to get this background in order to understand the dialogue which begins here and continues through chapter 37.

There are three rounds of speeches: (1) By Job, then Eliphaz, and Job answers him; (2) by Bildad, and Job answers him; and (3) by Zophar, and Job answers him. This is repeated three times with one exception—Zophar does not give a third speech. The dialogue is in the nature of a contest.

First Round	Chapter
Job	3
Eliphaz, First Discourse	4–5
Job's Answer	6–7
Bildad, First Discourse	8
Job's Answer	9–10
Zophar, First Discourse	11
Job's Answer	12–14
Second Round	
Eliphaz, Second Discourse	15
Job's Answer	16–17
Bildad, Second Discourse	18
Job's Answer	19
Zophar, Second Discourse	20
Job's Answer	21
Third Round	
Eliphaz, Third Discourse	22
Job's Answer	23–24
Bildad, Third Discourse	25
Job's Answer	26–31

Job's friends have been sitting with him for seven days. Finally Job explodes, under the critical and accusing eyes of his friends, with his tale of woe and a wish that he had never been born.

JOB'S FIRST DISCOURSE

After this opened Job his mouth, and cursed his day.

And Job spake, and said,

Let the day perish wherein I was born, and the night in which it was said, There is a man child conceived.

Let that day be darkness; let not God regard it from above, neither let the light shine upon it.

Let darkness and the shadow of death stain it; let a cloud dwell upon it; let the blackness of the day terrify it [Job 3:1–5].

This is a very beautiful speech, very flowery, but when you add it all up, boil it down, and strain it, he is simply saying, "I wish I hadn't been born." How many times have you said that? I'm of the opinion that many of us have said it, especially when we were young and something disappointed us. This is what Job is saying, only he is saying it in poetic language.

As for that night, let darkness seize upon it; let it not be joined unto the days of the year, let it not come into the number of the months.

Lo, let that night be solitary, let no joyful voice come therein.

Let them curse it that curse the day, who are ready to raise up their mourning.

Let the stars of the twilight thereof be dark; let it look for light, but have none; neither let it see the dawning of the day:

Because it shut not up the doors of my mother's womb, nor hid sorrow from mine eyes.

Why died I not from the womb? why did I not give up the ghost when I came out of the belly?

Why did the knees prevent me? or why the breasts that I should suck? [Job 3:6–12].

Job is saying loud and clear, "I wish I had never been born." It is interesting, my friend, that this attitude never solves any problems of this life. You may wish you had never been born, but you can't undo the fact that you have been born. You may wish that you could die, but you will not die by wishing. It is all a waste of time. It may help a person let off some steam. That seems to be what it does for Job now.

For now should I have lain still and been quiet, I should have slept: then had I been at rest,

With kings and counsellors of the earth, which built desolate places for themselves [Job 3:13–14].

They built great monuments or great pyramids for themselves.

Or with princes that had gold, who filled their houses with silver:

Or as an hidden untimely birth I had not been; as infants which never saw light [Job 3:15–16].

He wishes he had been stillborn. Job complains that this oblivion has been denied him. He describes death as the great equalizer. All sleep equally.

There are two things Job is saying in this chapter. He wishes that he had never been born. However, having been born, he wishes that he had died at birth. These are his two wishes in this chapter, and he finds no relief from his misery.

There the wicked cease from troubling; and there the weary be at rest.

There the prisoners rest together; they hear not the voice of the oppressor.

The small and great are there; and the servant is free from his master.

Wherefore is light given to him that is in misery, and life unto the bitter in soul;

Which long for death, but it cometh not; and dig for it more than for hid treasures;

Which rejoice exceedingly, and are glad, when they can find the grave?

Why is light given to a man whose way is hid, and whom God hath hedged in?

For my sighing cometh before I eat, and my roarings are poured out like the waters [Job 3:17–24].

He pictures death as being preferred to life. He says that life is such a burden. He doesn't want to live. He would rather die. Job says he would welcome death like a miner who is digging for gold and gives a shout of joy when he finds it. He is in a desperate, desolate condition.

For the thing which I greatly feared is come upon me, and that which I was afraid of is come unto me.

I was not in safety, neither had I rest, neither was I quiet; yet trouble came [Job 3:25–26].

Job had been dwelling in peace and prosperity in the land of Uz, and things had been going so well with him. He was living in the lap of luxury. Everyone was saying, "Look at Job. He certainly has a wonderful life." Job says, "At that very moment, I was living in fear. And the thing that I dreaded has come upon me." His tranquility even in his days of prosperity was disturbed by the uncertainty of life.

I think that is a fear of a great many people today. They fear that something terrible is going to happen to them. Our problem is that we grab for our security blanket instead of grabbing for the Savior. We ought to be using our Bible for our blanket instead of turning to other things. We need to *rest* upon the Word of God.

One would almost get the impression that Job has lost his faith. He actually has not. This is the bitter complaint of a man who is tasting the very dregs in the bottom of the cup of life. Trouble has come upon him and he does not understand at all why it should have come.

It is a monologue of complaint as his friends sit around him. The language is tremendous, but Job does not have the answer. It is black pessimism.

CHAPTERS 4–5

THEME: *The first discourse of Eliphaz, the voice of experience*

Job's three friends had been sitting with him for seven days, and they have been wagging their heads as if to say, "Mmm, it finally caught up with you!" It seems that Job could take all his suffering, but he couldn't take this attitude from his friends. He broke out in a monologue of complaint and whining. It is black pessimism and has no answer to the problem at all.

Now his three friends will begin to talk to him. The first will be Eliphaz and then Bildad and finally Zophar. The names of these men actually give us just a little pen picture of them.

Eliphaz means "God is strength" or "God is fine gold."

Bildad means "son of contention." He is a mean one, by the way. He is actually brutal and blunt and crude in his method.

Zophar means "a sparrow." He twitters. He has a mean tongue and makes terrible insinuations to Job.

The dialogue that takes place is a real contest. These friends are actually going to make an attack on Job, and he will respond. This is what we might call intellectual athletics. This type of thing was popular in that day. Today people go to a football game or a baseball, basketball, or hockey game—something athletic where the physical is demonstrated. In those days people gathered for intellectual contests. I think that by the time this dialogue was under way a great crowd had gathered, listening to what was taking place.

We want to think that those people were not civilized; yet they put the emphasis on the intellectual. And we consider ourselves to be such civilized people who have advanced so far, but we put the emphasis on the physical. We are not as superior to these ancient people as we would like to think.

Job has just broken out with a complaint. He is in the deepest, blackest pessimism that a man can be in. The Devil has stripped him of everything. He has nothing left to lean on, no place to turn. Even God seems very far removed from him at this particular time.

Eliphaz is the first to speak. His is the voice of experience. He is a remarkable man, and he relates a strange and mysterious experience. The key to what he has to say is found in verse 8, "Even as I have seen." Everything he has to say rests on that. He is the voice of experience. He has had a remarkable vision and has heard secrets that nobody else has ever heard.

Then Eliphaz the Temanite answered and said,

If we assay to commune with thee, wilt thou be grieved? but who can withhold himself from speaking? [Job 4:1–2].

He begins in a diplomatic sort of way, but one gets the feeling he has his tongue in his cheek. This is a sort of false politeness. He says to Job, "Do you mind if I say something?" Then he adds, "Regardless of whether or not you mind my saying something, I'm going to say it." And he does.

Behold, thou hast instructed many, and thou hast strengthened the weak hands.

Thy words have upholden him that was falling, and thou hast strengthened the feeble knees.

But now it is come upon thee, and thou faintest; it toucheth thee, and thou art troubled [Job 4:3–5].

He is saying to Job, "In the old days when you were in prosperity and plenty and in good health, you were a tower of strength to everybody else. You could advise them. You could speak to them and tell them what to do. You knew how to help those who were in trouble. But now something has happened to you, and you have folded up. You're just a paper doll; you're just a paper tiger. You were never real at all. The advice you gave to others—can't you follow it yourself?"

I would say that that is the problem a great many of us have today. Isn't it interesting that we can always tell the other person what he should do when troubles come to him? It is like the cartoon of two psychiatrists meeting one day. One looked at the other and said, "You are fine. How am I?" We are always analyzing the other fellow, telling how *he* is.

Eliphaz accuses Job of being an expert at that. In a very sarcastic manner he says, "Now it has happened to you, and what have you done? You folded up."

Is not this thy fear, thy confidence, thy hope, and the uprightness of thy ways? [Job 4:6].

"Isn't your own advice good enough for you? It helped others; now it ought to help you."

Now Eliphaz makes an insinuation to Job. But he does it in a polite way. We will find that Job's other two friends are more blunt and crude, especially old Zophar.

Remember, I pray thee, who ever perished, being innocent? or where were the righteous cut off? [Job 4:7].

He accuses Job of having a chink in his armor, of having an Achilles' heel. He says this would not have happened to Job if there hadn't been something radically wrong in his life, something that he is keeping secret. This is the argument. He is making an insinuation, and it's not true of Job. I hear this verse quoted even today, and it's not interpreted accurately, my friend.

Now we know this insinuation is wrong and is not true of Job, because at the beginning of the book God gave us that scene in heaven so that we might know Job and understand his character. These friends will be miserable comforters because they do not understand God, they do not understand Job, and they do not understand themselves.

There are too many people who try to deal with spiritual matters who are not qualified to do so. Very candidly, that is one of the reasons I am reluctant to counsel folk. My feeling is that if a person is a child of God—unless it is a technical matter, a theological matter, or some physical difficulty—it can be settled between the soul and God. We don't need to go to the third person. After all, we have an Intercessor with God. Job cried out for a daysman, an intercessor, and today we know we have that. "For there is one God, and one mediator between God and men, the man Christ Jesus" (1 Tim. 2:5). Now He's the One to whom a great many Christians ought to be going instead of a minister or a psychologist. And if the problem is physical, go to the doctor—and with that go to God also. As Eliphaz could speak from experience, I can also speak from experience and say that God does hear and answer prayer relative to our physical condition and relative to our spiritual condition. It is wonderful to see the way God will deal with Job before He is through with him.

Eliphaz is not going to be very helpful to Job.

Even as I have seen, they that plow iniquity, and sow wickedness, reap the same [Job 4:8].

Eliphaz is speaking from a very high pulpit and is looking down at Job when he says this. He insists there is something hidden in his life which he has not revealed. He is saying that Job is reaping what he sowed.

By the blast of God they perish, and by the breath of his nostrils are they consumed [Job 4:9].

This man is wrong. God disciplines His children, but He never destroys them. Eliphaz is like so many of us who give advice. We can tell someone else how he ought to do things, in a nice way, phrased in very attractive language, but what we say may not be accurate.

The roaring of the lion, and the voice of the fierce lion, and the teeth of the young lions, are broken.

The old lion perisheth for lack of prey, and the stout lion's whelps are scattered abroad [Job 4:10–11].

He is saying that those who sow evil seed are going to reap a harvest of evil, and they are going to perish like the young lions that have broken teeth and like the old lions that can no longer stalk their prey.

Now Eliphaz will say that this was impressed on him because he had a vision. He really tries to make your hair stand on end while he tells of this dream.

Now a thing was secretly brought to me, and mine ear received a little thereof [Job 4:12].

Draw closer now. Cup your ear and don't miss a thing of what is happening.

In thoughts from the visions of the night, when deep sleep falleth on men,

Fear came upon me, and trembling, which made all my bones to shake [Job 4:13–14].

Doesn't this sound mysterious? Isn't it bloodcurdling? The vision took place at night, in the dark.

Then a spirit passed before my face; the hair of my flesh stood up:

It stood still, but I could not discern the form thereof: an image was before mine eyes, there was silence, and I heard a voice, saying [Job 4:15–16].

My, how Eliphaz builds this up! It sounds so scary. It sounds so frightening. This is going to be something nobody's ever heard before.

This is something nobody ever knew before, because this man has had a vision. He has seen things. He has had a dream. It was dark and a spirit passed before him. What did it say?

Shall mortal man be more just than God? shall a man be more pure than his maker? [Job 4:17].

Now I don't know about you, but I must say I am disappointed. I thought that if a man had had such an experience he was really going to come up with something profound, something that none of us had ever heard before.

This is nothing *new*. I think he really exercised himself a little bit too much to come up with so little. It is like the old saying about the mountain that conceived and travailed and brought forth a mouse! I think that is what Eliphaz did. He's in great travail here, and you expect him to give birth to a great statement, a profound truth. He comes up with this: Shall a mortal man be more just than God? Of course not. Any of us knows that, and we didn't need a dream or a frightening nightmare to learn it. I don't think it was worth missing a night's sleep to come up with something so trite, so evident. There is really nothing profound here at all. Yet this is the voice of experience, and there are a lot of folks with the voices of experience today.

I'm in that very difficult spot myself as a retired preacher. Retired preachers can become a nuisance by giving advice—especially to young preachers. When I was young, I can remember how retired preachers would come up, put their arm around me and say, "Son, this is the way you should be doing it." The interesting thing was that they had not done it that way themselves. I find myself doing the same thing now. This very morning I met a young man who is candidating in a church I recommended to him. Before I could even think, I found myself telling him how he ought to do it. Finally I bit my tongue, got back in my car, told him that I would pray for him, and left it there. My, there is a danger in the voice of experience. May I say that Eliphaz was not being helpful to Job.

Let me hasten to say that I don't want to give the impression that Eliphaz and these other men are not stating profound, wonderful truths. The point is that they are not helping Job.

Behold, he put no trust in his servants; and his angels he charged with folly:

How much less in them that dwell in houses of clay, whose foundation is in the dust, which are crushed before the moth? [Job 4:18–19].

Even God's angels act rather foolishly. How much more foolish are we who live in houses of clay. There is not a better description of our bodies than that. We live in houses of clay. In 2 Corinthians 5 Paul called our bodies a tent, a feeble, frail tent which the wind will blow over. We live in houses of clay, and before long our houses fall in on us.

They are destroyed from morning to evening: they perish for ever without any regarding it.

Doth not their excellency which is in them go away? they die, even without wisdom [Job 4:20–21].

No matter how strong or beautiful our bodies may be, they are of brief duration. Eliphaz is stating truths that are remarkable coming from a period so early in history, but they are not helpful to Job. You see, it is easy to give out truth that is not pertinent, that is not geared into life. We don't need just any truth, but the truth that meets our need.

All of these friends will say some true things, some wonderful things. I enjoy reading this, and I hope you enjoy it. But it doesn't meet the need of Job. One feels like stopping these men and saying, "Don't talk any further because you're going down the wrong road. What you say is not helping this man."

Call now, if there be any that will answer thee; and to which of the saints wilt thou turn? [Job 5:1].

That is still a good question. To whom will you turn for help? I'm afraid saints are not able to help you. Apparently the patriarchs had already gone on at the time of Job. Probably Abraham and Isaac had died, possibly Jacob was still living. Abraham wasn't able to help; Isaac wasn't able to help—no one who had lived in the past was able to help. Well, which saint are you going to turn to?

For wrath killeth the foolish man, and envy slayeth the silly one.

I have seen the foolish taking root: but suddenly I cursed his habitation [Job 5:2–3].

He is saying that he has seen the foolish and the wicked prosper but finally they are brought down. That, by the way, is true. David was troubled by the prosperity of the wicked and writes, "I have seen the wicked in great power, and spreading himself like a green bay tree. Yet he passed away, and, lo, he was not: yea, I sought him, but he could not be found" (Ps. 37:35–36). David wondered why wicked men prospered while the godly men did not. He watched and noted that finally God brought down the wicked men.

It seemed like a long time before God brought down Hitler and got rid of him. It seemed long while we were living through it, but it was only a few years. Why doesn't God move against evil men today? Well, friend, God moves slowly. God will bring down the ungodly in His own time. He has all eternity ahead of Him.

Eliphaz is classifying Job as one of the foolish ones who took root and was flourishing before he was brought down.

His children are far from safety, and they are crushed in the gate, neither is there any to deliver them.

Whose harvest the hungry eateth up, and taketh it even out of the thorns, and the robber swalloweth up their substance.

Although affliction cometh not forth of the dust, neither doth trouble spring out of the ground;

Yet man is born unto trouble, as the sparks fly upward [Job 5:4–7].

We don't need to pour his last statement into a test tube to find out it is true. Man is born unto trouble. I don't think it is even debatable that the human family has adversity, calamity, sorrow, distress, anxiety, worry, and disturbance. All one needs to do is pick up the newspaper and read a partial report of the human family: fires, accidents, tragedies, wars, rumors of war. The song says, "Nobody knows the trouble I've seen," but really everyone does know because all people have trouble. We do not all have the same color, we are not all the same size, or the same sex, or have the same blood type, or the same I.Q., but we all have trouble. No one is exempt or immune or can get inoculated for trouble. Tears are universal. In fact, the word *sympathy* means "to suffer together," and that is the human symphony today—the suffering of mankind. In fact, a Hebrew word for man is *enash,* meaning "the miserable." That's man. There is nothing sure but death and taxes, we are told. We can add to this another surety: trouble. "Yet man is born unto trouble, as the sparks fly upward." The sparks fly upward according to a universal law, the law of thermodynamics. It isn't by chance or by luck. The updraft caused by heat on a cool night causes the sparks to fly upward.

Trouble and suffering and sin are basically the result of disobedience to God. "There is no peace, saith the LORD, unto the wicked" (Isa. 48:22). Man is trying to build a Utopia in sin, but it won't work. We cannot have the Millennium without the Prince of Peace. Man is trying to achieve peace in the world without the Prince of Peace. Therefore trouble comes to man, and the righteous *do* suffer, and the children of God *do* have trouble today.

Sometimes trouble comes to a child of God because of a stupid blunder. A woman once told me, "My husband is my cross." Well, no matter how bad he is, he is not her cross. She is the one who said yes. It was her stupid blunder. Your cross is something you take up gladly, my friend.

Trouble sometimes is a judgment of the Father upon His child. We are told, ". . . for if we would judge ourselves, we should not be judged" (1 Cor. 11:31). But if we do not judge ourselves, God will have to judge us.

Trouble is sometimes a discipline of the Father. We are told in Scripture, "For whom the Lord loveth he chasteneth, and scourgeth every son whom he receiveth" (Heb. 12:6). Moses who was living the life of Riley in the court of Pharaoh chose ". . . to suffer affliction with the people of God, than to enjoy the pleasures of sin for a season" (Heb. 11:25). It was a discipline for Moses. God could not have used him as a deliverer if he had not had forty years training down in the desert of Midian. Also Saul of Tarsus, the proud young Pharisee, came to know Christ, and God said of him, "For I will shew him how great things he must suffer for my name's sake" (Acts 9:16). God really put him through the mill! Trouble is a discipline of the Father.

Trouble comes to us sometimes for the purpose of teaching us to be patient and to trust God. Practical James says, "Knowing this, that the trying of your faith worketh patience" (James 1:3).

At other times trouble comes to us because God is putting the sandpaper on us to smooth the rough edges. We will see that Job comes to the realization that God is doing that for him: "But he knoweth the way that I take: when he hath tried me, I shall come forth as gold" (Job 23:10). He saw that God was putting sandpaper on him to smooth him down.

Then sometimes God permits trouble to come to us to get our minds and hearts fastened on Him. This is an explanation, I think, for many of us today.

There are good reasons, my friend, for trouble coming to a child of God. Therefore Eliphaz is accurate when he says, "Yet man is born unto trouble, as the sparks fly upward."

I would seek unto God, and unto God would I commit my cause:

Which doeth great things and unsearchable; marvellous things without number:

Who giveth rain upon the earth, and sendeth waters upon the fields:

To set up on high those that be low; that those which mourn may be exalted to safety.

He disappointeth the devices of the crafty, so that their hands cannot perform their enterprise.

He taketh the wise in their own craftiness: and the counsel of the froward is carried headlong.

They meet with darkness in the daytime, and grope in the noonday as in the night.

But he saveth the poor from the sword, from their mouth, and from the hand of the mighty.

So the poor hath hope, and iniquity stoppeth her mouth [Job 5:8–16].

What he is saying here—and he is saying it really in a beautiful way—is that God is faithful and God is good and God is just. While this is true, it doesn't reach the root of the problem of this man Job. Eliphaz actually is not even talking to Job.

Behold, happy is the man whom God correcteth: therefore despise not thou the chastening of the Almighty [Job 5:17].

I have heard this verse quoted again and again. Isn't it true? Of course, it is true, but Eliphaz was using it as a personal dig against Job. Chastening is not always the reason that God's people suffer, as we have seen. Sometimes one can use this verse as a little dagger to put into the heart of a friend. It is a nice way of saying, "You are having trouble because you've done wrong and God is correcting you." Well, that could be, but it may not be. Who are you to make such a judgment? Do you have a telephone into heaven? Has the Lord revealed some secret to you? There are people who like to speak *ex cathedra,* and they are not even the Pope! Some people think they have the last word on everything. Listen, friend, you cannot always speak to the problem of someone else, and someone else cannot always speak to your problem either. Although the statement of Eliphaz is true, it does not apply to Job.

For he maketh sore, and bindeth up: he woundeth, and his hands make whole [Job 5:18].

What a wonderful picture of God that is.

He shall deliver thee in six troubles: yea, in seven there shall no evil touch thee [Job 5:19].

You will notice this use of seven again in Proverbs 6:16 and, in fact, quite often throughout the Bible. It is not just a poetic expression. It means seven—not the number of perfection—the number of completeness. For instance, the seventh day was the completion of one week. Seven is the number of completeness here, as he gives the total spectrum of the trouble of man.

In famine he shall redeem thee from death: and in war from the power of the sword.

Thou shalt be hid from the scourge of the tongue: neither shalt thou be afraid of destruction when it cometh [Job 5: 20–21].

God will deliver you in these seven troubles: (1) In famine he shall redeem thee from death; (2) in war from the power of the sword; (3) from the scourge of the tongue. During the war in Vietnam we were given a body count in the daily news. I wonder what the body count from gossip would be in this day. The tongue has probably killed more people than war has. We need to pray that God will deliver us from the evil tongue. A woman in a church I served had a very evil tongue. I remember praying, "Oh God, don't let her hit me with that tongue." I found out that she did use her tongue against me. She was mean, but God protected me from being hurt by her. (4) God will deliver from the fear of destruction when it cometh—that is the typhoon, the tornado, the storm. When I was a boy it seemed like I spent half my life in a storm cellar in West Texas. God did deliver us, but He expected us to go to the storm cellars.

At destruction and famine thou shalt laugh: neither shalt thou be afraid of the beasts of the earth [Job 5:22].

(5) He delivers from famine. Have you ever stopped to think that generally wherever the gospel has gone, whether or not it has been widely accepted, you find one of the prosperous areas of the world? These nations are the "haves." I do not think that is an accident. I have often thought that with the food we send to "have not" countries should be prizes like we get in boxes of Crackerjacks. And the prize should be the Word of God. Blessing attends the reading of the Word. (6) Neither shalt thou be afraid of the beasts of the earth.

For thou shalt be in league with the stones of the field: and the beasts of the field shall be at peace with thee.

And thou shalt know that thy tabernacle shall be in peace; and thou shalt visit thy habitation, and shalt not sin.

Thou shalt know also that thy seed shall be great, and thine offspring as the grass of the earth.

Thou shalt come to thy grave in a full age, like as a shock of corn cometh in in his season [Job 5:23–26].

(7) The last trouble is death. Eliphaz speaks of death, not as an awful hideous monster, but as something welcome. There is a leveling out in death.

Lo this, we have searched it, so it is; hear it, and know thou it for thy good [Job 5:27].

This concludes the first discourse of Eliphaz. It has not met the need of Job. It hasn't touched him at all. As a matter of fact, Job is dismayed; he is alarmed, and he cries out for pity. He cries out for mercy and for help because Eliphaz was of no help to him at all.

CHAPTERS 6–7

***THEME:** Job's answer to Eliphaz*

But Job answered and said,

Oh that my grief were throughly weighed, and my calamity laid in the balances together! [Job 6:1–2].

Job is making a plaintive plea. He says, "I can't even tell you how terrible my grief is. I can't explain to you this awful thing that has happened to me." You can see that Eliphaz had not helped him at all. Just to say, "You have some secret sin and the thing for you to do now is to confess and get right with God," is not always the correct thing to say. Job is saying, "You need to recognize what my question is." Eliphaz had missed the point altogether. He said a lot of nice things, good things, true things, but he didn't help Job. It is like giving the answer, "Christ is the answer," when you don't know what the question is.

Job needs more than has been given him by Eliphaz. He is crying out like a wounded animal.

For now it would be heavier than the sand of the sea: therefore my words are swallowed up.

For the arrows of the Almighty are within me, the poison whereof drinketh up my spirit: the terrors of God do set themselves in array against me.

Doth the wild ass bray when he hath grass? or loweth the ox over his fodder? [Job 6:3–5].

Job says, "I am crying out and you can see my misery and you show no pity at all. You act as if I'm not in trouble. I wouldn't be crying out if I weren't." He points out that the long-eared donkey out in the field doesn't bray for something to eat when he is eating grass. So Job is saying that he wouldn't be crying out if there were nothing hurting him. He says, "I'm hurting and I'm hurting bad."

Can that which is unsavoury be eaten without salt? or is there any taste in the white of an egg?

The things that my soul refused to touch are as my sorrowful meat [Job 6:6–7].

"Sorrowful meat" is loathsome food.

Oh that I might have my request; and that God would grant me the thing that I long for!

Even that it would please God to destroy me; that he would let loose his hand, and cut me off! [Job 6:8–9].

He has hit bottom. He finds no help anywhere. He actually questions the justice of God. He is miserable. He wishes God would destroy him, get rid of him, let loose His hand, and cut him off. He wants to die.

Then should I yet have comfort; yea, I would harden myself in sorrow: let him not spare; for I have not concealed the words of the Holy One.

What is my strength, that I should hope? and what is mine end, that I should prolong my life? [Job 6:10–11].

He is saying, "I have nothing to live for."

Is my strength the strength of stones? or is my flesh of brass? [Job 6:12].

"I am weary. I can't stand any more."

Is not my help in me? and is wisdom driven quite from me? [Job 6:13].

Now listen to his cry.

To him that is afflicted pity should be shewed from his friend; but he forsaketh the fear of the Almighty [Job 6:14].

My friend should have shown pity, should have sympathized with me. But he didn't.

My brethren have dealt deceitfully as a brook, and as the stream of brooks they pass away [Job 6:15].

The meaning in the Hebrew is that they were like a mirage in the desert.

This is beautiful, poetic language. It is as if he says that he looked down the road and saw his three friends coming and said to himself, *Oh thank God, here come my friends. They will understand me and they will sympathize with me.* Their sympathy would be like an oasis in the desert, but it was only a mirage.

Which are blackish by reason of the ice, and wherein the snow is hid:

What time they wax warm, they vanish: when it is hot, they are consumed out of their place [Job 6:16–17].

He says they are like a pool that is covered with ice and snow. It is deceitful. You think you can walk on it, but when you step on it, you fall through. That is the type of friends they have turned out to be.

What a picture Job gives us!

I'm not sure but what Job's cry is the cry of the human predicament in our day. Man with all his comforts and his gadgets—oh, how lonesome, how restless, how unhappy he is! He is *Enash*, the miserable one. He needs more than gadgets; he needs *God*.

Now Job will say, "If you have something to tell me, *tell* me. I'm teachable."

Teach me, and I will hold my tongue: and cause me to understand wherein I have erred.

How forcible are right words! but what doth your arguing reprove?

Do ye imagine to reprove words, and the speeches of one that is desperate, which are as wind? [Job 6:24–26].

He says, "What you have said is good, but it doesn't touch my case at all. You're not diagnosing my condition."

I heard of a person who went to a doctor, and his case was diagnosed as arthritis. It turned out to be a cancer, but by the time the patient got into the hands of a cancer specialist, it was too late to do anything for him. That is the problem of Job. He says, "You have come and you have attempted to diagnose my case, but your diagnosis is wrong. You have said it is hidden sin, and it isn't that at all. Now if you diagnose it accurately and you have something helpful to say to me, say it and I'll listen to you."

Remember that these three friends didn't really know God, they didn't really know Job, and they didn't really know themselves. They didn't understand the true situation, and all three will come to the conclusion that Job had sinned and won't confess the truth. Since he won't confess his secret sin, he is being judged.

Is there not an appointed time to man upon earth? are not his days also like the days of an hireling?

As a servant earnestly desireth the shadow, and as an hireling looketh for the reward of his work:

So am I made to possess months of vanity, and wearisome nights are appointed to me [Job 7:1–3].

Job has no relief from his sorrow or from his pain. He is a very sick man, and his friends seem to ignore that. They have not offered him any comfort. Even his wife, his helpmeet, has suggested suicide to him. When his world caved in, he became a distraught and frustrated man to be pitied.

When I lie down, I say, When shall I arise, and the night be gone? and I am full of tossings to and fro unto the dawning of the day.

My flesh is clothed with worms and clods of dust; my skin is broken, and become loathsome.

My days are swifter than a weaver's shuttle, and are spent without hope [Job 7:4–6].

Job apparently felt he had an incurable disease and that the end was coming and was not far off. He probably did have such a disease. In all this his friends paid no attention to his problem. They have come to him but have not ministered to his need. They just didn't understand. It has been said that a friend is one who knows you and *still* loves you. These friends didn't really know Job. He says that at least his physical condition should have called forth some sympathy from them.

When I say, My bed shall comfort me, my couch shall ease my complaint;

Then thou scarest me with dreams, and terrifiest me through visions:

So that my soul chooseth strangling, and death rather than my life.

I loathe it; I would not live alway: let me alone; for my days are vanity [Job 7:13–16].

It seems that his fever drove him to periods of delirium and hallucinations.

What is man, that thou shouldest magnify him? and that thou shouldest set thine heart upon him?

And that thou shouldest visit him every morning, and try him every moment?

How long wilt thou not depart from me, nor let me alone till I swallow down my spittle? [Job 7:17–19].

He wishes he could just die in peace. He wishes that God would let him alone. He senses that he is being tried, but he hasn't any notion what is really behind all of this.

His reaction is the reaction of many. "Just leave me alone in my misery."

I have sinned; what shall I do unto thee, O thou preserver of men? why hast thou set me as a mark against thee, so that I am a burden to myself?

And why dost thou not pardon my transgression, and take away mine iniquity? for now shall I sleep in the dust; and thou shalt seek me in the morning, but I shall not be [Job 7: 20–21].

They have raised the question of Job's sin. Job doesn't claim to be guiltless. He admits he has sinned. But why should he be selected for this special attack as a notorious sinner? Why should his life be a burden when he is not that kind of a sinner? Why doesn't God show mercy on him? Why doesn't God pardon his sin and restore him?

While he admits that he is a sinner, he says that he is getting more than he deserves.

We can see in Job a breaking down of his integrity. When a man's integrity is broken down, he becomes an easy mark for Satan. This is the thing that happens to many a man today who attempts to fight life alone. He begins to hit the bottle or he drops into sin. Satan has a chance to attack him because the man's integrity has broken down. This is the situation with Job. Will Job break under all of this?

CHAPTER 8

***THEME:** Bildad's first discourse*

The next man who makes his attack upon Job is Bildad. He is what we would call a traditionalist. Bildad is a man who rests upon the past. His argument is: "For inquire, I pray thee, of the former age, and prepare thyself to the search of their fathers" (Job 8:8). It is as if he picks up the old rocks and stones of geology, looks at them and tells what happened years ago and from them predicts what will happen.

Actually, the evolutionist is really a traditionalist, which a great many people do not recognize. The evolutionist rests upon the past and assumes certain premises which he cannot prove. There are only two explanations for the origin of this universe: one is creation and the other is speculation. Evolution is speculation. It digs up a bone, attempts to date it and classify it as belonging to a certain period, and then relate it to the development of man. But who knows? This Book of Job is going to raise that very question. In Job 38:4 God asks Job, "Where wast thou when I laid the foundations of the earth? declare, if thou hast understanding." Bildad will use the argument of "when I was young," and "we've been doing it this way." He knew a lot of old sayings and proverbs and pious platitudes, but he actually offers nothing new at all. He is a more crude fellow than Eliphaz. He breaks in upon Job and hurts him a great deal. He doesn't help Job at all. This is Bildad who is supposed to have been his friend.

BILDAD RESTS HIS ARGUMENT ON TRADITION

Then answered Bildad the Shuhite, and said,

How long wilt thou speak these things? and how long shall the words of thy mouth be like a strong wind? [Job 8:1–2].

These men really get in some good ones. This is real repartee. This is a real rap session they are having here. They are brilliant men, by the way. Notice that Bildad puts the knife into Job and twists it a little. He says, "Job, listening to you is just like listening to the wind blowing. You're a windy individual." Actually, I would say they are all a little windy, including Job. We will see a little later that there is something wrong with Job, too.

So this remark by Bildad was good for a laugh at the expense of Job. A crowd had gathered around by this time. This was as interesting to people as a football game or a basketball game would be today. They were interested in an intellectual contest as we seem to be interested in physical contests. I wonder who are the more civilized people!

Doth God pervert judgment? or doth the Almighty pervert justice? [Job 8:3].

He is really saying, "Job, you are getting exactly what you had coming to you. You try to defend yourself, but it means that there is some great sin in your life and you are getting exactly what you deserve."

If thy children have sinned against him, and he have cast them away for their transgression [Job 8:4].

Now that is an awful thing to say. He is suggesting that the reason Job's children were destroyed was because they were sinners. I can't think of anything anyone could say that would hurt more than that. Bildad had no right to say that. We know (because God let us in on it from the beginning of the book) that his children were not destroyed for that reason.

If thou wouldest seek unto God betimes, and make thy supplication to the Almighty;

If thou wert pure and upright; surely now he would awake for thee, and make the habitation of thy righteousness prosperous [Job 8:5–6].

Job, if you were lily white, as you have given the impression, God would hear your prayer and heal and restore you. But as it is, there must be something radically wrong.

Though thy beginning was small, yet thy latter end should greatly increase [Job 8:7].

By the way, that is what is going to happen. When all of this is over, Job will greatly increase—God is going to double everything he had.

For inquire, I pray thee, of the former age, and prepare thyself to the search of their fathers [Job 8:8].

Bildad is going back to give the old evolutionary theory. He is going to say that everything works according to set laws. He will put down quite a few of those laws which are old sayings.

(For we are but of yesterday, and know nothing, because our days upon earth are a shadow:) [Job 8:9].

"We are but of yesterday and know nothing" is a true statement. Of course, Bildad doesn't really feel that *he* knows nothing; he means that Job knows nothing. However, the statement was true of Bildad, it is true of the evolutionists, and it is true of you and me. We are but of yesterday. Man is a "Johnny-come-lately" in God's universe. He hasn't been around very long. God has not seen fit to tell us what He was doing back in the millenniums before man arrived on the scene. Frankly, I'm not interested in the eternity past, but I am very interested in what He is going to be doing in the millions of years from today, because I expect to be around then.

Shall not they teach thee, and tell thee, and utter words out of their heart? [Job 8:10].

Bildad says that the past will teach us. Men try to take a few rocks and a few bones and then pretend they know all about the origin of the earth and its development. May I say to you that man is assuming more than he could possibly know.

Notice how different is the philosophy of the apostle Paul. He pointed to Christ and to the future: "I press toward the mark for the prize of the high calling of God in Christ Jesus" (Phil. 3:14). The only way we can learn about eternal things is from the Word of God.

Now Bildad gets more candid and more crude.

Can the rush grow up without mire? can the flag grow without water?

Whilst it is yet in his greenness, and not cut down, it withereth before any other herb [Job 8:11–12].

He tries to get very scientific here, but any third grader would know the answer. I've learned the answer here in California. I need to water my flags out by my back fence or they will not grow. That is not very profound wisdom. Who doesn't know this!

So are the paths of all that forget God; and the hypocrite's hope shall perish [Job 8:13].

Now he is accusing Job of being a hypocrite! He says Job has been covering up something. He says to Job, "You've been a hypocrite, just putting up a front."

Whose hope shall be cut off, and whose trust shall be a spider's web.

He shall lean upon his house, but it shall not stand: he shall hold it fast, but it shall not endure [Job 8:14–15].

That's as good as leaning on a spider's web. When trouble comes, it won't hold you.

Behold, God will not cast away a perfect man, neither will he help the evildoers [Job 8:20].

Now, wait a minute—is that actually true? God has certainly helped me although I have been an evildoer. He saved me, my friend. Will God "cast away a perfect man"? No, He won't. But where is the perfect man? There is none. The Scripture is clear on that score: ". . . There is none righteous, no, not one" (Rom. 3:10). Although what Bildad says is true, it is not true when you pour it into the test tube of life and pour the acid of experience upon it.

Till he fill thy mouth with laughing, and thy lips with rejoicing.

They that hate thee shall be clothed with shame; and the dwelling place of the wicked shall come to nought [Job 8:21–22].

He is telling Job that he has come to nothing because he is a great sinner. That is not very helpful for a man who is in the position of Job! You see, Bildad does not know God. He does not know Job. Neither does he really know himself. He is a traditionalist. He thinks that by scientific examination he can tell you how the world began. He is a smart boy, but he doesn't know. He cannot put himself in the place of God.

In the following chapter we will see that Job answers Bildad, and he does it very well, although he is getting awfully weary of these rounds of conversation.

CHAPTERS 9–10

***THEME:** Job's answer to Bildad*

Job makes it very clear that Bildad has not met his need at all. He was not even talking in the field of his problem. At this point he makes it clear that he makes no claim to perfection, and he knows that he cannot defend himself before God. What he needs is someone on his side to present his case. We will hear Job's longing for someone to be his mediator and his intercessor. In other words, we will hear Job's heart-cry for Christ.

Then Job answered and said,

I know it is so of a truth: but how should man be just with God? [Job 9: 1–2].

That is, much of what Bildad had said is true. The problem is that his words haven't met the need of Job, they haven't spoken to the problem of Job. "I know that in a general way your words are true," says Job, "but the question is 'How can I be just with God?'"

Job surely needed the gospel at this point. He needed to know how a man could be just with God. Job says he wants some questions answered, and his friends are not answering the questions.

If he will contend with him, he cannot answer him one of a thousand.

He is wise in heart, and mighty in strength: who hath hardened himself against him, and hath prospered? [Job 9:3–4].

Job says, "I don't pretend. If you think I am trying to put up a front before God, you are wrong. I know I cannot contend with Him. He could ask me a question and I would never be able to answer." Job wants an answer to his questions, and he wants God to answer him. God is far removed from him.

Which removeth the mountains, and they know not: which overturneth them in his anger.

Which shaketh the earth out of her place, and the pillars thereof tremble.

Which commandeth the sun, and it riseth not; and sealeth up the stars.

Which alone spreadeth out the heavens, and treadeth upon the waves of the sea [Job 9:5–8].

Here is a tremendous picture of God as the Creator. Job knows Him as the Creator but knows nothing about His tender mercy at this time.

Which maketh Arcturus, Orion, and Pleiades, and the chambers of the south.

Which doeth great things past finding out; yea, and wonders without number [Job 9:9–10].

We can see that Job knew something about the stars. However, he is not attempting to say that he is in the situation of his misery because he was born under a certain star. That is without a doubt one of the most foolish things men say. Shakespeare had the answer to that when Mark Antony said, "The fault, dear Brutus, is not in our stars, But in ourselves, that we are underlings." Job knew the stars did not account for his situation. He recognized God as the Creator of the stars.

Lo, he goeth by me, and I see him not: he passeth on also, but I perceive him not [Job 9:11].

Job knows God as the Creator of the universe, and he also knows God is a spirit, and Job cannot see Him at all.

If God will not withdraw his anger, the proud helpers do stoop under him.

How much less shall I answer him, and choose out my words to reason with him? [Job 9:13–14].

Job knows that he wouldn't stand a chance if he came into the presence of God. If God should speak to him, he wouldn't know what to answer.

If I had called, and he had answered me; yet would I not believe that he had hearkened unto my voice [Job 9:16].

Job couldn't believe that He was really listening to him.

For he breaketh me with a tempest, and multiplieth my wounds without cause.

He will not suffer me to take my breath, but filleth me with bitterness.

If I speak of strength, lo, he is strong: and if of judgment, who shall set me a time to plead? [Job 9:17–19].

Job asks, "How in the world can I plead my case before Him?"

If I justify myself, mine own mouth shall condemn me: if I say, I am perfect, it shall also prove me perverse [Job 9:20].

Job says, "If I try to pretend I am perfect, my own mouth will condemn me." However, we will find later on that Job has a high estimation of himself. He is not the man who said, "For I know that in me (that is, in my flesh,) dwelleth no good thing . . ." (Rom. 7:18). Job does not say that he is a perfect man before God, but he does contend that he is a pretty good man—in fact, a righteous man. Yet he recognizes that before God he would not be able to defend himself.

There are many men today who, because they do not know the Word of God, feel that they will be able to stand before God and meet His standards and are actually well-pleasing to Him.

I remember an oilman in Nashville, Tennessee. He was one of a group of businessmen with whom I used to play volleyball three times a week. He was a godless man although he was a church member. He and I were always on opposite sides, and he didn't like me to beat him. One night he had really been beaten, so he began to argue with me in the locker room. He said, "I heard you speak (I had a morning devotion on the radio in those days) about a religion that calls men sinners who need to come to Christ. I don't believe that stuff. I believe in helping people. In my business I give men jobs. I pay them money so they can buy beans to put on their tables. I think that is better than any religion you have to offer." How do you answer a man like that before a group of men all gathered in the locker room? Some of the men were church members, but most of them were godless and unsaved men. It was difficult to know how to answer that—until about a year later when we were in the locker room and that man was not there. He was in jail. He had been arrested for the way he had been conducting his business. He defrauded not only the government but also his own employees. I shall never forget that another of the men mentioned his name and said, "Well, I don't think he'd have much of a chance before God. He didn't do so well before Judge So-and-So the other day. They found out he really wasn't putting beans on the plates of his employees, but he was really taking them off their plates." That really shook those men. Very candidly, I saw several of them in my church services, and I even had the privilege of leading one of those men to the Lord. But the point is that men have a misconception of God. They think they are good enough to stand before Him. Job is saying in effect, "If I come into God's presence, He will think of something in me that I am not aware of, and I won't be able to answer Him."

JOB'S HEART-CRY FOR CHRIST

For he is not a man, as I am, that I should answer him, and we should come together in judgment [Job 9:32].

Job is saying in effect, "If He were a *man*, I could talk to Him." This is the reason God became a Man, my friend—so man could talk to Him and walk with Him and realize that he cannot meet God's standards. The only Man who ever met God's standards was the Lord Jesus Christ.

This is what makes some of the contemporary plays and literature such a curse. They insinuate that Jesus was not only a man, but that He was a sinful man! Liberalism has been saying this for years. However, they cannot find in the Word of God that there was any sin in the Lord Jesus Christ. They find the sin in their own dirty hearts, because Jesus was without sin.

Because Jesus was a Man, I can go to Him. He died for me on the cross! And He shows me by His life that I cannot meet God's standards, that I need a Savior. By His death He can save me. This is what poor old Job was longing for.

Neither is there any daysman betwixt us, that might lay his hand upon us both [Job 9:33].

Job's complaint was that there was no mediator between him and God. His cry is this: "Oh, if there were only Someone who could put His hand in the hand of God and who could put His other hand in my hand and bring us together. If He could do that, then I would have a mediator." In the New Testament Paul wrote to a young preacher, "For there is one God, and one mediator between God and men, the man Christ Jesus" (1 Tim. 2:5).

The song that says, "Put your hand in the hand of the Man from Galilee" is only half true. The Man of Galilee has another hand, and that hand is in the hand of God. Jesus is God, my friend; He is the God-Man. What a glorious, wonderful truth that is. Oh, how Job longed for Him!

My soul is weary of my life; I will leave my complaint upon myself; I will speak in the bitterness of my soul [Job 10:1].

Because Job has no mediator, no man to represent him before God, he will just speak in the bitterness of his soul. He is weary of life, and he is going to say exactly how he feels. He is plain and honest about his sad plight and his wretched condition.

I will say unto God, Do not condemn me; shew me wherefore thou contendest with me [Job 10:2].

God is going to answer him on this before we are through the book. God is going to show Job something about himself, something that all of us need to find out about ourselves.

Is it good unto thee that thou shouldest oppress, that thou shouldest despise the work of thine hands, and shine upon the counsel of the wicked? [Job 10:3].

Job cannot understand why he must suffer so while there are wicked men who are not suffering. By the way, that was the problem that confronted David. That is a problem that has confronted me. As a pastor I have wondered sometimes why God would let certain wonderful, godly men suffer while at the same time godless men—even men in the church—seemed to get by with sin. They seem to get by with it for a time, but I notice that in time God deals with these people. Even so, there are times when we all ask this question. You see, this book faces up to the questions of life. It is right down where the rubber meets the road.

Hast thou eyes of flesh? or seest thou as man seeth? [Job 10:4].

Job bewails his condition and his sad plight. He wonders whether God really sees him in his true condition.

Here is another reason that God became a man down here: now I have the assurance that there is a Man in the glory who understands me. Because He was a Man like I am, He knows exactly how I feel. There is not a pulsation that ever entered the human breast that Jesus Christ did not feel when He was here on this earth. My friend, He knows how I feel. He knows how *you* feel.

Are thy days as the days of man? are thy years as man's days,

That thou inquirest after mine iniquity, and searchest after my sin?

Thou knowest that I am not wicked; and there is none that can deliver out of thine hand [Job 10:5–7].

Job now begins to defend himself. He is not willing to admit that there is a great sin in his life. He says that he finds himself in a pretty awkward situation. "God knows that I am not wicked, and yet I cannot get out of His hand. I must go through all this—and I don't see why I should be put through this."

Job was a man who needed a little humility, and God is going to give him that humility. Have you ever noticed that humbleness and patience are qualities that God doesn't hand over to you on a silver platter with a silver spoon for you to lap it up? You don't become humble that way. Patience and humility are a fruit of the Holy Spirit produced in your life through trying experiences. God is going to produce both humility and patience in this man Job.

In the New Testament we hear about the patience of Job. James writes, ". . . Ye have heard of the patience of Job," but he also adds, "and have seen the end of the Lord; that the Lord is very pitiful, and of tender mercy" (James 5:11). It wasn't that Job was naturally a patient man—that quality would have increased his self-confidence and his conceit. Actually Job was not patient. We have seen that his patience broke down, and he is crying out to God in impatience. But when we see the "end of the *Lord*," that is, the outcome of the Lord's dealing with him, then we see that God was *making* him patient, and God was *giving* him humility. It is God who does this, you see.

I should have been as though I had not been: I should have been carried from the womb to the grave [Job 10:19].

Job is back at the thing he started with and will stay with it part of the way through this book. During this time of testing, death was something that he desired. He felt that death would put him out of his misery. It would get him away from this scene. He would welcome it as sleep, as something that would put him in a place of unconsciousness.

Now if you think you can draw something from this book to sustain the doctrine of soul sleep, you are entirely wrong. Job will say before we get through this book, "For I know that my redeemer liveth . . . yet in my flesh shall I see God" (Job 19:25–26). My friend, this book does not teach soul sleep at all.

But at this point, Job is wishing that he had never been born. He wishes for complete oblivion. That is something you can wish for, too. Job was not the only one who did that. Elijah wished it. Jonah wished it. The only thing is, it won't do you one bit of good. To wish you hadn't been born is a complete waste of time. And, by the way, wishing you were dead won't help either. No one ever died by wishing. I always suspect that most of us who say we wish we were dead don't really mean it. We are just talking. When people face death, they really want to live. I suspect that if Job had really faced up to it, he didn't really mean he wished he were dead either. But right now he is pouring out his soul, and there is a breaking down of the dignity of this man. God is going to need to get through to his heart.

A lot of God's saints today have proud, hard hearts. Sometimes God must deal with us as He dealt with Job.

CHAPTER 11

***THEME:** Zophar's first discourse*

Now we meet the last of Job's friends. His name is Zophar, and he is the legalist. He assumed (and rightly so as far as he goes) that God works according to measure, according to law. He pretends to know what God will do in a given circumstance.

He is different from Bildad who was the traditionalist. Bildad said you can go back and look at what has happened in the past and learn from it. He had a scientific mind. He is like the scientist who thinks he can look at rocks and tell you how old the earth is. Zophar has a scientific mind, too, but he puts the emphasis on the laws. If one would bring him up to date, he would be more or less an atheist. His philosophy is that the universe is run by laws. It is obvious that we cannot have law without somebody who makes the law. Nevertheless, Zophar assumes this physical universe is following laws.

Zophar is like the fellow who says, "Ask me another." He is the I-have-all-the-answers type. He is the voice of legalism. He holds that God is bound by laws and never operates beyond the circumference of His own laws. He is probably the senior member of the group, and he speaks with a dogmatic finality that is even more candid and crude than that of Bildad.

Then answered Zophar the Naamathite, and said,

Should not the multitude of words be answered? and should a man full of talk be justified? [Job 11:1–2].

He is saying that Job is covering his sin with words. Job has tried to make it clear that a man in his condition—suffering as he is—is not apt to put up a front. Zophar simply ignores that and says that Job is trying to talk his way out of his situation. It is true that there are men who are able to talk their way out of a situation and who are clever at manipulation by words. That is the way some lawyers win cases in court. It is really not a matter of justice being done but rather the cleverness of the lawyer and his manipulation. This is not true of Job.

Should thy lies make men hold their peace? and when thou mockest, shall no man make thee ashamed? [Job 11:3].

Zophar goes a step farther and actually accuses Job of lying. "Should thy lies make men hold their peace?" He has accused him of being a hypocrite, and now he accuses him of lying. That is even more crude than Bildad had been. Bildad had said that Job was a hypocrite but had never called him a liar.

Zophar is now going to assume the pious position of being on the inside with God. He thinks he knows what God will do under a certain circumstance. Of course, while he is on the inside with God, Job is on the outside, unable to know what God is doing. So Zophar feels that Job ought to listen to him because he has the final word and that his word is, in fact, the word of God.

For thou hast said, My doctrine is pure, and I am clean in thine eyes.

But oh that God would speak, and open his lips against thee [Job 11:4–5].

Since God wasn't speaking, Zophar speaks for Him.

I received a rather crude letter the other day. It was from a man who was rebuking me for a position that I held, which to him indicated I was not only a very ignorant and dogmatic man, but that I had no spiritual discernment whatsoever. Then he proceeded to give me his interpretation. When he finished, he said, "Now I am going to see whether you will listen to the Holy Spirit or not." Isn't that interesting? That man claimed to be the voice of the Holy Spirit. If I didn't listen to him, it meant I wasn't listening to God.

As I read his letter, I felt confident that he was totally unaware of the fact that he was doing the very thing he had accused me of doing! Supposing the man did have some inside information that I do not have access to, he certainly was not proceeding in a way that was helpful to me. In fact, his letter was not at all helpful to me and ended up in the "round file," which is the wastebasket. I put it there because it had no message for me.

I don't think Zophar had a message for Job.

And that he would shew thee the secrets of wisdom, that they are double to that which is! Know therefore that God exacteth of thee less than thine iniquity deserveth [Job 11:6].

And what he says to Job is really a blow, not a comfort. He tells Job that he is not even getting half of what he really has coming to him. Now that is a pretty hard statement. He says the fact that Job is suffering as much as he is shows that Job is a lot worse than his friends even dreamed he was.

Zophar is not very helpful to a man in Job's condition! We must remember that all this time Job is a sick man and is in desperate pain. He actually thinks he may expire at any moment and at times he hopes that he will die.

Canst thou by searching find out God? canst thou find out the Almighty unto perfection? [Job 11:7].

That is a great statement. It is a marvelous statement. But who doesn't know that? Job will tell him later that everyone knows that. No man can *discover* God; God is *revealed.* The only way you can know about God is what He is pleased to reveal of Himself to us. I have come to the conclusion that He has revealed very little of Himself to us. In fact, the little that He has revealed to us has some of us so awestruck and some so confused that we can see why He hasn't revealed more of Himself to us.

You cannot "find out God" by starting out like a Columbus in search of Him. Nor can you find God by going into space in a sputnik. I recall that the Russians published in their paper the fact that they hadn't discovered God in the early days of space exploration, and so they assumed He was not there. We can put little gadgets out in space, but they won't find God. To think they could find Him is absurd!

Man cannot look through a microscope or out into the heavens through a telescope and discover God. God must reveal Himself to man. This is a profound statement that Zophar makes, but it is nothing new to Job.

It is as high as heaven; what canst thou do? deeper than hell; what canst thou know?

The measure thereof is longer than the earth, and broader than the sea [Job 11:8–9].

He gives a lofty discourse about God which is tremendous. It just doesn't touch the need of Job.

If he cut off, and shut up, or gather together, then who can hinder him?

For he knoweth vain men; he seeth wickedness also; will he not then consider it?

For vain man would be wise, though man be born like a wild ass's colt [Job 11:10–12].

Of course, he is speaking of Job here—not of himself! He feels that he is the man who has the answer.

If thou prepare thine heart, and stretch out thine hands toward him;

If iniquity be in thine hand, put it far away, and let not wickedness dwell in thy tabernacles [Job 11:13–14].

Again he comes at Job on the basis that Job is hiding something, that there is secret sin in Job's life. All three of Job's friends assume that Job is covering up something. Job actually isn't aware of anything that he should put away; yet there is something as we shall see later.

For then shalt thou lift up thy face without spot; yea, thou shalt be stedfast, and shalt not fear:

Because thou shalt forget thy misery, and remember it as waters that pass away:

And thine age shall be clearer than the noonday; thou shalt shine forth, thou shalt be as the morning [Job 11:15–17].

Zophar is saying, "If you would just deal with the sin that is in your life and quit fighting it, God would hear and answer your prayers and restore you."

But the eyes of the wicked shall fail, and they shall not escape, and their hope shall be as the giving up of the ghost [Job 11:20].

He concludes by saying to Job, "You are going to come to the time when the judgment of God will be upon you unless you confess your secret sin." He predicts the absolute and complete judgment of Job.

That concludes Zophar's address which in reality is an attack upon Job. All three friends have now had their little say. Job's answer will be one of the lengthiest discourses in the book.

CHAPTERS 12–14

***THEME:** Job replies to his three friends*

This lengthy reply that Job makes in this section concludes the first round of discourses. Remember that in Job's day folk enjoyed intellectual competition—men pitting their minds against each other. Today it is not brain but brawn in athletic contests.

And Job answered and said,

No doubt but ye are the people, and wisdom shall die with you [Job 12:1–2].

Now there is a sarcastic statement and a pretty good one. Job says, "You fellows think you have all the answers. You are *the* people, and wisdom will die with you!" They were talking as if Job were a simpleton and they had all the answers.

But I have understanding as well as you; I am not inferior to you: yea, who knoweth not such things as these? [Job 12:3].

Job knows as much as they know. The problem is that they have not spoken to the situation as it really is. There is something important in these discourses that I want to call to your attention so you can be watching for it. Instead of leading Job to self-judgment, the three friends only minister to a spirit of self-vindication in Job. In other words, they make an attack on Job which forces him to come back with a defense of himself.

They did not introduce God into the scene. They did not speak of a God of mercy and a God of grace, but a God of law. Although He is a God of law, He is also a God of grace and mercy. They brought in experience and tradition and legality, but they didn't bring in *the truth*. When they brought their incriminations against Job, it caused him to defend himself and to declare that he was right. The minute Job started justifying himself he was not justifying God. Up to this point it looks as if Job is saying that God is wrong and that God is the One to be criticized.

This is a position which many people take today, even many Christian people. The friends should have led Job to condemn himself and to vindicate God. God has recorded all these discourses in His Word to reveal this truth. The utterances of Job will prove how far he was from that true brokenness of spirit and humility of mind which flows from being in the divine Presence. His friends never brought him to the place where he said as Paul said, "For I know that in me (that is, in my flesh) dwelleth no good thing," (Rom. 7:18) or, ". . . by the grace of God I am what I am" (1 Cor. 15:10).

There are too many Christians today who boast of who they are and what they have done and how much they give. It looks as if God is on the receiving side and they are on the giving side. It looks as if they, rather than God, are superior. My friend, we are not witnessing correctly for God—no matter how many people we buttonhole and tell about Jesus—unless you and I take the place where we are condemned and God is vindicated, and

God is to be praised and honored. This is a tremendous lesson in this book.

I am as one mocked of his neighbor, who calleth upon God, and he answereth him: the just upright man is laughed to scorn.

He that is ready to slip with his feet is as a lamp despised in the thought of him that is at ease [Job 12:4–5].

Job is a very sick man, but he is standing up to these three men. He tells them, "You fellows are in a comfortable position and you are able to give advice to me, but I am slipping, I am falling, and you have no word for me at all."

For years I served as a pastor and I realize now how a professional attitude enters into our lives. I would go to the hospital to visit a sick person, perhaps a dying person. I would pat him on the hand and say, "God will be with you," and I would pray for him and say, "God will lead you." Then I'd walk out. Well, the day came when I went to the hospital, not to visit someone, but to lie on that bed myself. When someone came to pray with me and walked out, I didn't walk out. I stayed there. My friend, I want to say to you, that is quite a different position to be in. Now I was in the other fellow's shoes. Now I was in bed and I was facing surgery. That is the time you need someone to help you and to comfort you. That is what Job is needing.

For the rest of the chapter, Job goes on to say that his friends do not have such superior wisdom. They are not the only ones who know about God. Job also knows about the power of God in the affairs of men.

Job now is bitter and sarcastic. His friends are not helping him at all, and he longs to appeal to God directly.

Lo, mine eye hath seen all this, mine ear hath heard and understood it.

What ye know, the same do I know also: I am not inferior unto you [Job 13:1–2].

He knows all the truths which his friends have expounded to him. They haven't told him anything new that he had not known before, and they have not helped him.

Surely I would speak to the Almighty, and I desire to reason with God [Job 13:3].

Job would like to bypass his friends and appeal to God directly. He wants to reason with God. Oh, if only someone had been there to tell Job about the grace and the mercy of God and how God wanted to help him.

But ye are forgers of lies, ye are all physicians of no value [Job 13:4].

He repeats that his friends have not been able to diagnose his case and that they are not helping him. They are like a doctor who has a patient with diabetes and says the cure would be to take out his lungs. They missed the whole point.

O that ye would altogether hold your peace! and it should be your wisdom [Job 13:5].

He tells them the best thing for them to do would be to keep quiet. He tells them that that would be smarter than what they were saying.

Hear now my reasoning, and hearken to the pleadings of my lips.

Will ye speak wickedly for God? and talk deceitfully for him? [Job 13:6–7].

He really speaks back to them. He says that when they are accusing him of committing some awful sin and that God is judging him, they are talking deceitfully for God. They are not representing God as they should. Job knows they are not God's direct representatives. They could have helped Job if they had brought him to the place where he could see himself as he really was. Instead, they put him on the defense. As a result, he is actually making a good case for himself. All of this makes it look bad for God. It looks as if God is to blame in all this.

Will ye accept his person? will ye contend for God?

Is it good that he should search you out? or as one man mocketh another, do ye so mock him?

He will surely reprove you, if ye do secretly accept persons [Job 13:8–10].

Job says that God is going to judge them for misrepresenting Him.

Shall not his excellency make you afraid? and his dread fall upon you?

Your remembrances are like unto ashes, your bodies to bodies of clay.

Hold your peace, let me alone, that I may speak, and let come on me what will.

Wherefore do I take my flesh in my teeth, and put my life in mine hand? [Job 13:11–14].

In the midst of all this, the faith of Job stands inviolate. He has experienced the onslaught of his friends who, by now, have actually become strangers to him, as we shall see.

Though he slay me, yet will I trust in him: but I will maintain mine own ways before him [Job 13:15].

This is Job's great statement of faith. Job's friends, you see, were accusing him of some gross secret sin such as immorality or dishonesty or some other sin of the flesh. Job is not guilty of anything like this. But here we begin to see the root of his problem. Job says that he will go into the presence of God and will defend himself there.

My friend, the minute you go into the presence of God to start defending yourself, you will lose your case. When you stand before Him, you can only plead guilty, because He knows you. You can't go into the presence of God with an attorney who by some clever routine can clear you of the accusation. No attorney can annul God's statement that all have sinned and come short of the glory of God, that there is none righteous, no, not one, and that the soul that sinneth shall die. God just doesn't change that at all. No smart lawyer can get you out of that. Nor are you going to stand before some softhearted and softheaded judge. You are going to stand before the God of this universe who is the moral Ruler. No one can maintain a case before Him. The thing to do is to go in and plead guilty and cast yourself upon the mercy of the court. You will find that God has a mercy seat. It is a mercy seat because the blood of Jesus Christ is on it. Christ paid the price for your sin. My friend, that is the *only* way you can escape the penalty.

You can see that Job desperately needs someone to represent God to him and keep him from trying to defend himself before Him. Someone needs to show him that he can cast himself on the mercy of God. This book has a tremendous message for us, as you can see.

He also shall be my salvation: for an hypocrite shall not come before him [Job 13:16].

There are glimmers of light that break through on this man's soul. He says, "He shall be my salvation." By the way, notice that it is the teaching of the Old Testament as well as the New Testament that God is our salvation. David held on to this fact, because David committed an awful sin. Of course he didn't *live* in sin, but he needed a Savior. He wrote, "He only is my rock and my salvation; he is my defence; I shall not be greatly moved" (Ps. 62:2). Salvation is not like a coin that you carry around in your pocket and might lose. Salvation is God. Today salvation is Jesus Christ. You either have Him or you don't have Him. You either trust Him or you don't trust Him. There are no other alternatives, friends. You stand on one side or the other. Either you are for Him or you are against Him. ". . . there is none other name under heaven given among men, whereby we must be saved" (Acts 4:12). He is the only "out" for the human family. It is marvelous that Job, who probably lived in the patriarchal age of the days of Abraham, Isaac, and Jacob, had a glimmer of light.

Hear diligently my speech, and my declaration with your ears [Job 13:17].

Job says, "Listen to me!"

Behold now, I have ordered my cause; I know that I shall be justified [Job 13:18].

Job thinks he has a good case even before God. He says that he knows he shall be justified, but he does not claim that on the grounds that Someone else obtained that justification for him.

There are people today who say, "Oh, I don't mind coming before God. I can stand on my good works." I have news for them: they have already been condemned before God. My friend, we are *all* sinners. We live in a world that is in rebellion against God because our hearts are evil. Not one of us is so important that God needs us in His program here on earth. He could get along without us very nicely. But, thank God, He loves us and He made a way for us to be justified. The Judge had mercy on us and sent His own Son to pay our penalty. That is the reason He can justify us.

Who is he that will plead with me? for now, if I hold my tongue, I shall give up the ghost [Job 13:19].

This is interesting. At the beginning Job said that he wanted to die. He wished he had never been born. Now he says that if he holds his tongue he shall give up the ghost. All right, Job, if you want to die, why don't you quit talking? You will notice he doesn't do that. He is going to talk. This is the way of little men—we all have a lot to say.

> **Only do not two things unto me: then will I not hide myself from thee.**
>
> **Withdraw thine hand far from me: and let not thy dread make me afraid [Job 13:20–21].**

Job is a frightened man.

> **Then call thou, and I will answer: or let me speak, and answer thou me [Job 13:22].**

He is telling God what to do. I'm afraid many of us do that. I hear so many people say they have unanswered prayers. No, there are no unanswered prayers. God always answers prayer and many times He answers "no." At least He has said "no" to most of my prayers, but that *is* an answer.

We must admit that a lot of our praying is really giving orders to God. We pray as if we are a top sergeant talking to a buck private in the rear ranks. We say, "You do that," or "You do it this way." But God doesn't move that way.

Job tries to tell God how He should handle his situation. But God says, "I am not moving according to your plan. I have a plan, and I am going to work it out in your life."

I had the privilege of speaking to a group of Christian college students at a state college, and I was rather amazed to hear some of these young people arguing about prayer. They said, "What's the use of praying because you can't change God." They felt there was no need for prayer. That reminded me of Job here. Their idea of prayer was that God should be the One who would come at their beck and call.

I tried to make it clear to them that the purpose of prayer is not to change God. Where did we ever get that idea? Do we think we can change God by prayer? God has already made His plan, and He has *all* the information. Neither can we tell Him anything in our prayer that He doesn't already know. The primary purpose of prayer is to change *us*. We often see a little motto—and I think it is partially true—that reads: "Prayer Changes Things." I think it does change things, but the important thing is that prayer changes us, my friend.

God is not a Western Union boy. Don't get the idea you just call Him to come and deliver a message for you or to you. That is what Job was trying to get Him to do here. I'm not pointing an accusing finger at Job, because I have done the very same thing.

> **How many are mine iniquities and sins? make me to know my transgression and my sin.**
>
> **Wherefore hidest thou thy face, and holdest me for thine enemy?**
>
> **Wilt thou break a leaf driven to and fro? and wilt thou pursue the dry stubble? [Job 13:23–25].**

Very candidly, Job is asking for a showdown with God. That is what he wants. He wants to know how many sins and iniquities he has so he will understand why he is being treated as he is. He says he is just like a leaf that has been driven to and fro and has been stepped on.

> **Thou puttest my feet also in the stocks, and lookest narrowly unto all my paths; thou settest a print upon the heels of my feet.**
>
> **And he, as a rotten thing, consumeth, as a garment that is moth eaten [Job 13:27–28].**

Job feels that he is just rotting away. He cannot see any point to his suffering at all.

JOB'S ELEGY ON DEATH

> **Man that is born of a woman is of few days, and full of trouble [Job 14:1].**

There is nothing any truer than that; trouble is the common denominator of mankind. All of us have had trouble. As Eliphaz had said, "Yet man is born unto trouble, as the sparks fly upward" (Job 5:7). Trouble is a language that the whole human family knows.

> **He cometh forth like a flower, and is cut down: he fleeth also as a shadow, and continueth not [Job 14:2].**

Job says that death is inevitable and that we must depart from this world. Life is like a shadow. When the sun goes down, what happens to the shadow? It is gone.

> **And dost thou open thine eyes upon such an one, and bringest me into judgment with thee? [Job 14:3].**

Like a flower that has been cut down, or as a shadow that disappears, is my life. And yet God sees me and deals with me.

> **Who can bring a clean thing out of an unclean? not one [Job 14:4].**

Then he goes on to state a great truth. We were all born sinners. David said, "Behold, I was shapen in iniquity and in sin did my mother conceive me" (Ps. 51:5). How could any of us be a sinless creature when we had a sinful father and a sinful mother? You cannot bring a clean thing out of an unclean. That is a universal rule.

Seeing his days are determined, the number of his months are with thee, thou hast appointed his bounds that he cannot pass [Job 14:5].

Job says that as a human being he feels that he is pretty well hemmed in. David wrote, ". . . though I walk through the valley of the shadow of death . . ." (Ps. 23:4). Was he referring to his death bed? No. From the very minute of birth when we start out in life we are walking through a canyon where the shadow of death is on us, and we keep going until it gets narrower and narrower and finally leads to death. We are always walking in the shadow of death! Someone has put it like this: "The moment that gives us life begins to take it away from us."

For there is hope of a tree, if it be cut down, that it will sprout again, and that the tender branch thereof will not cease.

Though the root thereof wax old in the earth, and the stock thereof die in the ground;

Yet through the scent of water it will bud, and bring forth boughs like a plant.

But man dieth, and wasteth away; yea, man giveth up the ghost, and where is he? [Job 14:7–10].

A man may have made a tremendous success down here, been a famous person, and then he is gone. Where is he? There may be a few monuments around for him. Maybe a street or two are named after him. What good is that? What does that amount to?

Here is a breakthrough that reveals the faith of Job.

If a man die, shall he live again? all the days of my appointed time will I wait, till my change come.

Thou shalt call, and I will answer thee: thou wilt have a desire to the work of thine hands [Job 14:14–15].

It has always been a big question with man. "If a man die, shall he live again?" Even in death Job knows that God is going to call him, and he will answer that call. In other words, God is not through with us at our death. Death is not the end of it all. We will hear Job say again later on: ". . . I know that my redeemer liveth, and that he shall stand at the latter day upon the earth: And though after my skin worms destroy this body, yet in my flesh shall I see God: Whom I shall see for myself, and mine eyes shall behold, and not another; though my reins be consumed within me" (Job 19:25–27).

This entire chapter is a great elegy on death. I recommend that you read it in its entirety.

CHAPTER 15

***THEME:** Second discourse of Eliphaz*

These men are pitting their minds one against another. Instead of seeing brawn pitted against brawn in athletic events, these folk liked to witness intellectual battles. We have completed one round of discourses. All three of the friends have spoken and Job has answered each of them. Now we start on the second round of discourses. We could say this is the second inning if we were talking about baseball, or we could call it the second half if we were talking about basketball or football.

Remember that Eliphaz is the spiritualist. He has had a dream and a vision. He feels that he has had a remarkable experience and should be heard.

Many of the testimonies we hear in our day have little value because they rest truth on experience. First of all we should have *truth*, which is the Word of God; then experience should come out of that. Many experiences do not coincide with God's Word. I have heard testimonies given by so-called Christians who have had a "great experience" that is no more scriptural than the telephone directory.

Eliphaz bases his words on experience, and it is mighty hard to deal with a fellow like that.

Then answered Eliphaz the Temanite, and said,

Should a wise man utter vain knowledge, and fill his belly with the east wind?

Should he reason with unprofitable talk? or with speeches wherewith he can do no good? [Job 15:1–3].

My, they are really slugging it out with words in this intellectual foray. He says, "My goodness, Job, you certainly are windy. You're just doing empty talking." Again you can see that he is not helping Job. Actually, he is attacking Job to try to break him down and make him confess. That is not the way to treat a man in trouble like Job is.

Yea, thou castest off fear, and restrainest prayer before God.

For thy mouth uttereth thine iniquity, and thou choosest the tongue of the crafty.

Thine own mouth condemneth thee, and not I: yea, thine own lips testify against thee [Job 15:4–6].

Eliphaz says that Job is his own accuser. He is really going after Job, as you can see.

Art thou the first man that was born? or wast thou made before the hills? [Job 15:7].

You speak as if you know something, Job.

Hast thou heard the secret of God? and dost thou restrain wisdom to thyself?

What knowest thou, that we know not? what understandest thou, which is not in us? [Job 15:8–9].

Again he is arguing from a wrong premise.

He tries to put Job in a very bad light. He does not bring Job to the place where he can see that he is a man who has a great lack and a great need. There is no comfort for Job from his friend.

With us are both the gray-headed and very aged men, much elder than thy father [Job 15:10].

Eliphaz defends himself and the two other friends by telling Job of their advantage of maturity over him. He says that wisdom is on their side and not on the side of Job. This is his argument here.

What is man, that he should be clean? and he which is born of a woman, that he should be righteous? [Job 15:14].

It is true that all men are sinners, but Eliphaz and his friends say this with the basic premise that Job has committed an awful, terrible sin and that he ought to bring it out in the open and confess it.

Behold, he putteth no trust in his saints; yea, the heavens are not clean in his sight [Job 15:15].

What he says about the heavens is also true. When the Lord Jesus Christ died, He did not die only to redeem mankind; but in His plan of redemption there is to be a new heaven and a new earth that will come because He has redeemed us. It is a true statement that the heavens are not clean in His sight.

How much more abominable and filthy is man, which drinketh iniquity like water? [Job 15:16].

That is also a true statement. If the heavens are filthy and need redeeming, how much more does man need redeeming! Although it is true, it is no more applicable to Job and his condition than it is to any other human being.

The wicked man travaileth with pain all his days, and the number of years is hidden to the oppressor.

A dreadful sound is in his ears: in prosperity the destroyer shall come upon him [Job 15:20–21].

Here again is the suggestion that Job is wicked and is hiding something from them.

We must admit, however, that these men did not have a contemporary false psychology which says there is really nothing wrong with man, that man has made a few mistakes, and his sin is really one of ignorance, but it really is nothing that couldn't be cured by rubbing a little "salve" on it. These men had a truer concept than our modern men who teach that man is a superior creature because he is the product of evolution, and so is not responsible to a Creator. Although these men did not have the answer to the problem of Job, many of the things they said were absolutely true.

Eliphaz, instead of being a comforter, is a debater. He is not adding anything new but is playing the same old record over again. He has no new information since his first speech.

CHAPTERS 16–17

THEME: *Job's answer to Eliphaz*

We will now hear Job answer Eliphaz for the second time. This is very much like a debate. First we hear one side, and then we hear from the other side. Actually it should not have been this way, because these men had come to be Job's comforters. Instead of being comforters they have become debaters. They are really attempting to beat him down, attempting to gain an intellectual victory over him. But they are not winning the debate. My feeling is that it is a standoff. Eventually a young man who has been standing by enters in and picks up the argument. Finally, God will break in on the scene. That, of course, is what Job needs and what Job wants.

Eliphaz has just played the same old record over again. He is the dreamer. He has had a vision. He is a spiritualist. He claims to have some inside information that no one else has, but he didn't get any advance information after his first speech. He just comes up with the same old thing.

Then Job answered and said,

I have heard many such things: miserable comforters are ye all [Job 16:1–2].

Job says, "You haven't said anything new to me. You haven't said a thing that I haven't already heard. Besides, you are miserable comforters."

These men, I am confident, were friends of Job, but they ended up in a debate. Job has his chance to give a rebuttal after each man speaks, which is what we have here now.

Shall vain words have an end? or what emboldeneth thee that thou answerest? [Job 16:3].

Job is saying, "I would have thought you would have been ashamed to speak as you have. Those are vain words, empty words. They do not meet the need."

Unfortunately, a great many sermons are like that. Some of them are not even Bible-centered and cannot be used by the spirit of God. Unless the spirit of God can use a sermon, it will come to naught. It will be a vain, empty thing. There is a lot of preaching in the world today that is absolutely meaningless as far as worship of God and expounding His Word are concerned. The same can be said for a lot of the singing—and the entire service—in some of our churches. The fault may lie with the preacher, but it doesn't always rest there; sometimes the congregation, the listeners, can be responsible for the breakdown that takes place.

I also could speak as ye do: if your soul were in my soul's stead, I could heap up words against you, and shake mine head at you [Job 16:4].

Job is telling them that if their situations were reversed, he could have given a little speech of condemnation against them.

Paul was concerned about this type of thing, and he wrote to believers in order to counteract it, "Brethren, if a man be overtaken in a fault, ye which are spiritual, restore such an one in the spirit of meekness; considering thyself, lest thou also be tempted" (Gal. 6:1). Don't go to debate with such a person. Don't go to preach at him. Restore him in the spirit of meekness, which was illustrated by our Lord when he washed the feet of those who were His own. He is still doing that today. When you and I confess our sins, ". . . he is faithful and just to forgive us our sins, and to cleanse us from all unrighteousness" (1 John 1:9). He still washes feet; that is, He still cleanses his own. But He also set us an example. If you are going to wash someone's feet, you can't put yourself above him, look down upon him, point your finger, and begin to preach at him. You will need to kneel down and take the place of a servant to wash feet. That is quite a bit different from arguing with the person.

It's too bad that these friends didn't come to Job in that way, but they didn't. They came preaching at him. Realizing that, he tells them that if he were in their position, he could do the same thing. He could shake his head at them and heap up words against them.

But I would strengthen you with my mouth, and the moving of my lips should assuage your grief [Job 16:5].

Job says that he would approach them in a different way. He says he would want to strengthen them. He would want to comfort them. He would want to "wash their feet," that is, restore them to fellowship—which is what they should have done for him.

Though I speak, my grief is not assuaged: and though I forbear, what am I eased? [Job 16:6].

Job is not helped at all.

But now he hath made me weary: thou hast made desolate all my company.

And thou hast filled me with wrinkles, which is a witness against me: and my leanness rising up in me beareth witness to my face [Job 16:7–8].

Job says, "You've made an old man out of me—you have filled me with wrinkles."

He teareth me in his wrath, who hateth me: he gnasheth upon me with his teeth; mine enemy sharpeneth his eyes upon me.

They have gaped upon me with their mouth; they have smitten me upon the cheek reproachfully; they have gathered themselves together against me.

God hath delivered me to the ungodly, and turned me over into the hands of the wicked [Job 16:9–11].

These men are the same as the *ungodly*. They are supposed to be friends to Job, but they treated him like an enemy. And do you know that there are Christians today who can be meaner to you than many of the unsaved people? There is nothing meaner than a Christian when he is mean. So Job classifies his friends as ungodly. You see, they think they are defending God, but in doing so they are unfair and even brutal in their accusations against Job.

I was at ease, but he hath broken me asunder: he hath also taken me by my neck, and shaken me to pieces, and set me up for his mark [Job 16:12].

Job recognizes that God has permitted this to happen to him. Many times when I was a boy and would go hunting, I would see the dog catch a rabbit. He would grab the rabbit by the nape of the neck and shake it—oh, how he would shake it! Apparently Job had seen that, too. Job said that that was how God was shaking him. God does that sometimes, friends.

His archers compass me round about, he cleaveth my reins asunder, and doth not spare; he poureth out my gall upon the ground [Job 16:13].

Thinking of the bitterness of gall, he is saying that his bitterness is poured out of him.

He breaketh me with breach upon breach, he runneth upon me like a giant [Job 16:14].

He says that God has been walking up and down on him like a giant. Job feels that God has made a door mat out of him, as it were. You couldn't find any more vivid description than Job gives us here.

Great writers of the past, novelists, poets, and essayists, have read and reread the Book of Job. Its language is superb. Its descriptions are magnificent. I would recommend it to you for your reading so that it becomes a part of you. The beauty of the language here is wonderful.

I have sewed sackcloth upon my skin, and defiled my horn in the dust.

My face is foul with weeping, and on my eyelids is the shadow of death [Job 16:15–16].

Have you noticed how close to death Job was? He wished for it, and yet he avoided it. He stood right on the threshold of death during all of this time. I think he felt that at any moment he might die. He was a sick man, a very sick man.

Not for any injustice in mine hands: also my prayer is pure [Job 16:17].

Now again we see emerging the thing in the heart and life of Job that needed to be dealt with. You see, his friends have not been leading him to a place where he would judge himself. Instead, they actually ministered to a spirit of self-vindication. They put him on the defensive. The minute Job started to defend himself, he put God at a disadvantage. Job justified himself instead of justifying God. The problem was that his friends condemned Job instead of leading Job to condemn himself. They were using the wrong approach with him.

The minute a person begins to defend himself, he puts himself in the position which John very candidly stated. "If we say that we have no sin, we deceive ourselves, and the truth is not in us . . . If we say that we have not sinned, we make him a liar, and his word is not in us" (1 John 1:8, 10). That makes God a liar. It puts God in the place of being blamed. It takes God from the position of being the Judge and puts Him down as the One who is judged, the guilty one, the criminal. A person then is bringing a charge against God.

There are actually many people who sit in judgment upon God. That is what Job is actually doing here. He is justifying himself by saying, "Not for any injustice in mine hands"—the minute he says that, he is also saying that God is wrong in letting this happen to him.

Job says, "Also, my prayer is pure." I have heard that same statement coming from Christians. Friend, I doubt whether any of us pray a pure prayer. That is the reason I always tell the Lord, "I am asking this in Jesus' name"—because I know that Vernon McGee would not get through on his own. Job thinks *he* would get through.

O earth, cover not thou my blood, and let my cry have no place [Job 16:18].

Now Job cries out in spectacular language. He asks the earth not to cover up his blood. If the blood of Abel cried out to God, then certainly Job thinks his blood ought to cry out to God.

Friend, God does not cover up blood. And God sees the blood that Christ shed, especially when you reject it.

Also now, behold, my witness is in heaven, and my record is on high [Job 16:19].

The Bible all the way through teaches that God keeps a record of us. There are those today who like to pooh-pooh such an idea. They say, "Can you imagine God up there sitting at a desk keeping books?" Friend, who said He is keeping books? God doesn't need to do that. If a mere man can make a little machine called a computer, don't you think God can have a way of keeping records that surpasses anything we can imagine? I am of the opinion that everything we have ever said, everything we have ever done, is recorded. I don't know about you, but I can say for myself that I don't ever want to see the record that is made of me. I am very happy that some of it is blotted out under the blood of Jesus Christ. Oh, thank God for that!

My friends scorn me: but mine eye poureth out tears unto God [Job 16:20].

This is the picture of Job as he sits there in that desolate place with tears streaming from his eyes. His friends stand around him and look at him in scorn and call him a hypocrite and accuse him of being a liar. They don't know him, they don't know God, and they don't know themselves.

O that one might plead for a man with God, as a man pleadeth for his neighbour! [Job 16:21].

Here is another of those cries of Job. How wonderful it is for believers to know that we have an Intercessor. We have an Advocate. We have an Attorney who represents us before God. Everything has been taken care of for us. We have One who pleads for us before God. "For there is one God, and one mediator between God and men, the man Christ Jesus" (1 Tim. 2:5). Friend, He would like to be your Advocate if He isn't already.

My breath is corrupt, my days are extinct, the graves are ready for me [Job 17:1].

Job knew about halitosis—bad breath—and he didn't have the mouthwashes we have today! What it really means is that he is very sick. The grave is ready for him. It is as if he were saying that he has one foot in the grave and the other on a banana peeling. He thinks he is dying.

Are there not mockers with me? and doth not mine eye continue in their provocation? [Job 17:2].

Here Job is dying, and his friends stand around and mock him. What a picture this is! These men who had come to comfort him are actually debating with him and condemning him. My friend, it is possible to be a hard-boiled Christian and not be very helpful to the poor sinners in this world.

We need to recognize that there are times for harsh words. God will be very harsh with Job, but He also is going to comfort him. God is going to help him and God is going to restore him. Oh, that you and I might see that God is a God of judgment, but that He is also the God of mercy and the God of grace.

Lay down now, put me in a surety with thee; who is he that will strike hands with me? [Job 17:3].

Job says that at least they could shake hands with him.

For thou hast hid their heart from understanding: therefore shalt thou not exalt them.

He that speaketh flattery to his friends, even the eyes of his childen shall fail [Job 17:4–5].

And he pleads that he does not want to be flattered. He doesn't want them to come to "butter him up." He continues in this vein and then concludes that he is on his deathbed.

If I wait, the grave is mine house: I have made my bed in the darkness [Job 17:13].

He never expects to leave that dump heap outside the city—he thinks it is his deathbed.

I have said to corruption, Thou art my father: to the worm, Thou art my mother, and my sister.

And where is now my hope? as for my hope, who shall see it?

They shall go down to the bars of the pit, when our rest together is in the dust [Job 17:14–16].

He says that corruption and decay are closer to him than his father or mother. His parents had brought him into the world, but now he is closer to death than he is to them. His body, which is so weary and so sick, is ready to return to the dust.

CHAPTER 18

***THEME:** The second discourse of Bildad*

This is now the second round for Bildad, the Shuhite. This is his rebuttal. The interesting thing is that he really hasn't anything new to contribute at all. You will recall that he is a traditionalist. He has a lot of old sayings and proverbs that he strings along like a string of beads. He will do that again here. He has a whole series of epigrams and pious platitudes and slick clichés. Some of them are good, but none of them throw light on Job's case.

Then answered Bildad the Shuhite, and said,

How long will it be ere ye make an end of words? mark, and afterwards we will speak.

Wherefore are we counted as beasts, and reputed vile in your sight? [Job 18:1–3].

To state it very bluntly Bildad is saying, "Job, if you would shut up, then we could speak. You should quit talking and start listening. You have been doing the talking when you should have been listening to us." Actually, all of them, Job and his friends, could have refrained from talking and been listening. But they were not prepared for the voice of God at this time. God is preparing Job to hear His voice, and later he will listen.

Bildad asks Job why he holds them in such contempt and why they are vile in his sight. The answer is obvious. This is the way they have been looking at Job. That is why I say that at this point it is a stand-off between Job and his friends. I think they have been glaring at each other during this debate. These men who had come to him as his friends are no longer his friends.

He teareth himself in his anger: shall the earth be forsaken for thee? and shall the rock be removed out of his place? [Job 18:4].

Bildad is asking, "Do you think God is going to run His universe just to suit you?" Bildad, you remember, is a traditionalist, and he rests everything on the past. He feels that anything that was true in the past is also good enough for today. That is the method which he uses.

"Job, can you not show some sense so that we may come to an understanding here? Do you think that your contempt for us as incompetent and your rage at divine dealings with you are going to release you now from the trap you are in?"

Yea, the light of the wicked shall be put out, and the spark of his fire shall not shine [Job 18:5].

Nothing truer could be spoken, but it does not apply to Job.

The light shall be dark in his tabernacle, and his candle shall be put out with him.

The steps of his strength shall be straitened, and his own counsel shall cast him down.

For he is cast into a net by his own feet, and he walketh upon a snare [Job 18:6–8].

"Job, you have been caught in a net like a fish, and it is not because we have done anything. We are supposed to be here to help you, and you don't listen to us. You are in that position because there is some secret sin in your life. You have walked into a trap."

The gin shall take him by the heel, and the robber shall prevail against him.

The snare is laid for him in the ground, and a trap for him in the way [Job 18:9–10].

The *gin* means a trap. "A trap will take you. You have been caught like a bear in a trap because you have been fooling around with the bait. If that weren't true, you wouldn't have been caught."

You can see that Bildad gives these little pious platitudes and works them like a geometry problem. First you take all the steps of the proof, then you come to the conclusion, and that's it. However, life is not quite like that. For one thing, it is easy in life to begin with some wrong premises. If the premises are accurate, one can come up with a good deduction. But if the premises are wrong, the conclusion will also be wrong. If A equals ten and you make it equal fifteen, you will not arrive at the correct answer to your problem—even if you use the right methods.

These men are all trying to put down their formulas, but they are putting the wrong premises into their formulas. Bildad comes up with a hard and fast rule which states that Job has walked into a trap, that it has been his own doing, and that it could not be otherwise. Another translation would be, "For he is sent into the net by his own feet and he walketh on the meshes."

Terrors shall make him afraid on every side, and shall drive him to his feet.

His strength shall be hunger-bitten, and destruction shall be ready at his side.

It shall devour the strength of his skin: even the firstborn of death shall devour his strength.

His confidence shall be rooted out of his tabernacle, and it shall bring him to the king of terrors.

It shall dwell in his tabernacle, because it is none of his: brimstone shall be scattered upon his habitation.

His roots shall be dried up beneath, and above shall his branch be cut off.

His remembrance shall perish from the earth, and he shall have no name in the street [Job 18:11–17].

He is saying that disease shall waste the body of the wicked. The fire of God will destroy his habitation, and his name shall be blotted out. His family shall perish—he will have neither son nor grandson. His desolation shall astonish future generations. All of this is true of the wicked, but it is not applicable to Job. A statement can be absolutely true, and yet have no application to an individual situation.

This is the reason, I feel, that a great deal of so-called "counseling" today is dangerous. I think there are many fine Christian psychologists; I know some of them, and I would recommend them. But, candidly, many psychologists often have premises which are not accurate, and for that reason they are not able to counsel.

These men are trying to counsel Job, but they are not able to do so. Bildad says the wicked are going to be judged. The wicked will be blotted out. That is true. Look in our own day to the fate of Hitler and Stalin and other dictators. As they lived, they died. Although his statement is true, Job is not that kind of man by any means.

He shall be driven from light into darkness, and chased out of the world [Job 18:18].

That is a figurative expression of the wicked, but it does not apply to Job.

He shall neither have son nor nephew among his people, nor any remaining in his dwellings.

They that come after him shall be astonied at his day, as they that went before were affrighted [Job 18:19–20].

Any man likes to have sons and daughters and grandchildren. They are a source of pride and satisfaction. Sometimes the wicked have more offspring than anyone else. Job, at this time, does not have one child left to him. They have all been slain. It is actually cruel for Bildad to talk in this way to Job. We shall see later on that God is going to make it up to Job and give him more children.

Surely such are the dwellings of the wicked, and this is the place of him that knoweth not God [Job 18:21].

So we see that Bildad gives a description of the wicked. He shows the position of the wicked and the end of the wicked. He classes Job with the wicked and tells him that he is at the end of the road. He says, "This is the way it is, Job, and the description fits you." Of course, if one looks at the circumstances, one must admit that it looks as if Job does fit this description. These friends simply could not believe that what had happened to Job could have happened for some other reason. They believe that he is wicked and that he is hiding some secret sin, and they will not accept any other reason for his suffering.

When Job answers them, he is going to say, "Can't you conceive it possible that God has entangled me in His net and left His action unexplained? There must be an explanation for it, but your explanation may not be right."

CHAPTER 19

***THEME:** Job's answer to Bildad*

As you can see, the mistake Job is beginning to make is this: he knows they are wrong, but their being wrong does not make him right. His attitude is wrong also. He has a wrong conception of God at this time, although light breaks in from time to time.

Then Job answered and said,

How long will ye vex my soul, and break me in pieces with words? [Job 19:1–2]

If this had been a physical combat like a football game, the coach would have said, "The opposition tore down our defense." Job's so-called friends have been breaking down his defense.

These ten times have ye reproached me: ye are not ashamed that ye make yourselves strange to me [Job 19:3].

The more they talked, the more alienated from Job they became. They were not right, but neither was Job. Job thought that, because they were wrong, he would be right. If Job's conscience and his life had been open in the presence of God, what position should he have taken? Let me make a suggestion: I think that he should not have replied to his friends at all. Unfortunately, most of us think we must defend ourselves.

I thank God for giving me the gift of preaching and teaching, but I will be very frank with you and say that it is a dangerous gift to have, because it puts you up where you can be shot at and where you can be criticized. People have asked me from time to time, "Why don't you defend yourself? Why don't you write a little book to defend yourself?" The answer is that I don't need to. As someone has stated it, your friends who know you don't need an explanation, and your enemies wouldn't believe you anyway.

I have learned that in time things pretty much answer themselves. I don't think a person needs to defend himself in these cases. My suggestion would be that Job should not have answered these friends at all. He should have simply bowed in sweet submission. I think he should have listened to what they had to say, then told them good-bye and shown them the front gate of the city. But Job was determined to vindicate himself.

I can think of some men whom time has vindicated. William Booth, the founder of the Salvation Army, was accused very cruelly. He sought to defend himself, but he needn't have done so. Time has shown the truth of the matter. The late Dr. M. R. DeHann was severely attacked when he was pastor of a church. There were those who sought to defend him, but he really didn't need any defense. Time has justified his actions and revealed the fact that those charges made against him were false indeed.

I personally think that Job should have taken the position of silence and that he should not have come out with this defense of himself. He has become alienated from them. If he had kept silent, he would not have had ten reproaches from them. Apparently he doesn't see that.

And be it indeed that I have erred, mine error remaineth with myself [Job 19:4].

"No one knows any error in me but myself." His friends are not able to point it out, and the implication is that he isn't aware of any error himself. Someone has said that the Lord did not make us perfect, but He made us blind to our errors. Although I don't think the Lord is responsible for that, I think the statement is probably true. We are not perfect, but most of us are blind to our faults. Job is a man who is blind to a great many of his faults.

If indeed ye will magnify yourselves against me, and plead against me my reproach:

Know now that God hath overthrown me, and hath compassed me with his net [Job 19:5–6].

Bildad has said that Job had walked into a net, but Job maintains that God has done this and that God hasn't given an explanation for it. Couldn't it be that God has done this for some reason that He has not explained to Job? Of course, but the friends are determined that their explanation is the right one.

Now he pleads with his friends.

Behold, I cry out of wrong, but I am not heard: I cry aloud, but there is no judgment.

He hath fenced up my way that I cannot pass, and he hath set darkness in my paths.

He hath stripped me of my glory, and taken the crown from my head.

He hath destroyed me on every side, and I am gone: and mine hope hath he removed like a tree.

He hath also kindled his wrath against me, and he counteth me unto him as one of his enemies [Job 19:7–11].

He says that God is treating him very harshly and that there must be an explanation for it. The purpose of God must be different from the explanation that his friends give to him, but Job confesses he doesn't know what that purpose is.

He goes on to tell how his brethren have forsaken him, his acquaintances are estranged from him, his friends have forgotten him, the maids that lived in his house count him as a stranger, his servants will not answer his call, and his wife is a stranger to him. Even the young children have despised him. He is so thin that his bone cleaves to his skin, and ". . . I am escaped with the skin of my teeth." (Job 19:20). He asks his friends for their pity.

Oh that my words were now written! oh that they were printed in a book!

That they were graven with an iron pen and lead in the rock for ever! [Job 19: 23–24].

Job wishes that his words were written out and put in a book. He would be willing for his worst enemy to write them. He would like them engraven in the rock so he could say, "Look, this is what my enemy says about me, and he has to praise me."

Would you want your worst enemy to write your biography? I'm not sure that I'd want even my best friend to write mine. I am satisfied to let my biography stand on God's books where it will be accurate, which is the important thing.

Now Job will express his great faith. His friends have been attempting to break him down, which is actually the Devil's subtle attempt. The Devil, through his friends, has been able to bring Job to the place where he is not humble but is still trying to vindicate himself before God. However, Job has not hit rock bottom yet. These friends have not broken him down completely. He has a living, real faith in God, and here he utters one of the great statements in the Bible. It is not only that the statement is great, but it is great because the man who said it is a sick man who is ready to expire. He has lost everything; he is under the discipline of Almighty God, and he feels the lash upon his back. Still he is able to say:

For I know that my redeemer liveth, and that he shall stand at the latter day upon the earth:

And though after my skin worms destroy this body, yet in my flesh shall I see God:

Whom I shall see for myself, and mine eyes shall behold, and not another; though my reins be consumed within me [Job 19:25–27].

When Job became ill and was in the shock of all his troubles, he said he wanted to die. He was not speaking of annihilation. He was speaking of the death which would get him away from his troubles. I think that is obvious. He knew he would be raised again. He knew that in his flesh he would see God. He knew that even if the worms destroyed his body after death, yet in his flesh he would see God. He believed in the *resurrection* of the dead.

Friends, these bodies of ours are going to return to the dust. The bodies of the dead in Christ will be put to sleep, but the spirit will go to be with Christ immediately. How wonderful this is!

Job again cries out to his friends, having made this great statement.

But ye should say, Why persecute we him, seeing the root of the matter is found in me?

Be ye afraid of the sword: for wrath bringeth the punishments of the sword, that ye may know there is a judgment [Job 19:28–29].

"Don't you fear the judgment of God for the things you have been saying to me?" In spite of all their accusations, Job has kept his faith. He believes the Redeemer is coming and that he himself is numbered with the redeemed.

CHAPTER 20

***THEME:** The second discourse of Zophar*

Zophar is the last man to speak in this round. We are in the second round of the debate, and Zophar is the third man in this round. We find that there will be a third round and that it is going to be a brief one. Zophar won't even get in on the third round. It will simply end in a standoff before Zophar has another chance to speak.

Remember that Zophar is the legalist. He believes that God works according to law and order. That is true, of course, but that throne of law and order in judgment has become a throne of grace. Zophar knew nothing about that.

I suppose today we would say that Zophar has the scientific mind. He thinks you pour life into the test tube and it will always come out a certain way. He is the one who says that things can never be changed, that all things continue as they have from the foundation of the world. He knows nothing of the grace of God.

He comes on strong. He is actually less impressive this time around than he was before, although he is more brutal and cruel than he was before. He is a hard slugger. He hits Job hard because he realizes this may be his last time around. Although he introduces nothing new, he pours out all that he has to pour out. He rests upon his seniority, and he resorts to the same legalism. He holds to the theory that Job is a very wicked person because of the law that the wicked must be punished. That will be his emphasis here.

Then answered Zophar the Naamathite, and said,

Therefore do my thoughts cause me to answer, and for this I make haste.

I have heard the check of my reproach, and the spirit of my understanding causeth me to answer [Job 20:1–3].

He sounds like a politician running for office. He says he is capable of answering. I never heard of a man running for office who didn't say he was more qualified than his opponent; he doesn't mind telling you that. When a man says that, he does lack modesty! Now this man Zophar comes on like a politician. He is going to present his case with the same type of an argument which he had used before. He says that he is going to repeat an age-established fact. Well, what is it?

Knowest thou not this of old, since man was placed upon earth [Job 20:4].

Here it is. Here is his specific conclusion, which he poured into the test tube of the past and found to be true.

That the triumphing of the wicked is short, and the joy of the hypocrite but for a moment? [Job 20:5].

This is his age-established fact. May I say to you, how short is short and how long is long? How long is the moment of the hypocrite? Sometimes it seems that the wicked hang on for a mighty long time. But it is true that finally they do come to judgment.

Though his excellency mount up to the heavens, and his head reach unto the clouds;

Yet he shall perish for ever like his own dung: they which have seen him shall say, Where is he? [Job 20:6–7].

He can get dramatic, too. "Though his excellency mount up to the heavens, and his head reach unto the clouds." The language is tremendous in this book. As I have said, people will read the Book of Job for its expressive language, even though they may not read any other book in the Bible.

Eventually the wicked perish. Some of our contemporary young people hear about Hitler and they do not simply say, "Where is he?" but they even ask, "Who was he?" They don't even recall him. I remember that when I was a little boy, people spoke of Kaiser Wilhelm as though he were the Devil incarnate. He is gone. All of them are gone. They had a long moment, but now they are gone.

He shall fly away as a dream, and shall not be found: yea, he shall be chased away as a vision of the night.

The eye also which saw him shall see him no more; neither shall his place any more behold him.

His children shall seek to please the poor, and his hands shall restore their goods [Job 20:8–10].

Very candidly, it seems to me that man is the greatest failure in God's universe. Consider the brevity of man. They tell us how old the rocks are—even the rocks that came from the moon. Man hasn't been around that long; he is a Johnny-come-lately in the universe. Friends, if there is not an eternity ahead of us, man is the most colossal failure that God has ever made. His life is brief. He flies away as a dream.

Dr. Bill Anderson, a great preacher in Dallas, Texas, was a tremendous inspiration to me when I was a student. He met one of his deacons on the street and somewhat surprised him with this unusual question. "Suppose when we get to heaven into the presence of God, we find that the Christian life wasn't essential to our getting there. What would be your viewpoint?" This deacon looked him straight in the eye and said, "If we get to heaven and find that all this business of the Christian life was nothing in the world but our own imagination, I'm going to say to the Lord that it was very much worthwhile. It was worth it all."

Now while I believe that is true—that the Christian life is worth it all for the here and now—even then there is a little tug of disappointment at our hearts if that is all there is. Why? Because we want eternity. God has set eternity in our hearts, because it is *there*, and man is going to move on into eternity.

Zophar is calling Job not only wicked, but a hypocrite. His whole speech describes the fall of a wicked man. He says such a man may attain eminence, but that just simply means that his fall is going to be greater. His implication is that that is what has happened to Job.

His bones are full of the sin of his youth, which shall lie down with him in the dust.

He hath swallowed down riches, and he shall vomit them up again: God shall cast them out of his belly.

Because he hath oppressed and hath forsaken the poor; because he hath vio-

lently taken away an house which he builded not;

Surely he shall not feel quietness in his belly, he shall not save of that which he desired.

There shall none of his meat be left; therefore shall no man look for his goods [Job 20:11, 15, 19–21].

He suggests that such a man is like fuel which will be consumed. He is like an evil vision which will disappear. His evil is like a sweet morsel that he keeps under his tongue, but it will turn to gall within him. It is like food that he eats, but God will compel him to disgorge his unjustly amassed fortune and will force him to make restitution to his victims.

When he is about to fill his belly, God shall cast the fury of his wrath upon him, and shall rain it upon him while he is eating [Job 20:23].

Although nothing could escape his greed, he will be reduced to poverty. Worst of all, God shall cast the fury of his wrath upon him.

All darkness shall be hid in his secret places: a fire not blown shall consume him; it shall go ill with him that is left in his tabernacle.

The heaven shall reveal his iniquity; and the earth shall rise up against him.

The increase of his house shall depart, and his goods shall flow away in the day of his wrath [Job 20:26–28].

"A fire not blown shall consume him." In other words, he will become a raging flame, and all his prosperity will go up in flames—there will be no avenue of escape.

He sums it by saying,

This is the portion of a wicked man from God, and the heritage appointed unto him by God [Job 20:29].

His implication, of course, is that the "wicked man" is Job. That is a pretty bitter dose for a man in Job's condition, but Job is ready to answer him. He is going to defend himself, and he comes on strong, as we shall see.

CHAPTER 21

***THEME:** Job's sixth answer*

Job is still able to come back with an answer. I think it would have been better if he had not tried to answer Zophar's brutal accusation, but he is going to defend himself again.

He tells them that he is growing weary of their false charges. He appeals his case to a higher court. He agrees with them that the wicked will be punished but insists that this does not apply to his case.

But Job answered and said,

Hear diligently my speech, and let this be your consolations.

Suffer me that I may speak; and after that I have spoken, mock on [Job 21: 1–3].

Job wants their attention and sarcastically says that he is going to console them.

As for me, is my complaint to man? and if it were so, why should not my spirit be troubled? [Job 21:4].

He is not taking his complaint to men; he is appealing to God.

Mark me, and be astonished, and lay your hand upon your mouth [Job 21:5].

In other words, "Shut up!"

Wherefore do the wicked live, become old, yea, are mighty in power?

Their seed is established in their sight with them, and their offspring before their eyes.

Their houses are safe from fear, neither is the rod of God upon them.

Their bull gendereth, and faileth not; their cow calveth, and casteth not her calf [Job 21:7–10].

Job is now going to point out a fallacy in their argument. The wicked do not always suffer in this life; in fact, they may prosper. They are not always cut off; sometimes they attain old age, their property remains intact, and their children are able to inherit it.

They send forth their little ones like a flock, and their children dance.

They take the timbrel and harp, and rejoice at the sound of the organ.

They spend their days in wealth, and in a moment go down to the grave [Job 21:11–13].

They may have a whole flock of children. They dance and are gay and rejoice. They have a good time, and they live it up. You may say that their fall is going to be apparent, but you are mistaken. Like others, they go down to the grave but without catastrophe striking them beforehand.

Job had been a rancher, and he points out that some of the wicked people are very prosperous cattlemen with big, prosperous families. I can remember when I was a boy in West Texas that some of the biggest drunkards in the neighborhood were also the biggest ranchers in the area. Where are they today? They are gone. Their sons apparently are following right in their footsteps, and they are going to disappear also. But they *do* prosper. Job calls attention to that.

You will remember that this was also an observation of David. He said, "I have seen the wicked in great power, and spreading himself like a green bay tree" (Ps. 37:35). However, David found, too, that God finally moves in judgment against the wicked.

We can look around in our own country today. We know certain family names that stand for money, and they have no reputation for godliness. We find them in politics and in high society. They don't seem to suffer as other people suffer. Maybe sometimes this causes you to wonder. It is as Job is saying here, the wicked do prosper.

Therefore they say unto God, Depart from us; for we desire not the knowledge of thy ways.

What is the Almighty, that we should serve him? and what profit should we have, if we pray unto him? [Job 21: 14–15].

They are godless. They don't want God. They insultingly say that they don't need God nor desire to know His ways. What could God give to them that they can't get for themselves?

Lo, their good is not in their hand: the counsel of the wicked is far from me [Job 21:16].

Job is saying, "I don't belong in that class. I am not one of the wicked. What you lay down as an inevitable truth does not always work out to be true. Besides, even if it were true, it does not apply to me!"

How oft is the candle of the wicked put out! and how oft cometh their destruction upon them! God distributeth sorrows in his anger [Job 21:17].

Those exclamation marks should probably be question marks—but either way, he is saying that the wicked have no more problems than the average person has.

They are as stubble before the wind, and as chaff that the storm carrieth away.

God layeth up his iniquity for his children: he rewardeth him, and he shall know it.

His eyes shall see his destruction, and he shall drink of the wrath of the Almighty [Job 21:18–20].

However, death is no respecter of persons, and the time comes when death knocks at the door of the wicked. There comes a time of judgment when "he shall drink of the wrath of the Almighty." So Job shows his friends that their proverbs are not always true, but that doesn't mean that God is not going to judge the wicked someday.

One time I heard a friend of mine say to a man who was apologizing for being drunk, "Don't apologize. You go ahead and drink it up now, boy, because in this life is the only place you can get it. Where you are going, they don't serve it. I don't blame you for getting all you can here." The wicked might as well enjoy every pleasure available to them, because this is their last chance. The wicked are going to be judged eventually.

Job is confident that God will judge the wicked—there is no question about that.

Have ye not asked them that go by the way? and do ye not know their tokens,

That the wicked is reserved to the day of destruction? they shall be brought forth to the day of wrath [Job 21:29–30].

The judgment of the wicked may not be until the Great White Throne judgment, but judgment will come eventually. God will permit the sinner to live it up down here if that's what he wants to do. You see, God is gracious. God is long-suffering. The goodness and the forbearance and the long-suffering of God should lead us to repentance.

I know that today we look at the rich who are enjoying life. The jet set goes from the United States to Europe and to Mexico from resort to resort. My, they really live it up, and God permits them to do it. But remember this: "The wicked is reserved to the day of destruction." We don't hear much said about that in these days.

This is the answer of Job to Zophar. May I say that it is a good answer. But we see that Job is still justifying himself. There is no thought of repentance in this speech by Job.

CHAPTER 22

THEME: *The third discourse of Eliphaz*

Here we come to the third inning, if you please. This is the third time that these men get into the arena to battle an intellectual battle. This kind of thing is not so attractive today. We had debate teams and that type of contest when I was going to college, but it was no more popular then than it is now.

Today we build bigger and better stadiums all over this country. It is a mighty poor city that doesn't have a gleaming, multi-million dollar stadium for athletic events. However, very little money goes for the intellectual and even less for the spiritual exercise. Here in Job it is an intellectual battle and a spiritual battle. You know, very few of us have ever been out on the football field carrying the ball or charging or blocking. Very few of us have ever gone up to bat in a major league, but all of us are out in the arena of life in a spiritual battle. This does not seem important to most people. They would rather go and sit in the bleachers and watch somebody else carry the ball. Well, my friend, you and I are fighting a spiritual battle. Paul tells us that we are wrestling and that the wrestling match is going on right now.

This kind of intellectual and spiritual battle excited the people in that day. We think they were uncivilized then. We are the ones who build the multi-million dollar stadiums for physical combat and fail to emphasize the intellectual combat.

You will remember that Eliphaz is the man who had the remarkable experience. He had a strange and mysterious vision. He is a spiritualist. He is the one who says, "I have seen."

Then Eliphaz the Temanite answered and said,

Can a man be profitable unto God, as he that is wise may be profitable unto himself? [Job 22:1–2].

The very nature of the question reveals that a man cannot be profitable to God. He is asking, "Job, you sure think a lot of yourself, but what do you suppose God thinks of you?" He thinks Job is acting as if God might derive some benefit from his behavior and that if God were not restraining him, he might become too strong for God—that God is holding Job back for this reason. Well, Eliphaz is certainly off target. And it is certainly not comforting to a man who at this moment does need help and light from heaven.

Eliphaz' question applies to some church members I have known who think they are profitable to God. Some folk seem to think they make a real contribution to God down here and that He is rather fortunate to have them on His team. They seem to think that when they get to heaven, heaven will really be improved because of who they are. We need to recognize that man is not profitable to God. We are all unprofitable, which means we are like a bunch of spoiled fruit. Jesus told a parable about service and He concluded, "So likewise ye, when ye shall have done all those things which are commanded you, say, We are unprofitable servants: we have done that which was our duty to do" (Luke 17:10).

Is it any pleasure to the Almighty, that thou art righteous? or is it gain to him, that thou makest thy ways perfect? [Job 22:3].

These men do sense a little chink in the armor of this man Job. It will be glaring and apparent in just a few chapters. The trouble is that they do not really make a correct diagnosis of the man, and they certainly do not know the remedy. They are not able to comfort him and bring him help as they should. The fact that Job claims to be a righteous man doesn't cause God to jump up and down with glee and throw His hat into the air.

I have a feeling that there are a great many professing Christians who rest so much upon themselves and who they are that they really are not trusting Christ. Let me emphasize that we bring no pleasure to the Almighty because we have been good little Sunday school boys and have pins for perfect attendance. A great many folk think that the Lord is delighted with that sort of thing. I don't think so. We need to recognize who we are, and we need to recognize our utter dependence upon God—our great need of Him. We are to be looking to Him instead of trying to impress Him with who we are and what we are doing.

Will he reprove thee for fear of thee? will he enter with thee into judgment? [Job 22:4].

Eliphaz asks Job, "Are you so righteous and so perfect that God has to be afraid to deal with you?" We need to understand that when God says Job was "perfect" it means he stood in a right relationship with God through sacrifice—we know he offered sacrifices for his sons and daughters. And certainly God was not afraid to deal with Job. Obviously, this man is having a very rough time.

Is not thy wickedness great? and thine iniquities infinite?

For thou hast taken a pledge from thy brother for nought, and stripped the naked of their clothing.

Thou hast not given water to the weary to drink, and thou hast withholden bread from the hungry [Job 22:5–7].

Eliphaz is indulging in a very mean thing here. Unfortunately there are some Christians today who indulge in this same type of thing. You see, when this tragedy struck Job, it caused many people to say, "I wonder what it is in his life?" Since they weren't able to pinpoint anything, the gossip began. Folk began to manufacture reasons. Before long they could spin quite a yarn out of a little piece of thread. That is exactly what Eliphaz is doing.

He has already accused Job of acting as if God might derive some benefit from his good behavior. Now he turns around and tells Job that his wickedness couldn't be greater. Eliphaz thinks he had just better tell Job all the things of which he is guilty. He is guessing, because none of these things are true. It is pure gossip. But look at the accusations he levies against Job.

Such treatment cannot help Job. It puts Job on the defensive. Instead of leading Job to defend God, it leads Job to defend himself. If Job becomes convinced that he is not guilty of these false accusations, then it leads him to think that God certainly must have made a mistake and that there is something wrong with God. That is the alternative way of thinking about it. The accusations of Eliphaz lead Job to this kind of defense.

Listen to the stories the gossips tell about Job. They make him sound like a real Mr. Scrooge!

But as for the mighty man, he had the earth; and the honourable man dwelt in it.

Thou hast sent widows away empty, and the arms of the fatherless have been broken.

Therefore snares are round about thee, and sudden fear troubleth thee;

Or darkness, that thou canst not see; and abundance of waters cover thee [Job 22:8–11].

Eliphaz implies that these are the things Job has done, and now the word is getting out. He goes on to warn Job that God is on high and takes note of all these things.

Is not God in the height of heaven? and behold the height of the stars, how high they are! [Job 22:12].

"Job, you have been doing these things as if God doesn't see you, but God does see you. Although you thought you were getting by with it, it is obvious now that you didn't get by with it." The entire argument rests upon the premise that Job has some secret sin in his life which nobody knows but God, and now God is dealing with him in judgment. This is the explanation for his illness and all the tragedy that has happened to him—according to the argument of Eliphaz.

He thinks Job conceives of God as One who does not know what is going on.

And thou sayest, How doth God know? can he judge through the dark cloud?

Thick clouds are a covering to him, that he seeth not; and he walketh in the circuit of heaven [Job 22:13–14].

"Job, you don't see Him, but He sees you and knows about you."

Hast thou marked the old way which wicked men have trodden?

Which were cut down out of time, whose foundation was overflown with a flood:

Which said unto God, Depart from us: and what can the Almighty do for them? [Job 22:15–17].

It is always the same old argument which we heard at the beginning. He rests everything upon some experience that he has had. He can say, "I have seen the wicked."

Now Eliphaz gives a gospel plea here, but it is something which Job didn't need, because he occupied a redeemed relationship. He could say, "I know that my redeemer liveth" (Job 19:25).

Acquaint now thyself with him, and be at peace; thereby good shall come unto thee [Job 22:21].

That is a marvelous, wonderful invitation, but it does not apply to Job. It is like many of the invitations given in churches today—there sits a congregation of redeemed folk (at least they think they are saved), and an invitation for salvation is given. It is almost meaningless in such circumstances and borders on the ridiculous. To ask Job to accept Christ when he had already accepted Christ is not the answer to his problem.

"Acquaint now thyself with him, and be at peace" is a gracious invitation and a good invitation. It is the invitation which God gives to us. The Lord Jesus said the same thing in the New Testament, "Come unto me, all ye that labour and are heavy laden, and I will give you rest" (Matt. 11:28). Eliphaz said this was the way to have peace with God. Also Paul says, "Therefore being justified by faith, we have peace with God through our Lord Jesus Christ" (Rom. 5:1).

"Thereby good shall come unto thee" is true also. However, we must remember that "good" means what will be good for us. Sometimes that means discipline when we need it.

Receive, I pray thee, the law from his mouth, and lay up his words in thine heart.

If thou return to the Almighty, thou shalt be built up, thou shalt put away iniquity far from thy tabernacles [Job 22:22–23].

These men just keep harping on the one theme: "Job, there is some secret sin in your life. Deal with it and turn to God." They are treating him as if he is not even related to God at all.

Then shalt thou lay up gold as dust, and the gold of Ophir as the stones of the brooks.

Yea, the Almighty shall be thy defence, and thou shalt have plenty of silver.

For then shalt thou have thy delight in the Almighty, and shalt lift up thy face unto God [Job 22:24–26].

Eliphaz is assuming that God is Job's enemy, but God is not Job's enemy. This is an attitude which is still one of the greatest deterrents in the preaching of the gospel. Men are sinners—this should be made very clear—but God today is not at enmity with this world. God is *reconciled* to this world. You and I don't need to do anything to reconcile God; Christ did this for us. God is reconciled and has His arms outstretched to a lost world, saying, "You can come to Me, but you must come My way. You must come by the One who told you 'I am the way, the truth, and the life. No man cometh unto the Father but by Me.' " If you come His way, you can come with boldness into the presence of God. God will meet you with a great welcome and abundance of spiritual blessing. Eliphaz is not representing God accurately, as you can see. Neither is he any help or comfort to Job.

CHAPTERS 23–24

***THEME:** Job's seventh answer*

This is the seventh time that Job answers his friends, and he expresses a deep longing for God. He would like to present his case before God. He is beginning to sense that he is in the sieve of God's testing and that God will bring him through his trials.

Then Job answered and said,

Even to-day is my complaint bitter: my stroke is heavier than my groaning [Job 23:1–2].

Job says, "You fellows see my condition, and you have heard my complaint. Actually, my condition is worse than it looks, and it is worse than I can tell you."

Oh that I knew where I might find him! that I might come even to his seat! [Job 23:3].

Job has a longing to come into the presence of God. It would be wonderful if his friends knew how to bring him into the presence of the throne of grace. He doesn't need a throne of judgment; he has already been there. And he has already been to the woodshed for discipline—there is no question about that. Now somebody needs to bring him into the presence of God.

I would order my cause before him, and fill my mouth with arguments [Job 23:4].

Job says that he wants to go into the presence of God, because he wants to defend himself. My friend, no one can go into God to defend himself. We all must go before God to plead guilty before Him. Every one of us is guilty. We will find that when Job does get into the presence of God, he will not defend himself. He will change his tune altogether.

I would know the words which he would answer me, and understand what he would say unto me [Job 23:5].

Job wonders what God would say to him. He wonders where he can find Him. I can assure you that any man who has that longing for God in his heart is going to find Him. God will meet him.

Will he plead against me with his great power? No; but he would put strength in me.

There the righteous might dispute with him; so should I be delivered for ever from my judge.

Behold, I go forward, but he is not there; and backward, but I cannot perceive him:

On the left hand, where he doth work, but I cannot behold him: he hideth himself on the right hand, that I cannot see him [Job 23:6–9].

God is not found by running around here and there. He is near, nearer than a hand, nearer than breathing. He is right close to you. Job says he has been running up and down trying to find God.

But he knoweth the way that I take: when he hath tried me, I shall come forth as gold [Job 23:10].

Now a little light is beginning to break on the soul of Job: "I am being tested for a purpose. I don't know what it is, and I don't understand it, but God is using this in my own life."

Friend, have you discovered in your own heart and in your own life that trouble will strengthen the fiber of your faith? Haven't you found that it has given you a moral character that you never had before? Have you experienced God's strength and comfort in the time of the storm? You know that God has never promised that we would miss the storm, but He has promised that we would make the harbor. And that is good enough for me.

My foot hath held his steps, his way have I kept, and not declined.

Neither have I gone back from the commandment of his lips; I have esteemed the words of his mouth more than my necessary food [Job 23:11–12].

Job has had a desire for the Word of God and apparently has been following God's Word. Here again is where God will teach us. Job did not understand or did not correctly interpret the Word of God. You know that some of the lessons in the Word of God cannot be learned just by studying them. They are learned by experience. Many of God's truths must be taught to us in that way.

As Job's answer continues through chapter 24, we see that he gets a little long-winded.

Eliphaz gave him the invitation, "Acquaint thyself with Him." So Job expressed his desire to find God. Job knows Him as Redeemer—he has called Him that. But he doesn't understand what is happening to him, and he needs the comfort and the help and the light from heaven, which has not been forthcoming from his friends.

Eliphaz had made a stab at trying to ferret out the secret sin which he thought was in the life of Job. The effect this has had upon Job is that it has put him even more on the defensive. In fact, it causes him now to raise another question: "Why is God so exacting with me? He apparently condones the actions of others who are really sinners and who are out in the open with their sins." This is the thrust of his argument in chapter 24.

Why, seeing times are not hidden from the Almighty, do they that know him not see his days?

Some remove the landmarks; they violently take away flocks, and feed thereof [Job 24:1–2].

Job now lists the open sins of other people. Some are dishonest. They remove the landmarks from the land.

They drive away the ass of the fatherless, they take the widow's ox for a pledge.

They turn the needy out of the way: the poor of the earth hide themselves together [Job 24:3–4].

They are not honest in their dealings, and they take advantage of other people, even those who are in need.

They reap every one his corn in the field: and they gather the vintage of the wicked [Job 24:6].

The corn crop of the wicked makes just as many bushels to the acre as does the crop of the righteous. Job is asking, "Why does this happen?"

They have committed murder, they have robbed, they have committed adultery; yet this whole evil group is permitted to go down to the grave like all others.

Drought and heat consume the snow waters: so doth the grave those which have sinned [Job 24:19].

Not only do they go down to the grave like others, but it seems that they are immune from justice in this life. In fact, it looks as if they are actually favored. Job looks at his own condition—he is sick and destitute, and he looks over at the wicked and sees them getting along nicely. He says, "I just don't understand it. I want to know why I am ferreted out, why I am the one who is being treated in this way."

And if it be not so now, who will make me a liar, and make my speech nothing worth? [Job 24:25].

Job's friends have not helped him. In fact, they have given him another cause for complaint.

As the pastor of churches and in my ministry I have heard one question, I would be willing to say, almost a thousand times: "Why does God let this happen to me?" One hears it over and over again. That is what Job is asking here. Why does God let this happen to me? Job's premise is: I am such a fine fellow and that crowd over there is wicked, so why me? It is the same question that comes into the minds of many people. Job does not understand God, and we will find that Job doesn't understand himself, either. And yet Job has a great faith in God with the limited knowledge that he has.

CHAPTER 25

***THEME:** Bildad's third discourse*

We are now going to have the final word from Bildad. Fortunately, it is brief. I think the light is beginning to dawn on Bildad. He is a very thoughtful and intelligent man. Perhaps he is beginning to think, *If Job is guilty, why doesn't he break under all this bombardment of argument that we have given to him?* He has still maintained his integrity. He stood up against it. Remember that Bildad is the traditionalist. He believes God follows certain laws. Things have been done this way for a thousand years, so why would there be a change? He is the scientist who pours life into the test tube, and says, "See, this is what happens every time." The Law of God is that He will punish sinners. And yet he wonders why Job doesn't break if he is a guilty sinner.

There are men today, both theologians and scientists, who speak so learnedly, especially about the creation of the earth. They seem to know exactly what God did under certain circumstances two billion years ago. We have a whole brainwashed generation, but I am, perhaps, one of the biggest skeptics you have ever known. This gross assumption of knowledge is simply not justified. My friend, they don't even know what is going to happen tomorrow, so how can they speak with such authority about what happened two billion years ago? I think they are simply kidding themselves and those who listen to them. I get a little weary of them all. Does anyone really know exactly what the first chapter of Genesis means? I think that if Moses were here today and could hear some of these scientific explanations, he would smile and say, "My, what those boys have learned since I wrote Genesis! They seem to know more than I knew about it."

Both Bildad and our contemporary intellectuals need to remember that God's ways are past finding out.

Then answered Bildad the Shuhite, and said,

Dominion and fear are with him, he maketh peace in his high places [Job 25:1–2].

He has an exalted notion of God, which is good.

Is there any number of his armies? and upon whom doth not his light arise? [Job 25:3].

A better translation would be, "Whom doth not his light pass?" In other words, God is the Supreme One.

How then can man be justified with God? or how can he be clean that is born of a woman? [Job 25:4].

Now here is a good question. It is a question he should have asked at the beginning. Although he has asked the right question, he doesn't have the right answer.

Behold even to the moon, and it shineth not; yea, the stars are not pure in his sight [Job 25:5].

Well, we have been to the moon now, and we have found that it is a pretty dirty place. It is covered with dust and dirt, volcanic ash—not a nice place to have a picnic. It is not as romantic up there as it is down here when the moon is shining and you're out with your girl for the first time. Mars seems to be no cleaner. The stars are not pure in His sight.

How much less man, that is a worm? and the son of man, which is a worm? [Job 25:6].

There are those who don't like to face that. I like it. People today talk about us having come from a worm. We haven't *come* from a worm, friends; we *are* worms. That is what we are now in God's sight.

How can a man who is born of woman be clean in God's sight? That's the question. It is a good question. It is the supreme question. Bildad did not have the answer. Only the Lord Jesus Christ has the answer to that question.

CHAPTERS 26–31

***THEME:** Job's eighth answer*

This is Job's longest speech. It includes chapters 26 through 31. Job professes his faith in God his Creator, and we begin to see his real problem.

But Job answered and said,

How hast thou helped him that is without power? how savest thou the arm that hath no strength?

How hast thou counselled him that hath no wisdom? and how hast thou plentifully declared the thing as it is? [Job 26:1–3].

"Bildad, you don't have an answer for me. Zophar, you didn't have the answer. Eliphaz, your answers didn't help me. You all had a lot of talk but no answers." They all have said many things that were good, but they were of no direct meaning nor did it communicate anything to Job, because none of them could answer the question of the *why* of Job's suffering.

To whom hast thou uttered words? and whose spirit came from thee? [Job 26:4].

"To whom hast thou uttered words?" You have finally come up with the right question, Bildad, but you have no answer; so who has been helped by all this talk?

Now Job really launches into his discourse. In it he will lay his soul bare. He has a lot to say, and some of it is really great. He moves into the area of the Creation and God as the Creator.

Dead things are formed from under the waters, and the inhabitants thereof.

Hell is naked before him, and destruction hath no covering.

He stretcheth out the north over the empty place, and hangeth the earth upon nothing [Job 26:5–7].

Much has been made of the fact that He "stretcheth out the north over the empty place." Folk have attempted to point out that there is a void in the north, that there are no stars in a certain place in the north. In fact, it was called a "hole in the north." However, since we have these very powerful telescopes, and especially the radio telescopes, we find that we cannot point a telescope in any direction in God's universe without finding it filled with stars—other universes. Job is saying that God reached out in space and covered it—He can cover the empty place.

Also space is a creation of God. Here is one star which God has created. Billions and billions of light years over yonder is another star, and God has also created that one. What keeps them from rubbing together or banging into each other like cars do on our freeways today? Well, God put space between them. What is space? Maybe some people would answer, "Nothing." Friend, it is something. I don't know what it is, but it is something, and God created it to hold heavenly bodies apart. It is like a lubricant that He uses to keep the universes from banging into each other.

Listen to the apostle Paul. "For I am persuaded, that neither death, nor life, nor angels, nor principalities, nor powers, nor things present [that's time], nor things to come [that's future], Nor height, nor depth [that's space], nor any other creature, shall be able to separate us from the love of God, which is in Christ Jesus our Lord" (Rom. 8:38–39). "Nor any other creature" is literally "nor any other created thing." Space is one of God's creations. Friend, that gives us something to turn over in our minds. What is space?

It takes a long time to go to the moon. What is all this expanse between the earth and the moon? Don't tell me it is nothing, because it is *something*. What is it? I don't know; I'm no authority on that. I simply know that we call it space, God created it, and it is out there serving His purpose.

He "hangeth the earth upon nothing." Who in the world told Job that? Remember that Job lived back in the age of the patriarchs, and yet this man knew that this earth is hanging out in space. That God suspends the huge ball of earth in space with nothing to support it but His own fixed laws is a concept unknown to ancient astronomers.

Job understood that He "hangeth the earth upon nothing." There is no foundation under it. If it fell, what direction would it go? We talk about gravity, but that is a pulling down toward the center of the earth. When you get out far enough into space, there is nothing pulling on anything. So where is down and where is up? And what keeps it hanging there in space? We get an answer in Colossians 1:17:

"And he is before all things, and by him all things consist." The word *consist* is the Greek *sunistemi,* meaning "to hold together." By Christ it all is held together. We are moving now into a great section of the Book of Job.

Job had a tremendous view of God as the Creator. Out there on the ash heap he was able to look at the stars at night, and he had spent time doing that in the past.

By his spirit he hath garnished the heavens; his hand hath formed the crooked serpent.

Lo, these are parts of his ways: but how little a portion is heard of him? but the thunder of his power who can understand? [Job 26:13–14].

God has garnished the heavens with stars. Probably the "crooked serpent" that Job mentions is a constellation out in the heavens. He is calling attention to the greatness of God as He is revealed in the heavens by His wonderful creation.

We see that Job knew God as a Creator; Job understood Him as a Redeemer; but Job did not know God as a Sustainer and the One who loved him. He did not understand that God would not let anything happen to him unless it would minister to him.

JOB CONDEMNS THE WICKED

We are approaching some of the really basic material of this book. The Book of Job reaches right down where we are, into the center of our lives. Beneath the suffering which Job went through there is a great lesson for him to learn. That is the reason I say that the main lesson of the Book of Job is not why believers suffer. Suffering is not the main issue of the book. Behind it all is the great teaching of *repentance,* repentance in a child of God.

When a sinner comes to God, is he to repent? Paul told the jailer at Philippi, ". . . Believe on the Lord Jesus Christ, and thou shalt be saved, and thy house" (Acts 16:31). Paul made no mention of repentance, but repentance is *in* that word *believe,* because when a sinner turns *to* Christ in faith, he also turns *away* from sin. In the case of the Philippian jailer, it was probably his idolatry from which he turned. That would be his repentance. Turning to Christ is the important part.

Many a child of God today and many a lost sinner are self-sufficient. Anyone who is self-sufficient needs to repent, as this book will reveal. This is the great lesson of the Book of Job.

Moreover Job continued his parable, and said,

As God liveth, who hath taken away my judgment; and the Almighty, who hath vexed my soul;

All the while my breath is in me, and the spirit of God is in my nostrils;

My lips shall not speak wickedness, nor my tongue utter deceit [Job 27:1–4].

I would like to give a translation here which may be helpful in bringing out the meaning. "As God liveth, who hath taken away my right, and the Almighty, who hath embittered my soul (all the while my breath is in me, and the Spirit of God is in my nostrils); my lips shall not speak unrighteousness, nor my tongue utter deceit." Job makes it very clear that he is undaunted and that he is determined. Zophar hasn't answered, and so Job keeps on talking, and he says, "I will never admit the charges that you three so-called friends have brought against me." On the contrary, he says:

God forbid that I should justify you: till I die I will not remove mine integrity from me [Job 27:5].

He is stubborn, isn't he? All his friends have been able to do is to make him more and more defensive. In defending himself there is no brokenness of spirit, no humility of mind. It makes it look as if God is the One who is unrighteous, while Job is perfectly all right. He says, "I will not remove mine integrity from me."

My righteousness I hold fast, and will not let it go: my heart shall not reproach me so long as I live [Job 27:6].

Listen to him! These friends have not led him to self-judgment but have only ministered to a spirit of self-defense. Job is vindicating himself. You see, God is not on the scene here. Job is being rather foolhardy in all this, because before it is over we will see that Job is down in dust and ashes before God.

There is a lesson for us to learn in all this. I certainly will grant that many things which his friends said to Job were truths. Also I am of the opinion that these men had the best intentions. Although they said things that were true, I don't think that they had *the* truth. They talked about experience and tradition and legality, but they never gave Job the *truth.* Having failed to do that, they built up the man's ego.

Let me repeat this because it is so important. They thought that Job had committed some secret sin, and they were trying to bring it out into the open. Job had not committed some great, secret sin, and he knew that they were wrong. Since they were wrong, Job assumed he was right. That is where Job made his mistake. The fact that his friends were wrong in no way made Job right. Job should have been in the presence of God where there would have been a brokenness of spirit. One of the purposes of trouble in our lives is to lead us into that brokenness of spirit before God.

Someone has said that trouble is like the sun. The sun shining on wax will melt it. The same sun shining on clay will harden it. That is the way trouble affects different people. Some will respond with a broken spirit. They just melt before the presence of God. Job isn't to that place yet. He is hard now, hard as nails in his own integrity.

"My righteousness I hold fast, and will not let it go: my heart shall not reproach me so long as I live." This is the position and condition of a lot of church members today. They feel exactly the same way. The assurance of salvation is wonderful to have, but, my friend, you can be a hardboiled sinner, thinking you have assurance of salvation, when all you have is a great big ego. You feel that you have it made. Well, Job thought he had it made, and he is going to find out otherwise very shortly.

Let mine enemy be as the wicked, and he that riseth up against me as the unrighteous [Job 27:7].

Job is putting everyone who disagrees with him over on the other side. They are his enemies. They are wicked and they are unrighteous. I tell you, that is a dangerous position for any man! Now Job is going to talk about the wicked and what is going to happen to them. Job will give a little lecture now. In the midst of all his own trouble, this man is going to give a lecture about the wicked.

For what is the hope of the hypocrite, though he hath gained, when God taketh away his soul?

Will God hear his cry when trouble cometh upon him?

Will he delight himself in the Almighty? will he always call upon God?

I will teach you by the hand of God: that which is with the Almighty will I not conceal [Job 27:8–11].

Job is saying that the wicked may prosper but God will eventually judge them.

The rich man shall lie down, but he shall not be gathered: he openeth his eyes, and he is not.

Terrors take hold on him as waters, a tempest stealeth him away in the night.

The east wind carrieth him away, and he departeth: and as a storm hurleth him out of his place [Job 27:19–21].

Riches will make no difference. If a man has been wicked, his life will go out like a flame that is blown out, like a candle blown out by a wind coming through a window. The time will come when—

Men shall clap their hands at him, and shall hiss him out of his place [Job 27:23].

Can you remember a time when millions saluted Mussolini? There came a day when people actually walked across his dead body and that of his paramour as they lay in the mud after their execution. The wicked shall be judged. There will come an end to their wickedness and to the glory they seem to have. But that doesn't answer Job's problem.

Job is still full of words.

POEM OF CREATION

He continues his discourse with one of the most beautiful poems of creation that you can find anywhere. It may not seem like poetry to us, but it is Hebrew poetry and it is beautiful. He deals with things that are absolutely wonderful. If we were studying poetry, I would spend a long time here.

Surely there is a vein for the silver, and a place for gold where they fine it.

Iron is taken out of the earth, and brass is molten out of the stone.

He setteth an end to darkness, and searcheth out all perfection: the stones of darkness, and the shadow of death [Job 28:1–3].

God has put silver and gold and iron and precious stones into the earth. It is difficult to find these things. I personally do not think that men have found the vastness of the treasures that are really in this old earth on which we live. I think this chapter is saying that clearly. It also suggests that there are precious stones which have never yet been discovered, which might be more valuable than the diamond.

The flood breaketh out from the inhabitant; even the waters forgotten of the foot: they are dried up, they are gone away from men.

As for the earth, out of it cometh bread: and under it is turned up as it were fire [Job 28:4–5].

Not only does the earth turn up precious stones, but also it produces food—bread for us to eat.

The stones of it are the place of sapphires: and it hath dust of gold.

There is a path which no fowl knoweth, and which the vulture's eye hath not seen:

The lion's whelps have not trodden it, nor the fierce lion passed by it [Job 28:6–8].

The birds fly over the earth and its mountains. There are veins of minerals down in the earth that the birds fly over and know nothing about, neither can the vulture see them. There must be precious stones and veins of riches and wealth which are completely unknown and untapped.

He putteth forth his hand upon the rock; he overturneth the mountains by the roots [Job 28:9].

God can cause the earthquake. He can change the topography of the land. He can expose those veins of riches in the earth that He wants to have exposed.

He cutteth out rivers among the rocks; and his eye seeth every precious thing.

He bindeth the floods from overflowing; and the thing that is hid bringeth he forth to light [Job 28:10–11].

Job has been talking about the minerals and the precious stones in the earth. There are things which are of even more value: wisdom and understanding. Job knows that God has placed the minerals in the earth, but where is the source of that precious commodity—wisdom?

But where shall wisdom be found? and where is the place of understanding?

Man knoweth not the price thereof; neither is it found in the land of the living.

The depth saith, It is not in me: and the sea saith, It is not with me [Job 28:12–14].

Job is telling his friends that they have not found wisdom.

I would like to voice an opinion on the basis of this passage. I do not believe that all of this probing of the ocean floor and space and every crevice in the earth is going to tell man anything relating to real wisdom and real knowledge concerning the origin of the earth. Man cannot find it there. He will not learn how it came into existence nor who put it into existence.

It cannot be gotten for gold, neither shall silver be weighed for the price thereof [Job 28:15].

We are paying billions of dollars to bring back rocks from the moon. Those are mighty expensive rocks, friend. But they are not telling man what he would like to know.

It cannot be valued with the gold of Ophir, with the precious onyx, or the sapphire.

The gold and the crystal cannot equal it: and the exchange of it shall not be for jewels of fine gold.

No mention shall be made of coral, or of pearls: for the price of wisdom is above rubies [Job 28:16–18].

The wisdom that Job hoped his friends would bring to him is a wisdom beyond the understanding of man.

The topaz of Ethiopia shall not equal it, neither shall it be valued with pure gold [Job 28:19].

Even the Bureau of Standards just can't evaluate it.

Whence then cometh wisdom? and where is the place of understanding?

Seeing it is hid from the eyes of all living, and kept close from the fowls of the air.

Destruction and death say, We have heard the fame thereof with our ears [Job 28:20–22].

We have heard about it, but even death ought to tell us *something*. It ought to tell us that there is something on the other side, and it ought to tell us that there is something we don't know. Men just step through the doorway of death, my friend, and they are not able to get word back to us. Houdini, the great magician, left a code with his wife before he died so that he could communicate with her after he was gone. Spiritualist after spiritualist came to Mrs. Houdini, claiming to have a message from him. She would say, "Give me the code." Not one of them was able to come up with the code, which means that no one heard from Houdini after he died. We just don't get word back from over there. That should tell us that there is something which we do not know today.

He goes on to say something very interesting:

> **When he made a decree for the rain, and a way for the lightning of the thunder [Job 28:26].**

For many years the critics said this was an incorrect statement; that everyone knows you see the lightning before you hear the thunder. But after it was discovered that sound waves do not travel as fast as light waves, they realized that the lightning is the flash from the crash of the thunder that takes place. How amazing that the writer of the Book of Job knew that it was the "lightning of the thunder"!

> **And unto man he said, Behold, the fear of the Lord, that is wisdom; and to depart from evil is understanding [Job 28:28].**

Job's friends were not able to probe this man's problem at all. We are going to see his secret sin revealed, but it is not anything that his friends suspected.

He is suffering from a bad case of perpendicular "I-itis." This is a very bad disease. It is a case when the little pronoun "I" becomes so important that all we can talk about is "I, I, I." We find that Job is filled with pride. This shows us that even a good man needs to repent. We will find in this chapter of twenty verses Job uses the personal pronoun "I" or "me" fifty-two times. Mark them in your Bible. You will be amazed. Job is wrapped up in himself. That is his big problem. We will see how it had affected his life. It affects the life of anyone when he gets all wrapped up in himself. Someone has said, "When you're wrapped up in yourself, it makes a mighty small package."

This chapter does not contain any form of a confession by Job. It is really his boasting. He has "I" trouble. There are many of *us* who have it, too. The perpendicular pronoun is the hub of the wheel of life for all of us. Everything is a spoke that goes out from us. We see no brokenness of spirit. There is not that broken and contrite heart, no admission of guilt, no confession, no feeling of guilt or failure.

His friends were not able to help him. They failed to see the real problem. They didn't know Job, and they didn't know themselves, and they certainly didn't know God. They believed that God sent trouble to Job only as a punishment, and they thought Job was just holding out. They roughed him up and were miserable comforters to him. Each one used a different approach, and yet they all came to the same conclusion.

We can sum up the methods of his friends. Eliphaz was the voice of experience. He used what would be called today the psychological approach. This is the approach of the power of positive thinking. It adopts a cheerful attitude. Bildad was the traditionalist and he used the philosophical approach. That would be the approach of several of the seminaries today. They use the philosophical approach, but that doesn't help anyone. Zophar was a religious dogmatist. He thought he knew all about God. He sounds like some of us fundamentalists, by the way. All of us would fall into the category of one of these friends. As we have seen, not one of his friends had been able to help him.

Now I do want to say on Job's behalf, as we move into this chapter, that he was a "perfect" man according to the standard which God had set up, which was sacrifice. He was a very wealthy man. He had all that it took to make this life agreeable. He had what it took to make him important in the world. We have seen that he was a religious man. He feared God. He had a concern for his children. He didn't put up a false front. He could be weighed on the scale of God's balance and not be called a hypocrite. So the insinuation of his friends was base and low. He was a genuine saint of God, a quickened soul, a child of God. His earthly cup of bliss had been full and running over. Then why should this man suffer?

Actually, the suffering is only incidental—although Job would never have told you that. The suffering in Job is about as important as the fish in the Book of Jonah, in which the real problem is between Jonah and Jehovah. Here the real problem is between Job and Jehovah. Even Satan, the enemy, is secondary.

The real problem is Job. He did not know himself, and he did not know God. Socrates has said, "Know thyself." That is important. Job didn't know himself. He was self-righteous and self-sufficient. He received all kinds of compliments from people, and there was a little of the self-adulation. There was a spiritual egotism in this man's life. We will see this clearly when God confronts him.

Job now is going to tell us about himself. He reviews his past. Chapter 29 is Job's "This is my life."

Moreover Job continued his parable, and said,

Oh that I were as in months past, as in the days when God preserved me [Job 29:1–2].

Job reminds me of a little tea party I heard about:

I had a little tea party
This afternoon at three.
'Twas very small—
Three guests in all,
Just I, Myself, and Me.
Myself ate all the sandwiches,
While I drank up the tea.
'Twas also I who ate the pie
And passed the cake to Me.
—Author unknown

When his candle shined upon my head, and when by his light I walked through darkness [Job 29:3].

Those were the good old days for Job.

As I was in the days of my youth, when the secret of God was upon my tabernacle [Job 29:4].

Here is a man who from his youth served God.

When the Almighty was yet with me, when my children were about me;

When I washed my steps with butter, and the rock poured me out rivers of oil;

When I went out to the gate through the city, when I prepared my seat in the street! [Job 29:5–7].

He was prosperous. Everything he touched turned to gold. Not only was he a prosperous man, but he was also a man of influence.

The young men saw me, and hid themselves: and the aged arose, and stood up.

The princes refrained talking, and laid their hand on their mouth.

The nobles held their peace, and their tongue cleaved to the roof of their mouth [Job 29:8–10].

The children would run and hide from him because he was such a great man. The old men would rise when they saw him coming, they would take off their hats and bow to him. When he came, all the others quit talking. Even the princes and the nobles were silent. They waited for Job to speak. Nobility didn't speak in his presence unless he asked them to do so.

When the ear heard me, then it blessed me; and when the eye saw me, it gave witness to me [Job 29:11].

He was voted the most valuable citizen by the city clubs of Uz in Chaldea. He was the outstanding citizen of the town.

Because I delivered the poor that cried, and the fatherless, and him that had none to help him [Job 29:12].

He provided pensions for the aged. He helped the poor.

The blessing of him that was ready to perish came upon me: and I caused the widow's heart to sing for joy [Job 29:13].

He took care of the widows. My, this man was thoughtful!

I put on righteousness, and it clothed me: my judgment was as a robe and a diadem [Job 29:14].

Job was adorned with good works. And people came to him for advice.

I was eyes to the blind, and feet was I to the lame [Job 29:15].

He was chairman of the board at the blind school, and he was a benefactor of the crippled children's home. My friend, this man Job was outstanding! How we need citizens like this.

I was a father to the poor: and the cause which I knew not I searched out [Job 29:16].

He made a thorough investigation before he gave to a cause. This is something which many believers do not do today. Job supported only that which he knew to be a worthy cause.

And I brake the jaws of the wicked, and plucked the spoil out of his teeth [Job 29:17].

He believed in civic righteousness and law and order. He was influential enough to bring it to pass. What a man he was!

Then I said, I shall die in my nest, and I shall multiply my days as the sand.

My root was spread out by the waters, and the dew lay all night upon my branch.

My glory was fresh in me, and my bow was renewed in my hand [Job 29:18–20].

Job said to himself, "I've got it made. I have everything I want for retirement. I'm going to die in my nest. I'll multiply my days as the sand and live to a ripe old age." I tell you, he thought he had everything. He had a wonderful family. He had good health. One can't think of anything that Job did not have.

Unto me men gave ear, and waited, and kept silence at my counsel.

After my words they spake not again: and my speech dropped upon them.

And they waited for me as for the rain; and they opened their mouth wide as for the latter rain [Job 29:21–23].

All the group sought out his advice. Before they would make a decision, they would contact Job and ask his advice. The governor of the state and the supreme court would talk things over with Job before they made a decision. I tell you, he was an outstanding man of great influence. They would hang on every word that Job said.

If I laughed on them, they believed it not; and the light of my countenance they cast not down.

I chose out their way, and sat chief, and dwelt as a king in the army, as one that comforteth the mourners [Job 29: 24–25].

Job sat at the very top of the totem pole of life. He dwelt in honor, affluence, and influence. He was a plutocrat and a tycoon. He was an ideal man, the goal toward which humanity is striving today. He lived the good life. He knew what abundant living really was.

But Job lived in a fool's paradise. He was in a Cinderella world; and when the clock struck midnight, his chariot turned into a pumpkin. Remember what he said in chapter 3: "For the thing which I greatly feared is come upon me, and that which I was afraid of is come unto me. I was not in safety, neither had I rest, neither was I quiet; yet trouble came" (Job 3:25–26). The bomb fell on his nest. He had dreaded something like this. He had feared that all of this material substance could be wiped out and taken from him in a moment, and it was. He had nothing to fall back on. Even his friends didn't cushion his fall. In fact, they made him fall with a terrible, resounding crash.

Job has been putting on his self-righteousness. Listen to him again in verse 14: "I put on righteousness, and it clothed me: my judgment was as a robe and a diadem." Fifty-two times he has used "I" and "me." We hear no confession, no admission of failure. We see nothing of a broken and contrite spirit in Job.

Chapter 30 continues his description of his present wretchedness and suffering.

But now they that are younger than I have me in derision, whose fathers I would have disdained to have set with the dogs of my flock [Job 30:1].

"I have told you how it used to be, but now—now these young scoundrels come around and throw rocks at me. They have no use for me. Let me tell you about the fathers of these kids. I wouldn't even have hired them to watch over my flock."

Yea, whereto might the strength of their hands profit me, in whom old age was perished?

For want and famine they were solitary; fleeing into the wilderness in former time desolate and waste [Job 30: 2–3].

He goes on to deride these scoundrels who now have no use for him.

And now am I their song, yea, I am their byword.

They abhor me, they flee far from me, and spare not to spit in my face [Job 30:9–10].

They are making up dirty little ditties about Job, and they ridicule him in song. He knew what it was to be the object of derision led by young hoodlums.

I don't know about you, but I am tired of listening to Job. First he was boasting about the outstanding man he had been. Now he is courting sympathy. "I was such a great fellow and now look at me." And who is to blame for this, my friend? Why, God is to blame.

There are a lot of Christians in that same position today. It is possible to be blaming God but to do it in a very pious way. "I had all those blessings. I was so active. I did kind things for people. But look at me now." Well, whatever it is that has happened, it is because God is good, never because God is not good. Whatever happens is because God is working out something beneficial in the life of a believer.

Job finally says,

My harp also is turned to mourning, and my organ into the voice of them that weep [Job 30:31].

His singing voice is the *harp*. All he can sing now is the "Desert Blues." The *organ* is his speaking voice, and he says all it can do is weep. He has a tear in his voice all the time. That is his condition now. He is asking for sympathy and certainly is a man to be pitied.

However, you will notice that there still is no brokenness of spirit. God has been put at a great disadvantage in this man's life. He is a proud man. He justifies himself instead of justifying God. In fact, he *blames* God. What is the problem of Job? It is pride. It is the same thing that caused Satan to fall. It was the sin in the Garden of Eden. It is that awful thing that eats like a cancer into the human heart. That awful sin of pride is there in the hearts and lives of all of us.

JOB CONCLUDES HIS SELF-DEFENSE

Now chapter 31 concludes Job's lengthy defense. It has been quite a slugging match! The three friends of Job, lined up against him, have attempted to beat him down into admitting that he had committed a great sin. Their logic, as we have seen, is that God would not have permitted him to suffer so, if he had not committed some terrible sin.

After going three rounds with him, they gave up, which is evident by the fact that the last man, Zophar, did not answer Job. When he did not step forward to make his rebuttal, Job continued to speak. Believe me, they had teed him off, and he came out of his corner fighting.

In defending himself, he must accuse God —it boils itself down to that. He is implying that God is wrong in punishing him. Probably the most foolish thing any person can do is to justify himself, inasmuch as God must impute sin. The minute you begin to justify yourself, God immediately will have to point the finger at you and say what you are. Real wisdom, and the correct position, is to condemn ourselves utterly and to cast ourselves upon God. When we do that, God becomes our justifier. There is nothing but *wrath* for the self-righteous. And there is nothing but *grace* for the self-judged. This is very important for us to remember in our own lives.

Humility is a quality that we admire and look for in others. A clipping from the *New York Times* regarding a contemporary boxing match underscores this fact: ". . . Ability to wear the trappings of humility is an occupational requirement in certain lines of work, particularly in politics and championship boxing. He who scorns them invites the vengeance of an outraged public. . . . We like our champions humble. After they have flattened some poor gaffer for our amusement, we want them to come to the microphone like Joe Louis and Rocky Marciano and say, 'He put up a good fight.' Muhammad Ali outrages us by coming to the microphone and calling a bum a bum."

May I say to you, it is a characteristic of human nature to be proud. Boxers are not the only ones guilty of pride. It just may be that they are a bit more brazen about it, but pride characterizes the human family.

The Book of Job is teaching us that when we come before God, He wants us to be real before Him. We can't put up a defense for ourselves. There is no possible use to try to build ourselves up as if we were some great person or had done some great thing. Nothing is more sure than that God will break down every such type of arrogance. The Day of the Lord will be against everything high and lifted up. So it is wisdom for us to take the low and broken place today, for it is the low place that gives us our best view of God and His salvation.

There is a great deal of this "coming forward" in response to an altar call which does not lead to real salvation, because of the fact that some folk come in *pride*.

I wonder if you have ever noted in the Word of God the references to this matter of being contrite and how God approves of it. "The LORD is nigh unto them that are of a broken heart; and saveth such as be of a contrite spirit" (Ps. 34:18). You see, real repentance involves taking that position. We need to recognize that just as David did. Listen to him in that great penitential psalm when he made his confession: "The sacrifices of God are a broken spirit: a broken and a contrite heart, O God, thou wilt not despise"

(Ps. 51:17). My friend, when you come to God to do business with Him, you do not come to God to trade with Him on equal terms and turn in your little goodness to Him. We need to recognize that we approach God through contrition. This is taught all through the Bible.

"For thus saith the high and lofty One that inhabiteth eternity, whose name is Holy; I dwell in the high and holy place, with him also that is of a contrite and humble spirit, to revive the spirit of the humble, and to revive the heart of the contrite ones" (Isa. 57:15). This matter of being humble and contrite is not a problem for the politicians and the boxers alone; it is a problem for all believers today, especially those who are in the Lord's service. I think that we can say that egotism and self-conceit are more detestable when they show themselves in the servants of the Lord Jesus Christ, the One who ". . . made himself of no reputation, and took upon him the form of a servant . . ." (Phil. 2:7). How unlike Him is pride in the lives of those who name His name and say they are believers. To reveal a hateful, unsubdued, self-displaying Christian profession and Christian service is atrocious. And in this final section Job is not very attractive.

Job has been doing a good job of patting himself on the back. He has told what an outstanding, influential, good man he was and then makes a play for sympathy for his present condition. As he concludes his discourse in this chapter, he is still claiming that he is a very good fellow.

I made a covenant with mine eyes; why then should I think upon a maid? [Job 31:1].

Job makes it very clear that he had lived a clean life. He didn't run around and chase women. He wants them to know he has not been guilty of ordinary sensual sins.

For what portion of God is there from above? and what inheritance of the Almighty from on high?

Is not destruction to the wicked? and a strange punishment to the workers of iniquity? [Job 31:2–3].

He is still pointing his finger at others who commit such things, and he says they are to be judged. He cannot see why he should be judged so severely when he is such a wonderful fellow. He is about to break his arm patting himself on the back.

Doth not he see my ways, and count all my steps?

If I have walked with vanity, or if my foot hath hasted to deceit;

Let me be weighed in an even balance, that God may know mine integrity [Job 31:4–6].

He is boasting of his integrity. Well, he is going to come into the presence of God before long, and he is going to really *see* himself—then he won't see much integrity.

If my step hath turned out of the way, and mine heart walked after mine eyes, and if any blot hath cleaved to mine hands;

Then let me sow, and let another eat; yea, let my offspring be rooted out.

If mine heart have been deceived by a woman, or if I have laid wait at my neighbour's door;

Then let my wife grind unto another, and let others bow down upon her.

For this is an heinous crime; yea, it is an iniquity to be punished by the judges [Job 31:7–11].

He says that if he has been unfaithful or untrue, let his wife be taken from him. He hasn't lived in sin as some other folks do. And I believe that all these things Job is saying are completely accurate. He was really a good man. But he has this terrible blind spot: pride. His friends have led him into a defense of himself and he just can't let up. He must boast about his goodness.

We see this same sort of thing today among Christians. For a child of God to boast and to live in pride is just as bad as getting a gun and murdering someone. Pride among Christians is one of the things that causes our churches to be so cold today. People sit in the pews and think that they are just all right. My friend, if you are in Christ Jesus, you are saved, but regardless of who you are, your life is not measuring up to God's standard—and neither is mine.

If I did despise the cause of my manservant or of my maidservant, when they contended with me;

What then shall I do when God riseth up? and when he visiteth, what shall I answer him? [Job 31:13–14].

Job was an employer, and he says that he was good to his employees. He was a capitalist who was good to labor. There should be more who could say that today. Of course, in our time the shoe is on the other foot, and labor is not too nice to the consumer today. Anyway, the point is that Job could say that he had been considerate of others.

If I have withheld the poor from their desire, or have caused the eyes of the widow to fail;

Or have eaten my morsel myself alone, and the fatherless hath not eaten thereof;

(For from my youth he was brought up with me, as with a father, and I have guided her from my mother's womb;)

If I have seen any perish for want of clothing, or any poor without covering;

If his loins have not blessed me, and if he were not warmed with the fleece of my sheep;

If I have lifted up my hand against the fatherless, when I saw my help in the gate:

Then let mine arm fall from my shoulder blade, and mine arm be broken from the bone [Job 31:16–22].

Job had certainly helped the poor. He had a poverty program long before anyone else ever had one. He took care of the orphans. He goes over all this ground again. He is boasting of all the things that he has done. I believe he really did them, too, but he is lifted up with pride about it. That is where he is in trouble. He is constantly saying, in effect, "I have been so good that God is unjust in treating me as He is. God is wrong."

My friend, we need to get to the place where we can praise His name above everything and can see ourselves down in the dust before Him.

If I rejoiced at the destruction of him that hated me, or lifted up myself when evil found him:

Neither have I suffered my mouth to sin by wishing a curse to his soul [Job 31:29–30].

Job says that he didn't rejoice when his enemy stubbed his toe and had trouble. He was not spiteful.

If I covered my transgressions as Adam, by hiding mine iniquity in my bosom:

Did I fear a great multitude, or did the contempt of families terrify me, that I kept silence, and went not out of the door?

Oh that one would hear me! behold, my desire is, that the Almighty would answer me, and that mine adversary had written a book.

Surely I would take it upon my shoulder, and bind it as a crown to me [Job 31:33–36].

He says he has not done anything in secret. He wishes his enemies would write out what they think of him, and he would be glad to wear it like a necktie or like a crown on his head so everyone could see it. He would walk up and down the streets and say, "Look, this is what my enemy says about me, and it is all *praise* for me." How Job is boasting! He has discussed everything about his life, but he has not made a confession of his pride.

Job is righteous in his own eyes, but Job is not righteous before God.

CHAPTERS 32–37

***THEME:** The discourse of Elihu*

There is a crowd standing around listening to these men talk. When Job is finished with his discourse, it is one of the members of this audience, Elihu, who picks up the discourse and carries on from then until God breaks into the discussion. During this time a storm gathers on the horizon. By the time we get to the end of Elihu's discourse, the storm breaks upon the group, and they all run for cover. Only Job is left there in the storm. It is then that God will deal with Job personally.

Now the three friends of Job are through. They fade into the distance. Frankly, I heave a sigh of relief. I am thankful they are through talking, and I hope they've gone home.

To all intents and purposes, Job has won the debate. But he hasn't won. Here stands a young man with something to say. He hasn't opened his mouth so far, which is unusual for a young man, but this is a very intelligent young man.

So these three men ceased to answer Job, because he was righteous in his own eyes [Job 32:1].

That, of course, is accurate—Job was righteous in his own eyes.

The three friends had not been able to give an answer to Job. They failed to meet his need in all their reasonings and in all their arguments. Eliphaz was the one who had referred to experience. Zophar was the legalist. Bildad put his arguments on the basis of human authority. None of them had been able to come up with a solution for Job. They had said many things that were true—they came up with a number of great truths—but they did not answer Job's problem. At the end of it all, Job remained righteous in his own eyes.

There was a value in this controversy. It is important for *us* to see that when two parties are divided over any issue, they can never reach an understanding unless there is a brokenness and a submissiveness and a willingness to be subdued and not to contend for self on the part of one or both of the parties involved. We find a lot of high-mindedness today, inside and outside the church, which is the cause of a great many of the problems that we have today. Job was a high-minded man. He has been touchy and tenacious and easily provoked, but his friends have been equally so. They have not been able to come to any kind of an understanding.

I think we ought to say on behalf of the friends of Job that they found no answer because there was no answer. Only God can answer a self-righteous individual. We will find that finally God did break in with an answer for Job. To anything else the unbroken heart can find a ready reply, but not to God, of course. Job's friends had no answer.

Now Elihu is going to break into the conversation. He doesn't have an answer for Job, but he comes closer than the others had come. And I do think that he prepares the way for God finally to break in upon this scene. Then God will give Job some information from "Headquarters" that all of us need.

Notice that Elihu is a Buzite (descended from Buz, Gen. 22:21), evidently a tribe of Arabs.

Then was kindled the wrath of Elihu the son of Barachel the Buzite, of the kindred of Ram: against Job was his wrath kindled, because he justified himself rather than God [Job 32:2].

Elihu speaks because he is angry, and he is angry on two counts. Job had spent his time justifying himself rather than God. This meant that he was actually saying, "God is wrong. God has made a big mistake with me." This aroused the anger of Elihu.

Also against his three friends was his wrath kindled, because they had found no answer, and yet had condemned Job [Job 32:3].

This was the second reason for his anger. The friends had not been able to put their finger on Job's real problem, and yet they were condemning Job.

Now Elihu had waited till Job had spoken, because they were elder than he [Job 32:4].

Things apparently were different in that day from what they are today. A modern young man would already have broken into the conversation. We find in our society that little Willie has center stage. I have noticed this with my grandson. I tell you, he is on center stage, up front all the time. We listen to him, and I'm not sure that that is wise.

When Elihu saw that there was no answer in the mouth of these three men, then his wrath was kindled [Job 32:5].

Elihu had waited. He thought these older men would come up with something very wise. I can remember when I was a young preacher that I was frightened to death of the gray heads in the congregation, because I thought they knew a great deal—probably much more than I did. However, I soon learned that length of days did not always indicate knowledge or depth of wisdom.

And Elihu the son of Barachel the Buzite answered and said, I am young, and ye are very old; wherefore I was afraid, and durst not shew you mine opinion.

I said, Days should speak, and multitude of years should teach wisdom [Job 32:6–7].

Notice this interesting comment:

But there is a spirit in man: and the inspiration of the Almighty giveth them understanding [Job 32:6–8].

Elihu doesn't have the same position with the Holy Spirit that believers have today. Apparently the Holy Spirit did not *indwell* believers in the Old Testament, but He did come *upon* certain men for the performance of certain functions. For example, Bezaleel was filled with the spirit of God (Exod. 31:2–3) who gave him the skill and the wisdom to make the articles of furniture for the tabernacle. The spirit of God came upon many men in the Old Testament. David prayed, ". . . Take not thy holy spirit from me" (Ps. 51:11), which would indicate that the Holy Spirit could depart from an Old Testament believer. There is no teaching in the Old Testament that men were indwelt by the spirit of God. Elihu recognizes that only the inspiration of the Almighty can give understanding to man. This means that there is only one sure authority, and that is the Word of God.

Great men are not always wise: neither do the aged understand judgment [Job 32:9].

The "inspiration of the Almighty giveth them understanding"—he recognizes that only God could provide an answer in Job's case.

Elihu is preparing the way for God to answer. Although he himself does not really have the answer, he recognizes that these other men did not have the answer either.

Therefore I said, Hearken to me; I also will shew mine opinion.

Behold, I waited for your words; I gave ear to your reasons, whilst ye searched out what to say.

Yea, I attended unto you, and, behold, there was none of you that convinced Job, or that answered his words [Job 32:10–12].

This, of course, is absolutely true.

Lest ye should say, We have found out wisdom: God thrusteth him down, not man [Job 32:13].

It disturbed Elihu because he felt that these men should have been able to answer Job. It disturbed him because Job stands vindicated, and in this position he feels very cocky and self-confident.

The literal meaning of the word *contrite* is "bruised." Now it is true that Job has been battered and bruised. He has been in the ring with Satan, and he has had three rounds with his friends. This man Job is coming out bruised, there is no question about that. But contrition comes from within a man. It is grief and penitence for sin.

David understood that, "The sacrifices of God are a broken spirit: a broken and a contrite heart, O God, thou wilt not despise" (Ps. 51:17). Job had been bruised, but he still was not contrite. However, God is not through with him yet.

Only God has the answer for self-righteousness, pride, and arrogance. Sometimes people come to me with this story: "I have a son who has gone to college, and he knows everything now. How can I answer a boy like that?" The answer is that only God can deal with a son who thinks he knows it all.

The minute that you and I become self-righteous we can be sure of one thing: we will be brought into the ring with God, and He is going to bruise us. He must treat us in that way, because it seems to require bruising to bring us to a realization of our sin and to a spirit of humility.

It was that spirit of humility which was demonstrated in the life of John Wesley. There is a somewhat humorous anecdote about his humility. It is said that Wesley was crossing a narrow bridge when he met an enemy right in the middle of it. It was impossible to pass, and his enemy drew himself up to his full height, and said, "I never give way to an ass!" Wesley looked at him for a minute, and then he answered, "Well, I always do," and he just backed off the little bridge and let the man go by. I guess that would be the best answer one could give in a case like that. Not many men would have been willing to back off, but Wesley was.

When I think of a really contrite spirit, I think of the confession of Horatius Bonar. He said, "I went to God to confess my coldness, my indifference, and my pride. After I had finished, I went back again to God and I repented of my repentance." My friend, that is true contrition to repent of your repentance! You see, it is very easy for us to be proud even of our repentance.

Elihu expected Job's friends to continue the debate.

When I had waited, (for they spake not, but stood still, and answered no more;)

I said, I will answer also my part, I also will shew mine opinion [Job 32:16–17].

Here we have the suggestion that it was Elihu who was the author of the Book of Job. Notice that he is using "I" when he gives this explanation, and it sounds as if he were writing the book.

For I am full of matter, the spirit within me constraineth me. [Job 32:18].

He is saying here that he is constrained from saying more. He really would like to say more, but he will not say it. Apparently the spirit of God held him back.

Unfortunately, many of us are high-minded. We are touchy and tenacious. We are easily provoked. We are ready to get into this business of vindicating ourselves, and we don't want anyone to rebuke us at all. There is not that softness of tone or delicacy of touch. We pour no oil on the troubled waters. We do not have that broken heart and weeping eye. We parade our own experience like Eliphaz. We indulge in a legal spirit like Zophar. We introduce human authority like Bildad. We do not demonstrate the spirit and the mind of Christ.

Remember that Proverbs 15:1 tells us that "A soft answer turneth away wrath: but grievous words stir up anger." Most of us forget that—or perhaps I am just talking about myself.

THE CREATOR INSTRUCTS THROUGH DISCIPLINE

Now Elihu has something to say.

Wherefore, Job, I pray thee, hear my speeches, and hearken to all my words.

Behold, now I have opened my mouth, my tongue hath spoken in my mouth [Job 33:1–2].

He is going to insist on several great truths.

My words shall be of the uprightness of my heart: and my lips shall utter knowledge clearly.

The spirit of God hath made me, and the breath of the Almighty hath given me life [Job 33:3–4].

My friend, this is a great truth. God is my Creator.

Elihu is going to speak by the spirit of God. He says that the other men haven't been able to answer Job, and now he is going to try.

Peter, in his first epistle, wrote, "If any man speak, let him speak as the oracles of God. . ." (1 Peter 4:11). I would like to write these words in the chapels of every seminary in this country. If a minister is not speaking for God (I don't mean to be crude, but I am going to say it anyway), he should shut up! He has no business talking. After I had been speaking in the San Francisco Bay area, a man said to me, "You sound very dogmatic." I said, "Yes, I'm glad it got through to you that I am dogmatic." "Well," he said, "there are other ways of looking at the Bible." I discovered that he was a legalist. He said, "Have you ever thought that there might be another explanation?" I told him, "Yes. There was a time when I thought there were several ways a man could come to God. But after many years of study I have come to the conclusion that the way God saves is by grace, and I am dogmatic about it. I am dogmatic about quite a few things in the Word of God—because the Word of God is dogmatic. I am dogmatic about the deity of Jesus Christ, that He is the Son of God. I am dogmatic about the fact that He is virgin born, that He performed miracles, that He died in a substitutionary death, that He rose bodily from the grave, that He ascended to heaven, that He is seated today at God's right hand, that He is the living Christ right now, and that He is coming back someday. Brother, I am dogmatic!" The fellow looked at me and said, "Then I guess there is no use of my talking with you." I said, "If you have a different viewpoint, you would be wasting your time, I can assure you." My friend, let me say it as Peter said it, "If any man speak, let him speak as the oracles of God." Of course there is such a thing as dogmatic ignorance. But the point I am making is that when you are quoting the Bible, if you are not sure it is the Word of God, then you have nothing to say at all. Unbelief is always dumb. It has nothing to say. I don't mean that it doesn't talk—it talks a great deal. But any ministry is powerless, valueless, and fruitless unless a man is speaking as the oracles of God.

If thou canst answer me, set thy words in order before me, stand up.

Behold, I am according to thy wish in God's stead: I also am formed out of the clay [Job 33:5–6].

Job has been wanting a man to represent him before God. This young fellow, Elihu, is willing to do that. He says, "I'm made of the same clay you are made of." He wants to stand as a mediator between Job and God. Obviously, he is not the man, but it reveals the great need for the incarnation of our Lord. He must be a Mediator so He must be God, but He must also be of the same clay as we are.

Behold, my terror shall not make thee afraid, neither shall my hand be heavy upon thee.

Surely thou hast spoken in mine hearing, and I have heard the voice of thy words, saying,

I am clean without transgression, I am innocent; neither is there iniquity in me [Job 33:7–9].

Elihu had been listening to all the preceding conversation and had heard that Job considered himself innocent and that he found fault with God. Now Elihu tells Job that God is greater than man and not responsible to man.

Behold, he findeth occasions against me, he counteth me for his enemy,

He putteth my feet in the stocks, he marketh all my paths.

Behold, in this thou art not just: I will answer thee, that God is greater than man [Job 33:10–12].

He makes the great statement that God is greater than man. It is a simple statement; yet it is great because so many folk take the place of God. Many Christians propose to tell you why certain things happen. Some Christians speak as if they have a private line into heaven—they get the latest right off the wire. I doubt that sincerely. There is a great deal that none of us know.

Why dost thou strive against him? for he giveth not account of any of his matters [Job 33:13].

Job needs to understand that God didn't need to report back to any board. He is not responsible to any group, nor is He subject to public opinion.

My friend, God is not responsible to either you or me. He doesn't have to give an answer to us. He is not accountable to us. Some people say, "Oh, why does God let this happen to me?" I don't know why, my friend; all I know is that God is not accountable to you. He doesn't have to tell you the reason why. He doesn't have to tell me the reason why. He has asked me to trust Him. He has never promised that He would take me out of the darkness, but He says, "Put your hand in My hand and I will lead you *through* the darkness." He has not promised to explain everything to us. He has asked us to trust Him!

For God speaketh once, yea twice, yet man perceiveth it not.

In a dream, in a vision of the night, when deep sleep falleth upon men, in slumberings upon the bed [Job 33:14–15].

We must recognize that since we have the completed Bible, we do not need to trust any dream that we have had. However, way out on the frontier where the gospel has not gone, I think you will find that God still uses this method.

Then he openeth the ears of men, and sealeth their instruction,

That he may withdraw man from his purpose, and hide pride from man [Job 33:16–17].

The problem with Job was that he had an awful disease—it was cancer of the spirit: pride. Oh, the proud heart of man! And I see it in my own life. Do you see it in yours? How we need to grovel in the dust and put on sackcloth and ashes because of the kind of folk we are. Elihu says here that God instructs men through discipline.

Job's false reasoning is a very simple thing. He did not understand the character of God; so he did not understand God's dealings with him. But God *was* dealing with Job, and He wanted to "hide pride" from him. He wanted to take pride out of that man's life. Job was a good man; he was a great man. But he was a low-down sinner just like you are and just like I am. Because we are sinners, pride creeps into our lives. For example, we get angry with individuals who dare criticize us. God "withdraweth not his eyes from the righteous . . ." (Job 36:7). We are in His hands, and we are under His eye continually. We are the objects of His deep and tender and unchanging love, but we are also the subject of His wise and moral government. He doesn't want spoiled brats as His children!

Lo, all these things worketh God oftentimes with man,

To bring back his soul from the pit, to be enlightened with the light of the living [Job 33:29–30].

God often instructs men through discipline. God uses it to deliver his soul from going into "the pit."

Mark well, O Job, hearken unto me: hold thy peace, and I will speak.

If thou hast any thing to say, answer me: speak, for I desire to justify thee.

If not, hearken unto me: hold thy peace, and I shall teach thee wisdom [Job 33:31–33].

God still wants to do the same thing for believers today. We need to consider the exhortation given us in Hebrews: "For consider him that endured such contradiction of sinners against himself, lest ye be wearied and faint in your minds. Ye have not yet resisted unto blood, striving against sin. And ye have forgotten the exhortation which speaketh unto you as unto children, My son, despise not thou the chastening of the Lord, nor faint when thou art rebuked of him" (Heb. 12:3–5). Then drop down to verse 11: "Now no chastening for the present seemeth to be joyous, but grievous: nevertheless afterward it yieldeth the peaceable fruit of righteousness unto them which are exercised thereby" (Heb. 12:11). There are three distinct ways in which we may meet the chastening of our Heavenly Father: (1) We can *despise* it as though His hand and His voice were not in it. We can ignore God. (2) We may *faint* under it. When we do that, it is real defeat. Job had had both these reactions, by the way. But what are we to do? (3) We are to be exercised by it so that it will produce the fruit of righteousness in our lives. God does permit trouble to come to His own, and He chastens every son whom He receives. That is the great purpose that is behind all that has been happening to Job. God is going to bring it to a tremendous consummation.

GOD NEVER DOES WICKEDLY

Now as we continue listening to Elihu in chapter 34, notice that for a man of his day he has real spiritual insight. He certainly is defending God in this matter. Up to this point the Lord was at a distinct disadvantage, because it looked as if the Lord were either punishing Job because of some great sin in his life, or, if there were no great sin in his life, then God was unjust. It looked as if the Lord would have to prove him to be a great sinner, but God didn't have to do that, as we shall see.

If Job could only have been shown by his friends that God was dealing with him—not in the sense of punishing him for his sin, but that God was using all of these instruments in attempting to take pride out of his life and reduce him to a plane where he could trust God, where he could respond even as little Samuel did, ". . . Speak; for thy servant heareth" (1 Sam. 3:10). Job was so busy defending himself that he couldn't see that God was using circumstances, people, the Sabeans, storms, even Satan himself as God's marvelous agencies to bring this man to a very gracious and a very wise end. God's mercy was actually being displayed. His mercy endureth forever! Job had lost sight of that, which removed him from God.

We need to recognize that God moves in *our* lives as believers. We get occupied with men and things and circumstances, and we look at them in reference to our lives instead of walking with God. We do not live above our circumstances but under them, and then our circumstances weigh us down.

A wonderful man of God, who is now with the Lord, was my friend in the ministry. He used to kid me and say, "McGee, your trouble is that you live under your circumstances and you don't live on top of them." Although he was kidding me, what he said was true. Actually, God permitted me to have cancer, and now I can see a purpose in it. Don't misunderstand me. I'm not being pious and saying, "I praise the Lord for my cancer." I do not. I'd get rid of it in the next minute if I could. But the point of it is that I recognize God has used this in my life.

When we let circumstances come between us and God, God is shut out, and as a result of that we lose the sense of His presence. We get to the place where there is worry and distress instead of peace in our souls, and we do not feel His fatherly hand upon us. We become fretful and impatient and irritable and faultfinding. We get far away from God and out of communion with Him. We do not see the hand of God in all our circumstances. All the while He wants to bring us back to Himself in brokenness of heart and humbleness of mind. This is the "end of the Lord," that for which He is striving in your life and in mine.

Elihu is the one who concludes man's attempted ministry to Job. Now Job will experience the direct ministry of God. There will be a threefold effect on him: it will change his relationship to God and to his friends and to himself. My friend, we all need to be changed within ourselves. The Lord will chasten for this purpose. God doesn't mind doing that, because it will bring us to that place of humility before God so that He can use us. God uses chastening for this purpose in our lives.

Furthermore Elihu answered and said,

Hear my words, O ye wise men, and give ear unto me, ye that have knowledge [Job 34:1–2].

Now Elihu turns to the three friends and has a word for them.

For the ear trieth words, as the mouth tasteth meat [Job 34:3].

As we taste something that we eat with our tastebuds, so also the ear tastes—it tastes words or "trieth words." Music is delightful to the ear; we taste it with our ears.

Let us choose to us judgment: let us know among ourselves what is good [Job 34:4].

Just as we like to taste something good, let's hear something that is good.

For Job hath said, I am righteous: and God hath taken away my judgment [Job 34:5].

Job has been saying that he is righteous and that God hasn't given him a fair trial. In other words, God is not fair to me.

Should I lie against my right? my wound is incurable without transgression [Job 34:6].

Job maintains that he has an incurable disease and didn't do anything to deserve it.

What man is like Job, who drinketh up scorning like water? [Job 34:7].

Job despised the chastening of the Lord. He felt that God had no right to treat him so. This attitude removed him far from God. Then he began to faint under the chastening—we are not to faint when we are rebuked of Him. God is doing all this to accomplish a good purpose in our lives.

Which goeth in company with the workers of iniquity, and walketh with wicked men [Job 34:8].

Job has joined the protesters outside of heaven. He is in company with the workers of iniquity and walks with wicked men. It is as if he is marching up and down with a placard that reads: "God is wrong and I am right." A lot of folk are doing that. Job has joined with those who are in rebellion against God.

For he hath said, It profiteth a man nothing that he should delight himself with God [Job 34:9].

Job might as well have said, "I have been serving God and being a nice little boy, and I expected to have a Sunday school pin. At Christmas I expected God to put a nice gift in my stocking. Instead, God put ashes in my stocking, and I don't think that God has been very nice to me in doing that." That was the attitude of Job, and it is the attitude of a lot of Christians today.

Therefore hearken unto me, ye men of understanding: far be it from God, that he should do wickedness; and from the Almighty, that he should commit iniquity [Job 34:10].

Again he is saying that *God* does not do *wrong*. Remember that Paul asked, "Is there unrighteousness with God? God forbid" (Rom. 9:14). My friend, it may sound ugly to say this, but if you say that God is wrong, then *you* are wrong. God is always right and you and I are the ones who are always wrong. No matter what God does, He is right. He doesn't have to report to you or me. He doesn't need to ask our permission to do something.

It is interesting today to find people who are willing to let criminals have their freedom to live as they choose, but they don't want God to have the freedom to run the universe the way He chooses. My friend, He will run it right, and He is not bound by your standards or my standards.

Yea, surely God will not do wickedly, neither will the Almighty pervert judgment [Job 34:12].

Now that is something you can write down in your little book and keep it there. God does not do wickedly. He will not permit a wrong act. If you want to go back in the Old Testament and find fault with God for getting rid of the Amorites, that is your privilege. But that doesn't make God wrong. He was right. Maybe you say, "I just don't see it." Well, maybe I don't either. But I know that God extended His grace to them for four hundred years and gave them time to repent, and only after that period of time did He wipe them out. God is always right. Reason from *that* point.

You see, our whole system of human thinking is based on reasoning from experience to the truth, and that is the reason so few of us ever arrive at truth. God reasons from truth, and He *is* the truth. The Lord Jesus said, ". . . I am . . . the truth"(John 14:6). When Pilate asked, ". . . What is truth? . . ." (John 18:38). *Truth* was standing right before him. Jesus is the Truth. We need to learn to reason from the truth to experience, which is what God does.

Who hath given him a charge over the earth? or who hath disposed the whole world?

If he set his heart upon man, if he gather unto himself his spirit and his breath [Job 34:13–14].

The point is that God has a care, God has a concern for man.

Surely it is meet to be said unto God, I have borne chastisement, I will not offend any more [Job 34:31].

If God has chastened you, then you ought to learn your lesson and not continue in your old way. Maybe God is attempting to develop something in your life. He won't let anything happen to you unless it accomplishes a worthy purpose.

That which I see not teach thou me: if I have done iniquity, I will do no more [Job 34:32].

If you have done iniquity, and you know the purpose of God's chastening is to get you away from sin, then for goodness' sake, learn the lesson and turn from the sin.

Let men of understanding tell me, and let a wise man hearken unto me.

Job hath spoken without knowledge, and his words were without wisdom [Job 34:34–35].

What is said of Job could be said of most of us. We do a lot of talking, but a great deal of it is "without knowledge" and "without wisdom." We are living in a day when we have what is known as rap sessions. I meet with a lot of groups, especially young people, who want to have a rap session. I welcome the opportunity, but I hear a lot of asinine and foolish things said. It wasn't only Job who spoke without knowledge. A lot of folk today speak without knowledge and some of them have a Ph.D. degree. A degree is no guarantee of knowledge or wisdom.

My desire is that Job may be tried unto the end because of his answers for wicked men.

For he addeth rebellion unto his sin, he clappeth his hands among us, and multiplieth his words against God [Job 34: 36–37].

What Elihu is saying is that he hopes God will try Job until Job will be able to defend *God* instead of defending himself.

GOD IS TEACHING JOB A LESSON

Elihu spake moreover, and said,

Thinkest thou this to be right, that thou saidst, My righteousness is more than God's? [Job 35:1–2].

The minute Job says that he is right and that he is suffering in spite of being right, God must be wrong. That is the inference one must draw from that type of reasoning.

Look unto the heavens, and see; and behold the clouds which are higher than thou.

If thou sinnest, what doest thou against him? or if thy transgressions be multiplied, what doest thou unto him? [Job 35:5–6].

This is the question that Job was raising. He was saying, "My little life is not affecting God." The wonder of it all is that it does affect Him. A sin is something that is almost infinite. Abraham sinned in the case of that little handmaid Hagar, and the world is still paying for that sin in the conflicts of the Middle East. He took the Egyptian at the suggestion of Sarah, but Abraham and Sarah were wrong. How wrong were they? The results of their wrong have gone on for four thousand years. Sin is an awful thing, and it does affect God.

Thy wickedness may hurt a man as thou art; and thy righteousness may profit the son of man [Job 35:8].

You are always a witness, my friend. You are a *preacher*, regardless of who you are. The mother of a drunken man asked me to talk to her son. Once when he went wobbling down the street, I detoured him into my study. I told him what a low-down, dirty ingrate he was and how he disgraced his mother, breaking her heart. He just sat there and took all of it. Then I said, "You preach by your life. You are a preacher." He stood up to fight me. I could call him anything in the world except a preacher. Well, my friend, you are a preacher! Your wickedness will hurt somebody, and your righteousness may help somebody.

By reason of the multitude of oppressions they make the oppressed to cry: they cry out by reason of the arm of the mighty.

But none saith, Where is God my maker, who giveth songs in the night [Job 35:9–10].

That is so wonderful! It is God who gives songs in the night. The only place of happiness is with God. Have you ever noticed the expression, "Blessed be the God and Father of our Lord Jesus Christ . . ." (Eph. 1:3)? What does that word *blessed* mean? It means "happiness." God is happy and He wants us happy. When Moses came down from the mountain, his face was shining because there was now forgiveness. There was now sacrifice for sin, and God would deal with man in grace.

John writes, "And these things write we unto you, that your *joy* may be full" (1 John 1:4). He is the One who gives songs in the night. The night clubs have songs. They are the blues and you *pay* for them and you have a headache the next morning. It is God alone who can bring happiness to you. That is so important. And Elihu had learned that way back there in the patriarchal period.

After we finish the discourse of Elihu, we will find that God will break through to Job. A storm will come up and break over Job, and out of that storm God will speak to him. It is through the storms of life that God wants to speak peace to you and me. Oh, let us not let circumstances come between our souls and our God!

GOD IS THE GREAT TEACHER

Elihu also proceeded, and said,

Suffer me a little, and I will shew thee that I have yet to speak on God's behalf [Job 36:1–2].

Elihu is defending God. He has—as all of us have—a limited knowledge of God. We are dealing with an infinite God, and we don't have all the answers.

That is the difficulty for a great many people today. A man said to me, "I can't believe." I asked, "What is it that you can't believe? Do you believe that Jesus died on the cross and that He rose again?" Yes, he believed that. "Well," I said, "then why can't you trust Him?" "There is so much else—creation, Jonah, Noah, and the miracles." Also he had all kinds of personal problems. Then he challenged me, "You made the statement that we are unbelievers because of our sin, but I *want* to be a believer." May I say that he is committing the real sin, and it is this: he is letting what he *doesn't* know disturb him from what he *does* know. My friend, if you know enough to trust Christ, these other things will adjust themselves.

Let me illustrate. As I write, I am sitting in a chair. Now there is a great deal about this chair that I do not know. To begin with, I don't know who made it. I don't even know the company that made it. I don't know much about the materials in the chair—what kind of wood it is, what kind of covering it has. I really know very little about this chair. But, friend, I know enough to sit down in it and trust myself to it.

Do you know that Christ died for you? Do you know He rose again? All right, then *trust* Him as your Savior. These other doubts will take care of themselves in time, I can assure you. If it were necessary for me to know more about this chair, I think I could find out. But all I need to know is just enough to sit in it. I know very little about an airplane, and I am even fearful when I get on one, but I walk aboard, sit down, and trust myself to it. That is all God asks us to do when we trust Christ. Too many of us let what we don't know disturb what we do know.

Now Elihu is quite limited in knowledge, as we shall see.

I will fetch my knowledge from afar, and will ascribe righteousness to my Maker [Job 36:3].

Paul said the same thing years later. He asked, ". . . Is there unrighteousness with God?" His answer was, "God forbid" (Rom. 9:14). God is righteous in all that He is and does.

Although Elihu is ascribing righteousness to God, he is also making it clear that God is so far removed from man that, actually, man cannot know Him. There is an element of truth in that, by the way. But what is it today that is separating us from God? Notice what Elihu is saying.

For truly my words shall not be false: he that is perfect in knowledge is with thee [Job 36:4].

That is, only God has perfect knowledge.

Behold, God is mighty, and despiseth not any: he is mighty in strength and wisdom.

He preserveth not the life of the wicked: but giveth right to the poor.

He withdraweth not his eyes from the righteous: but with kings are they on the throne; yea, he doth establish them for ever, and they are exalted [Job 36: 5–7].

The whole sense of what he is saying is simply that God is far removed from us. He is separated from us, and we cannot communicate with Him because He is so far from us. Elihu is *wrong* in that. And many folk today are wrong in that concept.

Listen to the words of Isaiah concerning that which separates man from God. It is not because of distance. It is not because God is great and we are small. It is not because He is infinite and we are finite. "But your iniquities have separated between you and your God, and your sins have hid his face from you, that he will not hear" (Isa. 59:2). He continues to describe their situation: "For your hands are defiled with blood, and your fingers with iniquity; your lips have spoken lies, your tongue hath muttered perverseness. None calleth for justice, nor any pleadeth for truth: they trust in vanity, and speak lies; they conceive mischief, and bring forth iniquity" (Isa. 59:3–4). God says these are the things that separate man from God.

Today there is no reason for you and me to be separated from God. The sin question has been settled forever. There is one Mediator between God and man, the man Christ Jesus, and today we can come to God through Him. The great cry of Job was for someone to make a connection for him with God. Elihu came nearer to this than anyone else, but he didn't make it. That is the reason God finally broke in on Job.

Then Elihu states that God is the great Teacher.

Behold, God exalteth by his power; who teacheth like him?

Who hath enjoined him his way? or who can say, Thou hast wrought iniquity? [Job 36:22–23].

Elihu felt that he couldn't communicate with Him, but he does say this: "No one can teach like God." As you know, this was the thing that marked out the Lord Jesus Christ when He came to this earth. He was the greatest Teacher of all. Even His enemies said, ". . . Never man spake like this man" (John 7:46). The teaching of the Lord Jesus is the greatest teaching that the world has ever known right down to this present hour.

It is a strange thing that people today who reject the Lord Jesus Christ still try to use His teachings. They talk about loving your neighbor. They talk about mercy. They talk about the Sermon on the Mount. You don't hear them trying to foster the teachings of Plato or Aristotle even though they were smart boys. No, the Lord Jesus still stands as the greatest Teacher. Elihu asked, "Who teacheth like Him?"

ELIHU CONCLUDES

Chapter 37 concludes what Elihu has to say. I am going to lift out only three verses from this final chapter:

Fair weather cometh out of the north: with God is terrible majesty.

Touching the Almighty, we cannot find him out: he is excellent in power, and in judgment, and in plenty of justice: he will not afflict.

Men do therefore fear him: he respecteth not any that are wise of heart [Job 37:22–24].

Again, he is inferring that God is so far removed from man that we just cannot communicate with Him. He is way up yonder, and we are way down here. However, we have already seen that it is not the greatness and majesty of God that has separated man from Him; it is man's sin.

This chapter clearly shows us that Elihu cannot be a prophet or a mediator for Job. That is one of the reasons that I have never specialized in counseling. If you want to know the truth, I don't know enough to be a counselor. I feel that a man who is going to pose as a counselor is sitting in the place of God. The friends of Job tried to be his counselors. They were trying to take the place of God in this man's life. Their problem was that their own knowledge was not adequate. We need to recognize counseling for what it is. It arises out of the experience and wisdom of another human being. The great breakdown in counseling is that no one is all-knowing, no one is omniscient. No counselor can know all the facts or have all the wisdom that is necessary.

As you know by now, I have cancer and it is necessary for me to have a good doctor. I wanted the very best, and I have a wonderful doctor. The thing I like about him is that he is not all-knowing or all-powerful. He isn't afraid to tell me, "I don't know." I like that. It makes him a human being. He does not put himself into the place of God. He is a fine Christian and is attempting to serve the Lord, so he doesn't try to usurp God's place.

Elihu really almost tried to move into God's place. He wanted to be a mediator for Job. But he breaks off here with the fact that he really doesn't know God as he should. He doesn't know how to approach God, and he is far removed from Him. That is why it is necessary for God to break through.

You will notice in verse 22 that he gives a little weather report. He says, "Fair weather cometh out of the north." Why do you suppose he said that? I think that during most of the discourse of Elihu a storm was forming over the horizon. It grew darker, and the storm began to advance. The wind was probably howling, and a few drops of rain were beginning to fall. It became a formidable storm, and the people were running for shelter. I think that after he finished his discourse, Elihu also took off and ran for shelter.

Job was left, alone.

CHAPTERS 38–42

***THEME:** Jehovah and Job*

We last saw Job left all alone. Now God breaks in on this man in his weakness. God meets him right at the point of his own inadequacy. God is so great!

JEHOVAH VS. JOB

The mark of a good teacher is that he begins where a student has left off. He will begin where the student is and will move up to where he wants to bring him. God is a teacher. He will teach Job here. The Lord Jesus Christ is also a teacher, the greatest teacher. He wants to teach us today.

Notice here as God teaches Job that He begins right where they left off—in nature. A storm is coming up, and God breaks in as the Creator. He begins there, and He will bring this man to where He wants to bring him.

The Lord Jesus also taught that way. I don't think the parables of the Lord Jesus were imagined. He would just stop and observe the lives of the people of that day, and that would be His parable. He would meet them where they were. For example, ". . . Behold, a sower went forth to sow" (see Matt. 13:3–9). There were little hills all through Palestine and, wherever He walked, He would see the sowers sowing the grain. Or, ". . . The kingdom of heaven is like unto leaven, which a woman took, and hid in three measures of meal . . ." (Matt. 13:33). That was a common experience, and Jesus had watched women do that over and over again. The Lord Jesus began his teaching where the people were, and then He brought them to where He wanted them to be.

We find this teaching principle all through the Word of God, which is the greatest teaching available to man. It begins where we are and teaches and brings us to where God wants us to be.

I tried to use this principle in my conference preaching. Whenever I came to a different city, I would buy the paper for a few days before the conference. Then I would begin speaking at the conference with some reference to a local situation—the race for mayor, some famous person visiting there, or some kind of scandal in that city. I would try to start with a casual remark about it, probably something humorous. Why? Because that is where the people lived.

So we find God breaking in right where Job is. I want to confess as we come to this part of the book that if I felt totally inadequate up to this point, now I don't even know what to say. I feel like just simply being quiet, closing my Bible and stopping. But we cannot do that, so we will simply read what God says, and I will make a few comments as we go along.

JEHOVAH SPEAKS TO JOB

Then the LORD answered Job out of the whirlwind, and said [Job 38:1].

God answers Job out of the whirlwind, out of that storm that has now broken upon Job. God is speaking to him as the Creator.

Who is this that darkeneth counsel by words without knowledge? [Job 38:2].

We will find that Job will finally be willing to say that he has uttered words without knowledge. That, my friend, is an awful sin. I think we have a lot of it today. Those talk programs on television not only commit this sin but most of them are the most asinine things imaginable. They accomplish nothing at all, but they make for entertainment and are prepared by some light-headed folk. God says, "Who is this that darkeneth counsel by words without knowledge?"

One man said he liked the dictionary because the stories in it were so short. Well, there are a great many people who pull a few words out of the dictionary and attempt to put them together. Whether they make sense or not doesn't seem to be the point as long as they are using big words.

Gird up now thy loins like a man; for I will demand of thee, and answer thou me.

Where wast thou when I laid the foundations of the earth? declare, if thou hast understanding [Job 38:3–4].

This is the verse that I have always wanted to put in the front of every book on geology, but they won't let me do it. It makes no difference whether the book was written by a Christian or a non-Christian; I think it should be put in the book. "Where wast thou when I laid the foundations of the earth? declare, if thou hast understanding." By the way, where were you? That is a good question.

What is it that holds this universe in space? And it is not standing still. You and I are on a little earth that is as unstable in itself as anything can be. There is nothing under it to hold it up. I don't even know which is under —what is down or up—as far as the universe is concerned. Why doesn't it start going in some direction? Why does it just go around and around? What keeps it going around and around? Apparently it has been doing this for millions of years. The question is, "Where wast thou when I laid the foundations of the earth?"

A geologist once took me up to a ridge in northern Arizona—I thought it was a ridge, but it was just sand. I couldn't understand why sand was piled up there. He kicked away the sand and under it was a petrified log. I asked, "My, where did this come from?" He said, "California." I said, "Who hauled it in here?" He answered, "It floated in here." Now if you look at that Arizona desert, it is hard to imagine that there was ever any water that could have floated that log. But, apparently that is what has happened. That log had floated in from California.

I asked, "When did that happen?" He said, "Well, about 250,000 years ago." And he said it like he had been there when the log arrived. Now it may be that he was right. I am not contradicting him and saying that he was wrong. I am saying that there are a lot of folk today who seem to know what took place millions and millions of years ago. God asks, "Where wast thou when I laid the foundations of the earth? declare, if thou hast understanding."

Who hath laid the measures thereof, if thou knowest? or who hath stretched the line upon it?

Whereupon are the foundations thereof fastened? or who laid the corner stone thereof [Job 38:5–6].

The Book of Job apparently comes from the period before any word of Scripture was written. God begins with Job at the point where He began with all men at that particular time —at the point of creation. Paul began at this same point when he talked about the revelation of God to all mankind. "For the wrath of God is revealed from heaven against all ungodliness and unrighteousness of men, who hold the truth in unrighteousness; Because that which may be known of God is manifest in them; for God hath shewed it unto them. For the invisible things of him from the creation of the world are clearly seen, being understood by the things that are made, even his eternal power and Godhead; so that they are without excuse" (Rom. 1:18–20).

It is all important for us to see that God was speaking to Job and to all men in that day through His creation. They were close enough to creation that there was no atheism. Instead, there was polytheism. They actually worshiped the creature rather than the Creator. This is what Paul went on to speak of in the first chapter of Romans (Rom. 1:21–23).

I am not going to attempt to develop this section here. It has to do with creation. It has to do with this physical universe that you and I live in today. And, as Paul says in Romans, creation speaks of God: the person of God, the power of God, and the wisdom of God. Creation reveals the greatness of our God. How great Thou art! This is the impression we are bound to get, as God speaks of the fact that He is the Creator and He knows much that man does not know.

When the morning stars sang together, and all the sons of God shouted for joy? [Job 38:7].

Actually, man is a "Johnny-come-lately" in God's universe. There was a joy in creation even before man was created.

My friend, if you are His son, you are going to have joy in your life. God wants you to have joy. "Blessed be the God and Father of our Lord Jesus Christ . . ." (Eph. 1:3). Blessed! The word is *happy*. God is happy. He's joyful and He wants us to be joyful. I hope that the joy of the Lord is your portion today. He wants it to be.

There are a couple of interesting verses here:

Hast thou entered into the treasures of the snow? or hast thou seen the treasures of the hail,

Which I have reserved against the time of trouble, against the day of battle and war? [Job 38:22–23].

Some fantastic interpretations have been drawn from these verses of how snow and hail will be used in warfare, but I am not about to get out on a limb with this. I do know that snow is what defeated Napoleon. Revelation 8:7 tells us that God will use hail in one of the judgments of the earth. But here God is simply making the point to Job that His creation is beyond the understanding of man. Only God can know these things.

He goes on to talk about the starry heavens:

Canst thou bind the sweet influences of Pleiades, or loose the bands of Orion?

Canst thou bring forth Mazzaroth in his season? or canst thou guide Arcturus with his sons?

Knowest thou the ordinances of heaven? canst thou set the dominion thereof in the earth? [Job 38:31–33].

What do we know about those tremendous stars out yonder in the heavens? I do not know how much the ancients knew about them, but apparently they knew a great deal more than we give them credit for knowing. It is my understanding that the Egyptians were able to accurately measure the distance to the sun. Therefore they must have had considerable knowledge.

Have you known God through His creation? Can you really know God through creation? I think God is making it very clear to Job that the creation reveals His greatness. One can know about God through His creation, but creation will not bring a man to a saving knowledge of God.

Chapter 38 has shown God in His past creation. Chapter 39 will reveal God in nature—God as the sustainer of His creation. This is His revelation through His creation right at the present.

Knowest thou the time when the wild goats of the rock bring forth? or canst thou mark when the hinds do calve? [Job 39:1].

God is the God of nature. Things happen in nature today because God makes them happen. Without God, nature would be dead; nothing would happen. There would be no spring, no summer, no fall, no winter, no storms, no movement in this universe. It would all come to a dead standstill if there were no Creator and Sustainer behind it. Think that one through. That is the point that God is making to this man Job. He is revealing His greatness.

Moreover the Lord answered Job, and said,

Shall he that contendeth with the Almighty instruct him? he that reproveth God, let him answer it [Job 40:1–2].

"Job, are you in a position to give God a lesson? Actually, Job, you have been speaking without knowledge." Job has been attempting to instruct God. He has been attempting to tell God something, and he is in no position to do that because he has been uttering words without knowledge. Now God wants an answer from Job.

Then Job answered the Lord, and said,

Behold, I am vile; what shall I answer thee? I will lay mine hand upon my mouth.

Once have I spoken; but I will not answer: yea, twice; but I will proceed no further [Job 40:3–5].

Job says, "I should have kept quiet. Now I see I am vile." Is this the man who said that he would maintain his integrity regardless of what happened? Is this the man who declared that he was a righteous man and that therefore there must be something wrong with God to let this happen to him? This same man is now saying that he is vile.

As someone has said, if we could see ourselves as God sees us, we couldn't stand ourselves. When we get into the presence of God, we will acknowledge that we are vile.

This appearance of God to Job had a threefold effect upon him. It had an effect upon his relationship to God, his relationship to himself, and his relationship to his friends. This is the man who has spoken without knowledge. His words were without wisdom. Now he wishes that he had kept his mouth shut. He becomes suddenly silent. He lays his hand over his mouth.

Then answered the LORD unto Job out of the whirlwind, and said,

Gird up thy loins now like a man: I will demand of thee, and declare thou unto me.

Wilt thou also disannul my judgment? wilt thou condemn me, that thou mayest be righteous? [Job 40:6–8].

The storm breaks in all of its fury, and God speaks out of the whirlwind. He continues His appeal to Job. God is asking Job, "Are you trying to say to Me that I am wrong?" Of course, God is not wrong. Eventually Job is going to be able to say to God, "I know that thou canst do every thing, and that no thought can be withholden from thee" (Job 42:2). Job is going to come a long way.

Actually, Job is already advancing. He had not known himself but has now come to the point where he has discovered that he is vile. When a man discovers that, he has come a long way. This is the first step Job takes as he comes to God.

The Lord again appeals to Job on the basis of His creation. "Job, look around. There are a lot of things that you don't know. How can you judge Me and My moral government of this universe?"

Many folk today come up with some asinine statements concerning God. I have heard Christians say some very foolish things about the Lord. Friend, we ought to be very careful what we say about Him. We should keep our words in the context of the Word of God.

It is quite obvious that Job actually did not know God. He has uttered words without knowledge. And when the Lord breaks in upon him, He asks him some more questions.

Canst thou draw out leviathan with an hook? or his tongue with a cord which thou lettest down?

Canst thou put an hook into his nose? or bore his jaw through with a thorn? [Job 41:1–2].

"Job, what do you really know about this great monster of the sea?" Today they are making a study of the great whales off the coast of California. They are doing many things, trying to find out about them. We've come a long way since the days of Job, and we still don't know all about those big fellows that are in the water.

What do we know about dinosaurs? I have heard this whimsy about the guide in the museum who gave a lecture to the crowd. When they came to the dinosaur he said, "This dinosaur is two million and six years old." A man came up to him and said, "Wait a minute. I'll accept the two million years, but where do you get the six years?" The guide answered, "Well, when I came to work here, that dinosaur was two million years old. I've been here six years now. So the dinosaur is now two million and six years old."

I ask again: what do we really know about dinosaurs? You can ask any real scholar in any field and he will admit that he is no authority—he hasn't mastered his field. He will frankly say that he is just beginning to learn.

May I say to you that no man is in any position to pass judgment on God. That is what God told Job way back yonder at the dawn of history.

JOB REPENTS

Now notice the effect upon Job:

Then Job answered the LORD, and said,

I know that thou canst do every thing, and that no thought can be withholden from thee [Job 42:1–2].

Is that the kind of God you have? Can He do anything?

There is the old saw about God: "Can God make a rock so big that He can't lift it?" That is like the question to Mr. Milquetoast, "Are you still beating your wife?" You see, there is no answer because you are caught whether you answer it yes or no. The question about God has no answer because God never does anything foolish. He always does that which is in the context of His character. He is always true to Himself. So you cannot tell God to do something that He cannot do. Do you know why not? Because, my friend, you are in no position to do that. God is not your errand boy. God is not going to jump through any hoop just because you hold it up.

Who is he that hideth counsel without knowledge? therefore have I uttered that I understood not; things too wonderful for me, which I knew not [Job 42:3].

Job admits he has been talking about things he doesn't know anything about. That is the way it was with our bull sessions in the college dorm. We would finish studying at night and would meet in some room and say, "What are we going to talk about?" I used to say, "Let's talk about something we don't know anything about. Then the sky's the limit. We can say anything we want to say." This is what Job has been doing. He has been talking about things he knows nothing about. He talked about things too wonderful for him, which he knew not. He has been talking without knowledge.

Hear, I beseech thee, and I will speak: I will demand of thee, and declare thou unto me.

I have heard of thee by the hearing of the ear: but now mine eye seeth thee.

Wherefore I abhor myself, and repent in dust and ashes [Job 42:4–6].

Now this man Job has a new conception of God. He is not in a position to question God in anything that He does. He is to trust Him. He is in a new relationship.

First, Job saw himself as he really was, and he came into a new relationship with himself. He saw himself as vile; he abhorred himself. Now he sees himself in a new relationship to God. He repents in dust and ashes.

Here are the steps of real repentance. This is the repentance that is in faith. First, you must see yourself as vile. Secondly, you must abhor yourself. Perhaps you have seen birds feeding on carrion in the wilderness. When you quit trusting yourself and quit trying to live on the old dead carcass of self and you turn to the living God, that is real repentance. What a wonderful thing it is!

Job recognizes the sovereignty of God. He confesses his sin and repents. God has accomplished His purpose in the life of Job. Job evidently realizes that the reason God has permitted him to suffer is to bring him to repentance. He sees himself in the light of the presence of God. "If we say that we have fellowship with him, and walk in darkness, we lie, and do not the truth: But if we walk in the light, as he is in the light, we have fellowship one with another, and the blood of Jesus Christ his Son cleanseth us from all sin" (1 John 1:6–7).

EPILOGUE

Finally, we find that Job also comes to a new relationship with his friends.

And it was so, that after the LORD had spoken these words unto Job, the LORD said to Eliphaz the Temanite, My wrath is kindled against thee, and against thy two friends: for ye have not spoken of me the thing that is right, as my servant Job hath.

Therefore take unto you now seven bullocks and seven rams, and go to my servant Job, and offer up for yourselves a burnt offering; and my servant Job shall pray for you: for him will I accept: lest I deal with you after your folly, in that ye have not spoken of me the thing which is right, like my servant Job.

So Eliphaz the Temanite and Bildad the Shuhite and Zophar the Naamathite went, and did according as the LORD commanded them: the LORD also accepted Job [Job 42:7–9].

Instead of fighting against his friends or debating them, he is now going to pray for them. He is going to offer a sacrifice for them. We are not to argue religion today or to fight among ourselves. What is it that we are to do? Paul writes, "Brethren, if a man be overtaken in a fault, ye which are spiritual, restore such an one in the spirit of meekness . . ." (Gal. 6:1). Job has a new relationship with himself, with God, and with his friends. Now God does something for Job.

And the LORD turned the captivity of Job, when he prayed for his friends: also the LORD gave Job twice as much as he had before [Job 42:10].

Now, how did God give Job twice as much? He used human means.

Then came there unto him all his brethren, and all his sisters, and all they that had been of his acquaintance before, and did eat bread with him in his house: and they bemoaned him, and comforted him over all the evil that the LORD had brought upon him: every man also gave him a piece of money, and every one an earring of gold [Job 42:11].

This is the way he got started. These friends staked him to a new beginning and, believe me, Job was a good business man. God gave him twice as much as he had had at the very beginning.

So the LORD blessed the latter end of Job more than his beginning: for he had fourteen thousand sheep, and six thousand camels, and a thousand yoke of oxen, and a thousand she asses.

He had also seven sons and three daughters [Job 42:12–13].

All of the animals were doubled. But it says here, "He had also seven sons and daughters." Someone will say, "God didn't double them." Yes, He did. You see, Job did not lose those sons and daughters who died. They were still his. He was yet to be with them. He is with them today.

We do not lose our loved ones in death. I have a little one up there. I used to tell people that I have two daughters, and they would look around and see only one. They would think there was something wrong with me. But, you see, I have one in heaven. Very frankly, I am not at all worried about my little one in heaven. I worry about the one on earth.

And he called the name of the first, Jemima; and the name of the second, Kezia; and the name of the third, Kerenhappuch.

And in all the land were no women found so fair as the daughters of Job: and their father gave them inheritance among their brethren [Job 42:14–15].

Now, friend, if you have quite a few daughters in your family and you are trying to think of a new name, I have a suggestion for you. Jemima would not be so good to use because there is a pancake mix sold in the United States called "Aunt Jemima." But how about Kerenhappuch? Wouldn't you like that for a name for a little girl? Or do you like Kezia?

After this lived Job an hundred and forty years, and saw his sons, and his sons' sons, even four generations.

So Job died, being old and full of days [Job 42:16-17].

We are told that after this Job lived 140 years. This puts him back in the age of the patriarchs. Even after all this had happened to him, he lived to see his sons and his sons' sons, even four generations. When he died, he was old and full of days.

BIBLIOGRAPHY

(Recommended for Further Study)

Archer, Gleason L. *The Book of Job*. Grand Rapids, Michigan: Baker Book House, 1982.

Blair, J. Allen. *Job: Living Patiently*. Reprint. Neptune, New Jersey: Loizeaux Brothers, 1966.

Darby J.N. *Synopsis of the Books of the Bible*. Addison, Illinois: Bible Truth Publishers, n.d.

Ellison, H. L. *A Study of Job: From Tragedy to Triumph*. Grand Rapids, Michigan: Zondervan Publishing House, n.d.

Epp, Theodore H. *Job—A Man Tried as Gold*. Lincoln, Nebraska: Back to the Bible Broadcast, n.d.

Gaebelein, Arno C. *The Annotated Bible*. 1917. Reprint. Neptune, New Jersey: Loizeaux Brothers, 1971.

Garland, D. David. *Job—A Study Guide Commentary*. Grand Rapids, Michigan: Zondervan Publishing House, 1971.

Gray, James M. *Synthetic Bible Studies*. Westwood, New Jersey: Fleming H. Revell Co., 1906.

Jensen, Irving L. *Job—A Self Study Guide*. Chicago, Illinois: Moody Press, 1975.

Mackintosh, C. H. *Miscellaneous Writings*. Reprint. Neptune, New Jersey: Loizeaux Brothers, 1976.

Ridout, Samuel. *The Book of Job*. Neptune, New Jersey: Loizeaux Brothers, 1919. (Very fine.)

Sauer, Erich. *The Dawn of World Redemption*. Grand Rapids, Michigan: Wm. B. Eerdmans Publishing Co., 1951. (An excellent Old Testament survey.)

Scroggie, W. Graham. *The Unfolding Drama of Redemption*. Grand Rapids, Michigan: Zondervan Publishing House, 1970. (An excellent survey and outline of the Old Testament.)

Unger, Merrill F. *Unger's Bible Handbook*. Chicago, Illinois: Moody Press, 1966. (A concise commentary on the entire Bible.)

Unger, Merrill F. *Unger's Commentary on the Old Testament*. Vol. 1. Chicago, Illinois: Moody Press, 1981. (A fine summary of each paragraph. Highly recommended.)

Zuck, Roy B. *Job*. Chicago, Illinois: Moody Press, 1978. (A fine summary—see the *Everyman's Bible Commentary* series.)

The Book of PSALMS

INTRODUCTION

The title in the Hebrew means *Praises* or *Book of Praises*. The title in the Greek suggests the idea of an instrumental accompaniment. Our title comes from the Greek *psalmos*. It is the book of worship. It is the hymn book of the temple.

Many writers contributed one or more psalms. David, "the sweet psalmist of Israel," has seventy-three psalms assigned to him. (Psalm 2 is ascribed to him in Acts 4:25; Psalm 95 is ascribed to him in Hebrews 4:7.) Also he could be the author of some of the "Orphanic" psalms. He was peculiarly endowed to write these songs from experience as well as a special aptitude. He arranged those in existence in his day for temple use. The other writers are as follows: Moses, 1 (90th); Solomon, 2; Sons of Korah, 11; Asaph, 12; Heman, 1 (88th); Ethan, 1 (89th); Hezekiah, 10; "Orphanic," 39 (David may be the writer of some of these). There are 150 psalms.

Christ (the Messiah) is prominent throughout. The King and the kingdom are the theme songs of the Psalms.

The key word in the Book of Psalms is *Hallelujah*, that is, *Praise the Lord*. This phrase has become a Christian cliché, but it is one that should cause a swelling of great emotion in the soul. Hallelujah, praise the Lord!

Psalms 50 and 150 I consider to be the key psalms. Psalm 50, a psalm of Asaph, probably tells more than any other. Psalm 150 is the hallelujah chorus—the word *hallelujah* occurs thirteen times in its six brief verses. It concludes the Book of Psalms and could be considered the chorus of all other psalms.

The Psalms record deep devotion, intense feeling, exalted emotion, and dark dejection. They play upon the keyboard of the human soul with all the stops pulled out. Very candidly, I feel overwhelmed when I come to this marvelous book. It is located in the very center of God's Word. Psalm 119 is in the very center of the Word of God, and it exalts His Word.

This book has blessed the hearts of multitudes down through the ages. When I have been sick at home, or in the hospital, or when some problem is pressing upon my mind and heart, I find myself always turning to the Psalms. They always bless my heart and life. Apparently down through the ages it has been that way. Ambrose, one of the great saints of the church, said, "The Psalms are the voices of the church." Augustine said, "They are the epitome of the whole Scripture." Martin Luther said, "They are a little book for all saints." John Calvin said, "They are the anatomy of all parts of the soul." I like that.

Someone has said that there are 126 psychological experiences—I don't know how they arrived at that number—but I do know that all of them are recorded in the Book of Psalms. It is the *only* book which contains every experience of a human being. The Psalms run the psychological gamut. Every thought, every impulse, every emotion that sweeps over the soul is recorded in this book. That is the reason, I suppose, that it always speaks to our hearts and finds a responsive chord wherever we turn.

Hooker said of the Psalms, "They are the choice and flower of all things profitable in other books." Donne put it this way, "The Psalms foretell what I, what any, shall do and suffer and say." Herd called the Psalms, "A hymn book for all time." Watts said, "They are the thousand-voiced heart of the church." The place Psalms have held in the lives of God's people testifies to their universality, although they have a peculiar Jewish application. They express the deep feelings of all believing hearts in all generations.

The Psalms are full of Christ. There is a more complete picture of Him in the Psalms than in the Gospels. The Gospels tell us that He went to the mountain to pray, but the Psalms give us His prayer. The Gospels tell us that He was crucified, but the Psalms tell us what went on in His own heart during the Crucifixion. The Gospels tell us He went back to heaven, but the Psalms begin where the Gospels leave off and show us Christ seated in heaven.

Christ the Messiah is prominent throughout this book. You will remember that the Lord Jesus, when He appeared after His resurrection to those who were His own, said to them, ". . . These are the words which I spake unto you, while I was yet with you, that all things must be fulfilled, which were written in the law of Moses, and in the prophets, and in the psalms, concerning me" (Luke 24:44). Christ is the subject of the Psalms. I think He is the object of praise in every one of them. I will not be able to locate Him in all of them, but that does not mean that He is not in each psalm; it only means that Vernon McGee is limited. Although all of them have Christ as the object of worship, some are technically called messianic psalms. These record the birth, life, death, resurrection, glory, priesthood, kingship, and return of Christ. There are sixteen messianic psalms that speak specifically about Christ, but as I have already said, all 150 of them are about Him. The book of Psalms is a hymn book and a HIM book—it is all about Him. As we study it, that fact will become very clear.

In a more restrictive sense, the Psalms deal with Christ belonging to Israel and Israel belonging to Christ. Both themes are connected to the rebellion of man. There is no blessing on this earth until Israel and Christ are brought together. The Psalms are Jewish in expectation and hope. They are songs which were adapted to temple worship. That does not mean, however, that they do not have a spiritual application and interpretation for us today. They certainly do. I probably turn to them more than to any other portion of the Word of God, but we need to be a little more exacting in our interpretation of the Psalms. For example, God is not spoken of as a Father in this book. The saints are not called sons. In the Psalms He is God the Father, not the Father God. The abiding presence of the Holy Spirit and the blessed hope of the New Testament are not in this book. Failure to recognize this has led many people astray in their interpretation of Psalm 2. The reference in this song is not to the rapture of the church but to the second coming of Christ to the earth to establish His kingdom and to reign in Jerusalem.

The imprecatory psalms have caused the most criticism because of their vindictiveness and prayers for judgment. These psalms came from a time of war and from a people who under law were looking for justice and peace on earth. My friend, you cannot have peace without putting down unrighteousness and rebellion. Apparently God intends to do just that, and He makes no apology for it. In His own time He will move in judgment upon this earth. In the New Testament the Christian is told to love his enemies, and it may startle you to read prayers in the Psalms that say some very harsh things about the enemy. But judgment is to bring justice upon this earth. Also there are psalms that anticipate the period when Antichrist will be in power. We have no reasonable basis to dictate how people should act or what they should pray under such circumstances.

Other types of psalms include the penitential, historic, nature, pilgrim, Hallel, missionary, puritan, acrostic, and praise of God's Word. This is a rich section we are coming to. We are going to mine for gold and diamonds here, my friend.

The Book of Psalms is not arranged in a haphazard sort of way. Some folk seem to think that the Psalms were dropped into a tub, shaken up, then put together with no arrangement. However, it is interesting to note that one psalm will state a principle, then there will follow several psalms that will be explanatory. Psalms 1–8 are an example of this.

The Book of Psalms is arranged in an orderly manner. In fact, it has been noted for years that the Book of Psalms is arranged and corresponds to the Pentateuch of Moses. There are Genesis, Exodus, Leviticus, Numbers, and Deuteronomy sections, as you will see in the outline which follows.

The correspondence between the Psalms and the Pentateuch is easily seen. For instance, in the Genesis section you see the perfect man in a state of blessedness, as in Psalm 1. Next you have the fall and recovery of man in view. Psalm 2 pictures the rebellious man. In Psalm 3 is the perfect man rejected. In Psalm 4 we see the conflict between the seed of the woman and the serpent. In Psalm 5 we find the perfect man in the midst of enemies. Psalm 6 presents the perfect man in the midst of chastisement with the bruising of his heel. In Psalm 7 we see the perfect man in the midst of false witnesses. Finally, in Psalm 8 we see the salvation of man coming through the bruising of the head. In Psalms 9–15 we see the enemy and Antichrist conflict and the final deliverance. Then in Psalms 16–41 we see Christ in the midst of His people sanctifying them to God. All of this will be seen as we go through the Book of Psalms.

Spurgeon said, "The Book of Psalms instructs us in the use of wings as well as words. It sets us both mounting and singing." This is the book that may make a skylark out of you instead of some other kind of a bird. This book has been called the epitome and anatomy of the soul. It has also been designated as the garden of the Scriptures. Out of 219 quotations of the Old Testament in the New Testament, 116 of them are from the Psalms. You will see 150 spiritual songs which undoubtedly at one time were all set to music. This is a book which ought to make our hearts sing.

OUTLINE

I. Genesis Section, Psalms 1–41
Man seen in a state of blessedness, fall, and recovery (Man in View)
A. Perfect Man (Last Adam), Psalm 1
B. Rebellious Man, Psalm 2
C. Perfect Man Rejected, Psalm 3
D. Conflict between Seed of Woman and Serpent, Psalm 4
E. Perfect Man in Midst of Enemies, Psalm 5
F. Perfect Man in Midst of Chastisement (Bruising Heel), Psalm 6
G. Perfect Man in Midst of False Witnesses, Psalm 7
H. Repair of Man Comes through Man (Bruising Head), Psalm 8
I. Enemy and Antichrist Conflict; Final Deliverance, Psalms 9–15
J. Christ in Midst of His People Sanctifying Them to God, Psalms 16–41

II. Exodus Section, Psalms 42–72
Ruin and Redemption (Israel in View)
A. Israel's Ruin, Psalms 42–49
B. Israel's Redeemer, Psalms 50–60
C. Israel's Redemption, Psalms 61–72

III. Leviticus Section, Psalms 73–89
Darkness and dawn (Sanctuary in View)
Tabernacle, temple, house, assembly and congregation in almost every psalm.

IV. Numbers Section, Psalms 90–106
Peril and protection (Earth in View)

V. Deuteronomy Section, Psalms 107–150
Perfection and praise of the Word of God

PSALM 1

THEME: *Two men, two ways, two destinies*

This is the psalm which opens the Genesis section. It begins with man instead of the material universe. This psalm talks about the blessed man, or the happy man. The blessed man is contrasted to the ungodly. It is also a picture of Christ, the last Adam, in the midst of ungodly sinners and the scornful. We sometimes think of the Lord as a man of sorrows and acquainted with grief, and for some strange reason many of the pictures that have been painted of Him reveal Him as a very sad-looking individual. It is true that Isaiah says He is a Man of Sorrows, but why don't you read on? In Isaiah you will find that Christ did not have any sorrows and griefs of His own. Isaiah 53:4 says, "Surely he hath borne our griefs, and carried our sorrows: yet we did esteem him stricken, smitten of God, and afflicted." It was *our* griefs, not His own, that He was carrying. He was the happy Christ. This is a picture of Him.

PRACTICE OF THE BLESSED MAN

Blessed is the man that walketh not in the counsel of the ungodly, nor standeth in the way of sinners, nor sitteth in the seat of the scornful [Ps. 1:1].

This verse states the *practice* of the blessed man. A little bit further in this psalm we will see the *power* of the blessed man, and finally his *permanency*. In this first verse we see the negative side of the practice of the blessed man. We are told what the happy man does *not* do. Here we see three positions or postures. Blessed is the man, or happy is the man, who does not walk in the counsel of the ungodly, nor stand in the way of sinners, nor sit in the seat of the scornful. The person who does these things is not a happy person. He goes through three stages. First he associates with the ungodly, then he gets in with sinners, and finally he joins in with the scornful.

There is definitely regression, deterioration, and degeneration here. The blessed man does not walk in the counsel of the ungodly. *Counsel* means "advice." He does not listen to the ungodly. Have you ever noticed that even the Lord Jesus never referred to His own reason or His own mind as the basis for a decision? Whatever He did was based on the will of God. He never said to His disciples, "Fellows, we are going into Galilee again. I have been thinking this over, and I am smarter than you fellows, and I think this is the best thing to do according to my point of view." That is not the way He approached His disciples. He always said, "I am going to Jerusalem because it is the will of my Father." He spent time with His Father and knew what His will was and moved into certain areas on that basis.

My friend, it is one thing to listen to counsel, and good counsel is fine, but certainly not the counsel of the ungodly. We are to walk by faith. Listening to the counsel of the ungodly is not walking by faith. Who are the ungodly? They are the people who just leave God out. There is no fear of God before their eyes. They live as though God does not exist. Around us today are multitudes of people like this. They get up in the morning, never turn to God in prayer, never thank Him for the food they eat or for life or health. They just keep moving right along, living it up. They are ungodly—they just leave God out.

The ungodly counsels the man, and now we find him standing in the way of sinners. It is the sinner who takes him from there. Sin means to "miss the mark." They don't quite live as they should. They are the ones the Scripture speaks of when it says, "There is a way which seemeth right unto a man, but the end thereof are the ways of death" (Prov. 14:12). Again the Scriptures say, "All the ways of a man are clean in his own eyes . . ." (Prov. 16:2). The sinner may think he is all right, but he is a *sinner*. God's Word says, "Let the wicked forsake his way, and the unrighteous man his thoughts. . ." (Isa. 55:7). Also it says, "All we like sheep have gone astray; we have turned every one to his own way; and the LORD hath laid on him the iniquity of us all" (Isa. 53:6). The Father laid on the Lord Jesus all the weight of our guilt. We are sinners. That's our picture.

The next step down from standing in the way of sinners is sitting in the seat of the scornful. The scorners are atheists. Now the sinner gets the young man to sit down. We are told that the third stage is that he sits in the seat of the scornful. The scornful is the atheist. He not only denies God, but he exhibits an antagonism and a hatred of God. This we see on every hand today. The scornful—they're the ones who are absolutely opposed to God. They don't want the Bible read in the public schools; they don't want it read anywhere for that matter. They deny the Word of God. May I say to you that there is nothing lower than to deny God. The drunkard in the gutter today is not nearly as low as the man who is denying God. And if you want to know God's attitude, here it is: "Surely he scorneth the scorners: but he giveth grace unto the lowly" (Prov. 3:34). God is opposed to the scornful, and He will scorn them. That's a very frightful picture, by the way, presented here.

Now this is the negative side. This is what the happy man does not do. In the next verse we see what the happy man *does* do.

But his delight is in the law of the LORD, and in his law doth he meditate day and night [Ps. 1:2].

You remember our Lord told about a man possessed with a demon, and when the demon went out of him the man cleaned up his life. He was swept and garnished—he had a new paint job. He was all cleaned up and he thought he was all right. But that demon still owned him. The demon wandered around, got tired of traveling, and returned. When he came back he brought some friends with him —seven other spirits more wicked than himself. And we're told that the last estate of the man was worse than the first. Many folk think that if they clean up their lives a little, that is all that is necessary. But notice, "his delight is in the law of the LORD." The delight of God's man is in the law of the Lord. In other words, he finds joy in the Word of God. I wish I could get the message over to folk that the Bible is a thrilling Book. It's not a burden; it's not boring. It is real delight to read and study the Word of God. Blessed is the man—*happy* is the man—whose delight is in the law of the Lord. Today the tragedy that has come to man—the tear, the sigh, the groaning, the heartache, the heartbreak, the broken homes, the ruined and wrecked lives—are the result of God's broken laws. The Word of God makes it very clear. "For this is the love of God, that we keep his commandments: and his commandments are not grievous" (1 John 5:3). His commandments for believers today are not only the Ten Commandments. And His commandments are not burdensome.

The idea that being saved by grace means that you can be lawless and live as you please is not the picture given to us in the Word of God. We are not to be lawless. "For, brethren, ye have been called unto liberty; only use not liberty for an occasion to the flesh, but by love serve one another" (Gal. 5:13). Liberty is not license by any means. Of course we don't keep the Ten Commandments to be saved, but that doesn't mean we are to break them. It means, my friend, that you cannot measure up to God's law. He demands perfection, and you and I don't have it. We have to come to God by faith. After we are saved by faith, we are to live on a higher plane than the law. We are to have in our lives the fruit of the Spirit, which is: love, joy, peace, long-suffering, gentleness, goodness, faithfulness, meekness, and self-control. We have the discipline and guidance of grace.

"His delight is in the law of the LORD; and in his law doth he meditate." *Meditate* is a very figurative word. It pictures a cow chewing her cud. I'm told that the cow has several compartments in her tummy. She can go out in the morning, graze on the grass when the dew is on it in the cool of the day. Then when it gets hot in the middle of the day, she lies down under a tree and begins to chew the cud. She moves the grass she had in the morning back up and now she masticates it, she goes over it again. That is what we do when we meditate. We go over what we have read. Thomas a Kempis put it rather quaintly: "I have no rest, but in a nook, with the Book." Way back in 1688 Bartholomew Ashwood said, "Meditation chews the cud." My, how that is needed today in the lives of believers. Remember that James spoke of the man who beholds his natural face in a mirror, then ". . . straightway forgetteth what manner of man he was" (James 1:24). We are to meditate on the Word of God (which is God's mirror that shows us what we really are). We are to allow the Word to shape our lives.

"And in his law doth he meditate day and night." My friend, God has no plan or program by which you are to grow and develop as a believer apart from His Word. You can become as busy as a termite in your church (and possibly with the same effect as a termite), but you won't grow by means of activity. You will grow by meditating upon the Word of God—that is, by going over it again and again in your thinking until it becomes a part of your life. This is the practice of the happy man.

POWER OF THE BLESSED MAN

Where does he get his power?

And he shall be like a tree planted by the rivers of water, that bringeth forth

his fruit in his season; his leaf also shall not wither; and whatsoever he doeth shall prosper [Ps. 1:3].

The happy man shall be like a tree planted by the rivers of water. The word *rivers* is the superlative in the Hebrew; it is a hyperbole for *abundance*. The blessed man is planted, given plenty of water, and becomes a tree. God's trees are "planted" trees. They are not wild-growing trees by any means. I think this picture refers to being born again. Isaiah 61:3 says, "To appoint unto them that mourn in Zion, to give unto them beauty for ashes, the oil of joy for mourning, the garment of praise for the spirit of heaviness; that they might be called *trees* of righteousness, the *planting* of the LORD, that he might be glorified." God does not use wild-grown trees. His trees are born again, taken up and set out in God's garden—set out by the rivers of water.

What does "rivers of water" mean? That is the Word of God. Somebody asks, "Are you sure about that?" Oh, I *know* it, because Isaiah 55:10–11 tells me, "For as the rain cometh down, and the snow from heaven, and returneth not thither, but watereth the earth, and maketh it bring forth and bud, that it may give seed to the sower, and bread to the eater: So shall my *word* be that goeth forth out of my mouth: it shall not return unto me void, but it shall accomplish that which I please, and it shall prosper in the thing whereto I sent it." God wants His Word to come down like rain. The radio is a fine way to do this—it scatters God's Word everywhere. We are to get out the Word of God. And it will produce something—it will cause trees to grow.

It provides drink and sustenance. It is also cleansing, and you can see this washing of water with the Word expressed by the psalmist in Psalm 104:16, which says, "The trees of the LORD are full of sap; the cedars of Lebanon, which he hath planted." Now the psalmist does not say that God's trees are *saps,* he says that they are full of sap. That "sap" is the Word of God—the trees of Lebanon which He has planted are full of the Word of God.

Each tree "bringeth forth his fruit in his season." It is interesting to note that God's trees don't bring forth fruit all of the time. They bring forth in their season, and the power is in the Word of God. I have heard the statement made in this day of activity and nervous action that the primary business of a Christian is soul-winning. I disagree with that. The Word of God does not say it. Second Corinthians 2:14–16 says, "Now thanks be unto God, which always causeth us to triumph in Christ, and maketh manifest the savour of his knowledge by us in every place. For we are unto God a sweet savour of Christ, in them that are saved, and in them that perish: To the one we are the savour of death unto death; and to the other the savour of life unto life. And who is sufficient for these things?" Well, I am not, but I do know this: I am called to give out the Word of God. It is the business of the Holy Spirit to bring people to Christ. We are experiencing multitudes of people coming to Christ through our radio program. I am amazed at it, but *we* don't do it. We just give out the Word of God, and when we do, our God causes us to triumph. Suppose nobody accepted Christ? Then we are a savour of life to those who are saved and a savour of death to those who perish. My responsibility is to give you the Word of God, and it is your responsibility to do something about it. When I was a pastor, I used to tell folk when I gave an invitation to receive Christ, "If you leave here unsaved, it's too bad because you can't go into God's presence saying you had not heard the gospel. I really have become your enemy because you cannot tell God that you had never heard His Word." It is your business to give it to the unsaved, my friend, and it is his business what he does with it. But he will have to be accountable to God. God tells us to get out the Word of God, and that is what I've been trying to do for many years. Some are saved, and some are not saved.

At Dr. George Truett's fiftieth anniversary as pastor of the First Baptist Church of Dallas, Texas, a very prominent lawyer came up to him after the morning service. He said, "George, you and I came to Dallas in the early days, in the horse-and-buggy days. I want to make a confession to you. As a young lawyer, I used to come in to hear you. You were a young preacher in those days, but you disturbed me. Many a time I went home after a Sunday night service and I couldn't sleep." But he said, "George, today you have become the greatest preacher in America, but I can sit and listen to you now, and you don't bother me at all." And he laughed and walked away.

I'd hate to be that lawyer. As brilliant as he is, he won't have much of a case to offer when he stands before Christ someday because he happened to have listened to one of the greatest preachers America ever produced. Dr. Truett was called the prince of the pulpit. For fifty years that lawyer listened to him. And at the end of fifty years he said, "You don't bother me at all." But Dr. Truett had discharged his responsibility.

The primary business of a Christian is not soul-winning, but getting out the Word of God, my friend. It "bringeth forth his fruit in his season." There is a time to get fruit. I have a little tangerine tree that overdid itself one year. It was loaded with tangerines. I know I picked two bushels off that tree, and there still were two more bushels there. But a month later there wasn't one tangerine on that tree. It only brings forth its fruit in its season. There is a season for fruitbearing. That is the reason there ought to be a long time of preparation, of sowing seed, of helping it to fructify. Just to hand out a tract here and there may have its value, but, my friend, we are in the business of giving out the living Word of God, and it needs to be tended. It takes time and care because fruit comes forth only at the right season.

He also says: "His leaf also shall not wither." Now the leaf is the outward testimony of the Christian. That is something that should be out all the time. God's trees are evergreens—they never lose their testimony. A friend of mine, while taking a course at a seminary in New York one summer, went to one of those famous churches in New York City one Sunday. He said, "I walked down on Sunday morning to this great church and saw over the entrance, carved in stone, these words: The Gate of Heaven. Then I saw underneath it a temporary sign: Closed During July and August." Too often this happens in the lives of individual believers, but it should not, my friend. You are always an evergreen. Your leaf is the outward testimony that you have in this world for Christ. All God's children are evergreens.

In addition to this he says, "whatsoever he doeth shall prosper." Back in the Old Testament God promised material blessings to His own. Those blessings are not promised to the believer today. If you have them, you can thank Him for more than He has promised. John Trapp put it like this: "Outward prosperity, if it follows close walking with God, is sweet. As the cipher when it follows a figure adds to the number, though it be nothing by itself." The important thing is to have Christ. That's number one. All material blessings are zero. If you don't have One before your zeroes, you have only a goose egg, friend. But if you put that One, who is Christ, before your material blessings, then you are blessed indeed. But remember that He has not promised material blessings in this age.

PERMANENCY OF THE BLESSED MAN

Notice the insecurity of the ungodly.

The ungodly are not so: but are like the chaff which the wind driveth away.

Therefore the ungodly shall not stand in the judgment, nor sinners in the congregation of the righteous [Ps. 1: 4–5].

Two men, two ways, two destinies. One is a dead-end street; it leads to death. The other leads to life. God says what is right and what is wrong. We are living in a day when folk are not sure what is right or wrong. God is sure. His Word does not change with every philosophy of a new generation.

For the Lord knoweth the way of the righteous: but the way of the ungodly shall perish [Ps. 1:6].

Perish simply means "lost." It is a word of finality, if you please. The wicked are going to perish; Proverbs 10:28 tells us: "The hope of the righteous shall be gladness: but the expectation of the wicked shall perish." We are admonished: "Enter ye in at the strait gate: for wide is the gate, and broad is the way, that leadeth to destruction, and many there be which go in thereat: Because strait is the gate, and narrow is the way, which leadeth unto life, and few there be that find it" (Matt. 7:13–14). The wide, broad way is like a funnel in that you enter at the big end and, as you continue, it becomes narrower and narrower and finally leads to death. You enter the narrow way by Christ, who is the way, the truth, and the life. As you continue, the way becomes broader and broader; and this way leads to life. In John 10:10 Christ says, ". . . I am come that they might have life, and that they might have it more abundantly." What a glorious picture of the blessed and happy man is presented in the first psalm!

PSALM 2

***THEME:** Drama of the ages—man's rebellion against God*

A noticeable feature in the Book of Psalms is the systematic arrangement. The first psalm presents the perfect man, the happy man. (And I believe it pictures the Lord Jesus Christ as the last Adam.) Now in contrast to the perfect man, the blessed man in Psalm 1, we see the rebellious man in Psalm 2. We call this the Genesis section of the Book of Psalms, and the parallel is striking. Genesis begins with the perfect man, the happy man, in the Garden of Eden. But he became the rebellious man who ran away from God, was no longer seeking Him, who had no capacity for Him. Now here in Psalm 2 we find the children of Adam—mankind.

Psalm 2 has been called the drama of the ages. It contains a decisive declaration concerning the outcome of events and forces that are in the world today. This psalm is divided more like a television program than a play. It is presented as if there were a camera on earth and one in heaven. We experienced something like this when we were treated to on-the-spot moon exploration by camera. It was quite exciting and dramatic.

When we come to the second psalm we find that the Spirit of God uses two cameras in a dramatic way beyond the imagination of man. First, the camera on earth comes on, and when it does, we hear the voices of the masses. We hear little man speaking his little piece and playing his part—as Shakespeare puts it, "A poor player that struts and frets his hour upon the stage" of life. Little man. Then the camera on earth goes off, the camera in heaven comes on, and we hear God the Father speak. After He speaks, the camera shifts to His right hand, and God the Son speaks His part. Then the camera in heaven goes off, the camera on earth comes on again, and God the Holy Spirit has the last word.

CAMERA FOCUS: MANKIND

Now let's watch this presentation. First, the camera on earth comes on, and we see mankind. He is put before us here in the first verse with this question:

> **Why do the heathen rage, and the people imagine a vain thing? [Ps. 2:1].**

Why do the heathen (Gentiles) rage, and the people (Jews) imagine a vain thing? The word *vain* here means "empty." It means that this which has so enraged the Gentiles, and which has brought together mankind in a great mass movement, a great protest movement, will never be fulfilled, will never be accomplished. It is an empty, futile thing that has brought mankind together.

Well, what is it?

> **The kings of the earth set themselves, and the rulers take counsel together, against the LORD, and against his anointed, saying [Ps. 2:2].**

"The kings of the earth set themselves" are the political rulers, "and the rulers take counsel together" are the religious rulers. Not only do you have the masses of mankind in this protest movement, but also the establishment has joined in with it. Here are the rulers, both religious and political, joining together.

Now what is it they are protesting? Whom are they against? "Against the LORD, and against his anointed." The word *anointed* here means "Messiah"—that is what it is in Hebrew. When the word is brought over in the Greek New Testament it is *Christos*, and in English "Christ." Here is a great worldwide movement that is against God and against Christ.

Now when did this movement begin? Scripture lets us know about this. Over in the fourth chapter of the Book of Acts, when the first persecution broke out against the church, we're told that the apostles, Peter and John, after they had been threatened, returned back to the church to give their report: "And when they heard that, they lifted up their voice to God with one accord, and said, Lord, thou art God . . ." (Acts 4:24).

We need to pause here just a moment because this is one of the things the church is not sure about today: "Lord, thou art God." Many people are not sure He is God. They wonder. The early church had no misgivings or questions.

". . . Lord, thou art God, which hast made heaven, and earth, and the sea, and all that in them is: Who by the mouth of thy servant David hast said, Why did the heathen rage, and the people imagine vain things?" (Acts 4:24–25). As you can see, they were quoting Psalm 2. "The kings of the earth stood up, and the rulers were gathered together against the Lord, and against his Christ" (Acts. 4:26). Now this is the Holy Spirit's interpretation: "For of a truth against thy holy child Jesus, whom thou hast anointed, both Herod, and Pontius Pilate, with the Gentiles, and the people of Israel, were gathered together" (Acts 4:27). Here is this movement, beginning, we are told by the Holy Spirit, back yonder when Pilate joined up with the religious rulers and Herod in order to put Jesus to death. This is a movement against God and Christ. It has been snowballing as it has come down through the centuries, and it will break out finally in a worldwide revolution against God and against Christ.

Now somebody says to me, "You really don't think the world is moving in that direction, do you?" May I say to you, I think it is. Someone comes to me and asks, "Dr. McGee, do you think the world is getting better?" I say, "Yes, I do." Somebody else comes and says, "Dr. McGee, don't you think the world is getting worse?" I say, "Yes, I do." "Well," you may say, "what in the world are you trying to do? Go with both crowds?" No, both are true. That is the same thing the Lord Jesus said in His parable of the tares (Matt. 13:24–39). The Lord Jesus said that He Himself is the sower and that He is sowing seed in the world. Then He said an enemy came in and sowed tares. The servants wanted to go in and pull up the tares. When I entered the ministry that is what I wanted to do. I was the best puller-upper of tares you've ever seen. But I soon found out that we're not called to pull up tares (I sure found that out the hard way!). That is the reason I don't try to straighten out anybody else. I'm having enough trouble with Vernon McGee, so I don't worry about the others. He will take care of them. But what He said was that the wheat is growing, the tares are growing, they are both growing together, and He will do the separating. He will take care of that.

Today the good is growing. Did you know that there is more Bible teaching going out today than in any period in the history of the world? We brag about the few radio stations that carry our Bible study, but other radio programs have been giving out the Word lots longer than we have. Across this land are many radio stations that are dedicated to the ministry of broadcasting the Word of God. The Word is going out today through many more avenues than it has ever gone out before. The wheat is growing. But I want to tell you, brother, the tares are growing also. Evil is growing. There is an opposition against God and Christ today that is unbelievable. I could give you many incidents of the enmity that I've encountered.

Somebody says, "I just can't quite buy that. I believe that over there on the other side of the Iron Curtain atheism is growing, but not on this side." Well, it is growing on the other side, and it is rather amazing. Did you know that you and I have seen in our lifetime (those of you who are as old as I am) a nation appear whose basic philosophy, basic political economy, is atheism? There has been nothing like that in the past. No nation of the ancient world, that great pagan world of the past, was atheistic. Not one. Somebody says, "I thought they were." No, they were the opposite. They were polytheistic. They worshiped many gods. None was atheistic. You see, they were too close to the mooring mast of revelation. Noah knew a man who knew Adam. When you are that close to it, you do not deny God. In Noah's day the world was filled with violence, but there wasn't an atheist in the crowd. When God gave the Ten Commandments, He didn't give any one of them against atheism. He gave two against polytheism: "Thou shalt have no other gods before me. Thou shalt not make unto thee any graven image, or any likeness of any thing that is in heaven above, or that is in the earth beneath, or that is in the water under the earth" (Exod. 20:3–4). He gave these two commandments against polytheism, none against atheism. Why? There were no atheists.

Now when you get to the time of David, you meet atheists, and there were a great many atheists by that time. David labels them, though. He says, "The *fool* hath said in his heart, There is no God . . ." (Ps. 14:1). The word *fool* in the Hebrew means "insane." The insane, the nutty individual, is the one who is the atheist. Of course he may be a Ph.D. in a university. The Bible says he is insane. It is insane for a man to say there is no God.

There is, I believe, as much opposition to Jesus Christ on this side of the Iron Curtain as there is on the other side of the Iron Curtain today. I believe that with all my heart. Somebody says, "Wait a minute. I hear many talk about Jesus, and how wonderful Jesus is." Have you ever stopped to think that the Jesus of liberalism, the Jesus the world thinks of, actually never lived? The Jesus of the Bible and the Jesus of liberalism are two different individuals. And the Jesus of liberalism never lived at all.

Let me give you an example of what I

mean. For many years when I was a pastor in downtown Los Angeles the leading liberal in this country pastored a church nearby. Actually I had great respect for him because he was one liberal who was honest. For instance, he would just come out and say he did not believe in the virgin birth. And if you don't believe it, I'd like for you to say it and not beat around the bush. He had a question-and-answer program on radio, I had a question-and-answer program on radio, and listeners would feed questions to both of us to set us in opposition. Every year we went through that same little ritual during the Christmas season. I always enjoyed it. So one time we both were invited to a banquet, and (I think it was done purposely) we were seated together. I got there first and sat down. I saw his name there. In a minute he came in. I felt somebody put his arm around me and say, "You know, Brother McGee, you and I ought to be much closer together. We preach the same Jesus," and he sat down. I said to him, "Are you sure we preach the same Jesus?" "Oh, don't we?" "I don't think so. Let me ask you some questions. Was the Jesus you preach virgin born?" "Of course not." "Well, the one I preach is virgin born. The Jesus you preach—did He perform miracles?" "I do not believe in miracles." "Well, the Jesus I preach performed miracles. The Jesus you preach—did He die on a cross for the sins of the world?" "Of course He died on a cross, but not for the sins of the world." "The Jesus I preach died a substitutionary, vicarious death for the sins of man. Do you believe that Jesus rose bodily?" "Oh, no, of course not." "Obviously then, you and I are not preaching about the same Jesus. Now I want to ask you a question." You see, these liberal men have called some of us fundamentalists "intellectual obscurantists." (Now whatever that is, it's terrible!) So I said to him, "Look, what are the documents or where are the documents for the Jesus you preach?" He laughed, just laughed and passed it off. "Of course we don't have any." "Now isn't that interesting. We have documents for the Jesus we preach, and you don't—yet you call us intellectual obscurantists. I'd like to know who is an intellectual obscurantist!"

May I say to you, my friend, the Jesus that the world believes in today doesn't even exist. He never lived. The Jesus we preach is the Jesus of the Bible, and that is the One against whom there is opposition in the world today. There is a tremendous build-up, a mighty crescendo of opposition against God and against Christ in this day in which we live.

Now how does it manifest itself? Exactly as He said it would. Notice again the second psalm. Hear what they are saying:

Let us break their bands asunder, and cast away their cords from us [Ps. 2:3].

What are some of the bands God has put on the human family? Marriage is one. God has made marriage for the welfare of mankind. Whether you are a Christian or not, God has given marriage to mankind. Today they not only *want* to get rid of it; they *are* getting rid of it. I was rather shocked two or three years ago. (I'm a square. I'm not really keeping up with it today, so I don't follow along in the way they are going in this modern thinking, relative to God, relative to man, and relative to the Word of God.) So I was startled at a young people's conference when the sweetest little girl got up in our question-and-answer period and said, "Dr. McGee, why does a young couple have to get married if they love each other? Why can't they just start living together?" God gave marriage, and God intends for it to be followed. But they say, "Let's break their bands asunder."

Also, "Let's cast away their cords from us." The Ten Commandments are cords. When somebody accuses me of saying that we don't need the Ten Commandments, they are wrong. We are not saved by keeping them—I tried it, and it won't work—but I'll say this: God gave them, and He gave them to protect mankind. They are thrown out the door today, and right now we are experiencing lawlessness in this country because of the fact that crime is not being punished. There has been a terrible toll of lives that would not have been sacrificed had laws been enforced. You see, we are living in a day when the prevailing philosophy is "Let us break their bands asunder, let's cast away their cords from us. We want to be free and do as we please." God says we can't make it that way. It won't work. We've got old evil natures that need to be restrained. But mankind is moving toward getting rid of all restraints today.

It is disturbing as we look at this world in which we are living. In the political world there is confusion. In the moral realm there is corruption. In the spiritual sphere there is compromise and indifference. And in the social sphere there is comfort. This affluent society never had it so easy, and their goal is to make it easier. We are living in that kind of a day. It is disturbing, and I'll be honest with you, I do worry about it a little.

CAMERA FOCUS: GOD THE FATHER

The question arises, How does *God* feel about this?

He that sitteth in the heavens shall laugh: the Lord shall have them in derision [Ps. 2:4].

What kind of laughter is this? Let me say at the outset that it is not the laughter of humor. He is not being funny.

Do not misunderstand me—there is humor in the Bible. The devil has really hit a home run by making people think that going to church is quite an ordeal. We are living in a day when folk think you can't have fun in church. I think the Bible is full of humor. Those of you who study with us through the Bible know we find a lot of it. There used to be a dear maiden lady at a church I served who never found any humor in the Bible. When I gave a message which cited some humorous incident, she used to come down, shake a bony finger under my nose and say, "Dr. McGee, you are being irreverent to find humor in the Bible." I said to her, "Don't you wish *you* could?" She's gone now to be with the Lord, and I certainly hope she's had a good laugh since she has been there because she has gone to the place where she can have a good time. She needs to have a good time—she never had one down here. There are too many Christians like that today. My friend, it is going to be thrilling to be with Him some day. We're going to have a wonderful time with Him. It's going to be fun, and I'm looking forward to that. God has a sense of humor, and there is humor in His Word.

"He that sitteth in the heavens shall laugh . . ." Since this is not the laughter of humor, what is it? Well, look at it from God's viewpoint—little man down there parading up and down, shaking his midget fist in Heaven's face and saying, "Come on out and fight me! I'm against you." God looks down at the puny little creature. It's utterly *preposterous*. It is so ridiculous! He looks down and laughs. "He that sitteth in the heavens shall laugh: the LORD shall have them in derision." It is so utterly ridiculous, my friend. Little men putting themselves in opposition to God won't be around very long. Mussolini did a lot of talking, and we haven't heard from him lately. Stalin did the same thing, and he is gone. Little man plays his brief role here on the stage of life, then his part is over. How ridiculous and preposterous for him to oppose God!

Then shall he speak unto them in his wrath, and vex them in his sore displeasure [Ps. 2:5].

This is the judgment that is coming upon this earth.

What effect will man's opposition have upon God's program? God is going forward to the accomplishment of His purpose. What little man does down here won't deter Him, detour Him, or defer Him at all. God did not read something in the morning paper that He didn't already know about. There is nothing that has surprised Him at all. He is moving according to His purpose. He has, I believe, a twofold purpose in this world. I think He has a heavenly purpose; I think He has an earthly purpose. Right now He is working on His heavenly purpose. The writer to the Hebrews expresses this: it is ". . . bringing many sons unto glory . . ." (Heb. 2:10). God today is calling out of this world a people to His name. That is His present purpose. However, God has another purpose, and it is stated here:

Yet have I set my king upon my holy hill of Zion [Ps. 2:6].

God is moving forward today undeviatingly, unhesitatingly, uncompromisingly to the establishment of that throne on which Jesus Christ will sit on this earth. I hear folk say, "If the Lord delay His coming." Where in the world did that idea come from? He is not delaying anything. He is going to come on schedule—*His* schedule, not mine, because I don't know when He is coming. He is running on schedule and nothing will stop Him, nothing can cause Him to change His plan.

CAMERA FOCUS: GOD THE SON

Now the camera in heaven shifts to God the Son on His right hand. God the Son speaks, "I will declare the decree." Those of you who have studied theology know that the Lord Jesus executes all the decrees of God.

I will declare the decree: the LORD hath said unto me, Thou art my Son; this day have I begotten thee [Ps. 2:7].

This is a verse that the Jehovah Witnesses use a great deal. I wish they would listen long enough to find out what it means. It would help them a great deal to find it has no reference to the birth of the Lord Jesus Christ—which they would see if only they would turn to the New Testament and let the Spirit of God interpret. This verse was quoted by the apostle Paul when he preached in Antioch of Pisidia. This was, I believe, one of his greatest sermons; and he was talking about the resurrection of Jesus Christ: "God hath fulfilled the same unto us their children, in that he hath raised up Jesus again; as it is also written in the second psalm, Thou art my Son, this day have I begotten thee" (Acts 13:33).

The reference in the second psalm is not to the *birth* of Jesus. He never was begotten in the sense of having a beginning. Rather, this is in reference to His *resurrection*. Christ was begotten out of Joseph's tomb. Jesus is the eternal Son of God, and God is the eternal Father. You cannot have an eternal Father without having an eternal Son. They were this throughout eternity. This is their position in the Trinity. It hasn't anything to do with someone being born, but it does have something to do with someone being begotten from the dead. It has to do with resurrection. I'm afraid the Jehovah's Witnesses have not heard this, but they could find, with a little honest searching, that the New Testament makes it very clear Jesus Christ is not a creature. He is the theanthropic Person. He is the God-man. Psalm 2:7 sustains this doctrine. God the Father continues:

Ask of me, and I shall give thee the heathen for thine inheritance, and the uttermost parts of the earth for thy possession [Ps. 2:8].

The scepter of this universe will be held by a Man with nail-pierced hands. He is the One who is yet to rule.

This verse is often used in missionary conferences. I suppose I have heard a dozen sermons on missions using this verse of Scripture—and probably you have—but it ought never go to a missionary conference. It hasn't anything to do with missions. I remember listening to a graduate of Union Seminary in New York City bring a missionary message using this verse. I was then a student in seminary. As a student I did something that was very impolite, very rude. I think I've got more sense than to do it today. I went up to him after he had preached the message, and I asked, "Doctor, why didn't you use the next verse?" He acted as if he didn't hear me, although I am sure he did, and began talking with somebody there. I said to him the second time, "Doctor, why didn't you use the next verse?" This time he turned his back on me, and just ignored me. Well, I should have left, but I didn't. I walked around in front, and I said to him, "Doctor, why didn't you use the next verse?" He looked me right straight in the eye and said, "Because it would have ruined a missionary sermon." And it sure would have!

Notice the next verse, the verse that follows it:

Thou shalt break them with a rod of iron; thou shalt dash them in pieces like a potter's vessel [Ps. 2:9].

Do you think this is the gospel of the grace of God we are to preach today? It is not. This passage hasn't any reference to Christ's first coming. This speaks of His second coming, when He comes to this earth to *judge*.

This is the way He will come the second time—to judge the earth. He has not asked me to apologize for Him, so I won't apologize. He says that He intends to come to this little planet and put down the rebellion that has broken out—and He will *break* them with the rod of iron. Maybe you don't like that. Well, you take it up with Him. He said it, and He is going to do it just that way.

Now I have a question to ask you, if you think He ought to do it the way some of our political leaders are suggesting. Suppose Jesus came back to this earth tomorrow, like He came some two thousand years ago, the man of Galilee, the carpenter of Nazareth, the gentle Jesus. Suppose He went to the Kremlin and knocked at the door. Whoever keeps the store over there would come and say, "Yes?" He would say, "I'm Jesus. I'm here to take over." Do you think they would say, "My, we have been waiting for you"? No, they'd put Him before a firing squad in the morning. My friend, how do you think He could take over if He came to Russia today? He would have to break them with a rod of iron, would He not? Apparently that is what He is going to do. Now suppose He goes to France. They don't want Him. Suppose He went down to Rome. I was there just a few weeks ago. I went over the Tiber and listened to a man speak. Although I could not understand what he was saying, I was told that he was telling the world how they ought to do it. He would like to take over. Suppose our Lord would go and knock on the door of the Vatican. The man with the long garment would come to the door, and the Lord Jesus would say, "I'm here to take over." What do you think he would say? I think he would say, "Now look, You've come a little too soon. I'm having trouble with some of my priests, but I'm going to work that out. I don't need You." I don't think he would want Him. Suppose He came to this country.

Suppose He went to the Democratic headquarters, or the Republican headquarters, and said, "I'm here to take over." They would say, "We're getting ready for a presidential campaign, we've already got our candidates; we don't need You." Now maybe you think their reaction would be different. Maybe you are saying, "Oh, they would take Him." Then *why* don't they take Him? They will not because they won't have Him! Suppose He went to the World Council of Churches today, and He said to Protestantism, "I'm here." Would they receive Him? Then why don't they receive Him today? When He comes the second time He will come exactly as God said: "Thou shalt break them with a rod of iron; thou shalt dash them in pieces like a potter's vessel." He intends to put down the rebellion when He comes to this earth the next time. Oh, my friend, this namby-pamby way of thinking that our God is not going to judge! You and I are living in a world that is moving to judgment day, and God *is* going to judge.

CAMERA FOCUS: GOD THE HOLY SPIRIT

The camera in heaven goes off. The camera on earth comes on. Now God the Holy Spirit speaks:

Be wise now therefore, O ye kings: be instructed, ye judges of the earth.

Serve the LORD with fear, and rejoice with trembling [Ps. 2:10–11].

One of the most startling things I have encountered in studying the Bible the past few years is a little thing like this: God, in the history of this world, has always gotten a message to the rulers of this world. Always. No exception. Down yonder in the land of ancient Egypt, there was a Pharaoh on the throne, and there was boy Joseph in prison. God kept him in prison so that at the right moment He could bring him out to make him the prime minister of Pharaoh at one of the most crucial periods in the history of the world. That is the way God does it. Down yonder when the first great world power, Babylon, came into existence, God put the man Daniel at the side of Nebuchadnezzar. He not only became his prime minister, but also he brought him to a saving knowledge of the living God. And God kept him there until Cyrus, the Persian, came to the throne. And Cyrus even made his *decree* in the name of the living God. Napoleon said that he was a man of destiny, that he was told God had raised him up. It is interesting how God has gotten His Word to the rulers of this earth and to those who are in high places. God the Holy Spirit says to the rulers: "Serve the LORD with fear, and rejoice with trembling."

Also He says:

Kiss the Son, lest he be angry, and ye perish from the way, when his wrath is kindled but a little. Blessed are all they that put their trust in him [Ps. 2:12].

The late Dr. George Gill used to tell us in class, " 'Kiss the Son' is the Old Testament way of saying, '. . . Believe on the Lord Jesus Christ, and thou shalt be saved . . .' (Acts 16:31)." "Kiss the Son."

Do you remember who kissed Him? Have you ever noted what our Lord said to Judas after he kissed Him? The theologians today argue about predestination and election and predetermination and foreknowledge, and that this man Judas could not help what he did since it had been prophesied he would do it. Now I'm going to let the theologians handle that. I'm just a poor preacher who doesn't know very much; so I stay away from those problems and let the theologians solve them. However, after I listen to them awhile I have a sneaking feeling they haven't solved them. Notice what the Bible says, and it is well to listen to the Bible rather than to the theologians. Remember at Jesus' betrayal when Judas led the mob out to apprehend Jesus in the garden, he said, "I'll identify him for you by kissing Him." So he came to Jesus and kissed Him. Have you noted what Jesus said to him? "And Jesus said unto him, Friend, wherefore art thou come? . . ." (Matt. 26:50). Why did He say that? Didn't He know why Judas had kissed Him? Of course He did. Then why did He call him *friend*? What did He mean? Let me suggest this. "Judas, you have just kissed Me, which has fulfilled prophecy, and has satisfied all the theologians who are going to come along. Now you are free to turn and accept Me, free to turn that kiss of betrayal into a kiss of acceptance. You can do that, Judas. You are a free moral agent." And the Spirit of God says, "Kiss the Son. Believe on the Lord Jesus Christ, and thou shalt be saved."

My friend, the Spirit of God today is in the world saying to mankind, "Kiss the Son before it is too late. Believe on the Lord Jesus Christ before it is too late." He is coming some day, and He is going to establish His kingdom here upon this earth. He is going to rule, and He is going to put down all rebellion.

He will bring peace and harmony to this little earth.

When I first went to Nashville, Tennessee, as a pastor, some friends, thinking they were doing me a favor, called me and said, "We have tickets for the symphony orchestra that's coming to town, and we want to take you as our guest." Well, I love music, but I know nothing about it; and I can't sing it—I always help congregational singing by keeping quiet. Frankly, I can't think of anything more boring than a whole evening of symphony! But I had to go because they were polite and I wanted to be polite, so I accepted graciously and went along. I had never been to a thing like that before, and I was impressed by what I saw. We went in, took our seats, and in a few moments the musicians began to drift out from the stage sides. They were in shirt sleeves for the most part, and each man went up to his instrument and started tuning it. The fellows with the fiddles too big to put under their chins sawed back and forth—oh, it sounded terrible. The fellows with the little ones they put under their chins squeaked up and down with those. The ones with the horns—oh my, nothing was in harmony. It was a medley of discordant, confused noise. Then after they got through with that kind of disturbance, they all disappeared again—went out through the wings. Another five minutes went by, when all of a sudden the lights in the auditorium went off, the lights on the platform came on, and the musicians walked out. This time they had on their coats. My, they looked so nice. Each one came out and stood or sat at his instrument. Then there was a hush in the auditorium, a spotlight was focused on the wings, and the conductor stepped out. When he did, there was thunderous applause for him. He bowed. Then he came up to the podium and picked up a thin little stick. He turned around again to the audience and bowed, then turned his back to the audience, lifted that little stick—total silence came over that auditorium, you could have heard a pin drop—then he brought that little stick down. And, my friend, there were goose pimples all over me. I never heard such music in all my life. Oh, what harmony, what wonderful harmony there was!

Today I live in a world where every man is tooting his own little horn. Every little group wants to be heard. Everybody wants to tell you what he thinks. Everybody is playing his own little fiddle, and I want to tell you, it's a medley of discord. Everything is out of tune. But one of these days the spotlight is going on, and the Lord Jesus Christ will come. When He comes to this universe, He is going to lift His scepter, and everything that is out of tune with Him is going to be removed. Then when He comes down with that scepter—oh, the harmony that will be in this universe! I'm thankful today that I do live in a universe where I can bow to Him, and I can bring this little instrument of my body, my life, into tune with Him. I can bow to Him, I can acknowledge Him, I can make Him my Savior and Lord.

PSALM 3

***THEME:** A morning prayer: the trials of the godly in Israel*

Psalms 3–7 form a bridge, which I think of as a stairway between two messianic psalms. Psalm 2 is the prophetic rejection of God's anointed, and Psalm 8 is His ultimate victory as Man. The psalms between furnish the glue that holds these two messianic psalms together. They primarily describe the godly remnant of Israel during the time of the absence of the Messiah from the earth, especially during that time which our Lord labeled the Great Tribulation period. In these five psalms we have the record of Israel's trials, sorrows, confusions, problems, and sins. We also see their confidence in God, the promises of God, and their prayers for deliverance.

Trials and sorrows are shared by all godly people, regardless of who they are or in what period of history they live. The comfort given in these psalms is for all of God's children. There are three ways to look at these psalms. The *primary* interpretation, of course, concerns the personal experience of David. Then there is a direct *application* to the godly remnant in the nation of Israel during the Great Tribulation. There is also an application to God's people everywhere at any time in the history of the world. If we look at the psalms from this point of view, they will become more meaningful to us.

Psalm 3 is called "A Psalm of David when he fled from Absalom his son." (The historical record is in 2 Samuel, chapters 15–18.) This title tells us about the contents of this psalm. It tells us what went on in the heart of David when he had to flee from Jerusalem when Absalom his son rebelled against him. This psalm came out of the personal experience of David. He was in a difficult situation. He had become an outcast and a fugitive from his own city Jerusalem, which is called the city of David. He had been driven from the people he ruled. Absalom, his son, was in rebellion against him and seeking his life. Absalom's intention was actually to put his father to death. Your heart cannot help but go out to David during this heartbreaking experience.

As David fled, the enemy was on the sidelines cursing him. Abishai, one of his mighty men said, "Let me run a spear through him." David said, "Oh, no." The prophet Nathan had told David that God would punish him for his sins. In 2 Samuel 12:11 Nathan said to David, "Thus saith the LORD, Behold, I will raise up evil against thee out of thine own house, and I will take thy wives before thine eyes, and give them unto thy neighbour. . . ." Why would this happen? Because David had sinned greatly, and he was not going to get away with it. God has graciously forgiven David and restored him, but David has to reap the results of his sin; and it is in his son's rebellion that he does it. We find that David's enemies have increased on all sides and that the hearts of the men of Israel followed Absalom. The Scripture tells us, ". . . The hearts of the men of Israel are after Absalom" (2 Sam. 15:13). Absalom was an attractive young man. He was a clever politician who was able to promise the people many good things which he would not have been able to deliver.

During the time of Absalom's rebellion there were many others who rose up against David. He went out of Jerusalem barefoot and weeping. He passed over Kidron. It looked as if there was no help for him at all.

With this background in mind, let us look at Psalm 3.

LORD, how are they increased that trouble me! many are they that rise up against me [Ps. 3:1].

David is speaking right out of his heart, friend, as he leaves Jerusalem.

Many there be which say of my soul, There is no help for him in God. Selah [Ps. 3:2].

Many said that David would find no help from God, that God had forsaken him. But God did not forsake him. When someone says to me, "I cannot understand how God put up with a man like David," I always feel like saying, "Well, if God put up with David, maybe He will put up with you and me." Be thankful that we have this kind of a God, friend. He puts up with folk like David, and He will forgive any believer who comes to Him in repentance. This doesn't mean that David did not pay for his sin, because he did.

At the end of the second verse we find the word *Selah*. There has been a great deal of discussion as to the meaning of this word. It occurs about seventy-one times in the Psalms. I believe the Psalms were set to music, to be played by an orchestra and sung by great choirs. I am sure that Jerusalem became famous throughout the world, and people came from near and far to hear the music and the singing of these psalms. I think *selah* was probably a musical rest, a musical pause. For the common layman who does not understand much about music it means, "Stop, look, and listen." That is the type of sign you have at railroad crossings. I remember the days when my dad would drive a buggy into Snyder, Texas, and I would sometimes go with him. He would always stop at the railroad crossing. There wouldn't be a train within ten miles of the place, but we always stopped, looked, and listened. When we come to these marvelous psalms, we should stop, look, and listen. *Selah* reminds us to do that. That is what we should do when we come to the Word of God.

The word *selah* probably ends the first stanza of this psalm. Now David says:

I laid me down and slept; I awaked; for the LORD sustained me.

I will not be afraid of ten thousands of people, that have set themselves against me round about [Ps. 3:5–6].

This has been called "a morning psalm." This is a good psalm with which to start the day. In spite of all the problems and troubles that David had, he trusted in the Lord. He could sleep at night. He wasn't able to get an aspirin tablet or a sedative to put him to sleep. He simply trusted in the Lord, pillowed his head on the promises of God, and went to sleep.

"I awaked; for the LORD sustained me." Then David says that he would not be afraid if ten thousands of people set themselves against him. Even though the whole world was against him, David says he will not be afraid.

Cromwell is considered by many to be the bravest man who ever lived. Someone asked him, "What is the explanation of your bravery?" Cromwell replied, "Because I fear God, I have no man to fear." Martin Luther also took that position. If there were more fear of God today, there would be less of this licking of men's boots. There are some men who go around with their tongues black because they spend so much time licking the boots of men. Why do they do it? There is no fear of God in them. The thing that gives you courage is to fear God. If you fear God, then you have no man to fear. David trusted in God.

Arise, O LORD; save me, O my God: for thou hast smitten all mine enemies upon the cheek bone; thou hast broken the teeth of the ungodly [Ps. 3:7].

It really hurts to get hit on the cheekbone. When you get hit there, it will really knock you out; and David had probably experienced that. He says that his enemies had been smitten on the cheekbone. God had also broken the teeth of the ungodly—they were not able to bite David anymore.

Salvation belongeth unto the LORD: thy blessing is upon thy people. Selah [Ps. 3:8].

Salvation unto the Lord—*belongeth* is a word which was inserted by the translators. This is a great Scripture. The Lord is the author of salvation. David never thought of salvation as a coin that you could put in your pocket and lose. He never thought it was something he would have to work out. Salvation was the *gift* of God. "Salvation . . . unto the LORD: thy blessing is upon thy people."

Then comes the word *selah*. We are to stop, look, and listen. David has said some wonderful things about God in this psalm. For example, in verse 3 David calls Him his "shield." As a shield, God covers those who are His own. In Ephesians 6:16 we are told to take the shield of faith, as believers. David knew something about what the shield would do—he used it a great deal. God was also his "glory." That is, David believed in the presence of God. The cloud of glory, you remember, was spread over Israel. It was a visible sign of the presence of God in the midst of His people. Today we walk by faith, and the glory of God is with us, friend; He makes Himself real to those who are His own. God was also the "uplifter" of David's head. How could that be? God promised to build David a house and give him a blessing, a glory, and a kingdom. David said, "He is going to lift my head." We may be down, my friend, but He is going to lift us up. This is a marvelous psalm, is it not?

PSALM 4

THEME: *An evening prayer: the plea of the Son of man and those who plead in His name*

This brief psalm divides itself like this: a cry—verses 1–3; a correction—verses 4–5; a confidence—verses 6–8.

The psalm has a musical inscription "To the chief Musician on Neginoth, A Psalm of David." Apparently a neginoth is some sort of instrument; it is the belief of many that it is a stringed instrument. Probably this psalm was played as a solo on a neginoth.

The psalm begins with a great cry—the refuge of the people of God in the time of trouble is always prayer. And God is their shield, as we have seen.

Hear me when I call, O God of my righteousness: thou hast enlarged me when I was in distress; have mercy upon me, and hear my prayer [Ps. 4:1].

Distress indicates pressure—the pressures of life are great. They are great in our day, and we need the encouragement that we find in the Word of God. "The LORD is nigh unto all them that call upon him, to all that call upon him in truth" (Ps. 145:18). Again in Psalm 50:15 we read, "And call upon me in the day of trouble: I will deliver thee, and thou shalt glorify me." In Isaiah 65:24 God tells us, "And it shall come to pass, that before they call, I will answer; and while they are yet speaking, I will hear." Psalm 18:6 is very personal: "In my distress I called upon the LORD, and cried unto my God: he heard my voice out of his temple, and my cry came before him, even into his ears." In Psalm 55:16 we are told, "As for me, I will call upon God; and the LORD shall save me." Psalm 86:7 says, "In the day of my trouble I will call upon thee: for thou wilt answer me." Finally, Psalm 91:15 says, "He shall call upon me, and I will answer him: I will be with him in trouble; I will deliver him, and honour him." The Bible is just filled with these wonderful promises. The cry of the psalmist in Psalm 4 is that God be with him.

O ye sons of men, how long will ye turn my glory into shame? how long will ye love vanity, and seek after leasing? Selah [Ps. 4:2].

Leasing is falsehood.

But know that the LORD hath set apart him that is godly for himself: the LORD will hear when I call unto him [Ps. 4:3].

How wonderful He is! God will hear our prayer.

Then he gives two verses of correction, which is sort of a warning.

Stand in awe, and sin not: commune with your own heart upon your bed, and be still. Selah [Ps. 4:4].

Stand in awe is better translated *tremble,* and do not sin. We don't see much trembling today.

Offer the sacrifices of righteousness, and put your trust in the LORD [Ps. 4:5].

Paul expressed this thought to the Ephesian Christians: "Be ye angry, and sin not: let not the sun go down upon your wrath" (Eph. 4:26).

Now notice his confidence and the assurance of faith.

There be many that say, Who will shew us any good? LORD, lift thou up the light of thy countenance upon us [Ps. 4:6].

Many folk say, "Nothing is right anymore." How we need the Lord to lift up the light of His countenance upon us!

Thou hast put gladness in my heart, more than in the time that their corn and their wine increased [Ps. 4:7].

David was like the rest of us—his heart failed in the time of trouble. Around him were unbelievers, his own people, who were mocking him, "God is not going to do anything for him." But God *did* do something for him. "Thou hast put gladness in my heart, more than in the time that their corn and their wine increased." David found that God was good to him. And God is good to us, my friend.

Notice how this evening psalm concludes:

I will both lay me down in peace, and sleep: for thou, LORD, only makest me dwell in safety [Ps. 4:8].

My friend, do you need a sleeping pill at night? Have you ever tried Psalm 4? It is lots better than any brand of sleeping pill you have used.

Oh, how wonderful these psalms are for us today, and how much they will mean to God's people in that coming day of trouble.

PSALM 5

***THEME:** A morning prayer: a cry of the godly in the time of great trouble*

Psalm 5 is included in the section which forms a stairway between two messianic psalms. This group of psalms (3–7) actually tells a story. They are, first of all, a picture of a personal experience of David. Secondly, they reveal prophetically the picture of the nation Israel during the Great Tribulation Period. Also they have very real applications for us today, for they involve great principles. They have messages for God's people in all ages and in all times.

This is a psalm written by David, and it has as its inscription: "To the chief Musician upon Nehiloth." Psalm 4 was on neginoth, a stringed instrument, and this one, nehiloth, is generally believed to have been a wind instrument, a flute. David, the sweet psalmist of Israel, set most of these psalms to music. Possibly a choir also sang this psalm to the accompaniment of flutes. Arthur Pridham states the tone and general character of this psalm very nicely: "It is a prayer of faith, sent up from a heart in which the discernment of God as the shield and rewarder of them that seek Him, is found in union with a very deep sense of the prevailing evil and ungodliness which daily present themselves to the contemplation of the faithful. Vexing of soul because of the abundance of iniquity is thus a leading feature in its general expression." Pridham also makes this very interesting statement: "Hence patience is wrought in tribulation. Joy abounds in the sure hope of a deliverance, which is deferred only by the councils of unerring love." This pretty well sums up this very magnificent psalm.

It is called a morning psalm, and notice how it begins:

> **Give ear to my words, O LORD, consider my meditation.**
>
> **Hearken unto the voice of my cry, my King, and my God: for unto thee will I pray.**
>
> **My voice shalt thou hear in the morning, O LORD; in the morning will I direct my prayer unto thee, and will look up [Ps. 5:1–3].**

Now let me give you a little different translation: "Give ear to my words, O Jehovah, give heed to my meditation. Listen to the voice of my cry, my King, and my God; for to thee do I pray. Jehovah, in the morning shalt thou hear my voice; in the morning will I come before thee, and expectantly look up." This psalm is a morning prayer—in the morning his voice would be lifted unto God. The morning is a mighty good time to lift your heart to God in prayer.

> **For thou art not a God that hath pleasure in wickedness: neither shall evil dwell with thee.**
>
> **The foolish shall not stand in thy sight: thou hatest all workers of iniquity.**
>
> **Thou shalt destroy them that speak leasing: the LORD will abhor the bloody and deceitful man.**
>
> **But as for me, I will come into thy house in the multitude of thy mercy: and in thy fear will I worship toward thy holy temple [Ps. 5:4–7].**

A little different translation at this point I think will be helpful for a better understanding of this passage. "For no God art thou whom wickedness can please. The evil man cannot dwell with thee. The arrogant shall not dare to stand before thine eyes. Thou hatest all workings of iniquity. Thou wilt destroy them that speak lies: the man of blood and deceit Jehovah abhorreth. As for me, through thy great mercy will I enter thy house. I will fall down, facing thy holy temple in fear."

This is the comfort of the godly. When you look about you today, you may have (as I do) a sinking feeling as you see the evil that is abroad and the iniquity that abounds. It is something that makes you sick at heart. What is the comfort of the godly in days like these? The psalmist tells us. The hatred that he has in his heart for evil reveals that he is on God's side. God also hates it. It also makes God sick to look down on this sinful world of today. Wickedness does not please God, nor will it please those who know God. Evil cannot dwell with Him, for ". . . God is light, and in him is no darkness at all" (1 John 1:5). Habakkuk said it like this (when the Lord told him that the Chaldeans were going to invade God's land): "Thou art of purer eyes than to behold evil, and canst not look on iniquity. . ." (Hab. 1:13). Wickedness may prosper for a time, but the day is surely coming which will bring destruction and eternal shame to those who practice lies and iniquity. God has made it very, very clear that there is a day of judgment coming, and evil is not going to prevail. God spells it out in Revelation 21:8 which says, "But the fearful, and unbelieving, and the abominable, and murderers, and whoremongers, and sorcerers, and idolaters, and all liars, shall have their part in the lake which burneth with fire and brimstone: which is the second death." Now I may sound like an antiquated preacher referring to a passage like this, but I believe that the judgment of God is coming upon this earth.

Lead me, O Lord, in thy righteousness because of mine enemies; make thy way straight before my face.

For there is no faithfulness in their mouth; their inward part is very wickedness; their throat is an open sepulchre; they flatter with their tongue [Ps. 5:8–9].

A different translation is: "Jehovah, lead me in thy righteousness because of my foes." He is saying, "My enemies are watching me. They want me to stumble and fall, but I want to glorify You." Therefore he is praying to God that He will not let him stumble and fall, and that He will lead him. He prays, "Make thy paths straight before me, for in their mouth is nothing trustworthy; they are inwardly full of depravity; their throat is an open sepulchre." By the way, this is quoted in Romans 3:13 by the apostle Paul. "They make their tongues smooth"—they are glib of tongue. They don't seem to know what the truth is, and they seldom tell it.

Destroy thou them, O God; let them fall by their own counsels; cast them out in the multitude of their transgressions; for they have rebelled against thee.

But let all those that put their trust in thee rejoice: let them ever shout for joy, because thou defendest them: let them also that love thy name be joyful in thee.

For thou, Lord, wilt bless the righteous; with favour wilt thou compass him as with a shield [Ps. 5:10–12].

Or to translate it another way: "Destroy them, O God, let them fall by their own counsels; cast them out in the multitude of their transgressions, for they have rebelled against Thee. And all who seek refuge with Thee shall rejoice; forever shall they shout for joy because of thy protection, and they shall exult in Thee and love Thy name, for Thou, Jehovah, will bless the righteous: with favour wilt Thou surround him as with a shield." Prayer is this man's resource and recourse when he looks at the wickedness all about him. He prays for that guidance which will enable him to walk in a way that will not bring disrepute upon the name of God.

In verse 10 the psalmist asks the Lord to destroy the enemy. This is the first imprecatory prayer recorded in the Psalms. Later on I will have time to develop that subject. There are certain prayers that David prayed where he asked God for justice; he asked God to intervene and bring judgment. Some of them are very harsh. Isaiah prayed that way in Isaiah 64:1–2, when he said, "Oh that thou wouldest rend the heavens, that thou wouldest come down, that the mountains might flow down at thy presence, As when the melting fire burneth, the fire causeth the waters to boil, to make thy name known to thine adversaries, that the nations may tremble at thy presence!" Judgment must fall some day upon the transgressors. Scripture makes it very clear that God will take vengeance.

The Lord, you remember, told the parable concerning the widow who took her case to an earthly judge, saying, ". . . Avenge me of mine adversary. And he would not for a while: but afterward he said within himself, Though I fear not God, nor regard man; Yet because this widow troubleth me, I will avenge her, lest by her continual coming she weary me. And the Lord said, Hear what the unjust judge saith. And shall not God avenge his own elect, which cry day and night unto him, though he bear long with them? I tell you that he will avenge them speedily . . ." (Luke 18: 3–8). And David in his day prayed for vengeance.

For a Christian to pray these prayers during these days I think is absolutely sinful. You say, "You don't mean that!" I certainly do mean it. This is where I think a proper interpretation of Scripture is essential. There are many people who want to get rid of this portion of the Word of God. There are even people who say this is not even God's Word because it is no expression for a Christian today. Well, who said it was? This is going to be for God's people during the Great Tribulation. In that day these people under law will pray this kind of prayer as they did in the past under law. And God intends to hear His people, and He intends to bring vengeance upon their enemies. We are to do things differently during this age. Matthew 5:44 says, "But I say unto you, Love your enemies, bless them that curse you, do good to them that hate you, and pray for them which despitefully use you, and persecute you." This is difficult to do, I will grant you that, but that is what the Lord asks us to do. In Romans 12:19 we are told, "Dearly beloved, avenge not yourselves, but rather give place unto wrath: for it is written, Vengeance is mine; I will repay, saith the Lord." God says that He will take care of any reprisals. When we get hit in the nose, it is human nature to want to hit back. But when we take matters into our own hands, we are not walking with Him by faith. God wants us to trust Him to take care of our enemies.

When the Lord Jesus Christ was here on earth and was so brutally treated, He did not strike back. He wants those who are His own in the church today to take that same position. But God has said, "Vengeance is mine; I will repay." God intends to take care of it some day.

This is a marvelous psalm. What a comfort it will be to God's people in the time of severe persecution!

PSALM 6

***THEME:** A cry for mercy*

The man in this psalm has looked all about him and has seen the wickedness on every hand. He has also looked in his own heart and recognized that he is not perfect before God at all. If the previous psalms and prayers had to do with morning and evening, this psalm has to do with the darkest night. This psalm is addressed to "The chief Musician on Neginoth upon Sheminith." We are introduced to a new term *sheminith.* It means "upon the octave," and there are those who believe it should be sung by male voices. Psalm 5 is an imprecatory psalm, and Psalm 6 is a penitential psalm, a cry of repentance, and plea for mercy.

O LORD, rebuke me not in thine anger, neither chasten me in thy hot displeasure.

Have mercy upon me, O LORD; for I am weak: O LORD, heal me; for my bones are vexed.

My soul is also sore vexed: but thou, O LORD, how long?

Return, O LORD, deliver my soul: oh save me for thy mercies' sake [Ps. 6:1–4].

The psalmist sees his own need. When he does, there is a wonderful cry of repentance. Next we have his confession.

For in death there is no remembrance of thee: in the grave who shall give thee thanks?

I am weary with my groaning; all the night make I my bed to swim; I water my couch with my tears.

Mine eye is consumed because of grief; it waxeth old because of all mine enemies [Ps. 6:5–7].

I think we have here a picture of David, and I think we have a picture of the Lord Jesus Christ. I think it is also a picture of Israel in the last days, and a picture of believers right now—you and me. What a psalm this is! This is a cry for mercy out of the very depths of despair. Only mercy can save us. We are told over and over again in the New Testament that God is *rich* in mercy. He has had to use a lot of His mercy on me, but He has some left over for you. He has plenty of mercy, and we certainly need it.

Isaiah 52:14 says of the Lord Jesus, ". . . his visage was so marred more than any man, and his form more than the sons of men." In Psalm 69:3 the Lord says, "I am weary of my crying: my throat is dried: mine eyes fail while I wait for my God." Again in Psalm 42:3 the Lord says, "My tears have been my meat day and night, while they continually say unto me, Where is thy God?" In Psalm 38:10 He says, "My heart panteth, my strength faileth me: as for the light of mine eyes, it also is gone from me." Finally, in Psalm 88:9 the Lord says, "Mine eye mourneth by reason of affliction: LORD, I have called daily upon thee, I have stretched out my hands unto thee." In all of these expressions, and I have given you only a very small segment, the Spirit of Christ speaks prophetically of His own suffering through which He would pass in the days of His humiliation.

His people, the nation Israel, that remnant in the Great Tribulation, will also pass through suffering. Today many of God's saints are passing through it. The great comfort is that *He* has been through it. These are the things that He has suffered, that He endured. Regardless of what you are going through today, *He* has already been through it, and He can comfort you. How wonderful it is to have a Savior like the Lord Jesus Christ.

> **Depart from me, all ye workers of iniquity; for the LORD hath heard the voice of my weeping [Ps. 6:8].**

Here is the answer to prayer:

> **The LORD hath heard my supplication; the LORD will receive my prayer [Ps. 6:9].**

In Hebrews 5:7 we are told concerning the Lord Jesus, "Who in the days of his flesh, when he had offered up prayers and supplications with strong crying and tears unto him that was able to save him from death, and was heard in that he feared." That is our confidence today. God will hear and answer our prayer when we are in deep trouble. Isn't that a comfort to you, friend? You may be in a very hard place right at the moment. If you are, this psalm is for you.

PSALM 7

***THEME:** A cry for revenge*

Someone has suggested that over this psalm should be written: "Shall not the Judge of all the earth do right?" (Gen. 18:25).

Notice that the inscription is "Shiggaion of David, which he sang unto the LORD, concerning the words of Cush the Benjamite." Although we cannot be dogmatic on the meaning of *shiggaion*, it is thought that it means "crying aloud." This is David crying aloud in song. How I would love to have heard him sing this psalm. This psalm is a *loud cry*. I think it reveals prophetically the persecution and the final suffering of the God-fearing remnant of Israel during the time of the Great Tribulation. It is the outcry against the "man of sin," a theme that is carried into the next psalm. Notice David's confidence in prayer:

> **O LORD my God, in thee do I put my trust: save me from all them that persecute me, and deliver me:**
>
> **Lest he tear my soul like a lion, rending it in pieces, while there is none to deliver [Ps. 7:1–2].**

Arno Gaebelein's translation reads: "Jehovah, my God, in thee I seek shelter. Save me from my pursuers, and rescue me, lest like a lion he tear my soul rending in pieces, and no one to deliver" (*The Book of Psalms*, p. 40). Who is that lion? That is Satan, whom Peter says is on the prowl. "Be sober, be vigilant; because your adversary the devil, as a roaring lion, walketh about, seeking whom he may devour" (1 Pet. 5:8).

Then he speaks of unjust persecution:

> **O LORD my God, if I have done this; if there be iniquity in my hands;**
>
> **If I have rewarded evil unto him that was at peace with me; (yea, I have delivered him that without cause is mine enemy:) [Ps. 7:3–4].**

Unjust and innocent suffering in this world is something I don't understand. I don't propose to understand it, but I want to say this to you: I know Somebody who does understand it, and He is going to explain it to us one day. There are things in my life and things in your life that we don't understand. I can't explain your trouble, because I don't even know why I have had to go through certain things; but He is going to explain it someday.

Now we come to the wonderful part. This is not the darkness of night as we saw in Psalm 6, but this is morning light.

> **Arise, O LORD, in thine anger, lift up thyself because of the rage of mine enemies: and awake for me to the judgment that thou hast commanded [Ps. 7:6].**

He cries for God to avenge and vindicate him.

God judgeth the righteous, and God is angry with the wicked every day [Ps. 7:11].

At the time I am writing this, we are in a time of the "new morality," which is really just old immorality. God doesn't go along with it; He is not changing His standards to conform to modern thought. Because of this, we can sing with David:

I will praise the LORD according to his righteousness: and will sing praise to the name of the LORD most high [Ps. 7:17].

My friend, God will deal with sin and wickedness, and He will finally eradicate it from His universe. Praise the Lord!

PSALM 8

THEME: *A messianic psalm emphasizing the humanity of Christ and His ultimate victory as Man*

Messianic psalms are so called because they are quoted in the New Testament in direct reference to the Lord Jesus Christ. Psalm 8 is quoted three times in the New Testament. In fact, the Lord Jesus Himself quoted from this psalm. In Matthew 21 we have recorded what is called the triumphal entry of Christ into Jerusalem. The children in the temple were saying, ". . . Hosanna to the son of David" (Matt. 21:9). The chief priests and the scribes said, "Do you hear what they are saying?" It was at this time that Jesus said, ". . . Yea; have ye never read, Out of the mouth of babes and sucklings thou hast perfected praise?" (Matt. 21:16). Our Lord was quoting Psalm 8:2. He was telling the chief priests and the scribes that it would be a good idea if they read this Scripture so that they would understand why the children were saying this.

The second quotation from this psalm is found in 1 Corinthians 15:27, the resurrection chapter: "For he hath put all things under his feet" (v. 6). It is quite obvious that this psalm does not refer to our day, as Paul explains: "For he hath put all things under his feet. But when he saith all things are put under him, it is manifest that he is excepted, which did put all things under him."

We today do not see all things put under Him, that is for sure. However, the most complete quotation is found in Hebrews 2:5–8, which makes it very clear that Psalm 8 refers to our Lord Jesus Christ: "For unto the angels hath he not put in subjection the world to come, whereof we speak. But one in a certain place testified, saying, What is man, that thou art mindful of him? or the son of man, that thou visitest him? Thou madest him a little lower than the angels; thou crownedst him with glory and honour, and didst set him over the works of thy hands: Thou hast put all things in subjection under his feet. For in that he put all in subjection under him, he left nothing that is not put under him. But now we see not yet all things put under him." Again it is called to our attention that you and I live in a day when all things are not put under Him. Obviously Psalm 8 looks to the future.

Read Hebrews 2:9: "But we see Jesus, who was made a little lower than the angels for the suffering of death, crowned with glory and honour; that he by the grace of God should taste death for every man." Psalm 8 is talking about Jesus.

Now this second great messianic psalm begins with the statement: "O LORD our Lord, how excellent is thy name in all the earth!" And the psalm closes with "O LORD our Lord, how excellent is thy name in all the earth!"

This is not a reference to the present hour in which we are living. God's name is not very excellent in the world today. Not long ago on the golf course I heard an old man, who was standing right on the threshold of eternity, use the name of the Lord in vain in a way that was absolutely uncalled for. Walking down the street I heard a very nicely dressed, refined looking, gentle-woman, who looked like a grandmother, swear. My, how she could swear! God's name is not very excellent today. The fact of the matter is that people today are not saying very much about God. I notice on the newscasts that God is never mentioned. He makes the news, too, but He is never brought into the picture. God is recognized in insurance policies that insure houses that are destroyed by fire or by an "act of God"! Do they think the Lord is running around destroying houses? That is the only publicity God gets today. It is all bad as far as He is concerned. He is being left out and left out purposely. His Word is not wanted in the schools. These broad-minded liberals, who believe that everybody should be heard, think pornography should be permitted because the liberties of people should not be curtailed. Well, friend, don't I have a share in that liberty? I would like to have prayer in schools for my grandchildren. How about you? I would like some public recognition of God. I would like to have prayer in public places. Have I no liberties any longer in this land of ours? No, God's name is not excellent today.

The other night I watched a thrilling travelogue on television. Some men climbed to the top of Mount Everest, and the wind at the top was terrific. That old mountain was really talking back to them, letting them know that man is nothing. But there was no mention of God. Mountains are just a bunch of dirt, rocks, and a few trees; they do not talk or become violent or make men feel little. It is the God who made the mountain who does that. It was God on top of Mount Everest who let those men know how really insignificant they were. But the men did not learn how great God is; they just talked about nature. May I say to you that God's name is not excellent in the world today. Not at all.

This first verse in Psalm 8 is a prophecy. It looks to the future, a glorious future. It is a messianic psalm in which we see God's Man. It emphasizes the humanity of Christ and His ultimate victory as Man. In Psalm 2 we saw man in rejection and man's rebellion against God. In Psalm 8 we see that man finally gains control of this earth, and the day will come when God's name will be excellent in all the earth.

At this point I should mention that this psalm is addressed to "the chief Musician upon Gittith." Both Psalm 81 and Psalm 84 are also dedicated to "The chief Musician upon Gittith." What does that mean? The "gittith" has generally been interpreted as a musical instrument, a type of lyre. A Jewish scholar said that the word *gittith* was taken from the name Gath, and it was an instrument known in Gath. You will recall that David found shelter in Gath when he was escaping from King Saul. He probably learned to play this strange instrument at that time and later introduced it to Israel. The Vulgate and the Septuagint translate the word *gittith* as "winepress." I think there is significance in that also, as Psalm 8 reveals the winepress of suffering that the Lord Jesus went into for you and me. As Man He tasted death for all men; He tasted the *bitterness* of the winepress. Later on, Isaiah will tell us that the Lord Jesus is coming from Edom. He says: "I have trodden the winepress alone; and of the people there was none with me: for I will tread them in mine anger, and trample them in my fury; and their blood shall be sprinkled upon my garments, and I will stain all my raiment" (Isa. 63:3). The juice of the grapes on His garments is not His own blood but that of His enemies. You see, if the blood of Christ means nothing to you now and you are not saved, you will have to be judged. It is either His blood or yours, my friend. That is the position of man in the world today.

Psalm 8 is a psalm of David. There are those who try to read into it "the death for the son," supposing that David wrote it at the time of the death of Bathsheba's infant son or on the occasion of the death of the giant Goliath. I mention all of these theories because this is a psalm that apparently has a great and deep meaning. I had a professor once who gave this psalm the title: "Stars and Sucklings." This psalm goes all the way from the heavens—the moon and the stars—to nursing children. Also this psalm goes along with Psalm 19, another nature psalm, which speaks of the Scriptures and the sun. But the sun is not mentioned here in Psalm 8 at all.

O LORD our Lord, how excellent is thy name in all the earth! who hast set thy glory above the heavens.

Out of the mouth of babes and sucklings hast thou ordained strength because of thine enemies, that thou mightest still the enemy and the avenger [Ps. 8:1–2].

The Lord made the truth of this verse clear when He said on earth, ". . . Verily I say unto you, Except ye be converted, and become as little children, ye shall not enter into the kingdom of heaven" (Matt. 18:3). It was children who cried, ". . . Hosanna to the son of David . . ." (Matt. 21:15) during His so-called triumphal entry into Jerusalem. Actually I do not consider it a triumphal entry. We must wait until He comes to earth again; then He will have a *real* triumphal entry. This is just a little picture of the fact that He is coming to earth again; and, when He does, He will establish His kingdom. In the meantime we must be converted and become as little children. I think this means that you and I must be born again and become little children. Like little children, we put aside all of our boasting and come in simple faith. How tremendous is the faith of a little child.

In this psalm we see the Lord as Creator. You have nature, the creation, and you have man, the creature. You have a relationship here.

When I consider thy heavens, the work of thy fingers, the moon and the stars, which thou hast ordained [Ps. 8:3].

"Which thou hast ordained" means that God put them in their places. In Southern California I often look at the moon and a star that is very bright when it gets over into the southwest—which means it is located out yonder over the South Pacific. I have often wondered why it is there. I know only that it is there because Jesus wants it to be there. He put it there. In my study I have certain things placed here and there. I have a book in a certain place—because that is where I want it. Now the stars are not arranged according to the way I want them—I might move that one out in the southwest—but they are placed where our Lord Jesus wants them to be. He is the One who is ordaining.

The heavens are the work of His fingers. It is interesting that when the Word speaks of salvation, it refers to the bared *arm* of the Lord: "Who hath believed our report? and to whom is the arm of the LORD revealed?" (Isa. 53:1). But when it speaks of the creation of the heavens and the earth, it calls it His *fingerwork*. As John Wesley put it, "God created the heavens and the earth and didn't half try." Creation was His finger-work, like the crocheting that a woman does.

God put His glory above His creation. It is great to us, and there is a glory in creation, but we don't worship His creation. We worship the Creator. His finger-work tells out His glory and His power.

What is man, that thou art mindful of him? and the son of man, that thou visitest him? [Ps. 8:4].

There are those still working on the problem of, "What is man?" Man is a complicated creature. He is a human being. He belongs to the human race, and there are people still trying to figure out how he got here. The Bible says that God created us and put us on earth. Then man went afoul, he turned aside, he disbelieved God, and he disobeyed Him. Why would God be mindful of man? Why didn't God just wipe man out and get rid of him?

Man is a great failure. We don't like to hear that. We want to hear about success. Sometimes I think the most difficult job in the world is to be a cancer specialist. Since I have had cancer, I have gotten pretty close to that group, and they are pessimists, as I see it. They don't have many success stories in their field. Well, man doesn't have a success story; he is really a miserable failure. He has gotten his world in a mess. The psalmist asks, "What is man, that thou art mindful of him?" I will tell you why man is important. Some two thousand years ago the Lord Jesus Christ visited him. He made a trip to earth and died on a cross to let us know that He loved us. He did not save us by love; He saved us by grace because we did not have anything to offer—we were not worth saving. Yet God the Son came to this earth. I don't know if there are any other planets which are inhabited—there may be—but I know that Christ has not been there to die on a cross. He came only here for that purpose.

For thou hast made him a little lower than the angels, and hast crowned him with glory and honour [Ps. 8:5].

When the Lord Jesus made Old Testament appearances, He came as *the* Angel of the Lord; but when He came to Bethlehem, He came much lower than that—He came to the level of man.

Thou madest him to have dominion over the works of thy hands; thou hast put all things under his feet [Ps. 8:6].

Man was given dominion over the works of God's hands, but man lost that. Man does not control this universe today. Science thought it had things under control, but now we find that science has polluted this earth; and it looks as if our earth will become a big garbage can. Science is responsible for polluting this earth. If you have been worshiping science and want to get out of the garbage can, you need a God who can help you.

"Thou madest him to have dominion . . . thou hast put all things under his feet"—but they haven't been put there yet, and won't be until Jesus returns.

All sheep and oxen, yea, and the beasts of the field;

The fowl of the air, and the fish of the sea, and whatsoever passeth through the paths of the seas [Ps. 8:7–8].

God made it all. He is the Creator. God made the beasts of the field, the fowl of the air, and the fish of the sea. God made it all. He is the Creator. He made you and me. In Romans 1:20 Paul says, "For the invisible things of him from the creation of the world are clearly seen, being understood by the things that are made, even his eternal power and Godhead; so that they are without excuse." We can see God's handiwork by simply looking around.

O Lord our Lord, how excellent is thy name in all the earth! [Ps. 8:9].

Not today, but someday the name of the Lord will be excellent in all the earth. In our time, we live in a universe that is groaning, travailing in pain, waiting for the redemption (Rom. 8:22). But God is above all creation. He has set His glory above the heavens. And up yonder is that Man who over two thousand years ago came down to this earth to be born in Bethlehem. He is seated now in glory at God's right hand. Only by faith will we be able to see Him.

"But we all, with open face beholding as in a glass the glory of the Lord, are changed into the same image from glory to glory, even as by the Spirit of the Lord" (2 Cor. 3:18). "Beloved, now are we the sons of God, and it doth not yet appear what we shall be: but we know that, when he shall appear, we shall be like him; for we shall see him as he is" (1 John 3:2). What a glorious prospect this is for the child of God!

Once again I would like to remind you that this is a messianic psalm. It emphasizes the humanity of Christ and His ultimate victory as Man. We have just stood on the fringe of this glorious psalm, friend, that sings praises to our Savior.

PSALMS 9–10

THEME: *Satan's man*

We were climbing an ascending stairway between the first two messianic psalms (2 and 8). Psalm 8 was the pinnacle, and now we are starting down the mountain on the other side. The descent will be through seven psalms that tell out a prophetic story. We will get glimpses of the suffering of the Jewish remnant at the end time and also a glimpse of the "man of sin," also called "the lawless one," who is yet to appear upon the earth.

Psalm 9 and Psalm 10 are very closely connected. There is a certain alphabetical structure, an acrostic, that is not seen in our translation, but which can be seen in the original. As a result, you will find that the Septuagint and the Vulgate put these two psalms together and consider them as one. This psalm is addressed to "the chief Musician upon Muth-labben." What does this word mean? It means "death for the son," a subject that some authors identify with Psalm 8 as we have seen. I think it is generally accepted to be the inscription for Psalm 9. This psalm is ascribed to David, the sweet singer of Israel. There are those who see the death of Goliath in this psalm. Others identify it with the death of Bathsheba's son. It means "death of the son, the firstborn"; and I rather think that it refers to what happened in the land of Egypt when Israel was delivered from slavery through the death of the firstborn of Egypt.

It begins with a note of praise.

I will praise thee, O Lord, with my whole heart; I will shew forth all thy marvellous works.

I will be glad and rejoice in thee: I will sing praise to thy name, O thou most High [Ps. 9:1–2].

This psalm begins with praise just as Psalm 7 begins with praise. As in the seventh psalm, so in Psalm 9 the praise is in anticipation of the coming victory so beautifully predicted in Psalm 8, when all things will be put under the feet of Him who was made a little lower than the angels. In fact, the first section of this psalm is a prophetic forecast of what earthly conditions will be when the Son of Man has received the throne in righteousness and in peace. In view of the future deliverance, we have this great song of praise in which all earthly people will join in that day. We have a picture of this in the Book of Revelation when that great company out of the nation Israel, the church, and the twenty-four elders will share in a time of great praise unto God.

When mine enemies are turned back,

they shall fall and perish at thy presence.

For thou hast maintained my right and my cause; thou satest in the throne judging right [Ps. 9:3–4].

Once again we move into the time of the kingdom that is mentioned in Psalm 8, when all things will be put under His feet. John Knox put it like this: "One with God is a majority." He was not so much concerned about having God on his side as he was making sure he was on God's side. The important thing to David was that his cause was right. Let's make sure, my friend, that we are on God's side.

Now he speaks of the coming judgment.

Thou hast rebuked the heathen, thou hast destroyed the wicked, thou hast put out their name for ever and ever [Ps. 9:5].

"Thou hast rebuked the heathen" is better translated, "Thou hast rebuked the nations." What a psalm this is!

O thou enemy, destructions are come to a perpetual end: and thou hast destroyed cities; their memorial is perished with them [Ps. 9:6].

This is a strong declaration of the judgment that is coming.

The question arises, Is there enough preaching today about judgment? I would say that there is enough preaching of a certain kind of judgment, but there are very few sermons on the subject of hell. Lately I have had the opportunity to hear more sermons than I have heard for years, and I notice two things about them. Most sermons are designed to comfort God's people. In fact, many sermons are geared for those who seem to have some sort of a complex or are just looking for a shoulder to cry on. However, a sermon I heard the other day was on the subject of hell; but the bitterness of the preacher came through. I feel that before a man preaches on hell he ought to search his own heart to make sure that the subject affects him—that his heart is broken because men are lost. An unbeliever made the following statement about Dwight L. Moody when he was told that Moody preached a sermon on hell: "I don't like to hear sermons on hell, but if there is any man who can preach on that subject, it is Dwight L. Moody." May I say to you, not only should there be sermons on hell, but the right kind of men should preach them. I suppose one of the reasons I don't preach more sermons on hell is because I think I should be deeply moved in my heart when I do talk about this subject.

The psalmist makes it clear that all the enemies of Israel are to be conquered. This is God's victory for the remnant that will be on His side. I think what we have here is the death of the son, the firstborn, in Egypt. This takes us right down to the place where anti-Semitism was born—it started in the land of Egypt. A new king in that land enslaved God's chosen people, and he tried to exterminate the whole race which would frustrate the grace and purpose of God in redemption. Ever since that time the nations have been Israel's enemies. They will continue to hate Israel until the day of deliverance comes. At this present moment there is a feeling of hatred toward the Jews.

In this next passage the kingdom and the throne of righteousness is established.

But the LORD shall endure for ever: he hath prepared his throne for judgment.

And he shall judge the world in righteousness, he shall minister judgment to the people in uprightness [Ps. 9:7–8].

"He shall judge the world in righteousness" —that is important. It is my feeling today that we are short on judges who will follow the law and assess a penalty when a penalty should be assessed. We have too many judges who are softhearted, and I sometimes think softheaded, who are trying to be popular. Righteousness is what is needed today. The One who makes the right is God. Right is not necessarily what you think or what I think. It was God who divided the light from the darkness. I have never been able to separate them. I have never gotten up before daylight, waved a wand, and brought up the sun. God does that. He is the One who declares what is right. If you don't think so, *you* are wrong. That is just the way it is. It is as simple as that. Someone has to make the rules. God makes the rules for this universe, and He is running it. God is going to be around for a long time, and I think He has that prerogative.

Now, moving down a few verses, we have a picture of the condition before Christ comes to establish His kingdom.

Have mercy upon me, O LORD; consider my trouble which I suffer of them that hate me, thou that liftest me up from the gates of death [Ps. 9:13].

"Have mercy upon me, O LORD"—I don't know about you, but I need mercy from God. You may question that since I said there will be justice when He comes. But, you see, justice has already been established in the person of the Lord Jesus Christ when He bore our sins, and He has been made unto us righteousness. What I need today is mercy, and mercy is extended to us in the person of Jesus Christ.

That I may shew forth all thy praise in the gates of the daughter of Zion: I will rejoice in thy salvation [Ps. 9:14].

And we need more folk to *rejoice* in God.

The heathen are sunk down in the pit that they made: in the net which they hid is their own foot taken [Ps. 9:15].

The *heathen* is better translated "nations"—"The nations are sunk down in the pit that they made."

Look at the nations of the world today. Even the great nations of the world, including our own nation, have sunk down into a pit. We seem to be caught. This is the condition of the world at the present hour.

The LORD is known by the judgment which he executeth: the wicked is snared in the work of his own hands. Higgaion. Selah [Ps. 9:16].

This is a tremendous verse!

The wicked shall be turned into hell, and all the nations that forget God [Ps. 9:17].

A cry goes out: "The wicked shall be turned into hell [Sheol, that is, unto *death*], and all the nations that forget God." This is a great principle that God has put down.

For the needy shall not alway be forgotten: the expectation of the poor shall not perish for ever [Ps. 9:18].

"The needy shall not alway be forgotten"—they are today. Oh, there are poverty programs, but the man at the top always seems to get it before it reaches the poor. The poor will receive justice when the Lord Jesus comes. You know, we poor people ought to be more interested in the Lord. There are so many people in poverty who are turning to political parties and certain political candidates for help. Unfortunately, they are not going to receive much help. What the candidates are trying to do is to get into office. The Lord Jesus is not running for office—He is King of kings and Lord of lords. He is not anxious to please any party or any group on this earth. When Christ came to earth the first time, He came to do God's will. Since He is God, when He comes again He is going to do His own will. My friend, "the needy shall not always be forgotten: the expectation of the poor shall not perish for ever." They are expecting a great deal from man, but only God will meet their need.

Arise, O LORD; let not man prevail: let the heathen be judged in thy sight [Ps. 9:19].

"Let the *nations* be judged"—the nations are yet to be judged, according to our Lord (Matt. 25:31–46), ". . . and he shall separate them one from another, as a shepherd divideth his sheep from the goats" (Matt. 25:32).

Put them in fear, O LORD: that the nations may know themselves to be but men. Selah [Ps. 9:20].

There are some today who feel that they are operating in the position of God. Remember that the inscription of this psalm is "Muthlabben," meaning death for the son. If you consider the son to be Goliath or Pharaoh, both of them are little pictures of the Antichrist who is yet to come. He will be Satan's man, and he will put himself in the position of God. God will ultimately put him down.

Now when we come to Psalm 10, we still see Satan's man, the man of the earth, which closely identifies Psalm 10 with Psalm 9.

Notice how the wicked one is described:

Why standest thou afar off, O LORD? why hidest thou thyself in times of trouble?

The wicked in his pride doth persecute the poor: let them be taken in the devices that they have imagined.

For the wicked boasteth of his heart's desire, and blesseth the covetous, whom the LORD abhorreth [Ps. 10: 1–3].

There are two things that characterize the wicked in these verses: pride and boasting. Do you want to know who the wicked are as you look around the world? They are those who are filled with pride, the "great" of the earth, who have no place for God in their lives. Also they do a great deal of boasting. I don't know how you feel, but I am not impressed by politicians and world leaders who are always boasting that they will solve the problems of the world. They remind me of what Aesop said about a mountain that travailed and brought forth a mouse! They boast of doing great things, but they accomplish practically nothing. What a picture we have here of the wicked and the "wicked one," the Antichrist, who will be the false messiah. He is identified in this psalm. Pride identifies him.

The wicked, through the pride of his countenance, will not seek after God: God is not in all his thoughts [Ps. 10:4].

"God is not in all his thoughts" is better translated: "All his thoughts are: there is no God." Antichrist will be an atheist.

In the time of David there began to emerge for the first time in history those who were atheists. There were no atheists at the beginning because they were too close to the mooring mast of revelation. After all, Noah knew a man who knew Adam. When you are that close to the time of creation, you are not apt to deny the existence of God. When the Ten Commandments were given, there was no commandment against atheism; but there was one against polytheism—the worship of many gods. The first commandment is: "Thou shalt have no other gods before me." The second commandment is: "Thou shalt not make unto thee any graven image, or any likeness of any thing that is in heaven above, or that is in the earth beneath, or that is in the water under the earth" (Exod. 20:3–4). There are two commandments against polytheism, and none against atheism because there were no atheists. However, David will mention atheism several times.

The Antichrist at the end times will be characterized by atheism, filled with pride and boasting.

His ways are always grievous; thy judgments are far above out of his sight: as for all his enemies, he puffeth at them.

He hath said in his heart, I shall not be moved: for I shall never be in adversity [Ps. 10:5–6].

This also characterizes man in our day—boasting of his prosperity and self-sufficiency. He feels no need of God.

Now notice something else that will characterize Antichrist:

Wherefore doth the wicked contemn God? he hath said in his heart, Thou wilt not require it [Ps. 10:13].

Not only does he not believe in God, but he despises Him. It is inconsistent to despise Someone who does not exist; apparently He has to exist to build up this kind of bitterness and hatred.

When he says, "Thou wilt not require it," he is saying that there is no judgment. There is a great multitude of people emerging in our contemporary culture who are saying there is no God, or, if He exists, He is too far away for them to bother with; and they are confident there will be no judgment. My friend, if you take that position, anything goes. It is that philosophy that is behind the movement to abolish capital punishment or any kind of punishment or any kind of imprisonment for a criminal. The argument I hear is that methods used today do not *reform* criminals. Whoever said that the purpose of punishment and prisons was to *reform*? It never was intended to reform; it was intended to *deter* crime. God gave these laws to protect the innocent. And God's judgment is inevitable upon the earth. The closer we get to it, the less man believes it is coming.

God is probably the most unpopular Person in the world right now. Why? Because the wicked are in the saddle. We are moving toward the time when the sin of man will lead to the "man of sin," this final Antichrist.

The LORD is King for ever and ever: the heathen are perished out of his land.

LORD, thou hast heard the desire of the humble: thou wilt prepare their heart, thou wilt cause thine ear to hear:

To judge the fatherless and the oppressed, that the man of the earth may no more oppress [Ps. 10:16–18].

"The man of the earth" is Antichrist.

These are remarkable psalms, my friend, because they amplify a great many truths which we get historically and prophetically in other portions of the Word of God.

PSALM 11

***THEME:** Testing of the righteous*

This is a wonderful little psalm of David, ascribed to the chief Musician. We are not told under what circumstances it was written, but obviously it came out of the persecution and trials in the life of David. I am going to give an extended quotation from J. J. Stewart Perowne because I think it is a remarkable statement to be coming from a man who was liberal in his theology.

> The singer is in danger of his life; and timorous and faint-hearted counsellors would fain persuade him to seek safety in flight. But, full of unshaken faith in God, he rejects their counsel, believing that Jehovah, the righteous king, though He tries His servants, does not forsake them. Not the righteous, but the wicked have need to fear. The Psalm is so short and so general in its character, that it is not easy to say to what circumstances in David's life it should be referred. The choice seems, however, to lie between his persecution by Saul and the rebellion of his son Absalom. Delitzsch decides for the last, and thinks the counsel (v. 1), "flee to your mountain," comes from the mouth of friends who are anxious to persuade the king to betake himself, as he had before done when hunted by Saul, to "the rocks of the wild goats" (1 Sam. 24:2). It is in favor, to some extent, of this view that the expression in v. 3, "when the foundations are destroyed," points to a time when lawful authority was subverted (*The Book of Psalms*, p. 166).

This is one time when I agree with a liberal. I think this psalm has reference to the time he fled from Absalom.

Here is another expression from the heart of this great king:

In the LORD put I my trust: how say ye to my soul, Flee as a bird to your mountain? [Ps. 11:1].

This is the advice psychologists will give you today. They will tell you that what you need to do is get away from your problems. Go off somewhere—what you need is a rest. Flee from your present circumstances, as a bird to the mountain. My friend, getting away from it all does not solve a thing. Years ago, in my southland, the lady of the house was complaining to her wonderful housekeeper about wanting to get away from it all. Her housekeeper said, "What are you trying to get away from? This beautiful home? Your lovely children? Your wonderful husband? No matter where you go, you are going to have to lug *yourself* along." You can never run away from yourself. How true that is! People would tell David, "Flee as a bird to your mountain," but that was not the way to solve his problems.

In our mechanical society and very monotonous culture it is very tiring to sit in an automobile for seven hours on a freeway. Flying in an airplane is a wonderful experience; but after you have been across the country and around the world, flying gets monotonous. You are way up in the air where there is not much to see or do. Actually, I think it is a good thing for a person to get away from the busy life and the noise of the city and the traffic to find a restful place to relax. But if you are trying to run away from your *problems* or from some situation that you ought to face, this is not good advice. You should not run away because of fear. Many who were counseling David to run away and to get out of the country were afraid for his life, because Absalom, this son of his, was trying to kill him.

For, lo, the wicked bend their bow, they make ready their arrow upon the string, that they may privily shoot at the upright in heart [Ps. 11:2].

Those who were following Absalom were willing to kill David if they had the opportunity. There was great bitterness on both sides. When Absalom came in battle against his father, David did not leave the land. David retreated in order to reconnoiter and then came against his son with his army. David gave specific instructions to his three captains: "Remember my boy Absalom and don't harm him. I want him safe." Absalom made a big mistake in fighting his father and the veterans who were with him, because David was a seasoned warrior and knew all the tricks of the trade. He knew how to fight in the woods and the mountains. Absalom and his men were not as experienced, and they lost. Not only was there bitterness on Absalom's side, it was also on David's side—although not in David's heart—but Joab, one of

David's captains, when he had the opportunity, put a dart through the boy and killed him. There was bitterness on both sides.

The death of his son broke David's heart. I don't think he ever recovered from that. When Absalom tried to take over, David fled from Jerusalem. Law and order had disappeared. No longer was there worship of the living and true God.

If the foundations be destroyed, what can the righteous do? [Ps. 11:3].

This is still a good question to ask. Today the authority of the Word of God is being challenged on every hand. As I write, we have the "new morality," which is sin that the Bible has condemned from the very beginning. The problem is, What can the righteous do? I will tell you what they can do. Listen to the psalmist:

The LORD is in his holy temple, the LORD'S throne is in heaven: his eyes behold, his eyelids try, the children of men [Ps. 11:4].

God is watching us today. He is testing us. And the only place we can turn is to Him. When the foundations are taken out from under us, the righteous have God to cling to.

Abraham reached that place. When it says that Abraham believed God, it means that Abraham threw his arms around God and just held on. He believed God. And these are days when we can believe God and hold on to Him. It is time for many of us who cannot sing the Hallelujah Chorus to at least say it. How wonderful is our God!

The LORD trieth the righteous: but the wicked and him that loveth violence his soul hateth [Ps. 11:5].

"The LORD trieth the righteous" is better translated "the Lord *tests* the righteous." God knows who are His own, and He will test His children. He tests me and He may be testing you. And that doesn't mean He hates us. He is testing us for our good and His glory.

"But the wicked and him that loveth violence his soul hateth." If you think God is just lovey-dovey, you had better read this and some of the other psalms again. God hates the wicked who hold on to their wickedness. I don't think God loves the devil. I think God hates him, and He hates those who have no intention of turning to Him. Frankly, I do not like this distinction that I hear today that, "God loves the sinner, but He hates the sin." God has loved you so much that He gave His Son to die for you; but if you persist in your sin and continue in that sin, you are the enemy of God. And God is your enemy. God wants to save you, and He will save you if you turn to Him and forsake your iniquity. Until then, may I say, God is not a lovey-dovey, sentimental, old gentleman from Georgia.

Upon the wicked he shall rain snares, fire and brimstone, and an horrible tempest: this shall be the portion of their cup [Ps. 11:6].

The cup of iniquity is filling up in our day. And God is allowing it to fill up; He is doing nothing to hinder it. The wicked are prospering. He makes it rain on the unjust as well as the just. In fact, it looks to me like they are getting more rain than anybody else. This is *their* day.

For the righteous LORD loveth righteousness; his countenance doth behold the upright [Ps. 11:7].

The Lord *loves* righteousness. In time of trouble when the foundations are removed, we are to look from earth to heaven—the upright will behold His face. What a wonderful picture this is!

PSALM 12

***THEME:** The godly in the midst of the godlessness of the Great Tribulation*

Prophetically, this psalm is like the preceding ones. It refers ultimately in its final fulfillment to the days of the Tribulation which will come upon Israel's godly remnant—also upon godly Gentiles—in that day.

In the opening verses we find a description of the apostasy in those days. You see, there is to be an apostasy in Israel as well as in the church.

Help, LORD; for the godly man ceaseth; for the faithful fail from among the children of men [Ps. 12:1].

It is easy to develop an Elijah complex today and say, "I am the only one left. I am the only one standing for God today." Many people develop that complex. It is not accurate, but it can happen when you see godlessness on every hand.

They speak vanity every one with his neighbour: with flattering lips and with a double heart do they speak [Ps. 12:2].

This is a day when Christians need to speak the truth. That is, we should not say one thing to a man's face and another thing when his back is turned. That is double-talk. It is being two-faced.

The LORD shall cut off all flattering lips, and the tongue that speaketh proud things:

Who have said, With our tongue will we prevail; our lips are our own: who is lord over us? [Ps. 12:3–4].

The psalmist goes after the proud in this psalm. They say, "We are going to say what we please." We are seeing that apostasy in the church is noted by pride like this. Jude predicted the coming apostasy, "These are murmurers, complainers, walking after their own lusts; and their mouth speaketh great swelling words, having men's persons in admiration because of advantage" (Jude 16). In other words, those in apostasy are a bunch of liars.

Now we see those who are God's people.

For the oppression of the poor, for the sighing of the needy, now will I arise, saith the LORD; I will set him in safety from him that puffeth at him [Ps. 12:5].

Or, better, the Lord says, "I will set him in safety at whom they puff." Today the enemy huffs and puffs like the wolf did in the story of the three little pigs. Two little pigs lost their homes because the big bad wolf blew them down. But the last little pig had a house that stood up under the huffing and puffing. The story of the three little pigs illustrates what David is saying here. God says, "I will set him in safety at whom they puff. I will hide him in the clefts of the rocks. I will put him in a place of safety."

The words of the LORD are pure words: as silver tried in a furnace of earth, purified seven times [Ps. 12:6].

Now the wicked boast and use flattery. You cannot believe what they say. But the words of the Lord are pure. That is one reason why we need to spend more time in the Word of God. It is the fortress into which God wants to put us.

Thou shalt keep them, O LORD, thou shalt preserve them from this generation for ever.

The wicked walk on every side, when the vilest men are exalted [Ps. 12:7–8].

We are living in a day like this, and it will be especially true during the time of the Great Tribulation. Listen to the prophet Isaiah when he says, "Hear the word of the LORD, ye that tremble at his word; Your brethren that hated you, that cast you out for my name's sake, said, Let the LORD be glorified [they said that in mockery]: but he shall appear to your joy, and they shall be ashamed" (Isa. 66:5). This is a wonderful picture given to us which describes the temple worship in Jerusalem at, I think, the end of the age. The Lord Jesus said in His day, when the enemy came to arrest Him, ". . . this is your hour, and the power of darkness" (Luke 22:53). We go through times when the enemy has the upper hand, but God won't let something happen to His own unless it will accomplish some worthwhile purpose in their hearts and lives.

PSALM 13

***THEME:** David's desperate plight*

This is a rather doleful section of the Book of Psalms. As we have said, Psalm 9 through Psalm 15 deal with that time of trouble which is coming—the Great Tribulation—and ones who figure during this time: Antichrist, and the Jewish remnant which will be true to God. It will be a time of great testing.

David has written this psalm out of his own trying experience, but it has a contemporary interpretation. Also it has a prophetic or chronological interpretation, reaching down into the end times after the church is removed from the earth.

David is being pursued as he writes this psalm—probably by King Saul. He may have been hiding at this time in the cave of Adullam while the Philistines were teamed up to hunt him out. Day after day he found himself in a desperate situation. In weariness of body and soreness of mind and heart he cries out to God:

> **How long wilt thou forget me, O Lord? for ever? how long wilt thou hide thy face from me? [Ps. 13:1].**

David sounds extremely pessimistic here. He feels that God has forsaken him, that he is on his own. What you have here, as Delitzsch describes it, is a long, deep sigh. "It comes finally from a relieved breast, by an already much more gentle and half-calmed prayer."

> **How long shall I take counsel in my soul, having sorrow in my heart daily? how long shall mine enemy be exalted over me? [Ps. 13:2].**

David is asking, "How long will this continue?" At this time David is a very weary man. Then he turns in prayer to God. This is his resource and his recourse.

> **Consider and hear me, O Lord my God: lighten mine eyes, lest I sleep the sleep of death [Ps. 13:3].**

David was in grave danger when he wrote this. He was afraid to go to sleep for fear that his enemy would kill him. Yet, he needed rest badly. So he asked the Lord to protect and give him sleep.

> **Lest mine enemy say, I have prevailed against him; and those that trouble me rejoice when I am moved [Ps. 13:4].**

The enemy would rejoice if he could get to David. The rejoicing of the enemy would not only be against David but also against God, so he prays that the enemy will not get the upper hand. After having heaved this awful sigh of sorrow, he continues in prayer, and he finally settles back in wonderful faith and trust in God. This is a beautiful psalm.

> **But I have trusted in thy mercy; my heart shall rejoice in thy salvation [Ps. 13:5].**

David did not think he was smart enough to get out of his predicament on his own. He took precautions, of course, but he knew only God could deliver him. God was his salvation.

> **I will sing unto the Lord, because he hath dealt bountifully with me [Ps. 13:6].**

My friend, wherever you are and whoever you are and however you are, you can still sing praises to God. As I write this, it is easy for me to praise Him. I just got a good report from my doctor about my physical condition. The Lord has been good to me and it is easy to praise Him, but I think of a man in Southern California who for years ignored God. Then he was stricken with cancer. He is flat on his back, but he has turned to the Lord through our radio program. Although he is in bad condition, a friend of mine who visited him told me, "It will rejoice your heart and humble you to visit this man and to see that in the midst of trouble he talks about how good God has been to him, how God has saved him, and how wonderful He is." When you can praise God in a spot like that, you have arrived. He may be farther along than I am.

And so in this psalm we have seen the desperate plight of David which mirrors the plight of God's people in the Great Tribulation.

PSALM 14

THEME: *Depravity of man in the last days—atheistic, filthy, rebellious*

This psalm is linked to the other psalms, especially Psalm 12. In that psalm you will recall that we saw the corruption of the last days. The godly man had ceased, it seemed; and the godless were in control. Corruption, wickedness, and lawlessness abounded. You may think it is a picture of this day, but if I may use the common colloquialism of the street, "You ain't seen nothin' yet." Wait until the Great Tribulation comes. By the way, I hope you don't see it, because God's own—those who are in the body of believers—are not going through the Great Tribulation. He has already said that He would keep them from "the hour of temptation, which shall come upon all the world, to try them that dwell upon the earth" (Rev. 3:10). The church, by which I mean the true believers, will leave before that time. This psalm certainly sets before us the corruption and wickedness of the last days, the end of the age.

Notice the marvelous arrangement of this psalm made by Bishop Horn. He divides this psalm into three parts: the corruption of the world, the enmity against the people of God, and the longing and prayer for salvation. This is the picture of Psalm 14. It is brief but very important.

THE CORRUPTION OF THE WORLD

The fool hath said in his heart, There is no God. They are corrupt, they have done abominable works, there is none that doeth good [Ps. 14:1].

The Hebrew word for "fool" in this verse is *nabal.* This may ring a bell in your thinking, because there was a man by the name of Nabal who was married to a lovely woman by the name of Abigail. His story is told in 1 Samuel 25. His name certainly characterized him accurately. He acted a fool. The word *nabal* may be translated "simple, silly, simpleton, fool, or madman."

I have a very intelligent friend who has been very successful in dealing with atheists. He was in a group of men one day when an atheist said, "I don't believe there is a God. Man doesn't have a soul, and when he dies, he dies like a dog." This man went on raving like a madman. My friend waited until the group began to break up and then approached this man. He said, "I understand you said that you are an atheist." Upon hearing these words the man launched into another tirade about his belief that there is no God. My friend said, "I would like to ask you a question. The Bible says, 'The fool hath said in his heart, There is no God.' The word *fool* means insane or mad. Either you were not sincere when you talked about God as you did and you were just talking for the benefit of the crowd, or you are a fool and a madman. I would like to know which one it is." The man turned and walked away. Knowing what we do about the universe today, only a madman would say that there is no God. Man has found that the universe works more accurately than any clock or watch he has been able to make. And there is no watch running around that "just happened"—some watchmaker made it. The universe that is timed more accurately than a watch tells us that there is a universe-maker. The *fool* has said in his heart that there is no God, and now the fool begins to appear on the scene. We have already had a glimpse of him in Psalm 10:4, where we read, "God is not in all his thoughts." A better translation of this is, "All of his thoughts are, 'There is no God!' " He exhibits the very depth of human depravity.

There are many people with Ph.D.s teaching in our universities today. Many of them are atheists. I want to say this carefully—the lowest that a man can sink in human depravity is to be an atheist. That is what the Word of God says. If you do not believe there is a God, you are a madman; you are crazy. You do not have any real sense. Having a high I.Q. is not enough. I used to teach with a man who had a Ph.D., and he didn't have sense enough to get out of the rain. I played golf with him one day when it began to rain. He looked at me and asked, "What shall we do?" He was really asking for information. What would any sensible person do when it starts pouring down rain? I said to him, "I think we had better get in out of the rain!" Even *I* knew that, but he didn't seem to know. So, you see, a scholastic degree doesn't prove a man's intelligence! "They are corrupt, they have done abominable works, there is none that doeth good." I believe you will find that most atheists are also great sinners. Gross immorality is generally one of their characteristics. A man who mixes with the college set told me, "It is amazing the number of Ph.D.s who claim to be atheists and who are living in gross immorality. And some of them actually live in filth—and I mean material, physical filth."

The LORD looked down from heaven upon the children of men, to see if there were any that did understand, and seek God [Ps. 14:2].

And what did He find?

They are all gone aside, they are all together become filthy: there is none that doeth good, no, not one [Ps. 14:3].

Paul quotes this verse in Romans 3:12, "They are all gone out of the way, they are together become unprofitable; there is none that doeth good, no, not one." Paul is not only speaking about atheists; he is speaking about everyone. This is a picture of you and me, friend. I am not an atheist, and I don't imagine you are, but we are sinners. We do not do *good*. The condition of man is corrupt, and the first three verses tell us the depths to which man can go.

ENMITY AGAINST THE PEOPLE OF GOD

They are not only against God, but they are against the people of God.

Have all the workers of iniquity no knowledge? who eat up my people as they eat bread, and call not upon the LORD.

There were they in great fear: for God is in the generation of the righteous.

Ye have shamed the counsel of the poor, because the LORD is his refuge [Ps. 14:4–6].

There is a lot of pretense upon the part of rich politicians today. A college professor, who is a friend of mine and who is liberal in his theology and in his politics, calls these politicians "limousine liberals." He said, "They don't know anything about what the *poor* man goes through, and yet they pretend to be liberal." They are like the rich man who always lets some crumbs fall off his table for the poor man to keep him satisfied (see Luke 16:20–21). I find no rich man today giving up his riches to help the poor. What little you and I accumulate he will tax to death; yet he somehow escapes taxation himself. God certainly knows human nature, does He not? This is a picture of them.

THE LONGING AND PRAYER FOR SALVATION

Now here is a note of triumph.

Oh that the salvation of Israel were come out of Zion! when the LORD bringeth back the captivity of his people, Jacob shall rejoice, and Israel shall be glad [Ps. 14:7].

This verse looks forward in anticipation to that glorious day when out of Zion will come salvation for Israel. In that day Jacob shall rejoice and Israel shall be glad. You cannot misunderstand this verse. Anyone who says that God does not have a future purpose for Israel is admitting that he doesn't know very much about the Psalms. He may try to avoid what is so clearly stated in other passages of the Word, but how can he deny that the heart cry and the joy of the psalmist is in the future when God establishes a kingdom on earth with Israel at the center?

PSALM 15

THEME: *Description of those who will be in the presence of God*

This is another brief psalm which will conclude the section which began with Psalm 9. If you review these psalms you will see a definite development. Psalms 9 and 10 picture Satan's man, who is characterized by pride, boasting, and self-sufficiency. Psalm 11 deals with the testing of the righteous. In Psalm 12 we see the godly in the midst of godlessness and the ultimate godlessness of the Great Tribulation. Psalm 13 mirrors the plight of God's people in the Great Tribulation. Psalm 14 shows us the depravity of man in the last days, with his atheistic attitude and his filthy and rebellious ways. Now Psalm 15 tells us about those who shall enter the kingdom. It describes those who are going to be in the presence of Jehovah.

> **LORD, who shall abide in thy tabernacle? who shall dwell in thy holy hill? [Ps. 15:1].**

There is only *one* holy hill; the Bible calls it Zion, which is in the land of Israel. He is talking about those who will enter the millennial kingdom, the kingdom Christ will establish on earth with Israel as the center.

> **He that walketh uprightly, and worketh righteousness, and speaketh the truth in his heart.**
>
> **He that backbiteth not with his tongue, nor doeth evil to his neighbour, nor taketh up a reproach against his neighbour.**
>
> **In whose eyes a vile person is contemned; but he honoureth them that fear the LORD. He that sweareth to his own hurt, and changeth not [Ps. 15: 2–4].**

"In whose eyes a vile person is contemned"—that is, despised. In our contemporary culture the opposite is often true; the vile person is honored, and the godly man is despised.

"He that sweareth to his own hurt, and changeth not" means that he will go on record for the truth and will not change his story to protect himself.

> **He that putteth not out his money to usury, nor taketh reward against the innocent. He that doeth these things shall never be moved [Ps. 15:5].**

In this psalm David is saying exactly what James said: "Yea, a man may say, Thou hast faith, and I have works: shew me thy faith without thy works, and I will shew thee my faith by my works" (James 2:18). I like the way John Calvin put it: "Faith alone saves, but faith that saves is not alone." Who is going to stand before God? Those who have had a faith in God that has produced a life of righteousness. At the time I write this, there is a great deal of talk about the soon coming of Christ, and yet I don't see much change in the lives of folk who say they are expecting Him. My friend, if you really believe Jesus is coming soon—or even if you believe you will someday stand before Him to give an account, you will make sure that you live your life in such a way that it will count for God. This is the real test that will prove whether or not you love Him and look for Jesus' return.

This is a tremendous psalm!

PSALM 16

***THEME:** The resurrection of the Messiah*

Psalms 16 through 24 form another segment that belongs together. In our songbooks today songs of like themes are grouped together—songs of praise, songs of repentance, etc., are in certain sections of our books. Well, this is how the Psalms are arranged in this songbook. The theme of these nine psalms is the prophecy of Christ blended with the prophecy of the faithful remnant.

Psalm 16 gives us the song of resurrection. This is the third messianic psalm. It touches on the life of Christ (v. 8), the death of Christ (v.9), the resurrection of Christ (v. 10), and the ascension of Christ (v. 11). The resurrection of Christ is quoted from this psalm in the New Testament in three different places.

This psalm is called a "Michtam of David." The word *Michtam* is of uncertain origin. Martin Luther translated it as "a golden jewel," which I think is close to the actual meaning. Psalms 56 through 60 are also called Michtam psalms.

The messianic meaning of this psalm is fully established by the testimony of the Holy Spirit in the New Testament, as we shall see.

Let us call this psalm the *Golden Jewel of David* because he is looking forward to the One coming in his line, the One of whom he could say, "This is all my salvation."

Preserve me, O God: for in thee do I put my trust [Ps. 16:1].

This reveals the wonderful voice of the Lord Jesus Christ when He said He had come to do the Father's will and had committed Himself completely to the Father (John 5:30). Christ purposely took a place of subjection on earth when He took upon Himself our humanity. Little man—and all of us are pretty little—becomes proud and tries to lift himself up. We have men in high positions today—politicians, statesmen, men of science, educators, and ministers, who almost take the place of God. But actually we are pretty small potatoes here on this earth. We don't amount to much. We were created lower than the angels (Heb. 2:6–7). I *have* to take that position, but Christ did not have to take it. He *willingly* became man. I am glad that I am a man, but I also need to recognize what man really is. I rejoice in what God is going to do for me, and with me, and to all those who believe in Him.

The psalmist says, "Preserve me, O God: for in thee do I put my trust." What a picture of the Lord Jesus Christ! It was a picture of David, and I trust it is also a picture of you and me.

O my soul, thou hast said unto the LORD, Thou art my Lord: my goodness extendeth not to thee [Ps. 16:2].

Have you ever ridden along in your car, walked in the mountains or by the seashore, looked up and said, "You are my Creator, my Redeemer, and my Lord"? Have you ever told Him that? I have a little grandson, and you cannot imagine what it means to an old man to have his grandson crawl up in his lap, put his little arms around him, and say, "You are my grandpa." It is quite wonderful. And we have a heavenly Father who made us in His image, and I am of the opinion He likes us to come to Him and tell Him, "You are my Lord." Have you told Him that lately? Don't be like the proud spoken of in Matthew 7:22–23: "Many will say to me in that day, Lord, Lord, have we not prophesied in thy name? and in thy name have cast out devils? and in thy name done many wonderful works? And then will I profess unto them, I never knew you: depart from me, ye that work iniquity." These people called Him "Lord" and did not even know Him. When I call Him "Lord," I want to *mean* it.

But to the saints that are in the earth, and to the excellent, in whom is all my delight [Ps. 16:3].

You see, He is the Lord to His saints on the earth—this privilege does not extend to everybody, as the next verse indicates.

Their sorrows shall be multiplied that hasten after another god: their drink offerings of blood will I not offer, nor take up their names into my lips [Ps. 16:4].

"Their sorrows shall be multiplied that hasten after another . . ." (you will notice that "god" is in italics in most Bibles because the word was supplied by the translators). It means that they "hasten after another" whom they think is God.

What a picture this is. The pagan had what he called his gods; in David's day they were Dagon and Baal. I am amused at folk who say they have no creed. A man said to me, "I don't believe in having a creed." I replied, "Yes, you do. Your creed is that you don't believe in having any creed." You cannot help but have a creed.

There used to be a church in downtown Los Angeles that had one whole side exposed to the street. On it there was a sign which said, "No creed, but Christ." Well, that was their creed and a good one, although it was oversimplification, and they weren't quite telling the truth to make a statement like that.

The LORD is the portion of mine inheritance and of my cup: thou maintainest my lot.

The lines are fallen unto me in pleasant places; yea, I have a goodly heritage [Ps. 16:5–6].

How wonderful—"the LORD is the portion of mine inheritance." The Lord came to earth and took His place, walking in a world of sin and sorrow. He was a perfect stranger down here. He rejoiced in Jehovah. There was peace and joy in His life.

He said, "My portion and my cup." What is the difference between a "portion" and a "cup"? My portion is what belongs to me—whether or not I enjoy it—it's mine. My cup is what I actually appropriate and make my own. For example, what is put on my grandson's plate at the dinner table is his portion. But frankly, he scatters it around and does not eat all of it; he only appropriates so much. He has a "portion" given to him, but his "cup" is what he actually consumes.

Many people in the world who have been blessed by God with all spiritual blessings do not enjoy them. Their cups do not run over. They don't have much in their cups. God wants us to *enjoy* life. Jesus said, ". . . I am come that they might have life, and that they might have it more abundantly" (John 10:10). He also said, "These things have I spoken unto you, that my joy might remain in you, and that your *joy* might be *full*" (John 15:11). Some of us have a little fun sometimes but not all the time. We need to be full of life and joy all of the time.

I will bless the LORD, who hath given me counsel: my reins also instruct me in the night seasons [Ps. 16:7].

What do you think about at night when you cannot sleep? The psalmist thought about the Lord.

Now we come to the verses that are quoted in the New Testament.

I have set the LORD always before me: because he is at my right hand, I shall not be moved.

Therefore my heart is glad, and my glory rejoiceth: my flesh also shall rest in hope.

For thou wilt not leave my soul in hell; neither wilt thou suffer thine Holy One to see corruption [Ps. 16:8–10].

This is the psalm of the resurrection of Jesus Christ. This was the heart of Peter's message on the day of Pentecost. "For David speaketh concerning him, I foresaw the Lord always before my face, for he is on my right hand, that I should not be moved: Therefore did my heart rejoice, and my tongue was glad; moreover also my flesh shall rest in hope: Because thou wilt not leave my soul in hell [*sheol* was the Hebrew word, meaning "the unseen world"], neither wilt thou suffer thine Holy One to see corruption. Thou hast made known to me the ways of life; thou shalt make me full of joy with thy countenance. Men and brethren, let me freely speak unto you of the patriarch David, that he is both dead and buried, and his sepulchre is with us unto this day [from where Peter was preaching in the temple area, they could see the tomb of David, and Peter undoubtedly pointed to it]. Therefore being a prophet, and knowing that God had sworn with an oath to him, that of the fruit of his loins, according to the flesh, he would raise up Christ to sit on his throne; He seeing this before spake of the resurrection of Christ, that his soul was not left in hell, neither his flesh did see corruption" (Acts 2:25–31). Peter said clearly that Psalm 16:8–10 spoke of the resurrection of Christ. There are several liberal expositors—Perowne is one of them—who say that Psalm 16 has no reference to the resurrection of Christ. When a liberal makes that statement, I have to consider what Simon Peter said. When Peter preached on the day of Pentecost, several thousand people turned to Christ and were saved, which brought about a revolution in the Roman Empire. With this in mind I feel like saying to the liberals, "How many are coming to the Lord through your ministry?" That is the real test. Simon Peter said that Psalm 16 refers to the resurrection of Jesus Christ, and I am taking his word for it.

Peter also said more on the day of Pentecost: "This Jesus hath God raised up, whereof we all are witnesses. Therefore being by the right hand of God exalted, and having received of the Father the promise of the Holy Ghost, he hath shed forth this, which ye now see and hear. For David is not ascended into the heavens: but he saith himself, The LORD said unto my Lord, Sit thou on my right hand, Until I make thy foes thy footstool. Therefore let all the house of Israel know assuredly, that God hath made that same Jesus, whom ye have crucified, both Lord and Christ" (Acts 2:32–36). Obviously Psalm 16 refers to the resurrection of the Lord Jesus Christ.

Paul also quoted from this psalm. In Acts 13:35–37 he says, "Wherefore he saith also in another psalm, Thou shalt not suffer thine Holy One to see corruption. For David, after he had served his own generation by the will of God, fell on sleep, and was laid unto his fathers, and saw corruption: But he, whom God raised again, saw no corruption." You see, Paul also said it was the psalm of Jesus' resurrection.

What we have in this psalm is quite remarkable. In verse 8 we have the life of Christ. "I have set the LORD always before me: because he is at my right hand, I shall not be moved." That, my friend, was the pathway He followed down here, and it is the pathway I want to follow.

Then in verse 9 we have the death of Christ: "Therefore my heart is glad, and my glory rejoiceth: my flesh also shall rest in hope." He died there upon the cross, knowing that God would raise Him from the dead.

Then we have the resurrection of Christ in verse 10: "For thou wilt not leave my soul in hell [that is, the grave]; neither wilt thou suffer thine Holy One to see corruption."

Then we have the ascension of Christ in verse 11:

Thou wilt shew me the path of life: in thy presence is fulness of joy; at thy right hand there are pleasures for evermore [Ps. 16:11].

As you can see, this is a wonderful resurrection psalm, and it is so used in the New Testament. The resurrection of Christ is definitely prophesied in this great messianic psalm.

PSALM 17

THEME: *A prayer of David when in great danger*

Psalm 17 is entitled, "A Prayer of David." The question is, When was it written? It seems to be a prayer that came out of his wilderness experience. It probably concerns the time when Saul and his men were almost upon him and came close to taking him. This psalm reveals David's trust in God, but in the final analysis it speaks primarily of the Lord Jesus Christ. This psalm can also be a prayer for us today when we find ourselves in similar situations of trial, anxiety, or danger. As we study this psalm, keep in mind that we are in a new series that speaks of Christ in prophecy. After all, this is a HIM book; it is all about Him.

Hear the right, O LORD, attend unto my cry, give ear unto my prayer, that goeth not out of feigned lips [Ps. 17:1].

This is a prayer of David—probably when he is being pursued by Saul—and his life is in danger. This prayer comes from his heart, and he says what he is really thinking. There will be no "put-on" in it; he is not going to speak with "feigned lips." In other words, there will be no insincerity in what he is saying.

Let my sentence come forth from thy presence; let thine eyes behold the things that are equal [Ps. 17:2].

He is willing for the Lord to balance things off. "Let thine eyes behold the things that are equal." I don't know about you, but I am not asking for justice from God; I am asking for mercy. What most of us need from Him is mercy.

Thou hast proved mine heart; thou hast visited me in the night; thou hast tried me, and shalt find nothing; I am purposed that my mouth shall not transgress [Ps. 17:3].

It is interesting to note that when God tested David, He *did* find something and, when He tested me, He also found something. I have a notion that when He tested you, He found something also. These words must first of all be applied to Christ.

When the psalmist speaks in verse 1, of the prayer that did not go out of "feigned lips" it is a perfect picture of our perfect Lord. Peter says of the Lord, "Who did no sin, neither was guile found in his mouth" (1 Pet. 2:22). Peter goes on to say about Him, "Who, when he was reviled, reviled not again; when he suffered, he threatened not; but committed himself to him that judgeth righteously" (1 Pet. 2:23).

Concerning the works of men, by the word of thy lips I have kept me from the paths of the destroyer [Ps. 17:4].

The "destroyer" is none other than Satan. Because of his presence in the world, every child of God should be alert. David was in enemy territory, and he was aware of that when he was hiding from Saul. And we are in enemy territory—the earth is Satan's bailiwick. To the church in Pergamos the Lord said, "I know thy works and where thou dwellest, even where Satan's seat [Satan's throne] is . . ." (Rev. 2:13). I don't know where you live today, but some of us think that Satan's throne is very close to Los Angeles.

Our Lord didn't fall into Satan's trap as we often do.

Hold up my goings in thy paths, that my footsteps slip not.

I have called upon thee, for thou wilt hear me, O God: incline thine ear unto me, and hear my speech [Ps. 17: 5–6].

Delitzsch translates verse 6 like this: "As such an one I call upon thee, and thou hearest me." David knew he was heard. The Lord Jesus Christ identified Himself with His own. When He prayed, God heard Him. We can be sure, my friend, that He hears and answers our prayers when we are in trouble.

Shew thy marvellous loving-kindness, O thou that savest by thy right hand them which put their trust in thee from those that rise up against them.

Keep me as the apple of the eye, hide me under the shadow of thy wings [Ps. 17:7–8].

Years before God had used a similar expression when He said to Israel, "Ye have seen what I did unto the Egyptians, and how I bare you on eagles' wings, and brought you unto myself" (Exod. 19:4). This is a picture of where we are placed—in the shadow of His wings. Years later the Lord Jesus said of Jerusalem: "O Jerusalem, Jerusalem, thou that killest the prophets, and stonest them which are sent unto thee, how often would I have gathered thy children together, even as a hen gathereth her chickens under her wings, and ye would not!" (Matt. 23:37). Notice it is "under her wings"—this is also the picture David is giving us.

From the wicked that oppress me, from my deadly enemies, who compass me about.

They are enclosed in their own fat: with their mouth they speak proudly.

They have now compassed us in our steps: they have set their eyes bowing down to the earth;

Like as a lion that is greedy of his prey, and as it were a young lion lurking in secret places [Ps. 17:9–12].

David is crying out to God. He knew that God had heard his prayer.

Arise, O LORD, disappoint him, cast him down: deliver my soul from the wicked, which is thy sword:

From men which are thy hand, O LORD, from men of the world, which have their portion in this life, and whose belly thou fillest with thy hid treasure: they are full of children, and leave the rest of their substance to their babes.

As for me, I will behold thy face in righteousness: I shall be satisfied, when I awake, with thy likeness [Ps. 17:13–15].

Here is David, hiding in a cave, and he calls out to God to deliver him. David knows that God is going to deliver him and that one day he will be in His presence. At the moment, however, the enemy seems to be so strong and powerful.

You and I as God's children look out on a world that is against us. We are like the little boy playing in a vacant lot who saw a big old weed growing there and decided to pull it out of the ground. As he was pulling, a man happened by, stopped, and watched him. The little fellow would pull on one side and grunt, then get on the other side and pull. Finally, with one great supreme effort the little fellow pulled, the roots of the weed gave way, and he fell back with a bump. For a few moments he sat there, shocked. The man who had been watching him said, "Son, that was a mighty big pull." The boy replied, "It sure was 'cause the whole world was pulling against me." My friend, that is the position of the child of God today, but we have a resource and a recourse by coming to our Heavenly Father. This is what our Lord did when He was on earth, and so did David when he was in real danger.

What a psalm to help those who are in trouble today—especially when we find we have enemies who are against us. Most of us who stand for God have enemies—we have enemies just like a dog has fleas! They seem to be a part of the Christian's life.

PSALM 18

THEME: *David's praise when God delivered him from the hand of Saul*

This is another wonderful psalm written by David. Many of the liberal expositors have found nothing in this psalm but David's experience, and they have said some wonderful things about it. I would like to quote from Perowne as an example:

> In this magnificent hymn the royal poet sketches in a few grand outlines the tale of his life—the record of his marvelous deliverances and of the victories which Jehovah had given him—the record, too, of his own heart, the truth of his affection towards God, and the integrity of purpose by which it had ever been influenced. Throughout that singularly chequered life, hunted as he had been by Saul before he came to the throne, and harassed perpetually after he became king by rivals, who disputed his authority, and endeavored to steal away the hearts of his people—compelled to flee for his life before his own son, and engaged afterward in long and fierce wars with foreign nations—one thing had never forsaken him, the love and the presence of Jehovah. By His help he had subdued every enemy, and now, in his old age, looking backward with devout thankfulness on the past, he sings this great song of praise to the God of his life *(The Book of Psalms*, p. 192).

Everything this expositor has said is true; he has given the local, contemporary interpretation of this psalm. This psalm is a duplication of 2 Samuel 22; and, when we studied that book, I touched upon it lightly but will deal with the contents a little more closely here.

There is a deeper meaning to this psalm than the expositor gave us. Some of the utterances that are called poetic figures are more than figures of speech. These utterances speak of the Son of God, the Anointed One of God, Christ our Savior in His sufferings. Someone has labeled this psalm "All the way from the jaws of death to Jehovah's throne."

We are living today in a world where a lot is said about love, and many think the subject of love is foreign to the Old Testament. Notice how this psalm opens:

> **I will love thee, O LORD, my strength [Ps. 18:1].**

When was the last time you told the Lord you loved Him? To tell Him you love Him is one of the most wonderful things you can do. Praise toward God begins because He loves us and has provided a salvation for us. He preserves us and by His providence watches over us.

Notice that the Lord is called "my strength."

> **The LORD is my rock, and my fortress, and my deliverer; my God, my strength, in whom I will trust; my buckler, and the horn of my salvation, and my high tower [Ps. 18:2].**

He calls the Lord his strength, his rock, his fortress, and his deliverer—in all of this He is his Savior, you see. Then he says again that He is his strength, He is his shield, his horn, and his high tower. He is my shield—He protects me. He is my horn, my power. By laying hold of the horns of the altar a person would be safe from his attackers. That is how we need to hold on to our God today. The Lord, our Savior, is our horn. He is our high tower. A high tower is also a good place for protection and a good place to get a vision and a perspective of life. Many of us need to go to the high tower. This verse contains excellent names for our God.

The word that interests me a great deal is the personal pronoun *my*. David says, "The LORD is *my* rock, and *my* fortress, and *my* deliverer." It is one thing to talk about the attributes of God and say He is omnipotent, but the important thing is to say He is *my* strength. It is one thing to say He is a shepherd. David could have said, "The Lord is *a* shepherd," and He is, but it is altogether different to say, "He is *my* shepherd."

I think I can illustrate what I am talking about. One day I went out to the airport to pick up my wife and grandson. She brought him back on a plane so that he would not have to travel from the East coast in a car. There were lots of little boys and girls at the airport. They were all precious children, and as I looked at them I smiled. Then all of a sudden here comes one that is different. Do you know what makes him different? He is *my* grandson. There were lots of grandparents there, and, oh, how sentimental we grandparents can become! Their grandchildren were just as special to them as mine was to me—all because of the little possessive pronoun *my*.

Can you say, "The Lord is *my* shepherd; He is *my* high tower; He is *my* horn; He is *my* shield; He is *my* strength; He is *my* deliverer; He is *my* rock; He is *my* fortress"?

I will call upon the LORD, who is worthy to be praised: so shall I be saved from mine enemies [Ps. 18:3].

Worship comes from the old Anglo-Saxon word *worth*. Worship is that which is extended to the one who is worthy. David sang, "I will call upon the LORD"—why? Because He "is worthy to be praised."

The sorrows of death compassed me, and the floods of ungodly men made me afraid [Ps. 18:4].

Once again the psalm reaches out and touches the Lord Jesus Christ. Bishop Horne saw something else in this psalm. Let me quote from him:

> Let us suppose King Messiah, like His progenitor of old, is seated upon the throne. From thence let us imagine Him taking a retrospective view of the sufferings He had undergone, the battles He had fought and the victories He had gained. With this before our minds, we shall be able in some measure, to conceive the force of the words "With all the yearnings of affection I will love Thee, O Jehovah, My strength, through My union with whom I have finished My work, and am now exalted to praise Thee in those who are redeemed." Whenever we sing this Psalm, let us think we are singing it in conjunction with our Saviour, risen from the dead; a consideration, which surely will incite us to do it with becoming gratitude and devotion. (Quoted in A. C. Gaebelein, *The Book of Psalms*, p. 82.)

What a picture! Friend, this happens to be a psalm we can join Him in singing.

Listen to him now, as he recounts his experiences—and I think this presents the life of David in a limited way, but more especially the life of the Lord Jesus who said, "The sorrows of death compassed me, the floods of ungodly men made me afraid."

The sorrows of hell [*Sheol*, the grave] compassed me about: the snares of death prevented [were round about] me.

In my distress I called upon the LORD, and cried unto my God: he heard my voice out of his temple, and my cry came before him, even into his ears [Ps. 18:5–6].

Notice again "*my* God." And what happened? God responded. And what happened when the Lord Jesus was brought back from the grave? The next few verses tell us. (In the following section the first person possessive pronoun changes to the third person, and it refers to the Lord.)

Then the earth shook and trembled; the foundations also of the hills moved and were shaken, because he was wroth [Ps. 18:7].

He was angry with sinful men for what they had done to His Son. The Gospels tell us that when the stone was rolled away from the sepulcher there was an earthquake. What else took place in the heavens which corresponds to the following verses we do not know.

There went up a smoke out of his nostrils, and fire out of his mouth devoured: coals were kindled by it.

He bowed the heavens also, and came down: and darkness was under his feet.

And he rode upon a cherub, and did fly: yea, he did fly upon the wings of the wind.

He made darkness his secret place: his pavilion round about him were dark waters and thick clouds of the skies [Ps. 18:8–11].

There was darkness on the day that the Lord Jesus Christ was crucified. Who did all of this?

The LORD also thundered in the heavens, and the Highest gave his voice; hail stones and coals of fire [Ps. 18:13].

This psalm began using the pronoun *my*. Then it changed at verse 7 and talked about what God has done. Now in this next verse it is "He and me." That may be bad grammar, but that is the way it is here—He and me!

He sent from above, he took me, he drew me out of many waters.

He delivered me from my strong enemy, and from them which hated me: for they were too strong for me [Ps. 18:16–17].

"He delivered *me* from my strong enemy." Oh, how you and I need a personal, vital relationship with God! Let's come to grips with Him. He has delivered us from the enemy. Do you need help today? Do you need a partner today? I want to recommend One to you. He will never desert you. He will never leave you alone. He will never forsake you. He says, ". . . lo, I am with you alway, even unto the end of the world" (Matt. 28:20). That is the reason that I depend on Him more than I depend on anyone. That is also the reason you should depend on Him instead of depending on any human being. Psalm 118:8 says, "It is better to trust in the LORD than to put confidence in man."

He delivereth me from mine enemies: yea, thou liftest me up above those that rise up against me: thou hast delivered me from the violent man [Ps. 18:48].

"The violent man" I think is Satan.

Therefore will I give thanks unto thee, O LORD, among the heathen, and sing praises unto thy name.

Great deliverance giveth he to his king; and sheweth mercy to his anointed, to David, and to his seed for evermore [Ps. 18:49–50].

God extends His mercy to us today. This marvelous psalm closes on a note of praise to God. Oh, that there might be praise in your mouth and mine, in your life and mine, in your heart and mine, toward our God! Praise to God. "O give thanks unto the LORD, for he is good: for his mercy endureth for ever. Let the redeemed of the LORD say so" (Ps. 107: 1–2). If the redeemed do not say the Lord is good, nobody else in the world will. The redeemed ought to say so. We need some "say-so" Christians.

PSALM 19

THEME: *The revelation of God in His creation, in His commandments, and in Christ*

This can be called a great psalm of creation. It has been divided by many scholars into two parts: creation and the revelation of Jehovah in the Law, that is, in His Word. I have attempted to divide the psalm into three parts: creation of the cosmos, the commandments, and Christ—I feel that He has a special place here in the subject of redemption, salvation, and the grace of God. We will find God revealed in His creation, in His commandments, and in His grace in Christ. This is all that God saw fit to give to man, and I do not think He has exhausted all the things He could tell us about Himself.

This is another psalm of David, and it is so called in the inspired text. Also there is a division right in the text: the first part (vv. 1–6) uses *El* for the name of God, meaning the "Mighty One." He is the Mighty One in creation—"In the beginning *Elohim* [*Elohim* is the plural of *El*] created the heavens and the earth" (see Gen. 1:1). *Elohim* is His name as the Creator. The second division begins at verse 7, "The law of the LORD is perfect"—and His name is Jehovah. It is so used seven times in this section, and the last time two other names are added, *Jehovah, Tzuri, Goeli*, meaning "Jehovah, my Rock, my Redeemer." (Common sense scholarship does not try to explain the difference in names by contending that it was written by two different authors. If the same common sense had been used in the study of the Pentateuch, some scholars would not have come up with the "Jehovist and Elohist" writers of the Pentateuch theory. The same writer wrote it, using the two names for God. The Psalms flood light on many sections of the Bible. I trust they bless your heart and life.

GOD IN CREATION

This is a morning psalm. It speaks of creation in the first six verses. Psalm 8 was a creation psalm, and in it we saw the moon and the stars. It was a night psalm. Psalm 19 is called a day psalm because it is the sun that is brought before us.

The heavens declare the glory of God; and the firmament sheweth his handiwork.

Day unto day uttereth speech, and night unto night sheweth knowledge.

There is no speech nor language, where their voice is not heard.

Their line is gone out through all the earth, and their words to the end of the world. In them hath he set a tabernacle for the sun,

Which is as a bridegroom coming out of his chamber, and rejoiceth as a strong man to run a race.

His going forth is from the end of the heaven, and his circuit unto the ends of it: and there is nothing hid from the heat thereof [Ps. 19:1–6].

Now I want to share with you the translation made by Dr. Arno C. Gaebelein, who was one of my teachers, and in whom I have great confidence. He was well acquainted with the great Hebrew and German scholars who made a thorough study of the Book of Psalms: "The heavens declare the glory of God and the expanse maketh known the work of His hands. Day unto day poureth forth speech, and night unto night showeth knowledge—there is no speech and there are no words, Yet their voice is heard. Their line is gone out through all the earth, and to the end of the earth their words; in them hath He set a tent for the sun. And he is as a bridegroom coming out of his chamber, He rejoiceth as a strong man to run the course. His going forth is from the end of the heavens, and his circuit unto the ends of them, and there is nothing hid from the heat thereof" (*The Book of Psalms*, p. 89).

This is a marvelous psalm. "The heavens declare the glory of God." Paul says it this way in Romans 1:20, "For the invisible things of him from the creation of the world are clearly seen, being understood by the things that are made, even his eternal power and Godhead; so that they are without excuse." The heavens tell out the wisdom of God, they tell out the power of God, and they tell out, I think, something of the plan and purpose of God. From the beginning creation has been the primitive witness of God to man, His creature.

In all the creeds of the church, including the Apostles' Creed, creation is ascribed exclusively to God the Father. But when you come to the New Testament, where there is an amplification even of the act of creation, you find that it is not exactly accurate to say that God the Father is the Maker of heaven and earth. The Trinity was involved in the creation of the earth. In fact, the word *Elohim* is a plural word in the Hebrew, and it speaks of the Trinity. The New Testament tells us that the Lord Jesus was the agent of creation, and the Holy Spirit came in and refurbished and revamped it: ". . . the spirit of God moved upon the face of the waters" (Gen. 1:2). The apostle John tells of another beginning: "In the beginning was the Word, and the Word was with God, and the Word was God. . . .All things were made by him; and without him was not any thing made that was made" (John 1:1–3). This is the Lord Jesus Christ. Colossians 1:16, speaking about the Lord Jesus, says, "For by him were all things created, that are in heaven, and that are in earth, visible and invisible, whether they be thrones, or dominions, or principalities, or powers: all things were created by him, and for him." The Lord Jesus was the agent in creation. The first chapter of Ephesians tells us that all the members of the Trinity were involved in our redemption: God the Father planned it, the Son paid for it, and the Holy Spirit protects it. This applies to God's creation as well: God the Father planned this universe; the Son carried out the plan, and He is the One who redeemed it; and the Holy

Spirit today is moving and brooding over this creation.

It is interesting to note that the sun is prominent and likened to a bridegroom coming out of his chamber. When I was in Jerusalem, every morning I could see the sun come up over the side of the Mount of Olives. What a thrill it was to see the light breaking on Jerusalem—the walls of the city, the high places first. It touched David's tomb on Mount Zion, then touched the tops of the buildings, and then moved to the temple area. It was thrilling, and it was a picture of another bridegroom, the Lord Jesus Christ, the Sun of Righteousness. Some day He is coming in glory to this earth, but before He comes, He is going to take His church out of the world. He is the Bright and Morning Star. The Bright and Morning Star always appears before the sun rises. What a picture we have here in creation! There is nothing quite like it. This wonderful, wonderful psalm pictures creation.

GOD IN HIS COMMANDMENTS

The law of the LORD is perfect, converting the soul: the testimony of the LORD is sure, making wise the simple.

The statutes of the LORD are right, rejoicing the heart: the commandment of the LORD is pure, enlightening the eyes.

The fear of the LORD is clean, enduring for ever: the judgments of the LORD are true and righteous altogether.

More to be desired are they than gold, yea, than much fine gold: sweeter also than honey and the honeycomb.

Moreover by them is thy servant warned: and in keeping of them there is great reward [Ps. 19:7–11].

Again let me give you Dr. Gaebelein's translation: "The Law of Jehovah is perfect, restoring the soul; the testimony of Jehovah is sure, making wise the simple. The precepts of Jehovah are right, rejoicing the heart; the commandment of Jehovah is pure, enlightening the eyes; the fear of Jehovah is clean, enduring for ever; the judgments of Jehovah are truth, they are altogether righteous. More to be desired than gold, than much fine gold, and sweeter than honey, and honey-comb. By them thy servant is warned, in keeping them the reward is great" *(The Book of Psalms*, p. 91).

Now notice what he says about the commandments:

1. They are *perfect*. The Law cannot save us because it is perfect and we are not. We cannot measure up to it, but there is nothing wrong with the Law. Paul, who set forth the grace of God, says this about the Law, "Wherefore the law is holy, and the commandment holy, and just, and good. Was then that which is good made death unto me? God forbid. But sin, that it might appear sin, working death in me by that which is good; that sin by the commandment might become exceeding sinful. For we know that the law is spiritual: but I am carnal, sold under sin" (Rom. 7: 12–14). There is nothing *wrong* with the Law, but it is an administration of death to us because there is something radically wrong with us. The Law was given to show us that we are sinners before God. The Law is perfect.

2. "The testimony of the LORD is *sure*." Don't bank on God changing to the "new" morality. God is not reading some of the new views of psychology, and He is not listening to the decisions that some judges are handing down. God is going to punish sin—He *says* that is what He is going to do. The testimony of the Lord is *sure*. Judgment is coming. The commandments reveal that.

3. "The statutes of the LORD are *right*." Someone says, "There are certain commandments I don't like." Well, maybe you don't like them, but God does. They are right. What makes them right? In a college sociology class years ago, I had a professor who was always saying, "Who is going to determine what is right? How do you know what is right?" I didn't know the answer then, but now I know that God determines what is right. This is His universe; He made it, and He made the rules. Maybe you do not like the law of gravitation, but I advise you not to fool with it. That is, if you go to the top of a ten-story building, don't step off, because God will not suspend the law of gravitation for you. It operates for everyone, doesn't it?

4. "The commandment of the LORD is *pure*." I tell you, it is pure. It will do something for you—ennoble you and lift you up.

5. "The fear of the LORD is *clean*." We are told that this word *fear* means "reverential trust." I believe it means more than that. It means *fear*. We do well to fear God, my friend. I loved my Dad, but I sure was afraid of him. He kept me in line, and I think, in the final analysis, that is what kept me out of jail. I knew that when I did wrong there would be

trouble. The fear of the Lord is clean; the fear of the Lord will clean you up. Fear of my Dad made me a better boy, but I still loved him.

6. "The judgments of the LORD are *true.*" Do you want to know what truth is? Pilate wanted to know. He asked our Lord, ". . . What is truth? . . ." (John 18:38), and Truth was standing right in front of him in the person of the Lord Jesus Christ.

7. "The judgments of the LORD are . . . *righteous.*" They are right. Whatever God does is right. This is a tremendous section. We ought to learn to love all of the Word of God—all of it. Several people have written to me because they think I am opposed to the Ten Commandments. Why, the Ten Commandments are wonderful; I am not opposed to them. I am opposed to Vernon McGee—he can't keep them. If you can keep them, then you can ask God to move over; and you can sit beside Him because you have made it on your own. But God says you cannot keep them, and I agree with Him. He told me I would not make it on my own, and I agree with Him. I have to come as a sinner to God.

THE GRACE OF GOD IN CHRIST

This brings us to the grace of God in Christ.

Who can understand his errors? cleanse thou me from secret faults.

Keep back thy servant also from presumptuous sins; let them not have dominion over me: then shall I be upright, and I shall be innocent from the great transgression.

Let the words of my mouth, and the meditation of my heart, be acceptable in thy sight, O LORD, my strength, and my redeemer [Ps. 19:12–14].

"Who can understand his errors?" Who can? I use subterfuge a great deal. My wife says I rationalize. In fact, I am pretty good at that. I can give excuses, but God won't accept them. God says that you cannot understand your errors. Just take His word for it that you are a sinner.

"Cleanse thou me from secret faults." Secret faults are the problem with a great many folk today. They are secret from themselves —they think they are not sinners.

"Keep back thy servant also from presumptuous sins . . . and I shall be innocent from the great transgression." Do you know what "the great transgression" is? It is the rejection of Jesus Christ, the One who is set before us in this psalm.

Now listen to the psalmist. This is a verse that you hear many times in a believer's prayer. "Let the words of my mouth, and the meditation of my heart, be acceptable in thy sight, O LORD, my strength, and my redeemer." Who was David's *strength*? Christ! Who was his redeemer? Christ. He is also *my* strength and *my* redeemer. He becomes that through the grace of God. What a wonderful psalm this is!

PSALM 20

***THEME:** Plea of Israel for the success of the Messiah*

This psalm is not classed as one of the messianic psalms, but I have labeled it such because it is a prophecy of the Messiah and His work of redemption. I think it is closely linked with the two psalms that follow it. In Israel these psalms were sung together in a liturgical way. Some scholars think they were chanted by the leaders of worship, the Levites, and by the assembled worshipers who responded antiphonally.

Bishop Horne said, concerning this prayer psalm: "The Church prayeth for the prosperity of the King Messiah, going forth to battle, as her champion and deliverer; for His acceptance by the Father, and for the accomplishment of His will" (quoted in A. C. Gaebelein, *The Book of Psalms*, pp. 93–94). Bishop Horne would have hit the nail right on the head if he had said "the remnant of Israel" instead of "church." This psalm really deals with Israel.

This is another psalm that tells out the grace of God.

The LORD hear thee in the day of trouble; the name of the God of Jacob defend thee [Ps. 20:1].

"The day of trouble" is when we want Him to hear us, isn't it?

This is a psalm of David. How did old Jacob get in here? By the grace of God. God never was ashamed to be called the God of Jacob. I would have been ashamed of Jacob because of some of the things he did. Maybe you have been ashamed of him, too, but God was not. God saved Jacob by His grace.

Send thee help from the sanctuary, and strengthen thee out of Zion [Ps. 20:2].

What sanctuary is this verse talking about? The church? No! The sanctuary in Jerusalem. Where is Zion? Maybe you are thinking of Zion, Illinois, or Zion, Utah; but David is not talking about those places—nor any church. Zion is in Israel, of course. Nothing could be clearer.

Remember all thy offerings, and accept thy burnt sacrifice; Selah [Ps. 20:3].

Dr. Gaebelein translates it like this: "He shall remember all Thine offerings, and accept Thy burnt offerings. Selah." Notice that he is not referring to our offerings, but to Christ's offering. He offered up in the days of His flesh, not only prayers and tears (Heb. 5), but finally His own body.

"Selah"—here is something for you to meditate on, to think about, in these days when there is so much trouble.

Grant thee according to thine own heart, and fulfil all thy counsel.

We will rejoice in thy salvation, and in the name of our God we will set up our banners: the LORD fulfil all thy petitions.

Now know I that the LORD saveth his anointed; he will hear him from his holy heaven with the saving strength of his right hand [Ps. 20:4–6].

The Father is going to hear the prayers of the Lord Jesus. Remember that He said, ". . . Father, I thank thee that thou hast heard me. And I knew that thou hearest me always . . ." (John 11:41–42). Christ is probably the only One whom the Father always hears and always answers.

Some trust in chariots, and some in horses: but we will remember the name of the LORD our God.

They are brought down and fallen: but we are risen, and stand upright.

Save, LORD: let the king hear us when we call [Ps. 20:7–9].

The "king" is for Israel. For us today He is Savior, and we pray in the name of Jesus.

"Save, LORD" is *Hosanna* in the Hebrew. This is a great Hosanna psalm. May God make it real to our hearts.

PSALM 21

***THEME:** The ascension of Christ*

This is another psalm which I consider messianic, although it is not on the list of messianic psalms that I gave in the introduction, nor is it quoted verbatim in the New Testament as referring to Christ. However, I don't think you can read it without coming to the judgment that it has reference to Him. In fact, Israel, from the beginning said this psalm spoke of the Messiah. The Targum, which is the Chaldean paraphrase of the Old Testament, and the Talmud teach that the king mentioned in this psalm is the Messiah. The great Talmud scholar, Rabbi Solomon Isaaci, known as Rashi, born in A.D. 1040, endorsed this interpretation but suggested that it should be given up because of Christians making use of this psalm as an evidence that Jesus of Nazareth is the Messiah. I feel that this is a very good testimony to the fact that this psalm does refer to the Lord Jesus.

It is interesting to note that this psalm is used by the liturgical churches that observe certain days such as Ascension Day. They use this psalm as commemorating the Ascension, that is, the return of the Lord Jesus to glory and His presence there as our Great High Priest. I don't know why those of us who are fundamental in the faith have paid so little attention to the ascension of Christ. We observe Christmas and Easter and the Day of Pentecost, but we forget the ascension of Christ. To me that is a great day. Well, this psalm gives us the opportunity to give some thought to our Lord's ascension. We will see Him as king in heaven, and we will see the judgment that is to come upon those who have rejected Him.

This is another psalm of David, according to the inspired text, and includes Christ's coming reign as king on the earth. This psalm was undoubtedly used in temple worship. Dr. J. J. Stewart Perowne has made this comment: "Each Jewish Monarch was but a feeble type of Israel's true King: and all the hopes and aspirations of pious hearts, however, they might have for their immediate object the then reigning Monarch, whether David himself or one of his sons, still looked beyond these to Him, who should be David's Lord as well as his son" (*The Book of Psalms*, p. 207). That is quite a testimony coming from a man who was liberal in his theology.

Now notice how this psalm opens.

> **The king shall joy in thy strength, O LORD; and in thy salvation how greatly shall he rejoice! [Ps. 21:1].**

Although David is speaking of his personal experience, the primary interpretation refers to the Lord Jesus Christ.

"The king shall joy in thy strength." In Hebrews 12:2 it was said of the Lord, ". . . who for the joy that was set before him endured the cross, despising the shame,"—and He ascended into heaven—"and is set down at the right hand of the throne of God." This verse speaks of the *joy* of our Lord in having wrought our salvation for us. He rejoices in the power and strength that have been bestowed upon Him. He has gone to heaven, and the angels and principalities have been made subject to Him. Today He is able to save to the uttermost those who come to God through Him (Heb. 7:25). This is a wonderful psalm.

> **Thou hast given him his heart's desire, and hast not withholden the request of his lips. Selah [Ps. 21:2].**

When the Lord made His final report to His Father in His High Priestly prayer in John 17, He said, ". . . Father, the hour is come; glorify thy Son, that thy Son also may glorify thee" (John 17:1). This prayer, and all of the Lord's other requests, have been and will be answered, as we see in this prayer. This is the prayer of ascension. He is at God's right hand. "Thou has given him his heart's desire." When He was here on earth, the Lord could say, "Father, I will that they also, whom thou hast given me, be with me where I am; that they may behold my glory, which thou hast given me: for thou lovedst me before the foundation of the world" (John 17:24). This prayer will be answered in the future when we are with Him. He came to earth to make this possible. The Father has not withheld the request of His Son's lips. "Selah"—this is something we ought to meditate about.

> **He asked life of thee, and thou gavest it him, even length of days for ever and ever.**
>
> **His glory is great in thy salvation: honour and majesty hast thou laid upon him.**
>
> **For thou hast made him most blessed for ever: thou hast made him exceeding glad with thy countenance [Ps. 21:4–6].**

Now notice Dr. Gaebelein's translation of these verses: "He asked life of Thee, Thou gavest it Him: length of days for ever and ever. His glory is great in Thy salvation; Honour and majesty hast Thou laid upon Him. For Thou hast made Him most blessed for ever: Thou dost delight Him with joy in Thy presence" (*The Book of Psalms*, p. 98).

The Lord Jesus Christ came to give His life a ransom for many down here. On earth you find Him in humiliation, and you find Him pleading again and again in prayer. He agonized in the Garden of Gethsemane. Psalm 102:23–24 says of the Lord: "He weakened my strength in the way; he shortened my days. I said, O my God, take me not away in the midst of my days: thy years are throughout all generations." He asked for life. He died in the very prime of life. He was thirty-three years old. He prayed, ". . . Father, if thou be willing, remove this cup from me: nevertheless not my will, but thine, be done" (Luke 22:42). In Hebrews 5:7 we are told: "Who in the days of his flesh, when he had offered up prayers and supplications with strong crying and tears unto him that was able to save him from death, and was heard in that he feared." How was He heard? He *died*! But God raised Him from the dead. Now He lives in His glorified human body for ever and ever. He is now at God's right hand. "His glory is great in Thy salvation." Oh, the glory that should accrue to Him because He saved you, and He saved me!

> **For the king trusteth in the LORD, and through the mercy of the most High he shall not be moved.**

Thine hand shall find out all thine enemies: thy right hand shall find out those that hate thee.

Thou shalt make them as a fiery oven in the time of thine anger: the Lord shall swallow them up in his wrath, and the fire shall devour them [Ps. 21:7–9].

Dr. Gaebelein translates it: "Thy hand shall find out all Thine enemies; Thy right hand shall find out those that hate Thee. Thou shalt make them as a fiery oven in the time of Thy coming" (*The Book of Psalms*, p. 99). Not only is He a God of salvation but, because of His death upon the cross for sinners, He is also a God of judgment. Those who have rejected Him are His enemies. You don't believe in hell? The Bible teaches it. If you don't believe there is a hell, you are in disagreement with the Bible.

A man once came to me and said, "I don't believe in hell." I replied, "Do you know that you are in disagreement with the Bible?" He said, "I don't care. I don't believe there is a hell." Well, I told him, "You will someday. The day will come when you will find that it is true." Hell is not a pleasant subject. Who said that it was? God does not take any delight in the lost. God's judgment is called His strange work. His wonderful work is salvation. He *wants* to save. If you won't come to Him His way, or if you don't want His salvation, then there is nothing but judgment that remains.

"Thou shalt make them as a fiery oven in the time of thine anger: the Lord shall swallow them up in his wrath, and the fire shall devour them." This verse is clear. Fire is fire, and judgment is judgment.

Their fruit shalt thou destroy from the earth, and their seed from among the children of men.

For they intended evil against thee: they imagined a mischievous device, which they are not able to perform.

Therefore shalt thou make them turn their back, when thou shalt make ready thine arrows upon thy strings against the face of them.

Be thou exalted, Lord, in thine own strength: so will we sing and praise thy power [Ps. 21:10–13].

In this marvelous psalm we see Christ's cross and suffering. He endured the cross ". . . for the *joy* that was set before him" (Heb. 12:2). His prayers have been answered. Now the King is in heaven. We see Him there crowned with glory and honor. He is there on behalf of His people. He is there in unspeakable joy and waiting for His manifestation and kingly glory.

I would like to give you another picture of the Lord Jesus Christ today. The first time He came to earth He was a man of sorrows and acquainted with grief. Somebody says, "Every picture I have ever seen of Him is a solemn, serious looking Christ." I don't care for the pictures that have been painted of Christ, and I know He doesn't look like that today. He is sitting at God's right hand, and His heart is filled with joy. He wants to communicate that joy to you and me. Oh, that we might get a glimpse of *Him* today! When the Lord was on earth, His enemies conspired against Him, but He trusted in Jehovah. In John's vision in Revelation 12 the dragon, representing Satan, wanted to devour the manchild, representing Christ. (The woman is Israel.) Before the dragon could devour the manchild, He was caught up to God and to His throne. That is where He is right now.

Also this psalm gives us a picture of judgment, which is amplified greatly in the Book of Revelation. That is a serious picture that is given to us there. Paul the apostle mentions it also in 2 Thessalonians 1:7–8: "And to you who are troubled, rest with us, when the Lord Jesus shall be revealed from heaven with his mighty angels, In flaming fire taking vengeance on them that know not God, and that obey not the gospel of our Lord Jesus Christ." This is a picture of the Lord's coming in judgment upon His enemies. 2 Thessalonians 1: 9–10 goes on to say, "Who shall be punished with everlasting destruction from the presence of the Lord, and from the glory of his power; When he shall come to be glorified in his saints, and to be admired in all them that believe (because our testimony among you was believed) in that day."

This is a glorious psalm of the Ascension of Christ. What is your relationship to Him today? If He is not your Savior, if you have not trusted the One who came down here to die, then judgment is coming upon you someday. But today He is filled with joy up yonder at God's right hand, because He has wrought out your salvation and mine. This wonderful ascension psalm makes very clear the glorious grace of God in Christ Jesus.

PSALM 22

***THEME:** The crucifixion of Christ*

There are several Scriptures with which I never feel adequate to deal. This is one of them. When we come to Psalm 22 I feel that we are standing on holy ground, and we should take off our spiritual shoes. This psalm is called the Psalm of the Cross. It is so named because it describes more accurately and minutely the crucifixion of Christ than does any other portion of the Word of God. It corresponds, of course, to the twenty-second chapter of Genesis and the fifty-third chapter of Isaiah.

We have many messianic psalms which are pictures of Christ. The first psalm, for instance, is a portrait of Christ in His character—who He is, His life, His practice. But in Psalm 22 we have an X-ray which penetrates into His thoughts and into His inner life. In this psalm we see the anguish of His passion; His soul is laid bare. In the Gospels is recorded the historical fact of His death, and some of the events which attended His crucifixion; but only in Psalm 22 are His thoughts revealed. It has been the belief of many scholars that actually the Lord Jesus, while on the cross, quoted the entire twenty-second psalm. I concur in this, because the seven last sayings that are given in the Gospels either appear in this psalm or the psychological background for them is here.

It is the custom in many churches to conduct a Good Friday service in which seven ministers bring messages from the seven last sayings of Christ from the cross. In the course of fifteen years, I have heard over one hundred men deal with these seven words. It is always a spiritual feast to hear how each man develops the subject, and always there are many new and profitable thoughts presented. However, we shall attempt to encompass all seven sayings in one message. And instead of standing beneath the cross and listening to Him, we are going to hang on the cross with Him. We shall view the crucifixion of Christ from a new position—from the cross itself. And we can look with Him on those beneath His cross, as He was hanging there, and see what went on in His heart and in His mind. We shall see what occurred in His soul as He became the sacrifice for the sins of the world. As He was suspended there between heaven and earth, He became the ladder let down from heaven to this earth so that men might have a way to God.

We were there, if you please, on that cross as He was made sin for us—He ". . . who knew no sin; that we might be made the righteousness of God in him" (2 Cor. 5:21). We were as truly on that cross when He died as we today are *in* Christ by faith. Peter put it like this: "Who his own self bare our sins in his own body on the tree, that we, being dead to sins, should live unto righteousness: by whose stripes ye were healed" (1 Pet. 2:24). Healed from sin!

"MY GOD, MY GOD, WHY HAST THOU FORSAKEN ME?"

Psalm 22 opens with the plaintive and desperate cry of this poor, lone Man, forsaken of God.

My God, my God, why hast thou forsaken me? why art thou so far from helping me, and from the words of my roaring? [Ps. 22:1].

There has been an attempt made to play down the stark reality and the bitter truth that He was forsaken of God. I hold an article written by a local minister who takes the position that Jesus was not forsaken. He attempts to translate, "Eli, Eli, lama sabachthani" to mean, "My God, my God, for this was I kept." His authority is the Peshitta, or the Syriac version. However, the Peshitta is not a good manuscript. It never has been used by any reputable translator, for it is not a good translation. Evidently it was made by some who had gone into a heresy at the very beginning. The value of it is that in many places it throws light on the customs in Palestine during that period. I have used it in that connection on several occasions, but never would I accept the translation. Actually, the Hebrew is very clear, and the Greek is very clear, and the Aramaic is very clear—in each language the cry means that Jesus was forsaken of God.

Now we have here—and this is something I want to emphasize from the very beginning—a record of His *human suffering*. We see Him hanging there as a man, ". . . the Lamb of God, which taketh away the sin of the world" (John 1:29). We get more light on this by turning to the Epistle to the Hebrews: "But we see Jesus, who was made a little lower than the angels [a little lower than the angels? Yes, made a man. Why?] for the suffering of death, crowned with glory and honour; that he by the grace of God should taste death for every man" (Heb. 2:9). That is what we are looking at—the One who left heaven's glory and became a Man. He became a Man to reveal God, yes, that is true; but most of all to redeem man. "Forasmuch then as the children are partakers of flesh and blood, he also himself likewise took part of the same; that through death he might destroy him that had the power of death, that is, the devil" (Heb. 2:14).

He could save no one by His life; it was His sacrificial death that saves. "And deliver them who through fear of death were all their lifetime subject to bondage. For verily he took not on him the nature of angels; but he took on him the seed of Abraham. . . .For in that he himself hath suffered being tempted, he is able to succour them [help them] that are tempted" (Heb. 2:15–16, 18). We see the Man Christ Jesus on the cross as the perfect Man. He had learned to rest upon God. He had learned to trust Him in all that He did. He said, ". . . I do always those things that please him" (John 8:29). But yonder in that desperate and despairing hour He was abandoned of God. There was no place to turn, either on the human plane or on the divine. He had no place to go. The Man Christ Jesus was forsaken. No other ever has had to experience that. No one. He alone.

Why did God forsake Him?

But thou art holy, O thou that inhabitest the praises of Israel [Ps. 22:3].

Why was He forsaken of God? Because on the cross in those last three hours, in the impenetrable darkness, He was made sin.

But none of the ransomed ever knew
How deep were the waters crossed;
Nor how dark was the night that the Lord
passed through
Ere He found His sheep that was lost.

He was forsaken for a brief moment. The paradox is that at that very moment God was in Christ reconciling the world unto Himself. And the Lord Jesus Himself said, "Behold, the hour cometh, yea, is now come, that ye shall be scattered, every man to his own, and shall leave me alone: and yet I am not alone, because the Father is with me" (John 16:32). The Father was with Him when He was in prison, the Father was with Him when He was being beaten, the Father was with Him when they nailed Him to the cross. But in those last three hours He made His soul an offering for sin, and it pleased the Father to bruise Him (see Isa. 53:10).

Forsaken. My friend, you do not know what that is; and I do not know what it is to be forsaken of God. The vilest man on this earth today is not forsaken of God. Anyone can turn to Him. But when Christ takes my sin upon Himself, He is forsaken of God.

"Why hast thou forsaken me?" It is not the *why* of impatience. It is not the *why* of despair; it is not the *why* of doubt. It is the human cry of intense suffering, aggravated by the anguish of His innocent and holy life. That awful and agonizing cry of the loneliness of His passion! He was alone. He was alone with the sins of the world upon Him.

"Why art thou so far from helping me, and from the words of my roaring?" (Ps. 22:1). Roaring? Yes. At His trial He was silent, ". . . as a sheep before her shearers is dumb, so he openeth not his mouth" (Isa. 53:7). When they beat Him, He said nothing; when they nailed Him to the cross, He did not whimper. But when God forsook Him, He roared like a lion. It was a roar of pain. Have you ever been in the woods when dogs attacked an animal? Have you heard the shriek of that animal? There is nothing quite like it. And that is what the writer is attempting to convey to us here. I think that shriek from the cross rent the rocks, for it had been His voice that had created them. Now the Creator is suffering! On that cross He cried like a wounded animal; His was not even a human cry, but like a wild, roaring lion. It was the plaintive shriek and the wail of unutterable woe as our sins were pressed down upon Him.

But I am a worm, and no man; a reproach of men, and despised of the people [Ps. 22:6].

What does He mean when He says, "I am a worm"? He has roared like a lion; now He says, "I am a worm." It is because He has reached the very lowest place. "He is despised and rejected of men; a man of sorrows, and acquainted with grief: and we hid as it were our faces from him; he was despised, and we esteemed him not" (Isa. 53:3). "I am a worm." The interesting thing is that the word used here for worm means the coccus worm, which was used by the Hebrews in dyeing all the curtains of the tabernacle scarlet red. When He said, "I am a worm," He meant more than that He had reached the lowest level. It was He who had said, ". . . though your sins be as scarlet, they shall be as white as snow . . ." (Isa. 1:18). Only His blood, my friend, can rub out that dark, deep spot in your life.

Lady Macbeth, sleepwalking that night, went up and down rubbing her hands, insane with the guilt of murder. She says, "All the perfumes of Arabia will not sweeten this little hand." And she was right; they could not. She seemed to be continually washing her hands as she rubbed them together, and she cried, "Out damned spot! out, I say!" (*Macbeth*, Act V, Scene 1).

My friend, there is only one thing that will take the spot of sin out of your life, that is the blood of Christ. The blood of the Lord Jesus, God's Son, cleanses from all sin. Only His blood.

"FATHER, FORGIVE THEM"

Will you look at that victim on the cross? His suffering is intensified by that brutal mob and hardened spectators that are beneath Him. Look through His eyes and see what He sees.

All they that see me laugh me to scorn: they shoot out the lip, they shake the head, saying,

He trusted on the LORD that he would deliver him: let him deliver him, seeing he delighted in him [Ps. 22:7–8].

Some criminals have been so detested that they have been taken from jail and lynched by a mob. But while the criminal was being executed, the mob would disperse. Tempers were cooled, and emotions were assuaged. But not this crowd! I think the lowest thing that ever has been said of religion was said of these Pharisees when the Lord Jesus Christ was dying: "And sitting down they watched him there" (Matt. 27:36). You have to be low to do that. In fact, you cannot get lower than that! The venom and vileness of the human heart were being poured out like an open sewer as they remained there and ridiculed Him in His death. After a snake has put its deadly fangs into its victim and emitted its poison, it will slither away in the grass. But not this crowd —not the human heart in rebellion against God.

"Then said Jesus, Father, forgive them: for they know not what they do . . ." (Luke 23:34). If He had not said that, this crowd would have committed the unpardonable sin. But they did not—He asked forgiveness for their sin. We know that the centurion in charge of the execution was saved; and a whole company of Pharisees, including Saul of Tarsus, who probably were in this crowd, were saved.

"WOMAN, BEHOLD THY SON!"

Now as He looks over the crowd He sees not only eyes of hate and antagonism, but He sees eyes of love. He sees His mother with John down there. "Now there stood by the cross of Jesus his mother . . ." (John 19:25). As Jesus looks at her, do you want to know what went on in His heart? He went back to Bethlehem at the time He was born, and He says to the Father:

But thou art he that took me out of the womb: thou didst make me hope when I was upon my mother's breasts.

I was cast upon thee from the womb: thou art my God from my mother's belly [Ps. 22:9–10].

". . . Woman, behold thy son!" (John 19:26). Yonder at the wedding at Cana in Galilee, she had asked Him to do something to show that He was the Messiah, that she was right when she said He was virgin born. She wanted Him to reveal Himself at this wedding. His answer to her at that time was, ". . . Woman, what have I to do with thee? mine hour is not yet come" (John 2:4). But there hanging on the cross: ". . . Woman, behold thy son!" His hour has come! The reason for His coming into the world is now being accomplished. This is the most important hour in the history of the world!

Then His attention moves back to those who are doing the crucifying.

Many bulls have compassed me: strong bulls of Bashan have beset me round [Ps. 22:12].

Describing these soldiers that were crucifying Him, He says they are like the bulls of Bashan; but He does not stop with that, for He is being devoured by wild animals—that is what His tormenters had become:

They gaped upon me with their mouths, as a ravening and a roaring lion [Ps. 22:13].

He is talking about Rome now—Rome crucified Him. He compares them to a roaring lion, for the lion was the picture of Rome.

Now notice His condition:

I am poured out like water, and all my bones are out of joint: my heart is like wax; it is melted in the midst of my bowels [Ps. 22:14].

This accurate description of crucifixion is remarkable when you consider that crucifixion was unknown when this psalm was written. The Roman Empire was not even in existence, and it was Rome that instituted crucifixion. Yet here is a picture of a man dying by crucifixion!

"I am poured out like water"—the excessive perspiration of a dying man out in that sun.

"All my bones are out of joint"—the horrible thing about crucifixion is that when a man began to lose blood, his strength ebbed from him, and all his bones slipped out of joint. That is an awful thing. It was terrible, terrible suffering.

Then He says something that is indeed strange, "My heart is like wax." He died of a broken heart. Many doctors have said that a ruptured heart would have produced what John meticulously recorded. "But one of the soldiers with a spear pierced his side, and forthwith came there out blood and water" (John 19:34). Let me paraphrase that. "I saw that Roman soldier put the spear in His side and there came out blood and water—not just blood but blood and water." John took note of that and recorded it. May I say to you, Jesus died of a broken heart.

"I THIRST"

As He is hanging there ready to expire, with excessive perspiration pouring from Him, He suffers the agony of thirst.

My strength is dried up like a potsherd; and my tongue cleaveth to my jaws; and thou hast brought me into the dust of death [Ps. 22:15].

Down beneath the cross they hear Him say, "I thirst."

For dogs have compassed me: the assembly of the wicked have enclosed me: they pierced my hands and my feet [Ps. 22:16].

"Dog" was the name for Gentiles. The piercing of His hands and feet is an accurate description of crucifixion.

I may tell all my bones: they look and stare upon me.

They part my garments among them, and cast lots upon my vesture [Ps. 22: 17–18].

He was crucified naked. It is difficult for us in this age of nudity and pornography to comprehend the great humiliation He suffered by hanging nude on the cross. They had taken His garments and gambled for ownership. My friend, He went through it all, crucified naked, that you might be clothed with the righteousness of Christ, and so be able to stand before God throughout the endless ages of eternity.

"FATHER, INTO THY HANDS I COMMEND MY SPIRIT"

But be not thou far from me, O LORD: O my strength, haste thee to help me.

Deliver my soul from the sword; my darling from the power of the dog [Ps. 22:19–20].

The word *darling* is better translated "my only one"—"This is my beloved Son . . ." (Matt. 3:17). "Deliver my soul from the sword; my *only one* from the power of the dog." Jesus is saying, ". . . Father, into thy hands I commend my spirit . . ." (Luke 23:46).

Save me from the lion's mouth: for thou hast heard me from the horns of the unicorns [Ps. 22:21].

One of the most remarkable statements is this: "thou hast heard me from the horns of the unicorns." To express intensity in the Hebrew, the plural is used—horns of the unicorns; but the thought is *one horn*.

For many years it was thought that the unicorn was a mythical animal, but recent investigation has revealed that it was an animal a size smaller than the elephant, very much like the rhinoceros, sometimes called a wild bull. Vicious and brutal, every one of them was a killer. And the thing that identified them was the fact that they had *one horn*. "Thou hast heard me from the horns of the unicorns"—*uni* means "one"—one horn. To me, my beloved, that is remarkable indeed; because the cross on which the Lord Jesus Christ was crucified was probably not the shaped cross that we see today. We think of a cross made of an upright with a crosspiece. Nowhere does Scripture so describe it.

There are two Greek words that are translated by the English word *cross*. One of them is the word *stauros*. You find it used in several places. For instance: ". . . Thou that destroyest the temple, and buildest it in three days, save thyself. If thou be the Son of God, come down from the cross" (Matt. 27:40). The word *cross* is *stauros*, meaning "one piece." It is interesting how accurate Scripture is, but how tradition has been woven into it in our thinking. Paul used the word *stauros* when he wrote: "For the preaching of the cross [*stauros*] is to them that perish foolishness; but unto us which are saved it is the power of God" (1 Cor. 1:18).

The second Greek word is *xulon*, which is translated by the English "cross" or "tree." It simply means a piece of wood. Paul also used this word: "And when they had fulfilled all that was written of him, they took him down from the tree [*xulon*], and laid him in a sepulchre" (Acts 13:29).

They took Him down from the tree! Does he mean an upright with a crosspiece? Now I am perfectly willing to go along with the popularly accepted shape of a cross, but for the sake of accuracy and to appreciate the exactness of this psalm, we need to brush aside tradition for a moment. Jesus said, "thou has heard me from the horns of the unicorns [the cross]." ". . . Into thy hands I commend my spirit . . ." (Luke 23:46).

Another thing that amazes me is that this word *xulon*, translated "tree" or "cross," is mentioned in the twenty-second chapter of Revelation as the tree of life! I believe that the tree on which Jesus died will be there, alive, throughout the endless ages of eternity, to let you and me know what it cost to redeem us.

Now when we come to verse 22 of this psalm, we see a radical change, a bifurcation. We have had the sufferings of Christ described for us; now we see the glory that should follow.

I will declare thy name unto my brethren: in the midst of the congregation will I praise thee [Ps. 22:22].

I think that He said this entire psalm on the cross. He did not die defeated; for when He reached the very end He said, "This is the gospel that will be witnessed to. I will declare thy name unto my brethren." And I see Peter in the midst of the Sanhedrin, composed of both Pharisees and Sadducees, saying to them, ". . . there is none other name under heaven given among men, whereby we must be saved" (Acts 4:12). "I will declare thy name unto my brethren."

"TODAY SHALT THOU BE WITH ME IN PARADISE"

My praise shall be of thee in the great congregation: I will pay my vows before them that fear him.

The meek shall eat and be satisfied: they shall praise the LORD that seek him: your heart shall live for ever [Ps. 22:25–26].

The thief on the cross said, ". . Lord remember me when thou comest into thy kingdom" (Luke 23:42). Christ says, "I'll pay my vows"—". . . Today shalt thou be with me in paradise" (Luke 23:43). The redeemed shall be there to praise, and the thief He was taking with Him that very day. Although he was a man unfit to even live down here, according to Rome's standard, the Lord Jesus makes him fit for heaven by His death on the cross.

"IT IS FINISHED"

There is a seventh word; it is His last.

They shall come, and shall declare his righteousness unto a people that shall be born, that he hath done this [Ps. 22:31].

"To a people that shall be born" includes you, my friend.

They shall declare *His* righteousness—not your righteousness, for God says it is filthy rags in His sight. How will they declare His righteousness? "That he hath done this." Some would translate it, "It is finished," the last word He spoke on the cross. And when He said it, it was but one word—*Tetelestai*! Finished! Your redemption is a completed package, and He presents it to you wrapped up with everything in it. He doesn't want you to bring your do-it-yourself kit along. He does not need that. When He died on the cross, He provided a righteousness that would satisfy a holy God. All He asks of you is that you receive this package, this gift of God, which is eternal life in Christ Jesus.

If you reject it, God must treat you as He treated His Son when He cried, ". . . My God, my God, why hast thou forsaken me?" (Mark 15:34). I am not here to argue about the temperature of hell: it will be hell for any man to be forsaken of God. Jesus Christ went through it that you might *never* have to utter that cry.

Psalm 22 reveals the heart of our Savior as He was made a sin offering in our behalf. He completed the transaction in triumph. He offers to us a finished redemption. We never shall be worthy of it; we cannot earn it: we cannot buy it—we must receive it as a gift. Over nineteen hundred years ago the Lord Jesus Christ did all that was needed to save us.

It is done. *Tetelestai*. Finished!

PSALM 23

THEME: *Christ as the great Shepherd*

Psalm 23, which is so popular, would be meaningless without Psalm 22, which leads me to say that we have a trilogy or triptych of psalms that belong together. They are Psalms 22, 23, and 24, and they are called the shepherd psalms. These three psalms present the following picture of our Lord: In Psalm 22 He is the Good Shepherd. The Lord Jesus Himself made the statement, "I am the good shepherd: the good shepherd giveth his life for the sheep" (John 10:11). Now here in Psalm 23 He is the Great Shepherd. Notice this title in the great benediction at the conclusion of the Epistle to the Hebrews: "Now the God of peace, that brought again from the dead our Lord Jesus, that great shepherd of the sheep, through the blood of the everlasting covenant, Make you perfect in every good work to do his will, working in you that which is well-pleasing in his sight, through Jesus Christ; to whom be glory for ever and ever. Amen" (Heb. 13:20–21). Psalm 23 reveals Him as the Great Shepherd. Next, we see Him in Psalm 24 as the Chief Shepherd. "And when the chief Shepherd shall appear, ye shall receive a crown of glory that fadeth not away" (1 Pet. 5:4).

To put it succinctly, in Psalm 22 we see the *cross*, in Psalm 23 the *crook* (the Shepherd's crook), and in Psalm 24 the *crown* (the King's crown). In Psalm 22 Christ is the *Savior*; in Psalm 23 He is the *Satisfier*; in Psalm 24 He is the *Sovereign*. In Psalm 22 He is the *foundation*; in Psalm 23 He is the *manifestation*; in Psalm 24 He is the *expectation*. In Psalm 22 He *dies*; in Psalm 23 He is *living*; in Psalm 24 He is *coming*. Psalm 22 speaks of the *past*; Psalm 23 speaks of the *present*; and Psalm 24 speaks of the *future*. In Psalm 22 He gives His *life* for the sheep; in Psalm 23 He gives His *love* to the sheep; in Psalm 24 He gives us *light* when He shall appear. What a wonderful picture we have of Christ in these three psalms!

Now let us zero in on Psalm 23, probably the most familiar passage there is in the Word of God. No portion in writing of any time or of any work has been so widely circulated. Jews, both Orthodox and Reformed, know this psalm. Christians of all denominations are acquainted with this psalm. The world has caught its beauty.

Much has been written about this psalm, although its six verses are short and simple. It is like the Gettysburg Address as far as brevity is concerned. Someone has said, "I do not care how much a man says, if he says it in a few words." Someone else has said, "If folk who do not have anything to say would refrain from saying it, it would be a better world." Psalm 23 has few words. There was a business executive years ago who had a little motto on the wall of his office for all to see. It said, If you have anything important to say, say it in five minutes. Well, it only takes about forty-five seconds to read Psalm 23. It is brief. It is not the language of philosophy. It is not the language of theology. It is not a legal or scientific document. It is sublimely simple and simply sublime.

Before we look at the text itself, there are some things we should consider about this psalm. It is agreed that David is the author, but the question has always been: Did he write it when he was a shepherd boy or when he was an aged king? It is important to know the answer. Dr. Frank Morgan has called this "The Song of the Old Shepherd." I like that, and I agree with him. David the king never forgot David the shepherd boy. In Psalm 23 you do not have the musings of a green, inexperienced lad but the mature deliberations of a ripe experience. You see, David, when he came close to the end of his life, looked back upon his checkered career. It was then that he wrote this psalm. The old king on the throne remembered the shepherd boy. Life had beaten, battered, baffled, and bludgeoned this man. He was a hardened soldier, a veteran who knew victory, privation, hardship. He knew song and shadow. He was tested and tried. Therefore in Psalm 23 we do not have the theorizing of immaturity but fruit and the mature judgment born of a long life.

This psalm begins by saying, "The LORD is my shepherd." By what authority do you say *my* shepherd? Is this psalm for everybody? I don't think so. Since Psalms 22, 23, and 24 go together and tell one story, you have to know the Lord Jesus Christ as the Good Shepherd who gave His life for the sheep before you can know Him as the Great Shepherd. You must know the Shepherd of Psalm 22 before you can come to Psalm 23 and say, "The LORD is *my* shepherd."

REVELATION OF THE SANCTUARY OF THE SHEPHERD'S SOUL

The LORD is my shepherd; I shall not want.

He maketh me to lie down in green pastures: he leadeth me beside the still waters [Ps. 23:1–2].

Notice "*my* shepherd . . . *I* shall not want . . . He maketh *me* lie down . . . he leadeth *me*." This is a "he and me" psalm. The emphasis is upon the fact that there is nothing between the man's soul and God. "The LORD is *my* shepherd."

Verse 1 is a declaration and a deduction. It is one thing to say, "The Lord is a shepherd"—many people say that, and it sounds good. But can you make it personal and say, "The LORD is *my* shepherd"? By the authority of His redemptive work, His death and resurrection, you can trust Him and call Him your Shepherd. It is also easy to say, "The Lord *will be* my shepherd," but David did not say that either. He said, "The LORD *is* my shepherd." This is his declaration.

"I shall not want"—notice that David does not say, I have not wanted, but "I shall not want." What is it that I need? Well, I need safety. I'm a sheep, a stupid little animal. Therefore, my Shepherd sees to it that I won't want for protection. He protects me. When a little sheep says, "I shall not want" and "I shall never perish," it is because it has a wonderful Shepherd. "I shall not want" looks into the future and gives assurance to the child of God. The security of the believer rests upon the Shepherd. And the believer's deduction rests upon his declaration.

A friend of mine who moved to Oregon once heard me talk about sheep. He said to me later, "Dr. McGee, you gave me the impression that sheep are nice, sweet little animals. You made them appear so helpless. I want to show you some sheep." He invited me to dinner. He gathered several sheep together, and after dinner we went out to look at them. As we watched them, he told me, "These sheep are stubborn, hardheaded, and pigheaded animals. Besides that, they are dirty and filthy." I said, "That's a picture of the human race." They do set us forth!

Not only do sheep need safety, they need sufficiency and satisfaction. "He maketh me to lie down in green pastures." That is sufficiency. Folk that know sheep tell us that a hungry sheep will not lie down. When sheep are lying down in green pastures, it means they have their tummies full. And Christ is our sufficiency. "And Jesus said unto them, I am the bread of life: he that cometh to me shall never hunger; and he that believeth on me shall never thirst" (John 6:35).

"He leadeth me beside the still waters." Sheep are frightened by turbulent water. And they don't like stagnant water. They don't want to drink where the hogs drink. All of this applies to the human family. We need rest in our day—not so much physical or mental rest, but rest of the soul. Remember what David said in Psalm 55:6: "Oh that I had wings like a dove! for then would I fly away, and be at rest." He wanted to get away from it all. But he found out that getting away from it all did not solve his problems. He had to learn to put his trust in the Lord, rest in Him, and wait patiently upon Him. The Lord Jesus says, "Come unto me, all ye that labour and are heavy laden, and I will rest you" (Matt. 11:28).

RECORD OF THE THOUGHTS OF THE SHEPHERD'S MIND

He restoreth my soul: he leadeth me in the paths of righteousness for his name's sake.

Yea, though I walk through the valley of the shadow of death, I will fear no evil: for thou art with me; thy rod and thy staff they comfort me [Ps. 23:3–4].

"He restoreth my soul." David knew what that was. David had sinned—he was that little lost sheep that had strayed from the fold, and his Shepherd had restored him.

"He leadeth me in the paths of righteousness for his name's sake." He leads, but we must follow. The Lord Jesus said to the religious rulers who were actually His enemies, ". . . I told you, and ye believed not: the works that I do in my Father's name, they bear witness of me. But ye believe not, because ye are not of my sheep, as I said unto you. My sheep hear my voice, and I know them, and they follow me" (John 10:25–27). Sheep will follow their own shepherd. That is the way you can tell the one to whom the sheep belong. In Jesus' day the shepherd never drove his sheep; he led them. That is no longer the case. When I have visited the land of Israel, I very seldom saw a shepherd walking ahead of his sheep. But in the time of Christ, the shepherd was with his sheep day after day. They knew him and they followed him. Our Shepherd leads us in right paths, and it is up to us to follow Him.

"Yea, though I walk through the valley of the shadow of death, I will fear no evil." Here is courage and comfort. Death is the supreme test of life. This is not just talking about the deathbed. Our human family lives in the shadow of death. When a person is born, he starts down a great canyon, and that canyon is the valley of the shadow of death. You are in it constantly. In Los Angeles they say that when you cross the street, you better move in a hurry because we have only the quick and the dead. If you are not quick, you will be dead. All of us walk in the shadow of death. As someone has said, the moment that gives you life begins to take it away from you. All of us are in death's valley. The shadow of death is on us. But, all the while I walk through that valley, I will fear no evil. This is the encouraging comfort He gives. If one of our loved ones dies as a child of God, this is our courage and comfort.

"I will fear no evil: for thou art with me." We can know that our Shepherd is with us at all times, and even at the time of death. And I want Him *with* me when my time comes to die.

"Thy rod and thy staff they comfort me." A rod was for defense, and a staff was for direction. He gives us gentle reproof and severe rebuke. He has a rod for our defense, but He also has a staff for our direction. He has a staff for the little old sheep that are bound to stray. That comforts me. Now that I am getting to be an old man, I look back on my life and I realize that indeed that rod is a comfort. He used it on me several times, and I thank Him for it because it got me back into the fold. We all need that.

REFLECTION OF THE HAPPINESS AND HOPE OF THE SHEPHERD'S HEART

Thou preparest a table before me in the presence of mine enemies: thou anointest my head with oil; my cup runneth over.

Surely goodness and mercy shall follow me all the days of my life: and I will dwell in the house of the LORD for ever [Ps. 23:5–6].

These two verses reflect the happiness and hope of the Shepherd's heart. "Thou preparest a table before me in the presence of mine enemies." Here we have felicity, fruitfulness, and fullness. All of that is undergirded with joy. What is that table today? I think it speaks of the Lord's table. At the time this psalm was written it spoke of God's promise to Israel of physical blessings; to us He promises spiritual blessings.

"Thou anointest my head with oil." That oil speaks of the Holy Spirit. We need that anointing today. We cannot face life alone.

"My cup runneth over." This is symbolic of joy. We need to be undergirded with joy today. The Lord says, ". . . I am come that they might have life, and that they might have it more abundantly" (John 10:10). The Lord wants our joy to be full. It reminds me of the little girl who said, "Lord, fill up my cup. I can't hold very much, but I can run over a whole lot." Oh, how this world needs Christians who are running over!

This brings us to the final verse of this psalm. Our Shepherd brings us all the way from the green pastures and the still waters to the Father's house. "Surely goodness and mercy shall follow me all the days of my life: and I will dwell in the house of the LORD for ever." In John 14:2–3 the Lord says to us, ". . . I go to prepare a place for you. And if I go and prepare a place for you, I will come again, and receive you unto myself; that where I am, there ye may be also." You know, we are not pedigreed sheep, and sheep are not worth much anyway, but we do have a wonderful Shepherd. Can you say at this moment, "The LORD is my shepherd"? If you can, all the wonderful promises of this psalm are yours. If He is the Shepherd who gave His life for the sheep and He is *your* Savior, this psalm is for you.

PSALM 24

***THEME:** Christ as the Chief Shepherd*

This is the psalm of the crown. It speaks of the coming of the Chief Shepherd. Tradition says it was composed by David and sung when he brought up the ark from Kiriath-jearim to Mount Zion (1 Chronicles 13:1–8). It was sung in an antiphonal way. It has been suggested that it was sung by the chorus of the procession and by solo voices. Josephus, the Jewish historian, says that seven choirs of singers and musicians marched before the ark as it was brought to Mount Zion where David had prepared a tabernacle for it until the temple was built. I think it will help us to appreciate the thrill of this psalm if we use the possible arrangement as suggested by Delitzsch and Gaebelein.

The psalm divides itself into two sections: the companions of the King who enter the kingdom (vv. 1–6), and the coming of the King to set up the kingdom (vv. 7–10).

It must have been wonderful to have heard this psalm sung in David's day.

COMPANIONS OF THE KING WHO ENTER THE KINGDOM

Chorus of the Procession

> **The earth is the LORD's, and the fulness thereof; the world, and they that dwell therein.**
>
> **For he hath founded it upon the seas, and established it upon the floods [Ps. 24:1–2].**

"The earth is the LORD'S." David speaks of Him again as the Creator. This earth belongs to Him. The earth does not belong to the Democrats or the Republicans. It does not belong to the president, whoever he might be. It does not belong to the Communists. There are so many people today who want to run this earth, but it belongs to God.

"He founded it upon the seas, and established it upon the floods." On the third day of creation God said, ". . . Let the waters under the heaven be gathered together unto one place, and let the dry land appear: and it was so. And God called the dry land Earth; and the gathering together of the waters called he Seas: and God saw that it was good" (Gen. 1:9–10). When God gathered the waters together, submerged land appeared out of the water. It was life out of death, and it speaks of resurrection.

Soloist

> **Who shall ascend into the hill of the LORD? or who shall stand in his holy place? [Ps. 24:3].**

Who shall stand in his holy place? The answer is in the next verse.

Answering Soloist

> **He that hath clean hands, and a pure heart; who hath not lifted up his soul unto vanity, nor sworn deceitfully [Ps. 24:4].**

If the only ones who are going to ascend into the hill of the Lord are those who have "clean hands and a pure heart," and those who have not "lifted up" their souls "unto vanity, nor sworn deceitfully," I guess I won't be there. That leaves me out. But I *am* going to be there, because I am going to be there *in Christ*. He has undertaken to present me before the throne of grace in His present priestly office because I have trusted Him as my Savior.

Chorus and Solo Voices

> **He shall receive the blessing from the LORD, and righteousness from the God of his salvation.**
>
> **This is the generation of them that seek him, that seek thy face, O Jacob. Selah [Ps. 24:5–6].**

Now picture this procession as it enters Jerusalem singing:

> **Lift up your heads, O ye gates; and be ye lift up, ye everlasting doors; and the King of glory shall come in [Ps. 24:7].**

A voice from the gates inquires: "Who is this King of glory?" And the chorus answers.

> **Who is this King of glory? The LORD strong and mighty, the LORD mighty in battle.**
>
> **Lift up your heads, O ye gates; even lift them up, ye everlasting doors; and the King of glory shall come in [Ps. 24:8–9].**

Another voice from the gates inquires: "Who is this King of glory?" And again the chorus answers—probably the full choir and orchestra.

Who is this King of glory? The LORD of hosts, he is the King of glory. Selah [Ps. 24:10].

I think this passage illustrates two events. First of all this is a picture of when the Lord returned to heaven. It is also a picture of His coming to earth again. "Lift up your heads, O ye gates; even lift them up, ye everlasting doors; and the King of glory shall come in." Who is He? The world does not know, but this psalm gives us the answer. The King of glory is "The LORD strong and mighty, the LORD mighty in battle." Then the gates are told to open up so that the King of glory might enter in. Well, He is not "in" today. The world has rejected Him. "Who is this King of glory?" He is the Lord of hosts, He is the Lord Jesus Christ. He is King of kings and Lord of lords. And He is the King of glory. The psalmist writes "Selah" at the conclusion—that is, think on this for a little while. This will bless your heart, my beloved.

PSALM 25

***THEME:** Plea for mercy and deliverance*

This psalm brings us to a new section. It begins a new series of fifteen psalms—25 through 39—which primarily record David's personal experience, but look also to the future when the godly remnant of Israel is in trouble. For the comfort of believers today they contain the balm of Gilead. The preceding psalms can be described as dramatic and, in my judgment, sensational. But the following fifteen psalms are more personal, quiet, and intimate. They have a wonderful message and impact for our lives today. They are applicable to the past, the present, and the future. Some of these psalms may not be so familiar, but they have much to say to us. We will only be hitting the high points, but there are many things to be learned. Often when I could not sleep, or when I was away from home and in a strange place, probably feeling a little lonely, I found myself turning to the book of Psalms, and particularly to this section, because it came out of the experience of a man who was going through a time of trouble. It has a prophetic element, and looks into the future to a time of trouble for the faithful remnant of Israel, but it provides comfort to saints of all ages.

Unto thee, O LORD, do I lift up my soul.

O my God, I trust in thee: let me not be ashamed, let not mine enemies triumph over me [Ps. 25:1–2].

This is a prayer that reveals the dependence that David had upon God. One day Israel will also experience this. The time will come when that remnant of Israel will find themselves in a position where there is no one upon whom they can depend but God. And it is good for us to come to that place also.

When David says, "Unto thee, O LORD, do I lift up my soul," he is getting right down to business. This is not just his voice talking, it is his *soul* speaking. He continues, "O my God, I trust in thee: let me not be ashamed, let not mine enemies triumph over me." Have you ever been in a place where everything seemed to be failure rather than success? You did not want to go down in crushing defeat, either in your personal life, or your business life, or your home or church life. "Let not mine enemies triumph over me." What a prayer! Is this how you pray?

Yea, let none that wait on thee be ashamed: let them be ashamed which transgress without cause [Ps. 25:3].

Now listen to his pleading.

Shew me thy ways, O LORD; teach me thy paths [Ps. 25:4].

There are *two* ways a man can go. He can go God's way or his own way. God gives us a choice. We can walk in the path of our choosing. "There is a way which seemeth right unto a man, but the end thereof are the ways of death" (Prov. 14:12). What a glorious thing it is to be able to call out to God and ask Him to show us the way we should go.

Lead me in thy truth, and teach me: for thou art the God of my salvation; on thee do I wait all the day [Ps. 25:5].

The psalmist is calling on God to show him the

way, to teach him the way. This leads me to say that this is what is known as an acrostic psalm. That is, it is built upon the Hebrew alphabet. Each verse begins with a letter of the Hebrew alphabet. Unfortunately, in English we miss it.

Remember, O LORD, thy tender mercies and thy loving kindnesses; for they have been ever of old [Ps. 25:6].

The psalmist speaks not only of the kindnesses of God but also of His loving kindnesses. It is difficult for me to distinguish between the two, but I think what a little girl once said in Sunday school is a good definition. She said, "When you ask your Mother for a piece of bread with butter on it, and she gives it to you, that is kindness. But when she puts jam on it without you asking her, that is loving kindness." I don't know of a better way to describe the difference. David could say this during a time of trouble, as will the godly remnant of Israel in their time of trouble. And this speaks to our hearts today. What was good for the saints of the past and will be good for the saints of the future is also good for us. I do not see how anyone could read the Psalms, or study the Epistle to the Romans, without seeing that God has a plan and purpose for the nation of Israel in the future. He is not yet through with His people.

Remember not the sins of my youth, nor my transgressions: according to thy mercy remember thou me for thy goodness' sake, O LORD [Ps. 25:7].

David asked God not only to remember His tender mercies and loving kindnesses, but now he asks Him to forget something. He says, "Remember not the sins of my youth" —forget them. Then he prays to God for goodness and mercy. God is rich in both of these. He has enough for you today, and there will be some left over for me. I don't know about you, but I am going to need a whole lot of mercy; and I would like to have a lot of goodness, too. "Surely goodness and mercy shall follow me all the days of my life" (Ps. 23:6).

EXPRESSION OF CONFIDENCE IN GOD

In the second section of this psalm David expresses his confidence and trust.

Good and upright is the LORD: therefore will he teach sinners in the way.

The meek will he guide in judgment: and the meek will he teach his way [Ps. 25:8–9].

God's goodness, His love, and His righteousness are revealed in His provision for salvation for you and me.

For thy name's sake, O LORD, pardon mine iniquity; for it is great [Ps. 25:11].

God forgives us for Christ's sake, never for *our* sake. You and I do not merit forgiveness. We know that God forgave David; and, if we trust in the Lord Jesus Christ, He will forgive us, too. An old blasphemer came to me one time with a sneer on his face and asked, "Why did God choose a man like David, who was such a big sinner?" I said to him, "You and I ought to take a great comfort in that. If God would save David, there just might be a chance that He would save you and me." Concerning His people in the future, God says of Israel in Jeremiah 31:34, ". . . I will forgive their iniquity, and I will remember their sin no more."

The secret of the LORD is with them that fear him; and he will shew them his covenant [Ps. 25:14].

There are so many people today who are just question marks as far as their Christian lives are concerned. They don't understand this or that verse of Scripture, and they don't understand why God does certain things. Their lack of understanding is almost a dead giveaway. They are constantly in a questioning state. But "the secret of the LORD is with them that fear him." When we walk with the Lord, many times we do not need to ask a question; we just put our hand in His and walk along. My daughter and I often used to go for walks. She was a regular question-box. She had to ask questions about everything along the way. Finally she would grow tired, I would pick her up, and she would put her arms around my neck. Question time was over. She just accepted everything from then on. I think many of us should forget about some of the questions we have and simply put our hand in His and walk with Him.

TROUBLE AND DELIVERANCE

As we come to the final section of this psalm, we are faced once again with that time of trouble that is coming for Israel in the future.

Mine eyes are ever toward the LORD; for he shall pluck my feet out of the net.

Turn thee unto me, and have mercy upon me; for I am desolate and afflicted.

The troubles of my heart are enlarged: O bring thou me out of my distresses [Ps. 25:15–17].

What a prayer this will be for the faithful remnant of Israel during the time of trouble that is coming. Also it is a good prayer for you and me when we experience times of trouble.

Look upon mine affliction and my pain; and forgive all my sins [Ps. 25:18].

When we are in trouble we are more apt to confess our sins!

Consider mine enemies; for they are many; and they hate me with cruel hatred.

O keep my soul, and deliver me: let me not be ashamed; for I put my trust in thee.

Let integrity and uprightness preserve me; for I wait on thee [Ps. 25:19–21].

Now hear the conclusion:

Redeem Israel, O God, out of all his troubles [Ps. 25:22].

This glorious prayer is, you see, primarily for the nation Israel and for the day of trouble that is coming upon the earth.

All of us who are God's children have trouble during our lifetimes. This is a prayer for us. O God, deliver us out of all our troubles.

Years ago, down south, a black deacon got up and gave a testimony about a verse of Scripture that was meaningful to him. He said the verse was, "It came to pass." Everyone looked puzzled, so the preacher said to him, "How is it that that particular verse means so much to you?" "Well," the deacon said, "when I am in trouble, I always get my Bible and read, 'It came to pass,' and I thank God that my troubles came to *pass*, and they did not come to *stay*." That may not be the exact interpretation of those words, but it expresses the truth of Scripture, and that is exactly what Psalm 25 is saying. "Redeem Israel, O God, out of all his troubles." I am sure that you can see that the primary interpretation is for the nation Israel, but we certainly can also pray this prayer for ourselves.

PSALM 26

***THEME:** Plea on the basis of personal righteousness*

In Psalm 25 David confessed his sins, and David was a great sinner. But in this psalm David talks about his righteousness. David did have righteousness. I don't know about you, but I have *perfect* righteousness—but it's not Vernon McGee's. First Corinthians 1:30 tells us, "But of him are ye in Christ Jesus, who of God is made unto us wisdom, and *righteousness*, and sanctification, and redemption." He has been made unto me righteousness as well as redemption. This is on the plus side of the ledger, and I stand complete in Him, accepted in the beloved. That is what it means to pray in His name. It is to present *His* work, *His* merit, and who *He* is with our requests.

Judge me, O LORD; for I have walked in mine integrity: I have trusted also in the LORD; therefore I shall not slide.

Examine me, O LORD, and prove me; try my reins and my heart [Ps. 26:1–2].

This is a marvelous psalm that speaks of David's walk. David committed a great sin, but David did not continue to live in sin. What David did once, the king of Babylon did every day. David's sin stands out like a lump of coal in a snowman because the rest of David's life was an example of godliness. He became a measuring stick for the kings who followed him. Every king was judged by whether or not he walked in the steps of his father David. If he followed David's example, he was accepted and proclaimed a good king.

This psalm reminds us of the first psalm. Notice how it reads: "Judge me, O LORD; for I have walked in mine integrity: I have trusted also in the LORD." It was because of his faith in the Lord that David did not slide. Not that he was so strong—he knew he wasn't—but he knew that when he trusted the Lord, the Lord would sustain him.

For thy lovingkindness is before mine eyes: and I have walked in thy truth.

I have not sat with vain persons, neither will I go in with dissemblers.

I have hated the congregation of evildoers; and will not sit with the wicked [Ps. 26:3–5].

This psalm is similar to Psalm 1 in content. David says, "I have walked in thy truth." This is a positive statement. Psalm 1 presents the negative side. "Blessed is the man that walketh *not* in the counsel of the ungodly" (v. 1). Furthermore, David states that he has "not sat with vain persons," nor "with dissemblers." David did not sit with false persons. As Psalm 1 put it, "Blessed is the man that walketh not in the counsel of the ungodly, nor standeth in the way of sinners, nor sitteth in the seat of the scornful" (v.1).

I will wash mine hands in innocency: so will I compass thine altar, O LORD [Ps. 26:6].

A man's faith needs to be backed up by a good life. How important this psalm is in this connection—maybe the reason this section of psalms is not so popular today is because they emphasize a *life* that is pleasing to God.

My foot standeth in an even place: in the congregations will I bless the LORD [Ps. 26:12].

"My foot standeth in an even place." That means that he is sure-footed now. He is established on the Rock. The "even place" speaks of that. When you are on the side of a slippery hill, you are apt to fall. A lot of Christians are in that position today. They are playing with evil. They get close to it. It reminds me of a little boy in the pantry. His mother heard a noise in the back of her kitchen and asked, "Willie, where are you?" The boy replied, "I am in the pantry." She asked, "What are you doing?" He said, "I am fighting temptation." That was not the place for Willie to fight temptation!

Many Christians today flirt with sin. Some time ago I received a letter from one of our radio listeners who wanted counsel. She wrote about how her husband had died, and a close friend of her husband became the one to handle the estate. It was necessary for her to meet with him often; and before long—as she put it—the chemistry between them began to react, and they began to care for each other. She felt uneasy about the situation and asked what she should do. In my reply to her, I wrote: "You are in a burning building. Jump out as quickly as you can." I advised her to leave that town and relocate. Later I received another letter from her that said after a couple of weeks of rationalizing she had followed my suggestion and moved to another town. Looking back on it, she said, "I know I would have fallen if I had stayed there." My friend, it is well to have your feet on even ground. Where are you standing today? The reason a great many people fall is because they are fighting temptation in the pantry!

PSALM 27

THEME: *Prayer*

This is a deeply spiritual psalm and one that is very familiar to many of God's people. The moment you read the first verse your face will probably light up with recognition. It divides itself naturally into two major divisions. The first six verses speak of the provision God makes for the encouragement and confidence of His own. The remainder of the psalm is a prayer for help and sustenance. It is not a psalm for the super-duper saints but has a message for many hearts and lives. It is a prayer of David and opens on this grand note:

FOUNDATION FOR PRAYER

The LORD is my light and my salvation: whom shall I fear? the LORD is the strength of my life; of whom shall I be afraid? [Ps. 27:1].

This again is a "He and me" psalm. "The LORD is *my* light and *my* salvation."

"He is my light." He is a holy God. He is the One who directs and guides me by the light of His Word. Later the psalmist will say, "Thy word is a lamp unto my feet, and a light unto my path" (Ps. 119:105).

He is "my salvation," which speaks of the love of God, because it was His love that provided a salvation for us. That salvation, of course, is only through Jesus Christ. "For God so loved the world, that he *gave* his only begotten Son, that whosoever believeth in him should not perish, but have everlasting life" (John 3:16). God didn't so love the world that He *saved* the world; God so loved the world that He provided a salvation for sinners. And we have to come to Him on that basis. That salvation is conditioned, as Simon Peter put it: ". . . There is none other name under heaven given among men, whereby we must be saved" (Acts 4:12). This is the same salvation that David is talking about. "The LORD is my light and my salvation"—my *light*, my *salvation*.

"The LORD is the strength of my life." God not only gives life, He also empowers us to *live* that life on earth. Is He the light of your life, the one who loves you and gives you strength, my friend?

"Of whom shall I be afraid?" John Knox said, "One with God is a majority." When Cromwell was asked why he did not fear anyone, he said, "I have learned that if you fear God, you have no one else to fear."

When the wicked, even mine enemies and my foes, came upon me to eat up my flesh, they stumbled and fell [Ps. 27:2].

David was probably looking back upon that time of his life when he was in much danger. He started out as a shepherd boy, and his life was in danger when he protected his sheep from a lion and a bear. That is something that a person does not do every day. I don't know about you, but I just don't meet a lion or a bear very often. When I do, they are on the other side of a cage. But there are people like lions and bears walking our streets today, many of them seeking to devour us. Also there is that old lion spoken of in 1 Peter 5:8, "Be sober, be vigilant; because your adversary the devil, as a roaring lion, walketh about, seeking whom he may devour."

Though an host should encamp against me, my heart shall not fear: though war should rise against me, in this will I be confident [Ps. 27:3].

David's confidence was in God, and this is the provision that God has made for His own today. Have you ever noticed that every time the Lord Jesus would break through to speak to His apostles after His resurrection He would say, "Fear not"? You and I have a resurrected Savior. Fear comes to us many times. I have a natural fear of heights; and when I am flying in that big bus in the sky, I say to the Lord, "You are with me. My confidence is in *You*."

MEDITATION ON PRAYER

One thing have I desired of the LORD, that will I seek after; that I may dwell in the house of the LORD all the days of my life, to behold the beauty of the LORD, and to inquire in his temple [Ps. 27:4].

This is a rich verse. David had whittled his life down to one point: "One thing have I desired of the LORD." Also Paul did that with his life. He said, ". . . but this one thing I do, forgetting those things which are behind, and reaching forth unto those things which are before, I press toward the mark for the prize of the high calling of God in Christ Jesus" (Phil. 3:13–14). In this day, whittle down your life, as you would whittle down a pencil, until you can write with it. Our lives are very complicated, so just keep whittling. Most of my life I felt like Martha in the kitchen. She was encumbered with much service (see Luke 10:40). Poor Martha reached for a pot to cook something in it; then she reached for a pan to boil something in it, and she reached for another container to put the potatoes in, and by that time something fell out of the cupboard. She became frustrated trying to do everything at once. How complicated life has become for many of us. We are frustrated, under tension and pressure all the time. It is wonderful to whittle your life down to what is important. It is a relief to reduce your life to the lowest common denominator. I hope you won't mind my speaking out of personal experience, but the happiest time of my ministry began when I retired from the pastorate; the most spiritually profitable time of my life began at that moment. I have seen more folk turn to Christ in this brief interval than in any other period of my life, and I have never rejoiced so. Do you know why? I have whittled my life down to the one thing I want to do—teach the Bible. That is all I am doing. My life has been whittled down to that, and I am enthusiastic about it. I believe this is what God wants me to do.

Now notice the "one thing" in David's life was "that I may dwell in the house of the LORD all the days of my life." Now I don't think David intended to take his sleeping bag into the tabernacle and stay there. But he wanted the ark, which was God's meeting place with His people, with him in Jerusalem. He went to great lengths to bring it to Jerusalem and erected a tabernacle for it and planned an elaborate temple for God. Why? Through that he had *access* to God. That was the "one thing" in David's life.

We have access to God through Christ, and this is the thing we ought to rejoice in. He is the One who will enable us to whittle our lives down to that one point. Paul gives us the eight benefits of being justified by faith in Romans 5:1–5. The second benefit Paul mentions is access to God: "By whom also we have *access* by faith into this grace wherein we stand, and rejoice in hope of the glory of God." What a wonderful thing it is to have access to God!

This is the one thing that was the aim of David's life. "One thing have I desired of the LORD, that will I seek after; that I may dwell in the house of the LORD all the days of my life, to behold the beauty of the LORD, and to inquire in his temple." In the house of God was the mercy seat. David needed mercy, and I need mercy—and I am sure you do also. In the house of God was an altar that spoke of the cross of Christ. This provided for David *access* into the presence of God. You and I can approach God through the Lord Jesus today. We have access into this marvelous grace. What a privilege is ours to have access to God!

No wonder this psalm has been such a wonderful blessing to God's people. Now notice this fifth verse:

For in the time of trouble he shall hide me in his pavilion: in the secret of his tabernacle shall he hide me; he shall set me up upon a rock [Ps. 27:5].

Where was the secret place of the tabernacle? It was inside the Holy of Holies. No one could go there but the high priest. Do you know what was in there? The ark of the covenant, which was only a box overlaid with gold; but upon the ark was the elaborate lid, which God designated as the mercy seat because blood was sprinkled upon it. Now in our day because the Lord Jesus has shed His blood, we have a mercy seat to which we can go. And that is where He hides us. What a secure place we have!

And now shall mine head be lifted up above mine enemies round about me: therefore will I offer in his tabernacle sacrifices of joy; I will sing, yea, I will sing praises unto the LORD [Ps. 27:6].

When we get this wonderful picture and recognize what He has done for us, it will put a song in our hearts. This leads him to pray the next verse.

DECLARATION OF PRAYER PROPER

Hear, O LORD, when I cry with my voice: have mercy also upon me, and answer me [Ps. 27:7].

You see, in that secret place there was *mercy*. And God has prepared that secret place for us today where we can receive the mercy of God.

When thou saidst, Seek ye my face; my heart said unto thee, Thy face, LORD will I seek [Ps. 27:8].

David puts the invitation in the Lord's mouth. When God said, "Seek ye my face," David said, "I have already responded. My heart said unto Thee, 'Thy face, LORD, will I seek.'" My friend, God has a longing for *you*. Do you respond to that? It is awful to live with a person who does not express his love. Marriage is not an arrangement whereby a woman gets a living and a man gets a cook. Marriage is a love relationship; if it is not that, it isn't anything. Our relationship to God should be like that. David's heart responded when God said, "I love you." David said, "*I* love *You*." When God said, "I want to have fellowship with you," David said, "*I* want to have fellowship with *You*."

Hide not thy face far from me; put not thy servant away in anger: thou hast been my help; leave me not, neither forsake me, O God of my salvation [Ps. 27:9].

When David sinned, he found out what it was like for God to hide His face from him. He lost his fellowship. He lost his joy. But he prayed, "Restore unto me the *joy* of my salvation."

The next verse has been misunderstood.

When my father and my mother forsake me, then the LORD will take me up [Ps. 27:10].

This verse has been misunderstood by critics. Even Delitzsch suggested that this verse could have been written by someone else. The reason that possibility is considered is because David's father and mother did not forsake him. But I do not think that is what David is saying here. You will notice that this is a temporal clause—"*When* my father and my mother." It would be better translated

"*Had* my father and my mother forsaken me, then the Lord will take me up." I wish the new revisions of the Bible would call attention to that fact. Probably your father and mother have not forsaken you—but *should* they do so, then the Lord would take you up.

Some wiseacre said, "When my father and my mother forsake me, then the *boy scouts* will take me up." I am afraid that many parents are letting organizations, including the church, raise their children. Even though you may be a member of a good Bible church, your children are *yours*. You are the one who should lead them to the Lord, not the Sunday school teacher or the preacher—*you*. And *you* are the one who should give them your time and attention.

> **Teach me thy way, O LORD, and lead me in a plain path, because of mine enemies [Ps. 27:11].**

David is saying, "I want a good testimony before the enemy, because I know he will criticize me. I want You to watch over me, Lord, and help me not to embarrass You by what I do."

> **Deliver me not over unto the will of mine enemies: for false witnesses are risen up against me, and such as breathe out cruelty [Ps. 27:12].**

I was brought up in a denomination that has since gone into liberalism. And I was a preacher in a denomination that has gone into liberalism. I always prayed to the Lord, "Do not let me fall into a position where I am at the mercy of church leaders or a church board." I was an active pastor from about 1930 to 1970. During that entire time of forty years, God never let me get into a position where I was at the mercy of men. That is what David is praying in this verse. My heart goes out to many ministers today who find themselves at the mercy of a church board or some hierarchy. I urge them to pray like David did, "Don't deliver me into the will of my enemies. Don't let them get me down and pin my shoulders to the mat, Lord." I think He will hear and answer that prayer.

REALIZATION OF PRAYER

> **I had fainted, unless I had believed to see the goodness of the LORD in the land of the living [Ps. 27:13].**

Even in the world today you can see the goodness of the Lord. How wonderful He is.

> **Wait on the LORD: be of good courage, and he shall strengthen thine heart: wait, I say, on the LORD [Ps. 27:14].**

There is a lot of heart trouble today among believers. It is known as faintheartedness, or the coward's heart. All of us have a little touch of it. How can this be cured? "Wait on the LORD; be of good courage." When we do that the Lord will strengthen our hearts. *He* is really the great heart specialist.

PSALM 28

THEME: *A cry in the time of trouble*

This wonderful little psalm contains a cry —David is in trouble here. And it is prophetic of Israel during the Tribulation. It is a prayer for judgment upon his enemies and praise for the deliverance he knows will come. This psalm is actually preliminary to the next one.

> **Unto thee will I cry, O LORD my rock; be not silent to me: lest, if thou be silent to me, I become like them that go down into the pit [Ps. 28:1].**

Israel knew about the "Rock." This Rock Israel rejected, as Moses lamented, ". . . then he [Israel] forsook God which made him, and lightly esteemed the Rock of his salvation" (Deut. 32:15). A rock is something to stand upon. It provides a sure foundation. The believer in our day also knows about that Rock. The apostle Paul wrote, "For other foundation can no man lay than that is laid, which is Jesus Christ" (1 Cor. 3:11).

> **Hear the voice of my supplications, when I cry unto thee, when I lift up my hands toward thy holy oracle [Ps. 28:2].**

The "holy oracle" was the mercy seat, which was in the tabernacle. The mercy seat Christ has provided is what you and I need to cling to today.

Blessed be the LORD, because he hath heard the voice of my supplications [Ps. 28:6].

God hears and answers prayer. As a result, David now says:

The LORD is my strength and my shield; my heart trusted in him, and I am helped: therefore my heart greatly rejoiceth; and with my song will I praise him.

The LORD is their strength, and he is the saving strength of his anointed.

Save thy people, and bless thine inheritance: feed them also, and lift them up for ever [Ps. 28:7–9].

God is power; He is mighty. And He is a shield for protection. He is power and protection. But you say, "Is He *my* power? Is He *my* protection?" He is if your heart trusts in Him. If you trust God, He will help you. He will hear and answer prayer.

What happens when He answers prayer? "With my song will I praise him." Oh, my friend, let's not forget to thank Him and praise Him when He answers our prayers!

He is "the saving strength of his anointed" —the "anointed" is the Messiah, Christ, who is so often mentioned in the Psalms as the coming Deliverer for Israel.

He concludes with this plea, "Save thy people," or another translation is "Shepherd thy people." The anointed One is their Shepherd who will "lift them up forever" when He comes. It reminds us of what Isaiah wrote, "He shall feed his flock like a shepherd: he shall gather the lambs with his arm, and carry them in his bosom, and shall gently lead those that are with young" (Isa. 40:11).

PSALM 29

***THEME:** The voice of the Lord in a thunderstorm*

The psalm before us is a nature psalm. It is not the first nature psalm, as we have already read Psalm 8: "When I consider thy heavens, the work of thy fingers, the moon and the stars, which thou hast ordained," which is a psalm to be read on a good clear night. Then we read Psalm 19, "The heavens declare the glory of God; and the firmament sheweth his handiwork." Then he likens the sun to a bridegroom coming out of his chamber. That is a daytime psalm. Now we come to a psalm that describes a storm. In this psalm is the gloom of the tempest, the clap of thunder, the flash of lightning, and terror on every side. Several years ago a hurricane which they named Camille hit the Gulf Coast. She hurled her might on the other side of New Orleans, around Gulfport, Mississippi. Camille caused millions of dollars worth of damage. In an apartment in that area, several couples decided to have a hurricane party. It was a great big beer bust, and I suppose they all got drunk. I understand that most of them were killed when the storm hit. It is too bad to go into eternity like that. I wish they had read Psalm 29 instead. My friend, if you are frightened in a storm, rather than trying to get your courage from a bottle, I suggest you read this magnificent psalm. It has a message in the time of storm.

The structure of this psalm is quite interesting. This is Hebrew poetry of the highest order. Ewald said of this psalm, "This psalm is elaborated with a symmetry of which no more perfect specimen exists in Hebrew." Delitzsch called it "The Psalm of seven thunders." Perowne said this about it: "This Psalm is a magnificent description of a thunderstorm. Its mighty march from north to south, the desolation and terror which it causes, the peal of thunder, the flash of lightning, even the gathering fury and lull of the elements, are vividly depicted."

So Psalm 29 is a song of Hebrew poetry describing a storm. Hebrew poetry is not attained by rhyming. When we think of poetry, we think of rhymes. We like the sentences to end in words that sound alike. Here is an example of one of our modern ditties: "I shoot the hippopotamus with bullets made of platinum. If I used lead ones, his hide were sure to flatten 'em!" That is not exactly Shakespeare, but it is our kind of poetry. Hebrew poetry is attained by what is known as parallelism, which is repeating a thought in a different way and generally amplifying and enlarging upon it.

The psalm sweeps along with all the freedom and majesty of a storm. There is sort of a lilting triumph here, a glorious abandon, a courageous exultation.

The first two verses are the prologue: "Give unto the LORD, O ye mighty, give unto the LORD glory and strength. Give unto the LORD the glory due unto his name; worship the LORD in the beauty of holiness." David lifts our thoughts to the very highest.

Now, the epilogue is the last two verses: "The LORD sitteth upon the flood; yea, the LORD sitteth King for ever. The LORD will give strength unto his people; the LORD will bless his people with peace." The storm with all its fury lashed across the land, but Jehovah was still in control. And, my friend, in the storms of life He is still in control.

Before we look at this psalm in detail, let me say a word about the subject (which is developed in vv. 3–10). Seven times the voice of the Lord is mentioned: "The voice of the LORD is upon the waters . . . the voice of the LORD is powerful . . . the voice of the LORD is full of majesty . . . the voice of the LORD breaketh the cedars" and so on.

Notice the setting of this psalm. David wrote it. He was an outdoorsman. He was not bottled up in an office. He was not held down to a throne. However, when this storm came, he was not outside; he was in Jerusalem, a city that was beautifully situated. David was in his cedar palace built on Mount Zion, the highest point. He could view the whole land. He could look to the northeast and see the clouds beginning to gather and watch as the storm was getting ready to break. I think most of us are acquainted with the geography of the Holy Land. If you are not, turn to the map in the back of your Bible that shows the location of Jerusalem.

As you look at your map, you will see that the Mediterranean Sea is on your left to the west. Up north there are two ranges of mountains: the Lebanon and the Anti-Lebanon. There is Mount Carmel up there at Haifa and Mount Hermon, the Sea of Galilee on the east, the Valley of Esdraelon, the Jordan River and the Dead Sea. Then there is Mount Ebal and Mount Gerizim in Samaria and the rugged terrain lying immediately north. Bethel, Ai, and Anathoth are just north of Jerusalem. In Jerusalem you look to the west and see Joppa, to the east you see Jericho, and to the south you see the wilderness of Judea, frightful and ominous. David and Amos knew how to survive in that wilderness—a bishop from San Francisco several years ago didn't know; and he perished there. From David's palace on Mount Zion, the highest point in the city of Jerusalem, he could look over this landscape.

PROLOGUE

Give unto the LORD, O ye mighty, give unto the LORD glory and strength.

Give unto the LORD the glory due unto his name; worship the LORD in the beauty of holiness [Ps. 29:1–2].

Notice that the psalm is addressed to the "mighty." I agree with Bishop Horne that "the prophet addresses himself to the 'mighty ones of the earth,' exhorting them to 'give' God the glory and to submit themselves to the kingdom of the Messiah."

SUBJECT

Now we come to the substance of the psalm. The thunderstorm sweeps over the entire land.

We have three strophes, or stanzas, here.

The voice of the LORD is upon the waters: the God of glory thundereth: the LORD is upon many waters.

The voice of the LORD is powerful; the voice of the LORD is full of majesty [Ps. 29:3–4].

That is the beginning of the storm. Way up in the northwest there is distant thunder and lightning. The storm is gathering. The storm begins to move down toward Jerusalem and the voice of Jehovah is the thunder. In the palace David sees the gathering storm. He hears the wind begin to blow. The clouds become black and angry. They hide the sun and it is dark at midday. There is the low rumble of thunder and the flash of lightning which is streaked and forked. This is not a summer shower. This is not an ordinary storm. It is like the hurricane Camille I mentioned earlier. The storm breaks on the Mediterranean Coast. The waves roll high and break with the sound of a cannon on the shore. The angry waves mount up, and then the storm strikes inland. You can see its mighty march from north to south. Jerusalem will not escape it—it comes closer and closer. "The voice of the Lord is powerful." You can now hear that thunder. It shakes everything. "The voice of the Lord is full of majesty"—it is awe-inspiring.

The voice of the LORD breaketh the cedars; yea, the LORD breaketh the cedars of Lebanon [Ps. 29:5].

As the thunder rolls and rumbles, Lebanon is shaken. The trees are struck by lightning. Mighty Mount Hermon is shaken like a dog shakes a rabbit. As the storm draws nearer to Jerusalem, its approach is majestic and awe-inspiring. It rolls along with the rhythm of the thunder and lightning over the hills. Here it comes, as it begins to roll.

He maketh them also to skip like a calf; Lebanon and Sirion like a young unicorn.

The voice of the LORD divideth the flames of fire [Ps. 29:6–7].

The lightning is near Jerusalem now. It pops and crackles like heavy guns in a battle. The storm breaks with all its fury. In Jerusalem the streets are deserted. Shutters are slammed. A hush settles over the city. It is the hush before the sledgehammer blow comes. Only the barking of a dog in the Kidron Valley can be heard. Suddenly it comes. Rain descends in torrents. Savage winds hurl themselves against the walls of Jerusalem. A shutter breaks loose. It bangs and makes a tremendous noise. David has been through this before. He waits patiently and listens to the voice of Jehovah.

The voice of the LORD shaketh the wilderness; the LORD shaketh the wilderness of Kadesh [Ps. 29:8].

Now David sees the storm passing over. It moves away, and the rains let up, and the winds die down. The storm is departing, and the people begin to open their shutters. The storm is departing from Jerusalem and advancing upon the wilderness of Judea to the south and west. Kadesh is down there. Soon the storm is spent in the wilderness of Sinai. The air is fresh, and David can hear the roar of water down in the Kidron Valley.

The voice of the LORD maketh the hinds to calve, and discovereth the forests: and in his temple doth every one speak of his glory [Ps. 29:9].

The storm did accomplish some good. Animals were frightened, causing some that were carrying young to give birth—there was no prolonged pain. It also caused some people to go to the temple who had not been there for a long time. They went to the temple to call upon God. The storm has died away and has disappeared in the south.

EPILOGUE

The LORD sitteth upon the flood; yea, the LORD sitteth King for ever [Ps. 29:10].

God was in charge of this storm all of the time, just as He was in charge of the flood.

The LORD will give strength unto his people; the LORD will bless his people with peace [Ps. 29:11].

The power of God in a storm is great, and it is He who gives strength during a storm. God can strengthen and enable us to go through the storms of life and know what peace is afterward. The storm with all of its fury may lash across the land, but Jehovah is still in control. In every storm of life He is in control, and He will bless His people with peace.

As we have gone through the Psalms, I have called attention to the fact that the Great Tribulation lies ahead for Israel, but God will see His people through it. Armageddon is ahead for these people. The enemy will come from the north and will cover the land, but God is in the storm, and He is in control. What a message this is for Israel.

This psalm has a message for us. We belong to a new creation. We do not belong to the old creation. We belong to the last Adam. "Therefore if any man be in Christ, he is a new creature [creation]: old things are passed away; behold, all things are become new" (2 Cor. 5:17). That is the reason I do not keep the Sabbath day—it belongs to the old creation. You hear the question: "When was the Sabbath day changed?" It was never changed. *We* have been changed and are now joined to a living Christ. Our new day to worship is the first day of the week, the day of resurrection. Adam was given dominion over creation, but he lost it. Christ has recovered it, and the old creation furnishes us with a pattern, an illustration, and the message is here for us today.

There are storms in the new creation, spiritual storms, storms that threaten to destroy us. If you are God's child, you have been through storms, or you are in a storm even now. The last Adam, Jesus Christ, is master of storms. He went through storms with His own. Once when He and His disciples were in a boat, a storm came up on the Sea of Galilee. "And there arose a great storm of wind, and the waves beat into the ship, so that it was now full. And he was in the hinder part of the ship, asleep on a pillow: and they awake him, and say unto him, Master, carest thou not that we perish? And he arose, and rebuked the wind, and said unto the sea, Peace, be still. And the wind ceased, and there was a great calm. And he said unto them, Why are ye so fearful? how is it that ye have no faith?" (Mark 4:37–40). In this instance the Lord quieted the storm, but He does not always do that. Sometimes He just whispers to us, "We are going to make it to the harbor." That is important.

I can think of many people who are in the storm today. There is a little Eskimo mother way up yonder in Alaska. She listens to our Thru the Bible Radio program. She lost a son in Vietnam. She is snowed in in the winter, and she wrote to tell me that listening to the Word being taught is helping to carry her through this difficult time. She is in a storm, but God will see her through it. One of these days the storm is going to be over.

I know of a family in Southern California which is going through a storm. A broker in San Francisco wrote and told me that he would have lost his mind if it was not for the fact that the Lord Jesus stood by him. I was in Flagstaff, Arizona, sometime ago and, while I was there, a storm gathered. By the time I was ready to leave on the train (I thank the Lord I was not flying), oh! the thunder, lightning, and the rain were furious. But before I arrived at my destination, the storm passed, and the moon came out. It was so wonderful, so beautiful. Are you going through a storm? There are two things you should remember: the storm will end, and the Lord will see you through it.

PSALM 30

THEME: *Hallelujah for healing*

This is a psalm and song at the dedication of the house of David. It is a song of praise and worship. After the storm of life is over, there is a song. Some Bible scholars have thought that David wrote this when he brought up the ark to Jerusalem and placed it in the tabernacle he had erected for it. Others have thought that it was written for the dedication of the threshing floor of Araunah, the area where the future temple was to be built. Still others believe it has a prophetic aspect and was David's expression of praise and thanksgiving when God promised to build him a house (2 Sam 7:11). It is interesting to note that in the modern Jewish ritual it is used at the Feast of *Chanukah*, the Feast of Dedication, which dates back to the time of the Maccabees.

I will extol thee, O LORD; for thou hast lifted me up, and hast not made my foes to rejoice over me.

O LORD my God, I cried unto thee, and thou hast healed me [Ps. 30:1–2].

It is my belief, and the belief of many others, that David was once as sick as Hezekiah, and God raised him up. We have no record of what his sickness might have been, but these verses tell us that God healed him. I like this psalm because God did the same thing for me. In fact, I consider this my psalm, because after having cancer, the Lord has permitted me to live. "O LORD my God, I cried unto thee, and thou hast healed me." Perhaps I should organize a chorus and call it "The Cancer Chorus," of those folk all across the country who have been attacked by the awful monster of cancer and God has sustained them.

O LORD, thou hast brought up my soul from the grave: thou hast kept me alive, that I should not go down to the pit [Ps. 30:3].

I don't know about you, but I could sing, or at least say, this psalm. It has a great deal of meaning to me.

Sing unto the LORD, O ye saints of his, and give thanks at the remembrance of his holiness [Ps. 30:4].

We "give thanks at the remembrance of his holiness." God didn't heal me because I am some special little pet of His. He didn't heal me because I am a teacher of the Bible. He did it because He is a holy God and He maintains His holiness. He recognizes my sins, and He has saved me by His grace. He hasn't lowered His standard one bit. Again I say, Hallelujah for healing; I praise Him, my Great Physician. I don't have to praise some great man or woman who claims to be a healer. I didn't go to a person like that. I went directly to the Great Physician. Oh, my friend, if you are sick, take your case to the Great Physician, and then call in the best doctor you can get—because our Great Physician gave him all the skill and wisdom he has (whether or not he recognizes that fact). God is holy. We ought to be thankful that we have a holy God who deals with us in grace.

For his anger endureth but a moment; in his favor is life: weeping may endure for a night, but joy cometh in the morning. [Ps. 30:5].

"His anger endureth but a moment." The storm will be over. Even if God judges me, His anger endures only for a moment. The Lord has taken me to the woodshed on two or three occasions. My dad used to take me to the woodshed, and I was accustomed to it. He died when I was fourteen years old. Shortly after that, I came to know the Lord as my Savior; and He has been taking me to the woodshed ever since. It is not pleasant to be punished, but His anger does not last forever; it only lasts for a moment.

I cried to thee, O LORD; and unto the LORD I made supplication.

What profit is there in my blood, when I go down to the pit? Shall the dust praise thee? shall it declare thy truth? [Ps. 30:8–9].

I told the Lord the same thing David did. I said, "Lord, I would love to stay in this life and teach Your Word. I am going to be with You a long time when I get to heaven, but I would love to stay on earth a little while longer." David talked like that, and I feel akin to him.

Friend, you will find a psalm that fits you. I believe that every person can find a psalm that will be just his size. This one is my size.

To the end that my glory may sing praise to thee, and not be silent. O LORD my God, I will give thanks unto thee for ever [Ps. 30:12].

There is nothing I could say to improve this verse. What David said, I want to say. I hope it is what you want to say, too. David's life had changed. He went from sickness to health, from mourning to gladness, and from silence to praise.

PSALM 31

***THEME:** A prayer of deliverance from trouble*

Most of the psalms are very unfamiliar; yet they comprise one of the richest portions of God's Word. My feeling is that if proper emphasis were given in this section, it would give a different perspective to Scripture, especially relative to God's purposes in the nation Israel.

Practically all of the psalms we have looked at so far have been written by David, and he probably composed the music that went with them. Each psalm has a special meaning for each of us. Here again we see the troubles of the godly. So far in the Psalms there has been a lot of that; but, after all, the godly do have a lot of troubles—at least the ones I know have troubles. Psalm 31 speaks particularly of the past troubles of David. Also it looks to the future and refers prophetically to the troubles that will come to the nation Israel in the Great Tribulation. Finally, it speaks of the present troubles that we have. This psalm has a message for you and for me. At night when I cannot sleep, I generally turn to the Psalms, particularly to this section. Here I find great comfort and help.

In thee, O LORD, do I put my trust; let me never be ashamed: deliver me in thy righteousness [Ps. 31:1].

"Deliver me in thy *righteousness*." David knew that God could not lower His standards in order to save sinners. Sin required a penalty; and, if the sinner did not pay it, someone else would have to pay it. God has a plan, and He can save sinners because Someone else has paid the penalty for sin. That Person is His Son, Jesus Christ. Because of this, David goes on to say:

Bow down thine ear to me; deliver me speedily: be thou my strong rock, for an house of defence to save me [Ps. 31:2].

We need a strong rock—not just some little pebble. "He saith unto them, But whom say ye that I am? And Simon Peter answered and said, Thou are the Christ, the Son of the living God. And Jesus answered and said unto him, Blessed art thou, Simon Bar-jona: for flesh and blood hath not revealed it unto thee, but my Father which is in heaven. And I say also unto thee, That thou art Peter, and upon this rock I will build my church; and the gates of hell shall not prevail against it" (Matt. 16: 15–18). The Rock upon which the church is built is Christ. "For other foundation can no man lay than that is laid, which is Jesus Christ" (1 Cor. 3:11). The Savior, Jesus Christ, is the strong Rock upon which we can rest. I am reminded of the little Scottish lady who was talking about her salvation and her assurance of it: "There are times when I am frightened and I tremble on the Rock, but the Rock never trembles under me." It is a strong Rock.

Now David is not yet through with the Rock. He has more to say. Maybe you could call this the first "rock" music, although it is a little different from the kind we hear today.

For thou art my rock and my fortress; therefore for thy name's sake lead me, and guide me [Ps. 31:3].

Is the Lord God your Rock? Is that where you are resting today? Is He your fortress? A fortress is for protection. You need that.

"Therefore for thy *name's sake* lead me, and guide me"—not because I am David the king, but for *His name's* sake.

Pull me out of the net that they have laid privily for me: for thou art my strength [Ps. 31:4].

"Pull me out of the net that they have laid privily [secretly] for me."

Into thine hand I commit my spirit: thou hast redeemed me, O LORD God of truth [Ps. 31:5].

At the scene of our Lord's crucifixion we are told, "And when Jesus had cried with a loud voice, he said, Father, into thy hands I commend my spirit: and having said thus, he gave up the ghost" (Luke 23:46). When Stephen, the first martyr, was stoned to death, we are told in Acts 7:59, "And they stoned Stephen, calling upon God, and saying, Lord Jesus, receive my spirit." It is interesting that down through the history of the church many martyrs have used that same expression. For instance, when the sentence of degradation was being executed upon John Huss, the bishop pronounced upon him these horrible words: "And now we commit thy soul to the devil." And John Huss, in great calmness, stood there and replied, "I commit my spirit into Thy hands, Lord Jesus Christ. Unto Thee I commend my spirit whom Thou hast redeemed." When Polycarp was being burned at the stake in Smyrna, these were also his words. Bernard used them; Jerome of Prague used them; Luther and Melancthon and many others have also used them. In fact, Martin Luther said, "Blessed are they who die not only for the Lord, as martyrs; not only in the Lord as believers, but likewise *with* the Lord, as breathing forth their lives in the words, into Thy hands I commend my spirit."

I will be glad and rejoice in thy mercy: for thou hast considered my trouble; thou hast known my soul in adversities [Ps. 31:7].

Dr. Gaebelein changed this verse a little: "Thou hast *seen* my troubles; Thou hast *seen* my soul in adversities." I like that better. Twice the psalmist says it. There is great comfort in knowing that God sees you in your trouble. Remember that God said to Moses when He wanted to deliver the children of Israel out of Egypt: ". . . I have surely *seen* the affliction of my people which are in Egypt, and have heard their cry by reason of their taskmasters; for I know their sorrows; And I am come down to deliver them out of the hand of the Egyptians . . ." (Exod. 3:7–8). The Lord had seen the affliction of His people. He had heard their groaning. He knew their condition, and He came down to deliver them.

The Gospels record the time the disciples were out on the Sea of Galilee in a boat when they were hit by a storm. It was the dead of night, and the waves were rolling high. They thought it was the end for them. But Mark says, concerning the Lord, "And he *saw* them toiling in rowing; for the wind was contrary unto them . . ." (Mark 6:48). I like that. He sees you and me today. He knows our troubles. What a comfort this is.

Now we come to a prayer.

Have mercy upon me, O LORD, for I am in trouble: mine eye is consumed with grief, yea, my soul and my belly [Ps. 31:9].

Are you in trouble, friend? Instead of whining and telling everybody else about it, why don't you go to the Lord? Say, "Lord, I am in trouble!" That is what David did.

My times are in thy hand: deliver me from the hand of mine enemies, and from them that persecute me [Ps. 31:15].

"My times are in thy hand" is an interesting expression. Many people go to fortune-tellers and have their palms read. They are told that this line means this and another line means something else. All of it is perfect nonsense, but it affords a living for some people; and for others who are trying to get rid of money it provides another way of getting rid of it. But our times are in Christ's hands. "My times are in thy hand"—and those are crucified hands. I can see my sin in His hands. And they are the tender hands of a Shepherd. He picked up a lost sheep and put it on His shoulders. My care and protection are in those hands. Some future day He is coming with blessing, and those hands will bless. I rejoice that my times are in His hands.

Make thy face to shine upon thy servant: save me for thy mercies' sake [Ps. 31:16].

"Make thy face to shine upon thy servant" is a lovely expression. A Hebrew commentator back in ancient times said, "The face of God is his Anointed, the Messiah." You see, God is a spirit. I don't know how He looks or how He feels or how He acts. But the Lord Jesus came down here to show us the Father. He is the face of God. Through Him we know God. It reminds me of the little girl whose mother took her upstairs and tucked her in bed for the night. Soon after she left her, the child began to whimper, and she called to her, "You go to sleep. God is up there with you." But the little girl wanted someone to stay with her. Once again her mother told her, "God is up there with you." To this the little girl replied, "I know, but I want somebody with a *face*!" My friend, that is what all of us need. All of us little children down here want Somebody with a face to be with us. Jesus Christ is God with a face. How wonderful!

Oh how great is thy goodness, which thou hast laid up for them that fear thee; which thou hast wrought for them that trust in thee before the sons of men! [Ps. 31:19].

How great is the goodness of the Lord! Have you ever told anyone how good God is? Psalm 107:1–2 says, "O give thanks unto the LORD, for he is good: for his mercy endureth for ever. Let the redeemed of the LORD say so, whom he hath redeemed from the hand of the enemy." I find that people like to talk about their neighbors or their children or their father and mother or relatives or their boss or their preacher, but not many people like to talk about the goodness of God. My, how good He is! When was the last time you told someone how good God is?

PSALM 32

***THEME:** A psalm of instruction*

This psalm has been called a spiritual gem; yet it has been misunderstood. The title is: "A Psalm of David, Maschil." *Maschil* means "to give instruction" or "to understand." This Hebrew word is used especially as it relates to the future of Israel. I can't help but think of the seminaries today that have gone intellectual, depending on high-powered personalities and promotional programs and that type of thing to sell themselves. They emphasize the intellectual. It would be nice if they would turn to this psalm and find out that God has a future for Israel, but it requires a little spiritual gumption to get the point.

I want you to see how the word *maschil* is used in connection with the nation Israel. In Daniel 11:33 we read, "And they that understand [*maschil*] among the people shall instruct many: yet they shall fall by the sword, and by flame, by captivity, and by spoil, many days." Again, in Daniel 11:35 we read, "And some of them of understanding [*maschil*] shall fall, to try them, and to purge, and to make them white, even to the time of the end: because it is yet for a time appointed." Daniel 12:3 says, "And they that be wise [*maschil*] shall shine as the brightness of the firmament; and they that turn many to righteousness as the stars for ever and ever." In Daniel 12:10

we read, "Many shall be purified, and made white, and tried; but the wicked shall do wickedly: and none of the wicked shall understand; but the wise [*maschil*] shall understand."

In the New Testament, the Lord Jesus, in speaking of the time of the trouble coming in the future for the nation Israel, says in Matthew 24:15, "When ye therefore shall see the abomination of desolation, spoken of by Daniel the prophet, stand in the holy place, (whoso readeth, let him understand [*maschil*]:)." The Lord was saying that when they see the abomination of desolation spoken of by Daniel the prophet, it is time to run for their lives. I don't know what the abomination of desolation is. I have read quite a few books by men who thought they knew what it is. It took some of them two or three chapters to make it clear that they didn't know what it is. I can say it in one sentence: I don't know what it is. I am not looking for the abomination of desolation; I am looking for the Lord Jesus Christ. Notice that at the end of Matthew 24:15 the Lord said, ". . . whoso readeth, let him *understand*."

In the Book of Revelation, chapters 6–18, we are told more about the Great Tribulation period. In Revelation 13, which tells us about two beasts and the world dictatorship that is coming, we read, "Here is wisdom. Let him that hath *understanding* count the number of the beast: for it is the number of a man; and his number is Six hundred threescore and six" (Rev. 13:18). Numerous books have been written about the number 666. Do you want to know what that number means? I can give you an answer: I don't know! Those who have written the books about the number 666 don't know either—they just think they know. It will be a day when God will reveal Himself to His people. Psalm 32 is a maschil psalm. It will be instruction for God's people in a future day. Right now it is a psalm of instruction for us.

Psalm 32 has been called a penitential psalm, that is, a confession of David. I disagree with that. Psalm 51 is David's prayer of confession after Nathan said to him, "Thou art the man" (2 Sam. 12:7). In that psalm he asks for forgiveness. In Psalm 32 is the record of the confession, the forgiveness received, and the blessedness of his complete restoration. In Psalm 51:12–13 David says, "Restore unto me the joy of thy salvation; and uphold me with thy free spirit. Then will I teach transgressors thy ways; and sinners shall be converted unto thee." David promises if the Lord will forgive him for his sin that he will teach sinners His ways. That is what David is doing in Psalm 32—instructing. So Psalm 32 is not a penitential psalm, but one of instruction.

Blessed is he whose transgression is forgiven, whose sin is covered [Ps. 32:1].

David is giving instruction here. He is telling us that he had made his confession to God, was forgiven, and had found complete restoration. He found shelter in God and was given a song of deliverance.

The word *blessed* in this verse means "happy." We have seen this word before in Psalm 1: "Blessed is the man that walketh not in the counsel of the ungodly, nor standeth in the way of sinners, nor sitteth in the seat of the scornful" (Ps. 1:1). The blessedness in Psalm 1 is that which only a perfect man can enjoy. I don't know about you, but I am not perfect. Psalm 1 actually speaks of the Lord Jesus who was the perfect man. "Blessed is the man that walketh not . . . that standeth not . . . and that sitteth not" (Paraphrase mine). That tells what the perfect man does not do. "But his delight is in the law of the LORD . . ." (v. 2). That Law condemns us. It did not condemn the Lord Jesus Christ. The law written in commandments and ordinances cannot give man blessedness. It demands a perfect obedience which man cannot attain, and thus it pronounces a curse on him. Galatians 3:10 tells us, "For as many as are of the works of the law are under the curse: for it is written, Cursed is every one that continueth not in all things which are written in the book of the law to do them." There is no man who can honestly say that he measures up to God's Law. If you can say that you measure up to the Law, then you can ask the Lord Jesus to move over from the right hand of God because that is your seat—you are perfect. Friend, neither you nor I are perfect, but the Lord Jesus Christ is perfect.

In Psalm 32:1 it is the blessedness of a man whose sin has been forgiven. Christ died for our sins; and, in His death as substitute for sinners, He met and satisfied the righteousness of God. So now the holy God can be a just God and a Savior—He can be just and the justifier of all those who believe in Jesus. When faith is exercised in Christ, it is counted for righteousness. In Romans 4:5 we read, "But to him that worketh not, but believeth on him that justifieth the ungodly, his faith is counted for righteousness." In this way thousands of Old Testament believers, beginning with Adam and Eve who looked for the Seed of the woman, were saved in anticipation of the finished work of the Lord Jesus Christ. David is expressing the blessedness, the happiness of a man whose sins had been forgiven.

Blessed is the man unto whom the LORD imputeth not iniquity, and in whose spirit there is no guile [Ps. 32:2].

God does not impute sin (or make sin over to the sinner) who trusts in Christ. That sin was put on Christ, "Who was delivered for our offences, and was raised again for our justification" (Rom. 4:25). "He knew no sin, but was made sin for us, that we might be made the righteousness of God in him" (2 Cor. 5:17, paraphrase mine). What a wonderful thing God has done for us in Christ!

David relates his experience in trying to hide his sin.

When I kept silence, my bones waxed old through my roaring all the day long [Ps. 32:3].

He had sat on the throne, looked around at the crowd, and said, "Nobody here knows what I have done. Nobody knows about my sin. I have hidden it pretty well." But David's conscience bothered him. In fact, this verse tells us that even his bones bothered him. He began to lose weight, and his friends around him became uneasy. They felt that he needed to see a doctor—that he was probably suffering from some serious disease. But he just kept going through this agony from day to day.

For day and night thy hand was heavy upon me: my moisture is turned into the drought of summer. Selah [Ps. 32:4].

If you are a child of God, you can sin, but you cannot get by with it. That is the difference between the saved and the unsaved man. If you are a man of the world, you can get by with your sin temporarily, but a child of God cannot. The hand of God was heavy upon David day and night. Paul says, "For if we would judge ourselves, we should not be judged. But when we are judged, we are chastened of the Lord, that we should not be condemned with the world" (1 Cor. 11:31–32). If we do not judge ourselves, then God is going to judge us. God takes His own child to the woodshed for punishment.

Sometime after David's sin, the prophet Nathan came to David to reprove him, and he said, "David, I have a little story to tell you." This is the story: ". . . There were two men in one city; the one rich, and the other poor. The rich man had exceeding many flocks and herds: But the poor man had nothing, save one little ewe lamb, which he had bought and nourished up: and it grew up together with him, and with his children; it did eat of his own meat, and drank of his own cup, and lay in his bosom, and was unto him as a daughter. And there came a traveller unto the rich man, and he spared to take of his own flock and of his own herd, to dress for the wayfaring man that was come unto him; but took the poor man's lamb, and dressed it for the man that was come to him. And David's anger was greatly kindled against the man; and he said to Nathan, As the LORD liveth, the man that hath done this thing shall surely die: And he shall restore the lamb fourfold, because he did this thing, and because he had no pity. And Nathan said to David, Thou art the man . . ." (2 Sam. 12:1–7). Then David confessed his sin.

I acknowledged my sin unto thee, and mine iniquity have I not hid. I said, I will confess my transgressions unto the LORD; and thou forgavest the iniquity of my sin. Selah [Ps. 32:5].

This is good instruction for you and me, is it not? If you are out of fellowship with God today, David in this verse tells about the way back. "If we confess our sins, he is faithful and just to forgive us our sins, and to cleanse us from all unrighteousness" (1 John 1:9).

For this shall every one that is godly pray unto thee in a time when thou mayest be found: surely in the floods of great waters they shall not come nigh unto him [Ps. 32:6].

When David refers to the "floods of great waters," I think he is referring to the flood of Noah's time. Noah was in the ark when the Flood came, and that flood which destroyed others simply lifted him up because he was in the ark. The waters of judgment could not reach Noah. There is going to be another time of great judgment coming upon the earth, but it will not be a flood of water; it will be fire. What can you do at a time like that?

Thou art my hiding place; thou shalt preserve me from trouble; thou shalt compass me about with songs of deliverance. Selah [Ps. 32:7].

This verse ends with the word *Selah,* which means "to stop, look, and listen." Think over what has been said. Selah is a musical rest, and I have a notion the orchestra did not play at this time, nor did the chorus sing. It was a time of silence so you could think over what had been sung. Think it over, friend. Have you lost fellowship with God? Do you need a hiding place? Well, God can be your hiding place.

I will instruct thee and teach thee in the way which thou shalt go: I will guide thee with mine eye [Ps. 32:8].

You have to be very close to the Lord if you are going to be guided with His eye.

Now God uses a humorous comparison.

Be ye not as the horse, or as the mule, which have no understanding: whose mouth must be held in with bit and bridle, lest they come near unto thee [Ps. 32:9].

There are many Christians who do not orbit in the will of God. They are way up in space; yet God will guide them by His overruling providence, as we learn in the little Book of Esther. He compares a believer who will not be led by God to an old hard-headed mule. It reminds me of the man in Texas who visited his friend who owned a little donkey. They hitched it to the wagon intending to take a ride and visit some mutual friends. Before they got in the wagon, the owner reached into the wagon, took out a two-by-four, and hit the donkey over the head. The man asked his friend, "Why in the world did you do that?" His friend replied, "I do that to get his attention." Many of us are like that donkey. That is why Scripture says, "Be ye not as the horse or as a mule, which have no understanding: whose mouth must be held in with a bit and bridle."

This psalm closes on a high note.

Many sorrows shall be to the wicked: but he that trusteth in the LORD, mercy shall compass him about.

Be glad in the LORD, and rejoice, ye righteous: and shout for joy, all ye that are upright in heart [Ps. 32:10–11].

Whoever you are and wherever you are, if you know the Lord Jesus Christ as your Savior, you can lift up your heart in great joy to God.

PSALM 33

***THEME:** A song of praise from a redeemed people*

In this psalm we find the praises of redeemed people. God is worshiped as the Creator and as providential Ruler. He is praised for His majestic and matchless grace. For the first time musical instruments are plainly mentioned in the text itself. This is one of the orphanic (orphan) psalms because the author's name is not given. It is one in this segment of psalms that David may not have written.

Rejoice in the LORD, O ye righteous: for praise is comely for the upright [Ps. 33:1].

We are to rejoice in the presence of God. This is a beautiful psalm of praise. It sounds like David, and it is possible that he could have written it.

Praise the LORD with harp: sing unto him with the psaltery and an instrument of ten strings [Ps. 33:2].

The psaltery is a stringed instrument resembling a zither.

Sing unto him a new song: play skilfully with a loud noise [Ps. 33:3].

We are to sing a new song unto the Lord. What is that new song? Several psalms speak of a new song that will be sung in the future. I think when the time comes to sing that new song there will be new singers also. I am going to have a new body, and I think I will be able to sing. I hope the Lord will let me sing in heaven. Revelation 5:9 says, "And they sung a new song, saying, Thou art worthy to take the book, and to open the seals thereof: for thou wast slain, and hast redeemed us to God by thy blood out of every kindred, and tongue, and people, and nation." The psalmist exhorts us to sing a song of praise to God because He is our *Creator*, but the new song we will sing in heaven will be because the Lord Jesus Christ is our *Redeemer*. In Revelation 14:3 we read, "And they sung as it were a new song before the throne, and before the four beasts, and the elders: and no man could learn that song but the hundred and forty and four thousand, which were redeemed from the earth." A new song will be sung in the future.

In this verse we are also told that we are to "play *skilfully.*" Friend, I believe that if you are going to sing before a group of people you should sing well. Church music is in a sad state today. I visit many churches and hear many people sing who do not have a gift for singing. You may not be a trained musician, but you should be dead sure that you can sing and that your voice is a gift of the Spirit which He can use for the profit and building up of the church. Otherwise your effort will be an exercise in futility. And don't try to hit a high "C" when you cannot even hit a high "A" or "B"—that is an exercise in futility also!

For the word of the LORD is right: and all his works are done in truth [Ps. 33:4].

Notice the *Word* of God and the *works* of God, meaning His creative works.

By the word of the LORD were the heavens made; and all the host of them by the breath of his mouth [Ps. 33:6].

The Word of God is powerful! I once saw a demonstration by a singer who broke two or three glasses by hitting a high note. God used *His* voice to create, not destroy. He brought the universe into existence by His word. He said, ". . . Let there be light: and there was light" (Gen. 1:3). There is power in light, electrical power and electronic power. Do you realize that all of that came into existence when God spoke? God *spoke* into existence all created things. Vegetation, animal life, and man were all created by God's word. What tremendous power there is in His Word! I don't know *how* He did it, but I do know that God did it, and that is the important thing.

The LORD bringeth the counsel of the heathen to nought: he maketh the devices of the people of none effect [Ps. 33:10].

The United Nations has selected to put up a verse like Isaiah 2:4 which says in part, ". . . and they shall beat their swords into plowshares, and their spears into pruninghooks: nation shall not lift up sword against nation, neither shall they learn war any more." They have used the wrong verse because it doesn't look to me like they are doing much beating—they are beating each other but not swords into plowshares. Instead, Psalm 33:10 should be written over the United Nations: "The LORD bringeth the counsel of the heathen [nations] to nought." That would be appropriate. Witness the past: the League of Nations, and before that, the Hague Conference on Peace, all came to naught. Do you know something else? I know I will be criticized for saying this, but the United Nations is also going to come to naught, because they have left God out.

Blessed is the nation whose God is the LORD; and the people whom he hath chosen for his own inheritance [Ps. 33:12].

This is a verse I would love to put up in Washington so that the president and all of Congress could see it.

The LORD looketh from heaven; he beholdeth all the sons of men [Ps. 33:13].

God sees the United Nations. He sees the president of the United States. He sees the Congress. He sees you. He sees me. No one escapes His eye.

There is no king saved by the multitude of an host: a mighty man is not delivered by much strength [Ps. 33:16].

Napoleon said that God is on the side of the greatest battalion, but he demonstrated he was wrong, because at the Battle of Waterloo Napoleon had the greatest battalion and lost. God is not on the side of the one who has the biggest bomb, either.

Behold, the eye of the LORD is upon them that fear him, upon them that hope in his mercy [Ps. 33:18].

How wonderful this is!

For our heart shall rejoice in him, because we have trusted in his holy name [Ps. 33:21].

When we trust in the name of God, our hearts will rejoice. May I make a suggestion? Why don't you saturate yourself with the Psalms? Instead of running around attending all of the conferences which tell you about new methods of running the Sunday school, running the church, or doing this or that, why don't you stay home and read the Psalms? When you are saturated with this portion of God's Word, it not only will bring comfort to your heart, it will solve 99.4 percent of the problems of the church. Oh, that it might become meaningful to you personally and be translated into shoe leather! This is a rich area of the Word of God.

PSALM 34

THEME: *A song of praise for deliverance*

This psalm has an explanation, which is part of the inspired text: "A Psalm of David, when he changed his behavior before Abimelech; who drove him away, and he departed." This provides me with a fine opportunity to illustrate something that the critic has used to discredit the Word of God, which has led many uninstructed folks away from believing in the integrity and the inerrancy of Scripture. The occasion for this psalm goes back to an incident that is recorded in the life of David. You will recall that King Saul was after David. This young man was fleeing for his life and hiding in one cave after another. He was in that region of wilderness down toward the Dead Sea, and not many people can survive in that area. I have been driven through it, but I would not want to drive through it alone. David was able to survive in that wilderness, but he did grow weary; and his faith got very weak. He thought he was going to be destroyed, so he went west to the land of the Philistines. The king of the Philistines received David at that time, but some of his men distrusted him. "And the servants of Achish said unto him, Is not this David the king of the land? did they not sing one to another of him in dances, saying, Saul hath slain his thousands, and David his ten thousands? And David laid up these words in his heart, and was sore afraid of Achish the king of Gath" (1 Sam. 21:11–12). David realized that he was in real danger there in enemy territory, so he acted like an insane man. The king was disgusted at having an insane man in his presence, and he sent him away. So David's life was spared at this time. When David escaped and returned to the wilderness of Israel to hide, I think he was lying there in the safety of a cave, thinking, *I should have trusted God.*

Now if you turn back to 1 Samuel 21 and read the record, you will note that the king of Gath is called Achish, and in Psalm 34 he is called Abimelech. The critic sees this and says that it is quite obvious this is not an inspired psalm of David, and that this is an error in the Bible. The problem with the critic is that he looks only where he wants to look. Abimelech is a general title of royalty, just as Pharaoh was a general title in Egypt.

When I was teaching in a Bible institute a young fellow brought this problem of Achish and Abimelech to me. He said he believed in the inspiration of the Scriptures, but this was obviously an error, and he was greatly distressed by it. Of course, it was simply a lack of knowledge on his part. Remember, when you think you find an error in the Bible, the problem is not with the Bible but with you. That is the problem the critics have today.

As we consider this psalm, think of it in the light of David's experience.

I will bless the LORD at all times: his praise shall continually be in my mouth [Ps. 34:1].

When you are in trouble, do you feel discouraged and defeated? David did. He kept running, running, running, and it looked like it would never come to an end. He lost heart and was discouraged. He thought, *One of these days I will be killed.* Yet he says, "I will bless the LORD at all times." My friend, I do pretty well in praising the Lord on a good sunshiny day and when things go right, but it is not so easy when things become difficult. Yet David could say, "His praise shall continually be in my mouth."

My soul shall make her boast in the LORD: the humble shall hear thereof, and be glad [Ps. 34:2].

David's attitude was a testimony for the Lord.

O magnify the LORD with me, and let us exalt his name together [Ps. 34:3].

I have thought about putting this verse on the letterhead we use at our *Thru the Bible Radio* headquarters. I want you to join with me in magnifying the Lord. We are going to find out in one of the psalms that the *Word* of God and the *name* of God are just about the same. Both are important. We want to get out the Word of God because it will magnify the name of the Lord. I would like to say with the psalmist, O magnify the Lord with me, and let us exalt His name together, in getting out the Word of God today.

The first three verses are sheer praise to God; they are the Hallelujah Chorus. Now he gives us the reason for his praise.

I sought the LORD, and he heard me, and delivered me from all my fears [Ps. 34:4].

How wonderful!

They looked unto him, and were lightened: and their faces were not ashamed.

This poor man cried, and the LORD heard him, and saved him out of all his troubles [Ps. 34:5–6].

How thankful David was for God's deliverance. And, friend, I thank God for the way He has led me. I am sure you do, too.

The angel of the LORD encampeth round about them that fear him, and delivereth them [Ps. 34:7].

The Angel of the Lord is mentioned only three times in the Psalms. He is mentioned in Psalm 34:7 and in Psalm 35:5–6 and that is all. I am not going to go into any detail about this subject, but I believe the Angel of the Lord is the preincarnate Christ. You do not find the Angel of the Lord in the New Testament because the Lord is no longer an angel, but a Man. When He appeared in the Old Testament as an angel, He was none other than the Lord Jesus Christ. In this verse the psalmist tells us that the "angel of the LORD encampeth round about them that fear him, and delivereth them." In Hebrews 13:5 the Lord Jesus says, ". . . I will never leave thee, nor forsake thee." In Matthew 28:20 the Lord says, ". . . lo, I am with you alway, even unto the end of the world. Amen."

Now David extends an invitation:

O taste and see that the LORD is good: blessed is the man that trusteth in him [Ps. 34:8].

David says, "If you don't believe what I have said is true, taste for yourself and see that the Lord is good." Blessed or *happy* is the man who trusts in the Lord. There is nothing like it.

David had been hunted by Saul for a long time. He had hid in caves and had become a rugged outdoorsman. He had seen the sight mentioned in the following verse.

The young lions do lack, and suffer hunger: but they that seek the LORD shall not want any good thing [Ps. 34:10].

David had seen hungry little lion cubs whining for something to eat. He also had seen that those who had sought the Lord had not lacked any good thing. If a lioness can take care of her little cubs, God can take care of you and me. David learned that by experience. This is putting Christianity into shoe leather, and we need it in shoe leather. I am tired of Sunday morning Christianity. People come to church, sing a few hymns, listen to the sermon, and sing the Doxology. That just about ends it for many folks. I love what a broker in San Francisco wrote—it was one of the nicest things anyone had said: "You do not sound like you are speaking behind a stained glass window." I thank God for that. There is nothing wrong with speaking behind stained glass windows—I did that for forty years—but I would rather that it sounded as if it came from the marketplace, the schoolroom, the office, and the workshop. David had experienced God's care. He knew it was real.

Keep thy tongue from evil, and thy lips from speaking guile [Ps. 34:13].

This is something that I need to learn. Perhaps you also need to learn it.

The eyes of the LORD are upon the righteous, and his ears are open unto their cry [Ps. 34:15].

God hears and answers prayer. It may not be the answer we were expecting, because sometimes He says no.

The face of the LORD is against them that do evil, to cut off the remembrance of them from the earth [Ps. 34:16].

There is a lot of sentimental rot today in dramatic productions of some old low-down sinner who deserts his wife and baby so he can live a life of sin. Maybe he becomes a thief or a murderer, but one day he comes home and finds his little child sick. He gets down by the side of the bed and prays. This kind of story brings boo-hoos all over the audience. I don't know about you, but it turns my tummy. Do you know why? God says, "I don't hear the prayer of a man like that." Such a person has no right to go to God and ask Him for anything *except* salvation. You don't even have to ask for forgiveness. He's got forgiveness for you. All you have to do is confess yourself a sinner and trust Christ as your Savior. He will automatically forgive you. ". . . Believe on the Lord Jesus Christ, and thou shalt be saved . . ." (Acts 16:31).

The LORD is nigh unto them that are of a broken heart; and saveth such as be of a contrite spirit [Ps. 34:18].

If a person is willing to take the place of humility, come to the Lord as a sinner and trust Him, the Lord will be near to him. Now if that old reprobate who got down by the bed and prayed for his sick child will acknowledge his sin and accept Jesus Christ as his Savior, then God will hear his prayer for his child. The Lord is near those who have a broken heart.

Many are the afflictions of the righteous: but the LORD delivereth him out of them all [Ps. 34:19].

No one is free from trouble—regardless of who he is. But when we are God's children we can expect God's deliverance. Oh, how good He is. Let's bless Him at all times, even as David did.

PSALM 35

THEME: *A plea for deliverance from his enemies*

This is a psalm that David wrote during the days of his persecution by King Saul. First Samuel 24 probably contains the background for this psalm. It is David's powerful appeal to a righteous God to execute judgment upon the enemies of God and the persecutors of His righteous people.

There are folk who say that this is not the kind of prayer a Christian should pray and that the Lord Jesus did not talk like this. However, the Lord Jesus did give a parable about a widow who went to a judge saying, "Avenge me of mine adversary." That judge took a long time to do it, but he finally saw that the widow got justice. It is a parable by contrast. God is not an unfeeling, hardhearted judge. God is gracious, wonderful, and eager to help His children, and we are to turn over to Him our grievances. And Paul gives believers this admonition: "Dearly beloved, avenge not yourselves, but rather give place unto wrath: for it is written, Vengeance is mine; I will repay, saith the Lord" (Rom. 12:19). You and I are not to take vengeance. We are to turn that over to God—it is His department. He will handle it better than either you or I will handle it.

I want to speak quite frankly. I have turned several people over to the Lord when what I wanted to do was smack them in the mouth. There is no use beating around the bush—I have that feeling sometimes. I know a man who is a liar; yet he pretends to be an outstanding Christian and carries a big Bible under his arm! God told me, "Vernon, don't hit him in the mouth. That would be wrong—you wouldn't be walking by faith. You trust Me. Vengeance is mine. I will repay." So I turned that man over to the Lord. I think the Lord will spank him. We need to learn to walk the pathway of faith.

When David wrote this psalm, he was in trouble. He was running away from Saul. Yet when David had an opportunity to kill Saul, he refused to do it. Saul knew that David had spared his life, and in 1 Samuel 24 Saul even said to him that he knew God had given the kingdom to David and admitted that David was more righteous than he was. Yet he continued to treat David as an enemy instead of bringing him home in peace.

David's imprecatory prayer is not only personal but prophetic. David's persecution pictures the remnant of Israel during the Tribulation period. The cry for righteous judgment will be answered when the Lord Jesus Christ comes the second time. He will execute judgment and will deliver God's elect.

Let them be confounded and put to shame that seek after my soul: let them be turned back and brought to confusion that devise my hurt.

Let them be as chaff before the wind: and let the angel of the LORD chase them [Ps. 35:4–5].

David wanted to turn it over to the Lord, you see.

Here is the second mention of the "angel of the LORD"—the first was in Psalm 34:7. Again let me say that I believe the Angel of the Lord is none other than the preincarnate Christ. He is the deliverer and the executor of judgment.

Let their way be dark and slippery: and let the angel of the LORD persecute them.

For without cause have they hid for me their net in a pit, which without cause they have digged for my soul.

Let destruction come upon him at unawares; and let his net that he hath hid catch himself: into that very destruction let him fall [Ps. 35:6–8].

This sounds extreme! It is an imprecatory prayer. I do think it is inconsistent for a Christian to pray a prayer like that today since God has told us to turn things over to Him. But if you think God is not going to take vengeance on evildoers, you are mistaken. He will do it without being vindictive. He will do it in justice and in righteousness and in holiness. We do well in turning over to God our grievances because He is going to make things right. This is a great psalm, a great comfort and solace for the soul of man.

Now listen to David after he has prayed that prayer.

And my soul shall be joyful in the LORD: it shall rejoice in his salvation.

All my bones shall say, LORD, who is like unto thee, which deliverest the poor from him that is too strong for him, yea, the poor and the needy from him that spoileth him? [Ps. 35:9–10].

At this time in David's life he was a very poor man. While he was in exile there came to him men who were in debt, men who were in distress, and men who were discontented. These were his companions, and they shared his rugged existence and his poverty. But God was with them, and He "delivered the poor from him that was too strong for him."

With hypocritical mockers in feasts, they gnashed upon me with their teeth [Ps. 35:16].

A mocker in that day was a court jester who was hired to amuse the guests at a banquet. In this case they would make fun of David for running away and hiding from Saul. They probably would say, "He could slay the giant Goliath, but he is afraid of King Saul."

Hypocritical mockers are about us today, and you will find them in the church. I was a pastor for a long time, and I have seen them. Since I am no longer a pastor, I am in a position to say some things that need to be said. Mockers hurt the testimony of the church. The church is the bride of Christ; God still has a purpose for her, and somebody needs to do some cleaning up on the inside. We are not to judge the world, but we are to judge the things inside the church. There are those who ridicule God's men, and they lie about God's men—doing it in a most pious way. They are hypocritical mockers. They are *jesters* in the court of God, ridiculing God's men.

My friend, it is good to know that although the righteous do suffer ridicule and even affliction, and although the enemy rejoices over their suffering, the end is always deliverance. In God's kingdom the righteous will have their share.

PSALM 36

THEME: *A picture of the wicked*

This psalm has the inscription of David as the "servant of Jehovah." The psalm gives us a view of the human heart, which is *wicked.* You may not believe this, but every human being has a wicked heart. Jeremiah 17:9 tells us, "The heart is deceitful above all things, and desperately wicked: who can know it?" Fortunately God has a remedy for heart trouble.

The transgression of the wicked saith within my heart, that there is no fear of God before his eyes [Ps. 36:1].

The Septuagint translation, which is the Greek translation made by the seventy in Egypt, of this verse reads, "The wicked hath an oracle of transgression in his heart." What is that oracle of transgression in the heart? It is the old nature that everyone has, the Adamic nature. In Matthew 15:19 the Lord Jesus Christ says, "For out of the heart proceed evil thoughts, murders, adulteries, fornications, thefts, false witness, blasphemies." It's an ugly brood that comes out of the human heart.

"There is no fear of God before their eyes" is quoted by Paul in Romans 3:18. This is a revelation of the wicked. "The wicked hath an oracle of transgression in his heart." That old evil nature has a hold on mankind. To those who say, "Let your conscience be your guide," I want to say, "Your conscience is not your guide." The Holy Spirit is your guide. Your conscience is like a barometer that will let you know if what you have done is right or wrong. Let the Holy Spirit be your guide. Your conscience is that which will prick you after you have done something wrong.

For he flattereth himself in his own eyes, until his iniquity be found to be hateful [Ps. 36:2].

Matthew Henry, in his commentary, makes a very interesting statement in this connection. He says that sinners are self-destroyed. "They are self-destroyers by being self-flatterers; Satan could not deceive them, if they did not deceive themselves. But will the cheat last always? No, the day is coming when the sinner will be undeceived, when his iniquity shall be found hateful." I think that one of the things the lost will have to live with throughout eternity is an old nature that he is going to learn to hate. That is the thing that will make his own little hell on the inside of his skin!

The words of his mouth are iniquity and deceit: he hath left off to be wise, and to do good [Ps. 36:3].

On the golf course I met a man, a fine-looking man who had retired from an excellent position. All that came out of his mouth was iniquity. In every breath he uttered he took God's name in vain. "The words of his mouth are iniquity and deceit."

He deviseth mischief upon his bed; he setteth himself in a way that is not good; he abhorreth not evil [Ps. 36:4].

In his bed he plans the evil he is going to do the next day. This is a frightful picture!

Now we have a picture of what God is:

Thy mercy, O Lord, is in the heavens; and thy faithfulness reacheth unto the clouds.

Thy righteousness is like the great mountains; thy judgments are a great deep: O Lord, thou preservest man and beast.

How excellent is thy lovingkindness, O God! therefore the children of men put their trust under the shadow of thy wings [Ps. 36:5–7].

What blessed, wonderful words these are. This is the God that man rejects. This is the God whom men do not fear. The wicked do not know this God, and they have no idea what it is like to be under His wings. That is the place where the righteous take refuge. I like to talk about the wings of Jehovah. In Exodus 19:4 God told Israel, "Ye have seen what I did unto the Egyptians, and how I bare you on eagles' wings, and brought you unto myself." Under His wings there is protection, security, rest, and the warmth of God's love. Jesus said, "O Jerusalem, Jerusalem, thou that killest the prophets, and stonest them which are sent unto thee, how often would I have gathered thy children together, even as a hen gathereth her chickens under her wings, and ye would not!" (Matt. 23:37). This is the God that many people are rejecting today!

Let not the foot of pride come against me, and let not the hand of the wicked remove me.

There are the workers of iniquity fallen: they are cast down, and shall not be able to rise [Ps. 36:11–12].

David prays that God will continue giving His mercy and grace to him so that he will not fall under the hand of the wicked. This is something that every believer should pray. We live in a wicked, mean world. My prayer has always been, "Oh, God, don't let me fall into the hands of the wicked."

PSALM 37

THEME: *A promise of future blessing*

This is a psalm of David. It is an experience of David and a promise of future blessing to the remnant of Israel written in the form of an acrostic. Each verse in this psalm begins with a letter of the Hebrew alphabet. There are forty verses in Psalm 37, which means that two verses would begin with each letter of the Hebrew alphabet. For example, two verses of this psalm begin with Aleph, two verses with Beth, two verses with Gimel, etc., right through the alphabet. That is the way we instruct our children. I still remember a book I got when I was a little fellow: "*A* is for apple, *B* is for baby, *C* is for cat," etc., with illustrating pictures for each. This psalm is constructed in a similar way. It has been a great blessing to God's people down through the years, although it is often misapplied.

Fret not thyself because of evildoers, neither be thou envious against the workers of iniquity.

For they shall soon be cut down like the grass, and wither as the green herb [Ps. 37:1–2].

The prosperity of evildoers troubled David a great deal. It is a subject that is dealt with in Psalm 73 and one that is presented elsewhere in the Old Testament. Why do the godless people seem to prosper? In the Old Testament, God promised believers *earthly* and *material* prosperity. He has not promised that to believers today. Our hope is in heaven, not on earth. But the hope of Israel was upon the earth. The man of that day looked about and saw the ungodly prosper. He could see the fields of the ungodly being watered by the rain and flourishing, while down the road a poor righteous man was having a hard time. It was difficult to understand the reason for this.

David came to the conclusion, as Asaph did in Psalm 73, that someday the wicked would be cut down just like the grass. A few years ago I had people in my congregation who could not understand why God would permit Hitler to do the things he was doing. Why, he almost won World War II. Why would God permit a man like Mussolini to do some of the things he did? But where are these men today? Just give God time. He will deal with the wicked. It is the *end* of the ungodly that we need to consider. If it disturbs you when you look around today and see the wicked prospering, there are several things you can do to solve your problem.

Trust in the LORD, and do good; so shalt thou dwell in the land, and verily thou shalt be fed [Ps. 37:3].

This was a promise to God's earthly people. He told them, "Don't worry about the wicked. You trust in Me, and I will take care of you."

Delight thyself also in the LORD; and he shall give thee the desires of thine heart [Ps. 37:4].

This was a promise for Israel, but it also applies to us today. I am not sure that He is going to bless your business, but He has already blessed you with spiritual blessings, and He will shower on you all of the spiritual blessings you can contain. Then notice what we are to do. We are to delight ourselves in the Lord.

Now, there is something else that we can do.

Commit thy way unto the LORD: trust also in him; and he shall bring it to pass [Ps. 37:5].

"Commit thy way unto the LORD." Many Christians criticize and find fault with God—they have not committed their way to the Lord.

"Trust also in him; and he shall bring it to pass." Give God time. He will work things out in your life. God is *good*, my friend. The heathen concept of God is as a terrible Being. Their idols are hideous. Many Christians view God that way. They think of Him as sort of a villain who will turn on you at any moment. He never will—He is your Friend. He loves you. He wants to save you, but you have to commit your way to Him.

Rest in the LORD, and wait patiently for him: fret not thyself because of him who prospereth in his way, because of the man who bringeth wicked devices to pass [Ps. 37:7].

Here is another thing to do: "Rest in the LORD, and wait patiently for him." How wonderful it is. When the wicked prosper, don't fret. When the ungodly bring their wicked devices to pass, don't let it disturb you. Don't get "uptight" about it.

Cease from anger, and forsake wrath: fret not thyself in any wise to do evil [Ps. 37:8].

"Cease from anger"—don't lose your temper.

If you do evil, don't think *you* can get by with it. If you are God's child, you will find yourself in deep trouble if you try to get by with evil.

For evildoers shall be cut off: but those that wait upon the LORD, they shall inherit the earth [Ps. 37:9].

God will see to it that those who wait upon the Lord will one day inherit the earth. The wicked are going to be cut off.

But the meek shall inherit the earth; and shall delight themselves in the abundance of peace [Ps. 37:11].

Someday the meek shall inherit the earth. The day will come when God will put His people on the earth. I heard a preacher say, "God is going to save so many people that there won't be enough room for them on earth, so He made heaven to take care of the overflow." Heaven is *not* for the overflow; it is for the church. Israel will inherit the earth. To make a statement like that preacher did is to hopelessly confuse the purposes of God.

The wicked have drawn out the sword, and have bent their bow, to cast down the poor and needy, and to slay such as be of upright conversation [Ps. 37:14].

The Scripture makes it clear that if you take the sword, that is the way you will perish.

A little that a righteous man hath is better than the riches of many wicked [Ps. 37:16].

Having traveled a lot in the course of my ministry, I have been in the homes of very poor saints and also in the homes of some very rich saints. It has been my experience that the happiest saints are those who do not have so much. God seems to see to that.

But the wicked shall perish, and the enemies of the LORD shall be as the fat of lambs: they shall consume; into smoke shall they consume away [Ps. 37:20].

The wicked are going to perish. Don't concern yourself with their prosperity. That is God's department, and He will take care of it.

The steps of a good man are ordered by the LORD: and he delighteth in his way [Ps. 37:23].

"The steps of a good man are ordered by the LORD," that is, they are *established* by the Lord on a foundation that is the Rock—and the Rock is Christ.

"He delighteth in his way." Does God delight in *you* today? God could point to Job—who was not sinless by any means—but God took delight in him.

The righteous shall inherit the land, and dwell therein for ever [Ps. 37:29].

This verse again tells us that God is going to make good His promise to Abraham and to the children of Israel. He promised them earthly blessings. He did not promise that to you and me. We are blessed with all spiritual blessings. You will be confused if you believe God has promised you earthly blessings. It is true that many Christians are blessed with material things, but that is surplus. It is an added blessing; and, if God has blessed you that way, you have a tremendous responsibility. I feel sorry for some of the rich saints who are not using their money the way God wants them to use it.

Mark the perfect man, and behold the upright: for the end of that man is peace.

But the transgressors shall be destroyed together: the end of the wicked shall be cut off [Ps. 37:37–38].

The "perfect man" is one who is perfect toward God in that he trusts God and rests upon His salvation. The end of the upright man is peace. God will see to that.

"The end of the wicked shall be cut off." The transgressors will be destroyed and the wicked shall be cut off. Mark that down. It is as sure as the law of gravitation.

PSALM 38

THEME: *A penitential psalm involving physical disease*

This is entitled "A Psalm of David, to bring to remembrance" and is classed as a penitential psalm. It is David's confession and concerns physical sickness. David is very ill. His body is wasting away. We have no record of his having this illness, but we have seen before that he thanked God for his healing.

O LORD, rebuke me not in thy wrath: neither chasten me in thy hot displeasure [Ps. 38:1].

David, in deep distress, prays that God will not judge him in anger.

For thine arrows stick fast in me, and thy hand presseth me sore [Ps. 38:2].

This is real conviction.

There is no soundness in my flesh because of thine anger; neither is there any rest in my bones because of my sin [Ps. 38:3].

David's physical sickness is the result of sin.

For mine iniquities are gone over mine head: as an heavy burden they are too heavy for me [Ps. 38:4].

You and I cannot carry our burdens, friend, and we especially cannot carry the burden of sin. We must give that burden to God.

My wounds stink and are corrupt because of my foolishness.

I am troubled; I am bowed down greatly; I go mourning all the day long.

For my loins are filled with a loathsome disease: and there is no soundness in my flesh.

I am feeble and sore broken: I have roared by reason of the disquietness of my heart [Ps. 38:5–8].

Disease, the result of his foolishness, is followed by mental anguish. In the first church in which I served, there was a doctor in the congregation. He called me into his office one day and showed me this psalm. He said, "There are many people who believe that David had a venereal disease. I was told that in medical school, but I do not agree with it." He asked me what I thought. Well, I agreed with him that I would not accept that diagnosis.

Regarding the prophetic aspect of this psalm, some have interpreted it as being a description of the condition of Christ on the cross, that when Christ bore our sins, He also bore our diseases and actually took in His own body all the diseases of mankind.

This could not be true, because disease is the result of sin, and there was no sin in Him. Concerning His birth, Luke 1:35 says, "And the angel answered and said unto her, The Holy Ghost shall come upon thee, and the power of the Highest shall overshadow thee: therefore also that *holy* thing which shall be born of thee shall be called the Son of God." He was holy—He was not born with a sin nature. Of Christ's earthly life the Father said, ". . . Thou art my beloved Son, in whom I am well pleased" (Mark 1:11). Toward the end of His life on earth the Lord Jesus said, "Which of you convinceth me of sin? . . ." (John 8:46). Jesus was holy, harmless, and separate from sin. He could not be the spotless Lamb offered for our sin if He were diseased—disease is the result of sin.

Christ was holy when He went to the cross. For the first three hours that Christ was on the cross, man did his worst; but in those last three hours God did His best, for Christ took upon Himself the sin of the world. It is at this point that we need to be careful. It was the *sin* of the world that Christ took. When we are told that He bore our diseases, it is the disease of sin. Simon Peter confirms this in 1 Peter 2:24: "Who his own self bare our sins in his own body on the tree, that we, being dead to sins, should live unto righteousness: by whose stripes ye were healed"—healed of what? Our diseases? No! We are healed of *sin*. He bore our sins on the cross and took care of the sin problem for us. He did not have a diseased body. Disease is the result of sin, and there was no sin in the Lord Jesus Christ. It is an awful, blasphemous thing to say that Jesus Christ was diseased when He hung on the cross.

Those of us who have endured illness and disease in our bodies can identify with David in this psalm. And it is the proper thing to do to first take your case to the Great Physician—and then make an appointment with the best doctor you can find. Let's be practical about this. All the skill and wisdom a doctor has comes from God, whether or not he acknowledges it.

PSALM 39

***THEME:** A psalm for funerals*

This remarkable psalm reveals to us the frailty, weakness, and the littleness of humanity. It sets before us the vanity of human existence. This psalm has been used at funerals a great deal, and it can be used so properly. There are those who have considered it probably "the most beautiful of all elegies in the Psalter." Dean Perowne has said: "The holy singer had long pent up his feelings; and though busy thoughts were stirring within him, he would not give them utterance. He could not bare his bosom to the rude gaze of an unsympathizing world. And he feared lest, while telling his perplexities, some word might drop from his lips which would give the wicked an occasion to speak evil against God. And when at last, unable to repress his strong emotion, he speaks to God and not to man, it is as one who feels how hopeless the problem of life is, except as seen in the light of God" (*The Book of Psalms*, p. 295). He speaks of this frailty and sinfulness, this weakness and littleness of mankind, with deep conviction. Candidly, human life is, without a doubt, the most colossal failure in God's universe. Apart from a relationship with God, my friend, it is rather meaningless. All is vanity—that is what you have to say under the sun. Without the Son of God it means nothing at all.

This is a psalm of David, and it is dedicated "To the chief Musician, even to Jeduthun." Who is Jeduthun? Perhaps he wrote the music for this psalm. He was one of three musical or choir directors connected with Israel's worship. Asaph and Heman were the other two men. David, the sweet singer of Israel, had associated with himself these three men in the ministry of music.

Now notice the beautiful words of this psalm.

I said, I will take heed to my ways, that I sin not with my tongue: I will keep my mouth with a bridle, while the wicked is before me [Ps. 39:1].

This psalm concerns a subject that David would rather not talk about with the man of the world. "He would not quite understand it, so I put a zipper on my mouth."

I was dumb with silence, I held my peace, even from good; and my sorrow was stirred [Ps. 39:2].

But David wanted to say something, and finally he opens his heart before God.

My heart was hot within me, while I was musing the fire burned: then spake I with my tongue [Ps. 39:3].

He speaks now to the Lord:

LORD, make me to know mine end, and the measure of my days, what it is; that I may know how frail I am [Ps. 39:4].

David recognizes the frailty of man and asks, "What is the purpose of life? What is it that gives meaning to existence?" This is a current question being asked by young people today and they are asking it with a bang. After World War II my generation wanted to settle down in peace. We wanted a nice little bungalow, one or two cars in the garage, and a chicken in the pot. We wanted to live in an affluent society and shut our eyes to everything else in order to escape responsibility. Things did not turn out the way we wanted them to. We got tied up in traffic snarls. Our lives became filled with tension. The young generation came along (even those who came from Christian homes), looked around and asked "Is this what life is all about? What is the meaning of life?" This was David's question.

Christians can live in such a way today that there is no meaning to life. If you are a Christian parent, are you living a life that is turning your children *on* to Jesus Christ, or are you turning them *off* to everything that is Christian? There are many vagrants drifting over the face of the earth who have left home and gotten into a lot of trouble because of the poor examples set before them. Many of them have come from "good homes"—from all outward appearances they were good homes—but these young folk looked at the lives of their parents and said, "They have no meaning."

Oh, this psalm is relevant to the contemporary generation. David prayed, "LORD, make me to know mine end, and the measure of my days, what it is"—give me purpose and meaning.

Behold, thou hast made my days as an handbreadth; and mine age is as nothing before thee: verily every man at his best state is altogether vanity. Selah [Ps. 39:5].

This verse ends with the word *Selah*—stop, look, and listen; think this over, friend. The brevity of human life on this earth ought to tell us something. If this life is all there is to human existence, it is a colossal failure. I would rather be a dinosaur or a redwood tree and hang around for awhile, because compared to them man's life is just a handbreadth.

Surely every man walketh in a vain shew: surely they are disquieted in vain: he heapeth up riches, and knoweth not who shall gather them [Ps. 39:6].

William Thackeray, an English novelist and a Christian, wrote a novel called *Vanity Fair*. I enjoyed that book. It is a brilliant satire on a little group of people, a clique that had its status symbols, played its little parts, and committed its little sins that are an awful stench in heaven. They lived and died with their littleness and their bickerings. That's life! "Surely every man walketh in a vain shew . . . he heapeth up riches, and knoweth not who shall gather them." Nothing has changed. Think of the Christians who gather fortunes down here and leave it for godless offspring, or they leave it to unworthy so-called Christian work. We see a great deal of this. The psalmist saw it and asked, "What is the purpose of it all?"

And now, Lord, what wait I for? my hope is in thee [Ps. 39:7].

David turned to God—"my hope is in thee." Friend, if you don't turn to God, you will not find the meaning of life.

Deliver me from all my transgressions: make me not the reproach of the foolish [Ps. 39:8].

David wanted to be a good example.

I was dumb, I opened not my mouth; because thou didst it [Ps. 39:9].

He did not want to express his thoughts to the crowd, because they are rather pessimistic.

Remove thy stroke away from me: I am consumed by the blow of thine hand [Ps. 39:10].

He was feeling the discipline of God in his life—and it was for a purpose. Oh, my friend, how we need to get a proper perspective of life! The grave is not its goal. Longfellow wrote, "Dust thou art, to dust returnest, was not spoken of the soul." Man is going on a long journey. Eternity is ahead. What glorious anticipation there should be!

Hear my prayer, O LORD, and give ear unto my cry; hold not thy peace at my tears: for I am a stranger with thee, and a sojourner, as all my fathers were [Ps. 39:12].

We are just pilgrims and strangers down here, but we don't think of it that way. We want to fix up our little corner of the earth and think it is going to be permanent. We want to wrap ourselves in a blanket of false security. May I say, at best we are pilgrims and strangers on earth, and that is the way we ought to live our lives. We are on a journey, and we seek a city ". . . whose builder and maker is God" (Heb. 11:10). Oh, to have a hope today! The psalmist says of God, "My hope is in thee."

O spare me, that I may recover strength, before I go hence, and be no more [Ps. 39:13].

That is, enable me to so live that my life will cause men and women to think on eternity. Enable me to live a life that will not turn folk away from God but draw them to Him. We hear a lot today about personal witnessing, but what about the testimony of our lives? Are people turning to God because of the way we are living, or are they turning away from God? I am confident that our lives are doing one or the other.

PSALM 40

***THEME:** A messianic psalm predicting the crucifixion of Christ*

Two messianic psalms, 40 and 41, conclude the Genesis section of the Psalms. They are called messianic psalms because they are so quoted in the New Testament, which makes them especially important.

I waited patiently for the LORD; and he inclined unto me, and heard my cry [Ps. 40:1].

This is a proper psalm to follow Psalm 39. All of these psalms go together; that is, you will note a continuity. There are those who feel that this psalm expresses the experience of David in his flight from Absalom, and that is accurate to a point. But this psalm is quoted in the Epistle to the Hebrews in a most remarkable way. In this psalm the One who celebrates in praise and thanksgiving the Resurrection, the triumph and Ascension is the Lord Jesus Himself. This is truly a messianic psalm. It reveals that the death of Christ was not a defeat at all. It was a great victory. When He says, "I waited patiently for the LORD; and he inclined unto me, and heard my cry," He is referring to His cry from the cross.

He brought me up also out of an horrible pit, out of the miry clay, and set my feet upon a rock, and established my goings [Ps. 40:2].

Christ's agony and death is likened to a horrible pit, a pit of destruction. We cannot conceive how terrible the death of Christ on the cross really was.

And he hath put a new song in my mouth, even praise unto our God: many shall see it, and fear, and shall trust in the LORD [Ps. 40:3].

This verse mentions a new song—we have read about a new song before—it is the song of redemption.

"Many shall see it, and fear, and shall trust in the LORD." What are they going to see? They will see the death and resurrection of the Lord Jesus Christ.

Blessed is that man that maketh the LORD his trust, and respecteth not the proud, nor such as turn aside to lies [Ps. 40:4].

Our Lord Jesus Christ is the example of a man who puts his trust in God, who does not respect the proud, and who does not turn aside to lies.

Many, O LORD my God, are thy wonderful works which thou hast done, and thy thoughts which are to us-ward: they cannot be reckoned up in order unto thee: if I would declare and speak of them, they are more than can be numbered [Ps. 40:5].

God has revealed what He thinks of us by sending His Son to die on the cross. At the time I am writing this, I often hear speculations as to the possibility of life on planets other than our own. I am certainly no expert in this field, but I think it may be possible that other planets are inhabited. But I can guarantee this: there will not be a *cross* on any of the planets out there in space. It was only here that the Son of God died on a cross. How wonderful! "Many, O LORD my God, are thy wonderful works which thou hast done, and thy thoughts which are toward *us*." My, how the cross reveals God's love for us!

Now the following is quoted in the Epistle to the Hebrews:

Sacrifice and offering thou didst not desire; mine ears hast thou opened: burnt offering and sin offering hast thou not required.

Then said I, Lo, I come: in the volume of the book it is written of me,

I delight to do thy will, O my God: yea, thy law is within my heart.

I have preached righteousness in the great congregation: lo, I have not refrained my lips, O LORD, thou knowest [Ps. 40:6–9].

This is a marvelous psalm that follows the preceding one which reveals the frailty of man.

"Sacrifice and offering thou didst not desire; mine ears hast thou opened." Now notice how this is quoted in Hebrews 10:5, "Wherefore when he cometh into the world, he saith, Sacrifice and offering thou wouldest not, but a body hast thou prepared me." Now, wait a minute. Is this misquoted? Critics of the Bible say, "Oh, here is an error, a contradiction in the Bible. In Psalm 40:6 it says, '. . . mine ears hast thou opened . . .'; and in Hebrews it says, '. . . a body hast thou prepared me.'"

The Holy Spirit is the author of the Bible. He wrote the Old Testament and the New Testament. He wrote both Psalms and Hebrews, and He has a perfect right to change His own writing. When He does, there is always a good reason.

Now let's consider the background. In Exodus 21 there is a law concerning servants and masters. If a man became a slave to another man, at the end of a certain period of time he could go free. Suppose during that period he met another slave, a woman, they fell in love and married and had children. When it was time for the man to go free, he could leave, but his wife and children could not go with him because she was a slave. What could this man do? He could decide that because he loved his master and his wife he would not leave. "Then his master shall bring him unto the judges; he shall also bring him to the door, or unto the door post; and his master shall bore his ear through with an awl; and he shall serve him for ever" (Exod. 21:6).

The psalmist is referring to this custom when he says, "mine ears hast thou opened." When the Lord Jesus came to this earth, did He have His ear thrust through with an awl? No, He was given a body. He took upon Himself our humanity. He identified Himself with us and He became a servant. And He became a sacrifice. "Sacrifice and offering thou didst not desire"—God did not delight in all the animal offerings in the Old Testament, but they pointed to the sacrifice of the Lord Jesus Christ.

Now notice what Isaiah says on this subject. "The Lord GOD hath opened mine ear, and I was not rebellious, neither turned away back" (Isa. 50:5). This verse is prophesying the humiliation of the Servant (Christ) who would come to earth. When the Lord Jesus came down to this earth and went to the cross, His ear wasn't "opened" or "digged"; He was given a body, and that body was *nailed* to a cross. My friend, He has taken a glorified body with nail prints in it back to heaven, and He will bear those nail prints and scars throughout eternity that you and I might be presented without spot or blemish before Him. You see, He did more than have His ear bored through with an awl; He gave His body to be crucified because He loved us and would not return to heaven without us.

My friend, this is a marvelous messianic psalm that reveals the crucifixion of the Lord Jesus Christ because He loved us.

PSALM 41

***THEME:** A messianic psalm predicting the betrayal of Judas*

This messianic psalm was written by David probably at the time he was betrayed by Ahithophel, his trusted counselor. Ahithophel sided with David's son Absalom when he led a rebellion against his father. Finally Ahithophel committed suicide by hanging himself (2 Sam. 17:23). Ahithophel foreshadows the betrayer of Christ, Judas Iscariot, and is so quoted by our Lord Himself.

This psalm opens with a blessing.

> **Blessed is he that considereth the poor: the LORD will deliver him in time of trouble [Ps. 41:1].**

It opens with "blessed" and closes with "blessed." It begins with, "Blessed is he that considereth the poor," and ends with, "Blessed be the LORD God of Israel." The word *blessed* as we have already seen, means "happy," so that the Genesis section of the Psalms (Psalms 1–41) begins with "happy" and closes with "happy."

Now notice the section that makes this a messianic psalm:

> **Yea, mine own familiar friend, in whom I trusted, which did eat of my bread, hath lifted up his heel against me [Ps. 41:9].**

Jesus quoted this verse in reference to Judas, "I speak not of you all: I know whom I have chosen: but that the scripture may be fulfilled, He that eateth bread with me hath lifted up his heel against me" (John 13:18). This verse was fulfilled in Judas, the one who betrayed the Lord Jesus. Peter also referred to it in Acts 1:16, "Men and brethren, this scripture must needs have been fulfilled, which the Holy Ghost by the mouth of David spake before concerning Judas, which was guide to them that took Jesus." We have something more here:

But thou, O LORD, be merciful unto me, and raise me up, that I may requite them [Ps. 41:10].

This verse is a reference to the resurrection of the Lord Jesus Christ. "Raise me up, that I may recompense them." In this Genesis section we have seen the death of Christ and His resurrection as well. But I want to make something startlingly clear: The death of Christ saves no one; it is the death and *resurrection* of Christ that saves. Paul explicitly defines the gospel in 1 Corinthians 15:3–4: "For I delivered unto you first of all that which I also received, how that Christ died for our sins according to the scriptures; And that he was buried, and that he rose again the third day according to the scriptures." Without the resurrection of the Lord there is no gospel.

Almost everyone has an opinion about the Lord Jesus. Jesus asked His disciples, ". . . Whom do men say that I the Son of man am? And they said, Some say that thou art John the Baptist: some, Elias; and others, Jeremias, or one of the prophets. He saith unto them, But whom say ye that I am? And Simon Peter answered and said, Thou art the Christ, the Son of the living God" (Matt. 16:13–16). Who do you say that Christ is? Many modern plays about Jesus leave Him on the cross or in the tomb. Thomas Jefferson left Him in the tomb in his moral teachings about Jesus. He concluded his book with a stone closing the tomb. There is no gospel there. That stone was rolled away and the Lord left the tomb. He was raised from the dead.

Because of the resurrection we can say:

Blessed be the LORD God of Israel from everlasting, and to everlasting. Amen, and Amen [Ps. 41:13].

This verse ends with a double amen. "Amen, and Amen" means that God put the finishing touches on our salvation when Christ rose from the dead, ascended into heaven, and sat down at the right hand of the throne of God. Christ finished the work of salvation for us. You don't have to add anything to it, but don't take away from the gospel by omitting the Resurrection. Without that there is no gospel.

This is the final psalm in the Genesis section. It has been well stated that the Book of Genesis is the entire Bible in miniature; that is, all the great truths of Scripture are germinal in Genesis. This first section of psalms covers the entire Book of Psalms in the same way. While the Book of Genesis concludes with a "coffin in Egypt," this Genesis section of Psalms closes on the high note of resurrection.

EXODUS SECTION

Ruin and Redemption (Israel in view)
Psalms 42–72

Psalms 42–72 comprise the Exodus section. As in the Book of Exodus, we will see God's people in a strange land, a suffering people away from the Land of Promise. The heel of a dictator is on them. You hear them groan and moan, and you hear the whip of the taskmaster falling upon them. They are in great trouble, which increases rather than decreases. Finally Israel's cries and groans are heard, and the Lord arises on behalf of His suffering people. He makes good His covenant to Abraham, Isaac, and Jacob. Then the Lord delivers them out of the land of Egypt. For example, in the first seven psalms (42–48) we find conditions as they were at the beginning of the Book of Exodus. But these psalms do not refer to the past; they look to the future and reveal the experiences of the remnant of Israel in the days that lie ahead. We will see God's chosen people away from Jerusalem; they are separated from the holy place and out of touch with Jehovah, just as they were in Egypt.

In the Genesis and Exodus sections of the Psalms there is an interesting contrast of the names of God. In the Genesis section the name *Jehovah* occurs 272 times, while the name *Elohim* occurs only fifteen times. In the Exodus section the name *Elohim* occurs 164 times, and the name *Jehovah* occurs only thirty times. What is the significance of this? These two personal names of God have different meanings. Elohim speaks of the fullness of God's divine power. The name *Jehovah* is involved in redemption. Jehovah is the One who keeps Israel.

We will find that David did not write as many of the psalms in this section as he did in the last one. David wrote nineteen of the psalms, and seven of them were written by the sons of Korah who were connected with the Levitical family. All of the psalms in this division are a prophetic picture of Israel in the last days.

In Psalms 42–44 we see the children of Israel in Egypt with Pharaoh ruling over them. Psalm 43 mentions the Antichrist, and Israel is mourning because of the oppression of the enemy. We find them crying out to God to deliver them, and deliverance comes to them. Psalm 45 is the great millennial psalm which speaks of the Lord Jesus coming to reign on the earth.

Something important for God's people to see is that the primary and fundamental interpretation of these psalms is applicable to the nation of Israel. They look to the future during the time of trouble called the Great Tribulation. Therefore, we need to be careful when we lift out a verse from one of the psalms to ask the question, "How does it really apply to us?" We can apply many of the psalms to our needs today. God's children, who are in trouble, can find real solace and comfort in them, but we must never forget that their primary application is to Israel. I think it is a terrible thing to exclude Israel from the plan and purpose of God for the future as many people do. It is almost like writing off a certain portion of God's Word, and saying, "Yes, I believe in the inspiration of Scripture that applies to me, but if it supposedly applies to other people that I am not concerned about, it is not the Word of God." There is danger today in that type of thinking.

Let us keep in mind that when the psalmist speaks of Israel he is not referring to the whole nation of Israel, for the entire nation is not in view. We see this distinction also in the word *church.* Is the church made up of all the names of people on membership rolls in every church regardless of the denomination? I don't think so. The church is made up of a body of believers who have trusted the Lord Jesus Christ as Savior. You don't become a member of the true church by joining a visible church and having your name put on a church roll or by going through a ceremony of some kind. Only a personal relationship with Christ can make you a member of the true church. We should always make a distinction between the organized church and what is generally called the *invisible* church. The remnant of the nation of Israel is not the entire nation, just as all members of the organized church do not make up the invisible church, or body of believers. It is the believing remnant of Israel that we will be looking at in this Exodus section of the Book of Psalms.

PSALMS 42–43

***THEME:** Heart cry of the God-fearing remnant*

This psalm presents the future suffering of the godly remnant of Israel during the Great Tribulation period. When Israel was in the land of Egypt (Exod. 12), God first redeemed them by blood. The blood of the Passover lamb was sprinkled on the doorposts of the houses by those who believed God. At night the death angel passed over the homes, and if blood was there no one died. This was redemption by *blood.* The second phase of redemption was at the Red Sea, and there it was redemption by *power*.

The inscription of this psalm is "Maschil, for the sons of Korah." *Maschil* means that it is a psalm of teaching, a psalm of understanding. You may recall that Korah led a rebellion during the period of Israel's wandering in the wilderness. God executed him because of his rebellion against the authority of Moses and Aaron, but his sons were spared. God made it very clear (Num. 26:9–11) that his sons did not die in God's judgment, but they continued their service before God. They are the ones who wrote these first few psalms of the Exodus section, which is quite wonderful.

Prophetically, this gives us a picture of the Great Tribulation period.

As the hart panteth after the water brooks, so panteth my soul after thee, O God.

My soul thirsteth for God, for the living God: when shall I come and appear before God? [Ps. 42:1–2].

Rather than going back to Egypt, I want to apply this to the future because there will be a time when these people, the Israelites, will be out of their land again. There are several excellent Bible expositors who believe that the present regathering of Jews in the land of Israel may eventuate in their dispersion again—that they will be put out of the land—perhaps in our day. The godly remnant is not in the land today. There are two groups in the land of Israel right now: one group we call the orthodox Jews who are waiting for their Messiah, expecting Him to come and wanting to rebuild the temple. The other group is not concerned with religious matters. They contend that a new era has begun. They have Egypt, the Arabs, and the United Nations to deal with.

The godly remnant of Israel, God's people, have a longing for God, as do God's people of all ages. They picture David. I think David could easily have said these words hiding in a cave overlooking a valley. He could have heard hunters and the barking of the dogs and, in a few minutes, a rustle in the bushes. David's men on guard duty became alert. There is a little spring near the opening of the cave, and soon a little deer, foaming at the mouth, his sides lathered, plunges his head into the water and takes a good deep drink. He waits a moment, listening, then he takes another drink.

Therefore the psalmist could say, "As the hart panteth after the water brooks, so panteth my soul after thee, O God." Is that the way you feel about God? There are those who claim that if you become very legalistic and keep the Ten Commandments you are pleasing to God. My friend, man is alienated from God; he needs more than the Ten Commandments. The Ten Commandments show us that we are *sinners*, and we are in rebellion against God. We have no desire or capacity for Him. We need, therefore, to be born again. We need to be brought into the family of God and to the place where we can say, not just as a verse in Scripture but from our hearts, "As the hart panteth after the water brooks, so panteth my soul after thee, O God."

This will be especially meaningful to the remnant of Israel, but it is meaningful right now to many of God's children.

My tears have been my meat day and night, while they continually say unto me, Where is thy God? [Ps. 42:3].

There was much weeping in the brickyards of Egypt and will be in the future. This will be the taunt during the Great Tribulation period: "Where is your God? When is Messiah coming?"

Why art thou cast down, O my soul? and why art thou disquieted in me? hope thou in God: for I shall yet praise him for the help of his countenance [Ps. 42:5].

He rebukes himself for his despondency and encourages himself to trust in God.

O my God, my soul is cast down within me: therefore will I remember thee from the land of Jordan, and of the Hermonites, from the hill Mizar.

Deep calleth unto deep at the noise of thy waterspouts: all thy waves and thy billows are gone over me [Ps. 42:6–7].

This is the language Jonah used in his prayer. "For thou hadst cast me into the deep, in the midst of the seas; and the floods compassed me about: all thy billows and thy waves passed over me" (Jonah 2:3). Jonah went down into the jaws of death. During the Great Tribulation Israel will think that destruction is upon them, but God will deliver them.

Yet the LORD will command his lovingkindness in the daytime, and in the night his song shall be with me, and my prayer unto the God of my life.

I will say unto God my rock, Why hast thou forgotten me? why go I mourning because of the oppression of the enemy? [Ps. 42:8–9].

Do you feel like that sometimes? I am sure that many of us do.

Why art thou cast down, O my soul? and why art thou disquieted within me? hope thou in God: for I shall yet praise him, who is the health of my countenance, and my God [Ps. 42:11].

In his desperate hour he turns to God. In their desperate hours the remnant will turn to God. There will be no help from the east, the west, the north, or the south. My help comes from the Lord, the maker of heaven and earth.

Psalm 43 is closely connected with Psalm 42. The godly remnant calls on God to act in their behalf.

Judge me, O God, and plead my cause against an ungodly nation: O deliver me from the deceitful and unjust man [Ps. 43:1].

This is the remnant of Israel speaking. The Antichrist is a liar. He will make a covenant with these people and then will break it in the midst of the "week." When this happens, their cry will be, "Deliver me from the deceitful and unjust man." I don't know if you have ever prayed this prayer or not, but I have said, "O God, don't let a dictator arise in the United States." There is grave danger of that. We need to ask God to deliver us from deceitful and unjust men. I certainly don't want him ruling over me, and we have had quite a few like that in our history. I am afraid the condition of our nation is due to the leadership and internal problems.

O send out thy light and thy truth: let them lead me; let them bring me unto thy holy hill, and to thy tabernacles [Ps. 43:3].

"Send out thy light and thy truth." What is the psalmist praying for? Jesus said, ". . . I am the light of the world: he that followeth me shall not walk in darkness, but shall have the light of life" (John 8:12). He also said, ". . . I am the way, the truth, and the life: no man cometh unto the Father, but by me" (John 14:6). These statements of the Lord Jesus Christ were not lost on His hearers, because if they knew He was the light and the truth, they would also know He was the Messiah who had come to deliver them. "Let them bring me unto thy holy hill, and to thy tabernacles." He wants to go back to Jerusalem. He wants to worship in the temple and to be brought back to God.

Why art thou cast down, O my soul? and why art thou disquieted within me? hope in God: for I shall yet praise him, who is the health of my countenance, and my God [Ps. 43:5].

Their prayers will be answered, and their long expected Messiah will return. At that time Ezekiel's prophecy will be fulfilled: "A new heart also will I give you, and a new spirit will I put within you: and I will take away the stony heart out of your flesh, and I will give you an heart of flesh. And I will put my spirit within you, and cause you to walk in my statutes, and ye shall keep my judgments, and do them. And ye shall dwell in the land that I gave to your fathers; and ye shall be my people, and I will be your God" (Ezek. 36: 26–28).

PSALM 44

***THEME:** Israel's cry during the Great Tribulation*

We come now to another maschil psalm, a psalm of instruction, and it is from the sons of Korah.

Although it is impossible to determine the historical condition in Israel that called forth this prayer, we do know the prophetic interpretation. This will be the final experience of the faithful remnant of Israel before their Messiah returns to deliver them.

We have heard with our ears, O God, our fathers have told us, what work thou didst in their days, in the times of old [Ps. 44:1].

Gideon said the same thing. "And Gideon said unto him, Oh my Lord, if the Lord be with us, why then is all this befallen us? and where be all his miracles which our fathers told us of, saying, Did not the Lord bring us up from Egypt? but now the Lord hath forsaken us, and delivered us into the hands of the Midianites" (Judg. 6:13). In that day of trouble, just when God is on the verge of delivering them again, Israel will refer to God's help in the past. God has intruded in history before, and He will do it again.

How thou didst drive out the heathen with thy hand, and plantedst them; how thou didst afflict the people, and cast them out [Ps. 44:2].

This refers to the time of Moses and Joshua. God evicted the inhabitants of Canaan because of their gross sin and planted His chosen people there.

For they got not the land in possession by their own sword, neither did their own arm save them: but thy right hand, and thine arm, and the light of thy countenance, because thou hadst a favour unto them [Ps. 44:3].

It was God who gave the land to the children of Israel. They did not capture it because of their own strength or cleverness.

For our personal application, "Thy right hand" is the mighty bared arm of God in salvation, revealed nineteen hundred years ago at the cross.

Then listen to this heart cry that comes from him:

Thou art my King, O God: command deliverances for Jacob [Ps. 44:4].

I hope you understand that "Jacob" is the man Jacob, and Jacob became the nation of Israel. When he cries, "Thou art my King, O God," he is talking about Israel's King. Our Lord Jesus is Israel's King, and He will return to deliver His suffering people. Of course there is application for us, but let's keep the Psalms in correct perspective so that they will be more meaningful to us.

Through thee will we push down our enemies: through thy name will we tread them under that rise up against us.

For I will not trust in my bow, neither shall my sword save me [Ps. 44:5–6].

In that day of tribulation the godly remnant is going to ask for revenge. They will be under Law, and they will have a right to do that.

Today we are to *pray* for those who deceitfully use us; we are told even to *love* our enemies. That is a very difficult thing to do, but we can turn our enemies over to the Lord. We are not to avenge ourselves because the Lord says, ". . . Vengeance is mine; I will repay . . ." (Rom. 12:19). There are many people we should turn over to the Lord, not only for salvation, but for reasons of vengeance. I am not talking about people who have caused us some personal grievance, but those who are trying to hinder the giving out of the Word of God. It is a terrible thing to try to blacken the name of a man or woman who stands for the things of God. You should be careful before you criticize your pastor. Make sure your facts are true. To some people a pastor represents God's cause on earth. They will judge God largely by what he says. If you discredit him, you discredit God in their eyes. I think this is why many young people have turned away from the Bible and the church. Many of them have grown up in Christian homes, and their parents have served "roast preacher" each Sunday. It is wrong to discredit a man who is giving out the Word of God. If things seem to be wrong, we should ask God to intervene rather than to try to take matters into our own hands.

Israel is in deep trouble. The enemy is raging against them; that "little horn" that Daniel mentioned ". . . shall wear out the saints of the Most High . . ." (Dan. 7:25). These are Jewish saints, and Antichrist makes war against them to overcome them. They are warned not to fight back. They refuse the mark of the beast, and they are killed in large numbers. In their distress they cry out to God. I think this will be the darkest moment in the history of the world.

Yea, for thy sake are we killed all the day long; we are counted as sheep for the slaughter [Ps. 44:22].

This verse is not a picture of the church right now, would you say? There are many believers suffering for Christ's sake; but by and large, the church is not under persecution. However, the remnant of Israel will be persecuted; and it is the remnant that is in view here. I want to keep that clear.

Awake, why sleepest thou, O Lord? arise, cast us not off for ever [Ps. 44:23].

Here is a cry for God to wake up. Well, God is not asleep. It is in their desperation that the remnant cries out. During the time of the Maccabees, between the Old and New Testaments, the enemies of Israel came to the foreground. As far as the past is concerned, it was the time that Israel suffered more than at any other time in their history; but it will be nothing compared to the suffering they will endure during the Great Tribulation period. During the Maccabean period there was a group of priests called the "wakers." They were the ones who cried out to God saying, "Awake, why sleepest thou, O Lord?" During this time people felt like God was asleep. But John Hyrcanus, one of the great Maccabees, a high priest, put an end to this practice. He asked the people, "Does the Deity sleep? Hath not the Scripture said, 'Behold, the keeper of Israel slumbereth and sleepeth not?' " You don't have to ask God to wake up even though there are times when you feel like it. In that future day the remnant will feel that He is asleep and say, "Awake, why sleepest thou, O Lord?" When that day comes, God will not be asleep. He will be ready to move. He will not cast off His people forever.

Wherefore hidest thou thy face, and forgettest our affliction and our oppression?

For our soul is bowed down to the dust: our belly cleaveth unto the earth.

Arise for our help, and redeem us for thy mercies' sake [Ps. 44:24–26].

From the darkest moment in the history of this world comes a cry from the remnant for God to redeem them for His mercies' sake. This is a plea for help and justice.

PSALM 45

***THEME:** The coming of Christ to establish His kingdom on this earth*

This is a messianic psalm and is so quoted in the Epistle to the Hebrews. This is another maschil psalm, that is, for instruction, written by the sons of Korah, and is inscribed "To the chief Musician upon Shoshannim," which means "lilies." It is a picture of Christ as the Messiah—He is the Lily of the Valley as well as the Rose of Sharon. In translating this, the Targumim adds, "Thy beauty, O King Messiah, is greater than that of the children of men."

This very wonderful psalm speaks of the second coming of Christ. This changes the tenor of the Psalms from the cry of a people in the anguish of tribulation to the glorious triumph of their coming King, as it is described in Revelation, chapter 19. Our Lord Jesus Christ spoke of it also (Matt. 24:29–30), and it is the hope of the world.

My heart is inditing a good matter: I speak of the things which I have made touching the king: my tongue is the pen of a ready writer [Ps. 45:1].

"My heart is inditing" means bursting forth or overflowing. There is something he *must* say and wishes he could *tell* it, because his tongue moves faster than his pen. That is true of many of us. Have you ever been excited about something and have tried to put it in a letter to a friend, and when you read it over you see how inadequate it is and wish you could *tell* it instead of write it? I had that experience a few minutes ago—I couldn't say what I wanted to say to a friend in a letter; so I called him by phone. Well, the psalmist couldn't call us by telephone, so we have Psalm 45 in printed form.

MESSIAH, HIS PERSON AND POWER

Thou art fairer than the children of men: grace is poured into thy lips: therefore God hath blessed thee for ever [Ps. 45:2].

This is a lovely psalm which is occupied with the person of Christ. Paul mentioned that: "But we all, with open face beholding as in a glass the glory of the Lord, are changed into the same image from glory to glory, even as by the Spirit of the Lord" (2 Cor. 3:18). My friend, we need to behold Him more.

In this psalm we are seeing Him, not as a Savior, but as a King.

Gird thy sword upon thy thigh, O most mighty, with thy glory and thy majesty [Ps. 45:3].

This is a picture of Christ coming forward, not as Savior, but as the King at His second coming. Israel expected Messiah to come to earth with a sword. The first time He came to earth He came without a sword. You will recall that when Jesus was arrested, one of His disciples drew his sword and cut off the ear of the servant of the high priest. And Jesus said, ". . . Put up again thy sword into his place: for all they that take the sword shall perish with the sword" (Matt. 26:52). In our day they are looking for the Messiah who will bring peace, without a sword, but Psalm 2:9 says of the Lord, "Thou shalt break them with a rod of iron; thou shalt dash them in pieces like a potter's vessel." Psalm 2 speaks of Christ's coming to earth the second time. In fact, it is quoted several times in the Book of Revelation in respect to His second coming.

When He returns, He is going to find the world in rebellion. The Antichrist will be in power. He will be persecuting God's people, both the remnant of Israel and that great company of Gentiles who turned to God.

"Grace is poured into his lips"—that is emphasized, but there will also be condemnation and judgment. I think we ought to be realistic, not idealistic. He will have to come in power and wrath against a world that is in rebellion against Him.

And in thy majesty ride prosperously because of truth and meekness and righteousness; and thy right hand shall teach thee terrible things [Ps. 45:4].

"Terrible things" means *awe-inspiring* things.

Notice, the Lord is riding to victory, and here are the three planks of His platform: truth, meekness, and righteousness. Do you know of any candidate today who uses these three planks in his platform? The candidates don't sound meek to me, and I wonder about the truth of their statements, and righteousness—well, the whole motive is to get elected, not to do right. How this poor nation needs a candidate who will speak truth, who exhibits a little meekness, and who goes all-out for righteousness. These are eternal principles of our Lord's kingdom. No president, leader, dictator, or king has ever come to power on this platform in the history of this world. This King is different. The character of Christ is truth; His words are truth—yet men call Him a liar. But all men are liars, not Christ. You won't hear the truth today in the halls of Congress, or in the marts of trade, or on Wall Street, or in our industrial complexes, or on our college campuses, or read it in the newspaper, or hear it on TV or radio—because all news is slanted. Unfortunately you can't even hear the truth in many of our churches. But our Lord is coming to power on the platform of truth and humility. Someone has said, "If you wish to astonish the whole world, tell the truth." That is the way our Lord is coming to power—it will be startling.

Thine arrows are sharp in the heart of the king's enemies; whereby the people fall under thee [Ps. 45:5].

This is a portrait of the King coming to earth.

MESSIAH, HIS GOVERNMENT AND GLORY

This is coronation day, and it is the key of this psalm.

Thy throne, O God, is for ever and ever: the sceptre of thy kingdom is a right sceptre [Ps. 45:6].

He is going to rule in righteousness. How the world needs a righteous ruler! Regarding His return to the earth, the Lord Jesus Himself said, "When the Son of man shall come in his glory, and all the holy angels with him, then shall he sit upon the throne of his glory" (Matt. 25:31). Not until then will we have peace on this earth. That is the need of the world. When Betsy Ross made the first American flag, George Washington expressed the wish that it would wave for a thousand years. We have recently celebrated our two hundredth anniversary, and already we are growing old as a nation. But the government of God is eternal.

Thou lovest righteousness, and hatest wickedness: therefore God, thy God, hath anointed thee with the oil of gladness above thy fellows [Ps. 45:7].

The Anointed One is Messiah, of which *Christ* is the Greek form. It is not a name, but it is His official title. The first time He came, He came as Prophet—the messenger and message of God—which refers to the past. In our day He is our Great High Priest at the right hand of God; that is His present ministry. But His second coming will be as King, the Messiah. This is for the future.

"God hath anointed thee with the oil of gladness." It is unfortunate that we tend to think of Him as a Man of Sorrows. I believe that He was the most joyous person on this earth when He was here.

That this is a messianic psalm referring to our Lord Jesus Christ is fully attested by the quotation of these two verses in the Epistle to the Hebrews: "But unto the Son he saith, Thy throne, O God, is for ever and ever: a sceptre of righteousness is the sceptre of thy kingdom. Thou hast loved righteousness, and hated iniquity; therefore God, even thy God, hath anointed thee with the oil of gladness above thy fellows" (Heb. 1:8–9). The critic who attempts to apply this psalm to Solomon or some unknown king fails to note that He is addressed as God. It is not conceivable that Solomon or any other king would be addressed as God. The entire first chapter of Hebrews presents our Lord Jesus in His exaltation, being the express image of God, far superior to angels, and seated at God's right hand.

All thy garments smell of myrrh, and aloes, and cassia, out of the ivory palaces, whereby they have made thee glad [Ps. 45:8].

He came to this earth that our joy might be full. And it was for "the joy that was set before him" that He endured the cross. Oh, how we as believers need to rejoice! The tribe of Judah, which means "praise," led the children of Israel in the wilderness march; yet they complained, they whined, they sang the desert blues when they should have been praising God. This is the same thing the church is doing in our day. My friend, believers should be praising God—not complaining! At Christmastime we sing the song, "Joy to the world! the Lord is come; Let earth receive her King." That is not a Christmas hymn at all; it refers to Christ's second coming and should not be relegated to a seasonal section of our hymbook.

Moving down in this wonderful psalm, we have a scene at court:

Kings' daughters were among thy honourable women: upon thy right hand did stand the queen in gold of Ophir [Ps. 45:9].

The church is not mentioned by name in the Old Testament, but I believe you see it in type or in figures of speech. I think most of the brides in the Old Testament are pictures of Christ and His bride, the church. Examples of this are Eve, Rebekah, and Ruth. Who is the queen in this verse? I believe she is a picture of the church, although she is not specifically identified, and Christ will lift her to the throne.

Hearken, O daughter, and consider, and incline thine ear; forget also thine own people, and thy father's house [Ps. 45:10].

We are to leave the world. We are not to love the world. We have been saved out of it. We are to cling to the Lord.

So shall the king greatly desire thy beauty: for he is thy Lord; and worship thou him [Ps. 45:11].

The church is to be made beautiful. All sin will be removed. What a prospect this is!

I will make thy name to be remembered in all generations: therefore shall the people praise thee for ever and ever [Ps. 45:17].

This verse speaks of the millennial kingdom. But the kingdom goes on into eternity after the Lord has made a few adjustments, which includes Satan being loosed for a time and then his being cast into the lake of fire and brimstone. This is a glorious psalm, and when it is put in proper perspective, it has great meaning for us today.

PSALM 46

***THEME:** God is our refuge, a song of the Millennium*

The next three psalms form a little cluster of prophetic pictures of the kingdom that is coming on this earth. Psalm 45 presented the coming of the King to establish His kingdom here upon this earth, the millennial kingdom. The following three psalms set before us this kingdom.

This psalm is "To the chief Musician for the sons of Korah, A Song upon Alamoth." The word *almah* is used in Isaiah 7:14 which says, "Therefore the Lord himself shall give you a sign; Behold, a virgin shall conceive, and bear a son, and shall call his name Immanuel." Evidently the word *alamoth* means "with virgins" and in this instance speaks of maidens' voices. This psalm is one of deliverance and will refer us to another great song of deliverance and victory that was sung when the children of Israel crossed the Red Sea. We are told that they sang the song of Moses, but who led the singing? I don't think Moses was a better song leader than I am, and I am no good at all; so Miriam, the prophetess, the sister of Moses and Aaron, took a timbrel in her hand and led the singing. The women went out after her with timbrels and with dances. As Moses and the children of Israel sang, ". . . Miriam answered them, Sing ye to the LORD, for he hath triumphed gloriously; the horse and his rider hath he thrown into the sea" (Exod. 15:21). So the song leader and the soloist on that occasion was Miriam, the sister of Moses. It was the celebration of a great victory.

Now when the future remnant of Israel is delivered from their enemies by the coming of Christ, they will celebrate a great victory. It is important to see this psalm in its proper setting. It belongs after Psalm 45 and with Psalms 47 and 48. To consider these psalms apart from each other is like the little boy who was asked to give a definition of a lie. In his explanation the little fellow put together two Scripture verses that were totally unrelated. He said, "A lie is an abomination unto the Lord, but a very present help in time of trouble." He misinterpreted the Scripture. We smile at the little boy, but we do the same thing by taking this psalm out of context.

Psalm 46 is a wonderful soprano solo. It is not the blues but a hallelujah chorus in which we see the sufficiency of God, the security of God, and the supremacy of God.

THE SUFFICIENCY OF GOD

God is our refuge and strength, a very present help in trouble.

Therefore will not we fear, though the earth be removed, and though the mountains be carried into the midst of the sea;

Though the waters thereof roar and be troubled, though the mountains shake with the swelling thereof. Selah [Ps. 46:1–3].

This is a very wonderful promise. Someone may challenge it and ask, "But how do you know it is true?" Well, it is true because the Bible says so. But it is more than theory with me. I have tried it and found it to be true. We are told, "O taste and see that the LORD is good: blessed is the man that trusteth in him" (Ps. 34:8). Jesus said, "If any man will do his will, he shall know of the doctrine, whether it be of God, or whether I speak of myself" (John 7:17). In times of trouble you can count on God. Christians fail to trust God in times of trouble because they know nothing about His sufficiency. They have not learned that He is sufficient. We need a God who does not fail us. God is sufficient in any circumstance.

"Though the earth be removed"—the removal of the earth would be the most extreme circumstance I can think of. Has the earth ever been taken out from under you? Have you ever been suspended in space? Most people think they are the only ones who have ever had trouble. Everyone has trouble, but God's people find God sufficient in time of trouble. Psalm 46 was Martin Luther's favorite psalm. When he wrote that great Reformation hymn, "A Mighty Fortress Is Our God," he probably had this in mind. God is our refuge, and our strength, and a very present help when we are in trouble. Men down through the ages have found this to be true.

THE SECURITY OF GOD

There is a river, the streams whereof shall make glad the city of God, the holy place of the tabernacles of the most High [Ps. 46:4].

Some expositors consider this river symbolic. I believe the river is a reality that speaks of the supply and the refreshment that God gives even today, and that river is the Word of God. In Psalm 1 we were told that the blessed man was planted by the rivers of water, which is the Word of God. Also the Scriptures mention a river that flows out from the house of God (Ezek. 47). And in the Book of the Revelation John saw ". . . a pure river of water of life, clear as crystal, proceeding out of the throne of God . . ." (Rev. 22:1).

God is in the midst of her; she shall not be moved: God shall help her, and that right early.

The heathen raged, the kingdoms were moved: he uttered his voice, the earth melted.

The LORD of hosts is with us; the God of Jacob is our refuge. Selah [Ps. 46:5–7].

"The heathen raged, the kingdoms were moved" is looking back on the convulsions of the Great Tribulation period. At the darkest hour, when the enemy came in like a flood, "he uttered his voice, the earth melted." Now the faithful remnant who were delivered sing His praises, "The LORD of hosts is with us; the God of Jacob is our refuge."

THE SUPREMACY OF GOD

Come, behold the works of the LORD, what desolations he hath made in the earth.

He maketh wars to cease unto the end of the earth; he breaketh the bow, and

cutteth the spear in sunder; he burneth the chariot in the fire [Ps. 46:8–9].

The Messiah has come to the earth in judgment. He is the One who makes wars to cease, breaks the bow, cuts the spear, and burns the chariot in the fire. This picture sets before us the last days on earth, when the One who is ". . . the stone cut out of the mountain without hands . . ." (whom Nebuchadnezzar saw in his vision in Dan. 2:45) will deal an annihilating blow upon this earth. We are told that after the Battle of Armageddon is over, the wreckage of warfare and the dead will be strewn everywhere. The works of God ought to tell man that there is a God. The prediction of peace on earth is here a blessed reality. The King has come and has put down all unrighteousness on the earth.

Be still, and know that I am God: I will be exalted among the heathen, I will be exalted in the earth.

The LORD of hosts is with us; the God of Jacob is our refuge. Selah [Ps. 46: 10–11].

"I will be exalted among the heathen [nations], I will be exalted in the earth"—this is God's purpose for the earth.

"Be still, and know that I am God." With the knowledge of this blessed truth we can be calm in time of trouble. There are storms blowing outside today. We are living in a mean old world, a wicked world. Tremendous changes are taking place. There are even convulsions in nature today. He tells us to be calm in the time of storm. Christ, you remember, was in a storm with His disciples, and He went to sleep. When they roused Him from His sleep, He had more trouble calming the disciples than He had calming the storm. Many of us are like those men. We don't know what it is to wait patiently before Him.

This is a psalm that will be a great blessing in the future, but it also is a comfort and a blessing for all of God's people today.

PSALM 47

***THEME:** Praise and worship in the Millennium*

This is the second of the little cluster of prophetic pictures of the millennial kingdom, which is established by the Lord Jesus Christ at His second coming. This is a continuation of praise and worship of Christ who is now King over all the earth.

O clap your hands, all ye people; shout unto God with the voice of triumph.

For the LORD most high is terrible; he is a great King over all the earth [Ps. 47:1–2].

"The LORD most high is terrible [awe-inspiring]; he is a great King over all the earth"—you see, Christ is reigning as King over all the earth; and as such, He is praised and worshiped.

My friend, before Christ can reign on this earth, He will have to put down all rebellion, self-conceit, arrogance, and the lawlessness of man against God. In Psalm 46 we saw the celebration of His coming in judgment, and now in Psalm 47 His kingdom is established and He is reigning on the earth.

He shall subdue the people under us, and the nations under our feet.

He shall choose our inheritance for us, the excellency of Jacob whom he loved. Selah [Ps. 47:3–4].

This is the appropriate time to sing, "Joy to the World!"

Joy to the world! the Lord is come;
Let earth receive her King;
Let every heart prepare Him room,
And heav'n and nature sing.

Joy to the world! the Saviour reigns;
Let men—their songs employ;
While fields and floods, rocks, hills
and plains
Repeat the sounding joy.

No more let sins and sorrows grow,
Nor thorns infest the ground;
He comes to make His blessings flow
Far as the curse is found.

He rules the world with truth and grace,
And makes the nations prove
The glories of His righteousness,
And wonders of His love.
—Isaac Watts

As you can see, this is not really a hymn that speaks of the birth of Christ; but it speaks of His second coming. There is going to be joy on the earth when He comes.

"Clap your hands; . . . shout unto God with the voice of triumph!" What a wonderful day that will be!

Not long ago I preached in a church where the people clapped their hands and were rather vociferous. Later someone asked me if all the noise did not disturb me. I replied, "No, it *helped* a great deal because they were right with me." I think that what many people call reverence today is really deadness. There is a lot of reverence in the cemetery—no one disturbs anybody or anything. I believe we need a little life in our services.

God is gone up with a shout, the LORD with the sound of a trumpet.

Sing praises to God, sing praises: sing praises unto our King, sing praises.

For God is the King of all the earth: sing ye praises with understanding.

God reigneth over the heathen: God sitteth upon the throne of his holiness.

The princes of the people are gathered together, even the people of the God of Abraham: for the shields of the earth belong unto God: he is greatly exalted [Ps. 47:5–9].

Let me give you Dr. Gaebelein's translation of this passage. "God is gone up amidst shouting, Jehovah amid the sound of a trumpet. Sing Psalms unto God! Sing Psalms unto our King, sing Psalms! For God is the King of all the earth—sing Psalms for instruction. God reigneth over the nations; God sitteth upon the throne of His holiness. The willing hearted of the people have gathered together with the people of the God of Abraham; for unto God belong the shields of the earth; He is greatly exalted" (*The Book of Psalms*, p. 207).

"God is gone up with a shout, the LORD with the sound of a trumpet"—that is, He has ascended amid shouting. And the fact that He ascended means He made a previous descent. The Lord came to earth nineteen hundred years ago, was born in Bethlehem, finished His work of salvation on earth, and then ascended to heaven—I think Psalm 24 refers to that. But in this psalm another ascension is spoken about. When Christ comes to earth the second time, He will establish His kingdom and be going back and forth to the New Jerusalem. I think that between the New Jerusalem and this earth there is going to be a freeway much busier than any of the California freeways—with one exception: there will be no traffic tie-ups. You will be able to move back and forth with freedom. Probably the Lord will descend and ascend at stated times during the Millennium and will display His visible glory upon the earth.

What a glorious, wonderful prospect this psalm predicts!

PSALM 48

***THEME:** Messiah's final victory upon the earth*

This is the last of the group of three millennial psalms. It celebrates the final and complete victory of the Messiah.

Great is the LORD, and greatly to be praised in the city of our God, in the mountain of his holiness.

Beautiful for situation, the joy of the whole earth, is mount Zion, on the sides of the north, the city of the great King.

God is known in her palaces for a refuge [Ps. 48:1–3].

Once again, I would like to give Dr. Gaebelein's translation. "Great is Jehovah, and greatly to be praised, in the city of our God, in His holy mountain. Beautiful in elevation, the joy of the whole earth, is the Mount Zion, the sides of the north, the city of the great King. God in her palaces hath made Himself known as a high tower" (*The Book of Psalms*, p. 208).

When it says Mount Zion, it means Mount Zion; and when it talks about the city of God in the holy mountain, it refers to Jerusalem.

Note the mention of "the sides of the north." This is an interesting expression. It probably speaks of a way of ascent and descent to this earth. There is a remarkable prophecy in Isaiah which mentions Satan in connection with "the sides of the north": "For thou hast said in thine heart, I will ascend into heaven, I will exalt my throne above the stars of God: I will sit also upon the mount of the congregation, in the sides of the north: I will ascend above the heights of the clouds; I will be like the most High" (Isa. 14:13–14). The "sides of the north" is apparently the route. Satan actually hoped to overthrow God!

This now is the conflict which is the last great battle that will take place on the earth:

For, lo, the kings were assembled, they passed by together.

They saw it, and so they marvelled; they were troubled, and hasted away [Ps. 48:4–5].

Notice Dr. Gaebelein's translation through verse 7: "For lo! the kings were gathered, they passed by together. They saw it and were amazed; they were terror stricken, they started to flee, trembling came upon them there, pains as a woman in travail. With the East wind Thou hast broken the ships of Tarshish" (*The Book of Psalms*, p. 209). I believe it describes the time after the thousand years of peace when the devil is released for a season: "And when the thousand years are expired, Satan shall be loosed out of his prison, And shall go out to deceive the nations which are in the four quarters of the earth, Gog and Magog, to gather them together to battle: the number of whom is as the sand of the sea. And they went up on the breadth of the earth, and compassed the camp of the saints about, and the beloved city: and fire came down from God out of heaven, and devoured them" (Rev. 20:7–9).

As we have heard, so have we seen in the city of the LORD of hosts, in the city of our God: God will establish it for ever. Selah [Ps. 48:8].

The people have heard and read all about this from their prophets, and now they are seeing the literal accomplishment of it all. It is the promised deliverance that down through the centuries God has assured them was coming. Finally it is realized.

We have thought of thy lovingkindness, O God, in the midst of thy temple.

According to thy name, O God, so is thy praise unto the ends of the earth: thy right hand is full of righteousness [Ps. 48:9–10].

In their millennial temple they will worship Him and meditate upon His lovingkindness to them.

This psalm concludes with a great hallelujah chorus.

Let mount Zion rejoice, let the daughters of Judah be glad, because of thy judgments.

Walk about Zion, and go round about her: tell the towers thereof.

Mark ye well her bulwarks, consider her palaces; that ye may tell it to the generation following.

For this God is our God for ever and ever: he will be our guide even unto death [Ps. 48:11–14].

With great joy they will walk about Jerusalem, noticing every part of it, and praise Him who is their God and guide of their lives. What praise this will be!

PSALM 49

***THEME:** The end of those who boast themselves in riches*

Psalm 49 concludes this first segment of the Exodus section of Psalms. We have seen the vindication of God's ways in connection with the wicked and the righteous. We have seen that God leads His people who are away from Him and out of the land. He has made known His intention of bringing His own to Himself and keeping them during the time of great trouble, just as He brought His people out of the land of Egypt when they were in bondage under a dictator.

Psalm 49 is designed to contrast the ways of God in dealing with the wicked and the righteous. It does not exactly philosophize about the uncertainty of riches, the shortness of life; it is not just a sweet little dissertation which bids us bear bravely our perils and our sufferings, and tells us that virtue is its own reward, and that justice will triumph at the end. Rather, this psalm shows us not only the vanity of riches but the *end* of those who boast themselves in riches. This psalm may sound a bit revolutionary to you according to the thinking of today, but it is one that should be given special consideration in the days in which we live.

Hear this, all ye people; give ear, all ye inhabitants of the world:

Both low and high, rich and poor, together.

My mouth shall speak of wisdom; and the meditation of my heart shall be of understanding.

I will incline mine ear to a parable: I will open my dark saying upon the harp [Ps. 49:1–4].

Or, as Dr. Gaebelein has translated them: "Hear ye this, all ye peoples, give ear, all ye inhabitants of the age, both low and high, rich and poor together! My mouth speaketh wisdom, and the meditation of my heart is understanding. I will incline mine ear to a parable. I will open my riddle upon the harp" (*The Book of Psalms*, p. 211).

What the psalmist is doing in this psalm, and will also do in the next one, is issuing a call to God's creatures to "hear." We are going to see this same thing when we come to the first chapter of Isaiah. We have already seen this in the Book of Deuteronomy. You will recall that when the Lord was ready to put His people in the land which He had promised, He called heaven and earth to witness that He was not only giving His people the land, but the conditions under which He was giving it to them. He used the form of a song. "Give ear, O ye heavens, and I will speak; and hear, O earth, the words of my mouth" (Deut. 32:1). This is the beginning of the song of Moses. In this song God calls heaven and earth to witness the conditions under which He is putting them in the land. At least eight hundred years later God is ready to put His people out of the land because of their sin. Again, in the Book of Isaiah, God calls heaven and earth to witness that putting His people out of the land is just and righteous (Isa. 1:2).

Now here is God's call to hear something that may be troubling you also, and it begins with a question:

Wherefore should I fear in the days of evil, when the iniquity of my heels shall compass me about? [Ps. 49:5].

Immediately you wonder who is asking the question. Is it the psalmist? Or is this question asked by the self-confident rich? Perhaps it is asked by the righteous who suffer unjustly at the hands of the wicked, or asked by the people today who are in want. I believe it is the question of a poor man. I was a poor boy, and I confess that I have always considered the rich with a little bit of suspicion. I question their motives. Why does God permit some people to become so rich? What is going to happen to them? Why do they get by with so much and seem not to have the same trouble as other men? There is a clique today in this country that is made up of the rich and influential. At election time they talk to us and tell *us* how wonderful, intelligent, and lovely we are because they want us to vote for their candidates. The question is, Why does God permit them to get by with so much? Why doesn't God do something about it? Let's see what this psalm has to say about this subject.

They that trust in their wealth, and boast themselves in the multitude of their riches;

None of them can by any means redeem his brother, nor give to God a ransom for him [Ps. 49:6–7].

No matter how rich a man is, he cannot buy salvation. He and I go to the counter for salvation. I have nothing with which to buy salvation. The rich man has money, but he cannot buy salvation with it. We are both on the same par. The rich man is excluded from redemption if he is deluded into thinking that he can either buy, do something, or give something to obtain his salvation. Romans 4:5 says, "But to him that worketh not, but believeth on him that justifieth the ungodly, his faith is counted for righteousness."

Now we come to a parenthesis.

(For the redemption of their soul is precious, and it ceaseth for ever:) [Ps. 49:8].

They don't have enough money to buy their salvation—no one has enough to buy his salvation.

That he should still live for ever, and not see corruption [Ps. 49:9].

Those who are rich will die just like everyone else. I think it was on the basis of this psalm that the Lord Jesus gave the parable about the rich man and Lazarus, the poor man, as recorded in Luke 16:19–31. No man, regardless of how rich he is, can redeem his (or another's) soul so that he can have eternal life.

For he seeth that wise men die, likewise the fool and the brutish person perish, and leave their wealth to others [Ps. 49:10].

I don't care who you are, or how much wealth you have accumulated, some day you will die and leave it all behind. You can take all your treasures and put them in a safety deposit box, or in a vault, or bury them in the earth; you can say, "This is mine. Nobody can take it away from me." You are right—no one can take it away from you, but there is Someone who can take *you* away from *it*. He is the Lord. One day death will knock at your door, and at that time you will be as poor as anyone. As the old bromide puts it, there is no pocket in a shroud.

Years ago when one of the Astors died, some of the eager relatives were waiting outside. When the lawyer came out, they asked, "How much did he leave?" The lawyer replied, "He left it *all*." He did not take anything with him. That is the first thing the psalmist observes—the rich "leave their wealth to others." Friend, you may be rich while you are here on earth, but you cannot buy salvation, nor can you extend your life on earth forever. Someday you will have to leave, and that bundle you made here will have to stay. That is one reason we encourage people to leave what they have accumulated to Christian work to get the Word of God out to needy hearts. That is what is important.

Their inward thought is, that their houses shall continue for ever, and their dwelling places to all generations; they call their lands after their own names [Ps. 49:11].

Many people try to perpetuate their names. I think it is interesting that the Rockefeller name is on buildings all over the world. People say, "My, wasn't he generous." In one sense that is pretty cheap advertising. I have never been able to pay enough money to have my name put in marble on a building—I don't want it there either. The point is that a name on a building doesn't mean much. One of these days the buildings are going to come down, and the individual will be forgotten.

Nevertheless man being in honour abideth not: he is like the beasts that perish [Ps. 49:12].

Men who have held high positions will go into the grave and return to dust just like everyone else.

This their way is their folly: yet their posterity approve their sayings. Selah [Ps. 49:13].

Now here is a very interesting expression:

Like sheep they are laid in the grave; death shall feed on them; and the upright shall have dominion over them in the morning; and their beauty shall consume in the grave from their dwelling [Ps. 49:14].

The word *grave* in verse 14 is "Sheol," or "the world of the dead." The rich, like sheep, are laid in Sheol. The literal rendering is: *death* is their shepherd. In contrast to this David said, "The *LORD* is my shepherd" (Ps. 23:1) and He is *life*. "He that hath the Son hath life; and he that hath not the Son of God hath not life" (1 John 5:12). The false shepherd is death. "Death shall feed on them." That is interesting. A shepherd should feed his sheep, but here is a shepherd who is eating his sheep.

We are also told that "their beauty shall consume in the grave [Sheol] from their dwelling." A person may spend a fortune in a beauty parlor. A person may put on all kinds of lotions, powders, and creams; but what they look like after a few years in the grave is not a pretty sight. I have seen several like that. Death is not a beautiful thing by any means.

But God will redeem my soul from the power of the grave [Sheol]: for he shall receive me. Selah [Ps 49:15].

"Selah" indicates a pause at this point so that you can think over what you have read. God alone is able to redeem your soul. The important thing in this life is not whether you are rich or poor. In the final analysis, when you move out into eternity, the important thing is whether or not you are redeemed, whether or not you are a child of God through faith in Christ:

Be not thou afraid when one is made rich, when the glory of his house is increased [Ps. 49:16].

Rich people today are getting away with murder, and with adultery, and with all kinds of things, and they are elected to office. Poor people are not getting a just deal in this world today. One of the reasons I cast my lot with the Lord Jesus is because He is going to judge the poor in righteousness. Some day I know I am going to get a fair deal.

For when he dieth he shall carry nothing away: his glory shall not descend after him.

Though while he lived he blessed his soul: and men will praise thee, when thou doest well to thyself.

He shall go to the generation of his fathers; they shall never see light.

Man that is in honour, and understandeth not, is like the beasts that perish [Ps. 49:17–20].

This is an interesting passage. We hear a great deal today about the theory that man has evolved from beasts and animals. The fact of the matter is that the Bible teaches the opposite. God created man in an upright position. God created man in His image. Man fell, and man can so live apart from God that he is like an animal in his life, and he is like an animal when he dies. Man does not evolve upward; he devolves downward. He is not on the upward trail at all. His inclination is to go down. That is natural with anything in this life. Everything, in my judgment, contradicts evolution. Nothing goes upward by itself; it all gravitates downward. The law of gravitation in the physical world pulls everything down. There is also a moral law of gravitation, which is immorality, and it will pull a man down.

My friend, let's not be disturbed when we see the wicked prospering.

PSALM 50

***THEME:** A psalm of judgment*

This is the first psalm of Asaph, a musician and one of the three great song leaders in the temple. Heman, Asaph, and Ethan were the three.

This is a great psalm of judgment. It reveals God coming in righteousness to judge His people and to judge the wicked.

The mighty God, even the LORD, hath spoken, and called the earth from the rising of the sun unto the going down thereof.

Out of Zion, the perfection of beauty, God hath shined.

Our God shall come, and shall not keep silence: a fire shall devour before him, and it shall be very tempestuous round about him [Ps. 50:1–3].

The introduction to this psalm proclaims that the mighty God is coming. What a glorious anticipation this should be for the child of God. Some day we shall *see* our Lord! That is the prospect for every believer.

He shall call to the heavens from above, and to the earth, that he may judge his people [Ps. 50:4].

When God is getting ready to judge, He wants plenty of witnesses to be there to make sure that He is righteous in all that He does. He says:

Gather my saints together unto me; those that have made a covenant with me by sacrifice [Ps. 50:5].

Those saints who have made a covenant with God by sacrifice are the Jews, the children of Israel.

And the heavens shall declare his righteousness: for God is judge himself. Selah [Ps. 50:6].

The Lord Jesus Christ is going to be the judge. "For the Father judgeth no man, but hath committed all judgment unto the Son" (John 5:22).

Hear, O my people, and I will speak; O Israel, and I will testify against thee: I am God, even thy God [Ps. 50:7].

If you had lived in Jerusalem when the temple was there and people worshiped in it, you probably would have asked, "Lord, are you criticizing these people? They come regularly to the temple, (which is the equivalent of every Sunday morning and evening service plus prayer meeting on Wednesday night). They are as busy as termites serving around the temple." Sure they were, but just going to church is not the most important thing. Of course it is important, but it will not establish a relationship with God. You had better establish that relationship through Christ so that your churchgoing can be pleasing to God.

I will not reprove thee for thy sacrifices or thy burnt offerings, to have been continually before me.

I will take no bullock out of thy house, nor he goats out of thy folds.

For every beast of the forest is mine, and the cattle upon a thousand hills [Ps. 50:8–10].

God says, "Did you really think you were giving Me something when you brought sacrifices to Me? Why, all the animals belong to Me anyway." This reminds us of the words of Jeremiah the prophet: "For I spake not unto your fathers, nor commanded them in the day that I brought them out of the land of Egypt, concerning burnt offerings or sacrifices: But this thing commanded I them, saying, Obey my voice, and I will be your God, and ye shall be my people: and walk ye in all the ways that I have commanded you, that it may be well unto you" (Jer. 7:22–23). The prophet Micah said something similar: "Wherewith shall I come before the LORD, and bow myself before the high God? shall I come before him with burnt offerings, with calves of a year old? Will the LORD be pleased with thousands of rams, or with ten thousands of rivers of oil? shall I give my firstborn for my transgression, the fruit of my body for the sin of my soul? He hath shewed thee, O man, what is good; and what doth the LORD require of thee, but to do justly, and to love mercy, and to walk humbly with thy God?" (Mic. 6:6–8).

If I were hungry, I would not tell thee: for the world is mine, and the fulness thereof [Ps. 50:12].

If the Creator were hungry, He certainly would not need to tell the creature about it!

And call upon me in the day of trouble: I will deliver thee, and thou shalt glorify me [Ps. 50:15].

God asks His people to come to Him. But God intends to judge the wicked. He is saying, "I didn't intend to let you get by with sin."

These things hast thou done, and I kept silence; thou thoughtest that I was altogether such an one as thyself: but I will reprove thee, and set them in order before thine eyes.

Now consider this, ye that forget God, lest I tear you in pieces, and there be none to deliver [Ps. 50:21–22].

My friend, God is not speaking only to Israel, He is speaking to us in our day also. He unmasks hypocrisy. Because God is silent does not mean that He approves. There is a day of reckoning coming. God says, "I will reprove thee, and set them [your sins] in order before thine eyes."

But God never ceases to be gracious. The way of salvation is mentioned.

Whoso offereth praise glorifieth me: and to him that ordereth his conversation aright will I shew the salvation of God [Ps. 50:23].

"To him that ordereth his conversation [his way] aright"—who confesses his sins to God—will be shown the way of salvation.

PSALM 51

***THEME:** David's great penitential psalm*

The superscription on many of the psalms is actually a part of the inspired Word of God. The title of Psalm 51 is self-explanatory, and it is essential to the understanding of this psalm. "To the chief Musician, A Psalm of David, when Nathan the prophet came unto him, after he had gone in to Bathsheba." The reference, of course, is to the great blot on David's life. It is not our intention to go into the lurid details of David's sin. Suffice it to say that David broke two of God's commandments. He broke the seventh commandment: "Thou shalt not commit adultery." He did with Bathsheba. He broke the sixth commandment: "Thou shalt not kill." He broke it indirectly in that he arranged for Uriah, the husband of Bathsheba, to be put in the front of the battle that he might be killed. And this was a dastardly and cold-blooded deal on the part of David, because Uriah was one of his mighty men and one of his most faithful followers—or he would never have gone into the front of the battle at David's command.

Now after this disgraceful incident, David did nothing, and he said nothing. Actually, both incidents would be considered business as usual down in Egypt, or in Babylon, or in Philistia, or in Edom, or in Moab. What David had done was a common practice and was more or less accepted. As a great preacher of the South said years ago, "When you put together a bunch of crooked sticks, they seem to straighten each other out." Have you ever noted that? And in this case when many monarchs engaged in things like this it gave it an air of not being as bad as it was. But it was as bad as God said it was.

On the surface it looked as if David had gotten by with it. But let's put down one thing: David was God's man, and David was not going to get by with it. The fact of the matter is, during the interval when he kept quiet, he was a tormented man. He told us later what really went on in his heart. Over in Psalm 32, David says this: "When I kept silence, my bones waxed old through my roaring all the day long" (Ps. 32:3). I think if you'd been in the court of David during that period when he was silent, you would have seen him age. This man went through awful anxiety. "For day and night thy hand was heavy upon me: my moisture is turned into the drought of summer" (Ps. 32:4). This describes his feelings during that interval.

Then God sent Nathan to David demanding an audience regarding an urgent matter. And Nathan approached the subject by telling David a story: "And the LORD sent Nathan unto David. And he came unto him, and said unto him, There were two men in one city; the one rich, and the other poor. The rich man had exceeding many flocks and herds: But the poor man had nothing, save one little ewe lamb, which he had bought and nourished up: and it grew up together with him, and with his children; it did eat of his own meat, and drank of his own cup, and lay in his bosom, and was unto him as a daughter. And there came a traveller unto the rich man, and he spared to take of his own flock and of his own herd, to dress for the wayfaring man that was come unto him; but took the poor man's lamb, and dressed it for the man that was come to him. And David's anger was greatly kindled against the man; and he said to Nathan, As the LORD liveth, the man that hath done this thing shall surely die: And he shall restore the lamb fourfold, because he did this thing, and because he had no pity" (2 Sam. 12:1–6).

Then we come to one of the most dramatic moments in the Word of God, and it reveals Nathan as one of the bravest men in Scripture: "And Nathan said to David, Thou art the man . . ." (2 Sam. 12:7). Nathan pointed his finger at David and said to him, "You're the man!"

When he said that, there were three courses open to David. He could deny the charge. He could say, "Nathan is entirely wrong and is attempting to smear me." Or he could have merely pointed his scepter at Nathan, without saying a word because the guards would have understood, and would have led Nathan out and summarily executed him. David would not have needed to say anything. And, I suppose, if it had been carried to any kind of tribunal (which in those days it would not have been), the "supreme court" would have handed down a decision that undue pressure was used by Nathan to extract a confession from David, and David would have been freed from all charges.

There was a third course open to David, and that was to admit the charge. David followed the latter course. He made confession of his sin. Now David was not just a man; he was the *king*. And the king can do no wrong; he is above reproach. No one points the finger at the king. But Nathan did. And the very interesting thing is that David confessed.

Now continuing with this encounter, let's pick up at verse 10, with Nathan giving him God's message: "Now therefore the sword shall never depart from thine house; because thou hast despised me, and hast taken the wife of Uriah the Hittite to be thy wife. Thus saith the LORD, Behold, I will raise up evil against thee out of thine own house, and I will take thy wives before thine eyes, and give them unto thy neighbour, and he shall lie with thy wives in the sight of this sun. For thou didst it secretly: but I will do this thing before all Israel, and before the sun. And David said unto Nathan, I have sinned against the LORD. And Nathan said unto David, The LORD also hath put away thy sin; thou shalt not die. Howbeit, because by this deed thou hast given great occasion to the enemies of the LORD to blaspheme, the child also that is born unto thee shall surely die" (2 Sam. 12:10–14).

This now is the background of Psalm 51, because after this, David went into the privacy of his own chamber and made the confession which this psalm records.

All the great men of God have confessed their sin before God. Augustine wrote his confessions. But Psalm 51 is one of the greatest confessionals that has ever been written.

Psalm 51 divides very nicely into three divisions: (1) Cry of Conscience and Conviction of Sin—verses 1–3; (2) Cry of Confession of Sin and Clemency (Compassion) of God—verses 4–8; (3) Cry for Cleansing and Communion—verses 9–19.

CRY OF CONSCIENCE AND CONVICTION OF SIN

Let us now listen to David's confession:

Have mercy upon me, O God, according to thy loving-kindness: according unto the multitude of thy tender mercies blot out my transgressions.

Wash me throughly from mine iniquity, and cleanse me from my sin.

For I acknowledge my transgressions: and my sin is ever before me [Ps. 51: 1–3].

Sin is always complicated. It never is simple. And there are several words that David uses to describe his sin. In the Scriptures God uses many more words than this to describe sin, by the way. Sin is that which is complicated; it is goodness that is simple. Let me give you an illustration. Suppose I were holding behind me a stick and I told you it was a crooked stick. How do you think it would look? No two people would think it looked like it really does. No two would agree because it could be crooked in a million different ways. But suppose I say that I hold a ruler behind me that is perfectly straight. Everyone would think of it in just one way. It can't be straight in more than one way. It is sin that is complicated; it is goodness that is simple.

David, first of all, called his sins *transgressions*. To transgress is to step over the boundaries of God. God has put up certain boundaries in this life. He has certain physical laws. He has certain moral laws. He has certain spiritual laws. Any time man attempts to step over any of them, he'll have to suffer the consequences. To do this is always called transgression.

Also David called his sin *iniquity*. And *iniquity* means that which is altogether wrong. You can't excuse it; you can't offer some sort of an apology for it; you can't in any way condone it. That's *iniquity*. Then there are two words translated with the English word *sin*. In verses 2 and 3 it is the Hebrew word *chattath*, meaning "sin offering." In verse 4 it is *chata*, translated in the Septuagint by the Greek word *hamartia*, meaning "to miss the mark." That's all—just miss the mark. We don't come up to God's standard, and it is in that sense that all of us today are sinners. None of us come up to the standard of God. "For all have sinned, and come short of the glory of God" (Rom. 3:23).

Then the word *evil* that is used here by David means that which is actually wrong. In our day we even have ministers who are trying to condone all kinds of immorality, but let it be understood that the Bible is still very clear on what is right and what is wrong. There are questionable areas on which the Bible is silent, I grant you, but there is also clear-cut black and clear-cut white. God is unmistakably certain on these things. *Evil* is that which is actually wrong. David uses this word to speak of the fact that he was wrong. He admitted it.

There is a dispensational aspect to this psalm, but I am not going to deal with that here. Actually, you cannot cram this psalm into one dispensation. It voices the experience of a man who is a member of the human family. This is the experience of a man in *any* dispensation—at any time since Adam and Eve left the Garden of Eden and on until eternity begins on this earth.

The experience of David is that he has come under deep conviction of sin. You and I cannot enter into the horror of the guilt of David. To him his sin was repugnant. He hated it, and he hated himself because he did it. He felt dirty all over. His conscience was outraged. And he had a feeling of guilt as big as the Rock of Gibraltar. There was anguish of soul in this man. Conscience was pointing an accusing finger at him, and there was a cry of conscience within, telling David he was *wrong*.

Now I know someone will say, "But conscience is not a good guide." That's true. But let's notice that conscience has a function; the function of conscience is not to tell us what is right or what is wrong. That is not the purpose of conscience. The purpose of conscience, and the function of it, is to tell us that we *are* right or that we *are* wrong. It doesn't tell us what is right and wrong. Let me give you an example in the New Testament. Paul uses it in his letter to the Corinthians: "Whatsoever is sold in the shambles, that eat, asking no question for conscience sake: For the earth is the Lord's, and the fulness thereof" (1 Cor. 10:25–26). Then he goes on to say: "Conscience, I say, not thine own, but of the other . . ." (1 Cor. 10:29). What Paul is saying is this: "As far as God is concerned whether you eat meat or you don't eat meat makes no difference. But if you go into the home of someone and meat is served to you, don't ask them where they bought it. If you knew they bought it at the heathen temple, then your conscience would tell you that you were wrong in eating it—because you may have a wrong influence. But if you don't know, if your host doesn't tell you, then it's not wrong for you to eat it." Conscience, you see, doesn't tell you *what* is wrong; it tells you that it *is* wrong. There are some folk who have a conscience about one thing and some have a conscience about something else. And it is dangerous for any person to violate his own conscience.

Now David's conscience was speaking to him, and the cry of his conscience was a conviction of sin. He was wrong, and there was no explanation he could offer at all. Listen to him:

For I acknowledge my transgressions: and my sin is ever before me [Ps. 51:3].

The king said he was wrong.

CRY OF CONFESSION OF SIN AND CLEMENCY (COMPASSION) OF GOD

The second division is the cry of confession of sin, and the clemency and compassion of God.

Against thee, thee only, have I sinned, and done this evil in thy sight: that thou mightest be justified when thou speakest, and be clear when thou judgest [Ps. 51:4].

David has been criticized because he made this statement. There are those who say he should not have said it was a sin against God; he should have said it was a sin against Bathsheba. Wasn't it? It sure was. Also it was a sin against his family, for he had a family at that time. It *was* a sin against them, and David should have said that, so the critics say. They also say that it was a sin against society and Jerusalem at that time, and it was. It was a sin against the nation of which he was king. He was breaking God's commandment. But, my friend, in the final analysis sin is always against God. Bathsheba is gone. I do not know where her family is. The society of that day has disappeared. Actually, the nation is no longer under the line of David. But that sin still stands on the escutcheon of the Word of God and against God.

Let's read the historical record again, as it is very important. This is what God said to David: "Now therefore the sword shall never depart from thine house; because thou hast despised me, and hast taken the wife of Uriah the Hittite to be thy wife" (2 Sam. 12:10). "And David said unto Nathan, I have sinned against the LORD. And Nathan said unto David, The LORD also hath put away thy sin; thou shalt not die. Howbeit, because by this deed thou hast given great occasion to the enemies of the LORD to blaspheme, the child also that is born unto thee shall surely die" (2 Sam. 12:13–14). For three thousand years now the enemy, the critic, has been pointing his finger at the Word of God and saying, "You mean to tell me that David is a man after God's own heart?" I heard this on Pershing Square in Los Angeles several years ago. A man had gathered around him a crowd—he was a disheveled, dirty-looking fellow, with a leer in his voice and on his face. He said to them, "Now they say God is holy!" Then he gave a suggestive laugh and made some filthy statements about David, and said, "They say He is a holy God!"

God said to David, "David, you've hurt Me." One night I went with some friends to Bughouse Square in Chicago (that corresponds to Pershing Square in Los Angeles, and that's a better name than Pershing Square, by the way), and there was the worst filth I've ever heard. I never have heard a man as filthy as he was. And who was he talking about? David. God said, "David, you've given great occasion to My enemies to blaspheme, and because of that the child will die, and the sword will never leave your house." And it never did. To his dying day David paid for his sin. Not only *that* child died, but the son he loved, the one he wanted to succeed him as king, also died. When David heard that his son Absalom had been killed in battle, he wrapped his mantle about his head, walked to the top of the wall, up those winding stairs, and as he went up he wept, ". . . O my son Absalom, my son, my son Absalom! would God I had died for thee, O Absalom, my son, my son!" (2 Sam. 18:33). David did not think Absalom was saved; he wanted him to live. My friend, David paid for his sin.

Now notice that David makes it very clear that this sin goes back to a sin nature.

> **Behold, I was shapen in iniquity; and in sin did my mother conceive me [Ps. 51:5].**

David, as well as the rest of us, came into the world with a sin nature. Paul, recognizing this, says to believers today, "Brethren, if a [Christian] man be overtaken in a fault, ye which are spiritual, restore such an one in the spirit of meekness; considering thyself, lest thou also be tempted" (Gal. 6:1). And Goethe said that he saw no fault committed which he too might not have committed. And Samuel Johnson said, "Every man knows that of himself which he dares not tell his dearest friend." Even Seneca, a pagan philosopher of Rome, said, "We must say of ourselves that we are evil, have been evil, and unhappily, I must add—shall be also in the future. Nobody can deliver himself; someone must stretch out a hand to lift him up." And the Word of God confirms this. Even the writer of Ecclesiastes says, "For there is not a just man upon earth, that doeth good, and sinneth not" (Eccl. 7:20). Also in the Book of Proverbs we read, "There is a generation that are pure in their own eyes, and yet is not washed from their filthiness" (Prov. 30:12). There are people who think they are all right, but they are not sensitive to sin. They are like the man in the far North who, as he got colder, wanted to rest. He felt very comfortable sitting down. But those with him knew what was happening to him—he was freezing to death. They wouldn't let him sit down but kept him moving so he would not die. Today there are many sitting in our churches so cold and so comfortable that they do not realize that in God's sight they are sinners. We not only need a Savior, but we need *cleansing.* Paul says, "For I know that in me (that is, in my flesh,) dwelleth no good thing . . ." (Rom. 7:18). David, you see, went right down to the root of the matter. He confessed that he had a sin nature.

David's confession continues:

> **Behold, thou desirest truth in the inward parts: and in the hidden part thou shalt make me to know wisdom [Ps. 51:6].**

God is not interested in what you have been on the surface. You may be baptized and be nothing more than a baptized sinner, still unsaved. You may be a member of a church, but, my friend, that is all exterior. You still could be lost. He says He desires truth on the inside.

The psalmist goes on:

> **Purge me with hyssop, and I shall be clean: wash me, and I shall be whiter than snow [Ps. 51:7].**

Follow me now very carefully. Here is without doubt one of the greatest passages in the Word of God. There are those who say that the reason David was forgiven was because he confessed his sin. If you say that, you've told only part of the story. That's not the reason. Turn back to the historical record: "And David said unto Nathan, I have sinned against the LORD. And Nathan said unto David, The LORD also hath put away thy sin; thou shalt not die" (2 Sam. 12:13). *God* took the first step: He sent Nathan. I think David would still be sitting over there keeping quiet if Nathan had not come in. Maybe he couldn't have kept it much longer—I don't know. But he didn't make the first step; God made the first step.

And how was God able to forgive him? Because He had revealed Himself. Now follow this closely. God revealed Himself to the nation Israel: "And the LORD passed by before him, and proclaimed, The LORD, The LORD God, merciful and gracious, longsuffering, and abundant in goodness and truth, Keeping mercy for thousands, forgiving iniquity and transgression and sin, and that will by no means clear the guilty; visiting the iniquity of the fathers upon the children, and upon the children's children, unto the third and to the fourth generation" (Exod. 34:6–7). Somebody asks, "Doesn't it go any further than that?" It sure does. It will keep going, but that is as far down as any man will be able to see—the third and fourth generations. A man may see his sin carried down that far. But I want you to notice here two things that are conflicting and contradictory. God says He forgives iniquity and He shows mercy. Then He turns right around and says, "that will by no means clear the guilty." There is a paradox. Listen to David again: "Purge me with hyssop, and I shall be clean: wash me, and I shall be whiter than snow." Hyssop was a little plant that grew on rocks in damp places. An interesting sidelight is a statement from a scientific journal that penicillin was found growing on hyssop. However, hyssop had to do with something penicillin can't cure: sin. Back in the Old Testament hyssop was used for three purposes. First, when God took the children of Israel out of Egypt, He said, "There is one thing you must do at the Passover. You are to take a lamb, slay it and take its blood in a basin out to the front door and, with bunches of hyssop, apply the blood to the doorposts and to the lintel, then go back inside." Second, when God was giving instructions for cleansing a leper, He told about taking two birds. One was to be slain; the live bird was taken with hyssop, dipped in the blood of the slain bird, and then let fly away. This portrays the death and resurrection of Christ. But the application of it was by hyssop. Third, when the people of Israel were on the wilderness march and one of them sinned, they couldn't stop and put up the tabernacle and offer a sacrifice. So provision was made for purification of sin by killing a red heifer, burning it (with hyssop added), gathering the ashes and taking them along on the wilderness march. When a man sinned, the ashes were put in water, then hyssop was used to sprinkle them on him. There was the application of a sacrifice that brought forgiveness.

You have to go to the cross to find the interpretation. On the cross the Son of God said, ". . . My God, my God, why hast thou forsaken me?" (Matt. 27:46). Why did He say that? I'll tell you why. Because *God cannot by any means clear the guilty*. He can't. He never will. And when the Lord Jesus Christ, on the cross, was made sin for us, He who knew no sin, that we might be made the righteousness of God in Him—when He was delivered for our offenses—God had to treat Him as He *must* treat sin. God spared Abraham's son; but God did not spare His own Son when He had my sin and your sin upon Him. He had to slay Him, because God *cannot* pardon the guilty. Let's be clear on that. He does not operate like our Supreme Court. God *hates* sin. God will punish sin. By no means will He clear the guilty. And His Son *died*.

On the cross Jesus also said, ". . . Father, forgive them . . ." (Luke 23:34). *Forgive* them! How can He forgive them? How can He extend *mercy* to thousands? How can He forgive iniquity? How can He forgive David? And how can He forgive you and me? "In whom we have redemption through his blood, the forgiveness of sins, according to the riches of his grace" (Eph. 1:7). And every time you find forgiveness in the New Testament, the blood of Christ is close by. God never forgives sin apart from the death of Christ. Never. *Never.* God is not forgiving sin because He is big-hearted. He forgives because His Son paid the penalty. And now with open arms He can say to you, "I can extend mercy to *you* because My Son died for you." Oh, David knew the way into the heart of God. David says, "Purge me with hyssop, and I shall be clean: wash me, and I shall be whiter than snow." It is the application of the death of Christ to the life.

CRY FOR CLEANSING AND COMMUNION

Notice now David's cry for cleansing and communion.

> **Hide thy face from my sins, and blot out all mine iniquities [Ps. 51:9].**

Blot out—David needed a spot remover. In getting ready to make an extensive trip, every little book and folder I read advised, "Be sure to take along a spot remover because you are going to get gravy on your suit." How in the world did they know me? But I appreciate their advice because I know I'll need a spot remover. All of us do. David needed a spot remover.

> **Create in me a clean heart, O God; and renew a right spirit within me [Ps. 51:10].**

The word for "create" here is the same word as is in Genesis 1:1: "In the beginning God created the heaven and the earth"—*bara*, out of nothing. "I need a new heart," David said. "Create in me a *new* heart," and the word *create* means "out of nothing." In other words, there was nothing in David's heart that God could use. He was not asking for renovation or reformation. He was asking for something new. Sometimes we hear the invitation, "Give God your heart." May I ask you, "What do you think God wants with that old dirty, filthy heart of yours?" He doesn't want it. God is not asking anybody to give Him his heart. He wants to give you a *new* one. That's what He wants to do. "Create in me a new heart" is what David is asking for. "For we are his workmanship, created in Christ Jesus unto good works, which God hath before ordained that we should walk in them"(Eph. 2:10). "Therefore if any man be in Christ, he is a new creature: old things are passed away; behold, all things are become new" (2 Cor. 5:17). Let God give you a new heart.

David has another request:

Cast me not away from thy presence; and take not thy holy spirit from me [Ps. 51:11].

The Spirit of God came upon David as king that he might be God's man. By the way, no Christian today can pray that prayer, because if you are indwelt by the Spirit of God, He will never leave you. You can grieve Him, you can quench Him, but you can never grieve Him away or quench Him away. We are told, "And grieve not the holy Spirit of God, whereby ye are sealed *unto the day of redemption*" (Eph. 4:30). Therefore no child of God can lose the Spirit of God. However, the Holy Spirit can be inoperative in a Christian's life, and that is what happened to David. He is asking that the Spirit of God may continue to work in his life.

Then he says,

Restore unto me the joy of thy salvation; and uphold me with thy free spirit [Ps. 51:12].

David did not lose his salvation. He lost the *joy* of his salvation, and he wanted communion with God restored. For he found out, as the prodigal son found out, that there is not nearly as much fun in the far country as there is in the Father's house.

He wanted all this for a purpose:

Then will I teach transgressors thy ways; and sinners shall be converted unto thee.

O Lord, open thou my lips; and my mouth shall shew forth thy praise [Ps. 51:13,15].

He wanted to praise God again.

Then shalt thou be pleased with the sacrifices of righteousness, with burnt offering and whole burnt offering: then shall they offer bullocks upon thine altar [Ps. 51:19].

He not only wanted to praise God, he wanted to please God.

The Lord Jesus went to dinner in the home of a Pharisee. A woman who had been saved came in there from the street. But Simon the Pharisee only knew her in the past, and he would have passed by on the other side rather than meet her on the street. But according to the custom of the day, when he had guests she had a right to come into his house and even stand and observe. She got to the place where our Lord was reclining (they used couches rather than chairs in that day), and she stood at His feet behind Him, weeping. She washed His feet with her tears, and wiped them with the hair of her head, and kissed His feet, and anointed them with ointment. Simon, His host, became critical. He began to find fault. And our Lord really rebuked him. He said, "When I came here you didn't even furnish Me water to wash My feet. You didn't even extend to Me the common courtesies. But this woman has not ceased to wash My feet with her tears. *She's* been forgiven. You have not" (Luke 7:44, paraphrase mine). Then He said to him, ". . . Her sins, which are many, are forgiven; for she loved much: but to whom little is forgiven, the same loveth little" (Luke 7:47). We *think* we are all right. My friend, God cannot clear the guilty, and He says you and I are *guilty* before Him. The only way he could save you and me is to give His Son to die. For the worst sinner in the world that is all that is needed. And this is the way you and I are saved also. ". . . To whom little is forgiven, the same loveth little." To whom much is forgiven—oh, He loves much.

What is the measure of *your* love? Well, it is your estimate of your own sins. Is it possible that you do not confess your sins? When was the last time you wept over your sins? When was the last time you cried out in the night because of your failures? Thank God, there is forgiveness with Him. But there needs to be confession on our part.

PSALM 52

***THEME:** Antichrist, the mighty man of mischief*

Psalm 52 begins a series of four psalms (52–55) which give a prophetic picture we get nowhere else of the coming of Antichrist, the Man of Sin, who will be a world dictator and dominate Israel during the Tribulation. Our Lord referred to him in the Olivet discourse. The prophet Daniel and the apostle Paul both speak of him.

These four psalms are *maschil,* or instruction, psalms. They give us deep spiritual truths concerning the future. Many wild things are being said today in the field of prophecy. There is fanaticism in the great department of eschatology, the doctrine of future things; and some things are being said that should not be said. Because of the anxiety and uncertainty of this day and age in which we live, many folk are turning to the Word of God. Prophetic conferences are springing up everywhere, sponsored by churches that never before were interested in prophecy. Many speakers are attempting to be sensational by making prophetic statements that have no foundation in the Word of God.

Now here this cluster of four psalms gives us accurate instructions relative to this "Man of Sin," the Antichrist who is coming.

Let me remind you that the superscription of the psalm is inspired; it is part of the psalm itself. It was written, "To the chief Musician, Maschil, A Psalm of David, when Doeg the Edomite came and told Saul, and said unto him, David is come to the house of Ahimelech." In other words, here is a man who betrayed David. David was hurt and betrayed by many men who professed to be his friends. We will see one of them in this particular section.

Boasting is a mark of the Antichrist.

Why boastest thou thyself in mischief, O mighty man? the goodness of God endureth continually [Ps. 52:1].

Here is a man who is boasting of his *sin.* When David sinned, he kept quiet because he was under deep conviction. When the man of the world sins, he loves it and boasts about it. A mark of the Antichrist is that he will brag about his sin. This is the big difference between the child of God and the child of the devil. The child of God may sin just like the man in the world, because they both have an old nature. The difference is that the man of God will not boast about it. He will hang his head in shame. He will hate himself. But the sinner brags about what he does, and the Man of Sin, the Antichrist, will be the epitome of that type of man. And all the sinners will love him for it, you see.

Thy tongue deviseth mischiefs; like a sharp razor, working deceitfully [Ps. 52:2].

God will tolerate the Man of Sin for a short period of time. For seven years the Antichrist's tongue will devise mischief.

Thou lovest evil more than good; and lying rather than to speak righteousness. Selah [Ps. 52:3].

You have heard it said of some people that they would rather tell a lie even when it would have been easier to tell the truth. That will be true of the Antichrist.

Thou lovest all devouring words, O thou deceitful tongue [Ps. 52:4].

This psalm has given us two names for the Man of Sin. In Psalm 52:1 he is called "mighty man." In this verse he is called a "deceitful tongue." You will not be able to believe a word he says. This is another one of his characteristics.

God shall likewise destroy thee for ever, he shall take thee away, and pluck thee out of thy dwelling place, and root thee out of the land of the living. Selah [Ps. 52:5].

The word *destroy* means "to beat down." The Antichrist will be a world dictator whom no one can stop, no one except God. When the Lord Jesus Christ returns to earth, He will beat down the Man of Sin.

The righteous also shall see, and fear, and shall laugh at him [Ps. 52:6].

When God brings the Antichrist into judgment, when He beats him down, and the one whom the peoples of the earth once feared will be laughed at, he will be the laughingstock of the universe.

Lo, this is the man that made not God his strength; but trusted in the abun-

dance of his riches, and strengthened himself in his wickedness [Ps. 52:7].

He will be a very rich man. Our country has come to the place where only a rich man can win an election to office. The politicians talk a great deal about Abraham Lincoln, but I doubt if he would be able to make it to the presidency in this day. The Antichrist will be able to make it to the top at the beginning because he will be a rich man.

In the midst of this, the child of God will be able to say:

But I am like a green olive tree in the house of God: I trust in the mercy of God for ever and ever.

I will praise thee for ever, because thou hast done it: and I will wait on thy name; for it is good before thy saints [Ps. 52:8–9].

This brief psalm gives us a prophetic picture of the Antichrist and of the believing remnant who will suffer under his persecution, then will worship and praise God when he is dethroned.

PSALM 53

***THEME:** The fool, foreshadowing Antichrist, denies the existence of God*

This psalm is the same as Psalm 14 as far as the translation is concerned, but there is something very interesting about it. It begins:

The fool hath said in his heart, There is no God. Corrupt are they, and have done abominable iniquity: there is none that doeth good [Ps. 53:1].

This psalm is "To the chief Musician upon Mahalath, Maschil, A Psalm of David." *Mahalath* has to do with sickness and sorrow, and it corresponds to the mournful condition of the last days when Antichrist is the ruler. He, of course, will be an atheist. The difference between Psalm 14 and Psalm 53 lies in the way the name of God is used. In Psalm 14 the name *Jehovah* is used four times and the name *Elohim* is used three times. Psalm 53 uses the name *Elohim* seven times. That is significant. Elohim is God's name as Creator. Now notice at what point atheism breaks through. It is relative to creation. The Bible, which is God's revelation, is denied and is no longer considered trustworthy, infallible, and inerrant. The first chapters of Genesis are branded as folklore and myth, even by some men who claim to be believers. Evolution is adopted as the explanation for the origin of all things. Many years ago an educator, who was president of one of the largest universities in this country, said, "We no longer take anything for granted, not even the existence of God." This is the spirit of Antichrist. He will deny the existence of the Father and the Son. First John 2:22 tells us the mark of the Antichrist: "Who is a liar but he that denieth that Jesus is the Christ? He is antichrist, that denieth the Father and the Son."

If you are going to come to God, you will have to come by faith. "But without faith it is impossible to please him; for he that cometh to God must believe that he is, and that he is a rewarder of them that diligently seek him" (Heb. 11:6). A number of years ago the Beatles (a rock music group) said, "We are more popular than Christ!" Of course that is not true. Such popularity lasts for only a short time. It is interesting how the Lord Jesus Christ has moved back into the spotlight, having been out of it for so long.

Atheism is a characteristic of Antichrist. In the last days the forces of atheism will be headed up by him. Of him Paul wrote: "Who opposeth and exalteth himself above all that is called God, or that is worshipped; so that he as God sitteth in the temple of God, shewing himself that he is God" (2 Thess. 2:4).

This psalm ends with an expression of longing on the part of the believing remnant.

Oh that the salvation of Israel were come out of Zion! When God bringeth back the captivity of his people, Jacob shall rejoice, and Israel shall be glad [Ps. 53:6].

How can anyone say that God is through with the nation of Israel after reading this verse?

"*When* God bringeth back the captivity of his people, Jacob shall rejoice, and Israel shall be glad." To deny that God has a future purpose for Israel is to deny the inerrancy and inspiration of Scripture. Yet men who say they are believers attempt to spiritualize this. A great company of Amillennialists (I studied in an amillennial seminary, and I know that crowd pretty well) have spiritualized the Book of Revelation instead of interpreting it literally. In my judgment, to spiritualize Scripture is practically to deny its inspiration. Now, my friend, God is not through with the nation of Israel. Listen to this verse again: "Oh that the salvation of Israel were come out of *Zion!* When God bringeth back the captivity of his people, *Jacob* shall rejoice, and *Israel* shall be glad." I think that even a child could understand what is being said here—that "Zion" means Zion, "Jacob" means Jacob, "Israel" means Israel, and "God" means God. This verse means exactly what it says. And God will answer this prayer. He will again deal with Israel as a nation.

PSALM 54

THEME: *A cry of faith in the time of Antichrist*

This marvelous little psalm is wedged in here, in the midst of all the troubles of the Great Tribulation, so that we can hear the cry of faith on the part of the remnant of God's people and of a great company of Gentiles, too.

Now note the historical background: "To the chief Musician on Neginoth, Maschil, A Psalm of David, when the Ziphims came and said to Saul, Doth not David hide himself with us?" From this introduction we discover several things. The neginoth was a stringed musical instrument. *Maschil* means that this is another psalm of instruction, a psalm of David. The Ziphims absolutely betrayed David. The Ziphims are also called Ziphites, and the record of their betrayal is found in 1 Samuel 23. When David learned that these people had told Saul where he was, he cried:

Save me, O God, by thy name, and judge me by thy strength.

Hear my prayer, O God; give ear to the words of my mouth [Ps. 54:1–2].

David was betrayed. And we are told that in the Great Tribulation period brother will betray brother. It will be a time again of awful betrayal.

It was a godless crowd that betrayed David. During the Tribulation period the godless Antichrist will be in power, and the Jewish remnant will suffer greatly under this Man of Sin.

For strangers are risen up against me, and oppressors seek after my soul: they have not set God before them. Selah [Ps. 54:3].

David was in deep distress, as will be the remnant during the Tribulation of the future.

This brief psalm concludes with an expression of confidence in the help of God.

Behold, God is mine helper: the Lord is with them that uphold my soul.

He shall reward evil unto mine enemies: cut them off in thy truth.

I will freely sacrifice unto thee: I will praise thy name, O LORD; for it is good.

For he hath delivered me out of all trouble: and mine eye hath seen his desire upon mine enemies [Ps. 54:4–7].

We know from the historical record that God did deliver David from the treacherous Ziphites, and the faithful remnant can rest in the confidence that God will deliver them also. God will surely keep His promises.

PSALM 55

***THEME:** The darkest days under Antichrist*

This psalm concludes this little cluster of four prophetic psalms that picture the Antichrist. Notice that this is another maschil psalm, which is a psalm of instruction. It pictures what I believe to be the darkest moment of the Tribulation period. The Antichrist, the Man of Sin, is fully portrayed here in a remarkable way, a way that many who are even students of prophecy have never considered.

This psalm is inscribed "To the chief Musician on Neginoth, Maschil, A Psalm of David." We are not told the exact background of this psalm, but I think we can make an educated guess. You will recall that David's own son, Absalom, led a rebellion against him. David was forced to leave Jerusalem. He found that many people were following his son, and he knew there would be trouble. In order that Jerusalem, his beloved city, would not be destroyed, he left it. He went back to the caves of the earth to hide. As David left his city, weeping, word was brought to him that Ahithophel, a member of his cabinet and close friend, had gone over to Absalom's side. He had betrayed David. We are told in 2 Samuel 15:30–31, "And David went up by the ascent of mount Olivet, and wept as he went up, and had his head covered, and he went barefoot: and all the people that was with him covered every man his head, and they went up, weeping as they went up. And one told David, saying, Ahithophel is among the conspirators with Absalom. And David said, O LORD, I pray thee, turn the counsel of Ahithophel into foolishness." And that is exactly what God did—He turned the counsel of Ahithophel into foolishness. Keep these things in mind as we hit the high points of this psalm.

Give ear to my prayer, O God; and hide not thyself from my supplication.

Attend unto me, and hear me: I mourn in my complaint, and make a noise [Ps. 55:1–2].

David is like the squeaking wheel that gets the grease. David says, "I am making a noise to Thee, Lord. I am crying out to Thee because I am in a desperate situation. I have been betrayed by a friend."

Because of the voice of the enemy, because of the oppression of the wicked: for they cast iniquity upon me, and in wrath they hate me.

My heart is sore pained within me: and the terrors of death are fallen upon me [Ps. 55:3–4].

David did not know but what he would be slain at that time, especially when those who had been so close to him had deserted him.

And I said, Oh that I had wings like a dove! for then would I fly away, and be at rest [Ps. 55:6].

At first, David was advised to fly away to his mountain, but he would not do it then. But now all seems lost. Even Ahithophel, his trusted advisor, has betrayed him. Does that remind you of something? It reminds me of Judas Iscariot who betrayed Christ. Also, it foreshadows the time when the nation will be betrayed by Antichrist.

Many of us have had the bitter experience of betrayal. I was a pastor for many years, and during those years I have had some wonderful people on my staff; but one or two of them have turned out to be like Ahithophel and Judas Iscariot. They betrayed me. When someone in whom you have placed your confidence betrays you, it hurts.

But it was thou, a man mine equal, my guide, and mine acquaintance [Ps. 55:13].

David is speaking, I believe, of his "familiar friend," Ahithophel. This is also a picture of the Antichrist who will betray the nation of Israel. He will pretend to be their friend, will make a covenant with them and then will betray them.

We took sweet counsel together, and walked unto the house of God in company [Ps. 55:14].

These are people who will pray with you and who will pray *for* you when you are with them. But when your back is turned, they will put a knife in it. There are people like that all around us. And if the Antichrist appeared tomorrow, he would have a following before the sun went down.

What David says next is imprecatory, I grant you, but listen to him:

Let death seize upon them, and let them go down quick into hell: for wick-

edness is in their dwellings, and among them [Ps. 55:15].

"Let them go down quick into hell" is literally, "Let them go alive down to Sheol!" In our contemporary society we often hear the frightful expression, *Go to hell.* That is an awful thing to say, and David almost said that relative to Ahithophel. In contrast to him, our Lord Jesus prayed for them who despitefully used Him and instructed us to do likewise.

As for me, I will call upon God; and the LORD shall save me.

Evening, and morning, and at noon, will I pray, and cry aloud: and he shall hear my voice [Ps. 55:16–17].

What a picture that gives of David's distress—"Evening, and morning, and at noon, will I pray, and cry aloud." My friend, one good thing your enemy will do for you is to cause you to pray more than you have ever prayed before!

Now notice this picture of Antichrist—oh, is he a liar! Remember that the Lord Jesus said the devil was a liar from the beginning (John 8:44), and Antichrist is right out of the pit of hell.

The words of his mouth were smoother than butter, but war was in his heart: his words were softer than oil, yet were they drawn swords [Ps. 55:21].

Ahithophel, pretending to be a friend to David, was plotting against him. He was a little adumbration of Antichrist.

Cast thy burden upon the LORD, and he shall sustain thee: he shall never suffer the righteous to be moved [Ps. 55:22].

Dear Christian friend, let me say to you: Turn your enemies over to God. "Dearly beloved, avenge not yourselves, but rather give place unto wrath: for it is written, Vengeance is mine; I will repay, saith the Lord" (Rom. 12:19). Turn over those who would betray you to the Lord. I was a pastor for over forty years, and I feel I can speak about this subject with some experience and knowledge. I have found that the Lord does a better job in dealing with my enemies than I can. He knows just *how* to do it. Cast your burden upon the Lord and He will take care of everything. During the days of the Great Tribulation, Israel will finally turn to the Lord because there will be no place else for them to turn.

But thou, O God, shalt bring them down into the pit of destruction: bloody and deceitful men shall not live out half their days; but I will trust in thee [Ps. 55:23].

What about *you* today? What about me? How are we going to live in the world today? Are we going to hate people and criticize them for what they do to us? Are we going to cry when we are betrayed and wronged? No! Let's start trusting in the Lord. That's the way out.

PSALM 56

***THEME:** David's fear and trust*

This psalm brings us to another delightful cluster of psalms (56–60) known as the michtam psalms. What does *michtam* mean? It speaks of that which is substantial, or enduring, or fixed. *Michtam* literally means "engraven" or "permanent." This word pictures that which is unmoveable, steadfast, stable and enduring. In Psalm 57:7 when David says, "My heart is fixed," that is a *michtam.*

Delitzsch called Psalm 56 "the cheerful courage of a fugitive." You will recall that in Psalm 55 David wished that he had the wings of a dove so that he could fly away and lodge in the wilderness (Ps. 55:6–7); in this psalm his desire is realized. The enemy is outside. However, David is in great danger; the wicked are on every side. But through it all God delivered him. The historical background of this psalm has to do with the Philistines capturing David at Gath. David's experience is a picture of the Great Tribulation period. All of these psalms have a prophetic undertone. Between the historical (David's experiences) and the prophetical (Israel's experience in the future), is a real message for us today. All of the Psalms have a message for our own hearts.

This psalm is inscribed "To the chief Musician upon Jonathelem-rechokim, Michtam of David, when the Philistines took him in Gath."

Be merciful unto me, O God: for man would swallow me up; he fighting daily oppresseth me.

Mine enemies would daily swallow me up: for they be many that fight against me, O thou most High [Ps. 56:1–2].

Now let me give you Dr. Gaebelein's translation of these verses—he was a Hebrew scholar. "Be gracious unto me, O God, for man would swallow me up; throughout the day fighting he oppresseth me. They are watching me and would swallow me up the whole day; for many are they that fight against me in pride" (*The Book of Psalms*, p. 232). David is surrounded by the enemy. He seems to be on a hot seat. What is he going to do in a bad spot like this?

What time I am afraid, I will trust in thee [Ps. 56:3].

Was David afraid? He certainly was. A couple heard me make the statement that when I travel by plane I do not enjoy the trip because there is fear in my heart. They thought there was something wrong with my faith in God. My friend, fear will bring out *faith* in your life. Listen to David, "What time I am afraid, I will trust in thee." These people who sit back comfortably and say, "I haven't any fear," may mean that they are insensitive to the circumstances and problems that really exist. Or they may have a foolish sort of faith. David admitted he was afraid, but he *trusted* the Lord to take care of him.

Can you have fear and faith at the same time? The Scripture says, "There is no fear in love; but perfect love casteth out fear: because fear hath torment. He that feareth is not made perfect in love" (1 John 4:18). Perfect love casts out fear. *Love* will do it. But you can have faith and still be afraid. I hope this will comfort some folks, because there are many foolish things being said which are not scriptural.

Thou tellest my wanderings: put thou my tears into thy bottle: are they not in thy book? [Ps. 56:8].

"The Lord counts my wanderings." The Lord knows about every trip you take and about every trip I take. I have thought about this many times while I have been studying the Psalms. Since I have been retired, I have gone from place to place for speaking engagements. Sometimes I ask my wife, "What did I speak about when we were in a certain place in Florida, or when we were in Texas, Washington, or the Hawaiian Islands?" I had forgotten, but the Lord has written all of that down. If I just had access to His book, it would be a great help.

"My tears have been put into thy bottle." A note in *The New Scofield Bible* concerning this subject says, "Sometimes, in olden days in the East, mourners would catch their tears in bottles (water skins) and place them at the tombs of their loved ones"—to show how much they had grieved. Let me add to that something John Bunyan, the tinker of Bedford, said, "God preserves our tears in a bottle, so that He can wipe them away." When I read that, I wished I had cried more. We need to weep more. Matthew Henry said, "The tears of God's persecuted people are bottled up, and sealed among God's treasures."

In God will I praise his word: in the LORD will I praise his word [Ps. 56:10].

Someone wrote to me and said, "You make too much of the Bible. You are everlastingly talking about the Word of God." That is what David did also. There are so few people who are praising His Word that I am going to try to make up for them.

In God have I put my trust: I will not be afraid what man can do unto me [Ps. 56:11].

How wonderful it is to have a resource and a recourse to God.

For thou hast delivered my soul from death: wilt not thou deliver my feet from falling, that I may walk before God in the light of the living? [Ps. 56:13].

David said, especially after his great sin, "I want to walk before God so that I won't slip up again." As far as the record is concerned, he did not slip up again, either. The king of Babylon committed that kind of sin every day of the year; it was commonplace for him. But it was not the practice of David. He said, "I want to walk before God." Today we are enjoined to walk in the Holy Spirit. ". . . Walk in the Spirit, and ye shall not fulfil the lust of the flesh" (Gal. 5:16). God has given us more than a walking stick. He has given us the indwelling Holy Spirit. To walk in the Spirit means to utterly and absolutely depend on the

Spirit of God. This gets right down to where the rubber meets the road. As we will see in our study of Galatians, we are to get down from our highchairs and start walking. We learn to walk in the Spirit as we learned to walk physically, by trying it. Of course we will fail time and time again, but we are to get up, dust ourselves off, and start out again. You will learn to walk in the Spirit if you *keep at* it and commit yourself to Him every day.

PSALM 57

THEME: *A cry for mercy*

This is the second michtam psalm, and it has an added title—*Al-taschith*, meaning "destroy not." As we get into this psalm we will see that it has real meaning. It is inscribed "To the chief Musician, Al-taschith, Michtam of David, when he fled from Saul in the cave."

David spent time in the caves along the Dead Sea by Engedi. It is below sea level and a hot spot during the summer; in the winter it is a delightful place. It is rugged country. The cave of Adullam is in that area also. It is the belief of many expositors that this psalm has reference to that cave of Adullam where David meditated on many of the psalms that he composed. In them we see that his sufferings foreshadowed the sufferings of Christ and those of the godly remnant during the time of Jacob's trouble. Also these psalms speak to us today, which is the wonder of the Word of God.

Be merciful unto me, O God, be merciful unto me: for my soul trusteth in thee: yea, in the shadow of thy wings will I make my refuge, until these calamities be overpast [Ps. 57:1].

I don't know about you, but my prayer is the same as David's, "O God, be merciful to me." I want God to be merciful to me. I don't want Him to be just with me and righteous. If He is, I am going to get a whipping. I want Him to be merciful and gracious to me. He is that kind of a God—rich in mercy. He has enough for me—and I am going to require a lot of it—but there will be enough for you also.

"In the shadow of thy wings will I make my refuge"—or as Dr. Gaebelein has it, "in the shadow of Thy wings will I find shelter." David experienced this shelter. The nation of Israel did not, however. In Matthew 23:37 the Lord Jesus said, "O Jerusalem, Jerusalem, thou that killest the prophets, and stonest them which are sent unto thee, how often would I have gathered thy children together, even as a hen gathereth her chickens under her wings, and ye would not!" Israel has not as yet come under His wings. Are you ready to come under His wings? In other words, be obedient to Him, to love Him—Jesus said, "If ye love me, keep my commandments" (John 14:15)—and to walk in the Spirit?

Now notice these wonderful statements:

He shall send from heaven, and save me from the reproach of him that would swallow me up. Selah. God shall send forth his mercy and his truth [Ps. 57:3].

This will be literally fulfilled for the faithful remnant when Christ returns in power and great glory; and they will say, ". . . Lo, this is our God; we have waited for him, and he will save us: this is the LORD; we have waited for him, we will be glad and rejoice in his salvation" (Isa. 25:9).

My soul is among lions: and I lie even among them that are set on fire, even the sons of men, whose teeth are spears and arrows, and their tongue a sharp sword [Ps. 57:4].

Satan goes up and down this world like a roaring lion seeking whom he may devour (1 Pet. 5:8), and he has a lot of little lions helping him, by the way.

Remember that these michtam psalms have to do with that which is permanent and enduring, that which is substantial and lasting.

My heart is fixed, O God, my heart is fixed: I will sing and give praise [Ps. 57:7].

Then notice this beautiful expression:

Awake up, my glory; awake, psaltery and harp: I myself will awake early [Ps. 57:8].

"I will wake the morning dawn" is Dr. Gaebelein's translation. What a beautiful expression! The night of sin and suffering is over.

Satan's rule is finished, and the morning has come. The Sun of Righteousness has risen with healing in His wings. How wonderful! What assurance we find in this psalm.

PSALM 58

***THEME:** An imprecatory prayer against the enemy*

Notice that this is another *al-taschith* as well as another michtam psalm. It means that there is something substantial and enduring here, and it means "destroy not."

Now it begins with a question, and who is asking it? I believe it is God who is speaking, using the pen of David.

> **Do ye indeed speak righteousness, O congregation? do ye judge uprightly, O ye sons of men [Ps. 58:1].**

Or, as Dr. Gaebelein translates it: "Is righteousness indeed silent? Do ye judges speak it? Do ye with uprightness judge the children of men?"

The day is going to come when the Lord is going to call on the judges to turn in their report. God is asking, "Is righteousness indeed silent? Do ye judges speak it?" They will have to answer these questions.

This is another imprecatory prayer. David's enemies are all around him.

> **The wicked are estranged from the womb: they go astray as soon as they be born, speaking lies.**
>
> **Their poison is like the poison of a serpent: they are like the deaf adder that stoppeth her ear;**
>
> **Which will not hearken to the voice of charmers, charming never so wisely.**
>
> **Break their teeth, O God, in their mouth: break out the great teeth of the young lions, O LORD [Ps. 58:3–6].**

David prays for six destructions to come upon his enemies in this psalm: (1) "Break out the great teeth of the young lions." We have already found that the enemy is like a lion. There are those who say that a Christian cannot pray this way. I have prayed that the Lord would absolutely deal with Satan. He is like a roaring lion, and I hope God breaks his teeth. I don't consider that unchristian at all. David is speaking of his enemies, and he is under law; so he is asking for justice.

Now he uses another figure of speech:

> **Let them melt away as waters which run continually: when he bendeth his bow to shoot his arrows, let them be as cut in pieces [Ps. 58:7].**

(2) Wickedness was like a flood! He asks that this flood of wickedness might just melt away. (3) "When he bendeth his bow to shoot his arrows, let them be as cut in pieces." The enemy is like a marksman who is shooting at him. What a picture we have here!

> **As a snail which melteth, let every one of them pass away: like the untimely birth of a woman, that they may not see the sun [Ps. 58:8].**

(4) "As a snail which melteth, let every one of them pass away." There is a certain snail in that country called a "slimeworm" which actually melts away in the heat of the sun. David is saying, "The enemy leaves a slimy trail, but evaporate him! Get rid of that slimy trail through the world." (5) "Like the untimely birth of a woman, that they may not see the sun." That is, may they not come to fruition in the things they plan in the evil womb of their mind. May it come to nought.

> **Before your pots can feel the thorns, he shall take them away as with a whirlwind, both living, and in his wrath [Ps. 58:9].**

(6) "Before your pots can feel the thorns, he shall take them away"—the twigs of the bramble bush are gathered together and put under the pot to heat it, then a wind comes along and blows them away. David says, "Oh, God, remove them before they can do their dirty work, before they can burn and sear."

This is a tremendous prayer.

PSALMS 59–60

THEME: *God's people surrounded by enemies*

Psalm 59 is closely linked with the two preceding psalms. It is also an *al-taschith* ("destroy not") and a michtam of David. Again in this psalm we see David surrounded by his enemies, and prophetically it describes the suffering remnant during the Tribulation, surrounded by enemies.

The inspired title of this psalm places it at the time Saul sent messengers, and they watched the house to kill David. The historical record is found in 1 Samuel 19.

> **Deliver me from mine enemies, O my God: defend me from them that rise up against me.**
>
> **Deliver me from the workers of iniquity, and save me from bloody men.**
>
> **For, lo, they lie in wait for my soul: the mighty are gathered against me; not for my transgression, nor for my sin, O LORD [Ps. 59:1–3].**

As is typical with David's psalms, it concludes with an expression of faith and trust in God's deliverance.

> **But I will sing of thy power; yea, I will sing aloud of thy mercy in the morning: for thou hast been my defence and refuge in the day of my trouble.**
>
> **Unto thee, O my strength, will I sing: for God is my defence, and the God of my mercy [Ps. 59:16–17].**

In the case of David, God did deliver him. My friend, God will not forsake those who are His own. The believing remnant of Israel will be delivered by the coming of Christ Himself, and He will judge the nations of the world.

Psalm 60 is the last of these michtam psalms and describes the time David was victorious over his enemies, the Edomites. The Edomites were soundly defeated and never rallied after that.

Prophetically it is the picture of the deliverance God will give to His people, the remnant of Israel, after the suffering of the Great Tribulation.

> **O God, thou hast cast us off, thou hast scattered us, thou hast been displeased; O turn thyself to us again [Ps. 60:1].**

Now here is the answer:

> **God hath spoken in his holiness; I will rejoice, I will divide Shechem, and mete out the valley of Succoth [Ps. 60:6].**

And how will it be accomplished?

> **Who will bring me into the strong city? who will lead me into Edom? [Ps. 60:9].**

"Who will bring me into the strong [or the fortified] city?" That is the question; now notice the answer:

> **Wilt not thou, O God, which hadst cast us off? and thou, O God, which didst not go out with our armies? [Ps. 60:10].**

God will restore His saints. In any age He will restore them—though they be in trouble and difficulty and even sin. My, isn't God good!

PSALM 61

THEME: *Cry and confidence of the godly*

The theme throughout this new cluster of psalms (61–68) is the cry and confidence of the godly. As you listen to the pleadings of the godly in these eight psalms, you will find beautifully described their steadfast confidence in the Lord. You will also see the Lord Jesus Christ in these psalms, as well as derive great help for yourself. Psalm 61 is "To the chief Musician upon Neginah, A Psalm of David." This is a psalm that you can play with a stringed instrument and would be appropriate for a guitar, because of the mournful undertone. It is a prayer from David's heart. This makes it different from the modern prayers we so often hear, which make our prayer meetings so stereotyped. All many of us do is turn in to the Lord a grocery list of the things we want. We ask Him to take them down off the shelf and give them to us so we won't have to go through the checkout stand

and pay for them. I think that attitude has killed prayer today. I believe in the organization, the mechanics, and the arrangement of prayer, but I also believe prayer should come from the *heart*. You seldom hear that deep heart cry in prayer any more, but you will find it in David's prayer.

Hear my cry, O God; attend unto my prayer.

From the end of the earth will I cry unto thee, when my heart is overwhelmed: lead me to the rock that is higher than I [Ps. 61:1–2].

David says, "From the end of the earth will I call upon Thee." When you pray, have you ever felt that God is way up in the heavens and you are way down here? David feels that he is at the end of the earth and God is way off yonder. He is trying to get closer. He wants to get to a Rock that is higher than he is. The reason I am opposed to this modern viewpoint of prayer is because the Jesus who is presented is not a superstar at all. He is just a man like I am. He is a rock that is no higher than I am. I need to be led to the Rock that is higher than I. The Word of God tells me that that Rock is Jesus Christ (1 Cor. 10:4), and He is a lot higher than I am! What a picture we have here of the Lord!

For thou hast been a shelter for me, and a strong tower from the enemy [Ps. 61:3].

What a comforting picture of God! He is a *shelter* from storms. He is a *strong tower* to protect us from our enemies.

I will abide in thy tabernacle for ever: I will trust in the covert of thy wings. Selah [Ps. 61:4].

Once again the word *wings* is mentioned in connection with God. The Lord Jesus also used this illustration when He spoke of gathering Jerusalem to Himself as a mother hen gathers her little ones under her wings to protect them.

For thou, O God, hast heard my vows: thou hast given me the heritage of those that fear thy name [Ps. 61:5].

David made vows; he promised God something. We *ask* things of God. Did you ever promise Him anything? (I have promised more than I have delivered, I know that.) You go to God continually and ask Him for something. Why don't you promise to do something for Him? David did, and God heard his vow.

Thou wilt prolong the king's life: and his years as many generations.

He shall abide before God for ever: O prepare mercy and truth, which may preserve him [Ps. 61:6–7].

Here he goes again asking for mercy. David needed the mercy of God. I believe that the closer we get to God, the more we realize that we can't bring Him down to our level, but we will see Him high and lifted up. Then we will be in the same position as Isaiah was when he had a vision of the Lord sitting upon His throne. We will recognize our uncleanness and our need of His mercy.

So will I sing praise unto thy name for ever, that I may daily perform my vows [Ps. 61:8].

Make your vows and then get close to God. Sing His praises, and He will help you fulfill your vows.

PSALM 62

***THEME:** The only psalm*

This is called the "only" psalm, not because there are no others—there are 149 others—but because the word *only* is significant. "Truly [better translated *only*] my soul waiteth upon God . . . He *only* is my rock and my salvation . . . they *only* consult to cast him down . . . wait thou *only* upon God . . . He *only* is my rock."

The superscription here is "To the chief Musician, to Jeduthun, A Psalm of David." Psalm 39 was also written to Jeduthun. He was one of the chief musicians. His name is mentioned several times in the Psalms. Apparently he led the orchestra and the choir when this psalm was used.

This is a simple psalm. It is one of simple faith. It reveals a faith and confidence in God that is akin to a child's faith in his parents.

Perowne gives us a wonderful statement concerning this psalm: "Scarcely anywhere do we find faith in God more nobly asserted, more victoriously triumphant; the vanity of man, of human strength and riches, more clearly confessed; courage in the midst of peril more calm and more unshaken, than in this Psalm, which is as forcible in its conception, and its language, as it is remarkable for the vigorous and cheerful piety it breathes" (*The Book of Psalms*, Vol. I, p. 442).

Although the inspired text does not give us this information, tradition tells us that this psalm came from the greatest heartbreak of David's life—the rebellion led by his son Absalom.

We turn to the historical record, and read this language: "And David went up by the ascent of mount Olivet, and wept as he went up, and had his head covered, and he went barefoot: and all the people that was with him covered every man his head, and they went up, weeping as they went up" (2 Sam. 15:30). That was a tragic time in the life of David. It was his dramatic moment, his time of crisis. Thomas Paine spoke of times that try men's souls. This time had come to the old king.

Absalom, David's son, is marching into Jerusalem. His entry is forcing a time of decision. There are some who are choosing David; others are choosing Absalom. It is a time when David has found who are the loyal and disloyal in the ranks. The betrayers and followers are well-marked. An important man is Ahithophel (related by marriage through Bathsheba to David), an astute statesman, a man of sagacity, of wonderful ability, a counselor upon whom David had leaned. Ahithophel has deserted and gone over to Absalom. It was a great grief to David when he found that this trusted man had deserted him. Then Ziba, the servant of Mephibosheth, came and said that his master, the son of Jonathan, whom David had befriended, had also betrayed him.

As David fled from the city, barefoot and weeping, there stood Shimei, a Benjamite, still loyal to former King Saul. From a heart of bitter hatred for David, he threw stones and heaped cursings upon the old king as he fled.

We see Absalom entering Jerusalem in triumph, and the same crowd that once shouted to the rafters for David is now shouting deliriously for Absalom. Centuries later the children of these people were the ones who shouted "Hosanna" to the Lord Jesus Christ, and shortly after cried, "Crucify him." David knew the sting of the voice of the mob, and Psalm 62 is the song of David in that hour of ignominy.

Here we find a man who has committed his way to God, one who is traveling in the spiritual stratosphere; a man who is living above the storms, shocks, and stresses of this life. And as we read this psalm which comes from his heart in this hour of darkness, this time of testing, this hour of defeat, we are amazed to find not one note of discouragement, nor suggestion of fear, nor word of distress. There is neither rancor nor bitterness welling up in the heart of the psalmist. He sings forth a song of salvation, a paean of praise, an opus of optimism. It is a song of sanguinity, a thesis of trust, and a work of wonder. How could David write such a Hallelujah chorus out of an experience so dark?

THE TEST OF FAITH

Truly my soul waiteth upon God: from him cometh my salvation [Ps. 62:1].

No doubt there were those around David—fanatics of those days—who urged that he stand his ground and thereby exhibit his faith, for he was God's anointed and God should overrule this whole matter. Not David! He said that his life was in God's hands, and it seemed best that he leave. David lived above the hue and cry of little men. He did not listen to pious shibboleths, for while little men cried for a miracle David avowed to walk in the dark, trusting God. O for a faith like that! A God-given faith! What others called defeat, to David was but a test of faith. David can retreat from Jerusalem and it is still going to sound like a victory.

He only is my rock and my salvation; he is my defence; I shall not be greatly moved [Ps. 62:2].

Zadok, the high priest, is come out to go with David. He is faithful and has brought the ark, a symbol to the Israelites of God's presence in their midst, and he is following David when the old king turns and, seeing the ark, commands Zadok to carry it back to the city, for ". . . if I shall find favour in the eyes of the LORD, he will bring me again, and shew me both it, and his habitation: But if he thus say, I have no delight in thee; behold, here am I, let him do to me as seemeth good unto him" (2 Sam. 15:25–26).

If I can but make this great truth clear so that it will live for you! Here is a man so wholly committed to God that he turns aside from any thought of merit in the ark, clinging only unto God and saying to Zadok that if it is God's will for him to come back to this city, he will be allowed to come back; if not, then he is in God's hands. He refuses to attempt to force God to do anything but determines to go the way God leads, regardless of the path. O, to live like that today!

How long will ye imagine mischief against a man? ye shall be slain all of you: as a bowing wall shall ye be, and as a tottering fence [Ps. 62:3].

David tells them that they are just running over him "as a bowing wall . . . and as a tottering fence." He says, "How long will ye imagine mischief against a man? ye shall be slain all of you." Here he is thinking of Ziba, servant of Mephibosheth, who did a dastardly thing, thinking he would gain favor with David. He said his master had deserted, which was not true.

Then he thinks of Ahithophel, his best friend and wisest of his counselors. Ahithophel went over to the other side in David's darkest hour. Here in this psalm David is speaking of Ahithophel prophetically as Judas Iscariot. Ahithophel was in the inner circle and was the man that David leaned upon.

David says that they are running over him as a mob runs over a fence, but he says it is all right if it is God's will.

They only consult to cast him down from his excellency: they delight in lies: they bless with their mouth, but they curse inwardly. Selah [Ps. 62:4].

Let us understand David's action under the bitter attack of Shimei. While David was on the throne, Shimei bowed like the rest of them; but, when he was free to express his heart of hatred, we find him cursing David and hurling rocks after him as he fled from Jerusalem. David had a loyal captain by the name of Abishai, a son of Zeruiah, who said to the king, ". . . Why should this dead dog curse my lord the king? let me go over, I pray thee, and take off his head" (2 Sam. 16:9).

My friend, if you want an example of what the Scripture means by ". . . Vengeance is mine; I will repay, saith the Lord" (Rom. 12:19), listen to David as he replies to his captain: "And the king said . . . so let him curse, because the LORD hath said unto him, Curse David. Who shall then say, Wherefore hast thou done so?" (2 Sam. 16:10). In other words, David tells him "God has permitted him to curse me; you let him curse me." Have you ever stopped to think, my friend, that God has given you certain enemies for a definite purpose to test you that you might become a better Christian? Do not become alarmed at the presence of enemies and difficulties that God has permitted to cumber your path. He is not bearing hard on you. Would that we would trust God to the extent that we would not cry out at a time like that!

THE TIME OF FAITH

When is the time of faith? Is it on a sunshiny day when there is not a cloud in your sky? Is it a time when everything is going exactly right, with nothing to mar your outlook? David's answer is that the best time to trust God is at the crisis moment of your life—

My soul, wait thou only upon God; for my expectation is from him [Ps. 62:5].

This is a Bible definition of prayer.

I once had a little card sent to me bearing a message that seemed rather important, so I kept it. Here it is: "True prayer is the Holy Spirit speaking in the believer, through the Son, to the Father." That is prayer; it is real prayer. "My expectation is from him." David is saying here that he is not making some wild prayer, some audacious statement, that he is not demanding that God do anything—"My expectation is from him." David is expecting God to put into his heart the thing that He wants done; therefore, he will be praying for the thing that is best.

We wonder again if some pious person around David might not have suggested to him that he was in such a tight place that they should have a prayer meeting. To this David would have said to them that his whole life was a life of prayer, "My expectation is from him." Here is the illustration that Paul had in mind when he said, "Pray without ceasing" (1 Thess. 5:17). Now by this Paul did not mean that you are to get on your knees and remain there twenty-four hours a day. But Paul did mean for you to get on your knees and pray and then live in the expectation of that prayer for twenty-four hours every day. So David is not going to call a prayer meeting. In fact, the amazing thing is that this psalm has no prayer in it at all. But we find that the entire psalm is in the atmosphere of prayer. He is a man so committed to God that his life and actions are that of prayer.

Now we see this old king going out of Jerusalem; we hear him weeping. But these exterior things fade away when we glimpse the depths of his heart, for he is a man who is committed to God and he will go with God regardless of what the outcome might be. Other men would have become bitter, but not David. He is saying something here that is tremendous: "My soul, wait thou *only* upon God; . . . my expectation is from him."

He only is my rock and my salvation: he is my defence; I shall not be moved [Ps. 62:6].

That is the central truth of the psalm. That is the central truth of David's life. That is the dynamo that ran his life. That is the thing that caused him to stand head and shoulders above other men on the horizon of history. It has caused him to cast a long shadow down the corridor of time. "He *only* is my rock."

When we come to the New Testament, we can see what the Lord Jesus means when He says this tremendous thing: "And whosoever shall fall on this stone shall be broken: but on whomsoever it shall fall, it will grind him to powder" (Matt. 21:44). Christ is that Rock, that Stone. There is coming a day when the Stone cut out without hands will fall on this earth. Today, you and I can fall on this Stone, and those who fall on it will be saved.

A little Scottish woman got up in a testimony meeting and gave this as her testimony: "You know, sometimes I tremmel [tremble] on the rock, but the rock never tremmels under me." Are you on this Rock? Whosoever falls on this Rock shall be saved. This is what Paul meant when he said, "For other foundation can no man lay than that is laid, which is Jesus Christ" (1 Cor. 3:11). David said, "He *only* is my rock. He is the One I am trusting. O, the throne is toppling, Jerusalem is in convulsions, the people have turned against me, but I am on the Rock!" David has learned that glorious lesson.

In God is my salvation and my glory: the rock of my strength, and my refuge, is in God.

Trust in him at all times; ye people, pour out your heart before him: God is a refuge for us. Selah [Ps. 62:7–8].

This is a very personal psalm. Notice that God is "*my* salvation . . . *my* glory . . . *my* strength . . . *my* refuge."

THE TRIUMPH OF FAITH

Surely men of low degree are vanity, and men of high degree are a lie: to be laid in the balance, they are altogether lighter than vanity [Ps. 62:9].

He has learned that one cannot trust the mob, for they are fickle. He has found that men of high degree, such as Ahithophel, are not to be trusted. They cannot be leaned upon. And this is the first thing that a new Christian must learn—not to look to men but to God. Many new Christians have become discouraged, disappointed, and disillusioned, for they have their eyes set upon a man. A young Christian told me recently that he had gotten his eyes on a man, and it had all but made shipwreck of his faith. David knew all of the time that he could not trust men, so his faith was fixed utterly upon God. He rested upon a Rock that could not be moved.

Then he tells us that we cannot trust in material things either:

Trust not in oppression, and become not vain in robbery: if riches increase, set not your heart upon them [Ps. 62:10].

And now hear the conclusion: Why is it that you can trust God?

God hath spoken once; twice have I heard this; that power belongeth unto God [Ps. 62:11].

Friend, you can trust God because He can do anything that requires power. He has all power, and He can do anything He wants to do! Power did not reside in David. He was simply a great king because God made of him a great king. Now He has permitted men to force him to leave Jerusalem; and, if it is not God's will that he return, then he will not go back. But he is resigning all to God for He alone is the One who has *all power*.

The mad rush to gain power is the destroying element in the world at this hour. In the effort to gain power, the bomb has been created. This form of power wreaks destruction. It is man's effort at power. But David says he has discovered that with real power there is another element that goes with it always:

Also unto thee, O Lord, belongeth mercy: for thou renderest to every man according to his work [Ps. 62:12].

If you have power, you ought to be able to exercise mercy. David is saying that his God who can exercise power is a God who can also exercise mercy. To Zadok he said that he wanted him to take back the mercy seat and place it in the temple, for he would find mercy with God.

At the very heart of Old Testament religion was the mercy seat. At the heart of the Christian faith today is mercy. "Come every soul by sin oppressed, there's mercy with the Lord." I think that is what Brother George Bennard meant when he wrote: "I'll cling to the old rugged cross." Mercy!

Friend, let me make a suggestion. This psalm simply states this precious relationship with God. David just pours out his heart to God. He talks to God and tells Him, "You are *my* salvation; You are *my* rock." So many people get uptight in a prayer meeting or in a church service. They feel oppression in prayer—they want to say the right things and use the right words. Public prayer is all right, but let me suggest that you go aside and be alone with God. Perhaps you can drive along in your car, or maybe you can find a good quiet corner in a room in your home. Find a place where you can be quiet before God. Then "take the lid off." There is a time to "gird up your loins," and there is a time to take off your girdle and just let yourself go before God. When I was in Pasadena, a ladies' group put a shaggy rug in my study. It was the first shaggy rug I ever had, and I liked it very much. I used to get down on that rug, on my face before God, and pour my heart out to Him. It did me good, and it will do you good. It is the best tonic you could have.

PSALM 63

***THEME:** Thirst for the Water of Life*

This is "A Psalm of David, when he was in the wilderness of Judah." This is a special psalm. It is an ointment that is poured out upon all kinds of sores. It is a bandage for bruises. It is a balm to put upon wounds to help them heal. It has been a marvelous psalm for the church. It speaks of the thirst for the Water of Life. Chrysostom said that it was ordained and agreed upon by the primitive fathers that no day should pass without the public singing of this psalm, and in the primitive church this psalm was sung every morning or every time there was a public gathering. They always began the morning service with it.

This psalm is the expression of wonderful thoughts.

O God, thou art my God; early will I seek thee: my soul thirsteth for thee, my flesh longeth for thee in a dry and thirsty land, where no water is;

To see thy power and thy glory, so as I have seen thee in the sanctuary [Ps. 63:1–2].

These two verses were translated by Dr. Gaebelein thus: "O God, Thou art my God; early do I seek Thee; my soul thirsteth for Thee, my flesh pineth for Thee, in a dry, thirsty land without water; as I gazed upon Thee in the Sanctuary, to see Thy power and glory" (*The Book of Psalms*, p. 251). It is faith, and faith alone, that can speak like this. God, the Eternal One, transcends all human thinking. He is the Creator. He is the Redeemer. He is my Father. It was He whom David sought. He knew what it was to be thirsty. He had hidden in caves down by the Dead Sea, and it is some of the driest land I have ever seen. California, Arizona, and New Mexico haven't anything that can touch that dry land around Engedi. It is a place where you can get thirsty! If you are ever over there, make sure that you have water with you. David's soul thirsted for God. Do you feel that way about Him? Do you have a love for Him, or has He become a burden to you? Oh, that we might thirst for Him!

Thus will I bless thee while I live: I will lift up my hands in thy name.

My soul shall be satisfied as with marrow and fatness; and my mouth shall praise thee with joyful lips [Ps. 63:4–5].

David is saying that he would rather have fellowship with God than have a gourmet dinner.

When I remember thee upon my bed, and meditate on thee in the night watches.

Because thou hast been my help, therefore in the shadow of thy wings will I rejoice [Ps. 63:6–7].

David thought about God—meditated upon Him—during the night when he couldn't sleep. My friend, meditating upon God's goodness is a lot better than counting sheep!

My soul followeth hard after thee: thy right hand upholdeth me [Ps. 63:8].

Oh, that *our* souls might follow hard after Him!

This is a great psalm. Remember, it is the psalm of the morning and was sung at every service of the early church. Maybe we can't sing it in our day—I don't know.

PSALM 64

THEME: *The evil may win, but God will judge them*

This psalm also has a historical background in the life of David, although we can't locate it exactly. Prophetically, it looks yonder in the future to the day when Israel will be in Great Tribulation and the godly remnant will use this psalm. Someone might say, "My, there certainly are a lot of psalms for the Day of Jacob's Trouble." Yes, there are, and the people are going to need every one of them. Also, this is a very fine psalm for you and me.

Hear my voice, O God, in my prayer: preserve my life from fear of the enemy.

Hide me from the secret counsel of the wicked; from the insurrection of the workers of iniquity [Ps. 64:1–2].

Once again, David is asking God to hide him. David prayed this kind of a prayer time and time again. His refuge was prayer. It was the only refuge he had. Prayer is the only refuge Israel will have in that day of tribulation.

This brief psalm concludes with David expressing his confidence in God. His God was his only hope.

But God shall shoot at them with an arrow; suddenly shall they be wounded.

So they shall make their own tongue to fall upon themselves: all that see them shall flee away.

And all men shall fear, and shall declare the work of God; for they shall wisely consider of his doing.

The righteous shall be glad in the LORD, and shall trust in him; and all the upright in heart shall glory [Ps. 64:7–10].

As I look at the world today, I have come to the conclusion that our hope is no longer in statesmen or politicians; our hope is no longer in science or education—they are all more or less failures. We are going to have to do what David did and what Israel will do in the future—start looking up. God is our only hope today.

PSALMS 65–66

THEME: *Songs of the Millennium*

"To the chief Musician, A Psalm and Song of David." It is known as a restoration psalm—". . . of restitution of all things, which God hath spoken by the mouth of all his holy prophets since the world began" (Acts 3:21). The "restitution of all things" does *not* mean that everyone is going to be saved. Those who hold the doctrine of restitutionalism use this verse to support their theory. Exactly what are the "all things" which are to be the subject of restitution? In Philippians 3:8 when Paul said, ". . . I count all things but loss . . ." did he mean all things in God's universe? Obviously not. So here, the "all things" are limited by what follows. "The times of restitution of all things, which God hath spoken by the mouth of all his holy prophets since the world began." The prophets had spoken of the restoration of Israel. Nowhere is there a prophecy of the conversion and restoration of the wicked dead.

Praise waiteth for thee, O God, in Sion: and unto thee shall the vow be performed [Ps. 65:1].

Sion is the same as Zion, and this verse is not speaking about a heavenly Zion. It is a geographical spot down here on earth. I have been to that place. I saw the sign that pointed the way to Mount Zion, and I went up there. And I didn't go to heaven that day, I assure you of that. It is a long hard pull up that elevation. When David speaks of Sion, he means that place.

Blessed is the man whom thou choosest, and causest to approach unto thee, that he may dwell in thy courts: we shall be satisfied with the goodness of thy house, even of thy holy temple [Ps. 65:4].

As a redeemed people, they express their happiness.

Thou visitest the earth, and waterest it: thou greatly enrichest it with the river of God, which is full of water: thou preparest them corn, when thou hast so provided for it.

Thou waterest the ridges thereof abundantly: thou settlest the furrows thereof: thou makest it soft with showers: thou blessest the springing thereof.

Thou crownest the year with thy goodness; and thy paths drop fatness.

They drop upon the pastures of the wilderness: and the little hills rejoice on every side.

The pastures are clothed with flocks; the valleys also are covered over with corn; they shout for joy, they also sing [Ps. 65:9–13].

Everything sings! This is a beautiful picture of the Millennium, when the desert blossoms like the rose and the earth at last is at peace.

Psalm 66 is "To the chief Musician, A Song or Psalm." Did David write it? We are not told, but he could have. We are not given any historical background for it at all, but many have guessed at what prompted its writing. It is a psalm of praise unto God and a wonderful psalm of worship.

O bless our God, ye people, and make the voice of his praise to be heard [Ps. 66:8].

This verse looks forward to that day in the future when Israel will be restored to the land. Ezekiel tells us that in that day they will offer sacrifices. What is the explanation of it? Just as they offered sacrifices in the Old Testament that pictured the *coming* of Christ, in the future they will offer sacrifices that will look *back* to Christ's coming. Every lamb will point to ". . . the Lamb of God which taketh away the sin of the world" (John 1:29).

PSALM 67

***THEME:** Blessing and praise for the Millennium*

This is one of the shortest prophetic psalms. It has only seven stanzas. Now I believe that numbers in Scripture have a meaning, but I also think you can go to seed in that direction. Seven seems to be not so much the number of perfection as the number of completeness; and, in a sense, when something is complete, perfection is always implied.

This psalm reveals the ultimate and final desire and purpose of God for this earth. It is a great psalm of the kingdom. It has been labeled by some (*The Expositor's Bible*, for example) as a missionary psalm. They give as its theme the outmoded, postmillennial interpretation of the church converting the world. Well, this is not a missionary psalm as such. Actually, the church is not in view at all. I do not believe we see the church in the Psalms except as a figure of speech or in a symbol. For example, we noted in Psalm 45 the church as ". . . the queen in gold of Ophir." This is a picture of the church with the Lord Jesus when He reigns on earth. Psalm 67 is a *prophetic* psalm. It looks beyond this age to the kingdom age. During the millennial kingdom you will see a converted world, a renovated world, a world in which God shall bless us, and all the ends of the earth shall fear Him. The curse will be removed and we will be able to sing songs of praise—even I will be able to sing the Hallelujah Chorus.

Now there is a difference between interpretation and application of Scripture. I am afraid that in wanting to be esoteric and intellectual, many theologians and Bible teachers have forgotten one of the simplest rules for the understanding of Scripture. And the simple rule is this: All Scripture is *for* us, but not all Scripture is *to* us. This psalm is *for* us, and not *to* us; and it gives us the perspective of missions. Now someone is going to say, "How can you possibly get missions into a psalm that looks beyond the church?" A great principle of hermeneutics (the science of interpretation) points out the difference between interpretation and application. *Interpretation* is definitive; it is like a mold—it is basic. That is, Scripture means *one* thing. It does not mean everything under the sun that you want it to mean. But there can also be an *application*, and the application may be elastic, although it must rest upon the interpretation if it is going to be accurate.

I can illustrate this in a simple way. A diamond, to be of practical value, must be cut, mounted in a proper setting, and worn on any finger it fits. Several years ago I was in Washington, D.C., for the first time. I went to the Smithsonian Institution, and among other things I saw the Hope diamond. I made an interesting observation. Many people were passing by the space exhibit, but everyone stopped to look at the Hope diamond. I suppose that reveals the covetousness in the hearts of all men. However, that diamond could not be worn on any finger, so it's of no practical value. If our country were invaded or some other terrible thing were to happen, I am told that the case in which the diamond rests would sink into a vault somewhere in the basement of that institution. As far as I can see, it is not doing anyone any good. It is of no personal worth at all. It is just a big diamond, ill-starred and ill-fated. To be useful it must be put in a setting. Scripture likewise must be put in a proper setting, which is interpretation. Then it must be placed on the finger of experience, and that is application. There is an old bromide that says, If the shoe fits you, put it on. If you come to one of these psalms and it speaks to your heart (and God can speak to you in all of them), then it has a message to apply to your life. For example, in the Book of Revelation the Lord Jesus spoke to seven churches in Asia. His message had a local interpretation and a local application. He concluded His messages by saying, "Hear!" That word is for the fellow who has ears. If you have ears, He is also talking to you. "He that hath an ear, let him hear what the Spirit saith unto the churches" (Rev. 3:13). There is an application for us in every one of the seven messages to the churches.

Psalm 67 is not a missionary psalm, I repeat, but it does contain some great principles that relate to God's missionary program for you and me.

Let us now summarize several interesting aspects of this psalm. "Bless us" is used three times. "Praise thee" is repeated four times. There are three persons or groups mentioned: (1) God is referred to fifteen times, and the Trinity is there. (2) The nation of Israel, which is the "us," is mentioned six times. (3) The "nations" are mentioned nine times—and that means foreigners, different peoples and races, different strata of society, and you and me.

Notice how this psalm begins.

God be merciful unto us, and bless us; and cause his face to shine upon us; Selah [Ps. 67:1].

This verse is a reference to the Trinity. It is a reference to the great threefold Trinitarian blessing that God gave the nation of Israel when He prepared them for the wilderness march. That blessing is found in Numbers 6:24–26, which says: "The LORD bless thee, and keep thee [refers to the Father]: The LORD make his face shine upon thee, and be gracious unto thee [refers to Jesus]: The LORD lift up his countenance upon thee, and give thee peace [the work of the Holy Spirit]."

As we have noted before, some of the teachers of Israel refer to the "face of God" as the Messiah; and this is the Messiah, that is Jesus, the Christ, God the Son, our Savior. So here we have the threefold blessing of God the Father, God the Son, and God the Holy Spirit. The conclusion to this blessing is found in Numbers 6:27, which says, "And they shall put my name upon the children of Israel; and I will bless them." This Aaronic blessing will be fulfilled in the Millennium.

That thy way may be known upon earth, thy saving health among all nations [Ps 67:2].

There will be no blessing for the earth until Israel is actually back in the land; and I do not mean as they are today, but in that day when the Lord puts them in the land. When that happens, Israel will be able to do what Isaiah speaks about in Isaiah 49:13, "Sing, O heavens; and be joyful, O earth; and break forth into singing, O mountains: for the LORD hath comforted his people, and will have mercy upon his afflicted." Verses 14–16 go on to say, "But Zion said, The LORD hath forsaken me, and my Lord hath forgotten me. Can a woman forget her sucking child, that she should not have compassion on the son of her womb? yea, they may forget, yet will I not forget thee. Behold, I have graven thee upon the palms of my hands; thy walls are continually before me." That is what God says concerning His people Israel. Either God meant what He said, or He did not; and, as far as I'm concerned, He meant it.

Let the people praise thee, O God; let all the people praise thee.

O let the nations be glad and sing for joy: for thou shalt judge the people righteously, and govern the nations upon earth. Selah [Ps. 67:3–4].

This is the marvelous promise God gave to Abraham: I will make you a blessing unto all peoples (Gen. 12:1–3). At His first coming the Lord Jesus made it very clear that salvation was of the Jews. At the Lord's second coming the earth will be converted. The greatest time of salvation, I believe, will be in the future. It is not possible for this passage to come true during this age; not until the Millennium will it come to pass. For Isaiah says, "And I will set a sign among them, and I will send those that escape of them unto the nations, to Tarshish, Pul, and Lud, that draw the bow, to Tubal, and Javan, to the isles afar off, that have not heard my fame, neither have seen my glory; and they shall declare my glory among the Gentiles" (Isa. 66:19). The day is coming when the world will be converted.

Let the people praise thee, O God; let all the people praise thee [Ps. 67:5].

What is the goal of God? Is it that we should get Israel back to the land? It would indeed be foolish just to be interested in getting them back into the land; but it would be no more foolish than to try to convert the whole world, for the church will not bring in the kingdom by preaching, I can assure you of that. Romans 11:25 makes it very clear: "For I would not, brethren, that ye should be ignorant of this mystery, lest ye should be wise in your own conceits; that blindness in part is happened to Israel, until the fulness of the Gentiles be come in." For how long? ". . . Until the fulness of the Gentiles be come in."

Then shall the earth yield her increase; and God, even our own God, shall bless us [Ps. 67:6].

The curse of sin will be removed from the earth, you see.

God shall bless us; and all the ends of the earth shall fear him [Ps. 67:7].

I want to make a comment that I believe is important. Suppose I should ask you, "What is the primary objective and purpose of missions?" What would your answer be? Someone might say, "The purpose of missions is to save souls." My response to that is that to save souls is not the purpose of missions. It is true that missions should result in the saving of souls, but that is not the primary purpose. Someone else might say, "We should preach the gospel to every creature in order that we might obey the command of our Lord Jesus

Christ. Those are our orders. We are to preach the gospel everywhere. We are to get the Word of God out to people around the globe." While this is true, it is not the primary motive of missions. It is close but, honestly, I don't think that is quite it. Let me again quote verses 5 and 7 together: "Let the people praise thee, O God; let all the people praise thee. . . . God shall bless us; and all the ends of the earth shall fear him" (that means reverential trust in God). What is the final goal of missions? "Let all the people praise thee." The chief end of missions is to *glorify God*. That is the engine that is to pull the train of every mission program and of every Christian enterprise. The engine is to glorify God, and that which follows it is this: preach the gospel, get the Word out so people can be saved. The whole purpose is to glorify God. I wonder if we have lost that objective today? It is in the catechism I had to learn: Question: "What is the chief end of man?" Answer: "The chief end of man is to glorify God and to enjoy Him forever." That is the purpose of man on earth. Why do you and I exist? Are we here only "to eat the meat and fish and leave behind an empty dish"? Is that all man is supposed to do? No, man is to glorify God. We glorify Him when we get His Word out. We glorify Him when we preach the gospel. We glorify Him when people are saved. But the *purpose* is to glorify God.

PSALM 68

***THEME:** Song of deliverance that ushers in the kingdom*

Here is a psalm of deliverance and victory. Whereas we saw the kingdom in Psalm 67, here we see the King in His glory and strength.

> **Let God arise, let his enemies be scattered: let them also that hate him flee before him [Ps. 68:1].**

This is a reference to Numbers 10:35. Each day when Israel was ready to begin the wilderness march, Moses would say, ". . . Rise up, LORD, and let thine enemies be scattered; and let them that hate thee flee before thee." What a wonderful way to begin the day's march!

The preceding psalm was a singing psalm, and this is another singing psalm—a song of triumph and glory!

> **Sing unto God, sing praises to his name: extol him that rideth upon the heavens by his name JAH, and rejoice before him [Ps. 68:4].**

"Sing unto God, sing praises to his name"—here, again, we see that man is to glorify Him, and God is moving toward that day when the earth will glorify Him. Men don't glorify God today; they take His name in vain.

> **Though ye have lien among the pots, yet shall ye be as the wings of a dove covered with silver, and her feathers with yellow gold [Ps. 68:13].**

The word *pots* should probably be changed to "sheepfolds." Deborah used that same Hebrew word in her prophetic song: "Why abodest thou among the sheepfolds, to hear the bleatings of the flocks? . . ." (Jud. 5:16). You will see that this was addressed to Reuben, because Reuben did not go out to battle. Evidently in both passages the word is used to describe an indifferent, an inactive, and a selfish condition. In this psalm it seems to have the same meaning—Israel was undecided and inactive. "Yet shall ye be as the wings of a dove"—the dove was a sacrificial bird and is a type of Christ. What a picture this gives us. Though they be negligent, though they are not moved by enthusiasm, yet the sacrifice of Christ will cover them.

This psalm could actually be called the psalm of the Ascension since we have a verse that is quoted in Ephesians 4:8: ". . . When he ascended up on high, he led captivity captive, and gave gifts unto men."

> **Thou hast ascended on high, thou hast led captivity captive: thou hast received gifts for men; yea, for the rebellious also, that the LORD God might dwell among them [Ps. 68:18].**

When the Lord Jesus Christ ascended to heaven after His death, I think He did two things. First, He took with Him to heaven all those saints of the past who were in paradise.

God had saved them on credit up to that time, but our Lord paid the redemptive price for them when He died on the cross. He took them (the spirits of just men made perfect) into the presence of God. Secondly, He gave gifts to men on earth so that today He carries on His work through those to whom He has given those gifts. Every person who is in the body of Christ has a gift—not all have the same gift, of course. As you can see, this is a marvelous verse.

But God shall wound the head of his enemies, and the hairy scalp of such an one as goeth on still in his trespasses.

The Lord said, I will bring again from Bashan, I will bring my people again from the depths of the sea [Ps. 68: 21–22].

These verses speak of a glorious victory for the future. The one referred to as the "hairy scalp" is the Antichrist. In spite of what the Antichrist will try to do, he will fail. God will bring His people from even the depths of the sea. This is Israel's restoration.

There is little Benjamin with their ruler, the princes of Judah and their council, the princes of Zebulun, and the princes of Naphtali [Ps. 68:27].

These verses are talking about the children of Israel. There are those today who believe that Great Britain is the ten lost tribes of Israel. Perhaps they think little Benjamin really refers to Big Ben in London. May I say to you that there are interpretations that are as wild as that today. Little Benjamin simply means the tribe of Benjamin. It does not mean anything else. But notice that little Benjamin has a great God.

O God, thou art terrible out of thy holy places: the God of Israel is he that giveth strength and power unto his people. Blessed be God [Ps. 68:35].

We also are little but have the same great God, and He gives us the strength and power we need. Blessed be God!

PSALM 69

***THEME:** The silent years in the life of Christ*

This is a great messianic psalm. It is another psalm of David, and it is unique because it deals with the silent years in the life of the Lord Jesus. It is also called a shoshannim, or lily, psalm because He is the Lily of the Valley as well as the Rose of Sharon, and He is altogether lovely. Next to Psalm 22 it is the most quoted psalm in the New Testament. Psalm 22 deals with the death of Christ; Psalm 69 deals with the life of Christ. I was drawn to this psalm when I was a student in college, and from that day to this it has been a favorite of mine. Psalm 22 is number one on the Hit Parade of the New Testament as far as quotes go, and Psalm 69 is second on the Hit Parade. It is quoted in the Gospel of John, in Romans, in Matthew, Mark, Luke, and Acts. Very candidly, I think there are many references to it which are not actual quotations. It is classified as an imprecatory psalm because verses 22–28 are what is known as an imprecatory prayer. Yet from that section the New Testament writers often quoted.

This psalm tells us about the silent years of Christ's childhood and young manhood, of which the Gospels tell us practically nothing. Dr. Luke tells us about an incident in the life of our Lord when He was twelve years old, and then we learn nothing else about Him until He is about thirty years old. What about that period of time? This psalm fills in some of the details. We see some of Christ's dark days in Nazareth and His dark hours on the cross. His imprecatory prayer is actually a cry for justice. This is the psalm of His humiliation and rejection. We begin with Him way up north at Nazareth. We hear the heart sob of a little boy, a teenager, a young man:

Save me, O God; for the waters are come in unto my soul [Ps. 69:1].

Notice how He suffered. His physical suffering on the cross was bad enough, but I think some of the things He suffered in His life on earth were almost unbearable. I am confident that multitudes of us would have ended our lives if we had gone through what He did during His lifetime.

But none of the ransomed ever knew
How deep were the waters crossed;
Nor how dark was the night that the Lord passed through
Ere He found His sheep that was lost.
("The Ninety and Nine"
—Elizabeth C. Clephane)

During our Lord's last three hours on the cross He became the Lamb of God that took away the sin of the world. It was then that He was made sin for us. Although He suffered all during His lifetime, as we shall see, there is no salutary or saving value in those sufferings as far as we are concerned. He took the place of humiliation, and He took it voluntarily. The limitation of Christ as a human being was a self-limitation. You and I would like to know more than we now know; we would like to expand our knowledge and our understanding. In contrast to this, when the Lord Jesus became a man, He contracted Himself, He humbled Himself. In this state He cries out:

I sink in deep mire, where there is no standing: I am come into deep waters, where the floods overflow me [Ps. 69:2].

These are the floods of suffering which started when the Lord was born in a stable, which was probably part of an inn. The stable was a better place to be born because no one could see what took place that night except the cows, the oxen, and the sheep. They were better than the leering crowd that filled the inn. But in the stable He began His life in suffering.

Now we go to Nazareth where He was brought up. We are told:

I am weary of my crying: my throat is dried: mine eyes fail while I wait for my God [Ps. 69:3].

During those thirty years there were times when His eyes were red with weeping. The next verse tells us why.

They that hate me without a cause are more than the hairs of mine head: they that would destroy me, being mine enemies wrongfully, are mighty: then I restored that which I took not away [Ps. 69:4].

This verse is quoted in John 15:25, "But this cometh to pass, that the word might be fulfilled that is written in their law, They hated me without a cause." The Lord quoted this verse and applied it to Himself. The enemies of the Lord hated Him without a cause; that is, there was no justification for their hatred. Romans 3:24 says, "Being justified *freely* by his grace through the redemption that is in Christ Jesus." Being justified freely is the same as being justified without a cause; the Lord did not find any merit in me. The Lord didn't say, "That fellow McGee down there is such a nice fellow, I'll justify him." You can be sure He didn't say that! Rather, He said, "He is a poor lost sinner." He justified me without a cause within me. Now this psalm tells us that they hated Jesus without a cause—they hated Him without a cause that I might be justified without a cause. What a wonderful truth this is!

O God, thou knowest my foolishness; and my sins are not hid from thee [Ps. 69:5].

How in the world can this verse apply to the Lord? You must remember that He came to earth as a human being. He was holy, harmless, undefiled, and separate from sinners. But the last few hours on the cross He became sin for us. That was the thing He was resisting in the Garden of Gethsemane. He prayed, "Let this cup pass." What cup? The cup of sin, which was *my* cup and *your* cup of iniquity. The sin that was put upon Him was awful for Him—it comes naturally for us—but because He was holy, His suffering was terrible.

Let not them that wait on thee, O Lord God of hosts, be ashamed for my sake: let not those that seek thee be confounded for my sake, O God of Israel.

Because for thy sake I have borne reproach; shame hath covered my face [Ps. 69:6–7].

There are two reasons He is bearing this: (1) They hated Him because of who He was, the same way the sinner hates the righteous person today. (2) He came to take a lowly, humble place on earth.

I am become a stranger unto my brethren, and an alien unto my mother's children [Ps. 69:8].

This verse tells me a lot I would not know otherwise. Mary had other children, which confirms the record in the Gospels. Perhaps one day her boys, Judas and Joses, said to her, "Mother, we heard somebody down the street talking, and they said that Jesus is not really our brother. They said that nobody knows who His father is." He became an alien unto His mother's children. Do you think it was a happy home in which He was raised? It may have been a very unhappy home.

Note how it reads: "An alien unto my *mother's* children"—not His father's children because Joseph was not His father. He was "an alien" because they were half-brothers and half-sisters. You see, this verse teaches the virgin birth of Christ.

For the zeal of thine house hath eaten me up; and the reproaches of them that reproached thee are fallen upon me [Ps. 69:9].

This is a verse which our Lord also quoted—in reference to the temple. In the temple the Lord found men who sold oxen, and sheep, and doves for offerings. He also found money changers there. He made a scourge of small cords and drove them all out. "And [he] said unto them that sold doves, Take these things hence; make not my Father's house an house of merchandise. And his disciples remembered that it was written, The zeal of thine house hath eaten me up" (John 2:16–17). My, these men were religious and as busy as termites; in fact, they were doing just about as much damage as termites would. Oh, they were busy, but they were far from God.

When I wept, and chastened my soul with fasting, that was to my reproach [Ps. 69:10].

When He would fast or weep, His brothers would ridicule Him for it. They would tell Him that He was just putting on an act.

I made sackcloth also my garment; and I became a proverb to them [Ps. 69:11].

Do you know what that proverb was? The word that circulated around was that He was illegitimate. You know what people would call Him today.

They that sit in the gate speak against me; and I was the song of the drunkards [Ps. 69:12].

Those who are "sitting in the gate" are the high officials of the town, the judges. You see, the best people in Nazareth also spoke against Him. Nazareth was a little town that would not accept the Lord Jesus because it would not believe the fact that He was the Son of God.

"I was the song of the drunkards"—the drunkards at the local bar made up dirty little ditties about Him and His mother. This was His life in Nazareth. It was not nice. Do you know why He endured all of this? He was raised in a town where He was called illegitimate in order that I might be a legitimate son of God. There is nobody in heaven who is going to point a finger at Vernon McGee and say that he is not God's son. Do you know why? Because the Son of God bore that for me on the cross; He paid the penalty for my sins. My friend, you have no notion what He endured for thirty years in order that you might have a clear title as a legitimate son of God.

But as for me, my prayer is unto thee, O LORD, in an acceptable time: O God, in the multitude of thy mercy hear me, in the truth of thy salvation [Ps. 69:13].

This verse is quoted in 2 Corinthians 6:2 which tells us, "For he saith, I have heard thee in a time accepted, and in the day of salvation have I succoured thee: behold, now is the accepted time; behold, now is the day of salvation."

The Gospel records tell us that our Lord prayed, but this psalm tells us *what* He prayed:

Deliver me out of the mire, and let me not sink: let me be delivered from them that hate me, and out of the deep waters.

Let not the waterflood overflow me, neither let the deep swallow me up, and let not the pit shut her mouth upon me.

Hear me, O LORD; for thy lovingkindness is good: turn unto me according to the multitude of thy tender mercies.

And hide not thy face from thy servant; for I am in trouble: hear me speedily.

Draw nigh unto my soul, and redeem it: deliver me because of mine enemies.

Thou hast known my reproach, and my shame, and my dishonour: mine adversaries are all before thee [Ps. 69:14–19].

We see His distress but also His assurance of deliverance and victory. Neither the deep nor the pit could hold Him. He was saved out of them.

The next two verses tell of our Lord's dark hours on the cross:

Reproach hath broken my heart; and I am full of heaviness: and I looked for some to take pity, but there was none; and for comforters, but I found none.

They gave me also gall for my meat; and in my thirst they gave me vinegar to drink [Ps. 69:20–21].

This, now, is His imprecatory prayer:

Let their table become a snare before them: and that which should have been for their welfare, let it become a trap [Ps. 69:22].

This is quoted by Paul in his Epistle to the Romans: "And David saith, Let their table be made a snare, and a trap, and a stumbling-block, and a recompence unto them: Let their eyes be darkened that they may not see, and bow down their back alway" (Rom. 11:9–10). Now there are some folk who consider the imprecatory prayers unchristian. But since it is quoted in the New Testament in reference to those who have rejected Christ, I see nothing unchristian about it. I feel that the imprecatory prayers have been greatly misunderstood. When we put them back into the position where they belong, we see they are judgment being pronounced upon the lost.

Let their habitation be desolate; and let none dwell in their tents [Ps. 69:25].

This is quoted by Peter in Acts 1:20 in reference to Judas Iscariot.

For they persecute him whom thou hast smitten; and they talk to the grief of those whom thou hast wounded.

Add iniquity unto their iniquity: and let them not come into thy righteousness.

Let them be blotted out of the book of the living, and not be written with the righteous [Ps. 69:26–28].

"Let them be blotted out of the book of the living" raises a question. There has been a great deal of debate on Revelation 3:5 which says, "He that overcometh, the same shall be clothed in white raiment; and I will not blot out his name out of the book of life, but I will confess his name before my Father, and before his angels." Apparently there is the book of creation, and when we are born we are recorded in that book—"Thine eyes did see my substance, yet being unperfect; and in thy book all my members were written, which in continuance were fashioned, when as yet there was none of them" (Ps. 139:16). Also there is a book of life for those who are saved. And there is the book of works. It would seem that the blotting out has to do with the works of the person who is already saved. There is no suggestion of a name being blotted out of the book of salvation. There have been many other explanations for this passage. Another one is this: When you are born, you are put in God's book of the living. I take it that you are a candidate for salvation. When you are blotted out of that book, you have crossed over the line and are no longer a candidate for salvation. Now here in Psalm 69 the "book of the living" is obviously the book of creation; and "not be written with the righteous" means that they will not be written in the book of salvation.

This psalm ends with a glorious song of praise.

I will praise the name of God with a song, and will magnify him with thanksgiving [Ps. 69:30].

The first time the Lord came to earth He came in humiliation. He is coming back to earth in exaltation. Those on earth will be the redeemed ones—they are the only ones that will be on this earth. And the only ones who will be in heaven are the redeemed. Friend, there are just two kinds of people in the world today. There are lost people and saved people—redeemed sinners and unredeemed sinners. You can distinguish quite easily which group you are in.

Then there is a verse about God's poverty program.

For the LORD heareth the poor, and despiseth not his prisoners [Ps. 69:33].

God is going to bring justice to this earth some day, but justice will not be realized until He returns.

Let the heaven and earth praise him, the seas, and every thing that moveth therein [Ps. 69:34].

What a Hallelujah chorus this will be when everything that moves praises Him!

PSALM 70

***THEME:** Urgent cry for deliverance*

This is a lovely little psalm of David. Its contents can also be found in the last five verses of Psalm 40. One of the critics has said, "It is a fragment accidentally inserted here." I will agree with the critic if he will take out the word *accidentally*. It is called a song of remembrance. Why repeat it here? Because my memory is not very good, and God knew it wouldn't be. I can imagine that God said, "By the time McGee gets to this point in the Book of Psalms he will have forgotten all about Psalm 40, so I'll repeat it." There are some things to remember here.

> **Make haste, O God, to deliver me; make haste to help me, O LORD [Ps. 70:1].**

This is a cry for immediate help. I like that.

> **But I am poor and needy: make haste unto me, O God: thou art my help and my deliverer; O LORD, make no tarrying [Ps. 70:5].**

I fall into that class of the poor and needy, and He wants me to know that He is my helper, my deliverer. My friend, God is *for* the poor and needy, and He is our helper in this day.

PSALM 71

***THEME:** A psalm for old age*

This psalm is an elegy, and it is a psalm for old age. It is obvious that the psalmist, possibly it was David, was an old man when he wrote this.

> **Deliver me, O my God, out of the hand of the wicked, out of the hand of the unrighteous and cruel man.**
>
> **For thou art my hope, O Lord GOD: thou art my trust from my youth [Ps. 71:4–5].**

He prays and trusts.

> **Cast me not off in the time of old age; forsake me not when my strength faileth [Ps. 71:9].**

This is a good psalm for us senior citizens. I find that this psalm means a little bit more to me than it did twenty years ago.

> **But I will hope continually, and will yet praise thee more and more.**
>
> **My mouth shall shew forth thy righteousness and thy salvation all the day; for I know not the numbers thereof.**
>
> **I will go in the strength of the Lord GOD: I will make mention of thy righteousness, even of thine only [Ps. 71: 14–16].**

Now notice another definite reference to old age:

> **Now also when I am old and greyheaded, O God, forsake me not; until I have shewed thy strength unto this generation, and thy power to every one that is to come [Ps. 71:18].**

Now, friend, if you are a senior citizen, let me say this to you: Don't go into a corner and sit in a rocking chair. God hasn't forsaken you, and right down to your dying days He has kept you on this earth for a *purpose*. To be candid, I am praying, "Lord, don't let me sit down in a rocking chair *permanently*." I love to sit in a rocking chair. Many of my friends across the country have a rocking chair in their homes with my name on it. They always drag it out when I come to visit. I enjoy a rocking chair—but I don't want to stay there all the time. I want to be active for the Lord right down to the end of my life.

> **I will also praise thee with the psaltery, even thy truth, O my God: unto thee will I sing with the harp, O thou Holy One of Israel.**
>
> **My lips shall greatly rejoice when I sing unto thee; and my soul, which thou hast redeemed [Ps. 71:22–23].**

As we grow old, let's not talk about our aches and pains, let's rejoice in the Lord and sing His praises.

> **My tongue also shall talk of thy righteousness all the day long: for they are**

confounded, for they are brought unto shame, that seek my hurt [Ps. 71:24].

It is all right to reminisce if we are talking about God's goodness. The psalmist says, "My tongue also shall talk of thy righteousness all the day long."

This is a wonderful psalm for us old folk!

PSALM 72

***THEME:** The King and the kingdom are coming*

This is called "A Psalm for Solomon." The critic claims that Solomon wrote it, but I don't believe it, because the concluding verse says this: "The prayers of David the son of Jesse are ended." This is a psalm of David written for his son, Solomon.

This psalm concludes what we call the Exodus section of the Psalms. The Book of Exodus concludes with the glory of the Lord filling the tabernacle, and this is a prophetic psalm in which the Messiah Himself comes and establishes His glorious kingdom on earth. Notice that He is the God of *righteousness*:

Give the king thy judgments, O God, and thy righteousness unto the king's son.

He shall judge thy people with righteousness, and thy poor with judgment.

The mountains shall bring peace to the people, and the little hills, by righteousness [Ps. 72:1–3].

Also verse 7:

In his days shall the righteous flourish; and abundance of peace so long as the moon endureth [Ps. 72:7].

Righteousness is the plank in the platform that no political candidate has ever had—as far as I can tell. The Lord Jesus will reign in righteousness some day. This psalm describes His glorious kingdom.

His name shall endure for ever: his name shall be continued as long as the sun: and men shall be blessed in him: all nations shall call him blessed.

Blessed be the LORD God, the God of Israel, who only doeth wondrous things.

And blessed be his glorious name for ever: and let the whole earth be filled with his glory; Amen, and Amen [Ps. 72:17–19].

Apparently God gave to David this great vision of the kingdom and the reign of Christ when the whole earth will be filled with His glory. This is what David had prayed for; so he says—

The prayers of David the son of Jesse are ended [Ps. 72:20].

David says, "My prayers are all ended; I am through praying." What David had prayed for will be realized. He had nothing more to pray for!

LEVITICUS SECTION

Darkness and Dawn (Sanctuary in View)
Psalms 73–89

As I said in the beginning, we are dividing the Book of Psalms according to the Pentateuch. The first forty-one psalms we call the Genesis section. Psalms 42–72 are known as the Exodus section. Now we come to Psalm 73 which brings us to the beginning of the Leviticus section. It corresponds to the Book of Leviticus because in this section—even in Psalm 73—the sanctuary is prominent. You see, the Book of Leviticus is the book of worship for the tabernacle and later for the temple. It is one of the greatest books in the Bible. Now as we come to this Leviticus section of the Book of Psalms, we find the emphasis upon the sanctuary and, in particular, on two aspects of the house of God. The Book of Leviticus emphasizes two things: that God is holy and that without shedding of blood there is no remission of sins—the key words are *holiness* and *sacrifice*. These two words will also figure largely in this Leviticus section of the Book of Psalms.

PSALM 73

THEME: *Perplexity about prosperity*

In this section are very wonderful psalms, and we begin with psalms of Asaph. Like David, this man was a musician. The first series of eleven psalms (73–83) was written by Asaph.

Truly God is good to Israel, even to such as are of a clean heart [Ps. 73:1].

Immediately our attention is drawn to the fact that "God is good to Israel." Does that mean that He is good to every Israelite? No! His goodness is limited to those who are of a clean heart. Who would they be? Those who have come with their sacrifices, those who have a desire to serve God and walk with Him. My friend, if you are saved, you want to walk with God and fellowship with Him. You want to have a clean heart. That follows just as day follows night. You cannot come to Christ and accept Him as your Savior and continue to live as you did before. If you do, I cannot believe that you were saved in the first place. That is the explanation, and I feel that we need to hold to that rather tenaciously in our day. We are in the presence of God on the basis that He has cleaned us up. When we receive Christ, we have forgiveness of sins; we are washed—it is a washing of water by the Word of God. We are not only washed by the blood of Christ, but we are washed by the Word of God. The Word of God sanctifies us, and then we want to walk well-pleasing to Him.

Now this man Asaph who came into God's presence and could say, "God is good to Israel," had a problem. I think his problem may be your problem also—it certainly has been mine. The problem is this: "Why does God permit the prosperity of the wicked? Why is it that God's people seem to suffer more?" Many times, as a pastor, I found myself puzzled. I saw God's people tried. I saw God's people suffer. I saw the prosperity of the wicked, and it was hard for me to understand it.

It was brought home to me when our first child was born. In the hospital God took that child. I only heard the cry of that little one. All she ever did in her life was cry. I shall never forget the day she died. Across the hall from where my wife was, there was a very wealthy couple who had a baby boy, and their rich friends came to celebrate with them. As I drove into the parking lot in my old beat-up Chevrolet, they all drove up in Cadillacs. They went into the hospital with their champagne and celebrated the birth of the little boy. He was a precious looking little baby—all they desired, I guess. I shall never forget that night. It was summertime, and I went out on a balcony that was there and cried out to God. To be honest with you, I don't know to this good day why God took our baby and left the baby across the hall. They have money, and, boy, they live it up! I have seen write-ups about them, and they have been in trouble several times. Their little boy is now an adult, as my daughter would be. After all these years, I still don't have the answer. You may be thinking, *You are a minister, and you don't have the answer?* No, I don't have the answer. *Then how can you comfort others?* Well, I'll tell you how. Although I don't have the answer, I know the One who does, and He has told me to walk with Him by faith. He tests me by putting me in the dark. Then I'll reach out my hand and take His. In His Word He tells me that I can trust Him. Someday He will explain the whys of life to me.

Asaph had a problem like that. Asaph has already said that God is good to Israel—that believing remnant of which he was a part—but this question really bothered him.

But as for me, my feet were almost gone; my steps had well nigh slipped.

For I was envious at the foolish, when I saw the prosperity of the wicked [Ps. 73:2–3].

Asaph said, "I looked around me at my nation, and I noticed that the wicked among my people were the ones prospering, and the godly were not."

For there are no bands in their death: but their strength is firm [Ps. 73:4].

"There are no bands in their death"—there are no pangs or pains in their death.

They are not in trouble as other men; neither are they plagued like other men.

Therefore pride compasseth them about as a chain; violence covereth them as a garment [Ps. 73:5–6].

I think again of the wealthy couple with the little boy baby; oh, how arrogant they were and filled with pride!

Their eyes stand out with fatness: they have more than heart could wish [Ps. 73:7].

These folk have everything. As I think of it, I don't think they have had the fun that I have had in this life, because when I got a new something or other, it sure was a joy to me. It wasn't a joy to them because they had it all along. "Their eyes stand out with fatness"—I hadn't thought of that until I studied this psalm. They had puffs under their eyes—they had been drinking too much and had too much night life. The mother of that little fellow would have been beautiful if her face had not shown so much sign of dissipation.

They are corrupt, and speak wickedly concerning oppression: they speak loftily [Ps. 73:8].

They don't mind walking on the poor. They insist that our children have to go to public schools, but their children do not. Everyone else must obey the law, but they somehow are exempt. As you look around you, this is something that can make you bitter.

They set their mouth against the heavens, and their tongue walketh through the earth [Ps. 73:9].

My, listen to these rich people on television today. They are the ones who make the news. "Their tongue walketh through the earth," and I know of nothing that enables it to walk better than television.

Therefore his people return hither: and waters of a full cup are wrung out to them [Ps. 73:10].

God's people are taxed to death. We are told that some rich folk pay no taxes at all. My, they really have it made!

And they say, How doth God know? and is there knowledge in the most High? [Ps. 73:11].

They are not interested in God, and they don't think He knows anything about them.

Behold, these are the ungodly, who prosper in the world; they increase in riches [Ps. 73:12].

Does that ever bother you? It bothers me.

Verily I have cleansed my heart in vain, and washed my hands in innocency [Ps. 73:13].

Asaph says, "I have attempted to live for God, and it looks like it does not pay."

For all the day long have I been plagued, and chastened every morning.

If I say, I will speak thus; behold, I should offend against the generation of thy children.

When I thought to know this, it was too painful for me [Ps. 73:14–16].

This problem worried Asaph. It gave him sleepless nights. Why do the wicked prosper?

Now we come to the answer:

Until I went into the sanctuary of God; then understood I their end [Ps. 73:17].

When Asaph went into the temple of God, he understood the "end" of the wicked. He gained insight into the *end* reserved for the wicked. This is the reason the Lord Jesus gave a parable about a rich man and a poor man to illustrate afterlife. It is recorded in Luke 16:19–31. It tells us that the day is going to come when God will judge the rich. That rich fellow ended up in a place of torment even though the liberal preacher pushed him right into heaven at the funeral. Nice things were said about him. They praised him for his gifts of charity, but his end was a place of torment. The poor man wasn't even given a decent burial—his body was thrown onto a dump heap. But God's pallbearers were waiting for him—they were angels—and they took him right into Abraham's bosom. You have to stay close to God today, friend, or you will become bitter and cynical as you see the injustice in the world. Asaph found his answer in the sanctuary. I don't know the answer to your question because I don't know the answer to mine, but I know Someone who does. He didn't say He would tell me right now. He said, "You trust *Me*. I've got the answer." Someday in His presence He is going to explain it all to us. Also I know that He is going to show me that what He did was *best*. I don't understand that either, but that is what He is going to do.

Until then—

> **Nevertheless I am continually with thee: thou hast holden me by my right hand [Ps. 73:23].**

I told you that He will take your hand. He took mine when my little girl died. He said, "Walk with me." That is the lesson I learned, and this is the lesson the psalmist learned.

> **Thou shalt guide me with thy counsel, and afterward receive me to glory [Ps. 73:24].**

I am with Him today. My life verse is Philippians 1:6, "Being confident of this very thing, that he which hath begun a good work in you will perform it until the day of Jesus Christ." Don't tell me that He won't, because He will; and that is the message of this psalm. "Thou shalt guide me with thy counsel, and afterward receive me to glory." I can't ask for anything better than that. So, no matter what happens, whether I understand it or not, I will simply trust Him; and, if you don't mind, I will go on with Him.

PSALM 74

THEME: *A cry for deliverance when the temple is defiled by the enemy*

In this psalm the temple is before us again, and this time it is being profaned. It is a maschil psalm, not of David but of Asaph, who is a Levite and a musician in the tabernacle.

> **O God, why hast thou cast us off for ever? why doth thine anger smoke against the sheep of thy pasture? [Ps. 74:1].**

The psalmist asks, "Why have You done this to us?" Then he cries out:

> **Remember thy congregation, which thou hast purchased of old; the rod of thine inheritance, which thou hast redeemed; this mount Zion, wherein thou hast dwelt [Ps. 74:2].**

He gives us the geographic location. The psalmist obviously is talking about the land of Palestine and the nation Israel.

> **Lift up thy feet unto the perpetual desolations; even all that the enemy hath done wickedly in the sanctuary [Ps. 74:3].**

Notice that it is the "sanctuary" that the enemy had profaned.

> **Thine enemies roar in the midst of thy congregations; they set up their ensigns for signs [Ps. 74:4].**

What has happened? This is prophetic of that terrible invasion by the forces of Antiochus Epiphanes. (He was a Syrian, in the family of one of the four generals who divided up the empire of Alexander the Great after his death). In 175 B.C. he plundered Jerusalem, profaned the temple by pouring the broth of a sow all over the holy vessels, and placed an image of Jupiter in the holy place. This was called the transgression of desolation in Daniel

8. In A.D. 70 the destruction by Titus the Roman who profaned the temple and leveled it to the ground was also a fulfillment. However there will be further fulfillment of Asaph's prophecy after the temple is rebuilt. During the Tribulation the final abomination of desolation will be revealed which will profane the holy place. You will notice that in spite of all of this persecution and discouragement a godly remnant will say:

For God is my King of old, working salvation in the midst of the earth [Ps. 74:12].

Now hear their prayer:

Remember this, that the enemy hath reproached, O LORD, and that the foolish people have blasphemed thy name [Ps. 74:18].

In other words, Israel is saying to God, "The enemy has taken us, and many of the people of our nation have been foolish—they have not turned to You." But there is a faithful remnant.

O deliver not the soul of thy turtledove unto the multitude of the wicked: forget not the congregation of thy poor for ever [Ps. 74:19].

The psalmist cries out, "O God, save us in the midst of trouble." He looks forward to that day of God's deliverance. No matter how bad your trouble is, my friend, He will also deliver you. He has delivered His people out of much worse situations than we have been in, and He will do even greater things for them in the future.

Arise, O God, plead thine own cause: remember how the foolish man reproacheth thee daily [Ps. 74:22].

This is a call to God to move in victory; it is a prayer that recognizes God's ability to do it.

This psalm is a prayer of Asaph. It is a maschil psalm, instructing you and me that we can trust God in all our troubles.

PSALM 75

THEME: *A song of deliverance*

This psalm is "To the chief Musician, Altaschith, A Psalm or Song of Asaph." Psalm 74 was a prayer of Asaph. Psalm 75 is a song of deliverance, a song of the triumph that will come; therefore, it is a psalm of faith.

Unto thee, O God, do we give thanks, unto thee do we give thanks: for that thy name is near thy wondrous works declare [Ps. 75:1].

Ultimately, God is going to protect His name on earth. What a wonderful, glorious truth this is which is put before us in this psalm!

When I shall receive the congregation I will judge uprightly [Ps. 75:2].

This verse should read, "For I will take hold of the set time; I will judge in uprightness." This means that when the Lord comes it will be at a set time. When our Lord walked on earth, He took the place of self-humiliation. It was as a man on earth that He said, "But of the day and hour knoweth no man, no, not the angels of heaven, but my Father only" (Matt. 24:36). The Lord is coming at that appointed time. You cannot rush Him. He will come at the predetermined time. No man knows the date or the hour, although there are a few prophetic teachers across the country today who seem to have a private wire to heaven and seem to know when the Lord is going to return. But I don't—and, of course, they don't either. The important thing to note is that there is a set time when the Lord Jesus is going to return.

For promotion cometh neither from the east, nor from the west, nor from the south [Ps. 75:6].

Where will help come from? Not from the east, west, or south. You will notice that no mention is made of the north, because that is the direction the enemy will come from. Only *God* will be able to deliver His people. Psalm 75 is a prayer of thanksgiving to God before the event even takes place! How wonderful these psalms are! I trust they are a blessing to your heart.

PSALM 76

THEME: *Prophecy of the Messiah upon the throne*

As we study these psalms, I trust that you have your Bible open before you, and that you will read the entire text. These psalms are not only the Word of God, but their arrangement is important. I am not going to insist that the arrangement is inspired, but you will miss a great deal of the message if you ignore the arrangement because they do tell a story. There is a message that develops in each series of psalms. You recall that Psalm 74 was a cry for help—"Arise, O God." Psalm 75 was a song of thanks for God's deliverance out of the clutches of the northern power. They couldn't get help from the east or west or south, and the north was where their trouble was coming from. Russia will come from the north to invade the land of Israel, which we believe will be during the Great Tribulation Period. Now Psalm 76 shows the Lord Jesus reigning in His kingdom as King-Priest, the true Melchisedek. Man on this earth is in subjection to Him.

In Judah is God known: his name is great in Israel.

In Salem also is his tabernacle, and his dwelling place in Zion [Ps. 76:1–2].

Reading from Dr. Gaebelein's translation, which I have used from time to time, these verses say, "In Judah God is known; in Israel His Name is great. In Salem is found His Tabernacle, and His dwelling place in Zion" (*The Book of Psalms*, p. 298). *Salem* is the ancient name for Jerusalem and means "the habitation of peace." Four geographical places are mentioned. None of these places have to do with California or any state in the union, or any other country. Judah, Israel, Salem (Jerusalem), and Zion are all in Israel in the Mideast. The fact that this psalm has a blessing for us lies in its application, not in its interpretation, and I believe that all Scripture is *for* us.

There brake he the arrows of the bow, the shield, and the sword, and the battle. Selah [Ps. 76:3].

This is the day the prophet spoke of when he said, ". . . they shall beat their swords into plowshares, and their spears into pruninghooks: nation shall not lift up sword against nation, neither shall they learn war any more" (Isa. 2:4). Until the Lord Jesus Christ reigns, you had better not apply that verse to the United Nations, because it doesn't fit. Isaiah is speaking about the peace that will come to this earth when Christ comes back. Until the sin of the human heart is either dealt with in redemption or judgment, there can never be peace on earth.

Thou art more glorious and excellent than the mountains of prey [Ps. 76:4].

Dr. Gaebelein translates this, "Thou art shining forth gloriously above the mountains of prey." The "mountains of prey" refer to Jerusalem. That city has been besieged twenty-seven times. It has certainly been a mountain of prey! The enemies have been there.

The Lord is going to judge the arrogant and the proud who have walked on earth and those who have come against the city of Jerusalem.

The stout-hearted are spoiled, they have slept their sleep: and none of the men of might have found their hands [Ps. 76:5].

Or, as Dr. Gaebelein has it, "Spoiled were the stout-hearted; they fell asleep in their sleep." "They fell asleep in their sleep" is an interesting expression. How can you do that? It means that the stouthearted were no longer alert or aware. The apostle John writes that the whole world lies asleep in the arms of the wicked one (1 John 5:19). And the Devil doesn't want the world to wake up. He says to Vernon McGee, "Hush! Don't give out the Word so loud. You'll wake them up." But, friend, I'm trying to wake up the babies by telling them that judgment is coming and also that there is salvation in Christ.

You will also notice that ". . . none of the men of might have found their hands." Waking out of sleep, they were like the Midianites in the days of Gideon when they were awakened by the sound of trumpets and saw the lights. They knew they had been taken, ". . . and all the host ran, and cried, and fled" (Jud. 7:21).

At thy rebuke, O God of Jacob, both the chariot and horse are cast into a dead sleep [Ps. 76:6].

When the Lord comes again, at His rebuke both the chariot and the horse will be brought down into a deep sleep. At that time the Lord will shine forth gloriously. Isaiah 60:1 speaks of that day, "Arise, shine; for thy light is come, and the glory of the LORD is risen upon thee." We sometimes sing a song with these words at Christmas. Actually, this verse has no fulfillment at Christmas, at the birth of Christ. It will be fulfilled when the Lord comes again to this earth. It will be a great day, but it is still in the future. Isaiah 4:5 tells us more about this day: "And the LORD will create upon every dwelling place of mount Zion, and upon her assemblies, a cloud and smoke by day, and the shining of a flaming fire by night: for upon all the glory shall be a defence." The glory that will be there will be the person of Christ.

The day of vengeance of our God will come.

Thou, even thou, art to be feared: and who may stand in thy sight when once thou art angry?

Thou didst cause judgment to be heard from heaven; the earth feared, and was still,

When God arose to judgment, to save all the meek of the earth. Selah [Ps. 76:7–9].

These verses can be translated, "Thou, Thou, must be feared, and who can stand before Thee when Thou art angry? From heaven Thou didst thunder forth in judgment—the earth feared and became silent, when God arose to judge, to save all the meek of the earth." In Revelation 6:17 John says, "For the great day of his wrath is come; and who shall be able to stand?"

When the Lord comes again to earth, all things are going to be put under His feet.

Surely the wrath of man shall praise thee: the remainder of wrath shalt thou restrain [Ps. 76:10].

"For the wrath of man praiseth Thee, Thou restrainest the remainder of wrath." God says that He lets man go only so far. However, during the Great Tribulation it seems that the Lord will remove all restraint and let man go to the limit. Today man is being restrained. The Restrainer is the Holy Spirit. Who else can restrain evil in the world today? God is going to make the wrath of man to praise Him.

Vow, and pay unto the LORD your God: let all that be round about him bring presents unto him that ought to be feared [Ps. 76:11].

The satanic raging against God and against His anointed, He will restrain. And, as Psalm 110:3 puts it, "Thy [His] people shall be willing in the day of thy [His] power." His people vow and *pay* their vows. The Gentile nations are in submission to Him. "The kings of Tarshish and of the isles shall bring presents: the kings of Sheba and Seba shall offer gifts. Yea, all kings shall fall down before him: all nations shall serve him" (Ps. 72:10–11).

What a day that will be! My, this is a great psalm.

PSALM 77

***THEME:** Perplexity about the mercy and goodness of God*

This psalm is "To the chief Musician, to Jeduthun, A Psalm of Asaph." You will remember that Jeduthun was the chief musician. Asaph wrote this psalm for him either to play or to sing. It reveals a time of deep soul-searching because of the perplexity in the minds of the people in that day. Faith has its problems, but faith can find the solution. The answer again is in the sanctuary. History reveals that God does not forget.

I cried unto God with my voice, even unto God with my voice; and he gave ear unto me.

In the day of my trouble I sought the Lord: my sore ran in the night, and ceased not: my soul refused to be comforted [Ps. 77:1–2].

A good time to seek the Lord is in the day of trouble. I received a letter from a man who had lost his position. He would never listen to our program until he was out of a job and had nothing to do. It was then that he got right down to the nitty-gritty and trusted the Lord as his Savior. It is well to cry to the Lord in the time of trouble.

"And he gave ear unto me." God will hear you, my friend, when you are in trouble. You can go to Him. He is *real*. Sometimes I hear a soloist sing, "It's real; it's real; I know it's real. . . ." The way they sing it and the way they live makes me wonder if it actually is real with them. My friend, it is real—not because I say it, or because it is written here, but because you find it out by experience. He has already told us to taste of the Lord and see whether He is good or not. Try this thing out.

"My sore ran in the night, and ceased not" —I don't think he was speaking of a physical sore but an open sore of the soul.

Here is another wonderful thing he did:

I call to remembrance my song in the night: I commune with mine own heart: and my spirit made diligent search [Ps. 77:6].

It is a wonderful thing to be able to sing in the night. I don't mean that you sing out loud and wake everybody up out of sleep. "I remember my song in the night." The night is the time when you wake up and worry. Problems loom large—everything in the dark looks bigger than it really is. That is the time to remember your song in the night.

Now he raises some perplexing questions:

Will the Lord cast off for ever? and will he be favourable no more?

Is his mercy clean gone for ever? doth his promise fail for evermore?

Hath God forgotten to be gracious? hath he in anger shut up his tender mercies? Selah [Ps. 77:7–9].

I would say that a practical atheist said these things, but I have asked the same questions. Maybe you have, too. Do you realize that there are many of us believers who practice atheism? We, and I include myself, act as if God does not exist, as if He does not hear our prayers, as though He has thrown us overboard. We live as though God is no longer favorable and has stopped expressing His grace. My friend, God is *good!* He wants to be gracious to you and to me. Regardless of what you have done, God wants to be good to you.

Thy way, O God, is in the sanctuary: who is so great a God as our God? [Ps. 77:13].

You will remember that as we began this Leviticus section of the Book of Psalms I pointed out that it is called such because it is anchored in the sanctuary, the Holy of Holies. "Thy way, O God, is in the sanctuary" is a reminder to us who are believers to not forsake ". . . the assembling of ourselves together, as the manner of some is . . ." (Heb. 10:25). We are enjoined today to meet with God's people. God does not want you or me to go off in a corner and enjoy the Word of God by ourselves. We are to share the Word with others so that we can grow together. I don't believe in super-duper saints. God won't let you get way ahead of your brothers and sisters. We are in the family of God and will have to share the Word and the blessing with each other. Therefore the way of God is in the *sanctuary*. If you are going to find the answers to your questions, you will have to meet with God's people.

I received a letter the other day from a Christian mother. She wrote: "God has given me and my husband five wonderful children to guide for Him. All of the children are saved except for the baby, who is seventeen months old. We are fortunate enough to be members of a Bible-teaching church, where the pastor is led by God instead of man. He is one of those precious men of God who has been rebuked and has had his life threatened because of his boldness for God. Our cup runs over with joy as we see God work in the hearts of people and change their lives." It is good to hear of a church like this. We hear a great deal of criticism of churches, but there are many Bible-believing churches still at work today. If you attend a church where the Word of God is preached and taught, you should fellowship there and grow with the congregation. You will find the answer to many of your questions. The way in which the Devil works is subtle. His attack today is not a frontal one. He attacks the men who stand for the Word. This is something of which we should take note.

Now here is a scene that has to do with the sea.

The waters saw thee, O God, the waters saw thee; they were afraid: the depths also were troubled.

The clouds poured out water: the skies sent out a sound: thine arrows also went abroad.

The voice of thy thunder was in the heaven: the lightnings lightened the world: the earth trembled and shook.

Thy way is in the sea, and thy path in the great waters, and thy footsteps are not known [Ps. 77:16–19].

This passage refers specifically to God's leading the people of Israel across the Red Sea.

Thou leddest thy people like a flock by the hand of Moses and Aaron [Ps. 77:20].

My friend, this has an application for us. God is able to deliver His people today from the flood tide of atheism and lawlessness and immorality. What a great, loving Shepherd He is!

PSALM 78

THEME: *The history of Israel from Moses to David*

This psalm is a maschil of Asaph, a psalm of instruction, covering Israel's history from Egypt to the time of David. In it we see the failure of the people and the faithfulness of God. It is a wonderful psalm, and it calls upon God to hear and answer.

First, it is the call of God to His people. He asks His people to listen to Him.

Give ear, O my people, to my law: incline your ears to the words of my mouth [Ps. 78:1].

This is a long psalm, and we can only hit the high points; but I urge you to read the entire psalm in your Bible. It will bless your heart.

The children of Ephraim, being armed, and carrying bows, turned back in the day of battle.

They kept not the covenant of God, and refused to walk in his law [Ps. 78:9–10].

This is a direct reference to when Ephraim did not go to battle, and God took note of it. In a larger sense, Ephraim is typical of the conduct of all Israel and of *all* of God's people. It was Israel then; it is the church today. And God's faithfulness is unchanged.

And they sinned yet more against him by provoking the most High in the wilderness.

And they tempted God in their heart by asking meat for their lust.

Yea, they spake against God; they said, Can God furnish a table in the wilderness? [Ps. 78:17–19].

Let me translate this a little differently to bring out the meaning: "And they sinned yet more against him by provoking the Most High in the wilderness. And they tested God in their heart by asking food according to their desire. Yes, they spoke against God; they said, 'Can God furnish a table in the wilderness?' " This represents the type of unbelief that is seen among believers today. It is practical atheism on the part of God's people.

Now notice what God did:

Man did eat angels' food: he sent them meat to the full [Ps. 78:25].

"Angels' food" is better translated *food of the mighty*—"Man did eat the food of the mighty; He sent them food to the full." He gave them all that they needed, yet they were doubting God and criticizing God.

This psalm of instruction concludes with this allusion to David:

He chose David also his servant, and took him from the sheepfolds:

From following the ewes great with young he brought him to feed Jacob his people, and Israel his inheritance.

So he fed them according to the integrity of his heart; and guided them by the skilfulness of his hands [Ps. 78: 70–72].

David is a type of Him who is David's Lord and David's Son. God was faithful to them, and He is faithful to us today, my friend.

PSALM 79

***THEME:** Future of Israel in the Great Tribulation*

This psalm is a prayer—not for you and me to pray, but for God's people, the nation Israel, in the Great Tribulation, which is the terrible day of trouble that is coming to them.

This is another psalm of Asaph, a great musician, who was probably the writer and arranger of them. He was contemporary with David and probably served as his assistant.

> **O God, the heathen are come into thine inheritance; thy holy temple have they defiled; they have laid Jerusalem on heaps [Ps. 79:1].**

Although this psalm was prophetic at the time it was written, it accurately pictures the siege of Nebuchadnezzar and the subsequent Babylonian captivity. Also the Maccabean period brought such a calamity. This prophecy's ultimate fulfillment will be during the Great Tribulation.

Prior to the Babylonian captivity, the false prophets were saying that God would never allow their destruction and captivity. However, the city that the false prophets had said could never be taken *was* taken, and the inhabitants were carried away into captivity. The temple they said could never be destroyed *was* destroyed. The city, of course, was Jerusalem, and the people were the children of Israel. This happened several times, and it caused these people to cry out to God. The temple, the sanctuary, is the very center of things. Remember that this section of the Psalms corresponds to the Book of Leviticus which has as its theme the worship centering about the tabernacle and later the temple.

> **The dead bodies of thy servants have they given to be meat unto the fowls of the heaven, the flesh of thy saints unto the beasts of the earth [Ps. 79:2].**

This horrible carnage was difficult for the people of Israel to understand. Why was God permitting this to happen to them? The false prophets had been continually telling them that it could not happen to God's people. Although the prophet Jeremiah had been faithfully giving God's warning of judgment to come, he had been discredited and labeled as a traitor to his nation. The Israelites could not understand why God had not protected them. This is still a question in our day. I understand that a great many Jews have become atheists because of the terrible persecution and suffering of their people in Germany during Hitler's dictatorship. Of course it is difficult for them to understand it. Maybe they have the same questions the psalmist has. But have they been faithful to God? Are they back in proper relationship with Him? Have they accepted their Messiah? Are they turning to Him? The answer, of course, is no. God has judged His people in the past and is judging them in our day. I feel that great judgment has come upon the church and will increase in the future. Judgment has come upon the nations of the world, nations like our own.

Hear their cry:

> **How long, LORD? wilt thou be angry for ever? shall thy jealousy burn like fire? [Ps. 79:5].**

The Jews cry out, "Aren't You going to let up on us, O Lord?"

Then they cry to God for forgiveness:

> **O remember not against us former iniquities: let thy tender mercies speedily prevent us: for we are brought very low [Ps. 79:8].**

They pray, "Don't remember our former iniquities." But how will He be able to rub them out and forget them? Only through the death of Christ. When Christ is rejected—whether it be by Jew or Gentile, rich or poor, bond or free, male or female, black or white, red or yellow—there is judgment. You have to meet Him in judgment or redemption; there are only two ways.

Now listen to the plaintive cry of these suffering people:

> **Help us, O God of our salvation, for the glory of thy name: and deliver us, and purge away our sins, for thy name's sake [Ps. 79:9].**

The children of Israel had been making the boast that God was among them and would deliver them. God had not delivered them, and they were being subjected to ridicule. The heathen were making fun of them.

Notice the note of thankfulness on which this psalm ends:

> **So we thy people and sheep of thy pas-**

ture will give thee thanks for ever: we will shew forth thy praise to all generations [Ps. 79:13].

In that coming kingdom their sorrows and their tears will be gone forever, and so there will be praise from generation to generation.

PSALM 80

THEME: *Prayer to the Shepherd of Israel*

In this series of psalms there is a continuation of thought, a prophetic development. The Septuagint version has the inscription: "the Assyrian," which has led some expositors to place this psalm in a later time. However, because it is definitely a psalm of Asaph, a contemporary of David, we know it was written during the time of the Davidic kingdom. The inscription is "To the chief Musician upon Shoshannim-Eduth," which means "lilies." We have seen before that a beautiful lilies' psalm mentions the Messiah, the Lord Jesus Christ. It is a plea to the Shepherd of Israel to lead them again.

Give ear, O Shepherd of Israel, thou that leadest Joseph like a flock; thou that dwellest between the cherubims, shine forth [Ps. 80:1].

The "Shepherd of Israel" is none other than the Lord Jesus Christ. We have had a simile of the sheep and the Shepherd before.

"Thou that leadest Joseph like a flock" refers to the wilderness journey of the tribes of Israel when they advanced toward the Promised Land to take possession of it. Jehovah, the Shepherd of Israel, was their leader. Joshua was their human leader, but he acted under the Captain of the Host of the Lord. The psalmist appeals to God who had met with these people in the Holy of Holies.

Before Ephraim and Benjamin and Manasseh stir up thy strength, and come and save us [Ps. 80:2].

Why would Ephraim, Benjamin, and Manasseh be mentioned? I think the answer can be found in Numbers 2:17–24. If you read this portion of Scripture, you will find that in placing the tribes around the tabernacle, these three tribes were immediately behind the ark in the order of the march. It was the ark that led the children of Israel through the wilderness. Just as God had led them once before, the cry comes to lead them again.

Turn us again, O God, and cause thy face to shine; and we shall be saved [Ps. 80:3].

This same refrain is repeated three times in this psalm (vv. 3, 7, 19). It is sort of a chorus.

O Lord God of hosts, how long wilt thou be angry against the prayer of thy people? [Ps. 80:4].

This is a brief elegy here. It is a lament, a sad part of the psalm, and includes verses 4–6. The psalmist feels God is angry because He does not answer the prayer of His people.

Thou feedest them with the bread of tears; and givest them tears to drink in great measure [Ps. 80:5].

This is one of the most remarkable verses in the Word of God. God has given His people "tears to drink" and tears for their bread—all they had to eat was tears. These are the tears of suffering. No nation has suffered as the children of Israel have suffered—and survived. Most other nations, had they been treated like the Jews, would have been exterminated and would have disappeared from the face of the earth. Israel has been drinking tears down through the centuries. Why? Israel has rejected the Shepherd. When the Lord was here, He beheld the city of Jerusalem and wept over it. Luke 19:41–44 tells us what He said as He wept, "And when he was come near, he beheld the city, and wept over it, Saying, If thou hadst known, even thou, at least in this thy day, the things which belong unto thy peace! but now they are hid from thine eyes. For the days shall come upon thee, that thine enemies shall cast a trench about thee, and compass thee round, and keep thee in on every side, And shall lay thee even with the ground, and thy children within thee; and they shall not leave in thee one stone upon another; because thou knewest not the time of thy visitation." This is a tremendous passage of Scripture and gives the reason the Jews have had tears to drink. On His way to the cross Jesus turned to some of the women in the crowd who were weeping and said, ". . . Daughters of Jerusalem, weep not for me, but weep for yourselves, and for your children" (Luke 23:28).

Turn us again, O God of hosts, and cause thy face to shine; and we shall be saved [Ps. 80:7].

That "face to shine" is none other than the face of Israel's Messiah, the Lord Jesus Christ.

Now here is another remarkable verse:

Thou hast brought a vine out of Egypt: thou hast cast out the heathen, and planted it [Ps. 80:8].

God brought the nation of Israel out of bondage in Egypt. God cast the heathen nations out of the land of Palestine and planted Israel, His vine, there. Israel built a temple in which to worship God. Then they were told that their temple would be destroyed and they would be put out of the land. Why? For the same reason that God put the heathen nations out of the land—they turned their backs upon God. The responsibility of Israel was greater than that of the heathen nations, because God had granted to them a privilege that no other nation had, which was the *visible presence* of God.

Thou preparedst room before it, and didst cause it to take deep root, and it filled the land [Ps. 80:9].

This verse is speaking about Israel, the vine that God brought forth out of Egypt and planted in the Promised Land.

The hills were covered with the shadow of it, and the boughs thereof were like the goodly cedars.

She sent out her boughs unto the sea, and her branches unto the river [Ps. 80:10–11].

The question arises:

Why hast thou then broken down her hedges, so that all they which pass by the way do pluck her? [Ps. 80:12].

For years, after God planted His vine, He put a hedge about the land. The people lived in the land for a good six hundred years. God did not permit any of the great nations of that day to destroy them. Egypt came against Israel and had victories but did not destroy them. The same was true of Syria and the Hittite nation. But the day came when God removed the hedge and let the enemies of Israel come in. Why? Because Israel had rejected the Shepherd of Israel.

Let thy hand be upon the man of thy right hand, upon the son of man whom thou madest strong for thyself [Ps. 80:17].

At God's right hand is the place of power. Who is at God's right hand? It is Israel's Messiah. David wrote, "The LORD said unto my Lord, Sit thou at my right hand, until I make thine enemies thy footstool" (Ps. 110:1). The Lord Jesus applied this to Himself when His enemies challenged His messianic claim (Matt. 22:44).

Back in Genesis 35 is the account of Rachel when she gave birth to her second son along the roadside that leads into Bethlehem. Benjamin was the baby, but she didn't call him that. When she looked upon that little fellow to whom she had given birth, she called him Ben-oni, which means "son of my suffering." But when Jacob looked upon him—I think the baby had eyes like his lovely Rachel—he said, "No, we won't call him Ben-oni, we'll call him Benjamin, because he is the *son of my right hand.*" Benjamin is a picture, a type of our Lord Jesus who came to earth the first time as the Son of suffering. But today He is at God's right hand. Of Him the Father said, "Sit thou at my right hand, until I make thine enemies thy footstool." And someday He will be returning from that position to this earth.

So will not we go back from thee: quicken us, and we will call upon thy name [Ps. 80:18].

A better translation would be: "So will not we go back from Thee, revive us, and we will call upon Thy name."

Now here is the chorus for the third time:

Turn us again, O LORD God of hosts, cause thy face to shine; and we shall be saved [Ps. 80:19].

In other words, "Restore us, O LORD God of hosts, cause Thy face to shine upon us." This is a wonderful, wonderful psalm!

PSALM 81

THEME: *A song of deliverance*

This psalm, like so many of the others, is linked to the one that preceded it. In other words, we have a continuous story. The prayer in the preceding psalm was not a prayer for Christians; it is for the time of Jacob's trouble at the end of the age. The great prayer for us today is, ". . . Even so, come, Lord Jesus" (Rev. 22:20). And in the meantime we're to ask Him to help us get out His Word.

It is a song of deliverance. It begins on a high note. It is a soprano solo. It is inscribed "To the chief Musician upon Gittith, A Psalm of Asaph."

Sing aloud unto God our strength: make a joyful noise unto the God of Jacob.

Take a psalm, and bring hither the timbrel, the pleasant harp with the psaltery.

Blow up the trumpet in the new moon, in the time appointed, on our solemn feast day.

For this was a statute for Israel, and a law of the God of Jacob [Ps. 81:1–4].

I think the key to this passage is in the blowing of the trumpet at the new moon. This is all very proper because the new moon appears before the Sun of Righteousness arises with healing in His wings. He is coming to deliver them. It is a beautiful picture of the Feast of Tabernacles. Israel had four feasts that came at the beginning of the year: the Passover, the Feast of Pentecost, the Feast of First Fruits, and then the Feast of Tabernacles. This psalm sounds like the Feast of Tabernacles, also called the Feast of Trumpets. "For this was a statute for Israel, and a law of the God of Jacob." It was a great day. And its fulfillment is still in the future.

Hear, O my people, and I will testify unto thee: O Israel, if thou wilt hearken unto me;

There shall no strange god be in thee; neither shalt thou worship any strange god [Ps. 81:8–9].

The Lord reminds them of the past.

I am the LORD thy God, which brought thee out of the land of Egypt: open thy mouth wide, and I will fill it [Ps. 81:10].

This is a promise to Israel, and we should leave it that way, but there is a spiritual lesson for us in this verse. God did not lead me out of Egypt; but He did save me out of sin, which is the "Egypt" of this world. Now God says, "Open wide your mouth, McGee, and I will fill it with spiritual blessings." And He has done just that. God has been *good* to me.

But my people would not hearken to my voice; and Israel would none of me [Ps. 81:11].

In other words, "Israel would have none of me." They still have not turned to God. There is not much difference between the Israel side and the Arab side as far as their relationship to God goes, and there is not much difference between that land and the United States. In fact, I think the United States is in the worst spiritual condition, yet we are telling the world how things ought to be done. Because of our own failure I believe our nation should be in sackcloth and ashes. As a people, as individuals, we need to turn to God.

PSALM 82

***THEME:** God judges the judges of His people*

This is a psalm that has been misunderstood. A critic who denies the deity of Christ will turn to this psalm and ridicule it. This is another prophetic psalm that looks to the future for God's earthly people, Israel. We see in connection with this the glory of the Lord—and it is wonderful when these two are brought together. This gives us a prophetic description of the judgment which God will execute during the Tribulation period when He saves the faithful remnant.

He begins on that note:

God standeth in the congregation of the mighty; he judgeth among the gods [Ps. 82:1].

"God standeth in the congregation of the mighty"—this hasn't happened yet, but He will stand there during the Millennium.

"He judgeth among the gods." Whom is He calling *gods?*

How long will ye judge unjustly, and accept the persons of the wicked? Selah [Ps. 82:2].

It is important to understand this verse of Scripture. Notice who are "the gods." God is calling the judges "gods" because they stand in His place and walk in His shoes, if I may use that expression.

Defend the poor and fatherless: do justice to the afflicted and needy.

Deliver the poor and needy: rid them out of the hand of the wicked [Ps. 82:3–4].

When the Lord Jesus Christ comes as the Judge of this earth, He is going to defend the poor, the fatherless, the afflicted, and the needy. One of the big arguments against capital punishment is that rich people never have to pay the penalty of their crimes, and poor people have to pay in full. The argument is that because of the inequality the penalty should be abolished. God is saying to the judges, "I want you to defend the poor and the fatherless." The current discussion of giving the poor an equal opportunity is not new; it is as old as the Book of Psalms. When the Lord Jesus, as Messiah, reigns on this earth, He will defend the poor and the fatherless, the afflicted and the needy. Today judges are standing in God's place, and they are to do the same thing.

Now here is an interesting verse:

They know not, neither will they understand; they walk on in darkness: all the foundations of the earth are out of course [Ps. 82:5].

Certainly the world today is being shaken and is in great turmoil, and one of the great problems has been the judges of the earth. It is very easy for a judge to be like Pilate, to wash his hands, and say, "I don't believe in that uncivilized method of punishing people by capital punishment." He thinks he can escape in that way. But when those who have broken the law come before him, he ought to remember that justice is blind. If a rich man has committed a crime that deserves capital punishment, it should be meted out just as it would be to a poor man who committed the same crime. Unfortunately, very few rich people have to pay for their crimes.

I have said, Ye are gods; and all of you are children of the most High [Ps. 82:6].

What does He mean, "Ye are gods"? The Lord Jesus Christ Himself quoted this verse when the Jews questioned His deity. They accused Him of blasphemy because He made Himself God. In John 10:33–37 we read, "The Jews answered him, saying, For a good work we stone thee not; but for blasphemy; and because that thou, being a man, makest thyself God. Jesus answered them, Is it not written in your law, I said, Ye are gods? If he called them gods, unto whom the word of God came, and the scripture cannot be broken; Say ye of him, whom the Father hath sanctified, and sent into the world, Thou blasphemest; because I said, I am the Son of God? If I do not the works of my Father, believe me not."

Jesus was telling these Jews that they were sitting in judgment and, when one sits in the place of judgment, he is taking the place of God. Many saints are guilty of that type of thing. They sit in judgment on other saints. Paul says, "But with me it is a very small thing that I should be judged of you, or of man's judgment: yea, I judge not mine own self. For I know nothing by myself; yet am I not hereby justified: but he that judgeth me is the Lord. Therefore judge nothing before the time, until the Lord come, who both will bring to light the hidden things of darkness, and will make manifest the counsels of the hearts: and then shall every man have praise of God" (1 Cor. 4:3–5). Paul is saying that he is going to stand before God someday; and, because of that, he doesn't even judge *himself*. My friend, when you start judging someone, you are acting for God, and you are a god when you have taken that position of judging. I am fearful of our nation with so many godless people seeking office. They know nothing of the background of this country which was founded upon the Word of God; they are not in spiritual tune with the founding of this nation.

Years ago I was greatly impressed by that judge in New York City who presided at the trial of a husband and wife who were charged with being spies. This judge was a Jew, and he said that the night before he handed down his judgment was spent in prayer. I was impressed with that. Why? He was going to hand down a harsh judgment; he was going to stand in the place of God when he made the decision. That judge was actually standing in the place of God when he judged the lives of these two people who would have to pay for their crime against the government. A man in that position ought to be a godly man. He should be a man of prayer. The big problem in our contemporary society is not so much with the criminal as it is with the judges and the breakdown of law and order. It is strange that the breakdown of law and order has begun with the law profession and not really with the criminal element.

Any time that you pass judgment on a person, you stand in the position of God. Parents ought to recognize that. What does God say to a little fellow growing up in a home? He says, "Children, obey your parents in all things: for this is well pleasing unto the Lord" (Col. 3:20). But wait a minute—what if his parents don't tell him to do the right things and don't bring him up the way they should? There are many parents like that today. God says, "I am going to hold them responsible. They are in My place. They occupy that position because I have said to that little boy, 'My son, hear the instruction of thy father, and forsake not the law of thy mother' " (Prov. 1:8). God help the father or the mother who does not lead their child in a godly pathway. Someone has asked the question, "What is worse than going to hell?" The answer given by a great preacher in the South years ago was this: "To go to hell and recognize the voice of your son and ask, 'Son, what are you doing here?' and hear him answer, 'Dad, I followed you!' "

This is a tremendous psalm. God says to the judges, "Be sure you judge accurately. Ye are gods, and all of you are children of the Most High."

But ye shall die like men, and fall like one of the princes [Ps. 82:7].

God reminds the judges, who stand in the place of God, that they are still human beings, and the day is coming when they will have to stand before God and be judged.

Arise, O God, judge the earth: for thou shalt inherit all nations [Ps. 82:8].

This will be a prayer of the nation Israel. I feel that I could join in that prayer. "O God, judge this earth. O God, You are going to inherit all the nations. This earth is Yours. You judge it." I believe this is a prayer all of us can pray in this day in which we live.

PSALM 83

THEME: *A cry for judgment*

This is "A Song or Psalm of Asaph." This is the last psalm of the Asaph series and a rather puzzling one. The fact of the matter is that you cannot fit it into the history of the nation of Israel. Since you cannot, the idea is to guess at it, and there have been some wild guesses. This is an imprecatory prayer, a cry for justice. The psalmist prays for God to deliver His people from their enemies.

Keep not thou silence, O God: hold not thy peace, and be not still, O God.

For, lo, thine enemies make a tumult: and they that hate thee have lifted up the head [Ps. 83:1–2].

Whoever the enemy is here, he hates God. But isn't that always the case with the enemy?

They have taken crafty counsel against thy people, and consulted against thy hidden ones.

They have said, Come, and let us cut them off from being a nation; that the name of Israel may be no more in remembrance [Ps. 83:3–4].

This refers to those who have plotted the destruction of the nation Israel. There are those who have tried to fit this psalm into the time of Jehoshaphat, and others who have attempted to fit it into other historical periods. The important thing for us to note is that the enemies of God express their hatred toward Him.

Now we begin with the section of this psalm that is difficult to fit into history.

For they have consulted together with one consent: they are confederate against thee:

The tabernacles of Edom, and the Ishmaelites; of Moab, and the Hagarenes;

Gebal, and Ammon, and Amalek; the Philistines with the inhabitants of Tyre;

Assur also is joined with them: they have holpen the children of Lot. Selah [Ps. 83:5–8].

"Assur" is Assyria. "The children of Lot" would be Moab and Ammon. The names in this portion of God's Word are His enemies. There is no place in history where they seem to fit in; and that makes it a very remarkable section, because it appears that these verses look to the future. Apparently these nations which were in existence at one time will appear again in the future.

At the present time Israel is surrounded by Arab nations who are apparently joined together not so much as Arabs but as Moslems. They are opposed to the nation Israel. It looks as though the nations mentioned in these verses will come back into existence during the last days. They are not in existence now, and there is nothing to which they correspond. This fact makes Psalm 83 a very remarkable passage of Scripture.

The remainder of this psalm is an imprecatory prayer. It asks for God's judgment. It is retrospective in the sense that the psalmist is saying, "Judge as You have done it in the past."

Do unto them as unto the Midianites; as to Sisera, as to Jabin, at the brook of Kison:

Which perished at En-dor: they became as dung for the earth [Ps. 83:9–10].

In the Book of Judges we read how God judged those nations. There are those who say that God will not judge that way in the future. He won't? He has judged that way in the past. God has not changed. What He has done in the past, He will do in the future. For that reason this is impressive.

Let me remind you that this is not the way we, as believers today, should pray. We should pray for our enemies—not that God would punish them, but that they might be converted, that they might turn to God.

This is a prayer for Israel to pray:

O my God, make them like a wheel; as the stubble before the wind [Ps. 83:13].

Do you remember reading about the great big wheel that the oxen used to pull around to beat out the grain and crush the stubble? The psalmist is saying, "Deal with our enemies that way, O Lord."

As the fire burneth a wood, and as the flame setteth the mountains on fire [Ps. 83:14].

In other words, "Be like a forest fire!"

Now note the conclusion:

That men may know that thou, whose name alone is JEHOVAH, art the most high over all the earth [Ps. 83:18].

I am convinced that the only way this world is going to know that God is *God* is for Him to move in judgment. The *goodness* of God ought to lead men to repentance, but it doesn't. If men were at all sensitive to the presence and person of God, it would lead them to His presence, but it actually drives them farther away from God. We are an affluent nation now. When we were a frontier nation, pioneering, fighting our way across to the West, we depended on God, but today we think we don't need Him. However, it looks to me as if we need Him desperately.

PSALM 84

***THEME:** A deep desire for God's house*

This is a psalm in which the Levitical emphasis is prominent. It is a psalm for the *sons* of Korah. The sons of Korah served in the tabernacle and later in the temple. Let's go back to 1 Chronicles 26 to see the background of this family. "Concerning the divisions of the porters: Of the Korhites was Meshelemiah the son of Kore, of the sons of Asaph" (1 Chron. 26:1). Then it gives a long list of that family of the Korhites. Now Korah, you may recall, led the rebellion against Moses, and he was judged for it. But now, by the grace of God, these descendants of his are serving in the tabernacle and in the temple of God. Then 1 Chronicles 26:12–13 says, "Among these were the divisions of the porters, even among the chief men, having wards one against another, to minister in the house of the LORD. And they cast lots, as well the small as the great, according to the house of their fathers, for every gate." A man was assigned to every gate. Lots were cast for the jobs. Strong, robust Levites guarded the tabernacle, and later they watched over every entrance to the temple. So the tabernacle and the temple are prominent in this psalm.

How amiable are thy tabernacles, O LORD of hosts!

My soul longeth, yea, even fainteth for the courts of the LORD; my heart and my flesh crieth out for the living God [Ps. 84:1–2].

Is this your heartcry today? Do you love to meet with God's people? I recognize that you don't get much fellowship in some churches today. In fact, you get more gossip and criticism than you get anything else. However, the place for fellowship is a church, and there are some *wonderful* churches throughout our land. I hope there is one in your neighborhood, where the Word of God is preached and Christ is exalted. If there is, that is where you should seek the fellowship of believers. That is where you will grow and be blessed.

Now this is lovely. These sons of Korah serving in the tabernacle and later in the temple saw this:

Yea, the sparrow hath found an house, and the swallow a nest for herself, where she may lay her young, even thine altars, O LORD of hosts, my King, and my God [Ps. 84:3].

I think the sparrows built nests around the temple. The man who wrote this psalm, as he looked up and saw them, said, "I want to dwell like that. I want to live that close to God." The Lord Jesus said to consider the little sparrows. They are not worth anything. In fact, you would like to get rid of them the way they chatter around and mess up everything. They are dirty little birds. The Lord Jesus said, "Are not two sparrows sold for a farthing? and one of them shall not fall on the ground without your Father" (Matt. 10:29). Not one sparrow falls but what the Father sees it. Actually, the language is stronger than that. He says that the sparrow falls into the lap of your Father. He knows all about it.

Behold, O God our shield, and look upon the face of thine anointed [Ps. 84:9].

The psalmist can say, "Behold, O God our shield." God is our shield. "And look upon the face of thine anointed." This is a reference to the Messiah. Christ, the Messiah, revealed the face of God on earth.

The sanctuary, as we saw in the Book of Leviticus, was the very center of the life of Israel. There was a day when the church was the center of the social life in this country. It is not even the center of religious life today, but it should be.

For a day in thy courts is better than a thousand. I had rather be a doorkeeper in the house of my God, than to dwell in the tents of wickedness [Ps. 84:10].

He says, "A day in Thy courts is better than a thousand days anywhere else. I had rather be a doorkeeper in the house of my God, than to dwell in the tents of wickedness," and that's what the sons of Korah were—doorkeepers. He says, "I would rather have *my* job than to be a rich man living far from God." There are some folk who look at their watches on Sunday morning to see if the preacher is going overtime. The psalmist says, "I'd rather spend one day in God's house than a thousand anywhere else." What a glorious psalm this is, and what a rebuke it is to many of us.

PSALM 85

THEME: *Future restoration of Israel*

This psalm is "To the chief Musician, A Psalm for the sons of Korah." Certain critics have attempted to identify this psalm with the return of the people to the land under Ezra and Nehemiah. Actually it has no reference to that at all. The reason critics do this is because they do not recognize the fact that the Psalms are prophetic.

We are in a section where we have several writers of the Psalms and the amazing thing is that these psalms have been put together to tell a story. Although I do not insist upon the inspiration of the arrangement, it certainly looks as if God had the oversight of it. We have seen that they appear in series—a cluster here and a cluster there—that present a prophetic picture. This psalm looks to the future, and I have no confidence in any translation or interpretation made by a man who does not believe this is the very Word of God. I feel like a certain minister in Southern California who says, "We might as well trust a lunatic for a lawyer, a quack for a physician, a wolf for a sheepdog, or an alligator for a babysitter, as to trust a modernist's translation of the Word of God or proclamation of the Word of God." I say amen to that. My feeling is that we need expositors who believe the Bible is the Word of God and God knows the future as well as He knows the past.

Now note this prophetic picture:

LORD, thou hast been favourable unto thy land: thou hast brought back the captivity of Jacob [Ps. 85:1].

Many critics assume that this verse refers to the return of the Jews to their land from the Babylonian captivity, but in reality only a small remnant returned to the land at that time. Less than sixty thousand people came back. The bulk of the people did not return. Rather than referring to the return after the Babylonian captivity, it looks forward to the kingdom age when God brings all of His people back into the land.

Thou hast forgiven the iniquity of thy people, thou hast covered all their sin. Selah [Ps. 85:2].

What a glorious picture this is! It can only refer to the future. It certainly did not depict the condition after the Babylonian captivity. If you think it does, read the Books of Ezra, Nehemiah, Haggai, Zechariah, and Malachi. Why, Malachi severely rebukes the people because their hearts are far from God. Oh, they were going to the temple and bringing sacrifices, but their hearts were far away from God. This psalm presents an entirely different picture.

Thou hast taken away all thy wrath: thou hast turned thyself from the fierceness of thine anger [Ps. 85:3].

This looks forward to the time when the judgments are over for Israel. The worst time for this nation and for the world is still in the future. The Great Tribulation is going to be global in its extent, and it will be a time of judgment. Satan will be turned loose, and the Holy Spirit will not be restraining evil. The lid will be taken off. The fellow who wants to paint the town red will have to have a brush that is big enough and plenty of paint to do it. God is going to let men go the limit, and then He is going to judge them.

For the child of God in this day, the judgment for sin is over. The sin question was settled when Jesus died on the cross for our sins. As the song writer put it, "The old account was settled long ago." But there is something that does trouble me: it is the fact that I will have to stand before the judgment seat of Christ, as will every believer, to give an account of my life and my works. Our works are going to be tried by fire. "Every man's work shall be made manifest: for the day shall declare it, because it shall be revealed by fire; and the fire shall try every man's work of what sort it is. If any man's work abide which he hath built thereupon, he shall receive a reward. If any man's work shall be burned, he shall suffer loss: but he himself shall be saved; yet so as by fire" (1 Cor. 3:13–15). I'm not sure about some of my works. No wonder that Paul didn't even judge himself because God alone can judge. I hope He will say, "Well done, thou good and faithful servant," but I'll have to wait and see.

During the Great Tribulation there is going to be brought together into a focal point everything in the way of judgment and evil, which is the reason I don't want to be here when it happens. And I don't think I will be here. To say that the church goes through that period is to miss entirely what is meant by the Great Tribulation.

Turn us, O God of our salvation, and cause thine anger toward us to cease.

Wilt thou be angry with us for ever? wilt thou draw out thine anger to all generations? [Ps. 85:4–5].

The day is coming when the suffering of these people will cease. As we saw in a previous psalm, their history has been one of tears to drink and tear-sandwiches to eat—that was their diet. The day is coming when it will be over. God will come and wipe away all of their tears.

Wilt thou not revive us again: that thy people may rejoice in thee? [Ps. 85:6].

Today we need revival in our churches for several reasons. One reason is there is a lack of *joy* in the lives of believers. It should be there, but it is not.

Shew us thy mercy, O LORD, and grant us thy salvation [Ps. 85:7].

This is something into which all of our hearts can enter. God hates evil and will judge it, but He is also a God of mercy and salvation to those who turn to Him.

I will hear what God the LORD will speak: for he will speak peace unto his people, and to his saints: but let them not turn again to folly [Ps. 85:8].

When God's final judgment of sin takes place, His people will no longer turn to folly. They will not return to their sins because sin will be removed from the universe.

Surely his salvation is nigh them that fear him; that glory may dwell in our land [Ps. 85:9].

There is no glory in Israel today. I love to visit that land, but I see nothing in the way of *glory* there, only a pile of rocks. Of course there are many places which are sacred to us as Christians.

Now this is one of the most remarkable verses in Scripture:

Mercy and truth are met together; righteousness and peace have kissed each other [Ps. 85:10].

"Mercy and truth" haven't met each other in our day. "Righteousness and peace have kissed each other"—they aren't even on speaking terms today. One of the reasons we cannot have *peace* in this world is because we do not have *righteousness* in the world. Things have to be right, my friend, before there can be peace in the world. Things are not "right" today—they are not right in my neighborhood, or anywhere, and maybe things are not right in our lives. Until things are right, there will be no peace on earth. This is a great verse!

Righteousness shall go before him; and shall set us in the way of his steps [Ps. 85:13].

When the Lord Jesus Christ reigns, He will reign in righteousness.

PSALM 86

THEME: *David prays for the future kingdom*

We have come now to another Davidic psalm, and it is a prayer of David.

It is remarkable in that it introduces another name for God. We have seen in former psalms that the names *Elohim*, which speaks of God as Creator, and *Jehovah*, which speaks of God as Savior, have been used. In this psalm another name for God appears seven times. It is *Adonai*, of which the English translation is "LORD." Adonai is the name of God which the pious Jew used (and still does) instead of Jehovah. When an orthodox Jew comes to the name Jehovah—the sacred tetragram *YHWH*—he doesn't pronounce it. In fact, the pronunciation has been lost, and today scholars debate about whether it should be pronounced Jehovah or Yahweh or something else. The orthodox Jew, considering the name Jehovah too sacred to voice, substitutes the name *Adonai*. Adonai refers to God as our Savior, the One who is the holy God, the One who has been able to extend mercy unto us.

Because Adonai occurs seven times in this psalm, it is considered a messianic psalm by some scholars. However, I do not think it could be called a messianic psalm in the strict sense of the word because of the nature of the prayer. For an example:

Teach me thy way, O LORD; I will walk in thy truth: unite my heart to fear thy name [Ps. 86:11].

There is no way that you can apply this verse to the Lord Jesus. He would never need to pray a prayer like this, because He *came* to do the Father's will. But this verse can apply to you and me. We need to be taught God's way and His truth. Our hearts need to be united to fear His name. Christ came to do the will of His Father, and He did it. It is different with us. F. W. Grant has made a remarkable statement in this regard: "This is indeed what is everywhere the great lack among the people of God. How much of our lives is not spent in positive evil, but frittered away and lost in countless petty diversions which spoil effectually the positiveness of our testimony for God! How few can say with the Apostle [Paul], 'This *one* thing I do.' We are on the road—not at least, intentionally off it—but we stop to chase butterflies among the flowers, and make no serious progress. How Satan must wonder when he sees us turn away from 'the kingdoms of the world and the glory of them,' *when* realized as his temptation, and yet yield ourselves with scarce a thought to endless trifles, lighter than a thistledown for which the child spends all his strength, and we laugh at him. If we examined our lives carefully in such an interest as this, how we would realize the multitude of needless anxieties, or self-imagined duties, of permitted relaxations, of 'innocent trifles,' which incessantly divert us from that in which alone is profit. How few perhaps would care to face such an examination day by day of the unwritten history of their lives."

There are many Christian workers today who are not in open sin, but they sure are lazy. They kill time doing this and that, and they are busy here and there, but the main business remains undone. They are not guarding the stuff, and they are not alert in serving the Lord. How we need to pray, "Unite my heart to fear thy name."

The psalmist's prayer that preceded it is, "Teach me thy way, O LORD," which is, I think, the solution for a wandering, divided heart. The first thing that the apostle Paul said after he was converted was, ". . . Lord, what wilt thou have me to do? . . ." (Acts 9:6). The psalmist had the answer, "Teach me thy way, O LORD." And the Lord has promised to teach His children, "I will instruct thee and teach thee in the way which thou shalt go: I will guide thee with mine eye" (Ps. 32:8).

"I will walk in thy truth" should be our response, which means we should walk in the light that the Word of God gives us.

Then He will receive the praise of our *whole* heart. When our heart is united and devoted to Him, the greater our praise will be.

I will praise thee, O Lord my God, with all my heart: and I will glorify thy name for evermore [Ps. 86:12].

PSALM 87

***THEME:** Zion, the city of God*

This psalm is "A Psalm or Song for the sons of Korah." Actually, I think it is a psalm *by* the sons of Korah. It is a song that deals with Zion, the city of God, and speaks of the glorious future of Jerusalem. The nations will come to Jerusalem to worship. I hear people today sing, "We're marching to Zion, that wonderful city of God." I am afraid that song is meaningless, because Zion is a geographical spot on this earth. When I was with a tour in Israel, several of us were in a car together riding toward Zion, which is the highest elevation in the city of Jerusalem. None of us could sing very well, but we sang as we rode along, "We're marching to Zion, that wonderful city of God." Actually we were riding, not marching, but at least we were headed for Zion.

His foundation is in the holy mountains [Ps. 87:1].

That is where the government of the world will one day be. Isaiah 2:2 tells us, "And it shall come to pass in the last days, that the mountain of the LORD'S house shall be established in the top of the mountains, and shall be exalted above the hills; and all nations shall flow unto it." Zechariah 2:10–11 says, "Sing and rejoice, O daughter of Zion: for, lo, I come, and I will dwell in the midst of thee, saith the LORD. And many nations shall be joined to the LORD in that day, and shall be my people: and I will dwell in the midst of thee, and thou shalt know that the LORD of hosts hath sent me unto thee."

Remember that we are still in the section that is known as the Leviticus section, and the tabernacle and temple are the very heart of it.

The LORD loveth the gates of Zion more than all the dwellings of Jacob.

Glorious things are spoken of thee, O city of God. Selah [Ps. 87:2–3].

This same view was expressed before in Psalm 48, "Great is the LORD, and greatly to be praised in the city of our God, in the mountain of his holiness. Beautiful for situation, the joy of the whole earth, is mount Zion, on the sides of the north, the city of the great King" (Ps. 48:1–2).

I will make mention of Rahab and Babylon to them that know me: behold Philistia, and Tyre, with Ethiopia; this man was born there [Ps. 87:4].

"Rahab" is not the harlot of Jericho, but Egypt (see Isa. 51:9; Ps. 89:10). It represents the southern world power, and "Babylon" represents the northern. The name *Rahab* means "tumult" and *Babylon* means "confusion"—the tumult and confusion of these nations will end when Christ is reigning in Zion. It is very interesting to see that Zion will be the birthplace of many nations. When the Lord Jesus Christ is there, the world will come up to Jerusalem, and many nations will be converted. Notice it mentions "Philistia, and Tyre, with Ethiopia." This is all tremendously interesting when we remember that as the gospel left the land of Israel and started down the highways of the world, the first convert was the Ethiopian eunuch (Acts 8). He was born again out there in the desert. But the psalmist here has reference to, I believe, the entire nation of Ethiopia, which will be converted in that future time.

And of Zion it shall be said, This and that man was born in her: and the highest himself shall establish her [Ps. 87:5].

The King of kings will make Zion the capital of the earth.

The LORD shall count, when he writeth up the people, that this man was born there. Selah [Ps. 87:6].

There will be many who will turn to the Lord in that day, recognizing that they were deceived by the Antichrist. What a glorious time this will be!

PSALM 88

***THEME:** Confidence in God in the midst of suffering*

This is "A Song or Psalm for the sons of Korah, to the chief Musician upon Mahalath Leannoth, Maschil of Heman the Ezrahite." It is a doleful psalm. Psalm 87 was all glory; this psalm is all gloom. It is a lamentation. It is the darkest wail of woe in the Book of Psalms.

O LORD God of my salvation, I have cried day and night before thee [Ps. 88:1].

The one ray of hope in this psalm is that He is the "God of my salvation," and the psalmist is holding on to that. It is mere speculation, of course, but this psalm has been applied to Job and to Uzziah who had leprosy and to Jeremiah in the dungeon and to Hezekiah when he was sick. But no matter who is in view, this psalm describes great suffering. Yet in all of his suffering and affliction he maintains his confidence in God as the God of his salvation. That is the great theme of this psalm.

I am afflicted and ready to die from my youth up: while I suffer thy terrors I am distracted [Ps. 88:15].

He is in a tough place. Wrath, death, the grave, and darkness are summed up together by the sufferer.

Thy fierce wrath goeth over me; thy terrors have cut me off.

They came round about me daily like water; they compassed me about together.

Lover and friend hast thou put far from me, and mine acquaintance into darkness [Ps. 88:16–18].

Unlike other psalms which begin with deep distress but end with the joy of deliverance, this psalm closes with the word *darkness*. Hengstenberg has this comment: "The Psalm ends with an energetic expression of its main thought—the immediate vicinity of death. The darkness is thickest at the end just as it is in the morning, before the rising of the sun."

PSALM 89

***THEME:** Psalm of the Davidic covenant*

This is the final psalm in the Leviticus section. *The New Scofield Reference Bible* calls it the psalm of the Davidic Covenant. I like that because it is what the psalm is all about. This great psalm was written by Ethan the Ezrahite. It is a maschil, which means it is one of instruction. Ethan was probably a singer who belonged to the tribe of Levi. The writer is not identified for us—purposely, I think—because it is the faithfulness of God that is exalted in this psalm. The faithfulness of God is mentioned ten times, which makes it obvious that the psalmist is emphasizing His faithfulness. The word *covenant* is mentioned four times, and with it God says, "I have sworn" three times. Also "I will not lie" occurs four times. It is quite a contrast to the previous psalm which was all gloom and no glory. This one is all glory and no gloom. It is a psalm of great excitement, and it rests upon the covenant that God made with David.

When we were studying 2 Samuel, we spent quite a bit of time in chapter 7 which records God's covenant with David. If you want to know how important it is, you will find it referred to again and again in the writings of the prophets, and here is a psalm devoted to it.

I will sing of the mercies of the LORD for ever: with my mouth will I make known thy faithfulness to all generations [Ps. 89:1].

Is God good to you? I am sure He is. He certainly is good to me, and because of that "I will sing of the mercies of the LORD for ever." Although I can't really sing, I am going to tell it out the best way I know how. The mercies of the Lord are wonderful!

"With my mouth will I make known thy faithfulness"—I'm glad he didn't say "sing" this time, because singing excludes me; but I can use my mouth to make known His faithfulness. My, how faithful He has been to me!

Notice the pronoun is "thy"—it is *God's* faithfulness. It is praise to God for His faithfulness to David. Then down in verse 24 we read, "But *my* faithfulness and *my* mercy shall be with him." The pronoun has changed because it is God speaking. All the references in this psalm, regardless of the pronoun used, refer to the faithfulness of God.

For I have said, Mercy shall be built up for ever: thy faithfulness shalt thou establish in the very heavens [Ps. 89:2].

God is faithful. Our salvation rests upon the death of Christ and the faithfulness of God in saving those who put their trust in Him. It is what *God says* that is important.

It reminds me of the little Scottish lady I have told you about. She had sent her boy away to school, and he had come home a skeptic. She was fixing breakfast for him one morning and telling him how God had saved her, how sure she was of it, and how wonderful His salvation was. Finally the son could stand it no longer. He blurted out, "Your little soul doesn't amount to anything! It is very small compared to this great universe. God could forget you and wouldn't even miss you." On and on he talked. Then there was silence. This little Scottish mother kept quiet for a while. She finished serving him breakfast and sat down to eat. Then she said, "Son, I have been thinking about it. Maybe you are right. It may be that my soul doesn't amount to anything, but if I lose my soul, God is going to lose more than I will lose." Her son asked, "What do you mean by that?" Her reply was this, "If I lose my soul—you've just said it doesn't amount to much—so I wouldn't lose much, but God would lose a great deal. He would lose His Word, His reputation, because He *said* He would save me!"

She was right. And God would lose His reputation if He did not make good His covenant to David. But God is faithful.

I have made a covenant with my chosen, I have sworn unto David my servant [Ps. 89:3].

God says He made a covenant with David.

And the heavens shall praise thy wonders, O LORD: thy faithfulness also in the congregation of the saints [Ps. 89:5].

"The heavens declare the glory of God; and the firmament sheweth his handiwork" (Ps. 19:1), but the faithfulness of God has more glory connected with it than that. "O LORD: thy faithfulness also in the congregation of the saints." His faithfulness toward *us* deserves our praise!

O LORD God of hosts, who is a strong LORD like unto thee? or to thy faithfulness round about thee? [Ps. 89:8].

We certainly get the impression that he is talking about the faithfulness of God.

I have found David my servant; with my holy oil have I anointed him [Ps. 89:20].

God says, "I will make good what I promised David at the time I anointed him."

God rests upon what He has promised David:

But my faithfulness and my mercy shall be with him: and in my name shall his horn be exalted [Ps. 89:24].

The "horn" speaks of his strength.

Also I will make him my firstborn, higher than the kings of the earth [Ps. 89:27].

God's covenant to David was that He would be sending One in his line. The covenant centers on the Lord Jesus Christ. Of Him God says, "Also I will make him my firstborn, higher than the kings of the earth." Look at this—it is wonderful. When God sent the Lord Jesus into this world, He came as the only begotten Son, and by His incarnation yonder at Bethlehem He became the Son of God. Thus He was revealed in His life of humiliation—God manifested in the flesh. And after He died a sacrificial death—for that is the reason He came from heaven—He became in *resurrection* the firstborn, the first begotten from the dead. He is speaking of the resurrected Christ: "Also I will make him my firstborn"—the resurrected Christ, the One who came back from the dead after He had died on the cross. It simply means that the scepter of this universe is in nail-pierced hands.

But we are told here that He is "higher than the kings of the earth." This means that He is Lord of lords and King of kings! The psalmist now is talking about the Lord Jesus. Therefore again He says:

My mercy will I keep for him for evermore, and my covenant shall stand fast with him [Ps. 89:28].

Now we must correctly divide the Word of Truth. Verses 29–32 cannot speak of Christ, but of David's posterity. Suppose that David's children forsake God. What will God do?

> **If his children forsake my law, and walk not in my judgments;**
>
> **If they break my statutes, and keep not my commandments;**
>
> **Then will I visit their transgression with the rod, and their iniquity with stripes [Ps. 89:30–32].**

Does it sound as though God is through with His children if they are not faithful to Him? No!

> **Nevertheless my lovingkindness will I not utterly take from him, nor suffer my faithfulness to fail [Ps. 89:33].**

Oh, my friend, I may be faithless; but my God is *faithful*. What wonderful assurance!

Next God takes an oath concerning the covenant He made with David:

> **My covenant will I not break, nor alter the thing that is gone out of my lips.**
>
> **Once have I sworn by my holiness that I will not lie unto David.**
>
> **His seed shall endure for ever, and his throne as the sun before me [Ps. 89: 34–36].**

At this very moment there is One sitting at the right hand of God who is coming to earth to sit on that throne of David. He is the Lord Jesus Christ, the Son of David.

> **It shall be established for ever as the moon, and as a faithful witness in heaven. Selah [Ps. 89:37].**

David will have a Son who will sit on the throne of this universe. That fact is as established as the moon is established in the heavens, and it looks like the moon is going to be there for a long time. God will make good His covenant with David.

> **Lord, where are thy former lovingkindnesses, which thou swarest unto David in thy truth? [Ps. 89:49].**

To these people who had gotten away from God at this time, it looked as if God had forgotten His covenant. But He hadn't forgotten His covenant. God is faithful. God has the Man to sit on David's throne.

NUMBERS SECTION

Peril and Protection (Earth in view)
Psalms 90–106

This begins the fourth section, the Book of Numbers in the "Pentateuch" of the Psalms. It opens with a prayer of Moses. It is the only psalm of Moses that we have. Moses was the first writer of the Bible, and you would naturally think that his psalm would be the first one. If you or I had arranged the Psalms, we probably would have placed it at the very beginning. But we did not do the arranging, and I am of the opinion that God supervised even the arrangement because Psalm 90 falls into place in such a wonderful way.

The Book of Numbers records the great tragedy of a generation dying in the wilderness, never reaching the goal, which was the Promised Land. How appropriate it is to begin this Numbers section with Psalm 90, the prayer of Moses.

PSALM 90

THEME: *The prayer of Moses*

The setting for this psalm is out there on the desert during Israel's wanderings. You recall that when the people of Israel came from the bondage of Egypt, they were led first to Mount Sinai where God gave them the Law. Then they went up to enter the Promised Land; but, instead of entering it, they turned back to that frightful desert. For thirty-eight years they wandered in the desert—until that generation died. Moses saw a lot of people die—over two million of them—and his psalm is the psalm of death.

To me it is a remarkable psalm. It was Martin Luther who wrote: "Just as Moses acts in teaching the law, so does he in this Psalm. For he preaches death, sin and condemnation, in order that he may alarm the proud who are secure in their sins, and that he may set before their eyes their sin and evil." My friend, that is the teaching of this psalm.

Notice how majestic and sublime it is as it opens:

> **LORD, thou hast been our dwelling place in all generations.**
>
> **Before the mountains were brought forth, or ever thou hadst formed the earth and the world, even from everlasting to everlasting, thou art God [Ps. 90:1–2].**

The word *everlasting* is figurative in the Hebrew. It means "*from* the vanishing point *to* the vanishing point." God is from the vanishing point in the past and reaches to the vanishing point in eternity future. Just as far as you can see, from vanishing point to vanishing point, He is still God. How majestic is this thought! Man is just one of God's creatures, an offspring, as it were. In the Book of Genesis Moses wrote, "So God created man in his own image, in the image of God created he him; male and female created he them" (Gen. 1:27). Then in Genesis 2:7 Moses said, "And the LORD God formed man of the dust of the ground, and breathed into his nostrils the breath of life; and man became a living soul." This psalm regards man as a created being, not as an evolved animal. He is a creature in a class by himself. He has a body that was taken from the ground, a body by which he is going to earn his living down here by the sweat of his brow until the day comes when it returns to the dust out of which God created it. That's the picture of man.

> **Thou turnest man to destruction; and sayest, Return, ye children of men [Ps. 90:3].**

God returns man's frail body to the dust, saying, "Go back to where you came from."

> **For a thousand years in thy sight are but as yesterday when it is past, and as a watch in the night [Ps. 90:4].**

Suppose, my friend, you live as long as Methuselah lived—almost a thousand years—that would be like just a watch in the night. It would be like the flight of a bird through a lighted room, coming out of the darkness through one window and going out another window into the darkness again. Even if you could live one thousand years, you wouldn't be very much. Life is so brief compared to eternity.

> **Thou carriest them away as with a flood; they are as a sleep: in the morning they are like grass which groweth up.**
>
> **In the morning it flourisheth, and groweth up; in the evening it is cut down, and withereth [Ps. 90:5–6].**

This is a picture of man. In the wilderness Moses saw over one million people die. He probably attended more funerals than anyone else. Man's body was taken from the ground, and Moses saw that body put back into the ground from which it had come.

This leads me to another subject. I have received several letters asking me what I think about cremation. I do not believe in cremation. I don't mean that God cannot raise up your body if you are cremated, but cremation is not a good testimony for a believer. Many unbelievers in Southern California want to be cremated and have their ashes scattered over the ocean. I knew an undertaker in Pasadena who was a pilot. He told me that many people wanted their ashes scattered over the ocean, and that was one of the services he provided. What is the motive of folk who want to be cremated and their ashes scattered over the ocean? Many of them don't want their bodies resurrected; they think that God will not be able to get their bodies back together again.

Christian friend, you give a testimony when you take your dead loved one who is in Christ and you bury him in the ground. In John 12:24 the Lord Jesus Christ said, "Verily, verily, I say unto you, Except a corn of wheat fall into the ground and die, it abideth alone: but if it die, it bringeth forth much fruit." This is the picture of the Lord's death and resurrection. When you bury your loved one, you are planting that body, expecting his resurrection some day. In the early days the cemetery was called two things: (1) an inn, a place where people sleep for a time, and (2) a field, a place where seed is planted. You do not *burn up* your seed! When you bury your dead, you are planting seed. Your testimony is that you believe God meant what He said when He promised resurrection, and you are looking forward to being reunited with that loved one some day.

Thou hast set our iniquities before thee, our secret sins in the light of thy countenance [Ps. 90:8].

Dr. Lewis Sperry Chafer used to say that secret sin on earth is open scandal in heaven. The angels are watching you; they see what you do down here.

For all our days are passed away in thy wrath: we spend our years as a tale that is told [Ps. 90:9].

In the Hebrew this verse is figurative: "We spend our years as a moan." We go through life moaning. If you do not know the Savior today and have no hope for eternity, you just don't have anything to live for, do you? You don't have purpose in life or any direction.

The days of our years are threescore years and ten; and if by reason of strength they be fourscore years, yet is their strength labour and sorrow; for it is soon cut off, and we fly away [Ps. 90:10].

Threescore years and ten is seventy years. Fourscore years is eighty years. If you make it to eighty years, you sure are going to have a lot of rheumatism and arthritis. I am finding this to be true already. What a picture this gives of us down here! If you live for eighty years, it is going to be uphill all the way. We talk about coming to the "sunset" of life, but that is when you start going uphill, not downhill. We just pass our days as a moan. It is well to have a future, and that is what the believer has when he puts his faith in Christ.

So teach us to number our days, that we may apply our hearts unto wisdom [Ps. 90:12].

It is Christ who is made unto us wisdom. "But of him are ye in Christ Jesus, who of God is made unto us wisdom, and righteousness, and sanctification, and redemption" (1 Cor. 1:30). If you have Christ, you have wisdom and hope.

And let the beauty of the LORD our God be upon us: and establish thou the work of our hands upon us; yea, the work of our hands establish thou it [Ps. 90:17].

Oh, to do something in this life that will have value in eternity!

My friend, Moses out there in the desert, pausing day after day in the wilderness march to bury someone, got a perspective on life that many of us do not have. What a beautiful and practical psalm this is!

PSALM 91

THEME: *Song of life and light*

As Psalm 90 was a psalm of death, so Psalm 91 is a psalm of life; it is a messianic psalm and gives a picture of the Lord Jesus Christ. However it reveals a wonderful place of protection and security for us. It is a psalm that is very popular among God's people, both old and young of all ages. Many have been greatly blessed by it.

Psalm 90 was a picture of the first man, Adam; and in Adam all die. It was a psalm of death. But Psalm 91 is a picture of the Lord from heaven, a truly messianic psalm and a psalm of life.

This is a psalm that was quoted by Satan. It is one he knows very well, as we shall see.

He that dwelleth in the secret place of the most High shall abide under the shadow of the Almighty.

I will say of the LORD, He is my refuge

and my fortress: my God; in him will I trust [Ps. 91:1–2].

This is beautiful language, my friend. "I will say of Jehovah, He is my refuge and my fortress." The One who is depicted for us in these verses is the same Man who was the blessed Man in Psalm 1—the Lord Jesus Christ—the perfect, holy, sinless Man. He *always* dwells in the secret place of the Most High. My problem is that I am there sometimes, but my stay is like it is in motels—only for a night or two at a time.

Surely he shall deliver thee from the snare of the fowler, and from the noisome pestilence [the pestilence that destroys].

He shall cover thee with his feathers, and under his wings shalt thou trust: his truth shall be thy shield and buckler.

Thou shalt not be afraid for the terror by night; nor for the arrow that flieth by day [Ps. 91:3–5].

A young man in my congregation claimed this verse as his when he went into military service. He felt that it brought him through combat safely.

Nor for the pestilence that walketh in darkness; nor for the destruction that wasteth at noonday [Ps. 91:6].

Another young man took this verse with him when he was in the Navy Air Corps. He was a very fine young man, and he retired as a commander. This was the verse he claimed as his.

A thousand shall fall at thy side, and ten thousand at thy right hand; but it shall not come nigh thee.

Only with thine eyes shalt thou behold and see the reward of the wicked [Ps. 91:7–8].

I believe these verses can be used by God's people, and many times God has made them real to His people; but they actually picture our Lord. I want to give you the statement of Dr. A. C. Gaebelein, a Bible teacher of the past generation. He had this to say about this passage: "Let us think of Himself first of all. There was no sin in Him, and that which is the result of sin, disease and death, had no claim on Him. In every way He was the perfect Man, and because He trusted in God His Father, walked in perfect obedience, the great fowler, Satan, could not catch Him nor the pestilence of destruction. Covered by His feathers, under His wings, the perfect Man on earth found His constant refuge. He knew no fear; that which befell others could never come nigh unto Him. And His own follow Him in the life of trust and obedience, claiming also the preservation and protection" (*The Book of Psalms*, p. 347). I pause to intrude with this: I think that the two young men I mentioned, who claimed verses from this psalm, had a perfect right to do so, and God made them real in their lives. Dr. Gaebelein continues: "Yet how true it is 'our body is dead on account of sin.' Fanaticism may claim all these statements as having an absolute meaning for the trusting child of God, experience teaches often the opposite. Because we are the failing and erring creatures of the dust we need discipline and have to pass through the tests of faith. Yet in it all the believer can be in perfect peace, knowing that all is well. 'Though He slay me, yet will I trust' is the summit of true faith and confidence in God" (*The Book of Psalms*, p. 347). This is quite a wonderful statement, is it not?

Because thou hast made the LORD, which is my refuge, even the most High, thy habitation;

There shall no evil befall thee, neither shall any plague come nigh thy dwelling [Ps. 91:9–10].

This pictures Christ, you see.

For he shall give his angels charge over thee, to keep thee in all thy ways.

They shall bear thee up in their hands, lest thou dash thy foot against a stone [Ps. 91:11–12].

This is the passage that the Devil quoted, and the interesting thing is that Satan knew this psalm applied to the Lord Jesus. He knew something a lot of theology professors don't know today. During the Lord's temptation, Satan said, "For it is written, He shall give his angels charge over thee, to keep thee." This statement is recorded in Luke 4:10; it seems that the Devil quotes Scripture for his purposes. Well, I don't think he can quote it, but he can misquote it, and in this case that is just what he did. He left out the words, "in all thy ways." The Lord Jesus Christ came to do the Father's will, and that meant to walk in His ways. He would have stepped out of the will of God if He had attempted to make the stones into bread, or if He had accepted the kingdoms of the world from Satan, or if He had cast Himself down from the pinnacle of the temple. To do any of that would have been out of the *way* of God. The promise is: "For he shall give his angels charge over thee, to keep thee in all *thy ways*."

Now in verse 14 there are two "becauses," and they are very important:

Because he hath set his love upon me, therefore will I deliver him: I will set him on high, because he hath known my name.

He shall call upon me, and I will answer him: I will be with him in trouble; I will deliver him, and honour him [Ps. 91:14–15].

You see, the perfect Man went into the jaws of death. He went down into the lowest parts of the earth, which meant death and the grave. Deliverance came on the third day when God raised Christ from the dead and gave Him glory. God says, "I will set him on high." What a picture we have of Christ in this psalm!

PSALM 92

***THEME:** Song of praise for the sabbath day*

This psalm bears the inscription: "A Psalm or Song for the sabbath day." It is a song of praise that naturally follows a messianic psalm. It tells of praise and worship and adoration—that's what the sabbath was given for. However, worship in this psalm is connected with an earthly sanctuary and actually looks forward to the day when, once again, an earthly sanctuary will be established in Jerusalem and God's redeemed people will worship there. The worship of believers today is a little bit different. The Lord said to the Samaritan woman, ". . . Woman, believe me, the hour cometh, when ye shall neither in this mountain, nor yet at Jerusalem, worship the Father . . . .But the hour cometh, and now is, when the true worshippers shall worship the Father in spirit and in truth: for the Father seeketh such to worship him" (John 4:21, 23). Believers today are made into a kingdom of priests unto God, not to serve Him in an earthly sanctuary, but to worship Him in spirit and in truth.

The psalm opens on this glorious note:

It is a good thing to give thanks unto the LORD, and to sing praises unto thy name, O most High [Ps. 92:1].

Do you want to do a good thing today? Do you want to do a good turn? All right, give thanks to the Lord right now wherever you are and sing praises to His name.

To shew forth thy lovingkindness in the morning, and thy faithfulness every night [Ps. 92:2].

You can thank Him in the morning; you can thank Him at night for His lovingkindness and faithfulness. I always thank Him in the morning. I must confess that I sometimes forget to thank Him at night, but I always thank Him early in the morning for a new day and for His lovingkindness that has brought me to a new day. At night, when you go to bed, you can thank Him for his *faithfulness* in bringing you through the day. I think it is quite an undertaking to bring Vernon McGee through any day. It is wonderful to have a God who will do that!

A brutish man knoweth not; neither doth a fool understand this [Ps. 92:6].

The New Scofield Reference Bible says, "A stupid man knoweth not, neither doth a fool understand this." They do not know about, nor understand, God's lovingkindness or faithfulness.

This is a millennial psalm which looks forward to the future, when the time of worship will once again be on the sabbath day. I don't worship on the sabbath; I worship on the first day of the week, because my Lord was *dead* on the sabbath day, but He came back from the dead on the first day of the week.

But thou, LORD, art most high for evermore [Ps. 92:8].

"Most high" is a millennial name for our God. This psalm is a great millennial psalm, but some verses look back in retrospect to earthly conditions. Man is pictured as brutish. He does not walk uprightly. He does not look up to God. He thinks he does, but he does not. He actually looks down and grovels in the filth of sin. He is a fool. He lacks good sense. He cannot understand because God says, "... [his] foolish heart was darkened" (Rom. 1:21). The brutish man denies God, and he lives like a brute. He lives like an animal—like a *pig*. Many people live as though God does not exist. They just eat, and sleep, and rest, and play, and work. That's it—that's life for them!

But what a beautiful picture we have brought before us here:

The righteous shall flourish like the palm tree: he shall grow like a cedar in Lebanon [Ps. 92:12].

The palm tree has been an emblem of victory, and the cedar tree denotes strength and seriousness. This is a picture of the righteous who are walking in fellowship with God even today.

PSALM 93

THEME: *Millennial psalm of sheer praise*

This is a brief psalm with only five verses. This little psalm, tucked between psalms 92 and 94, is a song of sheer praise because the King is reigning. It is a millennial kingdom psalm and speaks of the Lord who has come to reign gloriously over the earth.

The LORD reigneth, he is clothed with majesty; the LORD is clothed with strength, wherewith he hath girded himself: the world also is stablished, that it cannot be moved [Ps. 93:1].

"Jehovah reigneth"—this is the Lord Jesus. He is clothed with majesty. This is a psalm that will really have meaning when He comes to reign on this earth. All rebellious opposition will be broken down, and all those who have opposed God will be dethroned on the earth.

The floods have lifted up, O LORD, the floods have lifted up their voice; the floods lift up their waves [Ps. 93:3].

The flood tide of sin is over. Satan's head has been crushed.

The LORD on high is mightier than the noise of many waters, yea, than the mighty waves of the sea.

Thy testimonies are very sure: holiness becometh thine house, O LORD, for ever [Ps. 93:4–5].

What a wonderful time of rejoicing this will be!

PSALM 94

THEME: *A call upon God to intervene against the wicked*

Psalms 94 to 100 form a series of psalms that tell a consecutive story. These seven glorious psalms are kingdom songs celebrating the reign of the Messiah. They are a revelation of the Lord Jesus Christ and His reign on earth following the time of the Great Tribulation and all the trouble that comes upon man during that period.

Psalm 94 is a call upon God to intervene in righteousness against the wicked. It is a cry from the remnant in the time of trouble preceding the kingdom.

O LORD God, to whom vengeance belongeth; O God, to whom vengeance belongeth, shew thyself [Ps. 94:1].

"Shew thyself" or "shine forth, O God." Many people say, "O, if the Lord would only come." Well, He is coming, friend; but He is coming on His schedule, not on mine or any man's schedule. Then when He comes, He will take care of all those things that caused us suffering. For the present He simply says, "Take my hand, and walk in faith." Vengeance belongs to the Lord. He will repay. God will take care of things and set them right. There are a lot of things that need to be straightened out; and, when He comes to earth again in power and great glory, He will make things right. In the meantime, we are not to avenge ourselves. Turn those matters over to Him.

Understand, ye brutish among the people: and ye fools, when will ye be wise?

He that planted the ear, shall he not hear? he that formed the eye, shall he not see? [Ps. 94:8–9].

Once again God is speaking to the stupid and foolish man. God is Spirit. He does not have ears like we do, but He hears. He does not have eyes like we do, but He sees. The sinner down here on this earth seems to think he is getting away with sin. God sees; God hears, and He is able to keep a record of what man does. My friend, there are only two places for your sins: either they are on Christ, or they are on you. If they are on Christ, the judgment is passed; if they are not, you have only judgment to look forward to in the future. Those who are in Christ have the glorious prospect of life with Him to look forward to in the days ahead. My friend, if you have not yet come to Christ, you will have to stand before God in judgment.

When I said, My foot slippeth; thy mercy, O LORD, held me up [Ps. 94:18].

The psalmist says, "I would have slipped, but God held me up."

And he shall bring upon them their own iniquity, and shall cut them off in their own wickedness; yea, the LORD our God shall cut them off [Ps. 94:23].

The psalm concludes with the confidence that God has heard and will judge the wicked.

PSALMS 95–99

THEME: *Songs of joy*

Psalm 95 is just a delightful hymn of praise.

O come, let us sing unto the LORD: let us make a joyful noise to the rock of our salvation.

Let us come before his presence with thanksgiving, and make a joyful noise unto him with psalms.

For the LORD is a great God, and a great King above all gods [Ps. 95:1–3].

Then He is worshiped as the Creator:

In his hand are the deep places of the earth: the strength of the hills is his also.

The sea is his, and he made it: and his hands formed the dry land.

O come, let us worship and bow down: let us kneel before the LORD our maker [Ps. 95:4–6].

Psalm 96 is another wonderful psalm of praise when the Lord Jehovah, who is the Lord Jesus Christ, shall reign over the whole earth.

O sing unto the LORD a new song: sing unto the LORD, all the earth [Ps. 96:1].

We have already seen that this "new song" is the song of redemption. The Book of Revelation says we will sing it.

Here we have idolatry mentioned:

For the LORD is great, and greatly to be praised: he is to be feared above all gods.

For all the gods of the nations are idols: but the LORD made the heavens [Ps. 96:4–5].

Idolatry is referred to here because the Millennium will end all idolatry. There are men today who think themselves wondrously wise by turning to all kinds of religions. May I say to you that the day will come when atheism, deism, polytheism, and all of the cults will be done away with.

Give unto the LORD, O ye kindreds of the people, give unto the LORD glory and strength [Ps. 96:7].

The Lord Jesus Christ will fulfill prophecy, end idolatry, and banish Satan; then all creation will rejoice.

Psalm 97 is similar to Psalm 96 because its message is, "Joy to the world, the Lord is come."

The LORD reigneth; let the earth rejoice; let the multitude of isles be glad thereof [Ps. 97:1].

This is not a hymn of Christ's first coming to earth but of His second coming to earth.

Confounded be all they that serve graven images, that boast themselves of idols: worship him, all ye gods [Ps. 97:7].

"Gods" should be translated angels—compare Hebrews 1:6—"And again, when he bringeth in the first begotten into the world, he saith, And let all the angels of God worship him."

Psalm 98 is the second stanza of the new song of worship.

O sing unto the LORD a new song; for he hath done marvellous things: his right hand, and his holy arm, hath gotten him the victory [Ps. 98:1].

Psalm 99 is a song to the King whose throne is a throne of grace and mercy.

The LORD reigneth; let the people tremble: he sitteth between the cherubims; let the earth be moved [Ps. 99:1].

This is another great psalm of praise to God, the Mighty One. If you haven't formed the habit of praising God, you should. If you are going to heaven, you had better tune up, because you are going to spend a lot of time praising Him in heaven and the best place to tune up is down here. We are going to come to a psalm that says that the Lord is good—let the redeemed of the Lord say so, whom He hath redeemed from the hand of the enemy. That psalm looks to the future when we will praise Him during the Millennium. It is not the Millennium yet, but there is no reason why *we* should not praise Him today. Do you know why we should praise Him? Because He is wonderful, He is faithful, and His lovingkindness endures forever. He will always be good to me, and He will always be good to you. Doesn't this do something for you?

PSALM 100

***THEME:** Chorus of the hymn to Him*

This psalm is the grand finale of that wonderful little cluster of psalms that began with Psalm 94 and closes with this psalm. In this section we have seen the Lord Jesus Christ as King. Jehovah is King. In Psalm 93 we saw that, "The LORD reigneth, he is clothed with majesty . . ." (Ps. 93:1). This phrase speaks of the future and the time that the Lord will come again to earth. The first time He came to earth He did not come in majesty. He came, as George Macdonald put it, "a little baby thing that made a woman cry." He is coming to earth the next time, as we are told in this psalm, "clothed with majesty." Psalm 94:1 begins, "O LORD God, to whom vengeance belongeth. . . ." When the Lord comes to earth again, He will make things right. We could not do it because we would be vindictive; the Lord will not reign that way. He will vindicate, but He will not be vindictive. Then Psalm 95: "O come, let us sing unto the LORD: let us make a joyful noise to the rock of our salvation." Psalm 96: "O sing unto the LORD a new song: sing unto the LORD, all the earth." Psalm 97: "The LORD reigneth; let the earth rejoice . . . ." Psalm 98: "O sing unto the LORD a new song; for he hath done marvellous things. . . ." Psalm 99: "The LORD reigneth; let the people tremble. . . ."

Now we come to the great doxology, Psalm 100. This is the Hallelujah chorus at the conclusion of this series. It is the glorious finale of this very precious cluster of psalms. Listen to it:

Make a joyful noise unto the LORD, all ye lands.

Serve the Lord with gladness: come before his presence with singing [Ps. 100:1–2].

Once again I would emphasize the fact that God does not want you to come before Him to worship with a long face. There are times when we have long faces; problems beset us, temptations overcome us, or we come to God in repentance, asking Him for forgiveness. We cast ourselves upon Him. But none of that is worship. You worship God when you come to *praise* Him. He wants you to be happy. At the time of this writing most of the bars have what is called a "happy hour." I wish we had a "happy hour" in church, without the liquid. Let's tune up and get ready to worship the Lord. "Make a joyful noise unto the Lord, all ye lands." That includes everybody. That is universal praise. There is a time coming when the entire world will be able to sing, "Joy to the world, the Lord is come!"

"Serve the Lord with gladness: come before his presence with singing." This is a wonderful psalm of praise—praise Him, worship Him, glorify Him. Now that I am a retired preacher I find myself becoming an expert on telling young pastors how they should conduct their services. There is one criticism I want to make concerning my own ministry, and that is that I did not have enough praise included in the services. We ought to praise God more. We ought to worship God more. We ought to come joyfully into His presence.

This psalm is just like a great doxology. There are many doxologies in the Word of God. Believers can sing the one in Ephesians 1:3: "Blessed be the God and Father of our Lord Jesus Christ, who hath blessed us with all spiritual blessings in heavenly places in Christ." God has been good to us. He has given us *all* spiritual blessings, but some of us do not avail ourselves of them; we are keeping them in cold storage, waiting for a rainy day. Well, it is a rainy day today—regardless of how bright the sun is shining. Start using the blessing God has for you! Here is another wonderful doxology in the first chapter of the Revelation: ". . . Unto him that loved us, and washed us from our sins in his own blood, And hath made us kings and priests unto God and his Father; to him be glory and dominion for ever and ever" (Rev. 1:5–6). My, I don't know about you, but that just carries me into the clouds! The whole world is called upon to shout aloud their praises unto Jehovah and to sing the mighty Hallelujah chorus, because in that day the whole world will know Him.

In this next verse is something quite interesting—the homogenizing of God as the Creator and as the Redeemer.

Know ye that the Lord he is God: it is he that hath made us, and not we ourselves; we are his people, and the sheep of his pasture [Ps. 100:3].

There are a lot of people who do not know that the Lord is God. Many Christians are not aware of this fact. In the early Christian church when the first persecution broke out, the apostles came back to the church in Jerusalem and reported what was happening. Their report moved the church to pray, and they began their prayer by saying, "Lord, thou art God . . ." (Acts 4:24). Someone says, "That is easy to say." Yes, but the question is, Do you believe it today? There are many Christians who act as if He is not God.

"It is he that hath made us, and not we ourselves"—God is the Creator. We ought to worship Him because He is the Creator! He *made* this universe!

Not only do we worship Him as Creator, but "we are his people, and the sheep of his pasture." How do you become a sheep? You must be redeemed. This is a case where the Shepherd died for the sheep; the sheep did not die for this Shepherd. What sheep are being talked about in this psalm? The sheep are Israel. The Lord is their Shepherd too. The Lord Jesus told them that He had "other" sheep that were not part of the flock of Israel. "I am the good shepherd, and know my sheep, and am known of mine. As the Father knoweth me, even so know I the Father: and I lay down my life for the sheep. And other sheep I have, which are not of this fold: them also I must bring, and they shall hear my voice; and there shall be one fold, and one shepherd" (John 10:14–16). The Lord is the Shepherd of Israel; He is also my Shepherd and yours—if we belong to Him.

Enter into his gates with thanksgiving, and into his courts with praise: be thankful unto him, and bless his name [Ps. 100:4].

This is the way God wants you to come into His presence. Someone told me the other day that he attended the services of one of the great churches of the past and had never witnessed a place that was so dead. Do you know what the problem was? People were not coming to church with praise in their hearts. They did not come to the service with thankfulness in their hearts to God. They did not enter His gates with thanksgiving. If you go to church on Sunday to worship, make *sure* you go with thanksgiving and praise in your heart. If you fail to do that, you are not going to be very helpful to your church.

For the LORD is good; his mercy is everlasting; and his truth endureth to all generations [Ps. 100:5].

I don't know who you are, or why you are, or where you are, but I do know that God is *good* to you, and He is good to me. Oh, how *good* He is!

"His mercy is everlasting." He hasn't run out of it. Perhaps since He extended so much mercy to me, you thought He had exhausted His supply. He hasn't. He has a lot left for you. His mercy is everlasting. Like the flour in the barrel belonging to the widow that Elijah helped—it never runs out.

"His truth endureth to all generations." My, what a great psalm of praise this is!

PSALM 101

THEME: *Song to the King who rules in righteousness and judgment*

This is a Davidic psalm. It begins a little nest of six psalms (101–106) that speak of praise to the King. Guess who is the subject of the hymnbook? It is all about Him again, the Lord Jesus Christ. He is the King of righteousness and peace, and He is going to reign on this earth. This is a psalm that could not fit into David's reign at all, so it must be a prophetic psalm. It looks into the future to the Man whom God told David about—the Man who would be coming in David's line. It wasn't about Solomon or any other in the Davidic line until Jesus was born in Bethlehem, because He was of the house and lineage of David. The Lord Jesus is the Man about whom the psalmist is singing.

I will sing of mercy and judgment: unto thee, O LORD, will I sing [Ps. 101:1].

This psalm begins, as others have done, with singing praises to God. "I will sing of mercy and *justice* [rather than judgment]." Now mercy and justice don't get along together today. It is difficult for man to hold them in balance, but God can do it. And we can sing of mercy and justice, because it is "unto thee, O LORD, will I sing." He is the King of righteousness and He is the King of peace. What a wonderful One is presented here!

I will behave myself wisely in a perfect way. O when wilt thou come unto me? I will walk within my house with a perfect heart [Ps. 101:2].

I don't remember David ever walking like that. The One whom we see here is the Redeemer, the only-begotten of the Father. The King speaks as the Son of Man. Notice that He was the Son of Man on the earth. In His work as the Redeemer He was the only-begotten of the Father, but He took His place in subjection to God's will. He occupied a lower place while He was on earth, but He took it willingly. We attempt to get a higher place. He took a lower place in order that He might bring us to a higher place. Before His incarnation Christ said, "Then said I, Lo, I come (in the volume of the book it is written of me,) to do thy will, O God" (Heb. 10:7). While our Lord was on earth, He stated that His meat and drink were to do the will of the Father who sent Him, and He did *perfectly* His Father's will. He waited patiently for that hour called "My hour" when He wrought out your salvation and mine. Today He is at God's right hand and is still doing the will of His Father. He is waiting for that hour when the Father will send Him into the world again, because the Father has said, ". . . Sit thou at my right hand, until I make thine enemies thy footstool" (Ps. 110:1). We are told that ". . . when all things shall be subdued unto him, then shall the Son also himself be subject unto him that put all things under him, that God may be all in all" (1 Cor. 15:28). This verse has caused a great deal of discussion. What does it really mean? It means that after He reigns on this earth, subject to the Father, He is going back to His place in the Godhead, a member of the Trinity. But when He is on this earth it is said of Him, ". . . I will declare thy name unto my brethren, in the midst of the church will I sing praise unto thee" (Heb. 2:12).

Now notice how Christ is going to reign—and David never reigned like this:

A froward heart shall depart from me: I will not know a wicked person.

Whoso privily slandereth his neighbour, him will I cut off: him that hath an high look and a proud heart will not I suffer.

Mine eyes shall be upon the faithful of the land, that they may dwell with me: he that walketh in a perfect way, he shall serve me.

He that worketh deceit shall not dwell within my house: he that telleth lies shall not tarry in my sight.

I will early destroy all the wicked of the land; that I may cut off all wicked doers from the city of the LORD [Ps. 101:4–8].

Dr. Gaebelein translates these verses a little more clearly: "A perverse heart shall depart from Me, an evil person I will not recognize. Whosoever slandereth his neighbor, I will destroy; him with a lofty look and proud heart I will not suffer. Mine eyes shall be on the faithful of the land, that they may dwell with Me; He that walketh in a perfect way, he shall serve Me. He that is given to deceit shall not dwell within My house, he that speaketh lies shall not be established in My sight. Morning after morning will I destroy all the wicked of the land; that I may cut off all workers of iniquity from the City of Jehovah" (*The Book of Psalms*, p. 379). This is a picture of Christ's reign here on this earth. During the Millennium you will not be able to take your case to the Supreme Court, for the very simple reason that Christ is the Supreme Court. He is the only One who will judge. The Father has turned over all judgment to His Son, and He will judge everyone every morning. They will have to toe the mark. The Lord is going to be a dictator when He reigns on earth, and everyone will do His will.

Then they will sing a new song to the King who rules in righteousness and judgment.

PSALM 102

***THEME:** Prayer of trouble and sorrow*

This is a messianic psalm that pictures the Lord Jesus in Gethsemane. The writer of this psalm is not mentioned. Since there have been all sorts of guesses as to who wrote it, I will guess that it was David. The inspired inscription of this psalm is "A Prayer of the afflicted, when he is overwhelmed, and poureth out his complaint before the LORD." This psalm pictures the affliction and humiliation of our Lord in the Garden of Gethsemane. As we will soon find, the Holy Spirit has marked out this psalm as messianic in the New Testament.

Hear my prayer, O LORD, and let my cry come unto thee [Ps. 102:1].

Dr. Gaebelein's translation is: "Jehovah, hear My prayer and let My cry come unto Thee!" Here is a case where Jehovah prays to Jehovah! He came in humiliation; yet He was Jehovah manifested in the flesh. In Genesis we find a remarkable statement: "Then the LORD rained upon Sodom and upon Gomorrah brimstone and fire from the LORD out of heaven" (Gen. 19:24). In other words, Jehovah on earth asks Jehovah in heaven to bring down judgment. Dr. Gaebelein adds this comment: "But here in humiliation, facing His great work as the sin-bearer, the fellow of Jehovah (Zech. 13:7) cries unto Him 'that was able to save Him out of death.' We have here in prophecy 'the prayers and supplications with strong crying and tears' of Gethsemane (Heb. 5:7)." And He was heard. But we find here that the wrath of the holy and righteous God fell upon Him because He bore your sins and my sins.

What a glorious and wonderful psalm this is!

Now here we see the deepest woe and agony that man can have:

Mine enemies reproach me all the day; and they that are mad against me are sworn against me [Ps. 102:8].

This expresses the depth of despair.

Because of thine indignation and thy wrath: for thou hast lifted me up, and cast me down [Ps. 102:10].

The words *indignation* and *wrath* are the strongest terms you can use in the Hebrew language. The Lord endured this. Why? He did it ". . . for the *joy* that was set before him . . ." (Heb. 12:2).

But thou, O LORD, shalt endure for ever; and thy remembrance unto all generations.

Thou shalt arise, and have mercy upon Zion: for the time to favour her, yea, the set time, is come [Ps. 102:12–13].

He will have mercy upon *Zion!* And so it was ". . . for the joy that was set before him endured the cross, despising the shame . . ." (Heb. 12:2). He died, you see, for the nation Israel. John 11:51 mentions that it was necessary for one to die for the nation. And Christ did die for that nation.

And He is going to build Zion again when He appears in His glory—which will be at His second coming.

When the LORD shall build up Zion, he shall appear in his glory [Ps. 102:16].

Our Lord knew that through His sacrificial death Zion would ultimately be redeemed.

Of old hast thou laid the foundation of the earth: and the heavens are the work of thy hands.

They shall perish, but thou shalt endure: yea, all of them shall wax old like a garment; as a vesture shalt thou change them, and they shall be changed.

But thou art the same, and thy years shall have no end [Ps. 102:25–27].

The Holy Spirit quotes this passage in Hebrews 1:10–12, and we would not have known that Psalm 102 was a messianic psalm if it hadn't pleased the author of the Bible, the Spirit of God, to reveal the meaning of this section in the first chapter of Hebrews. Psalm 102 applies to the Lord Jesus Christ. It is His prayer of trouble and sorrow. This is the King in Gethsemane—His humiliation before His exaltation, as set forth in Hebrews 5:7, which says, "Who in the days of his flesh, when he had offered up prayers and supplications with strong crying and tears unto him that was able to save him from death, and was heard in that he feared." Because He suffered for us, He can sympathize with us. I like to think of Psalm 102 as the psalm of Gethsemane.

PSALM 103

***THEME:** A great psalm of praise for the tender mercies of God*

When Gustavus Adolphus entered Augsburg after his victory at Leipzig, he had this psalm read. It looks forward to a new day; in fact, it looks beyond the Millennium into eternity where it will find the fullness of fulfillment. In the past the nation of Israel turned to this psalm, today the godly Israelite turns to this psalm, and in the future he will also turn to this psalm. Individual believers today find it a real source of strength and light. It is a psalm of thanksgiving for things, and a psalm of praise for a Person—that Person is Christ. I suppose it was sung antiphonally. The psalm begins as a solo and ends in a symphony of universal praise. I have divided the psalm like this: (1) Admonition for the present; (2) Declaration concerning Jehovah; (3) Declaration concerning man; and (4) Proclamation for the future.

ADMONITION FOR THE PRESENT

Psalm 103 begins with an admonition for the present, and notice how personal it is.

Bless the LORD, O my soul: and all that is within me, bless his holy name.

Bless the LORD, O my soul, and forget not all his benefits [Ps. 103:1–2].

Twice we are told to bless the Lord, twice in the first two verses. This is a psalm that gets way down where we live; it reveals something to our hearts. The Polychrome Bible translates the first verse, "Bless the LORD, O my soul: and all that is deepest within me, bless his holy name." We are told to praise and glorify the Lord; yet when I read this psalm I recognize that the best I can do just doesn't quite make it. My soul goes out to Him but not like it should. My friend, I want to put up a warning signal. There is a real danger today of going to church, observing the ritual, and parroting pious platitudes. This is the thing God warned His people about in Isaiah 29:13, "Wherefore the Lord said, Forasmuch as this people draw near me with their mouth, and with their lips do honour me, but have removed their heart far from me, and their fear toward me is taught by the precept of men." It is nothing more than lip service. There is no submission to God's Word and His demands. They just follow the precepts of men. We see this in Judaism and Romanism; and it is pretty easy for Protestants to point a finger at them and say, "Look how dead their religion is!" My friend, how dead is your church and your personal worship? Oh, if only *my* praise could be pure and from the depths of my heart! That is what I long for and what we should all long for. There is a lot of chanting and ritualism today in church. It is easy to say that liberalism rejects all of the great truths of God's Word, but if we simply go to church and mouth these truths, it can also be said of us, "Men worship Me with their lips, but their hearts are far from Me." This psalm says, "*All* that is within me, bless his holy name." The flesh cannot do this. I am going to make a confession to you: I can't worship the Lord like I want to. Do you know why? This old flesh of mine can't rise to that level. It is only by the Holy Spirit that you and I can worship the Lord in spirit and in truth.

Let's not forget "all His benefits." He has been so *good* to us—how evident this is as we look back over the years.

DECLARATION CONCERNING JEHOVAH

Who forgiveth all thine iniquities; who healeth all thy diseases [Ps. 103:3].

I am of the opinion that this verse speaks of the kingdom age (there are many people who disagree with me), and I am very frank to say that this refers to physical as well as spiritual diseases. God has made it quite clear what He is going to do during the kingdom age. Isaiah 33:24 says, "And the inhabitant shall not say, I am sick: the people that dwell therein shall be forgiven their iniquity." I have been told that many of these "faith healers" emphasize salvation. I don't think they emphasize salvation at all. Instead they put it on the end of their services like a caboose. My friend, there can be no healing until the sins are forgiven. Disease is the result of sin; and, before healing can take place, the sin question must be settled. Christ was delivered for our offenses. He was raised for our justification. Not until we are justified by faith in Christ can we be forgiven. In 1 Peter 2:24 (a quote from Isaiah 53:5) we read, "Who his own self bare our sins in his own body on the tree, that we, being dead to sins, should live unto righteousness: by whose stripes ye were healed." Healed of what? Healed of your *sins*, my friend. That is the important thing.

Who redeemeth thy life from destruction; who crowneth thee with lovingkindness and tender mercies [Ps. 103:4].

We ought to recognize the fact that many of God's choicest servants have been ill and afflicted and have *never* been healed in this life. The apostle Paul was one of these. He had a thorn in his flesh. It may have been eye trouble. If anyone should have claimed healing, it seems to me he should have. Fanny Crosby was blind to her dying day. John Milton was blind. What about these people? Do you have the audacity to say that something was wrong with these people because they were not healed? It is wonderful to be healed, but that is not always God's plan. Understand one thing: some of God's choicest servants never experienced healing at all.

Who satisfieth thy mouth with good things; so that thy youth is renewed like the eagle's [Ps. 103:5].

I was very amused one day when I saw a "faith healer" on television. In fact, I was shocked because the picture I had seen of her looked very much like that of a high school girl. What I saw on television was not a high school girl—God had not renewed her youth. That will take place during the Millennium. In fact, I have a new body coming to me. I don't have it yet, but one day in the future it will be mine.

The LORD executeth righteousness and judgment for all that are oppressed.

He made known his ways unto Moses, his acts unto the children of Israel [Ps. 103:6–7].

God made known His *ways* to Moses, but all that the children of Israel saw were the miracles. They did not have much understanding. There are many people like them today who recognize certain truths, but they don't enter into the way of God. Oh, how important that is.

The LORD is merciful and gracious, slow to anger, and plenteous in mercy [Ps. 103:8].

What we need above everything else today is God's mercy.

DECLARATION CONCERNING MAN

He will not always chide: neither will he keep his anger for ever.

He hath not dealt with us after our sins; nor rewarded us according to our iniquities [Ps. 103:9–10].

My friend, if God would deal with us according to our sins and according to our iniquities, none of us would be saved.

For as the heaven is high above the earth, so great is his mercy toward them that fear him [Ps. 103:11].

Oh, how we need his mercy!

As far as the east is from the west, so far hath he removed our transgressions from us [Ps. 103:12].

The psalmist does not say, "As far as the north is from the south." That is quite a distance; but when you start moving from the east to the west, there is no end. When you start going west, you keep going west. When you go north, you eventually reach a point where you start going south, but when you go west, you never stop going west. That is how far God has removed our transgressions from us!

Like as a father pitieth his children, so the LORD pitieth them that fear him [Ps. 103:13].

God is so good to us, and we do not seem to recognize it.

For he knoweth our frame; he remembereth that we are dust [Ps. 103:14].

Dr. George Gill used to put it like this: "*God* remembers that we are dust. We forget it, and when dust gets stuck on itself, it is *mud*." That is a picture of man.

As for man, his days are as grass: as a flower of the field, so he flourisheth.

For the wind passeth over it, and it is gone; and the place thereof shall know it no more [Ps. 103:15–16].

We won't be here on earth very long, friend. Someone said to me the other day, "I notice you are getting a little gray." I replied, "I notice that you are, too." Do you know what God is trying to tell us? When God puts gray in your hair, He is saying, "You are not going to be here much longer." When you get arthritis and you have trouble getting up in the morning, that is a warning from God. He is saying, "You won't be around much longer. You need to get straightened out."

PROCLAMATION FOR THE FUTURE

But the mercy of the LORD is from everlasting to everlasting upon them that fear him, and his righteousness unto children's children [Ps. 103:17].

It is a wonderful thing to look into the future and know that God will always be *merciful* to us.

Bless the LORD, all his works in all places of his dominion: bless the LORD, O my soul [Ps. 103:22].

How glorious it will be when all creatures in His dominion will bless Him. This is universal worship when, as Dr. Gaebelein expresses it, "the mighty Hallelujahs will sweep the earth, will sweep the heavens, will come downward and upward, when all creation will join in, when everything which has breath will shout 'Hallelujah.' "

But in the meantime, let's not forget to "bless the LORD, O *my* soul."

PSALM 104

***THEME:** Praise to the God of creation*

This is a psalm of nature, or as *The New Scofield Reference Bible* puts it, "Praise to the God of creation." It begins:

Bless the LORD, O my soul. O LORD my God, thou art very great; thou art clothed with honour and majesty [Ps. 104:1].

This psalm speaks about the God of creation. It is a hymn to God in nature because He is Creator.

Who coverest thyself with light as with a garment: who stretchest out the heavens like a curtain [Ps. 104:2].

On the first day of creation God said, ". . . Let there be light: and there was light" (Gen. 1:3). The second day of creation is pictured in these words: "Who stretchest out the heavens like a curtain"—just as you would stretch out a tent. In the day this psalm was written, travelers, such as those with a camel caravan, would arrive at their stopping place for the night and stretch out their tents. Well, that is the way God stretched out the heavens. As He did this, He put a layer of water above (and sometimes it comes down pretty fast), and the clouds are His chariots.

Who layeth the beams of his chambers in the waters: who maketh the clouds his chariot: who walketh upon the wings of the wind [Ps. 104:3].

On the second day of creation God said, ". . . Let there be a firmament in the midst of the waters, and let it divide the waters from the waters" (Gen. 1:6).

Who laid the foundations of the earth, that it should not be removed for ever.

Thou coveredst it with the deep as with a garment: the waters stood above the mountains [Ps. 104:5–6].

On the third day of creation ". . . God said, Let the waters under the heaven be gathered together unto one place, and let the dry land appear: and it was so" (Gen. 1:9). He had put waters above them—the clouds that go over carry quite a bit of water—now He divides the land and the waters.

At thy rebuke they fled; at the voice of thy thunder they hasted away.

They go up by the mountains; they go down by the valleys unto the place which thou hast founded for them [Ps. 104:7–8].

On the fourth day God did not create the sun and moon; He simply said, ". . . Let there be lights in the firmament of the heaven to divide the day from the night; and let them be for signs, and for seasons, and for days, and years" (Gen. 1:14). The sun and moon are to regulate time here on this earth. We have this in verse 19:

He appointed the moon for seasons: the sun knoweth his going down [Ps. 104:19].

Ancient people learned that the sun and moon regulated seedtime and harvest on the earth. In the ruins of an Indian building in Arizona are two holes which were made in a wall. For a long time no one could figure out why they were there. They finally discovered that when you could look through both of those holes and see the moon it was time to plant corn. God gave us the moon for seasons—He says so. The sun and the moon move according to schedule. Don't tell me that we are living in a meaningless universe.

What did God create on the fifth day? That was the day animal life appeared.

So is this great and wide sea, wherein are things creeping innumerable, both small and great beasts.

There go the ships: there is that leviathan, whom thou hast made to play therein [Ps. 104:25–26].

"And God said, Let the waters bring forth abundantly the moving creature that hath life . . ." (Gen. 1:20). It became alive with living creatures and everything that is in the ocean.

Now, what about man?

Thou sendest forth thy spirit, they are created: and thou renewest the face of the earth [Ps. 104:30].

Man now is going to be put on the earth—his home is ready for him.

The glory of the LORD shall endure for ever: the LORD shall rejoice in his works [Ps. 104:31].

When His creation was finished, God looked upon it and saw that it was good.

He looketh on the earth, and it trembleth: he toucheth the hills, and they smoke.

I will sing unto the LORD as long as I live: I will sing praise to my God while I have my being [Ps. 104:32–33].

Man is on the earth, created to praise God. He has been put on earth, and he has an address: he lives at No. 1, Garden of Eden.

My meditation of him shall be sweet: I will be glad in the LORD [Ps. 104:34].

However—

Let the sinners be consumed out of the earth, and let the wicked be no more. Bless thou the LORD, O my soul. Praise ye the LORD [Ps. 104:35].

Man has sinned. So what will God do? He is going to remove him from the earth, my friend. Unless you are willing to turn to Christ, I can assure you of one thing: this earth will not be your permanent dwelling place. God will remove you to another place, and He has another address for you.

PSALMS 105–106

THEME: *Historic psalms*

Psalms 105 is a hymn to God in history from Abraham to Moses. I am confident that it was written by David because the first part of this psalm is the same as 1 Chronicles 16:8–22, which tells about the time David brought the tabernacle into Jerusalem. This psalm is a recitation of Israel's history.

O give thanks unto the LORD; call upon his name: make known his deeds among the people.

Sing unto him, sing psalms unto him: talk ye of all his wondrous works.

Glory ye in his holy name: let the heart of them rejoice that seek the LORD.

Seek the LORD, and his strength: seek his face evermore.

Remember his marvellous works that he hath done; his wonders, and the judgments of his mouth [Ps. 105:1–5].

He goes back in history and begins with the descendants of Abraham, and the covenant God made with Abraham, Isaac, and Jacob. Then He follows them through Joseph, down into the land of Egypt.

Israel also came into Egypt; and Jacob sojourned in the land of Ham [Ps. 105:23].

Then when His people were oppressed by the Egyptians—

He sent Moses his servant; and Aaron whom he had chosen.

They shewed his signs among them, and wonders in the land of Ham [Ps. 105:26–27].

Now here is an interesting comment—

Egypt was glad when they departed: for the fear of them fell upon them [Ps. 105:38].

"Egypt was glad when Israel departed"—they certainly were. They were glad to get Israel out of their hair after those plagues. Then God brought His people into the land. The psalmist recites Israel's history as something to sing praise about.

My friend, there is something wrong with you if you cannot look back through your life and find something to thank God for. As the final verse of this psalm says, "Praise ye the LORD."

Psalm 106 is another historic psalm, and a long one; it ends the Numbers section. It follows the children of Israel through the wilderness. It begins:

Praise ye the LORD. O give thanks unto the LORD; for he is good: for his mercy endureth for ever [Ps. 106:1].

This psalm also speaks about the confession of sins.

We have sinned with our fathers, we have committed iniquity, we have done wickedly [Ps. 106:6].

When you look back over your life, you have something to thank God for if you have turned to Jesus Christ as your Savior and asked Him to forgive your sins. You can *thank* God for your salvation. These psalms are marvelous, are they not? This psalm shows us Israel's failure and God's faithfulness. We ought to become saturated with these psalms.

DEUTERONOMY SECTION

Perfection and Praise of the Word of God
Psalms 107–150

Psalm 107 begins the Deuteronomy section of the Book of Psalms. Dr. Gaebelein makes this comment: "The fifth book written by Moses begins with a great retrospect in the plains of Moab, in which inspired Moses reviews God's gracious dealings with His people. They were then facing the land of promise, into which they were soon to enter. In the opening Psalm of this Deuteronomy section the remnant of Israel is seen prophetically regathered and about ready to enter the land. They are looking back over their age long experiences, how He led them, dealt with them, humbled them, preserved and kept them" (*The Book of Psalms*, p. 399).

Believers of all ages have shared experiences such as these in their personal lives, and they are applicable to you and me.

PSALM 107

THEME: *God is good*

This is a psalm that has been greatly misunderstood. I feel that an excellent commentator like Matthew Henry, who had wonderful things to say about this psalm, missed it because he did not see the prophetic aspect of it. I trust by now that you are seeing the deep meaning in these psalms when they are put in their proper context. It is the song of the wandering Jew when he reenters the Promised Land. Also this psalm has a special meaning for us in our day and has blessed the hearts of saints down through the ages.

This is a psalm I would like to see set to music. It divides itself naturally into four stanzas, and the chorus is repeated three times (vv. 8, 21, and 31).

THE PROVIDENCE OF GOD—HE DIRECTS PILGRIMS

My suggestion would be that this be sung as a tenor solo.

O give thanks unto the LORD, for he is good: for his mercy endureth for ever.

Let the redeemed of the LORD say so, whom he hath redeemed from the hand of the enemy [Ps. 107:1–2].

We need more "say so" Christians. Let the redeemed of the Lord *say so*. Don't go around complaining and criticizing. If you are a Christian, tell others how good God is. He *is* good, but He doesn't have a good name in the world today. God's reputation is bad—a reputation is what people think about you. God does not have many friends in court among the multitudes of people in the world—no champion, or defender, and few to testify on His behalf. There are few to take the witness stand and say a good word in His behalf. If you doubt that, look around. Consider the pagan and heathen religions. Their conception of God is terrifying. He is pictured as a god that will destroy, not save; a god that is difficult to approach, and takes no personal interest in his creatures, nor does he love them. The average person today lives in a land with a veneer of civilization, a modicum of education, with a little Christian culture smeared on like face cream. To him God is not a Person to be cultivated; He is kept at arm's length. He is not considered a good neighbor, and He is very hard to please. Most people think of God as sort of a policeman, waiting around the corner to catch them in some wrongdoing. A little girl accidentally gave the average conception of God when she recited a Scripture verse and got it a bit confused. She said, "If God be for you, you are up against Him." That is the thinking of many people.

If anyone is going to say that God is good, it will have to be His redeemed ones. *God is good.* That is not an axiom; it is a proposition that is subject to proof. It is not a cliché, nor a slogan; it is not propaganda. It is true.

And gathered them out of the lands, from the east, and from the west, from the north, and from the south [Ps. 107:3].

The Lord is gathering people from the east, west, north, and south. Who are they? God is talking about Israel.

They wandered in the wilderness in a solitary way; they found no city to dwell in.

Hungry and thirsty, their soul fainted in them.

Then they cried unto the LORD in their trouble, and he delivered them out of their distresses.

And he led them forth by the right way, that they might go to a city of habitation [Ps. 107:4–7].

Remember that Psalm 107 begins the Deuteronomy section of the Psalms and corresponds to the Book of Deuteronomy, the last book of the Pentateuch which was written by Moses. This section deals with the perfection and praise of God's Word. In Deuteronomy 28: 64–65, God already told the Israelites that they would be scattered because of their sins: "And the LORD shall scatter thee among all people, from the one end of the earth even unto the other; and there thou shalt serve other gods, which neither thou nor thy fathers have known, even wood and stone. And among these nations shalt thou find no ease, neither shall the sole of thy foot have rest: but the LORD shall give thee there a trembling heart, and failing of eyes, and sorrow of mind." This has been the picture of the Jews down through the ages when they disobeyed God and were out of their land. But God is going to gather them together once again and make good His promise to establish them in the land. This is a wonderful picture of the providence of God in the lives of His people.

It speaks of me also. God reached down in the wilderness of this world and saved me. He will do the same for you, if He hasn't already done so. This is a glorious picture of the providence of God in the lives of His ancient people—God is not through with the nation Israel. In fact, God is not through with you and He is not through with me. This section has a message for us.

THE PARDON OF GOD—HE DELIVERS PRISONERS

Let's make this a soprano solo. It begins on that high note of praise. In fact, it begins with this wonderful chorus:

Oh that men would praise the LORD for his goodness, and for his wonderful works to the children of men! [Ps. 107:8].

The chorus is at the beginning of this section rather than at the end.

As we move down into this psalm, we will notice that God delivers prisoners, and we will see a picture of a man in prison. It describes Israel in the time of trouble, the Great Tribulation that is coming. If a man is in prison at that time, God will deliver him and bring him back into the land. Think of the multitudes in prison in Germany during World War II, and all of them did not get out. I wonder how many of them thought of this psalm at that time?

Such as sit in darkness and in the shadow of death, being bound in affliction and iron [Ps. 107:10].

This is a description of the prisoner's helpless condition.

He brought them out of darkness and the shadow of death, and brake their bands in sunder.

Oh that men would praise the LORD for his goodness, and for his wonderful works to the children of men!

For he hath broken the gates of brass, and cut the bars of iron in sunder [Ps. 107:14–16].

Remember how God brought Simon Peter out of prison and how He delivered Paul and Silas at night. Also He has delivered us from the prison house of sin, and God has given us a pardon. God has a pardon for everyone, my friend. Someone might say, "If there is a pardon, why am I not forgiven?" Well, even in prison today a pardon must be *accepted.* I remember Dr. Harry Rimmer telling about a case in Pennsylvania in which a man was granted a pardon from prison by the governor, but he would not accept it. The prison officials were in a dilemma. What do you do when a man is granted a pardon and he will not accept it? Finally, an appeal was made to the judge, and he said, "The man will have to stay in prison." A person has to *accept* the pardon before he can be free.

The Lord has a pardon for you. In the Lord Jesus Christ we have forgiveness of sins and a pardon for our iniquities, but we have to accept it. Have you accepted your pardon yet? Are you delivered from sin and from the penalty for sin?

This psalm is a marvelous picture of God's mercy, and think what it is going to mean to Israel in the future! Many of them will be in prison, and God will deliver them and bring them back into their land.

THE PROTECTION OF GOD—HE DISSOLVES PROBLEMS

This should be a bass solo. It opens with that same chorus:

Oh that men would praise the Lord for his goodness, and for his wonderful works to the children of men! [Ps. 107:21].

And, my friend, let's *do* it!

And let them sacrifice the sacrifices of thanksgiving, and declare his works with rejoicing [Ps. 107:22].

God wants you and me to bring an offering of praise and thanksgiving when we come to Him. As a result, "We have an altar, whereof they have no right to eat which serve the tabernacle. For the bodies of those beasts, whose blood is brought into the sanctuary by the high priest for sin, are burned without the camp. Wherefore Jesus also, that he might sanctify the people with his own blood, suffered without the gate. Let us go forth therefore unto him without the camp, bearing his reproach. For here have we no continuing city, but we seek one to come. By him therefore let us offer the sacrifice of praise to God continually, that is, the fruit of our lips giving thanks to his name" (Heb. 13:10–15).

You do not have to wait to go to church to give God a sacrifice: that is, the fruit of your lips giving praise to God. What can you thank Him for? You can thank Him for His protection. He has brought you to this present hour.

They that go down to the sea in ships, that do business in great waters;

These see the works of the Lord, and his wonders in the deep [Ps. 107:23–24].

This matter of being a sailor in the days of the psalmist was a dangerous business. A man who went on a voyage couldn't be sure if he was coming back or not. He was more apt to commit himself to God than folk who board a great ship or a plane in our day. Many folk give it no thought at all, or they adopt the philosophy of fatalism and believe their day to die is predetermined. However, it is wonderful to be able to commit ourselves to God at a time like that.

THE POWER OF GOD—HE DELIGHTS HIS PEOPLE

Here now is the final stanza.

Oh that men would praise the Lord for his goodness, and for his wonderful works to the children of men! [Ps. 107:31].

This is a chorus, and we can all join in it because we need God's power in our lives today. It is said of Thomas Aquinas that one day he walked in on the pope while he was counting the money of the church. The pope said, "Sir Thomas, no longer can the church say to the lame man, 'Silver and gold have I none.' " Thomas wheeled around, started out of the room, and without looking back he replied, "That is right, sir. And no longer can the church say to the lame man, 'Rise up and walk.' " Today we are problem conscious, not power conscious. The early church was conscious of the power of God.

Many years ago the Standard Oil Company had a float in the Pasadena Rose Parade. It was a beautiful float—and I shall never forget it—decorated with American Beauty roses, the likes of which I had never seen before.

Right in the middle of the parade the float ran out of gas and had to be towed. Everyone laughed, because the Standard Oil Company float is the last one that should have run out of *gas!* It certainly should have had gas, and enough of it for the parade, but someone had forgotten to fill the tank, and there it was. As I looked at that poor, helpless float, and I heard everyone laughing, I felt sorry, because it was like the church of today. We are beautiful, decorated in style with all of our buildings, our programs, our services, and our propaganda, but we have no power. Power is what the church needs, and power is what each individual believer needs. One reason we are powerless is that we are not praising the Lord as we should.

Let them exalt him also in the congregation of the people, and praise him in the assembly of the elders [Ps. 107:32].

We need to praise God—praise goes before power. It puts gas in the tank and sends the rocket up yonder.

Whoso is wise, and will observe these things, even they shall understand the lovingkindness of the Lord [Ps. 107:43].

A little girl has defined lovingkindness. She said, "If you ask your mother for a piece of bread and butter, and she gives it to you, that is kindness. But if she puts jam on it without you asking her, that is lovingkindness." My friend, the lovingkindness of God is lavished upon us who belong to Him.

PSALM 108

***THEME:** Israel's praise and possession*

This is another psalm of David, and it is a very wonderful psalm. The first half is the same as Psalm 57, and the last is like Psalm 60. For this reason it has come under criticism and has been judged as a sort of patchwork. However, it is not that at all. If the portions of other psalms have been joined together, God has a purpose in it.

O God, my heart is fixed; I will sing and give praise, even with my glory [Ps. 108:1].

This is Israel's remnant, redeemed, brought home, praising and exalting the Lord. We saw this in the previous psalm. God is going to bring Israel back into the land. He will gather them from all over the world; and, when they are back in the land, they will praise and glorify God.

God hath spoken in his holiness; I will rejoice, I will divide Shechem, and mete out the valley of Succoth [Ps. 108:7].

These, I believe, are the words of the delivered remnant of Israel. They see themselves receiving their inheritance and dividing the land among the tribes. What a time of rejoicing that will be!

PSALM 109

THEME: *Messianic—the humiliation of Christ*

This psalm, "To the chief Musician, A Psalm of David," is a messianic psalm. It pictures the humiliation of Christ and is an imprecatory psalm. It has been called a Judas Iscariot psalm, because Simon Peter quoted from this psalm in reference to Judas: "For it is written in the book of Psalms, Let his habitation be desolate, and let no man dwell therein: and his bishopric let another take" (Acts 1:20). A "bishopric" is an overseership, and Simon Peter held an election to choose a man to take the place of Judas.

Now notice how this psalm describes Judas Iscariot.

> **Set thou a wicked man over him: and let Satan stand at his right hand.**
>
> **When he shall be judged, let him be condemned: and let his prayer become sin.**
>
> **Let his days be few; and let another take his office.**
>
> **Let his children be fatherless, and his wife a widow [Ps. 109:6–9].**

This indicates that Judas was married and had children.

> **Let his children be continually vagabonds, and beg: let them seek their bread also out of their desolate places [Ps. 109:10].**

You cannot find anything more dreadful than this imprecatory prayer, which was applied to Judas. As far as I know, no one is defending Judas Iscariot. (I have a notion, however, that certain contemporary judges and organizations would have declared Judas innocent and Jesus guilty!) The Word of God is very clear on the subject—Judas was a guilty man, and he was a lost man. This psalm makes the condition of being *lost* frightening. It is a terrible thing to be lost! In fact, the Lord Jesus said, ". . . but woe unto that man by whom the Son of man is betrayed! it had been good for that man if he had not been born" (Matt. 26:24). The Lord Jesus made it very clear that the condition of the lost is a terrible thing. In John 3:36, where He gave that wonderful invitation, He also gave the other side of it; He contrasted light and darkness: "He that believeth on the Son hath everlasting life: and he that believeth not the Son shall not see life; but the wrath of God abideth on him." I don't know how you can make that verse any stronger. The teaching that somehow or other folks who are lost are going to have a second chance, and that there is a larger hope, and that God may have another way, is completely foreign to the Word of God, which says that the wrath of God *abides* on the person who has not trusted Christ. Jesus Christ endured God's wrath for us on the cross. He did it for *us*, and our only way of salvation is to trust Him. If we do not, God's wrath will be upon us.

PSALM 110

THEME: *Messianic—the exaltation of Christ*

This psalm, like Psalm 109, is a messianic psalm. It speaks of the exaltation of Christ and begins with the ascension of Christ.

> **The LORD said unto my Lord, Sit thou at my right hand, until I make thine enemies thy footstool [Ps. 110:1].**

This psalm is remarkable because it sets forth the deity of Christ. You could not in any way consider this psalm and still deny His deity. This psalm is referred to many times in the New Testament (Acts 2:34, 35; Heb. 1:13; Heb. 5:6; 6:20; 7:21; 10:12–13).

At the time the enemies of Jesus were making their final onslaught upon Him, the Herodians, a political party, tried to trap Him by forcing Him to make a political statement that would mark Him as a traitor to Rome. When they failed to do that, the Sadducees, a liberal religious party, tried to trap Him with a ridiculous question regarding the Mosaic Law. When they failed, the Pharisees, a religio-political party, tried to trap Him. Jesus' answer puzzled the Pharisees; so while they huddled again to plan further strategy, Jesus asked them a question: "While the Pharisees were gathered together, Jesus asked them, Saying, What think ye of Christ? whose son is he? They say unto him, The son of David. He saith unto them, How then doth David in spirit call him Lord, saying, The LORD said unto my Lord, Sit thou on my right hand, till I make thine enemies thy footstool? If David then call him Lord, how is he his son? And no man was able to answer him a word, neither durst any man from that day forth ask him any more questions" (Matt. 22:41–46). Notice that Jesus asked a straightforward question: "What think ye of Christ?" The Pharisees answered that He was the Son of David. Upon hearing this answer, the Lord pointed them to Psalm 110 to show them their insufficient knowledge of that particular portion of Scripture which the Jews interpreted as messianic. This psalm, written by David, shows Jehovah talking to Messiah. David calls Messiah "my Lord"; and any Jew who admitted Messiah was David's descendant was faced with this psalm, where David calls Messiah his "Lord" and claims that He is superior. This showed that Messiah would be more than a king who would merely be a political ruler upon a throne. Also since David called Him "Lord" in this psalm, how can He be his son? The Lord cannot be his son by natural birth; it had to be by supernatural birth. This psalm is telling us that the Lord Jesus Christ, Israel's Messiah, was virgin born.

"The LORD said unto my Lord . . . ." This is an equal speaking to an equal. This is God speaking to God, if you please. Hebrews 1:13 says, "But to which of the angels said he at any time, Sit on my right hand, until I make thine enemies thy footstool?" This sets forth the deity of Jesus Christ, and it could not be given to us in any stronger fashion. When folk say that the Bible does not teach the deity of Jesus, they are not acquainted with this section of the Word of God, I can assure you.

The LORD shall send the rod of thy strength out of Zion: rule thou in the midst of thine enemies [Ps. 110:2].

This verse speaks of the coming of Christ to the earth to rule in Zion. Concerning this time Isaiah said, "And many people shall go and say, Come ye, and let us go up to the mountain of the LORD, to the house of the God of Jacob; and he will teach us of his ways, and we will walk in his paths: for out of Zion shall go forth the law, and the word of the LORD from Jerusalem" (Isa. 2:3). Jerusalem will be the center of the government on earth. God does have a purpose for Israel in the future.

Thy people shall be willing in the day of thy power, in the beauties of holiness from the womb of the morning: thou hast the dew of thy youth [Ps. 110:3].

During "the day of thy power" there will be the greatest turning to Jesus Christ that the world has ever seen. Spurgeon used to say, "God will have more people saved than there will be lost." It may not look like it today; so don't press your nose up against the window and be discouraged. God may not be doing so well today, but He is not through yet. He has a host of saved folk behind Him, and He has a great many ahead of Him. He has great plans for the future.

The LORD hath sworn, and will not repent, Thou art a priest for ever after the order of Melchizedek [Ps. 110:4].

Here is another very important truth: the Lord Jesus is a High Priest after the order of Melchizedek. This is developed in the Epistle to the Hebrews, because it is one of the greatest truths in the Word of God. At this point let me lift out just one portion from Hebrews: "As he saith also in another place, Thou art a priest for ever after the order of Melchisedec. Who in the days of his flesh, when he had offered up prayers and supplications with strong crying and tears unto him that was able to save him from death, and was heard in that he feared; Though he were a Son, yet learned he obedience by the things which he suffered; And being made perfect, he became the author of eternal salvation unto all them that obey him; Called of God an high priest after the order of Melchisedec" (Heb. 5:6–10). The priesthood of the Lord Jesus is superior to the Aaronic or Levitical priesthood of the Old Testament. These verses show both the deity and the humanity of the Lord Jesus Christ.

The Lord at thy right hand shall strike through kings in the day of his wrath.

He shall judge among the heathen [nations], he shall fill the places with the dead bodies; he shall wound the heads over many countries [Ps. 110:5–6].

You see, Christ is coming again in judgment. As Psalm 2:9 makes clear, "Thou shalt break them with a rod of iron; thou shalt dash them in pieces like a potter's vessel."

He shall drink of the brook in the way: therefore shall he lift up the head [Ps. 110:7].

I like what Dr. Gaebelein says about this verse; so let me quote him: "The passage places before us once more the humiliation and exaltation of our Lord. The humiliation is that He drank of the brook in the way. We are reminded of the three hundred warriors of Gideon, who went down on their knees and lapped water like dogs and who were later used and exalted through victory. But He went deeper than that. He drank of the deep waters of suffering and death. And therefore God has highly exalted Him. What a wonderful Psalm it is!" (*The Book of Psalms*, p. 415).

PSALM 111

***THEME:** Hallelujah for the works of God*

This is a hallelujah psalm for the works of God. And in the Hebrew it is a perfect acrostic, which we don't see in our English translation. This begins a series of three hallelujah psalms (111–113). This psalm praises God for His works and also for His redemption, which is the "new song" that will be sung in heaven. The old song is the song of creation; the new song is the song of redemption. Both are in this psalm.

Praise ye the LORD. I will praise the LORD with my whole heart, in the assembly of the upright, and in the congregation [Ps. 111:1].

"Praise ye the LORD" means Hallelujah. Now notice the works for which He is being praised:

The works of the LORD are great, sought out of all them that have pleasure therein.

His work is honourable and glorious: and his righteousness endureth for ever.

He hath made his wonderful works to be remembered: the LORD is gracious and full of compassion [Ps. 111:2–4].

The idea today of attributing the origin of this universe to natural causes takes away the glory from God the Father and the Lord Jesus Christ. It is robbing Him of His glory. It is as bad as denying the Lord's redemption or denying Him as Savior. If you accept Him as Savior, you also accept Him as Creator.

Now the psalmist mentions the redemption that we have, which is part of the hallelujah chorus:

He sent redemption unto his people: he hath commanded his covenant for ever: holy and reverend is his name [Ps. 111:9].

Here we find the word *reverend*. The holy God is the reverend God. That title should never be applied to a man. No preacher should be called "Reverend." This is a title for God alone.

God has a redemption for His people.

The fear of the LORD is the beginning of wisdom: a good understanding have all they that do his commandments: his praise endureth for ever [Ps. 111:10].

Oh, my friend, let's praise the Lord for His works. "The works of the LORD are great!" They are great in His creation and display His omnipotence and His eternal wisdom. They are even greater in His redemption, which reveals His righteousness, honor, and glory. Finally the day will come when redemption will be consummated and all things will be put under His feet; then the redeemed nations and creation itself will sing His praise. Hallelujah!

PSALM 112

***THEME:** Hallelujah for the righteousness of God*

This is another of the wonderful hallelujah psalms, and it also is written as an acrostic in the Hebrew—which, of course, we miss in our English translations. All twenty-two letters of the Hebrew alphabet are included in this psalm.

The emphasis is on praising God for His righteousness. Because of His righteousness, God must judge sin. Aren't you glad that God is who He is? Suppose He were the Devil and attempted to deceive us and destroy us? It is a horrible thing to even contemplate. But God is *good*. God is *righteous*, and for that very reason He has to deal with sin. The day will come when He will make things right, and I want Him to make things right. I would like the things in my own life to be straightened out, wouldn't you? This is something to praise Him for.

Praise ye the LORD. Blessed is the man that feareth the LORD, that delighteth greatly in his commandments [Ps. 112:1].

Don't despise His commandments. They are a mirror and will let you see who you really are. After broadcasting a series on the Ten Commandments, I received several letters from people who listened to the broadcasts. One man said, "I saw what an awful sinner I was. It was the thing that was separating me from God." A lady wrote and said that her sin was swearing. She would take God's name in vain. Then she turned to the Lord and had a remarkable conversion. It is all because she saw herself in God's mirror. That is what His commandments will do. Don't despise the commandments; but if you are honest, you know that you cannot be saved by keeping them. They reveal that you need a Savior.

Wealth and riches shall be in his house: and his righteousness endureth for ever [Ps. 112:3].

God will never run out of righteousness. He has a good supply of it. Our God is righteous.

Unto the upright there ariseth light in the darkness: he is gracious, and full of compassion, and righteous [Ps. 112:4].

"There ariseth light in the darkness." Why? Because God is gracious, compassionate, and righteous. We really do not know how *good* God is. If we did, we would sing the Hallelujah chorus more often.

Surely he shall not be moved for ever: the righteous shall be in everlasting remembrance [Ps. 112:6].

God is not going to lose sight of His own throughout eternity.

He hath dispersed, he hath given to the poor; his righteousness endureth for ever; his horn shall be exalted with honour [Ps. 112:9].

God is interested in the poor, and He has the only poverty program that is going to work. Unfortunately the Democrats, the Republicans, the Communists, and other groups are not interested in His program. They are going to solve the problem themselves. The real problem is that they do well by *themselves*, instead of doing well by the poor.

The wicked shall see it, and be grieved; he shall gnash with his teeth, and melt away: the desire of the wicked shall perish [Ps. 112:10].

The day is coming when wickedness will end —it will be gone forever. Hallelujah!

PSALM 113

***THEME:** A hallelujah chorus to God as Creator and Redeemer*

This psalm to the majesty of God opens the Hallel psalms (113–118), which were sung at the Passover feast, the Feast of Pentecost, the Feast of Tabernacles, and probably at all feasts of Israel.

This is a precious and delightful psalm of praise and worship.

Praise ye the LORD. Praise, O ye servants of the LORD, praise the name of the LORD [Ps. 113:1].

We should not take the Lord's name in vain; we should praise the Lord. It is a praise that will never be exhausted because it is to creation's Lord, to creation's Redeemer.

Blessed be the name of the LORD from this time forth and for evermore.

From the rising of the sun unto the going down of the same the LORD'S name is to be praised.

The LORD is high above all nations, and his glory above the heavens.

Who is like unto the LORD our God, who dwelleth on high,

Who humbleth himself to behold the things that are in heaven, and in the earth! [Ps. 113:2–6].

God is so high and lifted up that He has to stoop down in order to look into the heavens!

Now notice what God is going to do:

He raiseth up the poor out of the dust, and lifteth the needy out of the dunghill [Ps. 113:7].

He is the Savior, the Redeemer!

That he may set him with princes, even with the princes of his people.

He maketh the barren woman to keep house, and to be a joyful mother of children. Praise ye the LORD [Ps. 113:8–9].

Hallelujah! Praise the Lord! It is time, my friend, to praise the Lord.

There is one thing I hope to accomplish in this study of the Book of Psalms, and that is to get folk to praise the Lord. Oh, that God's people would *praise* Him! My friend, tell somebody today that God is good, then back it up with your experience of His goodness.

PSALM 114

***THEME:** God leads His dear children along*

This is another of the Hallel psalms (which begin or conclude with a Hallelujah). Psalms 113–118 were called the Egyptian Hallel psalms, and they were used at the Feasts of Passover, Pentecost, Tabernacles and Dedication. Apparently they were sung during the time the Passover was being celebrated. Some Bible scholars think three of them were sung at the beginning and three at the end. Others think they were sung intermittently during the Passover feast.

The psalm before us is a call to praise the wonderful God at whom we have been looking in Psalms 112 and 113. In Psalm 113, for instance, He is the Creator, He is the Redeemer, and He will be the Redeemer of creation. Because of this, we are to praise God. The Hallel psalms are for the purpose of praising God.

Notice that this psalm looks back to the time Israel was delivered from Egyptian bondage.

When Israel went out of Egypt, the house of Jacob from a people of strange language [Ps. 114:1].

When Abraham first went into the Land of Promise, he was a stranger. God told him that his people would go down to the land of Egypt where they would become a nation. Israel began as a nation in Egypt, and anti-Semitism was born in Egypt. The Bible tells of their sufferings, their hardships, their persecutions, and their troubles in Egypt. Then God remembered His covenant with them, heard their cry, looked upon the children of Israel, and had respect unto them. God delivered them from Egypt, and this psalm begins with the wilderness march.

Judah was his sanctuary, and Israel his dominion [Ps. 114:2].

God is speaking now of the whole nation being a tabernacle. God's original intention was that Israel would be a nation of priests—not just one tribe—which means they were to be priests for the world. I think that that is what will happen in the Millennium when Israel will serve in the earthly temple.

The sea saw it, and fled: Jordan was driven back [Ps. 114:3].

The children of Israel not only crossed the Red Sea, they also crossed the Jordan River (Josh. 3:13–17).

What ailed thee, O thou sea, that thou fleddest? thou Jordan, that thou wast driven back? [Ps. 114:5].

The God of creation (whom we saw in Psalm 113 with His omnipotent power) rolled back the Red Sea, and He also held back the waters of Jordan. These were miracles, and I don't think they can be explained on any other basis. When the children of Israel crossed the Red Sea they had been delivered from Egypt by blood—blood on the doorposts. When they crossed over Jordan they were separated from the wilderness and brought into the Promised Land. These are the two stages of redemption, and they illustrate the two stages of our redemption. The Lord Jesus, on the cross, has delivered us from the *penalty* of sin—that is for the past. He delivers us from the *power* of sin in the present—provided we meet His conditions—and He will deliver us from the *presence* of sin, which has not yet been realized. The crossing of the Red Sea and the crossing of the Jordan picture the two stages of redemption.

Tremble, thou earth, at the presence of the Lord, at the presence of the God of Jacob;

Which turned the rock into a standing water, the flint into a fountain of waters [Ps. 114:7–8].

You can see how appropriate the reading of this beautiful little psalm would be at the celebration of the Passover. It is a call to remembrance of God's mercy and power on behalf of His people.

PSALM 115

THEME: *Glory to God because He is the opposite of heathen idols*

This great psalm was sung in the Upper Room at the time our Lord commemorated the Passover with His disciples and instituted the Lord's Supper. It is thrilling to realize that the Lord Jesus Himself sang this and the other Hallel psalms.

We are not told who the writer is, but it is felt that it was written by someone who was celebrating the Remnant's return from the Babylonian captivity. It can be divided into three stanzas: (1) the congregation singing (vv. 1–8), (2) the Levites (vv. 9–11), and (3) the congregation (vv. 12–18). You may disagree with me, but it seems to me that it was divided like this.

Not unto us, O Lord, not unto us, but unto thy name give glory, for thy mercy, and for thy truth's sake [Ps. 115:1].

The nation Israel is here taking a very humble place, and they are trusting God. They had not been trusting Him, but they are here in the Great Tribulation and are moving toward the Millennium. You can see that singing this during the three feasts was bound to make an impression upon them.

The heathen round about them were ridiculing them, saying, "Where is your God?"

Wherefore should the heathen say, Where is now their God? [Ps. 115:2].

In other words, "You say He is your God: Why doesn't He deliver you?"

But our God is in the heavens: he hath done whatsoever he hath pleased [Ps. 115:3].

God allowed them to suffer because of their sin. It was according to His will, His plan, and His purpose. Israel is beginning to accept their circumstances from God.

Now listen to his apology against idolatry:

Their idols are silver and gold, the work of men's hands [Ps. 115:4].

Israel's God is in heaven. He is the Creator. He is a spirit. Man did not make Him. The gods of the heathen, on the other hand, were made out of silver and gold; they were the work of men's hands.

They have mouths, but they speak not: eyes have they, but they see not:

They have ears, but they hear not: noses have they, but they smell not [Ps. 115:5–6].

The heathen made their gods with all of the sense organs, but the gods don't use them; indeed, they cannot use them.

They have hands, but they handle not: feet have they, but they walk not: neither speak they through their throat [Ps. 115:7].

In other words, the gods of the heathen cannot help them. Isaiah gave possibly the finest satire against idolatry that you will find in the Scriptures. He says, speaking of men who are idolaters, "He heweth him down cedars, and taketh the cypress and the oak, which he strengtheneth for himself among the trees of the forest: he planteth an ash, and the rain doth nourish it. Then shall it be for a man to burn: for he will take thereof, and warm himself; yea, he kindleth it, and baketh bread; yea, he maketh a god, and worshippeth it; he maketh it a graven image, and falleth down thereto. He burneth part thereof in the fire; with part thereof he eateth flesh; he roasteth roast, and is satisfied: yea, he warmeth himself, and saith, Aha, I am warm, I have seen the fire: And the residue thereof he maketh a god, even his graven image: he falleth down unto it, and worshippeth it, and prayeth unto it, and saith, Deliver me; for thou art my god" (Isa. 44:14–17). When the idol is made, the man has to carry it on his back into town. Do you see the picture? A man is carrying his god. God says to man, "I am the Lord. I will carry you." Does your God carry you, or do you carry your god? To many people their religion is a burden, something that they have to carry on their shoulders. Does God carry you, or do you try to carry Him? If you have to carry your god, that is a modern form of idolatry.

The enemy has ridiculed God's people; now the Levites will answer those who ridicule:

O Israel, trust thou in the LORD: he is their help and their shield.

O house of Aaron, trust in the LORD: he is their help and their shield.

Ye that fear the LORD, trust in the LORD: he is their help and their shield [Ps. 115:9–11].

Some folks ask me, "What is the answer to atheism? What is the answer to materialism? What is the answer to all of the immorality around us?" Well, don't bother visiting a psychiatrist and lying on his couch. He doesn't have the solution. The answer is simple, so simple that many people have passed right by it: trust the Lord. That's the solution. In the midst of all the atheism, the materialism, and the immorality, trust the Lord. Rest in Him. Draw near to Him. Cast yourself upon Him. Oh, this is a wonderful psalm! It will bring you very close to the Lord.

Beginning with verse 12 the congregation answers. This is, more or less, an antiphonal psalm.

The LORD hath been mindful of us: he will bless us; he will bless the house of Israel; he will bless the house of Aaron [Ps. 115:12].

God will bless you, too. He will bless your friends, your house, your church, and your community, if only you will turn to Him. The thing that is so wonderful is that He is *mindful* of us. God has not forgotten me, and He has not forgotten you. I don't know your name and address, but He knows it. When I am in an airplane and look down and see all the subdivisions of a city, I think of the thousands of people who live there, and who knows them? Society is very impersonal. You are a number where you work and live; you are a number where you attend school, and you are a number to your government. But God knows *you*. God not only knows your number, He knows your name, and He knows all about you. Trust in Him.

He will bless them that fear the LORD, both small and great [Ps. 115:13].

This is a categorical, dogmatic statement. Either you believe what it says, or you don't believe it. If you believe it, what a difference it will make in your life!

The LORD shall increase you more and more, you and your children.

Ye are blessed of the LORD which made heaven and earth [Ps. 115:14–15].

He is the Creator.

The heaven, even the heavens, are the LORD's: but the earth hath he given to the children of men [Ps. 115:16].

Apparently God did not intend for man to live on the moon. When man journeys to the moon, he is more or less using God's property. He has given the earth to man.

The dead praise not the LORD, neither any that go down into silence [Ps. 115:17].

While we are here on earth we are to praise the Lord—here is where it counts.

But we will bless the LORD from this time forth and for evermore. Praise the LORD [Ps. 115:18].

Those who know Him will bless Him from this time forth and for evermore. Praise the Lord. Hallelujah! You don't mind saying that, do you? Even if you are a dignified Presbyterian or an Episcopalian, you should not mind praising the Lord. It won't hurt any of us to do that. Many of us have tensions and hang-ups. One of the best remedies is to open your heart to the Lord and praise His name. Talk to Him. It will help a great deal.

PSALM 116

***THEME:** A love song because God swallows death in victory*

This is one of the great psalms in Scripture. Some expositors place it next to Psalm 23 in greatness. It is a psalm of thanksgiving. Man is in distress and calls upon God, and God hears in mercy. It is a love song. It is a Hallel psalm. It is a simple psalm that speaks of the past sufferings of Christ in the presence of death. The night He was arrested and the day before He died the Lord sang this psalm. I wish I could have heard Him sing it! Some folk say they wish they could have heard our Lord speak; I would love to have heard Him *sing!* It was ". . . for the joy that was set before him [that He] endured the cross . . ." (Heb. 12:2) and He sang that last night with great joy!

It is a psalm that speaks of the future, of the deliverance of the faithful remnant during the Great Tribulation period. Also it speaks of the present and has a message for modern man, for the believer in this hour in which we live. This is what God wants us to know. It is a gracious word for those in distress and trouble. It will relieve your anxiety and dispel your doubts. The Lord Jesus sang this psalm the night before He was crucified. In verses 1–5, God hears. In verses 6–13, God helps. In verses 14–19, God is holy.

GOD HEARS

I love the LORD, because he hath heard my voice and my supplications [Ps. 116:1].

"I love the LORD"—remember that this is a love song. Have you ever told Him that you love Him? I feel that the most important thing in the Christian life is right at this point. Do you love the Lord Jesus? Do you love His person? Do you have a personal relationship with Him? Is there any communication with Him? Have you talked to Him today? Is He vital and real to you? The world is tired of that which is phoney, and aren't you tired of it too? The Scripture says, "We love him, because he first loved us" (1 John 4:19). "Whom having not seen, ye love; in whom, though now ye see him not, yet believing, ye rejoice with joy unspeakable and full of glory" (1 Pet. 1:8). The Lord said to Simon Peter, ". . . Lovest thou me?" (John 21:15–17). ". . . Unto him that loved us, and washed us from our sins in his own blood" (Rev. 1:5). To the church in Philadelphia the Lord said, "I will make them to come and worship before thy feet, and to know that I have loved thee"

(Rev. 3:9). Philadelphia represents the Bible-believing church today.

Now what is the basis for all of this? "I love the LORD, because he hath heard my voice." Are we to pray audibly? Well, it says, "he hath heard my voice," and that implies audible prayer. I like to talk to the Lord as I drive along in my car. (And, believe me, we need to talk to the Lord as we drive in Southern California these days!)

The sorrows of death compassed me, and the pains of hell [sheol] gat hold upon me: I found trouble and sorrow [Ps. 116:3].

This is the desperate situation of our Lord on the cross. He knew what He would go through—He sang about it the night before He died. Actually the sentence of death was upon us, but it became His sentence. He did not have to die. He laid down His life for you and me. No one took His life from Him.

Then called I upon the name of the LORD; O LORD, I beseech thee, deliver my soul [Ps. 116:4].

He cried out to the Lord, "Save Me." His prayer was heard.

Gracious is the LORD, and righteous; yea, our God is merciful [Ps. 116:5].

God is merciful, but God is righteous. He cannot just arbitrarily forgive sin. He has to be right when He does it. God is the moral Ruler of this universe. He has to be right; He has to be holy; He has to be just, but He also wants to be merciful. The only way was to pay the penalty for the sin of man. Now He says, "Come on, I can receive you."

GOD HELPS

The LORD preserveth the simple: I was brought low, and he helped me.

Return unto thy rest, O my soul; for the LORD hath dealt bountifully with thee [Ps. 116:6–7].

After a difficult, frustrating, pressure-filled day, we need to seek out a quiet place where we can confess our sins, read the Word, and talk with God. That is the sanctuary of the soul. Oh, how all of us need this—"Return unto thy rest, O my soul." This will enable us to walk out and face the world for God.

I will take the cup of salvation, and call upon the name of the LORD [Ps. 116:13].

Apparently this was the Passover cup being passed at this time. As they passed it around the group they would sing, "I will take the cup of salvation." They knew the Passover cup was pointing to the One who was coming. Our Lord sang this in the Upper Room. I have wondered if this was the cup about which He said, "You take this cup and drink it. I'll not take it until I drink it new in the kingdom, because I have a cup to drink tomorrow." Then out in Gethsemane He prayed that the cup would pass from Him. His holy nature rebelled against being made sin. Yet ". . . for the joy that was set before him [he] endured the cross. . ." (Heb. 12:2), and He took that cup joyfully the next day on the cross.

GOD IS HOLY

This brings us to the last section of this psalm which tells us that God is holy. His holiness is important. It is the reason He had to die for us.

Precious in the sight of the LORD is the death of his saints [Ps. 116:15].

Precious was the death of Christ to God. Precious will be the deaths of those who lay down their lives as martyrs during the Great Tribulation period, and many will do so. I am not sure but what we can apply this today. The death of God's children is precious in His sight.

O LORD, truly I am thy servant; I am thy servant, and the son of thine handmaid: thou hast loosed my bonds.

I will offer to thee the sacrifice of thanksgiving, and will call upon the name of the LORD [Ps. 116:16–17].

The only thing that you can give God is your thanksgiving. That is *all* He wants from you. God wants His children to be thankful. Have you ever thanked Him for your salvation? Have you thanked Him for this day? Oh, to come to the light of a new day—what a privilege it is!

Forgive me for a personal illustration. When my daughter married and left home, it was a very difficult time for me. When I watched her drive off with a "strange" man, I went back over her short life. In my ministry I have been away from home a great deal. After World War II when Youth for Christ was really moving, I honestly believed that revival was going to come to our nation. For two years I never was at home on Saturday night. I spoke for Youth for Christ from border to border and from coast to coast. I averaged five nights away from home each week. I recalled one time at the railroad station, as my daughter, a little tyke then, said to me, "Daddy, either we come down here to tell you good-bye or to come and get you." Then she looked up at me and asked, "Can't you stay home more?" Thinking of that, I wrote a letter to her in which I said, "I feel like I have failed you." A short time later when my wife and I were in the Hawaiian Islands, I received a letter from her. She wrote, "You did not fail me. I *thank* you for all you did for me." My friend, I would rather have that thank-you than a check for a million dollars. There is nothing that she could give me that I want—just that: "I thank you." Oh, how valuable that is!

My friend, *you* have nothing that God wants—nothing tangible. The psalmist sings, "I will offer to thee the sacrifice of thanksgiving." I'm going to *thank* Him. In case we miss the import of this, the writer to the Hebrews says, "By him therefore let us offer the sacrifice of praise to God continually, that is, the fruit of our lips giving thanks to his name" (Heb. 13:15). Oh, my friend, the *only* thing we can give to our God is our *thanks*, and how precious that is to our Heavenly Father!

PSALM 117

***THEME:** Hallelujah for the universal praise of God*

This is another Hallel psalm, and it is the shortest in the series. Let me remind you that the Hallel psalms (113—118) were sung at the three great feasts of the nation Israel: Passover, Pentecost, and Tabernacles.

At the Feast of Passover the cup was passed seven times, and between each passing those gathered would sing one of these hymns. Some expositors say that Psalms 113 and 114 were sung before the meal, and then Psalms 117 and 118 were sung after the meal. It doesn't matter how you arrange them, the important thing is that they were sung. Psalm 118 was the last psalm they sang. Matthew 26:30 tells us, "And when they had sung an hymn, they went out into the mount of Olives."

This is not only the shortest psalm, it is the shortest chapter in the Bible. Because of that there is a danger of passing over it altogether.

O praise the LORD, all ye nations: praise him, all ye people [Ps. 117:1].

"Praise the LORD" is "hallelujah."

For his merciful kindness is great toward us: and the truth of the LORD endureth for ever. Praise ye the LORD [Ps. 117:2].

These are remarkable verses that we should not pass over hurriedly. "Praise the LORD, all ye nations" is obviously prophetic. It looks to the future when all nations and races and tribes and tongues on every continent and in every nation will join together in praising Jehovah and will worship Him as Lord. Is there anything like that in the world today? Do you see any evidence of it in your neighborhood? Can you see that the world is turning to God? There was a time at the turn of the century, during the good old Victorian era and during the Gay Nineties, when it was thought that the Millennium was about to be ushered in. That was the heyday of postmillennialism, and a premillennialist in that day had to run for cover. They would have ridden anyone out of town on a rail who would have been pessimistic enough to say that a time of Great Tribulation was going to come upon the world! "Praise the LORD, all ye nations." I have a question to ask: Where are the nations that are singing praises unto Jehovah today? Where are the nations who worship and adore Him and are in submission to Him? The answer is easy—there are no nations today that fit that description. The message of the prophets was that one day the nations would praise and worship the Lord. In Zechariah 2:11 it says, "And many nations shall be joined to the LORD in that day, and shall be my people . . . ." Then in Zechariah 14:16 we read, "And it shall come to pass, that every one that is left of all the nations which came against Jerusalem shall even go up from year to year to worship the King, the LORD of hosts, and to keep the feast of tabernacles."

Evidently the worshiping of all nations is connected with the turning of Israel to God.

The next question is, When will all of this find fulfillment? I think the answer to that is in this little psalm before us. When will the nations praise Jehovah? Notice what it says in verse 2: "For his merciful kindness is great toward us." Who is the "us" in this phrase? It is Israel. The day is coming when God is going to be gracious to Israel. That day is in the future, at the end of the Great Tribulation period, when the Lord comes to earth for the second time and establishes His kingdom. Then He will be gracious to Israel and to all the nations on the earth. At that time Micah says (referring to God), "Thou wilt perform the truth to Jacob, and the mercy to Abraham, which thou hast sworn unto our fathers from the days of old" (Mic. 7:20). Then in Isaiah 54:7–8 we read, "For a small moment have I forsaken thee; but with great mercies will I gather thee. In a little wrath I hid my face from thee for a moment; but with everlasting kindness will I have mercy on thee, saith the LORD thy Redeemer." So, my friend, you can see that *this* psalm has reference to a future day when *all* the nations are going to praise the Lord.

Is there any inkling of this subject in the New Testament? Yes, Acts 15 records the meeting of the council at Jerusalem, which was made up of Jewish believers; and they could not understand why the prophecies of the Old Testament were not being fulfilled. At the end of the conference James got up and said, "Simeon hath declared how God at the first did visit the Gentiles, to take out of them a people for his name" (Acts 15:14). My friend, that is what God is doing in our day—taking out a people from among the Gentiles. He is making up His church from all races and tribes and tongues and bringing them together into one body. Now notice how James continues, "And to this agree the words of the prophets; as it is written, After this"—after what? After He takes the church out of the world. "I will return, and will build again the tabernacle of David, which is fallen down; and I will build again the ruins thereof, and I will set it up: That the residue of men might seek after the Lord, and all the Gentiles, upon whom my name is called, saith the Lord, who doeth all these things" (Acts 15:15–17). As you can see, the psalm before us looks to the future when every creature on this earth will render praise unto God.

It simply is not true that the nations today are praising God. You may see some evidence of it in your little corner of the world; but, in my little corner in Southern California, there is *no* evidence that everyone will turn to God. However, the time is coming when "God shall bless us; and all the ends of the earth shall fear him" (Ps. 67:7).

Psalm 117 is a tremendous psalm. It is like an atom bomb in the midst of the psalms, and when this little bomb explodes, you won't find a postmillennialist or an amillennialist anywhere, for it will blow them all away. The fulfillment of this psalm will come during the Millennium when Christ reigns on this earth—and not before. Oh, what a glorious time that will be! "Praise ye the LORD"—Hallelujah!

PSALM 118

THEME: *The hymn Christ sang with His disciples before His death*

This wonderful psalm is the last of the Hallel psalms; for this reason we know it was the psalm which our Lord sang with His disciples the night before His death.

In the Upper Room that night there was an air of informality but also of awe, an air of sadness and of joy and of anticipation. Our Lord ate the Passover feast with His disciples; then on the dying embers of a fading feast, He reared something new. Out of the ashes of the past, He took frail elements—bread and grape juice which will spoil in a few days, the weakest things in the world—and He raised a monument. It is not of marble, not of bronze, silver, or gold; it is *bread* and *juice.* That's all. But it speaks of Him. We know from the Old Testament that a lamb was to be eaten at the Passover feast. But in the Gospel record we hear nothing about the lamb, only the bread and fruit of the vine. Do you know why? It is because the Lamb was there serving them. He was on the way to the cross as the Lamb of God to die, and the bread and juice were to speak of Him until He comes again.

Psalm 118 is the psalm they sang together on that fatal night. The Gospels tell us, "When they had sung an hymn, they went out . . ." (Matt. 26:30). It is Psalm 118, which makes this psalm very important to us.

It is said that at the Passover feast, the cup went around the circle seven times. The seventh time it came to Him, our Lord said, "I'll not drink this cup with you," and He passed it on. "I'll drink it new with you in my Father's kingdom." He had already said that He would take the cup of salvation—and He took it yonder on the cross. Christ is the Lamb of God who shed His blood, and the cup is the new covenant of His blood. He drank the bitter cup that our cup might be sweet. Oh, how good God is to us!

O give thanks unto the LORD; for he is good: because his mercy endureth for ever.

Let Israel now say, that his mercy endureth for ever.

Let the house of Aaron now say, that his mercy endureth for ever [Ps. 118: 1–3].

And let Vernon McGee now say that His mercy endureth for ever. And let *you* say that His mercy endureth for ever. Let us all "give thanks unto the LORD, for he is good."

Let them now that fear the LORD say, that his mercy endureth for ever.

I called upon the LORD in distress: the LORD answered me, and set me in a large place.

The LORD is on my side; I will not fear: what can man do unto me? [Ps. 118: 4–6].

This is the song that our Lord sang. He went to the cross without fear. And He cried out, ". . . My God, my God, why hast thou forsaken me?" (Matt. 27:46). The mystery of it all is ". . . that God was in Christ, reconciling the world unto himself . . ." (2 Cor. 5:19).

The LORD taketh my part with them that help me: therefore shall I see my desire upon them that hate me.

It is better to trust in the LORD than to put confidence in man [Ps. 118:7–8].

Have you learned to put your confidence in the Lord, rather than in man? It is a marvelous lesson to learn. A prominent Los Angeles attorney and outstanding jurist told me, "When I was a young Christian, my Christian life was almost ruined. I had my eye on a man, and that man failed me. I found out then that I had made a mistake. I cannot put confidence in men." The psalmist says that it is better to trust in the Lord than to put confidence in man. On the night that our Lord sang these words He looked around at eleven men. One of them had already gone to betray Him. Those eleven men were going to forsake Him —they would be scattered like sheep that night. Don't put your confidence in men, my friend, they will let you down. Put your trust in the Lord.

It is better to trust in the LORD than to put confidence in princes.

All nations compassed me about: but in the name of the LORD will I destroy them.

They compassed me about; yea, they compassed me about: but in the name of the LORD I will destroy them.

They compassed me about like bees; they are quenched as the fire of thorns: for in the name of the LORD I will destroy them [Ps. 118:9–12].

"All nations compassed me about"—Rome was a polyglot nation, and Rome nailed our Lord to a cross. The day He died on a Roman cross, that nation was doomed. Its days were numbered. That great world empire that had existed for a millennium would pass off the stage of human events. (It will, however, come back by the way of Antichrist.)

The LORD is my strength and song, and is become my salvation [Ps. 118:14].

In this wonderful section we have praise for deliverance. It is a song of salvation.

The voice of rejoicing and salvation is in the tabernacles of the righteous: the right hand of the LORD doeth valiantly.

The right hand of the LORD is exalted: the right hand of the LORD doeth valiantly.

I shall not die, but live, and declare the works of the LORD [Ps. 118:15–17].

This is a reference to our Lord's resurrection. Also there is something else here: Israel is going to survive as a nation.

The LORD hath chastened me sore: but he hath not given me over unto death [Ps. 118:18].

That is, Christ came back from the dead. And Ezekiel 37 makes it clear that God will open the graves and bring out the nations of the world.

Open to me the gates of righteousness: I will go into them, and I will praise the LORD:

This gate of the LORD, into which the righteous shall enter [Ps. 118:19–20].

What is the gate of the Lord? Christ made it very clear when He said, "I am the door: by me if any man enter in, he shall be saved, and shall go in and out, and find pasture" (John 10:9). That door was the door to the sheepfold. The Lord also said, ". . . I am the way, the truth, and the life: no man cometh unto the Father, but by me" (John 14:6).

I will praise thee: for thou hast heard me, and art become my salvation [Ps. 118:21].

Now we have another figure of speech:

The stone which the builders refused is become the head stone of the corner [Ps. 118:22].

The stone in this verse refers to Christ Himself. Our Lord in Matthew 21:42 made that clear: ". . . Did ye never read in the scriptures, The stone which the builders rejected, the same is become the head of the corner: this is the Lord's doing, and it is marvellous in our eyes?" First Peter 2:6–8 says, "Wherefore also it is contained in the scripture, Behold, I lay in Sion a chief corner stone, elect, precious: and he that believeth on him shall not be confounded. Unto you therefore which believe he is precious: but unto them which be disobedient, the stone which the builders disallowed, the same is made the head of the corner, And a stone of stumbling, and a rock of offence, even to them which stumble at the word, being disobedient: whereunto also they were appointed." The stone is the Lord Jesus Christ.

This is the day which the LORD hath made; we will rejoice and be glad in it [Ps. 118:24].

What *day* is the psalmist talking about—some twenty-four-hour day? No. The word *day* can be used for a period of time, it can be used for a twenty-four-hour day, and it can be used for a peculiar type of thing—most anything. For example, we could say that this is the *day* of the automobile. Now what *day* is the psalmist referring to here? Well, he is talking about the day "which the LORD hath made," the day of salvation. That *day* has already been two thousand years long, and "we will rejoice and be glad in it." We rejoice in the day of salvation.

Now here we have the believing cry, Hosanna—"Save now" is the word *hosanna*. It is the word the multitudes used when our Lord came riding into Jerusalem:

Save now, I beseech thee, O LORD: O LORD, I beseech thee, send now prosperity.

Blessed be he that cometh in the name of the LORD: we have blessed you out of the house of the LORD [Ps. 118:25–26].

"Blessed be he that cometh in the name of the LORD" was quoted by our Lord after He cleansed the temple for the final time, then wept over Jerusalem. His words were, "Behold, your house is left unto you desolate. For I say unto you, Ye shall not see me henceforth, till ye shall say, Blessed is he that cometh in the name of the Lord" (Matt. 23: 38–39).

God is the LORD, which hath shewed us light: bind the sacrifice with cords, even unto the horns of the altar [Ps. 118:27].

This is a picture of the Lord Jesus Christ on the cross, a sacrifice for you and for me.

Thou art my God, and I will praise thee: thou art my God, I will exalt thee.

O give thanks unto the LORD; for he is good: for his mercy endureth for ever [Ps. 118:28–29].

My friend, I wish I could somehow express to you the fact that you and I ought to praise the Lord. In my flesh I am cabined and contained and have all kinds of hang-ups. I wish I could open up like a flower and express my praise and thanksgiving to my God! Oh, my friend, to fall down and worship Him, to praise *His* name and glorify *Him* is all important. He loved us and gave Himself for us. May our love today go out to him in adoration and praise.

PSALM 119

***THEME:** Praise to the Word of God*

We come now to the longest psalm and the longest chapter in the Bible. It has in it 176 verses, and every verse (with the possible exception of two verses) is praise to the Word of God. Oh, that you and I might put an emphasis upon the Word of God. As believers, we need to put the emphasis where God puts it. In our day there is too much emphasis upon programs and methods and ceremonies and church activities. Our emphasis should be on the Word of God, because that is the only thing He has promised to bless. He has never promised to bless me or my ministry or any other ministry, but He has promised to bless His Word.

The mechanics of this psalm, the arrangement of it, is indeed interesting. It was written with a great deal of care. It is an acrostic, but an acrostic that is a little different from any that we have seen before. Instead of having one verse that begins with each letter of the Hebrew alphabet (there are twenty-two letters in the Hebrew alphabet), there are eight verses for each letter of the Hebrew alphabet, beginning with *Aleph*, *Beth*, *Gimel*, and so forth, which gives us 176 verses in this psalm.

There are Bible students who feel that numbers in the Bible are very significant. I don't want to labor the point, but I do find it interesting that eight is the key number in this psalm, because under each letter of the Hebrew alphabet there are eight verses. The number eight in Scripture seems to be the number of resurrection. It was on the eighth day that our Lord came back from the dead—He was dead on the seventh day, the sabbath, and the eighth day, the first day of the week, He was resurrected. Many people think that God is through with Israel, but He is not through with them. Paul made that very clear in Romans 11:15: "For if the casting away of them be the reconciling of the world, what shall the receiving of them be, but life from the dead?" God is definitely not through with Israel. Just as the Lord Jesus came back from the dead, these people will be brought back as a nation in the Millennium. God would, in a very special way, save nations—oh, the multitudes that are yet to be saved! Spurgeon used to say, "God is going to win. There will be more saved than there will be lost." I believe that with all my heart, although as I look around me today I don't see it happening.

Many people get excited when they visit the land of Israel today, thinking they are seeing the fulfillment of prophecy. While it is true that Jews are returning to the land of Israel, it is not a fulfillment of Scripture, because they are returning in unbelief; they are not turning to God. I read recently of Jewish immigrants to Israel who were shocked by the atheism and lack of observance of the Jewish religion in Israel. It is true that there is no more a turning to God in Jerusalem than there is in my hometown or your hometown. But when God fulfills His prophecy, He will bring the Jews back to their land and it will be a resurrection of the nation, life from the dead. And, my friend, if you receive life from the dead—if you receive eternal life—it will come through the Word of God. "Being born again, not of corruptible seed, but of incorruptible, by the word of God, which liveth and abideth for ever" (1 Pet. 1:23). We are begotten by the Word of God that reveals Jesus Christ. God's Word will bring life to you, it will bring liberty to you, it will bring joy to you, and it will bring blessing to you.

This psalm has meant a great deal to believers down through the years. Late in life John Ruskin wrote, "It is strange that of all the pieces of the Bible which my mother taught me, that which cost me the most to learn, and which was to my childish mind most repulsive—the 119th Psalm—has now become of all the most precious to me in its overflowing and glorious passion of love for the Law of God."

William Wilberforce, the statesman who was converted in the Wesleyan movement, wrote in his diary, "Walked from Hyde Park corner, repeating the 119th Psalm in great comfort." What a wonderful statement. If you can't sleep at night, don't count sheep; count the letters of the Hebrew alphabet and read the verses of this psalm. It would mean a great deal to you.

In this wonderful psalm God's Word is designated by several terms: *word*, *saying*, *way*, *testimonies*, *judgments*, *precepts*, *commandments*, *law*, *statutes*, and *faithfulness*.

As we go through this psalm, I will lift out certain verses. We will begin with *Aleph* which is the first letter of the Hebrew alphabet.

ALEPH

Blessed are the undefiled in the way, who walk in the law of the LORD,

Blessed are they that keep his testimonies, and that seek him with the whole heart [Ps. 119:1–2].

Oh, that we would seek God with the whole heart—not halfheartedly. I get a little discouraged with some folk who start out with our "Thru the Bible" program with a great deal of zeal at first. Then they begin to let down, and before long they drop by the wayside. They are not like the man in Psalm 1:1, of whom it is said, "Blessed is the man that walketh not in the counsel of the ungodly, nor standeth in the way of sinners, nor sitteth in the seat of the scornful." Blessed is the man that walketh not, standeth not, sitteth not, but just keeps on walking—walking in the Spirit. "Blessed are they that keep his testimonies, and that seek him with the whole heart."

BETH

Wherewithal shall a young man cleanse his way? by taking heed thereto according to thy word [Ps. 119:9].

One thing that every young man should learn about today is the Word of God. They are taught everything else in school except the Bible. It is against the law to teach the Bible in school, but we need to get the Word of God to them.

Thy word have I hid in mine heart, that I might not sin against thee [Ps. 119:11].

Many people believe that this verse only means that Scripture should be memorized. I think memorizing God's Word is a wonderful thing, but some of the meanest little brats I have seen in Sunday school were the ones who could stand up and quote one hundred verses of Scripture. When the psalmist wrote, "Thy word have I hid in mine heart," I think he meant, "I obey it." That is the important thing. It is a wonderful thing to be able to stand up and by rote recite verse after verse —I'm not criticizing that; I'm in favor of Scripture memorization programs—but we also need to *obey* the Word. That is what the psalmist means by hiding it in your heart.

GIMEL

Open thou mine eyes, that I may behold wondrous things out of thy law [Ps. 119:18].

This is the verse I used to begin the "Thru the Bible" program years ago when I first taught it in a little weather-beaten church on the side of a red clay hill in Georgia. I used this verse as a theme for many years. This is a good one—"Open thou mine eyes, that I may behold wondrous things out of thy law [thy word]."

DALETH

In the *Daleth* section we read:

My soul cleaveth unto the dust: quicken thou me according to thy word [Ps. 119:25].

The tendency today is to pull downward. Everything pulls us down. Television—a marvelous intrument that could be used for God —does nothing but pull us down. Everything is geared that way. "My soul cleaveth unto the dust"—we gravitate in that direction. Not only will our body fall downward, but our soul is pulled downward in the world. How can we overcome it? "Quicken [revive] thou me according to thy word." This is another reason I have a five-year program of going through the Bible. If folk will stay in the Word of God for five years, it will keep them out of a lot of sin. The Word will revive us and lift us up.

HE

In the *He* section we read:

Teach me, O LORD, the way of thy statutes; and I shall keep it unto the end [Ps. 119:33].

Oh, to follow on with God, running the race with patience, looking unto Jesus.

VAU

Let thy mercies come also unto me, O LORD, even thy salvation, according to thy word [Ps. 119:41].

God's mercy is channeled to us—the pipe that brings it to us is the Word of God. Therefore, the psalmist says:

And I will delight myself in thy commandments, which I have loved [Ps. 119:47].

Does it give you joy to read the Word of God? Do you love the Bible? If you don't love God's Word, ask Him to give you a love for it. I did that for years. I prayed, "Lord, give me a love for your Word." I was not brought up in a home where I heard the Word of God, and it took me a long time to become interested in it.

ZAIN

Remember the word unto thy servant, upon which thou hast caused me to hope [Ps. 119:49].

In other words, "Fulfill thy promises to me, upon which thou hast caused me to hope."

CHETH

Thou art my portion, O Lord: I have said that I would keep thy words [Ps. 119:57].

This is literally, "My portion O Lord!" Spurgeon comments: "The poet is lost in wonder while he sees that the great and glorious God is all his own! Well, might he be so, for there is no possession like Jehovah himself."

At midnight I will rise to give thanks unto thee because of thy righteous judgments [Ps. 119:62].

Have you ever thanked God in the middle of the night for His Word? Well, wake up tonight and do it.

TETH

The proud have forged a lie against me: but I will keep thy precepts with my whole heart.

Their heart is as fat as grease; but I delight in thy law [Ps. 119:69–70].

Critics of the Bible need to go on a diet, or they may die of heart trouble. We need to stay close to the Word of God. It is marvelous for heart trouble!

JOD

Thy hands have made me and fashioned me: give me understanding, that I may learn thy commandments [Ps. 119:73].

God made us. He knows exactly what we need. One of our basic needs is His Word, and that is what the psalmist is talking about here. I notice that some of the manufacturers of automobiles say, "When your car needs repair, take it to us. We made it, and we know how to fix it." Well, that may be good advice also. I know for sure that you need to take yourself to the Lord and to His Word. He made you, and He knows what is good for you.

CAPH

This psalm speaks of one persecuted but not forsaken—

For I am become like a bottle in the smoke; yet do I not forget thy statutes [Ps. 119:83].

"A bottle in the smoke" undoubtedly refers to a wine skin "bottle" hung up in the fire, which would become blackened, parched, and cracked. What a picture of the one who endures long and severe persecution! But he was not forsaken because the Word of God was his stay.

LAMED

For ever, O Lord, thy word is settled in heaven [Ps. 119:89].

I have preached on this verse many times. "For ever, O Lord, thy word is settled in heaven"—His Word is in heaven; that is where the original copy is. I believe in the plenary, verbal inspiration of that copy, and I hold a good copy of it right in my hands. Actually it is settled in the *heavens*. Now heaven and earth may pass away, but where He is, it will never pass away.

MEM

O how love I thy law! It is my meditation all the day [Ps. 119:97].

He meditated in God's Word because he loved it, and then he loved it even more because he meditated in it.

I have more understanding than all my teachers: for thy testimonies are my meditation [Ps. 119:99].

When I taught a course in Bible at a Bible institute, I used to tell my students, "Don't you ever give me this verse or I'll give you an F in the course!" Seriously, humble believers who sit at the feet of Christ are often more skilled in the Word than a man who has a D.D. or a Ph.D. after his name.

NUN

Now here is a verse you may have heard all your life—

Thy word is a lamp unto my feet, and a light unto my path [Ps. 119:105].

Each of us should use the Word of God personally, practically, and habitually as we make our way through this dark world.

SAMECH

Now, again, let me lift out only one verse from this section:

I hate vain thoughts: but thy law do I love [Ps. 119:113].

How much time do you spend reading the newspaper, or reading trash, in comparison to the time that you spend reading the Bible? God is telling us, through the psalmist, that He hates vain thoughts. If you spend time in the Word of God, the day will come when you will not be interested in a lot of the trash that is published.

AIN

It is time for thee, LORD, to work: for they have made void thy law [Ps. 119:126].

This is a good prayer for us to pray today. I pray this prayer, "Lord, the world has forgotten you, and the world has forgotten your Word. Help us get it out today, and make the world conscious of your Word."

PE

Thy testimonies are wonderful: therefore doth my soul keep them [Ps. 119:129].

"Thy testimonies are wonderful"—full of wonderful revelations, commands, and promises. As Spurgeon has well said, "Jesus the eternal Word is called Wonderful, and all the uttered words of God are wonderful in their degree. Those who know them best wonder at them most."

The entrance of thy words giveth light; it giveth understanding unto the simple [Ps. 119:130].

Since I come under that classification, I want to know the Word.

TZADDI

Righteous art thou, O LORD, and upright are thy judgments [Ps. 119:137].

"Righteous art thou, O LORD"—we can rest in the truth of that when we cannot see the reasons for our trials and troubles. We may be confident of this sure and certain fact that God is righteous and His dealings with us are also righteous.

KOPH

I cried with my whole heart; hear me, O LORD: I will keep thy statutes.

I cried unto thee; save me, and I shall keep thy testimonies [Ps. 119:145–146].

When God saves you, He wants to put you on a new diet, a diet of the Word of God.

RESH

Plead my cause, and deliver me: quicken me according to thy word [Ps. 119:154].

The word *quicken* is better translated "revive." So the psalmist is saying, "Revive me according to Thy Word." The *only* thing that can revive us is God's Word. Dwight L. Moody said that the next great revival will be a revival of the Word of God. I hope that that is true, and we are seeing more and more interest in the Bible.

SCHIN

Princes have persecuted me without a cause: but my heart standeth in awe of thy word [Ps. 119:161].

The psalmist had more respect and awe for the Word of God than he did for the rulers of this world.

TAU

I have gone astray like a lost sheep; seek thy servant; for I do not forget thy commandments [Ps. 119:176].

As long as the Word of God is in your heart, my friend, as long as there is a longing deep within you to come to God, the Shepherd is out looking for you. He will put you on His shoulder and bring you back into the fold.

Psalm 119 is a glorious psalm. It glorifies the Word of God which is the foundation of all liberty. And it reveals the Savior—"If the Son therefore shall make you free, ye shall be free indeed" (John 8:36). Oh, what liberty the Word of God will give to your heart and life!

PSALM 120

***THEME:** The living conditions of the pilgrim*

This brings us to a new series in the Book of Psalms, a package of fifteen psalms (120—134), each called "A song of degrees" in our Bibles. What we have here is, as Martin Luther translated it, "the gradual psalms, songs of the higher choir." An outstanding Hebrew scholar has translated it, "Songs of the pilgrim caravans" or "on the homeward marches." These fifteen psalms were traveling songs, and I think they were used in two different ways. When the captives returned from Babylon, they sang them on the way to Jerusalem. This same use of the term "going up" is used in Ezra 7:9, which says, "For upon the first day of the first month began he [that is, Ezra] to go up from Babylon, and on the first day of the fifth month came he to Jerusalem, according to the good hand of his God upon him." This verse is speaking of Ezra's "going up" from Babylon to Jerusalem. However the most common use of these psalms was during the three times each year when they went, as God had commanded, up to Jerusalem to worship. God had required the males to go; and, when they went, they took their families along. As they started to Jerusalem from all over the civilized world—they were scattered at this time—they would sing these psalms. One day it would be one of the psalms, the next day another psalm; and as they came closer and higher, as they approached Jerusalem, they continued to sing them until they came to the final psalm, 134, when they would be standing in the sanctuary of the Lord singing His praises. This is the reason they are called songs of degrees or ascents and songs of the pilgrim caravans. You will recall that we have one incident, recorded by Dr. Luke, in the life of the Lord Jesus between the time of His virgin birth and the beginning of His ministry at the age of thirty years. The Lord, who was then twelve years old, went with His parents to Jerusalem to celebrate one of the feasts. A day's journey from Jerusalem, all of the caravans would meet so that they could go to Jerusalem together. It was a time of fellowship, of renewing friendships, talking over old times, and telling others how things were going. Then they would journey together to Jerusalem, singing these psalms. The place where the caravans met is still pretty well known today, and it was one day's journey out of Jerusalem. When the feast was over, the parents of the Lord Jesus found He was missing, and they had to return to the city to look for Him. The account is found in Luke 2:41–50.

Now you may be wondering if we can be sure these psalms were used this way. Yes, Psalm 122:3–4 gives us this information: "Jerusalem is builded as a city that is compact together: Whither the tribes go up, the tribes of the LORD, unto the testimony of Israel, to give thanks unto the name of the LORD." Yes, they were sung three times during the year —at the Feasts of Passover, Pentecost, and Tabernacles—as they traveled toward Jerusalem to return thanks to God, to worship Him, and to offer sacrifices.

There is a spiritual meaning in these fifteen psalms. It is interesting that many writers of the Talmud pointed out the fact that *life* is like this—it is an ascent. We come to God as sinners who are away from Him, separated, and alienated. We come to Him for salvation, and having come for salvation, we go on to sanctification as we grow in grace and in the knowledge of Christ; it is a constant going up. We are to be climbing in a spiritual way. My friend, you and I ought to be farther along today than we were last year.

Now we begin this journey with Psalm 120, and in this psalm we are looking at the pilgrim and we will find out where he lives.

> **In my distress I cried unto the LORD, and he heard me.**
>
> **Deliver my soul, O LORD, from lying lips, and from a deceitful tongue.**
>
> **What shall be given unto thee? or what shall be done unto thee, thou false tongue?**
>
> **Sharp arrows of the mighty, with coals of juniper.**
>
> **Woe is me, that I sojourn in Mesech, that I dwell in the tents of Kedar!**
>
> **My soul hath long dwelt with him that hateth peace.**
>
> **I am for peace: but when I speak, they are for war [Ps. 120:1–7].**

This is one of the most marvelous psalms that we have read, and it is relevant to the present hour, especially for the nation Israel. The pilgrim in this psalm said he lived "in Mesech in Kedar." Who was Mesech? He was one of the sons of Japheth. Genesis 10:2 tells us of "The sons of Japheth; Gomer, and Magog, and Madai, and Javan, and Tubal, and Meshech, and Tiras." From the sons of Japheth came the gentile nations, and Israel today is scattered among the Gentiles throughout the world. They dwell in "Mesech." "Kedar" was the son of Ishmael. Does that tell you anything? The pilgrim was living among the Arabs. That is rather up-to-date, is it not?

Notice that in verse 2 he cries, "Deliver my soul, O LORD, from lying lips, and from a deceitful tongue." It doesn't sound as if he is living in a good neighborhood, does it? They had mean tongues. The man who sojourned in Mesech had been maligned and lied about. I do believe that no people have been lied about, maligned, and persecuted as much as the Jews. We hear much about minority groups today, and the interesting thing is that the Jew has been able to make his way among all nations and peoples, but he has been criticized the entire time. Anti-Semitism has been real down through the ages; yet the Jew has been able to survive all of it. The Jews are a minority group among the Gentiles and among the people of the world; and they have lived in the place of gossip, quarrels, tensions, problems, and burdens. Also this can be said of you and me.

Now, not only did the pilgrim live among people with mean tongues, but he lived in a world of war: "My soul hath long dwelt with him that hateth peace. I am for peace: but when I speak, they are for war." That is rather up-to-date also, is it not? It is a wonder the higher critics, who like to give a late dating to Scripture, haven't suggested that this psalm was written in the present century. It certainly describes the Jews' current situation.

Now it is time to pack up his troubles in his old kit bag and start toward Jerusalem. However, the pilgrim leaves his burdens at home. He leaves his Mesech and his Kedar and starts for Jerusalem to worship his God. Jerusalem is the city of peace. It is not that today; it is rather a dangerous place to be, but it was different in the days of the pilgrim, and it will be different in the future.

PSALM 121

THEME: *The pilgrim sees the hills of Judea come into view*

This psalm is the next "song of degrees" or song of ascents as the pilgrim travels to Jerusalem to worship. We had a glimpse into his home situation which he had left as he started on his way. Now in this psalm he can see in the distance the hills of Jerusalem.

> **I will lift up mine eyes unto the hills, from whence cometh my help [Ps. 121:1].**

I think it would be well to change this verse because it is obviously a question rather than a statement. This man is not looking to the hills for his help; he is looking to God. "Shall I lift my eyes unto the hills? From whence cometh my help?" His answer is in the next verse:

> **My help cometh from the LORD which made heaven and earth [Ps. 121:2].**

His help comes from God, and not from the hills.

As the pilgrim draws near to Jerusalem, and it makes no difference if he comes from the north, east, south, or west, he will have to go through hills. The first time I went to Jerusalem, I came from the east, across the Jordan River; and I traveled through some pretty rugged country. The second time I went to Jerusalem, I came from Tel Aviv by bus and found that the hills were "hillier" than they were on the east. I have also approached Jerusalem from the north and south—no matter from what direction you approach Jerusalem, you are in the hills.

As the pilgrim comes to the place where he can see the hills of Judea, he sees places of heathen worship on the tops of the hills. That is where the heathen erected their altars. He says, "Shall I lift up mine eyes to the hills? From whence cometh my help?" It doesn't come from the tops of those hills. Jeremiah commented on this subject when he said, "Truly in vain is salvation hoped for from the hills, and from the multitude of mountains: truly in the LORD our God is the salvation of

Israel" (Jer. 3:23). This is in the song of the pilgrim as he draws near Jerusalem.

He will not suffer thy foot to be moved: he that keepeth thee will not slumber.

Behold, he that keepeth Israel shall neither slumber nor sleep [Ps. 121:3–4].

"He will not suffer thy foot to be moved" means that God won't allow you to totter. Those of us who are senior citizens begin to totter just a little—I notice that I am not as surefooted as I once was.

The sun shall not smite thee by day, nor the moon by night.

The Lord shall preserve thee from all evil: he shall preserve thy soul.

The Lord shall preserve thy going out and thy coming in from this time forth, and even for evermore [Ps. 121:6–8].

I would like to give you a different translation of verses 3–8 which will bring out something not seen in the King James Version. "He will not suffer thy foot to be moved: thy keeper will not slumber. Behold, neither slumbereth nor sleepeth the keeper of Israel. Jehovah is thy keeper. Jehovah is thy shade upon the right hand: the sun shall not smite thee by day nor the moon by night. The Lord shall keep thee from all evil. He shall keep thy soul. Jehovah shall keep thy going out and thy coming in from henceforth and forever" (Translation mine). This pilgrim is not looking to the hills for strength. He is looking to the Lord for help. Jehovah is his keeper.

You will notice that in verses 7 and 8 we are told that "the Lord shall preserve thee." This has to do with the wonderful keeping power of God. He preserves you. Peter said it like this, "Who are *kept* by the power of God . . ." (1 Pet. 1:5). There are two ways to preserve fruits or vegetables—in sugar or in vinegar. Many Christians are preserved both ways. Those preserved in sugar are nice sweet folks. The others are preserved in vinegar, and that speaks for itself.

The pilgrim is moving toward Jerusalem. He travels through the hills and camps along the route. Howard Johnson, the Holiday Inn, and the Ramada Inn hadn't built any motels yet; so the travelers going to Jerusalem had to camp along the way. And they were looking to Jehovah to keep them. What a glorious assurance that is! The psalm says, "My help cometh from the Lord. He won't let me totter and fall." There are other references to this in the Scriptures: Proverbs 3:26 says, "For the Lord shall be thy confidence, and shall keep thy foot from being taken." He won't let you fall. Psalm 37:24 says, "Though he fall, he shall not be utterly cast down: for the Lord upholdeth him with his hand." In 1 Samuel 2:9 Hannah said, "He will keep the feet of his saints. . . ." One of the last benedictions in the Bible occurs in the little epistle of Jude. "Now unto him that is able to keep you from falling [stumbling], and to present you faultless before the presence of his glory with exceeding joy, To the only wise God our Saviour, be glory and majesty, dominion and power, both now and ever. Amen" (Jude 24–25). He is able to keep us. He is the keeper of Israel and the keeper of His own today.

Notice that He keeps us both day and night. He doesn't slumber or sleep. When they camped for the night and were sleeping in a strange country, God didn't sleep—He was still watching over them.

"The sun shall not smite thee by day, nor the moon by night." They traveled at certain seasons when the sun was really hot—I know how hot that sun can be over there. But He said He would keep them in the scorching heat. But what about "the moon by night"? Well, I don't know exactly what is meant by that. However, I do know that the word *lunatic* comes from the Latin word for moon—*luna*, and it arose from the widespread belief that the rays of the moon affect the minds of men. I can remember that when I was young I used to take a girl out on a date and the moonlight had an effect on us. But God can keep you—He can keep you in the sunshine and the moonlight. "The Lord shall preserve thy going out and thy coming in from this time forth, and even for evermore."

PSALM 122

THEME: *The pilgrim comes within sight of Jerusalem*

This is the third song of degrees. In Psalm 120 we saw the Jew in distress; he was in a neighborhood that was unfavorable to him —he was being talked about and lied about. He leaves that, takes his family, and goes up to Jerusalem to celebrate one of the feasts of the Jews. In Psalm 121 he comes within sight of the Judean hills. He continues traveling until he reaches the wonderful city of Jerusalem. This is where the tribes come to celebrate the feasts of the Lord.

I was glad when they said unto me, Let us go into the house of the LORD.

Our feet shall stand within thy gates, O Jerusalem.

Jerusalem is builded as a city that is compact together:

Whither the tribes go up, the tribes of the LORD, unto the testimony of Israel, to give thanks unto the name of the LORD [Ps. 122:1–4].

The weary pilgrims after their long journey stand at last in the gates of their beloved Jerusalem. They lift their eyes to the temple—there it stands with its shining gold glittering in the bright sunlight. A glad cry passes from lip to lip, "Let us go into the house of the LORD!"

This beautiful psalm is also a prophecy. It is a millennial psalm looking forward to the time when all the tribes will go up to Jerusalem and assemble themselves for worship.

They have been out of their city for a long time. They actually do not have full possession of it today. They cannot build their temple on the temple site because the Mosque of Omar is there. All of the sacred places are pretty well covered by Gentiles. In Hosea 3:4–5 we read, "For the children of Israel shall abide many days without a king, and without a prince, and without a sacrifice, and without an image, and without an ephod, and without teraphim: Afterward shall the children of Israel return, and seek the LORD their God, and David their king; and shall fear the LORD and his goodness in the latter days."

There is going to be a millennial Jerusalem. And what will the returning tribes find? Dr. Gaebelein describes it this way: "A magnificent city compacted together, not only architecturally, a vast, a great, a beautiful city, but compacted together spiritually. Her warfare is over. She is no longer in strife and in danger of attack" (*The Book of Psalms*, p. 447). This will be the city of Jerusalem in the Millennium.

What a glorious prospect this psalm pictures!

PSALMS 123–125

THEME: *The pilgrims see the temple, then Mount Zion, and finally stand in the security of Jerusalem*

These are also a part of the pilgrim psalms and form a little cluster of three psalms that tell a story. Psalm 123 has been called "the eye of hope" because the temple comes into view, and the children of Israel turn their eyes to God in hope. The temple was a means of approach to God.

Unto thee lift I up mine eyes, O thou that dwellest in the heavens [Ps. 123:1].

The psalmist is making it very clear that God is not confined to the temple; He is not in a "box" in Jerusalem. The critic is wrong when he says that Israel considered Jehovah God a local deity who lived in their little temple in Jerusalem. The psalmist makes it abundantly clear that Israel did not believe any such thing. He addresses Him: "O thou that dwellest in the heavens." The pilgrim comes within sight of the temple, but it causes him to lift his eyes to heaven, knowing that God dwelt in the heavens. The temple was only a means of approach to God.

Behold, as the eyes of servants look unto the hand of their masters, and as

the eyes of a maiden unto the hand of her mistress; so our eyes wait upon the LORD our God, until that he have mercy upon us [Ps. 123:2].

When you are working for someone, you watch the clock and you watch the boss. You are sure to be working when he is watching you. How many of us live as though God is looking at us all the time? Well, He is. We are always under His eye.

Have mercy upon us, O LORD, have mercy upon us: for we are exceedingly filled with contempt [Ps. 123:3].

The children of Israel have been despised in the world, and now they are coming to Jerusalem. They are asking for mercy, knowing they are sinners and need God's mercy. They have not come to Jerusalem to pat themselves on the back.

Our soul is exceedingly filled with the scorning of those that are at ease, and with the contempt of the proud [Ps. 123:4].

Israel has now come to Jerusalem—the eye of hope. They are looking to the One who dwells in the heavens. I wonder if we are looking in that direction today?

Psalm 124 is a historical psalm. As Psalm 123 is the "eye of hope" looking to the future, so Psalm 124 is the eye of the past, reviewing the history of God's mercy to them in the past.

If it had not been the LORD who was on our side, now may Israel say;

If it had not been the LORD who was on our side, when men rose up against us:

Then they had swallowed us up quick, when their wrath was kindled against us [Ps. 124:1–3].

As the Israelites look back over their history, it is obvious that God has moved in their lives and made it possible for them to go up to Jerusalem to worship. For this they are giving thanks to God.

Then the waters had overwhelmed us, the stream had gone over our soul [Ps. 124:4].

These would be the waters of the Red Sea and the waters of the Jordan River and the waters of circumstances in which they found themselves many times.

Blessed be the LORD, who hath not given us as a prey to their teeth [Ps. 124:6].

They know it is God who has helped them.

Our help is in the name of the LORD, who made heaven and earth [Ps. 124:8].

The children of Israel are worshiping the Creator, "who made heaven and earth." This is a wonderful little psalm.

Now in Psalm 125, as the pilgrim sees Mount Zion, his heart is encouraged for the future. For our own hearts we can bring this up to date and say, "Being confident of this very thing, that he which hath begun a good work in you will perform it until the day of Jesus Christ" (Phil. 1:6). This has been called a "Song of Security" and is a prediction of Israel's national restoration.

They that trust in the LORD shall be as mount Zion, which cannot be removed, but abideth for ever [Ps. 125:1].

The pilgrims have come from all over the land and beyond the land. As they came they saw the mountains of Judea. Then they saw the hills around Jerusalem, and now they can actually see Mount Zion. They are moving toward Jerusalem and can see the city clearly.

As the mountains are round about Jerusalem, so the LORD is round about his people from henceforth even for ever [Ps. 125:2].

This is a wonderful psalm with blessed assurance that all who put their trust in Jehovah are like the unmovable, never-changing Mount Zion.

PSALM 126

***THEME:** A song of joy after their return from Babylonian captivity*

When the LORD turned again the captivity of Zion, we were like them that dream [Ps. 126:1].

It seemed too good to be true that they were able to return to Jerusalem. It was like a dream—they couldn't believe it.

Then was our mouth filled with laughter, and our tongue with singing: then said they among the heathen, The LORD hath done great things for them [Ps. 126:2].

Now they want to give a testimony to the world.

The LORD hath done great things for us; whereof we are glad [Ps. 126:3].

The remnant of Israel that returned to their land after the Babylonian captivity does not exhaust the meaning of this psalm. It also looks forward to their national restoration when their Messiah, the Lord Jesus Christ, returns.

Turn again our captivity, O LORD, as the streams in the south.

They that sow in tears shall reap in joy.

He that goeth forth and weepeth, bearing precious seed, shall doubtless come again with rejoicing, bringing his sheaves with him [Ps. 126:4–6].

Let me quote Dr. Gaebelein's comment at the conclusion of this psalm. "Beautiful is the ending of this Psalm of prophecy. We must think first of all of Him who came in humility and sowed His precious seed with tears, our Lord Jesus Christ. . . . Only His Father knows the many tears which He shed in His presence in secret prayer. . . . And it is perfectly proper to apply this to ourselves also. So let us weep and scatter the seed! 'Let us not be weary in well-doing; for in due season we shall reap, if we faint not' (Gal. 6:9)" (*The Book of Psalms*, p. 456).

PSALM 127

***THEME:** The vanity of building without God*

This is another great pilgrim psalm. It has been called "The Cotter's Saturday Night Song," which is probably as good as any name. It is a mighty crescendo. Here you come to the crest of the psalms. We are at the highest elevation when we reach the temple area and Mount Zion in Jerusalem, but this psalm carries us right into the heavenlies. This is a psalm that is applicable to us in our day, and it reveals an utter dependence upon God.

This psalm has been used on several important occasions. It was used at the inauguration of President Eisenhower. Two Bibles were used. One of them was George Washington's Bible, and it was opened at Psalm 127.

The inscription "A Song of degrees for Solomon" does not appear in the Septuagint Version. There are those who hold that the expression "my beloved" refers to Solomon, but the son of David mentioned here is not Solomon; He is none other than the Lord Jesus Christ Himself.

Except the LORD build the house, they labour in vain that build it: except the LORD keep the city, the watchman waketh but in vain.

It is vain for you to rise up early, to sit up late, to eat the bread of sorrows: for so he giveth his beloved sleep [Ps. 127: 1–2].

The word *vain* is used three times in these verses. My friend, everything is vain unless God is in it. Everything is dependent on Him and on His blessings. An old German proverb says, "Everything depends on the blessing of God." I wish we looked at things like that. This is why this psalm has been called "The Cotter's Saturday Night Song." The Lord Jesus Christ said, "Therefore take no thought, saying, What shall we eat? or, What shall we drink? or, Wherewithal shall we be clothed? (For after all these things do the Gentiles seek:) for your heavenly Father knoweth that ye have need of all these things. But seek ye first the kingdom of God, and his righteousness; and all these things shall be added unto you. Take therefore no thought for the morrow: for the morrow shall take thought for the things of itself. Sufficient unto the day is the evil thereof" (Matt. 6:31–34).

In this psalm we find a reference to children. When the pilgrim went to Jerusalem, he took his family to worship with him.

Lo, children are an heritage of the LORD: and the fruit of the womb is his reward [Ps. 127:3].

Here is the pilgrim, his wife, and his children, all of them are in Jerusalem to thank God.

As arrows are in the hand of a mighty man; so are children of the youth.

Happy is the man that hath his quiver full of them: they shall not be ashamed, but they shall speak with the enemies in the gate [Ps. 127:4–5].

His children will defend him. It is a comforting thing to have a child who will defend you and to have a whole little army of them is quite wonderful. The psalmist who wrote this knew nothing about the population explosion.

PSALM 128

***THEME:** Home sweet home*

Luther called this a "Marriage Song." It describes a happy family life and then gives the invocation of the Lord's blessing. It is God's picture of a happy family, and notice its foundation:

Blessed is every one that feareth the LORD; that walketh in his ways [Ps. 128:1].

What is it that makes a family happy? What foundation must be laid? There are all kinds of conferences for the family, especially the young family. They are to adopt certain methods and adjust themselves to certain procedures. My friend, you can never have a happy home until the fear of the Lord is in that home, until the members of the family walk day by day in the ways of the Lord. This idea of working things out psychologically simply will not work. It reminds me of the man who, when asked how he had lived so long, said it was because he had lived an outdoor life. He explained that when he and his wife got married they decided that every time they had a quarrel he would go outside. So, he said, "I have lived an outdoor life." Well, my friend, that is not the solution. There must be the fear of the Lord in the home.

For thou shalt eat the labour of thine hands: happy shalt thou be, and it shall be well with thee [Ps. 128:2].

The husband works and provides for his family.

Thy wife shall be as a fruitful vine by the sides of thine house: thy children like olive plants round about thy table [Ps. 128:3].

If there is a family altar, this is it. I do not like the present set-up of many family altars where it is a hit-and-miss proposition. The family comes together in a hurry, a few verses of Scripture are read, and then everyone starts out in a different direction. They are like the cowboy who mounted his horse and rode off in every direction. That seems to be the way the family altar is conducted in many instances. In this passage the husband, wife, and children gather about the table.

Behold, that thus shall the man be blessed that feareth the LORD [Ps. 128:4].

You cannot get away from the fact that, unless there is that reverential fear of God and obedience to Him, there will not be a happy home. Children know if their parents love the Lord, and if they serve Him, and if they obey Him, and if He is important in their lives. There is no substitute for the godly life. You can go to all of the conferences you want to, but you will never have a happy home until your relationship with God is right. When you get rightly related to God, it will amaze you how many of your problems will fall into place and take care of themselves.

The LORD shall bless thee out of Zion: and thou shalt see the good of Jerusalem all the days of thy life.

Yea, thou shalt see thy children's children, and peace upon Israel [Ps. 128: 5–6].

An interesting statement has been made in reference to this psalm, and I would like to pass it on to you. It says, "Before the fall, paradise was man's home. After the fall, the home was man's paradise." Home can be either paradise or the exact opposite of it.

This is a wonderful little family psalm.

PSALMS 129–130

***THEME:** Burned but not consumed*

In Psalm 129 the pilgrim reviews his youth and the hand of God upon him. It is also a picture of Israel burned but not consumed. The burning bush seen by Moses is the emblem of the miraculous preservation of God's people. What a picture we have here!

God has delivered the pilgrims, and they are in Jerusalem to worship.

Many a time have they afflicted me from my youth, may Israel now say:

Many a time have they afflicted me from my youth: yet they have not prevailed against me [Ps. 129:1–2].

Israel was not destroyed because God had preserved them.

Neither do they which go by say, The blessing of the LORD be upon you: we bless you in the name of the LORD [Ps. 129:8].

"The blessing of the LORD be upon you" should be incorporated not only into the home but also into business today. A man's religion and his right relationship to God should be an integral part of both his home life and his business life. Boaz was a businessman. When he spoke to his workers, he said to them, ". . . The LORD be with you. And they answered him, The LORD bless thee (Ruth 2:4). You don't find capital and labor talking like that to each other today.

Psalm 130 is closely linked to the preceding psalm. It has been called a Pauline psalm because it speaks of that which has to do with the mercy of God. God has delivered man out of the depths of sin and death, and He has done it not on the basis of man's works. On a certain occasion Martin Luther was asked what were the best psalms. He answered by saying "Psalmi Paulini," the Pauline psalms. When they wanted to know what the Pauline psalms were, he replied, "The thirty-second, the fifty-first, the one hundred and thirtieth, and the one hundred and forty-third." He explained that these psalms teach us that the forgiveness of sins is vouchsafed to all who believe without having any works of the law to offer. Therefore, they are Pauline psalms.

This psalm has been inscribed "De Profundis"—out of the depths.

Out of the depths have I cried unto thee, O LORD.

Lord, hear my voice: let thine ears be attentive to the voice of my supplications.

If thou, LORD, shouldest mark iniquities, O Lord, who shall stand? [Ps. 130:1–3].

Thank God that He is not going to judge us according to our iniquities. If God judged us that way, we would all be lost. It is because of His mercy that He saves us.

But there is forgiveness with thee, that thou mayest be feared.

I wait for the LORD, my soul doth wait, and in his word do I hope.

My soul waiteth for the Lord more than they that watch for the morning: I say, more than they that watch for the morning [Ps. 130:4–6].

The grace that saves us as Gentiles will save the nation of Israel also. The day is coming when Israel's cry out of the depths will be answered. Christ will return unto Zion and will turn away ungodliness from Jacob: "And so all Israel shall be saved: as it is written, There shall come out of Sion the Deliverer, and shall turn away ungodliness from Jacob: For this is my covenant unto them, when I shall take away their sins. As concerning the gospel, they are enemies for your sakes: but as touching the election, they are beloved for the fathers' sakes" (Rom. 11:26–28). During the Great Tribulation they will wait for the Lord to deliver them more than the watchers for the morning. You and I also are to wait for the rising of the Bright and Morning Star, the Lord Jesus Christ, when He comes for His own.

PSALM 131

***THEME:** Childlike faith and simplicity of the pilgrim*

This is another pilgrim psalm, a brief but very precious one. Notice that it is written by David.

> **Lord, my heart is not haughty, nor mine eyes lofty: neither do I exercise myself in great matters, or in things too high for me [Ps. 131:1].**

Do you remember Michal who was David's wife and Saul's daughter? She despised David and mocked him because of the way he took the ark into the tabernacle (2 Sam. 6:12–23). David told his wife that he would probably be even more contemptible in her eyes, because he was going to humble himself even more and get down in the dust before his God. Remember, he was king. We need to get down before our God today. When was the last time you got down on all fours before God? Very few of us practice that. It is the best exercise there is. It certainly will help you spiritually, and it may help you physically.

> **Surely I have behaved and quieted myself, as a child that is weaned of his mother: my soul is even as a weaned child.**
>
> **Let Israel hope in the Lord from henceforth and for ever [Ps. 131:2–3].**

Let me quote Dr. Gaebelein's comment on this beautiful psalm: "Here we find the description of an humble, a broken and contrite spirit. It has well been said, 'All virtues together are a body of which humility is the head.' How many Scriptures teach the great importance and value of such true humility" (*The Book of Psalms*, p. 462). Then he cites several references in Scripture: "Though the Lord be high, yet hath he respect unto the lowly: but the proud he knoweth afar off" (Ps. 138:6). "For thus saith the high and lofty One that inhabiteth eternity, whose name is Holy; I dwell in the high and holy place, with him also that is of a contrite and humble spirit, to revive the spirit of the humble, and to revive the heart of the contrite ones (Isa. 57:15). "Likewise, ye younger, submit yourselves unto the elder. Yea, all of you be subject one to another, and be clothed with humility: for God resisteth the proud, and giveth grace to the humble" (1 Pet. 5:5). "But let it be the hidden man of the heart, in that which is not corruptible, even the ornament of a meek and quiet spirit, which is in the sight of God of great price" (1 Pet. 3:4). "Humble yourselves in the sight of the Lord, and he shall lift you up" (James 4:10). And the Lord Jesus Himself said, "Come unto me, all ye that labour and are heavy laden, and I will give you rest [literally, I will rest you]" (Matt. 11:28).

The figure of a weaned child is very interesting. Dr. Gaebelein comments, "As the weaned child no longer cries, and frets, and longs for the mother's breast, but rests still and is contented, because the child knows it is with its mother; so the soul is weaned from all discontentment, ambitiousness and self-seeking, or any kind of selfishness, waiting on the Lord, finding rest and contentment only in Him" (*ibid.*, p. 463).

PSALM 132

***THEME:** A messianic psalm looking forward to the time Christ will be King in Jerusalem*

This is another pilgrim psalm that speaks of a rest on the promises of God, and faith becomes all important. There has always been a question about the authorship of this psalm. David is mentioned four times, but I do not believe he wrote it. Those of real scholarship question that David wrote it. Delitzsch says, "It is suited to the mouth of Solomon." Perowne says, "It is perfectly natural that Solomon should write a song for such an occasion, speaking of the earlier efforts made by his father to prepare a habitation for Jehovah." It is his belief that this psalm was composed by King Solomon when the ark of the covenant was removed out of the tent of habitation that David had prepared for it in Jerusalem, and which was now being moved into the temple that Solomon had built. This idea seems to fit in better with the contents of this psalm, and the only mention we have of the ark in the Psalms is here.

We need to note, however, that the son of David in this psalm is not Solomon, but the greater Son of David, the Lord Jesus Christ. With this as a background, let us look at this psalm. Now that the pilgrims are there in Jerusalem, they have come to the temple where the mercy seat is above the ark, the place where they can approach God.

> **LORD, remember David, and all his afflictions:**
>
> **How he sware unto the LORD, and vowed unto the mighty God of Jacob;**
>
> **Surely I will not come into the tabernacle of my house, nor go up into my bed;**
>
> **I will not give sleep to mine eyes, or slumber to mine eyelids.**
>
> **Until I find out a place for the LORD, an habitation for the mighty God of Jacob [Ps. 132:1–5].**

You will recall that in 2 Samuel 7 it was in David's heart to build God a house. You can see from this passage that this was the overwhelming ambition of his life. His one great, pulsating thought was that he might build a temple for the ark of God.

> **Arise, O LORD, into thy rest; thou, and the ark of thy strength [Ps. 132:8].**

This evidently was the song that they sang when the ark was moved into the temple that Solomon had built, and the glory of the Lord filled the temple as it had the tabernacle of old.

> **The LORD hath sworn in truth unto David: he will not turn from it; Of the fruit of thy body will I set upon thy throne [Ps. 132:11].**

This is a reference to the Lord Jesus Christ. Can we be sure of this? Yes, because David's children did not measure up to the description of the One who one day would sit upon the throne of David. In the Books of Kings and Chronicles you follow the line of David, and you will see one sinner after another sitting upon the throne. Very few were good kings, and only five of them saw revival come to the nation.

> **If thy children will keep my covenant and my testimony that I shall teach them, their children shall also sit upon thy throne for evermore [Ps. 132:12].**

But, you see, David's children did not keep God's covenant and testimony. That is the reason they were put out of their land and sent into captivity in Babylon. Even though the line of David sinned, God's covenant was not destroyed, and the time will come when the fruit of his body will sit upon his throne. That is what the New Testament speaks about when it opens with, "The book of the generation of Jesus Christ, the son of David, the son of Abraham" (Matt. 1:1). The Lord Jesus is the "Son of David" about whom the psalmist is writing.

> **For the LORD hath chosen Zion; he hath desired it for his habitation.**
>
> **This is my rest for ever: here will I dwell; for I have desired it.**
>
> **I will abundantly bless her provision: I will satisfy her poor with bread [Ps. 132:13–15].**

This prophecy is not fulfilled in Jerusalem in our day. I walked up on top of Mount Zion one day with a friend, and when he saw what was there, he said, "I wonder if it was worth the walk?" I told him, "I guess David and the Lord thought so, but there is something in the future that they can see and we do not see."

It is apparent that this is a psalm that the pilgrims would sing as they came to Jerusalem and the temple where God promised He would meet with His people.

PSALM 133

***THEME:** Rejoicing in the fellowship of believers*

This psalm is "A Song of degrees of David." It is short, but it is a beautiful gem. It has been called "A Psalm of Brotherhood," and it certainly is a psalm of fellowship. Not only did this pilgrim come to Jerusalem with his wife and children, but he is with friends. They are having a wonderful time of fellowship together. Remember that these pilgrims came from all over the then-known world, and they had been suffering persecution among unbelievers. What a joyful experience it is for them to be with their own people who are worshiping God with them.

> **Behold, how good and how pleasant it is for brethren to dwell together in unity! [Ps. 133:1].**

As believers, we are told to endeavor to ". . . keep the unity of the Spirit in the bond of peace" (Eph. 4:3). Believers are one in Christ. My friend, let's avoid being in a little exclusive clique. Unfortunately, we have a lot of cliques in our churches today. Many people would rather be big fish in little ponds than little fish in big ponds. How much better it is for all believers to "dwell together in unity!"

> **It is like the precious ointment upon the head, that ran down upon the beard, even Aaron's beard: that went down to the skirts of his garments [Ps. 133:2].**

This verse refers to the time that Aaron was anointed high priest. It also speaks of the priesthood of the Lord Jesus Christ. Someone has said that in this verse you have the fragrance of a lovely rose. This precious ointment was put on the priest to indicate that he was a priest unto God. We see that this is a picture of the Lord Jesus Christ. Not only is He King; He is also our High Priest. It is said of Him in Psalm 45:7 that He is anointed ". . . with the oil of gladness above [His] fellows." In Ezekiel 39:29 we read, "Neither will I hide my face any more from them: for I have poured out my spirit upon the house of Israel, saith the LORD GOD." Ezekiel speaks of a future day, and like that ointment that ran down on Aaron, so will God pour out His Spirit. This is the meaning, by the way, of Joel's prophecy of the outpouring of the Holy Spirit upon the Israel of a coming day, which was not fulfilled on the day of Pentecost. However, in our day we are baptized with the Holy Spirit, which puts us in the body of believers; and Christ is our Great High Priest. Since this is true, we should attempt to keep the unity the Holy Spirit made.

The psalmist concludes by saying that for brethren to dwell together in unity is—

> **As the dew of Hermon, and as the dew that descended upon the mountains of Zion: for there the LORD commanded the blessing, even life for evermore [Ps. 133:3].**

This psalm is a beautiful little gem.

PSALM 134

***THEME:** The pilgrim's final song of praise*

This is the final psalm in the pilgrim's progress. We have arrived. And in this psalm the pilgrim stands in the temple and lifts his voice in praise with the multitude. This is the grand amen, a threefold amen.

> **Behold, bless ye the LORD, all ye servants of the LORD, which by night stand in the house of the LORD.**
>
> **Lift up your hands in the sanctuary, and bless the LORD [Ps. 134:1–2].**

Again I remind you that this pilgrim has come from a place where he was under suspicion. People criticized him, maligned him, and lied about him. His neighborhood was not good. But now he has arrived in Jerusalem; he is standing in the sanctuary lifting up his hands and blessing the Lord.

> **The LORD that made heaven and earth bless thee out of Zion [Ps. 134:3].**

The pilgrim blesses God and, in turn, he is looking for the blessing of God to be upon his life. This is a great worship psalm and one that should be incorporated into our worship.

Let me venture a suggestion. The curse of being a retired preacher is that you always want to tell the other fellow how to conduct his service—whether you did it like that yourself or not. I know something about retired preachers, because several of them used to be in my congregations. Now I find myself one of them. As I look back on my ministry I realize my services were too formal. I believe worship today is entirely too formal. I do not believe that there should be fanatical outbreaks during the worship services, but there are some of us who cannot sing to express our thoughts. I have to stand in services just like a dummy. I can't sing—I can't carry a tune. My wife doesn't want me even to try to sing when I am standing with her in a service. She tells me that everybody turns and looks at me with not very pleasant looks when I try to sing. Sometimes I would just like to say, "Praise the Lord—Hallelujah" or "How wonderful is our God. God is good." We need some informality in our services and the freedom to express ourselves. Oh, my friend, let's not be stiff and stilted when we worship our God. Let's praise Him from our hearts.

PSALM 135

***THEME:** Praise the Lord*

We leave the pilgrim psalms now and come to songs of praise.

This is a hallelujah psalm. It begins with "Praise ye the LORD," and it ends with "Praise ye the LORD." This psalm is in a parentheses of "Hallelujahs." In it Israel praises God for the deliverance of the past. It is a great call to praise God.

> **Praise ye the LORD. Praise ye the name of the LORD; praise him, O ye servants of the LORD.**
>
> **Ye that stand in the house of the LORD, in the courts of the house of our God.**
>
> **Praise the LORD; for the LORD is good: sing praises unto his name; for it is pleasant [Ps. 135:1–3].**

We do not say enough that God is good. My friend, have you told anyone today that God is good? Oh, He *is* good! This is a call to praise Him.

> **Whatsoever the LORD pleased, that did he in heaven, and in earth, in the seas, and all deep places.**
>
> **He causeth the vapours to ascend from the ends of the earth; he maketh lightnings for the rain; he bringeth the wind out of his treasuries [Ps. 135:6–7].**

It is God who makes the weather. The weatherman does not make the weather, and the proof is that he does not always give us the correct report. He is not in touch with headquarters. He is in touch with a lot of scientific gadgets, and every now and then he comes up with an educated guess; but *God* makes the weather. He is the Creator. Not only does He make the weather, but He runs the universe as it pleases Him. Maybe you don't like it; if you don't, why don't you move out? Why don't you go to another universe or start one of your own and run it your way? This is God's universe, and if you are not satisfied with it, I suggest that somehow you become reconciled to it and accept the Creator because He is also the Redeemer of man today. We have many questions that God has not answered. And frankly, my friend, God does not have to answer our questions. He asks us to trust Him and live a life of faith.

The psalmist compares the living God with idols.

The idols of the heathen are silver and gold, the work of men's hands.

They have mouths, but they speak not; eyes have they, but they see not;

They have ears, but they hear not; neither is there any breath in their mouths.

They that make them are like unto them: so is every one that trusteth in them [Ps. 135:15–18].

My friend, you are going to be like your god. What do you worship? You worship something. It could be gold or silver; it doesn't have to be in the shape of an image or an idol either. Many people today worship gold and silver. That is covetousness and modern idolatry. Whatever your god is—if it is not the living and true God—he may have a mouth, but he cannot speak. He may have ears, but he cannot hear you. Only the living God can hear you. Because you will become like your god, it is a good idea to worship the true God. We ought to bless His name.

Blessed be the LORD out of Zion, which dwelleth at Jerusalem. Praise ye the LORD [Ps. 135:21].

He is worthy to be praised. This is a tremendous psalm!

PSALM 136

***THEME:** Thanks to God for His mercy*

This is another hallelujah psalm. It praises God's mercy in creation, in redemption, in fighting enemies, and for the future glory.

O give thanks unto the LORD; for he is good: for his mercy endureth for ever [Ps. 136:1].

The Lord has plenty of mercy. He will never run out of it.

O give thanks unto the God of gods: for his mercy endureth for ever.

O give thanks to the Lord of lords: for his mercy endureth for ever [Ps. 136: 2–3].

Every verse in this psalm mentions the mercy of God. It exalts God's mercy. In Ephesians 2:4 Paul says, "But God, who is rich in mercy, for his great love wherewith he loved us." I want mercy from God, and He is rich in it. I receive many letters from folks who tell me they have committed some sin. They ask, "Do you think God will forgive me?" Friend, He is rich in mercy. Have you called on Him? If you really want forgiveness, He will give it to you. He deals with us according to His mercy.

This is praise to God the Creator. And notice that every verse has the refrain: "for his mercy endureth for ever."

To him that by wisdom made the heavens: for his mercy endureth for ever.

To him that stretched out the earth above the waters: for his mercy endureth for ever.

To him that made great lights: for his mercy endureth for ever:

The sun to rule by day: for his mercy endureth for ever:

The moon and stars to rule by night: for his mercy endureth for ever [Ps. 136: 5–9].

The next section is praise to God for His mercy in delivering Israel from Egyptian bondage. And with every step of God's deliverance he repeats: "for his mercy endureth for ever." He concludes with God's mercy in giving them their land:

And gave their land for an heritage: for his mercy endureth for ever:

Even an heritage unto Israel his servant: for his mercy endureth for ever [Ps. 136:21–22].

The concluding section of this glorious psalm is as meaningful to you and me as it is to the people of Israel:

Who remembered us in our low estate: for his mercy endureth for ever:

And hath redeemed us from our enemies: for his mercy endureth for ever.

Who giveth food to all flesh: for his mercy endureth for ever.

O give thanks unto the God of heaven: for his mercy endureth for ever [Ps. 136:23–26].

I don't know about you, but I feel like saying "Hallelujah" again. How wonderful is our God. Learn to fall down before Him and worship Him. He is worthy. When you get down in the dust (and you have to get down to get up), He will lift you up with His mercy.

PSALM 137

***THEME:** Singing the Lord's song in a strange land*

Reading through the Book of Psalms is like driving on a divided highway through some lovely section of the countryside. We pass through new and beautiful scenery with a spectacular landscape on each side.

The beginning of each psalm is like coming to an intersection. We casually observe the highway marker, but we proceed at the same speed, and we have the feeling of sameness. On each side of the highway marker the view is very much the same. That is true especially after we leave Psalm 119. As we are traveling along the highway all of a sudden we come to Psalm 137. When we come to this psalm we begin to slow down because we see down the highway that three flares have been thrown down. In fact, these three flares are telling us to Stop—Look—Listen.

By way of introduction, will you note these three flares. The first one is marked STOP.

As we come to this psalm we find that it is designated an imprecatory psalm. Somebody says, "Well, a flare with that word on it wouldn't make me stop because I wouldn't know what it meant anyway." May I say to you that *imprecatory* simply means that it is a psalm that pronounces a curse. It is a psalm that voices a prayer or a wish for vengeance. Listen to this concluding verse: "Happy shall he be, that taketh and dasheth thy little ones against the stones"! That is a red flare, let me tell you! It is a shocker, and it causes a great deal of difficulty. Many folk detour around it. In fact, it would be very easy for me to avoid it, but I feel that this psalm is one that we should stop and look at.

There are several ways men have of dealing with this psalm. The liberal critics deal with it very simply: they reject it. They say that it does not belong in the Bible. It expresses feelings that are contrary to what they think it ought to say. Therefore they reject it. Of course, the method of the higher critic is to take out of the Bible what he likes and reject what he does not like. He is like the simple-minded country boy who bought a cow. After he had bought the cow he learned it cost something to feed the front end of the cow, but he got the milk from the back end of the cow. He decided to concentrate on the back end, and forget about the front end so he could make more money. You know what happened—his cow died. But he was a "higher critic." Higher critics take what they like and reject what they do not like. This philosophy does not satisfy, nor does it solve the problem at all.

Then there is another way of dealing with this. There are those who say, in a naive sort of way, "I believe the Bible from cover to cover"—yet they are ignorant of what is between the covers! This is the reason those of us who are conservative are accused of being anti-intellectual. Multitudes of conservative folk claim to believe the Bible but are ignorant of it. This is the reason I put such an emphasis on teaching the Word of God. It is one thing to say you believe it; it is another thing to know what it says.

This leads us to the third viewpoint. It is to believe the Bible from cover to cover, and attempt to understand it. It is to determine what God's meaning is, to discover what He had in mind when He recorded certain things. I want to know what I am believing, and be able to give a reason for the hope that is in me. Therefore with this attitude let us come to Psalm 137, an imprecatory psalm. Although it expresses something here that sounds very terrible on the surface, let's look at it and see what it really says.

The second flare tells us not only to stop, but to LOOK. That is, Psalm 137 deals with a particular portion of the history of God's chosen people. It is an historical psalm—which is very unusual. The historical books of the Old Testament do not record the history of the nation Israel during the seventy years of captivity in Babylon. There is no record of that captivity. It is true that Jeremiah prophesied about it, but he did not go with the captives to Babylon. Ezekiel was in Babylon, but he was prophesying to the captives there. We can only draw by inference the conditions of the people. He was concerned more with his visions than he was with history. Also Daniel was in Babylon during that period; but he was in the court, prophesying to the gentile rulers. We have no record from him at all concerning the captives. The seventy years of Babylonian captivity are a period of silence. It is a vacuum. It is a void as far as the historical books are concerned. The two Books of Kings and the two Books of Chronicles bring us right up to the Babylonian captivity and the destruction of Jerusalem. The next historical books, Ezra, Nehemiah, and Esther, pick up the story after the seventy-year captivity is over and the people are back in their land. The captivity in Babylon is passed over, because in God's plan His clock stops when His people are out of their land.For this reason we have no record of this period. This fact gives great emphasis to Psalm 137 because it is a bridge over the "Grand Canyon" of silence. It is like a vista point along the highway where you can pull off the road and look at scenery you have never seen before. We don't see very much, but we see something of this silent period.

Then the third flare that has been thrown down is LISTEN. It is a question that has been raised: "How shall we sing the LORD'S song in a strange land?" (Ps. 137:4). I'm not sure that this question can be answered for these people. I'm not sure today that it can be answered for you and me unless we are willing to meet certain conditions. How can we sing the Lord's song in a strange land?

Psalm 137 records the tragic yet tender experience of these people during the seventy years of captivity. You will find in this psalm bitter hatred and deep love. You will find a people that are overwhelmed and overpowered by their emotions. They feel very deeply about what is recorded here.

THE CENTRAL EXPERIENCE

Notice first of all the central experience of these people.

By the rivers of Babylon, there we sat down, yea, we wept, when we remembered Zion [Ps. 137:1].

The location is all important—"by the rivers of Babylon." These people have had an experience that no other people have had. From the land of Goshen to the ghettos of Europe they have known what it is to be away from their homeland, to be in a strange land. They know what it is to go all the way from the brickyards of Egypt to Babylonian canals. They know what it is to spend time in slave labor camps. By the rivers of Babylon was one place where they were persecuted, where they performed slave labor, a place where they suffered. By the rivers of Babylon.

The question arises: What were they doing there? To begin with, they had no business being there. God had put them in the Promised Land, and God had promised to keep them there as His witnesses as long as they were true to Him. What are they doing by the rivers of *Babylon?*

The rivers of Babylon are, of course, the canals. I think it is well accepted today that these are the people who dug those canals off the Tigris and Euphrates Rivers. Those canals threaded through that section to irrigate the land. These are the people who from sunup to sundown wearily dug through that dry desert terrain. "By the rivers of Babylon, there we sat down." What a picture of deep dejection. What a picture of despair. What a picture of dire desperation. "There we sat down." What else could they do? "Yea, we wept, when we remembered Zion." How woebegone can you get!

The Psalms are songs of praise. The Psalms express joy, wonderful faith, hope, and confidence. But not this psalm. This is the psalm in which they throw in the crying towel. "Yea, we wept, when we remembered Zion." This is no psalm of praise. This is a psalm of deep indigo, as blue as you can possibly get. "We wept, when we remembered Zion."

What a contrast between Jerusalem and Babylon! Jerusalem yonder in the hills, beautiful for situation. Babylon, down on a dry plain. The people are not there because they want to be there. They are there because their city has been destroyed. They are there because the Babylonians, a people stronger than they, had invaded their city, taken them captive, and herded them like animals, and put them on slave labor. Now they are homesick. "We wept, when we remembered Zion."

Why are they there? They are there because they have sinned. If you want the explanation from another weeping one of that period, turn to Jeremiah. He was a crybaby, but don't find fault with him because, you see, when God chose a man to pronounce His judgment upon them, He chose a man with a tender heart. It was Jeremiah who told them their city was to be destroyed. It was Jeremiah who said they were going into captivity. God didn't use a brutal man to give that brutal message. He didn't choose a harsh man to give a harsh message. He chose a man with the heart of a woman. Jeremiah says, "My eyes were a fountain of tears. This message broke my heart." God sent that kind of a man so they would know how He felt about it. Listen to him in Lamentations. "Jerusalem hath grievously sinned; therefore she is removed . . ." (Lam. 1:8). Why are these people down there on the banks of the canals in Babylon? They have *grievously* sinned. That is the reason they are there.

Now listen to them:

We hanged our harps upon the willows in the midst thereof [Ps. 137:2].

They have no heart for singing. They have quit singing now. They will not have a choir there. There won't be any song service there. They are wailing instead of singing. They have put their harps upon the willows; they won't be needing them anymore. They couldn't sing the songs of Zion by the rivers of Babylon! It was yonder at the temple in Jerusalem where they went to sing praises to God. Now by the rivers of Babylon they hanged up their harps. These instruments of praise they put up on the willow trees—weeping willows.

Today there are multitudes of Christians who have put their harps on the weeping willow trees. They have lost their song. They have no harp, but they are harping just the same about this and that.

Christian friend, have you lost your song? Maybe you can remember the joy you had when you first came to Christ. Have you lost your song today?

THE CRITICAL EXPERIENCE

For there they that carried us away captive required of us a song; and they that wasted us required of us mirth, saying, Sing us one of the songs of Zion [Ps. 137:3].

Now the people of Babylon had heard about the singing in Israel. The Israelites were world famous—as we shall see in a moment—for a very definite reason. And when it was heard that they were being brought to the canals outside the city of Babylon, that they were colonized there and put in slave labor camps, the 'Tanner Bus' company started running a tour out there because people wanted to see them. You see, Israel was world famous because in Jerusalem there was a temple to the living and true God. When visitors came to Jerusalem they found a people, not worshiping an image, but serving the living God, approaching Him through redemption and forgiveness of sins, and singing praises unto Him. They had never seen anything like it. They had never heard anything like it. The news of it spread throughout the world. The Queen of Sheba came from the *ends* of the earth when she heard of it. She thought the report couldn't be true. During Israel's feast seasons the people would gather together in Jerusalem, and they would sing these psalms. Probably all of the psalms were set to music. David arranged a choir and an orchestra with hundreds of musicians. It is estimated that there were times when one hundred thousand people gathered in and around that temple singing praises unto God! To hear them was a sensational experience. But now the temple was burned, Jerusalem lay in rubble, and the people were doing slave labor in Babylon. Many travelers came to Babylon saying something like this: "I was in Jerusalem during a feast day those people had. They were there from all over the world. They gathered around their temple over one hundred thousand strong. When that sacrifice was burned and the smoke ascended, out from the throats of those people rose a psalm that lifted me off the ground into the heavens! I have never heard anything like it!" (These people have been musicians, whether you like it or not, through the centuries—all the way from David, the sweet psalmist of Israel, to Meyerbeer, Offenbach, Fritz Kreisler, Felix Mendelssohn, George Gershwin, Paul Whiteman, Irving Berlin and to the present crop.)

When these people met together and sang praises to God, the world heard about it. God intended the world to hear about it. Now that they were captives in Babylon, the Babylonians said, "We're going out there and listen to a concert!" When they got out there the Babylonians saw the harps hanging on the willow trees; they saw these people sitting in deep dejection—instead of singing they were weeping. And with a sneer they said to them, "Sing us a song of Zion. We've been hearing about you. We thought you people could *sing!*" They taunted and ridiculed them, "Heist us a tune. Let's hear it."

Listen to them.

How shall we sing the LORD'S song in a strange land? [Ps. 137:4].

With a sob in their soul they said, "We've lost our song. You mock us when you tell us to sing you a song of Zion. Our Zion is back yonder in ashes and rubble and ruin. We can't sing anywhere but back there. How can we sing the Lord's song in a strange land?"

The interesting thing is that the Christian *is* to sing in a strange land. The people of Israel were not; they were perfectly right in refusing. To begin with, they *couldn't* sing. Neither did God ask them to sing where they were. They were to sing the songs of Zion *at* Zion. The child of God today is a pilgrim and stranger in this world. Centuries before this time the people of Israel were going through the wilderness, with slavery in Egypt behind them, on their way to the Promised Land. In the lead were the Levites carrying the ark, and they were singing. Immediately behind them came Judah, the tribe whose name means "praise." They went through the wilderness with praise on their lips. Today this is the way in which the child of God is to go through the wilderness of this world. Every Christian today should have a song in his heart. I don't say a song on his lips—David made it very clear that we're to make a joyful *noise* unto the Lord. It's best for some of us not to sing aloud. I don't sing in public; I sing privately for my own amusement, usually in the car alone. But we are to sing in a strange land. God has given us a song, the song of redemption.

Now there are reasons for people losing their song: First of all, there is the natural tendency. That is, the psychological factor. Psychologists tell us that some folk are sanguine in their nature. That is, they are smiling, joyful all the time regardless of the circumstances. Other people are the opposite. They are filled with melancholy. Some *races* are like that. The Scottish have a reputation of being the dour Scots. I do not know, but I think I must have enough Scottish blood to give me a pessimistic view of life. Conversely, the contribution the black race has made in our midst is that they are generally an optimistic race. Under very extreme circumstances they have revealed that. I heard the story of the black woman who was so radiant, regardless of circumstances, that they asked her what was her secret. She said, "Well, when I works, I works hard. When I rest, I sits loose, and when I worries, I goes to sleep." Isn't it wonderful to have that kind of nature that when you worry you go to sleep! But a great many folk today don't look joyful. Some of us don't feel like smiling all the time. We're not made that way.

The second factor is that discouragement and disappointment come to a great many Christians. Life buffets some people more than it buffets others. You know some Christians that seem to have more trouble than anyone else. Shakespeare calls it "the slings and arrows of outrageous fortune." Some people seem to get *more* of the slings and arrows of outrageous fortune. When I first came to Los Angeles, I went out and stood on a street corner, watching the faces of those who went by. Folk had come there from everywhere. They had come largely to improve their condition, for entertainment, and for relaxation. But you will see as many unhappy faces on the streets of Southern California as you will see any place in the world. As I watched, in the midst of the many unhappy faces, I saw the face of a woman that just stood out. I had never seen a face that had tragedy marked on it as hers did. I wondered about it. I was startled when the next Sunday morning I looked out at the faces in my congregation, and there she sat. I was even more startled when that morning after the benediction she came to me and said, "I must talk to you." And when she told her story I agreed that her face should have looked just as it did—the saddest face I have ever seen. The discouragements of life sometimes beat in upon even children of God, and they lose their song.

Then there is the third reason. Sometimes folk lose their song because of sin. You remember that David in his great confession, recorded in Psalm 51:12, cried, "Restore unto me the joy of thy salvation." David never did lose his salvation, but he certainly lost the joy of it. That is what he asked God to restore. And in Psalm 32 he spoke of that awful, oppressive period when his sin was unconfessed. He said that his bones ached and he could not sleep. What a picture!

It was said of the Lord Jesus Christ that He was a Man of Sorrows and acquainted with grief. But before you make Him out a sad person—for He was not—note that Isaiah makes it very clear that He bore *our* griefs and carried *our* sorrows (Isa. 53:4). When all the sorrow and all the grief of your sin and my sin was put upon Him, He was a Man of Sorrows. But He had none of His own, for He had no sin of His own. He was made sin for us, and He was made our sin offering, completely identified with your sin and mine.

Why are these people by the rivers of Babylon? I can answer it now. *They have sinned.* Why have they lost their song? They sinned, and sin will rob you of your song.

THE CROWNING EXPERIENCE

Notice now in conclusion the crowning experience of these people.

If I forget thee, O Jerusalem, let my right hand forget her cunning.

If I do not remember thee, let my tongue cleave to the roof of my mouth; if I prefer not Jerusalem above my chief joy [Ps. 137:5–6].

And under the taunting of that mob of curious Babylonians who said, "Come on, let's hear something," they said, "We can't sing." Then they made a pledge to God. They said, "O Jerusalem, if I ever forget you, may my tongue cleave to the roof of my mouth. I'll never, never, *never* forget Jerusalem."

This is the ray of hope that is here. This is repentance. This is a pledge of allegiance. This is saying, "We'll become obedient now to God, and we want back in the will of God. We want to go back to Jerusalem." This is their confession. "If I forget thee, O Jerusalem. . ."

Remember, O LORD, the children of Edom in the day of Jerusalem; who said, Rase it, rase it, even to the foundation thereof [Ps. 137:7].

Edom, their eternal enemy, was there at the time Jerusalem fell, and Edom got in the cheering section for Babylon. They got up there and shouted, "Tear it down! Destroy it! We want to get rid of that wicked city!" They remember that now—these people who had survived that experience—and what they are asking for is justice. It is a cry for justice.

Someone is going to say, "But that is not the Christian spirit." I grant you, it is not. But these people are under law; they are not under grace. They are under law that provided justice. We may have misunderstood our Lord when on the cross He said, "Father, forgive them; for they know not what they do . . ." (Luke 23:34). Do you think He is dismissing all of the sins of these people? If you do, you are wrong. All He is saying is, "Father, forgive them for this particular thing of crucifying Me. They don't know what they are doing here." That crime is not to be held against them, but they are still sinners. And they will have to come to God as sinners, as one of them did—Saul of Tarsus, who was probably there at the time. He had to come to Christ and receive forgiveness of sin.

Somebody may remark that Stephen when he died said, ". . . Lord, lay not this sin to their charge . . ." (Acts 7:60). That is true. Stephen is exhibiting the attitude believers should take. Paul expresses it: "Dearly beloved, avenge not yourselves, but rather give place unto wrath: for it is written, Vengeance is mine; I will repay, saith the Lord" (Rom. 12:19). What is the Christian spirit? The Christian spirit is this: avenge not yourself. Does that mean that nothing is to be done about it? No. God says this to you and me as Christians: "Have you been harmed or hurt? Don't you hit back. I want you to turn that over to Me. I'll handle it. Vengeance is Mine; I will repay." God is saying that He will not let them get by with it. You see, when you and I take matters in our own hands, we are forsaking the walk of faith. What we are really saying is, "Lord, I can't trust You to handle this. I'll handle this one myself." In other words, we really want to hurt Him in return. But God is saying, "You walk by faith. Turn this matter over to Me. I'm the God of justice." My friend, justice must prevail. It has to prevail.

Someone still protests, But this isn't like the New Testament. What do you mean it isn't like the New Testament? I read this in Revelation 6:9–10: "And when he had opened the fifth seal, I saw under the altar the souls of them that were slain for the word of God, and for the testimony which they held: And they cried with a loud voice, saying, How long, O Lord, holy and true, dost thou not judge and avenge our blood on them that dwell on the earth?" A cry for vengeance is not contrary, you see, to the New Testament. My friend, justice *must* prevail. Our God is just. Things must be made right.

How deeply do you feel about evil? Do you hate a mad dog that comes into the yard to bite one of your children? If you don't love your children, then you wouldn't mind even bringing the mad dog into your home and urging the children to pet him on the head.

But if you love your children, you will hate that mad dog.

It is said of our Lord when He comes the next time: "Thou lovest righteousness, and hatest wickedness . . ." (Ps. 45:7). You can't love righteousness without hating wickedness. You can't love God without hating Satan. You can't love that which is right without hating that which is wrong. How deeply, really, do you feel about evil?

These captives, down by the river in Babylon, felt very deeply, and all they were asking for was that justice might prevail.

O daughter of Babylon, who art to be destroyed; happy shall he be, that rewardeth thee as thou hast served us [Ps. 137:8].

This is the law of retribution. It is still a principle for the child of God today. "Be not deceived; God is not mocked: for whatsoever a man soweth, that shall he also reap" (Gal. 6:7). He won't reap something else, but he will reap the identical thing that he sowed.

What these people are saying is, "O God, let that thing happen to them that happened to us—" the law of retribution. Our Lord said it: ". . . they that take the sword shall perish with the sword" (Matt. 26:52).

Now we come to the real difficulty.

Happy shall he be, that taketh and dasheth thy little ones against the stones [Ps. 137:9].

This Israelite, sitting yonder by the canals of Babylon, dejected, despondent, being jeered and taunted to sing, says, "I can't sing." His mind goes back to the destruction of his beloved city and of God's temple. He thinks again of what took place. He can see that Edomite in the cheering section, urging the Babylonians on. He sees how the Babylonians had destroyed his city. And then happened that frightful, awful thing. His wife was holding their precious little one. That great big brutal Babylonian soldier came to her, wrested the baby out of her arms, took it by the heels, and—with her screaming—hit its head across the rock, dashing its brains out! Remembering that, he says, "Because there is a just God in heaven, somebody will do that to the Babylonians."

Whether you and I like it or not, it is already a matter of history that Cyrus the Great through his general did exactly to the Babylonians what the Babylonians had done to the people of Jerusalem.

Is this psalm for the Dark Ages? Is it outmoded in this enlightened day? Has man grown more civilized and loving so that this psalm is no longer relevant?

Today on every continent strife is being fomented. And the most tragic casualties are the children. Man's inhumanity to man makes this psalm very up-to-date. And there is coming a day when all hell will break loose in this world. I thank God there is a God in heaven who is a God of justice and righteousness, and He is going to put an end to sin. Also I am thankful that He is a God of mercy, that He is not like men, but is merciful. The cross yonder reveals His love; it reveals His holiness. My Savior took upon Himself my sin. God so loved me that He gave His Son to die in my place, because He must judge sin.

Oh, today, in this day of grace He is merciful. But don't let it deceive you—He is also holy, and He is righteous. Those who will not receive the Savior, those who will spurn His grace, those who will turn their backs on His mercy, will be judged. He makes no apologies to us in the twentieth century for doing that, because He has been patient with us. He has been gracious so long.

Have you availed yourself of His mercy?

PSALM 138

THEME: *A song of wholehearted praise*

We come from Psalm 137, where we saw the harps hanging on the willow trees, to the psalm before us where the harps are again in the hands of the godly and are being used for the praise and worship of Jehovah. In the previous psalm the children of Israel were in captivity, down by the irrigation canals in Babylon. There they put their harps on the willow trees and wept when they remembered Zion. But in Psalm 138 we have a wonderful prophetic hymn of praise which looks into the future when the believing remnant will take up their harps again and sing praise unto God.

This is a psalm of David. Because there is a reference to the temple (which was not in existence in David's day), David's authorship has been questioned. Well, the word *temple* could be translated "tabernacle" just as easily; and I believe it is speaking of the tabernacle and the days of David. After all, in the inspired text it is inscribed as a psalm of David.

I will praise thee with my whole heart: before the gods will I sing praise unto thee [Ps. 138:1].

Let me give you Dr. Gaebelein's translation: "I will give thanks unto Thee with my whole heart, before the gods will I sing praises unto Thee."

Notice "I will praise thee with my whole heart." One of the things that impressed me on a visit to Jerusalem was seeing the Jews at the Wailing Wall (Israel has access to the wall again). I saw many of them standing there, some of them with a little book in their hands going through a ritual, some of them actually butting their heads against the wall, and some of them actually wailing, which touches the heart. But a great deal that I saw was just like ritualistic "churchianity"—nothing but lip service. However, in that future time when the Jews have been through the period of Jacob's trouble, the Great Tribulation, and have been delivered out of it, there will no longer be lip service. It will be real heart worship—"I will praise thee with my whole heart." My friend, you and I need to examine our own hearts to see how we are worshiping God. Do we worship Him with our whole heart? One of the things which impressed me about Horatius Bonar was what he said when he went to God to repent of the coldness, the indifference, and the sin in his life. He said, "Then I went back to God and repented of my repentance." His first confession was merely lip service, and he repented of that. I think some of us ought to go to God in prayer on Monday morning and ask Him to forgive us for going to church on Sunday. We should pray, "Lord, forgive me for going to church yesterday. I sang the hymns, but my heart wasn't in it. I prayed, but it was a mere formality. I listened to the Word of God, but it had no effect on me. I criticized the preacher and others who were there, but I did not criticize myself. God, forgive me for going to church like that." This would be a good thing for many of us to pray.

"Before the gods will I sing praise unto thee." Luther and Calvin explain that the "gods" were angels of God—I don't think they were that. Others think that he was talking about the idol gods of the nations, and certainly he could be referring to them. However, anything in your life that is in place of God or is between you and God, is *your* god. We saw this word *gods* back in Psalm 82:6, and there it referred to the judges, those who are in the place of God, that is, His representatives on earth. I have always been mindful of the fact that as a teacher, preacher, and minister of the Word of God, I have a responsibility to God. Someday I will have to answer to Him, because it is my job to make the gospel clear. If those who know the Lord don't make the gospel clear, who will? When I look back upon my ministry, I see much failure, and I have many regrets; but some day I will be able to look into the face of God and say, "Lord, I preached Your Word the best I could." That is a great comfort, because I have been His representative here on this earth. So, you see, when David said, "Before the gods will I sing praise unto thee," he could have meant several things, and we cannot be sure exactly what he had in mind.

I will worship toward thy holy temple, and praise thy name for thy lovingkindness and for thy truth: for thou hast magnified thy word above all thy name [Ps. 138:2].

A better translation of the last part of this verse would be, "Thou hast magnified thy saying according to all thy name." In other words, God's Word is as good as He is. There is an old saying that a man is as good as his word. Well, God is as good as His Word. His character is behind what He has said. "Thou hast magnified thy saying in accordance with all thy name," or, "Thou hast fulfilled it in such a manner as to bring out all that Thy name implies." This is a very wonderful statement.

Though the Lord be high, yet hath he respect unto the lowly: but the proud he knoweth afar off [Ps. 138:6].

Dr. Gaebelein translates it, "For Jehovah is high, and regardeth the humble, but the proud He knoweth afar off." He is high and He is over all; yet He will condescend to the lowly. There is so much said in the Word of God about God's regarding the humble. Proud modern man doesn't seem to be an expert at displaying humility. In James 4:6 we read, "But he giveth more grace. Wherefore he saith, God resisteth the proud, but giveth grace unto the humble." We are told, "Humble yourselves therefore under the mighty hand of God, that he may exalt you in due time" (1 Pet. 5:6). There is a great deal said about humility in Scripture. It is something God takes note of and recognizes. David took a humble place. We read his words in Psalm 131:1, "Lord, my heart is not haughty, nor mine eyes lofty: neither do I exercise myself in great matters, or in things too high for me." In Isaiah 57:15 we are told, "For thus saith the high and lofty One that inhabiteth eternity, whose name is Holy; I dwell in the high and holy place, with him also that is of a contrite and humble spirit, to revive the spirit of the humble, and to revive the heart of the contrite ones." In 1 Peter 5:5 we read, "Likewise, ye younger, submit yourselves unto the elder. Yea, all of you be subject one to another, and be clothed with humility: for God resisteth the proud, and giveth grace to the humble." 1 Peter 3:4 tells us, "But let it be the hidden man of the heart, in that which is not corruptible, even the ornament of a meek and quiet spirit, which is in the sight of God of great price." All of these verses reveal how God regards humility.

The Lord will perfect that which concerneth me: thy mercy, O Lord, endureth for ever: forsake not the works of thine own hands [Ps. 138:8].

This is the Old Testament way of saying, "Being confident of this very thing, that he which hath begun a good work in you will perform it until the day of Jesus Christ" (Phil. 1:6).

PSALM 139

***THEME:** A song of praise to the attributes of God*

This psalm is "To the chief Musician, A Psalm of David." This is a theological psalm in that it reveals something of the attributes of God in relation to His creation. It reveals His omniscience, His omnipresence, and His omnipotence. These are what I call four-cylinder words, but they simply mean that God is all-knowing (omniscient), He is everywhere present (omnipresent), and He is all-powerful (omnipotent). God can do anything that is the object of His power. Sometimes the ridiculous question is asked, Can God make a rock so big that He cannot lift it? The answer to that is that God never does anything ridiculous.

This is a psalm that will answer several pertinent questions for us.

THE OMNISCIENCE OF GOD

O Lord, thou hast searched me, and known me [Ps. 139:1].

This speaks of the omniscience of God. He knows you. He knows me. He is the greatest psychologist. When you have a problem, it is not necessary to climb upon the psychiatrist's couch and tell him everything. Why don't you climb upon the couch of the Lord Jesus and just tell Him everything? You might as well tell Him because He knows all about you anyway. The psychiatrist still won't know you even after you have told him everything you can think of.

Thou knowest my downsitting and mine uprising, thou understandest my thought afar off.

Thou compassest my path and my lying down, and art acquainted with all my ways.

For there is not a word in my tongue, but, lo, O Lord, thou knowest it altogether [Ps. 139:2–4].

That word that was on your tongue—perhaps you wanted to rip out a good strong oath, but you didn't do it because of the presence of someone. God saw it on your tongue. He knows everything. "There is not a word in my tongue, but, lo, O LORD, thou knowest it altogether."

Thou hast beset me behind and before, and laid thine hand upon me.

Such knowledge is too wonderful for me; it is high, I cannot attain unto it [Ps. 139:5–6].

You may ask, How can God do that? I don't know, and the psalmist says *he* doesn't know. "Such knowledge is too wonderful for me; it is high, I cannot attain unto it." Actually the omniscience of God is not an occasion for terror but for comfort. He saved me and yet He knew me—that is the amazing thing about it. There are some people whom you accept and receive, and then in some way they disappoint you. You thought you knew them, but you really did not know them. God *knows* us and yet He will save us. How wonderful He is! God knew David, and David let Him down. But God knew something about David's faith that we could not see. He could see David's heart, and beneath the faith that failed was a faith that never failed. The Lord knew what Simon Peter was going to do. He even knew that Judas would betray Him. Even though we don't understand it, that is the omniscience of God. He knows everything.

THE OMNIPRESENCE OF GOD

Let's look at the omnipresence of God for a moment. No matter where you go, you cannot get away from God.

Whither shall I go from thy spirit? or whither shall I flee from thy presence?

If I ascend up into heaven, thou art there: if I make my bed in hell, behold, thou art there [Ps. 139:7–8].

"Hell" is Sheol (not hell), the region of the unseen and unknown. God is there. No matter where you go, He is there.

If I take the wings of the morning, and dwell in the uttermost parts of the sea [Ps. 139:9].

You won't get away from God even if you go to the moon. To me it was thrilling to hear those first three astronauts who went around the moon read the first chapter of Genesis on Christmas Eve. You don't run away from God, my friend, even if you go to the moon!

Even there shall thy hand lead me, and thy right hand shall hold me.

If I say, Surely the darkness shall cover me; even the night shall be light about me.

Yea, the darkness hideth not from thee: but the night shineth as the day: the darkness and the light are both alike to thee [Ps. 139:10–12].

A man once said to me, "Do you think we ought to confess our sins in detail to God?" I said, "Of course. Spell them out. He already knows about them anyway. He was present when you committed them; so you better agree with Him on the subject. Let Him know that you recognize it as sin." My friend, to confess your sin is to *agree* with God—God says it is sin and you agree with Him that it is sin.

For thou hast possessed my reins: thou hast covered me in my mother's womb [Ps. 139:13].

From the time we are conceived in the womb we never get away from the presence of God in this life.

He reinforces this truth in the next verse:

I will praise thee; for I am fearfully and wonderfully made: marvellous are thy works; and that my soul knoweth right well [Ps. 139:14].

God is everywhere, and man is a fabulous creature who has the attention of God constantly.

My substance was not hid from thee, when I was made in secret, and curiously wrought in the lowest parts of the earth.

Thine eyes did see my substance, yet being unperfect; and in thy book all my members were written, which in continuance were fashioned, when as yet there was none of them [Ps. 139:15–16].

Before the body was formed David says he was a person. He was a person as he was being formed in the womb. Even before the members of his body were formed, he was a person. The personhood is declared to take place at the very moment of conception.

This is very important in our day because of the question of abortion. I heard a minister of

PSALM 143

***THEME:** David's urgent appeal for help*

This is another marvelous prayer of David. It is an urgent appeal for help. David had no inhibitions, and he opened his heart to God. Oh, that we could learn to pray like that!

Hear my prayer, O LORD, give ear to my supplications: in thy faithfulness answer me, and in thy righteousness [Ps. 143:1].

David appeals to the faithfulness and righteousness of God for an answer. Isn't this exactly what believers are to do when they sin? "If we confess our sins, he is faithful and just to forgive us our sins, and to cleanse us from all unrighteousness" (1 John 1:9). "He is faithful and just [or righteous]." Like David, we appeal to God on the basis of His faithfulness and His righteousness. This psalm is a very wonderful prayer, and it can fit into your experience and mine.

This is also the plea of the nation Israel. This is their hope when they cry for help from God in their day of calamity. And God will not disappoint them.

God is not through with Israel. In Micah 7:20 we read, "Thou wilt perform the truth to Jacob, and the mercy to Abraham, which thou hast sworn unto our fathers from the days of old." In Exodus 2:24–25 we are told, "And God heard their groaning, and God remembered his covenant with Abraham, with Isaac, and with Jacob. And God looked upon the children of Israel, and God had respect unto them." Why did God have respect unto Israel? Because He is faithful and righteous.

In Romans Paul tells us what Israel's problem is today. "For they being ignorant of God's righteousness, and going about to establish their own righteousness, have not submitted themselves unto the righteousness of God" (Rom. 10:3). This is also the trouble the Gentiles have. They are working at a religion. They are trying to do something to please God. My friend, He has already *done* something for them. He sent His Son to the cross to pay the penalty for sin. You please Him when you accept what He has done for you. "For Christ is the end of the law for righteousness to every one that believeth" (Rom. 10:4).

I stretch forth my hands unto thee: my soul thirsteth after thee, as a thirsty land. Selah [Ps. 143:6].

I have watched it rain out on the desert on that sandy soil when it has rained and rained and *rained*, and that thirsty land just drinks it up. David says, "My soul thirsteth after thee, as a thirsty land."

Now hear David's cry:

Hear me speedily, O LORD: my spirit faileth: hide not thy face from me, lest I be like unto them that go down into the pit [Ps. 143:7].

David is saying to God, "You are my only help."

Cause me to hear thy lovingkindness in the morning; for in thee do I trust: cause me to know the way wherein I should walk; for I lift up my soul unto thee.

Deliver me, O LORD, from mine enemies: I flee unto thee to hide me.

Teach me to do thy will; for thou art my God: thy spirit is good; lead me into the land of uprightness [Ps. 143:8–10].

This reveals David's trust in God as his only refuge and his only hope.

"Teach me to do thy will; for thou art my God" should be the daily prayer of every child of God.

PSALM 144

***THEME:** Praise and prayer to God because of who He is*

This is another one of the psalms written by David. Some of the contents are similar to those in Psalm 18, which began, "I will love thee, O LORD, my strength. The LORD is my rock, and my fortress, and my deliverer; my God, my strength, in whom I will trust; my buckler, and the horn of my salvation, and my high tower" (Ps. 18:1–2). Further down in the psalm David said, "In my distress I called upon the LORD, and cried unto my God: he heard my voice out of his temple, and my cry came before him, even into his ears" (Ps. 18:6). This psalm was written out of one of David's experiences when he was delivered out of the hand of King Saul. Also it is prophetic, looking forward to that coming day when the children of Israel will suffer during the Great Tribulation. In this time of great distress they will turn to God in prayer. Also this psalm is applicable to all the saints during the centuries between David's time and the Great Tribulation period.

Blessed be the LORD my strength, which teacheth my hands to war, and my fingers to fight [Ps. 144:1].

What does David mean? There will be those who will immediately jump at this and say, "Look, the God of the Old Testament is warlike." My friend, if you had lived in David's day, you would have been a lot more comfortable knowing that you were protected from the enemy surrounding you and knowing that you *could* defend yourself.

It is entirely incorrect to say that the Lord Jesus Christ was a pacifist. He gives peace to the human heart, and peace with God through the forgiveness of sins; but He also said, ". . . a strong man armed keepeth his [house] palace . . ." (Luke 11:21), which is what David is saying in this psalm. It is true that our Lord is the Prince of Peace, but He has made it very clear that there will be no peace on this earth until He returns. In the meantime it is more comfortable to know that our nation has enough armaments to protect us. I only hope we don't get some fanatic in power who will get rid of our protection, maintaining that we can depend on the goodness of human nature to take care of us. That type of thinking brought many a nation down into the dust. Some of the Greek states tried it. They had an outstanding civilization, but they are in ruin and rubble today because they could not protect themselves.

My goodness, and my fortress; my high tower, and my deliverer; my shield, and he in whom I trust; who subdueth my people under me [Ps. 144:2].

David says that God is his goodness. If you and I have any righteousness, it is Christ. David says that God is also his Goodness, his Protector, his Fortress, his High Tower, his Deliverer, and his Shield. Although it is comforting to know that our nation has an arsenal to protect us, I also want to make sure that God is my protector, that He is my fortress, my high tower, my deliverer, and my shield.

"Who subdueth my people under me" is David speaking as a commander.

LORD, what is man, that thou takest knowledge of him! or the son of man, that thou makest account of him! [Ps. 144:3].

Why should God take note of little man? Frankly, man does not amount to very much.

Man is like to vanity: his days are as a shadow that passeth away [Ps. 144:4].

"Man is like to vanity" means that man is nothing without God, that life is purposeless without Him.

When I was a pastor in Nashville, a man walked into my study one day holding a rusty old gun—it looked like a .45 to me. He said, "If you can't give me a reason to live, I am going to kill myself." I replied, "Well, you sure are putting me on the spot; I can't think of any reason why you shouldn't kill yourself, but I do want to tell you that you are not going to solve your problem by taking your life. All you will be doing is removing your problem from earth and taking it to a place where there is no solution, because you will fix your eternal destiny. But here and now you can make a decision for God which will add purpose to your life, and you won't be in such a hurry to end it. Then, when you do die, you will go home to be with Christ, your Savior."

Life without God is quite empty. I have a newspaper clipping which tells about a Swedish man who inherited what is said to be the largest fortune in the world, $5 billion—that is a lot of money! But that man took his own life. His $5 billion dollars didn't keep him here. He found life rather purposeless. My friend, without Jesus Christ, without God, "man is like to vanity" and emptiness. Without God life has no purpose.

Now listen to David plead with God.

Bow thy heavens, O LORD, and come down: touch the mountains, and they shall smoke [Ps. 144:5].

This is a call for God to break into human events, for God to intrude into human history. This is confirmed in Isaiah 64:1–2 which says, "Oh that thou wouldest rend the heavens, that thou wouldest come down, that the mountains might flow down at thy presence, As when the melting fire burneth, the fire causeth the waters to boil, to make thy name known to thine adversaries, that the nations may tremble at thy presence!" God is going to intrude into human history one day. I don't want to take a fanatical position and say that He is going to do it tomorrow, or even in this century, but the fact is that He is going to do it.

Cast forth lightning, and scatter them: shoot out thine arrows, and destroy them [Ps. 144:6].

When the Lord comes again, He is coming in judgment. The whole tenor of Scripture, including the New Testament, is that the Lord is coming in judgment one day. There is no more vivid and dramatic picture of this than the one given in Revelation 19:11, where John saw heaven opened and beheld a white horse, ". . . and he that sat upon him was called Faithful and True, and in righteousness he doth judge and make war." That is a picture of the Lord Jesus Christ coming forth as a conqueror to conquer. Maybe you don't like this picture, but it is the picture that the Word of God presents.

At that time, the psalmist says:

I will sing a new song unto thee, O God: upon a psaltery and an instrument of ten strings will I sing praises unto thee [Ps. 144:9].

Not until after the Tribulation will the children of Israel be able to sing this new song unto their God.

PSALM 145

***THEME:** Praise for what God is and for what He does*

This is the last psalm that mentions David as the author. He may have written some of the psalms that do not name an author, but we cannot be sure. This psalm is an acrostic, which means that each verse begins with one of the letters of the Hebrew alphabet.

Immediately we run into a problem which the critics have latched onto—there are twenty-two Hebrew letters and only twenty-one verses in this psalm. The psalm begins with *Aleph,* the first letter of the alphabet, and ends with *Tau,* the final letter in the Hebrew alphabet; the missing letter is *Nun.* Some critics say that *Nun* was left out by some transcriber. I don't think that is the case at all. I believe it was left out for a very definite reason. From Psalm 145 to 150 we find that every one of them is a hallelujah psalm. It is an increasing crescendo. Why would one verse be left out of Psalm 145? I think it speaks of the fact that our praise is imperfect. I like what F. W. Grant has written relative to the omission of this one letter: "I cannot but conclude that the gap is meant to remind us that in fact the fulness of praise is not complete without other voices, which are not found here, and that these missing voices are those of the Church and the heavenly saints in general." You don't get all of the hallelujahs until you get to the nineteenth chapter of Revelation: "And after these things I heard a great voice of much people in heaven, saying, Alleluia; Salvation, and glory, and honour, and power, unto the Lord our God . . . . And again they said, Alleluia. And her smoke rose up for ever and ever . . . . And I heard as it were the voice of a great multitude, and as the voice of many waters, and as the voice of mighty thunderings, saying, Alleluia: for the Lord God omnipotent reigneth (Rev. 19:1, 3, 6). There is the missing hallelujah. The praise in this Psalm 145 is not quite complete—nor is it in any of the psalms. At the occasion of the birth of Jesus, the angels said, "Glory to God in the highest . . ." (Luke 2:14). Why? Because Jesus was born in

Bethlehem and there would be peace. But there hasn't been peace. We have never been able to sing the Hallelujah chorus perfectly yet. But there is coming a day when Christ will return to this earth. The day that He comes forth will be a great day, and then the Hallelujah chorus will be sung correctly and completely.

I will extol thee, my God, O king; and I will bless thy name for ever and ever.

Every day will I bless thee; and I will praise thy name for ever and ever [Ps. 145:1–2].

"Every day will I bless thee"—this is not for only one day in the week when we go to church but for every day. There are days when we don't feel like blessing Him. We sometimes sing, "We praise Him for all that is past, and trust Him for all that is to come." We can change that around and sing, "We trust Him for all that is past and praise Him for all that is to come."

This is a marvelous psalm of praise!

The LORD is gracious, and full of compassion; slow to anger, and of great mercy [Ps. 145:8].

We have a kind God. David had experienced the kindness of God, and it motivated him to show the same kindness of God to others.

The LORD is righteous in all his ways, and holy in all his works.

The LORD is nigh unto all them that call upon him, to all that call upon him in truth [Ps. 145:17–18].

Whoever you are and wherever you are, if you mean business with God, you can come into His presence through Christ. "The LORD is nigh [He is near] unto all them that call upon him." There are many folk who are stiff-arming God. That is one reason they go through a church ritual—they are escaping a personal confrontation with Him.

One of the great doctrines that the Reformation brought back to us was the doctrine of the "priesthood of believers." If you have trusted Jesus Christ as your Savior, you have direct *access* to God. If you are unsaved, God invites you to come to Him for salvation. God is available.

PSALM 146

***THEME:** A Hallelujah psalm, praise to God for His goodness*

The five psalms that conclude this great hymn book are all hallelujah psalms. Notice that they begin with "Praise ye the LORD" and end with "Praise ye the LORD," which means, of course, "hallelujah." No longer do they tell anything of persecution or suffering; there are no prayers for help or deliverance from the enemy; there are no imprecatory prayers. The night of sin and suffering is over. Weeping is past and joy has come in the morning of the Millennium (See Ps. 30:5).

Praise ye the LORD. Praise the LORD, O my soul [Ps. 146:1].

Not only should we praise God with our lips, but we should genuinely praise Him from the heart.

Put not your trust in princes, nor in the son of man, in whom there is no help [Ps. 146:3].

This verse describes the powerlessness of man. No lasting help can come from any human being whose body will one day return to the dust from which it was made, whether he be a prince or a common man.

Dr. A. C. Gaebelein told of a visit he had from an orthodox Jew. I'll let him tell it in his own words: "He stated that he had read the New Testament and found the title of Jesus of Nazareth so often mentioned as 'the son of man.' He then declared that there is a warning in the Old Testament not to trust the son of man. As we asked him for the passage he quoted from this Psalm, 'Trust not . . . in the son of man in whom is no salvation.' We explained to him that if our Lord had been only the son of man and nothing else, if He had not been Immanuel, the virgin-born Son of God, if it were not true as Isaiah stated it, that He is the child born and *the Son given,* there would be no salvation in Him. But He came God's Son and appeared in the form of man for our redemption. His argument showed the blindness of the Jew. The statement is given in this Psalm, that man is sinful, that there is no hope in man, he is a finite creature and turns to dust. There is but One in whom salvation and all man's needs is found, the God of Jacob, the loving Jehovah" (*The Book of Psalms*, p. 500–501).

In the closing verses of this psalm, "the LORD," meaning *Jehovah*, is mentioned eight times.

Happy is he that hath the God of Jacob for his help, whose hope is in the LORD his God:

Which made heaven, and earth, the sea, and all that therein is: which keepeth truth for ever:

Which executeth judgment for the oppressed: which giveth food to the hungry. The LORD looseth the prisoners:

The LORD openeth the eyes of the blind: the LORD raiseth them that are bowed down: the LORD loveth the righteous [Ps. 146:5–8].

God is the One who is in the *helping* business.

The LORD preserveth the strangers; he relieveth the fatherless and widow: but the way of the wicked he turneth upside down.

The LORD shall reign for ever, even thy God, O Zion, unto all generations. Praise ye the LORD [Ps. 146:9–10].

As Jehovah, He is Redeemer. As Creator, He is Elohim. The Psalms make this abundantly clear. "Praise ye the LORD"—Hallelujah!

PSALM 147

***THEME:** A hallelujah chorus because of God's goodness to the earth and to Jerusalem*

Praise ye the LORD: for it is good to sing praises unto our God; for it is pleasant; and praise is comely.

The LORD doth build up Jerusalem: he gathereth together the outcasts of Israel [Ps. 147:1–2].

As you can see, this has not yet been accomplished, but has a future fulfillment.

He healeth the broken in heart, and bindeth up their wounds [Ps. 147:3].

God will do this for those who have passed through the horrors of the Great Tribulation. And, friend, He does it for you and me.

He telleth the number of the stars; he calleth them all by their names [Ps. 147:4].

What a contrast! He who cares for our broken hearts is the same God who not only knows the number of the stars—a number so vast that no human figures can express it—but has a name for each one!

Praise the LORD, O Jerusalem; praise thy God, O Zion.

For he hath strengthened the bars of thy gates; he hath blessed thy children within thee.

He maketh peace in thy borders, and filleth thee with the finest of the wheat [Ps. 147:12–14].

The King has come to Jerusalem, the Lord Jesus Christ, the King of Peace. At this time the prediction of Isaiah will be fulfilled, "O thou afflicted, tossed with tempest, and not comforted, behold, I will lay thy stones with fair colours, and lay thy foundations with sapphires. And I will make thy windows of agates, and thy gates of carbuncles, and all thy borders of pleasant stones. And all thy children shall be taught of the LORD: and great shall be the peace of thy children" (Isa. 54: 11–13).

He hath not dealt so with any nation:

and as for his judgments, they have not known them. Praise ye the LORD [Ps. 147:20].

The nation of Israel is unique. They are the *only* people given the title "Chosen People." They are the only ones made custodians of the revelation of God. In His Word God says He has an eternal purpose for them.

We are to pray for the peace of Jerusalem, for the time that God will fulfill His promise to them.

PSALM 148

***THEME:** A hallelujah chorus of all God's created intelligences*

In this psalm praise begins with the heavenlies. What a great hallelujah chorus this will be when all God's created intelligences in heaven and in earth will praise Him!

Praise ye the LORD. Praise ye the LORD from the heavens: praise him in the heights.

Praise ye him, all his angels: praise ye him, all his hosts.

Praise ye him, sun and moon: praise him, all ye stars of light [Ps. 148:1–3].

The praise starts in the highest heaven, the third heaven, where it includes believers, I think.

Kings of the earth, and all people; princes, and all judges of the earth:

Both young men, and maidens; old men, and children:

Let them praise the name of the LORD: for his name alone is excellent; his glory is above the earth and heaven [Ps. 148:11–13].

Not only in the heavenlies, but on the earth as well, will His created beings praise Him. This is moving now to a mighty crescendo when heaven and earth will praise God!

PSALM 149

***THEME:** A hallelujah chorus because the kingdom has come through redemption by blood, and judgment by power*

Praise ye the LORD. Sing unto the LORD a new song, and his praise in the congregation of saints [Ps. 149:1].

We have already discussed the "new song" that is spoken of in the Book of Revelation. The new song will be about the fact that the Lord Jesus is our Redeemer.

Let Israel rejoice in him that made him: let the children of Zion be joyful in their King [Ps. 149:2].

He is our Redeemer and let us remember that He is our Creator. We should praise Him for that. When we climb to a mountaintop or walk down by the ocean, we can praise Him. When we are flying by plane is a good time to praise the Lord.

Now notice that we have here the judgment of the nations.

Let the high praises of God be in their mouth, and a two-edged sword in their hand;

To execute vengeance upon the heathen, and punishments upon the people;

To bind their kings with chains, and their nobles with fetters of iron;

To execute upon them the judgment written: this honour have all his saints. Praise ye the LORD [Ps. 149:6–9].

Let's keep in mind that when the Lord Jesus returns to this earth, He will not be welcomed by the nations of the world. He is coming to *judge* this earth. When He returns to this little planet, He will put down the rebellion that has broken out; and He will *break* them with the rod of iron. As it is said in Psalm 2, "Thou shalt break them with a rod of iron; thou shalt dash them in pieces like a potter's vessel" (Ps. 2:9). Oh, my friend, let's not be deluded by this namby-pamby way of thinking that our God is not going to judge. You and I are living in a world that is moving to a judgment day.

PSALM 150

THEME: *The grand finale of the hallelujah chorus, with choir and orchestra*

Praise ye the LORD. Praise God in his sanctuary: praise him in the firmament of his power.

Praise him for his mighty acts: praise him according to his excellent greatness.

Praise him with the sound of the trumpet: praise him with the psaltery and harp.

Praise him with the timbrel and dance: praise him with stringed instruments and organs.

Praise him upon the loud cymbals: praise him upon the high sounding cymbals.

Let every thing that hath breath praise the LORD. Praise ye the LORD [Ps. 150: 1–6].

WHAT IS WORSHIP?

First of all we will consider the object of worship. This will require that we answer, in a general sort of way, the question: What is worship? To do this we shall deal with one statement found in Psalm 150:1: "Praise ye the LORD." In this first aspect the emphasis is on "Praise ye the *LORD*." He is the object of worship.

The Psalms put the emphasis upon two things: the fact that He is the *Creator*, and the fact that He is the *Redeemer*. God made this earth on which we live, as well as the universe. This lovely sunshine that you are enjoying is His. He is the Creator. There is not a thing at your fingertips today that He did not make. He is worthy of our worship because He is the Creator. He is also worthy of our worship because He is the Redeemer. He is the *only* Creator, and He is the *only* Redeemer. You see, God works in a field where He has no competition at all. He has a monopoly on the field of creation and on the field of redemption. Because of this, He claims from all of His creatures their worship, their adoration, and their praise.

And the Scriptures say that God is a jealous God. I can't find where He asks me to apologize for Him for this. He has created us for Himself. He has redeemed us for Himself. On the human level, marriage is used to illustrate the believer's relationship to Christ. A husband, if he loves his wife, does not share her with other men. He is jealous of her. Her love is to be for him alone. So believers, called in Scripture the bride of Christ, are created solely for Him. He alone is to have our adoration; He alone is to have our praise. You will recall that John, on the Isle of Patmos, felt constrained to fall down and worship the angel who had been so helpful in bringing all of the visions before him, but the angel rebuked him and said, ". . . See thou do it not . . . worship God" (Rev. 22:9). He does not want even His angels worshiped; He does not want Mary worshiped; He wants none worshiped but Himself. He alone is *worthy* of worship. And Scriptures say there is coming a day when everything that has breath will praise the Lord. He has created everything that it might praise Him.

WHO IS TO WORSHIP?

God is the *object* of worship, but this question follows: Who can worship?

The psalmist said: "Let every thing that hath breath praise the LORD. Praise ye the LORD" (Ps. 150:6). The emphasis now is upon *ye*. He is saying to mankind, "Praise *ye* the LORD." God apparently created man for the purposes of fellowship with Himself and that man might praise Him. There is no other reason for man's existence. What is the chief end of man? Man's chief end is to glorify God and enjoy Him forever.

God created the universe that it might glorify Him. It was not brought into existence for you and me. In the ages past—how far back we do not know—Job said: "When the morning stars sang together, and all the sons of God shouted for joy" (Job 38:7). They were praising God. And the psalmist said: "For all the gods of the nations are idols: but the LORD made the heavens" (Ps. 96:5). He made the heavens that they might be a musical instrument to sing forth His praises throughout the eternal ages of the future. Although man was created for that high purpose, he got out of harmony, he got out of tune with God. He got out of fellowship with God. Perhaps Shakespeare expressed it when he gave to one of his characters in *The Merchant of Venice* these lines:

There's not the smallest orb which thou
  behold'st
But in his motion like an angel sings,
Still quiring to the young-eyed cherubims;
Such harmony is in immortal souls;
But whilst this muddy vesture of decay
Doth grossly close it in, we cannot hear it.
(Act V, Scene 1)

Today you and I are living in a created universe that is actually singing praises to God. But man is out of tune. Man is in discord. God's great purpose is to bring man back into the harmony of heaven.

Let us move on now into the realm of music, about which I know nothing, but have made careful inquiry. I am reliably informed that on every good pipe organ there are four principal stops. There is the main stop known as Diapason; then there is the Flute stop; another which is known as the String stop; and then that which is known as Vox Humana (the human voice). I am told that the Vox Humana stop is very seldom in tune. If you put it in tune while the auditorium is cold, it would be out of tune when the auditorium is heated. And if you put it in tune when the auditorium is heated, it would be out of tune when the auditorium got cold. My beloved, it is hard to keep Vox Humana in tune.

This great universe of God's is a mighty instrument. One day Jesus Christ went to the console of God's great organ, His creation, and He pulled out the stop known as Diapason. When He did this, the solar and stellar spaces broke into mighty song. Then He reached over and pulled out the Flute stop, and these little feathered friends, called birds, began to sing. Then when He reached out and pulled the String stop, light went humming across God's universe, and the angels lifted their voices in praise. Then He reached over and pulled out the Vox Humana—but it was out of tune. The great Organist was not only a musician, He knew how to repair the organ, so He left the console of the organ yonder in heaven, and He came down to this earth. Through redemption, the giving of His own life, He was able to bring man back into harmony with God's tremendous creation. And, my beloved, today the redeemed are the ones to lift their voices in praise. Only the redeemed are in tune. The psalmist sings: "O give thanks unto the LORD, for he is good: for his mercy endureth for ever. Let the redeemed of the LORD say so, whom he hath redeemed from the hand of the enemy" (Ps. 107:1–2). And, brother, if the redeemed don't say so, no one will! Oh, to be in tune with heaven! Today sin has intruded into this world and has taken man out of God's choir; but individuals can come back in—and many have—through Jesus Christ, the son of David (David, the sweet singer of Israel). The Lord Jesus Christ has brought man back into a redemptive and right relationship with his Creator and Redeemer so that man can lift his voice in praise to Him.

WHY WORSHIP?

Now we want to answer the question: Why worship?

At this point we move our emphasis over from "Praise *ye* the LORD" to "*Praise* ye the LORD." We move the accent over to the verb, to that which is active. "*Praise* ye the Lord."

Very few people actually worship God. There really is no such thing as public worship. It was the great Chrysostom who put it like this: "The angels glorify; men scrutinize; Angels raise their voices in praise; men in disputation; They conceal their faces with their wings; but man with a presumptuous gaze would look into thine unspeakable glory." Oh, today, how many actually go to the church to worship? Somebody, in a very facetious manner, said that some people go to church to eye the clothes, and others to close their eyes. I wonder how many go to church for the purpose of worshiping God. Worship is divine intoxication. If you don't believe that, there is a fine illustration of it in the Book of Acts. On the Day of Pentecost Simon Peter got up and preached a sermon. We talk a great deal about that sermon, but actually it was an explanation to the people that these Spirit-filled men were not drunk. Drunkenness was not the explanation. How many would get the impression that *we* are intoxicated with God today? We need an ecclesiastical ecstasy. We need a theological thrill in this day in which we live.

There are three words that we must associate with worship, and these three words denote an experience of the human heart and the human soul as it comes into God's presence to worship.

The first of these words is *prostration*. In the Orient people are accustomed to get down on their faces; in the West we talk a great deal about having a dignified service. Now don't misunderstand me. I am not contending for a posture of the body. Victor Hugo once said that the soul is on its knees many times, regardless of the position of the body. I am not trying to insist on a posture of the body, but we do need to have our *souls* prostrated before God. The two prominent Bible words are the Hebrew *hishtahaweh*, meaning "to bow the neck," and the Greek *proskuneo*, meaning "to bow the knee" to God. And today we need to bow before God in heaven. The Book of Revelation does not tell us much about heaven, but one thing we are sure about—every time we read of someone in heaven they are either getting down on their faces to worship God, or getting up off their faces from worshiping God. And, friend, if you don't like to worship God, you wouldn't like heaven because that is the thing with which they are occupied. Most of the time they are worshiping God, prostrating themselves down before Him. Beloved, we need that today.

When my spiritual life gets frayed and fuzzy at the edges and begins to tear at the seams, I like to get alone, get down on my face before Him, and pour out my heart to Him. Friend, when was the last time you got down on your face before God? When was the last time that you prostrated yourself before Him? Oh, it would do us *good*. It would take us out of the deep-freeze. It would deliver us from the shell in which we live. It would create within our hearts a different attitude if we would learn to prostrate our souls before God.

The second word that goes with worship is the word *adoration*. It is a term of endearment. There is passion in that word. "O worship the LORD in the beauty of holiness . . ." (Ps. 96:9). Worship is a love affair; it is making love to God. Michal, the first wife of David, resented his devotion to God. When King David brought the ark into Jerusalem, the record tells us: "So David and all the house of Israel brought up the ark of the LORD with shouting, and with the sound of the trumpet. And as the ark of the LORD came into the city of David, Michal Saul's daughter looked through a window, and saw king David leaping and dancing before the LORD; and she despised him in her heart" (2 Sam. 6:15–16). She despised him. Sure she did. She discovered that David loved God more than he loved her and that he was making love to God. Worship without love is like a flame without heat; it is like a rainbow without color; it is like a flower without perfume. Worship should have a spontaneity. It should not be synthetic. It should have an expectancy, a tenderness, and an eagerness in it. My friend, some types of worship compare to going downtown, sitting in a department store window, and holding the hand of a mannequin in there. It has no more life in it; it has no more vitality in it than that! Oh, to have a heart that goes out to God in adoration and in love to Him!

A young fellow wrote a love letter to his girl. He waxed eloquent and said: "I would climb the highest mountain for you. I would swim the widest river for you. I would crawl across burning sands of the desert for you." Then he put a P.S. at the end: "If it doesn't rain Wednesday night I will be over to see you." A whole lot of so-called worship is like that today. It will not take very much to keep us away from God.

In a marriage ceremony there is something I occasionally use. I think how sacred it is. The two being joined in marriage say, "With my body I thee worship."

The hero swam the Hellespont every evening to be with the one he loved. One evening he did not come. She knew something had happened, and the next day she found his lifeless body washed ashore. Oh, my friend, to have a heart that goes out to God in adoration. Gregory Nazianzen said, "I love God because I know Him; I adore Him because I cannot understand Him; I bow before Him in awe and in worship and adoration." Oh, have you found that adoration in your worship?

Then, last of all, there is *exaltation* in worship. And I do not mean the exaltation of God—we put God in His rightful place when we worship Him. When you and I are down on our faces before Him, we are taking the place that the creature should take before the Creator. I am not speaking here of the exaltation of God; rather, I am speaking now of the exaltation of man.

Humanism with its deadening philosophy has been leading man back to the jungle for about half a century, and we are not very far from the jungle. It is degrading to become a lackey, a menial. And think of the millions of people who got their tongues black by licking the boots of Hitler! Humanism did that. They turned their backs on God. And when man turns his back on God, he will worship a man. No atheist, no agnostic, has ever turned his back on God who did not get his tongue black by licking somebody's boots. There is nothing that will exalt man, there is nothing that will give dignity to man, like worshiping God.

Dr. Harry Emerson Fosdick wrote a sermon in the 1920s entitled "The Peril of Worshiping Jesus." In this message he said that men have tried two ways to get rid of Jesus: one by crucifying Him, the other by worshiping Him. The liberal doesn't like you to worship Jesus. My friend, *I* worship Him. He is my Lord; He is my God. I do not find it humiliating to fall down before Him. There is nothing as exalting and as thrilling as to get down on your face before Jesus Christ. In Acts, chapter 9, the record tells us that Paul fell into the dust of the Damascus Road, and the Lord Jesus dealt with him there. Then notice that He told him to arise—stand up on his feet. Only the Christian faith has ever lifted a man out of the dust and put him on his feet. In the first chapter of Revelation we read that John, on the Isle of Patmos, saw the glorified Christ. John says, "And when I saw him, I fell at his feet as dead. And he laid his right hand upon me, saying unto me, Fear not . . ." (Rev. 1:17). The creature now can come to the Creator. Man, who has been lost in sin, who has gone down and down, can come up and up and worship Christ.

During the seventeenth century Muretus, a great scholar of that day, was going through Lombardy when he suddenly became ill and was picked up on the street. They took him to the hospital, and, thinking he was a bum, the doctors said something like this, "Let's try an experiment on this worthless creature." They were speaking in Latin and had no notion their patient could understand them. But Muretus answered them in Latin, "Will you call one worthless for whom Jesus Christ did not disdain to die?" My friend, it is only Jesus Christ and the worship of Him that has lifted man up.

Man is yet to be restored to his rightful place some day, and brought back into harmony with heaven.

The Great Psalm 150 begins with the Son of God pulling out the stop Diapason: "Praise ye the LORD. Praise God in his sanctuary: praise him in the firmament of his power."

Then the Flute stop is pulled out: "Praise him with the sound of the trumpet: praise him with the psaltery and harp."

Then the String stop is pulled out: "Praise him with the timbrel and dance: praise him with stringed instruments and organs."

Then listen, my beloved: "Let every thing that hath breath praise the LORD." In the beginning God breathed life into man—soul and spirit—but man departed from God. Now there is coming a day when everything that has life, everything that has breath, shall praise the Lord. Even now in this day in which you and I are living we can lift our hearts and lives to Him in adoration and praise.

In my first pastorate, one of my officers thought he was doing me a favor by inviting me to the performance of a symphony orchestra. Now, I know nothing about music, and I do not understand it, but to be nice I went along. I sat there, and I learned something. Before the concert began, one hundred fifty or so musicians came out on the platform. Each one picked up his little instrument and began tuning it. I have never heard such bedlam in my life! Every musician was making his own particular little squeak, regardless of anyone else. Such a medley of noise—it sounded like a boiler factory. Then they all disappeared, and in a few moments they came back out, and the lights went off in the auditorium. It got very quiet. Then the spotlight was focused on the wings, and out stepped the conductor. He came to the podium, turned and bowed. There was great applause. Then it grew quiet again. He lifted the baton—you could have heard a pin drop—then he gave the down beat. My friend, you have never heard such music! Everything was in tune; everything was in harmony.

About me in this world I hear nothing but bedlam. Every man is playing his own little tune. But one of these days out from the wings will step the Conductor, the Lord Jesus Christ. And when He lifts His baton, out yonder at the end of God's universe those galactic systems will burst forth into song. Every bird, every angel, and then man, will join the heavenly chorus.

> "Praise ye the LORD. Praise God in his sanctuary: praise him in the firmament of his power. Praise him for his mighty acts: praise him according to his excellent greatness. Praise him with the sound of

the trumpet: praise him with the psaltery and harp. Praise him with the timbrel and dance: praise him with stringed instruments and organs. Praise him upon the loud cymbals: praise him upon the high sounding cymbals. Let every thing that hath breath praise the LORD. Praise ye the LORD."

In the meantime, while we are waiting for His return, you and I can bow before Him and bring our little souls into the harmony of heaven.

BIBLIOGRAPHY

(Recommended for Further Study)

Alexander, J. A. *The Psalms.* 1864. Reprint. Grand Rapids, Michigan: Zondervan Publishing House, 1964.

Gaebelein, Arno C. *The Annotated Bible.* 1917. Reprint. Neptune, New Jersey: Loizeaux Brothers, 1970.

Gaebelein, Arno C. *The Book of Psalms.* 1939. Reprint. Neptune, New Jersey: Loizeaux Brothers, 1965. (The finest prophetical interpretation of the Psalms.)

Grant, F. W. *The Psalms.* Neptune, New Jersey: Loizeaux Brothers, 1895. (Numerical Bible.)

Gray, James M. *Synthetic Bible Studies.* Old Tappan, New Jersey: Fleming H. Revell Co., 1906.

Ironside, H. A. *The Psalms.* Neptune, New Jersey: Loizeaux Brothers, n.d.

Jamieson, Robert; Fausset, A. R.; and Brown, D. *Commentary on the Bible.* 3 vols. Grand Rapids, Michigan: Wm. B. Eerdmans Publishing Co., 1945.

Jensen, Irving L. *The Psalms.* Chicago, Illinois: Moody Press, 1970. (A self-study guide.)

Morgan, G. Campbell. *Notes on the Psalms.* Old Tappan, New Jersey: Fleming H. Revell Co., 1947.

Olson, Erling C. *Meditations in the Psalms.* Neptune, New Jersey: Loizeaux Brothers, 1939. (Devotional.)

Perowne, J. J. Stewart. *The Book of Psalms.* 1882. Reprint. Grand Rapids, Michigan: Zondervan Publishing House, 1976.

Sauer, Erich. *The Dawn of World Redemption.* Grand Rapids, Michigan: Wm. B. Eerdmans Publishing Co., 1951. (An excellent Old Testament survey.)

Scroggie, W. Graham. *The Psalms.* Old Tappan, New Jersey: Fleming H. Revell Co., 1948. (Excelllent.)

Scroggie, W. Graham. *The Unfolding Drama of Redemption.* Grand Rapids, Michigan: Zondervan Publishing House, 1970. (An excellent survey and outline of the Old Testament.)

Spurgeon, Charles Haddon. *The Treasury of David.* 3 vols. Reprint. Grand Rapids, Michigan: Zondervan Publishing House, 1974. (A classic work and very comprehensive.)

Unger, Merrill F. *Unger's Bible Handbook.* Chicago, Illinois: Moody Press, 1966. (A basic tool for every Christian's library.)

Unger, Merrill F. *Unger's Commentary on the Old Testament.* Vol. 1. Chicago, Illinois: Moody Press, 1981. (A fine summary of each paragraph. Highly recommended.)